S0-BJP-359

Albert Huck

Synopse der drei ersten Evangelien

mit Beigabe der johanneischen Parallelstellen

Synopsis of the First Three Gospels

with the Addition of the Johannine Parallels

13. Auflage, völlig neu bearbeitet von

13th edition, fundamentally revised by

Heinrich Greeven

J. C. B. Mohr (Paul Siebeck) Tübingen 1981

Wichtige Hinweise. *Important Information.*

1. Zeilenabstand und Papierqualität sind in dieser Synopse so gewählt, daß der Benutzer reichlich Gebrauch von Farbstiften machen kann. Es sollte je eine Farbe festgelegt werden für den gemeinsamen Text von a) Mt-Mk-Lk, b) Mt-Lk, für das Sondergut von c) Mt, d) Mk und e) Lk. Was man selbst durchkoloriert hat, prägt sich dem visuellen Gedächtnis stärker ein.

2. Zum Verständnis des textkritischen Apparats halte man sich zunächst an die auf dem eingelegten Karton gegebene Kurzfassung des Abkürzungsverzeichnisses. Wo diese nicht ausreicht, führt das volle Verzeichnis weiter (S. XXXVIII ff.). Dort finden sich die Verweise auf die entsprechenden Paragraphen der Einleitung.

1. The spacing of the lines and the quality of the paper are so chosen for this Synopsis that the owner can make full use of coloured pencils. He should decide on one colour severally for the text common (a) to Mt-Mk-Lk, (b) to Mt-Lk, and for the passages peculiar to (c) Mt, (d) Mk and (e) Lk. What the user has himself marked in colour prints itself more strongly on his visual memory.

2. For the understanding of the textual apparatus the reader will rely, first, on the accompanying card with its short list of abbreviations. When this is not sufficient the full list gives more information (p. XXXVIII ff.). He will find there the references to the corresponding paragraphs of the Introduction.

CIP-Kurztitelaufnahme der Deutschen Bibliothek

Synopse der drei ersten Evangelien: mit Beig. d. johanneischen Parallelstellen = Synopsis of the first three gospels / Albert Huck. — 13. Aufl., völlig neu bearb. / von Heinrich Greeven. — Tübingen: Mohr, 1981. Einheitssacht.: Evangelia
ISBN 3-16-143032-8

NE: Huck, Albert [Bearb.]; Greeven, Heinrich [Bearb.]; EST; PT

1. Auflage,	bearbeitet	von Albert Huck	1892
2. ,,	,,	,, ,, ,,	1898
3. ,,	umgearbeitet	,, ,, ,,	1906
4. ,,	bearbeitet	,, ,, ,,	1910
5. ,,	,,	,, ,, ,,	1916
6. ,,	,,	,, ,, ,,	1922
7. ,,	,,	,, ,, ,,	1927
8. ,,	,,	,, ,, ,,	1931
9. ,,	völlig neu bearbeitet von H. Lietzmann/H. G. Opitz		1936
10. ,,	Photomech. Nachdruck der 9. Auflage		1950
11. ,,	,, ,, ,, 9. ,,		1970
12. ,,	,, ,, ,, 9. ,,		1975
13. ,,	völlig neu bearbeitet von H. Greeven		1981

Printed in Germany. Satz Ernst Klett, Stuttgart
Offsetdruck: Karl Grammlich, Pliezhausen
Einband: Großbuchbinderei Heinrich Koch, Tübingen

REVERENDISSIMO ORDINI THEOLOGORUM
UNIVERSITATIS RUPERTO-CAROLAE HEIDELBERGENSIS
ET
SENATUI ACADEMICO
ILLUSTRISSIMAE SANCTI ANDREAE APUD SCOTOS UNIVERSITATIS
AD SUMMUM GRADUM DOCTORIS THEOLOGIAE PROMOTUS
GRATISSIMO ANIMO
AUCTOR

Inhalt. *Contents.*

Vorwort. *Preface.*

Als Albert Hucks „Synopse der drei ersten Evangelien" 1892 erschien, war sie ausdrücklich dazu bestimmt, den Hörern und Lesern von HJHoltzmanns synoptischer Evangelien-Auslegung als Textbuch zu dienen. Diese allzu enge Bindung an eine bestimmte Position wurde aber bald (3. Aufl. 1906) aufgegeben, und so konnte „der Huck" mit der Zeit[1]) immer mehr das werden, was er bis heute geblieben ist: Eine vollständige und übersichtliche Darstellung der Tatbestände, aus denen sich die „Synoptische Frage" ergibt und die bei ihrer Lösung erklärt werden müssen. Wie seit langem, so ist auch heute — wo weithin anerkannte Theorien von neuem hinterfragt werden — dieses Buch um strikte Neutralität gegenüber den verschiedenen möglichen Antworten auf die Synoptische Frage bemüht. Für die wenigen Fälle, in denen dies anders erscheint — einfach weil jede mögliche Art der Anordnung einer bestimmten These zuzuneigen scheint —, erkläre ich ausdrücklich, daß keinerlei Vorentscheidung beabsichtigt ist. Auch die Anordnung der Spalten (Mt — Mk — Lk) folgt lediglich der heute üblichen Reihenfolge.

Die letzte Neubearbeitung des „Huck" liegt nun schon 45 Jahre zurück (9. Aufl. 1936; die 12. Aufl. 1975 war ein unveränderter Nachdruck). Bereits im Jahre 1952 trat der Verlag mit dem Vorschlag an mich heran, das seit dem Tode HLietzmanns (1942) verwaiste Buch neu zu bearbeiten. Aber es sollten 28 Jahre vergehen, bis diese Aufgabe erfüllt war. Das lag zum Teil daran, daß verschiedene akademische Ämter — u. a. wurde ich 1965 zum ersten Rektor der neugegründeten Ruhr-Universität Bochum gewählt — mich viel mehr Zeit kosteten, als ich vorausgesehen hatte. Aber der Hauptgrund für den hohen Zeitbedarf lag in der Sache selbst. Eine Rundfrage bei 290 Neutestamentlern in aller Welt ergab, daß die überwältigende Mehrheit der Stellungnahmen sich dagegen aussprach, den damaligen Nestle-Text (21. Aufl. 1952) der Neubearbeitung zugrundezulegen. Huck^9 hatte den bis dahin benutzten Tischendorf-Text (ed. octava maior), ohne darüber ein Wort zu verlieren (was ihm in nicht wenigen Besprechungen eine Rüge eintrug), zu etwa 85% an Nestle angeglichen. Dies zu übernehmen, konnte ich mich nicht entschließen. Damit aber stand ich vor der Notwendigkeit, eine neue Rezension des Evangelientextes vorzunehmen. Sie liegt dieser 13. Aufl. des „Huck" zugrunde. Die Begründung der Einzelentscheidungen hoffe ich, an anderer Stelle noch geben zu können.

Viele Fragen beantwortet auch der textkritische Apparat, der ebenfalls auf eine neue Grundlage gestellt wurde. Anstatt einer subjektiven Auslese von Fall zu Fall wurden konsequent in den Apparat aufgenommen:

(a) Varianten, die von anderen Textkritikern als Urtext angesehen worden sind.

---

[1]) Zur Bedeutung und Geschichte des „Huck" verweise ich auf meinen Bericht über 200 Jahre griechische Evangeliensynopse vor dem Griesbach-Kolloquium 1976 in Münster, englisch erschienen unter dem Titel "The Gospel Synopsis from 1776 to the present day" in: BOrchard-ThRWLongstaff (Hrsg.), "J. J. Griesbach: Synoptic and text-critical studies 1776-1976" = SNTS Monograph Series vol. 34, 1978, 22—49.

When Albert Huck's "Synopsis of the first three Gospels" appeared in 1892 it was expressly intended to serve the hearers and readers of HJHoltzmann's lectures on the Synoptic Gospels as a textbook. This association with a particular theory was, however, far too close and was soon (3rd edition, 1906) given up, so that Huck could in due course of time[1]) become the tool that it still is today, a clear and full presentation of the facts which give rise to the Synoptic problem and which must be explained by any solution of it. Theories formerly widely accepted are being questioned anew and as this book was long ago so it is today concerned to maintain a strict neutrality before the various suggested solutions of the Synoptic problem. For the few instances in which it appears otherwise (simply because each possible kind of arrangement seems to favour a particular theory) I expressly declare that no such attempt to preempt the solution is intended. Even the arrangement of the columns (Mt, Mk, Lk) merely follows the order of the Gospels which is customary today.

The last revising of "Huck" is now some 45 years behind us (9th edition, 1936; the 12th edition, 1975, was a reprint of the 9th). Already in 1952 the publisher approached me with the proposal that I should make a new edition of the book which since HLietzmann's death (1942) had been fatherless. But 28 years were to pass before this assignment was fulfilled. The reason for this was partly that various academic offices — among other things in 1965 I became the first elected rector of the new University of the Ruhr at Bochum — took up much more time than I had foreseen. The chief reason, however, for the need for more time lay in the undertaking itself. A questionnaire sent to 290 NT scholars throughout the world showed that the overwhelming majority of replies were expressly against using the current Nestle-text (21st edition, 1952) as the basis for the revision. Huck's ninth edition had without a word assimilated Tischendorf's text (ed. octava maior), which had been used hitherto, for about 85 percent to that of Nestle, a procedure which brought on him adverse comment in not a few reviews. I could not persuade myself to take this text over. In so doing I brought upon myself the obligation to make a new recension of the Gospel text. It serves as the basis for this thirteenth edition of Huck. I hope to be able to give the reasons for the various decisions involved in another place.

Many questions are answered in the critical apparatus which too is constructed on a new plan. Instead of making a subjective selection I have consistently taken into the apparatus:

(a) variants which have been regarded by other textual critics as original. In this way the user is free to make his own decision.

---

[1]) For the signifiance and history of Huck I refer to my report of 200 years of Greek Synopses of the Gospels. It was delivered at the Griesbach Colloquy in 1976 in Münster and appeared in English under the title "The Gospel Synopsis from 1776 to the present day" in BOrchard-ThRWLongstaff (ed.), "J. J. Griesbach: Synoptic and text-critical studies 1776-1976" = SNTS Monograph Series vol. 34, 1978, 22—49.

(b) Varianten — soweit griechisch bezeugt —, durch die ein Text (mehr oder weniger) an den einer Parallel-Perikope oder einer anderen, inhaltlich oder formal verwandten Stelle angeglichen wurde. Das Synoptische Problem spiegelt sich nämlich in der Textgeschichte genau wider, und zwar in der unaufhörlich wirksamen Harmonisierungs-Tendenz. Diesen Trend, und zB auch sein signifikantes Gefälle auf Mt hin, muß man sich stets vor Augen halten, wenn man textkritische Fragen in den synoptischen Evangelien angemessen untersuchen will. So erweist sich der Variantenbestand unter (b) als sachlich erforderlicher Bestandteil des Apparats einer Synopse; er ist hier lückenlos vorgeführt: andere harmonistische Varianten sind mir nicht bekannt geworden. Die hier etwa nicht erfaßten „interessanten" Varianten sind ohne Mühe dem Apparat eines beliebigen NT Graece zu entnehmen, das ich wohl in der Hand jeden Benutzers der Synopse voraussetzen darf.

Außer im Text und im Umfang des textkritischen Apparats unterscheidet sich die 13. Aufl. des „Huck" von ihrer Vorgängerin wie folgt:

1. Vergleichbarer Text aus dem Johannesevangelium — vor allem in der Leidensgeschichte — wurde beigedruckt, abgesetzt durch starke Umrandung.

2. Synoptische Paralleltexte im weiteren Sinn sind nicht mehr im Apparat zu finden wie bei Huck[9] (erster Apparat), sondern grundsätzlich in den Haupttext aufgenommen (zB Perikope *137.*). Alle aus anderem Zusammenhang stammenden Texte sind durch kursive Schrift kenntlich gemacht. Zur Raumersparnis wurden die früheren regelmäßigen Kolumnen durch Ausweitung und Verengung häufig zu gewundenen Schläuchen, was einem Zeitungsleser von heute aber kaum Schwierigkeiten bereiten dürfte.

3. Die Nebeneinanderstellung aller Formen einer Perikope, eines Logions oder dergleichen findet in der Synopse in der Regel nur an einer Stelle statt (Vollvergleich).

4. Die Gleichstellung der gleichen oder entsprechenden Worte in den Parallel-Kolumnen ist stärker präzisiert.

5. Verifizierbare alttestamentliche Zitate sind durch Fettdruck hervorgehoben, die Fundorte am Rande vermerkt.

6. Die Perikopen sind ab Mt1$_1$ durchlaufend gezählt (die früheren Nummern stehen in Klammern am Zeilenrand links von der Perikopen-Überschrift).

7. Textkritischer Apparat wird nicht wiederholt. Für die Textkritik kursiv gedruckter Texte muß deren Stammperikope aufgeschlagen werden, die jeweils angegeben ist.

8. Bei den in den Apparat aufgenommenen Varianten sind alle mir bekannten Zeugen angegeben; Schlüsse e silentio sind daher zulässig. Die griechischen Papyri werden wie üblich immer einzeln genannt; ebenso alle Majuskeln und etwa 80 in der Einleitung (III.B.2.c.) aufgeführte ausgewählte Minuskeln, sofern sie nicht in Summen-Sigeln (→ 9.) enthalten sind oder mit *Rpl* (III.B.2.i.) gehen. Die 1952 getroffene Auswahl spiegelt den damaligen, genauer: meinen persönlichen Wissensstand wider und konnte während der laufenden Arbeiten nur noch unwesentlich korrigiert werden. Sie ist lediglich praktisch orientiert und will kein Beitrag zur Bestimmung von Handschriften-Gruppen sein. Von den übrigen Minuskeln und den Lektionaren ist angegeben, was mir aus anderen Ausgaben bekannt wurde; sie sind nicht laufend verglichen.

9. Bei der Aufzählung der Einzelzeugen ist weithin von „Summen-Sigeln" Gebrauch gemacht (ℌ, **λ**, **φ** usw → III.B.2.g.; 3.a.1.). Diese Zeichen bezeichnen nicht, wie sonst, Text-Typen, -Familien oder dergleichen, sondern eine genau aufgezählte Reihe von Handschriften, deren Lücken ebenfalls in einer Liste genau angegeben werden.

(b) variants which are extant in Greek, where a passage has been assimilated in greater or less degree to a parallel pericope or to another passage related to it in content or form. The reason for this is that the Synoptic problem is mirrored precisely in the history of the text, namely in an unremitting tendency to harmonisation. We must always keep before our eyes this trend and especially the significant tendency to assimilate to Mt, if we wish appropriately to investigate textual questions in the Synoptic Gospels. So the variants included in (b) are an essential element in an apparatus to a synopsis. They are presented in the apparatus without omission; I know of no other harmonising variants. "Interesting" variants which are not included can easily be found in the apparatus of any Greek NT, I assume to be in the hands of each user of the Synopsis.

Apart from the text and the enlarged apparatus, the 13th edition of "Huck" is distinguished from its predecessor as follows:

1. Comparable texts from John, especially in the Passion Story, are printed in the appropriate place, marked off by thick lines.

2. Marginal parallels in the Synoptic Gospels are no longer to be found in the apparatus as in Huck 9th edition (first apparatus) but are generally included in the main body of the text (e. g. pericope *137.*). All texts derived from another context are distinguished by cursive type. To save space the columns, which in the former editions retained a regular size, are frequently so contracted and expanded that they become like winding streams, a procedure which should cause no difficulty to readers of today's newspapers.

3. As a rule the complete presentation of a text in all its parallel forms occurs only once (comparison in full).

4. Like and corresponding words in the parallel columns are more precisely related in position to their parallels.

5. Verifiable Old Testament quotations are distinguished by heavy type and the source is indicated in the margin.

6. The pericopes are continuously numbered from Mt1$_1$ (the former numbers are in brackets in the margin on the left of the title of the pericopes).

7. The textual apparatus is not printed more than once. For the apparatus to the texts printed in cursive, reference must be made to the principal occurrence of these passages which is indicated on each occasion.

8. For variants in the apparatus I have given all witnesses known to me; accordingly inferences *e silentio* are permissible. As usual Greek papyri are always separately indicated. I do the same, where they are not comprehended under group symbols (→ 9.), with all majuscules and some 80 selected minuscules which are listed in the introduction (III.B.2.c.) insofar as they do not go with *Rpl* (III.B.2.i.). The selection made in 1952 reflects the knowledge available then, or more exactly my own knowledge at the time and during the progress of the work could only be slightly corrected. It serves merely practical ends and is not intended to make any contribution to the determining of manuscript groups. For the remaining minuscules and the lectionaries I give only the information which was to be taken from other editions; they are not continuously quoted.

9. In indicating the separate witnesses I make use widely of comprehensive symbols ("group symbols", e. g. ℌ, **λ**, **φ** etc. → III.B.2.g.; 3.a.1.). Unlike practice elsewhere these symbols do not indicate text types or text families or the like, but a series of manuscripts which are precisely enumerated whose lacunae are exactly indicated in a list.

10. Das Zeugnis der kirchlichen Schriftsteller ist viel breiter herangezogen, zugleich aber strengen Maßstäben unterworfen worden: nur solche „Zitate" finden Berücksichtigung, bei denen hinreichend feststeht, daß sie dem betreffenden Evangelium zuzuordnen sind. Sicherung solcher Zitate durch den Kontext wird durch Fettdruck hervorgehoben (zB **Eu**).

11. Die Evangelien-Harmonien sind herangezogen, wo immer sie als Zeugen in Frage kommen, nicht nur für das Sondergut (→ III.B.11.b.).

12. Im zweiten Apparat wird der Stoff der apokryphen Evangelien und ähnliches breiter dargeboten, soweit es noch Verwandtschaft mit synoptischem Traditionsgut erkennen läßt. Insbesondere wird das coptische Thomasevangelium mit etwa einem Drittel seines Textbestandes herangezogen. Ich habe die betreffenden Stücke aus dem nur wenigen vertrauten Coptischen in das (Koine-)Griechische übertragen, das ich als einzige Sprache mit Sicherheit bei jedem Benutzer voraussetzen kann. (Hierzu vgl. Einleitung VII. → S. XXXVII). Aus dem gleichen Grunde ist, wo immer es tunlich erschien, auch für lateinischen Text das mutmaßliche griechische Äquivalent gesetzt.

Von der Rundfrage 1952 an habe ich mich ständig des Rats und der Hilfe meiner Fachkollegen erfreuen dürfen. Ohne den Beitrag anderer geringer anzuschlagen, möchte ich statt vieler hier Bo Reicke nennen, der mir sein Arbeits-Exemplar des „Huck" für längere Zeit überlassen hat. Für viele Anregungen, vor allem auch für die Gestaltung des textkritischen Apparats, sowie für die Sorgfalt und die unendliche Geduld, die er auf die Übersetzung verwendet hat, schulde ich besonderen Dank dem Bearbeiter der englischen Ausgabe dieser Synopse, George D. Kilpatrick, Oxford. Ebenso danke ich meinem Freund und langjährigen Betheler Kollegen, Helmut Krämer, herzlich für seinen unermüdlichen Rat in Fragen des Griechischen. Vom Institut für neutestamentliche Textforschung in Münster/Westfalen, dessen Wissenschaftlichem Beirat ich angehöre, ließen der Direktor, Kurt Aland, und seine Mitarbeiter mir dankenswerterweise jede erbetene Hilfe zuteil werden. Von den vielen Assistenten, die mir im Laufe der Jahre nicht nur in der Lehrtätigkeit, sondern auch bei der Synopse geholfen haben, verdienen hervorgehoben zu werden die Herren Dieter Müller, jetzt Pfarrer in Neumünster, und Martin Völkel, jetzt Pfarrer in Dortmund. Ganz ungewöhnliche und bei einem solchen Buch besonders dankenswerte Verdienste hat sich bei Erstellung des Manuskripts und Begleitung des Drucks durch die Korrekturen meine langjährige Lehrstuhl-Sekretärin, Frau Eleonore Kollmann, erworben. Tiefen Dank schulde ich auch den Verlegern, Dr. iur. h. c. Hans Georg Siebeck und seinem Sohn Georg Siebeck, die unendliche Geduld mit dem ständig Aufschub verlangenden Autor gehabt und ihm jederzeit Verständnis und Entgegenkommen bewiesen haben. Was er der stillen, namenlosen Gewissenhaftigkeit und Treue von Setzern und Druckern verdankt, möchte ich dem Benutzer nachdrücklich ins Bewußtsein rufen, auch wenn er es kaum ganz ermessen kann.

Dem Dank muß ich eine dringende Bitte anfügen. Sie richtet sich an alle Benutzer, besonders aber an die Fachkollegen: Teilen Sie bitte mir oder dem Verlag alle Versehen und Druckfehler mit, auf die Sie stoßen! Das ist keine routinemäßige Floskel, sondern ein wirklicher Hilferuf, ausgelöst durch die fast täglichen Erfahrungen, die ich während der Drucklegung machen mußte, eine Bitte, die ich nicht wagen würde, geschähe sie nicht zum Besten aller künftigen Benutzer und im Interesse der wissenschaftlichen Erforschung der synoptischen Evangelien.

Bochum, im Februar 1981.

10. The witness of ecclesiastical writers has been quoted more widely but at the same time has been strictly controlled; such "citations" are reported only where they can be ascribed to one definite Gospel. The confirmation of such citations through their context is emphasized with heavy type (e. g. **Eu**).

11. The witness of the Gospel harmonies is used wherever possible, not only for passages peculiar to one Gospel (→ III. B.11.b.).

12. In the second apparatus material from the Apocryphal Gospels and similar sources is given at greater length, insofar as it permits us to recognize relationships with the material in the Synoptic Gospels. In particular I have made use of about a third of the Coptic Gospel of Thomas. I have translated the relevant texts from the Coptic, with which language only few are acquainted, into Koine Greek, the only language which I can confidently assume in the users of the Synopsis. (cp. the Introduction VII. → p. XXXVII). For the same reason wherever it is practical I have given the conjectured Greek equivalent for Latin renderings also.

From my questionnaire of 1952 onward I have continued to enjoy the advice and help of my colleagues in their expertise. Without underrating the contribution of others, I will here mention the name of Bo Reicke who for a long time lent me his working copy of "Huck". For many pieces of advice, above all for the shaping of the textual apparatus, and for the carefulness and unending patience he has displayed in making the translation I owe particular thanks to George D. Kilpatrick, Oxford, who provided the English rendering of this Synopsis. Likewise I heartily thank Helmut Krämer, my friend and colleague for many years at Bethel, for his unwearying advice in matters of Greek. To the Institut für neutestamentliche Textforschung at Münster/Westfalia, on whose Advisory Board I serve, and to Kurt Aland and the research staff I am especially thankful for the assistence which I requested. Of the many assistants who have helped me in the course of the years not only in my teaching but also in making the Synopsis these deserve to be mentioned: Dieter Müller, now pastor in Neumünster, and Martin Völkel, now pastor in Dortmund. Mrs. Eleonore Kollmann, my professorial secretary for many years has rendered unusual service in the making of such a book for which I can only be especially grateful; she established the manuscript and watched over the printing and correction of the proofs. My deepest thanks are due to the publishers, Hans Georg Siebeck Dr. iur. h. c. and his son Georg Siebeck who have shown continuous patience to an author who continuously asked for delay and have at all times demonstrated their understanding and forthcomingness toward him. I would like emphatically to call to mind for the user, even if he can scarcely estimate the whole of it, what he owes to the silent conscientiousness and loyalty of printers und compositors unnamed as they are.

To these acknowledgements I must add a pressing request. It is directed to all users especially to the experts: "please notify me or the publishers of any mistake or misprint which you come across". This request is not a piece of conventional decoration but a real cry for help, called forth by the almost daily experiences which I had to undergo during the printing of the work, a request that I would not dare to make were it not to the advantage of all future users and in the interest of scholarly research in the Synoptic Gospels.

H. Greeven.

Einleitung. *Introduction.*

I. Die ältesten Zeugnisse für die synoptischen Evangelien.
I. The Oldest Testimonies to the Synoptic Gospels.

Das Nähere über die im folgenden mitgeteilten ältesten Bezeugungen unserer drei ersten Evv. und ihre Bewertung ist zu finden in den die Entstehung der Evangelien und die Geschichte des Kanons behandelnden Abschnitten der „Einleitungen in das NT" von Holtzmann, Jülicher, Zahn, Wickenhauser-Schmid, Goguel, Kümmel, Guthrey; vgl. außerdem: AHarnack, Die Entstehung des NT, 1914, 46ff. und ThZahn, Geschichte des neutestamentlichen Kanons I 1888, 840ff., II 1890, 1ff. (Neudrucke 1975). Der Text der von Euseb erhaltenen Zeugnisse ist gegeben nach der Ausgabe von ESchwartz-ThMommsen GCS, Bd. II: Die Kirchengeschichte 1903/09. Die in Klammern hinzugefügten Seitenzahlen sind die der kleinen Ausgabe 1908, ^{5}1952.

More about the oldest evidences, given below, for our first three Gospels and their value, is to be found in the sections dealing with the origins of the Gospels and the history of the canon in the Introductions to the NT by Holtzmann, Jülicher, Zahn, Moffat, Wikenhauser-Schmid, Goguel Kümmel, Guthrey; cf. also AHarnack, Die Entstehung des NT, 1914, 46ff. and ThZahn, Geschichte des neutestamentlichen Kanons I 1888, 840ff., II 1890, 1ff. (reprinted 1975). The text of the testimonies contained in Eusebius has been given from the edition by ESchwartz and ThMommsen GCS, vol. II: Die Kirchengeschichte 1903/09. The page numbers in brackets are those of the editio minor 1908, ^{5}1952.

1. Das Zeugnis des Papias, Bischofs von Hierapolis, Zeitgenossen Justins, bei Eusebius, hist. eccl. III 39$_{1.14-16}$ p. 284. 290f. (119. 121f.):

1. The evidence of Papias, bishop of Hierapolis, contemporary of Justin, in Eusebius, hist. eccl. III 39$_{1.14-16}$ p. 284. 290f. (119. 121f.):

1 Τοῦ δὲ Παπία συγγράμματα πέντε τὸν ἀριθμὸν φέρεται, ἃ καὶ ἐπιγέγραπται Λογίων κυριακῶν ἐξηγήσεως ...

14 Καὶ ἄλλας δὲ τῇ ἰδίᾳ γραφῇ παραδίδωσιν Ἀριστίωνος τοῦ πρόσθεν δεδηλωμένου τῶν τοῦ κυρίου λόγων διηγήσεις καὶ τοῦ πρεσβυτέρου Ἰωάννου παραδόσεις· ἐφ' ἃς τοὺς φιλομαθεῖς ἀναπέμψαντες, ἀναγκαίως νῦν προσθήσομεν ταῖς προεκτεθείσαις αὐτοῦ φωναῖς παράδοσιν, ἣν περὶ Μάρκου τοῦ τὸ εὐαγγέλιον γεγραφότος ἐκτέθειται διὰ τούτων·

15 „Καὶ τοῦθ' ὁ πρεσβύτερος ἔλεγεν· Μάρκος μὲν ἑρμηνευτὴς Πέτρου γενόμενος, ὅσα ἐμνημόνευσεν, ἀκριβῶς ἔγραψεν, οὐ „μέντοι τάξει τὰ ὑπὸ τοῦ κυρίου ἢ λεχθέντα ἢ πραχθέντα. οὔτε γὰρ ἤκουσεν τοῦ κυρίου οὔτε παρηκολούθησεν αὐτῷ, ὕστε„ρον δέ, ὡς ἔφην, Πέτρῳ· ὃς πρὸς τὰς χρείας ἐποιεῖτο τὰς διδασκαλίας, ἀλλ' οὐχ ὥσπερ σύνταξιν τῶν κυριακῶν ποιούμε„νος λογίων, ὥστε οὐδὲν ἥμαρτεν Μάρκος οὕτως ἔνια γράψας ὡς ἀπεμνημόνευσεν. ἑνὸς γὰρ ἐποιήσατο πρόνοιαν, τοῦ „μηδὲν ὧν ἤκουσεν παραλιπεῖν ἢ ψεύσασθαί τι ἐν αὐτοῖς."

16 Ταῦτα μὲν οὖν ἱστόρηται τῷ Παπίᾳ περὶ τοῦ Μάρκου· περὶ δὲ τοῦ Ματθαίου ταῦτ' εἴρηται·
„Ματθαῖος μὲν οὖν Ἑβραΐδι διαλέκτῳ τὰ λόγια συνετάξατο, ἡρμήνευσεν δ' αὐτὰ ὡς ἦν δυνατὸς ἕκαστος."

Textausgabe aller Papiasfragmente bei AHarnack-OvGebhardt, Patrum apostolicorum opera, ed. major I 2 ^{2}1878, 87ff.; EPreuschen, Antilegomena ^{2}1905, 91—99. 195—202 (Übersetzung); KBihlmeyer, Die apostolischen Väter I ^{2}1956 133—140; *Lit.*: RGG^{3} V 47f.; BAltaner-AStuiber, Patrologie ^{8}1978, 52f. 552 („Altaner"); WGKümmel, Einleitung in das NT, ^{19}1978, 27ff. („Kümmel").

The text of all Papias fragments is to be found in AHarnack-OvGebhardt, Patrum apostolicorum opera, ed. major I 2 ^{2}1878, 87ff.; EPreuschen, Antilegomena ^{2}1905, 91—99. 195—202 (German translation); KBihlmeyer, Die apostolischen Väter I ^{2}1956 133—140; *Lit.*: RGG^{3} V 47f.; BAltaner-AStuiber, Patrologie ^{8}1978, 52f. 552 ("Altaner"); WGKümmel, Einleitung in das NT ^{19}1978, 27ff. ("Kümmel").

2. Irenaeus, adv. haer. III 1$_{1}$ bei/*in* Eusebius h. e. V 8$_{2-4}$ p. 442f. (189f.):

2 Ὁ μὲν δὴ Ματθαῖος ἐν τοῖς Ἑβραίοις τῇ ἰδίᾳ αὐτῶν διαλέκτῳ καὶ γραφὴν ἐξήνεγκεν εὐαγγελίου, τοῦ Πέτρου καὶ τοῦ Παύ-
3 λου ἐν Ῥώμῃ εὐαγγελιζομένων καὶ θεμελιούντων τὴν ἐκκλησίαν· μετὰ δὲ τὴν τούτων ἔξοδον Μάρκος, ὁ μαθητὴς καὶ ἑρμηνευτὴς Πέτρου, καὶ αὐτὸς τὰ ὑπὸ Πέτρου κηρυσσόμενα ἐγγράφως ἡμῖν παραδέδωκεν· καὶ Λουκᾶς δέ, ὁ ἀκόλουθος Παύλου, τὸ
4 ὑπ' ἐκείνου κηρυσσόμενον εὐαγγέλιον ἐν βίβλῳ κατέθετο. ἔπειτα Ἰωάννης, ὁ μαθητὴς τοῦ κυρίου, ὁ καὶ ἐπὶ τὸ στῆθος αὐτοῦ ἀναπεσών, καὶ αὐτὸς ἐξέδωκεν τὸ εὐαγγέλιον, ἐν Ἐφέσῳ τῆς Ἀσίας διατρίβων.

3. Der Canon Muratori. Ein Fragment von 85 Zeilen in barbarischem Latein; das Werk ist verfaßt um 200, vielleicht noch etwas früher. Ob es eine Übersetzung aus dem Griechischen ist, läßt sich nicht entscheiden. Die Handschrift, ehemals dem Kloster Bobbio gehörig, befindet sich in Mailand auf der Bibliotheca Ambrosiana (Cod. Ambr. J. 101. Sup.), stammt aus dem 8. Jhdt. und ist 1740 zum erstenmal veröffentlicht worden von LAMuratori. Text bei EPreuschen, Analecta II ^{2}1910, 27ff.; HLietzmann, Kleine Texte Nr. 1 ^{2}1933, dessen Rekonstruktion

3. The Muratorian Canon. A fragment of 85 lines in barbarous Latin; the work is written about A.D. 200, perhaps somewhat earlier. It cannot be decided whether it is a translation from the Greek. The ms, at one time the property of the monastery of Bobbio, is in the Ambrosian library at Milan (Codex Ambr. Ambr. J. 101. Sup.), comes from the 8th century and was first published in 1740 by LAMuratori. The text in EPreuschen, Analecta II ^{2}1910, 27ff.; HLietzmann, Kleine Texte Nr. 1 ^{2}1933, whose reconstruction is printed here. *Lit.*: Altaner

hier abgedruckt ist. *Lit.*: Altaner 94. 560; Kümmel 434ff.; HFrhvCampenhausen, Die Entstehung der christlichen Bibel 1968, 282ff. Die die synoptischen Evv. betreffenden Anfangszeilen lauten:

94. 560; Kümmel 434ff.; HFrhvCampenhausen, Die Entstehung der christlichen Bibel 1968, 282ff. The opening lines concerning the Synoptic Gospels are as follows:

... (ali?)quibus tamen interfuit et ita posuit. Tertium evangelii librum secundum Lucam. Lucas iste medicus post ascensum
5 Christi, cum eum Paulus quasi ut iuris studiosum (itineris socium? litteris stud.?) secum adsumsisset, nomine suo ex opinione conscripsit, dominum tamen nec ipse vidit in carne. Et ideo prout assequi potuit ita et a nativitate Johannis incipit dicere.

4. Clemens Al., Hypotyposes, bei/*in* Eusebius, h. e. VI 14_{5-7} p. 550 (235).

5 Αὖθις δ' ἐν τοῖς αὐτοῖς ὁ Κλήμης βιβλίοις περὶ τῆς τάξεως τῶν εὐαγγελίων παράδοσιν τῶν ἀνέκαθεν πρεσβυτέρων τέθειται,
6 τοῦτον ἔχουσαν τὸν τρόπον· προγεγράφθαι ἔλεγεν τῶν εὐαγγελίων τὰ περιέχοντα τὰς γενεαλογίας. τὸ δὲ κατὰ Μάρκον ταύτην ἐσχηκέναι τὴν οἰκονομίαν. τοῦ Πέτρου δημοσίᾳ ἐν Ῥώμῃ κηρύξαντος τὸν λόγον καὶ πνεύματι τὸ εὐαγγέλιον ἐξειπόντος, τοὺς παρόντας, πολλοὺς ὄντας, παρακαλέσαι τὸν Μάρκον, ὡς ἂν ἀκολουθήσαντα αὐτῷ πόρρωθεν καὶ μεμνημένον τῶν λεχθέντων,
7 ἀναγράψαι τὰ εἰρημένα· ποιήσαντα δέ, τὸ εὐαγγέλιον μεταδοῦναι τοῖς δεομένοις αὐτοῦ· ὅπερ ἐπιγνόντα τὸν Πέτρον προτρεπτικῶς μήτε κωλῦσαι μήτε προτρέψασθαι.

5. Origenes bei/*in* Eusebius, h. e. VI 25_{3-6} p. 576 (245f.).

3 Ἐν δὲ τῷ πρώτῳ τῶν εἰς τὸ κατὰ Ματθαῖον, τὸν ἐκκλησιαστικὸν φυλάττων κανόνα, μόνα τέσσαρα εἰδέναι εὐαγγέλια μαρτύρεται, ὧδέ πως γράφων·

4 „ὡς ἐν παραδόσει μαθὼν περὶ τῶν τεσσάρων εὐαγγελίων, ἃ καὶ μόνα ἀναντίρρητά ἐστιν ἐν τῇ ὑπὸ τὸν οὐρανὸν ἐκκλησίᾳ „τοῦ θεοῦ, ὅτι πρῶτον μὲν γέγραπται τὸ κατὰ τόν ποτε τελώνην, ὕστερον δὲ ἀπόστολον Ἰησοῦ Χριστοῦ Ματθαῖον, ἐκδε-
5 „δωκότα αὐτὸ τοῖς ἀπὸ Ἰουδαϊσμοῦ πιστεύσασιν, γράμμασιν Ἑβραϊκοῖς συντεταγμένον· δεύτερον δὲ τὸ κατὰ Μάρκον, ὡς „Πέτρος ὑφηγήσατο αὐτῷ, ποιήσαντα, ὃν καὶ υἱὸν ἐν τῇ καθολικῇ ἐπιστολῇ διὰ τούτων ὡμολόγησεν φάσκων· »ἀσπάζεται
6 „ὑμᾶς ἡ ἐν Βαβυλῶνι συνεκλεκτὴ καὶ Μάρκος ὁ υἱός μου«· καὶ τρίτον τὸ κατὰ Λουκᾶν, τὸ ὑπὸ Παύλου ἐπαινούμενον εὐαγ- „γέλιον τοῖς ἀπὸ τῶν ἐθνῶν πεποιηκότα· ἐπὶ πᾶσιν τὸ κατὰ Ἰωάννην".

6. Eusebius, h. e. III 24_{5-8} p. 246 (102).

5 Ὅμως δ' οὖν ἐξ ἁπάντων τῶν τοῦ κυρίου διατριβῶν ὑπομνήματα Ματθαῖος ἡμῖν καὶ Ἰωάννης μόνοι καταλελοίπασιν· οὓς
6 καὶ ἐπάναγκες ἐπὶ τὴν γραφὴν ἐλθεῖν κατέχει λόγος. Ματθαῖός τε γὰρ πρότερον Ἑβραίοις κηρύξας, ὡς ἤμελλεν καὶ ἐφ' ἑτέρους ἰέναι, πατρίῳ γλώττῃ γραφῇ παραδοὺς τὸ κατ' αὐτὸν εὐαγγέλιον, τὸ λεῖπον τῇ αὐτοῦ παρουσίᾳ τούτοις ἀφ' ὧν ἐστέλλετο,
7 διὰ τῆς γραφῆς ἀπεπλήρου· ἤδη δὲ Μάρκου καὶ Λουκᾶ τῶν κατ' αὐτοὺς εὐαγγελίων τὴν ἔκδοσιν πεποιημένων, Ἰωάννην
8 φασὶ τὸν πάντα χρόνον ἀγράφῳ κεχρημένον κηρύγματι, τέλος καὶ ἐπὶ τὴν γραφὴν ἐλθεῖν ... Τοὺς τρεῖς γοῦν εὐαγγελιστὰς συνιδεῖν πάρεστιν μόνα τὰ μετὰ τὴν ἐν τῷ δεσμωτηρίῳ Ἰωάννου τοῦ βαπτιστοῦ κάθειρξιν ἐφ' ἕνα ἐνιαυτὸν πεπραγμένα τῷ σωτῆρι συγγεγραφότας αὐτό τε τοῦτ' ἐπισημηναμένους κατ' ἀρχὰς τῆς αὐτῶν ἱστορίας.

7. Hieronymus, Comm. in Mattheum, Praefatio, 26-39

Primus omnium Mattheus est publicanus cognomine Levi, qui evangelium in Judaea hebraeo sermone edidit: ob eorum vel maxime causam, qui in Jesum crediderant ex Judaeis et nequaquam legis umbram succedente evangelii veritate servabant.

Secundus Marcus interpres apostoli Petri et Alexandrinae ecclesiae primus episcopus, qui dominum quidem salvatorem ipse non vidit, sed ea quae magistrum audierat praedicantem iuxta fidem magis gestorum narravit quam ordinem.

Tertius Lucas medicus natione Syrus Antiochensis, cuius laus in evangelio, qui et ipse discipulus apostoli Pauli in Achaiae Boetiaeque partibus volumen condidit, quaedam altius repetens et, ut ipse in prooemio confitetur, audita magis quam visa describens.

Text nach/*according to* DHurst-MAdriaen, CCL 70, 1969, 2; cf. auch/*also* HLietzmann, l.c. 10; EPreuschen, Analecta II 83.

8. Zu den sogenannten antimarkionitischen Evangelien-Prologen, die de Bruyne und Harnack für alt (160—180) und von gemeinsamer Herkunft hielten, vgl. jetzt JRegul, Die antimarcionitischen Evangelienprologe = Aus der Geschichte der lateinischen Bibel, Heft 6, 1969. Er weist nach, daß die Prologe weder gemeinsamen Ursprungs noch antimarkionitischen Charakters sind und frühestens aus dem IV. Jhdt. stammen. Ein den andern entsprechender Mt-Prolog ist nicht bekannt. Der Lk-Prolog ist als einziger auch griechisch erhalten und wird nachstehend nach Regul (S. 16) aus der Minuskel 1828 abgedruckt. Zu Mk ist die von Regul (S. 29) mit I bezeichnete kürzere und ältere Textform dargeboten. *Lit.*: Kümmel 428.

8. For the so-called antimarcionite prologues to the Gospels which de Bruyne and Harnack held to be old (A.D. 160—180) and to have a common origin, compare now JRegul, Die antimarcionitischen Evangelienprologe = Aus der Geschichte der lateinischen Bibel, vol. 6, 1969. He proves that the prologues have neither a common origin nor yet an antimarcionite character but derive at the earliest from the IVth century. A Mt-Prologue, corresponding to the other prologues, is not known. The Lk-Prologue alone is known also in Greek and is printed below from the minuscule 1828 following Regul (p. 16). For Mk I give the shorter and older form of the text, called by Regul (p. 29) "I". *Lit.*: Kümmel 428

Der Markus-Prolog / *The Prologue to Mark*

... Marcus adseruit, qui colobodactylus est nominatus, ideo quod ad ceteram corporis proceritatem digitos minores habuisset. Iste interpres fuit Petri. Post excessionem ipsius Petri descripsit idem hoc in Italiae partibus evangelium.

Der Lukas-Prolog / *The Prologue to Luke*

Ἔστιν ὁ ἅγιος Λουκᾶς Ἀντιοχεύς, Σύρος τῷ γένει, ἰατρὸς τὴν τέχνην, μαθητὴς ἀποστόλων γενόμενος καὶ ὕστερον Παύλῳ παρακολουθήσας μέχρις τοῦ μαρτυρίου αὐτοῦ δουλεύσας τῷ κυρίῳ ἀπερισπάστως, ἀγύναιος, ἄτεκνος, ἐτῶν ὀγδοήκοντα τεσσάρων ἐκοιμήθη ἐν Θήβαις τῇ μητροπόλει τῆς Βοιωτίας πλήρης πνεύματος ἁγίου.

Οὗτος προυπαρχόντων ἤδη εὐαγγελίων, τοῦ μὲν κατὰ Ματθαῖον ἐν τῇ Ἰουδαίᾳ ἀναγραφέντος, τοῦ δὲ κατὰ Μάρκον ἐν τῇ Ἰταλίᾳ, οὗτος προτραπεὶς ὑπὸ πνεύματος ἁγίου ἐν τοῖς περὶ τὴν Ἀχαίαν τὸ πᾶν τοῦτο συνεγράψατο εὐαγγέλιον δηλῶν διὰ τοῦ προοιμίου τοῦτο αὐτό, ὅτι πρὸ αὐτοῦ ἄλλα ἐστὶ γεγραμμένα καὶ ὅτι ἀναγκαῖον ἦν τοῖς ἐξ ἐθνῶν πιστοῖς τὴν ἀκριβῆ τῆς οἰκονομίας ἐκθέσθαι διήγησιν ὑπὲρ τοῦ μὴ ταῖς Ἰουδαϊκαῖς μυθολογίαις περισπᾶσθαι αὐτοὺς μήτε ταῖς αἱρετικαῖς καὶ κεναῖς φαντασίαις ἀπατωμένους ἀστοχῆσαι τῆς ἀληθείας· ὡς ἀναγκαιοτάτην οὖν οὖσαν εὐθὺς ἐν ἀρχῇ παρειλήφαμεν τὴν τοῦ Ἰωάννου γέννησιν, ὅς ἐστιν ἀρχὴ τοῦ εὐαγγελίου πρόδρομος τοῦ κυρίου γενόμενος καὶ κοινωνὸς ἔν τε τῷ καταρτισμῷ τοῦ εὐαγγελίου καὶ τῇ τοῦ βαπτίσματος διαγωγῇ καὶ τῇ τοῦ πνεύματος κοινωνίᾳ. ταύτης τῆς οἰκονομίας μέμνηται προφήτης ἐν τοῖς δώδεκα.

Καὶ δὴ μετέπειτα ἔγραψεν ὁ αὐτὸς Λουκᾶς Πράξεις Ἀποστόλων· ὕστερον δὲ Ἰωάννης ὁ ἀπόστολος ἐκ τῶν δώδεκα ἔγραψεν τὴν Ἀποκάλυψιν ἐν τῇ νήσῳ Πάτμῳ καὶ μετὰ ταῦτα τὸ εὐαγγέλιον.

II. Der Text der Synopse. *II. The Text of the Synopsis.*

1. Vom Evangelientext ist für die 13. Auflage der Huck'schen Synopse eine völlig neue Rezension hergestellt worden. Sie weicht je Kapitel durchschnittlich neunmal vom Greek New Testament ^{3}1975 (= Nestle-Aland ^{26}1979) ab — orthographische und itazistische Varianten nicht gerechnet.

2. In aufrechter Schrift („Gill") ist der durchlaufende Text jedes der drei Evv. gedruckt; auf ihn beziehen sich die Angaben am Kopf der Seite. Auch die beigedruckten Jo-Texte stehen in dieser Schrift. Stücke, die von anderswoher zum Vergleich abgedruckt sind, haben schräge Schrift („*Kursive*"). Wörtliche Zitate aus dem AT sind **fett** gedruckt und am Rande vermerkt.

3. Parallele Texte sind in gleich breiten Kolumnen so angeordnet, daß gleiche oder entsprechende Worte möglichst genau an der gleichen Stelle der Kolumne erscheinen. Die so fortlaufend entstehenden Lücken sind ein Hinweis auf Textverwandtschaft. Parallele Textteile ohne Lücken im Druckbild sind entweder völlig gleich oder völlig verschieden.

22.

4. Der gesamte Stoff ist in fortlaufend numerierte Perikopen eingeteilt. Die Perikopen-Nummern erscheinen in schräger Schrift mit einem Punkt dahinter (zB ***22.***). Sie sind das Hauptmittel für die Querverweise; darum werden sie laufend am Kopf der Seite vermerkt. Die früheren (ab Huck ^{4}1910) Perikopen-Nummern, auf die in der Literatur bisweilen Bezug genommen ist, stehen in der Überschriftszeile am linken Rande in Klammern.

[*85.*]

5. Parallele Texte werden nur an einer Stelle der Synopse vollzählig nebeneinandergestellt (Ausnahmen: Ahnentafel Jesu; Bergpredigt/Feldrede). Auf diesen „Vollvergleich" wird an den anderen Stellen jedesmal mit der umrandeten Perikopen-Nummer (zB [*85.*]) neben dem betreffenden Text — bei ganzen Perikopen außerdem auch rechts neben der Überschrift — hingewiesen (vgl. zB ***99.*** mit ***69.*** und ***163.***). Bietet die Vollvergleichs-Perikope nur die Mt- oder Lk-Parallele, so steht der Hinweis in der ersten bzw. dritten, andernfalls in der mittleren Spalte.

6. Aus dem Jo-Ev. sind alle Texte aufgenommen, die mit den synoptischen formal oder inhaltlich vergleichbar sind. Sie stehen stark umrandet rechts neben der Lk-Spalte. Auch die Jo-Texte sind nach Möglichkeit gleichgestellt (3. ←).

7. Sind mehrere Texte aus dem gleichen Ev. nebeneinandergestellt, so sind sie durch punktierte Linien getrennt (zB ***26.***).

...

8. Drei Punkte (...) vor oder nach einem Text bedeuten, daß

1. For the 13th edition of Huck's Synopsis I have made a quite new recension of the text of the Gospels. On the average it departs some nine times in each chapter from the Greek New Testament ^{3}(1975) = Nestle-Aland ^{26}(1979), orthographical and itacistic variants not being taken into account.

2. The continuous text of each of the three Gospels is printed in upright type ("Gill"); to it refers the information at the top of the page. The texts from John which are printed with the Synoptic Gospels are in the same type. Passages from elsewhere which are printed for comparison are in *cursive* type. Verbal citations from the OT are in **heavy** type and are indicated in the margin.

3. Parallel texts are so arranged in columns of equal width that the same or corresponding words appear as nearly as possible in the same place in the column. The gaps which have come into being in this way in the continuous text are an indication of relationship between the passages. Parallel passages in the text which have no gaps in the print are either completely the same or completely different.

4. The whole text is divided into continuously numbered pericopes. The pericope numbers are in cursive type followed by a full stop (e. g. ***22.***). They are the principal means for cross references; for this reason they are continuously indicated at the top of the page. The earlier pericope numbers which were indicated from Huck ^{4}1910 onwards, to which reference is made from time to time in literature on the subject, are in brackets on the same line with the heading in the left margin.

5. Parallel passages are printed in full, side by side only once (exceptions: the Genealogies, the Sermon on the Mount/the Sermon on the Plain). At all other places reference is made to the "comparison in full" i. e. the pericope, where the texts are all printed in full, by means of pericope numbers enclosed in an ablong (e. g. [*85.*]) beside the relevant text — in the case of complete pericopes it is placed in addition to the right of the heading (cp. e. g. ***99.*** with ***69.*** and ***163.***). Where only parallels from Mt and Lk are printed in full, then the indication stands in the first or third column, otherwise it stands in the middle (i. e. second) column.

6. From Jo I have included all texts which are comparable with the Synoptic Gospels in form or content. They are printed in thick lines on the right of the Lk column. The texts from Jo are also so arranged as far as possible that word corresponds to word in the parallel (3. ←).

7. If more texts from the same Gospel are printed one beside another, then they are separated by lines of dots (e. g. ***26.***).

8. Three dots before or after a passage indicate that a prece-

ein vorangehender bzw. anschließender Teil des Verses oder Satzes weggelassen ist. Drei Punkte zwischen zwei Texten machen darauf aufmerksam, daß sie in ihrem Ev. nicht unmittelbar aufeinander folgen.

9. Vers- und Kapitelzahlen stehen in Klammern — (^{47}), (*7*), vgl. ***143.***, ***89.*** —, wenn der Vers bzw. das Kapitel nach Unterbrechung wieder einsetzt.

10. Auf flüchtigere Wort- oder Sachparallelen in anderen Perikopen wird durch „*cf.*" mit Perikopennummer hingewiesen, zB „*cf. 222.*" in Perikope ***221.***, und umgekehrt.

11. Zur Orthographie.

a. Nichtgriechische Wörter, die nicht dekliniert werden, bleiben ohne Akzente und Spiritus (nach dem Vorgang von Rahlfs' Septuaginta-Ausgabe).

b. Grundsätzlich ist -ρρ- verdoppelt (Bl.-Debr. § 11,1), ν in συν- assimiliert, bewegliches ν nach ε und ι stehen gelassen (Ausnahme: -σιν dat. pl., → c.), steht γιν- (nicht γιγν-), λήμψω (nicht λήψω).

c. Den jeweils ältesten Zeugen folge ich beim Schwanken zwischen attischen, Koine- und anderen Formen in den folgenden und ähnlichen Fällen: in der Deklination bei -ρας/-ρης, -αρχος/-αρχης, κλεῖς/κλεῖδας, πλείονας/πλείους, -σι/-σιν (dat. pl.); bei εὐθύς/εὐθέως; in der Konjugation bei Unregelmäßigkeiten in Augment und Reduplikation, beim Wechsel zwischen 1. und 2. Aorist und Futur sowie bei -ον/-α usw im 2. Aor. Akt. und Med.; außerdem bei Schwanken zwischen σπυρίς/σφ-, πλέων/πλεί-, ἀμφιέζω/-άζω, ἀποκτείνω/-έννω/-έννυμι, ἐδυνήθην/-άσθην, ἔδυν/-υσα, ἔσθω/-ίω, ἤκουσιν/-ασιν, ῥήγνυμι/ῥήσσω, εἶτα/-εν, ἕνεκα/-εν.

d. Bei der Elision ἀλλ' (statt ἀλλά) habe ich mich nach Bl.-Debr. ^{15}1979 § 17 gerichtet, in vielen anderen Fällen (zB ἑόρακα statt ἑώ-) nach PKatz (Bespr. von Bl.-Debr. ^{9}1954 in ThLZ 82, 1957, 110—115 und Bespr. von Nestle-Aland ^{23}1957 ebda 83, 1958, 313—318; vgl. Ders. = PWalters, The Text of the Septuagint, 1973, 73 u. ö.).

ding or following portion of the text has been left out. Three dots between two passages warn us that they do not follow each other immediately in their Gospel.

9. Verse and chapter numbers are in brackets (^{47}), (*7*), cp. ***143.***, ***89.***, if the verse or chapter is resumed after an interruption.

(^{47}) (*7*)

10. Minor parallels in wording or meaning within other pericopes are referred to by "*cf.*" and the number of the pericope, e. g. "*cf. 222.*" in pericope ***221.*** and vice versa.

cf. 222.

11. Orthography.

a. Non-Greek words which are not declined are printed without accents and breathings (I follow the precedent of Rahlfs' edition of the Septuagint).

b. Regularly -ρρ- is printed (Bl.-Debr. § 11,1), ν in συν- is assimilated, movable ν after ε and ι is retained (exception: -σιν dat. pl., → c.), we print γιν-, not γιγν- and λήμψω, not λήψω.

c. I follow the oldest witnesses available in the fluctuation between Attic, Koine and other forms in the following and similar instances: in declension between -ρας/-ρης, -αρχος/-αρχης, κλεῖς/κλεῖδας, πλείονας/πλείους, -σι/-σιν (dat. pl.); between εὐθύς/εὐθέως; in conjugation in irregularities in augment and reduplication, in the variation between first and second aorist and future, between -ον/-α etc. in the second aorist active and middle; in addition in the fluctuation between σπυρίς/σφ-, πλέων/πλεί-, ἀμφιέζω and -άζω, ἀποκτείνω/-έννω/-έννυμι, ἐδυνήθην/-άσθην, ἔδυν/-υσα, ἔσθω/-ίω, ἤκουσιν/-ασιν, ῥήγνυμι/ῥήσσω, εἶτα/-εν, ἕνεκα/-εν.

d. For elision with ἀλλά (ἀλλ') I have followed Bl.-Debr. ^{15}1979 § 17 and in many other instances (e. g. ἑόρακα instead of ἑώ-) PKatz (review of Bl.-Debr. ^{9}1954 in ThLZ 82, 1957, 110—115 and review of Nestle-Aland ^{23}1957 ibid. 83, 1958, 313—318 and under the name of PWalters, The Text of the Septuagint, 1973, 73 and elswhere).

III. Der erste Apparat. *III. The First Apparatus.*

1. Der 1. App. enthält eine Auswahl der in der Überlieferung bezeugten Abweichungen (Varianten) vom Text dieser Synopse (= *txt*). Aufgenommen wurden:

a. Alle Varianten, die in den Ausgaben von Tischendorf (octava maior 1869), Westcott-Hort (1881), v. Soden (1913), Merk (^{9}1964), Nestle-Aland (^{25}1963), im Greek New Testament (^{3}1975) und von einigen anderen Textkritikern als Urtext angenommen worden sind. Sie sind durch ● hervorgehoben. Wo ich selbst nur bis zu einem „non liquet" gelangt bin, steht ◆, d. h.: diese Variante kann ebensogut den Urtext darstellen wie *txt*.

b. Alle griechisch bezeugten Varianten, die — ob erkennbar absichtlich oder nicht — den *txt* mehr oder weniger einer andern Textstelle angleichen (vgl. das Vorwort S. VI).

c. Griechisch nicht bezeugte Varianten, wenn sie für die Beurteilung der Varianten unter a. und b. (←) aufschlußreich sind.

2. Nicht als Varianten wurden behandelt:

a. Die unter II.11.c. und d. (←) aufgeführten Wechselformen.

b. Alle itazistischen Schreibungen (ι statt η, ει, οι; ε statt αι; ο statt ω und umgekehrt; υ statt οι). Vielmehr wurden alle Itazismen nach den Schulregeln korrigiert, es sei denn, daß sie verschiedene Deutungen erlaubten (z. B. παρενεγκαι Lk22₄₂).

c. Wechsel zwischen ὃς ἄν/ὃς ἐάν und ähnliches, αὐτοῦ/ἑαυ-, ἐκχύνω/-ννω, κἀγώ/καὶ ἐγώ, κἀκεῖ/καὶ ἐκεῖ, οὕτω/-ως.

1. The 1st app. contains a selection of the variants to the text of this Synopsis (= *txt*). It contains:

txt

a. all the variants from this *txt* in the text of Tischendorf (octava maior 1869), Westcott and Hort (1881), von Soden (1913), Merk ^{9}(1964), Nestle-Aland^{25} (1963), the Greek New Testament^{3} (1975) and variants preferred by some other textual critics as being original. They are marked by ●. Where I have been able only to decide *non liquet* I have put ◆, i. e. this variant has just as good claim to be original as the *txt*.

● ◆

b. all variants extant in Greek which, deliberately or not, assimilate the text more or less closely to that of another passage in the Synoptic Gospels (see the preface p. VI).

c. variants not extant in Greek if they are relevant to decisions about variants in a. and b. (←).

2. Readings are not treated as variants, if they are

a. alternative forms detailed under II.11.c. and d. (←).

b. itacisms (ι for η, ει and οι; ε instead of αι; ο instead of ω and vice versa). Instead all itacisms are corrected according to the rules of grammar unless they admit of alternative interpretations (e. g. παρενεγκαι Lk22₄₂).

c. variations between ὃς ἄν/ὃς ἐάν and similarly; αὐτοῦ/ἑαυ-, ἐκχύνω/-ννω, κἀγώ/καὶ ἐγώ, κἀκεῖ/καὶ ἐκεῖ, οὕτω/-ως.

— | **3.** Textkritische Angaben zur gleichen Stelle im *txt* werden durch „—", solche zu verschiedenen Stellen durch „|" getrennt. Varianten zu verschiedenen Textstellen können sachlich zusammengehören; sie werden gleichwohl getrennt aufgeführt, wenn damit bessere Übersichtlichkeit gewonnen wird.

4. Jede textkritische Angabe teilt eine Abweichung vom *txt* mit und nennt die bisher bekannten Zeugen dafür. Variantenteil und Zeugenteil sind jeweils durch einen Doppelpunkt (:) getrennt.

A. Der Variantenteil.

1. Zur eindeutigen Darstellung der Variante dient das dem *txt* entnommene Lemma (eigentlich: das Herausgegriffene), das durch die Variante entweder

] **a.** ersetzt, zB αυτος] ο Ιησους (] = „wird ersetzt durch"),

\+ *prm* **b.** erweitert, zB αυτος + δε oder αυτος *prm* (= praemittit) και (= και αυτος) (doch → h.),

om **c.** ausgelassen, zB *om* αυτος (auch: αυτος] *om*) oder

∼ **d.** umgestellt wird, zB ∼ αυτος και.

In a.—c. ist Lemma das αυτος, in d. das και αυτος des *txt* (entsprechend bei drei und mehr Worten nach ∼). Außer wenn ... (→ f.) steht, bilden die Worte nach ∼ im *txt* (oder in der Hauptvariante) eine geschlossene Folge.

e. Differiert die Variante vom *txt* nur in Wortteilen, so wird dies durch Sperrung angezeigt: α ν ε λ θ ο ν τ ω ν statt εξελθοντος] ανελθοντων. Als Lemma gilt jedoch das εξελθοντος des *txt*.

f. Das Lemma kann räumlich getrennte Textteile zusammenfassen, zB γαρ ... εφη] δε ... ελεγεν (d. h.: statt γαρ τοις μαθηταις εφη hat die Variante δε τοις μαθηταις ελεγεν). Der zwischen den beiden Textteilen liegende *txt* ist nicht betroffen (→ dagegen 3.b.). Mehrere auf das gleiche Lemma bezogene Varianten werden durch „—" getrennt. Jede auf ein „—" folgende Variante bezieht sich unmittelbar auf das Lemma zurück, das nach dem letzten vorhergehenden „|" (bzw. fetter Verszahl) angegeben ist; beachte jedoch d. und e. (←).

g. Dabei kann der unmittelbare Kontext des Lemmas einbezogen werden, zB παντα] ταυτα: ABC — ∼ παντα γαρ: DEF d. h.: ABC lesen ταυτα statt παντα; DEF behalten παντα, aber das im *txt* davorstehende γαρ wird umgestellt (eine Neu-Hinzufügung von γαρ müßte mit „+ γαρ" angezeigt werden).

h. Oft gibt das Lemma vor + (b. ←) lediglich die Stelle für die mit + angezeigte Erweiterung an, auch für Zeugen, in denen das Lemma-Wort selbst fehlt, zB δε + αυτοις: ABC(*om* δε) — d. h.: AB haben an dieser Stelle δε αυτοις, C nur αυτοις.

i. Werden die Zeugen für den *txt* genannt, so stehen sie am Schluß der Anmerkung, eingeleitet durch „*txt*:". Wenn die Angabe nichts enthielte außer bloßem „*txt*: *Rpl*" (→ B.2.i.), so ist sie in der Regel weggelassen.

2. Nebenformen, Weiterbildungen usw. von Varianten werden nicht als selbständige, sondern als Untervarianten dargestellt. Diese Unterscheidung dient lediglich darstellungstechnischen Zwecken und sagt nichts über die Bedeutung einer Variante aus. Untervarianten (= Varianten von Varianten) stehen in runden

() Klammern (), und zwar

a. im Variantenteil mit entsprechender Klammer im Zeugenteil (die eine Klammer enthält nur Variantentext, die andere nur Zeugen-Angaben), zB

1. ∼ πολλοις αλλοις(*om*) λογοις: AB(C) — d. h.: C hat die gleiche Umstellung wie A und B, läßt jedoch αλλοις (nur dieses! → d.2.) aus.

3. Textual notes to the same place in the *txt* are separated by an horizontal stroke (—); such notes as relate to different places are separated by a vertical stroke (|). Variants to different places in the *txt* can belong together; however, they are presented separately if this makes for greater clarity.

4. Every textual note in the apparatus reports a departure from the *txt* and details the witnesses for it as far as they are known. The variant and the witnesses to it are always separated by a colon (:).

A. The Variants.

1. In order to give an unambiguous presentation of the variant the lemma (originally = that which is taken) is taken from the *txt*. It is either

a. replaced by the variant as in αυτος] ο Ιησους (] = is replaced by);

b. enlarged e. g. αυτος + δε or αυτος *prm* (= praemittit) και (= και αυτος) (but → h.);

c. left out e. g. *om* αυτος (also αυτος] *om*) or

d. rearranged e. g. ∼ αυτος και.

In a.—c. the lemma is αυτος; in d. the lemma is και αυτος from the *txt* (correspondingly for three or more words after ∼). Unless ... (→ f.) occurs, the words following ∼ form a continuous passage also in the *txt* (or in the principle variant).

e. If the variant differs from the *txt* only in part of the word, this is indicated by spacing: α ν ε λ θ ο ν τ ω ν instead of εξελθοντος] ανελθοντων. εξελθοντος in the *txt* is, however, reckoned as the lemma.

f. The lemma can bring together portions of the *txt* which are not continuous with each other, e. g. γαρ ... εφη] δε ... ελεγεν (i. e. instead of γαρ τοις μαθηταις εφη we have the variant δε τοις μαθηταις ελεγεν). The portion of the *txt* which lies between the two words, γαρ and εφη, is not affected (different from 3.b. →). Where the same lemma has more than one variant the variants are separated by means of a horizontal stroke "—". Each variant following "—" refers immediately back to the lemma which is printed after the last preceding vertical stroke "|" or verse number in black type; but observe d. and e. (←).

g. The immediate context of the lemma may be implied, e. g. παντα] ταυτα: ABC — ∼ παντα γαρ: DEF i. e. ABC read ταυτα instead of παντα; DEF retain παντα but change the position of γαρ which immediately precedes it in the *txt* (an addition of γαρ would have to be indicated by "+ γαρ").

h. Often the lemma before + (b. ←) merely gives the place for the enlargment indicated by +, even for witnesses in which the word serving as lemma is itself lacking, e. g. δε] + αυτοις: ABC(*om* δε) i. e. AB have here δε αυτοις but C only αυτοις.

i. If the witnesses for the *txt* are named, then they stand at the conclusion of the note and are introduced by "*txt*:". If this indication should consist only in a mere note "*txt*: *Rpl*" (→ B.2.i.), then as a rule it would be omitted.

2. Alternative forms and developments etc. of variants are not presented as independent, but as dependent variants. This distinction serves merely the purposes of presentation and has nothing to say about the significance of a variant. Dependent variants (i. e. variants to variants) are put in round brackets and in particular

a. in the part giving the variant with corresponding brackets in the part giving the witnesses (one set of brackets contains only the text of the variant the other set only the witnesses) e. h.

1. ∼ πολλοις αλλοις(*om*) λογοις: AB(C), i. e. C has the same change of order as A and B, but omits αλλοις (only this word, → d.2.);

2. ~ πολλοις λογοις (+ και): A(B)C — d. h.: B hat die gleiche Umstellung wie A und C, läßt jedoch ein και folgen.

3. ~ πολλοις λογοις (*et om* ο Ιησους): (A)BC — d. h.: A hat die gleiche Umstellung wie B und C, läßt jedoch das ο Ιησους des *txt* aus.

4. ~ πολλοις(αλλοις) λογοις: A(BC) — d. h.: B und C haben die gleiche Umstellung wie A, ersetzen jedoch πολλοις durch αλλοις (Klammer in Kontaktstellung! → d.1.).

5. πολλοις +(*prm*) αλλοις: AB(C) — d. h.: A und B fügen αλλοις hinter πολλοις ein, C davor.

6. ~ πολλοις αλλοις(*om*) λογοις: (A, *et* λο. + ετεροις)B(C) — d. h.: ABC stellen um, aber A und C lassen αλλοις aus (→ d.2.), wofür A nach λογοις einfügt: ετεροις (zu dieser Varianten-Anzeige im Zeugenteil → c.bb.3.).

b. nur im Variantenteil (die Klammer nennt außer dem Variantentext auch die Zeugen), zB

1. ~ πολλοις λογοις (+ και: B): ABC — identisch mit a.2. (←); B, der Zeuge für „+ και", bleibt im Zeugenteil ohne Klammer, da vorher schon erwähnt.

2. ~ πολλοις(αλλοις: BC) λογοις: ABC — identisch mit a.4. (←); BC bleiben im Zeugenteil ohne Klammer.

c. nur im Zeugenteil;

aa. die Klammer enthält Variantentext und Zeugen, zB

1. ~ πολλοις λογοις: A(+ και: B)C — identisch mit a.2. und b.1. (←).

2. ~ πολλοις λογοις: A(πολλοις] αλλοις: BC) — identisch mit a.4. und b.2. (←).

bb. die Klammer enthält nur den Variantentext. Dann betrifft sie nur den in Kontaktstellung unmittelbar vorhergehenden Zeugen (Zeugengruppe; doch → bb.2.), zB

1. ~ πολλοις αλλοις λογοις: ABC(*om* αλλοις) — identisch mit a.1. (←).

2. ~ πολλοις λογοις: ABC *Lvg*[4](+ και) *Cs*[1:9](+ παλιν) — d. h.: vier Vulgata-Hss haben ein Äquivalent für και, eine von neun sah. Hss hat παλιν nach der auch von ABC bezeugten Umstellung.

3. ~ πολλοις λογοις: A(*et om* ο Ιησους)BC — identisch mit a.3. (←).

4. πολλοις + αλλοις: ABC(~) — identisch mit a.5. (←). Besteht das Lemma oder, wie hier, die Hauptvariante nur aus zwei Worten, so werden diese nach ~ bzw. (~) nicht wiederholt. So ist (~) immer zu verstehen, wenn nur zwei Worte genannt sind. Dagegen

5. λογοις] λογοις τοιουτοις πολλοις: AB(~)C — d. h.: wie A und C fügt auch B τοιουτοις πολλοις hinzu, allerdings mit einer hier nicht mitzuteilenden Umstellung, die jedoch den Zeugenwert für den Zusatz nicht beeinträchtigt.

cc. die Klammer enthält nur Zeugen, ohne daß — wie bei a. (←) — im Variantenteil eine Klammer mit nur Variantentext als Entsprechung auftritt, zB ~ πολλοις λογοις: AB(C) — d. h.: C ist zwar Zeuge der Umstellung, bietet aber gleichzeitig eine Abweichung, die hier nicht mitgeteilt wird, bisweilen weil sie sachlich nicht zur Variante gehört, meist aber deshalb, weil sie aus einer vorhergehenden oder folgenden Anmerkung ersichtlich ist.

d. 1. Folgt auf ein Wort des Variantentextes *ohne Zwischenraum* („Kontaktstellung") Text in *runden* Klammern, so bedeutet das: in einer Untervariante tritt der Klammertext anstelle des letzten Wortes — nur dieses! — vor der Klammer.

2. ~ πολλοις λογοις (+ και): A(B)C, i. e. B has the same change of order as A and C, but adds και at the end;

3. ~ πολλοις λογοις (*et om* ο Ιησους): (A)BC, i. e. A has the same change of order as BC, but omits ο Ιησους from the *txt*;

4. ~ πολλοις(αλλοις) λογοις:: A(BC), i. e. B and C have the same change of order as A, but substitute αλλοις for πολλοις (brackets in immediate sequence, → d. 1.);

5. πολλοις +(*prm*) αλλοις: AB(C), i. e. AB add αλλοις after πολλοις, C adds it before;

6. ~ πολλοις αλλοις(*om*) λογοις: (A, *et* λο. + ετεροις)B(C), i. e. ABC have the change in order, but AC omit αλλοις (→ d.2.), and in addition A adds ετεροις after λογοις. (For this indication of a variant in the part for witnesses → c.bb.3.); or

b. brackets are used only in the part giving the variant (within the brackets both the variant and the witnesses for it are given) e. g.

1. ~ πολλοις λογοις (+ και: B): ABC. This annotation has the same significance as that in a.2. (←); B, the witness for + και remains unbracketed in the part giving the witnesses, since it is already mentioned.

2. ~ πολλοις(αλλοις: BC) λογοις: ABC, identical with a.4. (←); BC are unbracketed in the part for the witnesses; or

c. brackets are used only in the part giving the witnesses; either

aa. the brackets enclose the text of the variant and the witnesses thereto, e. g.

1. ~ πολλοις λογοις: A(+ και: B)C, identical with a.2. and b.1. (←).

2. ~ πολλοις λογοις: A(πολλοις] αλλοις: BC), identical with a.4. and b.2. (←); or

bb. the brackets enclose only the text of the variant. In this case they concern only the witness (or group of witnesses, but → bb.2.) immediately preceding, e. g.

1. ~ πολλοις αλλοις λογοις: ABC(*om* αλλοις), identical with a. 1. (←).

2. ~ πολλοις λογοις: ABC *Lvg*[4](+ και) *Cs*[1:9](+ παλιν), i. e. four Vulgate mss have an equivalent for και, one out of nine sah. mss has παλιν after the change in order which occurs also in ABC.

3. ~ πολλοις λογοις: A(*et om* ο Ιησους)BC, identical with a.3. (←).

4. πολλοις + αλλοις: ABC(~), identical with a.5. (←). If the lemma or, as here, the principal variant consists of only two words, then these words are not repeated after ~ or (~) respectively. We must always understand the sign (~) in this way when only two words are given.

(~)

5. On the contrary λογοις] λογοις τοιουτοις πολλοις: A B(~)C, i. e. like AC, B adds τοιουτοις πολλοις, but with a change in order which is not detailed at this point. It does not modify the the testimony of B for this addition; or

cc. the brackets contain only witnesses without there being in the part for variants corresponding brackets with only the text of the variant (as described earlier, a. ←), e. g. ~ πολλοις λογοις: AB(C), i. e. C is indeed a witness for the transposition but at the same time has a departure from the text that is not indicated here, sometimes because it does not belong to the substance of the variant, but mostly because it can be inferred from a preceding or following note.

d. 1. If there follows immediately, without anything intervening, on a word in the variant text a text in round brackets, then this has the following meaning: in a dependent variant the last word before the brackets is replaced by the text in brackets.

2. Ebenso bezieht sich (*om*) stets nur auf das letztvorhergegangene Wort.

e. Bei umfangreicheren Varianten, meist Erweiterungen, werden die Untervarianten unmittelbar anschließend in eckigen Doppelklammern ⟦...⟧ aufgeführt, wobei der Text der Hauptvariante dieselbe Rolle spielt wie sonst der *txt*.

⟦ ⟧

3. Abkürzung.

a. Einzelne Worte.

1. Abkürzung durch Punkt wird aufgelöst durch das nächstvorhergehende Wort mit gleichem Wortanfang. Als „vorhergehend" gelten zunächst die Anmerkungen zum betreffenden Vers, sodann der *txt* (zB App. zu Lk251: ταυ. = ταυτα wie am Anfang der Anmerkung, ρημ. dagegen = ρηματα wie im *txt*).

2. Bei Präfixen und Endungen kann, wenn die Beziehung eindeutig ist, der Rest des Wortes durch Bindestrich ersetzt werden, zB εξηλθεν(αν-) statt εξηλθεν(ανηλθεν), ελευσεται] -ονται statt ελευσεται] ελευσονται, εβαλλον(-λ-) statt εβαλλον(εβαλον).

b. Größere Textteile.

Eine zusammenhängende Partie des *txt* oder einer Variante kann durch Anfangs- und Endwort, verbunden durch waagerechten Strich, dargestellt werden, zB (1) και[1]—κυριος] εφη δε statt και παλιν αποκριθεις ελεγεν και τουτω ο κυριος] εφη δε oder (2) ~ εδιδασκεν εν—θεου statt εν τω ιερω του θεου εδιδασκεν] εδιδασκεν εν τω ιερω του θεου.

4. Parallelen-Hinweise.

a. Der Darbietung der Variante folgt in der Regel ein Hinweis auf die Stellen, denen der *txt* durch die Variante mehr oder weniger angenähert wird. Der Hinweis wird angekündigt durch „‖", bei allgemeiner gebrauchten Redewendungen durch „*cf.*".

cf.

b. In der Reihe der Parallelstellen stehen diejenigen aus dem gleichen Ev. — mit der bloßen Verszahl, falls aus der gleichen Perikope, sonst mit Kapitel- und Verszahl — voran. Dann folgen die übrigen Evv. in der üblichen Reihenfolge. Abweichung von dieser Reihenfolge bzw. von Kapitel- und Versfolge bedeutet, daß die Vorangestellten die engere Parallele bieten.

c. Die Paralleltexte, die in der gleichen Perikope — oder im zugehörigen Vollvergleich (II.5.←)! — beigedruckt sind, werden mit dem bloßen Evangelistennamen, nur erforderlichenfalls mit Vers- oder Kapitel- (und Vers-)Zahl zitiert.

d. Ist der Text einer Parallele ohne jedes Schwanken (auch in den Übersetzungen und Schriftstellern) überliefert („*nfl*" = non fluctuat), so wird dies durch **halbfetten** Druck des ersten Buchstabens bzw. der ersten Zahl der Parallelen-Angabe hervorgehoben; **M**k3**2**4.28 Lk17**2**1.23 bedeutet zB: beide Mk- und der zweite der Lk-Verse sind an dieser Stelle *nfl*. Gegebenenfalls wird auch **p** halbfett gedruckt (→ e. und f.).

nfl

e. ‖p bedeutet, daß alle in der betreffenden Perikope oder im zugehörigen Vollvergleich (! c. ←) beigedruckten synoptischen Parallelstellen verglichen werden sollen. Trifft das gleiche auf eine beigedruckte Jo-Parallele zu, so wird sie neben p nicht besonders genannt.

p

f. p nach einer Synoptikerstelle oder einem sie vertretenden ← (→ g.) bedeutet: alle bei dieser Stelle in Stammperikope oder Vollvergleich beigedruckten Parallelen, zB (fingiert): Im Apparat zu *171.* Lk1230 würde ‖p 31p Mk1014 **M**t1211p bedeuten: Mt 68.32 Lk1231 Mt633 (so wegen **47.**) Mk1014 (hervorgehoben durch

2. In the same way (*om*) refers only to the last preceding word.

e. In more comprehensive variants, mainly additions, the dependent variants are introduced in double square brackets ⟦—⟧, immediately following the text to which they relate, so that the text of the principle variant plays the same part as the *txt* itself otherwise does.

3. Abbreviation.

a. Separate words.

1. Words abbreviated with a full stop are to be completed from the nearest preceding word with the same beginning in the app. to the same verse. If we cannot find the word in the app., then we look for it in the *txt*, e. g. we have in the app. to Lk251: ταυ. = ταυτα in the preceding part oi the app., while ρημ. in the same note stands for the ρηματα of the *txt*.

2. With prefixes and endings the rest of the word can be replaced by a hyphen, if the reference is unambiguous, e. g. εξηλθεν(αν-) instead of εξηλθεν(ανηλθεν), ελευσεται] -ονται instead of ελευσεται] ελευσονται, εβαλλον(-λ-) instead of εβαλλον(εβαλον).

b. Larger Portions of the Text.

A continuous portion of the text or of a variant can be represented by means of the first and last word joined by a horizontal line, e. g. (1) και[1]—κυριος] εφη δε instead of και παλιν αποκριθεις ελεγεν και τουτω ο κυριος] εφη δε or (2) ~ εδιδασκεν εν—θεου instead of εν τω ιερω του θεου εδιδασκεν] εδιδασκεν εν τω ιερω του θεου.

4. The Indication of Parallels.

a. As a rule there follows on the detailing of a variant an indication of the passages to which the variant assimilates the *txt*. This is generally shown by means of "‖", but with widely used expressions by means of "*cf.*".

b. In the series of parallel passages there come first the passages from the same Gospel. Chapter numbers are given only for passages from other pericopes. Then there follow the passages from the other Gospels in the usual sequence. Departures from this sequence or from the sequence of chapters and verses indicate that the passages which come first provide a closer parallel.

c. Parallel passages which are printed adjacently in the same pericope — or in the place where the appropriate parallels are given in full (II.5. ←)! — are cited merely with the name of the Gospel; only when it is particularly required are they provided with verse or chapter numbers.

d. If the text of a parallel passage is handed down without any variation (this includes the ancient translations and authors) ("*nfl*" = non fluctuat), then this is emphasized by printing the first letter or number in the indication of the parallel in **half-thick** type; **M**k3**2**4.28 Lk17**2**1.23 means that both verses in Mk and the second in Lk are *nfl* in that passage. On such occasions p as well is printed in half-thick type: **p** (→ e. and f.).

e. ‖p means that we must compare all Synoptic parallels in the relevant pericope or in the place where the appropriate parallels are given in full (c. ←). In this case no especial reference is made to any parallels that there may be in the text of Jo printed adjacently.

f. p following a Synoptic passage or an arrow which represents it (→ g.) indicates all parallels printed adjacently to this passage in the original pericope or in the place where the parallels are given in full, e. g. (invented examples): in the apparatus to Lk1230 (*171.*) ‖p 31p Mk1014 **M**t1211p would mean: Mt68.32

Voranstellung: engere Parallele als) Mt1211 *nfl* (d. ←) Lk 1315145 (beigedruckt in ***82.***).

g. ‖← (bzw. *cf.* ←) bedeutet: alles nach dem letzten vorhergehenden ‖ (bzw. *cf.*) Aufgezählte. Das letzte vorhergehende ‖ (bzw. *cf.*) kann auch in der Anmerkung zu einem früheren Vers stehen. Mk ← bedeutet: die vorher zuletzt genannte Mk-Stelle, gegebenenfalls auch in früheren Versen. Die Wiederholung durch ← betrifft auch den *nfl*-Charakter (Halbfettdruck) einer Stelle (d. ←).

h. Wo erforderlich, wird bei AT-Stellen unterschieden zwischen MT (= masoretischer Text) und LXX (= Septuaginta-Übersetzung), zB Ps224 MT oder Ps847 LXX.

i. Parallelstellen in runden Klammern — zB (Lk41p) — beziehen sich auf die vorhergehende in runden Klammern angegebene Untervariante (2.a. und b. ←).

Lk1231 Mt633 (so because of **47.**) Mk1014 (emphasized by being printed in advance: a closer parallel than) Mt1211 *nfl* (d. ←) Lk1315 145 (printed adjacently in ***82.***).

g. ‖← (or *cf.* ←) indicates everything enumerated after the last preceding instance of ‖ (or *cf.*). The last preceding ‖ (or *cf.*) can also stand in the annotation to an earlier verse. Mk ← means: the last previously mentioned Mk passage, which may be found also in a previous verse. Where ← indicates the parallels it implies also the *nfl* character (halfthick type) of a passage (d. ←).

‖← *cf.*←

Mk←

h. Where it is required, for OT passages I distinguish between MT (= masoretic text) and LXX (= the Septuagint translation), e. g. Ps224 MT or Ps847 LXX.

MT, LXX

i. Parallel passages in round brackets, e. g. (Lk41p), relate to a subordinate variant already indicated in round brackets (2.a. and b. ←).

B. Der Zeugenteil.

1. Allgemein.

a. Die Zeugen werden, nach Sprachen gruppiert, in folgender Reihenfolge aufgeführt (in Klammern der zugehörige Kennbuchstabe): griechische (ohne Kennbuchstabe), lateinische (*L*), syrische (*S*), coptische (*C*), armenische (*Arm*), georgische (*Geo*), äthiopische (*Aeth*), arabische (*Arab*), gotische (*Got*), altslawische (*Slav*). Als letzte Gruppe folgen die (älteren) Evangelien-Harmonien aller Sprachen (*Δ*).

b. Innerhalb der sprachlichen Gruppen werden, in folgender Reihenfolge, aufgeführt

1. die Hss des *laufenden Evangelientextes*. Dabei bedeutet

M*: die ursprüngliche Schrift der Hs.
M^{1}: eine Korrektur durch den ursprünglichen Schreiber.
M^{c}: eine Korrektur durch eine spätere Hand (→ M^{s}).
M^{m}: eine Randnotiz („Marginalie") zur Stelle, die nicht als Korrektur gekennzeichnet ist (→ M^{s}).
M^{cap}: die manchen Hss vorangestellten Kapitellisten mit Inhaltsangabe.
M^{cmt}: den marginalen oder interlinearen Kommentar der Hs.
M^{Od}: die in Vollbibeln zuweilen anzutreffenden Hymnen des AT und NT (aus NT: Lk146-55.68-79 214.29-32).
M^{s}: Text einer später ergänzten Lücke („Supplement") der Hs (vgl. auch Lückenlisten → V.). Dieser Text wird — ebenso wie der von M^{c} und M^{m} — gegebenenfalls bei der Hss-Gruppe aufgeführt, zu der M gehört, ist jedoch nicht in die betreffende Summensigel einbegriffen (→ 2.f. und g.).
M^{sch}: ein Scholion, eine gelehrte Anmerkung in M zur Stelle.
M(*spat.*): M hat an dieser Stelle einen freien Raum gelassen.
M^{t}: der Text der Hs, wo sie Randbemerkungen oder Kommentar hat.
M^{v} (videtur = „offensichtlich"): der angegebene Text ist in M trotz Beschädigung mit annähender Sicherheit auszumachen, zB aus Raumgründen.
M?: die angegebene Lesung ist wegen Beschädigung unsicher.
$א^{a}$, $א^{b}$ ...: verschiedene Korrektoren von א (→ IV.a.).
B^{2}, B^{3} ...: verschiedene Korrektoren von B (→ IV.a.).
D': Codex D (→ IV.a.), wo sein lat. Text (= d, → IV.b.) abweicht, ohne an dieser Stelle genannt zu sein.
F^{W}: → bei F (IV.a.).
$\mathfrak{H}$⟨W⟩ ($\mathfrak{H}$'⟨W⟩): alle (die restlichen) in dem Summensigel $\mathfrak{H}$ (→ 2.g.) zusammengefaßten Hss mit Ausnahme von W. W geht in diesem Fall entweder mit *Rpl*, oder seine Lesung ist nicht

B. The Witnesses.

1. General Principles.

a. The witnesses are grouped according to languages and introduced in the following order (the relevant indicators are in brackets): Greek (without an indicator), Latin (*L*), Syriac (*S*), Coptic (*C*), Armenian (*Arm*), Georgian (*Geo*), Ethiopic (*Aeth*), Arabic (*Arab*), Gothic (*Got*), Old Slavonic (*Slav*). These are followed by the last group, the older Gospel Harmonies in all their languages (*Δ*).

L
S C Arm
Geo Aeth
Arab Got
Slav Δ

b. Within the language groups are introduced in order as follows:

1. the mss of the *continuous* Gospel text. The following abbreviations are used:

M*: the original writing of the ms;
M^{1}: a correction by the original scribe;
M^{c}: a correction by a later hand (→ M^{s});
M^{m}: a marginal note to the passage concerned which is not distinguished as a correction (→ M^{s});
M^{cap}: the list of chapters given at the beginning of many mss which serves as a table of contents;
M^{cmt}: the commentary in the margin or between lines in the ms;
M^{Od}: the collection of hymns from the OT and NT (NT: Lk 146-55.68-79 214.29-32) which occurs from time to time in complete Bibles;
M^{s}: the text of a later supplement in a lacuna of the ms (cf. the list of such lacunae → V.). M^{s}, just like M^{c} and M^{m}, is quoted in the ms group to which M belongs. It is however not indicated under the appropriate group symbol (← 2.f. and g.);
M^{sch}: a scholion, a learned annotation ad loc. in M;
M(*spat.*): M has at this point left an empty space;
M^{t}: the text of M where it has marginal notes or a commentary;
M^{v} (videtur = apparently): the text which is inferred with approximate certainty, e. g. from considerations of space, to be that of M despite damage to the ms;
M?: the reported reading is uncertain because of damage to the ms;
$א^{a}$, $א^{b}$ ...: various correctors of א (→ IV.a.);
B^{2}, B^{3} ...: various correctors of B (→ IV.a.);
D': Codex D (→ IV.a.) where its Lat. text (=d, → IV. b.) is different, but is not reported at this place;
F^{W}: → under F (IV.a.);
$\mathfrak{H}$⟨W⟩ ($\mathfrak{H}$'⟨W⟩): all (or the remaining) mss comprehended in the group symbol $\mathfrak{H}$ (→ 2.g.) with the exception of W. W goes in this case either with *Rpl*, or its reading is not worth men-

* 1 c m cap cmt Od s sch (*spat.*) t v ? $א^{a\ b}$ $B^{2\ 3}$ D' F^{W} ⟨ ⟩

erwähnenswert. Also: ⟨...⟩ = „ausgenommen ..."; bisweilen auch „im Gegensatz zu", zB *C*⟨f⟩ = alle sah. und boh. Hss im Gegensatz zu den fajj. (obwohl f nicht in das Summensigel *C* einbegriffen ist, → 5.e.).

[ ] [M]: die Hs fehlt an dieser Stelle.

{ } {M}: die Hs (meist 𝔓) läßt wegen Beschädigung mehrere Lesungen zu (s. auch → c.).

Näheres über die einzelnen Hss ist den Listen (→ IV.) zu entnehmen.

2. die *Perikopenbücher*, — nur die griech. In den Übersetzungen werden die Perikopenbücher zu den Hss des laufenden Textes gestellt.

3. die Evangelien-Zitate der *Schriftsteller*.

aa. Die Schr. werden nur notiert, soweit hinreichend deutlich ist, daß sie aus einem bestimmten Ev. zitieren wollen (zB durch ausdrückliche Nennung des Evangelisten, durch den Kontext oder auch eine Variante, die ausschließlich für das betreffende Ev. bezeugt ist). **Halbfett** erscheint der Schr.-Name (zB **Or**, PsAu), wenn der Kontext die betreffende Variante sichert (zB durch Kommentierung). Widersprechen verschiedene Zitate des gleichen Schr. einander, so wird das Zahlenverhältnis angegeben (zB Au$^{2:7}$ = Augustin an zwei von im ganzen sieben Stellen). Zu Au^{cmt} und Au^{lm} vgl. das Abkürzungs-Verzeichnis (→ VIII.).

Or

bb. Ist die handschriftliche Überlieferung einer Schr.-Stelle gespalten, so wird die Variante wie eine weitere Stelle gezählt (Au$^{2:7}$ kann also auch bedeuten: Augustin an einer und in der Variante zu einer zweiten von *sechs* Stellen). Diese geringe Ungenauigkeit wird zugunsten der Raumeinsparung in Kauf genommen, und weil es wichtiger ist, das Vorkommen einer Variante bei dem betreffenden Schr. überhaupt anzuzeigen, als ihr relatives Gewicht anzudeuten.

cc. Dem Zeugnis der Evv.-Zitate kommt im allgemeinen der gleiche Rang zu wie dem der Masse der Minuskeln. Die Abschreiber haben nachweislich oft den ihnen geläufigen Text einkorrigiert, besonders in dem der Auslegung vorangestellten (und ursprünglich oft nur anzitierten) Lemma, dem dann die Auslegung nicht mehr entspricht. Kann man jedoch in solchen Fällen die Variante für einen bestimmten Schr. sichern, so gewinnt sein Zeugnis große Aussagekraft für Alter und Lokalisierung der Variante.

dd. Ist eine Lesart bei einem Schr. nicht durch seinen eigenen Text, sondern nur durch die Nachricht eines anderen Schr. belegt, so tritt das Zeichen des Gewährsmanns als Exponent zum Namen des Erstgenannten, zB Mcn^{Ep} *L*Mcn^{Te} = Marcion nach dem Zeugnis des Epiphanius bzw. des Tertullian. Der Name des Gewährsmanns erscheint daneben nur dann nochmals, wenn er halbfett (aa. ←) zu drucken ist oder auch an anderer Stelle für die betreffende Variante zeugt.

ee. Erwähnt ein Schr. mehrere Varianten des Evv.-Textes, so bezeugt er auch für die von ihm verworfenen, daß sie zu seiner Zeit und in seinem Bereich existierten.

ff. Zu den einzelnen Schr. siehe die Liste (→ VI.).

{ } **c.** Gegebenenfalls umfaßt eine Klammer mehrere sprachliche Gruppen oder Teile davon. In geschweiften Klammern {...} stehen außer den beschädigten Hss (b.1. ←) vor allem solche Zeugen der Übersetzungssprachen, für deren Lesart das griech. Äquivalent nicht hinreichend sicher ist; zB bedeutet {*L*a}: *L*a entspricht zwar am wörtlichsten dem angeführten griech. Text, könnte aber auch auf eine andere Form desselben zurückgehen. Wird diese andere Form ebenfalls angeführt, so erscheint dort ein leeres {} als Hinweis. Nicht selten sind die hier als leer ange-

tioning. So: ⟨...⟩ = "excepted ..."; sometimes also = "contrary to ...", e. g. *C*⟨f⟩ = all Sah. and Boh. mss contrary to the Fayy. (although f is not included in the group symbol *C*, → 5.e.);

[M]: the ms is missing at this point;

{M}: the ms (usually 𝔓) can be read in various ways because of damage (see also → c.).

More particulars about the individual mss are to be got from the lists (→ IV.).

2. the *lectionaries*, — only in Greek. In the versions the lectionaries are reckoned with the mss of the continuous text.

3. the Gospel quotations in the various *authors*.

aa. Authors noticed only insofar as it is sufficently clear that they intend to quote from one definite Gospel (e. g. through the express naming of a particular Gospel, through the context or through a variant reading which is exclusive to the relevant Gospel). The author's name appears in **half thick** type (e. g. **Or**, PsAu) if the context guarantees (e. g. by its comments) the relevant variant. If different quotations by the same author conflict with each other, then the proportion is given (the number of occasions where Au supports the reading is given against the total number of times where Au quotes the passage, e. g. Au$^{2:7}$). For Au^{cmt} and Au^{lm} s. the list of Abbreviations (→ VIII.).

bb. If the ms tradition of a passage in an author is divided, then the variant is reckoned as an additional witness (Au$^{2:7}$ can therefore mean as well: Augustine in one passage and in the variant to a second of *six* passages). This slight inexactitude has to be taken as a concession to the need to save space and because it is more necessary to indicate the presence of a variant in the relevant author than to describe its relative importance.

cc. The witness of the Gospel quotations has in general the same level of importance as that of the mass of minuscules. The copyists have often demonstrably corrected the text to that which was current in their day, particularly in the lemma (whose beginning was often alone quoted originally), to which the exposition no longer corresponds. In such a contradiction, e. g. between lemma and commentary, if we can determine what was the text that the author had in mind, then his testimony gains in significance for the dating and locating of that text.

dd. If we know of one form of the text of an author only from the report of another writer, then the symbol for this other author appears as exponent to the name of the first named author, e. g. Mcn^{Ep} *L*Mcn^{Te} = Marcion according to the evidence of Epiphanius and of Tertullian. The name of the guarantor appears beside this again only if it is to be printed in half thick type (aa. ←) or testifies in another place also to the appropriate variant.

ee. Variants of the Gospel text, mentioned but rejected by an author, are witnessed by him all the same, as they existed at his time within his reach.

ff. For the separate authors consult the list (→ VI.).

c. A bracket can include several language groups or parts of them. In the tailed brackets {...} I give in particular (apart from the damaged mss, b.1. ←) such witnesses from the versions whose renderings cannot be related to a definite Gr. equivalent; e. g. {*L*a} indicates that *L*a corresponds most closely in wording to the Gr. text in question, but could however go back to another form of the text. If this other form is also mentioned, then it has with it empty brackets {} as an indication of this. Not uncommonly the brackets which are here assumed to be empty are

nommenen Klammern auch durch einen Zeugen besetzt, der eher auf die andere Variante zurückgeht, ohne die erste ganz auszuschließen: {*La*} und {*Cs*^{5}} verweisen gegenseitig aufeinander. Gibt es mehrere solcher zweifelhaften Fälle beim gleichen Lemma, so erhalten die zusammengehörigen Klammern den gleichen Exponenten: $\{\}^1$ verweist auf $\{\ldots\}^1$, $\{\}^2$ auf $\{\ldots\}^2$ usw.

Über einige Fälle, in denen die Übersetzungen keinen Zeugenwert haben, →10.

2. Griechische Zeugen.

a. *Papyri*, II.—VII. (sc. Jahrhundert). Bezeichnung: $\mathfrak{P}^{1.2.3\ldots}$, davon rund 40 mit Evv.-Text. Auf Papyrus in Majuskelschrift geschrieben, fast immer in Ägypten gefunden, meist sehr fragmentarisch (Ausnahmen: $\mathfrak{P}^{45.66.75}$), daher häufig „^{v}" oder {...} (1.b.1. ←). Alle Papyri sind im Apparat berücksichtigt. Ihre herkömmliche — sachlich nicht (mehr) ganz berechtigte — besondere Zählung ist beibehalten: sie erscheinen jeweils am Anfang der gr. Zeugen, obwohl viele von ihnen einer der unten (→ f.) genannten Gruppen zuzuweisen wären.

b. *Majuskel*-Hss (Unzialen), IV.-XI. Bezeichnung: ℵ**(01)** A**(02)** B**(03)** ... Ω**(045) 047 050 053** ... im ganzen rund 170. Alle auf Pergament geschrieben, 36 davon später abgewaschen und neu überschrieben (Palimpseste, untere Schrift), eine **(0196)** auf abgewaschenem Pergament (Palimpsest, obere Schrift). Vollständigen Text, d. h.: keine Lücken, die mehr als *einen* ganzen Vers umfassen, haben in allen vier Evv. nur: ℵ B K M S U **055 0211**. Außerdem sind vollständig in Mt-Mk-Lk: W Δ, in Mt-Mk-Jo: E, in Mk-Lk-Jo: Θ, in Mk-Lk: A V, in Lk-Jo: Γ Λ Ψ Ω, in Mt: Σ, in Mk: Y, in Lk: D L **047**, in Jo: O **0141**. Viele Majuskeln bestehen nur aus Einzelblättern oder Fragmenten. Bei manchen besteht die Möglichkeit, daß sie aus Perikopenbüchern stammen. Alle sind, soweit bekannt, im Apparat berücksichtigt.

c. *Minuskel*-Hss, ab IX. Bezeichnung: 1 2 3 ..., im ganzen rund 2700, davon rund 2000 mit Evv.-Text. Auf Pergament oder Papier (ab XII.) in Minuskelschrift geschrieben. Meist vollständige Hss des NT oder der Evv., kaum Einzelblätter oder Fragmente. Folgende Minuskeln sind im Apparat, soweit bekannt, ständig berücksichtigt:

occupied by a witness which seems rather to correspond to the other form without entirely excluding the first: {*La*} and {*Cs*^{5}} refer to each other. If there are more such doubtful instances in the same lemma, then the relevant brackets display the same exponents: $\{\}^1$ refers to $\{\ldots\}^1$, $\{\}^2$ to $\{\ldots\}^2$ etc.

For some cases where the versions have no value as witnesses → 10.

2. Greek Witnesses.

a. *Papyri*, II.-VII. (understand "century"). Designation: $\mathfrak{P}^{1.2.3\ldots}$ of which some forty contain Gospel texts. Written on papyrus in majuscule hands, almost always found in Egypt, most are very small pieces (exceptions $\mathfrak{P}^{45.66.75}$) and so frequently qualified with "^{v}" or {...} (1.b.1. ←). All papyri are noticed in the apparatus. Their separate enumeration as papyri which we have inherited is retained though it is not in principle justified. They stand at the beginning of the Gr. witnesses, although many of them are to be referred to one of the groups named below (→ f.).

b. *Majuscule* mss (uncials), IV.-XI. Designation: ℵ**(01)** A**(02)** B**(03)** ... Ω**(045) 047 050 053** ... in all some 170. All are written on parchment. 36 of them (palimpsests) were later washed clean and inscribed anew (the under writing is the Gospel text), one text **(0196)** was inscribed on a parchment already washed clean (the upper writing is the Gospel text). Complete texts, i. e. with no gaps which contain more than one whole verse are extant in all four Gospels only in ℵ B K M S U **055 0211**. In addition W Δ are complete in Mt-Mk-Lk, E in Mt-Mk-Jo, Θ in Mk-Lk-Jo, A V in Mk-Lk, Γ Δ Ψ Ω in Lk-Jo, Σ in Mt, Y in Mk, D L **047** in Lk, O **0141** in Jo. Many majuscules consist of only single leaves or fragments. It is possible that a number of them derive from lectionaries. All are noticed in the apparatus as far as they are known.

c. *Minuscule* mss, from IX. onward. Designation: 1 2 3 ..., in all about 2700 of which some 2000 contain the Gospels. Written in minuscule script on parchment or paper (from XII.). Most are complete mss of the NT or of the Gospels, scarcely any single leaves or fragments. The following minuscules are regularly noticed in the apparatus as far as they are known:

1	124	517	828	1194	1604
7	131 (Mk1—5 Lk)	543	872 (Mk)	1207	1606
13	157	544	892	1223	1675
22	160	565 (Mk)	945	1241 (Lk Jo)	1689
27	174 (Mt Lk Jo)	579 (Mk Lk Jo)	954	1278	2191
28	179	659	983	1293	2193
33	209	692	990	1342	
69	230	700	1010	1391	
71	267	788	1071	1402	
115	346	826	1082	1424	
118	349	827	1188 (Lk Jo)	1582	

Der größte Teil der übrigen Minuskeln ist bisher nur in wenigen Stichkapiteln durchgeprüft.

d. *Perikopenbücher* (Lektionare), vereinzelt schon ab IV., zahlreich ab VIII. Bezeichnung: *l*1 *l*2 *l*3 ..., im ganzen rund 1900. Auf Pergament (auch Palimpsest, untere oder obere Schrift) oder Papier (ab XIII.) in Majuskel- (bis XII., vereinzelt bis XV.) oder Minuskelschrift (ab IX.) geschrieben.

Die Perikopenbücher enthalten in ihrem ersten Teil (Synaxarion) die gottesdienstlichen Lesungen a) aus den Evv., b) aus dem übrigen NT für die Sabbat- und Sonntage, später für alle Tage

The text of the largest part of the remaining minuscules has been tested up to the present only in a few specimen chapters.

d. *Lectionaries*, occasionally already from the IV. and numerous from the VIII. Designation: *l*1 *l*2 *l*3 ..., in all about 1900.

*l*1 *l*2

Written on parchment (including the top or underwriting of palimpsests) or paper (from XIII.) in majuscule (until XII., occasionally until XV.) or minuscule script (from IX.).

The lectionaries contain in their first part (Synaxarion) the liturgical lections a) from the Gospels, b) from the rest of the NT, for Saturday and Sunday, later for all week days in the

der Woche, im Verlaufe des beweglichen, vom Osterdatum bestimmten Kirchenjahres. Der zweite Teil (Menologion) bietet für jeden Kalendertag und den — örtlich oft verschiedenen — Kalenderheiligen, beginnend mit dem Jahresanfang (1. Sept.), ebensolche Lesungen. Die Perikopenanfänge und -enden sind meist mit liturgischer Einleitung und Schluß versehen (zB „Zu jener Zeit sprach Jesus ...“ und „Wer Ohren hat zu hören, der höre!“).

Die gleiche Perikope kann in einem Perikopenbuch mehrfach vorkommen, sogar mehrfach in Synaxarion und/oder Menologion. In solchen Fällen heißt $l547^1$ bzw. $l547^2$, daß die betreffende Variante sich unter den mehrfachen Vorkommen des Textes in *l*547 nur ein- bzw. zweimal findet. Stimmen alle Vorkommen überein, so steht lediglich *l*547. Diese Fälle sind nicht häufig, weil sich wiederholende Perikopen in den Lektionaren oft durch Verweisungen ersetzt sind.

Die große Masse der Perikopenbücher ist bisher noch weniger erschlossen und erforscht, als es die Minuskeln sind (c. ←). Daher mußte ich mich darauf beschränken, im Apparat dasjenige

l^{pc} l^{al}

anzuführen — manchmal auch in l^{pc}, l^{al} usw. (→ VIII.) zusammengefaßt —, was mir bekannt geworden ist. Ein völliger Verzicht, wie ihn v. Soden übt, schien nicht mehr vertretbar, seitdem Colwell und seine Schüler die ersten Ergebnisse ihrer Lektionarforschungen vorgelegt haben.

e. Evv.-*Zitate* aus gr. *Schriftstellern* (1.b.3. ←). Bei den gr. Zeugen werden nur die gr. Schriften des betreffenden Autors berücksichtigt. Zitate aus Übersetzungen erscheinen bei den entsprechenden sprachlichen Gruppen. Es gibt zB neben Ir (= gr. Irenäus) auch *L*Ir, neben Eu (= gr. Euseb) auch *S*Eu.

f. Gr. Majuskeln und Minuskeln, die häufiger zusammengehen, werden aus Gründen der Übersichtlichkeit in *Gruppen* angeführt. Bei der Abgrenzung dieser Gruppen wurden die Ergebnisse der textkritischen Familienforschung zwar zum großen Teil benutzt, doch wird keine endgültige Zuweisung im Einzelfall beansprucht. Lediglich praktische Überlegungen, besonders Raumgründe, ließen es geboten erscheinen, aus der Ähnlichkeit gewisser Hss Nutzen zu ziehen (vgl. besonders über Summensigeln → g.). Folgende Hss werden in Gruppen zusammengefaßt

†

und in der hierunter angegebenen Reihenfolge aufgeführt († = lückenhaft):

course of the variable ecclesiastical year determined by the variable date of Easter. The second part (Menologion) provides corresponding lections for each day in the calendar, i. e. for the saints of the calendar, often varying according to locality, starting with the beginning of the year (1st September). The beginning and ending of lections are mostly provided with liturgical introductions and conclusions (e. g. “At that time Jesus spoke ...” and “He who has ears to hear let him hear”).

The same lection can occur more than once in the same lectionary either in the Synaxarion or in the Menologion or in both, e. g. $l547^1$ or $l547^2$ means that the variant in question appears only once or twice in the frequent occurrences of the lection in *l*547. If all occurrences agree then we merely have *l*547. These cases are not many because recurring lections are often replaced by a cross reference in the lectionary.

The great majority of lectionaries have up to the present been even less explored and investigated than the minuscules have been (c. ←). So I must limit myself to reporting in the apparatus what had become known to me, often comprehended under the symbols l^{pc}, l^{al} etc. (→ VIII.). A total rejection such as v. Soden made seems no longer possible since Colwell and his pupils have published the first results of their research in the lectionaries.

e. Gospel *quotations* from the Greek authors (1.b.3. ←).

Among the Gr. witnesses only the writings of the relevant author surviving in Gr. are taken into account. Quotations from translations of these authors appear in the corresponding language group. We have, e. g. beside Ir (= the Gr. Irenaeus) also *L*Ir, beside Eu (= the Gr. Eusebius) also *S*Eu.

f. Gr. majuscules and minuscules which often agree are presented in *groups* for the sake of clarity. In determining the membership of these groups, though the results of the investigation into family groupings were used to a great extent, yet we lay claim to no final ascription to a family for individual mss. Merely practical considerations, particularly those of space, seemed to require that we make use of the similarity between certain mss (cp. particularly on group symbols → g.). The following mss are grouped together and appear in the annotations in the order in which they are given below († = with gaps):

1) Ägyptische oder Hesych-Gruppe/*Egyptian or Hesychius group*:
Voll-Hss/*Complete mss*: ℵBC†L(**019**)†W†(Lk1₁—8₁₂ Jo)X†Z†(Mt)Δ(Mk)Ψ†(Mk)-33†-579†(Mk Lk Jo)-892†-1241(Lk Jo).
Fragmente, in Klammern („mit ...“) andere Teile der gleichen Hs/*Fragments with other parts of the same ms in brackets* (“*with...*”):
Q(Jo)T(mit/*with*) **0113-0125-0139**)Ξ-**054-059**(mit/*with* **0215**)-**060-065-068-070**(mit/*with* **0110-0124-0178-0179-0180-0190-0191-0202**)-**071-073**(mit/*with* **084**)-**083**(mit/*with* **0112-0235**)-**085-086-091-099-0100**(mit/*with* *l*963?)-**0109-0114**(mit/*with* *l*965?)-**0118-0128-0163-0164-0170-0177-0184-0193-0200-0204-0237-0238-0239-0260**-*l*1355.

2) Cäsarea-Gruppe/*Caesarean group* (Majuskeln und Minuskeln außer 3)—5)/*majuscules and minuscules except for* 3)—5)):
N†O†W†(Mk5₃₁—fin.)Θ(Mk)Λ(Lk Jo)Σ†Φ-28†-544-565(Mk)-700-1071-1604.

λ

3) Lake-Gruppe/*Lake group* (Kennbuchstabe/*indicator*: λ):
1-22†-118†-131(Mk1—5 Lk)-209-872(Mk)-1278-1582-2193.

ϕ

4) Ferrar-Gruppe/*Ferrar group* (Kennbuchstabe/*indicator*: ϕ):
13†-69†-124-174†(Mt Lk Jo)-230†-346†-543†-788†-826-828†-983†-1689-*l*547.

σ

5) Soden-Gruppe/*Soden group* (Kennbuchstabe/*indicator*: σ):
M-7-27†-71-115†-160-179†-267†-349†-517†-659-692†-827†-945-954†-990†-1010†-1082†-1188 (Lk Jo)-1194-1207†-1223-1293†-1391†-1402-1424†-1606-1675†-2191†.

Auf einen Kennbuchstaben für die „Cäsarea-Gruppe“ wurde wie bei der ägyptischen Gruppe verzichtet; die streng eingehaltene Reihenfolge dürfte Mißverständnisse ausschließen.

In Klammern hinter den Hss wird angezeigt, daß sie, auch wenn sie mehr enthalten, nur mit den in Klammern stehenden Evv.(-Teilen) der Gruppe angehören, unter der sie aufgeführt

As with the Egyptian group we do not supply an indicator for the Caesarean group; the strictly observed order of witnesses should exclude misunderstandings.

Brackets placed after the mss in 1)—5) indicate that even when they contain more, the mss belong only in the parts of the Gospels given in brackets, to the group under which they are

sind. W zB gehört nur in Lk11—812 und Jo zur ägyptischen, in Mk531—fin. zur Cäsarea-, mit dem Rest dagegen zu keiner Gruppe.

Innerhalb der gleichen Gruppe stehen Buchstaben ohne Zwischenraum, Zahlen mit Bindestrich, zB BCX-**068**-579-1241.

g. In *Summensigeln* werden aus Raumgründen innerhalb der Gruppen solche Hss zusammengefaßt, die häufiger zusammengehen. Jedes Summensigel vertritt eine genau angegebene Reihe von Hss, nämlich:

listed; e. g. W belongs to the Egyptian group only in Lk11—812 and Jo, in Mk531—fin. to the Caesarean and in the remainder to no one group.

Within the same group capitals are printed without intervals and numbers with a hyphen e. g. BCX-**068**-579-1241.

g. Under the "*group symbols*" are comprehended such mss as agree more frequently. Each group symbol represents a series of mss which are exactly indicated, to wit:

ℌ = ℵBL†W†(Lk11—812 Jo)Z†(Mt)Δ(Mk)Ψ†(Mk)-33†-579†(Mk Lk Jo)-892†-1241(Lk Jo) **ℌ**
λ = 1-118†-131(Mk1—5 Lk)-209 (Lake-Kerngruppe/*the corc of the Lake group*) **λ**
λλ = 1-22†-118†-131(Mk1—5 Lk)-209-872(Mk)-1278-1582-2193 (vollständige Lake-Gruppe/*the complete Lake group*) **λλ**
φ = 13†-69†-124-346†-543†-788†-826-828†-983† **φ**
σ = 517†-954†-1424†-1675† **σ**

(Beachte: **λ**, **φ**, **σ** sind streng zu unterscheiden von den Kennbuchstaben λ, φ, σ).

Die Summensigeln bezeichnen also nicht — wie **ℌ**, **λ**, **φ** bei Nestle-Aland^{25} — einen Text*typ*, sondern ersetzen eine Vielzahl präziser Einzelangaben. Damit jederzeit genau festgestellt werden kann, welche Einzel-Hss an einer bestimmten Stelle hinter der Summensigel stehen, ist in Ergänzung der vorstehenden Aufzählung eine Lückenliste (→ V.a.) für die mit † bezeichneten Zeugen beigegeben.

Bieten nicht alle, sondern nur die Mehrzahl der zB von **ℌ** vertretenen Zeugen eine Variante, so steht bei dieser **ℌ**' (= Rest von **ℌ**), wenn die abweichenden Zeugen mit ihrer Variante eigens aufgeführt werden. Gehen sie jedoch mit *Rpl* (→ i.) oder ist ihre Abweichung hier nicht genannt, so stehen sie in ⟨ ⟩ hinter **ℌ**, zB **ℌ**⟨B-33⟩ = alle **ℌ**-Zeugen außer B und 33 (s. auch 1.b.1.← zu **ℌ**⟨W⟩).

Gehen weitere Hss der gleichen Gruppe mit den von der Summensigel vertretenen, so werden sie an die Summensigel unmittelbar angeschlossen, zB (1) **ℌ**X-*l*1355 = alle zur Stelle vorhandenen **ℌ**-Hss und außerdem X und *l*1355 — oder (2) **σ**⟨517⟩-M-71 = die zur Stelle vorhandenen **σ**-Hss außer 517, dazu M und 71.

h. Hss, die *keiner* der Gruppen 1)—5) (f. ←) zugeordnet sind, werden im Anschluß an die Gruppen aufgeführt, zuerst die Majuskeln, dann die Minuskeln. Von den letzteren werden 157 und 1342(Mk) besonders genannt, die übrigen, sofern es mehrere sind zusammengefaßt in *pc* = pauci (rund 2—10 Minuskeln), *al* = alii (rund 10—20 M.), *mu* = multi (rund 20—30 M.), *pm* = permulti (über 30 M.).

i. *Rpl* — d. h. Reliqui (maiusculi) + plerique (minusculi) — umfaßt die zur gleichen Stelle bei keiner andern Variante — auch nicht bei *txt*: — genannten gr. Majuskeln (alle) und Minuskeln (vollständig, soweit oben c. ← aufgeführt). Außerdem ist in *pl* die Mehrzahl der Lektionare enthalten, wenn nicht (sehr selten) l^{pl} bei einer anderen Variante steht. Bisweilen stehen *R* und *pl* auch getrennt, bei verschiedenen Varianten.

Rpl ist in der Regel mit dem Text identisch, der schließlich im byzantinischen Reich zur Herrschaft kam, nach v. Sodens Vorgang vielfach auch „Koine" genannt.

3. Lateinische Zeugen (Kennbuchstabe: *L*).

a. 1. Von den *Altlateinern* werden die folgenden Evangelien-Hss gegebenenfalls unter dem Summensigel (2.g. ←) „vl" (= vetus latina) zusammengefaßt: a† $a^{2\dagger}$ b† c e† f† ff^{1}(Mt) $ff^{2\dagger}$ g^{1}(Mt) h†(Mt) i†(Mk Lk) k†(Mt Mk) l† n†(Mt Mk Jo) q† $r^{2\dagger}$ z†(= „aur" bei Nestle-Aland und anderen). In Klammern stehen die Evv., die in den

(Note that **λ φ σ** are to be strictly distinguished from the indicators λ φ σ).

The group symbols, therefore, do not indicate a textual type (as do **ℌ λ φ** in Nestle-Aland^{25}), but represent a larger body of precisely detailed information. In order that at any time we can establish exactly which individual mss are included under the group symbol at a definite place, we have provided a list of lacunae (→ V. a.) for the witnesses marked by † in the preceding enumeration.

If the majority, but not all, the witnesses represented by **ℌ** give a variant, then we use the symbol **ℌ**' (= the remainder of **ℌ**) where the dissentient witnesses and their readings are expressly listed. If, however, they agree with *Rpl* (→ i.) or their variation is not detailed here, then they are placed in ⟨...⟩ after **ℌ**, e. g. **ℌ**⟨B-33⟩ = all **ℌ** witnesses except B and 33 (see also 1.b.1. ← at **ℌ**⟨W⟩).

ℌ'

If additional mss of the same group go with those mss represented by the group symbol, then they follow immediately on the group symbol, e. g. (1) **ℌ**X-*l*1355 = all **ℌ** mss extant at this place and in addition X and *l*1355, or (2) **σ**⟨517⟩-M-71 = the **σ** mss extant at this place, except 517, and in addition M and 71.

h. Mss which are assigned to none of the groups 1)—5) (f. ←) are given next after the groups, first the majuscules and then the minuscules. Of these last 157 and 1342 (Mk) especially are named, but the remainder, as far as more than one are concerned, are comprehended under *pc* = pauci (about 2—10 minuscules), *al* = alii (about 10—20 minuscules). *mu* = multi (about 20—30 minuscules), *pm* = permulti (over 30 minuscules).

pc
al mu
pm

i. *Rpl* — i. e. Reliqui (maiusculi) + plerique (minusculi) — embraces all the Gr. majuscules and, amongst others, all the minuscules which have been detailed above (c. ←) — except those reported for any other variant or for the *txt* of the relevant passage. In addition the majority of the lectionaries is included in *pl*, if l^{pl} does not occur with another variant (which happens rarely). From time to time *R* and *pl* are also printed separately after different variants.

Rpl
pl
l^{pl}

Rpl is as a rule identical with the text which finally became dominant in the Byzantine empire, often called "Koine" in keeping with v. Soden's precedent.

3. Latin Witnesses (Indicator: *L*).

L

a. 1. Among the *Old Latin* witnesses the following Gospel mss, if they are not enumerated separately, are included under the group symbol (2.g. ←) "vl" (= vetus latina): a† $a^{2\dagger}$ b† c e† f† ff^{1}(Mt) $ff^{2\dagger}$ g^{1}(Mt) h†(Mt) i†(Mk Lk) k†(Mt Mk) l† n†(Mt Mk Jo) q† $r^{2\dagger}$ z†(= "aur" in Nestle-Aland and other editions). The names

vl

betreffenden Hss vorhanden sind bzw. altlat. Text bieten. Für die lückenhaften Hss (†) ist eine Lückenliste (→ V.b.) beigegeben. Sie führt alle Lücken auf, die mindestens einen ganzen Vers umfassen. Kleinere Lücken sind im Apparat durch [ ] angezeigt, zB [n].

2. Von den übrigen, meist sehr fragmentarischen oder beschädigten altlat. Hss und Perikopenbüchern werden jeweils besonders genannt: β j μ o p π r^1 s t v 23 31 32 36 37 38 39 40 41 42 43 56 59 61 65 76 77 78 250.

3. Einige weitere Evv-Hss haben nur schwachen vl-Einschlag. Deshalb werden aufgeführt:

d nur, wenn von D(griech.) verschieden;
g^2 „ „ „ vg oder vg' (→ b.) verschieden;
30 „ „ „ vg „ vg' „
δ „ „ „ vg „ vg' und gleichzeitig von Δ(griech.) verschieden.

4. Auf das Fehlen von ek in Mt und Mk sowie von e in Lk und Jo wird wegen Alter und Bedeutung dieser „afrikanischen" Zeugen jeweils besonders hingewiesen, zB e[k] ab30 oder vl[ek] $r^1$41 (sowie regelmäßig, wenn mehr als drei vl-Zeugen angeführt werden). Sind e und/oder k als Zeugen zu nennen, so stehen sie zusammen mit Abstand vor den übrigen altlat. Zeugen, die alphabetisch geordnet folgen.

vg

b. 1. Die auf Hieronymus zurückgehende jüngere lat. Übersetzung, die sogenannte *Vulgata* (= vg), ist nach der Ausgabe von Wordsworth-White zitiert. Ist der Text dieser Ausgabe ohne Varianten, so steht „vg". Gibt es aber abweichende Hss, so werden diese nicht benannt, sondern gezählt, zB vg^4; der Rest ist dann vg' (2.g.Abs.3. ←). Haben einige Hss hier nicht genannte Varianten, so wird dies durch $vg^{\langle 4\rangle}$ (= vg außer 4 Hss) angezeigt. Verteilen sich die vg-Zeugen auf mehr als zwei Varianten, so steht vg' für die höchste Zahl, zB vg^7 — vg^4 — vg' = 7 — 4 — die übrigen (mindestens 8) vg-Hss.

2. Da es auch in vg-Hss Lücken gibt, ist die Zahl der von Wordsworts-White zu den einzelnen Stellen angeführten Zeugen nicht überall gleich. Sie schwankt zwischen 24 und 18, beträgt aber im Durchschnitt etwa 22.

c. Die Namen der lat. *Schriftsteller*, die aus den Evv. zitieren, folgen auf die Hss oder, falls solche nicht zu nennen sind, unmittelbar auf den Kennbuchstaben *L*. Nach dem Summensigel *L* oder *L*[..] (→ d.1.) steht jedoch ein Komma, ehe die Schr. folgen. Es ist somit zu unterscheiden zwischen „*L*Au" (= Augustin) und „*L*, Au" (= alle lat. Hss, dazu Augustin).

d. 1. Der Kennbuchstabe *L* kann auch als *Summensigel* (2.g. ←) gebraucht werden. In diesem Fall umfaßt *L* alle unter a. und b. (←) genannten Hss. In den Formen „*L*'", „*L*⟨..⟩" und „*L*," ist *L* immer Summensigel, emtsprechend *S*, *C* … (→ III.B.4.,5. ..)

2. Wird *L* als Summensigel gebraucht, so entfallen alle Hinweise auf in *L* enthaltene bedingte oder zweifelhafte Zeugen (zB b^v, a?) sowie auf die sonst besonders aufzuführenden Hss (a.2. und 3. ←). Wenn nicht mehr als *eine* vl-Hs von *L*' abweicht, gibt es keine Hinweise auf Lücken (a.1. am Ende ←). Lediglich das gänzliche Fehlen der „Afrikaner" (ek in Mt Mk, e in Lk Jo) wird nach a.4. (←), die Abweichung von d gegenüber D nach a.3. (←) vermerkt.

S

4. Syrische Zeugen (Kennbuchstabe: *S*).

Ssc

a. Die beiden Hss der *altsyrischen* Übersetzung, *S*s (Sinaiticus IV./V. Pal) und *S*c (Curetonianus V.) werden als erste hinter dem Kennbuchstaben *S* aufgeführt. Ihr Fehlen wird stets angezeigt (doch → e.); zusätzlich gibt Liste V.c. (→) Auskunft über die größeren (mindestens einen ganzen Vers umfassenden)

of the Gospels which are extant in the mss concerned or offer an Old Lat. text are in brackets. For mss with lacunae (†) a list of lacunae is provided (→ V.b.). It includes all lacunae which embrace a whole verse or more. Smaller lacunae are indicated in the apparatus through [ ], e. g. [n].

2. Of the remaining Old Lat. mss and lectionaries, for the most part very fragmentary and damaged, the following are cited where they are extant: β j μ o p π r^1 s t v 23 31 32 36 37 38 39 40 41 42 43 56 59 61 65 76 77 78 250.

3. Some further Gospel mss have only a weak vl element. On this account the following are cited

d only when it differs from D(Gr.)
g^2 „ „ „ „ „ vg or vg' (→ b.)
30 „ „ „ „ „ vg or vg'
δ „ „ „ „ „ vg or vg' and at the same time from Δ(Gr.).

4. Because of the age and significance of these "African" witnesses as a rule special reference is made to the absence of ek in Mt-Mk and of e in Lk-Jo, e. g. e[k] ab30 or vl[ek] $r^1$41 (this is done regularly if more than three vl witnesses are cited). Where e and/or k are to be given as witnesses they stand together separately before the remaining Old Lat. witnesses which follow in alphabetical order.

b. 1. The younger Lat. version, named the *Vulgate* (= vg) which goes back to Jerome is quoted according to Wordsworth and White's edition. If its text is without variants, then we have only "vg". If however mss have a variant, then they are not named but counted e. g. vg^4; the remaining mss are vg' (2.g.3rd section ←). If some mss have variants which are not reported here, then this is indicated by $vg^{\langle 4\rangle}$ (= vg except 4 mss). If the vg witnesses are divided among more than two variants, then vg' stands for the highest number of mss e. g. vg^7 — vg^4 — vg' = 7 — 4 — the remaining vg mss (at least 8).

2. Since there are lacunae in vg mss also, the number of the witnesses cited by Wordsworth and White at the various places is not throughout the same. They vary between 24 and 18 but average about 22.

c. The names of the Lat. *authors* who quote from the Gospels follow on the mss or, if these are not cited, immediately on the indicator *L*. After the group symbol *L* or *L*[..] (→ d.1.) follows a comma before the authors' names. We have in this way to distinguish between *L*Au (= Augustine) and L,Au (= all Lat. mss, as well as Augustine).

d. 1. The indicator *L* can also be used as a *group symbol* (2.g. ←). In this case *L* embraces all mss named under a. and b. (←). In the forms "*L*'", "*L*⟨..⟩" and "*L*," *L* is always the group symbol. The same is to be said about *S*, *C* … (→ III.B.4.,5…).

2. If *L* is used as the group symbol, we drop all references to conditional or doubtful witnesses contained in *L* (e. g. b^v, a?) and to mss which are otherwise detailed in addition (a.2. and 3. ←). If only one vl ms departs from *L*, no indication of lacunae is given (a.1. at the end ←). Only the complete absence of the African mss (ek in Mt-Mk, e in Lk-Jo) is recorded according to a.4. (←) and the departure of d over against D according to a.3. (←).

4. Syriac Witnesses (Indicator: *S*).

a. The two mss of the *Old Syriac* version *S*s (Sinaiticus IV./V. Pal) and *S*c (Curetonianus V.) are the first to be given after the group indicator *S*. Their absence is always indicated (but → e.); in addition list V.c. (→) gives information about larger gaps (which contain at least one entire verse). Editions: (*S*s)

Lücken. Ausgaben: (*S*s) ASLewis, The Old Syriac Gospels, 1910; (*S*c) FCBurkitt, Evangelion da-Mepharreshe, 1904 (mepharreshe = getrennte, im Gegensatz zu Tatians Diatessaron = Harmonie).

b. Die sogenannte *Peschitta* („die einfache", die syr. „Vulgata"), geht wohl zurück auf die Bibelrevision des Bischofs Rabbula von Edessa († 435). Sie wird zitiert nach der Ausgabe von GHGwilliam, Tetraevangelium sanctum, 1901: = *S*p. Die einzelnen dort verwerteten Hss (ab V.) werden wie bei *L*vg (3. b.1. ←) nicht genannt, sondern gezählt. Ihre Zahl schwankt zwischen 10 und 31, hält sich jedoch meist zwischen 15 und 23. Varianten sind hier, anders als bei *L*vg, selten. Zitierungsweise wie bei *L*vg (3.b.1. ←).

c. Die *Harclensis* oder Heracleensis (*S*h) ist eine in 30—40 Hss (ab VII.) erhaltene — möglicherweise auf eine ältere (Philoxeniana) zurückgehende — Übersetzung, die A.D. 616 von Bischof Thomas von Charkel (Heraclea) unter Heranziehung von zwei oder drei gr. Hss mit Randnotizen und textkritischen Zeichen versehen und „herausgegeben", d. h. mit diesem Apparat durch Abschreiber vervielfältigt wurde. Die *S*h und ihr Apparat werden notiert nach der Ausgabe von JWhite, Sacrorum evangeliorum versio syriaca Philoxeniana, Oxford 1778. Dabei bedeuten

*S*h: den übereinstimmenden Text aller *S*h-Zeugen.
Sh^{m} (Sh^{mgr}): eine (gr.) Randnotiz in *S*h.
Sh^{t}: den Haupttext in *S*h im Unterschied zu Sh^{m}.
Sh^{+}: das Wort (die Wortgruppe) ist in *S*h durch „asteriscus" als Zusatz aus den gr. Hss gekennzeichnet. Im Zweifesfall wird der betreffende Textteil hinzugesetzt, zB *S*h αυτου⁺.
Sh^{-}: das Wort (die Wortgruppe) ist in *S*h durch „obelus" als Überschuß gegenüber gr. Textüberlieferung gekennzeichnet. Im Zweifelsfall wie Sh^{+}.
Sh^{Brs}: der in den "Notae" von JWhite besonders verglichene Codex Barsalibaeus (Dionysius Barsalibi, Bischof von Amida, Mesopotamien, XII.).
Sh^{Bdl}: ein ebenda verglichener Codex Bodleianus.
Sh^{Brs+} wie Sh^{+} usw.

d. Die *syropalästinische* Übersetzung (*S*j, j = Jerusalem) ist bisher fast nur aus Perikopenbüchern und Fragmenten davon bekannt (ab VI.). Sie repräsentiert den westaramäischen Dialekt der Christen des V. Jahrhunderts in Palästina. Es bedeuten

*S*j: die gesamte vorhandene syropal. Überlieferung.
Sj^{a}: Cod. Vaticanus Syr. 19, A.D. 1030.
Sj^{b}: Cod. Sinaiticus, Kath. Kloster, A.D. 1104.
Sj^{c}: „ „ , „ „ , A.D. 1118.
Sj^{d}: "Remains of another lectionary", 6 Bl., mit Sj^{b} zusammengebunden.
Sj^{a-d} herausgegeben von ASLewis-MDGibson, The Palestinian Syriac Lectionary, 1899.
Sj^{k}: Cod. Climaci rescriptus (VI.), herausgegeben von ASLewis, Horae Semiticae VIII, 1909.
Sj^{l}: Fragmente aus Londoner und St. Petersburger Lektionaren, herausgegeben von JPNLand, Anecdota Syriaca IV, 1875. $Sj^{b} + Sj^{l} = Sj^{b.l}$ zum Unterschied von Sj^{bl} (→).
Sj^{f}: Fragmente, herausgegeben von FSchulthess, Christlich-palästinische Fragmente aus der Omajjaden-Moschee zu Damaskus, 1905; HDuensing, Christlich-paläst.-aramäische Texte und Fragmente, 1906.
Sj^{b1} oder Sj^{b2} steht, wenn der Text mehrfach in Sj^{b} vorkommt und die betreffende Variante nur ein- oder zweimal bezeugt ist (2.d. ←). Ebenso wird bei den Fragmenten-Sammlungen Sj^{l} und Sj^{f} verfahren.

ASLewis, The Old Syriac Gospels 1910; (*S*c) FCBurkitt, Evangelion da-Mepharreshe, 1904 (mepharreshe = separated in opposition to Tatian's Diatessaron = Harmony).

*S*p

b. The so-called *Peshitta* ("simple", the Syr. Vulgata) may go back to the revision of the Bible by bishop Rabbula of Edessa († 435). It is quoted from the edition by GHGwilliam, Tetraevangelium sanctum, 1901 = *S*p. As with *L*vg (3.b.1. ←) the the individual mss (from V.) used in it are not named separately but are counted. Their number varies between 10 and 31 and lies usually between 15 and 23. Unlike *L*vg it has few variants. The same rules obtain for its citation as with *L*vg (3.b.1. ←).

*S*h

c. The *Harclean* or Heracleensis version (*S*h) survives in 30—40 mss (from VII.), perhaps a revision of an older translation, the Philoxenian. It was made by Thomas of Harkel (Heraclea) in A.D. 616, using two or three Gr. mss. It was provided with marginal notes and textual symbols and "published", i. e. copied with this apparatus in large number by scribes. *S*h and its apparatus are recorded according to the edition of JWhite, Sacrorum evangeliorum versio syriaca Philoxeniana 1778. I have used the following abbreviations:

*S*h: the text of all witnesses to *S*h when they agree.
Sh^{m}: a marginal note in *S*h (Sh^{mgr}: the same in Gr.).
Sh^{t}: the text of *S*h in distinction from Sh^{m}.
Sh^{+}: the word or phrase is marked in *S*h with an asterisk as an addition from the Gr. mss. In doubtful cases the relevant portion of the text is added, e. g. *S*h αυτου⁺. (Sh^{+})
Sh^{-}: the word or phrase is indicated in *S*h by an obelus as marking a longer text in comparison with that of the Gr. mss. In doubtful cases the same provision is made as with Sh^{+}. (Sh^{-})
Sh^{Brs}: the codex Barsalibaeus, collated separately in the "Notae" of JWhite (Dionysius Barsalibi bishop of Amida in Mesopotamia XII.).
Sh^{Bdl}: a Bodleian codex collated by the same.
Sh^{Brs+} as with Sh^{+} etc.

*S*j

d. *S*j (j = Jerusalem): the *Palestinian Syriac* version is known up to now almost entirely from lectionaries and their fragments (from VI.). It represents the West Aramaic dialect used by Christians in Palestine in the fifth century. These symbols are used:

*S*j: the whole extant evidence of the Palestinian Syr. version.
Sj^{a}: Cod. Vaticanus Syr. 19, A.D. 1030.
Sj^{b}: Cod. Sinaiticus, St. Catherine's Monastery, A.D. 1004.
Sj^{c}: „ „ , „ „ „ , A.D. 1118.
Sj^{d}: "Remains of another lectionary", 6 leaves bound up with Sj^{b}.
Sj^{a-d} were published by ASLewis-MDGibson, The Palestinian Syriac Lectionary, 1899.
Sj^{k}: Cod. Climaci rescriptus (VI.), published by ASLewis, Horae Semiticae VIII, 1909.
Sj^{l}: Fragments from lectionaries at London and St. Petersburg, published by JPNLand, Anecdota Syriaca IV, 1875. $Sj^{b} + Sj^{l} = Sj^{b.l}$ in distinction from Sj^{bl} (→).
Sj^{f}: Fragments published by FSchulthess, Christlich-palästinische Fragmente aus der Omajjaden-Moschee zu Damaskus, 1905, and by HDuensing, Christlich-paläst.-aramäische Texte und Fragmente, 1906.
Sj^{b1}, or Sj^{b2}, is used if the text appears more than once in Sj^{b} and the variant in question occurs only once or twice in the witness (2.d. ←). The same procedure is followed in the collections of fragments Sj^{l} and Sj^{f}.

e. Als *Summensigel* (2.g. ←) umfaßt *S* alle unter a.—c. (←) genannten Zeugen; *S*j (d. ←) dagegen wird immer besonders aufgeführt. Zu *S*,j (= alle syr. Hss einschl. *S*j) vgl. *L*,Au (3.c. ←). Hinweise auf fragliche oder nur bedingt heranzuziehende sowie lückenhafte Zeugen entfallen bei *S* als Summensigel wie bei *L*. Lediglich das gleichzeitige Fehlen der beiden Altsyrer wird stets vermerkt: *S*[sc] = alle *S*p-Zeugen und die Harclensis, während beide Altsyrer fehlen (vgl. 3.d.2. ←).

C

5. Coptische Zeugen (Kennbuchstabe: *C*).

Aus der Vielzahl der *copt*ischen (= spät-ä*gypt*ischen) Dialekte sind größere Mengen von Evv.-Hss in sahidischer (→ a.) und bohairischer (→ b.) Sprache auf uns gekommen. Fajjumischer, akhmimischer und subakhmimischer Evangelientext (→ d.) ist nur in ganz wenigen Zeugen erhalten. In der Abgrenzung und Benennung der Dialekte gibt es (noch) keinen allgemeinen Konsensus. Die hier gegebene Einteilung erschien handlich und erhebt keinen Anspruch auf Unanfechtbarkeit.

*C*s

a. 1. Die *sahidische* (oberägyptische, thebaische) Übersetzung (*C*s) ist mit größeren zusammenhängenden Textpartien nur in drei Hss erhalten:

PBodmer XIX (Mt14$_{28}$—fin. R1$_{1}$—2$_{3}$), IV./V., hrsg. RKasser, Bibliotheca Bodmeriana, 1962.

PPalau 181 (Lk), 182 (Mk), V. erste Hälfte, hrsg. HQuecke, Papyrologica Castroctaviana Bd. 6 und 4, 1977. 1972.

Cod. Pierpont Morgan 569 (4 Evv.), IX., photographische Ausgabe von HHyvernat, Bibliothecae Pierpont Morgan codices coptici Tom. IV, 1922.

2. Daneben gibt es hunderte kleinerer weitverstreuter Fragmente (V.—XIV.), in unsäglich mühevoller Kleinarbeit gesammelt, zu einem laufenden Evangelientext zusammengefügt und — anonym — veröffentlicht von GHorner: The Coptic Version of the NT in the Southern Dialect ..., 1911. Horners Material wurde durch zahlreiche spätere Publikationen (ua von EAWBudge, WECrum, WCTill, KWessely) beträchtlich vermehrt. Jedoch können die Fragmente unmöglich einzeln aufgeführt werden.

3. Statt dessen werden sie gezählt, und zwar immer genau (also etwas anders als *L*vg und *S*p): Ist *C*s gespalten, so wird bei jeder Variante die Zahl der *C*s-Hss angezeigt, zB Cs^{4} — Cs^{7} (niemals Cs^{1}!). Wird nur eine von mehreren Varianten aufgeführt, so steht zB $Cs^{4:9}$ = vier von im ganzen neun *C*s-Zeugen (niemals $Cs^{\langle 5 \rangle}$!). Die Gesamtzahl der Hss zu einer Stelle schwankt bei *C*s besonders weit, nämlich zwischen 1 und etwa 15. Ihre Kenntnis ist für die Bewertung der einzelnen Bezeugung daher unentbehrlich.

4. Korrekturen sind in den sah. Evv.-Hss selten. Horner (Bd. 3, 374) berichtet, nur eine seiner (rekonstruierten) Hss sei einer planmäßigen Korrektur unterzogen worden. Wo eine Korrektur auftritt, wird sie wie ein zusätzlicher Zeuge gezählt (ähnlich wie 1.b.3.bb. ←).

*C*b

b. 1. Die *bohairische* (unterägyptische, memphitische) Übersetzung (*C*b) ist in vielen Voll-Hss erhalten. GHorner, The Coptic Version of the NT in the Northern Dialect ..., Oxford 1898, hat 46 z. T. lückenhafte Hss (ab IX.) und 9 kleinere Fragmente veröffentlicht, indem er die Oxforder Hs Huntington 17 (A.D. 1174) wortgetreu abdruckt und die Abweichungen der übrigen davon im Apparat vermerkt. Da sich 15 seiner Hss als getreue Abschriften einer anderen vorhandenen erweisen und somit keinen selbständigen Zeugenwert haben, werden sie bei Übereinstimmung mit ihrer Vorlage außer Betracht gelassen, bei Abweichung jedoch ebenso wie Korrekturen in den Hss behandelt, nämlich wie selbständige Zeugen (a.4. ←).

e. *S* as a *group symbol* (2.g. ←) embraces all witnesses named under a.—c. (←), but *S*j (d. ←) is always separately indicated. For S, j (= all Syr. mss including *S*j) cp. *L*,Au (3.c. ←). If *S* is used as a group symbol, then as with *L* we dispense with references to witnesses which are doubtful or which can only be cited conditionally or contain lacunae. Only the absence at the same time of both Old Syr. mss is always noted: *S*[sc] = all witnesses for *S*p and the Harclean while both Old Syriac witnesses are lacking (cp. 3.d.2. ←).

5. Coptic Witnesses (Indicator: *C*).

From the multitude of *Copt*ic (= late E*gypt*ian) dialects a large number of Gospel mss in Sahidic (→ a.) and Bohairic (→ b.) have come down to us. Fayyumic, Akhmimic and sub-Akhmimic (→ d.) texts of the Gospels survive only in quite few witnesses. In delimiting and naming these dialects there is still no general consensus. The distribution here employed seemed to me convenient and makes no claim to infallibility.

a. 1. The *Sahidic* (upper Epyptian, Thebaic) version (*C*s) is contained for large portions of continuous text only in three mss:

PBodmer XIX (Mt14$_{28}$—fin.; R1$_{1}$—2$_{3}$), IV./V., published by RKasser, 1962.

PPalau 181 (Lk), 182 (Mk), first half of V., published by HQuecke, Papyrologica Castroctaviana, vol. 6 and 4, 1977. 1972.

Cod. Pierpont Morgan 569 (4 Gospels) IX., photographic reproduction (edition) by HHyvernat, Bibliothecae Pierpont Morgan codices coptici Tome IV, 1922.

2. In addition there are hundreds of small scattered fragments (V.—XIV.) collected and fused with indescribably arduous work into a continuous text of the Gospels and, without giving his name, published by GHorner, The Coptic Version of the NT in the Southern Dialect ..., 1911. Horner's material was considerably added to by numerous later publications (among others by EAWBudge, WECrum, WCTill, KWessely). However it would be impossible to indicate the fragments individually.

3. Instead they are always exactly numbered (and so somewhat differently from *L*vg and *S*p): if *C*s is divided, then the number of *C*s mss is indicated with each variant, e. g. Cs^{4} — Cs^{7} (never Cs^{1}!). If only one variant out of several is quoted, then we have e. g. $Cs^{4:9}$ = four out of nine *C*s mss in all (never $Cs^{\langle 5 \rangle}$!). The total number of mss at any one passage varies considerably with *C*s, i. e. between 1 and about 15. Knowledge of this number is therefore indispensable for the assessment of the evidence at various places.

4. Corrections in Sah. mss are rare, Horner (vol. 3, 374) informs us that only one of his reconstructed mss has undergone systematic correction. Where there is a correction it is counted as an additional witness (similarly as at 1.b.3.bb. ←).

b. 1. The *Bohairic* (lower Egyptian, Memphitic) version (*C*b) is preserved in many complete mss. GHorner, The Coptic Version of the NT in the Northern Dialect ... 1898, has published 46 mss (from IX.), some of them with lacunae, and 9 smaller fragments. He has printed the Oxford ms Huntington 17 (A.D. 1174) word for word and given the variants of the other mss in the apparatus. Since 15 of his mss are shown to be exact copies of other mss now extant and so have no independent value they are left out of account when they agree with their exemplars, but, when they disagree with them, they are treated like corrections in the mss, i. e. like independent witnesses (a.4. ←).

2. Auch boh. Zeugen sind nach Horners grundlegendem Werk zusätzlich ans Licht gekommen. Der bei weitem wichtigste von ihnen ist PBodmer III (Jo Gn1₁—4₂), IV., hrsg. RKasser, CSCO 177, 1958. Diese Hs ist 500(!) Jahre älter als die älteste bisher bekannte und widerlegt die vorher lange herrschende Meinung, die boh. Übersetzung sei wesentlich später entstanden als die sah.

3. Die boh. Hss werden auch nur gezählt wie *L*vg und *S*p (3.b.1. und 4.b. ←; s. auch 5.b.1. am Ende ←), doch wird PBodmer III (2. ←) stets genannt, wo er vorhanden ist. So bedeutet

*C*b: alle boh. Zeugen.

Cb^{+B} (Cb'^{+B}): alle (die restlichen) boh. Zeugen einschließlich PBodmer.

$Cb^{\langle B\rangle}$ ($Cb'^{\langle B\rangle}$): alle (die restlichen) boh. Zeugen im Gegensatz zu PBodmer.

Cb^{B}: PBodmer (allein).

Cb^{B4}: PBodmer und 4 boh. Hss.

S. auch → e.

c. Die Zählziffern ¹ ² ··· sowie das Restzeichen ' beziehen sich ohne Rücksicht auf ( ) immer auf das letztvorhergegangene *C*s oder *C*b, zB Cs^2(*om* και: s^7b')$^6a^v$ = zwei sah., sechs boh. Hss und offensichtlich die akhm. Überlieferung haben die angegebene Lesart, sieben sah. und der Rest der boh. Hss lassen και aus.

d. Von der *fajjumischen* (mittelägyptischen, basmurischen) (*C*f), der *akhmimischen* (*C*a) und der *subakhmimischen* (Ca^s) Übersetzung gibt es fast nur kleinere Fragmente. Eine Ausnahme bilden zwei größere Hss-Reste von

*C*f: PMichigan 3521 (Jo6₁₁—15₁₁), IV./1., hrsg. EMHusselmann, 1962.

Ca^s: Ein Papyrus-Codex (Jo), 350/375 A.D., hrsg. HThompson. The Gospel of St. John according to the earliest Coptic manuscript. British School of Archaeology in Egypt and Egyptian Research Account 29, 1924.

e. Als *Summensigel* (2.g. ←) faßt *C* alle unter a. und b. (←) genannten Hss außer PBodmer zusammen. Dieser wird ebenso besonders aufgeführt wie die unter d. (←) genannten Zeugen für $Cfaa^s$. Es bedeutet somit

C^{+B} (C'^{+B}): alle (die restlichen) sah. und boh. Hss, dazu PBodmer.

$C^{\langle B\rangle}$ ($C'^{\langle B\rangle}$): alle (die restlichen) sah. und boh. Hss im Gegensatz zu PBodmer.

$C^{\langle B\rangle}aa^s$: alle sah., boh., akhm. und subakhm. Hss im Gegensatz zu PBodmer.

C⟨f⟩: alle sah. und boh. Zeugen, im Gegensatz zu den fajj.

6. Armenische Zeugen (Kennbuchstaben: *Arm*).

a. Der arm. Evv.-Text wurde nach der Ausgabe von JZohrab, NT ... armenice editum, Venedig 1805, herangezogen. Die von Z. benutzten Hss werden in seinem Apparat fast niemals namentlich, sondern nur unbestimmt angegeben: „eine Hs", „einige", „viele Hss". Nur ein Cod. Venetus von A.D. 1319 wird bisweilen besonders genannt. Außerdem wird die Ausgabe von Oskan (Uscanus) häufig zitiert, deren Text aber erheblich an den der lat. Vulgata (*L*vg) angeglichen ist.

b. Auch *Arm* dient als Summensigel (2.g. ←), wenn die handschriftliche Überlieferung zusammengefaßt werden soll. Dagegen ist *Arm*Cr ein Zitat in der arm. Übersetzung einer Schrift des Cyrill von Alexandria (3.c. ←).

c. Im einzelnen bedeutet

Arm^V: Codex arm. Venetus, A.D. 1319

Arm^1: eine einzelne arm. Hs } nach Zohrab
Arm^{pc}: wenige arm. Hss } nach Zohrab
Arm^{mu}: viele arm. Hss } nach Zohrab

2. Some Boh. witnesses have also come to light since Horner's fundamental work. By far the most important of them has been published by RKasser, Papyrus Bodmer III Evangile de Jean et Genèse 1₁—4₂ en bohaïrique, CSCO 177, 1958. This ms (IV.) is 500 years older than the oldest hitherto known ms and overthrows the opinion previously long dominant that the Boh. version came into being substantially later than the Sah.

3. The Boh. mss are enumerated in the same way as *L*vg and *S*p (3.b.1. and 4.b. ←; see also 5.b.1. at the end ←), but PBodmer III (2. ←) is always cited where it is extant. In this

*C*b = all Boh. witnesses.

Cb^{+B} (Cb'^{+B}) = all (or, the remaining) Boh. witnesses including PBodmer.

$Cb^{\langle B\rangle}$ ($Cb'^{\langle B\rangle}$) = all (or, the remaining) Boh. witnesses in opposition to PBodmer.

Cb^{B} = PBodmer alone.

Cb^{B4} = PBodmer and 4 Boh. mss.

See also → e.

c. The numbers ¹ ² ··· as well as ', the symbol for the remainder, refer, without regard to ( ), to the nearest preceding *C*s or *C*b, e. g. Cs^2(*om* και: s^7b')$^6a^v$ = two Sah. and six Boh. mss and apparently the Akhm. represent the reading in question, while seven Sah. and the rest of the Boh. mss leave out και.

d. From *Fayyumic* (Middle Egyptian, Basmurian) (*C*f), *Akhmimic* (*C*a) and *sub-Akhmimic* (Ca^s) we have for the most part only small fragments. The more extensive remains of two mss form an exception:

$Cfaa^s$

*C*f: PMichigan 3521 (Jo6₁₁—15₁₁), IV./1., edited by EMHusselmann, 1962.

Ca^s: a papyrus codex (Jo) 350/375 A.D., edited by HThomson, The Gospel of St. John according to the earliest Coptic ms. British School of Archaeology in Egypt and Egyptian Research Account 29, 1924.

e. *C* as a *group symbol* (2.g. ←) embraces all mss named under a. and b. (←) except PBodmer. This ms is separately introduced like the witnesses for $Cfaa^s$ mentioned under d. (←). So the following symbols are to be understood as indicated:

C^{+B} (C'^{+B}): all (the remaining) Sah. and Boh. mss and PBodmer.

$C^{\langle B\rangle}$ $C'^{\langle B\rangle}$): all (the remaining) Sah. and Boh. mss in opposition to PBodmer.

$C^{\langle B\rangle}aa^s$: all Sah., Boh., Akhm. and sub-Akhm. mss in opposition to PBodmer.

C⟨f⟩: all Sah. and Boh. witnesses in opposition to the Fayy.

6. Armenian Witnesses (Indicator: *Arm*).

a. The evidence of the Arm. Gospel text is taken from the edition of JZohrab, NT ... armenice editum, Venice 1805. The mss used by Z. are almost never cited by name but only in general terms ("one ms", "some", "many mss"). Only a Cod. Venetus of A.D. 1319 is separately named from time to time. In addition the edition of Oskan (Uscanus) is often quoted, whose text, however, is considerably assimilated to the Vulgate (*L*vg).

b. *Arm* serves too as *group symbol* (2.g. ←) if the ms tradition is to be presented as a whole. *Arm*Cr however is a quotation in the Arm. Version of a writing of Cyril of Alexandria (3.c. ←).

c. The following symbols are used:

Arm^V: Codex arm. Venetus, A.D. 1319

Arm^1: a single Arm. ms } according to Zohrab
Arm^{pc}: a few Arm. mss } according to Zohrab
Arm^{mu}: many Arm. mss } according to Zohrab

Arm^0: Oskans Ausgabe von 1666
Arm: alle arm. Hss
Arm': alle übrigen arm. Hss
Neben *Arm* und *Arm*' wird *Arm*^{0} nicht genannt, auch wenn er mit ihnen geht.

d. Über die Zitierung oder Nicht-Zitierung von *Arm* → 9.

7. Georgische Zeugen (Kennbuchstaben: *Geo*).

a. Das Zeugnis der georg. Hss wurde mangels eigenen Zugangs zu dieser Sprache einer besonders um wörtliche Genauigkeit bemühten Übersetzung ins Lat. entnommen: JMolitor, Synopsis latina evangeliorum ibericorum antiquissimorum secundum Matthaeum, Marcum, Lucam, CSCO 256, Louvain 1965; Derselbe, Das Adysh-Tetraevangelium neu übersetzt und mit altgeorg. Paralleltexten verglichen (hier: Jo), Oriens Christianus 44, 1960, 1—16; 45, 1961, 1—19; 46, 1962, 1—18; 47, 1963, 1—15. Außer den von Molitor benutzten Voll-Hss sind auch die von ihm (CSCO 166, 1956; 39 frgm.) und JNBirdsall (Or. Chr. 55, 1971, 62ff.; 1 frgm.) herausgegebenen und ins Lat. übersetzten sogenannten Chanmeti- und Haemeti-Fragmente der Evv. berücksichtigt, die einen sprachlich altertümlichen Text bieten.

b. Alle 4 Evv sind in folgenden Hss enthalten:
Geo^1 = Adysh-Tetraevangelium (A.D. 897),
Geo^A = Opiza- „ (A.D. 913),
Geo^B = Tbeth- „ (A.D. 995),
Geo^C = Urbnisi- „ (X.).
Geo^L = Fragment eines Perikopenbuchs (Mk14 33-38), in *Geo*^{1} hinter Jo.

Die Chanmeti- und Haemeti-Fragmente werden mit dem einheitlichen Zeichen *Geo*^{ch} dargestellt.

c. Als *Summensigel* (2.g. ←) umfaßt *Geo* die 4 Hss *Geo*$^{1\ A\ B\ C}$, von denen *Geo*^{A} und ^{B} unter *Geo*^{2} zusammengefaßt werden. *Geo*^{C} wird jedoch nur herangezogen, wenn sowohl *Geo*^{A} als auch *Geo*^{B} fehlen, und ist dann wie diese in *Geo* enthalten. Es bedeutet somit
Geo (*Geo*'): alle (die restlichen) Tetraevangelien (b. ←).
Geo$^{\langle B \rangle}$: alle Tetraevangelien außer *Geo*^{B} (Tbeth).
Geo^{ch}: ein Chanmeti- oder Haemeti-Text (allein).
Geo^{ch2}: zwei Chanmeti- oder Haemeti-Texte.
Geo^{1ch}: *Geo*^{1} (Adysh), dazu ein Chanmeti-(usw)-Text.
Geo^{+ch}: alle Tetraevangelien, dazu ein Chanmeti-(usw)-Text.

d. Über die Zitierung oder Nichtzitierung von *Geo* → 9.

8. Äthiopische (*Aeth*), arabische (*Arab*), gotische (*Got*) und altslawische (altbulgarische) (*Slav*) Zeugen.

Der Evv.-Text dieser Übersetzungen wurde mehr oder weniger regelmäßig herangezogen, wie er aus den App. anderer Ausgaben zu entnehmen war. Eine eigene planmäßige Überprüfung fand nicht statt. Über Zitierung oder Nichtzitierung → 9.

9. Sekundär-Übersetzungen.

a. Im Unterschied zu der lat., syr. und copt. gelten die in 6.—8. (←) aufgezählten alten Übersetzungen als sekundär. Sie gehen erwiesenermaßen oder — trotz aller Umstrittenheit doch — möglicherweise auf eine nichtgriechische Vorlage zurück, auch wenn sie später an Hand gr. Hss durchkorrigiert wurden. Stimmt eine Variante in einer Sekundär-Übersetzung mit (einer) ihrer nichtgr. Vorlage(n) überein, so steht sie im Verdacht, von der letzteren abhängig zu sein, und hat keinen selbständigen Zeugenwert. In diesem Falle wäre die Anführung im Apparat nutzloser Ballast. Das gleiche gilt für *Aeth*, *Arab*, *Got* und *Slav* aus zeitlichen oder geographischen Gründen, wenn sie mit *Rpl* gehen.

Arm^0: Oskan's edition of 1666
Arm: all Arm. mss
Arm': all remaining Arm. mss
Arm^0 is not mentioned beside *Arm* and *Arm*' even if it agrees with them.

d. On the citing, or not citing, of *Arm* → 9.

7. Georgian Witnesses (Indicator: *Geo*).

a. Because I lack command of Georg. I have taken the evidence of Georg. mss from a Lat. rendering particularly concerned about verbal accuracy: JMolitor, Synopsis latina evangeliorum ibericorum antiquissimorum secundum Mt. Mk, Lk, CSCO 256, 1965; the same, Das Adysh-Tetra-Evangelium neu übersetzt und mit altgeorg. Paralleltexten verglichen (Jo1—21 in:) Oriens Christianus 44—47, 1960—1963. In addition to these complete mss Molitor published and translated into Lat. 39 fragments (CSCO 166, 1956) and JNBirdsall one further fragment (Or. Chr. 55, 1971, 62ff.), all of them giving Gospel texts in an linguistically archaic character (Chanmeti and Haemeti).

b. All four Gospels are contained in the following mss:
Geo^1 = Adysh Tetraevangelium (A.D. 897),
Geo^A = Opiza „ (A.D. 913),
Geo^B = Tbeth „ (A.D. 995),
Geo^C = Urbnisi „ (X.).
Geo^L = a fragment of a lectionary book (Mk14 33-38) in *Geo*^{1} after Jo.

The Chanmeti and Haemeti fragments are represented by a uniform symbol *Geo*^{ch}.

c. *Geo* as a *group symbol* (2.g. ←) embraces the 4 mss *Geo*$^{1\ A\ B\ C}$ of which *Geo*^{A} and ^{B} are included under *Geo*^{2}. *Geo*^{C} is only used when both *Geo*^{A} and ^{B} are lacking and like them is contained in *Geo*. Therefore
Geo (*Geo*') = all (the remaining) Tetraevangelia (b. ←).
Geo^B = all Tetraevangelia except *Geo*^{B} (Tbeth).
Geo^{ch} = one Chanmeti or Haemeti text alone.
Geo^{ch2} = two Chanmeti or Haemeti texts.
Geo^{1ch} = *Geo*^{1} (Adysh) and one Chaemeti (etc.) text.
Geo^{+ch} = all Tetraevangelia and one Chaemeti (etc.) text in addition.

d. On the citing, or not citing, of *Geo* → 9.

8. Ethiopic (*Aeth*), Arabic (*Arab*), Gothic (*Got*) and Old Slavonic (Old Bulgarian) (*Slav*) Witnesses.

The Gospel text of these versions is cited more or less regularly as far as I was able to abstract it from the apparatus of other editions, but I have not tested their evidence systematically for myself. On the citing, or not citing, of these versions → 9.

9. Secondary Versions.

a. In distinction from the Lat., Syr. and Copt. versions the old versions recorded in 6.—8. (←) rank as secondary. Either demonstrably or, despite all dispute, possibly they go back to a non-Greek exemplar, even if they are later corrected from Gr. mss. If a secondary version agrees in a variant with its non-Gr. exemplar, then it is suspected of being dependent on it and has no independent value as a witness. In this case its appearance in the apparatus would be a purposeless taking up of space. The same holds true for *Aeth*, *Arab*, *Got* and *Slav* for reasons of time or geography if they agree with *Rpl*.

b. Es werden daher *nicht* aufgeführt
Arm, wenn es mit *Sp* übereinstimmt;
Geo, „ „ „ *Sp* oder *Arm* „ ;
Aeth, wenn es mit *Sp* oder *Rpl* übereinstimmt;
Arab, „ „ „ *Sp* „ *Rpl* „ ;
Got, „ „ „ *Rpl* „ ;
Slav, „ „ „ *Rpl* „ .

c. Ist *Sp* im Hinblick auf seine gr. Vorlage *mehrdeutig* und steht daher {*Sp*} bei der einen, {} bei (einer) anderen Variante(n), so ist *Arm* usw bei allen diesen Varianten — abgesehen von besonders begründeten Ausnahmefällen — fortgelassen. Dies tritt auch dann ein, wenn *Sp* wegen notorischer Mehrdeutigkeit (zB im Falle ουρανοι/ουρανος) ganz unerwähnt blieb. Das gleiche gilt für {*Arm*} mit Wirkung auf *Geo*.

d. Ist *Sp* dagegen *gespalten* und steht daher *Sp*' bei der einen, *Sp*⁴, *Sp*² usw bei anderen Varianten, so bekommen die von *Sp* abhängigen Übersetzungen wieder Gewicht und werden zitiert. Sie geben nämlich dem Überlieferungsstrang innerhalb *Sp*, dem sie zustimmen, erhöhte Relevanz. Entsprechendes gilt für *Arm* mit Bezug auf *Geo*.

e. Die Sekundär-Übersetzungen (6.—8. ←) sind immer angeführt, wenn sie selbst gespalten sind.

10. Bemerkungen zum Zeugenwert der Übersetzungen.

a. Die älteren Übersetzungen (in Klammern: das Jhdt ihrer Entstehung) ins Lateinische (Mitte II.), Syrische (II./III.) und Coptische (III./1.) sind, auch wenn die erhaltenen Hss aus späteren Jhdten stammen, oftmals indirekte Zeugen für eine Zeit, aus der wir wenige oder gar keine gr. Hss besitzen. Das kann ihnen unter Umständen — besonders für die Lokalisierung einer Lesart — einen hohen Zeugenwert verleihen.

b. Geringer ist, aufs Ganze gesehen, der Zeugenwert der oben (9.a. ←) als sekundär bezeichneten Übersetzungen. Ihr Alter und ihr Ursprung ist immer noch umstritten; doch wird heute weithin folgendes angenommen:
Gotische Übersetzung: Mitte IV., aus dem Gr.
Äthiopische „ : IV. oder VII./VIII., aus dem Gr. oder Syr.?
Armenische „ : V., aus dem Gr. oder Syr.?
Georgische „ : V.?, aus dem Gr. oder Arm.?
Arabische „ : VII./VIII., aus dem Gr. oder Copt.?
Altslawische „ : IX., aus dem Gr.

Alle diese Übersetzungen sind im Laufe der Zeit mit griech. Hss verglichen und oft nach ihnen korrigiert worden. So können sie ebenso gut wertvolle Lesarten enthalten wie eine späte gr. Minuskel.

c. Die sprachliche Verschiedenheit vom Gr. nimmt den Übersetzungen in bestimmten Fällen jeden Zeugenwert, zB im
Lat.: 1) Es gibt keinen Artikel, nur selten wird er durch ein Pronomen angedeutet; also kein Zeugenwert für Ἰησοῦ gegen τοῦ Ἰησοῦ.
2) Singularisches Prädikat nach einem Neutrum plur. ist nicht möglich.
3) Infinitiv mit vorangehendem εἰς τό oder τοῦ wird in einen Nebensatz umgebildet.
Syr.: 1) = Lat. 1), 2), 3).
2) Partizipialkonstruktionen müssen aufgelöst werden.
3) Oft ist der Unterschied zwischen Sing. und Plur. nur aus einem — später hinzugefügten — Zeichen (Sejâmê) zu entnehmen und daher für den ältesten Textbestand nicht auszumachen.
4) „Himmel" ist im Syr. ein plurale tantum; kein Zeugenwert für τῶν οὐρανῶν gegen τοῦ οὐρανοῦ.

b. For this reason I do not cite
Arm if it agrees with *Sp*;
Geo „ „ „ „ *Sp* or *Arm*;
Aeth if it agrees with *Sp* or *Rpl*;
Arab „ „ „ „ *Sp* or *Rpl*;
Got „ „ „ „ *Rpl*;
Slav „ „ „ „ *Rpl*.

c. If *Sp* is ambiguous in reference to its Gr. exemplar and so {*Sp*} occurs with one variant and {} with one or more others, then *Arm* etc. is left out with all these variants, apart from exceptions for which there are special reasons. This also applies if *Sp* is not quoted for well known reasons (e. g. in the case of ουρανοι/ουρανος). The same is true for {*Arm*} with reference to *Geo*.

d. If *Sp* is divided and *Sp*' occurs with one and *Sp*⁴, *Sp*² etc. with other variants, then the versions dependent on *Sp* gain in significance and are quoted. They give increased relevance to the strand of tradition within *Sp* with which they agree. This is correspondingly true for *Arm* with reference to *Geo*.

e. The secondary versions (6.—8. ←) are always cited if they are themselves divided.

10. Notes on the Value of the Versions as Witnesses.

a. The older translations (I give in brackets the century in which they were made) into Latin (mid II.), Syriac (II./III.) and Coptic (III./1.) are, even if the surviving mss come from later centuries, often indirect witnesses for a time when we have few or no Gr. mss. In some circumstances, especially where the localisation of a reading is concerned, this can bestow a high value as a witness on our versions.

b. Regarded as a whole, the value as witnesses of the translations described above as secondary (9.a. ←) is less. Their age and their origin is still always contested, but today the following is widely assumed:
Gothic translation mid IV. from Greek
Ethiopic „ IV. or VII./VIII. from Gr. or Syr.?
Armenian „ V. from Gr. or Syr.?
Georgian „ V.? from Gr. or Arm.?
Arabic „ VII./VIII. from Gr. or Copt.?
Old Slavonic „ IX. from Gr.

In course of time all these translations were compared with Gr. mss, and often corrected from them. Just as well as a late Gr. miniscule they can contain valuable readings.

c. Their linguistic differences from the Gr. deprives the translations in certain cases of all value as witnesses, e. g. in
Lat.: 1) Since there is no article it is seldom rendered in Lat., e. g. by a pronoun; the Lat. has no value as a witness for Ἰησοῦ against τοῦ Ἰησοῦ.
2) A singular verb is not possible after a neuter plural subject.
3) An infinitive after εἰς τό or τοῦ is rendered with a subordinate clause.
Syr.: 1) = Lat. 1) 2) 3).
2) Participial constructions must be resolved.
3) Often the difference between sing. and plur. is to be inferred only from Sejâmê, a sign added later and so is not to be detected in the oldest texts.
4) "Heaven" occurs in Syr. only in the plural. So Syr. is no witness for τῶν οὐρανῶν against τοῦ οὐρανοῦ.
5) The rendering of an historic present by a present occurs almost only with "say" (λέγει etc.).

5) Wiedergabe eines praesens historicum kommt fast nur bei „sagen" (λέγει etc.) vor.

6) Voranstellung von αὐτοῦ etc. vor einem Substantiv ist nicht möglich.

7) Für καὶ ... καί, οὔτε ... οὔτε gibt es kein Äquivalent; statt dessen wird die einfache Partikel verwendet.

Copt.: 1) = Lat. 2).

2) = Syr. 2), 6), 7).

3) Es gibt kein praesens historicum.

4) „Alle" steht immer voran; kein Zeugenwert für πάντα ταῦτα gegen ταῦτα πάντα.

5) Das nähere und das entferntere Objekt steht *nach* dem Verbum; kein Zeugenwert für εἶπεν αὐτῷ gegen αὐτῷ εἶπεν.

Arm.: 1) = Lat. 2).

2) Gebrauch des Artikels ist weithin verschieden vom Gr.

3) In „all diese" u. ä. steht das Pronomen voran; kein Zeugenwert für ταῦτα πάντα gegen πάντα ταῦτα.

4) Weiterführendes δέ wird häufig durch „und" oder überhaupt nicht wiedergegeben.

5) Das Mittel oder Werkzeug steht im bloßen Instrumentalis; kein Zeugenwert für ὕδατι statt ἐν ὕδατι.

6) Die Zeitangabe (Wann?) wird durch i + Locativ wiedergegeben; kein Zeugenwert für ἐν καιρῷ gegen καιρῷ.

7) Der Gen. partitivus wird fast immer durch i + Ablativ wiedergegeben; kein Zeugenwert für εἷς ἐκ τῶν ... gegen εἷς τῶν ...

Volle Nachahmung der gr. Wortstellung ist nur im Lat. weitgehend möglich. Ebenso ist die Wiedergabe von ἤδη in den nichtlat. Sprachen immer schwankend.

d. In den vorstehend angeführten Fällen ist die betreffende Übersetzung häufig, aber nicht immer weggelassen; bisweilen ist ihre Wiedergabe wegen benachbarter Varianten wissenswert. Die in 9.b. (←) genannten Auslassungen sind dagegen konsequent ausgeführt.

e. Genauere Auskunft über die Übersetzungen und ihre textkritische Verwertbarkeit geben KAland (Hrsg.), Die alten Übersetzungen des NT, die Kirchenväterzitate und Lektionare = ANTF 5, 1972; BMMetzger, The Early Versions of the NT, 1977, 83ff. 141ff. 171ff. 199ff. 240ff. 362ff. 388ff. 431ff.

Δ

11. Das Zeugnis der Evangelien-Harmonien
(Kennbuchstabe: Δ).

a. Obwohl sie selbst durchweg zu den nichtgriechischen Sprachgruppen gehören — lediglich in Δg (→ c.) haben wir ein kleines gr. Δ-Fragment —, sind die Harmonien zusammengefaßt ans Ende der Zeugen-Aufzählung gestellt. Das verlangt die Sonderstellung, die sie gemeinsam gegenüber den Evv.-Hss, den Perikopenbüchern und den Evv.-Zitaten der Schr. einnehmen. Daß sie ausnahmslos auf Tatians Diatessaron zurückgehen, wird heute kaum noch angenommen.

b. Bei harmonistischen Varianten haben die Harmonien keinen eigenen Zeugenwert. Die Verschmelzung der parallelen Texte zu einem einzigen ist ihre erklärte Absicht, sie müssen also harmonisieren. Dennoch erlauben sie in bestimmten Fällen Rückschlüsse auf den Text der „getrennten" Evv., dann nämlich, wenn es sich handelt um

1. Varianten innerhalb des Sonderguts der einzelnen Evangelisten.

2. Varianten, die in der ganzen sonstigen Überlieferung ausschließlich für ein bestimmtes der an dieser Stelle zusammengearbeiteten Evv. bezeugt sind.

3. Varianten, die nicht aus den unmittelbaren Parallel-Perikopen stammen, sondern aus ähnlichen Partien in anderen Peri-

6) The placing of αὐτοῦ (gen.) etc. before a substantive is not possible.

7) There are no equivalents for καὶ ... καί, οὔτε ... οὔτε; instead a single particle is used.

Copt.: 1) = Lat. 2).

2) = Syr. 2), 6), 7).

3) There is no historic present.

4) "All" always precedes; Copt. has no value as a witness for πάντα ταῦτα against ταῦτα πάντα.

5) The direct and the indirect object stand after the verb; Copt. has no value as a witness for εἶπεν αὐτῷ against αὐτῷ εἶπεν.

Arm.: 1) = Lat. 2).

2) The use of the article is widely different from Gr.

3) In "all these" etc. the pronoun comes first and so Arm. has no value as a witness for ταῦτα πάντα against πάντα ταῦτα.

4) Merely connective δέ is frequently rendered by "and" or not at all.

5) The means or instrument is in the simple instrumental; the Arm. is no witness for ὕδατι against ἐν ὕδατι.

6) The indication of time ("when") is rendered by i + locative; the Arm. has no value as a witness for ἐν καιρῷ against καιρῷ.

7) The partitive genitive is almost always rendered by i + ablative; the Arm. has no value as a witness for εἷς ἐκ τῶν ... against εἷς τῶν ...

The complete reproduction of the Greek order of words is possible only in Latin to any great extent. In the same the rendering of ἤδη is always varying in the languages other than Lat.

d. In the cases mentioned above the relevant version is often omitted but not always; sometimes its rendering is worth knowing because of neighbouring variants. The omission mentioned in 9.b. (←) are on the other hand always consistently observed.

e. More about the versions and their value as witnesses is to be found in KAland (ed.), Die alten Übersetzungen des NT, die Kirchenväterzitate und Lektionare = ANTF 5, 1972; BMMetzger, The Early Versions of the NT, 1977, 83ff. 141ff. 171ff. 199ff. 240ff. 362ff. 388ff. 431ff.

11. The Witness of the Gospel Harmonies
(Indicator: Δ).

a. Although they themselves belong throughout to the groups of non-Greek witnesses (only Δg is a small fragment in Greek, → c.), the Harmonies as a whole are placed at the end of the enumeration of witnesses. This is required by the distinctive position that they occupy in common over against the Gospel mss, the lectionaries and the quotations of the Gospels in ancient writers. That they go back without exception to Tatian's Diatessaron is hardly assumed any more nowadays.

b. For harmonizing variants the Harmonies have no particular value as witnesses. Their declared purpose is to fuse parallel texts into one single text and so they have to harmonize. Yet they permit us in particular cases to draw conclusions about the text of the "separate" Gospels especially if it is a matter of

1. variants within the passages peculiar to one of the Gospels.

2. variants which are witnessed in the rest of the whole tradition exclusively in only one Gospel of those used at this point.

3. variants which do not derive from immediately parallel passages, but must have been intruded from similar parts of

..kopen eingedrungen sein müssen. Dabei muß allerdings gleichzeitig die Bedingung zu 2. (←) erfüllt sein.

c. Die Harmonien werden in alphabetischer Reihenfolge ihrer Sigeln angeführt (zu den einzelnen Hss → IV.c.):

Δa: Die arabische Übersetzung von Tatians Diatessaron durch 'Abu'l Farag ibn at-Tayyib († A.D. 1043). Hss: Δa^{A} und ^{B} zitiert nach ACiasca, Tatiani evangeliorum harmoniae arabice 1888 (mit lat. Übersetzung); Δa^{E} zitiert nach ASMarmardji, Diatessaron de Tatien 1935 (mit franz. Übersetzung). Weitere Hss sind bekannt, aber — außer einigen Fragmenten aus Beirut (1331/32 A.D.) — nicht publiziert.

Δad: Althochdeutsche Harmonie, zitiert nach ESievers, Tatian, lateinisch und altdeutsch ^{2}1892.

Δg: Gr. Δ-Fragment (= **0212** bei Aland, ANTF 1 → IV.a.), enthaltend Stoff aus Perikope *265.* und *266.*, zitiert nach CHKraeling, A Greek Fragment of Tatian's Diatessaron from Dura. Studies and Documents 3, 1935.

Δi: Harmonien in toskanischem (Δi^{T}) und venetischen (Δi^{V}) Dialekt, zitiert nach VTodesco-AVaccari-MVattasso, Il Diatessaron in volgare italiano 1938 (Abdruck der einzigen Δi^{V}-Hs und Rezension des Δi^{T}-Textes auf Grund von 6 voll-, 9 teilkollationierten und 7 gelegentlich herangezogenen Hss). Δi^{T2} = zwei der Δi^{T}-Hss; Δi$^{T(M)}$ = Hs M der Δi^{T} Rezension (→ IV.c.).

Δl: Lat. Harmonien Δl^{ADFG}, zitiert nach HJVogels, Beiträge zur Geschichte des Diatessaron im Abendland = Neutestamentliche Abhandlungen VIII 1, 1919 (Kollation von Δl^{AD} gegen *L*vg nach Wordsworth-White; Proben aus weiteren Hss); ERanke, Codex Fuldensis (Δl^{F}) 1868; ESievers (Δl^{G} s. zu Δad ←). Mit Δl$^{ms(s)}$ werden eine (oder mehrere) der von Vogels in Proben verglichenen Hss besonders erwähnt.

Δmd: Mitteldeutsche Harmonien, zitiert nach CGerhardt, Das Leben Jhesu, Corpus sacrae scripturae neerlandicae medii aevi, Series minor I 4, 1970 (Abdruck einer Züricher Hs: Δmd^{Z}; Kollation von 5 weiteren Hss: Δmd^{NWU,MV} und einem Grazer Fragment: Δmd^{G}). Beide Gruppen, Δmd^{ZNWUG} und Δmd^{MV}, gehen auf Δn (→) zurück.

Δme: Die mittelengl. "Pepysian Gospel Harmony", hrsg. MGoates 1922. Sie gibt eine — meist verkürzende — Paraphrase des Δ-Textes, wobei fast alle Logien in indirekte Rede verwandelt werden.

Δn: Mittelniederländische Harmonien, Δn^{CHgHrLS}, zitiert nach den Ausgaben von JBergsma, De Levens van Jezus in het Middelnederlandsch 1895 (Abdruck von Δn^{L} und ^{S}, Kollation von Δn^{Hg}); DPlooij, The Liège Diatessaron, Verhandelingen der Koninklijke Nederlandse Akademie van Wetenschapen, 1929—70 (Δn^{L} mit engl. Übersetzung); CCdeBruin, Het Luikse Diatessaron, Corpus ... (Δmd ←) I 1, 1970 (Δn^{L} mit engl. Übersetzung); Ders., Het Haarense Diatessaron, Corpus ... I 2, 1970 (Δn^{Hr}); Ders., Het Diatessaron van Cambridge, Corpus ... I 3, 1970 (Δn^{C} mit einer großen Lücke, → IV.c.). Δn umfaßt alle Hss mit Ausnahme von Δn^{C}, wo sie fehlt.

Δp: Persische Harmonie, hrsg. GMessina, Diatessaron persiano, Biblica et Orientalia 14, 1951 (mit italienischer Übersetzung).

ΔE: Kommentar Efrems zu Tatians Diatessaron, aus dem syr. Ur- und dem arm. Übersetzungstext zitiert nach LLeloir, Saint Ephrem. Commentaire de l'évangile concordant. Texte syriaque (ΔE^{s} mit lat. Übersetzung) 1962; Ders., Saint Ephrem, Commentaire .... Version arménienne (ΔE^{a}), CSCO 137 (dazu lat. Übersetzung: CSCO 145) 1953 (1954).

d. Auch Δ dient als *Summensigel* (2.g. ←). Es umfaßt als solche alle unter c. (←) aufgeführten Zeugen mit folgenden Ausnahmen:

other pericopes. In any such case the conditions mentioned in 2. (←) must be fulfilled.

c. The Harmonies are introduced in the alphabetical sequence of their symbols (for the separate mss → IV.c.):

Δa: the Arabic translation of Tatian's Diatessaron by 'Abu'l Farag ibn at-Tayyib († A.D. 1043). Mss Δa^{A} and ^{B} cited according to ACiasca, Tatiani evangeliorum harmoniae arabice 1888 (with Lat. translation), Δa^{E} from ASMarmardji, Diatessaron de Tatien 1935 (with french translation). More mss are known but except for a few fragments from Beirut (A.D. 1331/32) have not been published.

Δad: Old High German Harmony from ESievers, Tatian, lateinisch und altdeutsch ^{2}1892.

Δg: Gr. Δ fragment (**0212** in Aland ANTF 1, → IV.a.) containing material from pericopes *265.* and *266.*, from CHKraeling, A Greek Fragment of Tatian's Diatessaron from Dura, Studies and Documents 3, 1935.

Δi: Harmonies in Tuscan (Δi^{T}) and Venetian (Δi^{V}) dialects from VTodesco-AVaccari-MVattasso, Il Diatessaron in volgare italiano 1938 (a reproduction of the one ms of Δi^{V} and a recension of the text of Δi^{T} using 6 fully collated 9 partly collated and 7 occasionally cited mss). Δi^{T2} = 2 of the Δi^{T} mss; Δi$^{T(M)}$ = ms M of the Δi^{T} recension (→ IV.c.).

Δl: Lat. Harmonies Δl^{ADFG}, from HJVogels, Beiträge zur Geschichte des Diatessaron im Abendland, Neutestamentliche Abhandlungen VIII 1, 1919 (collation of Δl^{AD} against Wordsworth and White's edition of *L*vg; test passages from additional mss); ERanke, Codex Fuldensis (Δl^{F}) 1868; ESievers (Δl^{G}, see to Δad ←). Δl^{ms} (Δl^{mss}) indicates one (or more) of Vogel's additional mss.

Δmd: Middle German Harmonies from CGerhardt, Das Leben Jhesu, Corpus sacrae scripturae neerlandicae medii aevi, Series minor I 4, 1970 (printed from a Zürich ms Δmd^{Z}, and collated with 5 additional mss Δmd^{NWU,MV} and with a fragment in Graz Δmd^{G}). Both groups Δmd^{ZNWUG} and Δmd^{MV} go back to Δn (→).

Δme: the Middle English Harmony from MGoates, The Pepysian Gospel Harmony, 1922. This provides a paraphrase of a Δ text mostly in abbreviated form in which nearly all logia are changed into indirect speech.

Δn: Middle Dutch Harmonies Δn^{CHgHrLS}, quoted from the editions of JBergsma, De Levens van Jesus in het Middelnederlandsch 1895 (a reprint of Δn^{L} and ^{S} with a collation of Δn^{Hg}); DPlooij, The Liège Diatessaron, Verhandelingen der Koninklijke Nederlandse Akademie van Wetenschapen 1929—70 (Δn^{L} with an Engl. translation); CCdeBruin, Het Luikse Diatessaron, Corpus ... (Δmd ←) I 1, 1970 (Δn^{L} with an Engl. translation); the same, Het Haarense Diatessaron, Corpus ... I 2, 1970 (Δn^{Hr}); the same, Het Diatessaron van Cambridge, Corpus ... I 3, 1970 (Δn^{C} with a large gap, → IV.c.).
Δn embraces all mss with exception of Δn^{C} where it is lacking.

Δp: Persian Harmony as in GMessina, Diatessaron persiano, Biblica et Orientalia 14, 1951 (with Italian translation).

ΔE: Ephrem's commentary on Tatian's Diatessaron quoted from the Syr. original and from the Arm. translation as in LLeloir, Saint Ephrem, Commentaire de l'évangile concordant. Texte syriaque (ΔE^{s} with Lat. translation) 1962; the same, Saint Ephrem, Commentaire .... Version arménienne (ΔE^{a}), CSCO 137 (with Lat. translation CSCO 145), 1953 (1954).

d. Δ serves also as a *group symbol* (2.g. ←). It embraces as such all witnesses brought forward under c. (←) with the following exceptions:

1. die nicht voll kollationierten Hss von Δi^{T}.
2. die nur in Proben herangezogenen Hss von Δl.
3. Δme wegen seines paraphrasierenden Charakters. Doch steht häufig Δ<me> (Δ'<me>) als Hinweis auf eine Besonderheit von Δme gegenüber allen übrigen Harmonien.
4. ΔE, weil Efrem in seiner Kommentierung des Diatessarons nur ab und zu den Text zitiert, also keinen durchgehenden Vergleich erlaubt.

1. mss of Δi^{T} which are not fully collated;
2. mss of Δl used only in test passages;
3. Δme because of its paraphrastic character. But Δ<me> (Δ'<me>) is frequently used to indicate the peculiar character of Δme against all other Harmonies.
4. ΔE permits of no continuous comparison because in his commentary on the Diatessaron Ephrem quotes the text only here and there.

IV. Liste der im 1. Apparat ständig berücksichtigten Hss.
IV. List of Mss regularly cited in Apparatus 1.

Alle Hss — abgesehen von den Papyri — sind auf gewöhnliches Pergament geschrieben, sofern nichts anderes angegeben ist (Pu = Purpur-Pergament; Pap = Papier; Pal = Palimpsest, untere Schrift; Pal^2 = Palimpsest, obere Schrift).

IV./2. = IV. Jahrhundert, 2. Hälfte.

† = die Hs hat Lücken durch Blattverluste oder -beschädigungen. Evv.† = alle 4 Evv. haben Lücken; Mt Mk Lk Jo† = nur Jo hat Lücken; Jo1† = Fragment(e) aus Jo1.

Jo104-7 = zusammenhängender Text; von den vv. 4 und 7 sind mindestens Teile erhalten.

gr.-lat.(copt.) = die Hs enthält sowohl den gr. wie den lat. (copt.) Evv.-Text: Bilingue.

(K) = die Hs ist mit einem Kommentar ausgestattet.

Korr.(Gre) = Korrekturen nach Gregory, Textkritik (→ a.).

Zu den Hss der nicht-lat. Übersetzungen s. die entsprechenden Abschnitte (B.4.ff. ←).

All mss apart from papyri are written on common parchment unless otherwise stated (Pu = purple parchment; Pap = paper; Pal = palimpsest, the under writing; Pal^2 = palimpsest, the upper writing).

IV./2. = IV. century 2nd half.

† = the ms has lacunae either through loss of leaves or through damage. Evv.† = all 4 Gospels have gaps; Mt Mk Lk Jo† = only Jo has lacunae; Jo1† = fragment or fragments from Jo1.

Jo104-7 = continuous text; at least parts of vv. 4 and 7 are exstant.

gr.-lat.(copt.) = the ms contains both the Greek and Latin (Copt.) Gospel text; bilingual ms.

(K) = the ms is provided with a commentary.

Korr.(Gre) = correctors according to Gregory, Textkritik (→ a.).

For mss of the Versions other than Latin s. the relevant sections (B.III.4.ff. ←).

a. Griechische Hss.

Näheres s. in der offiziellen „Kurzgefaßten Liste der griech. Hss des NT" von Kurt Aland, ANTF 1, 1963, fortgesetzt mit ANTF 3, 1969, 7—37; Bericht der Stiftung zur Förderung der neutestamentlichen Textforschung für 1970/71, 1972, 14—19; Dass. für 1972/74, 1974, 8—13; Dass. für 1975/76, 1977, 10—16. Genaueres bei CRGregory, Textkritik des NT 1909, 18ff., 127ff., 387ff., 1017ff., 1084ff., 1093ff., 1211ff. und in den bei Aland, Kurzgef. Liste S. 9—11 aufgeführten Fortsetzungen von Gregorys Liste.

a. Greek Mss.

For more details see the official "Kurzgefaßte Liste der griech. Hss des NT" by Kurt Aland, ANTF 1, 1963, and its supplements in ANTF 3, 1969, 7—37; Bericht der Stiftung zur Förderung der neutestamentlichen Textforschung für 1970/71, 1972, 14—19; Dass. für 1972/74, 1974, 8—13; Dass. für 1975/76, 1977, 10—16. More information in CRGregory, Textkritk des NT 1909, 18ff., 127ff., 387ff., 1017ff., 1084ff., 1093ff., 1211ff. and in the supplements to Gregory's list enumerated in Aland's Kurzgefaßte Liste p. 9—11.

Nr. in Gre-Aland	Alter/*Date* Material	Inhalt/*Content*
$\mathfrak{P}^{1}$	III.	Mt 11-9.12-20.23
$\mathfrak{P}^{2}$	VI.	Jo 1212-15 (gr.-copt.)
$\mathfrak{P}^{3}$	VI./VII.	Lk 736-45 1038-42
$\mathfrak{P}^{4}$	III.	Lk 158-59.62—21.6.7 38—42.29-32.34-35 53-8.30—616
$\mathfrak{P}^{5}$	III.	Jo 123-31.33-41 1614-30 2011-17.19-20.22-25
$\mathfrak{P}^{6}$	IV.	Jo 101-2.4-7.9-10 111-8.45-52 (gr.-copt.)
$\mathfrak{P}^{7}$	IV.-VI.?	Lk 41-2 (verloren/*lost*)
$\mathfrak{P}^{19}$	IV./V.	Mt 1032—115
$\mathfrak{P}^{21}$	IV./V.	Mt 1224-26.31-33
$\mathfrak{P}^{22}$	III.	Jo 1525—162.21-32
$\mathfrak{P}^{25}$	IV./2.	Mt 1832-34 191-3.5-7.9-10
$\mathfrak{P}^{28}$	III.	Jo 68-12.17-22
$\mathfrak{P}^{35}$	IV.?	Mt 2512-15.20-23
$\mathfrak{P}^{36}$	VI.	Jo 314-18.31-32
$\mathfrak{P}^{37}$	III./IV.	Mt 2619-52
$\mathfrak{P}^{42}$	VII./VIII.	Lk 154-55 229-32 (gr.-copt.)
$\mathfrak{P}^{44}$	VI./VII.	Mt 171-3.6-7 1815-17.19 258-10 Jo 93-4 108-14 1216-18
$\mathfrak{P}^{45}$	III.	Mt 2034-32 2113-19 2541—2639 Mk 436-40 516-26.38—63.16-25.36-50 73-15.25—81.10-26.34—98.18-31 1127—121.5-8.13-19.24-28 Lk 631-41.45—77 926-41.45—101.6-22.26—111.6-25.28-46.50—1212.18-37.42—131.6-24.29—1410.17-33 Jo 107-25.31—1110.18-36.43-57 Act 427 *etc.*
$\mathfrak{P}^{46}$	ca 200	… 1K 11 …
$\mathfrak{P}^{52}$	II./1.	Jo 1831-34.37-38
$\mathfrak{P}^{53}$	III.	Mt 2629-40 …
$\mathfrak{P}^{55}$	VI./VII.	Jo 131-33.35-38

IV. Liste der ständig berücksichtigten Handschriften. *IV. List of Manuscripts regularly cited.*

Nr. in Gre-Aland	Alter/*Date* Material	Inhalt/*Content*
$\mathfrak{P}^{59}$	VII.	Jo 1 26.28.48.51 2 15-16 11 40-52 12 25.29.31.35 17 24-26 18 1-2.16-17.22 21 7.12-13.15.17-20.23
$\mathfrak{P}^{60}$	VII.	Jo 16 29—19 26†
$\mathfrak{P}^{62}$	IV.	Mt 11 25-30 (gr.-copt.)
$\mathfrak{P}^{64(+67)}$	ca 200	Mt 3 9.15 5 20-22.25-28 26 7.10.14-15.22-23.31-33
$\mathfrak{P}^{66}$	III./1.	Jo 1 1—6 11.35—14 26.29-30 15 3-26 16 2-4.6-7.11—20 22.25—21 9
$\mathfrak{P}^{67}$	*cf.* $\mathfrak{P}^{64}$	
$\mathfrak{P}^{69}$	III.	Lk 22 41.45-48.58-61
$\mathfrak{P}^{70}$	III.	Mt 11 26-27 12 4-5
$\mathfrak{P}^{71}$	IV.	Mt 19 10-11.17-18
$\mathfrak{P}^{73}$	VII.?	Mt 25 43 26 2-3
$\mathfrak{P}^{75}$	III./1.	Lk 3 18-22.33—4 2.34-42.44—5 10.37—6 4.10—7 32.35-43.45—17 15.19—18 18 22 4—fin. Jo 1 1—11 45.48-57 12 3—13 1.8-9.14 14 8-30 15 6-8
$\mathfrak{P}^{77}$	II./III.	Mt 23 30-34.35-39
$\mathfrak{P}^{82}$	III./IV.	Lk 7 32-34.37-38
$\mathfrak{P}^{86}$	IV./1.	Mt 5 13-16.22-25
$\mathfrak{P}^{88}$	IV.	Mk 2 1-26

Nr. in Gre-Aland	Alter/*Date* Material	Inhalt/*Content* — (Name)
ℵ (01)	IV.	Vollbibel/*Complete Bible.* Korr. (Gre): $\aleph^{1}$(1. Hand), $\aleph^{a}$(IV.), $\aleph^{b}$(VI.), $\aleph^{c}$(VII., = $\aleph^{ca}$, wo nicht/*unless* $\aleph^{cb}$ (VII.) davon zu unterscheiden ist/*is to be distinguished* — (Sinaiticus)
A **(02)**	V.	Vollbibel/*Complete Bible.* Mt† Mk Lk Jo† — (Alexandrinus)
B **(03)**	IV.	Vollbibel/*Complete Bible.* Korr. (Gre): B^{1}(1. Hand), B^{2}(IV.), B^{3}(X./XI.) — (Vaticanus)
C **(04)**	V. Pal	Vollbibel/*Complete Bible.* Evv.† Korr. (Gre): C^{1}(1. Hand), C^{2}(VI., Palästina?), C^{3}(IX., Byzanz?). In Zweifelsfällen steht/*in doubtful cases I use* C^{c} — (Ephraemi rescriptus)
D **(05)**	VI.	Mt† Mk† Lk Jo† Act† (gr.-lat.) — (Bezae)
D **(06)**	VI.	… 1K 11 … (gr.-lat.) — (Claromontanus)
D^{abs1}	IX.	… 1K 11 … (gr.-lat.) Abschrift von/*copy of* **06**
E **(07)**	VIII.	Mt Mk Lk† Jo
E **(08)**	VI.	Act 1 … (gr.-lat.)
F **(09)**	IX.	Evv.† F^{W} = Teile, die zu Wetsteins Zeit noch vorhanden waren/*parts still extant in Wetstein's day*
F **(010)**	IX.	… 1K 11 … (gr.-lat.) — (Augiensis)
G **(011)**	IX.	Evv.†
G **(012)**	IX.	… 1K 11 … (gr.-lat.) — (Boernerianus)
H **(013)**	IX.	Evv.†
K **(017)**	IX.	Evv.
L **(019)**	VIII.	Mt† Mk† Lk Jo† (→ V. a.)
M **(021)**	IX.	Evv.
N **(022)**	VI. Pu	Evv.†
O **(023)**	VI. Pu	Mt† Lk† Jo
P **(024)**	VI. Pal	Evv.†
P **(025)**	IX. Pal	… 1K 11 …
Q **(026)**	V. Pal	Lk† Jo†
R **(027)**	VI. Pal	Lk†
S **(028)**	A.D. 949	Evv.
T **(029)**	V.	**+ 0113-0125-0139**: Lk† Jo† (gr.-copt.)
U **(030)**	IX.	Evv.
V **(031)**	IX.	Mt† Mk Lk Jo†
W **(032)**	V.	Mt Mk Lk Jo† (→ V. a.) — (Freerianus)
X **(033)**	X.	Evv.† (K)
Y **(034)**	IX.	Mt† Mk Lk† Jo†
Z **(035)**	VI. Pal	Mt† (→ V. a.)
Γ **(036)**	X.	Mt† Mk† Lk Jo
Δ **(037)**	IX.	Mt Mk Lk Jo† (gr.-lat.)
Θ **(038)**	IX.	Mt† Mk Lk Jo — (Koridethi)
Λ **(039)**	IX.	Lk Jo
Ξ **(040)**	VI. (VIII.) Pal	Lk† (K)
Π **(041)**	IX.	Evv.†
Σ **(042)**	VI. Pu	Mt Mk†
Φ **(043)**	VI. Pu	Mt† Mk†
Ψ **(044)**	VIII./IX.	Mk† Lk Jo (→ V. a.)
Ω **(045)**	IX.	Mt† Mk† Lk Jo

Nr. in Gre-Aland	Alter/*Date* Material	Inhalt/*Content*
047	VIII.	Mt† Mk† Lk Jo†
050	IX.	Jo† (K)
053	IX.	Lk 1f.† (K)
054	VIII.	Jo†
055	XI.	Evv. (K)
058	IV.	Mt 18†
059	IV./V.	**+ 0215**: Mk 15†
060	VI.	Jo 14†
063	IX.	**+ 0117**: Lk† Jo†
064	VI. Pal	**+ 074-090**: Mt† Mk†
065	VI. Pal	Jo†
067	VI. Pal	Mt† Mk†
068	V. Pal	Jo†
069	V.	Mk 10f.†
070	VI.	**+ 0110-0124-0178-0179-0180-0190-0191-0202**: Lk† Jo† (gr.-copt.)
071	V./VI.	Mt 1f.†
072	V./VI. Pal	Mk 2f.†
073	VI.	**+ 084**: Mt 14f.†
074		s. **064**
078	VI. Pal	Mt† Lk 18† Jo†
079	VI. Pal	Lk†
080	VI. Pu	Mk 9f.†
083	VI./VII.	**+ 0112-0235**: Mk† Jo†
084		s. **073**
085	VI.	Mt†
086	VI. Pal	Jo† (gr.-copt.)

Nr. in Gre-Aland	Alter/*Date* Material	Inhalt/*Content*
087	VI.	+ **092b**: Mt† Mk 12† Jo 18†
089	VI.	+ **092a**: Mt 26†
090		s. **064**
091	VI.	Jo†
092a		s. **089**
092b		s. **087**
094	VI. Pal	Mt 24†
099	VII.	Mk 16†
0100	VII.	(+ *l*963?): Jo† (gr.-copt.)
0101	VIII.	Jo†
0102	VII./VIII.	+ **0138**: Mt† Lk†
0103	VII. Pal	Mk 13f.†
0104	VII. Pal	Mt 23† + ? Mk 1† + ?
0105	X.	Jo†
0106	VII.	+ **0119**: Mt†
0107	VII.	Mt 22f.† Mk 4f.†
0108	VII.	Lk 11†
0109	VII.	Jo†
0110		s. **070**
0112		s. **083**
0113		s. T **(029)**
0114	VIII.	(+ *l*965?): Jo† (gr.-copt.)
0115	VIII.	Lk 9f.†
0116	VIII. Pal	Mt† Mk 13f.† Lk 3f.†
0117		s. **063**
0118	VIII.	Mt 11†
0119		s. **0106**
0124		s. **070**
0125		s. T **(029)**
0126	VIII.	Mk 5f.†
0128	IX.	Mt 25†
0130	IX. Pal	Mk2† Lk 1f.† (gr.-copt.)
0131	IX.	Mk†
0132	IX. Pal	Mk 5†
0133	IX. Pal	Evv.†
0134	VIII. Pal	Mk†
0135	IX. Pal	Mt† Mk† Lk†
0136	IX.	+ **0137**: Mt† (gr.-arab.)
0137		s. **0136**
0138	IX.	Mt†
0139		s. T **(029)**
0141	X.	Jo (K)
0143	VI.	Mk 8†
0144	VII.	Mk 6f.†
0145	VII.	Jo 6†
0146	VIII.	Mk 10†
0147	VI.	Lk 6†
0148	VIII.	Mt 28†
0154	IX.	Mk 10f.†
0155	IX.	Lk†
0160	IV.	Mt 26†
0161	VIII. Pal	Mt 22†
0162	IV.	Jo 2†
0164	VI./VII.	Mt 13† (gr.-copt.)
0167	VII.	Mk 6†
0170	V./VI.	Mt 6†
0171	IV.	Lk 22†
0177	X.	Lk 1f.† (gr.-copt.)
0178—0180		s. **070**
0181	IV.	Lk 9f.†

Nr. in Gre-Aland	Alter/*Date* Material	Inhalt/*Content*
0182	V.	Lk 19†
0184	VI.	Mk 15† (gr.-copt.)
0187	VI.	Mk 6†
0188	VII.	Mk 11†
0190—0191		s. **070**
0196	IX. Pal	Mt 5† Lk 24†
0197	IX. Pal[2]	Mt†
0200	VII.	Mt 11† (gr.-copt.)
0202		s. **070**
0204	VII.	Mt 24† (gr.-copt.)
0210	VII.	Jo 5f.†
0211	IX.	Evv.
0212		→ IV.c. Δg (III.B.10.c. ←)
0213	V./VI.	Mk 3†
0214	IV.	Mk 8†
0215		s. **059**
0216	V.	Jo 8f.†
0217	V.	Jo 11f.†
0218	V.	Jo 12†
0231	IV.	Mt 26f.†
0233	VIII. Pal	Jo 2† (Evv.†?)
0234	VIII.	Mt 28† Jo 1†
0235		s. **083**
0237	VI.	Mt 15† (gr.-copt.)
0239	VII.	Lk 2† (gr.-copt.)
0242	IV.	Mt†
0249	X. Pal	Mt 25†
0250	VIII. Pal	Evv.†
0253	VI.	Lk 10†
0255	IX.	Mt 26f.†
0260	VI.	Jo 1† (gr.-copt.)
0263	VI.	Mk 5†
0265	VI.	Lk 7†
0266	VI.	Lk 20†
0269	IX. Pal	Mk 6†
0274	V.	Mk†
1[eap]	XII.	NT⟨Ap⟩
7[e]	XII.	Evv.
13	XIII.	Evv† (→ V.a.)
22	XII.	Evv† (→ V.a.)
27	X.	Mt† Mk Lk Jo†
28	XI.	Mt† Mk Lk† Jo†
33	IX.	NT⟨Ap⟩ (→ V.a.)
69	XV. z.T. Pap	NT† (→ V.a.)
71	XII.	Evv.
115	X.	Evv.†
118	XIII.	Evv.† (→ V.a.)
124	XI.	Evv.
131	XIV.	NT⟨Ap⟩
157	XII.	Evv.
160	1123	Evv.
179	XII.	Mt Mk Lk Jo†
209	XIV.	NT
230	1013	Mt Mk Lk Jo†
267	XII.	Evv.†
346	XII.	Evv.† (→ V.a.)
349	1322 Pap	Mt Mk† Lk Jo†
517	XI./XII.	NT† (→ V.a.)

IV. Liste der ständig berücksichtigten Handschriften. *IV. List of Manuscripts regularly cited.*

Nr. in Gre-Aland	Alter/*Date* Material	Inhalt/*Content*
543	XII.	Evv.† (→ V.a.)
544	XIII.	Evv.
565	IX. Pu	Mt† Mk Lk† Jo†
579	XIII.	Evv.† (→ V.a.)
659	XII.	Evv.
692	XII.	Mt Mk Lk†
700	XI.	Evv.
788	XI.	Evv.† (→ V.a.)
826	XII.	Evv.
827	XIII.	Mt Mk Lk Jo†
828	XII.	Evv.† (→ V.a.)
872	XII.	Mt† Mk Lk Jo†
892	IX.	Evv.† (→ V.a.)
945	XI.	NT⟨Ap⟩
954	XV.	Evv.
983	XII.	Mt Mk Lk Jo†
990	XIV.	Evv.
1010	XII.	Mt Mk Lk† Jo†
1071	XII.	Evv.
1082	XIV.	Mt† Mk Lk Jo
1188	XI./XII.	Evv.
1194	XI.	Evv.
1207	XI.	Evv.
1223	X.	Evv.
1241	XII.	NT⟨Ap⟩† (→ V.a.)
1278	XII.	Evv.
1293	XI.	Evv.†
1342	XII./XIII.	Mt† Mk Lk† Jo
1391	XIII.	Evv.†
1402	XII.	Evv.
1424	IX./X.	NT† (→ V.a.) (K)
1582	949	Evv.† (→ V.a.)
1604	XIII.	Evv.
1606	XIII.	Evv.
1675	XIV. Pap	Evv.† (→ V.a.)
1689	1200	Evv.
2191	XII.	Mt Mk Lk Jo† + NT'⟨Ap⟩
2193	X.	Evv.
*l*547	XIII.	(s. III.B.2.f.4. ←)
*l*963	XI.	s. **0100**
*l*965	IX.	s. **0114**

b. Lateinische Hss.

Vgl. das „Verzeichnis der Sigel" von Bonifatius Fischer in: Vetus Latina. Die Reste der altlateinischen Bibel, Bd. 1, 1949 S. 11—14 mit Nachtrag 1 (1950); Ders.: The Latin Versions, in: BMMetzger, The Early Versions of the NT, 1977, 461.

b. Latin Mss.

Cf. Bonifatius Fischer "Verzeichnis der Sigel" in: Vetus Latina. Die Reste der altlateinischen Bibel, vol. 1, 1949 p. 11—14 (Supplement 1950); Ders.: The Latin Versions, in: BMMetzger, The Early Versions of the NT, 1977, 461.

Sigel/*Sign* Nr. (Fischer)	Alter/*Date* Material	Inhalt/*Content* — (Name)
a (3)	IV.	Evv.† (→ V.b.) — (Vercellensis)
a^2 (16)		→ n
b (4)	V./2.	Evv.† (→ V.b.) — (Veronensis)
β (26)	VII.	Lk 1f.†
c (6)	XII./XIII.	NT — (Colbertinus)
d (5)	V.	Mt† Mk† Lk Jo† Act 1 ... (gr.-lat., s. D, IV.a. ←) (→ V.b.) — (Bezae)
δ (27)	IX.	Mt Mk Lk Jo† (gr.-lat., s. Δ, IV.a. ←)
e (2)	V.	Evv.† (→ V.b.) — (Palatinus)
f (10)	VI./1.	Mt† Mk† Lk Jo (→ V.b.) — (Brixianus)
ff^1 (9)	X.	Evv. Act Jc—Jd — (Corbeiensis 1)
ff^2 (8)	V.	Evv.† (→ V.b.) — (Corbeiensis 2)
g^1 (7)	IX./1.	NT — (Sangermanensis 1)
g^2 (29)	X.	Evv. — (Sangermanensis 2)
h (12)	V./2.	Mt† (→ V.b.) — (Claromontanus)
i (17)	V./2. Pu	Mk† Lk† (→V.b.) — (Vindobonensis)
j (22)	VI./1. Pu	Lk 24† Jo† — (Sarzanensis)
k (1)	IV./V.	Mt† Mk† (→ V.b.) — (Bobiensis)
l (11)	VII./VIII.	Evv.† (→ V.b.) — (Rehdigeranus)
μ (—)	V.	Mt 9f.†
n (16)	V.	+ a^2: Mt† Mk† Lk† (a^2) Jo† (→ V.b.) — (Sangallensis)
o (16)	VII.	Mk 16† (= n^s)
p (20)	VIII.	Jo 11†
π (18)	VII. Pal	Mt† Lk† Jo†
q (13)	VII.	Evv.† (→ V.b.) — (Monacensis)
r^1 (14)	VII./1.	Evv.† — (Usserianus 1)
r^2 (28)	VIII./IX.	Evv.† (→ V.b.) — (Usserianus 2)
s (21)	V./2.	Lk†
t (19)	VI. Pal	Mk†
v (25)	VII.	Jo 19f.†
z (15)	VII.	Mt† Mk Lk† Jo (→ V.b.) = „aur" in Nestle-Aland^{26} etc. — (Aureus)
23	V.	Jo 7†
30	VIII.	Evv. — (Gatianus)
31	VI.?	Evv.-*l*, z.T. vl
32	ca 500 Pal	Evv.-*l*, z.T. vl
36	V.	Lk 23f.† (lat.-got.)
37	VIII.	Mt† (= Hi^{lm})
38	IX.	Mt† (= Hi^{lm})
39	IX./1.	Evv.-frgm. in *L*Eu^{can}
40	X.	Evv.-frgm. in *L*Eu^{can}
41	VIII./1.	Mt†
42	IX.	Evv.-frgm. in Iuv^m
43	VIII.	Evv. — (Book of Dimma)
56	XI.	NT (z.T. vl in Act ... 1K ....) — (Toletanus)
59	XIII.	NT⟨Evv.⟩ (verschollen/*lost*) — (Demidovianus)
61	IX./1.	NT — (Book of Armagh)
65	VIII.	NT⟨Evv. Act⟩

Sigel/*Sign* Nr. (Fischer)	Alter/*Date* Material	Inhalt/*Content* — (Name)
75 (d^p)	V./VI.	... 1K ... (gr.-lat., s. D (**06**), IV. a. ←) — (Claromontanus)
76 (e^p)	IX.	... 1K ... (gr.-lat., s. D^{abs1}, IV. a. ←) — (Sangermanensis)
77 (g^p)	IX.	... 1K ... (gr.-lat., s. G (**012**), IV. a. ←) — (Boernerianus)
78 (f^p)	IX.	... 1K ... (gr.-lat., s. F (**010**), IV. a. ←) — (Augiensis)
250	IX.	Psalter(gr.), ^{Od}(gr.-lat.)

c. Harmonien.

Angaben über die Publikation der hierunter aufgeführten Hss sind dem Abschnitt über die Harmonien (III.11.c. ←) zu entnehmen.

[*163.*(*163*†.)] = der Stoff der Perikope *163. fällt* (z. T.) in eine Lücke der Hs.

c. Harmonies.

For more information about the publication of mss enumerated below see the chapter on the witness of the Harmonies (III.11.c. ←).

[*163.*(*163*†.)] = the material of pericope *163.* is (partly) lost in a lacuna.

Sigel *Sign*	Bibliothek *Library* — Signatur	Alter *Date*	Bemerkungen *Remarks*
Δa^{A}	Roma, Vat. Arabo 14	XII.	
Δa^{B}	„ „ Borg. Arabo 250	XIV.	
Δa^{E}	Kairo, St. Etienne	XIX./1.	unveröffentlicht/*unpublished*
Δad	St. Gallen, Stift Nr. 56 in folio	IX./2.	lat.-ad. → Δl^{G}
Δg	New Haven, Yale Un. PDura 10	III.	
$\Delta i^{T(L)}$	Firenze, Riccardiana 2335	XIV./2.	voll kollationiert/*fully collated*
$\Delta i^{T(P)}$	Roma, Vat. Pal. lat. 56	XIV.	„ „
$\Delta i^{T(Q)}$	„ „ Barb. lat. 3971	XIV.	„ „ [*22*†. *104.-106. 108. 109*†. *110.-116. 121.-130. 168*†.]
$\Delta i^{T(R)}$	„ „ lat. 7654	XIV.	voll kollationiert/*fully collated* [*1.-20. 22*†. *23. 29. 133.-145. 147.-150. 170. 176. 177. 186.-188*†. *189. 191. 201.-203.*]
$\Delta i^{T(S)}$	Siena, Communale I, V 9	XIV.	voll kollationiert/*fully collated*
$\Delta i^{T(T)}$	Firenze, Centrale II, VIII 50	XIV./XV.	„ „
$\Delta i^{T(G)}$	„ Riccardiana 1304	XV.	z. T. kollationiert/*partly collated*
$\Delta i^{T(H)}$	„ „ 1334	XV.	„ „
$\Delta i^{T(J)}$	„ „ 1356	1372	„ „
$\Delta i^{T(K)}$	„ „ 1749	XIV.	„ „
$\Delta i^{T(M)}$	Modena, Estense 0.3.22.	XIV.	„ „
$\Delta i^{T(Y)}$	Firenze, Laurenziana 27,12	XIV.	„ „
$\Delta i^{T(Z)}$	„ „ 27,14	1427	„ „
$\Delta i^{T(\Theta)}$	„ Centrale II, X 39	XIV.	„ „
$\Delta i^{T(\Pi)}$	„ „ Pal. 73	XIV./XV.	„ „
Δl^{A}	München, Staatsbibliothek 23977	XIV.	
Δl^{D}	„ „ 10025	XIII.	
Δl^{F}	Fulda, Landesb. Bonif. 1	540/46	
Δl^{G}	cf. Δad (←)		
Δmd^{G}	Graz, Univ. Pergament/*parchment* frgm.	XIV.	
Δmd^{M}	München, Staatsbibliothek Cgm 532	1367	
Δmd^{N}	Nürnberg, Stadtbibliothek Cent 651	1293	
Δmd^{U}	Hamburg, Staatsb. Cod. theol. 1066	1411	
Δmd^{V}	Berlin, Stiftg. Preuß. Kulturbesitz Germ. Qu. 503	XIV.	
Δmd^{W}	„ „ „ Germ. Qu. 987	1409	
Δmd^{Z}	Zürich, Zentralb. C 170 App. 56	XIII./XIV.	
Δme	Cambridge, Magdalen Coll. Pepys 2489	ca 1400	
Δn^{C}	„ Univ. Dd 12.25	XIII./XIV.	[*26. 60.-69. 76.-82. 84. 93*†.*-95. 97.-121. 123.-133. 135.-150. 152. 154.-159. 163.-167. 170. 173. 174. 176.-178. 180. 182.-196. 199.-208. 211.-223. 226.*]
Δn^{Hg}	den Haag, Kon. Bibl. M 421	1473	
Δn^{Hr}	Haaren, Groot Seminar	ca 1400	
Δn^{L}	Liège Univ. Nr. 437	XIII./2.	
Δn^{S}	Stuttgart, Landesb. Cod. theol. 8° 140	1332	

Sigel *Sign*	Bibliothek *Library*	Signatur	Alter *Date*	Bemerkungen *Remarks*
Δp	Firenze, Medic. XVII. (81)		1567	
ΔE^{s}	Dublin, A. Chester Beatty 709		ca 500	
ΔE^{a}	Venetia, Mechitar. 495		1195	ms A (Leloir)
	„ „ 312		1195	ms B (Leloir)

V. Liste der Lücken *V. List of Lacunae*

in den unter Summensigeln zusammengefaßten Hss.

1. In die Listen sind alle Lücken aufgenommen, die mindestens einen ganzen Vers umfassen. Kleinere Lücken sind, sofern sie eine Variante berühren, im Apparat vermerkt: [...].

2. Mt816† = v. 16 fehlt nur zum Teil. Genauer Wortlaut wird nur gegeben, wenn irrige Rückschlüsse aus *Rpl* und Summensigeln möglich wären.

3. [und] bezeichnen den Anfang und das Ende der Lücke, wenn dadurch ein Wort verstümmelt ist, zB discipu]li^{2} = die Lücke reicht bis zum zweiten Vorkommen von „discipuli" im betreffenden Vers; mit „li" geht der erhaltene Text weiter.

4. Von den Lücken (durch Beschädigung) sind die Auslassungen der Hss zu unterscheiden; letztere sind in den Lückenlisten nicht berücksichtigt.

5. (s) = von späterer Hand ergänzt.

in the mss comprehended under "group symbols".

1. Included in the list are all lacunae which contain at least one whole verse. Smaller lacunae are indicated in the apparatus through [...].

2. Mt816† = v. 16 is lacking only in part. A more exact wording is quoted only where mistaken conclusions might be drawn from *Rpl* and the group symbols.

3. [, and], indicate the beginning and the end of a lacuna if a word is mutilated by it; e. g. discipu]li^{2} = the lacuna extends to the second appearance of "discipuli" in the relevant verse. The extant text continues with "li".

4. We have to distinguish between the lacunae (caused by damage) and the omissions, deliberate or not, of the mss; these last are not entered in the list of lacunae.

5. (s) = supplied by a later hand.

a. Griechische Hss. a. Greek Mss.

ℌ = ℵBLW(Lk 11—812 Jo) Z(Mt) Δ(Mk) Ψ(Mk)-33-579(Mk Lk Jo)-892-1241(Lk Jo).
Ohne Lücken / *Without lacunae*: ℵBW(Lk 11—812 Jo) Δ(Mk)-1241(Lk Jo).
Lücken in / *Lacunae in*
L: **Mt** 422—514; 2817 ι[δοντες—20 **Mk** 1016 τας—30†; 152—τα ιδια 20 **Jo** 2115†—24.
W: **Jo** 11—511(s).
Z: **Mt** 11—17†; 26†—13†. 20†—43. 13†—545†; 615 ανθρ.—ακαν]θων 716; 86†—1040†; 1118†—1242; 1311 βασι[λειας—εσκαν]δαλ. 57; 1419†—1512. 23†—178. 18—26†; 187—ανεγνωτε 194. 12†—υπαγε 21. 28†—αμπε]λωνα 207; 218†—23†. 30 εγω—36. 45 αρχιερ[εις—οτι 2216. 25†—αγαπ. 37; 233†—13†. 23 και^{1}—2415†. 26—αυ]των 251. 11†—2621†. 29 υμω[ν εν τη—62†. 71 ουτος—2820.
Ψ: **Mk** 11—σοι μιαν 95.
33: **Mk** 931 αυτον—1111†; 1311 εν—1460† **Lk**(137—1944 mut.); 2138†—απηγ]αγον 2326.
579: **Mk** 328†—καλην 48; 616—27(s) **Jo** 2015 κηπουργος—2125.
892: **Jo** 106†—1218†; 1423†—2125.

λ = 1-118-131(Mk 1—5 Lk)-209; **λλ** = **λ** + 22-872(Mk)-1278-1582-2193.
Ohne Lücken / *Without lacunae*: 1-131-209-872(Mk)-1278-2193.
Lücken in / *Lacunae in*
22: **Mt** 11—212†; 421†—σε 525 **Jo** 1422†—1627†.
118: **Mt** 11—62(s) **Lk** 1335 υμιν^{1}—1420†(s); 187†—199†(s) **Jo** 1625†—2125(s).
1582: **Mt** 53†—19†(s); 2229†—233†; [**Jo** 87†—11†(s)].

ϕ = 13-69-124-346-543-788-826-828-983.
Ohne Lücken / *Without lacunae*: 124-826.
Lücken in / *Lacunae in*
13: **Mt** 11—22; 2633—52†; 2726†—289† **Mk** 120 απηλθον—και^{2} 45 **Jo** 1619†—1711†; 212—25.
69: **Mt** 11—και 1815.
346: **Jo** 326†—752†.
543: **Mt** 1211†—139 **Mk** 84 ποθεν—βαπτ. 28 **Lk** 1520†—οταν 169 **Jo** 222†—46†; 52†—43†; 1121†—συνηγ. 47.
788: **Jo** 438†—542†; 2120†—25.
828: **Lk** 1021 ταυ[τα—1334.
983: **Jo** 1133†—199†.

σ = 517-954-1424-1675.
Lücken in / *Lacunae in*
517: **Lk** 215 οι ποιμενες—46; 642 εκβαλειν[το καρ.^{3}— **Jo** 2125.
954: **Mt** 2712†—27 **Mk** 11—10(s).
1424: **Mt** 123†—216†.
1675: **Mt** 11—25†; 1831 ουν—1918†.

b. Lateinische Hss.

Der Wortlaut des Lückentextes ist zum schnelleren Zurechtfinden nach der Vulgata (Nestle ^{7}1952) gegeben; wo dies nicht möglich war, ist Jülichers „Itala" zugrunde gelegt.

b. Latin Mss.

For quicker reference the wording of the text in the lacunae is given according to the Vulgate (Nestle ^{7}1952); where this was not possible I have taken Jülicher's "Itala" as a basis.

vl = a b c e f ff^1(Mt) ff^2 g^1(Mt) h(Mt) i(Mk Lk) k(Mt Mk) l n(Mt Mk Jo) q r^2 z
Ohne Lücken / *Without lacunae*: c ff^1 g^1.
Lücken in / *Lacunae in*
a: **Mt** 16autem^2—7; 135—non6; 2143†(*om*^{v} 44)—45†; 2234—37; 2449 et bibat—251†. 2—12†. 13 nescitis—quin]que16; **Mk** 122†—languori]bus34; 417†—24. 25 ab illo—28†. 31 in terra^2—34†. 34†—mitte]bat37. 41 ma[re—spiri]tum 52. 5†—me7. 9 mu[lti—depreca-ban]tur 12. 14 et egressi—16†. 17†—19†; 1515 volens—vos in167. 7 Galilaeam—20(s.); **Lk** 11†—4†. 6†—9†. 9†—13†. 39†—41. 42†—45†; 114 in—6†. 9†—aut 11. 12†—26†; 1237 ministrabit—59.
b: **Mt** 11—11†; 1512†—daemonio22; 2318†—27†; **Mk** 1311 datum—16†. 27 congregabit—hic 1424. 45 r[abbi—47†. 50 om[nes—52†. 53 Jesum—56†. 58—1620; **Lk** 1926—2129†; **Jo** 744†—811.
e: **Mt** 11—1249†; 1358†—cum detinuis?] set 143. 3 sui[...—6†. 7†—9†; 2449 cum ine[...—lapidem 282; **Mk** 11—sec. sunt 20; 48 in—sollicitudi]nes 19; 610—il]lum libenter 1237. 40†—...]tem dixit 132. 3 interroga[bant—24†. 27 te[rrae—33†. 36†—1620; **Lk** 830 at ille—48†; 114 siquidem—24†; **Jo** 1812†—25†.
f: **Mt** 816†—26†; **Mk** 125—hora 1332; 1453 convene[runt—61.
ff^2: **Mt** 11—similis 1116; **Mk** 918 dentibu[s—20†. 23. 24. 28—29†. 31 resurget—tacebant34; **Lk** 948 nam—1020†; 1145†—126; **Jo** 1716—189†; 2023†—218†.
h: **Mt** 11—314; 1433†—novem 1812.
i: **Mk** 11—egent 217; 329 non—aliud44; 101 docebat—32; 1436†—1533†. 40 de—1620; **Lk** 11—106†; 1422 factum—29†; 164†—10; 2311—2453.
k: **Mt** 310 fruc[tum—41†; 1417†—1520†. 36 suis— **Mk** 88†. 11†—13. 17—quin]que^1 19.
l: **Mt** 11—215†; **Mk** 1620; **Lk** 1128—ingressus37; **Jo** 11—16†; 632†—61†; 1156†—1210†; 1334†—1422; 153†—15†; 1613†—2125.
n: **Mt** 11—171†. 4 audita [est—g]enibus14; 1820†—adu]lescens 1920; 214—2656†. 75 verbi—273†. 4†—san]guinis 8. 9—12†. 12†—61. 64 di-[cant—66†; 283†—cum8; **Mk** 11—713†. 25 spiritu[m—pr]ius 27. 31 Decap.—eum^2 832; 910†—triduo 132. 20†—1522†; 1614—20; **Jo** 11—1913†. 17 locum—24†. 42†—2125.
q: **Mt** 315 implere—languorem 423; 525 tradat^1—ele]mosyna 64. 28†—77; **Mk** 17 dignus[...—ingressus21; 155†—veniat36; **Lk** 2323 instabant—dei35; 2411†—et] ossa39; **Jo** 1011—1238; 219†—17†. 18†—20†.
r^2: **Mt** 11—18†; 26†—et^1 424; 529 gehennam—137†; 141†—quem 1613; 1831 eius—1926†; 2618†—venit45; 2758 cor[pus^2—2820; **Mk** 324†—arum]nae 419; 531†—613; 1517†—ei41; **Lk** 11—13†; 25 discess.—318†; 639 in—disci]puli 711; 1154 insi[diantes—1245†; 1418†—1525†; 1616—agro 177; 1911—qui38; 2235†—59†; 2314†— **Jo** 512†; 625†—87†; 103†—2125.
z: **Lk** 218 nolite—29.

c. Die altsyrischen Hss.

Der Wortlaut wird in Anlehnung an den griechischen *txt* gegeben.

c. The Old Syriac Mss.

The wording is given according to the Greek *txt*.

Lücken in / *Lacunae in*

Ss (Sinaiticus):
Mt 610†—83†; 124 εφαγεν—6†. 25†—30†; 1615†—1711†; 2025—2120†; 2515†—16. 20†—25†. 27—31; 287†—20 **Mk** 11—12†. 44†—221†; 417†—θαλασσα 41; 526†—65† **Lk** 116†—38†; 528†—611 **Jo** 11—25†. 47†—215; 438—56†. 25†—46†; 1831 ουδενα—1940†.
Sc (Curetonianus):
Mt 823—1031; 2325†— **Mk** 1617† **Lk** 11—248†; 316†—733†; 1613—ουαι δε 171; 2444†—53 **Jo** 142 ειπεν—εισελθειν35; 819†—1410†. 12†—15†. 19†—21†. 24†—26†. 29†—2125.

VI. Kirchliche Schriftsteller. *VI. The Christian Authors.*

Abkürzung/ *Abbreviation*	Orig. Sprache/ *Language* g = gr. l = lat. s = syr. c = copt.	Name (PsAug etc. s. Aug etc.) B = Bischof von / *Bishop of* v. = von / *of* in (): Lebensort(e) / *place(s) of life*	Zeit / *Time* vor / *before* nach / *later than*
Ad	g	„Adamantius" = Dialogus contra Marcionitas	nach 235
Af	s	Afrahat (Persien/*Persia*)	† nach 345
Am	l	Ambrosius B Mailand/*Milan*	† 397
Amm	g	Ammonius (Alexandria)	V.
Amph	g	Amphilochius B Iconium (Lykaonien)	† nach 394
Amst	l	„Ambrosiaster" (= PsAm)	366/384
AnBal	c	Anonymus copt. (PDeir el-Bala'izah)	VII./VIII.
And	g	Andreas B Gortyna (Kreta)	† 740
AnMt	l	„Opus imperfectum", Anonymi (PsChr) in Mt comm.	V./1.
Ant	g	Antiochus monachus S. Sabae (Jerusalem)	VI./VII.
Antp	g	Antipater B Bostra (Prov. Arabia)	V.
Ap	g	Apelles Marcionita (Rom, Alexandria)	II./III.
APh	g	Acta Philippi	V./1.
APi	g	Acta Pilati	V./1.
APP	g	Acta Petri et Pauli	III.(?)
Ar	l	Arnobius iunior (N-Afrika, Rom)	† nach 455
Arius	g	Arius Presb. (Alexandria)	† 336
ATh	s	Acta Thomae	III.
Ath	g	Athanasius B Alexandria	295—373
Athg	g	Athenagoras (Athen)	II.
Au	l	Augustinus B Hippo Regius (N-Afrika)	354—430
PsAu	l	„Speculum". Liber de divinis scriptis	V.
Bas	g	Basilius B Caesarea Cappadociae	330—379
Bas^{S}	g	Basilius B Seleucia Isauriae	† ca 468
Brn	g	Barnabae epistula	115/140
Brs	s	Dionysius Barsalibi B Amida (Mesopotamien)	† 1171
Cad	l	Cassiodorus (Italien)	† ca 580
PsCae	g	„Erotapocriseis" (Caesarius: Bruder von/*brother of* Gr^{Na})	VI./1.
Can	l	Iohannes Cassianus (Ägypten, S-Gallien)	† 430/435
CAp	g	„Constitutiones Apostolorum"	ca 380
Cat	g	Catenen-Commentare (zB Cat^{Ox} = ed. Oxon.)	
Chr	g	Iohannes Chrysostomus B Konstantinopel (cf. AnMt)	† 407
ChriSt	l	Christianus („Druthmar") v. Stablo (Belgien)	ca 840/880
Chrm	l	Chromatius B Aquileia (N-Italien)	IV./V.

Abkürzung/ *Abbreviation*	Orig. Sprache/ *Language* g = gr. l = lat. s = syr c = copt.	Name (PsAug etc. s. Aug etc.) B = Bischof von / *Bishop of* v. = von / *of* in (): Lebensort(e) / *place(s) of life*	Zeit / *Time* vor / *before* nach / *later than*
Chrn	g	„Chronikon paschale"	VII./1.
Cl	g	Clemens B Alexandria	† vor 205
1Cl	g	Clemens B Rom (ad Corinthios 1)	I.
2Cl		s. PsCl	
PsCl	g	ad Corinthios 2	II.
	g	Homiliae, Recognitiones, ad virgines	III.
Co	g	Cosmas Indicopleustes (Alexandria, Syrien)	VI.
Cp	l	Cyprianus B Carthago	† 258
Cr	g	Cyrillus B Alexandria	† 444
Cr^{I}	g	Cyrillus B Jerusalem	† nach 381
Da	g	Iohannes Damascenus	† vor 754
DAp	g	„Didaskalia Apostolorum"	III./1.
Ddy	g	Didymus Caecus (Alexandria)	313—398
Dgn	g	ad Diognetum epistula	II./2.
DialTA	g	„Dialogus Timothei et Aquilae"	V.(?)
Did	g	„Didache" (Doctrina XII Apostolorum)	II./1.
Dio^{Al}	g	Dionysius B Alexandria	† 264/265
Dio^{Ar}	g	(Ps)Dionysius Areopagita	V./2.
Diod	g	Diodorus B Tarsus (Kilikien)	† vor 394
EAe	g	Ev. Aegyptorum	II./1.
EAr	arab.	Ev. infantiae Arabicum	vor VII.
EEb	g	Ev. Ebionaeorum	II.
Ef	s	Efrem Syrus (Nisibis, Edessa)	† 373
EH	g	Ev. sec. Hebraeos	II./1.
EIc	g	Protev. Iacobi	ca 200
EN	s(?)	Ev. Nazaraeorum	II.
EP	g	Ev. Petri	II.
Ep	g	Epiphanius B Salamis (Zypern)	† 403
EpAp	c	Epistula Apostolorum	II.
ETh^{I}	g	Ev. Thomae (ev. infantiae)	II./2.(?)
ETh^{II}	c	Ev. Thomae (+ gr. frgm.)	II./2.
Eu	g	Eusebius B Caesarea (Palästina)	† 399
Euch	l	Eucherius B Lyon (S-Gallien)	† 450/455
Eug	l	Eugippius (Noricum, Italien)	† nach 533
Eul	g	Eulogius B Alexandria	† nach 607
Eutha	g	Euthalius (Agypten, Sardinien)	IV.(VII.?)
Euthy	g	Euthymius Zigabenus (Konstantinopel)	† nach 1118
Fac	l	Facundus B Hermiane (N-Afrika)	† nach 571
Fau^{M}	l	Faustus Manichaeus (^{Au}) B Mileve (N-Afrika)	IV./V.

Abkürzung/ *Abbreviation*	Orig. Sprache/ *Language* g = gr. l = lat. s = syr. c = copt.	Name (PsAug etc. s. Aug etc.) B = Bischof von/ *Bishop of* v. = von/ *of* in (): Lebensort(e)/ *place(s) of life*	Zeit/ *Time* vor/ *before* nach/ *later than*
Fau^{R}	l	Faustus B Riez (S-Gallien)	† 490/500
Faustin	l	Faustinus Presb. (Rom)	IV.
Fil	l	Filastrius B Brescia (N-Italien)	† vor 392
Fu	l	Fulgentius B Ruspe (N-Afrika)	467—533
Gau	l	Gaudentius B Brescia (N-Italien)	† nach 406
Gel	l	Gelasius v. Cycicus (Bithynien)	V.
Gr^{Na}	g	Gregorius B Nazianz (Kappadozien)	† ca 390
Gr^{Ny}	g	Gregorius B Nyssa (Kappadozien)	† 394
GrTh	g	Gregorius Thaumaturgus B Neocäsarea (Pontus)	† ca 270
Haimo	l	Haimo monachus (Auxerre) *vel* B Halberstadt (Sachsen)	IX.
Hes	g	Hesychius Presb. (Jerusalem)	† nach 450
Hgm	g	Hegemonius (Syrien)	IV.
Hgs	g	Hegesippus (Korinth, Rom)	II.
Hi	l	Hieronymus (Antiochia, Konstantinopel, Rom, Bethlehem)	† 419/420
Hil	l	Hilarius B Poitiers (W-Gallien)	† 367
Hip	g	Hippolytus B in Rom	† 235
HM	g	Historia Monachorum in Aegypto	IV.
HPass	l	Historia passionis Domini (Theol. Sammel-Hs Bischoff)	XIV.
Iac	s	Iacobus Nisibenus (Syrien)	† 338
PsIg	g	Pseudo-Ignatianen	IV.
Ir	g	Irenaeus B Lyon (S-Gallien)	II.
Is^{M}	s	Ischo'dad v. Merv B Hedatta (Persien)	IX.
Isai	g	Isaias Abbas (Skete, Ägypten)	IV.
Isd	g	Isidorus (Pelusium, Ägypten)	ca 360 - ca 435
Iu	g	Iustinus Martyr (Sichem, Rom)	† ca 165
Iul	g	Iulius Africanus (Emmaus)	† nach 240
Iuv	l	Iuvencus (Spanien)	IV.
Lac	l	Lactantius (Nicomedia, Trier)	† nach 317
Leo	l	Leo I. Papa	† 461
Leont	g	Leontinus Byzantinus	VI./1.
LG	s	„Liber Graduum" (Mesopotamien)	IV. (?)
Luc	l	Luciferus v. Cagliari (Sardinien)	† 370/377
Mac^{J}	g	Macarius iunior (Alexandria)	† ca 394
Mac^{M}	g	Macarius B Magnesia (Prov. Asia)	IV./V.
Mac^{S}	g	Macarius senior *vel* Aegyptus (Skete)	† ca 390
Marcos	g	Marcosii, Marci Gnostici discipuli ($^{Hip. Ir}$)	II./III.
Marcl	g	Marcellus B Ankyra	† ca 374
Max^{C}	g	Maximus Confessor (Konstantinopel, N-Afrika)	† 622
Max^{T}	l	Maximus B Turin	† 408/423
Mcn	g	Marcion Haereticus (Sinope, Rom)	II.
Meth	g	Methodius (Lykien, Pamphylien)	III./IV.
MPol	g	Martyrium Polycarpi	ca 160
Naas	g	Naasseni Gnostici (^{Hip})	II./III.
Non	g	Nonnus v. Panopolis (Ägypten)	† nach 431
Nov	l	Novatianus Presb. (Rom)	† nach 251
Oec	g	Oecumenius Rhetor (Asia minor)	VI./1.
Ol	g	Olympiodorus Diaconus (Alexandria)	VI.
Opt	l	Optatus B Mileve (N-Afrika)	† vor 400
Or	g	Origenes (Alexandria, Cäsarea)	† 253/254
Oro	l	Paulus Orosius (N-Afrika, Palästina)	† nach 418
Ores	g	Oresiesis (Tabbanisi, Ägypten)	IV.
Pau^{M}	l	Paulinus (Mailand/*Milan*)	V./1.
Pau^{N}	l	Paulinus B Nola (Italien)	† 431
Pel	l	Pelagius (Rom, Carthago, Palästina)	† ca 420(?)
Pet	l	Petilianus B Cirta (Numidien)	V.
Phlp	g	Iohannes Philoponus (Alexandria)	† nach 565
Phlst	g	Philostorgius (Konstantinopel)	V.
Pho	g	Photius Patriarcha (Konstantinopel)	IX.
Phoe	l	Phoebadius B Agen (S-Gallien)	† nach 392
Pie	g	Pierius (Alexandria)	† nach 309
Pld	g	Palladius B Helenopolis (Ägypten, Bithynien)	† vor 431
Pol	g	Polycarpus B Smyrna	† 156
Pos	l	Possidius (Calama, Numidien)	IV./V.
Pris	l	Priscillianus B Avila (Spanien)	† 385
Procl	g	Proclus Patriarcha (Konstantinopel)	† 446
Procp	g	Procopius (Gaza, Palästina)	† ca 538
PS	c	„Pistis Sopia"	III./2.
Pt^{A}	g	Petrus B Alexandria	† 311
Pt^{L}	g	Petrus Laodicenus	VII.

Abkürzung/ *Abbreviation*	Orig. Sprache/ *Language* g = gr. l = lat. s = syr. c = copt.	Name (PsAug etc. s. Aug etc.) B = Bischof von/*Bishop of* v. = von/*of* in (): Lebensort(e)/ *place of life*(s)	Zeit/*Time* vor/*before* nach/*later than*
Pt^{R}	l	Petrus Rigensis	XII.
Ptl	g	Ptolemaeus Gnosticus (^{Ep})	II.
Qu	l	Quodvultdeus B Carthago	† ca 453
Ru	l	Rufinus (Aquileia)	† 410
Sch	c	Schenute (Atripe, Ägypten)	† 466
Sed	l	Sedulius (Gallien, Italien)	V.
SedScot	l	Sedulius Scotus (Irland, Liège, Köln)	† nach 858
Sev	g	Severus Patriarcha (Antiochia, Alexandria)	† 538
Sr	g	Serapion B Thmuis (Ägypten)	† nach 362
Svn	g	Severianus B Gabala (Syrien)	† nach 408
Te	l	Tertullianus (Carthago)	† nach 220
Thd^{A}	g	Theodotus B Ankyra	V.
Thd^{C}	g	Theodoretus B Cyrus (Syrien)	† ca 466
Thd^{M}	g	Theodorus B Mopsuestia (Kilikien)	† 428

Abkürzung/ *Abbreviation*	Orig. Sprache/ *Language* g = gr. l = lat. s = syr. c = copt.	Name (PsAug etc. s. Aug etc.) B = Bischof von/*Bishop of* v. = von/*of* in (): Lebensort(e) *place(s) of life*	Zeit/*Time* vor/*before* nach/*later than*
Thi	g	Theophilus B Antiochia	† ca 181
Thy	g	Theophylactus B Achrida (Serbien)	XI.
Ti	g	Titus B Bostra (Prov. Arabia)	† 371
TMti	g	Traditiones Matthiae (^{Cl})	II.
Tyc	l	Tyconius Donatista (N-Afrika)	IV.
Val	g	Valentini discipuli (^{Ir})	II.
Vic^{A}	g	Victor Presb. (Antiochia)	nach 500
Vic^{P}	l	Victorinus B Pettau (Pannonien)	† 304
Vic^{R}	l	Victorinus Rhetor (Rom)	† nach 362
Vic^{T}	l	Victor B Tannuna (N-Afrika)	† nach 566
Vig	l	Vigilius B Thapsus (N-Afrika)	V.

VII. Der zweite Apparat. *VII. The Second Apparatus.*

Der 2. Apparat bietet das außerkanonische Material, soweit es irgendeine, sei es auch noch so ferne Verwandtschaft mit synoptischen Perikopen oder Einzelversen erkennen läßt. Die Texte sind immer dort abgedruckt, wo das gesamte synoptische Material zusammengestellt erscheint („Vollvergleich"). An den Parallelstellen finden sich regelmäßig Querverweise. Den vollen Nachweis aller im 2. Apparat abgedruckten Texte enthält das Verzeichnis S. 285.

In der Zuteilung und Zählung der Fragmente judenchristlicher Evv. ist PVielhauer, Judenchristliche Evv. in: EHennecke-WSchneemelcher, Neutestamentliche Apokryphen [4]1968, 75ff. zugrunde gelegt.

Für das coptische Thomas-Ev. habe ich Text und Zählung der Leidener Ausgabe von 1959 benutzt. Nochmals sei betont, daß meine Übersetzung aus dem Coptischen nicht eine — nach wie vor umstrittene — griechische Vorlage rekonstruieren, sondern lediglich einen Zugang zu dem coptischen Original schaffen will, der jedem Benutzer der griechischen Synopse offensteht. Deshalb ist mein Text auch stets durch „(*transl.*)" eingeführt und kursiv gesetzt, während die uns bekannten griechischen Fragmente (POxy 1, 654, 655) gesondert in normaler Schrift stehen (vgl. zB 2. App zu *105.*).

The 2nd app. gives the extra canonical material so far as we can recognize a relationship, however remote, with Synoptic pericopes or individual verses. The texts are always printed in the place where the whole Synoptic material is collected ("comparison in full"). At the parallel passages there are regularly cross references. The full indication of all texts printed in the 2nd apparatus is contained in the list on p. 285.

In the ascription and numbering of the fragments of the Jewish-Christian Gospels I have taken PVielhauer, Judenchristliche Evangelien in: EHennecke-WSchneemelcher, Neutestamentliche Apokryphen [4]1968, 75ff. as a basis.

For the Gospel of Thomas in Coptic I have used the text and numbering of the Leiden edition of 1959. Let me stress here that my translation from the Coptic is not intended to reconstruct the Greek exemplar, now as formerly a subject of controversy, but merely to provide an approach to the Coptic original that is available to each user of the Greek Synopsis. For this reason my text is always introduced by "(*transl.*)" and is printed in cursive type, while the Greek fragments known to us (POxy 1, 654, 655) are printed in normal type separately (e. g. cf. the 2nd app. to *105.*).

VIII. Abkürzungen, Zeichen. *Abbreviations, Symbols.*

In (...): Abschnitte der Einleitung / *Sections of the Introduction.*

Biblische Bücher/*Books of the Bible*: Gn Ex Lv Nu Dt Jos Jdc Rth 1.2Sm 1.2Rg 1.2Chr Esr Neh Esth; Job Ps Prv Eccl Ct; Is Jr Thr Ez Dn Hos Joel Am Ob Jon Mch Nah Hab Zph Hgg Zch Ml; Jdth Sap Tob Sir Bar 1-4Mcc. — Mt Mk Lk Jo; Act; R 1.2K G E Ph Kol 1.2Th 1.2T Tt Phm; H; Jc 1.2P 1-3J Jd; Ap.

Schriftsteller / *Authors* s. Liste / *list* (VI. ←).

Buchstaben / *Letters*

A, B, C ...: gr. Majuskeln / *Gr. uncials* (III.B.2.b.; IV.a.; V.a.)
a, b, c ...: altlat. Hss / *Old Lat. mss* (III.B.3.a.; IV.b.; V.b.)
23a, 23b, 23c ...: das frühere, mittlere oder spätere Vorkommen des Wortes oder Ausdrucks in v. 23 / *the first, later or last appearance of a word or expression in v.* 23 (23a ist also nicht ein bestimmter, grammatisch abgrenzbarer erster Teil von v. 23 / 23a *therefore is not a first part of v.* 23 *which can be grammatically delimited*)
$ℵ^{a}$, $ℵ^{b}$, $ℵ^{c}$ ...: verschiedene Korr. von / *different corr. of* ℵ (IV.a.)
Sj^{a}, *Sj*^{b} ...: die verschiedenen Hss von / *different mss of S*j (III. B.4.d.)
a. a. O.: am angeführten Ort / *at the same place*
Act: = Acta: → Jo
A.D.: Anno Domini
ad loc.: zur Stelle / *commenting on this passage*
äth.: äthiopisch
Aeth: KB/SS für die äth. Zeugen / *Ind./GS for the eth. witnesses* (III.B.8.9.10.b.), ed. Rom.(^{ro}), Pell Platt(^{pp}), ms Paris.(^{ms})
Agr.: Agraphon
akhm./Akhm.: akhmimisch / *Akhmimic* (III.B.5.d.)
al = alii: ca 10—20 gr. Minuskeln / *Gr. minuscules* (III.B.2.h.)
Altaner: s. I.1. (←)
ANTF: Arbeiten zur neutestamentlichen Textforschung (hrsg. KAland)
apocr.: apokryph / *apocryphal* (Ev. apocr. = Evangelium apocryphum)
App./app.: Apparat(e) / *apparatus(es)*
arab./Arab.: arabisch / *Arabic*
Arab: KB/SS für die arab. Zeugen / *Ind./GS for the arab. witnesses* (III.B.8.9.10.b.)
arm./Arm.: armenisch / *Armenian*
Arm: KB/SS für die arm. Zeugen / *Ind./GS for the Arm. witnesses Arm*^{V}, *Arm*^{0} ... (III.B.6.9.10.b.c.)
AT: Altes Testament / *Old Testament*

B: in der Liste der Schr. / *in the list of the authors*: Bischof von / *bishop of*
Bd.: Band, Bände / *volume, -es*
Bl.: Blatt, Blätter / *leaf, leaves*
Bl.-Debr.: FBlaß-ADebrunner-FRehkopf, Grammatik des neutestamentlichen Griechisch ^{15}1979
boh./Boh.: bohairisch / *Bohairic* (III.B.5.b.)
bzw.: beziehungsweise / *respectively*

C: KB/SS für die copt. Zeugen / *Ind./GS for the coptic witnesses Cs, C*b ... (III.B.5.e.; 10.a.c.)
M^{c}: Korr. der Hs M / *a corr. of ms M* (III.B.1.b.1.)
ca: rund, ungefähr / *about*
Eu^{can}: die Canones des Euseb / *the canons of Eusebius*
M^{cap}: die in vielen Hss den einzelnen Evv. vorangestellten Kapitellisten mit Inhaltsangabe / *the list of the chapters and their contents, preceding the text of the individual Gospels in many mss*
cf.: = confer: vergleiche / *compair*
cf. ad: Verweise innerhalb der App. / *references within the apparatuses*
cj.: = conjecit: vermutete / *conjectured*
^{cmt}: Kommentar in einer Hs, marginal oder interlinear / *the commentary, in margin or interlinear, of a ms* (zB/*e.g.*: X^{cmt}, im Gegensatz zu / *to be distinguished from* X^{t}, dem Text von / *the text of* X); oder in einem Schr. / *or in an author* (zB/*e.g.*: Or^{cmt}, im Gegensatz zu / *to be distinguished from* Or^{lm}, dem / *the* Lemma in Or)
Cod.: Codex (Cod. Evv.: Codex evangeliorum)
Codd.: Codices (Codd. NT: Codices Novi Testamenti)
col.: Kolumne / *column*
copt./Copt.: coptisch / *Coptic*
corr.: → Korr.
cp.: vergleiche / *compair*

Dass.: dasselbe Werk / *the same book*
Ders.: derselbe Autor / *the same writer*
d. h.: das heißt / *that is*

ebda: ebenda / *at the same place*
ed.: = editio, editor, -es: Auflage, Hrsg. / *edition, editor, -s*
e. g.: = exempli gratia: zB / *for example*
engl./Engl.: englisch / *English*
et: und / *and*; verbindet gemeinsam auftretende Varianten / *connects variants which appear together* (III.A.2. a.3.6.)
etc.: = et cetera: und so weiter / *and so on*
Eth.: *Ethiopic*
Ev., Evv.: Evangelium, -ien / *Gospel, -s*; in Hss-Listen / *mss lists*: Evv. = 4 Evv.

f., ff.: der (die) folgende(n) / *the following v.* (*vv.*) etc.
fajj./fayy.: fajjumisch / *Fayyumic* (III.B.5.d.)
fin.: = finis: Ende (des Ev.) / *end* (*of the Gospel*)
fol.: = folium, -ia: Blatt, Blätter / *leaf, leaves*
frgm.: Fragment(e) / *fragment(s)*

Geo: KB/SS für die georg. Zeugen / *Ind./GS for the Georg. witnesses Geo*^{A}, *Geo*^{B} ... (III.B.7.9.10.b.)
georg./*Georg*.: georgisch / *Georgian*
Got: KB/SS für die gotischen Zeugen / *Ind./GS for the Gothic witnesses* (III.B.8.9.10.b.)
gr./Gr.: griechisch / *Greek*
Gre: CRGregory (IV.a.)
GS: Summensigel / *group symbol*

𝔊: SS für Zeugen der ägyptischen oder Hesych-Gruppe / *GS for witnesses of the Egyptian or Hesychius group* (III.B.2.g.)
Hrsg., hrsg.: Herausgeber, herausgegeben von / *editor, edited by*
Hs, Hss: Handschrift, -en / *manuscript, -s*

ibid.: = ibidem: ebenda / *at the same place*
i. e.: = id est: das heißt / *that is*
Ind.: Kennbuchstabe / *Indicator*
init.: Anfang / *beginning*

Jhdt: Jahrhundert / *century*

Jo: Johannes-Ev. / *Gospel of John*

Jo, ohne Kapitel- und Verszahl / *without chapter and verse number*: die bei dieser Perikope oder im zugehörigen Vollvergleich (II.5.) abgedruckte(n) Jo-Parallele(n) / *the parallel(s) from Jo printed adjacently to this pericope or to the appropriate comparison in full* (II.5.). Ebenso / *the same with* Mt, Mk, Lk, Act, 1K

Jo: die betreffende Stelle ist *nfl* / *the relevant passage is nfl* (III.A.4.d.)

Jo6: der hier oder im zugehörigen Vollvergleich (II.5.) abgedruckte Text aus Jo 6 / *the text from Jo 6 printed here or in the comparison in full* (II.5.)

Jo4: v. 4 des in der gleichen Perikope abgedruckten Jo-Textes / *v. 4 of the Jo text printed in the same pericope*

1K = 1. Korintherbrief / *1st Corinthians*: s. Jo (←)

KB: Kennbuchstabe / *Indicator*

Korr.(Gre): Korrektoren / *correctors* (laut / *according to* Gre)

Kümmel: s. I.1. (←)

L: KB/SS für die lat. Zeugen / *Ind./GS for the Lat. witnesses* La, *L*vg, *L*vl ... (III.B.3.d.)

*l*1, *l*2 ...: Lektionare / *lectionaries* (III.B.2.d.)

l^{pc}: ca 2—10 andere Lektionare / *other lectionaries*

l^{al}: ca 10—20 andere Lektionare / *other lectionaries*

l^{mu}: ca 20—30 andere Lektionare / *other lectionaries*

l^{pm}: über / *more than* 30 andere Lektionare / *other lectionaries*

l^{pl}: die meisten / *most of the* anderen Lektionare / *other lectionaries*

l^{12}: 12 andere Lektionare / *other lectionaries*

lat./Lat.: lateinisch / *Latin*

l. c. = loco citato: a. a. O. (←)

lin.: Zeile / *line*

Lit.: Literatur-Nachweis bei / *for the literature see*

Lk = Lukas-Ev. / *Gospel of Luke*: s. Jo (←)

^{lm}: Lemma in einem Schr.-Kommentar / *in an author's commentary* s. ^{cmt} (←)

^{m}: Marginal(Rand-)lesart, die nicht Korrektur sein will / *a marginal reading which is not intended to be a correction*, zB / *e.g.* G^{m}, im Gegensatz zu / *to be distinguished from* G^{t} = Text von / *of* G

Mk = Markus-Ev. / *Gospel of Mark*: s. Jo (←)

ms, mss: Handschrift, -en / *manuscript, -s*

Mt = Matthäus-Ev. / *Gospel of Matthew*: s. Jo (←)

MT nach AT-Stellen / *after quotations from the OT*: Masoretischer Text / *the Masoretic text* (III.A.4.h.)

mu = multi: ca 20—30 gr. Minuskeln / *Gr. minuscules* (III.B.2.h.)

mut. = mutilatus: verstümmelt / *mutilated*

nfl non fluctuat: das betreffende Textstück ist ohne jede Variante / *the passage in question has no variants* (III. A.4.d.)

Nr.: Nummer / *number*

NT: Neues Testament / *New Testament*

Od = Odae: Hymnen des AT und NT / *hymns of the OT and NT* (III.B.1.b.1.)

om: läßt (lassen) aus / *omit(s)*

OT: *Old Testament*

Oxy: Oxyrhynchus, Fundstätte zahlreicher Papyri / *where many papyri were found*

P: Papyrus, POxy = Papyrus Oxyrhynchus etc.

$\mathfrak{P}^{1.2}$ ...: gr. Papyri des NT / *Gr. papyri of the NT* (III.B.2.a.)

p: Parallelstelle(n) / *parallel passage(s)*

‖p: die hier oder im zugehörigen Vollvergleich (II.5.) abgedruckte(n) synotische(n) Parallele(n) / *the Synoptic parallel(s) printed here or with the appropriate comparison in full* (III.A.4.e.)

Mt 10₂p: Mt 10₂ und die dort oder im zugehörigen Vollvergleich (II.5.) abgedruckte(n) synoptische(n) Parallele(n) / *Mt 10₂ and the Synoptic parallel(s) printed adjacently to this passage or with the appropriate comparison in full* (III.A.4.f.)

p: die Parallele(n) ist (sind) *nfl* / *the parallel(s) is (are) nfl* (III.A.4.d.)

p.: Seite / *page*

Pal: Palimpsest untere Schrift / *the under writing* (III.B. 2.b.)

Pal^{2}: Palimpsest obere Schrift / *the upper writing*

Pap: Papier / *paper*

pc = pauci: ca 2—10 gr. Minuskeln / *Gr. minusculus* (III.B.2.h.)

pl = plerique: die meisten gr. Minuskeln und — sofern nicht l^{pl} bei einer konkurrierenden Variante steht — Lektionare / *most of the Gr. minuscules and, unless* l^{pl} *occurs with another variant, most of the lectionaries* (III.B.2.i.)

pm = permulti: über 30 gr. Minuskeln / *more than 30 Gr. minuscules* (III.B.2.h.)

prm = praemittit, -unt: schickt, -en voran / *adds, add before* (III.A.1.b.)

Ps vor einem Schr.-Namen / *before an author's name*: Schriften, die ihm fälschlich zugeschrieben werden / *writings wrongly ascribed to him*

Pu: Purpur-Pergament / *purple parchment*

R = reliqui (maiusculi): die übrigen gr. Majuskeln / *the remaining Gr. uncials* (III.B.2.i.)

r° = recto: Vorderseite (Papyrusfasern horizontal) eines Blattes / *front page of a leaf (with the horizontal papyrus fibres)*

S.: Seite / *page*

S: KB/SS für die syr. Zeugen / *Ind./GS for the Syr. witnesses* *S*s, *S*c ... (III.B.4.e.)

s.: siehe / *see*

(s) oder / *or* ^{s} = suppletus: aufgefüllt / *completed*; zB / *e.g.* Mt 28 6-20(s) oder / *or* D^{s}: dieser verlorene Teil der Hs, oder D an dieser Stelle, wurde durch eine spätere Hand ergänzt / *this lost part or the ms, or D at this place, was later completed by another hand*

sah./Sah.: sahidisch / *Sahidic* (III.B.5.a.)

sc. = scilicet: nämlich / *to wit*

^{sch} = scholion: gelehrte Anmerkung / *learned annotation*; zB / *e.g.* 238^{sch} = ein Scholion der Minuskel 238 zu der betreffenden Stelle / *a scholion in the minuscule* 238 *on this passage*

Schr.: Schriftsteller / *author(s)*

sic = „so!": Hinweis auf ungewöhnliche Schreibweise, Fehler usw / *an indication of an unusual orthography, mistake etc.*

sim = similiter: ähnlich / *similarly*
Slav: KB/SS für die altslavischen Zeugen / *Ind./GS for the Old Slavonic witnesses* (III.B.8.9.10.b.)
spat. = spatium: Zwischenraum / *space* (III.B.1.b.1.)
subakhm./sub-Akhm.: subakhmimisch / *sub-Akhmimic* (III.B. 5.d.)
syr./Syr.: syrisch / *Syriac*
SS: Summensigel / *group symbol*

M^t: Text der Hs M, wenn sie Marginalnotizen (^{m}) oder Kommentar (^{cmt}) hat / *text of the ms M, if there are marginal notes* (^{m}) *or a commentary* (^{cmt})
ThLZ: Theologische Literaturzeitung
Ti: CvTischendorf, NT Graece, ed. octava critica maior 1869
tom.: Band, Bände / *volume, -es*
transl.: Übersetzung / *translation*
txt: der im Haupttext dieser Synopse gedruckte Wortlaut / *the wording printed in the main text of this synopsis*

usw: und so weiter / *and so on*

v., vv.: Vers, -se / *verse, -es*
M^v = videtur: offensichtlich / *apparently*
v^o = verso: Rückseite (Papyrusfasern vertikal) eines Blattes / *back page of a leaf* (*with the vertical papyrus fibres*)
vel: oder / *or*
vl, vg: s. *L* (←)
vgl.: vergleiche / *compair*
vol.: Band, Bände / *volume, -es*

F^W: s. IV.a. F (←)

zB: zum Beispiel / *for example*
z.T.: zum Teil / *partly*

ℵ: Cod. Sinaiticus, gr. Majuskel / *Gr. uncial* (IV.a.)
β, δ, μ, π: altlat. Hss / *Old Lat. mss* (III.B.3.a.2.)
Γ, Δ, Θ, Λ, Ξ, Π, Σ, Φ, Ψ, Ω: gr. Majuskeln / *Gr. uncials* (III.B. 2.b.; IV.a.)
Δ: KB/SS für die Evv.-Harmonien / *Ind./GS for the Gospel Harmonies Δ*a, *Δ*ad ... (III.B.11.d.)
λ: KB für die Zeugen der Lake-Gruppe / *Ind. for the witnesses of the Lake group* 1-22 ... (III.B.2.f.)
λ: SS für die Lake-Kerngruppe / *GS for the core of the Lake group* (III.B.2.g.)
λλ: SS für die vollständige Lake-Gruppe / *GS for the complete Lake group* (III.B.2.g.)
σ: KB für die Zeugen der Soden-Gruppe / *Ind. for the witnesses of the Soden group* M-7 ... (III.B.2.f.)
σ: SS für Zeugen der Soden-Gruppe / *GS for witnesses of the Soden group* (III.B.2.g.)
ϕ: KB für die Zeugen der Ferrar-Gruppe / *Ind. for the witnesses of the Ferrar group* 13-69 ... (III.B.2.f.)
ϕ: SS für Zeugen der Ferrar-Gruppe / *GS for witnesses of the Ferrar group* (III.B.2.g.)

Andere international gebrauchte Abkürzungen / *other abbreviations used internationally* (zB. / *e.g.* dat.pl., CCL, GSC) werden als bekannt vorausgesetzt / *are supposed to be known.*

Zahlen / *Numbers*

I., II. ...: Teil / *Chapter* I., II. ... dieser Einleitung / *of this Introduction*
I., II. ...: erstes, zweites ... Jhdt / *1st, 2nd ... century*
IV./V. = im IV. und/oder V. Jhdt / *in the IVth and/or Vth century*
V./1.: fünftes Jhdt, 1. Hälfte / *5th century, 1st half*
LXX: nach AT-Stellen / *after quotations from the OT*: Text, gegebenenfalls auch Kapitel- und Verszählung der Septuaginta / *the text and, where they differ, the chapter and verse numbers of the Septuagint* (ed. Rahlfs)
30. 31. ...: Hss der / *mss of the* Vetus Latina (vl; III.B.3.a.2.)
1154: in den Hss- und Schr.-Listen / *in the lists of mss and authors*: A.D. 1154 (430/465 = zwischen / *between* 430 & 465 A.D.)
10$_{14}$: Kapitel 10 v. 14 / *chapter 10 v. 14*; falls / *if* „*nfl*" (←): **10**$_{14}$
$_{15}$: v. 15 des gleichen Kapitels / *of the same chapter*; falls / *if* „*nfl*" (←): **15**
1, 2 ...: gr. Minuskeln / *Gr. minuscules* 1, 2 ... (III.B.2.c.)
0141: Bezeichnung für die gr. Majuskeln ab **046**, vorher Buchstaben / *designation for the Gr. majusculus from* **046** *onward*; *instead of the lower numbers capital letters are used* (III.B.2.b.)
M^1: Korrektur in M durch erste Hand / *correction in M by the first hand* (III.B.1.b.1.)
$B^{2.3}$: verschiedene Korr. von B / *different corr. of* B (IV.a.)
vg^2: 2 Vulgata-Hss / *2 mss of the Vulgate*
$Cs^{3+1?}$: 3 sah. Hss und eine weitere sah., deren Lesung unsicher ist / *3 Sah. mss and one additional Sah. ms, whose reading is uncertain*
$και^2$: das zweite και in dem betreffenden V. / *the second* και *in the relevant v.* (→ ∩)
$^{14}και$: και in v. 14 (→ ∩)
$\{\}^2$: → {}
^{2}1910: 2. Auflage / *2nd edition* 1910
1°, 2° ...: an der ersten, zweiten ... Stelle / *on the 1st, 2nd ... appearance*
*l*1, *l*2 ...: gr. Perikopenbücher / *Gr. lectionaries* (III.B.2.d.)
$l43^1$ $l43^2$: die betreffende Perikope erscheint in *l*43 mehrfach, jedoch mit Varianten / *the relevant pericope appears in l43 a number of times, but there are variants* (III.B. 2.d.Abs. / *section* 3)
l^{12}: 12 Lektionare / *lectionaries*
(156) links neben der Perikopen-Überschrift / *on the left of the titel of a pericope*: Perikopen-Nummer / *pericope number* in Huck$^{9-12}$

Klammern / *Brackets*

(...) = Untervariante / *subvariant* (III.A.2.a.—c.); über (...) in Kontaktstellung / *about* (...) *following immediately a word* s. III.A.2.d.
[...] = Zeuge fehlt an dieser Stelle wegen Beschädigung / *the witness is missing here because of damage*; zB / *e.g.* [C](III.B.1.b.1.); *L*[ek] (III.B.3.a.4.)
= die alten Texterweiterungen / *the old additions to the text*, zB / *e.g.* [Mk 16$_{14}$] [Jo 8$_5$]
im 2. App. / *in the 2nd app.*: der abgedruckte Text hat eine Lücke / *the text of the ms has a lacuna*, zB / *e.g.* βασ[...]νων oder / *or* ...]ηκεν εις τ[...
...] = wird ersetzt durch / *is replaced by* (III.A.1.a.)

⟨...⟩ = außer, im Gegensatz zu / *except, in opposition to* (III.B.1.b.1.)
im 2. App. / *in the 2nd app.*: vom Hrsg. ergänzte Textteile / *passages supplied by the ed.*

{...} = Lesung bzw. gr. Äquivalent unsicher / *the reading of the text or the Gr. equivalent are uncertain* (III.B.1.b.1.; c.). Die Zahlen $\{\}^1$ $\{\}^2$ usw bezeichnen nur die Zusammengehörigkeit von Klammern und beziehen sich niemals auf ihren Inhalt / *the numbers* $\{\}^1$ $\{\}^2$ *etc. indicate only how the brackets belong together and do not refer to their contents*

⟦...⟧ = mehrere Untervarianten zu einer umfangreichen Hauptvariante / *several subvariants to a comprehensive main variant* (III.A.2.e.)

Interpunktionen / *Punctuation Marks*

. (Punkt / *full stop*): Abkürzungszeichen / *abbreviation mark* (III.A.3.a.1.)

, (Komma): trennt Varianten des (der) gleichen Zeugen / *separates variants of the same witness(es)*
macht *L S* ... zu Summensigeln / *turns L S ... into group symbols* (III.B.3.d.1.)

; (Semikolon): trennt Varianten verschiedener Zeugen / *separates variants of different witnesses*

: (Doppelpunkt / *colon*): leitet vom Varianten- zum Zeugenteil über / *separates the section of the variants from that of the witnesses*

! oder / *or* (!) (Ausrufungszeichen / *exclamation mark*): = sic (←)

? (Fragezeichen / *interrogation mark*): Lesung unsicher / *wording is in doubt* (III.B.1.b.1.); auch / *also* $C^{3+1?}$

Sonstige Zeichen / *Other Symbols*

▭ verweist auf diejenige Perikope, wo alle hierher gehörigen Parallelen abgedruckt sind (Vollvergleich) / *refers to that pericope where all relevant parallels are printed* (*comparison in full*), zB / *e.g.* **99.**

↑ ↓ im Haupttext / *in the main text*: s. oben, unten / *s. above, below*

↓ im 1. App. verweist auf den 2. / *in the 1st app. refers to the 2nd app.*

- zwischen gr. Hss (und SS) verbindet die Hss der gleichen Gruppe / *between Gr. mss* (*and GS*) *connects the mss of the same group* (III.B.2.f.)

- vor oder nach einem gr. Wort ersetzt einen aus dem Kontext ersichtlichen Wortteil / *before or after a Gr. word represents a part of the word which is to be supplied from the context* (III.A.3.a.2.)

| grenzt eine zusammengehörige Variantengruppe gegen eine andere ab / *separates a group of variants which belong together from another group*

— trennt zusammengehörige Varianten / *separates variants which belong together* (III.A.1.f.)

— zwischen zwei gr. Worten in Kontaktstellung / *between two Gr. words in immediate juxtaposition* (zB / *e.g.* αυτος—οικω): der zwischen αυτος und οικω stehende Text ist mitbetroffen / *the text between* αυτος *and* οικω *is involved* (III.A.3.b.)

... zwischen zwei gr. Worten / *between two Gr. words* (zB / *e.g.* γραμματεις ... πρεσβυτεροι): der zwischen γρ. und πρ. stehende Text ist nicht betroffen / *the text between* γρ. *and* πρ. *is not involved* (III.A.1.f.). Zu ... im Haupttext / *for ... in the main text* s. II.8.

←, → = s. oben, unten / *s. above, below*

‖ kündigt den Hinweis auf die Parallel-Stelle(n) an, der (denen) der *txt* durch die betreffende Variante angenähert erscheint / *indicates the reference to the parallel passage(s), to which the "txt" seems to be approximated through the relevant variant* (III.A.4.a.)

‖←, Lk← = Wiederholung der letzten vorhergegangenen Parallelen-Angabe bzw. der zuletzt genannten Lk-Stelle(n) / *indicates the same parallel(s) which is (are) given after the last preceding ‖ or Lk* (III.A.4.g.)

←p = Parallele(n), beigedruckt oder im Vollvergleich, zu der (den) mit ← wiederholten Stelle(n) / *parallel(s), printed adjacently or in the comparison in full, to the passage(s) indicated by* ← (III.A.4.f.)

● = von andern Hrsg. als Urtext angenommen / *held to be the original text by other authors*

◆ = der im *txt* gebotenen Fassung gleichwertig / *as probable as the wording given in the "txt"*

/ = vel: oder / *or*

< = verschrieben aus, entstanden aus / *miscopied from, originated from*

+ = fügt, -en hinzu / *adds, add*

∼ = stellt, -en um / *rearranges, -e.* Zu / *For* (∼) s. III.A.2.c.bb.4.5.)

∩ = der Abschreiber hat einen Sprung gemacht / *the copyist has made a jump* (zB / *e.g.* και$^2\cap^3$ = vom zweiten zum dritten / *from the 2nd to the 3rd* και oder / *or* $^{42}\cap^{43}$ αυτος = von / *from* αυτος in v. 42 zu / *to* αυτος in v. 43)

† = lückenhaft / *with gaps* (III.B.2.f.g.; 3.a.; IV.; V.2.)

* bezeichnet den später veränderten Originaltext einer Hs / *designates the original text which was later altered of a ms* (zB / *e.g.* B*)

⁺ & ⁻ = asteriscus & obelus s. Sh^+ & Sh^- (III.B.4.c.)

' = Rest / *remainder*; steht nach SS, wenn andere durch die SS repräsentierten Zeugen mit anderen Varianten aufgeführt sind / *is added to the GS, if other witnesses represented by the GS are cited with other variants* (III.B.2.g. Abs. / *section* 3)

† = gestorben / *died*

Die Vorgeschichten. *The Infancy Narratives.*

A. Die matthäische Vorgeschichte. *The Matthean Infancy Narrative.* **Matth 1. 2.**

(—)

1. Die Ahnentafel Jesu. *The Genealogy of Jesus.*

Matth 1 1–17	Luk *3* 23–34 *(19.)* in umgekehrter Reihenfolge *(in the reverse order)*	
1 Βίβλος γενέσεως Ἰησοῦ Χριστοῦ υἱοῦ Δαυιδ υἱοῦ Αβρααμ.		
2 Αβρααμ ἐγέννησεν τὸν Ισαακ,	34 *Αβρααμ*	**2-6:** 1Chr2 1-15
Ισαακ δὲ ἐγέννησεν τὸν Ιακωβ,	*Ισαακ*	
Ιακωβ δὲ ἐγέννησεν τὸν Ἰούδαν καὶ τοὺς ἀδελφοὺς αὐτοῦ,	*Ιακωβ*	**3-6:**
3 Ἰούδας δὲ ἐγέννησεν τὸν Φαρες καὶ τὸν Ζαρε ἐκ τῆς Θαμαρ,	33 *Ἰούδα*	Rth4 18-22
Φαρες δὲ ἐγέννησεν τὸν Εσρωμ,	*Φαρες*	
Εσρωμ δὲ ἐγέννησεν τὸν Αραμ,	*Εσρωμ, Αρνι*	
4 Αραμ δὲ ἐγέννησεν τὸν Αμμιναδαβ,	*Αδμιν*	
Αμμιναδαβ δὲ ἐγέννησεν τὸν Ναασσων,	*Αμιναδαβ*	
Ναασσων δὲ ἐγέννησεν τὸν Σαλμων,	32 *Ναασσων*	
5 Σαλμων δὲ ἐγέννησεν τὸν Βοες ἐκ τῆς Ραχαβ,	*Σαλα*	
Βοες δὲ ἐγέννησεν τὸν Ιωβηδ ἐκ τῆς Ρουθ,	*Βοος*	
Ιωβηδ δὲ ἐγέννησεν τὸν Ιεσσαι,	*Ιωβηδ*	
6 Ιεσσαι δὲ ἐγέννησεν τὸν Δαυιδ τὸν βασιλέα.	*Ιεσσαι*	
Δαυιδ δὲ ἐγέννησεν τὸν Σολομῶνα ἐκ τῆς τοῦ Οὐρίου,	31 *Δαυιδ*	**7-12:**
7 Σολομὼν δὲ ἐγέννησεν τὸν Ροβοαμ,	*Ναθαμ*	1Chr3 10-19
Ροβοαμ δὲ ἐγέννησεν τὸν Αβια,	*Ματταθα*	
Αβια δὲ ἐγέννησεν τὸν Ασαφ,	*Μεννα*	
8 Ασαφ δὲ ἐγέννησεν τὸν Ιωσαφατ,	*Μελεα*	
Ιωσαφατ δὲ ἐγέννησεν τὸν Ιωραμ,	30 *Ελιακιμ*	
Ιωραμ δὲ ἐγέννησεν τὸν Ὀζίαν,	*Ιωναμ*	
9 Ὀζίας δὲ ἐγέννησεν τὸν Ιωαθαμ,	*Ιωσηφ*	
Ιωαθαμ δὲ ἐγέννησεν τὸν Αχαζ,	*Ἰούδα*	
Αχαζ δὲ ἐγέννησεν τὸν Ἑζεκίαν,	*Συμεων*	
10 Ἑζεκίας δὲ ἐγέννησεν τὸν Μανασσῆ,	29 *Λευι*	
Μανασσῆς δὲ ἐγέννησεν τὸν Αμως,	*Μαθθατ*	
Αμως δὲ ἐγέννησεν τὸν Ἰωσίαν,	*Ιωριμ*	
11 Ἰωσίας δὲ ἐγέννησεν τὸν Ἰεχονίαν καὶ τοὺς ἀδελφοὺς αὐτοῦ ἐπὶ τῆς μετοικεσίας	*Ελιαζερ, Ἰησοῦ,* 28 *Ηρ,*	
Βαβυλῶνος.	*Ελμαδαμ, Κωσαμ, Αδδι,*	
12 Μετὰ δὲ τὴν μετοικεσίαν Βαβυλῶνος Ἰεχονίας ἐγέννησεν τὸν Σελαθιηλ,	*Μελχι,* 27 *Νηρι*	
Σελαθιηλ δὲ ἐγέννησεν τὸν Ζοροβαβελ,	*Σαλαθιηλ*	
13 Ζοροβαβελ δὲ ἐγέννησεν τὸν Αβιουδ,	*Ζοροβαβελ*	

Mt 1,8 Οζ.] Οχοζιαν, Οχοζιας γεννα(*om*) τον Ιωας, Ιω. γεννα(*om*) τον Αμεσσιαν, Αμεσσιας γεννα(*om*) τον Αζαριαν(Οζιαν) τον καλουμενον(κληθεντα) Οζιαν(Αζαριαν), Αζαριας ο και (*om* Αζ. ο κ.) *et om* ^{9}δε^{1}‖1Chr3 11f. *cf. ad* Lk3 24: Ep^{1}(^{1}) (*om* Αζ. τ. καλ. ... Αζ. ο και: *Sc* Af) *Aeth* **11** Ιωσ. + δε εγεννησεν τον Ιωακιμ, Ιωα.‖2Chr36 8 *cf.*←: 33 Σ-1604 **λ**-1582 ϕ230 σM-71(∼^{10} ... Ιωα. Ιωα. ... Ιωσ. ^{11}Ιωσ.)-954 U Θ *al l*54 *L*Ir *Sh*$^{+}$j Af *Geo*

Αβιουδ δὲ ἐγέννησεν τὸν Ελιακιμ,
Ελιακιμ δὲ ἐγέννησεν τὸν Αζωρ,
14 Αζωρ δὲ ἐγέννησεν τὸν Σαδωκ,
Σαδωκ δὲ ἐγέννησεν τὸν Αχιμ,
Αχιμ δὲ ἐγέννησεν τὸν Ελιουδ,
15 Ελιουδ δὲ ἐγέννησεν τὸν Ελεαζαρ,
Ελεαζαρ δὲ ἐγέννησεν τὸν Μαθθαν,

Μαθθαν δὲ ἐγέννησεν τὸν Ιακωβ,
16 Ιακωβ δὲ ἐγέννησεν τὸν Ιωσηφ τὸν ἄνδρα
Μαρίας, ἐξ ἧς ἐγεννήθη Ἰησοῦς ὁ λεγόμενος Χριστός.

Ρησα
Ιωανὰν
26 *Ιωδα*
Ιωσηχ
Σεμειν, Ματταθίου
Μααθ, 25 *Ναγγαι, Εσλι,*
Ναουμ, Αμως, Ματταθίου, 24 *Ιωσηφ, Ιανναι,*
Μελχι, Λευι
Ματθατ, 23 *Ηλι*
Ιωσηφ

17 πᾶσαι οὖν αἱ γενεαὶ ἀπὸ Αβρααμ ἕως Δαυιδ γενεαὶ δεκατέσσαρες, καὶ ἀπὸ Δαυιδ ἕως τῆς μετοικεσίας Βαβυλῶνος γενεαὶ δεκατέσσαρες, καὶ ἀπὸ τῆς μετοικεσίας Βαβυλῶνος ἕως τοῦ Χριστοῦ γενεαὶ δεκατέσσαρες.

(—) 2. Die Geburt Jesu. *The Birth of Jesus.* **Matth 1** 18–25

18 Τοῦ δὲ Ἰησοῦ Χριστοῦ ἡ γένεσις οὕτως ἦν. μνηστευθείσης τῆς μητρὸς αὐτοῦ Μαρίας τῷ Ιωσηφ, πρὶν ἢ συνελθεῖν αὐτοὺς εὑρέθη ἐν γαστρὶ ἔχουσα ἐκ πνεύματος ἁγίου. 19 Ιωσηφ δὲ ὁ ἀνὴρ αὐτῆς, δίκαιος ὢν καὶ μὴ θέλων αὐτὴν παραδειγματίσαι, ἐβουλήθη λάθρᾳ ἀπολῦσαι αὐτήν. 20 ταῦτα δὲ αὐτοῦ ἐνθυμηθέντος, ἰδοὺ ἄγγελος κυρίου κατ' ὄναρ ἐφάνη αὐτῷ λέγων· Ιωσηφ υἱὸς Δαυιδ, μὴ φοβηθῇς παραλαβεῖν Μαρίαν τὴν γυναῖκά σου· τὸ γὰρ ἐν αὐτῇ γεννηθὲν ἐκ πνεύματός ἐστιν ἁγίου. 21 τέξεται δὲ υἱόν, καὶ καλέσεις τὸ ὄνομα αὐτοῦ Ἰησοῦν· αὐτὸς γὰρ σώσει τὸν λαὸν αὐτοῦ ἀπὸ τῶν ἁμαρτιῶν αὐτῶν. 22 τοῦτο δὲ ὅλον γέγονεν ἵνα πληρωθῇ τὸ ῥηθὲν ὑπὸ κυρίου διὰ τοῦ προφήτου λέγοντος· 23 **ἰδοὺ ἡ παρθένος ἐν γαστρὶ ἕξει καὶ τέξεται υἱόν, καὶ καλέσουσιν τὸ ὄνομα αὐτοῦ Εμμανουηλ,** ὅ ἐστιν μεθερμηνευόμενον **μεθ' ἡμῶν ὁ**

Is7 14
Is8.10 LXX

Mt 1,16 τον²—Χρ.] ω μνηστευθεισα (+ ην) παρθενος Μαριαμ (+ η) εγεννησεν Ιησουν τον λεγομενον (*om* τ. λεγ.) Χριστον‖Lk1 27: ϕ⟨124⟩-*l*547(*om* τον) Θ *L*ag¹(*sim.*: vl')(*om* τ. λεγ.: k[e] d) Amst PsChr Gau (*S*c) — ● Ιωσηφ, ω εμνηστευμενη ην παρθενος Μαριαμ, εγεννησεν Ιησουν τον λεγομενον Χριστον‖←: DialAT¹:⁴?↓ *S*s Brs — *txt*: 𝔓¹ *Rpl* DialAT¹:⁴↓ *L*fff¹z vg *S*'j *C*s(b *Arm*) | τον²—Μ.] ω μνηστευθεισα Μαρια‖←: DialAT¹:⁴↓ — τον μνηστευσμενον Μαριαμ‖←: DialAT¹:⁴↓ | Μαρ. + ω εμνηστευμενη ην παρθενος Μαρια‖←: *Arm* | εξ—Χρ.] η εγεννησεν Ιησουν τ. λ. Χριστον: *C*b | Ιη.—Χρ.] ο Χρ. ο υιος του θεου‖16 16: DialAT¹:⁴↓ **19** παραδ.] ● δειγμ.: 𝔓¹ ℵ^a(b?)BZ λ1-1582 Eu¹ — *txt*: *Rpl* Ep Eu² *S*h^mgr
20 ∼ εφ. κ. ον.‖2 13.19: ϕ'-828(∼ αυτω κ. ον.)⟨124-346⟩-1689 Θ (=828: EIc↓ Ep) *L*vl⟨fff¹⟩ vg¹ | εφ.] φαινεται‖←: 892 ϕ124 σ1424-1606 Chr EIc↓ *L*k[e] | αυτω] τω Ιωσηφ‖←: 892 Θ(*om* Ιω.²) 280 Chr *L*g¹ vg¹ *S*c *C*b⟨1⟩ **21** δε + σοι‖Lk1 13: EIc↓ *S*sc | καλεσει‖Lk1 31: L *L*g¹ Am *Arm*¹ **22** *om* ολ.‖21 4: Ep *L*Ir³:⁴ *S*sc **23** καλεσεις‖Lk1 31 Is7 14 LXX: σ1391 D *l*184 Eu *C*b² — καλεσει‖Lk1 31 Is7 14 MT: *L*dff² — κληθησεται‖Lk1 32.35: *L*vg¹ Ir¹:³ Pris Te *S*c

---

Mt1 16 *cf.* DialAT (76.88): (fol.93r°) ... ὁ Ἰουδαῖος εἶπεν· ἔστιν μὲν οὖν καὶ ἐν τῇ παλαιᾷ (sc. διαθήκῃ) γενεαλογία· καὶ ἐν τῇ νέᾳ δέ ἐστιν ἐν τῷ κατὰ Ματθαία(!), οὕτως δὲ περιέχει· ὅτι Ιακωβ ἐγέννησεν τὸν Ιωσηφ, τὸν ἄνδρα Μαρίας, ἐξ ἧς ἐγεννήθη Ἰησοῦς ὁ λεγόμενος Χριστός. καὶ Ιωσηφ ἐγέννησεν τὸν Ἰησοῦν τὸν λεγόμενον Χριστόν, περὶ οὗ νῦν ὁ λόγος, φησίν· ἐγέννησεν ἐκ τῆς Μαρίας. ὁ Χριστιανὸς εἶπεν· ὀρθῶς καὶ κατὰ τάξιν μέλλεις λέγειν ... οὕτως γέγραπται, ἀρξάμενος γὰρ ἀπὸ τοῦ Αβρααμ, ὅτι Αβρααμ, φησίν, ἐγέννησεν Ισαακ ... (fol.93v°) ... Ιακωβ δὲ τὸν Ιωσηφ, ᾧ μνηστευθεῖσα Μαρία, ἐξ ἧς ἐγεννήθη Ἰησοῦς ὁ λεγόμενος Χριστός ... (88 fol.113r°) ... Ιακωβ δὲ ἐγέννησεν τὸν Ιωσηφ, τὸν μνηστευσάμενον Μαριαμ, ἐξ ἧς ἐγεννήθη ὁ Χριστὸς ὁ υἱὸς τοῦ θεοῦ.

Mt1 19-24 *cf.* EIc14 1-2: Καὶ ἐφοβήθη ὁ Ιωσηφ σφόδρα καὶ ἠρέμησεν ἐξ αὐτῆς, διαλογιζόμενος αὐτὴν τί ποιήσει. καὶ εἶπεν Ιωσηφ· 'ἐὰν αὐτῆς κρύψω τὸ ἁμάρτημα, εὑρεθήσομαι μαχόμενος τῷ νόμῳ κυρίου. καὶ ἐὰν αὐτὴν φανερώσω τοῖς υἱοῖς Ισραηλ, φοβοῦμαι μήπως ἀγγελικόν ἐστιν τὸ ἐν ἑαυτῇ, καὶ εὑρεθήσομαι παραδιδοὺς ἀθῷον αἷμα εἰς κρίσμα θανάτου. τί οὖν αὐτὴν ποιήσω; λάθρᾳ αὐτὴν ἀπολύσω ἀπ' ἐμοῦ.' καὶ κατέλαβεν αὐτὸν νύξ. ²Καὶ ἰδοὺ ἄγγελος κυρίου φαίνεται αὐτῷ κατ' ὄνειρον λέγων· 'μὴ φοβηθῇς τὴν παῖδα ταύτην· τὸ γὰρ ἐν ἑαυτῇ ὂν ἐκ πνεύματός ἐστιν ἁγίου. τέξεται δέ σοι υἱὸν καὶ καλέσεις τὸ ὄνομα ἑαυτοῦ Ἰησοῦν· αὐτὸς γὰρ σώσει τὸν λαὸν αὐτοῦ ἐκ τῶν ἁμαρτημάτων αὐτῶν.' καὶ ἀνέστη Ιωσηφ ἀπὸ τοῦ ὕπνου καὶ ἐδόξασεν τὸν θεὸν τοῦ Ισραηλ τὸν δόντα αὐτῷ τὴν χάριν αὐτοῦ. καὶ ἐφύλασσε τὴν παῖδα.

θεός. [24] διεγερθεὶς δὲ Ιωσηφ ἀπὸ τοῦ ὕπνου ἐποίησεν ὡς προσέταξεν αὐτῷ ὁ ἄγγελος κυρίου, καὶ παρέλαβεν τὴν γυναῖκα αὐτοῦ· [25] καὶ οὐκ ἐγίνωσκεν αὐτὴν ἕως οὗ ἔτεκεν υἱόν· καὶ ἐκάλεσεν τὸ ὄνομα αὐτοῦ Ἰησοῦν.

(—) 3. Die Weisen aus dem Morgenland. *The Visit of the Magi.* Matth 2 1-12

[1] Τοῦ δὲ Ἰησοῦ γεννηθέντος ἐν Βηθλεεμ τῆς Ἰουδαίας ἐν ἡμέραις Ἡρῴδου τοῦ βασιλέως, ἰδοὺ μάγοι ἀπὸ ἀνατολῶν παρεγένοντο εἰς Ἱεροσόλυμα [2] λέγοντες· ποῦ ἐστιν ὁ τεχθεὶς βασιλεὺς τῶν Ἰουδαίων; εἴδομεν γὰρ αὐτοῦ τὸν ἀστέρα ἐν τῇ ἀνατολῇ, καὶ ἤλθομεν προσκυνῆσαι αὐτῷ. [3] ἀκούσας δὲ ὁ βασιλεὺς Ἡρῴδης ἐταράχθη, καὶ πᾶσα Ἱεροσόλυμα μετ' αὐτοῦ, [4] καὶ συναγαγὼν πάντας τοὺς ἀρχιερεῖς καὶ γραμματεῖς τοῦ λαοῦ ἐπυνθάνετο παρ' αὐτῶν ποῦ ὁ Χριστὸς γεννᾶται. [5] οἱ δὲ εἶπαν αὐτῷ· ἐν Βηθλεεμ τῆς Ἰουδαίας· οὕτως γὰρ γέγραπται διὰ τοῦ προφήτου· [6] **καὶ σὺ Βηθλεεμ, γῆ Ἰούδα, οὐδαμῶς ἐλαχίστη εἶ ἐν τοῖς ἡγεμόσιν Ἰούδα· ἐκ σοῦ γὰρ ἐξελεύσεται ἡγούμενος, ὅστις ποιμανεῖ τὸν λαόν μου τὸν Ισραηλ.** [7] τότε Ἡρῴδης λάθρᾳ καλέσας τοὺς μάγους ἠκρίβωσεν παρ' αὐτῶν τὸν χρόνον τοῦ φαινομένου ἀστέρος, [8] καὶ πέμψας αὐτοὺς εἰς Βηθλεεμ εἶπεν· πορευθέντες ἐξετάσατε ἀκριβῶς περὶ τοῦ παιδίου· ἐπὰν δὲ εὕρητε, ἀπαγγείλατέ μοι, ὅπως κἀγὼ ἐλθὼν προσκυνήσω αὐτῷ. [9] οἱ δὲ ἀκούσαντες τοῦ βασιλέως ἐπορεύθησαν· καὶ ἰδοὺ ὁ ἀστήρ, ὃν εἶδον ἐν τῇ ἀνατολῇ, προῆγεν αὐτοὺς ἕως ἐλθὼν ἐστάθη ἐπάνω οὗ ἦν τὸ παιδίον. [10] ἰδόντες δὲ τὸν ἀστέρα ἐχάρησαν χαρὰν μεγάλην σφόδρα. [11] καὶ ἐλθόντες εἰς τὴν οἰκίαν εἶδον τὸ παιδίον μετὰ Μαρίας τῆς μητρὸς αὐτοῦ, καὶ πεσόντες **προσεκύνησαν αὐτῷ,** καὶ ἀνοίξαντες τοὺς θησαυροὺς αὐτῶν **προσήνεγκαν** αὐτῷ **δῶρα, χρυσὸν καὶ λίβανον** καὶ σμύρναν. [12] καὶ χρηματισθέντες κατ' ὄναρ μὴ ἀνακάμψαι πρὸς Ἡρῴδην, δι' ἄλλης ὁδοῦ ἀνεχώρησαν εἰς τὴν χώραν αὐτῶν.

> 7 41 f.: ... μὴ γὰρ ἐκ τῆς Γαλιλαίας ὁ Χριστὸς ἔρχεται; [42] οὐχὶ ἡ γραφὴ εἶπεν ὅτι ἐκ **τοῦ σπέρματος Δαυιδ,** καὶ **ἀπὸ Βηθλεεμ** τῆς κώμης ὅπου ἦν Δαυιδ, ὁ Χριστὸς **ἔρχεται**;

Mch5 2 2Sm7 12 Ps89 4f.

Ps72 10f. Is60 6

Mt 1,24 διεγ.] ● εγ.‖2 13f.20f.: ℵBC*Z-071 **λ**-1582 399 Ep — *txt*: *Rpl* PsAth Ep *L*vl'(μονογενη: g[2] vg[1])' Au Hi *S*'j[a] PsAth Ef *Arm*' **25** υιον] τον υιον αυτης τον πρωτοτοκον‖Lk2 7: — τον υιον τ. πρ.‖←: L D[c] *L*dq *Arm*[1] *Aeth* — τον υιον (+ αυτης): *S*c *C*(s)b (AnBal) — αυτω υιον: *S*s — *txt*: ℵBZ-071[v]-33 λ1-1582 φ230-788 *L*k[e a]bcg[1] Am *S*j[bck] **2,9** εστα.] εστη: *Rpl* EIc↓ Eu[1] Or — *txt*: ℵBC-33 **λ**-1582 D 399 Eu[1] Or **11** ειδ.] ευρον‖8 Lk2 16: 892 *pm* *L*bcff[1]g[1]z vg Au Sed

Jo 7,42 *cf. ad 223.*

---

3. cf. EIc21 1-4: Καὶ ἰδοὺ Ιωσηφ ἡτοιμάσθη τοῦ ἐξελθεῖν ἐν τῇ Ἰουδαίᾳ, καὶ θόρυβος ἐγένετο μέγας ἐν Βηθλεεμ τῆς Ἰουδαίας. ἦλθωσαν γὰρ μάγοι λέγοντες· 'ποῦ ἐστιν ὁ βασιλεὺς τῶν Ἰουδαίων; εἴδομεν γὰρ τὸν ἀστέρα αὐτοῦ ἐν τῇ ἀνατολῇ καὶ ἤλθαμεν προσκυνῆσαι αὐτῷ.' [2] καὶ ἀκούσας ὁ Ἡρῴδης ἐταράχθη καὶ ἔπεμψεν ὑπηρέτας πρὸς τοὺς μάγους· καὶ μετεπέμψατο καὶ τοὺς ἀρχιερεῖς καὶ ἀνέκρινεν αὐτοὺς ἐν τῷ πραιτωρίῳ λέγων αὐτοῖς· 'πῶς γέγραπται περὶ τοῦ Χριστοῦ; ποῦ γεννᾶται;' λέγουσιν αὐτῷ· 'ἐν Βηθλεεμ τῆς Ἰουδαίας· οὕτως γὰρ γέγραπται.' καὶ ἀπέλυσεν αὐτούς. καὶ ἀνέκρινεν τοὺς μάγους λέγων αὐτοῖς· 'τί εἴδετε σημεῖον ἐπὶ τὸν γεννηθέντα βασιλέα;' καὶ εἶπον οἱ μάγοι· 'εἴδομεν ἀστέρα παμμεγέθη λάμψαντα ἐν τοῖς ἄστροις τούτοις καὶ ἀμβλύναντα αὐτούς, ὥστε τοὺς ἀστέρας μὴ φαίνεσθαι. καὶ οὕτως ἔγνωμεν ὅτι βασιλεὺς ἐγεννήθη τῷ Ισραηλ, καὶ ἤλθομεν προσκυνῆσαι αὐτῷ.' καὶ εἶπεν αὐτοῖς Ἡρῴδης· 'ὑπάγετε καὶ ζητήσατε, καὶ ἐὰν εὕρητε ἀπαγγείλατέ μοι, ὅπως κἀγὼ ἐλθὼν προσκυνήσω αὐτῷ.' [3] καὶ ἐξῆλθον οἱ μάγοι. καὶ ἰδοὺ ὃν εἶδον ἀστέρα ἐν τῇ ἀνατολῇ προῆγεν αὐτοὺς ἕως εἰσῆλθαν ἐν τῷ σπηλαίῳ, καὶ ἔστη ἐπὶ τὴν κεφαλὴν τοῦ παιδίου. καὶ ἰδόντες αὐτὸν οἱ μάγοι ἑστῶτα μετὰ τῆς μητρὸς αὐτοῦ Μαρίας, ἐξέβαλον ἀπὸ τῆς πήρας αὐτῶν δῶρα χρυσὸν καὶ λίβανον καὶ σμύρναν. [4] καὶ χρηματισθέντες ὑπὸ τοῦ ἀγγέλου μὴ εἰσελθεῖν εἰς τὴν Ἰουδαίαν, διὰ ἄλλης ὁδοῦ ἀνεχώρησαν εἰς τὴν χώραν αὐτῶν. (22) [1] Τότε ... (*cf. ad 6.* Lk1 21)

3. cf. EN frgm.28 (SedScot Mt): Ita nanque refert evangelium, quod secundum Ebreos praetitulatur: Intuitus Joseph oculis vidit turbam viatorum comitantium venientium ad speluncam et dixit: 'Surgam et procedam foras inobviam eis.' Cum autem processisset, dixit ad Simonem Joseph: 'Sic mihi videntur isti, qui veniunt, augures esse. Ecce enim omni momento respiciunt in caelum et inter se disputant. Sed et peregrini videntur esse, quoniam et habitus eorum differt ab habitu nostro. Nam vestis eorum amplissima est, et color fuscus est eorum densius, et pilea habent in capitibus suis et molles mihi videntur vestes eorum, et in pedibus eorum sunt saraballae. Et ecce steterunt et intendunt in me, et ecce iterum coeperunt huc venientes ambulare.' Quibus verbis liquide ostenditur non tres tantum viros, sed turbam viatorum venisse ad Dominum, quamvis iuxta quosdam eiusdem turbae praecipui magistri certis nominibus Melchus, Caspar, Phadizarda nuncupentur.

(—) **4.** Von Bethlehem nach Nazareth. **Matth 2** 13–23

The Flight into Egypt, the Massacre of the Innocents, and the Return.

[13] Ἀναχωρησάντων δὲ αὐτῶν, ἰδοὺ ἄγγελος κυρίου φαίνεται κατ' ὄναρ τῷ Ιωσηφ λέγων· ἐγερθεὶς παράλαβε τὸ παιδίον καὶ τὴν μητέρα αὐτοῦ, καὶ φεῦγε εἰς Αἴγυπτον, καὶ ἴσθι ἐκεῖ ἕως ἂν εἴπω σοι· μέλλει γὰρ Ἡρῴδης ζητεῖν τὸ παιδίον τοῦ ἀπολέσαι αὐτό. [14] ὁ δὲ ἐγερθεὶς παρέλαβεν τὸ παιδίον καὶ τὴν μητέρα αὐτοῦ νυκτὸς καὶ ἀνεχώρησεν εἰς Αἴγυπτον, [15] καὶ ἦν ἐκεῖ ἕως τῆς τελευτῆς Ἡρῴδου· ἵνα πληρωθῇ τὸ ῥηθὲν ὑπὸ κυρίου διὰ τοῦ προφήτου λέγοντος· **ἐξ Αἰγύπτου ἐκάλεσα τὸν υἱόν μου.** (Hos11₁)

[16] Τότε Ἡρῴδης ἰδὼν ὅτι ἐνεπαίχθη ὑπὸ τῶν μάγων ἐθυμώθη λίαν, καὶ ἀποστείλας ἀνεῖλεν πάντας τοὺς παῖδας τοὺς ἐν Βηθλεεμ καὶ ἐν πᾶσι τοῖς ὁρίοις αὐτῆς ἀπὸ διετοῦς καὶ κατωτέρω, κατὰ τὸν χρόνον ὃν ἠκρίβωσεν παρὰ τῶν μάγων. [17] τότε ἐπληρώθη τὸ ῥηθὲν διὰ Ἰερεμίου τοῦ προφήτου λέγοντος· [18] **φωνὴ ἐν Ραμα ἠκούσθη, κλαυθμὸς καὶ ὀδυρμὸς** πολύς· **Ραχηλ κλαίουσα τὰ τέκνα αὐτῆς, καὶ οὐκ ἤθελεν παρακληθῆναι, ὅτι οὐκ εἰσίν.** (Jr31₁₅)

[19] Τελευτήσαντος δὲ τοῦ Ἡρῴδου, ἰδοὺ ἄγγελος κυρίου φαίνεται κατ' ὄναρ τῷ Ιωσηφ ἐν Αἰγύπτῳ [20] λέγων· ἐγερθεὶς παράλαβε τὸ παιδίον καὶ τὴν μητέρα αὐτοῦ, καὶ πορεύου εἰς γῆν Ισραηλ· τεθνήκασιν γὰρ οἱ ζητοῦντες τὴν ψυχὴν τοῦ παιδίου. [21] ὁ δὲ ἐγερθεὶς παρέλαβεν τὸ παιδίον καὶ τὴν μητέρα αὐτοῦ καὶ ἦλθεν εἰς γῆν Ισραηλ. [22] ἀκούσας δὲ ὅτι Ἀρχέλαος βασιλεύει τῆς Ἰουδαίας ἀντὶ Ἡρῴδου τοῦ πατρὸς αὐτοῦ ἐφοβήθη ἐκεῖ ἀπελθεῖν· χρηματισθεὶς δὲ κατ' ὄναρ ἀνεχώρησεν εἰς τὰ μέρη τῆς Γαλιλαίας, [23] καὶ ἐλθὼν κατῴκησεν εἰς πόλιν λεγομένην Ναζαρετ· ὅπως πληρωθῇ τὸ ῥηθὲν διὰ τῶν προφητῶν ὅτι **Ναζωραῖος** κληθήσεται. (Jdc13₅ (Is11₁?))

B. Die lukanische Vorgeschichte. *The Lucan Infancy Narrative.* **Luk 1. 2.**

(—) **5.** Der Prolog. *The Prologue.* **Luk 1** 1–4

[1] Ἐπειδήπερ πολλοὶ ἐπεχείρησαν ἀνατάξασθαι διήγησιν περὶ τῶν πεπληροφορημένων ἐν ἡμῖν πραγμάτων, [2] καθὼς παρέδοσαν ἡμῖν οἱ ἀπ' ἀρχῆς αὐτόπται καὶ [15 27: καὶ ὑμεῖς δὲ μαρτυρεῖτε, ὅτι ἀπ' ἀρχῆς μετ' ἐμοῦ ἐστε.] ὑπηρέται γενόμενοι τοῦ λόγου, [3] ἔδοξε κἀμοὶ παρηκολουθηκότι ἄνωθεν πᾶσιν ἀκριβῶς καθεξῆς σοι γράψαι, κράτιστε Θεόφιλε, [4] ἵνα ἐπιγνῷς περὶ ὧν κατηχήθης λόγων τὴν ἀσφάλειαν.

Mt 2,13 ∼ κ. ον. φαι.‖1 20: (B)C-33-892 700 σ27-71 K Π 157 (372) *al* | φαι.] εφανη‖←: B 372 {*L*, Au} — ωφθη‖Lk1 11: Ep {} **14** εγ.] διεγ.‖1 24: 33 D **17** δια] υπο (+ κυριου δια)‖22 31 (1 22 2 15): *Rpl* (D) φ*l*547 (*Lz*) *S*h^{m} — *txt*: ℌ⟨L⟩C σ71 W 157 *pc* *L*vl'[e] vg *S*ph^{t} **19** ∼ κ. ον. φαι.‖1 20: *Rpl* *L*vg^{2} *S*h — *txt* (φαι.] εφανη): ℵBZ Σ λ-1582 φ-174 D 157 1574 *l*54 *L*(vl[e])37.38 (vg') Au **21** εγ.] διεγ.‖1 24: 33 D | ● εισηλθ.‖Ex12 25 Lv14 34 19 23: ℵBC 157 *pc* Eu(επανηλθ.) *Cs* — *txt*: *Rpl* *L*, Au *S*,j **22** ● ∼ τ. πα. αυ. Η. *cf.* Mk1 20 11 10: ℵBC* W *Aeth* — *txt*: *Rpl* Eu *L*, Au *S*,j *C* **23** δια] υπο‖22 31 1 22 2 15: ℵ^{b} 472 | του προφητου‖5.17 33: σ349 *L*abcfff^{1}l(Ησαιου τ. πρ.) vg^{2} *Cs*$^{4:8}$ b^{1} *Δ*a i^{T} l^{AD} md⟨Z⟩ n^{HgHrS} p

---

Mt2 13 *cf.* Ev. apocr.(?) PCai 10735r°: ἄγγελος κ(υρίο)υ ἐλάλησεν· Ἰω[σηφ, ἐγερθεὶς] παράλαβε Μαρίαν τὴν γ[υναῖκά σου καὶ] φεῦγε εἰς Αἴγυπτον κοι[...]...[...] πᾶν δῶρον καὶ ἐὰν [...] φίλους αὐτοῦ καθ[...] βασιλέως λ[...]ειο[... (*cf. ad 7.* Lk1 36)

Mt2 15.23 *cf.* EN frgm.1 (Hi ill. 3): Porro ipsum Hebraicum (*sc.* evangelium) habetur usque hodie in Caesariensi bibliotheca ... Mihi quoque a Nazaraeis ... describendi facultas fuit. In quo animadvertendum, quod ubicumque evangelista ... veteris scripturae testimoniis abutitur, non sequatur septuaginta translatorum auctoritatem, sed Hebraicam. e quibus illa duo sunt: ex Aegypto vocavi filium meum, et: quoniam Nazaraeus vocabitur.

Mt2 16 *cf.* EIc22 1-2: (*cf. ad 3.*) ... Τότε Ἡρώδης ἰδὼν ὅτι ἐνεπαίχθη ὑπὸ τῶν μάγων ὀργισθεὶς ἔπεμψεν αὐτοῦ τοὺς φονευτὰς λέγων αὐτοῖς ἀνελεῖν πάντα τὰ βρέφη ἀπὸ διετίας καὶ κάτω. [2] καὶ ἀκούσασα ἡ Μαρία ὅτι τὰ βρέφη ἀναιρεῖται, φοβηθεῖσα ἔλαβεν τὸν παῖδα καὶ ἐσπαργάνωσεν αὐτὸν καὶ ἔβαλεν ἐν φάτνῃ βοῶν (*cf.* Lk2 7).

(—) ***6.*** **Verheißung der Geburt des Täufers.** ***The Promise of the Baptist's Bi*****ı** ***h.*** **Luk 1** 5-25

5 Ἐγένετο ἐν ταῖς ἡμέραις Ἡρῴδου βασιλέως τῆς Ἰουδαίας ἱερεύς τις ὀνόματι Ζαχαρίας ἐξ ἐφημερίας Αβια, καὶ γυνὴ αὐτῷ ἐκ τῶν θυγατέρων Ααρων, καὶ τὸ ὄνομα αὐτῆς Ελισαβετ. 6 ἦσαν δὲ δίκαιοι ἀμφότεροι ἐναντίον τοῦ θεοῦ, πορευόμενοι ἐν πάσαις ταῖς ἐντολαῖς καὶ δικαιώμασιν τοῦ κυρίου ἄμεμπτοι. 7 καὶ οὐκ ἦν αὐτοῖς τέκνον, καθότι ἦν ἡ Ελισαβετ στεῖρα, καὶ ἀμφότεροι προβεβηκότες ἐν ταῖς ἡμέραις αὐτῶν ἦσαν.

8 Ἐγένετο δὲ ἐν τῷ ἱερατεύειν αὐτὸν ἐν τῇ τάξει τῆς ἐφημερίας αὐτοῦ ἔναντι τοῦ θεοῦ, 9 κατὰ τὸ ἔθος τῆς ἱερατείας ἔλαχε τοῦ θυμιᾶσαι εἰσελθὼν εἰς τὸν ναὸν τοῦ κυρίου, 10 καὶ πᾶν τὸ πλῆθος ἦν τοῦ λαοῦ προσευχόμενον ἔξω τῇ ὥρᾳ τοῦ θυμιάματος. 11 ὤφθη δὲ αὐτῷ ἄγγελος κυρίου ἑστὼς ἐκ δεξιῶν τοῦ θυσιαστηρίου τοῦ θυμιάματος. 12 καὶ ἐταράχθη Ζαχαρίας ἰδών, καὶ φόβος ἐπέπεσεν ἐπ' αὐτόν. 13 εἶπεν δὲ πρὸς αὐτὸν ὁ ἄγγελος· **μὴ φοβοῦ,** Ζαχαρία, **διότι εἰσηκούσθη** ἡ δέησίς **σου,** καὶ **ἡ γυνή σου** Ελισαβετ **γεννήσει υἱόν σοι, καὶ καλέσεις τὸ ὄνομα αὐτοῦ** Ἰωάννην· 14 καὶ ἔσται χαρά σοι καὶ ἀγαλλίασις, καὶ πολλοὶ ἐπὶ τῇ γενέσει αὐτοῦ χαρήσονται. 15 ἔσται γὰρ μέγας ἐνώπιον τοῦ κυρίου, καὶ **οἶνον καὶ σικερα οὐ μὴ πίῃ,** καὶ πνεύματος ἁγίου πλησθήσεται ἔτι ἐκ κοιλίας μητρὸς αὐτοῦ, 16 καὶ πολλοὺς τῶν υἱῶν Ισραηλ ἐπιστρέψει ἐπὶ κύριον τὸν θεὸν αὐτῶν· 17 καὶ αὐτὸς προελεύσεται ἐνώπιον αὐτοῦ ἐν πνεύματι καὶ δυνάμει **Ἠλίου, ἐπιστρέψαι καρδίας πατέρων ἐπὶ τέκνα** καὶ ἀπειθεῖς ἐν φρονήσει δικαίων, ἑτοιμάσαι κυρίῳ λαὸν κατεσκευασμένον. 18 καὶ εἶπεν Ζαχαρίας πρὸς τὸν ἄγγελον· **κατὰ τί γνώσομαι** τοῦτο; ἐγὼ γάρ εἰμι πρεσβύτης καὶ ἡ γυνή μου προβεβηκυῖα ἐν ταῖς ἡμέραις αὐτῆς. 19 καὶ ἀποκριθεὶς ὁ ἄγγελος εἶπεν αὐτῷ· ἐγώ εἰμι Γαβριηλ ὁ παρεστηκὼς ἐνώπιον τοῦ θεοῦ, καὶ ἀπεστάλην λαλῆσαι πρός σε καὶ εὐαγγελίσασθαί σοι ταῦτα· 20 καὶ ἰδοὺ ἔσῃ σιωπῶν καὶ μὴ δυνάμενος λαλῆσαι ἄχρι ἧς ἡμέρας γένηται ταῦτα, ἀνθ' ὧν οὐκ ἐπίστευσας τοῖς λόγοις μου, οἵτινες πληρωθήσονται εἰς τὸν καιρὸν αὐτῶν. 21 καὶ ἦν ὁ λαὸς προσδοκῶν τὸν Ζαχαρίαν, καὶ ἐθαύμαζον ἐν τῷ χρονίζειν ἐν τῷ ναῷ αὐτόν. 22 ἐξελθὼν δὲ οὐκ ἐδύνατο λαλῆσαι αὐτοῖς, καὶ ἐπέγνωσαν ὅτι ὀπτασίαν ἑόρακεν ἐν τῷ ναῷ· καὶ αὐτὸς ἦν διανεύων αὐτοῖς, καὶ διέμενεν κωφός.

23 καὶ ἐγένετο ὡς ἐπλήσθησαν αἱ ἡμέραι τῆς λειτουργίας αὐτοῦ, ἀπῆλθεν εἰς τὸν οἶκον αὐτοῦ. 24 μετὰ δὲ ταύτας τὰς ἡμέρας συνέλαβεν Ελισαβετ ἡ γυνὴ αὐτοῦ, καὶ περιέκρυβεν ἑαυτὴν μῆνας πέντε, λέγουσα 25 ὅτι οὕτως μοι πεποίηκεν ὁ κύριος ἐν ἡμέραις αἷς ἐπεῖδεν ἀφελεῖν ὄνειδός μου ἐν ἀνθρώποις.

Dn10₁₂
Gn17₁₉
1Sm1₁₁ LXX
Jdc13₄ Nu6₃
Ml3₂₂f. Sir48₁₀
Gn15₈

Lk 1,5 Ηρ. + του‖Mt2₁: *Rpl* Ep Eu — *txt*: ℵBLWΞ 544 R Ψ **9** κυ.] θεου‖Mt26₆₁ K3₁₆.₁₇: C*-579 1071-1604 **σ**-179-827-1194 D' Ψ **0211** *pc l*883 *l*1642 Chr *S*(*om*: s[c])j *Δ*ad i^{T} md^{NUWZ} n$^{⟨L⟩}$ p **13** *om* σοι‖Mt 1₂₁: 579 λ1 D' 273 Antp *L*Or *Δ*i^{V} me **15** του κυ.] ● κυ.‖1₇₆: ℌ⟨BW-892⟩C 544 **λ**-1278-1582 σ7-659-945-990-1194 A Γ^{v} Ω *al l*47 Cr Or — τ. θεου‖1₉ 12₆ 16₁₅: 700-1071-1604 **φ** **σ**⟨954⟩ F^{W} Θ Ψ 157 *pc* *Δ*i md$^{⟨M⟩}$ n p **17** προελ.] προπορευσ.‖1₇₆: σ945 F^{v}(πορ.) *al l*33 *l*44 | αυτου] κυριου‖←: Δ **21** ● ∼ αυτ. εν τ. ναω: *Rpl* — *om* εν τω ναω: 544 σ1207 *pc* *Δ*i^{V} me — *txt*: BLWΞ-579 Ψ 565 **25** ● *om* ο‖1₅₈: ℵC LW-33 D *pc*

Lk1₈-₁₁ *cf.* EIc8₃: Καὶ εἰσῆλθεν ὁ ἱερεὺς λαβὼν τὸν ιβ´ κώδωνα εἰς τὰ ἅγια τῶν ἁγίων καὶ ηὔξατο περὶ αὐτῆς (*sc.* τῆς Μαρίας). καὶ ἰδοὺ ἄγγελος κυρίου ἔστη λέγων· 'Ζαχαρία Ζαχαρία, ἔξελθε καὶ ἐκκλησίασον τοὺς χηρεύοντας τοῦ λαοῦ, καὶ ἐνεγκάτωσαν ἀνὰ ῥάβδον, καὶ ᾧ ἐὰν ἐπιδείξῃ κύριος ὁ θεὸς σημεῖον, τούτῳ ἔσται γυνή.'

Lk1₂₀ *cf.* EIc10₂: ... τῷ δὲ καιρῷ ἐκείνῳ Ζαχαρίας ἐσίγησεν, καὶ ἐγένετο ἀντὶ αὐτοῦ Σαμουηλ, μέχρι ὅτε ἐλάλησεν Ζαχαρίας...

Lk1₂₁ *cf.* EIc23₁-₃ 24₁f.: Ὁ δὲ Ἡρώδης ἐζήτει τὸν Ἰωάννην, καὶ ἀπέστειλεν ὑπηρέτας ἐν τῷ θυσιαστηρίῳ πρὸς Ζαχαρίαν λέγων αὐτῷ· 'ποῦ ἀπέκρυψας τὸν υἱόν σου; ... [2]... οἶδας ὅτι τὸ αἷμά σου ὑπὸ τὴν χεῖράν μού ἐστιν;' ... [3]καὶ ἀποκριθεὶς εἶπεν· 'μάρτυς εἰμὶ τοῦ θεοῦ. ἔχε μου τὸ αἷμα. τὸ δὲ πνεῦμά μου ὁ δεσπότης δέξεται, ὅτι ἀθῷον αἷμα ἐκχύνεις εἰς τὰ πρόθυρα τοῦ ναοῦ κυρίου.' Καὶ περὶ τὸ διάφαυμα ἐφονεύθη Ζαχαρίας, καὶ οὐκ ᾔδεισαν οἱ υἱοὶ Ισραηλ πῶς ἐφονεύθη. (24)[1] ἀλλὰ τὴν ὥραν τοῦ ἀσπασμοῦ ἀπῆλθασιν οἱ ἱερεῖς, καὶ οὐκ ἀπήντησεν αὐτοῖς κατὰ τὸ ἔθος ἡ εὐλογία τοῦ Ζαχαρίου. καὶ ἔστησαν οἱ ἱερεῖς προσδοκῶντες τὸν Ζαχαρίαν τοῦ ἀσπάσασθαι αὐτὸν ἐν εὐχῇ καὶ δοξάσαι τὸν ὕψιστον θεόν. [2]χρονίσαντος δὲ αὐτοῦ ἐφοβήθησαν πάντες. τολμήσας δέ τις ἐξ αὐτῶν εἰσῆλθεν εἰς τὸ ἁγίασμα καὶ εἶδεν παρὰ τὸ θυσιαστήριον κυρίου αἷμα πεπηγὸς καὶ φωνὴν λέγουσαν· 'Ζαχαρίας ἐφόνευται καὶ οὐκ ἐξαλειφθήσεται τὸ αἷμα αὐτοῦ ἕως ἔλθῃ ὁ ἔκδικος.' καὶ ἀκούσας τῶν λόγων τούτων ἐφοβήθη καὶ ἐξῆλθεν καὶ ἀνήγγειλεν τοῖς ἱερεῦσιν ἃ εἶδεν καὶ ἤκουσεν. [3]καὶ τολμήσαντες ... (*cf. ad 224.* Mt23₃₅p)

(—) **7.** Verheißung der Geburt Jesu. *The Annunciation.* **Luk 1** 26–38

[26] Ἐν δὲ τῷ μηνὶ τῷ ἕκτῳ ἀπεστάλη ὁ ἄγγελος Γαβριηλ ἀπὸ τοῦ θεοῦ εἰς πόλιν τῆς Γαλιλαίας ᾗ ὄνομα Ναζαρετ, [27] πρὸς παρθένον ἐμνηστευμένην ἀνδρὶ ᾧ ὄνομα Ιωσηφ, ἐξ οἴκου Δαυιδ, καὶ τὸ ὄνομα τῆς παρθένου Μαριαμ. [28] καὶ εἰσελθὼν πρὸς αὐτὴν εἶπεν· χαῖρε, κεχαριτωμένη, ὁ κύριος μετὰ σοῦ. [29] ἡ δὲ ἐπὶ τῷ λόγῳ διεταράχθη, καὶ διελογίζετο ποταπὸς εἴη ὁ ἀσπασμὸς οὗτος. [30] καὶ εἶπεν ὁ ἄγγελος αὐτῇ· μὴ φοβοῦ, Μαριαμ· εὗρες γὰρ χάριν παρὰ τῷ θεῷ. [31] καὶ **ἰδοὺ συλλήμψῃ ἐν γαστρὶ καὶ τέξῃ υἱόν, καὶ καλέσεις τὸ ὄνομα αὐτοῦ** Ἰησοῦν. [32] οὗτος ἔσται μέγας καὶ υἱὸς ὑψίστου κληθήσεται, καὶ δώσει αὐτῷ κύριος ὁ θεὸς **τὸν θρόνον Δαυιδ** τοῦ πατρὸς αὐτοῦ, [33] **καὶ βασιλεύσει** ἐπὶ τὸν οἶκον Ιακωβ **εἰς τοὺς αἰῶνας**, καὶ τῆς βασιλείας αὐτοῦ **οὐκ ἔσται τέλος.** [34] εἶπεν δὲ Μαριαμ πρὸς τὸν ἄγγελον· πῶς ἔσται τοῦτο, ἐπεὶ ἄνδρα οὐ γινώσκω; [35] καὶ ἀποκριθεὶς ὁ ἄγγελος εἶπεν αὐτῇ· πνεῦμα ἅγιον ἐπελεύσεται ἐπὶ σέ, καὶ δύναμις ὑψίστου ἐπισκιάσει σοι· διὸ καὶ τὸ γεννώμενον ἅγιον κληθήσεται υἱὸς θεοῦ. [36] καὶ ἰδοὺ Ελισαβετ ἡ συγγενίς σου καὶ αὐτὴ συνειληφυῖα υἱὸν ἐν γήρει αὐτῆς, καὶ οὗτος μὴν ἕκτος ἐστὶν αὐτῇ τῇ καλουμένῃ στείρᾳ· [37] ὅτι **οὐκ ἀδυνατήσει παρὰ τοῦ θεοῦ πᾶν ῥῆμα.** [38] εἶπεν δὲ Μαριαμ· ἰδοὺ ἡ δούλη κυρίου· γένοιτό μοι κατὰ τὸ ῥῆμά σου. καὶ ἀπῆλθεν ἀπ' αὐτῆς ὁ ἄγγελος.

Is714 (v. 31) — Is96 Mch47 (v. 32–33) — Gn1814 (v. 37)

(—) **8.** Besuch der Maria bei Elisabeth. *The Visitation.* **Luk 1** 39–56

[39] Ἀναστᾶσα δὲ Μαριαμ ἐν ταῖς ἡμέραις ταύταις ἐπορεύθη εἰς τὴν ὀρεινὴν μετὰ σπουδῆς εἰς πόλιν Ἰούδα, [40] καὶ εἰσῆλθεν εἰς τὸν οἶκον Ζαχαρίου καὶ ἠσπάσατο τὴν Ελισαβετ. [41] καὶ ἐγένετο ὡς ἤκουσεν τὸν ἀσπασμὸν τῆς Μαρίας ἡ Ελισαβετ, ἐσκίρτησεν τὸ βρέφος ἐν τῇ κοιλίᾳ αὐτῆς, καὶ ἐπλήσθη πνεύματος ἁγίου ἡ Ελισαβετ, [42] καὶ ἀνεφώνησεν φωνῇ μεγάλῃ καὶ

Lk 1,27 οικ. + και πατριας‖24: ℵCL 28-700-1071-1604 **λ**⟨209⟩-22-1582 σ71-517-692-1194-1675 F^{W} U *al* Chr Chrn Eu Gr^{Th} Δi^{V}(*om* οικ. και) **28** ● σου + ευλογημενη συ εν γυναιξιν(+ και ευλογημενος ο καρπος της κοιλιας σου)‖42: *Rpl* (1071 *pc*) EIc↓ Eu *L*'(30) Te *S*[sc] Af Cb^{3} *Δ* — *txt*: 𝔥⟨33-892⟩ 700 λ1-131-1582 Ψ (*om* [15]αγιου—[38]σου: Ω; ∩?) **0130**^{v} *pc l*44 Chrn Da Pt^{A} *Sj C*' *Arm* **29** δε + ιδουσα‖12: *Rpl L*' Am Au^{2} *S*[sc] Cb^{5} *Δ*a ad 1^{FG} — + ακουσασα: σ1194 EIc↓ Lvg^{11} Au^{2} *Δ*i 1^{AD} md me n⟨L⟩ — *txt*: 𝔥⟨33-892⟩X 1604 λ1-131-1582 D Ψ *pc* And Chrn Da *Sj C*' *Arm Δ*p | διετα.] ετα.‖12: D *pc* Or | διελογ. + εν εαυτη λεγουσα(*om*)‖1217 Mt167f.: X-33-892-1241 (28-1604 D) F^{W} Ψ EIc↓ *pc* (*pc*) And *S*[sc]$p^{1}h^{m}$ (*C*sb^{1} *Arm* Δn^{L} p) **36** ● συνειληφεν: ℵBLWΞ-892 157 *pc L S*[sc]j *Cs* **39** ταυ.] εκειναις‖21: 28 σ1424 H^{*v} *L*Or *S*s[c]pj *Cb* Δi^{T} 1p **42** ανεφ. φω.] ανεβοησεν φω.‖Mt2746 Mk1534: ℵC-33-892 28-544-1071 λ2193 **φ**-*l*547 σ71-115-517-1207-1424-1606 Θ 157 *p* — ● ανεφ. κραυγη *cf.* Ap1418: 𝔥'Ξ 565 Or — *txt*: *Rpl* Chrn Cr

---

Lk128-38 *cf.* EIc111-3: καὶ ἔλαβεν τὴν κάλπιν καὶ ἐξῆλθεν γεμίσαι ὕδωρ. καὶ ἰδοὺ φωνὴ λέγουσα αὐτῇ· ‘χαῖρε κεχαριτωμένη· ὁ κύριος μετὰ σοῦ· εὐλογημένη σὺ ἐν γυναιξίν.’ καὶ περιέβλεπεν τὰ δεξιὰ καὶ τὰ ἀριστερὰ Μαρία πόθεν αὕτη εἴη ἡ φωνή. καὶ ἔντρομος γενομένη εἰσήει εἰς τὸν οἶκον αὐτῆς καὶ ἀναπαύσασα τὴν κάλπιν ἔλαβεν τὴν πορφύραν καὶ ἐκάθισεν ἐπὶ τοῦ θρόνου καὶ ἧλκεν τὴν πορφύραν. [2] Καὶ ἰδοὺ ἔστη ἄγγελος ἐνώπιον αὐτῆς λέγων· ‘μὴ φοβοῦ, Μαρία· εὗρες γὰρ χάριν ἐνώπιον τοῦ πάντων δεσπότου. συλλήμψῃ ἐκ λόγου αὐτοῦ.’ ἡ δὲ ἀκούσασα Μαρία διεκρίθη ἐν ἑαυτῇ λέγουσα· ‘ἐγὼ συλλήμψομαι ἀπὸ κυρίου θεοῦ ζῶντος ὡς πᾶσα γυνὴ γεννᾷ;’ [3] καὶ ἰδοὺ ἄγγελος ἔστη λέγων αὐτῇ· ‘οὐχ οὕτως, Μαρία. δύναμις γὰρ θεοῦ ἐπισκιάσει σοι· διὸ καὶ τὸ γεννώμενον ἅγιον κληθήσεται υἱὸς ὑψίστου. καὶ καλέσεις τὸ ὄνομα αὐτοῦ Ἰησοῦν· αὐτὸς γὰρ σώσει τὸν λαὸν αὐτοῦ ἐκ τῶν ἁμαρτιῶν αὐτῶν.’ καὶ εἶπεν Μαρία· ‘ἰδοὺ ἡ δούλη κυρίου κατενώπιον αὐτοῦ. γένοιτό μοι κατὰ τὸ ῥῆμά σου.’

Lk136 *cf.* Ev. apocr.(?) PCai 10735v°: ...] ἑρμηνευέτω σοι.’ ὁ [δὲ ἀρχιστράτηγός] φησι τῇ παρθένῳ· ‘ἰδοὺ [Ελισαβετ ἡ συγ]γενής σου καὶ αὐτὴ συν[είληφε καὶ ἕκτο]ς ἐστὶ μὴν αὐτῇ τῇ κα[λουμένῃ στείρᾳ.’ ἐν] τῷ ἕκτῳ, ὅ ἐστιν [Θωθ, μηνὶ ἡ] μ(ήτ)ηρ ἄρα Ἰω]άννην συνέλαβε. [ἔδει δὲ προκηρύσ]σειν τὸν ἀρχιστρά[τηγον Ἰωάννην τὸ]ν οἰκέτην προβαδί[ζοντα τῆς τοῦ] κ(υρίο)υ αὐτοῦ] παρουσίας [... (*cf. ad 4.* Mt213)

8. cf. EIc122f.: Χαρὰν δὲ λαβοῦσα Μαρία ἀπῄει πρὸς τὴν συγγενίδα αὐτῆς Ελισαβετ καὶ ἔκρουσεν πρὸς τὴν θύραν. καὶ ἀκούσασα ἡ Ελισαβετ ἔρριψεν τὸ κόκκινον καὶ ἔδραμεν πρὸς τὴν θύραν καὶ ἤνοιξεν αὐτῇ καὶ εὐλόγησεν αὐτὴν καὶ εἶπεν· ‘πόθεν μοι τοῦτο ἵνα ἡ μήτηρ τοῦ κυρίου μου ἔλθῃ πρὸς ἐμέ; ἰδοὺ γὰρ τὸ ἐν ἐμοὶ ἐσκίρτησεν καὶ εὐλόγησέν σε.’ ἡ δὲ Μαρία ἐπελάθετο τῶν μυστηρίων ὧν ἐλάλησεν Γαβριηλ ὁ ἄγγελος· καὶ ἠτένισεν εἰς τὸν οὐρανὸν καὶ εἶπεν· ‘τίς εἰμι ἐγὼ ὅτι ἰδοὺ πᾶσαι αἱ γυναῖκες τῆς γῆς μακαριοῦσίν με;’ [3] καὶ ἐποίησεν τρεῖς μῆνας πρὸς τὴν Ελισαβετ. καὶ ἡμέρᾳ ἀφ' ἡμέρας ἡ γαστὴρ αὐτῆς ὤγκουτο. καὶ φοβηθεῖσα ἡ Μαρία ἦλθεν ἐν τῷ οἴκῳ αὐτῆς καὶ ἔκρυβεν αὐτὴν ἀπὸ τῶν υἱῶν Ισραηλ ...

ε

ἶπεν· εὐλογημένη σὺ ἐν γυναιξίν, καὶ εὐλογημένος ὁ καρπὸς τῆς κοιλίας σου. 43 καὶ πόθεν μοι τοῦτο ἵνα ἔλθῃ ἡ μήτηρ τοῦ κυρίου μου πρός με; 44 ἰδοὺ γὰρ ὡς ἐγένετο ἡ φωνὴ τοῦ ἀσπασμοῦ σου εἰς τὰ ὦτά μου, ἐσκίρτησεν ἐν ἀγαλλιάσει τὸ βρέφος ἐν τῇ κοιλίᾳ μου. 45 καὶ μακαρία ἡ πιστεύσασα ὅτι ἔσται τελείωσις τοῖς λελαλημένοις αὐτῇ παρὰ κυρίου.

> 3 29: ... ὁ δὲ φίλος τοῦ νυμφίου, ὁ ἑστηκὼς καὶ ἀκούων αὐτοῦ, χαρᾷ χαίρει διὰ τὴν φωνὴν τοῦ νυμφίου. αὕτη οὖν ἡ χαρὰ ἡ ἐμὴ πεπλήρωται.

46 Καὶ εἶπεν Μαριαμ·

Μεγαλύνει **ἡ ψυχή μου τὸν κύριον,** — **46-55:** 1Sm2 1-10
47 καὶ **ἠγαλλίασεν** τὸ πνεῦμά μου **ἐπὶ τῷ θεῷ τῷ σωτῆρί μου·** — Hab3 18
48 ὅτι **ἐπέβλεψεν ἐπὶ τὴν ταπείνωσιν τῆς δούλης αὐτοῦ.** — 1Sm1 11
ἰδοὺ γὰρ ἀπὸ τοῦ νῦν **μακαριοῦσίν με** πᾶσαι αἱ γενεαί· — Gn30 13
49 ὅτι ἐποίησέν μοι μεγαλεῖα ὁ δυνατός.
καὶ **ἅγιον τὸ ὄνομα αὐτοῦ,** — Ps111 9
50 καὶ **τὸ ἔλεος αὐτοῦ εἰς γενεὰς καὶ γενεὰς** — Ps103 17
τοῖς φοβουμένοις αὐτόν.
51 Ἐποίησεν κράτος **ἐν βραχίονι** αὐτοῦ, — Ps89 11
διεσκόρπισεν ὑπερηφάνους διανοίᾳ καρδίας αὐτῶν·
52 **καθεῖλεν δυνάστας** ἀπὸ **θρόνων** καὶ **ὕψωσεν ταπεινούς,** — Sir10 14 Job12 19 Ez21 31
53 **πεινῶντας ἐνέπλησεν ἀγαθῶν** καὶ πλουτοῦντας ἐξαπέστειλεν κενούς. — Ps107 9
54 **ἀντελάβετο Ισραηλ παιδὸς αὐτοῦ,** — Is41 8f. Ps98 3
μνησθῆναι ἐλέους,
55 **καθὼς ἐλάλησεν πρὸς τοὺς πατέρας ἡμῶν,** — Mch7 20 2Sm22 51
τῷ Αβρααμ καὶ τῷ σπέρματι αὐτοῦ ἕως αἰῶνος.

56 Ἔμεινεν δὲ Μαριαμ σὺν αὐτῇ ὡς μῆνας τρεῖς, καὶ ὑπέστρεψεν εἰς τὸν οἶκον αὐτῆς.

(—) *9.* Die Geburt des Täufers. *The Birth of the Baptist.* **Luk 1** 57–80

57 Τῇ δὲ Ελισαβετ ἐπλήσθη ὁ χρόνος τοῦ τεκεῖν αὐτήν, καὶ ἐγέννησεν υἱόν. 58 καὶ ἤκουσαν οἱ περίοικοι καὶ οἱ συγγενεῖς αὐτῆς ὅτι ἐμεγάλυνεν κύριος τὸ ἔλεος αὐτοῦ μετ' αὐτῆς, καὶ συνέχαιρον αὐτῇ. 59 καὶ ἐγένετο ἐν τῇ ἡμέρᾳ τῇ ὀγδόῃ ἦλθον περιτεμεῖν τὸ παιδίον, καὶ ἐκάλουν αὐτὸ ἐπὶ τῷ ὀνόματι τοῦ πατρὸς αὐτοῦ Ζαχαρίαν. 60 καὶ ἀποκριθεῖσα ἡ μήτηρ αὐτοῦ εἶπεν· οὐχί, ἀλλὰ κληθήσεται Ἰωάννης. 61 καὶ εἶπον πρὸς αὐτὴν ὅτι οὐδείς ἐστιν ἐκ τῆς συγγενείας σου ὃς καλεῖται τῷ ὀνόματι τούτῳ. 62 ἐνένευον δὲ τῷ πατρὶ αὐτοῦ τὸ τί ἂν θέλοι καλεῖσθαι αὐτό. 63 καὶ αἰτήσας πινακίδιον ἔγραψεν λέγων· Ἰωάννης ἐστὶν τὸ ὄνομα αὐτοῦ. καὶ ἐθαύμασαν πάντες. 64 ἀνεῴχθη δὲ τὸ στόμα αὐτοῦ παραχρῆμα καὶ ἡ γλῶσσα αὐτοῦ, καὶ ἐλάλει εὐλογῶν τὸν θεόν. 65 καὶ ἐγένετο ἐπὶ πάντας φόβος τοὺς περιοικοῦντας αὐτούς, καὶ ἐν ὅλῃ τῇ ὀρεινῇ τῆς Ἰουδαίας διελαλεῖτο πάντα τὰ ῥήματα ταῦτα, 66 καὶ ἔθεντο πάντες οἱ ἀκούσαντες ἐν τῇ καρδίᾳ αὐτῶν, λέγοντες· τί ἄρα τὸ παιδίον τοῦτο ἔσται; καὶ γὰρ χεὶρ κυρίου ἦν μετ' αὐτοῦ.

67 Καὶ Ζαχαρίας ὁ πατὴρ αὐτοῦ ἐπλήσθη πνεύματος ἁγίου καὶ ἐπροφήτευσεν λέγων·

68 **Εὐλογητὸς κύριος ὁ θεὸς τοῦ Ισραηλ,** — Ps41 14 *etc.*
ὅτι ἐπεσκέψατο καὶ ἐποίησεν **λύτρωσιν τῷ λαῷ αὐτοῦ,** — Ps111 9
69 καὶ **ἤγειρεν κέρας σωτηρίας** ἡμῖν — Ps18 3 132 17 1Sm2 10

Lk 1,43 με] ● εμε: ℵ*B Θ EIc↓ — **49** ● μεγαλα: ℵ*BLW D* GrTh {*L*' Or} — *txt*: *Rpl* Chrn *Le* {*S*,j} — **55** εως αι.] ● εις τον αιωνα‖Mt21 19 Mk3 24 11 14 Jo3 14: 𝔓^{42} *Rpl* (*om* τον: 579) Chrn *L*' — *om*: σ1223 — *txt*: C-1241 544-700-1071 **λ**-1582-2193 **φ**⟨124⟩-*l*547 σM-517-990-1194-1606 A^{Od} F S Ψ *pm* *l*932 (*l*1345) *l*1346 *l*1347 *l*1348 *l*1349 *l*1350 GrTh *L*r^{1}z30 vg^{8} — **60** κλη. + το ονομα αυτου‖1 13.31 Mt1 23.25: C* D 213 *S*j *C*b^{5}(καλειτε) — **63** το ον. αυ.] ● ον. αυτου (-ω)‖Jo1 6: 𝔓^{4v} B*Ξ(L-579) 700 Or^{1}(') — **64** η γλ.] ελυθη ο δεσμος της γλωσσης‖Mk7 35: 1071 λ1-2193 (D Or *L*abcff^{2}r^{1}z *S*s[c]) — **66** ταις καρδιαις‖21 14: ℌ⟨ℵB-33⟩ D Θ *pc* *Le* *S*j^{c} *Arm* *Δ*a ad

ἐν οἴκῳ **Δαυιδ** τοῦ παιδὸς αὐτοῦ,

70 καθὼς ἐλάλησεν διὰ στόματος τῶν ἁγίων ἀπ᾽ αἰῶνος προφητῶν αὐτοῦ,

Ps106 10 18 18 — 71 σωτηρίαν **ἐξ ἐχθρῶν** ἡμῶν **καὶ ἐκ χειρὸς** πάντων **τῶν μισούντων** ἡμᾶς,

Mch7 20 — 72 ποιῆσαι **ἔλεος μετὰ τῶν πατέρων ἡμῶν**

Ps105 8 106 45 — καὶ **μνησθῆναι διαθήκης** ἁγίας **αὐτοῦ,**

Jr11 5 Gn22 16 — 73 **ὅρκον ὃν ὤμοσεν πρὸς Αβρααμ** τὸν πατέρα ἡμῶν,

τοῦ δοῦναι ἡμῖν 74 ἀφόβως ἐκ χειρὸς ἐχθρῶν ῥυσθέντας

λατρεύειν αὐτῷ 75 ἐν ὁσιότητι καὶ δικαιοσύνῃ

ἐνώπιον αὐτοῦ πάσαις ταῖς ἡμέραις ἡμῶν.

76 Καὶ σὺ δέ, παιδίον, προφήτης ὑψίστου κληθήσῃ·

Ml3 1 Is40 3 — προπορεύσῃ γὰρ **πρὸ προσώπου κυρίου ἑτοιμάσαι ὁδοὺς** αὐτοῦ,

77 τοῦ δοῦναι γνῶσιν σωτηρίας τῷ λαῷ αὐτοῦ

ἐν ἀφέσει ἁμαρτιῶν αὐτῶν,

78 διὰ σπλάγχνα ἐλέους θεοῦ ἡμῶν,

ἐν οἷς ἐπεσκέψατο ἡμᾶς ἀνατολὴ ἐξ ὕψους,

Is9 1 Ps107 10 — 79 **ἐπιφᾶναι τοῖς ἐν σκότει καὶ σκιᾷ θανάτου καθημένοις,**

Is59 8 — τοῦ κατευθῦναι τοὺς πόδας ἡμῶν εἰς **ὁδὸν εἰρήνης.**

80 Τὸ δὲ παιδίον ηὔξανεν καὶ ἐκραταιοῦτο πνεύματι, καὶ ἦν ἐν ταῖς ἐρήμοις ἕως ἡμέρας ἀναδείξεως αὐτοῦ πρὸς τὸν Ισραηλ.

(—) **10.** Die Geburt Jesu. *The Birth of Jesus.* **Luk 2** 1-20

1 Ἐγένετο δὲ ἐν ταῖς ἡμέραις ἐκείναις ἐξῆλθεν δόγμα παρὰ Καίσαρος Αὐγούστου ἀπογράφεσθαι πᾶσαν τὴν οἰκουμένην. 2 αὕτη ἀπογραφὴ πρώτη ἐγένετο ἡγεμονεύοντος τῆς Συρίας Κυρηνίου. 3 καὶ ἐπορεύοντο πάντες ἀπογράφεσθαι, ἕκαστος εἰς τὴν ἑαυτοῦ πόλιν. 4 ἀνέβη δὲ καὶ Ιωσηφ ἀπὸ τῆς Γαλιλαίας ἐκ πόλεως Ναζαρετ εἰς τὴν Ἰουδαίαν εἰς πόλιν Δαυιδ ἥτις καλεῖται Βηθλεεμ, διὰ τὸ εἶναι αὐτὸν ἐξ οἴκου καὶ πατριᾶς Δαυιδ, 5 ἀπογράψασθαι σὺν Μαριαμ τῇ ἐμνηστευμένῃ αὐτῷ γυναικί, οὔσῃ ἐγκύῳ. 6 ἐγένετο δὲ ἐν τῷ εἶναι αὐτοὺς ἐκεῖ ἐπλήσθησαν αἱ ἡμέραι τοῦ τεκεῖν αὐτήν, 7 καὶ ἔτεκεν τὸν υἱὸν αὐτῆς τὸν πρωτότοκον, καὶ ἐσπαργάνωσεν αὐτὸν καὶ ἀνέκλινεν αὐτὸν ἐν φάτνῃ, διότι οὐκ ἦν αὐτοῖς τόπος ἐν τῷ καταλύματι· 8 Καὶ ποιμένες ἦσαν ἐν τῇ χώρᾳ τῇ αὐτῇ ἀγραυλοῦντες καὶ φυλάσσοντες φυλακὰς τῆς νυκτὸς ἐπὶ τὴν ποίμνην αὐτῶν.

Lk 1,69 ● *om* του ‖ 1 54: 𝔓^{4} ℌ⟨33-1241⟩ D *pc* Cr Or **70** δια—αγ.] προς τους πατερας ημων των ‖ 1 55: **047** **75** ● πασας τας ημερας ‖ Mt28 20: *Rpl* Chrn Or *La* Ir — *txt*: 𝔓^{4}(ᵛ*om* ταις) BLW-579 565 *L*' **76** προ προσ.] ● ενωπιον ‖ 1 17: 𝔓^{4} ℵBW-**0177** Or *L*Or — *txt*: *Rpl* Chrn Ep Or *L*, Ir *S*,j **77** αυτων] ημων(εμων) ‖ 1 141 K15 3: C-579 28-1071-1604 **λ**⟨131⟩-1582-2193 ϕ1689 **σ**-M-27-115-1188-1194 A R U Θ Ψ (2355) *pc* *l*1345 *l*1346 *l*1348 *l*1350 (*L*g^{2}250 vg^{2}) *Arm*^{pc} *Geo*^{2} — *om* ‖ 3 3 24 47 Mt26 28 Mk1 4: ϕ174-983 *pc* *C*b$^{\langle 7\rangle}$ **78** ● επισκεψεται: 𝔓^{4v}(επι[...) ℵ*BL(επεσκ.!)W-**0177** Θ {*L*vg^{1}} *S*' *C*⟨b^{1}⟩ *Arm* *Geo*^{1} *Δ*a E^{a3} — *txt*: 𝔓^{4v} *Rpl* Chrn Cr Gr^{Ny} {*L*'Ir} *S*hj *Arm*^{0} *Geo*^{2} *Δ*ad i^{T} l md n$^{\langle Hg\rangle}$ E^{a1} **80** πνευ. + πληρουμενον σοφιας ‖ 2 40: 213 **2,2** ● αυτη + η: *Rpl* Chrn Eu — *txt*: ℵ*(∼ εγ. πρ.)B-**0177** 700 λ131 ϕ543 D(∼ εγ. απ. πρ.) *pc* *l*1596 **3** εαυ.] ιδιαν ‖ Mt9 1: *Rpl* Chrn — *txt*: ℵ^{c}(*-των)BLWΞ-**0177**-579 D Ψ Eu | πολ.] πατριδα ‖ 4 23 Mt13 54 Mk6 1: ϕ983 — χωραν ‖ Mt2 12: C* *L*30 *S*s[c] **5** εμν.—γυν.] ● *om* γυν. ‖ 1 27: ℵ*B*C*ᵛ LWΞ-**0177** 700 λ1-22-131-1582-2193 D* 565 *l*1596 Eu *L*e aβf(*om* αυτ. γυν.: r$^{1.2}$) Or *S*pj *C* *Δ*a i^{T} md n' p — *om* εμν. ‖ Mt1 20.24: *L*bcz *S*s[c] *Δ*n^{L} — *txt*: *Rpl* Chrn *L*' *S*h *Δ*ad l **7** *om* τ. πρω. ‖ Mt1 25: W *Δ*n^{L}

---

2 1-5 *cf.* EIc17 1f.: Κέλευσις δὲ ἐγένετο ἀπὸ Ἀόστου τοῦ βασιλέως ἀπογράψασθαι ὅσοι εἰσὶν ἐν Βηθλεεμ τῆς Ἰουδαίας. καὶ εἶπεν Ιωσηφ· ‘ἐγὼ ἀπογράψομαι τοὺς υἱούς μου. ταύτην δὲ τὴν παῖδα τί ποιήσω; πῶς αὐτὴν ἀπογράψομαι; γυναῖκα ἐμήν; ἐπαισχύνομαι. ἀλλὰ θυγατέρα; οἶδαν οἱ υἱοὶ Ισραηλ ὅτι οὐκ ἔστιν θυγάτηρ μου. αὕτη ἡ ἡμέρα κυρίου ποιήσει ὡς βούλεται.’ 2 καὶ ἔστρωσεν τὸν ὄνον καὶ ἐκάθισεν αὐτὴν καὶ ἧλκεν ὁ υἱὸς αὐτοῦ καὶ ἠκολούθει Σαμουηλ ...

2 7 *cf.* EIc22 2 (*cf. ad* 4. Mt2 16)

[9] καὶ ἄγγελος κυρίου ἐπέστη αὐτοῖς καὶ δόξα κυρίου περιέλαμψεν αὐτούς, καὶ ἐφοβήθησαν φόβον μέγαν. [10] καὶ εἶπεν αὐτοῖς ὁ ἄγγελος· μὴ φοβεῖσθε· ἰδοὺ γὰρ εὐαγγελίζομαι ὑμῖν χαρὰν μεγάλην, ἥτις ἔσται παντὶ τῷ λαῷ, [11] ὅτι ἐτέχθη ὑμῖν σήμερον σωτήρ, ὅς ἐστιν Χριστὸς κύριος, ἐν πόλει Δαυιδ. [12] καὶ τοῦτο ὑμῖν σημεῖον, εὑρήσετε βρέφος ἐσπαργανωμένον καὶ κείμενον ἐν φάτνῃ. [13] καὶ ἐξαίφνης ἐγένετο σὺν τῷ ἀγγέλῳ πλῆθος στρατιᾶς οὐρανίου αἰνούντων τὸν θεὸν καὶ λεγόντων·

[14] δόξα ἐν ὑψίστοις θεῷ καὶ ἐπὶ γῆς εἰρήνη ἐν ἀνθρώποις εὐδοκίας.

[15] Καὶ ἐγένετο ὡς ἀπῆλθον ἀπ' αὐτῶν εἰς τὸν οὐρανὸν οἱ ἄγγελοι, οἱ ποιμένες εἶπον πρὸς ἀλλήλους· διέλθωμεν δὴ ἕως Βηθλεεμ καὶ ἴδωμεν τὸ ῥῆμα τοῦτο τὸ γεγονὸς ὃ ὁ κύριος ἐγνώρισεν ἡμῖν. [16] καὶ ἦλθαν σπεύσαντες, καὶ ἀνεῦραν τήν τε Μαριαμ καὶ τὸν Ιωσηφ καὶ τὸ βρέφος κείμενον ἐν τῇ φάτνῃ· [17] ἰδόντες δὲ ἐγνώρισαν περὶ τοῦ ῥήματος τοῦ λαληθέντος αὐτοῖς περὶ τοῦ παιδίου τούτου. [18] καὶ πάντες οἱ ἀκούσαντες ἐθαύμασαν περὶ τῶν λαληθέντων ὑπὸ τῶν ποιμένων πρὸς αὐτούς· [19] ἡ δὲ Μαρία πάντα συνετήρει τὰ ῥήματα ταῦτα συμβάλλουσα ἐν τῇ καρδίᾳ αὐτῆς. [20] καὶ ὑπέστρεψαν οἱ ποιμένες δοξάζοντες καὶ αἰνοῦντες τὸν θεὸν ἐπὶ πᾶσιν οἷς ἤκουσαν καὶ εἶδον καθὼς ἐλαλήθη πρὸς αὐτούς.

(—)

11. Beschneidung Jesu und Darstellung im Tempel. Luk 2 21–40
The Circumcision of Jesus and the Presentation in the Temple.

[21] Καὶ ὅτε ἐπλήσθησαν ἡμέραι ὀκτὼ τοῦ περιτεμεῖν αὐτόν, καὶ ἐκλήθη τὸ ὄνομα αὐτοῦ Ἰησοῦς, τὸ κληθὲν ὑπὸ τοῦ ἀγγέλου πρὸ τοῦ συλλημφθῆναι αὐτὸν ἐν τῇ κοιλίᾳ.

[22] Καὶ **ὅτε ἐπλήσθησαν αἱ ἡμέραι τοῦ καθαρισμοῦ** αὐτῶν κατὰ τὸν νόμον Μωυσέως, ἀνήγαγον αὐτὸν εἰς Ἱεροσόλυμα παραστῆσαι τῷ κυρίῳ, [23] καθὼς γέγραπται ἐν νόμῳ κυρίου ὅτι **πᾶν ἄρσεν διανοῖγον μήτραν ἅγιον τῷ κυρίῳ** κληθήσεται, [24] καὶ τοῦ δοῦναι θυσίαν κατὰ τὸ εἰρημένον ἐν τῷ νόμῳ κυρίου, **ζεῦγος τρυγόνων ἢ δύο νοσσοὺς περιστερῶν.** Lv12 6 · Ex13 2.12.15 · Lv12 8

[25] Καὶ ἰδοὺ ἦν ἄνθρωπος ἐν Ιερουσαλημ ᾧ ὄνομα Συμεων, καὶ ὁ ἄνθρωπος οὗτος δίκαιος καὶ εὐλαβής, προσδεχόμενος παράκλησιν τοῦ Ισραηλ, καὶ πνεῦμα ἦν ἅγιον ἐπ' αὐτόν· [26] καὶ ἦν αὐτῷ κεχρηματισμένον ὑπὸ τοῦ πνεύματος τοῦ ἁγίου μὴ ἰδεῖν θάνατον πρὶν ἢ ἴδῃ τὸν Χριστὸν κυρίου. [27] καὶ ἦλθεν ἐν τῷ πνεύματι εἰς τὸ ἱερόν· καὶ ἐν τῷ εἰσαγαγεῖν τοὺς γονεῖς τὸ

Lk 2,9 επεσ.] εφανη‖Mt1 20: σ990 *L*Ir *S*s[c](+ επιστας) *C*s *Arm* *Δ*i^{V} | φοβ. μεγ.] σφοδρα‖Mt17 6 27 54: B — + σφο.‖Mt2 10: W *C*b⟨1⟩ **10** φοβ. + υμεις‖Mt28 5: **σ**-1188 Chrn *Geo*^{2} **11** κυριου‖2 26: *L*βr$^{1.2}$ vg^{1} *S*j *Δ*E^{a} **14** εν^{2}] *om*: 372 PsAth Ir Or *L*βr^{1} Ath Au Ir Or *S*Ef^{2} *Geo*^{1} *Δ*'⟨me⟩ — και: *S*s[c]ph(και⁻εν) Af Ef^{1} *Geo*^{2} *Δ*a p E^{a} | ● ευδοκια (∼ ευδ. ανθ.): A^{Od} *Rpl* Ath PsAth^{3} PsBas CAp Chr Co Cr Cr^{I} Ddy Ep Eu Gr^{Na} GrTh Or Procl Thd^{A}(Ps-?) *S*(')hj^{abcf3}(^{1} + σου) Af PsAth Ef Iac *C*b *Arm* *Δ*a p E^{a} — *txt*: ℵ*BW A D 372 PsAth^{1} Cr^{I} Ir Or *L*, Ath Au Ir Or *C*s *Got* *Δ*'⟨me⟩ **15** ● αγγ. + και οι ανθρωποι(+ εκεινοι): *Rpl* *L*q (*S*h) — + και εκ.: *L*c — *txt* (+ και): ℵBLWΞ-(579) 700-1071 λ1-22-1278-1582-2193 Θ (1365) *pc* *l*1043 *l*1596 *l*1663 Eu *L*'Au Or *S*'j *C* *Δ* | ειπ.] ● ελαλουν‖4 36 6 11 Act26 31: BW 565 *l*1596 *L*fz vg Au *S*s[c] *C*s | αλλ. + λεγοντες‖4 36 Act←: ℵ *L*abff^{2} lvg^{2} *S*p *C*s$^{1:7}$b⟨3⟩ *Δ*a i^{T} n^{L} **17** δε + προσεκυνησαν και‖Mt2 11: 544 | *om* τουτ.‖Mt2 8: Λ-544-700 λ1-131-1582-2193 ϕ124-788-*l*547 D Θ *pc* *l*53 *L*e afr^{1} *S*s[c]p *C* *Δ*a md n^{CHgS}p **18** εθαυμαζον‖1 21 4 22: 1604 D *pc* *L*e f (*S*s[c]j) *C*b^{1} *Δ*i **19** διετηρ.‖2 51: 1573 | *om* ταυτα‖51: B *pc* *S*p^{1} **21** ημ. οκ.] αι ημ. (+ αι) οκ.‖1 23 26.22: 33-579-1241 28-544-1071 **ϕ**⟨124⟩-*l*547 σ7 (D 1012) *al* Amph *S*h^{m} {*C*b⟨1⟩} — αι οκ.(*om*) ημ.‖←: λ118-209 157 565 (Eu) {} | αυτον^{1}] το παιδιον‖1 59: 33-892 28-544 **ϕ**-*l*547$^{1:2}$ σM-990-1194 D E G H V Γ(αυτο το π.) Ω 157 *mu* Amph Chrn Or *L* e βg^{2}r^{1}30 vg^{8} *S*s[c]pj *Δ*⟨i^{V}⟩ **25** *om* ιδ.‖66 Mk3 1: N ϕ*l*547 D *S*s[c]pj^{ac} *Geo*^{2} *Δ*a i^{T} n^{CL} p | ● ∼ ανθ. ην‖14 2: ℵBW-892 **σ**⟨954⟩ 713 Or *L*bfff^{2}lz vg' *S*' *Arm*^{pc} — *om* ην: ϕ983-1689 F^{W} 243 *S*j^{b} — *txt*: *Rpl* PsAth *L*e aβcqr^{1} vg^{2} *S*hj^{ac} *Arm*' *Geo* **26** πρ. η ιδη] εως αν ιδη‖9 27p: ℵ* *pc* Or *L*e *S*s[c]pj *Δ*a p E^{a} — πρ. αν ιδη: B-579 ϕ1689 F^{W} Θ *pc* — ● πρ. η αν(να!) ιδη: ℵ^{c}(L)X-33-892 R Ψ *pc* — πρ. ιδη: W λ118-209 σ1223-1424 *pc* *l*47 — πρ. ιδειν‖2 26 1 Mt26 34 Jo4 49: **ϕ**-*l*547 — πρ. η ιδειν‖Mt1 18 Mk14 30: 1241 N-544 σ1207 K Π *pc* Cr^{I} | κυριον‖2 11: Λ *L*bc(θεον: ff^{2}) *C*s$^{2:5}$bf *Δ*ad md^{MVW} n^{HgHrS} (∼ κυ. Χ.: E^{a})

Lk2 26 *cf.* EIc24 4: (*cf. ad 2 24.* Mt23 35) ... μετὰ δὲ τὰς τρεῖς ἡμέρας ἐβουλεύσαντο οἱ ἱερεῖς τίνα ἀναστήσουσιν εἰς τὸν τόπον τοῦ Ζαχαρίου. Καὶ ἀνέβη ὁ κλῆρος ἐπὶ Συμεων· οὗτος γὰρ ἦν ὁ χρηματισθεὶς ὑπὸ τοῦ ἁγίου πνεύματος μὴ ἰδεῖν θάνατον ἕως ἂν τὸν Χριστὸν ἐν σαρκὶ ἴδῃ.

παιδίον Ἰησοῦν τοῦ ποιῆσαι αὐτοὺς κατὰ τὸ εἰθισμένον τοῦ νόμου περὶ αὐτοῦ, 28 καὶ αὐτὸς ἐδέξατο αὐτὸ εἰς τὰς ἀγκάλας καὶ εὐλόγησεν τὸν θεὸν καὶ εἶπεν·

29 νῦν ἀπολύεις τὸν δοῦλόν σου, δέσποτα,
κατὰ τὸ ῥῆμά σου ἐν εἰρήνῃ·
Is40 5 — 30 ὅτι **εἶδον** οἱ ὀφθαλμοί μου **τὸ σωτήριόν σου,**
Is52 10 — 31 ὃ ἡτοίμασας **κατὰ πρόσωπον πάντων τῶν λαῶν,**
Is49 6.9 46 13 — 32 **φῶς εἰς ἀποκάλυψιν ἐθνῶν**
καὶ **δόξαν** λαοῦ σου **Ισραηλ.**

33 καὶ ἦν ὁ πατὴρ αὐτοῦ καὶ ἡ μήτηρ θαυμάζοντες ἐπὶ τοῖς λαλουμένοις περὶ αὐτοῦ. 34 καὶ εὐλόγησεν αὐτοὺς Συμεων καὶ εἶπεν πρὸς Μαριαμ τὴν μητέρα αὐτοῦ· ἰδοὺ οὗτος κεῖται εἰς πτῶσιν καὶ ἀνάστασιν πολλῶν ἐν τῷ Ισραηλ καὶ εἰς σημεῖον ἀντιλεγόμενον, 35 καὶ σοῦ δὲ αὐτῆς τὴν ψυχὴν διελεύσεται ῥομφαία, ὅπως ἂν ἀποκαλυφθῶσιν ἐκ πολλῶν καρδιῶν διαλογισμοί.

36 Καὶ ἦν Ἅννα προφῆτις, θυγάτηρ Φανουηλ, ἐκ φυλῆς Ασηρ· αὕτη προβεβηκυῖα ἐν ἡμέραις πολλαῖς, ζήσασα μετὰ ἀνδρὸς ἔτη ἑπτὰ ἀπὸ τῆς παρθενίας αὐτῆς, 37 καὶ αὐτὴ χήρα ἕως ἐτῶν ὀγδοήκοντα τεσσάρων, ἣ οὐκ ἀφίστατο τοῦ ἱεροῦ νηστείαις καὶ δεήσεσιν λατρεύουσα νύκτα καὶ ἡμέραν. 38 καὶ αὐτῇ τῇ ὥρᾳ ἐπιστᾶσα ἀνθωμολογεῖτο τῷ θεῷ καὶ ἐλάλει περὶ αὐτοῦ πᾶσιν τοῖς προσδεχομένοις λύτρωσιν Ιερουσαλημ.

39 Καὶ ὡς ἐτέλεσαν ἅπαντα τὰ κατὰ τὸν νόμον κυρίου, ἐπέστρεψαν εἰς τὴν Γαλιλαίαν εἰς πόλιν ἑαυτῶν Ναζαρεθ. 40 τὸ δὲ παιδίον ηὔξανεν καὶ ἐκραταιοῦτο πληρούμενον σοφίας, καὶ χάρις θεοῦ ἦν ἐπ' αὐτό.

(—) *12.* Der zwölfjährige Jesus. *The Child Jesus in the Temple.* Luk 2 41–52

41 Καὶ ἐπορεύοντο οἱ γονεῖς αὐτοῦ κατ' ἔτος εἰς Ιερουσαλημ τῇ ἑορτῇ τοῦ πάσχα. 42 καὶ ὅτε ἐγένετο ἐτῶν δώδεκα, ἀναβαινόντων αὐτῶν κατὰ τὸ ἔθος τῆς ἑορτῆς, 43 καὶ τελειωσάντων τὰς ἡμέρας, ἐν τῷ ὑποστρέφειν αὐτοὺς ὑπέμεινεν Ἰησοῦς ὁ παῖς ἐν Ιερουσαλημ, καὶ οὐκ ἔγνωσαν οἱ γονεῖς αὐτοῦ. 44 νομίσαντες δὲ αὐτὸν εἶναι ἐν τῇ συνοδίᾳ ἦλθον ἡμέρας ὁδὸν καὶ

Lk 2,27 ειθ.] εθος‖2 42: D **28** ● αγκ. + αυτου: *Rpl* PsAth Chrn Cr^{I} Or *L*' Ir *S*,j *C* — *txt*: ℵ BLW σ*27* Π *pc* Cr^{I} Ir Or *L*abff^{2}(*om* εις τ. αγκ.)lz **35** διαλογ. + πονηροι‖Mt15 19: ℵ* **39** ● υπεστρ.‖1 56 2 20.45 4 14: *Rpl* — *txt*: ℵ*(-εν)BWΞ-579 | ● εις^{2} + την: *Rpl* — *txt*: ℵ*BW λ1-131-1582-2193 ϕ346 D* | Ναζ. + καθως ερρεθη δια του προφητου οτι Ναζωραιος κληθησεται‖Mt2 23: D *La* **40** εκρ. + πνευματι‖1 80: *Rpl* Ep *L*fqr^{1}z PsCae *S*' *C*b^{4} *Δ*a p — + ηλικια‖52: *L*vg^{1} *S*j — *txt*: (∼ εκρ. ... ηυξ.): ℵBLW (D) Cl Cr Or *L*'(ebcff^{2}) Au *S*s[c] *C*' *Arm* *Δ*i l md n | *om* πλη. σοφ.‖1 80: ϕ983-1689 *pc* | ● σοφια‖52: ℵ^{c}BLW-33 Ψ 157 *l*44 **42** εορ. + των αζυμων‖22 1: X D 213 *L*e ac **43** επιστρ.‖2 39: 270 *pc*

---

12. cf. ETh^{I}19 1-5: Ὄντος δὲ αὐτοῦ δωδεκαετοῦς ἐπορεύοντο οἱ γονεῖς αὐτοῦ κατὰ τὸ ἔθος εἰς Ιερουσαλημ εἰς τὴν ἑορτὴν τοῦ πασχα μετὰ τῆς συνοδίας αὐτῶν, καὶ μετὰ τὸ πασχα ὑπέστρεφον εἰς τὸν οἶκον αὐτῶν. καὶ ἐν τῷ ὑποστρέφειν αὐτοὺς ἀνῆλθε τὸ παιδίον Ἰησοῦς εἰς Ἱεροσόλυμα· οἱ δὲ γονεῖς αὐτοῦ ἐνόμισαν αὐτὸν ἐν τῇ συνοδίᾳ εἶναι. 2 Ὁδευσάντων δὲ ὁδὸν ἡμέρας μιᾶς, ἐζήτουν αὐτὸν ἐν τοῖς συγγενέσιν αὐτῶν, καὶ μὴ εὑρόντες αὐτὸν ἐλυπήθησαν, καὶ ὑπέστρεψαν πάλιν εἰς τὴν πόλιν ζητοῦντες αὐτόν. καὶ μετὰ τρίτην ἡμέραν εὗρον αὐτὸν ἐν τῷ ἱερῷ καθεζόμενον ἐν μέσῳ τῶν διδασκάλων καὶ ἀκούοντα καὶ ἐρωτῶντα αὐτούς. προσεῖχον δὲ πάντες καὶ ἐθαύμαζον, πῶς παιδίον ὑπάρχων ἀποστομίζει τοὺς πρεσβυτέρους καὶ διδασκάλους τοῦ λαοῦ, ἐπιλύων τὰ κεφάλαια τοῦ νόμου καὶ τὰς παραβολὰς τῶν προφητῶν. 3 Προσελθοῦσα δὲ ἡ μήτηρ αὐτοῦ Μαρία εἶπεν αὐτῷ· 'ἱνατί τοῦτο ἐποίησας ἡμῖν, τέκνον; ἰδοὺ ὀδυνώμενοι ἐζητοῦμέν σε.' καὶ εἶπεν αὐτοῖς ὁ Ἰησοῦς· 'τί με ζητεῖτε; οὐκ οἴδατε ὅτι ἐν τοῖς τοῦ πατρός μου δεῖ εἶναί με;' 4 Οἱ δὲ γραμματεῖς καὶ Φαρισαῖοι εἶπον· 'σὺ εἶ μήτηρ τοῦ παιδίου τούτου;' ἡ δὲ εἶπεν· 'ἐγώ εἰμι.' καὶ εἶπον αὐτῇ· 'μακαρία σὺ εἶ ἐν γυναιξίν, ὅτι ηὐλόγησεν ὁ θεὸς τὸν καρπὸν τῆς κοιλίας σου· τοιαύτην γὰρ δόξαν καὶ τοιαύτην ἀρετὴν καὶ σοφίαν οὔτε εἴδομεν οὔτε ἠκούσαμέν ποτε.' 5 Ἀναστὰς δὲ Ἰησοῦς ἠκολούθησεν τῇ μητρὶ αὐτοῦ, καὶ ἦν ὑποτασσόμενος τοῖς γονεῦσιν αὐτοῦ. ἡ δὲ μήτηρ αὐτοῦ διετήρει πάντα τὰ γενόμενα. ὁ δὲ Ἰησοῦς προέκοπτεν σοφίᾳ καὶ ἡλικίᾳ καὶ χάριτι· ...

12. cf. EAr 50.53 (*transl.* Fleischer): *Et cum factus esset annorum duodecim, duxerunt eum Hierosolymam ad festum. finito autem festo ipsi quidem reverterunt, sed dominus Jesus remansit in templo inter doctores et seniores et eruditos ex filiis Israelis, quos de scientiis varia interrogabat, et vicissim eis respondebat. dixit enim illis: 'Messias cuius est filius?' responderunt illi: 'filius*

ἀνεζήτουν αὐτὸν ἐν τοῖς συγγενεῦσιν καὶ τοῖς γνωστοῖς, 45 καὶ μὴ εὑρόντες ὑπέστρεψαν εἰς Ιερουσαλημ ἀναζητοῦντες αὐτόν. 46 καὶ ἐγένετο μετὰ ἡμέρας τρεῖς εὗρον αὐτὸν ἐν τῷ ἱερῷ καθεζόμενον ἐν μέσῳ τῶν διδασκάλων καὶ ἀκούοντα αὐτῶν καὶ ἐπερωτῶντα αὐτούς· 47 ἐξίσταντο δὲ πάντες οἱ ἀκούοντες αὐτοῦ ἐπὶ τῇ συνέσει καὶ ταῖς ἀποκρίσεσιν αὐτοῦ. 48 καὶ ἰδόντες αὐτὸν ἐξεπλάγησαν, καὶ εἶπεν πρὸς αὐτὸν ἡ μήτηρ αὐτοῦ· τέκνον, τί ἐποίησας ἡμῖν οὕτως; ἰδοὺ ὁ πατήρ σου κἀγὼ ὀδυνώμενοι ἐζητοῦμέν σε. 49 καὶ εἶπεν πρὸς αὐτούς· τί ὅτι ἐζητεῖτέ με; οὐκ ᾔδειτε ὅτι ἐν τοῖς τοῦ πατρός μου δεῖ εἶναί με; 50 καὶ αὐτοὶ οὐ συνῆκαν τὸ ῥῆμα ὃ ἐλάλησεν αὐτοῖς. 51 καὶ κατέβη μετ' αὐτῶν καὶ ἦλθεν εἰς Ναζαρεθ, καὶ ἦν ὑποτασσόμενος αὐτοῖς. καὶ ἡ μήτηρ αὐτοῦ διετήρει πάντα τὰ ῥήματα ἐν τῇ καρδίᾳ αὐτῆς. 52 καὶ Ἰησοῦς **προέκοπτεν** σοφίᾳ καὶ ἡλικίᾳ καὶ **χάριτι παρὰ θεῷ καὶ ἀνθρώποις.**

1Sm226 Prv34

Lk 2,48 εζη.] ● ζητουμεν: ℵ*B ϕ69 *l*253^{v} *C* *Arab*EAr↓ **51** συνετη.‖219: σ1424 *l*1 Or | ρημ. + ταυτα‖219 165: *Rpl* (*om* τα ρημ.: S; *om* παντα: σ1424) *L*' Or *S*cp^{1}h *C*' *Geo* *Arab*EAr↓ *Δ*' + ταυ. συμβαλλουσα‖219: ℵ^{c} X(-αλου-) 1071 σ71-692 *pc* *l*1 *l*14 Eu *C*b^{6} — + αυτου: Or *La*(r^{1}) *Δ*p — *txt*: ℵ*BW σM-990 D *Le* *S*'j *Δ*E^{a} **52** ● προεκ. + εν τη *cf.* G114: ℵL Cr Or — + εν *cf.*←: Ath Cr Ep$^{2:5}$ Or — + τη: BW-579 | ∼ηλ. κ. σοφ.‖240: L-579 D 1012 Amph^{ct} Ath^{1} PsAth^{1} Cr Ep^{3} Gr^{Ny} Or Thd^{C} *L*vl'r^{1} vg^{1} Hi Or Vic^{P} *S*'j *C*b *Arab*EAr↓ *Δ*a n^{L} — *txt*: *Rpl* Ath^{2} PsAth^{1} Cr Ep^{2} ETh^{I}↓ Or *Lf* vg' Au Or *S*h PsAth *C*s *Arm*, PsAth *Δ*ad i^{T} l md$^{\langle Z\rangle}$ n'

Davidis.' 'quare ergo', inquit, 'in spiritu vocat illum dominum suum, cum dicit: dixit dominus domino meo: sede ad dextram meam, ut hostes tuos vestigiis pedum tuorum subiiciam?' rursus dixit ei princeps doctorum: 'legistine libros?' 'et libros', inquit dominus Jesus, 'et ea quae in libris continentur.' et explicavit libros et legem et praecepta et statuta et mysteria quae in libris prophetarum continentur, res quas nullius creaturae intellectus assequitur. dixit ergo doctor ille: 'ego hactenus talem scientiam nec consecutus sum nec audivi: quis tandem, putas, puer iste erit?' ... 53 Dum haec et alia inter sese loquebantur, adfuit domina hera Maria, postquam ipsum quaerens triduum cum Josepho circumivit. Videns ergo eum inter doctores sedentem perque vices ipsos rogantem et respondentem, dixit illi: 'mi fili, quare ita fecisti nobis? ecce ego et pater tuus te magno cum labore quaerimus.' at ille: 'quare', inquit, 'me quaeritis? nonne scitis decere me ut in domo patris mei verser?' sed ipsi non intellexerunt verba quae eis dixerat. tunc doctores illi rogarunt Mariam, hiccine ipsius esset filius, et annuente ipsa: 'o te felicem', dixerunt, 'Maria, quae hunc talem peperisti.' reversus autem cum eis Nazareth in omnibus rebus morem eis gerebat. et mater eius conservabat omnia verba ista in corde suo. dominus vero Jesus proficiebat statura et sapientia et gratia apud Deum et homines.

I. Die galiläische Periode. *The Galilean Period.*

Matth 3—18 = Mark 1—9 = Luk 3 1—9 50.

(1)

13. Der Täufer. *John the Baptist.*

Matth 3 1–6

[1] Ἐν ταῖς ἡμέραις ἐκείναις

παραγίνεται

Ἰωάννης ὁ βαπτιστὴς κηρύσσων ἐν τῇ ἐρήμῳ

cf. v. 5 ↓ τῆς Ἰουδαίας [2] καὶ λέγων· μετανοεῖτε· ἤγγικεν γὰρ ἡ βασιλεία τῶν οὐρανῶν. [3] οὗτος γάρ ἐστιν ὁ ῥηθεὶς διὰ Ἠσαΐου τοῦ προφήτου λέγοντος·

Ex 23 20 Ml 3 1

*11 10 (77.): ... **ἰδοὺ ἐγὼ ἀποστέλλω τὸν ἄγγελόν μου πρὸ προσώπου σου, ὃς κατασκευάσει τὴν ὁ-***

Mark 1 1–6

[1] Ἀρχὴ τοῦ εὐαγγελίου Ἰησοῦ Χριστοῦ.

[4] *ἐγένετο*

Ἰωάννης βαπτίζων ἐν τῇ ἐρήμῳ καὶ κηρύσσων βάπτισμα μετανοίας εἰς ἄφεσιν ἁμαρτιῶν. **21.**

[2] καθὼς γέγραπται ἐν τῷ Ἠσαΐᾳ τῷ προφήτῃ·

ἰδοὺ ἐγὼ ἀποστέλλω τὸν ἄγγελόν μου πρὸ προσώπου σου, ὃς κατασκευάσει τὴν ὁ-

Luk 3 1–6

[1] Ἐν ἔτει δὲ πεντεκαιδεκάτῳ τῆς ἡγεμονίας Τιβερίου Καίσαρος, ἡγεμονεύοντος Ποντίου Πιλάτου τῆς Ἰουδαίας, καὶ τετραρχοῦντος τῆς Γαλιλαίας Ἡρῴδου, Φιλίππου δὲ τοῦ ἀδελφοῦ αὐτοῦ τετραρχοῦντος τῆς Ἰτουραίας καὶ Τραχωνίτιδος χώρας, καὶ Λυσανίου τῆς Ἀβιληνῆς τετραρχοῦντος, [2] ἐπὶ ἀρχιερέως Ἅννα καὶ Καϊάφα,

ἐγένετο ῥῆμα θεοῦ

ἐπὶ Ἰωάννην τὸν Ζαχαρίου υἱὸν ἐν τῇ ἐρήμῳ. [3] καὶ ἦλθεν εἰς πᾶσαν περίχωρον τοῦ Ἰορδάνου κηρύσσων βάπτισμα μετανοίας εἰς ἄφεσιν ἁμαρτιῶν,

[4] ὡς γέγραπται ἐν βίβλῳ λόγων Ἠσαΐου τοῦ προφήτου·

*7 27 (95.): ... **ἰδοὺ ἀποστέλλω τὸν ἄγγελόν μου πρὸ προσώπου σου, ὃς κατασκευάσει τὴν ὁ-***

(Jo) 1 6: ἐγένετο ἄνθρωπος, ἀπεσταλμένος παρὰ θεοῦ, ὄνομα αὐτῷ Ἰωάννης.

Mt 3,1 ◆ εν^{1} + δε‖Lk: *Rpl* *L'* Au *S*ph *C'* — *txt*: L NΣ-28-700 σM-7-267-659-945-990-1010-1194-1391 D E K S V Δ Π Ω *mu* *L*k[e] bfff^{1}g^{1}q vg^{3} Hil *S*sc(και εν) *C*b^{7} *Arm* *Aeth* **2** ● *om* και‖Mk1 15: ℵB *L*g^{2}q30 vg^{2} Hil *Aeth* | *om* γαρ‖←: 544 φ13 *pc* *S*pj^{b} **3** δια] υπο (+ κυριου δια)‖(1 22 2 15) 22 31: *Rpl* (*L* Ir) *S*h — εν: *S*sc *Aeth* — *txt*: ℵBC-33 700 **λ**-1582 **φ**⟨346⟩-174-*l*547 D W *pc* *L*, Au *S*pj

Mk 1,1 Ιη. Χρ.] Ιη.: 28 — *prm* του κυριου (+ ημων): (*L*vg^{3}) *S*[sc]j^{abc} — *om*: 237^{sch} 238^{sch} 259^{sch} *L*vg^{1} Ir$^{1:3}$ | ● Χρ. + υιου του(*om*) θεου: *Rpl* (ℵ^{a}BL D W) Cr *L*[ek] Am Au Hi Ir^{2} *S*[sc] *C*s^{6}b *Geo*^{2} *Δ*p — *txt*: ℵ* Θ-28 *pc* Bas Cr^{I} Ir Or Sr Svn Ti *L*Hi Ir^{1} Or Vic^{P} *S*j *C*s^{2} *Geo*^{1} **2** καθ.] ως‖Lk: *Rpl* Ep Ir Or^{1} — *txt*: 𝔥⟨579-892⟩ Θ-565-700-1071 λ1-209 σ692 K Π *pc* Bas Or^{1} Sr Svn Ti | *om* τω^{1}‖**p**: Θ-700-1071 **λ** ⟨118⟩-22 σ115 D *pc* Ep Ir Or$^{2:4}$ Sr Svn Ti Vic^{A} | *om* ιδ.—σου^{2}‖**p**: Bas Ep *L*Vic^{P} | ● *om* εγω‖Lk: B Θ-28-565 D *L*[ek]⟨30 vg^{1}⟩ Hi Ir *S*[sc]p$^{\langle 3\rangle}$ *C*s$^{7:9}$b$^{\langle 1\rangle}$

Lk 3,1 *om* δε^{1}‖Mt: ℵ^{ca}X-579 N-28-1071 φ13-124-543-788-*l*547 σ71-115-267-692-990-1194-1606-1675 H K Ψ *al* Chrn Or^{2} | Καισ. + Αυγουστου‖2 1: X **3** ● πασ. + την‖7 17 4 14 Mt3 5 14 35 Mk1 28: *Rpl* (∼ την πασ.: φ124) Chrn Eu Or^{1} — *txt*: BLW-579 N A Ψ Or^{3} **4** ως] καθως‖Mk: C Eu | προφ. + λεγοντος‖Mt: *Rpl* (λεγων: φ13-543-826-828) Chrn *L*fqr^{1} *S'*j *C*b^{1} *Geo*^{2ch} — *txt*: 𝔥⟨33⟩700 **λ**-1582-2193 φ124-788 σ990-1424 D Δ Eu Or *L'* *S*sc *C'* *Arm* *Geo*^{1}

---

13. cf. EEb frgm.3.2 (Ep haer. 30,13,6 (*cf.* 14,3).4(: ... ἐγένετο ἐν ταῖς ἡμέραις Ἡρῴδου βασιλέως τῆς Ἰουδαίας (+ ἐπὶ ἀρχιερέως Καϊάφα) ἦλθεν (+ τις) Ἰωάννης (+ ὀνόματι) βαπτίζων βάπτισμα μετανοίας ἐν τῷ Ἰορδάνῃ ποταμῷ, ὃς ἐλέγετο εἶναι ἐκ γένους Ααρων τοῦ ἱερέως, παῖς Ζαχαρίου καὶ Ελισαβετ· καὶ ἐξήρχοντο πρὸς αὐτὸν πάντες ... [4]... ἐγένετο Ἰωάννης βαπτίζων, καὶ ἐξῆλθον πρὸς αὐτὸν Φαρισαῖοι καὶ ἐβαπτίσθησαν καὶ πᾶσα Ἱεροσόλυμα. καὶ εἶχεν ὁ Ἰωάννης ἔνδυμα ἀπὸ τριχῶν καμήλου καὶ ζώνην δερματίνην περὶ τὴν ὀσφῦν αὐτοῦ, καὶ τὸ βρῶμα αὐτοῦ, φησίν, μέλι ἄγριον, οὗ ἡ γεῦσις ἦν τοῦ μαννα, ὡς ἐγκρὶς ἐν ἐλαίῳ.

Matth: *δόν σου* ... (3) **φωνὴ βοῶντος ἐν τῇ ἐρήμῳ· ἑτοιμάσατε τὴν ὁδὸν κυρίου, εὐθείας ποιεῖτε τὰς τρίβους** αὐτοῦ.

Mark: δόν σου· [3] **φωνὴ βοῶντος ἐν τῇ ἐρήμῳ· ἑτοιμάσατε τὴν ὁδὸν κυρίου, εὐθείας ποιεῖτε τὰς τρίβους** αὐτοῦ,

Luk: *δόν σου* ... (4) **φωνὴ βοῶντος ἐν τῇ ἐρήμῳ· ἑτοιμάσατε τὴν ὁδὸν κυρίου, εὐθείας ποιεῖτε τὰς τρίβους** αὐτοῦ· [5] **πᾶσα φάραγξ πληρωθήσεται καὶ πᾶν ὄρος καὶ βουνὸς ταπεινωθήσεται, καὶ ἔσται τὰ σκολιὰ εἰς εὐθεῖαν καὶ αἱ τραχεῖαι εἰς ὁδοὺς λείας·** [6] **καὶ ὄψεται πᾶσα σὰρξ τὸ σωτήριον τοῦ θεοῦ.**

Jo 1 23: ἔφη· ἐγὼ **φωνὴ βοῶντος ἐν τῇ ἐρήμῳ· εὐθύνατε τὴν ὁδὸν κυρίου,** καθὼς εἶπεν Ἠσαΐας ὁ προφήτης.

Is 40 3 — Is 40 4f.

Matth: cf. v. 1 ↑

Mark: [4] ἐγένετο Ἰωάννης βαπτίζων ἐν τῇ ἐρήμῳ καὶ κηρύσσων βάπτισμα μετανοίας εἰς ἄφεσιν ἁμαρτιῶν.

Luk: cf. v. 2f. ↑

Matth: [4] αὐτὸς δὲ ὁ Ἰωάννης εἶχεν τὸ ἔνδυμα αὐτοῦ ἀπὸ **τριχῶν** καμήλου **καὶ ζώνην δερματίνην περὶ τὴν ὀσφῦν αὐτοῦ·** ἡ δὲ τροφὴ ἦν αὐτοῦ ἀκρίδες καὶ μέλι ἄγριον. [5] τότε ἐξεπορεύετο πρὸς αὐτὸν Ἱεροσόλυμα καὶ πᾶσα ἡ Ἰουδαία καὶ πᾶσα ἡ περίχωρος τοῦ Ἰορδάνου, [6] καὶ ἐβαπτίζοντο ἐν τῷ Ἰορδάνῃ ὑπ' αὐτοῦ ἐξομολογούμενοι τὰς ἁμαρτίας αὐτῶν.

Mark: *[6] ἦν δὲ Ἰωάννης ἐνδεδυμένος* ***τρίχας*** *καμήλου* ***καὶ ζώνην δερματίνην περὶ τὴν ὀσφῦν αὐτοῦ,*** *καὶ ἔσθων ἀκρίδας καὶ μέλι ἄγριον.* [5] καὶ ἐξεπορεύετο πρὸς αὐτὸν πᾶσα ἡ Ἰουδαία χώρα καὶ οἱ Ἱεροσολυμῖται πάντες, καὶ ἐβαπτίζοντο ὑπ' αὐτοῦ ἐν τῷ Ἰορδάνῃ ποταμῷ ἐξομολογούμενοι τὰς ἁμαρτίας αὐτῶν.

Luk: *[3] καὶ ἦλθεν εἰς πᾶσαν περίχωρον τοῦ Ἰορδάνου* ...

2Rg 1 8

Matth: cf. v. 4 ↑

Mark: [6] ἦν δὲ Ἰωάννης ἐνδεδυμένος **τρίχας** καμήλου **καὶ ζώνην δερματίνην περὶ τὴν ὀσφῦν αὐτοῦ,** καὶ ἔσθων ἀκρίδας καὶ μέλι ἄγριον.

2Rg 1 8

(2)

14. Bußpredigt des Täufers. *John's Preaching of Repentance.*

Matth 3 7–10

[7] Ἰδὼν δὲ πολλοὺς τῶν Φαρισαίων καὶ Σαδδουκαίων ἐρχομένους ἐπὶ τὸ βάπτισμα αὐτοῦ εἶπεν αὐτοῖς· γεννήματα ἐχιδνῶν, τίς ὑπέδειξεν ὑμῖν φυγεῖν ἀπὸ τῆς μελλούσης ὀργῆς;

23 33 (224.): ὄφεις, γεννήματα ἐχιδνῶν, πῶς φύγητε ἀπὸ τῆς κρίσεως τῆς γεέννης;

Luk 3 7–9

[7] Ἔλεγεν οὖν τοῖς ἐκπορευομένοις ὄχλοις βαπτισθῆναι ὑπ' αὐτοῦ· γεννήματα ἐχιδνῶν, τίς ὑπέδειξεν ὑμῖν φυγεῖν ἀπὸ τῆς μελλούσης ὀργῆς;

Mt 3,5 Ιερ.] πασα η(*om*) Ιερ. ‖ (23) Mk: (892) λ-22-1582 (σ349-517) *pc* (*pc*) Or *Lk*[e] al vg¹ *Cs*¹(∼ πασα Ιερ. και)$^{:10}$ *Arm Aeth* **6** ● Ιορ. + ποταμω ‖ p: ℵBC-33 Σ λ-22-1582 ϕ346 σM-71-1424 W Δ 157 *mu* Or *Lq S*,j *Cs*⁹b *Arm*' — *txt*: *Rpl L*' Hil *Cs*¹ *Arm*^{mu} *Geo* **7** πολ. + οχλους ‖ p: σ1424 | βαπ. αυ.] ● *om* αυ.: ℵB Or *L*Hil *Cs*$^{5+1v}$ — βαπτισθηναι: *S*pj *Cs*¹

Mk 1,2 σου² + εμπροσθεν σου(μου) ‖ Mt11 10p(Ml3 1): *Rpl* (478) Eu Pho Svn *L*fff²g²l 30 vg⁹ Hi *S*h *Cs*³(²)b' *Arm*' *Geo* — *txt*: ℵBL ΘΦ-700 D K P W Π *pc* Or *L*'[ek] Hi Ir *S*[sc]pj *Cs*³b⁵ *Arm*^{pc} **3** αυτ. + πασα φαραγξ πληρωθησεται και παν ορος και βουνος ταπεινωθησεται, και εσται παντα τα σκολια εις ευθειαν και η τραχεια εις πεδιον· και οφθησεται η δοξα κυριου, και οψεται πασα σαρξ το σωτηριον του θεου (+ ημων)· οτι κυριος ελαλησεν. φωνη λεγοντος· βοησον. και ειπα· τι βοησω; οτι(*om*) πασα σαρξ χορτος, και πασα η δοξα αυτης(*om*) ως ανθος χορτου· εξηρανθη ο χορτος, και ο ανθος εξεπεσεν, το δε ρημα κυριου μενει εις τον αιωνα ‖ Lk Is40 4-8 LXX: W (*Lc*) **4** ● Ιω. + ο ‖ 614.24 Mt: ℌ⟨579⟩-*l*1353 566 1342 *C*b⟨1⟩ *Geo*¹ | ερη. + της Ιουδαιας ‖ Mt: 157 | ● *om* και ‖ p: B-33-892 73 *C*sb² **5** ∼ εν τ. Ι. ποτ. υπ αυ. ‖ p: *Rpl La S*h *Cs*$^{7:8}$b — *txt*: ℌ⟨Δ-579⟩-*l*1353 1241 Or¹ *L*'[ek] *S*[sc]j | εν—ποτ.] εις τον Ιορδανην ‖ 19: 28-565 *L*[ek] bdff²r¹tz | *om* ποτ. ‖ p: Θ-700 ϕ*l*547 D W Eu Or¹ *L*[ek] acq vg¹ *S*[sc]p⟨4⟩ **6** ην δε] ● και ην: ℌ⟨Δ-579⟩-*l*1353 565^{m} 245 *L*blqr¹t vg' *Sj Cs*²b² — *txt*: *Rpl L*[ek] acff² vg¹ *S*[sc] *Cs*$^{4+1v}$b'⟨2⟩ | Ιω.] ● ο Ι.: *Rpl* — *txt*: Δ-33 Φ-1071 ϕ⟨69-124-788⟩-230-*l*547 σM-7-115-517-1606-1675 A D E F G K U V W Π 157 *al*

Lk 3,5 ● ευθειας ‖ 4: BΞ-892 D *pc l*32 Or³ {*L*' Ir Leo} *Arm* — ευθεια: ϕ983-1689 σ1194 {} Chrn¹ — *txt*: *Rpl* Chrn¹ *Le* df(?)lqr¹30 *S*,j *C*

Jo 1,23 *om* εγω ‖ p Is40 3: ϕ69 440 *L*vg¹ | ευθ.] ετοιμασατε ‖ ←: ϕ124-*l*547 *pc* Cr *Lc*(δ)fff²q vg² *Sc*[s] *C*b² | κυ. + ευθειας ποιειτε τας τριβομς αυτου(του θεου ημων) ‖ p (Is40 3): W^{s} Or (*Le*)

Matth 3 8-10	Mark	Luk 3 8-9	Jo
8 ποιήσατε οὖν καρπὸν ἄξιον τῆς μετανοίας· 9 καὶ μὴ δόξητε λέγειν ἐν ἑαυτοῖς· πατέρα ἔχομεν τὸν Αβρααμ· λέγω γὰρ ὑμῖν ὅτι δύναται ὁ θεὸς ἐκ τῶν λίθων τούτων ἐγεῖραι τέκνα τῷ Αβρααμ. 10 ἤδη δὲ ἡ ἀξίνη πρὸς τὴν ῥίζαν τῶν δένδρων κεῖται· πᾶν οὖν δένδρον μὴ ποιοῦν καρπὸν καλὸν ἐκκόπτεται καὶ εἰς πῦρ βάλλεται.	*7 19 (53.): πᾶν δένδρον μὴ ποιοῦν καρπὸν καλὸν ἐκκόπτεται καὶ εἰς πῦρ βάλλεται.*	8 ποιήσατε οὖν καρποὺς ἀξίους τῆς μετανοίας· καὶ μὴ ἄρξησθε λέγειν ἐν ἑαυτοῖς· πατέρα ἔχομεν τὸν Αβρααμ· λέγω γὰρ ὑμῖν ὅτι δύναται ὁ θεὸς ἐκ τῶν λίθων τούτων ἐγεῖραι τέκνα τῷ Αβρααμ. 9 ἤδη δὲ καὶ ἡ ἀξίνη πρὸς τὴν ῥίζαν τῶν δένδρων κεῖται· πᾶν οὖν δένδρον μὴ ποιοῦν καρπὸν καλὸν ἐκκόπτεται καὶ εἰς πῦρ βάλλεται.	8 39: ἀπεκρίθησαν καὶ εἶπαν αὐτῷ· ὁ πατὴρ ἡμῶν Αβρααμ ἐστιν ... 15 5 f.: ... οὗτος φέρει καρπὸν πολύν, ... 6 ... ἐβλήθη ἔξω ὡς τὸ κλῆμα καὶ ἐξηράνθη, καὶ συνάγουσιν αὐτὸ καὶ εἰς τὸ πῦρ βάλλουσιν, καὶ καίεται.

(3)

15. Standespredigt des Täufers. *John's Ethical Teaching.* **Luk 3 10-14**

10 Καὶ ἐπηρώτων αὐτὸν οἱ ὄχλοι λέγοντες· τί οὖν ποιήσωμεν; 11 ἀποκριθεὶς δὲ ἔλεγεν αὐτοῖς· ὁ ἔχων δύο χιτῶνας μεταδότω τῷ μὴ ἔχοντι, καὶ ὁ ἔχων βρώματα ὁμοίως ποιείτω. 12 ἦλθον δὲ καὶ τελῶναι βαπτισθῆναι καὶ εἶπον πρὸς αὐτόν· διδάσκαλε, τί ποιήσωμεν; 13 ὁ δὲ εἶπεν πρὸς αὐτούς· μηδὲν πλέον παρὰ τὸ διατεταγμένον ὑμῖν πράσσετε. 14 ἐπηρώτων δὲ αὐτὸν καὶ στρατευόμενοι λέγοντες· τί ποιήσωμεν καὶ ἡμεῖς; καὶ εἶπεν αὐτοῖς· μηδένα διασείσητε μηδὲ συκοφαντήσητε, καὶ ἀρκεῖσθε τοῖς ὀψωνίοις ὑμῶν.

(4. 5)

16. Messianische Verkündigung des Täufers. *John's Messianic Preaching.*

Matth 3 11-12 — Mark 1 7-8 — Luk 3 15-17

Luk 3 15	Jo
15 Προσδοκῶντος δὲ τοῦ λαοῦ καὶ διαλογιζομένων πάντων ἐν ταῖς καρδίαις αὐτῶν περὶ τοῦ Ἰωάννου, μήποτε αὐτὸς εἴη ὁ	1 19 f. 25-27: Καὶ αὕτη ἐστὶν ἡ μαρτυρία τοῦ Ἰωάννου, ὅτε ἀπέστειλαν οἱ Ἰουδαῖοι ἐξ Ἱεροσολύμων ἱερεῖς καὶ Λευίτας ἵνα ἐρωτήσωσιν αὐτόν· σὺ τίς εἶ; 20 καὶ ὡμολόγησεν καὶ οὐκ ἠρνήσατο, καὶ ὡμολόγησεν ὅτι οὐκ εἰμὶ ἐγὼ ὁ Χριστός ... 25 καὶ ἠρώτησαν αὐτὸν καὶ εἶπαν αὐτῷ· τί

Mt 3,8 καρπους αξιους‖p: L-33 28 ϕ828 σ267-1010-1194-1675 U *al* *L*ag^{2} vg^{1} Luc$^{1:2}$ Or *S*scpj **9** δοξ.] αρξησθε‖p: ϕ983-1689 σ1424 *S*(*om*: sc)j **10** δε + και‖p: *Rpl* *L*30 *S*h — *txt* (*om* δε): ℵBC-33 700 λ1-1582 σM D^{s} W Δ *L*' *S*(sc)p *C*sb'(^{2}) | του δενδρου‖Lk13 6-9: 472 Hip *L*Or | *om* ουν‖19: Hip Or *L*vg^{2} Cp *S*(και παν: s)j *C*b^{5} | πυρ] το π.‖Jo: Or *C* | βαλλ. + και καιεται‖Jo: 157

Lk 3,8 καρπον αξιον‖p: W D *pc* *L*e r^{1} *S*h^{t} *C*b *Geo* *Aeth* *Go* | αρξ.] δοξητε(-σθε)‖p: L (Γ) Ψ (*pc*) *L*a vg^{1} — αρξητε‖p: 2145 **9** *om* και^{1}‖p: D 713 *L*⟨c⟩ Ar Luc Or *S*pj *C* | του δενδρου‖13 6-9: 579 *L*vg^{3} | ουν] *om*‖Mt19: 237 *L*bff^{2}z vg^{1} *C*s$^{4:6}$b^{7} *Arm* — δε: *L*c *S*c | καρπους καλους‖8 Mt7 17f.: D' | *om* καλ.‖13 9: 𝔓^{4} Or *L*aff^{2}z vg^{9} *C*b | πυρ] το π.‖Jo: ϕ69 **12** βαπ. + υπ αυτου‖3 7 Mt3 13: CX 544-1071-1604 σ517-1207-1223-1606 K Π **047** *pm* *L*Or *S*h^{-}j *C*sb^{6} **15** *om* του^{2}‖Mt11 7p: Ξ-579-1241 700 λ1-1582-2193 ϕ-174 σ659-990-1606 D *pc* *l*54 Eu

Jo 1,19 ● απεστ. + προς αυτον: BC*-33-892^{c} 1071 σ1010-1293 Ψ *al* Cat Chr Cr *L*abcz *S*' *C*s^{6}b^{+Bv} *Geo*' *Δ*a i^{V} p — Ιου. + πρ. αυ.: σ954 — Ιερ. + πρ. αυ.: *S*j — ιερ. + πρ. αυ.: *Δ*n^{C} — Λευ. + πρ. αυ.: 𝔓^{66cv} X-579 544 ϕ-*l*547 σ945 A Θ *al* *L*' Au *S*h *Geo*^{A} *Δ*'(πρ. Ιωαννην: i^{T} l^{AD}) — *txt*: 𝔓$^{66*.75}$ *Rpl* Or *C*s^{1}(?) *Δ*ad l^{FG} n^{L} **20** ● ∼ εγω ουκ ειμι‖Mt24 5p: 𝔓$^{66.75}$ 𝔥⟨W^{s}-892-1241⟩C*X A Δ **0141** Chr Cr Or *L*e abff^{2}qr^{1}30 *S*c[s]j *Arm* — *om* εγω: Π *pc* — *txt*‖Act13 25: *Rpl* Cr Ep Hip *L*' Au *S*' **15,6** εβλ.] εκβληθη(-θησεται)‖12 31 Mt8 12p: L-(579)-1241 (544)-1071 **λ**⟨1⟩ ϕ346(-ηθητε)-543 G 397 (*L*e cfz vg$^{\langle 1 \rangle}$ *S*hj *C*b^{+B} fa^{s} Sch) | εξη.] ξηρανθη(-θησεται): L (544 *L*acfg^{2}q30? vg^{4} *S*hj) | ● αυτα‖Mt13 30: *Rpl* *L*' *S*h j$^{abc1.df}$ *C*'a^{s} — *txt*: 𝔓^{66v} ℵLWX-33 1071 **λ** **ϕ**-230-*l*547 σ71-1188-1223-1293 A D K Δ Π Ψ **0141** *mu* Cr *L*e g^{2} qr^{1}z vg^{6} *S*'j^{c1} *C*b^{1+B} Sch | *om* το^{2}‖Mt10.19 Lk: X-579 σ71 D H 1242 Cr Thd^{C} | εμβαλουσιν‖Lk12 5: 33 *L*ag^{2}q30 vg^{8} *C*sa^{s}

Matthew	Mark	Luke	John 1:25–27	John 1:31 / 1:15	John 1:33 / 1:30
		Χριστός, [16] ἀπεκρίνατο λέγων	οὖν βαπτίζεις εἰ σὺ οὐκ εἶ ὁ Χριστὸς οὐδὲ Ἠλίας οὐδὲ ὁ προφήτης;		
	[7] Καὶ ἐκήρυσσεν	πᾶσιν ὁ Ἰωάννης·	[26] ἀπεκρίθη αὐτοῖς ὁ Ἰωάννης		1 33:
[11] Ἐγὼ μὲν ὑμᾶς βαπτίζω ἐν ὕδατι εἰς μετάνοιαν·	λέγων· ... [8] *ἐγὼ ἐβάπτισα ὑμᾶς ὕδατι ...*	ἐγὼ μὲν ὕδατι βαπτίζω ὑμᾶς·	λέγων· ἐγὼ βαπτίζω ἐν ὕδατι· μέσος ὑμῶν στήκει ὃν ὑμεῖς οὐκ οἴδατε,	1 31: ... ἦλθον ἐγὼ ἐν τῷ ὕδατι βαπτίζων.	... ὁ πέμψας με βαπτίζειν ἐν ὕδατι ...
ὁ δὲ ὀπίσω μου ἐρχόμενος ἰσχυρότερός μού ἐστιν,	([7]) ἔρχεται ὁ ἰσχυρότερός μου ὀπίσω μου,	ἔρχεται δὲ ὁ ἰσχυρότερός μου,	[27] ὁ ὀπίσω μου ἐρχόμενος,	1 15: ... ὁ ὀπίσω μου ἐρχόμενος	1 30: ... ὀπίσω μου ἔρχεται ἀνὴρ
οὗ οὐκ εἰμὶ ἱκανὸς τὰ ὑποδήματα βαστάσαι·	οὗ οὐκ εἰμὶ ἱκανὸς κύψας λῦσαι τὸν ἱμάντα τῶν ὑποδημάτων αὐτοῦ.	οὗ οὐκ εἰμὶ ἱκανὸς λῦσαι τὸν ἱμάντα τῶν ὑποδημάτων αὐτοῦ·	οὗ οὐκ εἰμὶ ἐγὼ ἄξιος ἵνα λύσω αὐτοῦ τὸν ἱμάντα τοῦ ὑποδήματος.	ἔμπροσθέν μου γέγονεν, ὅτι πρῶτός μου ἦν.	ὃς ἔμπροσθέν μου γέγονεν, ὅτι πρῶτός μου ἦν.

Mt 3,11 ∼ βαπ. υμ.^{1} ‖ p: *Rpl* Max^C *L*vl'[ek] 30 vg^5 Cp^1 Hil — *txt* (∼ εν υδ. βαπ.): ℌ⟨L-892⟩ 700 **λ**-1582 **ϕ**⟨346⟩-174 230-*l*547 σ990-1010 W Chr Cr^1(^{1} Or) Iu *L*ff^{1}l vg' Cp^1 | *om* εις μετ. ‖ p: 998 | ικα.] αξιος ‖ Jo27 Act13$_{25}$: Chr | τα υπ.] τον ιμαντα του υποδηματος ‖ p: Chr | υπ. + αυτου ‖ p: 237 | βασ.] λυσαι ‖ **p** Act←: Chr

Mk 1,7 ερχ.] εγω μεν υμας βαπτιζω(εβαπτισα) εν υδατι (+ εις μετανοιαν ‖ Mt), ερχ. δε ‖ 8p: D *L*[ek] (a)ff^2(εις υδωρ, *om* δε)r^1(∼ βα. υμ.) | ∼ οπ. μου ο ισ. μου ‖ Mt: D *L*ar^1 *S*[sc] *C* — *om* ο ισ. μου ‖ Jo Act13$_{25}$: *l*184 — *om* οπ. μου ‖ Lk: Δ ϕ983-1689-*l*547 σ1424 *pc* *L*[ek] ff^{2}t vg^1 | ικ.] αξιος ‖ Jo Act←: ϕ*l*547 | *om* κυψ. ‖ Lk Jo27 Act←: Θ-28-565-1071 ϕ124-230-788 D 256 *L*[ek] abcff^{2}g^{2}r^{1}t vg^2 | του υποδηματος ‖ Jo Act←: L-892 W 1241 *L*Au Ru *S*[sc]hj^b *C* | *om* αυ. ‖ Mt: 245

Lk 3,16 απεκ.—Ι.] επιγνους τα διανοηματα αυτων ειπεν ‖ 5$_{22}$ 11$_{17}$: D — ειπεν αυτοις: *S*c | ∼ ο Ι. πα. λεγ.: *Rpl* ⟨D⟩ *S*h — ο Ι. λεγ. πα.: 544 K *pc* *L*' *S*j^a {} — Ι. πα. λεγ.: ϕ69-174 σ71-692 E *pc* — πα. ο Ι. λεγ.(+ αυτοις) ‖ Jo: X-33 λ1-131-1582-2193 σ945-1194(*om* ο) (472) *pc* *C*b'(^{1}) — πα. λεγ.: ϕ124-788-*l*547 *L*a(∼: bff^{2}l) vg^1(^{1}*om* πασ.) *S*s(+ αυτοις) *Arm* — ο Ι. λεγ. ‖ Jo: 1241 Γ *pc*(+ αυτοις: *S*pj^{bc}) *C*s^{1}b^4 — ο Ι.: Eu — *txt* (∼ πα. λεγ.): 𝔓^4 ℵ*(^{c}L-579)BW-892 Or *L*e c(∼ λεγ. ο Ι. πα.)r^1 {*C*s^8} | πασ.] απασ.: *Rpl* (*om*: 1241 Γ 472) — *txt*: ℌ'⟨33 892⟩Ξ N λ1-131-1582-2193 σ945-1194 K Θ *pc* | *om* μεν ‖ Mk Jo: 700 D 713 *S*scpj^a | υδ.—υμ.] υμ. βαπ. εν υδ. ‖ Mt Jo: λ1-131-1582 **ϕ**'(-τιζων: 346-*l*547) D 1012 *L*e r^1 Am — βαπ. υμ. εν υδ. ‖ ←: **047** *pc* *L*f vg^1 Or *S*'j *C* — υμ. (+ εν) υδ. βαπ. ‖ Mt: Θ *pc* *L*a(-τισω)bcff^2(q vg^1 Am) — *txt*: *Rpl* (*prm* εν: 700 713) Or *L*l(∼ υμ. βαπ.)r^{2}z vg' *S*h | υμας^1 + εις μετανοιαν ‖ Mt: C-892 1071 **σ**⟨945⟩ D *L*vl⟨fr^{2}z⟩r^{1}30 vg^4 Am | ερχ.—μου] ο δε ερχομενος ισχ. μου εστιν ‖ Mt: D *L*l | ο ισ. μου +(*prm*) οπισω μου ‖ p Act13$_{25}$: L 1604 σ1424 *pc* *l*7 *l*47 *S*(s[c])p^7 | ικ. + κυψας ‖ Mk: X-579 1071 **ϕ**-*l*547 σM *pc* | του υποδηματος ‖ Jo Act←: D *L*HM *C* | *om* αυ. ‖ Mt: D 482 *Arm*$^{\langle pc\rangle}$

Jo 1,15 ερχ. + ος ‖ 30: ℵ*W^s Eu *L*c *C*b^1 **25** *om* ο^2 ‖ Mk6$_{15}$p Lk7$_{39}$: σ267 Δ *C*b^3 **26** απεκρινατο ‖ Lk: L-**083**-33-579 σ1194 U **0141** *pc* Cat Or | εγω + μεν ‖ Mt Lk: **ϕ** σ659 **063** *pc* Chr *L*vl⟨e af⟩r^1 vg^1 Cp *S*j *C*s$^{9:10}$b^4 *Aeth* | βαπ. + υμας ‖ Lk Mk: **0113**(ημ-) N-1071 σ1010 Δ Θ *pc* *L*abff^2(∼)lq30 Cp *S*p^{1}h$^+$ *C*⟨b^2⟩ *Arm* *Aeth* **27** ερχ. + ος εμπροσθεν μου γεγονεν (+ οτι πρωτος μου ην) ‖ 15: *Rpl* (28 213) (*om* ος: *pc*) Chr Cr *L*'(*om* ος: e a Cp^1)^1 Au^1 *S*'j *C*b^2 — *txt*: 𝔓$^{5.66.75}$ ℌ⟨892⟩C*W^s-**083**-**0113** N-1071 **λ**⟨118⟩ Ψ **0141** 660 *l*19 *l*20 Cr Non Or *L*bl Au^1 *S*sc *C*' *Arm* *Aeth* | ∼ εγω ουκ ειμι ‖ Mt24$_5$p: *Rpl* *L*' Au^1 *S*' — *om* εγω ‖ **p** Act13$_{25}$: 𝔓$^{5v.66*.75}$ ℵCL N-1071 ϕ826-983 Chr Or^2 *L*qz vg^4 Cp *S*scj {*C*} *Arm* *Aeth* — *txt* (∼ αξ. εγω): 𝔓^{66c} ℌ'⟨892⟩W^{s}X-**083**-**0113**-(1241) ϕ13-69-543-788-(828) σ1010-1293 Ψ **0141** Or^4(^{1}) *L*(a) Au^2 {} | αξ.] ικανος ‖ Mt Mk Lk: 𝔓$^{66.75}$ 472 Chr^{ct} | ∼ τ. ιμ. τ. υπ. αυ. ‖ Mk Lk: 𝔓^{66} 185 *L*vl'⟨c⟩ vg^6 Au — *om* αυ. ‖ Mt: **063** *L*ff^{2}lz | υπ. + εκεινος(αυτος) υμας βαπτισει εν πνευματι αγιω και πυρι ‖ Mt Lk: (N) σ71-954 E F G *al* *Aeth* **31** ● *om* τω ‖ 26.33 Mt Mk Lk: 𝔓$^{66.75}$ ℌCW^s-**083**-**0260** Λ-1071 **λ** ϕ69-124-174-788-*l*547 **σ**-1223 G P Θ Ψ *al* Cat Chr Cr Or *C* **33** υδ.] τω υδ. ‖ 31: X **λ** Or *C*s$^{4:12}$

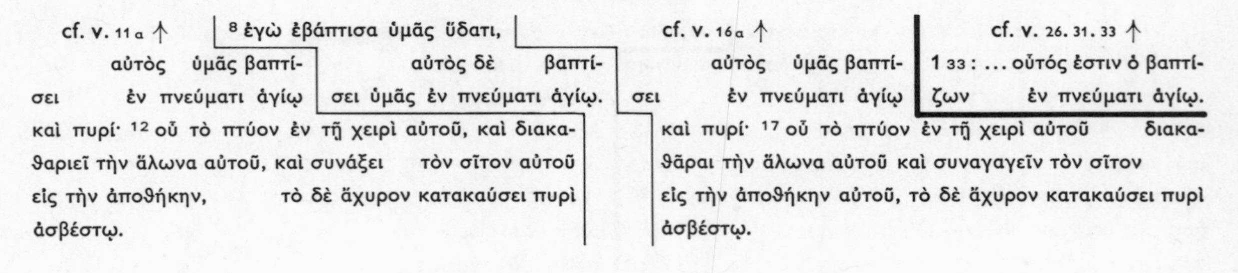
cf. v. 11a ↑ αὐτὸς ὑμᾶς βαπτίσει ἐν πνεύματι ἁγίῳ καὶ πυρί· [12] οὗ τὸ πτύον ἐν τῇ χειρὶ αὐτοῦ, καὶ διακαθαριεῖ τὴν ἅλωνα αὐτοῦ, καὶ συνάξει τὸν σῖτον αὐτοῦ εἰς τὴν ἀποθήκην, τὸ δὲ ἄχυρον κατακαύσει πυρὶ ἀσβέστῳ.

[8] ἐγὼ ἐβάπτισα ὑμᾶς ὕδατι, αὐτὸς δὲ βαπτίσει ὑμᾶς ἐν πνεύματι ἁγίῳ.

cf. v. 16a ↑ αὐτὸς ὑμᾶς βαπτίσει ἐν πνεύματι ἁγίῳ καὶ πυρί· [17] οὗ τὸ πτύον ἐν τῇ χειρὶ αὐτοῦ διακαθᾶραι τὴν ἅλωνα αὐτοῦ καὶ συναγαγεῖν τὸν σῖτον εἰς τὴν ἀποθήκην αὐτοῦ, τὸ δὲ ἄχυρον κατακαύσει πυρὶ ἀσβέστῳ.

cf. v. 26. 31. 33 ↑ 1 33: ... οὗτός ἐστιν ὁ βαπτίζων ἐν πνεύματι ἁγίῳ.

(5) *17.* Die Gefangennahme des Täufers. *John's Imprisonment.* **Luk 3 18–20** **124.**

124. [18] Πολλὰ μὲν οὖν καὶ ἕτερα παρακαλῶν εὐηγγελίζετο τὸν λαόν· [19] ὁ δὲ Ἡρῴδης ὁ τετράρχης, ἐλεγχόμενος ὑπ' αὐτοῦ περὶ Ἡρῳδιάδος τῆς γυναικὸς τοῦ ἀδελφοῦ αὐτοῦ καὶ περὶ πάντων ὧν ἐποίησεν πονηρῶν ὁ Ἡρῴδης, [20] προσέθηκεν καὶ τοῦτο ἐπὶ πᾶσιν, κατέκλεισεν τὸν Ἰωάννην ἐν φυλακῇ.

(6) *18.* Die Taufe Jesu. *The Baptism of Jesus.*

Matth 3 13–17

[13] Τότε παραγίνεται ὁ Ἰησοῦς ἀπὸ τῆς Γαλιλαίας ἐπὶ τὸν Ἰορδάνην πρὸς τὸν

Mark 1 9–11

[9] Καὶ ἐγένετο ἐν ἐκείναις ταῖς ἡμέραις ἦλθεν Ἰησοῦς ἀπὸ Ναζαρετ τῆς Γαλι-

Luk 3 21–22

[21] Ἐγένετο δὲ ἐν τῷ βαπτισθῆναι ἅπαντα τὸν λαὸν καὶ Ἰησοῦ

Mt 3,11 *om* κ. πυρι ‖ Mk Jo: *Rpl* (*om* αυτος—πυ.: ϕ828) Euth Or[1] Thi *L*vg[1] *S*j — *txt*: 𝔥⟨892⟩C Σ-700 λ-22 ϕ'-174-230-*l*547 σM-945-1194-1606-1675 D[s] K U W Γ Δ Π 157 *pm* Cr Chr Iu Or[1] *L*'[ek] Cp *S*'(∼ πυ. ... πν. αγ.: s) Cr *C* **12** *om* αυ.[3] ‖ Lk: L-892 1604 ϕ13-543-788-983-1689 σ⟨517⟩-7-27-659-990 E U 157 *al* Cl Cr Ddy Iu *L*[ek] abff[1] g[1]q vg[4] Am Ar *S* *C*PS | αποθ. + αυτου ‖ 13₃₀ Lk: 𝔥⟨ℵ-33⟩ 1071-1604 ϕ828 σ659-1391-1424 E U W 157 *al* Cr *L*[ek] bff[1]g[1] vg[5] Am *S* *C*PS

Mk 1,8 *om* εγω—υδ. (*cf. ad* 7) ‖ p: D *L*aff[2]r[1] — εγω + μεν ‖ p: *Rpl* (∼ εβαπ. υμ. μεν: Θ) *L*fl vg[1] *S*h *C*s[4] *Aeth* — *txt*: 𝔥⟨Δ-892⟩-*l*1353 565 ϕ69-124-174-788 Or *L*'[ek] Au *S*'[sc]j *C*s[2]b | εβαπ.] βαπτιζω ‖ **p** Jo26: 565 (-σω) ϕ983-1689 *pc* *L*[ek] bcflt vg[6] *C*s[5:6] *Aeth* | ∼ υμ. εβαπ. / βαπ. ‖ Mt: 565 ϕ-*l*547 *pc* | υδ.] ● εν υδ. ‖ Mt Jo: *Rpl* ⟨D⟩ *L*vl'[ek]⟨aff[2]r[1]⟩g[2]t30 vg[2](¹ εις υδωρ) Hip — *txt*: 𝔥⟨L-579⟩ Θ H 1342 *al* Or *L*vg' Au | υδ. + εις μετανοιαν ‖ Mt: σ1082 *pc* | ● *om* εν ‖ 8a: BL *L*[ek] btz vg⟨6⟩ Au | αγ. + και πυρι ‖ p: Φ σ827 P *pc* *S*[sc]h⁺ *C*s[2:8]

Lk 3,16 *om* κ. πυρι ‖ Mk Jo: σ1194 1574 *C*s[1:9] **17** διακ. ... συναγ.] ◆ και διακαθαριει ... συναξει ‖ Mt: *Rpl* *L*' Or *C*b[6] — *txt*: 𝔓[4] ℵ*B *L*e a(συναγει) *C*' *Arm* | *om* αυτου[3] ‖ Mt: σ990 D *pc* *L*e *C*b[7] **19** περι[1]] δια ‖ p: σ1424 | γυν. + Φιλιππου ‖ p: CWX-33-579 544-1071-1604 λ118-209-1582 ϕ174 σ517 A K Π Ψ *al* *S*ph *C*s[2:7]b *Arm*[pc] *Geo* **20** ● κατεκλ. *prm* και ‖ p: 𝔓[57v] *Rpl* *L*' *S* — *txt*: ℵ*BΞ D *L*e br[2]30 | εν + τη ‖ Mk 6₂₇ p: 𝔓[75v] *Rpl* — *txt*: 𝔓[4] ℵBLΞ-**0124** Λ-544 λ1 σM-990 D K Π *al* Eu

Jo 1,33 ουτ.] αυτος ‖ Mt Mk Lk: σ⟨1424⟩ A *L*ebqr[1] Or *S*sc *Arm* — εκεινος: *Aeth* | αγ. + και πυρι ‖ Mt Mk: C* Non Or[4:6] *C*s

---

18. cf. EEb frgm.4 (Ep haer. 30, 13, 7f.): Καὶ μετὰ τὸ εἰπεῖν πολλὰ ἐπιφέρει ὅτι· τοῦ λαοῦ βαπτισθέντος ἦλθεν καὶ Ἰησοῦς καὶ ἐβαπτίσθη ὑπὸ τοῦ Ἰωάννου. καὶ ὡς ἀνῆλθεν ἀπὸ τοῦ ὕδατος, ἠνοίγησαν οἱ οὐρανοὶ καὶ εἶδεν τὸ πνεῦμα τὸ ἅγιον ἐν εἴδει περιστερᾶς κατελθούσης καὶ εἰσελθούσης εἰς αὐτόν. καὶ φωνὴ ἐκ τοῦ οὐρανοῦ λέγουσα· 'σύ μου εἶ ὁ υἱὸς ὁ ἀγαπητός, ἐν σοὶ ηὐδόκησα,' καὶ πάλιν· 'ἐγὼ σήμερον γεγέννηκά σε.' καὶ εὐθὺς περιέλαμψε τὸν τόπον φῶς μέγα. ὃν ἰδών, φησίν, ὁ Ἰωάννης λέγει αὐτῷ· 'σὺ τίς εἶ, κύριε;' καὶ πάλιν φωνὴ ἐξ οὐρανοῦ πρὸς αὐτόν· 'οὗτός ἐστιν ὁ υἱός μου ὁ ἀγαπητός, ἐφ' ὃν ηὐδόκησα.' [8] καὶ τότε, φησίν, ὁ Ἰωάννης προσπεσὼν αὐτῷ ἔλεγεν· 'δέομαί σου, κύριε, σύ με βάπτισον·' ὁ δὲ ἐκώλυσεν αὐτὸν λέγων· 'ἄφες, ὅτι οὕτως ἐστὶ πρέπον πληρωθῆναι πάντα.'

Mt 3₁₃f. *cf.* EN frgm.2 (Hi Pel. 3,2): Ecce mater domini et fratres eius dicebant ei: 'Ioannes baptista baptizat in remissionem peccatorum: eamus et baptizemur ab eo.' dixit autem eis: 'quid peccavi, ut vadam et baptizer ab eo? nisi forte hoc ipsum quod dixi ignorantia est.'

Matth	Mark	Luk	Jo	Jo
'Ιωάννην τοῦ βαπτισθῆναι ὑπ' αὐτοῦ. 14 ὁ δὲ Ἰωάννης διεκώλυεν αὐτὸν	λαίας			
λέγων· ἐγὼ χρείαν ἔχω ὑπὸ σοῦ βαπτισθῆναι, καὶ σὺ ἔρχῃ πρὸς μέ;				
15 ἀποκριθεὶς δὲ ὁ Ἰησοῦς εἶπεν πρὸς αὐτόν· ἄφες ἄρτι· οὕτως γὰρ πρέ-				
πον ἐστὶν ἡμῖν πληρῶσαι πᾶσαν δικαιο-				
σύνην. τότε ἀφίησιν αὐτόν. 16 βαπτι-	καὶ ἐβαπτί-	βαπτι-		
σθεὶς δὲ ὁ Ἰησοῦς	σθη εἰς τὸν Ἰορδάνην ὑπὸ Ἰωάννου.	σθέντος καὶ προσευχομένου		
ἀνέβη εὐθὺς ἀπὸ τοῦ ὕδα-	10 καὶ εὐθὺς ἀναβαίνων ἐκ τοῦ ὕδα-			
τος· καὶ ἰδοὺ ἠνεῴχθη-	τος εἶδεν σχιζομέ-	ἀνεῳχθῆ-		
σαν αὐτῷ οἱ οὐρανοί,	νους τοὺς οὐρανοὺς	ναι τὸν οὐρανόν,	1 32.34:	1 33: ... ἐφ'
καὶ εἶδεν τὸ	καὶ τὸ	22 καὶ καταβῆναι τὸ	... τεθέαμαι τὸ	ὃν ἂν ἴδῃς τὸ
πνεῦμα τοῦ θεοῦ	πνεῦμα ὡς περιστερὰν	πνεῦμα τὸ ἅγιον σωμα-	πνεῦμα	πνεῦμα
καταβαῖνον ὡσεὶ περι-	καταβαῖνον	τικῷ εἴδει ὡς περι-	καταβαῖνον ὡς περι-	καταβαῖνον
στεράν,		στερὰν	στερὰν ἐξ οὐρανοῦ, καὶ	καὶ
ἐρχόμενον ἐπ' αὐτόν·	εἰς αὐτόν·	ἐπ' αὐτόν,	ἔμεινεν ἐπ' αὐτόν.	μένον ἐπ' αὐτόν, ...
17 καὶ ἰδοὺ φωνὴ	11 καὶ φωνὴ ἐγέ-	καὶ φωνὴν	34 κἀγὼ	
ἐκ τῶν οὐρανῶν	νετο ἐκ τῶν οὐρανῶν·	ἐξ οὐρανοῦ	ἑόρακα, καὶ μεμαρτύ-	

Mt 3,14 ● *om* Ιωα.: ℵ*B Eu *Cs* **15** προς αυ.^{1}] ● αυτω *cf.* 1617 2121 *etc.*: 𝔓^{64v} B φ⟨346⟩-174-230-*l*547 *pc l*184 Eu *L*[ek] | αυ.^{2} + et cum baptizaretur (+ Iesus) lumen ingens (magnum) circumfulsit (fulgebat) de aqua ita ut timerent omnes qui advenerant (congregati erant): *La*(g^{1}) *cf.* EEb↓ Iu↓ *L*PsCp *S*Brs Ef Is^{M} **16** ● ∼ ευ. ανεβη‖Mk: ℵB 28-700 λ-1582 D^{s} W *pc l*1354 Chr Hip *L*'[ek] Au PsChr *S*c(*om* ευ.: s)p *C* — *txt*: *Rpl* *L*dh PsAu *S*h (j) *Arm* | ● *om* αυτω‖Lk: ℵ*B *l*211 *l*1043 *l*1627 Eu Ir$^{1v:2}$ *L*32 vg^{2} PsAm Hil Ir$^{1:2}$ PsVig$^{1:2}$ *S*sc *Cs* | ● *om* το ... του^{2}‖Lk418 Is611 Gn12: ℵB Ir$^{1:1(+1v)}$ *C*s$^{1:9}$b$^{⟨1⟩}$ | καταβ. + εκ του ουρανου‖Jo32: D^{s} 372 *L*[ek] abcg$^{1.2}$hl 30 vg^{3} PsAm Hil *S*h(∼ ως περ. εκ τ. ου.) | ωσει] ως‖p: D^{s} Eu Ir$^{1:2}$ | ερχ.] ● και ερχ.‖Jo32f.: *Rpl* Chr Eu Ir^{1+1v} *L*fl vg^{7} PsAu^{1} *S*' *Geo*^{1} — και εμεινεν(μενον)‖Jo32(33): *l*183 (Eu) Hip *S*scj — *om*: *Cs Geo*^{B} — *txt*: ℵB *L*'[ek] Au PsAu^{1} Hil Ir *C*b | επ] εις‖Mk: D^{s} *pc* Eu Ir **17** φω. + εγενετο‖pLk935: *l*49 *L*vg^{1} *S*p^{3} *C*b$^{⟨1⟩}$ — + ηκουσθη‖218: *L*h *S*sc | του ουρανου‖Lk: W Ir(εξ ουρ.) *L*bh vg^{1} Ir

Mk 1,10 εκ] απο‖Mt: *Rpl* — *txt*: 𝔥⟨Δ⟩ Θ-28-565 φ-*l*547 D W *pc l*20 *l*44 *l*47 *l*49 | σχ.] ηνοιγμενους‖**p**: D *L*[ek] *S*[sc]j *Cs Geo* | πν. + του θεου‖Mt: 700 *pc l*251 *L*[ek] g^{2} vg^{1} Or *Arm Geo*^{2} | ως] ωσει‖←: 33-892 ΣΦ-565 λ φ σM P W 157 1342 *pm* | ∼ καταβ. (+ απο του ουρανου) ως περ.‖← (Jo32): Σ σ1402 (W) 157 | εις] επ‖p: *Rpl* — *txt*: B φ⟨983⟩ D 837 | εις] και μενον επ‖Jo: ℵ-33 σ27-71-179 W *pc l*253 *L*blr^{2}tz30 vg$^{⟨1⟩}$ *C*b^{7} *Aeth* | αυτ. + και μενον‖←: *L*ff^{2} **11** και + ιδου‖Mt: 565 1574 *C*s$^{3:5}$ | ● *om* εγεν.‖←: ℵ* Θ-28-565 D 1574 *l*184 *L*[ek] ff^{2}t *Geo*^{1} | ουρ. + ηκουσθη‖Mt 218: Θ-28-565 *Geo*^{1} — + λεγουσα‖Mt: σ179 1342 *pc L*[ek] cfl *S*[sc]p^{5}j *C*b^{1}

Lk 3,22 ως] ωσει‖Mt: *Rpl* — *txt*: 𝔓$^{4.75v}$ 𝔥⟨892⟩-**0124** σ692-1194 D 1012 Or | επ] εις‖Mk: D | εξ] εκ του‖p: D | ουρανων‖p: **0124** φ69 **047** *pc L*l

Jo 1,32 ∼ ως περ. κατ.‖Mk: ℵ (Ep) *L*e abr^{1} vg *S*c | ως περ.] εν ειδει περιστερας‖Lk: Ep | ως] ωσει‖Mt: 𝔓^{66} *Rpl* — *txt*: 𝔓^{75} 𝔥⟨892-1241⟩CW^{s}-**083** N-700 λ22 φ124-174-230-*l*547$^{1:2}$ σ7-659-945-1010-1207-1293 A E F G H S V Γ Θ Ψ Ω 565 *pm* Or **33** *om* και μεν.‖Mk Lk Mt: 565 Or *L*Eu

---

Mt315 *cf.* Iu dial. 88,3: ... κατελθόντος τοῦ Ἰησοῦ ἐπὶ τὸ ὕδωρ καὶ πῦρ ἀνήφθη ἐν τῷ Ἰορδάνῃ, καὶ ἀναδύντος αὐτοῦ ἀπὸ τοῦ ὕδατος ὡς περιστερὰν τὸ ἅγιον πνεῦμα ἐπιπτῆναι ἐπ' αὐτὸν ἔγραψαν οἱ ἀπόστολοι αὐτοῦ τούτου τοῦ Χριστοῦ ἡμῶν.

Mt316f.p *cf.* EH frgm.2 (Hi Is ad 112): Factum est autem cum ascendisset dominus de aqua, descendit fons omnis spiritus sancti, et requievit super eum, et dixit illi: 'fili mi, in omnibus prophetis exspectabam te, ut venires et requiescerem in te. Tu es enim requies mea, tu es filius meus primogenitus, qui regnas in sempiternum.'

Lk322 *cf.* Iu dial. 88,8; 103,6: ... τὸ πνεῦμα οὖν τὸ ἅγιον καὶ διὰ τοὺς ἀνθρώπους, ὡς προέφην, ἐν εἴδει περιστερᾶς ἐπέπτη αὐτῷ, καὶ φωνὴ ἐκ τῶν οὐρανῶν ἅμα ἐληλύθει, ἥτις καὶ διὰ Δαυειδ λεγομένη, ὡς ἀπὸ προσώπου αὐτοῦ λέγοντος ὅπερ αὐτῷ ἀπὸ τοῦ πατρὸς ἔμελλε λέγεσθαι· 'υἱός μου εἶ σύ, ἐγὼ σήμερον γεγέννηκά σε'... (103,6) καὶ γὰρ οὗτος ὁ διάβολος ἅμα τῷ ἀναβῆναι αὐτὸν ἀπὸ τοῦ ποταμοῦ τοῦ Ἰορδάνου, τῆς φωνῆς αὐτῷ λεχθείσης· 'υἱός μου εἶ σύ, ἐγὼ σήμερον γεγέννηκά σε' ἐν τοῖς ἀπομνημονεύμασι τῶν ἀποστόλων γέγραπται προσελθὼν αὐτῷ καὶ πειράζων ...

	Matth	Mark	Luk	Jo
Is421 442 Ps27	λέγουσα· οὗτός ἐστιν **ὁ υἱός μου ὁ ἀγαπητός, ἐν ᾧ εὐδόκησα.**	138. **σὺ εἶ ὁ υἱός μου ὁ ἀγαπητός, ἐν** σοὶ **εὐδόκησα.**	γενέσθαι· **υἱός μου εἶ σύ, ἐγὼ σήμερον γεγέννηκά σε.**	ρηκα ὅτι οὗτός ἐστιν ὁ υἱὸς τοῦ θεοῦ.

(7)

19. Die Ahnentafel Jesu. *The Genealogy of Jesus.* 1.

1 1–16 *(1.)*

[1] *Βίβλος γενέσεως Ἰησοῦ Χριστοῦ υἱοῦ Δαυιδ υἱοῦ Αβρααμ.* [2] *Αβρααμ ἐγέννησεν τὸν Ισαακ, Ισαακ δὲ ἐγέννησεν τὸν Ιακωβ, Ιακωβ δὲ ἐγέννησεν τὸν Ἰούδαν καὶ τοὺς ἀδελφοὺς αὐτοῦ,* [3] *Ἰούδας δὲ ἐγέννησεν τὸν Φαρες καὶ τὸν Ζαρε ἐκ τῆς Θαμαρ, Φαρες δὲ ἐγέννησεν τὸν Εσρωμ, Εσρωμ δὲ ἐγέννησεν τὸν Αραμ,* [4] *Αραμ δὲ ἐγέννησεν τὸν Αμμιναδαβ, Αμμιναδαβ δὲ ἐγέννησεν τὸν Ναασσων, Ναασσων δὲ ἐγέννησεν τὸν Σαλμων,* [5] *Σαλμων δὲ ἐγέννησεν τὸν Βοες ἐκ τῆς Ραχαβ, Βοες δὲ ἐγέννησεν τὸν Ιωβηδ ἐκ τῆς Ρουθ, Ιωβηδ δὲ ἐγέννησεν τὸν Ιεσσαι,* [6] *Ιεσσαι δὲ ἐγέννησεν τὸν Δαυιδ τὸν βασιλέα. Δαυιδ δὲ ἐγέννησεν τὸν Σολομῶνα ἐκ τῆς τοῦ Οὐρίου,* [7] *Σολομὼν δὲ ἐγέννησεν τὸν Ροβοαμ, Ροβοαμ δὲ ἐγέννησεν τὸν Αβια, Αβια δὲ ἐγέννησεν τὸν Ασαφ,* [8] *Ασαφ δὲ ἐγέννησεν τὸν Ιωσαφατ, Ιωσαφατ δὲ ἐγέννησεν τὸν Ιωραμ, Ιωραμ δὲ ἐγέννησεν τὸν Ὀζίαν,* [9] *Ὀζίας δὲ ἐγέννησεν τὸν Ιωαθαμ, Ιωαθαμ δὲ ἐγέννησεν τὸν Αχαζ, Αχαζ δὲ ἐγέννησεν τὸν Ἑζεκίαν,* [10] *Ἑζεκίας δὲ ἐγέννησεν τὸν Μανασσῆ, Μανασσῆς δὲ ἐγέννησεν τὸν Αμως, Αμως δὲ ἐγέννησεν τὸν Ἰωσίαν,* [11] *Ἰωσίας δὲ ἐγέννησεν τὸν Ἰεχονίαν καὶ τοὺς ἀδελφοὺς*

1Chr317 — 31-34: 1Chr21-15 — 32-33: Rth418-22

Luk 3 23–38

[23] Καὶ αὐτὸς ἦν Ἰησοῦς ἀρχόμενος ὡσεὶ ἐτῶν τριάκοντα, ὢν υἱός, ὡς ἐνομίζετο, Ιωσηφ, τοῦ Ηλι [24] τοῦ Μαθθατ τοῦ Λευι τοῦ Μελχι τοῦ Ιανναι τοῦ Ιωσηφ [25] τοῦ Ματταθίου τοῦ Αμως τοῦ Ναουμ τοῦ Εσλι τοῦ Ναγγαι [26] τοῦ Μααθ τοῦ Ματταθίου τοῦ Σεμειν τοῦ Ιωσηχ τοῦ Ιωδα [27] τοῦ Ιωαναν τοῦ Ρησα τοῦ Ζοροβαβελ τοῦ Σαλαθιηλ τοῦ Νηρι [28] τοῦ Μελχι τοῦ Αδδι τοῦ Κωσαμ τοῦ Ελμαδαμ τοῦ Ηρ [29] τοῦ Ἰησοῦ τοῦ Ελιαζερ τοῦ Ιωριμ τοῦ Μαθθατ τοῦ Λευι [30] τοῦ Συμεων τοῦ Ἰούδα τοῦ Ιωσηφ τοῦ Ιωναμ τοῦ Ελιακιμ [31] τοῦ Μελεα τοῦ Μεννα τοῦ Ματταθα τοῦ Ναθαμ τοῦ Δαυιδ [32] τοῦ Ιεσσαι τοῦ Ιωβηδ τοῦ Βοος τοῦ Σαλα τοῦ Ναασσων [33] τοῦ Αμιναδαβ

Mt 3,17 ουτ. εστ.] συ ει‖pPs27: D^{s} Ir *La* *S*scj

Mk 1,11 συ ει] ουτος εστιν‖Mt: σ179 *pc l*47 *l*183 *l*184 Ep | σοι] ω‖←: *R* 579 1071 λ872-1278 φ230-*l*547 **σ**-945-1010 *al l*49 *l*184 Ep(εφ ον) *L*bdfz vg' Hi *S*h^{m},j *C* *Arm*^{pc} — *txt*: 𝔊' ΘΣ-28-565-700 **λ**-22 **φ** σM-7-267-1082-1391 D K P U Ω **074** *pl* *L*vl'[ek] t vg^{1} Am *S*'[sc] *Arm*'

Lk 3,22 γεν. + λεγουσαν‖Mt: *Rpl* *L*fff^{2}g^{2}qz30 *S*'j *C*b^{1} — + προς αυτον λεγ.: Λ **φ**⟨124-788⟩ *pc* — *txt*: 𝔓^{4} 𝔊⟨33⟩-**0124** σ990-1424 D *L*' Am *S*s[c] *C*' | υιος—γεγ. σε] ◆ συ ει ο υιος μου ο αγαπητος εν σοι(ω) ευδοκησα‖p: 𝔓^{4}*Rpl* (X *pc*) Eu^{2}(^{1}) *L*'(f) Au^{1} *S*h('j *C*') *Arm* *Geo*(*om* ο αγ.) — ουτος εστιν ο υιος μ. ο αγ. εν ω(σοι) ευδ.‖Mt: 1574 (*L*r^{2}) *C*b^{1} — *txt*‖Ps27: D APP CAp **C**l DAp Dgn EEb↓ Iu↓ Meth *L*ab(*om* ει)cff^{2}lr^{1} Amst Au^{4} PsAu Fau Hil Iuv Lac Tyc **23** *om* 23-38‖Mk Mt: 579 | *om* ωσει ετ. τρ.‖p: 213 | Ιω. + του Ιακωβ‖Mt: 1604 σ1194 D Θ *S*j | *om* του Ηλι—^{38}του θεου‖Mk Mt: W | *om* του Ηλι‖Mt: D 4 273 *L*c(*om* του Η. ^{24}του Μ. του) *S*j^{c} **24** Ματθατ—^{31}Ναθαμ] Μαθθαν του Ελεαζαρ του Ελιουδ του Ιαχειν του Σαδωκ του Αζωρ του Ελιακειμ του Αβιουδ του Ζοροβαβελ του Σαλαθιηλ του Ιεχονιου του Ιωακειμ του Ελιακειμ του Ιωσεια του Αμως του Μανασση του Εζεκεια του Αχας του Ιωαθαν του Οζεια του Αμασιου του Ιωας του Οχοζιου του Ιωραμ του Ιωσαφαδ του Ασαφ του Αβιουδ του Ροβοαμ του Σολομων‖Mt: D | Ματθ(*vel sim.*)αν‖Mt15: LX-1241 N-544-700 **λ**-1582 **φ**⟨124⟩ σM-1194-1207-1223-1424-1606 D K U Γ Δ *pm* *S*h — Ματθ(*vel sim.*)α‖←: 33 σ517-954 *al l*16 *l*184 *L*r^{2} vg^{2} **30** Ιωραμ‖Mt8: σ1194 *l*14 *C*s$^{1:9}$ **32** Σα.] Σαλμων‖Mt4f. 1Chr211: *Rpl* *L* *S*' *C*b' *Arm*^{pc} — Σαλμαν‖Rth420f.: 1604 λ1-131(-αναν)-1582-2193 **φ**⟨124⟩ Chrn *Arm*' — *txt*: 𝔓^{4} ℵB *S*s[c]j *C*sb^{2} *Aeth*

Jo 1,34 θεου + του ζωντος‖Mt1616: 472 1093

Lk323 *cf.* EEb frgm.1 (Ep haer. 30,13,2): … ἐμφέρεται ὅτι· ἐγένετό τις ἀνὴρ ὀνόματι Ἰησοῦς, καὶ αὐτὸς ὡς ἐτῶν τριάκοντα, ὅς ἐξελέξατο ἡμᾶς. καὶ ἐλθὼν … (*cf. ad 23.*)

αὐτοῦ ἐπὶ τῆς μετοικεσίας Βαβυλῶνος. [12] Μετὰ δὲ τὴν μετοικεσίαν Βαβυλῶνος Ἰεχονίας ἐγέννησεν τὸν Σελαθιηλ, Σελαθιηλ δὲ ἐγέννησεν τὸν Ζοροβαβελ, [13] Ζοροβαβελ δὲ ἐγέννησεν τὸν Αβιουδ, Αβιουδ δὲ ἐγέννησεν τὸν Ελιακιμ, Ελιακιμ δὲ ἐγέννησεν τὸν Αζωρ, [14] Αζωρ δὲ ἐγέννησεν τὸν Σαδωκ, Σαδωκ δὲ ἐγέννησεν τὸν Αχιμ, Αχιμ δὲ ἐγέννησεν τὸν Ελιουδ, [15] Ελιουδ δὲ ἐγέννησεν τὸν Ελεαζαρ, Ελεαζαρ δὲ ἐγέννησεν τὸν Μαθθαν, Μαθθαν δὲ ἐγέννησεν τὸν Ιακωβ, [16] Ιακωβ δὲ ἐγέννησεν τὸν Ιωσηφ τὸν ἄνδρα Μαρίας, ἐξ ἧς ἐγεννήθη Ἰησοῦς ὁ λεγόμενος Χριστός.

τοῦ Αδμιν τοῦ Αρνι τοῦ Εσρωμ τοῦ Φαρες τοῦ Ἰούδα [34] τοῦ Ιακωβ τοῦ Ισαακ τοῦ Αβρααμ τοῦ Θαρα τοῦ Ναχωρ [35] τοῦ Σερουχ τοῦ Ραγαυ τοῦ Φαλεκ τοῦ Εβερ τοῦ Σαλα [36] τοῦ Καιναμ τοῦ Αρφαξαδ τοῦ Σημ τοῦ Νωε τοῦ Λαμεχ [37] τοῦ Μαθουσαλα τοῦ Ενωχ τοῦ Ιαρετ τοῦ Μαλελεηλ τοῦ Καιναμ [38] τοῦ Ενως τοῦ Σηθ τοῦ Αδαμ τοῦ θεοῦ.

34-35: 1Chr1 24-27

36-38: 1Chr1 1-4

(8)

20. Die Versuchung Jesu. *The Temptation.*

Matth 4 1-11

[1] Τότε ὁ Ἰησοῦς ἀνήχθη εἰς τὴν ἔρημον ὑπὸ τοῦ πνεύματος πειρασθῆναι ὑπὸ τοῦ διαβόλου. [2] καὶ νηστεύσας **ἡμέρας τεσσεράκοντα καὶ τεσσεράκοντα νύκτας** ὕστερον ἐπείνασεν.

[3] καὶ προσελθὼν αὐτῷ ὁ πειράζων εἶπεν· εἰ υἱὸς εἶ τοῦ θεοῦ, εἰπὲ ἵνα οἱ λίθοι οὗτοι ἄρτοι γένωνται. [4] ὁ δὲ ἀποκριθεὶς εἶπεν· γέγραπται·

Mark 1 12-13

[12] Καὶ εὐθὺς τὸ πνεῦμα αὐτὸν ἐκβάλλει εἰς τὴν ἔρημον. [13] καὶ ἦν ἐν τῇ ἐρήμῳ τεσσεράκοντα ἡμέρας πειραζόμενος ὑπὸ τοῦ σατανᾶ, καὶ ἦν μετὰ τῶν θηρίων,

Luk 4 1-13

[1] Ἰησοῦς δὲ πλήρης πνεύματος ἁγίου ὑπέστρεψεν ἀπὸ τοῦ Ἰορδάνου, καὶ ἤγετο ἐν τῷ πνεύματι ἐν τῇ ἐρήμῳ [2] ἡμέρας τεσσεράκοντα πειραζόμενος ὑπὸ τοῦ διαβόλου. καὶ οὐκ ἔφαγεν οὐδὲν ἐν ταῖς ἡμέραις ἐκείναις, καὶ συντελεσθεισῶν αὐτῶν ἐπείνασεν.

[3] εἶπεν δὲ αὐτῷ ὁ διάβολος· εἰ υἱὸς εἶ τοῦ θεοῦ, εἰπὲ τῷ λίθῳ τούτῳ ἵνα γένηται ἄρτος. [4] καὶ ἀπεκρίθη πρὸς αὐτὸν ὁ Ἰησοῦς· γέγραπται ὅτι

Ex 24 18 *etc.* 1Rg 19 8

Mt 4,1 ∼ υπο τ. πν. εις τ. ερ.‖Lk: ℵ-892 **σ**-349 K 157 Ath *S*scpj *Geo*[1] **2** *om* κ. τεσσ. νυ.‖p: **λ** σ27-1606 *S*c | ● ∼ νυ. τεσσ.‖2a: *Rpl L S*h — *txt*: ℵ-892 D *L*Au (∼ τεσσ. ημ. κ. τεσσ. νυ. *S*spj) *Aeth* **3** ● ∼ προσελθ. ο πειρ. ειπ. αυτω *cf.* 8 19 13 10.27 Lk: 𝔥⟨L⟩-*l*1355 700 **λ**-1582 **ϕ**-174-*l*547 σ1391 D'(-ηλθεν ... και ειπ.) W 157 *L*ff[1]lz vg' Au *S*p *C*b'([2] *om* αυτω) *Δ*a — *txt*: *Rpl L*vl' vg[5] Sed *S*'j *C*s[7+2v] *Δ*n'([C] *om* αυτω) | ειπ. + αυτω *cf.*←: *L*abcdg[1.2]h30 vg[5] *S*scj *C*s *Δ*n[L] **4** δε + Ιησους‖p: ϕ983-1689 (∼ απεκ. δε ο: D 372; *et om* ο: 372) *L*bcfg[1]h *S*sc *Aeth* | ειπ. + αυτω‖p: 157 *pc L*c vg[3] Ar *S*scj[c] *C*b⟨7⟩ | γεγ. + οτι‖p6: 700 ϕ1689 **σ**⟨954⟩-349 713 *L*vg[1] *S*,j *Geo*[1] — + γαρ(+ οτι)‖(p)6p.10: 471 *L*(30) vg[2]

Mk 1,12 πν. + το αγιον‖Lk: D **13** ∼ ημ. τεσσ.‖Mt Lk Ex 24 18 34 28 Dt 9 9 *etc.* 1R 19 8: *Rpl L*cff[2] vg[1] *S* — *txt*: 𝔥⟨Δ⟩ ϕ983-1689 σ349-517 W Or *L*vl'[ek]r[1]t vg' *Geo Aeth* | ημ. + και τεσσ. νυκτας(∼ νυ. τε.)‖Mt(Ex Dt 1Rg←): 𝔥⟨ℵBΔ⟩ **ϕ**⟨69-124⟩ (σM **047**) 837 (*pc*) Eu *L*(c)lr[1.2]z vg⟨1⟩ (*S*h[m]) *C*b(*om* τεσσ.[2]) *Aeth* | σατ.] διαβολου‖p: 892 Θ σ179 *L*g[2]

Lk 3,33 Αδμιν τ. Αρνι] Αραμ‖Mt 3f.: 33 1071 σ7-267-659-1194(-αβ)-1424 A D E G H U Π Ω *al l*184 *L*' *S*p *Geo*[2] — Αδμ. τ. Αραμ (+ του Ιωραμ)‖Mt 3f.(8): {} ϕ174-(230) **0102** *pc* (*pc*) — Αραμ του Αδμ. τ. Αρνι (+ του Ιωραμ)‖←: 1604 λ1-(22)-131-(1278) Θ (*pc*) *Arm Geo*[1] — Αραμ του Ιωραμ‖←: *Rpl* Chrn *Le* b *S*h — *txt*: {𝔓[4]} ℵBLX-1241 1604 λ1582-2193 **ϕ**(Αρηι) Γ157 (Αρμιν: *S*s[c]j) *C* **4,1** αγ.] ων‖p: Ath | ∼ εις την ερημον εν τ. πν.‖Mt: σ71-692 | εν τ. πν.] υπο του πνευματος‖Mt: N-700 *L*ac30 vg[2] Or — *om*‖p: 107 *L*b | εν τ. ερ.] εις την ερμον‖Mt Mk 12: *Rpl* PsAth Bas PsBas Ddy Thd[C] *Le* cflr[2] vg' Or *S C*s[3]b — *txt*: 𝔓[4.7] 𝔥⟨33⟩ σ990 D *L* vl'r[1]30 vg[11] Or *C*s[6] **2** τεσσ. + και νυκτας τεσσ.‖Mt: σ71-692 Γ 1047 *C*b[2] *Aeth* | πειρασθηναι‖Mt: 472 | διαβ.] σατανα‖Mk: D 243 *Le* r[2](sabula) *S*s[c] | ουδεν + ουδε επιεν‖12 29 17 28p: Λ-(1071) **ϕ**-230-1689 **0116**[v] *pc Arm* | αυτ. + υστερον‖Mt: *Rpl* Cr *L*fff[2]qr[1] *S*' *C*b[6](∼ επειν. υσ.) — *txt*: ℵBLW-579 ϕ788 σ990 D Θ 139 *L*' *S*s[c] *C*' *Arm Aeth* **3** τω—αρ.] ινα οι(ο) λιθοι(-ος) ουτοι(-ος) αρτοι(-ος) γενωνται (-ηται)‖p: D *l*31 *L*r[1.2]z vg[2] (*C*s[1:11]) | ∼ αρ. γεν.‖p: 1555 2145 *L*cf vg⟨2⟩ **4** απεκρ.] αποκριθεις‖p: D 59 *L*vg[1] | *om* πρ. αυτ.‖p: D *pc S*p[1] *C*b[2] | *om* ο I.‖p: Ψ | I. + και ειπεν‖p: σ1424(∼ κ. ειπ. πρ. αυ. ο I.) D(*om* και) 1012 *L*abff[2]lq30 *S*p | γεγρ. + γαρ‖10p Mt 10: ϕ124 | *om* οτι‖p: 579-1241 700-1071 **ϕ** σ1424 D *L*r[1]

	Matth	Luk
Dt 83	**οὐκ ἐπ' ἄρτῳ μόνῳ ζήσεται ὁ ἄνθρωπος, ἀλλ' ἐπὶ παντὶ ῥήματι ἐκπορευομένῳ διὰ στόματος θεοῦ.**	**οὐκ ἐπ' ἄρτῳ μόνῳ ζήσεται ὁ ἄνθρωπος.**
	[5] τότε παραλαμβάνει αὐτὸν ὁ διάβολος εἰς τὴν ἁγίαν πόλιν, καὶ ἔστησεν αὐτὸν ἐπὶ τὸ πτερύγιον τοῦ ἱεροῦ, [6] καὶ λέγει αὐτῷ· εἰ υἱὸς εἶ τοῦ θεοῦ, βάλε σεαυτὸν	*[9] ἤγαγεν δὲ αὐτὸν εἰς Ἰερουσαλημ καὶ ἔστησεν ἐπὶ τὸ πτερύγιον τοῦ ἱεροῦ, καὶ εἶπεν αὐτῷ· εἰ υἱὸς εἶ τοῦ θεοῦ, βάλε σεαυτὸν ἐντεῦθεν*
Ps 91 11f.	κάτω· γέγραπται γὰρ ὅτι **τοῖς ἀγγέλοις αὐτοῦ ἐντελεῖται περὶ σοῦ** καὶ	*κάτω· [10] γέγραπται γὰρ ὅτι* ***τοῖς ἀγγέλοις αὐτοῦ ἐντελεῖται περὶ σοῦ τοῦ διαφυλάξαι σε,*** *[11] καὶ ὅτι*
Dt 616	**ἐπὶ χειρῶν ἀροῦσίν σε, μήποτε προσκόψῃς πρὸς λίθον τὸν πόδα σου.** [7] ἔφη αὐτῷ ὁ Ἰησοῦς· πάλιν γέγραπται· **οὐκ ἐκπειράσεις κύριον τὸν θεόν σου.**	***ἐπὶ χειρῶν ἀροῦσίν σε, μήποτε προσκόψῃς πρὸς λίθον τὸν πόδα σου.*** *[12] καὶ ἀποκριθεὶς εἶπεν αὐτῷ ὁ Ἰησοῦς ὅτι εἴρηται·* ***οὐκ ἐκπειράσεις κύριον τὸν θεόν σου.***
	[8] πάλιν παραλαμβάνει αὐτὸν ὁ διάβολος εἰς ὄρος ὑψηλὸν λίαν, καὶ δείκνυσιν αὐτῷ πάσας τὰς βασιλείας τοῦ κόσμου καὶ τὴν δόξαν αὐτῶν, [9] καὶ εἶπεν αὐτῷ· ταῦτά σοι πάντα δώσω,	[5] καὶ ἀναγαγὼν αὐτὸν ἔδειξεν αὐτῷ πάσας τὰς βασιλείας τῆς οἰκουμένης ἐν στιγμῇ χρόνου. [6] καὶ εἶπεν αὐτῷ ὁ διάβολος· σοὶ δώσω τὴν ἐξουσίαν ταύτην ἅπασαν καὶ τὴν
	cf. v. 8 ↑	δόξαν αὐτῶν, ὅτι ἐμοὶ παραδέδοται καὶ ᾧ ἐὰν θέλω δίδωμι αὐτήν·
	ἐὰν πεσὼν προσκυνήσῃς μοι.	[7] σὺ οὖν ἐὰν προσκυνήσῃς ἐνώπιον ἐμοῦ, ἔσται σοῦ πᾶσα.
	[10] τότε λέγει αὐτῷ ὁ Ἰησοῦς· ὕπαγε, σατανᾶ·	[8] καὶ ἀποκριθεὶς ὁ Ἰησοῦς εἶπεν αὐτῷ·
Dt 59 613 1020	γέγραπται γάρ· **κύριον τὸν θεόν σου προσκυνήσεις καὶ αὐτῷ** μόνῳ **λατρεύσεις.**	γέγραπται· **προσκυνήσεις κύριον τὸν θεόν σου καὶ αὐτῷ** μόνῳ **λατρεύσεις.**

Mt 4,5 εστησ.] ◆ ιστησιν‖5a: *Rpl Shj* — *txt*(‖p): ℵBCZ-33-*l*1355 **λ**-1582 D P Eu *S*' **6** σεαυ. + εντευθεν‖p: *C* Σ Θ Eu PsIg *L*Ar *S*sh^{m}j *C*s(∼ κατω εντ.)b *Arm Geo*^{1} **8** δεικ.] εδειξεν‖**p**: D 372 | τ. κοσ.] της γης *cf.* 1725 Ap172: 1093 *S*h **9** ειπ.] ● λεγει‖6.8: *Rpl* — *txt*: ℵBCZ-33 **φ**⟨124⟩-174-*l*547 D *L Aeth* **10** υπαγε + οπισω μου(*om*)‖**16**23 Mk833: *Rpl* Ath Iu *L*bhl(acff^{1}g$^{1.2}$z vg^7) Am *S*s(μου] σου)ch$^+$ LG *C*s^{4}b^2 *Arm Geo*^{2} *Δ*n^{HrL} (E^a) — *txt*: ℵBC-892 Σ-700 λ1-22-1582 **φ**⟨346-828-983⟩ σ 71-1223 K P S V W Δ *pc* PsIg Or Pt^A *L*k[e] f vg' Ir Hi Hil Te *S*pj *C*s^{2}b' *Geo*^{1} *Δ*'⟨p⟩ | *om* γαρ‖p: 247 *L*k[e] ff^{1}hz vg^{10} Ir$^{1:2}$ Te

Lk 4,4 ανθρ. + αλλ επι παντι ρηματι(+ εκπορευομενω δια στοματος) θεου‖pDt83: *Rpl* (544-1071 λ118-209 σ1194-1424 157 *pc l*^{pl} Thy) (επι] εν: 892 φ983-1689 D **0102** *pc*) *L S*' (*C*b^{12}) *Arm* (*Aeth*) — *txt*: ℵBLW-1241 φ788 *S*s[c] *C*' **5** ∼ 9-12.5-8‖p: *L*(a)bcflqr^1 vg^1 Am | αυτον + ο διαβολος‖p: *Rpl* Cr *L*' Hil *S*h *C*b^2 — + ο σατανας‖p: *S*' — *txt*: ℵBLW-1241 700 λ1-131-1582- 2193 σ990 D *pc* Cr *L*e (a) *C*' *Arm* | εδει. *prm* εις ορος υψηλον (+ λιαν)‖**p**: *Rpl* (**φ** σ990 D *pc*) (*om* υψ.: W) *L*e(=W) fff^{2}qr^2(clr^{1v} vg^4 Hil) *S*' *C*s^5(^{1v}) (^{1} εις + το, *om* υψ.)b^9 — *txt*: ℵBL-1241 Cr *L*bz vg' *S*s[c] *C*s^{3}b' | της οικ.] του κοσμου‖p: 1241 D *pc* Or *L*fμ Or — της γης‖Mt1725 Ap172: W Or **6** αυτων + εαν προσκυνησης μοι‖p: φ124 | αυτην] αυτα‖p: 1604 Cr Ir *L*⟨a vg^1⟩ **7** προσκ.] πεσων πρ.‖**p**: 700-1604 **λλ**⟨118-209⟩ φ346 σ1223 157 *al l*17 Cr *L*vl⟨cr^{2}z⟩r^1 vg^3 *C*s$^{1:11}$b^1 *Arm* — πρ. μοι‖p: ℵ | σου] σοι‖p: 28-700 φ346 σ1194-1675 157 *pm* Cr *S*s[c] *C* | πασα] παντα‖p: W-579 *al* Cr *L*vl'⟨e⟩r^1 vg — ταυτα‖p: 1071 *l*51 *L*b(παν. σου ταυ.) — ολα αυτης‖p: 28 **8** ∼ ειπ. αυ. ο Ι.‖Mt7.10: 544 σM^t-517-1223-1424 A K Π *al l*48 *L*vl'(*om* αυ.: l)r^1 *Aeth* — ∼ αυ. ειπ. ο Ι.‖←: *Rpl* (*om* ο: B) — ∼ αυ. ο Ι. ειπ.: Λ-28 σ1606 D Ψ *S*h *Arm* — ∼ ο Ι. αυ. ειπ.: **φ**' — *txt* (*om* αυ.): ℌ⟨B⟩Ξ 1071-1604 **λ**-1582-2193 φ543-826-983 σM^m-990 F 157 *al l*34 *L*(e) fr^{2}z vg *S*' *C*b'(^{2}) | γεγ. *prm* υπαγε σατανα‖p: 98 *C*b^1 — *prm* υπαγε οπισω μου σατανα‖pMt1623 Mk833: *Rpl L*e(*om* μου) blqr^1 *S*h *C*b^7 — *txt*: ℌΞ 700 **λλ** φ788 σ990 D *pc* Or *L*' *S*' *C*' | γεγ. + γαρ‖p: Λ-1071-1604 **φ**⟨788⟩-230 σ7-71-267-659-692-1194 U Δ Ψ **0116** *al L*bq vg^1 | ∼ κυ.—σου προσκ.‖**p**Dt613 1020: ℌΞ Λ-1071-1604 **λ**-1582 **φ**-230 σ7-517-659-990-1606 D F **0116** *al l*48 *l*49 Cr Or *L*' Or *S*' *C*b — *txt*: *Rpl* (προσκυν.] αγαπ.‖1027p: *L*ar^1) *S*s[c] *C*s *Arm*

Mt4sp *cf.* EN frgm.3 (Cod. Evv. 566^m): Τὸ Ἰουδαϊκὸν οὐκ ἔχει· εἰς τὴν ἁγίαν πόλιν, ἀλλ'· ἐν Ιερουσαλημ.

Mt48p *cf.* EH frgm.3 (Or hom. Jr 15,4; Jo 2,12,87): ἄρτι ἔλαβέ με ἡ μήτηρ μου, τὸ ἅγιον πνεῦμα, (+ ἐν μιᾷ τῶν τριχῶν μου : Jo) καὶ ἀν(ἀπ- : Jo)ήνεγκέ με εἰς τὸ ὄρος τὸ μέγα τὸ (*om:* Jo) Θαβωρ.

(Hi Mi *ad* 77): modo tulit me mater mea, sanctus spiritus, in uno capillorum meorum.

(Hi Is *ad* 409ff.; Ez *ad* 1613): modo me tulit(arripuit: Ez) mater mea, spiritus sanctus.

Matth: cf. v. 5–7 ↑

11 τότε ἀφίησιν αὐτὸν ὁ διάβολος, καὶ ἰδοὺ ἄγγελοι προσῆλθον καὶ διηκόνουν αὐτῷ.

Mark: καὶ οἱ ἄγγελοι διηκόνουν αὐτῷ.

Luk: 9 ἤγαγεν δὲ αὐτὸν εἰς Ιερουσαλημ καὶ ἔστησεν ἐπὶ τὸ πτερύγιον τοῦ ἱεροῦ, καὶ εἶπεν αὐτῷ· εἰ υἱὸς εἶ τοῦ θεοῦ, βάλε σεαυτὸν ἐντεῦθεν κάτω· 10 γέγραπται γὰρ ὅτι **τοῖς ἀγγέλοις αὐτοῦ ἐντελεῖται περὶ σοῦ τοῦ διαφυλάξαι σε,** 11 καὶ ὅτι **ἐπὶ χειρῶν ἀροῦσίν σε, μήποτε προσκόψῃς πρὸς λίθον τὸν πόδα σου.** 12 καὶ ἀποκριθεὶς εἶπεν αὐτῷ ὁ Ἰησοῦς ὅτι εἴρηται· **οὐκ ἐκπειράσεις κύριον τὸν θεόν σου.** 13 καὶ συντελέσας πάντα πειρασμὸν ὁ διάβολος ἀπέστη ἀπ' αὐτοῦ ἄχρι καιροῦ.

Ps 91 11f.
Dt 6 16

(9)

21. Jesu Auftreten in Galiläa. *Jesus' First Preaching in Galilee.*

Matth 4 12–17 — **Mark 1** 14–15 — **Luk 4** 14–15

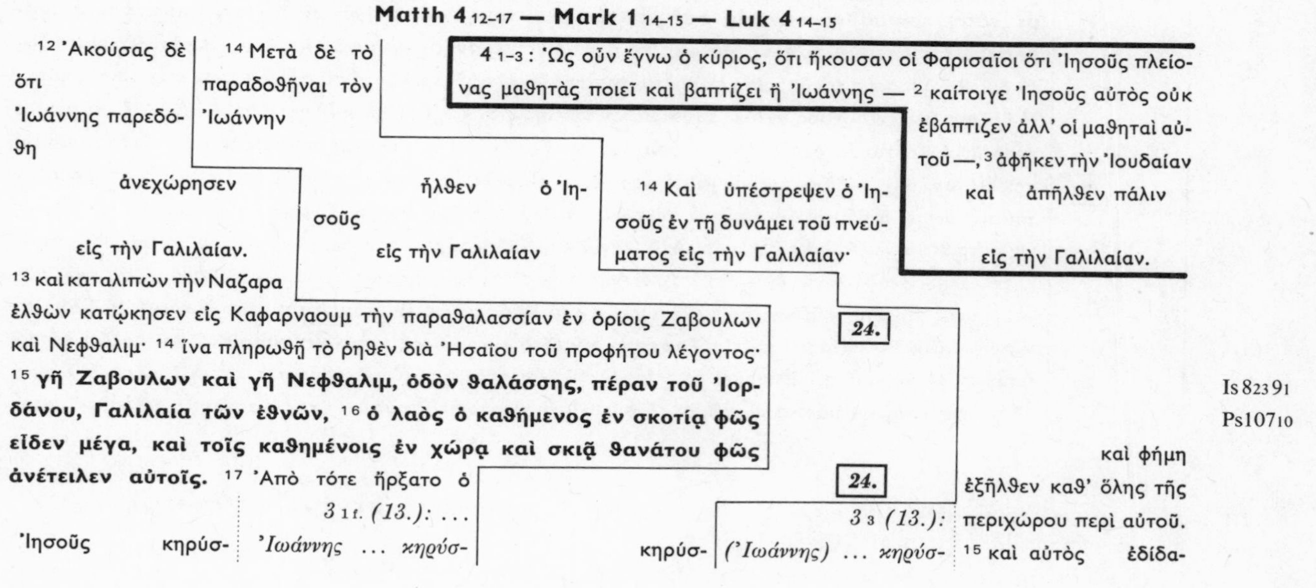

Matth: 12 Ἀκούσας δὲ ὅτι Ἰωάννης παρεδόθη ἀνεχώρησεν εἰς τὴν Γαλιλαίαν. 13 καὶ καταλιπὼν τὴν Ναζαρα ἐλθὼν κατῴκησεν εἰς Καφαρναουμ τὴν παραθαλασσίαν ἐν ὁρίοις Ζαβουλων καὶ Νεφθαλιμ· 14 ἵνα πληρωθῇ τὸ ῥηθὲν διὰ Ἠσαΐου τοῦ προφήτου λέγοντος· 15 **γῆ Ζαβουλων καὶ γῆ Νεφθαλιμ, ὁδὸν θαλάσσης, πέραν τοῦ Ἰορδάνου, Γαλιλαία τῶν ἐθνῶν,** 16 **ὁ λαὸς ὁ καθήμενος ἐν σκοτίᾳ φῶς εἶδεν μέγα, καὶ τοῖς καθημένοις ἐν χώρᾳ καὶ σκιᾷ θανάτου φῶς ἀνέτειλεν αὐτοῖς.** 17 Ἀπὸ τότε ἤρξατο ὁ Ἰησοῦς κηρύσ-

3 1f. (13.): ... Ἰωάννης ... κηρύσ-

Mark: 14 Μετὰ δὲ τὸ παραδοθῆναι τὸν Ἰωάννην ἦλθεν ὁ Ἰησοῦς εἰς τὴν Γαλιλαίαν κηρύσ-

24.

3 3 (13.): (Ἰωάννης) ... κηρύσ-

Luk: 14 Καὶ ὑπέστρεψεν ὁ Ἰησοῦς ἐν τῇ δυνάμει τοῦ πνεύματος εἰς τὴν Γαλιλαίαν·

24.

καὶ φήμη ἐξῆλθεν καθ' ὅλης τῆς περιχώρου περὶ αὐτοῦ. 15 καὶ αὐτὸς ἐδίδα-

Jo: 4 1–3: Ὡς οὖν ἔγνω ὁ κύριος, ὅτι ἤκουσαν οἱ Φαρισαῖοι ὅτι Ἰησοῦς πλείονας μαθητὰς ποιεῖ καὶ βαπτίζει ἢ Ἰωάννης — 2 καίτοιγε Ἰησοῦς αὐτὸς οὐκ ἐβάπτιζεν ἀλλ' οἱ μαθηταὶ αὐτοῦ —, 3 ἀφῆκεν τὴν Ἰουδαίαν καὶ ἀπῆλθεν πάλιν εἰς τὴν Γαλιλαίαν.

Is 8 23 9 1
Ps 107 10

Mt 4,11 *om* ιδου ‖ Mk: Eu *Ss* **12** δε + ο Ιησους ‖ p: *Rpl* (*om* ο: 892 σ1424 *l*184) Ep *L*vl'30 vg⁹ Gau Hil *S*' (κυριος l.: j) *C*b⁹ — *txt*: ℌ‹L›C* 700 ϕ*l*547 σ945 D *pc* Eu Or *Lk*[e] ff¹ vg' Au *Ss C*' **13** ελθ. κατ.] ηλθεν ‖ Lk4 31 Mk1 21: Ep¹:¹³ *Ss* **14** ινα] οπως ‖ 2 23 8 17 13 35: 213 Eu | δια] υπο ‖ 2 2 31 1 22 2 15: Σ 697 **16** ● σκοτει ‖ Lk1 79 Is9 1: *Rpl* Eu Or'(¹-τω) — *txt*: ℵᵇB D(*prm* τη) W

Mk 1,13 *om* οι ‖ Mt: 33-579 Σ σM-7-267-349-517-659-1606 A **074** 157 *al l*34 *l*48 *l*184 **14** μετα δε] ● και με.: B D' *L*aff² vg¹(+ δε) *Ss*[c] *C*b⁴ *Geo*² — κ. εγενετο με.: *Lc* vg¹

Lk 4,9 εστ. + αυτον ‖ p: *Rpl L' S C Arm*ᵖᶜ — *txt*: ℌ‹33-1241›Ξ 700 σ990 1093 *Le* Or *Arm*' | ειπ.] λεγει ‖ p: σ‹349›-1188 | *om* εντευ. ‖ p: 28-544 σ7-659-1194 E G H *pc l*184 *Lz* vg¹ Or — ∼ κατω εντ. ‖ p: ϕ69-788-983 σ1424 *pc C* — *om* κατω: 251 *L*acl *Ss*[c] **10** *om* του—σε ‖ p: 243 *L*bz Or **11** *om* οτι ‖ p: *Rpl L*br¹ Or *S' C'* — *om* και οτι: 16 *L*alz Or *C*b¹ *Geo* — *om* και: σ990 *Le* cff²30 vg³ — *txt*: ℌ‹579›Ξ 1604 λ‹131›-1582 ϕ σM-1223-1424 A K Θ Ψ **0116** 157 *mu L*fqr² vg' *Sh C*b⁷ **12** *om* οτι ‖ p: ℵᵃW σ990 D *pc l*184 *L*'‹a› (οτι] και: ff²) *Ss*[c]p | ειρ.] γεγραπται ‖ p: W D *pc L*vl‹r² z›r¹ Or — *om*: 243 *l*184 *Ss*[c] **14** φημη] η φ. ‖ Mt9 26: 472 *C*sb'(⁷ η ζητησις) **15** εδιδ. + αυτους ‖ Mt13 54 Mk2 13: 1200 *Ss*[c]

Jo 4,1 κυ.] ● Ιησους (*et om* l. 1b): ℵ-1241 (Λ) λ-22 σ1010-1223-1293 D Θ **086** (472) *pm* Chr Ep *L*'(j) ‹vg¹› *S*(cp)hᵗ *C*b'f *Arm* — *txt*: 𝔓⁶⁶·⁷⁵ *Rpl* Cr Non *L*fq *Ss*(*om* l. 1b)hᵐ *C*sb¹ *Geo* **3** Ιου. + γην ‖ 3 22: λ ϕ σ945 D *pc* Ep *Le* (∼: ad)bff²r¹30 *Arm Geo*¹ *Aeth*

σειν καὶ λέγειν· μετανο- εῖτε· ἤγγικεν γὰρ ἡ βασιλεία τῶν οὐρανῶν. cf. v. 17a ↑	*σων ...* *² καὶ λέγων· μετανο-* *εῖτε·* *ἤγγικεν γὰρ ἡ βασιλεία* *τῶν οὐρανῶν.* *cf. v. 2a* ↑	σων τὸ εὐαγγέλιον τοῦ θεοῦ ¹⁵ λέγων, ὅτι πε- πλήρωται ὁ καιρὸς καὶ ἤγγικεν ἡ βασιλεία τοῦ θεοῦ· μετανοεῖτε καὶ πιστεύ- ετε ἐν τῷ εὐαγγελίῳ.	*σων βάπτισμα* *μετανο-* *ίας* *εἰς ἄφεσιν* *ἁμαρτιῶν.*	σκεν ἐν ταῖς συναγω- γαῖς αὐτῶν, δοξαζό- μενος ὑπὸ πάντων.

(10)

22. Verwerfung in Nazareth. *The Rejection at Nazareth.* Luk 4 16–30 **121.**

Is 61 1f. 58 6 — 1Rg 17 9 — **121.**

¹⁶ Καὶ ἦλθεν εἰς Ναζαρα, οὗ ἦν τεθραμμένος, καὶ εἰσῆλθεν κατὰ τὸ εἰωθὸς αὐτῷ ἐν τῇ ἡμέρᾳ τῶν σαββάτων εἰς τὴν συναγωγήν, καὶ ἀνέστη ἀναγνῶναι. ¹⁷ καὶ ἐπεδόθη αὐτῷ βιβλίον τοῦ προφήτου Ἠσαΐου, καὶ ἀναπτύξας τὸ βιβλίον εὗρεν τόπον οὗ ἦν γεγραμμένον· ¹⁸ **πνεῦμα κυρίου ἐπ' ἐμέ, οὗ εἵνεκεν ἔχρισέν με· εὐαγγελίσασθαι πτωχοῖς ἀπέσταλκέν με, κηρύξαι αἰχμαλώτοις ἄφεσιν καὶ τυφλοῖς ἀνάβλεψιν, ἀποστεῖλαι τεθραυσμένους ἐν ἀφέσει,** ¹⁹ **κηρύξαι ἐνιαυτὸν κυρίου δεκτόν.** ²⁰ καὶ πτύξας τὸ βιβλίον ἀποδοὺς τῷ ὑπηρέτῃ ἐκάθισεν· καὶ πάντων οἱ ὀφθαλμοὶ ἐν τῇ συναγωγῇ ἦσαν ἀτενίζοντες αὐτῷ. ²¹ ἤρξατο δὲ λέγειν πρὸς αὐτοὺς ὅτι σήμερον πεπλήρωται ἡ γραφὴ αὕτη ἐν τοῖς ὠσὶν ὑμῶν. ²² καὶ πάντες ἐμαρτύρουν αὐτῷ καὶ ἐθαύμαζον ἐπὶ τοῖς λόγοις τῆς χάριτος τοῖς ἐκπορευομένοις ἐκ τοῦ στόματος αὐτοῦ, καὶ ἔλεγον· οὐχὶ υἱός ἐστιν Ιωσηφ οὗτος; ²³ καὶ εἶπεν πρὸς αὐτούς· πάντως ἐρεῖτέ μοι τὴν παραβολὴν ταύτην· ἰατρέ, θεράπευσον σεαυτόν· ὅσα ἠκούσαμεν γενόμενα εἰς τὴν Καφαρναουμ, ποίησον καὶ ὧδε ἐν τῇ πατρίδι σου. ²⁴ εἶπεν δέ· αμην ὑμῖν λέγω ὅτι οὐδεὶς προφήτης δεκτός ἐστιν ἐν τῇ πατρίδι αὐτοῦ. ²⁵ ἐπ' ἀληθείας δὲ λέγω ὑμῖν ὅτι πολλαὶ χῆραι ἦσαν ἐν ταῖς ἡμέραις Ἠλίου ἐν τῷ Ισραηλ, ὅτε ἐκλείσθη ὁ οὐρανὸς ἐπὶ ἔτη τρία καὶ μῆνας ἕξ, ὡς ἐγένετο λιμὸς μέγας ἐπὶ πᾶσαν τὴν γῆν, ²⁶ καὶ πρὸς οὐδεμίαν αὐτῶν ἐπέμφθη Ἠλίας εἰ μὴ **εἰς Σαρεπτα τῆς Σιδωνίας** πρὸς **γυναῖκα χήραν.** ²⁷ καὶ πολλοὶ λεπροὶ ἦσαν ἐν τῷ Ισραηλ ἐπὶ Ἐλισαίου τοῦ προφήτου, καὶ οὐδεὶς αὐτῶν ἐκαθαρίσθη εἰ μὴ Ναιμαν ὁ Σύρος. ²⁸ καὶ ἐπλήσθησαν πάντες θυμοῦ ἐν τῇ συναγωγῇ ἀκούοντες ταῦτα, ²⁹ καὶ ἀναστάντες ἐξέβαλον αὐτὸν

Mt 4,17 λεγ. + οτι‖Mk: Eu *Lk*[e] | *om* μετ. ... γαρ‖10 7 Mk Lk10 9.11: Cr Iu Or$^{2:6}$ Vic^{A} *Lk*[e] *S*sc — *om* γαρ‖Mk: σ1604 *S*j^{bc} *C*s$^{1:5}$b^{1}

Mk 1,14 ευα. + της βασιλειας (*et om* τ. θε.)‖Mt4 23: *Rpl* (*pc*) *L*vl'[ek] (z30)r^{1} vg'(^{2}) *S*p *C*b^{11} — *txt*: 𝔥⟨Δ⟩ Θ-28-565 λ1-209 ϕ69-788-983 1012 1342 Or *L*bcff^{2}t vg^{1} *S*' *C*' *Arm* **15** λεγ.] ● και λεγ.: *Rpl* *L*lr^{2}z vg'$^{\langle 2\rangle}$ *S*' *C*b' — ● *om*: ℵ* Or *L*(∼ οτι—θε. λεγ.: c) vg^{1} *S*s[c] — *txt*: ℵ^{a} Σ-28-1071 σ267-827-945 A D E F G H S U V Γ Ω **047 074 0133** *al* *l*34 *L*vl'[ek] r^{1}t vg^{1} *C*s^{1}b^{1} | του θ.] των ουρανων‖p: W *Aeth*

Lk 4,16 N.] ● την N.‖Mt4 13: *Rpl* Eu — *txt*: 𝔥⟨33⟩Ξ Λ-700 λ1-131-1582 ϕ788 σ945-990-1223 D Δ Θ *al* *l*184 Cr | εις τ. συν.] εν τη συναγωγη‖p: 1071 *L*acff^{2} vg^{2} | *om* και αν. αναγν.‖p: σ267 *pc* *l*18 *l*33 *l*48 *l*49 *l*183 *l*251 *l*260 *Δ*n^{L} — ∼ ¹⁷και—βιβ. Ησ. τ. προφ. ¹⁶και αν. αναγν.: 1604 λ1-22-131 Θ *l*44 *l*258 *S*s[c]j *Arm* **17** ∼ βιβ. Ησ. τ. πρ.‖3 4 Mt3 3 4 14 *etc.*: *Rpl* *L*vl'r^{1}vg^{1} *S*,j *C*sb^{2} *Δ*' — ο προφητης Ησαιας: D 1654 — *txt*: 𝔥⟨1241⟩Ξ **ϕ**⟨124⟩-*l*547 σ267-990 Θ Ψ *pc* *L*abq vg' Or *Δ*l^{FG} | τοπ.] ● τον τ.: *Rpl* — *om*: *pc* *L*e — *txt*: ℵLWΞ-33 157 *pc* **22** ουχι] ουχ‖Mt Mk: *Rpl* — *om*: Γ — *txt*: 𝔥⟨33-892⟩ N-700 λ1278 **ϕ**⟨124-346-788⟩ σ990 D Ψ 157 *pc* | υι. εστ. Ι. ουτ.] ουτ. εστ. ο υι. Ι.‖p: *Rpl* *L*vl'r^{1}30(∼ ο υι. εστ.: 1 vg')^{7} Au(*om* εστ.) *S*,j *C*s^{1v}b — ο υι. εστ. Ι. ουτ.: 579(∼ Ι. εστ.) **ϕ**⟨124⟩ Cr^{1} (του Ι.) — *txt*: 𝔥'⟨33-892⟩ N(∼ ουτ. εστ. Ι.)-700 ϕ788 D(∼ Ι. εστ.) Cr^{1} *L*e(= D) a(*om* εστ.) *C*s^{8} **23** εις την] εν τη‖Mt11 21p: *Rpl* — εν‖←: 579 NΛ-544 σ945-1223 A K Π *mu* *l*49 *l*53 Ep — εις *cf.* 4 31 7 1 Mt4 13 *etc.*: L **ϕ**⟨983⟩ D — *txt*: 𝔥'⟨33-1241⟩ 700 161 **24** δε + αυτοις‖p: σ990 213 *L*e vg^{1} *S*s[c] *C*b$^{\langle 4\rangle}$ | αμ.] ο Ιησους αμ.‖p: σ990 *L*vl'⟨e afr^{2}⟩r^{1}(+ αμην) vg^{1} — αμ. αμην *cf.* Jo1 51 *etc.*: 700-1604 D **047** *pc* *L*ff^{2} | ● ∼ λεγω υμ. *cf.* **12**37 18 17.29 **21**32 *etc.*: *Rpl* (*om* υμ.: Θ **047**) *L*⟨e⟩ *S*'j — *txt*: Λ-28-700 ϕ230 σ692-1207 A E G H V Γ **0102** *al* *S*h | πατ. αυτ.] ιδια πατ.‖Jo4 44: **047** *l*55 CAp *C*sb^{2} **25** ● *om* οτι *cf.* Mt5 18 6 2 Mk10 15 *etc.*: *Rpl* *L*' *Δ*ad l n^{HgHrS} p — *txt*: 𝔥⟨B-1241⟩X Λ-700-1071-1604 **λ**-1582 **ϕ**⟨124⟩-230-*l*547 σ517-692-945-990-1194-1223 Θ Ψ Ω *mu* *l*53 *l*184 Bas *L*e fl Or *S*,j *Δ*a i^{T} **28** και] οι δε‖6 11: D *L*e *C*s$^{7:8}$ **29** εξεβ.] εξηγαγον‖Mk15 20p: 1071

121. ἔξω τῆς πόλεως, καὶ ἤγαγον αὐτὸν ἕως ὀφρύος τοῦ ὄρους ἐφ' οὗ ἡ πόλις ᾠκοδόμητο αὐτῶν, ὥστε κατακρημνίσαι αὐτόν· 30 αὐτὸς δὲ διελθὼν διὰ μέσου αὐτῶν ἐπορεύετο.

7 30: ἐζήτουν οὖν αὐτὸν πιάσαι, καὶ οὐδεὶς ἐπέβαλεν ἐπ' αὐτὸν τὴν χεῖρα, ὅτι οὔπω ἐληλύθει ἡ ὥρα αὐτοῦ. 10 39: ἐζήτουν οὖν αὐτὸν πάλιν πιάσαι· καὶ ἐξῆλθεν ἐκ τῆς χειρὸς αὐτῶν.

(11)

23. Berufung der ersten Jünger. *The Call of the First Disciples.*

Matth 4 18–22

18 Περιπατῶν δὲ παρὰ τὴν θάλασσαν τῆς Γαλιλαίας εἶδεν δύο ἀδελφούς, Σίμωνα τὸν λεγόμενον Πέτρον καὶ Ἀνδρέαν τὸν ἀδελφὸν αὐτοῦ, βάλλοντας ἀμφίβληστρον εἰς τὴν θάλασσαν· ἦσαν γὰρ ἁλεεῖς. 19 καὶ λέγει αὐτοῖς· δεῦτε ὀπίσω μου, καὶ ποιήσω ὑμᾶς ἁλεεῖς ἀνθρώπων. 20 οἱ δὲ εὐθέως ἀφέντες τὰ δίκτυα ἠκολούθη-

Mark 1 16–20

16 Καὶ παράγων παρὰ τὴν θάλασσαν τῆς Γαλιλαίας εἶδεν Σίμωνα καὶ Ἀνδρέαν τὸν ἀδελφὸν Σίμωνος ἀμφιβάλλοντας ἐν τῇ θαλάσσῃ· ἦσαν γὰρ ἁλεεῖς. 17 καὶ εἶπεν αὐτοῖς ὁ Ἰησοῦς· δεῦτε ὀπίσω μου, καὶ ποιήσω ὑμᾶς γενέσθαι ἁλεεῖς ἀνθρώπων. 18 καὶ εὐθέως ἀφέντες τὰ δίκτυα ἠκολούθη-

5 10 f. (29.): 10 b ... καὶ εἶπεν πρὸς τὸν Σίμωνα ὁ Ἰησοῦς· μὴ φοβοῦ· ἀπὸ τοῦ νῦν ἀνθρώπους ἔσῃ ζωγρῶν ...

1 38 f.: στραφεὶς δὲ ὁ Ἰησοῦς καὶ θεασάμενος αὐτοὺς ἀκολουθοῦντας λέγει αὐτοῖς· τί ζητεῖτε; οἱ δὲ εἶπαν αὐτῷ· ραββι, ...ποῦ μένεις; 39 λέγει αὐτοῖς· ἔρχεσθε καὶ ὄψεσθε. ἦλθαν οὖν καὶ εἶδαν ποῦ μένει, καὶ παρ'

Mt 4,18 περιπ.] παραγων‖p: D Eu *Lvl*[e]⟨flz⟩ *S*sj Eu | περ. δε] και περ.‖p: L 259 *S*scpj | *om* δυο—λεγ.‖p: σ1194 **19** αυτ. + ο Ιησους‖Mk: C^2 157 Cr *Lach* vg^5 PsAu *S*cp | υμ. + γενεσθαι‖Mk: $ℵ^b$-33 D 157 *pc* Cr *L*'⟨h⟩ Euch *Sp*

Mk 1,16 κ. παρ.] περιπατων δε‖p: *Rpl S*h^t — κ. περιπ.‖p: *S*' *Cs*^{1} — παρ. δε‖p: 28-565-700 ϕ983 *S*h^m *Cs*^{1} — *txt*: ℌ⟨Δ-579⟩ ϕ' D 1342 *pc L Cs*^{1}b *Arm*(*om* κ.) *Geo Aeth* | Σιμωνα + τον λεγομενον Πετρον‖p: 488 *Lg*^{2}(*om* τ. λε.) | Σιμωνος] αυτου‖Mt: 33-579 Θ-28 σ1424-1606 D G W Γ 1342 *al L*' *S*' *Cs*^{1}b^2 *Geo*^{2} — ● του Σ.: Δ-1241 λ' ϕ-230 A E^c *al* *l*48 {} — αυτου του Σ.: *Rpl* (*om* του: λ131 *S*h) — *txt*: ℌ' 565-700 σM {*Lar*^{1} *Cs*^{2}b'} *Arm Geo*^{1} | αμφ.] βαλλοντας αμφιβληστρον‖Mt: 579-892-1241 1071 ϕ230 σM 157 E^c Γ Π^c *pl* — αμφιβλ. (-ρα) βαλλ.‖p: 700 (λ) 1342 — αμφιβα. αμφιβλ.‖p: *R* ϕ22 565^m — αμφιβα. τα δικτυα‖18p Lk5 4f.: Θ-28-565^t ϕ D — *txt*: ℵBL-33 σ27-71-692 **074 0133** | εις την θαλασσαν‖p: 579-892-1241 28-544-565 ϕ-230 σ179-349-517-827-945-1194-1223 K(*-σση) *pc Lvl*[ek]⟨r^1⟩t vg⟨1⟩ **17** *om* ο Ι.‖Mt: Φ ϕ230 σ1194 *Lvg*^{1} | *om* γεν.‖Mt: 579 28-544-700-1071 λ ϕ13-69 σ115-517-1606 *pc Lbr*^{1} *Ss*[c]p *C*⟨b^3⟩ *Geo*^{2} **18** τα δικ.] ● τ. δ. αυτων: *Rpl Lfl* vg^1 *S Csb*^{2} — παντα‖Lk 11: D *Lvl*' — *txt*: ℌ⟨Δ-579⟩C Θ-28-565-700(τα λινα) ϕ⟨124⟩ σ-27-349-517-659-1194 W 1342 *pc Lr*^{2}tz vg' *Cb*' *Arm* | ηκολουθουν‖2 14p: B

Jo 1,38 στρ. δε] ● στρ.: ℵ*-**083** Λ λ22 ϕ124-230 σM-1207 E F H V Γ Ω *pc Lj*^{v}(+ ουν) *Arm* — και στρ.‖Lk 22 61: 1187 *Le* q *S*'j *Cb*^{1} — *txt*: 𝔓$^{5v.66.75}$ *Rpl* Or Cr *L*' *Sh C*' **39** οψ.] ιδετε‖1 46 11 34: *Rpl* Ep Or *L Cs*$^{7(+1?)}$b *Geo* — *txt*: 𝔓$^{5v.66.75}$ BC*LW^s-**083**-33-579 λ Ψ **063** *pc* Or Non *S Cs*$^{2(+2?)}$ **7,30** πιασ. + και εξηλθεν εκ της χειρος(χωρας) αυτων‖10 39: (Λ) ϕ⟨124⟩ Θ 262 (1555) *Geo*^{1} | τας χειρας‖44 Lk 20 19 Mt 26 50 Mk 14 46: W N-1071 λ ϕ174 σ1010-1194-1293 G **053** *pc* Non *L*⟨r^1⟩ Ir *S*scph^{Brs} *Cb*$^{⟨1⟩B}$ *Arm*^{pc} *Geo*^{2} **10,39** εξηλ.] ουδεις επεβαλεν επ αυτω την χειρα. εξηλ. ουν‖7 30: 1241

Lk 4 30p *cf.* Ev. apocr.(?) PEg 2 frgm.1r^o 5–7: ... ἔ]λκω[σιν] β[αστάσαντες δὲ] λίθους ὁμοῦ λι[θάζω]σι[ν αὐ]τόν· 6 καὶ ἐπέβαλον [τὰς] χεῖ[ρας] αὐτῶν ἐπ' αὐτὸν οἱ [ἄρχον]τες [ἵ]να πιάσωσιν καὶ παρ[αδῶ]σω[σι]ν τῷ ὄχλῳ· καὶ οὐκ ἠ[δύναντο] αὐτὸν πιάσαι ὅτι οὔπω ἐ[ληλύθει] αὐτοῦ ἡ ὥρα τῆς παραδό[σεως]. 7 αὐτὸς δὲ ὁ κ(ύριο)ς ἐξελθὼν [ἐκ τῶν χει]ρῶν ἀπένευσεν ἀπ' [αὐτῶν]. 8 Καὶ [ἰ]δοὺ λεπρὸς ... (*cf. ad 57.*)

23. cf. EEb frgm.1 (Ep haer. 30, 13, 2f.; *cf. ad 19.* Lk 3 23): ... καὶ ἐλθὼν εἰς Καφαρναουμ εἰσῆλθεν εἰς τὴν οἰκίαν Σίμωνος τοῦ ἐπικληθέντος Πέτρου καὶ ἀνοίξας τὸ στόμα αὐτοῦ εἶπεν· 3 'παρερχόμενος παρὰ τὴν λίμνην Τιβεριάδος ἐξελεξάμην Ἰωάννην καὶ Ἰάκωβον υἱοὺς Ζεβεδαίου καὶ Σίμωνα καὶ Ἀνδρέαν καὶ Θαδδαῖον καὶ Σίμωνα τὸν ζηλωτὴν καὶ Ἰούδαν τὸν Ἰσκαριώτην, καὶ σὲ τὸν Ματθαῖον καθεζόμενον ἐπὶ τοῦ τελωνίου ἐκάλεσα, καὶ ἠκολούθησάς μοι. ὑμᾶς οὖν βούλομαι εἶναι δεκαδύο ἀποστόλους εἰς μαρτύριον τοῦ Ισραηλ.'

Matth	Mark	Luk	
σαν αὐτῷ. [21] καὶ προβὰς ἐκεῖθεν εἶδεν ἄλλους δύο ἀδελφούς, Ἰάκωβον τὸν τοῦ Ζεβεδαίου καὶ Ἰωάννην τὸν ἀδελφὸν αὐτοῦ, ἐν τῷ πλοίῳ μετὰ Ζεβεδαίου τοῦ πατρὸς αὐτῶν καταρτίζοντας τὰ δίκτυα αὐτῶν· καὶ ἐκάλεσεν αὐτούς. [22] οἱ δὲ εὐθέως ἀφέντες τὸ πλοῖον καὶ τὸν πατέρα αὐτῶν ἠκολούθησαν αὐτῷ.	σαν αὐτῷ. [19] καὶ προβὰς ὀλίγον εἶδεν Ἰάκωβον τὸν τοῦ Ζεβεδαίου καὶ Ἰωάννην τὸν ἀδελφὸν αὐτοῦ καὶ αὐτοὺς ἐν τῷ πλοίῳ καταρτίζοντας τὰ δίκτυα. [20] καὶ εὐθὺς ἐκάλεσεν αὐτούς· καὶ ἀφέντες τὸν πατέρα αὐτῶν Ζεβεδαῖον ἐν τῷ πλοίῳ μετὰ τῶν μισθωτῶν ἀπῆλθον ὀπίσω αὐτοῦ.	[10a] *ὁμοίως δὲ καὶ* *Ἰάκωβον καὶ Ἰωάννην υἱοὺς Ζεβεδαίου, ...* [11] *καὶ καταγαγόντες τὰ πλοῖα ἐπὶ τὴν γῆν, ἀφέντες ἅπαντα ἠκολούθησαν αὐτῷ.*	αὐτῷ ἔμειναν τὴν ἡμέραν ἐκείνην· ...

(12) **24.** Jesus in der Synagoge zu Kapernaum. *Jesus in the Synagogue at Capernaum.*

	Mark 1 21–28	**Luk 4** 31–37	
4 13 *(21.): καὶ καταλιπὼν τὴν Ναζαρα ἐλθὼν κατῴκησεν εἰς Καφαρναουμ τὴν παραθαλασσίαν ...* *7* 28f. *(56.): Καὶ ἐγένετο ὅτε συνετέλεσεν ὁ Ἰησοῦς τοὺς λόγους τούτους, ἐξεπλήσσοντο οἱ ὄχλοι ἐπὶ τῇ διδαχῇ αὐτοῦ·* [29] *ἦν γὰρ διδάσκων αὐτοὺς ὡς ἐξουσίαν ἔχων, καὶ οὐχ ὡς οἱ γραμματεῖς αὐτῶν.*	[21] Καὶ εἰσπορεύονται εἰς Καφαρναουμ· καὶ εὐθὺς τοῖς σάββασιν ἐδίδασκεν εἰς τὴν συναγωγήν. [22] καὶ ἐξεπλήσσοντο ἐπὶ τῇ διδαχῇ αὐτοῦ· ἦν γὰρ διδάσκων αὐτοὺς ὡς ἐξουσίαν ἔχων, καὶ οὐχ ὡς οἱ γραμματεῖς.	[31] Καὶ κατῆλθεν εἰς Καφαρναουμ πόλιν τῆς Γαλιλαίας. καὶ ἦν διδάσκων αὐτοὺς ἐν τοῖς σάββασιν. [32] καὶ ἐξεπλήσσοντο ἐπὶ τῇ διδαχῇ αὐτοῦ, ὅτι ἐν ἐξουσίᾳ ἦν ὁ λόγος αὐτοῦ.	2 12: Μετὰ τοῦτο κατέβη εἰς Καφαρναουμ αὐτὸς καὶ ἡ μήτηρ αὐτοῦ καὶ οἱ ἀδελφοὶ καὶ οἱ μαθηταὶ αὐτοῦ, καὶ ἐκεῖ ἔμειναν οὐ πολλὰς ἡμέρας. 7 46: ἀπεκρίθησαν οἱ ὑπηρέται· οὐδέποτε ἐλάλησεν οὕτως ἄνθρωπος, ὡς οὗτος ὁ ἄνθρωπος.

Mt 4,21 εκειϑ. + ολιγον‖Mk: 1604 Δ 1573 *L*h *S*h *C*s(*om* εκ.) **22** *om* ευϑ.‖Lk: 544 *pc* *L*k[e] abg$^{1.2}$h vg^{1} *S*s | το πλ.] τα δικτυα (+ αυτων)‖20p: 126 *L*(bcg^{1})ff^{1}hlz vg'(^{5} *S*c *C*s) *Geo*^{2}(το δικτυον) *Δ*ad i l md'(^{CMUZ}) n | *om* και—αυτων‖Lk: 122 *L*z *S*c

Mk 1,19 προβ. + εκειϑεν (*et om* ολιγ.)‖Mt: *Rpl* (ℵ* Σ)(∼ ολ. εκ.: 33) *L*cflr^{2} vg' *S*h *Arm* — *txt*: BL-579-892 Θ-28-565 **λ** **ϕ**124-788 σ349-517 D W *L*vl'[ek] r^{1}t vg^{1} *S*' *C* | *om* και^{3} αυτ.‖Mt: 1342 *L*c {*C*b^{6}} | δικ. + αυτων‖Mt: C^{2}-1241 1071 λ872 σM-945-1223-1606 K Γ Π **074** *mu* *L*vg^{2} *S*'h^{+} *C*⟨b^{3}⟩ *Geo*^{2} **20** *om* ευϑ.‖Mt: Δ Θ-700 **ϕ**124-788 W *L*bcff^{2}t *S*p *Geo*^{2} | και^{2}] οι δε ευϑεως‖Mt: 1342 *Geo* — και ευϑεως(-υς): Δ Θ-(565)-700 (**ϕ**')-124 W 472 (837) *L*cff^{2} *S*p | αφεν. + τα δικτυα και‖Mt: Θ | απη. οπ. αυ.] ηκολουϑησαν αυτω‖**p**: σ1424 D W *L* | **21** τ. σαβ.] εν τ. σαβ.‖Lk: C-892 G Ω *pc* *l*48 | εδ. εις τ. συν.] ● εισελϑων εις τ. σ. εδ.: *Rpl* (∼: 33 **ϕ**124) *L*'(*om* εις τ. σ.: lz) *S*h *C*b^{4} *Arm* *Geo*^{2} — ∼ εις τ. σ. εδ.: Δ *l*^{pl} — *txt*: ℵC(∼ εδ. εν τ. σαβ.)L-892 28-565 **ϕ**' 837 Or *S*(= C)j *C*' *Geo*^{1} | εδ. + αυτους‖Lk: Θ-700 D 1342 *L*'⟨t⟩(τον λαον: c) Au *S*h^{+} *Arm* *Geo*^{2} | συν. + αυτων *cf.* 139 Mt4 23 9 35 *etc.* Lk 4 15: Δ-892 1546 *S*p *C*b^{1} *Geo*^{2} **22** εξε. + οχλοι‖Mt: 1574 | γρα. + αυτων‖Mt: C-33-579 Σ σM D *al* *l*48 *L*cfg^{2} *S*,j *C*s$^{1:3}$b^{4}

Lk 4,31 Γ. + την παραϑαλασσιαν εν οριοις Ζαβουλων και Ναφϑαλειμ‖Mt4 13: D | *om* αυτ.‖Mk: σ990 485 *pc* *S*p' *C*s$^{4:6}$b$^{\langle 1\rangle}$

Jo 2,12 κατε.] ηλϑεν‖Mk1 14: 713 Ep *L*f *C*b^{4} | κατε. + ο Ιησους‖322 Mk1 14: λ1 σ954-1010-1293 *pc* *L*f (κυριος I.: *S*[sc]j) *Arm*$^{\langle 1\rangle}$ *Geo* | Καφ. + ο Ιησους: *C*b^{2} | *om* αυτου^{1}‖Mt12 46p: W^{s}(∼ μαϑ. ... μητ. ... αδ.) | ● αδ. + αυτου‖←: 𝔓^{66c} *Rpl* Or Ep *L*' *S*[sc],j *C*⟨b^{1}⟩a^{s} — *txt*: 𝔓$^{66*.75}$ BL-083-**0162** 1071 Ψ **0141** Chr Or *L*e ac(*om* κ. οι αδ.: q) vg^{1} | *om* αυτου^{2}: L-**083** Or | **7,46** ● ουτος + λαλει (*et om* ο ανϑρ.^{2}): 𝔓^{66} ℵ* (D) 495(∼: *pc*) *L*(cz vg^{2})^{5} *S*'j *Δ*a (i) l^{AD} n^{L} — *om* ως—ανϑρ.^{2}($^{1}\cap^{2}$?): 𝔓$^{66c.75}$ ℵ^{c}BLTW *pc* Cr *C*b — *txt*: *Rpl* Chr Thd^{C} *L*'(*om* ως: ff^{2}) *S*h *C*sb^{B}a^{s} *Arm* *Δ*'

Mark 1,23–27:

23 καὶ εὐθὺς ἦν ἐν τῇ συναγωγῇ αὐτῶν ἄνθρωπος ἐν πνεύματι ἀκαθάρτῳ, καὶ ἀνέκραξεν 24 λέγων· τί ἡμῖν καὶ σοί, Ἰησοῦ Ναζαρηνέ; ἦλθες ἀπολέσαι ἡμᾶς. οἶδά σε τίς εἶ, ὁ ἅγιος τοῦ θεοῦ. 25 καὶ ἐπετίμησεν αὐτῷ ὁ Ἰησοῦς λέγων· φιμώθητι καὶ ἔξελθε ἐξ αὐτοῦ. 26 καὶ σπαράξαν αὐτὸν τὸ πνεῦμα τὸ ἀκάθαρτον καὶ φωνῆσαν φωνῇ μεγάλῃ ἐξῆλθεν ἐξ αὐτοῦ. 27 καὶ ἐθαμβήθησαν ἅπαντες, ὥστε συζητεῖν πρὸς ἑαυτοὺς λέγοντας· τί ἐστιν τοῦτο; διδαχὴ καινὴ κατ' ἐξουσίαν· καὶ τοῖς πνεύμασι τοῖς ἀκαθάρτοις ἐπιτάσσει, καὶ ὑπακούουσιν αὐτῷ.

Luk 4,33–36:

33 καὶ ἐν τῇ συναγωγῇ ἦν ἄνθρωπος ἔχων πνεῦμα δαιμονίου ἀκαθάρτου, καὶ ἀνέκραξεν φωνῇ μεγάλῃ· 34 ἔα, τί ἡμῖν καὶ σοί, Ἰησοῦ Ναζαρηνέ; ἦλθες ἀπολέσαι ἡμᾶς. οἶδά σε τίς εἶ, ὁ ἅγιος τοῦ θεοῦ. 35 καὶ ἐπετίμησεν αὐτῷ ὁ Ἰησοῦς λέγων· φιμώθητι καὶ ἔξελθε ἀπ' αὐτοῦ. καὶ ῥῖψαν αὐτὸν τὸ δαιμόνιον εἰς τὸ μέσον ἐξῆλθεν ἀπ' αὐτοῦ μηδὲν βλάψαν αὐτόν. 36 καὶ ἐγένετο θάμβος ἐπὶ πάντας, καὶ συνελάλουν πρὸς ἀλλήλους λέγοντες· τίς ὁ λόγος οὗτος, ὅτι ἐν ἐξουσίᾳ καὶ δυνάμει ἐπιτάσσει τοῖς ἀκαθάρτοις πνεύμασιν καὶ ἐξέρχονται;

Jo 6 69: καὶ ἡμεῖς πεπιστεύκαμεν καὶ ἐγνώκαμεν ὅτι σὺ εἶ ὁ ἅγιος τοῦ θεοῦ.

4 24 (28.): καὶ ἀπῆλθεν ἡ ἀκοὴ αὐτοῦ εἰς ὅλην τὴν Συρίαν· ...

28 ἐξῆλθεν δὲ ἡ ἀκοὴ αὐτοῦ εὐθὺς πανταχοῦ εἰς ὅλην τὴν περίχωρον τῆς Γαλιλαίας.

37 καὶ ἐξεπορεύετο ἦχος περὶ αὐτοῦ εἰς πάντα τόπον τῆς περιχώρου.

4 14 (21.): ... καὶ φήμη ἐξῆλθεν καθ' ὅλης τῆς περιχώρου περὶ αὐτοῦ.

Mk 1,23 *om* ευθ.‖p: *Rpl L S* — *txt*: ℌ⟨Δ-892⟩ λ⟨118⟩ Or *Sj C* | ∼ εν τ. συν. αυ. ην‖p: C Or | *om* αυτ.‖p: L-579 D *pc Le*[k] bcff²t *C*⟨b⁴⟩ | ανεκ. + φωνη μεγαλη‖p: 1071 1241 **24** ● λεγ. + εα‖p: *Rpl* Cr Or *Sh Arm Geo*' — *txt*: ℵ*B Θ-28-565 D W *pc L*, Au *S*'j *C Geo*ᴮ | ηλθ. + ωδε‖Mt8₂₉: W(∼ απολ. ημ. ωδε) *Lc* — + προ καιρου‖←: Catᴼˣ | ● οιδαμεν‖←: ℵLΔ-892 Catᴼˣ Cr Or *L*Eug Hgm Hil Ir Pauᴹ Sed *C*b — *txt*: *Rpl L S*,j *Cs* | αγ.] υιος‖5₇p: Or **25** εξ] απ‖p: L-33-579 ΘΣ-544-565-700-1604 φ828 σ349-517-945-1194-1223 H *al l*48 | εξ αυ.] εκ(απο) του ανθρωπου(+ το) πνευμα(+ το) ακαθαρτον‖5₈p: (Θ-565ᵐ) D W 330 *Le*[k] bcff²g²qr¹30(*om* πν. ακ.: lr²z vg')³ **26** φωνησαν] κραξαν‖23p Lk5₇: *Rpl* — *txt*: ℌ⟨Δ⟩ 1342 Or | εξ] απ‖p: CΔ-33 ΘΣ σM-945-1424 D W *pc* **27** ωστε συζ.] και συνεζητουν‖p: W *Le*[k] bcff²qr¹ *S*(*om*: s[c])p *Geo*¹(*om* και) | πρ. εαυ.] ● αυτους: ℵB *Le*[k] bff²q *Sj* — πρ. αλληλους: σ1194 *S*' *C* — πρ. αυτ.: L-892 Φ-28-565 G S W Ω 1342 372 {} — *txt*: *Rpl* {*L*'} *S*h | λεγοντες‖p: CΔᶜ-33 Θ-544-1604 φ346-543 σM-115-179-267-1082-1391-1402 A E W 157 *al* | *om* τι εστ. του. D W 1342 *pc l*49 *l*211 *Le*[k] bcff²qr¹ᵛ *Ss*[c] *Arm Aeth* | διδ.—και²] τις η διδ. η καινη αυτη οτι κατ. εξ. και‖p: *Rpl L*' *S*'(*prm* και: p) *Geo*ᴬ('*om* και) — τις η καινη διδ. αυτη οτι κ. εξ. και: φ A(∼ αυ. διδ.) 837 (καινη + η) *l*48 *l*76 *Arm* — τις η διδ. εκεινη(*om*) η καινη αυτη η εξουσια(+ -στικη αυτου και) οτι και(*om*): D (W) — τις η (+ καινη: q) διδ. αυτη κ. εξ. και(*om*: c) οτι: *Le*[k] b(c)ff²(q)r¹ — διδ. καινη αυτη (+ οτι) κ. εξ. και(*om*): 579 (Θ)-565 λ — *txt*: ℵBL-33 700(∼ καινη διδ., *et* διδ. + οτι) *Cs*b(καινη + οτι) **28** εξη. δε] ● και εξη.‖p Mt9₂₆ Lk7₁₇: ℌ'(+ δε: 579)C ΘΣ-700 σM-7-267-349-659 D W 1342 *pc l*48 *l*49 *l*184 *L*' *S*'j *Cs*¹ᵛ(² *om* και)b — *txt*: *Rpl L*(*om* 28: b)f *S*h | ευθ. παντ.] ευθ.‖p: *Rpl L*' *S*' — παντ.‖p: 579 W 213 *Le*[k] bq *Sj C*b' *Aeth* — παλιν: *L*vg¹ — *om*‖p: ℵ*-33 Θ-28-565-700 λ φ230 σ349-517 *pc L*cff²r¹ *Ss*[c] *C*b¹ *Arm* — *txt* (-χη): (ℵᶜL)BC-892 φ 1342 *Cs*b⁶ | τ. Γ.] του Ιορδανου‖Lk3₃ Mt3₅: 28 — *om*‖Lk: 495

Lk 4,33 ανεκ.] εκραζεν‖Mk3₁₁ 5₇ Mt8₂₉: σ1194 | *om* φω. μεγ.‖p Mk3₁₁p Mt←: 33 | μεγ. + λεγων‖p4₄₁ Mk3₁₁: *Rpl* Ath *L S*'j — ℌ⟨33-892⟩Ξ 700 σ990 V Or *Ss*[c] *C* **34** *om* εα‖Mk: 33 D *pc L Ss*[c]j *C Aeth* | ημιν] εμοι‖8₂₈ Mk5₇: 251 2533 *C*b⁸ *Geo*¹ | ηλ. + προ καιρου‖Mt8₂₉: 1071 *l*32 *Le* bcr¹ | απολ. ημ.] ημ. ωδε απ.‖←: D 68 | οιδαμεν‖←: 892 Ψ Ath *L*Hgm *Arm* | αγ. θ.] υιος θ.‖4₄₁ 8₂₈p Mk3₁₁: 579 — αγ. θ. υι.‖←: *Lc* **35** απ¹] εξ‖p: 𝔓⁷⁵ *Rpl* — *txt*: ℵBLWΞ-579 700 λ-1582-2193 φ-230 σ71-1194-1424 D V *al* Or | απ²] εξ‖p: 𝔓⁷⁵ σM-1223 Γ 1093 | *om* μηδ. βλ. αυ.‖p: W **36** τις + εστιν‖pJo7₃₆: U *L* | εξερ.] υπακουουσιν αυτω‖p: ℵᵃ **37** εξεπ. ηχ.] εξηλθεν η ακοη‖4₁₄ Mk Mt: D *La Cs*

Jo 6,69 *cf. ad 135.*

(13) **25.** Heilung der Schwiegermutter des Petrus. *The Healing of Peter's Wife's Mother.*

8 14–15 (59.)	**Mark 1** 29–31	**Luk 4** 38–39
[14] *Καὶ*	[29] Καὶ εὐθὺς ἐκ τῆς συναγωγῆς	[38] Ἀναστὰς δὲ ἀπὸ τῆς συναγωγῆς
ἐλθὼν ὁ Ἰησοῦς εἰς τὴν οἰ-	ἐξελθόντες ἦλθον εἰς τὴν οἰ-	εἰσῆλθεν εἰς τὴν οἰ-
κίαν Πέτρου	κίαν Σίμωνος καὶ Ἀνδρέου μετὰ Ἰακώ-	κίαν Σίμωνος.
εἶδεν τὴν πενθερὰν	βου καὶ Ἰωάννου. [30] ἡ δὲ πενθερὰ	πενθερὰ δὲ
αὐτοῦ βεβλημένην καὶ πυρέσ-	Σίμωνος κατέκειτο πυρέσ-	τοῦ Σίμωνος ἦν συνεχομένη πυρετῷ
σουσαν·	σουσα, καὶ εὐθὺς λέγουσιν αὐτῷ	μεγάλῳ, καὶ ἠρώτησαν αὐτὸν
[15] *καὶ*	περὶ αὐτῆς. [31] καὶ προσελθὼν	περὶ αὐτῆς. [39] καὶ ἐπιστὰς ἐπάνω αὐτῆς
ἥψατο τῆς χειρὸς αὐ-	ἤγειρεν αὐτὴν κρατήσας τῆς χειρός·	ἐπετίμησεν τῷ πυρετῷ,
τῆς, καὶ ἀφῆκεν αὐτὴν ὁ πυρετός· καὶ	καὶ ἀφῆκεν αὐτὴν ὁ πυρετός,	καὶ ἀφῆκεν αὐτήν· πα-
ἠγέρθη, καὶ διηκόνει αὐτῷ.	καὶ διηκόνει αὐτοῖς.	ραχρῆμα δὲ ἀναστᾶσα διηκόνει αὐτοῖς.

(14) **26.** Krankenheilungen am Abend. *The Sick Healed at Evening.*

8 16 (60.)			**Mark 1** 32–34		**Luk 4** 40–41
[16] *Ὀψίας δὲ γενομένης*			[32] Ὀψίας δὲ γενομένης, ὅτε ἔδυ		[40] Δύνον-
	4 24 (28.): ...	*14 35 (127.): ...*	ὁ ἥλιος,	*6 55 (127.): ...*	τος δὲ τοῦ ἡλίου
προσήνεγκαν	*καὶ προσήνεγκαν*	*καὶ προσήνεγκαν*	ἔφερον πρὸς	*καὶ ἤρξαντο ἐπὶ*	
αὐτῷ	*αὐτῷ πάντας*	*αὐτῷ πάντας*	αὐτὸν πάντας	*τοῖς κραβάττοις*	ἅπαντες ὅσοι
	τοὺς κακῶς ἔχον-	*τοὺς κακῶς ἔχον-*	τοὺς κακῶς ἔχον-	*τοὺς κακῶς ἔχον-*	εἶχον ἀσθενοῦν-
	τας ποι-	*τας ...*	τας cf. v. 34 ↓	*τας περιφέρειν, ὅ-*	τας νόσοις ποι-
	κίλαις νόσοις καὶ		καὶ	*που ἤκουον ὅτι*	κίλαις ἤγαγον αὐ-
	βασάνοις συνεχο-		τοὺς	*ἐστίν.*	τοὺς πρὸς αὐτόν·
δαιμονιζο-	*μένους, δαιμονιζο-*		δαιμονιζο-		

Mk 1,29 *om* ευθ.‖p: D W *L*e[k] cff^{2}r^{1}z *S*s[c]p *Geo*^{2} | εξελθων *et* ηλθεν‖p: B-579 ΘΣ-565-700 **λ**⟨118⟩-22-1278 **ϕ** σ349-517-1675 D W 1342 *pc* *L*vl'[k] (ηλθον: l)r^{1}30 vg^5 *S*s[c]pj *C*(-οντες *et* -εν: s$^{1:2}$)b^5 *Geo*^{2} **30** Σιμ.] του Σ.‖Lk: LΔ 565-700-1071 **λ ϕ** σM-179-945-1402 *pm* | *om* ευθ.‖Lk: W *L*bcff^{2}qr^1 vg^1 *S*s[c]p *Geo*^{2} **31** χει. + αυτης‖Mt: *Rpl* *L*'*S*ph *C* *Geo*^{B} — ηγ.—χει.] εκτεινας την χειρα κρατησας(και επιλαβομενος) ηγ. αυ.‖141p(Lk144): D (W) *L*bqr^1 — *txt*: ℵBL *Geo*' | αφη. *prm* ευθεως: Σ σ1402 1970 *L*' *S*' — ● πυρ. + ευθ. (∼ ευθ. ο πυρ.)‖Lk: *Rpl* (σ247 *L*bq) *S*h — *txt*: 𝔖⟨Δ⟩C 28-700 **λ** σ517 W Θ 1342 *pc* *L*e[k] *C* | και^3 + ηγερθη και‖Mt: σ1082-1391 *pc* *L*(αναστασα‖Lk: e[k]) c *S*s[c]p^{1}h$^+$ *C*s$^{2:4}$b^4 *Geo*^{2} | αυτοις] αυτω‖Mt: 579 W *L*e[k] d *Geo*^{B} **32** ● εδυσεν: B 28 σ349-517 D | προσεφε.‖Mt: 579 {*L*⟨bq⟩} | εφε. + παντες(-ας)‖Lk: 28-565 **ϕ**'(346 566) 837 | πρ. αυ. παντας] αυτω πα.‖Mt: 1574 *C*sb$^{\langle 6\rangle}$ — *om* πρ. αυ.‖ 655: 716 *S*s[c] — *om* πα.‖←Lk: 28 ϕ828 *L*ff^2 | εχ. + νοσοις ποικιλοις‖34Lk: D *L*e[k] bcff^{2}qr^1 vg^3 *S*s[c] | *om* κ. τ. δαιμ.‖Lk: W *L*r^{1}30 vg^2 *S*s[c]

Lk 4,38 απο] εκ‖Mk: *Rpl* — *txt*: 𝔓^{75} 𝔖⟨892⟩CΞ N-700 **λ**-22-1582-2193 **ϕ** σ990 D Q *pc* Or | εισῃ.] ηλθεν‖p: σ945-1223 D Y Π *al* *l*19 | Σιμ.^{1} + και Ανδρεου‖Mk: D *L*bcff^{2}lr^1 vg^2 Am | πενθ. δε] η δε π.‖Mk: C λ131-1278 *pc* — η π. δε‖Mk: λ1-1582 σ517-945-954 *pc* | *om* του‖Mk: X *pc* | *om* μεγ.—αυτης‖Mt: 255 — *om* ηρω.—^{39}αυτης‖Mt: *S*s[c] **39** αυτην + ο πυρετος‖p: ℵ 1012 *l*48 Cr *Le* | παρ. δε] και π.(∼)‖p: CL 2533 *L*⟨e a⟩ *S*s[c]p (*C*b^2 *Geo*) | αυτοις] αυτω‖Mt: N-28 ϕ174 *Le* *C*b^1 *Geo*$^{1.B}$ **40** απ.] ● παντες: *Rpl* Or — *txt*: BC-579 700 **λ**-1582-2193 σ990 Θ 157 | ηγ.] εφερον‖Mk: D

---

25. cf. EEb frgm.1 (*cf. ad 23.*)

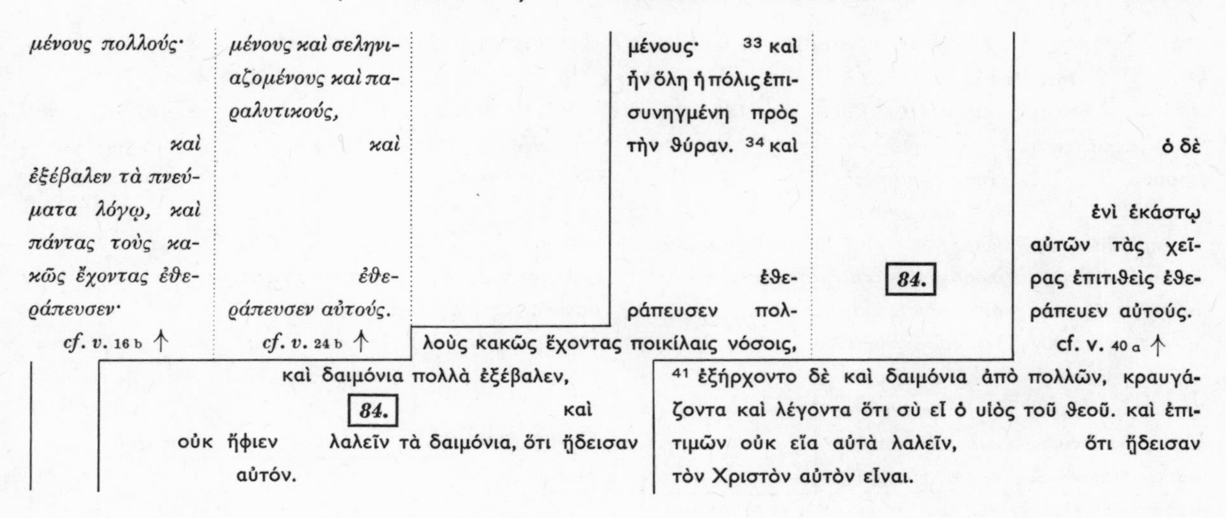

μένους πολλούς· *καὶ ἐξέβαλεν τὰ πνεύματα λόγῳ, καὶ πάντας τοὺς κακῶς ἔχοντας ἐθεράπευσεν·*
cf. v. 16 b ↑

μένους καὶ σεληνιαζομένους καὶ παραλυτικούς, καὶ ἐθεράπευσεν αὐτούς.
cf. v. 24 b ↑

μένους· [33] καὶ ἦν ὅλη ἡ πόλις ἐπισυνηγμένη πρὸς τὴν θύραν. [34] καὶ ἐθεράπευσεν πολλοὺς κακῶς ἔχοντας ποικίλαις νόσοις, καὶ δαιμόνια πολλὰ ἐξέβαλεν, **84.** καὶ οὐκ ἤφιεν λαλεῖν τὰ δαιμόνια, ὅτι ᾔδεισαν αὐτόν.

84. ὁ δὲ ἑνὶ ἑκάστῳ αὐτῶν τὰς χεῖρας ἐπιτιθεὶς ἐθεράπευεν αὐτούς.
cf. v. 40 a ↑
[41] ἐξήρχοντο δὲ καὶ δαιμόνια ἀπὸ πολλῶν, κραυγάζοντα καὶ λέγοντα ὅτι σὺ εἶ ὁ υἱὸς τοῦ θεοῦ. καὶ ἐπιτιμῶν οὐκ εἴα αὐτὰ λαλεῖν, ὅτι ᾔδεισαν τὸν Χριστὸν αὐτὸν εἶναι.

(15) *27.* **Aufbruch von Kapernaum.** ***Jesus' Departure from Capernaum.***

Mark 1 35–38

[35] Καὶ πρωῒ ἔννυχα λίαν ἀναστὰς ἐξῆλθεν καὶ ἀπῆλθεν εἰς ἔρημον τόπον, κἀκεῖ προσηύχετο. [36] καὶ κατεδίωξεν αὐτὸν Σίμων καὶ οἱ μετ' αὐτοῦ, [37] καὶ εὑρόντες αὐτὸν λέγουσιν αὐτῷ ὅτι πάντες ζητοῦσίν σε. [38] καὶ λέγει αὐτοῖς· ἄγωμεν ἀλλαχοῦ εἰς τὰς ἐχομένας κωμοπόλεις, ἵνα καὶ ἐκεῖ κηρύξω· εἰς τοῦτο γὰρ ἐξῆλθον.

Luk 4 42–43

[42] Γενομένης δὲ ἡμέρας ἐξελθὼν ἐπορεύθη εἰς ἔρημον τόπον· καὶ οἱ ὄχλοι ἐπεζήτουν αὐτόν, καὶ ἦλθον ἕως αὐτοῦ, καὶ κατεῖχον αὐτὸν τοῦ μὴ πορεύεσθαι ἀπ' αὐτῶν. [43] ὁ δὲ εἶπεν πρὸς αὐτοὺς ὅτι καὶ ταῖς ἑτέραις πόλεσιν εὐαγγελίσασθαί με δεῖ τὴν βασιλείαν τοῦ θεοῦ, ὅτι ἐπὶ τοῦτο ἀπεστάλην.

Mk 1,33 ● ∼ η πο. ολη: *Rpl S* — *txt* (*om* ολη): 𝔊'⟨א*Δ⟩(579)C Θ-1071 σ7-349-517 D 1342 *l*36 *l*48 (*l*184) *l*158 *L* **34** πολλους] παντας τους ‖32 Mt16.24.35: σ349 *pc* | *om* ποικ. νο. ‖32 6 55 Mt16.35: א* L-892 1574 (*S*s[c]*om* κακ.—νο.) | αυτ.] τον Χριστον αυτ. ειναι ‖Lk: C-892-1241 σ115-517-827-954-1675 *L*vg¹ — ● αυτ. (+ τον) Χ. ειν. ‖Lk: (א^c)BL-33^v ΘΣ-28-(544-700)-565 **λ**-22 (**φ**) σ(M)-349-692 (G) W 1342 *al* (*al*) *l*^pl *L*l vg² *S*h⁺ (*C*s¹b) *Arm Aeth* — *txt*: *Rpl L' S' C*s¹ **35** *om* αναστ. ‖**p**: D' *pc* Lac *S*s[c] **36** ● κατεδιωξαν: *Rpl L*vl' vg² *S Cs Geo*² — *txt*: אB Θ-28-565-700-1071 σM S U Ω *l*53 *l*184 *L*lr²(?)z *S*j *C*b *Arm Geo*¹ | Σ.] ● ο Σ.: *Rpl* — ο τε Σ.: Θ **φ**-*l*547 D(*om* ο) K Π *mu* — *txt*: 𝔊⟨Δ⟩ Φ W *pc l*48 **37** ευρ. αυ. λεγ.] ● ευρον αυ. και λεγ.: אBL-892 *L*e[k] *C*s¹b³ *Aeth* **38** εξηλ.] εληλυθα ‖Jo18 37: Δ-892 28-565 **φ** σ71-349-659-692-954-1082-1194-1207 W Ω **047 090**(ελεﾚη-) *pm l*47 *l*49 *L S*'h^m *C*b' — εξεληλ. ‖←: *Rpl* {} — *txt*: 𝔊'C Θ σ179 1342 *S*h^t j {*C*sb⁷}

Lk 4,40 επιτιθ.] επιθεις (∼ επιθ. τ. χ.) ‖Mt19 15: *Rpl* (אC) Or *L*a (*C*b *Aeth*) — *txt*: BWΞ-1241 λ2193 **φ**⟨124-983⟩ σ7-267 D Q *pc l*18 *l*19 *L'* | εθεραπευσεν ‖p Mt12 15 Mk3 10: *Rpl* Or¹ *C* — *txt*: BW D Y Ψ *pc* Or¹ *L S Arm* **41** ● εξηρχετο: 𝔓^75v *Rpl* — *txt*: אCX-33-1241 1071-1604 **λ**-1582-2193 **φ**346 σ267-659-1194-1606 Θ *pc* Or | απο πολ.] πολλων(-α) ‖(p): אW-1241 (28)-1604 **λ**⟨131⟩-1582 σ27-1194-1424-1675 **047** (1200) *pc* (*L*b) | κραυ.] ● κραζοντα ‖Mk3 11 5 7 p 9 26: *Rpl* — *txt*: W 565-700 λ118-1278 **φ** σ7-71-267-692 A D E G H Q U V Γ Δ Ω^c **047** 157 *pm l*184 Or | *om* οτι¹ ‖Mt16 16 p: σ517-1223-1424 *L*e abcff²r¹z vg² *S*s[c]h *Δ*a | ει + ο Χριστος ‖9 20 p Mt26 63 p Jo11 27: *Rpl* (*om* ο υι. τ. θε. ‖Mk8 29: 1574) *L*fq *S' C*b⁸ *Δ*a — *txt*: 𝔓^75v 𝔊⟨892⟩CXΞ 700 **φ**788 σ990 D F R *pc* Or *L'* Te Vic^P *S*s[c]j *C' Arm Δ*l^AD md n **42** επεζ.] εζητ. ‖Mk3 7: 544-700-1604 E G H K Π *pm* **43** οτι² ε. του.] ε. του. γαρ ‖p: D *L*e r¹ | επι] εις ‖**p**: *Rpl* — *txt*: 𝔓^75 אBLW-579 700 **φ** σ990 | ● απεσταλμαι *cf.* 4 18 13 34 Jo16 *etc.*: *Rpl* Cat — *txt*: 𝔓^75 𝔊CX **λ**'(απεσταλ[*spat.*]: 118)-1582-2193 **φ** σ990 D *pc*

(16) **28.** Wanderpredigt in Galiläa. *Preaching and Healing in Galilee.*

Matth 4 23–25		Mark 1 39		Luk 4 44	
[23] Καὶ	*9 35 (70.): Καὶ*	*6 6b (122.): Καὶ*	[39] Καὶ	[44] Καὶ	*8 1 (97.): ... καὶ*
περιῆγεν ὁ	*περιῆγεν ὁ*	*περιῆγεν*	ἦλθεν	ἦν	*αὐτὸς διώδευεν*
Ἰησοῦς	*Ἰησοῦς τὰς πό-*				*κατὰ πό-*
	λεις πάσας καὶ τὰς	*τὰς*			*λιν καὶ*
ἐν ὅλῃ τῇ Γαλιλαίᾳ,	*κώμας,*	*κώμας κύκλῳ*			*κώμην*
διδάσκων ἐν ταῖς	*διδάσκων ἐν ταῖς*	*διδάσκων.*	κηρύσσων εἰς τὰς	κηρύσσων εἰς τὰς	
συναγωγαῖς αὐ-	*συναγωγαῖς αὐ-*		συναγωγὰς αὐ-	συναγωγὰς	
τῶν καὶ κηρύσσων	*τῶν καὶ κηρύσσων*		τῶν εἰς ὅλην τὴν	τῆς	*κηρύσσων*
τὸ εὐαγγέλιον	*τὸ εὐαγγέλιον*		Γαλιλαίαν	Ἰουδαίας.	*καὶ εὐαγγελιζόμε-*
τῆς βασιλείας	*τῆς βασιλείας*				*νος τὴν βασιλείαν*
καὶ θεραπεύων	*καὶ θεραπεύων*		καὶ τὰ δαιμόνια ἐκ-		*τοῦ θεοῦ ...*
πᾶσαν νόσον καὶ	*πᾶσαν νόσον καὶ*		βάλλων.		
πᾶσαν μαλακίαν ἐν τῷ λαῷ. [24] καὶ	*πᾶσαν μαλακίαν.*	*cf. 122.*			

ἀπῆλθεν ἡ ἀκοὴ αὐτοῦ εἰς ὅλην τὴν Συρίαν· καὶ προσήνεγκαν αὐτῷ πάντας τοὺς κακῶς ἔχοντας ποικίλαις νόσοις καὶ βασάνοις συνεχομένους, δαιμονιζομένους καὶ σεληνιαζομένους καὶ παραλυτικούς, καὶ ἐθεράπευσεν αὐτούς. [25] καὶ ἠκολούθησαν αὐτῷ ὄχλοι πολλοὶ ἀπὸ τῆς Γαλιλαίας καὶ Δεκαπόλεως καὶ Ἱεροσολύμων καὶ Ἰουδαίας καὶ πέραν τοῦ Ἰορδάνου.

24. *26.* *84.*

(17) **29.** Der Fischzug des Petrus. *The Miraculous Draught of Fishes.* Luk 5 1–11

Luk 5	Jo 21
[1] Ἐγένετο δὲ ἐν τῷ τὸν ὄχλον ἐπικεῖσθαι αὐτῷ καὶ ἀκούειν τὸν λόγον τοῦ θεοῦ, καὶ αὐτὸς ἦν ἑστὼς παρὰ τὴν λίμνην Γεννησαρετ, [2] καὶ εἶδεν δύο πλοιάρια ἑστῶτα παρὰ τὴν λίμνην· οἱ δὲ	21 1–11 : Μετὰ ταῦτα ἐφανέρωσεν ἑαυτὸν πάλιν ὁ Ἰησοῦς τοῖς μαθηταῖς ἐπὶ τῆς θαλάσσης τῆς Τιβεριάδος· ἐφανέρωσεν δὲ οὕτως· [2] ἦσαν ὁμοῦ Σίμων Πέτρος καὶ Θωμᾶς ὁ λεγόμενος Δίδυμος καὶ Ναθαναηλ ὁ ἀπὸ

Mt 4,23 ● *om* ο Ι.‖MkLk: B *l*20 *Lk*[e] *S*s *C*s — ∼ εν—Γ. ο Ι.: *Rpl* — *txt*: ℵC-33-892 **λ**-1582 **ϕ**346 σ517 157 *pc* D *pc* l^{pl} Eu *L*' *S*'j(κυριος Ι.) *C*b | εν ολη τ. Γ.] ● ολην την Γαλιλαιαν‖35 Mk6: *Rpl* (εις ολην Γ.: *l*184) Eu — *txt*: ℵ*(*om* ολη)BC 157 *l*20 | διδ. + αυτους‖729 Mk122: ℵ* *Arm*'(*om* εν²—αυτων) | *om* εν τ. λαω‖35 101: **ϕ**983-1689 **24** εξηλθεν‖926 Mk128 Lk414 717: ℵC-33-892 **λ**-1582 *al* Or *S*h^{m}j *Arm* | ● συνεχ. + και: *Rpl L S*phj *C*s — *txt*: BC-892 **ϕ**⟨346⟩-174 Eu *C*b | εθερ. αυ.] παντας εθ.‖816 1215: D *L*(*om* k[e]) abcg¹h *S*scj | αυτους + λογω‖88p.16: **047**

Mk 1,39 ηλ.] ην‖Lk44: *Rpl L S* — *om et* εκηρυσσεν: *C*b¹ *Geo* — *txt*: ℵBL-892 Θ *l*1632 *S*j *C*' *Aeth* | κηρ.] διδασκων‖6Mt: 1574 | εις τ. συ.] εν ταις συναγωγαις‖Mt: *Rpl L* — *txt*: 𝔥⟨33⟩C ΘΦ(εις] εν)-28-565 **λ ϕ** σ115-179-349-517-827 A D K W Π **090 0104** 157 1342 *al l*1632

Lk 4,44 εις τ. συ.] ● εν ταις συναγωγαις‖Mt: *Rpl* — *txt*: 𝔓⁷⁵ 𝔥⟨L-33-1241⟩ **ϕ** σ⟨517⟩-990-1188 D Q Ψ *pc* l^{pl} | της Ι.] αυτων‖p: σ-1188 506 *l*34 *l*48 *l*1231 — ● της Γαλιλαιας‖Mt23 Mk39: *Rpl L S*ph^{m} *C*b$^{6(+1?)}$ — των Ιουδαιων *cf.* Act13 5 14 1 *etc.*: W 713 *l*18 — *txt*: 𝔓^{75v} 𝔥⟨33⟩C **λλ**⟨2193⟩ σ71-692-990 Q R 157 *pc* l^{pl} *S*' *C*' **5,1** τ. οχ. επικ.] συναχθηναι τ. οχ.‖Mt13 2 Mk4 1: ℵ(*om* αυτω) *C*b **2** πλοι.] ● πλοια‖3.7 Jo3 *etc.*: 𝔓⁷⁵ *Rpl* — *txt*: C*L-33-1241 1071 (πλοι[*spat.*]α: λ1 σ-7-1188 A Q R Ψ **047** *pc*

Jo 21,1 ● *om* ο: BC — *om* ο Ι.: σM D Chr *Le* vg¹

Jo21 2f. *cf.* EP14,59f.: (*cf. ad 275.*) ... ἡμεῖς δὲ οἱ δώδεκα μαθηταὶ ..., καὶ ἕκαστος ... εἰς τὸν οἶκον αὐτοῦ. [60]ἐγὼ δὲ Σίμων Πέτρος καὶ Ἀνδρέας ὁ ἀδελφός μου λαβόντες ἡμῶν τὰ λίνα ἀπήλθαμεν εἰς τὴν θάλασσαν, καὶ ἦν σὺν ἡμῖν Λευεὶς ὁ τοῦ Ἀλφαίου, ὃν κύριος[...

103.

ἁλεεῖς ἀπ' αὐτῶν ἀποβάντες ἔπλυναν τὰ δίκτυα. [3] ἐμβὰς δὲ εἰς ἓν τῶν πλοίων, ὃ ἦν τοῦ Σίμωνος, ἠρώτησεν αὐτὸν ἀπὸ τῆς γῆς ἐπαναγαγεῖν ὀλίγον· καθίσας δὲ ἐκ τοῦ πλοίου ἐδίδασκεν τοὺς ὄχλους. [4] ὡς δὲ ἐπαύσατο λαλῶν, εἶπεν πρὸς τὸν Σίμωνα· ἐπανάγαγε εἰς τὸ βάθος, καὶ χαλάσατε τὰ δίκτυα ὑμῶν εἰς ἄγραν. [5] καὶ ἀποκριθεὶς ὁ Σίμων εἶπεν αὐτῷ· ἐπιστάτα, δι' ὅλης νυκτὸς κοπιάσαντες οὐδὲν ἐλάβομεν· ἐπὶ δὲ τῷ ῥήματί σου χαλάσω τὰ δίκτυα. [6] καὶ τοῦτο ποιήσαντες συνέκλεισαν πλῆθος ἰχθύων πολύ· διερρήσσετο δὲ τὰ δίκτυα αὐτῶν. [7] καὶ κατένευσαν τοῖς μετόχοις ἐν τῷ ἑτέρῳ πλοίῳ τοῦ ἐλθόντας συλλαβέσθαι αὐτοῖς· καὶ ἦλθον, καὶ ἔπλησαν ἀμφότερα τὰ πλοῖα ὥστε βυθίζεσθαι αὐτά. [8] ἰδὼν δὲ Σίμων Πέτρος προσέπεσεν τοῖς γόνασιν Ἰησοῦ λέγων· ἔξελθε ἀπ' ἐμοῦ, ὅτι ἀνὴρ ἁμαρτωλός εἰμι, κύριε. [9] θάμβος γὰρ περιέσχεν αὐτὸν καὶ πάντας τοὺς σὺν αὐτῷ ἐπὶ τῇ ἄγρᾳ τῶν ἰχθύων ἧ συνέλαβον, [10] ὁμοίως δὲ καὶ Ἰάκωβον καὶ Ἰωάννην υἱοὺς Ζεβεδαίου, οἳ ἦσαν κοινωνοὶ τῷ Σίμωνι. καὶ εἶπεν πρὸς τὸν

23.

Σίμωνα ὁ Ἰησοῦς· μὴ φοβοῦ· ἀπὸ τοῦ νῦν ἀνθρώπους ἔσῃ ζωγρῶν. [11] καὶ καταγαγόντες τὰ πλοῖα ἐπὶ τὴν γῆν, ἀφέντες ἄπαντα ἠκολούθησαν αὐτῷ.

Κανα τῆς Γαλιλαίας καὶ οἱ τοῦ Ζεβεδαίου καὶ ἄλλοι ἐκ τῶν μαθητῶν αὐτοῦ δύο. [3] λέγει αὐτοῖς Σίμων Πέτρος· ὑπάγω ἁλιεύειν. λέγουσιν αὐτῷ· ἐρχόμεθα καὶ ἡμεῖς σὺν σοί. ἐξῆλθον καὶ ἀνέβησαν εἰς τὸ πλοῖον, καὶ ἐν ἐκείνῃ τῇ νυκτὶ ἐπίασαν οὐδέν. [4] πρωΐας δὲ ἤδη γινομένης ἔστη Ἰησοῦς ἐπὶ τὸν αἰγιαλόν· οὐ μέντοι ᾔδεισαν οἱ μαθηταὶ ὅτι Ἰησοῦς ἐστιν. [5] λέγει οὖν αὐτοῖς ὁ Ἰησοῦς· παιδία, μή τι προσφάγιον ἔχετε; ἀπεκρίθησαν αὐτῷ· οὔ. [6] ὁ δὲ εἶπεν αὐτοῖς· βάλετε εἰς τὰ δεξιὰ μέρη τοῦ πλοίου τὸ δίκτυον, καὶ εὑρήσετε. ἔβαλον οὖν, καὶ οὐκέτι αὐτὸ ἑλκύσαι ἴσχυον ἀπὸ τοῦ πλήθους τῶν ἰχθύων. [7] λέγει οὖν ὁ μαθητὴς ἐκεῖνος ὃν ἠγάπα ὁ Ἰησοῦς τῷ Πέτρῳ· ὁ κύριός ἐστιν. Σίμων οὖν Πέτρος, ἀκούσας ὅτι ὁ κύριός ἐστιν, τὸν ἐπενδύτην διεζώσατο, ἦν γὰρ γυμνός, καὶ ἔβαλεν ἑαυτὸν εἰς τὴν θάλασσαν· [8] οἱ δὲ ἄλλοι μαθηταὶ τῷ πλοιαρίῳ ἦλθον, οὐ γὰρ ἦσαν μακρὰν ἀπὸ τῆς γῆς ἀλλ' ὡς ἀπὸ πηχῶν διακοσίων, σύροντες τὸ δίκτυον τῶν ἰχθύων. [9] ὡς οὖν ἀπέβησαν εἰς τὴν γῆν, βλέπουσιν ἀνθρακιὰν κειμένην καὶ ὀψάριον ἐπικείμενον καὶ ἄρτον. [10] λέγει αὐτοῖς ὁ Ἰησοῦς· ἐνέγκατε ἀπὸ τῶν ὀψαρίων ὧν ἐπιάσατε νῦν. [11] ἀνέβη Σίμων Πέτρος καὶ εἵλκυσεν τὸ δίκτυον εἰς τὴν γῆν μεστὸν ἰχθύων μεγάλων ἑκατὸν πεντήκοντα τριῶν· καὶ τοσούτων ὄντων οὐκ ἐσχίσθη τὸ δίκτυον.

Lk 5,2 επλ.] ● απεπλ.: *Rpl*(-ον: *pc l*7 *l*13 *l*17; επεπλ.: *l*7; υπεπλ.: *l*80) — ● επλυνον: BW-892 D 91 *L S*,j[al](*om et* [2]∩[6] δικ.: j[bc]) *C* — *txt*: 𝔓[75v] 𝔥'⟨33⟩C*X φ174 Q *pc* | δικ. + αυτων‖Mt4 21: 238 *pc l*47 *l*183 *L*acr[1] *S*'h⁻j *C* **3** πλοιαριων‖2: *pc* | ◆ *om* του[1] *cf.* 4 38a Mk9 41 1K11 12 34: 𝔓[75] ℵBLW-579 D 157 **4** *om* εις[2] αγ.‖Jo6: **λ**-22-1582 *pc* **5** ● *om* ο *cf.* Mk1 36: 𝔓[75] ℵ(∼ ειπ. Σ.)BL σ1424 Δ | ● *om* αυτω: 𝔓[4v.75] ℵB 700 σ990 *L*e *C*b *Δ*i l[AD] p — *txt*: *Rpl L*' *S*,j *C*s *Δ*' | ● ολ. + της *cf.* Mt20 6 Act13 49: *Rpl* — *txt*: 𝔓[75] 𝔥⟨579-892-1241⟩ λ131 A Ψ *pc* | τ. δικ.] ● το δικτυον‖Jo6.8: *Rpl L*' — *txt*: 𝔓[75] 𝔥⟨33-1241⟩ 700 **λ**-1582-2193 D Θ *pc L*(e) cqr[2]z Am *C* **6** τ. δικ.] ● το δικτυον‖←: *Rpl L*e br[2] vg — *txt*: 𝔓[75] 𝔥⟨33⟩ **λ**-1582-2193 σ990 D Θ *pc* Eu *L*vl'r[1] *C* | αυτ. + ωστε μη δυνασθαι αναγαγειν αυτο‖←: 28 S Ω *al* **7** ● μετο. + τοις: *Rpl* — *txt*: 𝔓[4v.75] 𝔥⟨33-892-1241⟩ 700 λ1582-2193 D Ψ *pc* | ωστε + ηδη‖Mk4 37: C* {} *Δ*a i[V] l[AD] md me n[CHgL] — + παρα τι‖←: D *L*e cg[2]r[1] vg[1] {*S*'h[m]j} | βυθ. + υπο των κυματων‖Mt8 24 14 24: 1573 **8** γον.] ποσιν‖8 14 17 16 Mk7 25 5 22: 579 **λ**-1582-2193 D 872 *pc L*e c *S*s[c]p *C Δ*a i p | I.] ● του I.: CLX-33-579(τ. κυριου)-1241 Λ-1071 **λ**-1582 **φ**-230 σM-990-1293 A F Θ Ψ 157(= 579) *al* — αυτου *et* ∼ αυ. τοις πο.: D *L*e — *txt*: 𝔓[4.75] *Rpl*
10 ομοιως—[11]απα.] ησαν δε κοινωνοι αυτου(*om*) Ιακωβος κ. Ιωαννης υιοι Ζεβ. ο δε (+ ο Ιησους) ειπεν αυτοις(τω Σιμωνι)· δευτε και (*om* δευ. κ.) μη γινεσθε αλιεις ιχθυων· ποιησω γαρ υμας αλιεις ανθρωπων. οι δε ακουσαντες παντα κατελειψαν επι της γης και‖5 28 Mt4 19p: D (*L*e) **11** απα.] παντα‖5 28 Mt19 27 Mk10 28: ℵBL-579 λ131 φ174-983 **σ**-990-1188 D *pc*

Jo 21,3 εξηλ.] ● εξ. ουν.: 𝔥⟨BW⟩X N λ209 φ983-1689 D G Θ Π[c] *pc C*b[B] — και εξ.: 1071 A P Ψ *L*' *S*'(h και[+])j *C*b' *Geo*[1] — *txt*: *Rpl* Cr[I] *L*e aq vg[4] *C*s[6]([1]+ δε) *Arm Geo*[2] | πλοι. + ευθυς‖Mt14 22p Mk8 10: *Rpl* Cr *S*hj — *txt*: 𝔥⟨1241⟩C*X N **λ φ**⟨124-346⟩ D Δ Θ Ψ **0141** *pc* Cr[I] *L S*' *C*[+B] | επια.] εκοπιασαν‖Lk5: ℵ* **4** *om* ηδη‖Mt27 1: ℵ* λ209 **φ**⟨983⟩ 565 *l*150 *L*e acqr[1]z *S*s[c]p *C*[+B] | γιν.] γενομενης‖←: *Rpl L*' *C*c[3+1v]b[B] {*Arm*} — *txt*: BC*L λ2193 σ71-1010 A E *pc L*q *C*b' **5** ο I.] ● I.: ℵB — *om*: W A*[v] *L*a *S*s[c] — ο κυριος I.: *S*j[ac](*om* I.: j[b]) **6** ο δε ειπ.] ● λεγει‖10: ℵ*W *L*bcr[1]z (ειπ.: vg')[5] *S*'j *C*'[+B](*prm* και: b[1]) *Δ*a l — *txt*: 𝔓[66v] *Rpl* Cr[I] *L*e afq *S*h | ευρ. + οι δε ειπον· δι ολης (+ της) νυκτος εκοπιασαμεν και (εκ. και] κοπιασαντες) ουδεν ελαβομεν. επι δε τω σω ονοματι(ρηματι) βαλουμεν‖Lk5: 𝔓[66v] ℵ[c](ολ. + της) (Cr[I]) *L*vg[4] *C*s **8** τω + αλλω‖Lk7: ℵ* | πλοι.] πλοιω‖Lk7: W P **11** ● αν. + ουν: 𝔥⟨33-1241⟩CX N-1071 λ1-22 Θ Ψ *pc* Cr[I] *L*r[1] vg[3] *S*hj *C* — + δε: *C*b[B] — και αν.: *S*' *Δ*a me — τοτε αν.: *L*c vg[1] *Δ*ad i[T] md n — *txt*: *Rpl L*' *Arm Δ*i[V] l p

Die Bergpredigt. *The Sermon on the Mount.*

Matth 5—7.

(18)

30. Einleitung. *Introduction.*

Matth 5 1–2		6 17.20a (*84.*; *86.*)
1 Ἰδὼν δὲ τοὺς ὄχλους ἀνέβη εἰς τὸ ὄρος· καὶ καθίσαντος αὐτοῦ προσῆλθαν αὐτῷ οἱ μαθηταὶ αὐτοῦ· 2 καὶ ἀνοίξας τὸ στόμα αὐτοῦ ἐδίδασκεν αὐτοὺς λέγων·	*cf.* *85.*	*17 Καὶ καταβὰς μετ' αὐτῶν ἔστη ἐπὶ τόπου πεδινοῦ, καὶ ὄχλος πολὺς μαθητῶν αὐτοῦ, καὶ πλῆθος πολὺ τοῦ λαοῦ ... 20a Καὶ αὐτὸς ἐπάρας τοὺς ὀφθαλμοὺς αὐτοῦ εἰς τοὺς μαθητὰς αὐτοῦ ἔλεγεν·*

(19)

31. Die Seligpreisungen. *The Beatitudes.*

	Matth 5 3–12	6 20b–23 (*86.*)
	3 μακάριοι οἱ πτωχοὶ τῷ πνεύματι, ὅτι αὐτῶν ἐστιν ἡ βασιλεία τῶν οὐρανῶν.	*20b μακάριοι οἱ πτωχοί, ὅτι ὑμετέρα ἐστὶν ἡ βασιλεία τοῦ θεοῦ.*
Is 61 2	4 μακάριοι οἱ **πενθοῦντες,** ὅτι αὐτοὶ **παρακληθήσονται.**	*21b μακάριοι οἱ κλαίοντες νῦν, ὅτι γελάσετε.*
Ps 37 11	5 μακάριοι οἱ **πραεῖς,** ὅτι αὐτοὶ **κληρονομήσουσιν τὴν γῆν.**	
	6 μακάριοι οἱ πεινῶντες καὶ διψῶντες τὴν δικαιοσύνην, ὅτι αὐτοὶ χορτασθήσονται.	*21a μακάριοι οἱ πεινῶντες νῦν, ὅτι χορτασθήσεσθε.*
	7 μακάριοι οἱ ἐλεήμονες, ὅτι αὐτοὶ ἐλεηθήσονται.	
Ps 24 4	8 μακάριοι οἱ **καθαροὶ τῇ καρδίᾳ,** ὅτι αὐτοὶ τὸν θεὸν ὄψονται.	
	9 μακάριοι οἱ εἰρηνοποιοί, ὅτι υἱοὶ θεοῦ κληθήσονται.	
	10 μακάριοι οἱ δεδιωγμένοι ἕνεκα δικαιοσύνης, ὅτι αὐτῶν ἐστιν ἡ βασιλεία τῶν οὐρανῶν.	
	11 μακάριοί ἐστε ὅταν	*22 μακάριοί ἐστε ὅταν μισήσωσιν ὑμᾶς οἱ ἄνθρωποι, καὶ*

Mt 5,4 ● ∼ 5.4: 33 D Bas Chr Eu$^{can\,v}$ Gr^{Ny} Or *L*vl'[e] Hi Hil *S*c Af Ef *Δ*' — *txt*: *Rpl* Chr **Or** *L*bfqr^{2} vg PsChr Hil Te *S*'j *C*,Sch *Δ*a p | πεν. + νυν‖p: ℵ^{b}-33-892 Chr Ddy^{v} *L*30 *S*j^{ab} *C*b Sch *Aeth* | *om* αυτ.‖p: 700 Eu **9** ● οτι + αυτοι‖5-8: *Rpl* *L*k[e] f30 vg^{5} Au^{19} PsAu^{1} Cp$^{2:3}$ Or *S*'j *C* *Arm* *Geo*^{A} — *txt*: ℵC ϕ⟨346-828-983⟩ D Ddy *L*' Au^{16} PsAu^{1} Hil *Sp* *Geo*^{B}

Mt5 3 *cf.* ETh^{II} 54 (*cf. ad 86.* Lk6 20)

Mt5 6p *cf.* ETh^{II} 69b (*transl.*): *μακάριοι οἱ πεινῶντες, ὅτι χορτασθήσεται (ἵνα -ασθῇ?) ἡ κοιλία τοῦ θέλοντος.*

Mt5 8.10 *cf.* ETh^{II} 69a (*transl.*): *Λέγει Ἰησοῦς· μακάριοι οἱ δεδιωγμένοι ἐν τῇ καρδίᾳ αὐτῶν· ἐκεῖνοί εἰσιν οἱ γνόντες τὸν πατέρα ἐπ' ἀληθείας.*

Mt5 11p *cf.* ETh^{II} 68 (*transl.*): *Λέγει Ἰησοῦς· μακάριοί ἐστε ὅταν μισήσωσιν ὑμᾶς καὶ διώξωσιν ὑμᾶς· καὶ οὐχ εὑρεθήσεται ὁ(?) τόπος ὅπου ἐδίωξαν ὑμᾶς.*

ὀνειδίσωσιν ὑμᾶς καὶ διώξωσιν καὶ εἴπωσιν πᾶν πονηρὸν καθ' ὑμῶν ἕνεκα ἐμοῦ. [12] χαίρετε καὶ ἀγαλλιᾶσθε, ὅτι ὁ μισθὸς ὑμῶν πολὺς ἐν τοῖς οὐρανοῖς· οὕτως γὰρ ἐδίωξαν τοὺς προφήτας τοὺς πρὸ ὑμῶν.

86.

ὅταν ἀφορίσωσιν ὑμᾶς καὶ ὀνειδίσωσιν καὶ ἐκβάλωσιν τὸ ὄνομα ὑμῶν ὡς πονηρὸν ἕνεκα τοῦ υἱοῦ τοῦ ἀνθρώπου. [23] χάρητε ἐν ἐκείνῃ τῇ ἡμέρᾳ καὶ σκιρτήσατε· ἰδοὺ γὰρ ὁ μισθὸς ὑμῶν πολὺς ἐν τῷ οὐρανῷ· κατὰ τὰ αὐτὰ γὰρ ἐποίουν τοῖς προφήταις οἱ πατέρες αὐτῶν.

(20) *32.* Gleichnisse vom Salz und vom Licht. *Parables about Salt and Light.*

Matth 5 13–16

[13] Ὑμεῖς ἐστε τὸ ἅλας τῆς γῆς· ἐὰν δὲ τὸ ἅλας μωρανθῇ, ἐν τίνι ἁλισθήσεται; εἰς οὐδὲν ἰσχύει ἔτι εἰ μὴ βληθὲν ἔξω καταπατεῖσθαι ὑπὸ τῶν ἀνθρώπων.

[14] Ὑμεῖς ἐστε τὸ φῶς τοῦ κόσμου. οὐ δύναται πόλις κρυβῆναι ἐπάνω ὄρους κειμένη· [15] οὐδὲ καίουσιν λύχνον καὶ τιθέασιν αὐτὸν ὑπὸ τὸν μόδιον, ἀλλ' ἐπὶ τὴν λυχνίαν, καὶ λάμπει πᾶσιν τοῖς ἐν τῇ οἰκίᾳ. [16] οὕτως λαμψάτω τὸ φῶς ὑμῶν ἔμπροσθεν τῶν ἀνθρώπων, ὅπως ἴδωσιν ὑμῶν τὰ καλὰ ἔργα καὶ δοξάσωσιν τὸν πατέρα ὑμῶν τὸν ἐν τοῖς οὐρανοῖς.

9 50 *(146.)*

[50] καλὸν τὸ ἅλας· ἐὰν δὲ τὸ ἅλας ἄναλον γένηται, ἐν τίνι αὐτὸ ἀρτύσετε; ...

14 34–35 *(185.)*

[34] καλὸν οὖν τὸ ἅλας· ἐὰν δὲ καὶ τὸ ἅλας μωρανθῇ, ἐν τίνι ἀρτυθήσεται; [35] οὔτε εἰς γῆν οὔτε εἰς κοπρίαν εὔθετόν ἐστιν· ἔξω βάλλουσιν αὐτό. ὁ ἔχων ὦτα ἀκούειν ἀκουέτω.

107.

8 12: ... ἐγώ εἰμι τὸ φῶς τοῦ κόσμου ...

11 33 *(167.): Οὐδεὶς λύχνον ἅψας εἰς κρύπτην τίθησιν οὐδὲ ὑπὸ τὸν μόδιον, ἀλλ' ἐπὶ τὴν λυχνίαν, ἵνα οἱ εἰσπορευόμενοι τὸ φέγγος βλέπωσιν.*

(21) *33.* Jesu Stellung zum Gesetz. *The Law and the Prophets.*

Matth 5 17–20

[17] Μὴ νομίσητε ὅτι ἦλθον καταλῦσαι τὸν νόμον ἢ τοὺς προφήτας· οὐκ ἦλθον καταλῦσαι ἀλλὰ πληρῶσαι. [18] αμην γὰρ λέγω ὑμῖν, ἕως ἂν παρέλθῃ ὁ οὐρανὸς καὶ ἡ γῆ,

234.

16 17 *(190.)*

[17] εὐκοπώτερον δέ ἐστιν τὸν οὐρανὸν καὶ τὴν γῆν

Mt 5,11 ∼ διω. ... ονει.‖p: 33 D *L*k[e] h Au Cp *S*c Eu *C*b *Aeth* | πον. + ρημα‖12 35f.: *Rpl* Or *L*q *S*'j[cf] *C*Sch *Δ*a p — *txt*: ℵB D Cr Ep *L*' Au PsAu Hil Luc Te *S*scj[ab] Eu *C* *Aeth* *Δ*'⟨me⟩ | ● υμων + ψευδομενοι: *Rpl* CAp Chr Ep Or[1] *L*' Au[4] *S*'(∼ ψ. κ. υμ.: c)j *C* *Δ*'⟨me⟩ — *txt*: D Ddy Or[1] *L*k[e a]bc g[1]h Au[1] PsAu Hil Luc Te *S*s Eu *Δ*i[V] | εμου] δικαιοσυνης‖10: D *L*k[e] abcg[1] Hil — του ονοματος μου‖19.29 Lk21 12: *S*sc *Δ*i[V] **12** οτι] ιδου γαρ‖p: *l*49 | τ. ουρ.] τω ουρανω‖p: D *pc* *L*k[e] abh Hil Luc Te | υμ.[2] + οι πατερες (αδελφοι) αυτων‖p: U *L*(k[e]) bc Te *S*s(*om* τ. προ υμ.)c(∼ οι πατ. υμων τ. προφ. τ. προ υμ.) **13** δε + και‖Lk: 713 **15** λαμ.] φαινει‖Jo1 5: σ945 Thd[C] **17** ουκ] ου γαρ‖9 13: Or

---

Mt5 13; Lk14 35 *cf.* ETh[II] 93 (*cf. ad 49.*)

Mt5 14b *cf.* ETh[II] 32 (POx 1,7): Λέγει Ἰ(ησοῦ)ς· πόλις οἰκοδομουμένη ἐπ' ἄκρον [ὄ]ρους ὑψηλοῦ[ς?] καὶ ἐστηριγμένη οὔτε πε[σ]εῖν δύναται οὐδὲ κρυ[β]ῆναι.

(*transl.*): *Λέγει Ἰησοῦς· πόλις οἰκοδομουμένη ἐπ' ἄκρον ὄρους ὑψηλοῦ ἐστηριγμένη οὖσα οὐ πεσεῖν δύναται οὐδὲ κρυβῆναι δυνήσεται.*

Mt5 15p *cf.* ETh[II] 33b (*cf. ad 107.* Mk4 21)

Mt5 17 *cf.* EAe (Cl Strom. III 9,63): 'ἦλθον καταλῦσαι τὰ ἔργα τῆς θηλείας.' θηλείας μέν· τῆς ἐπιθυμίας, ἔργα δέ· γένεσιν καὶ φθοράν.

EEb frgm.6 (Ep haer. 30,16,5): ... 'ἦλθον καταλῦσαι τὰς θυσίας ...' (*cf. ad 81.* Mt12 7).

Mt5 18p *cf.* ETh[II] 11 (*cf. ad 234.* Mt24 35)

ἰῶτα ἓν ἢ μία κεραία οὐ μὴ παρέλθῃ ἀπὸ τοῦ νόμου, ἕως ἂν πάντα γένηται. [19] ὃς ἐὰν οὖν λύσῃ μίαν τῶν ἐντολῶν τούτων τῶν ἐλαχίστων καὶ διδάξῃ οὕτως τοὺς ἀνθρώπους, ἐλάχιστος κληθήσεται ἐν τῇ βασιλείᾳ τῶν οὐρανῶν· ὃς δ' ἂν ποιήσῃ καὶ διδάξῃ, οὗτος μέγας κληθήσεται ἐν τῇ βασιλείᾳ τῶν οὐρανῶν. [20] λέγω γὰρ ὑμῖν ὅτι ἐὰν μὴ περισσεύσῃ ὑμῶν ἡ δικαιοσύνη πλεῖον τῶν γραμματέων καὶ Φαρισαίων, οὐ μὴ εἰσέλθητε εἰς τὴν βασιλείαν τῶν οὐρανῶν.

234. *παρελθεῖν ἢ τοῦ νόμου μίαν κεραίαν πεσεῖν.*

(22)

34. Vom Töten. *On Murder.* **Matth 5** 21–26

Ex20 13 Dt5 17

[21] Ἠκούσατε ὅτι ἐρρέθη τοῖς ἀρχαίοις· **οὐ φονεύσεις**· ὃς δ' ἂν φονεύσῃ, ἔνοχος ἔσται τῇ κρίσει. [22] ἐγὼ δὲ λέγω ὑμῖν ὅτι πᾶς ὁ ὀργιζόμενος τῷ ἀδελφῷ αὐτοῦ ἔνοχος ἔσται τῇ κρίσει· ὃς δ' ἂν εἴπῃ τῷ ἀδελφῷ αὐτοῦ ρακα, ἔνοχος ἔσται τῷ συνεδρίῳ· ὃς δ' ἂν εἴπῃ μωρέ, ἔνοχος ἔσται εἰς τὴν γέενναν τοῦ πυρός. [23] ἐὰν οὖν προσφέρῃς τὸ δῶρόν σου ἐπὶ τὸ θυσιαστήριον κἀκεῖ μνησθῇς ὅτι ὁ ἀδελφός σου ἔχει τι κατὰ σοῦ, [24] ἄφες ἐκεῖ τὸ δῶρόν σου ἔμπροσθεν τοῦ θυσιαστηρίου, καὶ ὕπαγε πρῶτον διαλλάγηθι τῷ ἀδελφῷ σου, καὶ τότε ἐλθὼν πρόσφερε τὸ δῶρόν σου.

11 25 *(215.): καὶ ὅταν στήκετε προσευχόμενοι, ἀφίετε εἴ τι ἔχετε κατά τινος, ...*

[25] Ἴσθι εὐνοῶν τῷ ἀντιδίκῳ σου ταχὺ ἕως ὅτου εἶ μετ' αὐτοῦ ἐν τῇ ὁδῷ· μήποτέ σε παραδῷ ὁ ἀντίδικος τῷ κριτῇ καὶ ὁ κριτὴς τῷ ὑπηρέτῃ, καὶ εἰς φυλακὴν βληθήσῃ· [26] αμην λέγω σοι, οὐ μὴ ἐξέλθῃς ἐκεῖθεν ἕως ἂν ἀποδῷς τὸν ἔσχατον κοδράντην.

12 58 f. *(175.): ὡς γὰρ ὑπάγεις μετὰ τοῦ ἀντιδίκου σου ἐπ' ἄρχοντα, ἐν τῇ ὁδῷ δὸς ἐργασίαν ἀπηλλάχθαι ἀπ' αὐτοῦ, μήποτε κατασύρῃ σε πρὸς τὸν κριτήν, καὶ ὁ κριτής σε παραδώσει τῷ πράκτορι, καὶ ὁ πράκτωρ σε βαλεῖ εἰς φυλακήν.* [59] *λέγω σοι, οὐ μὴ ἐξέλθῃς ἐκεῖθεν ἕως καὶ τὸ ἔσχατον λεπτὸν ἀποδῷς.*

(23)

35. Vom Ehebruch. *On Adultery.* **Matth 5** 27–30

Ex20 14 Dt5 18

[27] Ἠκούσατε ὅτι ἐρρέθη· **οὐ μοιχεύσεις.** [28] ἐγὼ δὲ λέγω ὑμῖν ὅτι πᾶς ὁ βλέπων γυναῖκα πρὸς τὸ ἐπιθυμῆσαι αὐτὴν ἤδη ἐμοίχευσεν αὐτὴν ἐν τῇ καρδίᾳ αὐτοῦ. [29] εἰ δὲ ὁ ὀφθαλμός σου ὁ δεξιὸς σκανδαλίζει

Mt 5,18 νομ. + και(η) των προφητων‖17: Σ-565 φ⟨346⟩-*l*547 Θ *al* *L*Ir (*S*j) Af *Arm* *Δ*p **20** ∼ η δικ. υμ.‖61: *Rpl* (^{19a}∩^{20}ουρ.: D) Cl^{1} *L*, PsCp Or — *txt*: 𝔓^{64v} ℌ⟨33⟩ 28-700 φ⟨346-983⟩-174 σM-27-267-945-990-1223-1293-1391-1402 E K V W Γ Δ Θ Π Ω **047** 157 *pm* Cl^{1} Ddy Iu **22** ● αυτ.^{1} + εικη: *Rpl* PsAth Bas Chr Cr Ir PsIu Or *L*vl' vg^{3} Au^{6} PsAu^{1} Cp Ep Ir Luc Or *S*,j *C* *Δ*a p — *txt*: 𝔓^{64v} ℵ*B σ1424^{m} Δ^{c} Ω *pc* PsAth PsBas Eu Or *L*r^{2}z vg' Au^{1} PsAug^{1} Can Cp^{1} Hi Ir^{1} Or Te *Aeth* *Δ*'⟨i^{V}(^{21}∩^{22}κρ.) me⟩ | ειπη^{2} + τω αδελφω αυτου‖22a.b: L 700 **λ**-1582 φ⟨346⟩-174 Θ *pc* *L*ff^{1}30 *S*sc *C*b *Arm* *Δ*i^{V} md n p **25** κριτης + σε παραδω‖p: *Rpl* *L*' Au *S*'(και^{1}∩^{2}: s) *C*, PS *Geo*^{A} — *txt*: 𝔓^{64v} ℵB-892 **λ**-1582 φ⟨346-828⟩-174 Chr Cl Ep *L*k[e] Ar Hil Ir *S*j *Arm* *Geo*^{B} *Aeth* **26** *om* αν‖p: 33 σ945-1207-1606 *pc*

Mt5 22 *cf.* EN frgm.4 (Cod. N.T. 1424^{m}): Τὸ εἰκῇ ἔν τισιν ἀντιγράφοις οὐ κεῖται οὐδὲ ἐν τῷ Ἰουδαϊκῷ.

Mt5 23 *cf.* EH frgm.6 (Hi Ez *ad* 18 7): Et in evangelio, quod iuxta Hebraeos Nazaraei legere consueverunt, inter maxima ponitur crimina, qui fratis sui spiritum contristaverit. *Cf.* frgm.5 (Hi Eph *ad* 5 4): Ut in hebraico quoque evangelio legimus dominum ad discipulos loquentem: et nunquam, inquit, laeti sitis, nisi cum fratrem vestrum videritis in caritate.

σε, ἔξελε αὐτὸν καὶ βάλε ἀπὸ σοῦ· συμφέρει γάρ σοι ἵνα ἀπόληται ἓν τῶν μελῶν σου καὶ μὴ ὅλον τὸ σῶμά σου βληθῇ εἰς γέενναν. [30] καὶ εἰ ἡ δεξιά σου χεὶρ σκανδαλίζει σε, ἔκκοψον αὐτὴν καὶ βάλε ἀπὸ σοῦ· συμφέρει γάρ σοι ἵνα ἀπόληται ἓν τῶν μελῶν σου καὶ μὴ ὅλον τὸ σῶμά σου εἰς γέενναν ἀπέλθῃ. **145.**

(24)

36. Von der Ehescheidung. *On Divorce.* 201.

Matth 5 31–32		*16* 18 *(190.)*	
[31] Ἐρρέθη δέ· ὃς ἂν **ἀπολύσῃ** τὴν γυναῖκα αὐτοῦ, **δότω αὐτῇ ἀποστάσιον.** [32] ἐγὼ δὲ λέγω ὑμῖν ὅτι πᾶς ὁ ἀπολύων τὴν γυναῖκα αὐτοῦ παρεκτὸς λόγου πορνείας ποιεῖ αὐτὴν μοιχευθῆναι, καὶ ὃς ἐὰν ἀπολελυμένην γαμήσῃ, μοιχᾶται.	**201.**	[18] *πᾶς ὁ ἀπολύων τὴν γυναῖκα αὐτοῦ καὶ γαμῶν ἑτέραν μοιχεύει, καὶ ὁ ἀπολελυμένην ἀπὸ ἀνδρὸς γαμῶν μοιχεύει.*	Dt24 1

(25)

37. Vom Schwören. *On Swearing.* **Matth 5** 33–37

[33] Πάλιν ἠκούσατε ὅτι ἐρρέθη τοῖς ἀρχαίοις· **οὐκ ἐπιορκήσεις, ἀποδώσεις δὲ τῷ κυρίῳ τοὺς ὅρκους σου.** [34] ἐγὼ δὲ λέγω ὑμῖν μὴ ὀμόσαι ὅλως· μήτε ἐν **τῷ οὐρανῷ**, ὅτι **θρόνος ἐστὶν τοῦ θεοῦ·** [35] μήτε ἐν **τῇ γῇ**, ὅτι **ὑποπόδιόν ἐστιν τῶν ποδῶν αὐτοῦ·** μήτε εἰς Ἱεροσόλυμα, ὅτι **πόλις** ἐστὶν **τοῦ μεγάλου βασιλέως·** [36] μήτε ἐν τῇ κεφαλῇ σου ὀμόσῃς, ὅτι οὐ δύνασαι μίαν τρίχα λευκὴν ποιῆσαι ἢ μέλαιναν. [37] ἔστω δὲ ὁ λόγος ὑμῶν ναὶ ναί, οὒ οὔ· τὸ δὲ περισσὸν τούτων ἐκ τοῦ πονηροῦ ἐστιν.

23 22 *(224.)*: *καὶ ὁ ὀμόσας ἐν τῷ οὐρανῷ ὀμνύει ἐν τῷ θρόνῳ τοῦ θεοῦ καὶ ἐν τῷ καθημένῳ ἐπάνω αὐτοῦ.*

Lv19 12 Ps50 14 · Is66 1 · Ps48 3

Mt 5,29 *om* γαρ ‖ 18 8f. Mk9 43.45.47: *L*k[e] | βλη. εις γ.] εις γ. βλη.: D^v(^{21}⌒^{30}βαλε—γεε.) *L*fff^{1}lz vg' — εις γ. απελθη ‖ 30: *L*vl'(*om* απε.: k[e]) vg^2 — απε. εις γ. ‖ Mk9 43: *S*s(⌒ = D)c | γεε.] την γ. ‖ 5 22 18 9 Mk9 43.45.47: L ϕ983 σ1606 273 *pc* *l*48 | γεε. + του πυρος ‖ 5 22 18 9: 4 273 Ad(*om* του) *L*30 *C*s$^{3:7}$ *Aeth* **30** ∼ η χε. σου η δεξ. ‖ 29: Θ(*om* η^1) **ϕ**⟨346⟩-174 | *om* γαρ ‖ 18 8f. Mk9 43.45.47: *L*k[e] ff^{1}32 vg^5 PsAu *C*s$^{1:7}$b^2 | και μη] η ‖ ←: ℵ* *L*⟨k[e]⟩ Luc | εις γ. απε.] βληθη εις γ. ‖ 29 18 9 Mk9 45.47: *Rpl* *L*f30 vg^1 *S*' *C*s — απε. εις γ. ‖ 29: σ517-1675 D(*cf ad* 29) 372 *L*'(*om* απε.: k[e]) Luc *S*c(s *cf. ad* 29)j — *txt*: ℌ⟨L⟩ **λ**-22 157 *pc* *C*b | γεε.] την γ. ‖ 22 18 9 Mk9 43.45.47: L 273 | γεε. + του πυρος ‖ 22 18 9: *C*s$^{2:7}$ *Aeth* **31** αποστ.] βιβλιον αποστασιου ‖ **19** 7**p**: 1604 *pc* *L*cfff^{1}lz vg {*S*,j *Δ*⟨me p⟩} **32** πας ο απ.] ος(οστις) αν απολυση ‖ 31 19 9p: 28 ϕ230-346 D E S U V **0250** *pm* Chr^2 **Or** *L*k[e] abg^{1}h Au^7 *S*sc *C*s^{2}b *Arm*^{pc} *Δ*i^T — *txt*: *Rpl* Chr^1(ο γαρ απ.) Cl(*om* πας) *L*' Au^4 PsAu *S*'j *C*s^5 *Arm*' *Δ*'⟨me p⟩ | μοιχευθ.] μοιχασθαι ‖ Mk10 12: *Rpl* — *txt*: ℌ⟨L⟩ **λ**-1582 **ϕ**-174 D W Θ **0250** 660 Chr Cl **Or** Thi | ος εαν … γαμ.] ο … γαμησας ‖ 32a 19 9 Lk16 18: B (*om* ο: ϕ828-983-1689 *pc*) 80 *l*184(ο] ος) *l*185 *l*1579

37 εσ.—ου^2] εστω (+ δε) το ναι υμων ναι (+ ναι) και το ου υμων ου ‖ Jc5 12: *C*s$^{1:4}$(b^1) | ο λογ. υμ.] υμων ‖ ←: *l*184 Chr Cl Ddy Iu Or — υμιν: Chr | ναι ναι] το ναι ναι και το ‖ ←: Θ 213 Chr Cl PsCl Cr Ddy Eu Gr^{Ny} Iu {*L*bg^{1}h Ir *S*scpj *Δ*i$^{T2:7}$} — το ν. ν. το ‖ ←: *l*148 Ep — ν. ν. και ‖ ←: L 237 PsBas Or {}

(26) 38. Von der Wiedervergeltung. *On Retaliation.*

Ex21 24 Dt19 21 Lv24 20

Matth 5 38–42	6 29–30 (88.)
[38] Ἠκούσατε ὅτι ἐρρέθη· **ὀφθαλμὸν ἀντὶ ὀφθαλμοῦ καὶ ὀδόντα ἀντὶ ὀδόντος.** [39] ἐγὼ δὲ λέγω ὑμῖν μὴ ἀντιστῆναι τῷ πονηρῷ· ἀλλ' ὅστις σε ῥαπίσει εἰς τὴν δεξιάν σου σιαγόνα, στρέψον αὐτῷ καὶ τὴν ἄλλην· [40] καὶ τῷ θέλοντί σοι κριθῆναι καὶ τὸν χιτῶνά σου λαβεῖν, ἄφες αὐτῷ καὶ τὸ ἱμάτιον· [41] καὶ ὅστις σε ἀγγαρεύσει μίλιον ἕν, ὕπαγε μετ' αὐτοῦ δύο. [42] τῷ αἰτοῦντί σε δός, καὶ τὸν θέλοντα ἀπὸ σοῦ δανείσασθαι μὴ ἀποστραφῇς.	*[29] τῷ τύπτοντί σε ἐπὶ τὴν σιαγόνα πάρεχε καὶ τὴν ἄλλην, καὶ ἀπὸ τοῦ αἴροντός σου τὸ ἱμάτιον καὶ τὸν χιτῶνα μὴ κωλύσῃς. [30] παντὶ αἰτοῦντί σε δίδου, καὶ ἀπὸ τοῦ αἴροντος τὰ σὰ μὴ ἀπαίτει.*

(27) 39. Von der Feindesliebe. *On Loving One's Enemies.*

Lv19 18

Matth 5 43–48	6 27.28.35.32.33.36 (88.)
[43] Ἠκούσατε ὅτι ἐρρέθη· **ἀγαπήσεις τὸν πλησίον σου** καὶ μισήσεις τὸν ἐχθρόν σου. [44] ἐγὼ δὲ λέγω ὑμῖν, ἀγαπᾶτε τοὺς ἐχθροὺς ὑμῶν καὶ	*[27] ... ἀγαπᾶτε τοὺς ἐχθροὺς ὑμῶν, καλῶς ποιεῖτε τοῖς μισοῦσιν ὑμᾶς, [28] εὐλογεῖτε τοὺς καταρωμένους ὑμᾶς,*

Mt 5,39 οστ. σε ραπ.] τω ραπιζοντι σε ‖p: Ep | ● ραπιζει: ℵB-33 Σ-700 σ1424 W *l*48 — *txt* (οστ.] εαν τις): *Rpl* Ad Bas (PsBas) Chr^{1}(^{2}) Eu (Ptl^{Ep}) *L*,Or *C* | εις] επι ‖p: *Rpl* — *txt*: ℵ*B Σ-544 ϕ230-983-1689 σ1194 W *al* Ad Bas PsBas Chr Ep Eu Or | *om* δεξ. ‖p: D Ad Or *L*k[e] *S*sc Af Ef | ● *om* σου ‖**p**: ℵ-33-892 Σ-544 **λ**-22-1278-1582 ϕ230-346-983-1689 σ27-945-990-1010-1675 157 *pm* Ad Bas PsBas Chr Ep Or *L*afh vg^{1} — ● ∼ σι. σου: B D Eu {} — *txt*: *R* 28-700 **ϕ**'-174 *pm* {*L*' *C*} **42** τω] παντι τω ‖p: Iu *L*k[e] abfg^{1}h Cp | δος] διδου ‖p: *Rpl* — *txt*: ℵB-892 **ϕ**⟨346-543-828⟩ D W Cl
44 υμων + ευλογειτε τους καταρωμενους υμας(υμιν), καλως ποιειτε τοις μισουσιν υμας ‖p: *Rpl* (D) (τους μισουντας: *pc*) CAp Chr *L*cfh *S*'j Af *Geo*^{A}(^{B} *om* τ. μισ. υμ.) — + ευλ. τ. κατ. υμ. ‖p: 1071 213 *l*871 Athg(*om* υμ.) *L*Cad Luc Te *S*Af *C*b^{10} *Geo*^{1} — + καλ. π. τ. μισ. υμ. ‖p: 243 *pc* *L*' Can Cp^{1} — *txt*: ℵB **λ**-1582 *pc* Ad Eu Or Thi *L*k[e] Cp^{2} Ir *S*sc *C*' | *om* και ‖p: W Athg *C*b^{1}

---

38. (*et 39.*) *cf.* Did12-5: Ἡ μὲν οὖν ὁδὸς τῆς ζωῆς ἐστιν αὕτη· πρῶτον ἀγαπήσεις τὸν θεὸν τὸν ποιήσαντά σε, δεύτερον τὸν πλησίον σου ὡς σεαυτόν· πάντα δὲ ὅσα ἐὰν θελήσῃς μὴ γίνεσθαί σοι, καὶ σὺ ἄλλῳ μὴ ποίει. [3] τούτων δὲ τῶν λόγων ἡ διδαχή ἐστιν αὕτη· εὐλογεῖτε τοὺς καταρωμένους ὑμῖν καὶ προσεύχεσθε ὑπὲρ τῶν ἐχθρῶν ὑμῶν, νηστεύετε δὲ ὑπὲρ τῶν διωκόντων ὑμᾶς· ποία γὰρ χάρις, ἐὰν ἀγαπᾶτε τοὺς ἀγαπῶντας ὑμᾶς; οὐχὶ καὶ τὰ ἔθνη τὸ αὐτὸ ποιοῦσιν; ὑμεῖς δὲ ἀγαπᾶτε τοὺς μισοῦντας ὑμᾶς, καὶ οὐχ ἕξετε ἐχθρόν. [4] ἀπέχου τῶν σαρκικῶν καὶ σωματικῶν ἐπιθυμιῶν. ἐάν τίς σοι δῷ ῥάπισμα εἰς τὴν δεξιὰν σιαγόνα, στρέψον αὐτῷ καὶ τὴν ἄλλην, καὶ ἔσῃ τέλειος· ἐὰν ἀγγαρεύσῃ σέ τις μίλιον ἕν, ὕπαγε μετ' αὐτοῦ δύο· ἐὰν ἄρῃ τις τὸ ἱμάτιόν σου, δὸς αὐτῷ καὶ τὸν χιτῶνα· ἐὰν λάβῃ τις ἀπὸ σοῦ τὸ σόν, μὴ ἀπαίτει· οὐδὲ γὰρ δύνασαι. [5] παντὶ τῷ αἰτοῦντί σε δίδου καὶ μὴ ἀπαίτει· πᾶσι γὰρ θέλει δίδοσθαι ὁ πατὴρ ἐκ τῶν ἰδίων χαρισμάτων.

Mt542p *cf.* ETh^{II} 95 (*transl.*): *[Λέγει Ἰησοῦς·] ἐὰν ἔχητε ἀργύριον, μὴ δανείζετε, ἀλλὰ δίδοτε [...] παρ' οὗ οὐκ ἀπολήμψεσθε αὐτά.*

cf. Act2035: ... ὅτι αὐτὸς εἶπεν· μακάριόν ἐστιν μᾶλλον διδόναι ἢ λαμβάνειν.

39. (*et 38.*) *cf.* Did12-5 (*cf. ad 38.*)

Mt544p *cf.* Ev. apocr. (POxy 1224 fol. 2r^{o} col. 1): κ]αὶ π[ρ]οσεύχεσθε ὑπὲρ [τῶν ἐχθ]ρῶν ὑμῶν. Ὁ γὰρ ... (*cf. ad 144.* Mk940) προσεύχεσθε ὑπὲρ τῶν διωκόντων ὑμᾶς· [45] ὅπως γένησθε υἱοὶ τοῦ πατρὸς ὑμῶν τοῦ ἐν οὐρανοῖς, ὅτι τὸν ἥλιον αὐτοῦ ἀνατέλλει ἐπὶ πονηροὺς καὶ ἀγαθοὺς καὶ βρέχει ἐπὶ δικαίους καὶ ἀδίκους. [46] ἐὰν γὰρ ἀγαπήσητε τοὺς ἀγαπῶντας ὑμᾶς, τίνα μισθὸν ἔχετε; οὐχὶ καὶ οἱ τελῶναι τὸ αὐτὸ ποιοῦσιν; [47] καὶ ἐὰν ἀσπάσησθε τοὺς ἀδελφοὺς ὑμῶν μόνον, τί περισσὸν ποιεῖτε; οὐχὶ καὶ οἱ ἐθνικοὶ οὕτως ποιοῦσιν; [48] **ἔσεσθε** οὖν ὑμεῖς **τέλειοι** ὡς ὁ πατὴρ ὑμῶν ὁ οὐράνιος τέλειός ἐστιν.

προσεύχεσθε περὶ τῶν ἐπηρεαζόντων ὑμᾶς ... [35] *... ἔσεσθε υἱοὶ ὑψίστου, ὅτι αὐτὸς χρηστός ἐστιν ἐπὶ τοὺς ἀχαρίστους καὶ πονηρούς ...* [32] *καὶ εἰ ἀγαπᾶτε τοὺς ἀγαπῶντας ὑμᾶς, ποία ὑμῖν χάρις ἐστίν; καὶ γὰρ οἱ ἁμαρτωλοὶ τοὺς ἀγαπῶντας αὐτοὺς ἀγαπῶσιν.* [33] *καὶ ἐὰν ἀγαθοποιῆτε τοὺς ἀγαθοποιοῦντας ὑμᾶς, ποία ὑμῖν χάρις ἐστίν; καὶ οἱ ἁμαρτωλοὶ τὸ αὐτὸ ποιοῦσιν ...* [36] *γίνεσθε οἰκτίρμονες, καθὼς καὶ ὁ πατὴρ ὑμῶν οἰκτίρμων ἐστίν.*

Dt18 13

(28)

40. Vom Almosen. *On Almsgiving.* **Matth 6 1–4**

[1] Προσέχετε δὲ τὴν δικαιοσύνην ὑμῶν μὴ ποιεῖν ἔμπροσθεν τῶν ἀνθρώπων πρὸς τὸ θεαθῆναι αὐτοῖς· εἰ δὲ μή γε, μισθὸν οὐκ ἔχετε παρὰ τῷ πατρὶ ὑμῶν τῷ ἐν τοῖς οὐρανοῖς.

Mt 5,44 διω. υμ.] επηρεαζοντων υμ.‖p: ϕ*l*547 *pc l*185 Or[1] *Geo*[1] *Got* — επηρ. υμ.(*om*) και διω. υμ.‖p: *Rpl* (D σ954 157) (*om* υμ.[2]: 33) CAp Chr Eu *L*(abh)cf vg[1] *S*'j[ab](c = 33) Af *Geo*[2] — διω. (+ υμ.) και επηρ. υμ.‖p: *L*'(g[1] vg[1])(*om* υμ.: vg[1]) Can Cp[1] — *txt*: ℵB **λ**-1582 Ad Athg Cat Eu Or[2] Thi *Lk*[e] Cp[3] Ir *S*sc *C Aeth* **45** οτι] οστις: 1573 *pc* Eu {} — ● ος: 372 Athg PsCl Mcn[Ep] {*L*⟨k[e] vg[2]⟩ Cp Hil Ir Mcn[Te] Or *S*,j *Δ*a ad i l[AD] md n} **46** αγαπη.] αγαπατε‖p: **σ**⟨954⟩ *pc* | *om* ουχι‖p: ℵ* Thi *S*s | το αυτο] τουτο(ταυτα): 1604 **λ** Thi *L*'(g[1] Luc Cp[1])[1] *S*'j *Δ*'⟨a me⟩ — ουτως‖47: Z-33 D *Lk*[e] h Cp[1] Luc *S*sc(∼) *C Geo*[1] *Aeth Δ*n[L] p — *txt*: *Rpl L*Cp[1] *Arm Geo*[2] **47** αδ.] ● φιλους: L-33 Σ-28-700 ϕ346 σM-349-517-692 *R* 157 *pm* Bas *L*fh Luc *S*h *Arm Δ*i[V] md(2° *cf. ad* 47b) n[L](C[Hr] 2°) — *txt*: ℌ' **λ**-22-1582 **ϕ**-174-230-*l*547 D *pl L*' Cp *S*([46]∩[47]ποιου.: s)cpj *C*,f *Δ*a ad i[T] l md(1° *cf. ad* 47b) n(C[Hr] 1°)[HgS] p | εθν.] τελωναι‖46: *Rpl L*h Cp[1] *S*p *Arm*(+ και οι αμαρτωλοι) *Geo*[2] *Δ*a (αμαρτ.: i[V]) — *txt*: ℌ⟨L⟩ 1071-1604 **λ**-22-1582 σ349 (εθνη)-1424-1675 D *pc* Bas *L*' Cp[1] *S*'j *C*,f *Geo*[1] *Aeth Δ*'⟨me n[L]⟩ | ουτ.] ◆ το αυτο‖46: ℌ⟨L⟩ Σ-28-700 **ϕ**-174-230-*l*547 **λ**-1582 σ349-1194-1424-1675 D U W *al l*48 *L*Cp Luc *Arm Geo*[2] *Aeth Δ*n[L] — τουτο: 1604 λ22 Bas[1] *L*' (ταυτα: g[1]) *S*pj[ac] *C*s[1+1v] *Δ*'⟨i[V] me⟩ — *txt*: *Rpl* Bas[1] *L*h *S*chj[b] *C*bf *Geo*[1] | ποιου. + και εαν ασπασησθε τους φιλους υμων μονον τι περισσοτερον(-σσον: 230-788) ποιειτε; ουχι και οι εθνικοι(τελωναι: 788) ουτως(το αυτο: 230-788) ποιουσιν: ϕ174-(230-788) (*sim.*: *Δ*md n[C Hr], *cf. ad* 47a) **48** εσε.] γινεσθε‖p: 157 Ath[1:2] Chr Cl Ddy Gr[Ny] Thd[C] | ως] καθως και‖p: Bas[1] PsBas — ως και‖p: 1241 *pc* Chr *L*cfff[1]lz vg Au[6] Cp[1] Or — ωσπερ: *Rpl* (+ και: ϕ346) {} Bas[2] — *txt*: ℌ Σ-544-700 **λ**-1582 **ϕ**' **σ**⟨954⟩-1293 *pc* Ath Chr Ddy Eu {*L*vl' Au[7] Cp[1] Hi} | ουρ.] εν τοις ουρανοις‖5 45.16 6 1.9: *Rpl* (*om* τοις: D*) Bas[1] Ddy[1] *L*bcg[1]h Au[4] Luc Te *Δ*a i[V] — *txt*: ℌ Σ-28-544-1071-1604 **λ**-1582 **ϕ** σ7-349-517-1293-1424 E U W 157 *mu* Ath Bas[2] Chr Ddy[1] Or *L*' Au[3] Cp *Arm Δ*'⟨i[T2:9] me⟩(*om*: l[A] n[L]) **6,1** δικ.] ελεημοσυνην‖2.3: *Rpl* Ath PsAth Or *Lk*[e] f *S*h *Arm Δ*a p — δοσιν: ℵ[a] *S*s *C* — *txt*: ℵ*B-892 **λ**-1582 σ1424 D **0250** *pc* Or *L*' Au Hi Hil *S*'j *C*f(?) *Δ*'⟨i[V] me⟩

---

40. (*41. 43.*) *cf.* ETh[II] 6 (POxy 654,5): Ἐξ]ετάζουσιν αὐτὸν ο[ἱ μαθηταὶ αὐτοῦ καὶ λέ]γουσιν· πῶς νηστεύ[σομεν, καὶ πῶς προσευξό]μεθα καὶ πῶς [ἐλεημοσύνην ποιήσομεν, κ]αὶ τί παρατηρήσ[ομεν ὅταν δειπνῶμε]ν; λέγει Ἰη(σοῦ)ς· [μὴ ψεύδεσθε καὶ ὅ τι μισ]εῖται μὴ ποιεῖτ[ε· πάντα γὰρ ἔσται πλήρ]ης ἀληθείας ἀν[τὶ τοῦ οὐρανοῦ· οὐδὲν γάρ ἐστι]ν ἀ[π]οκεκρ[υμμένον ὃ οὐ φανερὸν ἔσται· μα]κάρι[ός] ἐστιν [ὁ ταῦτα μὴ ποιῶν. πάντα γὰρ ἐν φανερ]ῷ ἔστ[αι παρὰ τῷ πατρὶ ὃς ἐν τῷ οὐρανῷ ἐστ]ιν.

(*transl.*): *Ἠρώτησαν αὐτὸν οἱ μαθηταὶ (καὶ) εἶπον αὐτῷ· θέλεις νηστεύσωμεν; καὶ πῶς προσευξώμεθα (καὶ) ποιήσωμεν ἐλεημοσύνην καὶ τί παρατηρήσωμεν βρωμάτων(?); λέγει Ἰησοῦς· μὴ ψεύδεσθε καὶ ὅ τι μισεῖτε μὴ ποιεῖτε. πάντα γὰρ φανερὰ ἔμπροσθεν τοῦ οὐρανοῦ· οὐδὲν γάρ ἐστιν κρυπτὸν ὃ οὐ γνωσθήσεται καὶ οὐδὲν κεκαλυμμένον ὃ οὐ ἀποκαλυφθήσεται.*

cf. ETh[II] 14 (*transl.*): *Λέγει Ἰησοῦς αὐτοῖς· ὅταν νηστεύητε γεννήσετε ὑμῖν ἁμαρτίαν· καὶ ὅταν προσεύχησθε κατακρινοῦσιν ὑμᾶς· καὶ ὅταν ποιῆτε ἐλεημοσύνην κακοποιήσετε τὰ πνεύματα ὑμῶν (= ὑμᾶς αὐτούς?)· καὶ εἰς ἣν ...* (*cf. ad 153.* Lk10 8)

2 Ὅταν οὖν ποιῇς ἐλεημοσύνην, μὴ σαλπίσῃς ἔμπροσθέν σου, ὥσπερ οἱ ὑποκριταὶ ποιοῦσιν ἐν ταῖς
συναγωγαῖς καὶ ἐν ταῖς ῥύμαις,
ὅπως δοξασθῶσιν ὑπὸ τῶν ἀνθρώπων·
αμην λέγω ὑμῖν, ἀπέχουσιν τὸν μισθὸν αὐτῶν.
3 σοῦ δὲ ποιοῦντος ἐλεημοσύνην μὴ γνώτω ἡ ἀριστερά σου τί ποιεῖ ἡ δεξιά σου, 4 ὅπως ᾖ σοῦ ἡ ἐλεημοσύνη ἐν τῷ κρυπτῷ·
καὶ ὁ πατήρ σου ὁ βλέπων ἐν τῷ κρυπτῷ αὐτὸς ἀποδώσει σοι.

(29)

41. Vom Beten. *On Prayer.* **Matth 6** 5-6

5 Καὶ ὅταν προσεύχησθε, οὐκ ἔσεσθε ὡς οἱ ὑποκριταί· ὅτι φιλοῦσιν ἐν ταῖς συναγωγαῖς καὶ ἐν ταῖς
γωνίαις τῶν πλατειῶν ἑστῶτες προσεύχεσθαι,
ὅπως ἂν φανῶσιν τοῖς ἀνθρώποις·
αμην λέγω ὑμῖν, ἀπέχουσιν τὸν μισθὸν αὐτῶν.

Is26 20 LXX 2Rg 4 33

6 σὺ δὲ ὅταν προσεύχῃ, **εἴσελθε εἰς τὸ ταμιεῖόν σου καὶ κλείσας τὴν θύραν σου** πρόσευξαι τῷ
πατρί σου τῷ ἐν τῷ κρυπτῷ·
καὶ ὁ πατήρ σου ὁ βλέπων ἐν τῷ κρυπτῷ ἀποδώσει σοι.

(29.30)

42. Das Unser-Vater. *The Lord's Prayer.* **Matth 6** 7-15

7 Προσευχόμενοι δὲ μὴ βατταλογήσητε ὥσπερ οἱ ἐθνικοί· δοκοῦσιν γὰρ ὅτι ἐν τῇ πολυλογίᾳ αὐτῶν
εἰσακουσθήσονται. 8 μὴ οὖν ὁμοιωθῆτε αὐτοῖς· οἶδεν
γὰρ ὁ πατὴρ ὑμῶν ὧν χρείαν ἔχετε πρὸ τοῦ ὑμᾶς αἰτῆσαι
αὐτόν. 9 οὕτως οὖν προσεύχεσθε ὑμεῖς·

47.

11 2-4 *(160.):*

εἶπεν δὲ αὐτοῖς· ὅταν προσεύχησθε, λέγετε·

Mt 6,4 ● *om* αυτος‖66.19: 𝔥 544 **λ**-22-1582 **φ**⟨346⟩-174-230 σ1424 K U Θ 157 *al l*3 *l*5 *l*7 *l*12 *l*13 *l*32 *l*46 *l*303 *l*1627 *l*1632 *l*1663 *l*1963 *l*^{7} Chr Or *L*' Cp *S*sc *C*,f *Arm* *Δ*'⟨me⟩ — *txt*: *Rpl* (∼ απ. σοι αυ.: 700 σ1223) *L*hq *S*'j *Δ*i$^{T3:6}$ md^{MV} | σοι + εν τω φανερω‖Mk4 22 Lk8 17: *Rpl* CAp Chr *L*vl' Au PsAu PsChr Or *S*'j *Δ*a p — *txt*: ℵBZ-33 544 **λ**-22-1582 **φ**983-1689 D *pc* Or *L*k[e] ff^{1}z31.32 vg Au Chrm Cp Hi *S*c *C*,f *Δ*'⟨me⟩ **5** προσευχη, ... εση‖6: *Rpl* *L*k[e]q *S*'(*om* 5: s) *C*f *Arm*' *Geo*^{2} *Δ*a p — *txt*: ℵBZ-892(-σθε, ... εση) **λ**-22-1582 Or Chr *L*' *S*h^{m}j *C* *Arm*^{pc} *Aeth* *Got* *Δ*'⟨me⟩ | ως] ωσπερ‖62.7: *Rpl* Or — *txt*: 𝔥⟨L⟩ D | ● *om* αν‖62.16: 𝔥 544 **λ**-1582 **φ**⟨346⟩-174-*l*547 σ1293-1424-1606 D K Π Ω *al l*27 *l*44 *l*184 *l*303 *l*1634 *l*1963 Or Chr^{1} — *txt*: *Rpl* Chr^{1} | ● υμ. + οτι: *Rpl* Or^{1} *L*f *S*,j *Δ*a i^{V} n^{L} p — *txt*: 𝔥⟨L⟩ 28-544-700 **λ**-1582 **φ**⟨346⟩-174-230-*l*547 D **047** *pc* Chr Or^{1} *L*' Au *Arm* *Aeth* *Δ*'⟨i^{T} me⟩ **6** *om* τω^{2}‖64: 700-1604 λ1-1582 **φ**⟨346⟩ D *pc* *L* *S*sc *C*b$^{\langle 9\rangle}$f(?) *Δ*⟨me⟩ | αποδ. *prm* αυτος‖64: 1241 *l*32 *L*h *Δ*i$^{T3:7}$ | σοι + εν τω φανερω‖Mk4 22 Lk8 17: *Rpl* *L*vl' *S*'j^{ac} *Δ*a p — *txt*: ℵBZ **λ**-22 D PsCl Eu Or *L*k[e] ff^{1}z31.32 vg Am Hi *S*scj^{b} *C*,f *Δ*'⟨me⟩ **7** εθν.] υποκριται‖62.5.16: B σ1424 *S*c *Geo*^{1} *Δ*(εθν. και υπ.: md n')^{L}

Mt6 3 *cf.* ETh^{II} 62 (*transl.*): ... *ὅ τι ἂν ποιήσῃ ἡ δεξιά σου, μὴ γνώτω ἡ ἀριστερά σου τί ποιεῖ.*

41. cf. ETh^{II} 6. 14 (*cf. ad 40.*)

Mt6 7-13 *cf.* Did8 2f (*cf.* CAp 7,1–22): Μηδὲ προσεύχεσθε ὡς οἱ ὑποκριταί, ἀλλ' ὡς ἐκέλευσεν ὁ κύριος ἐν τῷ εὐαγγελίῳ αὐτοῦ (μηδὲ—αὐτοῦ] ὅταν δὲ προσεύχησθε, μὴ γίνεσθε ὡς οἱ ὑποκριταί, ἀλλ' ὡς ὁ κύριος ἡμῖν ἐν τῷ εὐαγγελίῳ αὐτοῦ διετάξατο: CAp), οὕτως προσεύχεσθε· Πάτερ ἡμῶν ὁ ἐν τῷ οὐρανῷ (τ. οὐ.] τοῖς οὐρανοῖς: CAp), ἁγιασθήτω τὸ ὄνομά σου· ἐλθέτω ἡ βασιλεία σου· γενηθήτω τὸ θέλημά σου ὡς ἐν οὐρανῷ καὶ ἐπὶ [+ τῆς: CAp) γῆς· τὸν ἄρτον ἡμῶν τὸν ἐπιούσιον δὸς ἡμῖν σήμερον· καὶ ἄφες ἡμῖν τὴν ὀφειλὴν (τ. ὀφ.] τὰ ὀφειλήματα: CAp) ἡμῶν, ὡς καὶ ἡμεῖς ἀφίεμεν τοῖς ὀφελέταις ἡμῶν· καὶ μὴ εἰσενέγκῃς ἡμᾶς εἰς πειρασμόν, ἀλλὰ ῥῦσαι ἡμᾶς ἀπὸ τοῦ πονηροῦ· ὅτι σοῦ ἐστιν (+ ἡ βασιλεία καί: CAp) ἡ δύναμις καὶ ἡ δόξα εἰς τοὺς αἰῶνας (+ αμην: CAp). [3]τρὶς τῆς ἡμέρας οὕτω προσεύχεσθε.

Πάτερ ἡμῶν ὁ ἐν τοῖς οὐρανοῖς,
ἁγιασθήτω τὸ ὄνομά σου·
[10] ἐλθέτω ἡ βασιλεία σου·
γενηθήτω τὸ θέλημά σου
ὡς ἐν οὐρανῷ καὶ ἐπὶ γῆς·
[11] τὸν ἄρτον ἡμῶν τὸν ἐπιούσιον δὸς ἡμῖν σήμερον·
[12] καὶ ἄφες ἡμῖν τὰ ὀφειλήματα ἡμῶν,
ὡς καὶ ἡμεῖς ἀφήκαμεν τοῖς ὀφειλέταις ἡμῶν·
[13] καὶ μὴ εἰσενέγκῃς ἡμᾶς εἰς πειρασμόν,
ἀλλὰ ῥῦσαι ἡμᾶς ἀπὸ τοῦ πονηροῦ.
[14] ἐὰν γὰρ
ἀφῆτε τοῖς ἀνθρώποις τὰ παραπτώματα αὐτῶν, ἀφήσει καὶ ὑμῖν ὁ πατὴρ ὑμῶν ὁ οὐράνιος·
[15] ἐὰν δὲ μὴ ἀφῆτε τοῖς ἀνθρώποις, οὐδὲ ὁ πατὴρ ὑμῶν ἀφήσει τὰ παραπτώματα ὑμῶν.

18 35 (*150.*): *οὕτως καὶ ὁ πατήρ μου ὁ οὐράνιος ποιήσει ὑμῖν, ἐὰν μὴ ἀφῆτε ἕκαστος τῷ ἀδελφῷ αὐτοῦ ἀπὸ τῶν καρδιῶν ὑμῶν.*

Πάτερ,
ἁγιασθήτω τὸ ὄνομά σου·
ἐλθέτω ἡ βασιλεία σου·

[3] τὸν ἄρτον ἡμῶν τὸν ἐπιούσιον δίδου ἡμῖν τὸ καθ' ἡμέραν·
[4] καὶ ἄφες ἡμῖν τὰς ἁμαρτίας ἡμῶν,
καὶ γὰρ αὐτοὶ ἀφίομεν παντὶ ὀφείλοντι ἡμῖν·
καὶ μὴ εἰσενέγκῃς ἡμᾶς εἰς πειρασμόν.

11 25 (*215.*):
καὶ ὅταν στήκετε προσευχόμενοι, ἀφίετε εἴ τι ἔχετε κατά τινος, ἵνα καὶ ὁ πατὴρ ὑμῶν ὁ ἐν τοῖς οὐρανοῖς ἀφῇ ὑμῖν τὰ παραπτώματα ὑμῶν.

(31)

43. Vom Fasten. *On Fasting.* **Matth 6** 16–18

[16] Ὅταν δὲ νηστεύητε, μὴ γίνεσθε ὡς οἱ ὑποκριταὶ σκυθρωποί· ἀφανίζουσιν γὰρ τὰ πρόσωπα αὐτῶν,
ὅπως φανῶσιν τοῖς ἀνθρώποις νηστεύοντες·
αμην λέγω ὑμῖν, ἀπέχουσιν τὸν μισθὸν αὐτῶν.
[17] σὺ δὲ νηστεύων ἄλειψαί σου τὴν κεφαλὴν καὶ τὸ πρόσωπόν σου νίψαι, [18] ὅπως μὴ φανῇς τοῖς ἀνθρώποις νηστεύων ἀλλὰ τῷ πατρί σου τῷ ἐν τῷ κρυφαίῳ·
καὶ ὁ πατήρ σου ὁ βλέπων ἐν τῷ κρυφαίῳ ἀποδώσει σοι.

Mt 6,12 οφειλη.] παραπτωματα ‖ 14f. Mk11 25: Or$^{1:3}$ — οφ. και παρ.: *L*h Hil | αφηκ.] αφιεμεν / -ομεν ‖ p: *Rpl* Did↓ Or^{1} *L*'(*om*: a^{v}) Au Cp Hil *S*j *C* *Arm* — αφησομεν(-ιωμεν): *L*ff^{1} *S*c[s] (*Geo*^{1}) — *txt*: ℵ*BZ λ1-22-1582 PsBas Gr^{Ny} Or^{2} *L*vg^{5} *S*' Ef *C*f *Geo*^{2} **14** ∼ υμιν και ‖ p: D *L*k[e] bcfg$^{1.2}$hq Au$^{5:11}$ *S*c[s]j *C*s | ουρ.] εν τοις ουρανοις ‖ 61.9 Mk: 700 Θ *l*1963 *L*k[e] abcfg^{1}hq | ουρ. + τα παραπτωματα υμων (*et om* ο ουρ.) ‖ 15 Mk: L 1604 ϕ13-826-828-983 *pc* *l*1663 Eu *L*cff^{1}g^{1}lz31 vg Au^{3}(^{6} Fau^{R}) *S*j *C*s$^{6:7}$b **15** ● ανϑ. + τα παραπτωματα αυτων ‖ 14: *Rpl* PsChr *L*b(*om* αυτ.)fg^{2}q30 vg^{2} Au^{2} *S*'j *C*' Sch *Arm* *Δ*p(ανϑ.] αλλοις, *om* αυτ.) — *txt*: ℵ-892 **λ**-22-1582 D *L*' Au^{5} *S*p *C*b^{8}f^{v} *Got* *Δ*a ad (τ. ανϑ.] τ. αλλοις: i^{T}, αυτοις: i^{V}) l md n^{C}(' *om* τ. ανϑ.) | υμ.^{1} + ο ουρανιος ‖ 14: σM-267-1391-1606 *pc* *L*g^{2}30 vg^{3} *S*j^{c} *C*s$^{3:7}$ *Arm*^{0} *Aeth* *Δ*n^{Hr} — + ο εν τοις ουρανοις ‖ 61.9: *L*vg^{1} Au$^{1:7}$ | αφησει + υμιν (*et om* τα παρ. υμ.) ‖ 14 Mk: σ1293 1606 D *pc* *L*vl⟨lz⟩30 Au^{1}(^{4})$^{:7}$ *S*,j *C* *Geo*⟨B⟩ *Δ*'⟨me p⟩(i^{V} n^{L}) **16** ως] ωσπερ ‖ 62.7: *Rpl* — *txt*: ℵB-892 **λ**-1582 D Δ 471 | οπως + αν ‖ 65: Δ 252 | ● υμιν + οτι: *Rpl* *L*' Au^{1} *S*,j *Δ*'⟨me⟩ — *txt*: ℵB **λ**-22-1582 ϕ124-174-788-983 D **047** *pc* *L*k[e] abfhq vg^{1} Au^{2} *Arm* *Geo*^{2} *Aeth* *Δ*l^{AD} md n⟨L⟩ **17** κεφ. + ελαιω ‖ Lk 746: 157 *l*1663 *C*b^{1} *Δ*a$^{BE⟨A⟩}$ p **18** *om* τω^{2} ‖ 64: λ22(*om* εν τω) D *C*b^{1} | κρυ.^{1} *et* ^{2}] κρυπτω ‖ 64.6: *Rpl* — κρυ.^{1}] ουρανω: *Δ*i$^{T2:6V}$ n^{L} — *txt*: ℵB λ1-22-1582 D^{c}(*^{v} 1° εν κρυφια) *pc* | σοι + εν τω φανερω ‖ Mk4 22 Lk8 17: 1604 **λ**⟨1⟩ ϕ124-230-346-543-*l*547 E Δ 157 *al* *l*333 *l*374 *l*950 *l*1231 *l*1564 *l*1663 *L*k[e] abcg^{1}h *S*j^{c} *Arm*^{pc} *Geo* *Aeth* *Δ*p E^{a}

Mt6 11 *cf.* EN frgm.5 (Hi Mt *ad* 6 11): In evangelio, quod appellatur secundum Hebraeos, pro *supersubstantiali pane* repperi *mahar*, quod dicitur crastinum, ut sit sensus: panem nostrum crastinum, i. e. futurum, da nobis hodie.

43. cf. ETh^{II} 6. 14 (*cf. ad 40.*)

(32)

44. Vom Schätzesammeln. *On Treasures.*

Matth 6 19–21	*12 33-34 (171.)*
[19] Μὴ θησαυρίζετε ὑμῖν θησαυροὺς ἐπὶ τῆς γῆς, ὅπου σὴς καὶ βρῶσις ἀφανίζει, καὶ ὅπου κλέπται διορύσσουσιν καὶ κλέπτουσιν· [20] θησαυρίζετε δὲ ὑμῖν θησαυροὺς ἐν οὐρανῷ, ὅπου οὔτε σὴς οὔτε βρῶσις ἀφανίζει, καὶ ὅπου κλέπται οὐ διορύσσουσιν οὐδὲ κλέπτουσιν. [21] ὅπου γάρ ἐστιν ὁ θησαυρός σου, ἐκεῖ ἔσται καὶ ἡ καρδία σου.	[33] ... *ποιήσατε ἑαυτοῖς βαλλάντια μὴ παλαιούμενα, θησαυρὸν ἀνέκλειπτον ἐν τοῖς οὐρανοῖς, ὅπου κλέπτης οὐκ ἐγγίζει οὐδὲ σὴς διαφθείρει·* [34] *ὅπου γάρ ἐστιν ὁ θησαυρὸς ὑμῶν, ἐκεῖ καὶ ἡ καρδία ὑμῶν ἔσται.*

(33)

45. Parabel vom Auge. *The Single Eye.*

Matth 6 22–23	*11 34-36 (167.)*
[22] Ὁ λύχνος τοῦ σώματός ἐστιν ὁ ὀφθαλμός. ἐὰν οὖν ᾖ ὁ ὀφθαλμός σου ἁπλοῦς, ὅλον τὸ σῶμά σου φωτεινὸν ἔσται· [23] ἐὰν δὲ ὁ ὀφθαλμός σου πονηρὸς ᾖ, ὅλον τὸ σῶμά σου σκοτεινὸν ἔσται. εἰ οὖν τὸ φῶς τὸ ἐν σοὶ σκότος ἐστίν, τὸ σκότος πόσον.	[34] *ὁ λύχνος τοῦ σώματός ἐστιν ὁ ὀφθαλμός σου. ὅταν ὁ ὀφθαλμός σου ἁπλοῦς ᾖ, καὶ ὅλον τὸ σῶμά σου φωτεινόν ἐστιν· ἐπὰν δὲ πονηρὸς ᾖ, καὶ τὸ σῶμά σου σκοτεινόν.* [35] *σκόπει οὖν μὴ τὸ φῶς τὸ ἐν σοὶ σκότος ἐστίν.* [36] *εἰ οὖν τὸ σῶμά σου ὅλον φωτεινόν, μὴ ἔχον μέρος τι σκοτεινόν, ἔσται φωτεινὸν ὅλον ὡς ὅταν ὁ λύχνος τῇ ἀστραπῇ φωτίζῃ σε.*

(34)

46. Vom Doppeldienst. *On Serving Two Masters.*

Matth 6 24	*16 13 (188.)*
[24] Οὐδεὶς δύναται δυσὶ κυρίοις δουλεύειν· ἢ γὰρ τὸν ἕνα μισήσει καὶ τὸν ἕτερον ἀγαπήσει, ἢ ἑνὸς ἀνθέξεται καὶ τοῦ ἑτέρου καταφρονήσει. οὐ δύνασθε θεῷ δουλεύειν καὶ μαμωνᾷ.	[13] *οὐδεὶς οἰκέτης δύναται δυσὶ κυρίοις δουλεύειν· ἢ γὰρ τὸν ἕνα μισήσει καὶ τὸν ἕτερον ἀγαπήσει, ἢ ἑνὸς ἀνθέξεται καὶ τοῦ ἑτέρου καταφρονήσει. οὐ δύνασθε θεῷ δουλεύειν καὶ μαμωνᾷ.*

Mt 6,20 ουδε κλ.] και κλ.‖619: ℵ-892 *pc* *L*abfg^{1}hq Am PsAm Au$^{2:7}$ Cp$^{2:6}$ Gaud *S*c[s]j *C*⟨b^1⟩ — *om*‖p: W *L*k[e] Au$^{1:7}$ Cp$^{2:6}$ **21** εστιν] εσται‖21b: 273 Chrm$^{1:2}$ *L*k[e] bcfg^{1}hq30 vg^1 PsAm Au$^{4:12}$ Cp *S*c[s]p^1 *C*s | εσται] εστιν‖21a: *L*ff^{1}l vg$^{\langle 7\rangle}$ Au$^{5:11}$ *S*pj | ● σου^1 *et* ^{2}] υμων‖p: *Rpl* *L*f *S*,j *C*b^7(^{1} 1°) — *txt*: ℵB 1582 *pc* *L*'Au Cp Te *S*Ef *C*' **22** οφ.^{1} + σου‖p: B 372 Ath *L*⟨f vg^9⟩ Au$^{4:5}$ Hil Or | *om* ουν‖p: ℵ* *pc* *L*acff^{1}lqz vg Au$^{3:4}$ *S*c[s] *C*s^1(^{1} *et* + δε)$^{:9}$b^1 | ∼ ο οφ. σου απ. η‖p: *Rpl* GrTh *L*vl'[e] vg^1 Au^2 — *txt*: ℵB Φ σ954-1207-1223-1293 W *pc* *L*fff^{1}lz vg' Au^3 **24** ουδ. + οικετης‖**p**: L Φ Δ *pc*

Mt620p *cf.* ETh^{II} 76 (*transl.*): (*cf. ad 114.* Mt1345f.) ... *ζητεῖτε καὶ ὑμεῖς τὸν θησαυρὸν αὐτοῦ (*sc. τοῦ *ἀνθρώπου ἐμπόρου) τὸν ἀνέκλειπτον, ὅπου σὴς οὐκ ἐγγίζει φαγεῖν οὐδὲ σκώληξ ἀφανίζει.*

45. cf. ETh^{II} 24 (*transl.*): ... *λέγει αὐτοῖς· ὁ ἔχων ὦτα ἀκουέτω. φῶς ἐστιν ἐν ἀνθρώπῳ φωτεινῷ καὶ φωτίζει πάντα τὸν κόσμον· εἰ δὲ μὴ φωτίζει σκότος ἐστίν* (*cf. ad 103.* Mt139).

46. cf. ETh^{II} 47a (*transl.*): *Λέγει Ἰησοῦς· οὐδεὶς ἄνθρωπος δύναται καθίζειν ἐπὶ δύο ἵππους ἢ τείνειν δύο τόξα, καὶ οὐδεὶς οἰκέτης δύναται δυσὶ κυρίοις δουλεύειν, ἢ τὸν ἕνα τιμήσει καὶ τὸν ἕτερον ὑβρίσει.* ^{b}*οὐ πίνει...* (*cf. ad 66.* Lk539)

(35)

47. Vom Sorgen. *On Earthly Cares.*

Matth 6 25–34

[25] Διὰ τοῦτο λέγω ὑμῖν, μὴ μεριμνᾶτε τῇ ψυχῇ ὑμῶν τί φάγητε, μηδὲ τῷ σώματι ὑμῶν τί ἐνδύσησθε. οὐχὶ ἡ ψυχὴ πλεῖόν ἐστιν τῆς τροφῆς καὶ τὸ σῶμα τοῦ ἐνδύματος; [26] ἐμβλέψατε εἰς τὰ πετεινὰ τοῦ οὐρανοῦ, ὅτι οὐ σπείρουσιν οὐδὲ θερίζουσιν οὐδὲ συνάγουσιν εἰς ἀποθήκας, καὶ ὁ πατὴρ ὑμῶν ὁ οὐράνιος τρέφει αὐτά· οὐχ ὑμεῖς μᾶλλον διαφέρετε αὐτῶν; [27] τίς δὲ ἐξ ὑμῶν μεριμνῶν δύναται προσθεῖναι ἐπὶ τὴν ἡλικίαν αὐτοῦ πῆχυν ἕνα; [28] καὶ περὶ ἐνδύματος τί μεριμνᾶτε; καταμάθετε τὰ κρίνα τοῦ ἀγροῦ, πῶς αὐξάνουσιν· οὐ κοπιῶσιν οὐδὲ νήθουσιν. [29] λέγω δὲ ὑμῖν ὅτι οὐδὲ Σολομὼν ἐν πάσῃ τῇ δόξῃ αὐτοῦ περιεβάλετο ὡς ἓν τούτων. [30] εἰ δὲ τὸν χόρτον τοῦ ἀγροῦ σήμερον ὄντα καὶ αὔριον εἰς κλίβανον βαλλόμενον ὁ θεὸς οὕτως ἀμφιέννυσιν, οὐ πολλῷ μᾶλλον ὑμᾶς, ὀλιγόπιστοι; [31] μὴ οὖν μεριμνήσητε λέγοντες· τί φάγωμεν; ἤ· τί πίωμεν; ἤ· τί περιβαλώμεθα; [32] πάντα γὰρ ταῦτα τὰ ἔθνη ἐπιζητοῦσιν· οἶδεν γὰρ ὁ πατὴρ ὑμῶν ὁ οὐράνιος ὅτι χρῄζετε τούτων ἁπάντων. [33] ζητεῖτε δὲ πρῶτον τὴν βασιλείαν τοῦ

12 22–31 *(171.)*

[22] Εἶπεν δὲ πρὸς τοὺς μαθητὰς αὐτοῦ· διὰ τοῦτο λέγω ὑμῖν, μὴ μεριμνᾶτε τῇ ψυχῇ τί φάγητε, μηδὲ τῷ σώματι τί ἐνδύσησθε. [23] ἡ γὰρ ψυχὴ πλεῖόν ἐστιν τῆς τροφῆς καὶ τὸ σῶμα τοῦ ἐνδύματος. [24] κατανοήσατε τοὺς κόρακας, ὅτι οὔτε σπείρουσιν οὔτε θερίζουσιν, οἷς οὐκ ἔστιν ταμιεῖον οὐδὲ ἀποθήκη, καὶ ὁ θεὸς τρέφει αὐτούς· πόσῳ μᾶλλον ὑμεῖς διαφέρετε τῶν πετεινῶν. [25] τίς δὲ ἐξ ὑμῶν μεριμνῶν δύναται προσθεῖναι ἐπὶ τὴν ἡλικίαν αὐτοῦ πῆχυν; [26] εἰ οὖν οὐδὲ ἐλάχιστον δύνασθε, τί περὶ τῶν λοιπῶν μεριμνᾶτε; [27] κατανοήσατε τὰ κρίνα, πῶς αὐξάνει· οὐ κοπιᾷ οὐδὲ νήθει· λέγω δὲ ὑμῖν, οὐδὲ Σολομὼν ἐν πάσῃ τῇ δόξῃ αὐτοῦ περιεβάλετο ὡς ἓν τούτων. [28] εἰ δὲ ἐν ἀγρῷ τὸν χόρτον ὄντα σήμερον καὶ αὔριον εἰς κλίβανον βαλλόμενον ὁ θεὸς οὕτως ἀμφιέζει, πόσῳ μᾶλλον ὑμᾶς, ὀλιγόπιστοι. [29] καὶ ὑμεῖς μὴ ζητεῖτε τί φάγητε καὶ τί πίητε, καὶ μὴ μετεωρίζεσθε· [30] ταῦτα γὰρ πάντα τὰ ἔθνη τοῦ κόσμου ἐπιζητοῦσιν· ὑμῶν δὲ ὁ πατὴρ οἶδεν ὅτι χρῄζετε τούτων· [31] πλὴν ζητεῖτε τὴν βασιλείαν

6 8 *(42.): ... οἶδεν γὰρ ὁ πατὴρ ὑμῶν ὧν χρείαν ἔχετε πρὸ τοῦ ὑμᾶς αἰτῆσαι αὐτόν.*

Mt 6,25 μεριμνησητε‖31.34: ϕ⟨346⟩-174 σ1424 *pc* Ath$^{1:2}$ Chr Eu | φαγ. + ● και τι πιητε‖Lk12 29: *Rpl* Bas *L*PsAu Hi *S'* *Cs*^{2}{^{1}}(^{1} *om* και) *Geo*^{A} *Δ*a i^{V} p(*om* και) — + η τι πι.‖31: B-33 Φ λ118-209 ϕ⟨346⟩-174 σ27 W 157 Ath Eu Max^{C} Or *L*cfg^{1}hqz *Cs*^{1}{}b *Arm* *Geo*^{1}(^{B} *om* τι) — *txt*: ℵ-892 λ1-22-1582 *pc* Ath Chr Cl Cr Ep Eu Iu Meth *L'* Au Hil *Sc*[s]j *Cs*^{2} *Aeth* *Δ'*⟨me⟩ | *om* υμων^{2}(*et*^{1})‖p: ℵ* Ath$^{1:2}$ *Lk*[e] b Au^{2}(^{3})$^{:8}$ **26** ου ... ουδε ... ουδε] ουτε ... ουτε ... ουδε‖p: 892-(ου ... ουτε ... ουτε: 1241) **28** αυξανει ου κοπια ουδε νηθει‖p: *Rpl* Bas — ∼ νηθ. ... κοπ.: Θ *Sc*[s] — ου ξενουσιν (= ξαιν.) ουδε νηθουσιν ουδε κοπιωσιν: ℵ*^{v} Ath Chr ETh^{II}↓ — *txt*: ℵ^{1}B-33(νηφ-) 1071(αυξανει) λ-22-1582 *pc* **29** *om* οτι‖p: W **30** ου πολ.] ποσω‖p: Δ *L* *Sc*[s] *C* **32** ∼ ταυ. γαρ πα.‖p: ℵ-892 ΝΣ-544 ϕ⟨346⟩-174 σ27-1402 Δ Θ **047** 157 Or *pc* *l*60 *l*183 *L'*(*om* πα.: k[e] ab PsAm$^{3:6}$ Cp) Au *Sc*[s] *Aeth* | τα εθ.] οι εθνικοι‖5 47: σ1424 — + του κοσμου‖p: 713 Chr$^{1:2}$ *Sc*[s]p^{3} | γαρ^{2}] δε‖Lk: ℵ^{c} *L*abcg^{1} PsAm Au$^{1:4}$ PsAu Cp$^{3:6}$ *Sp* *C*b$^{\langle 5\rangle}$ | *om* ο ουρ.‖8 Lk: ℵ 28 *pc* Cl *L*⟨fh⟩ Au PsAu Cp$^{3:5}$ *Sc*[s] *C*b *Geo*^{B} **33** *om* πρω.‖p: 61 Chr *L*b | τ. θε.] αυτου‖p: 440 *pc* *L*Cp$^{1:5}$ *S*Af *C* *Aeth* — των ουρανων: 301 Chr$^{4:8}$ Cl — ● *om*: ℵB(∼ δικ. ... βασ.) PsAth(βασ. κ. τ. δικ. τ. θε.) Eu *Lk*[e](= PsAth)g^{2}l vg^{3} PsAu Cp$^{3:5}$

Mt6 25–30p *cf.* ETh^{II} 36 (POxy 655 I): ... ἀ]πὸ πρωῒ ἕ[ως ὀψὲ μήτ]ε ἀφ' ἑσπ[έρας ἕως π]ρωῒ μήτε [τῇ τρυφῇ ὑ]μῶν τί φά[γητε μήτε] τῇ στ[ολῇ ὑμῶν] τί ἐνδύ[ση]σθε. [πολ]λῷ κρεί[σσον]ές ἐ[στε] τῶν [κρί]νων ἅτι[να α]ὐξάνει(ο)ὐ ξα[ί]νει Skeat, ZNW 37, 212) οὐδὲ ν[ή]θ]ει μ[ηδ]ὲν ἔχοντ[α ἔ]νδ[υ]μα. τί ἐν[δεῖτε] καὶ ὑμεῖς; τίς ἂν προσθ(εί)η ἐπὶ τὴν εἱλικίαν ὑμῶν; αὐτὸ[ς δ]ώσει ὑμεῖν τὸ ἔνδυμα ὑμῶν.

Mt6 25p *cf.* ETh^{II} 36 (*transl.*): *Λέγει Ἰησοῦς· μὴ μεριμνᾶτε ἀπὸ πρωῒ ἕως ὀψὲ μήτε ἀφ' ἑσπέρας ἕως πρωῒ τί ἐνδύσησθε.*

Mt6 33p *cf.* Agr. (Or orat. 14,1; 2,2 *etc.*): ... αἰτεῖτε τὰ μεγάλα, καὶ τὰ μικρὰ προστεθήσεται ὑμῖν· καὶ αἰτεῖτε τὰ ἐπουράνια, καὶ τὰ ἐπίγεια προστεθήσεται. — (Cl strom. I 24,158): αἰτεῖσθε, γάρ φησιν, τὰ μεγάλα, καὶ τὰ μικρὰ ὑμῖν προστεθήσεται. — (Eu Ps *ad* 16,1 LXX): ὁ σωτὴρ ἐδίδασκεν λέγων· αἰτεῖσθε τὰ μεγ. κ. τὰ μικ. προστεθ. ὑμῖν.

θεοῦ καὶ τὴν δικαιοσύνην αὐτοῦ, καὶ ταῦτα πάντα προστεθήσεται ὑμῖν.
[34] μὴ οὖν μεριμνήσητε εἰς τὴν αὔριον· ἡ γὰρ αὔριον μεριμνήσει ἑαυτῆς· ἀρκετὸν τῇ ἡμέρᾳ ἡ κακία αὐτῆς.

αὐτοῦ, καὶ ταῦτα προστεθήσεται ὑμῖν.

(36)

48. Vom Richten. *On Judging.*

Matth 7 1–5

[1] Μὴ κρίνετε, ἵνα μὴ κριθῆτε·
[2] ἐν ᾧ γὰρ κρίματι κρίνετε κριθήσεσθε, καὶ ἐν ᾧ μέτρῳ μετρεῖτε μετρηθήσεται ὑμῖν. [3] τί δὲ βλέπεις τὸ κάρφος τὸ ἐν τῷ ὀφθαλμῷ τοῦ ἀδελφοῦ σου, τὴν δὲ ἐν τῷ σῷ ὀφθαλμῷ δοκὸν οὐ κατανοεῖς; [4] ἢ πῶς ἐρεῖς τῷ ἀδελφῷ σου· ἄφες ἐκβάλω τὸ κάρφος ἀπὸ τοῦ ὀφθαλμοῦ σου, καὶ ἰδοὺ ἡ δοκὸς ἐν τῷ ὀφθαλμῷ σου; [5] ὑποκριτά, ἔκβαλε πρῶτον τὴν δοκὸν ἐκ τοῦ ὀφθαλμοῦ σου, καὶ τότε διαβλέψεις ἐκβαλεῖν τὸ κάρφος ἐκ τοῦ ὀφθαλμοῦ τοῦ ἀδελφοῦ σου.

4 24 (107.): … ἐν ᾧ μέτρῳ μετρεῖτε μετρηθήσεται ὑμῖν, καὶ προστεθήσεται ὑμῖν …

6 37. 38. 41. 42. (89.)

[37] Καὶ μὴ κρίνετε, καὶ οὐ μὴ κριθῆτε· καὶ μὴ καταδικάζετε, καὶ οὐ μὴ καταδικασθῆτε. ἀπολύετε, καὶ ἀπολυθήσεσθε· [38] δίδοτε, καὶ δοθήσεται ὑμῖν· μέτρον καλὸν πεπιεσμένον σεσαλευμένον ὑπερεκχυννόμενον δώσουσιν εἰς τὸν κόλπον ὑμῶν· τῷ γὰρ αὐτῷ μέτρῳ ᾧ μετρεῖτε ἀντιμετρηθήσεται ὑμῖν … [41] τί δὲ βλέπεις τὸ κάρφος τὸ ἐν τῷ ὀφθαλμῷ τοῦ ἀδελφοῦ σου, τὴν δὲ δοκὸν τὴν ἐν τῷ ἰδίῳ ὀφθαλμῷ οὐ κατανοεῖς; [42] πῶς δύνασαι λέγειν τῷ ἀδελφῷ σου· ἀδελφε, ἄφες ἐκβάλω τὸ κάρφος τὸ ἐν τῷ ὀφθαλμῷ σου, αὐτὸς τὴν ἐν τῷ ὀφθαλμῷ σου δοκὸν οὐ βλέπων; ὑποκριτά, ἔκβαλε πρῶτον τὴν δοκὸν ἐκ τοῦ ὀφθαλμοῦ σου, καὶ τότε διαβλέψεις τὸ κάρφος τὸ ἐν τῷ ὀφθαλμῷ τοῦ ἀδελφοῦ σου ἐκβαλεῖν.

(37)

49. Von der Entweihung des Heiligen. *On Casting Pearls before Swine.* **Matth 7 6**

[6] Μὴ δῶτε τὸ ἅγιον τοῖς κυσίν, μηδὲ βάλητε τοὺς μαργαρίτας ὑμῶν ἔμπροσθεν τῶν χοίρων, μήποτε καταπατήσουσιν αὐτοὺς ἐν τοῖς ποσὶν αὐτῶν καὶ στραφέντες ῥήξωσιν ὑμᾶς.

Mt 6,33 *om* και τ. δικ. αυ.‖p: 482 *pc* *l*184 *l*187 Chr$^{1:2}$ *L*Cp$^{1:4}$ *Geo*^{B} — *om* παντα‖p: σ990 *L* Hil
7,1 κριθ. + μη καταδικαζατε και ου μη καταδικασθητε‖p: L | ινα] και ου‖p: 28 *pc* **2** *om* εν^{2}‖**p**: Hip | αντιμετρηθ.‖p: ΝΣΦ-544 λ22 **φ**-174-*l*547 σ659-1194-1606 Θ 157 *pm* Hip *L*cfff^{1}g^{1}hz30 vg^{11} Au$^{8:12}$ Hi Luc *S*j **3** εν^{2}—δοκ.] δοκ. την εν—οφ.^{2}‖p: ℵ ΝΣ-544 **φ***l*547 *pc* Chr **4** σου^{1} + αδελφε‖p: ℵ *L*g^{2} vg^{2} *C*s$^{4:5}$ | απο] ● εκ: ℌ⟨L⟩ ΝΣ-28 **λ**-1582 **φ**⟨346⟩-174 σ945-1194-1424-1606 *pc* **5** ● ∼ εκ^{1}—σου^{1} τ. δοκ.: ℵBC | εκ^{2}—οφ.^{2}] το εν τω οφθαλμω‖3 Lk: Σ ETh^{II}(Oxy)↓ **6** ● -πατησωσιν‖6b: *Rpl* Cl Ddy Or — *txt*: ℌ⟨ℵ-892⟩CX ΝΣ-1604 **φ**⟨346⟩-174 W Θ 157 *pc* | ρηξουσιν‖6a: 33 ΝΣ

Mt7 1f.p *cf.* 1Cl13 2 (*cf. ad 89.* Lk6 37f.)

Mt7 2 *cf.* Agr. (Iu dial. 47,5): διὸ καὶ ὁ ἡμέτερος κύριος Ἰησοῦς Χριστὸς εἶπεν· ἐν οἷς ἂν ὑμᾶς καταλαβῶ, ἐν τούτοις καὶ κρινῶ.

Mt7 3-5p *cf.* ETh^{II} 26 (POxy 1,1): … καὶ τότε διαβλέψεις ἐκβαλεῖν τὸ κάρφος τὸ ἐν τῷ ὀφθαλμῷ τοῦ ἀδελφοῦ σου.
(*transl.*): *Λέγει Ἰησοῦς· τὸ κάρφος τὸ ἐν τῷ ὀφθαλμῷ τοῦ ἀδελφοῦ σου βλέπεις, τὴν δὲ δοκὸν τὴν ἐν τῷ ὀφθαλμῷ σου οὐ βλέπεις. ὅταν ἐκβάλῃς τὴν δοκὸν ἐκ τοῦ ὀφθαλμοῦ σου, τότε διαβλέψεις ἐκβαλεῖν τὸ κάρφος ἐκ τοῦ ὀφθαλμοῦ τοῦ ἀδελφοῦ σου.*

Mt7 5 *cf.* EN frgm.6 (*cf. ad 54.* Mt7 21ff.)

Mt7 6 *cf.* ETh^{II} 93 (*transl.*): *Μὴ δῶτε τὸ ἅγιον τοῖς κυσίν, μήποτε βληθῇ εἰς τὴν κοπρίαν· μὴ βάλητε τοὺς μαργαρίτας τοῖς χοίροις, μήποτε ποιήσωσιν αὐτὸ[…*
cf. Ev. apocr. POxy 840 lin. 33f. (*cf. ad 224.* Mt23 25f.)

(38)

50. Von der Gebetserhörung. *The Answer to Prayer.*

Matth 7 7–11

⁷ Αἰτεῖτε, καὶ δοθήσεται ὑμῖν· ζητεῖτε, καὶ εὑρήσετε· κρούετε, καὶ ἀνοιγήσεται ὑμῖν. ⁸ πᾶς γὰρ ὁ αἰτῶν λαμβάνει, καὶ ὁ ζητῶν εὑρίσκει, καὶ τῷ κρούοντι ἀνοιγήσεται. ⁹ ἢ τίς ἐστιν ἐξ ὑμῶν ἄνθρωπος, ὃν αἰτήσει ὁ υἱὸς αὐτοῦ ἄρτον, μὴ λίθον ἐπιδώσει αὐτῷ; ¹⁰ ἢ καὶ ἰχθῦν αἰτήσει, μὴ ὄφιν ἐπιδώσει αὐτῷ; ¹¹ εἰ οὖν ὑμεῖς πονηροὶ ὄντες οἴδατε δόματα ἀγαθὰ διδόναι τοῖς τέκνοις ὑμῶν, πόσῳ μᾶλλον ὁ πατὴρ ὑμῶν ὁ ἐν τοῖς οὐρανοῖς δώσει ἀγαθὰ τοῖς αἰτοῦσιν αὐτόν.

11 9–13 (162.)

⁹ ... αἰτεῖτε, καὶ δοθήσεται ὑμῖν· ζητεῖτε, καὶ εὑρήσετε· κρούετε, καὶ ἀνοιγήσεται ὑμῖν. ¹⁰ πᾶς γὰρ ὁ αἰτῶν λαμβάνει, καὶ ὁ ζητῶν εὑρίσκει, καὶ τῷ κρούοντι ἀνοιγήσεται. ¹¹ τίνα δὲ ἐξ ὑμῶν τὸν πατέρα αἰτήσει ὁ υἱὸς ἰχθῦν, μὴ ἀντὶ ἰχθύος ὄφιν αὐτῷ ἐπιδώσει; ¹² ἢ καὶ αἰτήσει ᾠόν, μὴ ἐπιδώσει αὐτῷ σκορπίον; ¹³ εἰ οὖν ὑμεῖς πονηροὶ ὑπάρχοντες οἴδατε δόματα ἀγαθὰ διδόναι τοῖς τέκνοις ὑμῶν, πόσῳ μᾶλλον ὁ πατὴρ ὁ ἐξ οὐρανοῦ δώσει πνεῦμα ἅγιον τοῖς αἰτοῦσιν αὐτόν.

16 24: ... αἰτεῖτε, καὶ λήμψεσθε ...

(39)

51. Die Goldene Regel. *The Golden Rule.*

Matth 7 12

¹² Πάντα οὖν ὅσα ἐὰν θέλητε ἵνα ποιῶσιν ὑμῖν οἱ ἄνθρωποι, οὕτως καὶ ὑμεῖς ποιεῖτε αὐτοῖς· οὗτος γάρ ἐστιν ὁ νόμος καὶ οἱ προφῆται.

222.

6 31 (88.)

³¹ καὶ καθὼς θέλετε ἵνα ποιῶσιν ὑμῖν οἱ ἄνθρωποι, ποιεῖτε αὐτοῖς ὁμοίως.

Mt 7,9 *om* εστιν *cf.* Lk17₇: BL 28-544 λ118 σ659-1207-1424 *pc* Chr^{1} *L*bcg^{1}h32$^{1:2}$ Au^{1} — *txt*: *Rpl* Chr^{3} *L*' Au^{1}(^{1} εσται) Cp | ανθ.] πατηρ‖p: Chr — *om*‖627p Lk17₇ 11₅ 14₂₈: *S*c[s] *C*s$^{1:10}$ | ον αιτ.] ● ον(ο *vel* ος) εαν/αν αιτ.: *Rpl* (φ⟨346⟩ σM) Chr^{1} *L*' Au Cp *S*h — *txt*: ℵ*BC Θ Chr^{1}(∼) *L*abc g^{1}h *S*'j *C* **10** η και] ● και εαν/αν: *Rpl* Chr *S*' — η και(*om*) εαν: 544 φ'⟨124-788⟩ σM-1402-1675 K S Π Ω *pm* *L*,(Cp) *S*(c[s])j *Geo*' — η: 892 *C*'(*om* και: b^{1}) *Geo*^{B} — *txt*: ℵBC λ-1582 φ983-1689 σ1424(*om* η) *pl* PsCl *Arm* | αυτω + και εαν ωον μη σκορπιον επιδωσει αυτω‖p: 1241 *L*vg^{1} **11** οντ.] υπαρχοντες‖p: ΝΟΣ | *om* δομ.‖11b: L *L*ff^{1}l 32 vg$^{\langle 5\rangle}$ — ∼ αγ. δομ.: λ-1582 Cl *L*Cp | εν τ. ουρ.] εξ ουρανου‖p: Or **12** ουτως] ομοιως‖p: *L*h — *om*: *l*183 — υμεις + ομοιως‖p: 892^{m} 157 485

Jo 16,24 αιτησασθε‖15₇: 𝔓^{66} ℵ*W-579 σ1194

Mt7₇f.p *cf.* EH frgm.4b (Cl strom. V 14,96): Ἴσον γὰρ τούτοις ἐκεῖνα δύναται· οὐ παύσεται ὁ ζητῶν ἕως ἂν εὕρῃ. εὑρὼν δὲ θαμβήσεται, θαμβηθεὶς δὲ βασιλεύσει, βασιλεύσας δὲ ἀναπαήσεται. — frgm.4a (Cl strom. II 9,45) ... ᾗ κἀν τῷ καθ' Ἑβραίους εὐαγγελίῳ· ὁ θαυμάσας βασιλεύσει, γέγραπται, καὶ ὁ βασιλεύσας ἀναπαήσεται.

cf. ETh^{II} 2 (POxy 654,1): Λέγει Ἰησοῦς·] μὴ παυσάσθω ὁ ζη[τῶν τοῦ ζητεῖν ἕως ἂν] εὕρῃ. καὶ ὅταν εὕρῃ [θαμβηθήσεται, καὶ θαμ]βηθεὶς βασιλεύσει κα[ὶ βασιλεύσας ἀναπα]ήσεται.

(*transl.*): *Λέγει Ἰησοῦς· μὴ παυσάσθω ὁ ζητῶν τοῦ ζητῆσαι ἕως ἂν εὕρῃ. καὶ ὅταν εὕρῃ θαμβηθήσεται, καὶ θαμβηθεὶς [spat.] θαυμάσει καὶ βασιλεύσει ἐπὶ τὰ πάντα.*

cf. ETh^{II} 92 (*transl.*): *Λέγει Ἰησοῦς· ζητεῖτε καὶ εὑρήσετε ...*

cf. ETh^{II} 94 (*transl.*): *..] Ἰησοῦς· ὁ ζητῶν εὑρήσει [καὶ τῷ κρούοντι] ἀνοιγήσεται.*

51. cf. Did12: ... πάντα δὲ ὅσα ἐὰν θελήσῃς μὴ γίνεσθαί σοι, καὶ σὺ ἄλλῳ μὴ ποίει (*cf. ad 38.*).

cf. ETh^{II} 6 (POxy 654,5): ... καὶ ὅ τι μισ]εῖται (= -τε) μὴ ποιεῖτ[ε ... (*cf. ad 40.*)

(*transl.*): ... *καὶ ὅ τι μισεῖτε μὴ ποιεῖτε* ... (*cf. ad 40.*)

(40)

52. Die enge Pforte. *The Two Ways.*

Matth 7 13–14

[13] Εἰσέλθατε διὰ τῆς στενῆς πύλης· ὅτι πλατεῖα ἡ πύλη καὶ εὐρύχωρος ἡ ὁδὸς ἡ ἀπάγουσα εἰς τὴν ἀπώλειαν, καὶ πολλοί εἰσιν οἱ εἰσερχόμενοι δι' αὐτῆς· [14] τί στενὴ ἡ πύλη καὶ τεθλιμμένη ἡ ὁδὸς ἡ ἀπάγουσα εἰς τὴν ζωήν, καὶ ὀλίγοι εἰσὶν οἱ εὑρίσκοντες αὐτήν.

13 24 (179.)

[24] *ἀγωνίζεσθε εἰσελθεῖν διὰ τῆς στενῆς θύρας, ὅτι πολλοί, λέγω ὑμῖν, ζητήσουσιν εἰσελθεῖν καὶ οὐκ ἰσχύσουσιν.*

(41)

53. Falsche Propheten. *False Prophets.*

Matth 7 15–20

[15] Προσέχετε ἀπὸ τῶν ψευδοπροφητῶν, οἵτινες ἔρχονται πρὸς ὑμᾶς ἐν ἐνδύμασι προβάτων, ἔσωθεν δέ εἰσιν λύκοι ἅρπαγες. [16] ἀπὸ τῶν καρπῶν αὐτῶν ἐπιγνώσεσθε αὐτούς. μήτι συλλέγουσιν ἀπὸ ἀκανθῶν σταφυλὰς ἢ ἀπὸ τριβόλων σῦκα; [17] οὕτως πᾶν δένδρον ἀγαθὸν καρποὺς καλοὺς ποιεῖ, τὸ δὲ σαπρὸν δένδρον καρποὺς πονηροὺς ποιεῖ. [18] οὐ δύναται δένδρον ἀγαθὸν καρποὺς πονηροὺς ποιεῖν, οὐδὲ δένδρον σαπρὸν καρποὺς καλοὺς ποιεῖν. [19] πᾶν δένδρον μὴ ποιοῦν καρπὸν καλὸν ἐκκόπτεται καὶ εἰς πῦρ βάλλεται. [20] ἄρα γε ἀπὸ τῶν καρπῶν αὐτῶν ἐπιγνώσεσθε αὐτούς.

90.

6 44.43 (90.)

[44] *ἕκαστον γὰρ δένδρον ἐκ τοῦ ἰδίου καρποῦ γινώσκεται· οὐ γὰρ ἐξ ἀκανθῶν συλλέγουσιν σῦκα, οὐδὲ ἐκ βάτου σταφυλὴν τρυγῶσιν . . .*

[43] *Οὐ γάρ ἐστιν δένδρον καλὸν ποιοῦν καρπὸν σαπρόν, οὐδὲ πάλιν δένδρον σαπρὸν ποιοῦν καρπὸν καλόν.*

14.

Mt 7,13 οτι] τι‖14: λ118^{c}(*και τι) *L*abhlq32 Au$^{3:6}$ Cp Hi Luc *Arm*^{pc} | ● *om* η πυλη: ℵ* *pc* Cl Eu Hip Naas Or *L*k[e] abch vg^{2} Au^{3} PsAu Cp Luc Or — *txt*: *Rpl* PsAth Chr Or *L*' Au^{2} Fu Or *S*,j *C* *Δ*⟨me⟩
14 τι] ● οτι‖13: ℵ*B*(+ δε)X 700^{c}-1071 λ1^{c}-118^{c} ϕ828-*l*547 σ1010 157 *pc l*10 *l*32 *l*76 *l*1043 *l*1627 Naas Or Thd^{C} *L*vg^{1} Cp^{1} Gau *C*(+ δε: s^{9})b *Arm*^{pc} *Geo*^{1ch} — *om* λ118*(*spat.*) σ1391(στενη + δε) 2148 *C*s^{1} *Δ*n^{C} — και: λ209 *l*47 Chr *Δ*md n' — *txt*: *Rpl*(+ δε: λ1582*^{v}) *L*' Cp^{1} Fau^{R} Luc Or *S*,j Ef *Arm*' *Geo*^{2} *Δ*'⟨i^{V} me⟩ | ● *om* η πυλη: 544 *pc* PsAth Cl PsCl Eu Hip Mac^{M} Naas Or$^{3:4}$ *L*k[e] ah Cp
15 ● προσε. + δε‖10 7 16 11: *Rpl* *L*fq vg^{1} *S*h *C*s^{5}b *Geo*^{1} — + ουν: *C*s^{1} — *txt*: ℵB 544 ϕ124-174-788-1689 σ945-1424-1606 Ω *pc l*184 *L*' *S*'j *C*s^{5} *Geo*^{2ch2}
16 απο^{1}] εκ‖**p12**33: Iu *L*k[e] c vg^{2} Au$^{6:7}$ PsAu | σταφυλην‖p: *Rpl* Bas^{1} *L*Au^{1} Luc *Arm* — *txt*: ℵBC^{c}(*-ληνας)-892 **λ**-22-1582 Bas^{1} PsBas Chr Ep *L*,Ar Au^{7} Or
18 ποιειν^{1} *et* ^{2}] ποι. ... ενεγκειν *cf.* Jo12 24 15 2 *etc.*: ℵ* *L* Or — ● ενε. ... ποι. *cf.*←: B Or — ● ενε. ... ενε.: *l*1043 Ad Or *L*Ad^{1} Te *Geo* {*Δ*a n^{HgL}} — *txt*: *Rpl* (-ησαι^{1} *et* ^{2}: 713 Ep) *L*,Ad^{1} Or *S*j^{ab} *Δ*'{p}⟨me⟩ | καρπον πονηρον‖p: Or *C* | ουδε + παλιν‖p: L | καρπον καλον‖p 3 10 p: 348 *pc* Or *C* *Geo*
19 παν + ουν‖3 10 Lk 3 9: C^{c}LZ-33 Φ ϕ⟨124-346⟩-*l*547 σ7-1391 157 *pm* *L*bcg^{1}h30 *S*c[s] *C*sb^{2}
20 απο] εκ‖**12**33 Lk 6 44: C **047** *L*⟨k[e] f⟩ Au$^{3:4}$ PsAu Or

---

Mt7 16p *cf.* ETh^{II} 45 (*cf. ad 90.* Lk 6 44f.)

Mt7 18p *cf.*? ETh^{II} 43 (*cf. ad 90.* Lk 6 43)

(42) *54.* Warnung vor Selbsttäuschung. *Warning against Self-Deception.* Matth 7 21–23

[21] Οὐ πᾶς ὁ λέγων μοι· κύριε κύριε, εἰσελεύσεται εἰς τὴν βασιλείαν τῶν οὐρανῶν, ἀλλ' ὁ ποιῶν τὸ θέλημα τοῦ πατρός μου τοῦ ἐν τοῖς οὐρανοῖς. [22] πολλοὶ ἐροῦσίν μοι ἐν ἐκείνῃ τῇ ἡμέρᾳ· κύριε κύριε, οὐ **τῷ** σῷ **ὀνόματι ἐπροφητεύσαμεν,** καὶ τῷ σῷ ὀνόματι δαιμόνια ἐξεβάλομεν, καὶ τῷ σῷ ὀνόματι δυνάμεις πολλὰς ἐποιήσαμεν; [23] καὶ τότε ὁμολογήσω αὐτοῖς ὅτι οὐδέποτε ἔγνων ὑμᾶς· **ἀποχωρεῖτε ἀπ' ἐμοῦ οἱ ἐργαζόμενοι τὴν ἀνομίαν.**

6 46 (90.): τί δέ με καλεῖτε· κύριε κύριε, καὶ οὐ ποιεῖτε ἃ λέγω;

13 26 f. (179.): τότε ἄρξεσθε λέγειν· ἐφάγομεν ἐνώπιόν σου καὶ ἐπίομεν, καὶ ἐν ταῖς πλατείαις ἡμῶν ἐδίδαξας· Jr27 15 14 14

[27] καὶ ἐρεῖ· λέγω ὑμῖν, οὐκ οἶδα πόθεν ἐστέ· ***ἀπόστητε ἀπ' ἐμοῦ πάντες ἐργάται ἀδικίας.*** Ps69

(43) *55.* Schlußgleichnisse. *Hearers and Doers of the Word.*

Matth 7 24–27

[24] Πᾶς οὖν ὅστις ἀκούει μου τοὺς λόγους τούτους καὶ ποιεῖ αὐτούς, ὁμοιωθήσεται ἀνδρὶ φρονίμῳ, ὅστις ᾠκοδόμησεν αὐτοῦ τὴν οἰκίαν ἐπὶ τὴν πέτραν. [25] καὶ κατέβη ἡ βροχὴ καὶ ἦλθαν οἱ ποταμοὶ καὶ ἔπνευσαν οἱ ἄνεμοι καὶ προσέπεσαν τῇ οἰκίᾳ ἐκείνῃ, καὶ οὐκ ἔπεσεν· τεθεμελίωτο γὰρ ἐπὶ τὴν πέτραν. [26] καὶ πᾶς ὁ ἀκούων μου τοὺς λόγους τούτους καὶ μὴ ποιῶν αὐτοὺς ὁμοιωθήσεται ἀνδρὶ μωρῷ, ὅστις ᾠκοδόμησεν αὐτοῦ τὴν οἰκίαν ἐπὶ τὴν ἄμμον. [27] καὶ κατέβη ἡ βροχὴ καὶ ἦλθον οἱ ποτα-

6 47–49 (91.)

[47] Πᾶς ὁ ἐρχόμενος πρός με καὶ ἀκούων μου τῶν λόγων καὶ ποιῶν αὐτούς, ὑποδείξω ὑμῖν τίνι ἐστὶν ὅμοιος. [48] ὅμοιός ἐστιν ἀνθρώπῳ οἰκοδομοῦντι οἰκίαν, ὃς ἔσκαψεν καὶ ἐβάθυνεν καὶ ἔθηκεν θεμέλιον ἐπὶ τὴν πέτραν· πλημμύρης δὲ γενομένης προσέρρηξεν ὁ ποταμὸς τῇ οἰκίᾳ ἐκείνῃ, καὶ οὐκ ἴσχυσεν σαλεῦσαι αὐτὴν διὰ τὸ καλῶς ᾠκοδομῆσθαι αὐτήν. [49] ὁ δὲ ἀκούσας καὶ μὴ ποιήσας ὅμοιός ἐστιν ἀνθρώπῳ οἰκοδομήσαντι οἰκίαν ἐπὶ τὴν γῆν χωρὶς θεμελίου, ᾗ προσέρρηξεν ὁ ποτα-

Mt 7,21 *om* τοις‖12 50 18 14: *Rpl* Bas EN↓ — *txt*: 𝔋<L>C **λ**-1582 **φ**124 **σ**<954>-349-1293 Θ 157 *al* Cr Ddy Iu Naas **22** επροφ. *prm* εφαγομεν και επιομεν και‖p: Iu^{1}(^{1} *et om* επροφ.—ον.^{3}) Or *L*Hi *S*c[s](+ τω σω ον.) **23** ομολ.] ερω‖p: EN↓ Iu Or *L*k[e] acg^{1}h PsAm Au$^{3:4}$ Cp$^{2:3}$ *S*c[s] *Arm* | εμου + παντες‖p Ps69: L **φ**<346> **σ**<945>-659 U Θ **047** *pc* *L*b30 vg^{3} Au$^{2:14}$ Cp$^{4:7}$ Hil Or *Arm* | εργ. τ. αν.] εργαται της ανομιας‖p: σ1606 *pc* Iu Or (^{1} *prm* οτι εστε) *L*achq Au$^{3:16}$ Or **24** *om* ουν‖p: X-892 σ517 K *L*k[e] a Euch Luc *S*c[s] *C*s$^{1:9}$b^{2} *Arm* | *om* τουτ.‖p: B*Σ-544 σ1424 *L*k[e] ag^{1} vg^{1} Au$^{2:10}$ PsAu Cp Ddy Euch Hil *S*j *C*b^{1} | ομ.] ομοιωσω αυτον‖Lk7 31 13 18.20: *Rpl* *L*k[e] fhq Ar Au^{7} PsAu Cp Hil Luc *S*'j *C*b<1> — ομοιος εστιν‖p: *L*abcg^{1}z Au^{1} Ddy Euch — *txt*: 𝔋<L> Φ-700-1071 **λ**-22-1582 **φ**<346> Θ *pc* PsBas Chr Cr Or *L*' Am Au^{2} *S*ph^{m}j *C*s **25** προσεκοψαν‖27: σ1424 *pc* *L*vl<ff^{1}lz> Ar Au$^{7:10}$ Cp — προσερρηξαν‖**p**: Σ Θ Eu **26** ο ακου. … ποι.] οστις ακουει … ποιει‖24 **φ**<346> Θ | *om* τουτους‖Lk4 7: 700 *L*k[e] f Ar Au$^{4:10}$ Cp Luc *S*j | ομ.] ομοιος εστιν‖p: Or *L*abcg^{1}hq vg^{2} Au$^{1:8}$ PsAu *Aeth*

Mt7 21p: *cf.* Ev. apocr. (PEg 2 fol. 1r°; *cf. ad 90.* Lk6 46p)

Mt7 21ff. *cf.* EN frgm.6 (Cod. N.T. 1424^{m} *ad* Mt7 5!): Τὸ Ἰουδαϊκὸν ἐνταῦθα οὕτως ἔχει· ἐὰν ἦτε ἐν τῷ κόλπῳ μου καὶ τὸ θέλημα τοῦ πατρός μου τοῦ ἐν οὐρανοῖς μὴ ποιῆτε, ἐκ τοῦ κόλπου μου ἀπορρίψω ὑμᾶς.

(2Cl4 5): … εἶπεν ὁ κύριος· ἐὰν ἦτε μετ' ἐμοῦ συνηγμένοι ἐν τῷ κόλπῳ μου καὶ μὴ ποιῆτε τὰς ἐντολάς μου, ἀποβαλῶ ὑμᾶς καὶ ἐρῶ ὑμῖν· ὑπάγετε ἀπ' ἐμοῦ, οὐκ οἶδα ὑμᾶς πόθεν ἐστέ, ἐργάται ἀνομίας.

μοὶ καὶ ἔπνευσαν οἱ ἄνεμοι καὶ προσέκοψαν τῇ οἰκίᾳ ἐκείνῃ, καὶ ἔπεσεν, καὶ ἦν ἡ πτῶσις αὐτῆς μεγάλη.

μός,
καὶ εὐθὺς συνέπεσεν, καὶ ἐγένετο τὸ ῥῆγμα τῆς οἰκίας ἐκείνης μέγα.

(44)

56. Nachwort. *The End of the Sermon.* Matth 7 28–29

[28] Καὶ ἐγένετο ὅτε συνετέλεσεν ὁ Ἰησοῦς τοὺς λόγους τούτους, ἐξεπλήσσοντο οἱ ὄχλοι ἐπὶ τῇ διδαχῇ αὐτοῦ· [29] ἦν γὰρ διδάσκων αὐτοὺς ὡς ἐξουσίαν ἔχων, καὶ οὐχ ὡς οἱ γραμματεῖς αὐτῶν.

24.

7 1 (92.): Ἐπειδὴ ἐπλήρωσεν πάντα τὰ ῥήματα αὐτοῦ ...

(45)

57. Heilung des Aussätzigen. *The Healing of a Leper.*

Matth 8 1–4

[1] Καταβάντος δὲ αὐτοῦ ἀπὸ τοῦ ὄρους ἠκολούθησαν αὐτῷ ὄχλοι πολλοί. [2] καὶ ἰδοὺ λεπρὸς προσελθὼν προσεκύνει αὐτῷ λέγων· κύριε, ἐὰν θέλῃς, δύνασαί με καθαρίσαι. [3] καὶ ἐκτείνας τὴν χεῖρα ἥψατο αὐτοῦ λέγων· θέλω, καθαρίσθητι. καὶ

Mark 1 40–45

[40] Καὶ ἔρχεται πρὸς αὐτὸν λεπρὸς παρακαλῶν αὐτὸν καὶ γονυπετῶν λέγων αὐτῷ ὅτι ἐὰν θέλῃς δύνασαί με καθαρίσαι. [41] καὶ σπλαγχνισθεὶς ἐκτείνας τὴν χεῖρα αὐτοῦ ἥψατο καὶ λέγει αὐτῷ· θέλω, καθαρίσθητι. [42] καὶ

Luk 5 12–16

[12] Καὶ ἐγένετο ἐν τῷ εἶναι αὐτὸν ἐν μιᾷ τῶν πόλεων καὶ ἰδοὺ ἀνὴρ πλήρης λέπρας· καὶ ἰδὼν τὸν Ἰησοῦν, πεσὼν ἐπὶ πρόσωπον ἐδεήθη αὐτοῦ λέγων· κύριε, ἐὰν θέλῃς, δύνασαί με καθαρίσαι. [13] καὶ ἐκτείνας τὴν χεῖρα ἥψατο αὐτοῦ εἰπών· θέλω, καθαρίσθητι. καὶ

Mt 7,27 προσερρηξαν ‖ p: C **λ**-22-1582 σM Θ *al* — προσεπεσαν ‖ 25: σ71-692 *pc* *L*ff^{1} lz vg Au$^{1:4}$ *S*h^{m} — προσεκρουσαν: **ϕ**⟨346⟩ **28** συνετ.] ● ετελησεν: 𝔥⟨L⟩C Σ-700 **λ**-1582 ϕ124-788 **σ**⟨954⟩-349 W Γ *al* *l*184 *l*1604^{v} Chr Or | l. + παντας ‖ p 26 1: λ1278 σM *pc* *Cs*$^{1:8}$b^{4} *Arm Geo*^{2} **29** αυτων] αυτ. και(η) οι Φαρισαιοι ‖ Lk 5 30: C*-33 W *pc* Eu *L*'(ff^{1})(κ. των Φαρισαιων: g^{2}) Au^{1} Hil *S Geo*^{A} *Δ*'⟨me p⟩(*om* αυτ.: ad md^{V} n; ∼ Φ. ... γρα.: n^{L}) — κ. οι Φ. αυτων: *L*k[e](∼ Φ. ... γρα.) b *Arm*^{O}(*om* αυτ.) — *om* ‖ Mk 1 22: *Rpl* *L*Au^{1} — *txt*: 𝔥'⟨L⟩C^{2} Σ-1604 **λ**-22-1582 **ϕ**⟨346⟩ K Δ Θ Π *al* Chr Eu *L*f Au^{2} *S*j *C Arm Geo*' *Aeth*

Mk 1,40 κ. γον.] + αυτον(-τω) ‖ 10 17 Mt 17 14: *Rpl* (1071 ϕ983-1689 σ27-945-1010 *pc*) *S*j *Cs*^{1} *Geo*^{B} — *om* ‖ Mt 8 5: B ϕ124-230-*l*547 σ659-827 D G W Γ **0104** *pc* *l*26 *l*211 *l*303 *l*952 *l*956 *l*1627 *L*abcff^{2}r^{1}z vg^{1} *Cs*^{2} — *txt*: ℵL-579-892 Θ-565 **λ**⟨131⟩ σ71-692-1402 *pc* *L*' Au *S* *C*b *Geo Got* | λεγ.] ● και λ.: *Rpl* *L*vl'r^{1} vg^{1} *S*,j *C*b^{7} — ειπεν: *L*flr^{2} vg Au — *txt*: ℵ*B ϕ69 *L*e[k] q *C* | οτι] κυριε ‖ **p**: CL-892 ΘΣ-700 W 1342 *L*e[k] cff^{2} vg^{6} *S*j — οτι κυ. ‖ p: *Cs*$^{2:3}$b$^{\langle 9\rangle}$ — κυ. οτι: B — *om* ‖ p: D 238 *L*'Au *S*p$^{\langle 7\rangle}$ | θελ. + κυριε ‖ p: Φ-28-565-1071 ϕ124-*l*547 **090** *pc* **41** και^{1}] ● ο δε Ιησους: *Rpl* *L*' *S*,j(κυριος Ι.) *Cs*^{1}(∼)b^{6} — *txt*: ℵB-892 D *L*e[k] abff^{2}r^{1} *Cs*^{1}b' | σπ.] ● οργισθεις: D *L*aff^{2}r^{1} *Δ*E$^{s.a}$ — *om* ‖ **p**: *L*b | ∼ ηψ. αυ. ‖ Mt Lk: *Rpl* — αυ. ηψ. αυτου ‖ p: D *L S*,j — *txt*: ℵBL-892 *pm* | και λε.] λεγων ‖ p: 565 **ϕ**'(*prm* και: 346) W 1342 *Cs* | *om* αυτω ‖ Mt Lk: ℵ **λ**⟨118⟩-22 ϕ1689 W 1342 *L*cff^{2} *S*p *Cs*$^{2:3}$b^{2}

Lk 5,12 πλ. λεπ.] λεπρος ‖ **p**: D — + (προσ)ελθων ‖ p: σ517-(1424)-1675 (*S*s[c]p) | και ιδ.] ● ιδ. δε ‖ 5 8 8 28.47: ℵB-579 ϕ124 σ990 *L*e — ιδ.: 700 19 *L*fr^{2}z31 vg^{1} *S*s[c]pj **13** ειπ.] ● λεγων ‖ Mt Mk: 𝔥CX **ϕ** σ990 D Θ *pc* Cr — *txt*: *Rpl*

---

57. cf. Ev. apocr. (PEg 2 fol. 1r° 8—10): (*cf. ad 22.* Lk 4 30) ... [8] Καὶ [ἰ]δοὺ λεπρὸς προσελθ[ὼν αὐτῷ] λέγει· ‘διδάσκαλε Ἰη(σοῦ) λε[προῖς συν]οδεύων καὶ συνεσθίω[ν αὐτοῖς] ἐν τῷ πανδοχείῳ ἐλ[έπρησα] καὶ αὐτὸς ἐγώ· ἐὰν [ο]ὖν [σὺ θέλῃς] καθαρίζομαι.’ [9] ὁ δὴ κ(ύριο)ς [ἔφη αὐτῷ]· ‘θέλ[ω] καθαρίσθητι·’ [καὶ εὐθέως ἀ]πέστη ἀπ’ αὐτοῦ ἡ λέπ[ρα. [10] ὁ δὲ κ(ύριο)ς εἶπεν αὐτῷ·] ‘πορε[υθεὶς ἐπίδειξον σεαυτὸ]ν τοῖ[ς ἱερεῦσι ...

Matth 8: εὐθέως ἐκαθαρίσθη αὐτοῦ ἡ λέπρα. [4] καὶ λέγει αὐτῷ ὁ Ἰησοῦς· ὅρα μηδενὶ εἴπῃς, ἀλλὰ ὕπαγε σεαυτὸν **δεῖξον τῷ ἱερεῖ** καὶ προσένεγκον τὸ δῶρον ὃ προσέταξεν Μωυσῆς, εἰς μαρτύριον αὐτοῖς.

Mark 1: εἰπόντος αὐτοῦ εὐθὺς ἀπῆλθεν ἀπ' αὐτοῦ ἡ λέπρα, καὶ ἐκαθαρίσθη. [43] καὶ ἐμβριμησάμενος αὐτῷ εὐθὺς ἐξέβαλεν αὐτόν, [44] καὶ λέγει αὐτῷ· ὅρα μηδενὶ μηδὲν εἴπῃς, ἀλλὰ ὕπαγε σεαυτὸν **δεῖξον τῷ ἱερεῖ** καὶ προσένεγκε περὶ τοῦ καθαρισμοῦ σου ἃ προσέταξεν Μωυσῆς, εἰς μαρτύριον αὐτοῖς. [45] ὁ δὲ ἐξελθὼν ἤρξατο κηρύσσειν πολλὰ καὶ διαφημίζειν τὸν λόγον, ὥστε μηκέτι αὐτὸν δύνασθαι φανερῶς εἰς πόλιν εἰσελθεῖν, ἀλλ' ἔξω ἐπ' ἐρήμοις τόποις ἦν· καὶ ἤρχοντο πρὸς αὐτὸν πάντοθεν.

Luk 5: εὐθέως ἡ λέπρα ἀπῆλθεν ἀπ' αὐτοῦ. [14] καὶ αὐτὸς παρήγγειλεν αὐτῷ μηδενὶ εἰπεῖν, ἀλλὰ ἀπελθὼν **δεῖξον** σεαυτὸν **τῷ ἱερεῖ** καὶ προσένεγκε περὶ τοῦ καθαρισμοῦ σου καθὼς προσέταξεν Μωυσῆς, εἰς μαρτύριον αὐτοῖς. [15] διήρχετο δὲ μᾶλλον ὁ λόγος περὶ αὐτοῦ, καὶ συνήρχοντο ὄχλοι πολλοὶ ἀκούειν καὶ θεραπεύεσθαι ἀπὸ τῶν ἀσθενειῶν αὐτῶν· [16] αὐτὸς δὲ ἦν ὑποχωρῶν ἐν ταῖς ἐρήμοις καὶ προσευχόμενος.

Lv 13 49

(46)

58. Der Hauptmann von Kapernaum. *The Centurion's Servant.*

Matth 8 5–13: [5] Εἰσελθόντος δὲ αὐτοῦ εἰς Καφαρναουμ προσῆλθεν αὐτῷ ἑκατόνταρχος παρακαλῶν αὐτὸν [6] καὶ λέγων· κύριε, ὁ παῖς μου βέβληται ἐν τῇ οἰκίᾳ παραλυτικός, δεινῶς βασανιζόμενος.

7 1–10 (92.): [1] *Ἐπειδὴ ἐπλήρωσεν πάντα τὰ ῥήματα αὐτοῦ εἰς τὰς ἀκοὰς τοῦ λαοῦ, εἰσῆλθεν εἰς Καφαρναουμ.* [2] *ἑκατοντάρχου δέ τινος δοῦλος κακῶς ἔχων ἤμελλεν τελευτᾶν, ὃς ἦν αὐτῷ ἔντιμος.* [3] *ἀκούσας δὲ περὶ τοῦ Ἰησοῦ ἀπέστειλεν πρὸς αὐτὸν πρεσβυτέρους τῶν Ἰουδαίων, ἐρωτῶν αὐτὸν ὅπως ἐλθὼν διασώσῃ τὸν δοῦλον αὐτοῦ.* [4] *οἱ δὲ παραγενόμενοι πρὸς τὸν Ἰησοῦν παρεκάλουν αὐτὸν σπουδαίως,*

4 46–53: Ἦλθεν οὖν πάλιν εἰς τὴν Κανα τῆς Γαλιλαίας, ὅπου ἐποίησεν τὸ ὕδωρ οἶνον. καὶ ἦν τις βασιλικὸς οὗ ὁ υἱὸς ἠσθένει ἐν Καφαρναουμ· [47] οὗτος ἀκούσας ὅτι Ἰησοῦς ἥκει ἐκ τῆς Ἰουδαίας εἰς τὴν Γαλιλαίαν, ἀπῆλθεν πρὸς αὐ-

Mt 8,3 εκαθ. + απ‖p: σ659 S *pc* *S*sc **4** μηδ. + μηδεν‖Mk: Γ *pc* | ∼ δει. σε.‖Lk5 14 17 14: 1396 Chr2:3 | τοις ιερευσιν‖Lk17 14: Ev. apocr.v↓ *Lh* *S*j *Δ*n p Es.a | δωρ. + σου‖p5 23: ΝΣ ϕ174 σ990 *pc* *l*54 Ep *L*c Hil *S*p7j *C*s3:6b⟨7⟩ *Geo* **5** ● εκατονταρχης (= 8)‖13: ℵ*-892 σ71-1424 W

Mk 1,42 ● *om* ειπ. αυ.‖**p**: ℵBL-892 565 ϕ⟨124-346⟩ σ827 D W *pc* *L*e[k] abcff2r1 vg1 *S*' *C* — *txt*: *Rpl* *L*' *S*hj *Arm* | ∼ η λε. απηλ. απ αυ.‖Lk: C-579-892 σ517-827 *pc* | *om* και εκαθ.‖Lk: W Ev. apocr.v↓ *L*e[k] b **43** *om* 43‖**p**: W *L*(*om* εμβ.—ευθ.: e[k]) bcz **44** *om* μηδεν‖7 36 Mt Lk: ℌ⟨B-579⟩ 565-700 ϕ⟨346⟩-*l*547 σ349-659-945-954-1194-1223 A D W 1342 *al* *L* *S*[sc]p *C* | ∼ δει. σεαυ.‖Lk5 14 17 14: D W(εαυ.) | α] ο‖Mt: 579 Θ-700 σ517-1424 W *pc* Lac *S*jab *C*b4('το δωρον ο) — καθως(καθα)‖Lk: C*-(33 1342) *S*[sc]pjc (*C*s2:3) **45** ● ∼ εις πολ. φαν.: ℌ⟨BD-579⟩C 28-565-1071 ϕ124 *pc* *Geo*1 | επ] εν‖p: *Rpl* — *txt*: ℌ⟨33-579⟩ 28-565 ϕ124 W 1342 | παντ. + και ελαλει αυτοις τον λογον‖2 2: 579

Lk 5,13 η λε. απη. απ αυ.] απη. απ αυ. η λε.‖p: 579 544 157 *pc* *L*vg1 — απη. απ αυ. η λε. αυτου(*om*)‖p: *S*s[c]p6('+ και εκαθαρισθη) (*Arm*) — απη. η λε. (+ αυτου) απ αυ.: ϕ⟨124⟩ (*S*p1) *Arm* *Aeth* — εκαθ. η λε. αυ.‖Mt: 46 126(λε. + απ) — εκαθ.‖Mt: D *L*e — *txt* (λε. + αυτου): *Rpl* *L*'(bff2lqr130 vg1) *S*h *C*s7(1)b'(1) **14** *om* αυτος‖**p**: W *L*e (αυτω + ο Ἰησοῦς: r1 *S*s[c])p | αλλα απ.] απελθε δε και‖p: D *L*e a | τοις ιερευσιν‖17 4: Ev. apocr.↓ *L*bff2 *Δ*n p Es.a | προσεν. + το δωρον‖Mt: X *L*bc *S*p5 *Arm* | καθως] α‖p: 2 245(καθαπερ) | εις μα. αυ.] ινα εις μα. η (D* ην) υμιν τουτο‖21 13: Dc McnEp(∼) *L*vl'⟨fz⟩(υμ.) αυτοις: e l vg1; *om* τουτο: e l Te) Am *S*s[c](= e) | αυτοις + και τοις εθνεσιν‖Mt 10 18 24 14: *l*18 — + ο δε εξελθων ηρξατο κηρυσσειν και διαφημιζειν τον λογον, ωστε μηκετι δυνασθαι αυτον φανερως εις πολιν εισελθειν, αλλα εξω ην εν ερημοις τοποις· και συνηρχοντο προς αυτον· και ηλθεν παλιν εις Καφαρναουμ‖Mk1 45 2 1: D **15** λογ.] ηχος‖4 37: 579 *L*a *S*s[c]p | ακ. + αυτου‖15 1 21 38: σM *pc* *L*ff2r1 *S*s[c]p *C*

Jo 4,46 κ. ην] ● ην δε: ℌ⟨BWs-579⟩-**083** N-1071 D **0141** *pc* Chr Cr *L*e bfff2lqr1z Gau *C*b⟨1⟩ **47** απη.] ● ηλθεν‖Mt15 25 p: ℵ*C-33-1241 **λ** ϕ-*l*547 *pc* Chr *L*vl'r1 *S*c[s] *Arm* *Aeth* — *txt*: 𝔓66.75 *Rpl* *L*cfq vg *S*'j *C*+Bas

7 καὶ λέγει αὐτῷ· ἐγὼ ἐλθὼν θεραπεύσω αὐτόν.

8 καὶ ἀποκριθεὶς ὁ ἑκατόνταρχος ἔφη· κύριε, οὐκ εἰμὶ ἱκανὸς ἵνα μου ὑπὸ τὴν στέγην εἰσέλθῃς· ἀλλὰ μόνον εἰπὲ λόγῳ, καὶ ἰαθήσεται ὁ παῖς μου. 9 καὶ γὰρ ἐγὼ ἄνθρωπός εἰμι ὑπὸ ἐξουσίαν, ἔχων ὑπ' ἐμαυτὸν στρατιώτας, καὶ λέγω τούτῳ· πορεύθητι, καὶ πορεύεται, καὶ ἄλλῳ· ἔρχου, καὶ ἔρχεται, καὶ τῷ δούλῳ μου· ποίησον τοῦτο, καὶ ποιεῖ. 10 ἀκούσας δὲ ὁ Ἰησοῦς ἐθαύμασεν καὶ εἶπεν τοῖς ἀκολουθοῦσιν· αμην λέγω ὑμῖν, παρ' οὐδενὶ τοσαύτην πίστιν ἐν τῷ Ισραηλ εὗρον. 11 λέγω δὲ ὑμῖν ὅτι πολλοὶ **ἀπὸ ἀνατολῶν καὶ δυσμῶν** ἥξουσιν καὶ ἀνακλιθήσονται μετὰ Αβρααμ καὶ Ισαακ καὶ Ιακωβ ἐν τῇ βασιλείᾳ τῶν οὐρανῶν· 12 οἱ δὲ υἱοὶ τῆς βασιλείας ἐκβληθήσονται εἰς τὸ σκότος τὸ ἐξώτερον· ἐκεῖ

Ps107 3

λέγοντες ὅτι ἄξιός ἐστιν ᾧ παρέξῃ τοῦτο· 5 ἀγαπᾷ γὰρ τὸ ἔθνος ἡμῶν καὶ τὴν συναγωγὴν αὐτὸς ᾠκοδόμησεν ἡμῖν. 6 ὁ δὲ Ἰησοῦς ἐπορεύετο σὺν αὐτοῖς. ἤδη δὲ αὐτοῦ οὐ μακρὰν ἀπέχοντος ἀπὸ τῆς οἰκίας, ἔπεμψεν πρὸς αὐτὸν φίλους ὁ ἑκατόνταρχος λέγων αὐτῷ· κύριε, μὴ σκύλλου· οὐ γὰρ ἱκανός εἰμι ἵνα ὑπὸ τὴν στέγην μου εἰσέλθῃς· 7 διὸ οὐδὲ ἐμαυτὸν ἠξίωσα πρὸς σὲ ἐλθεῖν· ἀλλὰ εἰπὲ λόγῳ, καὶ ἰαθήτω ὁ παῖς μου. 8 καὶ γὰρ ἐγὼ ἄνθρωπός εἰμι ὑπὸ ἐξουσίαν τασσόμενος, ἔχων ὑπ' ἐμαυτὸν στρατιώτας, καὶ λέγω τούτῳ· πορεύθητι, καὶ πορεύεται, καὶ ἄλλῳ· ἔρχου, καὶ ἔρχεται, καὶ τῷ δούλῳ μου· ποίησον τοῦτο, καὶ ποιεῖ. 9 ἀκούσας δὲ ταῦτα ὁ Ἰησοῦς ἐθαύμασεν αὐτόν, καὶ στραφεὶς τῷ ἀκολουθοῦντι αὐτῷ ὄχλῳ εἶπεν· λέγω ὑμῖν, οὐδὲ ἐν τῷ Ισραηλ τοσαύτην πίστιν εὗρον. 13 29.28 (179.): καὶ ἥξουσιν ***ἀπὸ ἀνατολῶν καὶ δυσμῶν καὶ*** *ἀπὸ* ***βορρᾶ*** *καὶ νότου, καὶ ἀνακλιθήσονται ἐν τῇ βασιλείᾳ τοῦ θεοῦ. 28 b ... ὑμᾶς δὲ ἐκβαλλομένους ἔξω ... 28 a ἐκεῖ*

τὸν καὶ ἠρώτα ἵνα καταβῇ καὶ ἰάσηται αὐτοῦ τὸν υἱόν· ἤμελλεν γὰρ ἀποθνῄσκειν. 48 εἶπεν οὖν ὁ Ἰησοῦς πρὸς αὐτόν· ἐὰν μὴ σημεῖα καὶ τέρατα ἴδητε, οὐ μὴ πιστεύσητε. 49 λέγει πρὸς αὐτὸν ὁ βασιλικός· κύριε, κατάβηθι πρὶν ἀποθανεῖν τὸ παιδίον μου. 50 λέγει αὐτῷ ὁ Ἰησοῦς· πορεύου, ὁ υἱός σου ζῇ. ἐπίστευσεν ὁ ἄνθρωπος τῷ λόγῳ ὃν εἶπεν αὐτῷ ὁ Ἰησοῦς, καὶ ἐπορεύετο. 51 ἤδη δὲ αὐτοῦ καταβαίνοντος οἱ δοῦλοι ὑπήντησαν αὐτῷ λέγοντες ὅτι ὁ παῖς αὐτοῦ ζῇ. 52 ἐπύθετο οὖν τὴν ὥραν παρ' αὐτῶν ἐν ᾗ κομψότερον ἔσχεν· εἶπον οὖν αὐτῷ ὅτι ἐχθὲς ὥραν ἑβδόμην ἀφῆκεν αὐτὸν ὁ πυρετός. 53 ἔγνω οὖν ὁ πατὴρ ὅτι ἐκείνῃ τῇ ὥρᾳ ἐν ᾗ εἶπεν αὐτῷ ὁ Ἰησοῦς·

Mt 8,7 ● *om* και: B 700 *l*47 *Lk*[e] bg¹hq vg⁵ *S*' Csb³ *Geo*² — *txt*: *Rpl L*' *S*hj *C*b' *Geo*¹ | αυτω + ο Ἰησοῦς ‖Jo: *Rpl L*' *S*'j Csb³ — *txt*: ℵB-892 *pc Lk*[e] *S*s *C*b' **8** και απ.] ● απ. δε: ℵ* B-33 *pc C*s — *om* και‖Jo: *Lk*[e] *S*j^b *C*b¹ *Arm* — *txt*: *Rpl* Cr *L*' *S*hj^ac *C*b' | ● εκατ. *cf. ad* 5 | ικ.] αξιος‖Lk4 Jo1 27: ϕ(*om*: 13-826)-543 | ∼ υπο τ. στε. μου‖p: Θ *l*1604 **9** εξου. + τασσομενος‖p: ℵB *pc l*211 Chr¹:⁴ *L*vl[e]⟨fff¹l⟩g²30 vg⁸ Au²:³ Hil Or **10** δε + ταυτα‖p: ΝΣ *l*50 *C*s¹:⁶ *Geo* | ακολ. + αυτω(-ον)‖p: C-33-892 ΝΣ ϕ13-543-826-(828-983) σ1424 157 *pc L S*,j | παρ ουδ.] ● ουδε(ουδεποτε)‖p: *Rpl* Chr *L*'Au⁷ Hil Or *S*sph^t (*Arm Geo*¹) — ουδε παρ ουδενι: λ118 *L*g¹ *S*h^m *Aeth* — *txt*: B-892 **λ**(*om* παρ: 118) W *Lk*[e] aq vg² Au¹ *S*cj *C Geo*² *Aeth* | ● ∼ εν τ. Ι. τοσ. πι.‖p: *Rpl* Chr *L*f vg¹ *S*' *Geo*'(^B ∼ ευ. τοσ. πι.) — *om* εν τ. Ι.: **λ** — *txt* (∼ ευ. εν τ. Ι.): B-(892) W *pc L*' Au Or *S*s(j) *C Aeth* **11** ∼ ηξ. απο—δυσ.‖Lk13 29: Eu Iu *L*Cp **12** εις—εξωτ.] εξω‖Lk13 28: Chr — εξω εις—εξωτ.‖←: 1093

Jo 4,47 ηρω. + αυτον‖Lk Mt: *Rpl L*' {*S*,j *C*^{+B}a^s} *Arm*^pc — *om* κ. ηρ.: G **047** — *txt*: 𝔓66.75 𝔊⟨579⟩CW^s-**083** 1071 ϕ69 σ1010-1223 D **086 0141** *pc* Chr *Le* alq vg¹ {} *Arm*' *Geo* **49** τον παιδα‖p51: ℵ **50** επιστ.] και επ.‖53 2 11: *Rpl L*vl' r¹ vg¹ *S*,j *C*b'^{+Bv}f *Δ*a i me (τοτε επ.: md n') — επ. δε: L-**083**-892 **0141** *pc* — *txt*: 𝔓66.75 ℵBW^s-1241 σ1010 D *pc L*cl vg' Csb² *Δ*ad l n^L | ον] ● ω: 𝔓66 *Rpl* — *txt*: 𝔓75 ℵ^cBCLW^s-**083** A F Θ Ψ *pc* **51** απηντ.‖Lk17 12: *Rpl* Or — *txt*: 𝔓66 𝔊⟨892⟩C N-1071 **λ** **ϕ** σ1010-1194-1207-1223 D K W^s Θ Ψ *pc* Chr | λεγ.] και απηγγειλαν (+ αυτω) λεγ.: 𝔓66 *Rpl* {*L*'(a vg¹ *S* Csfa^s) *Arm Geo*² (*Aeth*) *Δ*a ad l n'} — και ανηγγ. λεγ.: 33 544 **λ** σ1223 K Π *pc* {} — και ηγγ. αυτω: D *L*b *Δ*i^T p — ● και ηγγ.: ℵ — αγγελλοντες: *L*r¹ — *txt* (+ αυτω): 𝔓75 𝔊'⟨W^s⟩ N σ1010-1293 185 Chr *S*j *C*b'^{+B}(¹) *Geo*¹ *Aeth Δ*i^V (md n^L) **52** επυνθανετο‖Mt2 4: 579 **ϕ**-*l*547 σ1223 **053** Chr *L*acdfq vg *S*hj *Geo* | ∼ παρ αυ. την ω.‖←: *Rpl* (+ εκεινην: *pc*) Chr *L*vl'r¹^v30 vg¹ *S*h Csb'^{+B}fa^s *Arm Aeth* — την ω. εκ.‖53 Mt13: 𝔓75 B σ1194(*om* εκ.) *C*b¹ — *txt*: 𝔓66 ℵCW^s-579 N **λ** **ϕ**'-543^v-*l*547 σ945-1010-1223 A D K U Θ Π Ψ *al Le* a^vbcq vg' | αυτου] αυτην‖Mk13 1p: B Λ

ἔσται ὁ κλαυθμὸς καὶ ὁ βρυγμὸς τῶν ὀδόντων. [13] καὶ εἶπεν ὁ Ἰησοῦς τῷ ἑκατοντάρχῃ· ὕπαγε, καὶ ὡς ἐπίστευσας γενηθήτω σοι. καὶ ἰάθη ὁ παῖς ἐν τῇ ὥρᾳ ἐκείνῃ.

ἔσται ὁ κλαυθμὸς καὶ ὁ βρυγμὸς τῶν ὀδόντων, ... (7) [10] *καὶ ὑποστρέψαντες εἰς τὸν οἶκον οἱ πεμφθέντες εὗρον τὸν ἀσθενοῦντα δοῦλον ὑγιαίνοντα.*

ὁ υἱός σου ζῇ· καὶ ἐπίστευσεν αὐτὸς καὶ ἡ οἰκία αὐτοῦ ὅλη.

(47)

59. Heilung der Schwiegermutter des Petrus. **Matth 8** 14–15 [*25.*]
The Healing of Peter's Wife's Mother.

[14] Καὶ ἐλθὼν ὁ Ἰησοῦς εἰς τὴν οἰκίαν Πέτρου εἶδεν τὴν πενθερὰν αὐτοῦ βεβλημένην καὶ πυρέσσουσαν· [15] καὶ ἥψατο τῆς χειρὸς αὐτῆς, καὶ ἀφῆκεν αὐτὴν ὁ πυρετός· καὶ ἠγέρθη, καὶ διηκόνει αὐτῷ. [*25.*]

(48)

60. Krankenheilungen am Abend. *The Sick Healed at Evening.* **Matth 8** 16–17

[16] Ὀψίας δὲ γενομένης προσήνεγκαν αὐτῷ δαιμονιζομένους πολλούς· καὶ ἐξέβαλεν τὰ πνεύματα λόγῳ, καὶ πάντας τοὺς κακῶς ἔχοντας ἐθεράπευσεν· [17] ὅπως πληρωθῇ τὸ ῥηθὲν διὰ Ἠσαΐου τοῦ προφήτου λέγοντος· **αὐτὸς τὰς ἀσθενείας ἡμῶν ἔλαβεν καὶ τὰς νόσους ἐβάστασεν.** [*26. 84.*] Is53 4

(49)

61. Verschiedene Nachfolger. *Two Claimants to Discipleship.*

Matth 8 18–22 [*118.*]

[18] Ἰδὼν δὲ ὁ Ἰησοῦς πολλοὺς ὄχλους περὶ αὐτὸν ἐκέλευσεν ἀπελθεῖν εἰς τὸ πέραν.

[19] καὶ προσελθὼν εἷς γραμματεὺς εἶπεν αὐτῷ· διδάσκαλε, ἀκολουθήσω σοι ὅπου ἐὰν ἀπέρχῃ. [20] καὶ λέγει αὐτῷ ὁ Ἰησοῦς· αἱ ἀλώπεκες φωλεοὺς ἔχου-

9 57–60 *(152.)*

[57] *Καὶ πορευομένων αὐτῶν ἐν τῇ ὁδῷ εἶπέν τις πρὸς αὐτόν· ἀκολουθήσω σοι ὅπου ἐὰν ἀπέρχῃ.* [58] *καὶ εἶπεν αὐτῷ ὁ Ἰησοῦς· αἱ ἀλώπεκες φωλεοὺς ἔχου-*

Mt 8,13 ● εκατονταρχω‖5.8 Lk2.6: ℵ^{b}-33 NΦ **λ**-22-1582 ϕ174 σ267-659-1194 U Δ *pm* Bas^{S} | *om* και^{2}‖Lk17 19 Mk10 52: ℵB Φ-544 *pc* Bas *L*k[e] abg$^{1.2}$hq30 vg^{5} Ir Or *S*'Eu *C* *Δ*a n^{Hr} — *txt*: *Rpl* Bas^{S} Or *L*' Or *S*hj *Arm* | παις + αυτου‖Jo4 51: *Rpl* Bas^{S} *L*30 *S*,Eu *C*s^{6} — *txt*: ℵB-33 **λ**-22-1582 Bas *L*'Au *S*j *C*s^{1}b | εν τ. ω. εκ.] απο της ωρας εκεινης‖9 22 15 28 17 18: C-33 NΣ-544 σ1010-1606 Δ Θ **0250** *pc* *l*950 *l*1627 Bas Bas^{S} Chr Eu *L*abcg$^{1.2}$hq30 Au *S*j *C*s$^{5:8}$b^{3} *Δ*l^{AD} | εκεινη + και υποστρεψαντες οι πεμφθεντες εις τον οικον ευρον τον ασθενουντα δουλον υγιαινοντα‖p: ϕ124^{m} — + και υποστρεψας ο εκατονταρχος εις τ. οικ. αυτου εν αυτη τη ωρα ευρεν τον παιδα υγιαινοντα‖p: ℵCX-33 NΣΦ-544 **λ**-22-1582 ϕ230-983 σM-1194-1391 E S U Θ *L*g^{1} *S*hj Eu *Aeth* ⟦εκατονταρχης‖13: *pc* | *om* εν αυ. τ. ωρα‖p: S *Aeth* — *om* αυτη: ϕ983 | τ. παι.] αυτον: 33 NΣ *pc* — + αυτου‖Jo4 51: Φ σM-1194-1391 *pc* *S*Eu⟧ **14** εισελθ.‖Lk: 892 σ71-1391 *pc* | βεβ. + επι κλινης‖9 2 Mk7 30: Φ 713 **15** και^{2} + παραχρημα‖Lk: 157 {*S*sc} — + ευθυς‖←: ϕ⟨983⟩ {} | αυτω] αυτοις‖p Lk8 2: *Rpl* *L*'Au *S*scp^{3} *C*b *Arm*^{mu} — *txt*: ℵ*BCX N(-ον) Σ-700 ϕ174-*l*547 σ71 E G K S U V W Γ Θ Π *L*k[e] q vg^{1} *S*'j *C*s *Arm*' *Geo* **16** πνευ. + ακαθαρτα *cf.* 10 1 12 43 *etc.*: Δ(-τος!) *L*abcg^{2}hqz30 vg^{8} Hil *C*s$^{4:6}$b **17** δια] υπο‖22 31 1 22 2 15: σ349-517 Chr | ελα.] ηρε‖Jo1 29: σ659 **18** πολ. οχ.] ● οχλους: ℵ* **λ**⟨118⟩-22 *L*Au^{1}(τους οχ.: 1365 *l*186 *C*b) — ● οχλον: B *C*s^{7} — πολυν οχλον (~): 544 ϕ983-1689 σ1424 (W) *al* *L*(cg^{1}) PsAu^{1} {}^{1} (*C*s^{1} *Geo*^{2})^{1} *Δ*n^{L}{}^{2} — *txt* (~): *Rpl* (L'Au^{1} PsAu^{1} Hil) {(*S*)j}^{1} (*Arm*) *Δ*ad i^{T} l^{FG}{a md n' p}^{2} **19** διδ. + αγαθε‖Mk10 17 Lk18 18: **047**

Mt8 20p *cf.* ETh^{II} 86 (*transl.*): *Λέγει Ἰησοῦς· [αἱ ἀλώπεκες ἔχου]σιν τοὺς [φωλεοὺς αὐτῶν] καὶ τὰ πετεινὰ ἔχει [τὴν] κατασκήνωσιν αὐτῶν, ὁ δὲ υἱὸς τοῦ ἀνθρώπου οὐκ ἔχει ποῦ τὴν κεφαλὴν αὐτοῦ κλίνῃ καὶ ἀναπαύσηται.*

σιν καὶ τὰ πετεινὰ τοῦ οὐρανοῦ κατασκηνώσεις, ὁ δὲ υἱὸς τοῦ ἀνθρώπου οὐκ ἔχει ποῦ τὴν κεφαλὴν κλίνῃ.
21 ἕτερος δὲ τῶν μαθητῶν εἶπεν αὐτῷ· κύριε, ἐπίτρεψόν μοι πρῶτον ἀπελθεῖν καὶ θάψαι τὸν πατέρα μου. 22 ὁ δὲ Ἰησοῦς λέγει αὐτῷ· ἀκολούθει μοι, καὶ ἄφες τοὺς νεκροὺς θάψαι τοὺς ἑαυτῶν νεκρούς.

σιν καὶ τὰ πετεινὰ τοῦ οὐρανοῦ κατασκηνώσεις, ὁ δὲ υἱὸς τοῦ ἀνθρώπου οὐκ ἔχει ποῦ τὴν κεφαλὴν κλίνῃ.
59 εἶπεν δὲ πρὸς ἕτερον· ἀκολούθει μοι. ὁ δὲ εἶπεν· ἐπίτρεψόν μοι ἀπελθόντι πρῶτον θάψαι τὸν πατέρα μου. 60 εἶπεν δὲ αὐτῷ· ἄφες τοὺς νεκροὺς θάψαι τοὺς ἑαυτῶν νεκρούς, σὺ δὲ ἀπελθὼν διάγγελλε τὴν βασιλείαν τοῦ θεοῦ.

(50) *62.* Der Seesturm. *Stilling the Tempest.* **Matth 8** 23–27 *118.*

23 Καὶ ἐμβάντι αὐτῷ εἰς πλοῖον, ἠκολούθησαν αὐτῷ οἱ μαθηταὶ αὐτοῦ. 24 καὶ ἰδοὺ σεισμὸς μέγας ἐγένετο ἐν τῇ θαλάσσῃ, ὥστε τὸ πλοῖον καλύπτεσθαι ὑπὸ τῶν κυμάτων· αὐτὸς δὲ ἐκάθευδεν. 25 καὶ προσελθόντες οἱ μαθηταὶ ἤγειραν αὐτὸν λέγοντες· κύριε, σῶσον, ἀπολλύμεθα. 26 καὶ λέγει αὐτοῖς· τί δειλοί ἐστε, ὀλιγόπιστοι; τότε ἐγερθεὶς ἐπετίμησεν τοῖς ἀνέμοις καὶ τῇ θαλάσσῃ, καὶ ἐγένετο γαλήνη μεγάλη. 27 οἱ δὲ ἄνθρωποι ἐθαύμασαν λέγοντες· ποταπός ἐστιν οὗτος, ὅτι καὶ οἱ ἄνεμοι καὶ ἡ θάλασσα αὐτῷ ὑπακούουσιν;

118.

(51) *63.* Die Besessenen von Gadara. *The Gadarene Demoniacs.* **Matth 8** 28–34 *119.*

28 Καὶ ἐλθόντος αὐτοῦ εἰς τὸ πέραν εἰς τὴν χώραν τῶν Γαδαρηνῶν ὑπήντησαν αὐτῷ δύο δαιμονιζόμενοι ἐκ τῶν μνημείων ἐξερχόμενοι, χαλεποὶ λίαν, ὥστε μὴ ἰσχύειν τινὰ παρελθεῖν διὰ τῆς ὁδοῦ ἐκείνης. 29 καὶ ἰδοὺ ἔκραξαν λέγοντες· τί ἡμῖν καὶ σοί, υἱὲ τοῦ θεοῦ; ἦλθες ὧδε πρὸ καιροῦ βασανίσαι ἡμᾶς; 30 ἦν δὲ μακρὰν ἀπ' αὐτῶν ἀγέλη χοίρων πολλῶν βοσκομένη. 31 οἱ δὲ δαίμονες παρεκάλουν αὐτὸν λέγοντες· εἰ ἐκβάλλεις ἡμᾶς, ἀπόστειλον ἡμᾶς εἰς τὴν ἀγέλην τῶν χοίρων. 32 καὶ εἶπεν αὐτοῖς· ὑπάγετε. οἱ δὲ ἐξελθόντες ἀπῆλθον εἰς τοὺς χοίρους· καὶ ἰδοὺ ὥρμησεν πᾶσα ἡ ἀγέλη κατὰ τοῦ κρημνοῦ εἰς τὴν θάλασσαν, καὶ ἀπέθανον

119.

Mt 8,21 απ. και] απελθοντι‖p: 157 — *txt*: 𝔋⟨L⟩C **λ**-1582 *al* | **22** ● *om* I.‖p: ℵ-33 *L*k[e] bcq *S*s | λεγ.] ειπεν‖p: *Rpl* | ακο.—νεκ.^{2}] αφες—νεκ.^{2} συ δε ακο. μοι‖p: Cl *S*sc
23 εμβαινοντος αυτου‖Mk5 18: Σ *L*⟨k[e]⟩ | ● εις + το‖←Mk: *Rpl C Arm* — *txt*: ℵ^{b}BC-33-892 **λ**-22-1582 **φ**-*l*547^1 σ349-517-659-990-1207-1223-1606 **047** *pc l*32 *l*183 *l*184 *l*185 *l*333 *l*950 *l*1761 *Got* **24** ∼ εγε. μεγ.‖28 2: Γ *pc* Eu *Geo* | κυμ. + ην γαρ ο ανεμος εναντιος αυτοις‖Mk6 48p: 1604 *pc L*(g^{2}30 vg^2; ^{1} *et* ∼ ην—αυτοις ωστε)^2 *S*j **25** οι μαθ.] ● *om*‖p: ℵB-33^v-892 L' Hi Or *C* — + αυτου: CX ΣΦ-544-1604 **λ**-1582 σ7-517-945-990 W Θ *pl L*bg^{1}q30 vg^3 *S*,j *Geo*' — *txt*: L 700 λ22 **φ**-174-230-*l*547 σM-71-349 *R* 157 *pm l*76 *l*150 *l*185 *l*299 *l*950 *l*1231 *l*1579 *l*1599 *l*1627 *l*1663 *l*1761 Eu *L*h *Arm Geo*^{B} | σω. + ημας(+ οτι)‖14 30: *Rpl* (Δ) Chr Cr^I Eu *L*'(vg^2) Or *S*(s[c])ph(j) *C*(sb^3)'(^{2} + με) (*Geo*) *Aeth* *Δ*⟨me p⟩ — *txt*: 𝔋⟨L-33⟩C **λ**-1582 **φ**⟨124-983⟩-*l*547 **26** τω ανεμω‖**p**: ℵ* **λ**-22 **φ**-*l*547 *L*abg$^{1.2}$hlq vg^8 *C*s$^{1:4}$b^4 | *om* μεγ.‖Lk: *l*55
27 ∼ υπα. αυ.‖p: *Rpl* Chr *L*,Au Hil Or *S* — 𝔋⟨L⟩ λ1-1582 W Θ Eu *S*j **28** ελθοντι αυτω‖Lk27: *Rpl* Ath — -ντων αυτων‖Lk26: ℵ* *Arm*' — *txt*: ℵ^{b}BC-33-892 Φ **λ**-1582 **φ**⟨983⟩ σ1010 Θ *pc Arm*^{pc} | Γεργεσηνων‖Lk: *Rpl* Ath PsAth Ep Or *S*h^{m}j *C*b *Geo*^{2} — Γερασηνων‖Mk: Or *L*, Hil *S*h^m *C*s — *txt*: ℵ*(Γαζ-)BCΣ φ174 σM-1010-1606 Δ(Γαραδ-) Θ *pc* Ep Or *S*' *Geo*^{1} **29** *om* ιδ.‖MkLk: σ1424 Ep *L*vl⟨ff^{1}q⟩ vg^1 *S*s[c]pj *C*b^3 | ανεκρα.‖Lk Mk1 23p: σ1606 | εκρ. + φωνη μεγαλη‖**p**: φ124 *S*s[c] | λεγ. + εα‖Lk4 34: PsAth | σοι + Ιησου‖p: *Rpl* Ep *L*vl'30 vg^8 *C*p^1 *S*'j *C*sb^9 — *txt*: 𝔋C **λ**-1582 φ174-983-1689 σ517-1391 *pc* PsAth Or *L*k[e] ff^1 vg' *C*p^1 Oro *S*s[c] *C*b' | θε. + του ζωντος‖16 16: σ1424 | *om* ωδε‖Mk1 24p: 1604 1093 Ad PsAth Ep *L*bg^{1}hz vg^1 Oro | προ—ημας] ημ. απολεσαι προ κ.‖←: ℵ* 713 *L*vg^2 *C*b$^{⟨6⟩}$ — απολ. ημ. και προ κ. βασ.‖←: W **30** βοσκομενων‖Lk: X W *pc L*vl⟨ff^{1}lz⟩ vg^3 *C*b **31** απ. ημ.] επιτρεψον ημιν απελθειν‖Mk Mt: *Rpl L*fhq *S*' — *txt* (*om* ημ.): 𝔋⟨L⟩ λ1-22(+ απελθ.)-(118-209)-1582 Θ Ep *L*' Can *S*s[c]j *C Aeth*
32 ειπ.—υπα.] επετρεψεν αυτοις (+ και ειπ. υπα.)‖p: σ(517)-1424-(1675) | τ. χοι.] την αγελην των χοιρων‖31: *Rpl L*fh *S*hj *Arm* — *txt*: 𝔋⟨L⟩C **λ**-22-1582-σ1010 *al L*' *S*' *C* | *om* ιδ.‖p: σ1424 *S*,j | *om* πασα‖p: 471 *pc* | αγε. + των χοιρων‖31: *Rpl C*b — *txt* (∼ η αγε. πασα): 𝔋⟨L⟩(C) ΝΣΦ-1604 **λ**-1582 **φ**⟨543⟩-174-*l*547 σM-267-1010-1424 W Δ Θ *al L S*,j *C*s | θαλ.] λιμνην‖Lk: σ1424

ἐν τοῖς ὕδασιν. [33] οἱ δὲ βόσκοντες ἔφυγον, καὶ ἀπελθόντες εἰς τὴν πόλιν ἀπήγγειλαν πάντα καὶ τὰ τῶν δαιμονιζομένων. [34] καὶ ἰδοὺ πᾶσα ἡ πόλις ἐξῆλθεν εἰς συνάντησιν τῷ Ἰησοῦ, καὶ ἰδόντες αὐτὸν παρεκάλεσαν ὅπως μεταβῇ ἀπὸ τῶν ὁρίων αὐτῶν. | 119. |

(52) 64. Heilung des Gichtbrüchigen. *The Healing of a Man Sick of the Palsy.*

Matth 9 1-8	Mark 2 1-12	Luk 5 17-26
[1] Καὶ ἐμβὰς εἰς πλοῖον διεπέρασεν, καὶ ἦλθεν εἰς τὴν ἰδίαν πόλιν.	[1] Καὶ [119.] εἰσελθὼν πάλιν εἰς Καφαρναουμ δι' ἡμερῶν ἠκούσθη ὅτι εἰς οἶκόν ἐστιν. [2] καὶ συνήχθησαν πολλοί, ὥστε μηκέτι χωρεῖν μηδὲ τὰ πρὸς τὴν θύραν, καὶ ἐλάλει αὐτοῖς τὸν λόγον.	[17] Καὶ ἐγένετο ἐν μιᾷ τῶν ἡμερῶν καὶ αὐτὸς ἦν διδάσκων, καὶ ἦσαν καθήμενοι Φαρισαῖοι καὶ νομοδιδάσκαλοι οἳ ἦσαν ἐληλυθότες ἐκ πάσης κώμης τῆς Γαλιλαίας καὶ Ἰουδαίας καὶ Ιερουσαλημ· καὶ δύναμις κυρίου ἦν εἰς τὸ ἰᾶσθαι αὐτόν.
[2] καὶ ἰδοὺ προσέφερον αὐτῷ παραλυτικὸν ἐπὶ κλίνης βεβλημένον.	[3] καὶ ἔρχονται πρὸς αὐτὸν παραλυτικὸν φέροντες αἰρόμενον ὑπὸ τεσσάρων.	[18] καὶ ἰδοὺ ἄνδρες φέροντες ἐπὶ κλίνης ἄνθρωπον ὃς ἦν παραλελυμένος, καὶ ἐζήτουν αὐτὸν εἰσενεγκεῖν καὶ θεῖναι ἐνώπιον αὐτοῦ.
	[4] καὶ μὴ δυνάμενοι προσεγγίσαι αὐτῷ διὰ τὸν ὄχλον, ἀπεστέγασαν τὴν στέγην ὅπου ἦν, καὶ ἐξορύξαντες χαλῶσιν τὸν κράβαττον ὅπου ὁ παραλυτικὸς κατέκειτο.	[19] καὶ μὴ εὑρόντες ποίας εἰσενέγκωσιν αὐτὸν διὰ τὸν ὄχλον, ἀναβάντες ἐπὶ τὸ δῶμα διὰ τῶν κεράμων καθῆκαν αὐτὸν σὺν τῷ κλινιδίῳ εἰς τὸ μέσον ἔμπροσθεν τοῦ Ἰησοῦ.
καὶ ἰδὼν ὁ Ἰησοῦς τὴν πίστιν αὐτῶν εἶπεν τῷ παραλυτικῷ· θάρσει, τέκνον,	[5] ἰδὼν δὲ ὁ Ἰησοῦς τὴν πίστιν αὐτῶν λέγει τῷ παραλυτικῷ· τέκνον,	[20] καὶ ἰδὼν τὴν πίστιν αὐτῶν εἶπεν· ἄνθρωπε,

Mt 8,33 βοσ. + ιδοντες το γεγενημενον‖Lk: 1396 | ανηγγ.‖Mk: φ⟨346⟩ **34** *om* ιδ.‖p: *Ss*[c]p | ● υπαντησιν‖8 28p 25 1.6: ℵB-33 λ-1582 Θ 399 (απαντ.: 489) | παρεκ. + αυτον‖p: 472 1574 *L*bg$^{1.2}$h vg^{3} {*S*,j *C*} *Geo*^{1} **9,1** εις^{1} + το‖Mk 5 18: *Rpl* Chr^{1} *C*b *Δ*a i^{T} n^{S} — *txt*: ℌC^{3}X 1604 λ-1582 φ-*l*547 σ7-945-1207-1391-1606-1675 V^{m} Θ **047** *al* Chr^{1} Or *Cs* *Δ*ad i^{V} n'⟨^{L}⟩ **2** *om* ιδου‖Mk: 238 *L*aq *Ss*[c]pj

Mk 2,1 εις οι.] ● εν οικω: ℌ⟨Δ-579⟩ ΘΣ-1071 D W 1342 **2** ● και^{1} + ευθεως: *Rpl* *L*e[k] acfff^{2}qr^{1} vg^{1} *S*h — *txt*: 𝔓^{88v} ℌ⟨Δ⟩ Θ-700 W 1342 *L*' Au *S*[sc]pj *C* **3** και^{1} + ιδου ανδρες‖Lk Mt: 28-565 W *Cs*$^{3:4}$ | ∼ φε. παρ.‖p: C*-579 ΘΣ-565-700 λ φ⟨983⟩-*l*547 D G W(φε.] βασταζοντες εν κραβαττω) 1342 *pc* *L*vl'[k]g^{2}r^{1}(= W) vg^{2} *S*hj — ● ∼ φε. πρ. αυ. παρ.‖Mt: 𝔓^{88} ℌ'⟨Δ⟩ 1071 1396 *L*vg' Au *S*[sc]p *C* — *txt*: *Rpl* *S*j^{k}(+ αυτω) **4** ● προσενεγκαι‖Lk Mt: 𝔓^{88} ℵBL-33(-κειν)-892 Θ *l*48 *L*flr^{2}z vg$^{\langle 1\rangle}$ Au *S*[sc]p^{1}hj *Cs*$^{4:5}$b *Aeth* | αυτω] αυτον‖Lk: 892 φ13 σ827 488 *L*f vg^{1} *C*b' — αυτον αυτω‖Lk: 2145 *L*l(∼: r^{2}z) vg' Au *S*[sc]hj^{k}(αυτον τω κυριω Ιησου: j^{abc}) *Cs*$^{2:3}$b^{5} — *om*: D K **047** *L*'r^{1} vg^{1} | οπου^{2}] εφ ο‖Lk 25: Γ *pc* *l*184 {*L*'} — εφ ου‖←: 33 Θ-565 φ⟨124-983⟩ 1342 {} — εφ ω‖← *Rpl* {} — εις ον: W — *txt*: ℵBL-892 D' **047** *L*a **5** ιδ. δε] ● και ιδ.‖p: 𝔓^{88} ℌ⟨Δ-579⟩C Θ-28-565-700 φ-*l*547 1342 *L*e[k] vg^{1} *S*[sc]j *Cs*$^{1:4}$b *Geo*^{2ch} *Aeth* | *om* ο I.‖Lk: 892 *L*vg^{1} | παρ. + θαρσει‖Mt: C

Lk 5,17 και^{2}—διδ.] αυτου διδασκοντος‖20 1: D *L*e c *Ss*[c]p | διδ. + εν μια των συναγωγων‖13 10: φ | εληλ.] συνελ.‖Mk: 33 λ⟨118⟩-22-1582-2193 φ A* D *l*49 Cr *L*a *Arm* *Got* | κωμ.] χωρας‖Mk 1 5: W | *om* και δυν.—αυτον‖Mk: 1241 | αυτον] αυτους‖Mt 13 15 *cf.* Lk 4 40 Mt 4 24 19 2 *etc.*: *Rpl* *L* *S*' *C*b *Δ*a n^{HgLmS}p — παντας‖6 19 8 16 Mt 12 15: K Cr *S*j *Δ*md^{V} — *txt*: ℌ⟨33-892-1241⟩Ξ 544 Cr *Ss*[c] *Cs* *Aeth* *Δ*md' n^{Hr} **18** ∼ ανθ. επι κλ.‖Mt: λ22 *Ss*[c]p^{1} **19** αυτ.^{1}] αυτω‖Mk: σM U^{c} 2533 | δια τ. κερ.] αποστεγασαντες τους κεραμους οπου ην‖Mk: D *L*b vg^{1} | αυτ. συν τ. κλ.] τον κραβαττον συν τω παραλυτικω‖Mk: D | του I.] παντων‖Mk 2 12: B **20** και ιδ.] ιδ. δε‖Mk: 1071 D *L*e r^{1} *Sp* *Cs*$^{5:6}$b^{1} | ιδ. / δε + ο Ιησους‖p: C 1071 λ131 (αυτ. + ο I.) φ D(*om* ο) S 161 *l*30 *l*60 *L*ff^{2}r^{1} *Sp* *Arm*^{pc} | ειπ.] λεγει‖Mk: D | ειπ. + τω παραλυτικω‖p: C φ124-174 D *pc* Cr *L*f *S*' *C*b *Aeth* — + αυτω‖p: *Rpl* *S*hj *Arm* — *txt*: ℌ⟨892-1241⟩Ξ Θ-700 λ⟨118⟩-1582-2193 φ788 σ990 130 *L*' *Cs* | ανθ.] τω ανθρωπω‖p: λ⟨118⟩-1582-2193 *L*e(εκεινω τ. αν.) abclqr^{1} vg^{1} *S*j^{c} — τεκνον‖Mt Mk: φ124-174 — *om*: 157 *Aeth*

ἀφίενταί σου αἱ ἁμαρτίαι. ^{3} καὶ ἰδού τινες τῶν γραμματέων εἶπαν ἐν ἑαυτοῖς· οὗτος βλασφημεῖ.

^{4} καὶ εἰδὼς ὁ Ἰησοῦς τὰς ἐνθυμήσεις αὐτῶν εἶπεν· ἱνατί ἐνθυμεῖσθε πονηρὰ ἐν ταῖς καρδίαις ὑμῶν; ^{5} τί γάρ ἐστιν εὐκοπώτερον, εἰπεῖν· ἀφίενταί σου αἱ ἁμαρτίαι, ἢ εἰπεῖν· ἔγειρε καὶ περιπάτει; ^{6} ἵνα δὲ εἰδῆτε

ἀφίενταί σου αἱ ἁμαρτίαι. ^{6} ἦσαν δέ τινες τῶν γραμματέων ἐκεῖ καθήμενοι καὶ διαλογιζόμενοι ἐν ταῖς καρδίαις αὐτῶν· ^{7} τί οὗτος οὕτως λαλεῖ; βλασφημεῖ· τίς δύναται ἀφιέναι ἁμαρτίας εἰ μὴ εἷς ὁ θεός; ^{8} καὶ εὐθὺς ἐπιγνοὺς ὁ Ἰησοῦς τῷ πνεύματι αὐτοῦ ὅτι οὕτως διαλογίζονται ἐν ἑαυτοῖς, λέγει αὐτοῖς· τί ταῦτα διαλογίζεσθε ἐν ταῖς καρδίαις ὑμῶν; ^{9} τί ἐστιν εὐκοπώτερον, εἰπεῖν τῷ παραλυτικῷ· ἀφίενταί σου αἱ ἁμαρτίαι, ἢ εἰπεῖν· ἔγειρε καὶ ἆρόν σου τὸν κράβαττον καὶ περιπάτει; ^{10} ἵνα δὲ εἰδῆτε

ἀφέωνταί σοι αἱ ἁμαρτίαι σου. ^{21} καὶ ἤρξαντο διαλογίζεσθαι οἱ γραμματεῖς καὶ οἱ Φαρισαῖοι λέγοντες· τίς ἐστιν οὗτος ὃς λαλεῖ βλασφημίας; τίς δύναται ἁμαρτίας ἀφεῖναι εἰ μὴ μόνος ὁ θεός; ^{22} ἐπιγνοὺς δὲ ὁ Ἰησοῦς τοὺς διαλογισμοὺς αὐτῶν, ἀποκριθεὶς εἶπεν πρὸς αὐτούς· τί διαλογίζεσθε ἐν ταῖς καρδίαις ὑμῶν; ^{23} τί ἐστιν εὐκοπώτερον, εἰπεῖν· ἀφέωνταί σοι αἱ ἁμαρτίαι σου, ἢ εἰπεῖν· ἔγειρε καὶ περιπάτει; ^{24} ἵνα δὲ εἰδῆτε

Mt 9,2 ● αφεωνται ‖ Lk20.23 747f.: *Rpl* Chr Ddy Or^{1} *L*abcg^{1}hq — *txt*: ℵB {D(-ιοντε)} 372 Ir Or^{1} *L*' (αφεθησ.: 30 vg^{1}) Au Cp Hil *Aeth* | σου αι αμ.] σοι αι αμ. ‖ Lk: D' Δ^{c} *pc* Chr^{1} Or *Lk*[e] Au^{1} — σοι αι αμ. σου ‖ Lk: *Rpl* Ddy *L*' Au^{1} *S*,j *C* — σου αι αμ. σου: N σM-954 Ω *pc* — *txt*: 𝔥⟨L⟩ C 1604 **λ**-1582 W Δ* *l*50 Chr^{4} PsOr *L*Cp **4** κ. ειδ.] ● κ. ιδων ‖ 2p: *Rpl* *L*' *S*s[c]j^{b}(*om* και) *C*b *Aeth* *Δ*i^{V} l^{AD} md n^{L} — ιδ. δε ‖ Lk: NΣ *pc* *L*ah *S*j^{ac} — ειδ. δε ‖ 12₂₅ Lk: σ71-1194 Θ *S*p *C*s *Geo*^{2}(*om* δε) — *txt*: B 700 **λ**-1582 ϕ*l*547 σM-945-954-1207-1424-1606 Π *pc* Chr *l*76 *l*184 *l*313 *l*1627 *l*1761 *S*h *Arm* *Geo*^{1} *Aeth* *Got* | τ. ενθ.] τους διαλογισμους ‖ p: **λ**-22-1582 *pc* | ειπ. + αυτοις ‖ p 12₂₅: NΣ **ϕ**⟨983⟩ D Θ *pc* *l*183 *L*ch vg^{1} *S*s[c]pj *C*sb^{3} | ● ινατι + υμεις (∼ ενθ. υμ.): *Rpl* (σ1010 *pc*) *S*hj — *txt*: 𝔥⟨L-33⟩C 1604 **λ**-22-1582 D *pc* Chr **5** *om* γαρ ‖ Mk Lk: **λ**⟨1⟩ σM-945-1010-1606 K U Π *pc* *L*⟨fg^{1}h vg^{2}⟩ Can Qu *S*s[c] *Arm* *Aeth* | ειπ.^{1} + τω παραλυτικω ‖ 6 Mk: ϕ124 σ1606 1170 | ● αφεωνται ‖ Lk20.23 747f.: *Rpl* *L*abcg$^{1.2}$h — αφιωνται: {} *Geo*(*vel* -εθησονται) — *txt* (-ιον-): ℵ{(*)}^{c}B {(D)} 372 *L*' Can *Aeth* | σου αι αμ.] σοι αι αμ. ‖ Lk: *Rpl* *L*bdz vg$^{⟨9⟩}$ Can — σοι αι αμ. σου ‖ Lk: σ954-1675 *pc* *l*47 *L*' *S*,j — *txt*: 𝔥⟨33⟩CX Φ-700 ϕ*l*547 σM-71-692 D E F G K V W Θ *al* *Lk*[e]

Mk 2,5 αφεωνται ‖ Lk5₂₀.₂₃ 747f.: D' *Rpl* Cl *L*bfq — *txt*(-ιον-): B(Δ)-33 (Θ)-28-565 1342 *pc* *L*' *Got* | σου αι αμ.] σοι αι αμ. ‖ Lk: C* λ22 **090** *Le*[k] bff^{2}lr^{1}z vg' — σοι αι αμ. σου: Lk ‖ *Rpl* *L*vl' vg^{6} *S*[sc],j *C* — σου αι αμ. σου: 1071 **ϕ**'⟨983⟩-*l*547 σM-27 Ω — *txt*: 𝔓^{88} 𝔥' Θ-565 **λ** ϕ69 σ517 D' G W 1342 *pc* **6** αυτ. + λεγοντες(και λεγ.) ‖ Lk: 565 D W 575 *l*251 *L*(e[k] cff^{2})abr^{1} vg^{1} *C*b^{1}(^{4} ελεγον) **7** βλασφημιας ‖ Lk: *Rpl* *Le*[k]c *S*[sc],j *C*b' — *txt*: 𝔓^{88} ℵBL D 372 *L*'⟨bq⟩ *C*sb^{5} | αφειναι ‖ Lk: W **8** *om* ευθ. ‖ p: 28-565 σ1391 D W 64 *L*abcff^{2}g^{2}qr^{1} vg^{2} *S*[sc]p | λεγ.] ειπεν ‖ Mt Lk: *Rpl* *L*vl'r^{1} vg^{1} — *txt*: 𝔓^{88}? 𝔥⟨Δ-579⟩ W **0130** 1342 *Le*[k] fr^{2} vg' | *om* αυτ. ‖ Mt: B Θ λ872 102 *L*ff^{2} | *om* ταυτα ‖ Lk: L W Θ *pc* *Le*[k] bcff^{2}q *S*[sc]j^{bk} **9** τι + γαρ ‖ Mt: σ1424 W *C*s | *om* τω παρ. ‖ p: 33 W **047** *Le*[k]a *S*[sc]j^{c} *C*s$^{2:4}$ | αφεωνται ‖ Lk5₂₀.₂₃ 747f.: *Rpl* *L*b — *txt*: ℵB 28-565 1342 *L*'(∼ εγει. *etc.* ... αφιε. *etc.*: adff^{2}r^{1}) | σου αι αμ.] σοι αι αμ. ‖ Lk: CΔ Φ-1071 λ22-131 ϕ983-1689 σ945-1223-1606 A D S Γ **090** **0130** *al* *Le*[k] (dr^{1})lz vg' — σοι αι αμ. σου ‖ Lk: σ1194 *L*vl'(aff^{2}) vg^{7} *S*[sc],j *C* — σου αι αμ. σου: 544 ϕ13-*l*547 **047** *pc* — *txt*: 𝔓^{88} *Rpl* *L*b | *om* εγει.: **047** *L*r^{2} | *om* και^{1} ‖ 11 Jo8: CL-33-579 Σ-565-700 **λ** σ349-517-827-1424 D' **047** 157 1342 Ddy *L*flqr^{2}30 *S*[sc]pj *C*b$^{⟨4⟩}$ | *om* και^{1}— κρα. ‖ **p**: 544 ϕ828-983-1689 σ692 W *Le*[k] bc | ● ∼ τ. κρα. σου ‖ 11 Jo8 5 11 Lk24: 𝔓^{88} 𝔥⟨Δ-33⟩C ΘΣ-565-700-1071 **λ** **ϕ**⟨828-983⟩-*l*547 σM-7-179-267-659-827-1606 A D K Π 1342 *al* Ddy | περιπ.] ● υπαγε (+ εις τον οικον σου) ‖ 11p: 𝔓^{88} ℵLΔ-(33)-892 (D) **0130** (1588) *L*(aff^{2}g^{2}r^{1} vg^{3})^{1} *C*b (*Arm*) *Δ*i^{V}(va a la toa via) — *txt*: *Rpl* *L*' *S*[sc],j *C*s

Lk 5,20 σου αι αμ. σου] σου αι αμ. ‖ p: ℵW-579 D' F^{W} *pc* Cr *L*l — σοι αι αμ.: 1241 *l*184 — σου αι αμ. σου: σ990-1606-1675 59 *l*32 *l*34 *l*47 *l*1564 *l*1627 — *txt*: *Rpl* *L*' *S*,j *C* **21** γρα. + αυτων ‖ 30 Mt7₂₉: Γ *pc* | Φ. + εν ταις καρδιαις αυτων ‖ Mk: D *L*bc(∼ λεγ. εν τ. κ. αυ.)ff^{2}lq vg^{1} | τις—ος] τι ουτος ‖ Mk: D Ep$^{1:2}$ | ∼ αφ. αμ. ‖ 24p Mk: *Rpl* *L*' *S*,j — *txt*: BLΞ-579 565 **λ**⟨131⟩-22-1582 D Cr *Le* c | ● αφιεναι ‖ 24p Mk: *Rpl* — *txt*: BΞ D Cr | μον.] εις ‖ Mk: C^{3}X 28 D'(*om* ο) Ψ *pc* Cr *L*ar^{1} *S*h^{m} *C*b(εις μον.) **22** *om* αποκ. ‖ p: C D *pc* *l*32 *L*vl⟨e fq⟩r^{1}30 vg^{1} *C*s$^{3:6}$ *Aeth* | ειπ.] λεγει ‖ Mk: D | πρ. αυ.] αυτοις ‖ Mk: σ1424 D *pc* *l*44 *l*48 | διαλογιζ. + πονηρα ‖ Mt: D(∼ εν—υμ. πο.) *Le* clr^{1} *S*j *Aeth* **23** ειπ. + τω παραλυτικω ‖ Mk: 243 998 | σοι αι αμ. σου] σου αι αμ. ‖ p: ℵW 1604(∼ αι αμ. σ.) D Θ *pc* *l*48 — σοι αι αμ.: N Ψ *Le* dfz vg' — σου αι αμ. σου: CX-33-1241 Λ ϕ346 σ990 F^{W} *pc* — *txt*: *Rpl* *L*vl'r^{1}30 vg^{5} *S*,j *C*

Matth 9:

ὅτι ἐξουσίαν ἔχει ὁ υἱὸς τοῦ ἀνθρώπου ἐπὶ τῆς γῆς ἀφιέναι ἁμαρτίας, τότε λέγει τῷ παραλυτικῷ· ἐγερθεὶς ἆρόν σου τὴν κλίνην καὶ ὕπαγε εἰς τὸν οἶκόν σου. [7] καὶ ἐγερθεὶς ἀπῆλθεν εἰς τὸν οἶκον αὐτοῦ. [8] ἰδόντες δὲ οἱ ὄχλοι ἐφοβήθησαν καὶ ἐδόξασαν τὸν θεὸν τὸν δόντα ἐξουσίαν τοιαύτην τοῖς ἀνθρώποις.

Mark 2:

ὅτι ἐξουσίαν ἔχει ὁ υἱὸς τοῦ ἀνθρώπου ἀφιέναι ἐπὶ τῆς γῆς ἁμαρτίας, λέγει τῷ παραλυτικῷ· [11] σοὶ λέγω, ἔγειρε ἆρον τὸν κράβαττόν σου καὶ ὕπαγε εἰς τὸν οἶκόν σου. [12] καὶ ἠγέρθη καὶ εὐθὺς ἄρας τὸν κράβαττον ἐξῆλθεν ἐναντίον πάντων, ὥστε ἐξίστασθαι πάντας καὶ δοξάζειν τὸν θεὸν λέγοντας ὅτι οὕτως οὐδέποτε εἴδομεν.

Luk 5:

ὅτι ὁ υἱὸς τοῦ ἀνθρώπου ἐξουσίαν ἔχει ἐπὶ τῆς γῆς ἀφιέναι ἁμαρτίας, εἶπεν τῷ παραλελυμένῳ· σοὶ λέγω, ἔγειρε καὶ ἄρας τὸ κλινίδιόν σου πορεύου εἰς τὸν οἶκόν σου. [25] καὶ παραχρῆμα ἀναστὰς ἐνώπιον αὐτῶν, ἄρας ἐφ' ὃ κατέκειτο, ἀπῆλθεν εἰς τὸν οἶκον αὐτοῦ δοξάζων τὸν θεόν. [26] καὶ ἔκστασις ἔλαβεν ἅπαντας, καὶ ἐδόξαζον τὸν θεόν, καὶ ἐπλήσθησαν φόβου λέγοντες ὅτι εἴδομεν παράδοξα σήμερον.

Jo 5 8 f.:

λέγει αὐτῷ ὁ Ἰησοῦς· ἔγειρε ἆρον τὸν κράβαττόν σου καὶ περιπάτει. [9] καὶ εὐθέως ἐγένετο ὑγιὴς ὁ ἄνθρωπος, καὶ ἦρεν τὸν κράβαττον αὐτοῦ καὶ περιεπάτει: ...

(53)

65. Berufung des Levi und Zöllnermahl. *The Call of Levi.*

Matth 9 9–13

Mark 2 13–17

[13] Καὶ ἐξῆλθεν πάλιν παρὰ τὴν θάλασσαν· καὶ πᾶς ὁ ὄχλος ἤρχετο πρὸς αὐτόν, καὶ ἐδίδασκεν αὐτούς.

Luk 5 27–32

[27] Καὶ μετὰ ταῦτα ἐξῆλθεν,

Mt 9,6 ∼ ο υι. τ. αν. εξ. εχ.‖Lk: 33 D *L C* | ∼ αφ. επι τ. γης‖Mk: W | *om* τοτε‖MkLk: σM-517 *pc Sp* | εγερ.] ● εγειρε‖5p: B 372 *L'* Can *C*b *Arm* — εγει. και‖5LkMkJo: D *Lk*[e] aff^{1}g$^{1.2}$h30 vg^6 Hil *Cs Aeth* — *txt*: *Rpl L*q | υπα.] πορευου‖Lk: ℵ* **8** οχ. εφο.] ανθρωποι εθαυμασαν‖827: ϕ174 σ1223 — οχ. εθαυ.‖33 827: *Rpl* (*om* εθαυ. και: X *Lf*) *S*h *Arm Δ*ad i^T — *txt*: ℌ⟨L⟩ λ-22-1582 σ⟨349⟩ D W *pc L'* Au Hil *S'*j *C* | εδοξαζον‖Lk: 565 *Ss*[c] *C*b^6 *Geo*

Mk 2,10 ● ∼ επι τ. γ. αφ. αμ.‖p: 𝔓88 ℌ'C Σ-544-700-1071 λ118-209 ϕ230-*l*547 σM-7-267-827-1207-1402 D H **090 0130** 1342 *al l*60 *l*69 *l*70 *l*76 *l*150 *l*211 *l*299 *l*303 *l*333 *l*1127 *l*1663 *l*1761 *L'*(*om* επι τ. γ.: bq) *S*[sc]pj *Cs*^{2}b — ● ∼ αφ. αμ. επι τ. γ.‖p: B Θ Φ σ1194 157 *pc l*185 *L*Mcn *Cs*^{1} *Aeth* — *txt*: *Rpl* (*om* επι τ. γ.: W *pc*; αμαρτιαν: ϕ13) Bas *S*h | λεγ.] τοτε λεγ.‖Mt: Σ **11** *om* σοι λεγω‖Mt: W *pc l*184 *Le*[k] bc | εγερθεις‖Mt: σ827 *pc* | εγ. + και‖9Lk: *Rpl L*cd vg^7 *S*h *Cs*$^{1:4}$ — *txt*: 𝔓88 ℌ⟨Δ⟩C Θ-28-565-1071 ϕ13-788 σ349-517 D Γ *pc L'*(*om* εγ.: r^2) *S*[sc]pj *C*b | ∼ σου τ. κρα.‖9: 245 1093 *l*184 | υπα.—σου^2] περιπατει‖9p: 1588 *l*184 — + και περιπ.‖←: 1515 **12** *om* ευθ.‖Mt: Θ W(ο δε εγερθεις και) 1342 *Le*[k] bcq | απηλθεν‖p: W(∼ ε. παν. απη.) *L* | εναν.] ● εμπροσθεν‖Mt26 70 G2 14: 𝔓88 ℌ'⟨Δ⟩ 700 σ1606(εμπ. εναν.) W — ενωπιον‖Lk: 33 ΘΦ-28-1071 σ348-517 **090** *pc* | δοξ.] εδοξαζον‖Lk Mt: 495

Lk 5,24 ∼ εξ. εχ. ο υ. τ. αν.‖MtMk: *Rpl* Cr Mcn^{Ep} *Le* ac *S*,j *Cs*^{1}b — *txt*: BLWΞ 544 σ1223 K Π *al* Cr *L' Cs*^{5} | αφειναι‖21: L D* | ειπ.] λεγει‖p: σ1424 D *pc l*183 | παραλυτικω‖p: ℌ⟨B-892⟩CXΞ N-700-1071 ϕ-230-*l*547 σ⟨954⟩M-945-990 D F^W Θ Ψ 157 *pc l*47 *l*60 *l*184 *l*196 *l*259 *l*1564 Cr | *om* σοι λεγω‖Mt: 1279 *l*1663 *Le* vg^1 *Arm*^{V} *Geo*^{1} | αρ. ... πορ.] αρον ... και πορ.‖p: ℵ σ1424 D 157 *pc L'* — *om* αρ.—σου^1‖23: *Le* | το κλ.] τον κραβαττον‖Mk: σ D *Lcr*^{1} — την κλινην‖Mt: 579 | πορ.] υπαγε‖p: 579 *pc l*44 **25** αυτων] παντων‖Mk: W* ϕ'-174 157 *pc l*47 *l*1963 *La Arm* — αυτ. παντ.‖Mk: ϕ124 *pc Cs*$^{1:6}$ | εφ ο κατε.] την κλινην‖Mt6: D *Le Sp Cs* — *prm* το κλινιδιον‖←Mk: 243 *L*abcr^1 vg^1 *S*hj *Aeth* **26** απ.] παντας‖Mk: ϕ230 *pc l*12 *l*47 *l*49 | ∼ και^3—φοβ. και^2—τ. θ.‖Mt: A | επλ. + απαντες‖428: 716 *l*1963 *L*d vg^1 **27** μετα τ. εξ.] ελθων και παλιν παρα την θαλασσαν τον επακολουθουντα οχλον εδιδασκεν‖Mk: D

Jo 5,8 εγ. + και‖Mk9: A D K Π *pc Le* abff^{2}jr^1 vg^7 *Csa*^{s} *Aeth* | ∼ σου τ. κρα.‖←Mt: 1241 | περιπ.] υπαγε(*prm* περιπ.) εις τον οικον σου‖p: 33 1071 (*pc*) Ep(υπ.] πορευου) (*Sc*) *Arm*(*om* εις—σου) **9** ● *om* και ευθ.‖Mt: ℵ — *om* ευθ.‖←: W^s D *L*lz *Arm* | και^2 + ηγερθη και‖Mk: ℵ *Le* abj^v {*S*sph$^+$} *Ca*^{s} *Geo*^{1}(*om* και) — + εγερθεις‖Mt: λ ϕ-*l*547 D *L*ff^2 {}

Matth	Mark	Luk	
9 Καὶ παράγων ὁ Ἰησοῦς ἐκεῖθεν εἶδεν ἄνθρωπον καθήμενον ἐπὶ τὸ τελώνιον, Μαθθαῖον λεγόμενον, καὶ λέγει αὐτῷ· ἀκολούθει μοι. καὶ ἀναστὰς ἠκολούθει αὐτῷ.	14 καὶ παράγων εἶδεν Λευὶν τὸν τοῦ Ἁλφαίου καθήμενον ἐπὶ τὸ τελώνιον, καὶ λέγει αὐτῷ· ἀκολούθει μοι. καὶ ἀναστὰς ἠκολούθει αὐτῷ.	καὶ ἐθεάσατο τελώνην ὀνόματι Λευὶν καθήμενον ἐπὶ τὸ τελώνιον, καὶ εἶπεν αὐτῷ· ἀκολούθει μοι. 28 καὶ καταλιπὼν πάντα ἀναστὰς ἠκολούθει αὐτῷ.	
10 καὶ ἐγένετο αὐτοῦ ἀνακειμένου ἐν τῇ οἰκίᾳ, καὶ ἰδοὺ πολλοὶ τελῶναι καὶ ἁμαρτωλοὶ ἐλθόντες συνανέκειντο τῷ Ἰησοῦ καὶ τοῖς μαθηταῖς αὐτοῦ.	15 καὶ γίνεται κατακεῖσθαι αὐτὸν ἐν τῇ οἰκίᾳ αὐτοῦ, καὶ πολλοὶ τελῶναι καὶ ἁμαρτωλοὶ συνανέκειντο τῷ Ἰησοῦ καὶ τοῖς μαθηταῖς αὐτοῦ· ἦσαν γὰρ πολλοί, καὶ ἠκολούθουν αὐτῷ.	29 καὶ ἐποίησεν δοχὴν μεγάλην Λευὶς αὐτῷ ἐν τῇ οἰκίᾳ αὐτοῦ· καὶ ἦν ὄχλος πολὺς τελωνῶν καὶ ἄλλων οἳ ἦσαν μετ' αὐτῶν κατακείμενοι.	*15 1f. (186.): Ἦσαν δὲ αὐτῷ ἐγγίζοντες πάντες οἱ τελῶναι καὶ οἱ ἁμαρτωλοὶ ἀκούειν αὐτοῦ.*
11 καὶ ἰδόντες οἱ Φαρισαῖοι ἔλεγον τοῖς μαθηταῖς αὐτοῦ· διὰ τί	16 καὶ οἱ γραμματεῖς τῶν Φαρισαίων ἰδόντες ὅτι ἤσθιεν μετὰ τῶν ἁμαρτωλῶν καὶ τελωνῶν, ἔλεγον τοῖς μαθηταῖς αὐτοῦ· ὅ τι	30 καὶ ἐγόγγυζον οἱ Φαρισαῖοι καὶ οἱ γραμματεῖς αὐτῶν πρὸς τοὺς μαθητὰς αὐτοῦ λέγοντες· διὰ τί	*2 καὶ διεγόγγυζον οἵ τε Φαρισαῖοι καὶ οἱ γραμματεῖς λέγοντες· ὅ τι*

Mt 9,9 *om* εκ.‖p: ℵ*L ϕ*l*547 σ71-692 *Lvg*^{1} *C*b^{1} | λεγομ.] ονοματι‖Lk: S Eu *L*⟨k[e]⟩ *S*s[c]p Eu *C* | ● ηκολουθησεν‖4 20p.22 Lk5 11 Jo1 37: *Rpl* Eu Or *L S*,j Eu *C* — *txt*: ℵ-892 1604 **λ**-1582 σ1010 D *pc Geo* **10** *om* κ. ιδου‖p: 700 *S*s[c]p | *om* ελθ.‖p: ℵ* 243 *l*50 Eu *La S*Eu *C*s$^{1:4}$b^{1} **11** ελε.] ● ειπον: *Rpl Lk*[e] *S*p^{6}h *C*s *Geo*^{2} — *txt*: ℌC 1604 **λ**-1582 σ517-1010-1675 W *L*' *S*j *C*b *Geo*^{1}

Mk 2,14 παρ. + ο Ιησους‖Mt: 1604 ϕ230-346 σ27-179-267-945-1194-1223-1391-1402 F G H Γ Ω *al* — + εκειθεν‖Mt: ϕ174 1093 *Geo* | Λ.] Ιακωβον‖3 18: Θ-565 **ϕ**⟨346-983⟩ D Pho *Le*[k] abcff^{2}r^{1} vg^{1} *Δ*a E^{a} | ● ηκολουθησεν‖1 18 Mt4 20.22p Jo1 37: 𝔓^{88} *Rpl L S*[sc],j *C* — *txt*: C*-892 **λ** W *pc* **15** γιν.] εγενετο‖Mt: *Rpl* (εγ. + εν τω‖Lk24 30: 579) — *txt*: 𝔓^{88} ℵBL-33 565-700 W 1342 | γιν. κατ. αυ.] ανακειμενων αυτων‖Mt: W *l*253^{1}(αυτου ανακειμενου) | *om* αυτου^{1}‖Mt: W *L*bc | και^{2} + ιδου‖Mt: 579 ϕ174 *l*253^{1} | αμ. + ελθοντες‖Mt: C* A | ηκολουθησαν‖Mt**8**1 **12**15 **14**13 **20**29 *etc.*: *Rpl L*vl'r^{1} *S*[sc],j *C*s — *txt*: 𝔓^{88} ℌ⟨33-579⟩ 565 **0130** 258 *L*lr^{2}z vg *C*b *Arm* **16** ● *om* οι: ℵL Δ-33 | κ. οι—Φ.] κ.(*om*) οι (+ δε) γρα. και οι Φαρισαιοι‖Lk Mt: *Rpl* (700) *L*'(e[k] acff^{2}r^{1}) *S*[sc] *C*(s)b' (*Arm*) *Geo*^{2ch} *Got*(*om* οι^{2}) — *txt*: (ℵ)B(LΔ-33) 28 ϕ124-*l*547 W **0130**^{v}(*om* και) *L*b *S*j(Φ.] Ιουδαιων) (*om* και: *C*b^{3} *Geo*^{1}) | *om* ιδ.—τελω.^{1}‖Lk Mt: W *Le*[k] | ιδ.] και ιδ.‖Mt: 𝔓^{88} ℵLΔ-33 *C*b — και ειδαν: D *L*br^{1} | οτι ησθ.] ● οτι εσθιει‖16b p: B-33-579(+ πινει) *L*bdr^{1}(∼ με. τ. τε. κ. αμ. εσθ.: ff^{2}) *C*sb' *Geo*$^{ch.2}$ — αυτον εσθιοντα: *Rpl L*afq — *txt*: 𝔓^{88} ℵL Θ(εσθιεν!) D *L*'⟨e[k]⟩ *C*b^{5} *Geo*^{1} | ● ∼ τελ.^{1} … αμ.^{1}‖16b Mt Lk30: *Rpl L*f(ff^{2})l *S*[sc],j *C*s^{3}b' — *txt*: 𝔓^{88} BL*^{v}-33-892 Θ-565 D *L*'⟨e[k]⟩ *C*s^{4}b^{5} *Aeth* | ο τι] δια(*om*) τι‖Mt Lk30: ℵ(Θ) D W *l*253 {*L*,Au} *S*(p)j — ● τι οτι: *Rpl S*[sc]h *Arm* — *txt*: BCL-33 σ1424 1342 *pc* {}

Lk 5,27 και^{2} + παραγων‖**p**: ϕ*l*547 D | εθ.] ειδεν‖**p**: 544 σ945-990-1223 A D Π^{c} *pc* | τελ. ον. Λ.] Λευει τον του Αλφαιου‖Mk: D | ειπ.] λεγει‖Mt Mk: ℵ ϕ⟨124⟩ D *pc l*50 *l*184 *l*1627 *Arm* **28** αναστ.] και αν.‖p: 2145 | ● ηκολουθησεν‖5 11p Jo1 37: *Rpl L*'*S*s^{v}[c]phj *C* — *txt*: BLWΞ-892 700 ϕ69 D *La Geo* **29** τω οικω‖19 5: ℵ 544 σ945-990-1223 K Π *al l*32 | αλλ.] αμαρτωλων‖p: WX N-1071 **σ**-1188 *pc C*b^{1} *Aeth* | ανακειμ.‖p: Λ ϕ230 D *pc* **30** διεγογγ.‖15 2 19 7: 998 *pc* | ∼ γρα. αυτ. … Φ.‖Mk: *Rpl* (∼ κ. οι Φ. αυτων: λ131) Bas *L*r^{1}(= 131) *S*[sc] *C*s^{1}b^{1} — *txt*: ℌCΞ 700 λ1-1582-2193 D R 157 *L*' *S*j *C*s^{4}b' *Arm* | *om* αυτων‖15 2: ℵX 1071 **λ**' ϕ788 D F 213 *l*1564 *l*1627 *Le*[k] fff^{2}l *S*[sc]pj *C*

Mt9 11f.p *cf.* Ev. apocr. (POxy 1224 fol. 2v° col. 2): οἱ δὲ γραμματεῖς κ[αὶ Φαρισαῖ]οι καὶ ἱερεῖς θεασάμ[ενοι αὐ]τὸν ἠγανάκτουν [ὅτι σὺν ἁμαρ]τωλοῖς ἀνὰ μέ[σον κεῖται. ὁ] δὲ Ἰη(σοῦς) ἀκούσας [εἶπεν· 'οὐ χρείαν ἔχ]ουσιν οἱ ὑ[γιαίνοντες ἰατροῦ] …

Matth	Mark	Luk	
μετὰ τῶν τελωνῶν καὶ ἁμαρτωλῶν ἐσθίει ὁ διδάσκαλος ὑμῶν;	μετὰ τῶν τελωνῶν καὶ ἁμαρτωλῶν ἐσθίει καὶ πίνει;	μετὰ τῶν τελωνῶν καὶ ἁμαρτωλῶν ἐσθίετε καὶ πίνετε;	*οὗτος ἁμαρτωλοὺς προσδέχεται καὶ συνεσθίει αὐτοῖς;*
[12] ὁ δὲ ἀκούσας εἶπεν· οὐ χρείαν ἔχουσιν οἱ ἰσχύοντες ἰατροῦ ἀλλ' οἱ κακῶς ἔχοντες.	[17] καὶ ἀκούσας ὁ Ἰησοῦς λέγει αὐτοῖς ὅτι οὐ χρείαν ἔχουσιν οἱ ἰσχύοντες ἰατροῦ ἀλλ' οἱ κακῶς ἔχοντες·	[31] καὶ ἀποκριθεὶς ὁ Ἰησοῦς εἶπεν πρὸς αὐτούς· οὐ χρείαν ἔχουσιν οἱ ὑγιαίνοντες ἰατροῦ ἀλλ' οἱ κακῶς ἔχοντες·	
[13] πορευθέντες δὲ μάθετε τί ἐστιν· **ἔλεος θέλω καὶ οὐ θυσίαν.** οὐ γὰρ ἦλθον καλέσαι δικαίους ἀλλὰ ἁμαρτωλούς.	*81.* οὐκ ἦλθον καλέσαι δικαίους ἀλλὰ ἁμαρτωλούς.	[32] οὐκ ἐλήλυθα καλέσαι δικαίους ἀλλὰ ἁμαρτωλοὺς εἰς μετάνοιαν.	Hos66

(54)

66. Die Fastenfrage. *The Question about Fasting.*

Matth 9 14–17	**Mark 2** 18–22	**Luk 5** 33–39
	[18] Καὶ ἦσαν οἱ μαθηταὶ Ἰωάννου καὶ οἱ Φαρισαῖοι νηστεύοντες. καὶ ἔρχονται	
[14] Τότε προσέρχονται αὐτῷ οἱ μαθηταὶ Ἰωάννου λέγοντες·	καὶ λέγουσιν	[33] Οἱ δὲ εἶπαν πρὸς
διὰ τί ἡμεῖς καὶ οἱ Φαρισαῖοι νηστεύομεν πολλά,	αὐτῷ· διὰ τί οἱ μαθηταὶ Ἰωάννου καὶ οἱ μαθηταὶ τῶν Φαρισαίων νηστεύουσιν,	αὐτόν· οἱ μαθηταὶ Ἰωάννου νηστεύουσιν πυκνὰ καὶ δεήσεις ποιοῦνται, ὁμοίως

Mt 9,11 ∼ αμ. ... τελ.‖Mk16a: D Cr $Cs^{1:5}$ | εσθ.] + και πινει‖Mk Lk30: 544 ϕ346-1689 σM *pm* Lg^2 vg^1 Geo^2 — εσθιετε και πινετε‖Lk30 Mk: *S*s[c] | *om* ο διδ. υμ.‖Mk: *L*(εσθ.] sedes (< edit?): k[e]) a *S*s[c] **12** δε + Ιησους‖p: *Rpl L S*'j(κυριος Ι.) *C*b — *txt*: ℵB-892 σ1010 D **047** *pc* *S*s[c] *C*s | ειπ. + αυτοις‖p: *Rpl L*afhq *S*'j *C*b — *txt*: ℵBCX-892 σ1424 D *pc* *L*' *S*s[c]p^1 *C*s **13** ηλ.] εληλυθα‖Lk: F | αμ. + εις μετανοιαν‖Lk: *Rpl* Bas^2 PsBas $Lcg^{1.2}$ vg^3 Au Hil *S*s[c]h^mj Csb^{12} — *txt*: ℵB NΣΦ-1604 **λ**-22-1582 ϕ174 σ990-1223 D S V W Γ Δ *pc* Bas^1 Brn *L*' *S*' Cb^{12} PS **14** πολ.] πυκνα‖Lk: $ℵ^a$ *L*' Hil *S*s[c] — ● *om*‖Mk: ℵ*B σ27-71-692-1194 Cs^{1+1v} Geo^2 — *txt*: *Rpl* Bas *L*k[e] *S*'j Cs^5b Geo^1

Mk 2,16 ∼ αμ.^{2} ... τελ.^{2}‖16a: D $Lar^2$30 $Cs^{3:7}$ $Arm^{⟨pc⟩}$ *Aeth* | εσθιετε κ. πινετε‖Lk30: (Θ)Σ-565-700 ϕ124-*l*547 σ349-517 G *pc* *S*[sc]j $Arm^{⟨pc⟩}$ | ● *om* κ. πιν.‖Mt: ℵB Θ D W 1342 *pc l*302 *L*e[k] abff^{2}r^{1}z vg^1 | πιν. + ο διδασκαλος υμων (∼ ο δ. υμ. εσθ. κ. π.)‖Mt: ℵ(C)LΔ-(579) 1071(*om* υμ.) ϕ69-346-788 σ827-1391-1606 1342 *pc* *L*(τι + ο δ. υμ.: c)f(l)r^{2}z vg$^{⟨1⟩}$ Au (*sim* *C*⟨s$^{1:7}$⟩ *Aeth*) **17** *om* αυτ.‖Mt: 𝔓^{88} 28 **λ** D W *L*abcff^{2}qr^1 vg^1 | ● *om* οτι‖**p**: *Rpl L S*[sc],j — *txt*: 𝔓^{88} BΔ Θ-565-700-1071 713 | ισχ.] υγιαινοντες‖Lk: σ827 *L*⟨bq⟩ | ουκ] ου γαρ‖Mt: CL 1071 σ349-517-1082-1391-1424 1342 *pc* *L*cfff^{2}lr^{2}z vg$^{⟨1⟩}$ *S*[sc]p^1 $Cs^{5:8}$b$^{⟨2⟩}$ | ηλθ.] εληλυθα‖Lk: W | αμ. + εις μετανοιαν‖Lk: *Rpl L*acr^1 vg^2 *S*j Af Cs^2b^{11} $Geo^{ch.2}$ — *txt*: 𝔓^{88} 𝔥⟨33⟩ ΘΣ Φ-28-565-700 **λ**⟨131⟩-22 σ517-1223-1424 157 1342 A D K W Π *al* *L*' Au *S*[sc] Cs^4b' Geo^1 **18** οι Φ.] ● οι των Φαρισαιων‖18b Lk: *Rpl L*al vg^2 *S*p^{9}h^m Cs^2b^8 *Geo* — *txt*: 𝔓^{88} ℵBC Θ-565 **ϕ**⟨346⟩ σM-945-1223-1424-1675 A D K Π 157 1342 *al* *L*' Au *S*[sc]p^{9}h^t Cs^2b' *Arm* Geo^{ch} | και^5—Φ.] και οι Φαρισαιοι‖Mt: Θ *pc* *L*aff^{2}g^2 *C*b' *Arm* — *om*‖Lk: A — *om* μαθ.^{3}‖Lk: *Rpl*(*om* οι μαθ.^{3}: Δ W) *L*'(∼ Φ.^{2} ... Ι.^{2}: b) Au *S*'[sc] — *txt*: 𝔓^{88} 𝔥'⟨579⟩C* 565-1071 *L*e[k] *S*h^{m}j Csb^6 *Aeth*

Lk 5,31 πρ. αυ.] αυτοις‖Mk: LΞ-33 *pc l*48 Bas *L*f — *om*‖Mt: 72 *L*l | υγ.] ισχυοντες‖p: 1604 **ϕ**⟨124⟩ σ71-692-1424 Ψ *pc l*44 *C* | εχ.] πασχοντες‖Mt17 15: σ1606 1229 **32** ουκ] ου γαρ‖Mt: *l*47 *L*f vg^4 Hi *S*j$^{abc⟨1⟩}$ *C*b$^{⟨7⟩}$ | ελη.] ηλθον‖p: C^3-579-892 28 **λ**-1582-2193 σ1424 D 157 *pc l*47 **33** αυτ. + δια τι‖**p**: *Rpl L S*[sc],j Cb^8 — *txt*: 𝔓^4 𝔥⟨ℵ*-579⟩Ξ 157 *C*' | Ι. + και οι μαθηται των Φαρισαιων (*cf.* 33b)‖Mk: D 91 (*om* οι μα.: *L*vl⟨e[k]fr^1⟩) | πυκ.] πολλα‖Mt: 1200 *S*[sc]hj | *om* ομ.‖p: 1241 700 ϕ788 | *om* ομ.—Φ. (*cf.* 33a): σ115 D *pc* *L*vl⟨e[k]fr^1⟩

Mt9 14f.p *cf.* ETh^{II} 104 (*transl.*): *Εἶπον [αὐτῷ]· δεῦρο προσευχώμεθα σήμερον καὶ νηστεύωμεν. λέγει Ἰησοῦς· τίνα γὰρ ἁμαρτίαν πεποίηκα ἢ ἐν τίνι νενίκημαι; ἀλλ' ὅταν ὁ νυμφίος ἐξέλθῃ ἐκ τοῦ νυμφῶνος, τότε νηστεύσουσιν καὶ προσεύξονται.*

Matth 9,14–17	Mark 2,18–22	Luk 5,33–37
οἱ δὲ μαθηταί σου οὐ νηστεύουσιν;	οἱ δὲ σοὶ μαθηταὶ οὐ νηστεύουσιν;	καὶ οἱ τῶν Φαρισαίων, οἱ δὲ σοὶ ἐσθίουσιν καὶ πίνουσιν.
15 καὶ εἶπεν αὐτοῖς ὁ Ἰησοῦς· μὴ δύνανται οἱ υἱοὶ τοῦ νυμφῶνος πενθεῖν, ἐφ' ὅσον μετ' αὐτῶν ἐστιν ὁ νυμφίος;	19 καὶ εἶπεν αὐτοῖς ὁ Ἰησοῦς· μὴ δύνανται οἱ υἱοὶ τοῦ νυμφῶνος, ἐν ᾧ ὁ νυμφίος μετ' αὐτῶν ἐστιν, νηστεύειν; ὅσον χρόνον ἔχουσιν τὸν νυμφίον μετ' αὐτῶν, οὐ δύνανται νηστεύειν.	34 ὁ δὲ εἶπεν πρὸς αὐτούς· μὴ δύνασθε τοὺς υἱοὺς τοῦ νυμφῶνος, ἐν ᾧ ὁ νυμφίος μετ' αὐτῶν ἐστιν, ποιῆσαι νηστεῦσαι;
ἐλεύσονται δὲ ἡμέραι ὅταν ἀπαρθῇ ἀπ' αὐτῶν ὁ νυμφίος, καὶ τότε νηστεύσουσιν.	20 ἐλεύσονται δὲ ἡμέραι ὅταν ἀπαρθῇ ἀπ' αὐτῶν ὁ νυμφίος, καὶ τότε νηστεύσουσιν ἐν ἐκείνῃ τῇ ἡμέρᾳ.	35 ἐλεύσονται δὲ ἡμέραι, καὶ ὅταν ἀπαρθῇ ἀπ' αὐτῶν ὁ νυμφίος, τότε νηστεύσουσιν ἐν ἐκείναις ταῖς ἡμέραις. 36 ἔλεγεν δὲ καὶ παραβολὴν πρὸς αὐτοὺς ὅτι
16 οὐδεὶς δὲ ἐπιβάλλει ἐπίβλημα ῥάκους ἀγνάφου ἐπὶ ἱματίῳ παλαιῷ· αἴρει γὰρ τὸ πλήρωμα αὐτοῦ ἀπὸ τοῦ ἱματίου, καὶ χεῖρον σχίσμα γίνεται.	21 οὐδεὶς ἐπίβλημα ῥάκους ἀγνάφου ἐπιρράπτει ἐπὶ ἱμάτιον παλαιόν· εἰ δὲ μή, αἴρει τὸ πλήρωμα ἀπ' αὐτοῦ τὸ καινὸν τοῦ παλαιοῦ, καὶ χεῖρον σχίσμα γίνεται.	οὐδεὶς ἐπίβλημα ἀπὸ ἱματίου καινοῦ σχίσας ἐπιβάλλει ἐπὶ ἱμάτιον παλαιόν· εἰ δὲ μή γε, καὶ τὸ καινὸν σχίσει καὶ τῷ παλαιῷ οὐ συμφωνήσει τὸ ἐπίβλημα τὸ ἀπὸ τοῦ καινοῦ.
17 οὐδὲ βάλλουσιν οἶνον	22 καὶ οὐδεὶς βάλλει οἶνον	37 καὶ οὐδεὶς βάλλει οἶνον

Mt 9,14 μαθ. σου] σοι μαθ.‖p: σM 478 **15** πεν.] νηστευειν‖p: D W *pc* Chr *L*vl⟨k[e]⟩ Ar *S*ph^{m} *C*sb^{2} | οσον + χρονον‖Mk: λ1278 σ517-659-1675 *al l*49 | νηστ. + εν εκειναις ταις ημεραις‖Lk Mk: D Bas *L*abcg^{1}hq vg^{4} Ar *S*h^{m} **16** *om* δε‖Mk: V *pc* *S*s[c]pj *C*s^{1}b$^{\langle 6\rangle}$ | αγν. + ραπτει‖Mk: ϕ983(*om* επιβα.)-1689 | ιματιον παλαιον‖p: 713 {*L*⟨fh⟩ Ar} | ιματιου + του παλαιου‖Mk: L *L*cq Hi *S*s[c]j *C*b^{1}

Mk 2,18 σοι μαθ.] μαθ. σου‖Mt: ℵΔ(∼) Θ-28-1071 E 255 *L*c | *om* μαθ.^{4}‖Lk: 𝔓^{88}(νηστευουσιν^{1}⌒^{2}) B 565 *pc* *C*b$^{\langle 3\rangle}$ **19** ∼ μετ. αυ. εστ. ο νυ.‖Mt: 892 565-700 **047** *L*bcg^{2}qr$^{1(?).2}$30 vg^{3} | νηστ.^{1}] ποιησαι νηστ.‖Lk: 1574 | *om* εν ω—εστιν: *C*s$^{3:5}$ — *om* οσον—νηστ.^{2}(⌒?)‖p: 33 700 **λ** ϕ983-1689 σ827-1082 D U W *pc* *L*vl⟨cfqz⟩r^{1} vg^{4} *S*[sc]p^{3}(' + ου) *Geo*$^{ch.2}$ | ∼ μεθ εαυτων εχ. τ. νυ.‖Mt: *Rpl* *L*fqz *S*[sc]h *C*b^{8} *Arm* — ∼ μεθ εαυτ. τ. νυ.: λ131 ϕ124 σ115-179-1082-1391 **047** *L*c vg$^{\langle 4\rangle}$ — *txt* (● μεθ εαυτ.): (𝔓^{88}) ℵBC(L)-892 Θ-28-565 *C*s$^{2:5}$b' **20** εκειναις ταις ημεραις‖Lk: *Rpl* *L*' *C* *Geo* — *txt*: 𝔋 ΘΣΦ-565 λ1-209-872 **ϕ**⟨124⟩ σ1223 (∼ τ. ημ. εκ.) A D K W Π *al* *L*ff^{2}ilr^{2}q vg^{9} *S*[sc],j *Geo*^{ch} **21** ουδ. + δε‖Mt: Σ-28 σM-179 D G *al* *L*acff^{2} *S*[sc]h^{m} *C*s$^{1:4}$ | επιρ.] επιβαλλει‖p: σ945-1223 213 | ιματιω παλαιω‖Mt: *Rpl* (*om* επι: **ϕ**⟨828⟩-W 472 — *txt*: 𝔓^{88} 𝔋⟨Δ-579⟩C 544 σ115 D 1342 *pc* | μη] μηγε‖Lk: Δ-33 ΘΣ-28-565-700 λ872 ϕ346 σ7-267-659-827 K Y Π 1342 *al* | αιρ.] αρει‖Lk: H *L*di vg *C*s | *om* απ‖Mt: C ΘΦ-565-700-1071 λ22-118 σM E F G H S U V Y Γ Π^{c} Ω *pl* *S*p | *om* το^{2}—παλαιου‖Mt: 544 255

Lk 5,33 σοι + μαθηται‖p: **σ**⟨517⟩-1188 D(μα. σου) 2533 *L*e[k] bcfff^{2}r^{1} *C*b$^{\langle 1\rangle}$ *Geo* *Aeth* | εσ. και πι.] ου νηστευουσιν‖Mt Mk: **σ**-1188 **34** ● ο δε + Ιησους‖p: 𝔓^{4} 𝔋CXΞ 1071 **λ**-1582 **ϕ** σ7-267-659-945-990-1207-1223 D R 157 *pc* *L*f *S*h^{m}j *C*s(*om* δε)b *Aeth* — *txt*: *Rpl* *L*' *S*'[sc] | πρ. αυ.] αυτοις‖p: 1093 *L*⟨e[k] ac⟩ | δυνανται οι υιοι *et om* ποιη.‖p: ℵ* D 348 (τους υιους *et* εστ. + ποιη.) *L*e[k] abcff^{2}30 (= 348) vg^{3} *C*s$^{1:5}$ | εν ω—εστιν] εφ οσον χρονον εχουσιν τον νυμφιον μεθ εαυτων‖p: D *L*e[k] | ● νηστευειν‖Mk Mt: *Rpl* — *txt*: ℵ^{c}BXΞ-1241 28 *pc* **35** *om* και^{1}‖p: ℵCL-579-892 **λ** **ϕ**-174 σM-1606 F Θ 157 *pc* *L*' *S*[sc] *C* — *txt*: *Rpl* *L*a30 vg^{11} | τοτε] και τ.‖Mt Mk: ℵΔ-579-1241 28 **λ** **ϕ** σM-1606 F Θ 157 *L*vl⟨ar^{2}⟩30 vg^{3} *S*[sc]p^{1}j *Arm*^{pc} *Aeth* **36** *om* απο^{1}‖p: *Rpl* *L*adf *Geo* — *txt*: 𝔓^{4} 𝔋⟨579⟩XΞ 700 **λλ** ⟨2193⟩ **ϕ** D 157 *pc* *L*'Am *S*[sc],j *C* | *om* σχισας‖p: *Rpl* *L* *S*h *Arm* — *txt*: 𝔓^{4} 𝔋Ξ **λλ** D Θ Ψ 157 *pc* *S*[sc]pj *C*sb$^{\langle 1\rangle}$ | επιβα.] επιρραπτει‖Mk: Ψ | ∼ επιβα. επιβλ. απο ιμ. καιν. σχ.‖Mt: **047** | ιματιω παλαιω‖Mt: σM Γ 475 *L*a | σχιζει … συμφωνει‖p: *Rpl* (σχιζεται: R) *L*' {*C*b$^{\langle 3\rangle}$} — *txt*: 𝔓^{4} 𝔋'CX(-φωνουσιν: 579; -φωνει: 1241 σ945)-659 A(σχιζει) D Ψ 157 *pc* *L*e[k] ar^{1}(= 1241: 30 vg^{1}) *C*s {}

Mt9₁₅bp *cf.* ETh^{II} 38. (*cf. ad 105.*)

Mt9₁₆f.p *cf.* ETh^{II} 47c (*transl.*): (*cf. ad* Lk5₃₉) … ^{c}*καὶ οὐ βάλλουσιν οἶνον νέον εἰς ἀσκοὺς παλαιούς, ἵνα μὴ ῥαγῶσιν, οὐδὲ βάλλουσιν οἶνον παλαιὸν εἰς ἀσκὸν νέον, ἵνα μὴ ἀπολέσῃ αὐτόν. οὐκ ἐπιρράπτουσιν ἐπίβλημα παλαιὸν ἐπὶ ἱμάτιον καινόν, ἐπεὶ σχίσμα γενήσεται.*

Matth	Mark	Luk
νέον εἰς ἀσκοὺς παλαιούς· εἰ δὲ μή γε,	νέον εἰς ἀσκοὺς παλαιούς· εἰ δὲ μή,	νέον εἰς ἀσκοὺς παλαιούς· εἰ δὲ μή γε,
ῥήγνυνται οἱ ἀσκοί,	ῥήσσει ὁ οἶνος τοὺς ἀσκούς,	ῥήξει ὁ οἶνος ὁ νέος τοὺς ἀσκούς,
καὶ ὁ οἶνος ἐκχεῖται καὶ οἱ ἀσκοὶ	καὶ ὁ οἶνος ἐκχεῖται καὶ οἱ ἀσκοὶ	καὶ αὐτὸς ἐκχυθήσεται καὶ οἱ ἀσκοὶ
ἀπόλλυνται. ἀλλὰ βάλλουσιν οἶνον	ἀπολοῦνται. ἀλλὰ οἶνον	ἀπολοῦνται. [38] ἀλλὰ οἶνον
νέον εἰς ἀσκοὺς καινούς, καὶ ἀμφότεροι	νέον εἰς ἀσκοὺς καινούς.	νέον εἰς ἀσκοὺς καινοὺς βλητέον.
συντηροῦνται.		[39] καὶ οὐδεὶς πιὼν παλαιὸν θέλει νέον·
		λέγει γάρ· ὁ παλαιὸς χρηστός ἐστιν.

(55)

67. Die Tochter des Jairus und das blutflüssige Weib. **Matth 9** 18–26 [*120.*]
Jairus' Daughter and the Woman with the Issue of Blood.

[18] Ταῦτα αὐτοῦ λαλοῦντος αὐτοῖς, ἰδοὺ ἄρχων εἷς ἐλθὼν προσεκύνει αὐτῷ λέγων· ἡ θυγάτηρ μου ἄρτι ἐτελεύτησεν· ἀλλὰ ἐλθὼν ἐπίθες τὴν χεῖρά σου ἐπ' αὐτήν, καὶ ζήσεται. [19] καὶ ἐγερθεὶς ὁ Ἰησοῦς ἠκολούθησεν αὐτῷ καὶ οἱ μαθηταὶ αὐτοῦ. [*120.*]

Mt 9,17 *om* γε‖Mk: B | ρη. οι ασ.] ρησσει ο οινος (+ ο νεος) τους ασκους ‖ Mk (Lk): (D) *Lk*[e] g^{1}μ Ar *Ss*[c]j | εκχ.—απολ.] απολλυται και οι ασκοι ‖ Mk: D *Lk*[e] a(-ολειται, *om* κ. οι ασ.)μ Ar | απολουνται ‖ p: *Rpl* *Lvl'*g^{2}30 vg^{4} {} — *txt*: ℵB 700 λ-1582 ϕ⟨543⟩-174 σ517 Θ *al* *Lfl* vg' Ar {*S*,j} *C* | ∼ οινον^{2} ν. εις ασ. βαλλ. καιν. (∼ καιν. βαλλ.) ‖ Lk: ℵ(ασ. καιν. βλητσον)C 1604 (= ℵ) σ(7)-517-(659)-1010-1293-1424 *pc* *l*49 *l*184 (*L*) *Aeth*(*om* βαλλ. ‖ Mk) | οινον^{2} ν. βαλλ. ‖ Lk: 892 | *om* κ. αμφ. συντ. ‖ p: S **18** αυτοις] τοις οχλοις ‖ p: σM *pc* | *om* ιδ. ‖ Mk: σ1293 *Sp* | εις ελθ.] ● εις προσελθ. ‖ 19 16 *cf.* 8 19 Mk12 28: ℵ^{b}B *L'* Hil {*S*pj *C*sb^{1}} — ● τις προσελθ.(-ηλθεν): C^{c}L (544) ϕ'⟨124-788 (346-*l*547)-174 σ71-267-659-1391-1402 (F) G U *Lg*^{1} vg^{1} {}^{1} — προσελθ.: ℵ* 157 — τις ελθ.: Γ *pc* *Lk*[e] h {}^{2} — ελθ.: Δ *Lq* — *txt* (*vel* εισελθ.): *Rpl* Bas *Lf* Au {*S'* *Cb'* *Aeth*}^{2} | ● λεγ. + οτι ‖ Mk: *Rpl* Bas^{1} *Lq* *Sh* *Geo* — + κυριε ‖ 8 2.6 Lk5 12: σM *pc* *L*fff^{1}h30 vg^{11} Hil *Sj*^{b} — *txt*: ℵ-33-892 λ-1582-2193 ϕ-*l*547 D **047** *pc* Bas^{1} Chr *L'*Au *S'*j^{ac} | *om* σου ‖ Mk: Σ σ71-692 *L*ablq vg$^{\langle 7\rangle}$ **19** ∼ ηκ. αυτω ο I.: ϕ174 *Lk*[e] *Aeth* | ● ηκολουθει ‖ p: ℵC-33 1604 D *pc* *L'* Hil — *txt* (-ησαν): *Rpl* (σM E 157 *pc* *l*49 *l*184) Bas *Lk*[e] f *S'*(p$^{\langle 1\rangle}$)j *C* *Arm* (*Geo* *Aeth*) | *om* και^{2}: σM *l*184

Mk 2,22 μη] μηγε ‖ p: CL-33-579 ΘΣ σM^{c}-827-1675 1342 *l*48^{2} | ● ρηξει ‖ Lk: 𝔓^{88} ℌ⟨Δ-579⟩C* Θ-565 D *L*(a)bilr$^{1.2}$tz vg$^{\langle 5\rangle}$ *Cs* | ρησσ.—ασκους^{2}] διαρρησσονται οι ασκοι ‖ Mt: W 1342(ρηγνυ-) *La*(ραγησονται) *Cb*^{1} | οινος^{1} + ο νεος ‖ Lk: *Rpl* (ο νε. οι.: λ118-209 *pc*) *Le*[k] ft30 *S*hj *Geo*^{2ch} — *txt*: 𝔓^{88} ℌ⟨Δ-33⟩C* Θ-28-565-700 ϕ⟨124-346⟩ D *pc* *L'*(*om* ο οι.: ab) *S'* *C* *Geo*^{1} | ο οινος^{2}] αυτος ‖ Lk: 579 *Lvg*^{1} | εκχ.] ● απολλυται: 𝔓^{88} B-892 *Cb* — εκχυθησεται ‖ Lk: 579 *Lc*flqr^{2}z30 vg^{10} {} *Cs* *Geo*$^{ch.A}$ — *om*: D *Lvl'*[k]r^{1}t — *txt*: *Rpl* *Lvg'* {*S*,j} *Geo'* | απολ.] απολλυνται ‖ Mt: Θ(-ολυ-) ϕ124 W *pc* {*S*} *Geo'* — ● *om*: 𝔓^{88} BL-892 489 *Cb*$^{\langle 1\rangle}$ — *txt*: *Rpl* *L* {} *Cs* *Geo*^{A} | *om* αλλα—καιν.: D *L*abff^{2}ir^{1}t *Cb*^{1} | καιν. + βαλλουσιν ‖ Mt: W *Le*[k] f (αλλα + βα.: *S'* *C*) *Aeth* *Got* — + βλητεον ‖ Lk: 𝔓^{88} *Rpl* *Lc*lqr^{2}z vg *S*hj *Arm* *Aeth* — *txt*: ℵB-892 | βαλλ./βλητ. + και αμφοτεροι συντηρουνται ‖ Mt: *l*36 *Le*[k] fr^{2}30 vg^{5}(^{2} -ηθησονται)

Lk 5,37 *om* γε ‖ Mk: W | ρηξ.] ρησσει ‖ Mk: C Γ Δ *pc* *Lb*flqr^{2} *Cs*{b} *Arm* — ρηγνυσιν: 𝔓^{4} | *om* ο νεος ‖ Mk: ℵ 1071 *pc* | αυτ.] ο οινος ‖ p: 213 1038 *Le*[k] cf *S*[sc]p (αυτ. ο οι.) **38** βλη.] βαλλουσιν ‖ Mt: ℵ*(-ηται: W) D Mcn *Lvl'*⟨r^{2}⟩(∼ βα. οι. ν. εις ασ. κ.: e[k]; βαλου-: d)r^{1} *S*[sc]p *C* | βλη./βαλ. + και αμφοτεροι συντηρουνται(-ρηθησοντ.) ‖ Mt: *Rpl* (τηρουνται: D) *L* *S*[sc] *Cb*^{3} *Geo*^{A}(') — *txt*: 𝔓$^{4.75v}$ ℌ⟨892⟩ 700 λ⟨118⟩-1582-2193 157 301 *Sj* *C'* **39** *om* 39 | p: D Amm^{sect} Eu^{can} Mcn *Lvl*⟨fqr^{2}z⟩ | ● *om* και *cf.* 11 33 Mt6 24p Mk2 1: 𝔓^{4} ℵ^{c}B-579-892-1241 700 | ● παλαιον + ευθεως: *Rpl* (∼ θ. ν. ευ.: 28) *Lf*qr^{2}z vg *S*[sc] *C*ETh^{II}↓ *Δ*a ad i^{T} l n^{L} — *txt*: 𝔓$^{4.75v}$ ℌ⟨33-892⟩C λ-1582-2193 *Sj* *C* *Arm* *Aeth* *Δ*md me n' p | ● χρηστοτερος: *Rpl* (ευχρη.: 1093) *Lf*qr^{2}z vg *S*hj *Arm* — *txt*: 𝔓^{4} ℌ⟨33-579-892⟩ 157 225 *S*[sc]p *C*

Lk5 39 *cf.* ETh^{II} 47b (*transl.*): (*cf. ad 46.*) ... ^{b}*οὐ πίνει ἄνθρωπος οἶνον παλαιὸν καὶ εὐθέως ἐπιθυμεῖ πιεῖν οἶνον νέον.* ^{c}*καὶ οὐ* ... (*cf. ad* Mt9 16f.)

[20] καὶ ἰδοὺ γυνὴ αἱμορροοῦσα δώδεκα ἔτη προσελθοῦσα ὄπισθεν ἥψατο τοῦ κρασπέδου τοῦ ἱματίου αὐτοῦ· [21] ἔλεγεν γὰρ ἐν ἑαυτῇ· ἐὰν μόνον ἅψωμαι τοῦ ἱματίου αὐτοῦ, σωθήσομαι. [22] ὁ δὲ Ἰησοῦς στραφεὶς καὶ ἰδὼν αὐτὴν εἶπεν· θάρσει, θύγατερ, ἡ πίστις σου σέσωκέν σε. καὶ ἐσώθη ἡ γυνὴ ἀπὸ τῆς ὥρας ἐκείνης. **120.**

[23] καὶ ἐλθὼν ὁ Ἰησοῦς εἰς τὴν οἰκίαν τοῦ ἄρχοντος καὶ ἰδὼν τοὺς αὐλητὰς καὶ τὸν ὄχλον θορυβούμενον [24] ἔλεγεν· ἀναχωρεῖτε· οὐ γὰρ ἀπέθανεν τὸ κοράσιον ἀλλὰ καθεύδει. καὶ κατεγέλων αὐτοῦ. [25] ὅτε δὲ ἐξεβλήθη ὁ ὄχλος, εἰσελθὼν ἐκράτησεν τῆς χειρὸς αὐτῆς, καὶ ἠγέρθη τὸ κοράσιον. [26] καὶ ἐξῆλθεν ἡ φήμη αὐτῆς εἰς ὅλην τὴν γῆν ἐκείνην.

(56) *68.* Heilung zweier Blinden. *Two Blind Men Healed.* Matth 9 27-31 **207.**

[27] Καὶ παράγοντι ἐκεῖθεν τῷ Ἰησοῦ ἠκολούθησαν αὐτῷ δύο τυφλοὶ κράζοντες καὶ λέγοντες· ἐλέησον ἡμᾶς, υἱὲ Δαυιδ. [28] ἐλθόντι δὲ εἰς τὴν οἰκίαν προσῆλθαν αὐτῷ οἱ τυφλοί, καὶ λέγει αὐτοῖς ὁ Ἰησοῦς· πιστεύετε ὅτι δύναμαι τοῦτο ποιῆσαι; λέγουσιν αὐτῷ· ναί, κύριε. [29] τότε ἥψατο τῶν ὀφθαλμῶν αὐτῶν λέγων· κατὰ τὴν πίστιν ὑμῶν γενηθήτω ὑμῖν. [30] καὶ ἠνεῴχθησαν αὐτῶν οἱ ὀφθαλμοί. καὶ ἐνεβριμήθη αὐτοῖς ὁ Ἰησοῦς λέγων· ὁρᾶτε μηδεὶς γινωσκέτω. [31] οἱ δὲ ἐξελθόντες διεφήμισαν αὐτὸν ἐν ὅλῃ τῇ γῇ ἐκείνῃ. **207.**

(57) *69.* Heilung eines stummen Dämonischen. Matth 9 32-34 **99.**
The Healing of a Dumb Demoniac.

[32] Αὐτῶν δὲ ἐξερχομένων, ἰδοὺ προσήνεγκαν αὐτῷ ἄνθρωπον κωφὸν δαιμονιζόμενον. [33] καὶ ἐκβληθέντος τοῦ δαιμονίου ἐλάλησεν ὁ κωφός. καὶ ἐθαύμασαν οἱ ὄχλοι λέγοντες· οὐδέποτε ἐφάνη οὕτως ἐν τῷ Ἰσραηλ. [34] οἱ δὲ Φαρισαῖοι ἔλεγον· ἐν τῷ ἄρχοντι τῶν δαιμονίων ἐκβάλλει τὰ δαιμόνια. **99.**

(58) *70.* Die Aussendung der Zwölf. *The Mission of the Twelve.* Matth 9 35—10 16 **122.**

[35] Καὶ περιῆγεν ὁ Ἰησοῦς τὰς πόλεις πάσας καὶ τὰς κώμας, διδάσκων ἐν ταῖς συναγωγαῖς αὐτῶν καὶ κηρύσσων τὸ εὐαγγέλιον τῆς βασιλείας καὶ θεραπεύων πᾶσαν νόσον καὶ πᾶσαν μαλακίαν. [36] ἰδὼν δὲ **28.**

Mt 9,20 ∼ετη δω.‖Lk: 248 1093 *Lk*[e] c Ar | ετη + εχουσα εν τη ασθενεια‖Jo5 5: L | *om* του κρ.‖Mk: ϕ1689 *Lk*[e] abcg^1 vg Ar **21** εαυ. + οτι‖Mk: 1574 *Geo*^{A} | *om* μον.‖Mk: ℵ* 1574 *Lag*^{2}h *Ss*[c]p^1 *Aeth* | αψ. + του κρασπεδου (*et om* τ. ιμ.)‖20 Lk44a: (ϕ')-983-1689 σ1391 157 *Lg*^{2} *C* **22** ● *om* Ι.: ℵ* D 1355 *Lk*[e] abcq *Ss*[c] | επιστρ.‖Mk: *Rpl* — *txt*: ℌ⟨L⟩ ΝΣ-1604 ϕ⟨346⟩ σ1010-1293 D *l*183 *al* | σε + πορευου εις ειρηνην‖Lk Mk: σ1424 *Lc* | εσω.] ιαθη‖Lk47: 892 σ1424 713 *Lk*[e] *Ss*[c]p **24** ελεγ.] λεγει‖Mk: *Rpl Arm* — ειπεν‖Lk: 1093 *Lk*[e] cg^{1}h *Cs* — *txt*: ℌ⟨L⟩ Σ λ-1582 ϕ D *L'* *S*,j *C*b | ελεγ./ειπ./λεγ. + αυτοις‖Mk: *Rpl Lfg*^{1} *S* — *txt*: ℌ⟨L⟩ ΝΣ λ-1582 ϕ D *L'* *Sj C Aeth* | *om* το κο.‖Lk: 301 331 | αυτ. + ειδοτες οτι απεθανεν‖Lk: ℵ* 61 *Cs*$^{3:4}$ **25** ηγειρεν‖Mk1 31 9 27: ϕ σ517-1424 *Sj* **26** αυ.] ● αὔτη: *Rpl L*,Au *S Geo*$^{ch.B}$ *Δ*a ad i l^{FG} md n — αυτου: σ71-1424 D *pc* {} *C*sb^1 *Geo*^{1}(αυτη αυτου)^A *Aeth* — *txt*: ℵC-33 ΝΣ λ-1582-2193 ϕ124 Θ 157 1195 {*Sj*} *C*b'$^{\langle 2?\rangle}$ *Aeth* **27** ● *om* αυτ.: B-892 D Chr *Lk*[e] | ημ. + κυριε‖20 30f.: Ν ϕ⟨124-346⟩ σ1010 *pc l*47 *l*50 *l*183 *Lg*^{2} *Sp*^{1} *Geo*^{B} — + Ιησου‖Mk Lk: Σ σ1293 *pc* | ● υιος (ο υι. υ.)‖20 30: B G U W Y Π *pl* (700 *pc*) — *txt*: ℌ'C ΝΣΦ-28-1604 λ-22-1582 ϕ-174-230-*l*547 σM-27-71-659-1293-1424-1606 *R* (ο υιε = ω υιε?: Δ) 157 *pm* Or **29** οφθ.] ομματων‖20 34: D Θ **0250** **30** και^1 + παραχρημα‖p: Φ ϕ124 *Lag*^{1}h *Ss*[c]pj *Geo*^{2} *Δ*a i^V me p | ενεβριμησατο‖Jo11 33: *Rpl* — *txt*: ℵB*-892 λ-22-1582 *pc* **31** εις ολην την γην ειεκνην‖9 26: 713 *Lacg*$^{1.2}$hlz vg^{10} **32** ● *om* ανθ.‖12 22 Mk7 32: ℵB-892 ϕ124-788 σ71-692 *pc* *Ss*[c](+ τινα)p *C* **35** *om* ο Ι.‖Mk6 6: 16 1579 *Lvg*^{2} | μαλ. + εν τω λαω‖4 23: *Rpl Lcg*^{1} vg^1 *Sj Arm* — *txt*: ℵ^{b}BC-33-892 ΝΣ λ-22-1582 ϕ788 σ692 D S W Δ **047** 157 *pc L'* Au *S C* | μαλ./λαω + και πολλοι ηκολουθησαν αυτω *cf.* 4 25 8 1: ℵ*(*om* πο.)L Φ ϕ⟨124-788⟩ σ7-517-1010-1293 *pc Labg*^{1}h *Sj*$^{1\langle abc\rangle}$

τοὺς ὄχλους ἐσπλαγχνίσθη περὶ αὐτῶν, ὅτι ἦσαν ἐσκυλμένοι καὶ ἐρριμμένοι **ὡσεὶ πρόβατα μὴ ἔχοντα ποιμένα.** [37] τότε λέγει τοῖς μαθηταῖς αὐτοῦ· ὁ μὲν θερισμὸς πολύς, οἱ δὲ ἐργάται ὀλίγοι· [38] δεήθητε οὖν τοῦ κυρίου τοῦ θερισμοῦ ὅπως ἐκβάλῃ ἐργάτας εἰς τὸν θερισμὸν αὐτοῦ.

125. Nu27 17 2Chr18 16

10 [1] καὶ προσκαλεσάμενος τοὺς δώδεκα μαθητὰς αὐτοῦ ἔδωκεν αὐτοῖς ἐξουσίαν πνευμάτων ἀκαθάρτων, ὥστε ἐκβάλλειν αὐτὰ καὶ θεραπεύειν πᾶσαν νόσον καὶ πᾶσαν μαλακίαν. [2] τῶν δὲ δώδεκα ἀποστόλων τὰ ὀνόματά ἐστιν ταῦτα· πρῶτος Σίμων ὁ λεγόμενος Πέτρος καὶ Ἀνδρέας ὁ ἀδελφὸς αὐτοῦ, Ἰάκωβος ὁ τοῦ Ζεβεδαίου καὶ Ἰωάννης ὁ ἀδελφὸς αὐτοῦ, [3] Φίλιππος καὶ Βαρθολομαῖος, Θωμᾶς καὶ Μαθθαῖος ὁ τελώνης, Ἰάκωβος ὁ τοῦ Ἁλφαίου καὶ Θαδδαῖος, [4] Σίμων ὁ Καναναῖος καὶ Ἰούδας ὁ Ἰσκαριώτης ὁ καὶ παραδοὺς αὐτόν.

122. *85.*

[5] τούτους τοὺς δώδεκα ἀπέστειλεν ὁ Ἰησοῦς παραγγείλας αὐτοῖς λέγων· εἰς ὁδὸν ἐθνῶν μὴ ἀπέλθητε, καὶ εἰς πόλιν Σαμαριτῶν μὴ εἰσέλθητε· [6] πορεύεσθε δὲ μᾶλλον πρὸς τὰ πρόβατα τὰ ἀπολωλότα οἴκου Ισραηλ. [7] πορευόμενοι δὲ κηρύσσετε λέγοντες ὅτι ἤγγικεν ἡ βασιλεία τῶν οὐρανῶν. [8] ἀσθενοῦντας θεραπεύετε, νεκροὺς ἐγείρετε, λεπροὺς καθαρίζετε, δαιμόνια ἐκβάλλετε· δωρεὰν ἐλάβετε, δωρεὰν δότε. [9] μὴ κτήσησθε χρυσὸν μηδὲ ἄργυρον μηδὲ χαλκὸν εἰς τὰς ζώνας ὑμῶν, [10] μὴ πήραν εἰς ὁδὸν μηδὲ δύο χιτῶνας μηδὲ ὑποδήματα μηδὲ ῥάβδον· ἄξιος γὰρ ὁ ἐργάτης τῆς τροφῆς αὐτοῦ.

129.

[11] εἰς ἣν δ' ἂν πόλιν ἢ κώμην εἰσέλθητε, ἐξετάσατε τίς ἐν αὐτῇ ἄξιός ἐστιν· κἀκεῖ μείνατε ἕως ἂν ἐξέλθητε. [12] εἰσερχόμενοι δὲ εἰς τὴν οἰκίαν ἀσπάσασθε αὐτήν· [13] καὶ ἐὰν μὲν ᾖ ἡ οἰκία ἀξία, ἐλθέτω ἡ εἰρήνη ὑμῶν ἐπ' αὐτήν· ἐὰν δὲ μὴ ᾖ ἀξία, ἡ εἰρήνη ὑμῶν πρὸς ὑμᾶς ἐπιστραφήτω. [14] καὶ ὃς ἂν μὴ δέξηται ὑμᾶς μηδὲ ἀκούσῃ τοὺς λόγους ὑμῶν, ἐξερχόμενοι τῆς οἰκίας ἢ τῆς πόλεως ἐκείνης ἐκτινάξατε τὸν κονιορτὸν τῶν ποδῶν ὑμῶν. [15] αμην λέγω ὑμῖν, ἀνεκτότερον ἔσται γῇ Σοδόμων καὶ Γομόρρων ἐν ἡμέρᾳ κρίσεως ἢ τῇ πόλει ἐκείνῃ.

78.

Mt 9,36 περι αυ.] επ αυτους ‖ Mk6 34: σ517-659-1424 *l*49 *l*184 | *om* εσκ. και ερ. ‖ ←: N | ωσει] ως ‖ ←: CL-33-892 NΣ-544-700-1604 **λ**-1582 ϕ124-174-230-788 σM-517-945-1010-1293-1391-1402-1424 D F Y Θ 157 *pm* *l*184 Bas Chr **10,1** μαλ. + εν τω λαω ‖ 4 23: L σ7 157 *pc* *l*19 Cr *L*bg^{1} *S*j^{b} **2** Ια.] ● και Ι. ‖ Mk3 17p: ℵ*B 661 *L*d *S*h^{m} **3** Θαδ.] ● Λεββαιος ο επικληθεις Θ.: *Rpl* (Λ. ο και Θ.: C*^{v}; Λ. ο και επ. Θ.: σ954) *L*f *S*'j^{ab} — Θ. ο επ. Λ.: ϕ'⟨983⟩-*l*547 — ● Λ.: D 122 Hes *L*k[e] μ Au Or *S*j^{1} — Ιουδας Ιακωβου: *S*s[c](∼ ^{4}Σι. ο Κα. ^{3}Ιου. Ια.) — Ιου. ζηλωτης: *L*abg^{1}hq — *txt*: ℵB-892 ϕ124-788 *pc* *l*185 EEb↓ *L*' *C* **4** *om* ο^{2} ‖ p: *Rpl* — *txt*: ℵ^{b}(* ο Ιου.)B-33 Φ-544-700-1604 **λ** ϕ124 σM-990-1010-1223 K S Δ Θ Π Ω **047** 157 *mu* EEb↓ | Ισκαριωθ ‖ p: C σ1424 *l*150 (Scarioth: *L*abcff^{1}g^{1}hμz30) | Ισκ.] Σιμωνος Ισκαριωτου ‖ Jo6 71 13 26: Or | ο ... παραδους] ος ... παρεδωκεν ‖ Mk3 19: L **ϕ**-174 **σ**⟨954⟩ Or | *om* και^{2} ‖ Lk6 16: F *l*184 *L*vl[e]⟨af⟩μ *S*,j^{a1v} **7** *om* οτι ‖ Lk9: B 1604 *S*s[c] | οτι + μετανοειτε ‖ 3 2 4 17: 1604 (∼: 59 251) *C*s$^{8:9}$ | ηγγ. + γαρ ‖ ←: *C*s$^{8:9}$ — + εφ υμας ‖ Lk9: NΣ σ267 *l*49 **9f.** μηδε$^{1-5}$] μητε$^{1-5}$ ‖ Lk9 3: L 700(-δε^{1}) **ϕ** D **10** μη] μητε ‖ ←: 700 D *L*k[e] Au$^{1:4}$ *S*s[c]pj *C*s$^{8:9}$ | της τρ.] του μισθου ‖ Lk7 1T5 18: 892 σM-1402-1675 K Π 565 *L*vl⟨k[e] lz⟩ *S*h^{m} **11** *om* η κω. ‖ Lk8: 700 **λ** (D) *L*k[e] abff^{1}h Hil *S*s[c] | εξετα. + πρωτον ‖ Lk10 5: 157 | μενετε ‖ Mk Lk9 4 10 7: X 28 243 | εξελθ. + εκειθεν ‖ Mk Lk9 4: NΣ σ1293 *L*c vg^{1} **12** αυτ. + λεγοντες· ειρηνη τω οικω τουτω ‖ p: ℵ*L Φ-1604 **λ**-22-1582 ϕ346 σ7-349-517-945-1010-1293-1391-1402 D W Θ *pm* *l*7 *l*49 *l*184 *L*⟨k[e] l vg^{5}⟩ *S*j *Arm* **13** *om* μεν ‖ p: σ349-1424 238 *L*vl[e]⟨ff^{1}lz⟩ *Geo*^{1}(^{2}+ ουν) | εαν^{2}—αξ.] ει δε μη γε ‖ p: D *S*s[c] | προς] ● εφ ‖ p: ℵB-892 1604 ϕ174 σ1010-1293 W *pc* Chr *S*s[c]p | επιστ.] ανακαμψει ‖ p: 243 **14** οσοι ... δεξωνται ... ακουσωσιν ‖ Lk9 5: L Σ *L*k[e](ακουση) bcg^{1}h *Aeth* | ● εξερ. + εξω *cf.* 21 17 Act16 13 H13 13: 𝔇' 1604 **σ**⟨954⟩-7-659-1010-1293-1391 D Θ *pc* *l*7 *l*49 *L* {*S*j} — + απο ‖ Lk9 5: 1579 — + εκ *cf.* 27 53 Mk5 2 7 31 *etc.*: L *pc* — *txt*: *Rpl* {*S*} | *om* της οι. η(∩?) ‖ Lk9 5: D *Arm*$^{\langle pc\rangle}$ | πολ. + η κωμης ‖ 11: ℵ-892 **ϕ**⟨124-788⟩ *L*g^{2} vg^{3} *S*pj(*om* πολ. η) | εκτ. + και ‖ Lk11: σ71-692 | ● κον. + εκ ‖ Lk9 5: ℵC-33-892 1604 σ27-71-692-1010-1223-1293 157 *pc* *L* *S*p *Arm* | υμων + επ αυτη ‖ Lk9 5 Act13 51: 544 251(-την) 1588

Mt9 37f.p *cf.* ETh^{II} 73 (*transl.*): *Λέγει Ἰησοῦς· ὁ μὲν θερισμὸς πολύς, οἱ δὲ ἐργάται ὀλίγοι· δεήθητε δὲ τοῦ κυρίου ἵνα ἐκβάλῃ ἐργάτας εἰς τὸν θερισμόν.*

Mt10 2ff. *cf.* EEb frgm.1 (*cf. ad 23.*)

16 ἰδοὺ ἐγὼ ἀποστέλλω ὑμᾶς ὡς πρόβατα ἐν μέσῳ λύκων· γίνεσθε οὖν φρόνιμοι ὡς οἱ ὄφεις καὶ ἀκέραιοι ὡς αἱ περιστεραί.

(59) *71.* Das Schicksal der Jünger. *The Afflictions of the Disciples.* **Matth 10** 17–25 *229.*

17 Προσέχετε δὲ ἀπὸ τῶν ἀνθρώπων· παραδώσουσιν γὰρ ὑμᾶς εἰς συνέδρια, καὶ ἐν ταῖς συναγωγαῖς αὐτῶν μαστιγώσουσιν ὑμᾶς· 18 καὶ ἐπὶ ἡγεμόνας δὲ καὶ βασιλεῖς ἀχθήσεσθε ἕνεκεν ἐμοῦ, εἰς μαρτύριον αὐτοῖς καὶ τοῖς ἔθνεσιν. 19 ὅταν δὲ παραδῶσιν ὑμᾶς, μὴ μεριμνήσητε πῶς ἢ τί λαλήσητε· δοθήσεται γὰρ ὑμῖν ἐν ἐκείνῃ τῇ ὥρᾳ τί λαλήσητε· *229.* 20 οὐ γὰρ ὑμεῖς ἐστε οἱ λαλοῦντες, ἀλλὰ τὸ πνεῦμα τοῦ πατρὸς ὑμῶν τὸ λαλοῦν ἐν ὑμῖν. 21 παραδώσει δὲ ἀδελφὸς ἀδελφὸν εἰς θάνατον καὶ πατὴρ τέκνον, καὶ **ἐπαναστήσονται** τέκνα ἐπὶ γονεῖς καὶ θανατώσουσιν αὐτούς. (Mch7 6) 22 καὶ ἔσεσθε μισούμενοι ὑπὸ πάντων διὰ τὸ ὄνομά μου· ὁ δὲ ὑπομείνας εἰς τέλος, οὗτος σωθήσεται. 23 ὅταν δὲ διώκωσιν ὑμᾶς ἐν τῇ πόλει ταύτῃ, φεύγετε εἰς τὴν ἑτέραν· αμην γὰρ λέγω ὑμῖν, οὐ μὴ τελέσητε τὰς πόλεις τοῦ Ισραηλ ἕως ἂν ἔλθῃ ὁ υἱὸς τοῦ ἀνθρώπου. 24 οὐκ ἔστιν μαθητὴς ὑπὲρ τὸν διδάσκαλον οὐδὲ δοῦλος ὑπὲρ τὸν κύριον αὐτοῦ. 25 ἀρκετὸν τῷ μαθητῇ ἵνα γένηται ὡς ὁ διδάσκαλος αὐτοῦ, καὶ ὁ δοῦλος ὡς ὁ κύριος αὐτοῦ. *89.* εἰ τὸν οἰκοδεσπότην Βεελζεβουλ ἐπεκάλεσαν, πόσῳ μᾶλλον τοὺς οἰκιακοὺς αὐτοῦ.

(60) *72.* Aufforderung zum furchtlosen Bekenntnis. *Exhortation to Fearless Confession.*

Matth 10 26–33		*12* 2–9 *(169.)*
26 Μὴ οὖν φοβηθῆτε αὐτούς· οὐδὲν γάρ ἐστιν κεκαλυμμένον ὃ οὐκ ἀποκαλυφθήσεται, καὶ κρυπτὸν ὃ οὐ γνωσθήσεται. 27 ὃ λέγω ὑμῖν ἐν τῇ σκοτίᾳ, εἴπατε ἐν τῷ φωτί· καὶ ὃ εἰς τὸ οὖς ἀκούετε, κηρύξατε ἐπὶ τῶν	*107.*	2 *οὐδὲν δὲ συγκεκαλυμμένον ἐστὶν ὃ οὐκ ἀποκαλυφθήσεται, καὶ κρυπτὸν ὃ οὐ γνωσθήσεται.* 3 *ἀνθ' ὧν ὅσα ἐν τῇ σκοτίᾳ εἴπατε, ἐν τῷ φωτὶ ἀκουσθήσεται· καὶ ὃ πρὸς τὸ οὖς ἐλαλήσατε ἐν τοῖς ταμιείοις, κηρυχθήσεται ἐπὶ τῶν*

Mt 10,16 *om* εγω‖Lk10 3: σ1207 *L*ff^{1} **17** *om* δε‖7 5: 28 D 280 Or *L*k[e] acg^{1} *S*s[c]j^{b} *C*s$^{6:10}$ *Arm Geo*^{2} *Δ*a ad i md n p | *om* γαρ‖Mk: 16 *L*vg^{1} *S*s[c] *C*s$^{1:8}$ | εις τας συναγωγας‖p: D' **18** ηγεμονων‖Mk: D(*om* δε κ. βασ.) | *om* δε‖Mk: LX 544-700 λ1278 σ659 F G Δ *al l*47 Or *L*Or *C*s | αχ.] σταθησεσθε‖Mk: D 485 *L*vl[e]⟨flz⟩ Hil Or *S*s[c] **20** ~ εστε υμ.‖Mk: σ1293 *L*c Or **23** αν] ● *om*: ℵ*BX 248 — ου: ℵ^{c} 544 *pc* **26** κεκα.] συγκεκα.‖p: 28 ϕ *l*49 — κεκρυμμενον *cf.* Lk 18 34: X 700 399 **27** εις] προς‖p: 28-700 σM *pc* Bas$^{1:2}$ | κηρυχθησεται‖p: L

Mt10 16a *cf.* 2Cl5 2: λέγει γὰρ ὁ κύριος· ἔσεσθε ὡς ἀρνία ἐν μέσῳ λύκων.
cf. PsTt (492f.): ipso exortante domino: Audite me, inquid, quos elegi agnos et nolite timere lupos.

Mt10 16b *cf.* ETh^{II} 39 (POxy 655 IIb): (*cf. ad 224.* Mt23 13) ... ὑμεῖς] δὲ γεί[νεσθε φρόνι]μοι ὡ[ς οἱ ὄφεις καὶ ἀ]κέραι[οι ὡς αἱ περιστε]ρα[ί.
(*transl.*): (*cf. ad 224.* Mt23 13) ... *ὑμεῖς δὲ γίνεσθε φρόνιμοι ὡς οἱ ὄφεις καὶ ἀκέραιοι ὡς αἱ περιστεραί.*
cf. EN frgm.7 (Cod. N.T. 1424^{m}): Τὸ Ἰουδαϊκόν· ὑπὲρ ὄφεις.

Mt10 26p *cf.* ETh^{II} 5f. (*cf. ad 107.* Mk4 22p; *ad 40.*)

Mt10 27p *cf.* ETh^{II} 33a (POxy 1,8): Λέγει Ἰ(ησοῦ)ς· ⟨ὃ⟩ ἀκούεις [ε]ἰς τὸ ἓν ὠτίον σου, το[ῦτο κήρυξον ἐπὶ τῶν δωμάτων]
(*transl.*): *Λέγει Ἰησοῦς· ὃ ἀκούσεις εἰς τὸ οὖς σου, εἰς τὸ ἄλλο οὖς κήρυξον (-ξατε?) ἐπὶ τῶν δωμάτων ὑμῶν.* [b] *Οὐδεὶς ...* (*cf. ad 107.* Mk4 21)

δωμάτων. [28] καὶ μὴ φοβεῖσθε ἀπὸ τῶν ἀποκτεννόντων τὸ σῶμα, τὴν δὲ ψυχὴν μὴ δυναμένων ἀποκτεῖναι· φοβεῖσθε δὲ μᾶλλον τὸν δυνάμενον καὶ ψυχὴν καὶ σῶμα ἀπολέσαι ἐν γεέννῃ. [29] οὐχὶ δύο στρουθία ἀσσαρίου πωλεῖται; καὶ ἓν ἐξ αὐτῶν οὐ πεσεῖται ἐπὶ τὴν γῆν ἄνευ τοῦ πατρὸς ὑμῶν. [30] ὑμῶν δὲ καὶ αἱ τρίχες τῆς κεφαλῆς πᾶσαι ἠριθμημέναι εἰσίν. [31] μὴ οὖν φοβεῖσθε· πολλῶν στρουθίων διαφέρετε ὑμεῖς.

[32] πᾶς οὖν ὅστις ὁμολογήσει ἐν ἐμοὶ ἔμπροσθεν τῶν ἀνθρώπων, ὁμολογήσω κἀγὼ ἐν αὐτῷ ἔμπροσθεν τοῦ πατρός μου τοῦ ἐν οὐρανοῖς· [33] ὅστις δ' ἂν ἀρνήσηταί με ἔμπροσθεν τῶν ἀνθρώπων, ἀρνήσομαι αὐτὸν κἀγὼ ἔμπροσθεν τοῦ πατρός μου τοῦ ἐν οὐρανοῖς.

δωμάτων. [4] *λέγω δὲ ὑμῖν τοῖς φίλοις μου, μὴ φοβηθῆτε ἀπὸ τῶν ἀποκτεινόντων τὸ σῶμα καὶ μετὰ ταῦτα μὴ ἐχόντων περισσότερόν τι ποιῆσαι.* [5] *ὑποδείξω δὲ ὑμῖν τίνα φοβηθῆτε· φοβήθητε τὸν μετὰ τὸ ἀποκτεῖναι ἔχοντα ἐξουσίαν ἐμβαλεῖν εἰς τὴν γέενναν. ναὶ λέγω ὑμῖν, τοῦτον φοβήθητε.* [6] *οὐχὶ πέντε στρουθία πωλοῦνται ἀσσαρίων δύο; καὶ ἓν ἐξ αὐτῶν οὐκ ἔστιν ἐπιλελησμένον ἐνώπιον τοῦ θεοῦ.* [7] *ἀλλὰ καὶ αἱ τρίχες τῆς κεφαλῆς ὑμῶν πᾶσαι ἠρίθμηνται. μὴ φοβεῖσθε· πολλῶν στρουθίων διαφέρετε.*

21 18 *(229.): καὶ θρὶξ ἐκ τῆς κεφαλῆς ὑμῶν οὐ μὴ ἀπόληται.*

[8] *λέγω δὲ ὑμῖν, πᾶς ὃς ἂν ὁμολογήσῃ ἐν ἐμοὶ ἔμπροσθεν τῶν ἀνθρώπων, καὶ ὁ υἱὸς τοῦ ἀνθρώπου ὁμολογήσει ἐν αὐτῷ ἔμπροσθεν τῶν ἀγγέλων τοῦ θεοῦ·* [9] *ὁ δὲ ἀρνησάμενός με ἐνώπιον τῶν ἀνθρώπων ἀπαρνηθήσεται ἐνώπιον τῶν ἀγγέλων τοῦ θεοῦ.*

137.

(61)

73. Zwiespalt unter den Nächsten. *Division in Households.*

Matth 10 34–36

[34] Μὴ νομίσητε ὅτι ἦλθον βαλεῖν εἰρήνην ἐπὶ τὴν γῆν· οὐκ ἦλθον βαλεῖν εἰρήνην ἀλλὰ μά-

12 51–53 *(174.)*

[51] *δοκεῖτε ὅτι εἰρήνην παρεγενόμην δοῦναι ἐν τῇ γῇ; οὐχί, λέγω ὑμῖν, ἀλλ' ἢ*

Mt 10,28 φοβ.[1]] ● φοβηθητε‖p26: *Rpl* Ath[1] PsAth[2] Eu[1] Or — *txt*: ℵCLX 700 **ϕ**-174 σM-7-349-517-692 E F G K U V 157 *al* Ath[1] PsAth[1] Ddy Eu[1] | φοβ.[2]] ● φοβηθητε‖←: *Rpl* Ath Cr Ddy Ep Meth Or — *txt*: ℵBC-892 σ349-1010-1293 W *pc* | *om* μαλ.‖p: σ1424 Eu *C*b | απ. εν γε.] βαλειν εις γεενναν‖p: PsCl *L*Cp[1:5] Ir Hil *S*s[c] **29** πωλουνται‖p: D | υμ. + του εν τοις(*om*) ουρανοις‖32f.: 892 (544)-1604(*om* του) *pc* Ath (PsAth Chr) Cr[I] Or(*om* υμ.) *L*bff[1]g[1.2]hz vg[3] Ar Eu Or *C*s[2:3]b **30** υμ.—κεφ.] αλλα και—κεφ. υμων‖p: D *L*vl[e]<flqz> *C*s[1:3] *Aeth* | κεφ. + υμων‖p: L *S*s[c](*om* τ. κεφ.)p *C* | ηρ. εισιν] ηριθμηνται‖Lk7: 28 **σ**<954>-659 *l*49 *l*184 **31** φοβ.] φοβηθητε‖26: *Rpl* — *txt*: 𝔥 Σ-1604 **λ**-1582 D W 157 *pc* Or | φοβ. + αυτους‖26: **ϕ**<124-788> σM-1675 W *L*g[1] vg[4] *C*s **32** *om* ουν‖p: X ϕ124-788 *pc* *l*184 *L*32 Cp Hil *S*s *C*b *Geo* | καγω εν αυ.] αυτον κ.‖33: 𝔓[19](∼) L 544 | ● εν[3] +τοις‖69516: BCX ΣΦ-1604 **ϕ**<828-983>-*l*547 K V Ω *pc* Cr Eu Or[1] — *txt*: 𝔓[19] *Rpl* Cl Or[2] **33** απαρνηση.‖p: C **λ**-1582 **ϕ** Θ *pc* Or[2:3] *C*s[3:4] | απαρνησο.‖p: **λ**-1582 Or[2:3] *C*s[4:5] | ● ∼ καγω αυ.‖32: 𝔓[19] 𝔥<L> Σ **λ**-1582 **σ**<1424>-692-945 D W Δ Θ **047** *pc* Ad PsAth Or[2] *S*scj[c] *Arm* — *txt*: *Rpl* Or[3] *S*' | ● εν + τοις‖69516: BX-892 ϕ124-788-828 σ517-1675 V Ω *pc* Ad[1] PsAth Cr Ep Or[1] — *txt*: 𝔓[19] *Rpl* Ad[1] Or[2]

Mt1028p *cf.* 2Cl54: εἶπεν ὁ Ἰησοῦς τῷ Πέτρῳ· μὴ φοβείσθωσαν τὰ ἀρνία τοὺς λύκους μετὰ τὸ ἀποθανεῖν αὐτά· καὶ ὑμεῖς μὴ φοβεῖσθε τοὺς ἀποκτέννοντας ὑμᾶς καὶ μηδὲν ὑμῖν δυναμένους ποιεῖν, ἀλλὰ φοβεῖσθε τὸν μετὰ τὸ ἀποθανεῖν ὑμᾶς ἔχοντα ἐξουσίαν ψυχῆς καὶ σώματος τοῦ βαλεῖν εἰς γέενναν πυρός.

cf. Iu apol. I 19,6f.: ... Ἰησοῦν Χριστὸν ἔγνωμεν εἰπόντα· .... [7] Καί· μὴ φοβεῖσθε τοὺς ἀναιροῦντας ὑμᾶς καὶ μετὰ ταῦτα μὴ δυναμένους τι ποιῆσαι, εἶπεν, φοβήθητε δὲ τὸν μετὰ τὸ ἀποθανεῖν δυνάμενον καὶ ψυχὴν καὶ σῶμα εἰς γέενναν ἐμβαλεῖν.

Mt1032p *cf.* 2Cl32: λέγει δὲ καὶ αὐτός· τὸν ὁμολογήσαντά με ἐνώπιον τῶν ἀνθρώπων, ὁμολογήσω αὐτὸν ἐνώπιον τοῦ πατρός μου.

73. cf. Agr. (Iu dial. 35,3): εἶπεν γάρ (sc. Ἰησοῦς Χριστός)· ... (Mt245) ... καί· ἔσονται σχίσματα καὶ αἱρέσεις. καί· ... (Mt715) ... καί· ... (Mt2424.11). (*cf.* 1K1118f.)

cf. ETh[II] 16 (*transl.*): *Λέγει Ἰησοῦς· τάχα δοκοῦσιν οἱ ἄνθρωποι ὅτι ἦλθον βαλεῖν εἰρήνην ἐπὶ τὸν κόσμον, καὶ οὐκ οἴδασιν ὅτι ἦλθον βαλεῖν διαμερισμοὺς ἐπὶ τὴν γῆν, πῦρ, μάχαιραν, πόλεμον. πέντε γὰρ ἔσονται ἐν οἴκῳ· τρεῖς ἔσονται ἐπὶ δυσὶ καὶ δύο ἐπὶ τρισίν, ὁ πατὴρ ἐπὶ τῷ υἱῷ καὶ ὁ υἱὸς ἐπὶ τῷ πατρί. καὶ στήσονται αὐτοὶ μόναχοι (= μόνοι).*

χαιραν. [35] ἦλθον γὰρ διχάσαι ἄνθρωπον κατὰ **τοῦ πατρὸς** αὐτοῦ καὶ **θυγατέρα κατὰ τῆς μητρὸς αὐτῆς** καὶ **νύμφην κατὰ τῆς πενθερᾶς αὐτῆς,** [36] καὶ **ἐχθροὶ τοῦ ἀνθρώπου οἱ οἰκιακοὶ αὐτοῦ.**

Mch76

διαμερισμόν. [52] *ἔσονται γὰρ ἀπὸ τοῦ νῦν πέντε ἐν ἑνὶ οἴκῳ διαμεμερισμένοι, τρεῖς ἐπὶ δυσὶν καὶ δύο ἐπὶ τρισὶν* [53] *διαμερισθήσονται, πατὴρ ἐπὶ υἱῷ καὶ* ***υἱὸς*** *ἐπὶ* ***πατρί,*** *μήτηρ ἐπὶ θυγατέρα καὶ* ***θυγάτηρ ἐπὶ τὴν μητέρα,*** *πενθερὰ ἐπὶ τὴν νύμφην αὐτῆς καὶ* ***νύμφη ἐπὶ τὴν πενθεράν.***

(62) 74. Bedingungen der Nachfolge. *The Conditions of Discipleship.* Matth 10 37-39

[37] Ὁ φιλῶν πατέρα ἢ μητέρα ὑπὲρ ἐμὲ οὐκ ἔστιν μου ἄξιος· καὶ ὁ φιλῶν υἱὸν ἢ θυγατέρα ὑπὲρ ἐμὲ οὐκ ἔστιν μου ἄξιος· [38] καὶ ὅς οὐ λαμβάνει τὸν σταυρὸν αὐτοῦ καὶ ἀκολουθεῖ ὀπίσω μου, οὐκ ἔστιν μου ἄξιος. [39] ὁ εὑρὼν τὴν ψυχὴν αὐτοῦ ἀπολέσει αὐτήν, καὶ ὁ ἀπολέσας τὴν ψυχὴν αὐτοῦ ἕνεκεν ἐμοῦ εὑρήσει αὐτήν.

137.

14 26f. (185.): εἴ τις ἔρχεται πρός με καὶ οὐ μισεῖ τὸν πατέρα αὐτοῦ καὶ τὴν μητέρα καὶ τὴν γυναῖκα καὶ τὰ τέκνα καὶ τοὺς ἀδελφοὺς καὶ τὰς ἀδελφάς, ἔτι δὲ καὶ τὴν ἑαυτοῦ ψυχήν, οὐ δύναται εἶναί μου μαθητής. [27] *ὅστις οὐ βαστάζει τὸν σταυρὸν ἑαυτοῦ καὶ ἔρχεται ὀπίσω μου, οὐ δύναται εἶναί μου μαθητής. 17 33 (198.): ὃς ἐὰν ζητήσῃ τὴν ψυχὴν αὐτοῦ περιποιήσασθαι, ἀπολέσει αὐτήν, καὶ ὃς ἐὰν ἀπολέσῃ, ζῳογονήσει αὐτήν.*

(63) 75. Schluß der Rede. *End of the Discourse.* Matth 10 40—11 1

[40] Ὁ δεχόμενος ὑμᾶς ἐμὲ δέχεται, καὶ ὁ ἐμὲ δεχόμενος δέχεται τὸν ἀποστείλαντά με. [41] ὁ δεχόμενος προφήτην εἰς ὄνομα προφήτου μισθὸν προφήτου λήμψεται, καὶ ὁ δεχόμενος δίκαιον εἰς ὄνομα δικαίου μισθὸν δικαίου λήμψεται. [42] καὶ ὃς ἐὰν ποτίσῃ ἕνα τῶν μικρῶν τούτων ποτήριον ψυχροῦ μόνον εἰς ὄνομα μαθητοῦ, αμην λέγω ὑμῖν, οὐ μὴ ἀπολέσῃ τὸν μισθὸν αὐτοῦ.

143.

9 41 (144.): ὃς γὰρ ἂν ποτίσῃ ὑμᾶς ποτήριον ὕδατος ἐν ὀνόματι, ὅτι Χριστοῦ ἐστε, αμην λέγω ὑμῖν ὅτι οὐ μὴ ἀπολέσῃ τὸν μισθὸν αὐτοῦ.

11 [1] Καὶ ἐγένετο ὅτε ἐτέλεσεν ὁ Ἰησοῦς διατάσσων τοῖς δώδεκα μαθηταῖς αὐτοῦ, μετέβη ἐκεῖθεν τοῦ διδάσκειν καὶ κηρύσσειν ἐν ταῖς πόλεσιν αὐτῶν.

Mt 10,35 ανθ.] υιον‖p: D *pc* *Lvl*⟨k[e] f⟩ vg[1](υι. ανθ.) Hil Pris *Ssc* | *om* αυτης([1] *et*)[2] ‖(p): 700 (Eu *LIr*) **38** λαμ.] αιρει‖1624 Mk834 Lk923: Or[1]([2] αρη) *LCp*[2:4] *C* | αξ. + ειναι μαθητης‖p: Or (*om* αξ. ει.: *Lk*[e] c Cp[2:5]) **39** και ο] ο δε‖1625 Mk← Lk←: D *LTe* *Cb*[4](⟨6⟩ *om* δε) *Aeth* | εμου + και του ευαγγελιου‖Mk←: 213 | ευρη.] ουτος σωσει‖Mk← Lk←: λ⟨1⟩ **40** και ο] ο δε‖Lk1016: ℵ* **41** ο δεχ.[1]] ος γαρ αν δεξηται‖185 Mk937 Lk948: Cl[1:2] *Ss* | ο δεχ.[2]] ος αν δεξ.‖←: Cl[1:2] **42** ποτι.] δεξηται‖←: Cl[1:2] | μικ.] ελαχιστων‖2545: D 59 *L*, Au[5]([3]τουτ.] μου) Cp | τουτ. + ελαχ.‖←: σ1424-1675 157 | ποτη. + υδατος (*et om* ψυ.)‖(p): D(∼ ψυ. υδ.: Cl Or) *Lvl*[e a]⟨k⟩ Au Cp Hil *Ssc*(j[b]) *C Arm Geo*[1A] *Aeth* | *om* μον.‖p: 544 σ1675 D E Cl *L*Au Cp[1:2] Hil *Ssc Geo*[B] *Aeth* | υμ. + οτι‖p: 440 655 *Labchz S*,j

---

Mt1037f.p *cf.* ETh[II] 55.101 (*transl.*): *Λέγει Ἰησοῦς· ὅστις οὐ μισεῖ τὸν πατέρα αὐτοῦ καὶ τὴν μητέρα αὐτοῦ οὐ δυνήσεται εἶναί μου μαθητής. καὶ ὅστις οὐ μισεῖ τοὺς ἀδελφοὺς αὐτοῦ καὶ τὰς ἀδελφὰς αὐτοῦ καὶ οὐ βαστάζει τὸν σταυρὸν αὐτοῦ ὡς κἀγώ, οὐκ ἔσται μου ἄξιος ...* [101] *"Οστις οὐ μισεῖ τὸν πα[τέρα] αὐτοῦ καὶ τὴν μητέρα αὐτοῦ ὡς κἀγὼ οὐ δυνήσεται εἶναί μου μ[αθητή]ς. καὶ ὅστις οὐ φιλεῖ τὸν [πατέρα αὐτοῦ κα]ὶ τὴν μητέρα αὐτοῦ ὡς κἀγὼ οὐ δυνήσεται εἶναί μου μ[αθητή]ς· ἡ γὰρ μήτηρ μου ἡ [.....] ἡ δὲ [μήτηρ μου] ἡ ἀληθινὴ δέδωκεν ἐμοὶ τὴν ζωήν.*

(64)

76. Anfrage des Täufers. *The Baptist's Question.*

Matth 11 2–6

[2] Ὁ δὲ Ἰωάννης ἀκούσας ἐν τῷ δεσμωτηρίῳ τὰ ἔργα τοῦ Χριστοῦ, πέμψας διὰ τῶν μαθητῶν αὐτοῦ [3] εἶπεν αὐτῷ· σὺ εἶ ὁ ἐρχόμενος, ἢ ἕτερον προσδοκῶμεν; [4] καὶ ἀποκριθεὶς ὁ Ἰησοῦς εἶπεν αὐτοῖς· πορευθέντες ἀπαγγείλατε Ἰωάννῃ ἃ ἀκούετε καὶ βλέπετε· [5] **τυφλοὶ ἀναβλέπουσιν** καὶ χωλοὶ περιπατοῦσιν, λεπροὶ καθαρίζονται καὶ κωφοὶ ἀκούουσιν, καὶ νεκροὶ ἐγείρονται καὶ **πτωχοὶ εὐαγγελίζονται·** [6] καὶ μακάριός ἐστιν ὃς ἐὰν μὴ σκανδαλισθῇ ἐν ἐμοί.

7 18–23 (*94.*)

[18] Καὶ ἀπήγγειλαν Ἰωάννῃ οἱ μαθηταὶ αὐτοῦ περὶ πάντων τούτων. καὶ προσκαλεσάμενος δύο τινὰς τῶν μαθητῶν αὐτοῦ ὁ Ἰωάννης [19] ἔπεμψεν πρὸς τὸν κύριον λέγων· σὺ εἶ ὁ ἐρχόμενος, ἢ ἄλλον προσδοκῶμεν; [20] παραγενόμενοι δὲ πρὸς αὐτὸν οἱ ἄνδρες εἶπαν· Ἰωάννης ὁ βαπτιστὴς ἀπέστειλεν ἡμᾶς πρὸς σὲ λέγων· σὺ εἶ ὁ ἐρχόμενος, ἢ ἄλλον προσδοκῶμεν; [21] ἐν ἐκείνῃ τῇ ὥρᾳ ἐθεράπευσεν πολλοὺς ἀπὸ νόσων καὶ μαστίγων καὶ πνευμάτων πονηρῶν, καὶ τυφλοῖς πολλοῖς ἐχαρίσατο βλέπειν. [22] καὶ ἀποκριθεὶς εἶπεν αὐτοῖς· πορευθέντες ἀπαγγείλατε Ἰωάννῃ ἃ εἴδετε καὶ ἠκούσατε· ὅτι ***τυφλοὶ ἀναβλέπουσιν,*** *χωλοὶ περιπατοῦσιν, λεπροὶ καθαρίζονται, κωφοὶ ἀκούουσιν, νεκροὶ ἐγείρονται,* ***πτωχοὶ εὐαγγελίζονται·*** *[23] καὶ μακάριός ἐστιν ὃς ἐὰν μὴ σκανδαλισθῇ ἐν ἐμοί.*

Is61₁LXX

(65)

77. Jesu Zeugnis über den Täufer. *Jesus' Testimony to the Baptist.*

Matth 11 7–19

[7] Τούτων δὲ πορευομένων ἤρξατο ὁ Ἰησοῦς λέγειν τοῖς ὄχλοις περὶ Ἰωάννου· τί ἐξήλθατε εἰς τὴν ἔρημον θεάσασθαι; κάλαμον ὑπὸ ἀνέμου σαλευόμενον; [8] ἀλλὰ τί ἐξήλθατε ἰδεῖν; ἄνθρωπον ἐν μαλακοῖς ἠμφιεσμένον; ἰδοὺ οἱ τὰ μαλακὰ φοροῦντες ἐν τοῖς οἴκοις τῶν βασιλέων εἰσίν. [9] ἀλλὰ τί ἐξήλθατε; προφήτην ἰδεῖν; ναὶ λέγω ὑμῖν, καὶ περισσότερον προφήτου. [10] οὗτός ἐστιν περὶ οὗ γέγραπται· **ἰδοὺ ἐγὼ ἀποστέλλω τὸν ἄγγελόν μου πρὸ προσώπου** σου, **ὃς κατασκευάσει τὴν ὁδόν** σου ἔμπροσθέν

13.

7 24–28.31–35 (*95.*)

[24] Ἀπελθόντων δὲ τῶν ἀγγέλων Ἰωάννου ἤρξατο λέγειν πρὸς τοὺς ὄχλους περὶ Ἰωάννου· τί ἐξεληλύθατε εἰς τὴν ἔρημον θεάσασθαι; κάλαμον ὑπὸ ἀνέμου σαλευόμενον; [25] ἀλλὰ τί ἐξεληλύθατε ἰδεῖν; ἄνθρωπον ἐν μαλακοῖς ἱματίοις ἠμφιεσμένον; ἰδοὺ οἱ ἐν ἱματισμῷ ἐνδόξῳ καὶ τρυφῇ ὑπάρχοντες ἐν τοῖς βασιλείοις εἰσίν. [26] ἀλλὰ τί ἐξεληλύθατε ἰδεῖν; προφήτην; ναὶ λέγω ὑμῖν, καὶ περισσότερον προφήτου. [27] οὗτός ἐστιν περὶ οὗ γέγραπται· ***ἰδοὺ ἀποστέλλω τὸν ἄγγελόν μου πρὸ προσώπου*** *σου,* ***ὃς κατασκευάσει τὴν ὁδόν*** *σου* ***ἔμπροσθέν***

Ex23₂₀ Ml3₁

Mt 11,2 δια] δυο ‖ p: *Rpl* Or *L'* *S*h^{m}j *C*b *Geo*^{A} — *om, et* τους μαθητας: *L*k[e] abcfh Hil *S*sc *Geo'* — *txt*: 𝔊⟨L-892⟩C Σ ϕ124-174-788 D P W Δ Θ *pc* *L*q *S'* *C*s **4** ακ. ... βλε.] ∼ ‖ p: L *pc* Or^{1} *S*scj^{ab} *C*b — ηκουσατε ... ειδετε ‖ p: *L*fff^{1}g^{1}hlqz vg *S*j^{c} — ειδ. ... ηκ. ‖ p: Or^{1} — ηκ. ... βλε.: *L*ad **5** *om* και^{1} ‖ p: Z-892 σ1675 Δ *pc* Bas^{S} *L*⟨k[e] abq⟩ Cp *C* *Arm* *Geo*$^{\langle A\rangle}$ *Aeth* | *om* και^{3} ‖ p: *Rpl* *L'* *C* *Geo'* — ∼ πτω. ευα. κ. νεκ. εγ.: ϕ-*l*547 Θ *S*sc — *txt*: 𝔊⟨33⟩ Φ λ1-1582 ϕ174-230 D P W Δ *pc* Bas^{S} *L*abg^{1}q30 vg^{5} *S*'j *Geo*$^{B.ch}$ **7** εξεληλυθατε ‖ p: F Δ **8** εξεληλυθατε ‖ p: F 1574 | μαλακοις + ιματιοις ‖ p: *Rpl* (μαλακιοις: λ1 59) Chr *L*bfhl vg^{1} *S*,j *C* — *txt*: ℵBZ D(*om* εν^{1}) *l*47 *L'* | βασιλειων ‖ p: ΝΟΣ **λ**⟨1⟩-1278 σ71-349-517-692 E F G K S V Π *pm* | ● *om* εισ.: ℵ*B **9** εξεληλυθατε ‖ p: 892 F W Or | ◆ ∼ ιδ. προφ. ‖ 8 Lk: *Rpl* Chr^{1m} Cr *L*, Amst Hil *S*,j *C*s *Aeth* — *txt*: ℵ*B^{cv}Z-892 W Chr^{ct} Or *C*b *Aeth* **10** ● ουτ. + γαρ ‖ 3₃: *Rpl* *L'S'*j *C'* — *txt*: ℵBZ-892 D *L*k[e] bg^{1} *S*sc *C*b^{4} | *om* εγω ‖ p: Z ϕ*l*547 σ1402 Chr *L*cff^{1} g^{2} vg^{5} Am *S*sc *C*b *Geo*

Mt11₇f.p *cf.* ETh^{II} 78 (*transl.*): *Λέγει Ἰησοῦς· διὰ τί ἐξήλθατε εἰς τὸν ἀγρόν; θεάσασθαι κάλαμον σαλευόμενον ὑπὸ τοῦ ἀνέμου καὶ θεάσασθαι ἄνθ[ρωπον ἐν] μαλακοῖς ἱματίοις ἠμφιεσμένον; [ἰδοὺ οἱ] βασιλεῖς [ὑμῶν] καὶ οἱ μεγιστᾶνες ὑμῶν οὗτοι φοροῦσιν τὰ [ἱμάτια] τὰ μαλακά· καὶ οὐ δυνήσονται γνῶναι τὴν ἀλήθειαν.*

σου. [11] αμην λέγω ὑμῖν, οὐκ ἐγήγερται ἐν γεννητοῖς γυναικῶν μείζων Ἰωάννου τοῦ βαπτιστοῦ· ὁ δὲ μικρότερος ἐν τῇ βασιλείᾳ τῶν οὐρανῶν μείζων αὐτοῦ ἐστιν. [12] ἀπὸ δὲ τῶν ἡμερῶν Ἰωάννου τοῦ βαπτιστοῦ ἕως ἄρτι ἡ βασιλεία τῶν οὐρανῶν βιάζεται, καὶ βιασταὶ ἁρπάζουσιν αὐτήν. [13] πάντες γὰρ οἱ προφῆται καὶ ὁ νόμος ἕως Ἰωάννου ἐπροφήτευσαν· [14] καὶ εἰ θέλετε δέξασθαι, αὐτός ἐστιν Ἠλίας ὁ μέλλων ἔρχεσθαι. [15] ὁ ἔχων ὦτα ἀκουέτω.

[16] τίνι δὲ ὁμοιώσω τὴν γενεὰν ταύτην; ὁμοία ἐστὶν παιδίοις καθημένοις ἐν ταῖς ἀγοραῖς ἃ προσφωνοῦντα τοῖς ἑτέροις [17] λέγουσιν· ηὐλήσαμεν ὑμῖν καὶ οὐκ ὠρχήσασθε, ἐθρηνήσαμεν καὶ οὐκ ἐκόψασθε. [18] ἦλθεν γὰρ Ἰωάννης μήτε ἐσθίων μήτε πίνων, καὶ λέγουσιν· δαιμόνιον ἔχει. [19] ἦλθεν ὁ υἱὸς τοῦ ἀνθρώπου ἐσθίων καὶ πίνων, καὶ λέγουσιν· ἰδοὺ ἄνθρωπος φάγος καὶ οἰνοπότης, τελωνῶν φίλος καὶ ἁμαρτωλῶν. καὶ ἐδικαιώθη ἡ σοφία ἀπὸ τῶν ἔργων αὐτῆς.

139.

σου. [28] *λέγω ὑμῖν, μείζων ἐν γεννητοῖς γυναικῶν προφήτης Ἰωάννου οὐδείς ἐστιν· ὁ δὲ μικρότερος ἐν τῇ βασιλείᾳ τοῦ θεοῦ μείζων αὐτοῦ ἐστιν.*
16 16 *(190.): ...* [16 b] *ἀπὸ τότε ἡ βασιλεία τοῦ θεοῦ εὐαγγελίζεται καὶ πᾶς εἰς αὐτὴν βιάζεται ...*
[16 a] *Ὁ νόμος καὶ οἱ προφῆται μέχρι Ἰωάννου· ...*

7 31*: τίνι οὖν ὁμοιώσω τοὺς ἀνθρώπους τῆς γενεᾶς ταύτης, καὶ τίνι εἰσὶν ὅμοιοι;* [32] *ὅμοιοί εἰσιν παιδίοις τοῖς ἐν ἀγορᾷ καθημένοις καὶ προσφωνοῦσιν ἀλλήλοις λέγοντες· ηὐλήσαμεν ὑμῖν καὶ οὐκ ὠρχήσασθε· ἐθρηνήσαμεν καὶ οὐκ ἐκλαύσατε.* [33] *ἐλήλυθεν γὰρ Ἰωάννης ὁ βαπτιστὴς μὴ ἄρτον ἔσθων μήτε οἶνον πίνων, καὶ λέγετε· δαιμόνιον ἔχει.* [34] *ἐλήλυθεν ὁ υἱὸς τοῦ ἀνθρώπου ἐσθίων καὶ πίνων, καὶ λέγετε· ἰδοὺ ἄνθρωπος φάγος καὶ οἰνοπότης, φίλος τελωνῶν καὶ ἁμαρτωλῶν.* [35] *καὶ ἐδικαιώθη ἡ σοφία ἀπὸ τῶν τέκνων αὐτῆς πάντων.*

(66) *78.* Wehe über die galiläischen Städte. *Woes on the Cities of Galilee.*

Matth 11 20–24

[20] Τότε ἤρξατο ὀνειδίζειν τὰς πόλεις ἐν αἷς ἐγένοντο αἱ πλεῖσται δυνάμεις αὐτοῦ, ὅτι οὐ μετενόησαν· [21] οὐαί

10 13–15.12 *(153.)*

[13] *Οὐαί*

Mt 11,11 γυ. + προφητης(-των)‖p: (σ1010) *L*bcg^{1}h σ1010 | καθ. εν τ. αγ.] εν αγοραις(-ρα) καθ.‖(p): *Rpl* (28 **047** *pc* Ddy) — καθ. εν αγοραις(-ρα)‖(p): CL ΝΣΦ-(544) **ϕ**-174 σM-(349-990-1010-1293) W Δ (**047**) *pc* — *txt*: $\mathfrak{H}$' λ1-1582 D(τη αγορα) *l*184 | α προσφ.] (*cf. ad* 17) και προσφωνουσιν‖p: *Rpl* *L*vl' *S*' — α προσφωνουσιν: C 544 Ddy(-νει) *L*k[e] *S*h^m *C* *Geo* — *txt*: ℵBZ-892 λ1 **ϕ** σ7-267-659-1293-1391-1424-1675 D Θ 399 *L*ff^{1}lz vg | τ. ετερ. (= εταιρ.!)] αλληλοις‖p: *L*abcfff^{2}g^{1}hq *C*b — ετερα προς ετερα‖p: Ddy — + αυτων: *Rpl* *S* *C*s *Geo*' — *txt*: ℵBZ **λ**-1582 D Θ *L*' *Geo*^{B} **13** εως] μεχρι‖p: *l*184 **16** παι. + τοις‖p: **17** λεγ.] (*cf. ad* 16) και λεγ.: *Rpl* *L*ff^{2}g^1 *S*' — λεγοντες‖p: 544 Ddy *L*k[e] abfhq *C* — *om*: *L*g^2 *S*s — *txt*: ℵBZ-892 λ1-1582 **ϕ** **σ**⟨954⟩-7-267-659-1293-1391 D Θ *L*' | εθρ. + υμιν‖17a p: *Rpl* Ddy *L*abff^{2}hq30 vg^4 Au^1 *S* *Δ*a i md n p — *txt*: ℵBZ-892 λ1-1582 D Cl *L*' Au^2 *C* *Δ*ad l | εκο.] εκλαυσασθε‖p: W **18** γαρ + προς υμας‖21 3: L(*om* γαρ) **ϕ** σ517-659-1391-1402-1675 Θ *pc* *l*49 Eu *S*ch | I. + ο βαπτιστης‖p: Φ ϕ346 (∼ ο βα. I.) — + εν οδω δικαιοσυνης‖21 3: Ep **19** ∼ φιλ. τελ.‖p: ℵL 28 **ϕ**⟨124⟩ 157 *pc* Cl$^{1:2}$ *L*cff^{2}h Au | απο + παντων‖p: **ϕ** *pc* *L*k[e] | εργ.] τεκνων‖p: *Rpl* Chr *L*, Au Hil *S*sch^m *C*s^5 *Arm*' *Aeth* — *txt*: ℵB* ϕ124-230-788 W 2145 *L*Hi *S*' *C*s^{2}b *Arm*^{pc} *Aeth*

Mt11 11p *cf.* ETh^{II} 46 (*transl.*): *Λέγει Ἰησοῦς· ἀπὸ Αδαμ ἕως Ἰωάννου τοῦ βαπτιστοῦ ἐν γεννητοῖς γυναικῶν οὐδείς μείζων ἐστὶν Ἰωάννου τοῦ βαπτιστοῦ, ἵνα μὴ κατεαγῶσιν (= ἐκλίπωσιν? cf.* Is38 14) *οἱ ὀφθαλμοὶ αὐτοῦ. εἶπον δὲ ἐγώ· ὃς ἂν μικρὸς ᾖ ἐν ὑμῖν, γνώσεται τὴν βασιλείαν καὶ μείζων ἔσται Ἰωάννου.*

Mt11 12 *cf.* EN frgm.8 (Cod. N.T. 1424^m): Τὸ Ἰουδαϊκὸν διαρπάζεται ἔχει.

Mt11 15 *cf.* ETh^{II} 24.63.65.96 (*cf. ad 103.* Mt13 9)

Mt11 20f.p *cf.* EN frgm.27 (Hist. Lk-Ct. fol. 56r^o): *Besaida*, in qua sanavit paraliticum cata Johannem. In his civitatibus multae virtutes facte sunt, quae evangelium secundum Hebreos quinquaginta ter(!) virtutes in his factas enumerat.

σοι, Χοραζιν· οὐαί σοι, Βηθσαιδαν· ὅτι εἰ ἐν Τύρῳ καὶ Σιδῶνι ἐγένοντο αἱ δυνάμεις αἱ γενόμεναι ἐν ὑμῖν, πάλαι ἂν ἐν σάκκῳ καὶ σποδῷ μετενόησαν. 22 πλὴν λέγω ὑμῖν, Τύρῳ καὶ Σιδῶνι ἀνεκτότερον ἔσται ἐν ἡμέρᾳ κρίσεως ἢ ὑμῖν. 23 καὶ σύ, Καφαρναουμ, μὴ **ἕως οὐρανοῦ ὑψωθήσῃ; ἕως ᾅδου καταβιβασθήσῃ**· ὅτι εἰ ἐν Σοδόμοις ἐγενήθησαν αἱ δυνάμεις αἱ γενόμεναι ἐν σοί, ἔμεινεν ἂν μέχρι τῆς σήμερον. 24 πλὴν λέγω ὑμῖν ὅτι γῇ Σοδόμων ἀνεκτότερον ἔσται ἐν ἡμέρᾳ κρίσεως ἢ σοί.

10 15 (70.): αμην λέγω ὑμῖν, ἀνεκτότερον ἔσται γῇ Σοδόμων καὶ Γομόρρων ἐν ἡμέρᾳ κρίσεως ἢ τῇ πόλει ἐκείνῃ.

σοι, Χοραζιν, οὐαί σοι, Βηθσαιδα· ὅτι εἰ ἐν Τύρῳ καὶ Σιδῶνι ἐγενήθησαν αἱ δυνάμεις αἱ γενόμεναι ἐν ὑμῖν, πάλαι ἂν ἐν σάκκῳ καὶ σποδῷ καθήμενοι μετενόησαν. 14 πλὴν Τύρῳ καὶ Σιδῶνι ἀνεκτότερον ἔσται ἐν τῇ κρίσει ἢ ὑμῖν. 15 καὶ σύ, Καφαρναουμ, μὴ ***ἕως τοῦ οὐρανοῦ ὑψωθήσῃ; ἕως ᾅδου καταβιβασθήσῃ*** *...* Is14 13.15

12 λέγω ὑμῖν ὅτι Σοδόμοις ἐν τῇ ἡμέρᾳ ἐκείνῃ ἀνεκτότερον ἔσται ἢ τῇ πόλει ἐκείνῃ.

(67)

79. Jubelruf. *Jesus' Thanksgiving to the Father.*

Matth 11 25–27

25 Ἐν ἐκείνῳ τῷ καιρῷ ἀποκριθεὶς ὁ Ἰησοῦς εἶπεν· ἐξομολογοῦμαί σοι, πάτερ, κύριε τοῦ οὐρανοῦ καὶ τῆς γῆς, ὅτι ἔκρυψας ταῦτα ἀπὸ σοφῶν καὶ συνετῶν, καὶ ἀπεκάλυψας αὐτὰ νηπίοις· 26 ναί, ὁ πατήρ, ὅτι οὕτως εὐδοκία ἐγένετο ἔμπροσθέν σου. 27 πάντα μοι παρεδόθη ὑπὸ τοῦ πατρός μου, καὶ οὐδεὶς ἐπιγινώσκει τὸν υἱὸν εἰ μὴ ὁ πατήρ, οὐδὲ τὸν πατέρα τις ἐπιγινώσκει εἰ μὴ ὁ υἱὸς καὶ ᾧ ἐὰν βούληται ὁ υἱὸς ἀποκαλύψαι.

10 21–22 (155.)

21 Ἐν αὐτῇ τῇ ὥρᾳ ἠγαλλιάσατο τῷ πνεύματι τῷ ἁγίῳ καὶ εἶπεν· ἐξομολογοῦμαί σοι, πάτερ, κύριε τοῦ οὐρανοῦ καὶ τῆς γῆς, ὅτι ἀπέκρυψας ταῦτα ἀπὸ σοφῶν καὶ συνετῶν, καὶ ἀπεκάλυψας αὐτὰ νηπίοις· ναί, ὁ πατήρ, ὅτι οὕτως ἐγένετο εὐδοκία ἔμπροσθέν σου. 22 πάντα μοι παρεδόθη ὑπὸ τοῦ πατρός μου, καὶ οὐδεὶς γινώσκει τίς ἐστιν ὁ υἱὸς εἰ μὴ ὁ πατήρ, καὶ τίς ἐστιν ὁ πατὴρ εἰ μὴ ὁ υἱὸς καὶ ᾧ ἐὰν βούληται ὁ υἱὸς ἀποκαλύψαι.

3 35: Ὁ πατὴρ ἀγαπᾷ τὸν υἱόν, καὶ πάντα δέδωκεν ἐν τῇ χειρὶ αὐτοῦ. 17 2: καθὼς ἔδωκας αὐτῷ ἐξουσίαν πάσης σαρκός, ... 10 15: καθὼς γινώσκει με ὁ πατὴρ κἀγὼ γινώσκω τὸν πατέρα, ... 17 25 f.: ... ἐγὼ δέ σε ἔγνων, καὶ οὗτοι ἔγνωσαν ὅτι σύ με ἀπέστειλας. 26 καὶ ἐγνώρισα αὐτοῖς τὸ ὄνομά σου καὶ γνωρίσω, ...

Mt 11,21 εγενηθησαν ‖ p23: 33-892 σ⟨954⟩-7-1391 157 *l*49 | σπο. + καθημενοι(-αι) ‖ p: ℵC-33-(892 λ1-22-1278-1582 σ⟨954⟩-7-1391-1402)-945(καθεζομενον) U (Δ *al l*49) *pc* (Bas) *Sh Cb*[1] PsCae Chr[2:4] Max[C] — *txt*: ℵB 28 ϕ124-174-788 D W Δ Θ 157 *pc l*184 PsCae Chr[1:4] | **23** ουρ.] του ουρ. ‖ p: *Rpl* | ● καταβηση ‖ Is14 15 LXX: B D W 372 Chr[1:3] *L*, Ir *Ssc Cs Arm Aeth Got* — *txt*: ℵBC 1604 λ1-1582 σ517-1391-1424 D 157 *l*49 | εγενοντο ‖ 21: *Rpl* Chr — **24** υμιν] σοι ‖ 24b: *S*' *Cb*[1] — *om*: *Lk*[e] *Ssc* | σοι] υμιν ‖ 24a.22: σM[m]-659-1424 D *Lvl*[e]⟨flz⟩ Ir *Cs*[1:7]b[5] *Arm*[pc] **25** *om* ο I. ‖ p: 245 | απεκρυψ. ‖ p: *Rpl* Ir — *txt*: 𝔓[62] ℵB D *pc* PsCl **26** ~ εγεν. ευδ. ‖ p: *Rpl* Chr *L*' Hil — *txt*: 𝔓[62] ℵB-33-892 λ1-1582 W Θ *Lk*[e] ff[1] **27** επιγ.[1]] γινωσκει ‖ p: 𝔓[70] C σ71-692 *pc* Cl[1:8] Ddy Iu[1:3] Or | τ. υιον] τις εστιν ο υιος ‖ p: σ1010-1391 | *om* τις επιγ.[2] ‖ p: 1279 Cl[6:8] Ep[6:10] Ir Iu *L*Ir[5:6] *Sc* Ir | επιγ.[1] *et* [2](1)] οιδεν ‖ Jo8 19 7 28f.: (Ad[1]) Ath Bas Cr Ep[4](4)[:10] *L* Te — εγνω ‖ Jo17 25: (Ad[1]) Cl[6:8] Ddy Eu (Ep[2:10] Ir Iu[2:3]) Or *Lvl*⟨k[e] dff[1]h⟩30 (Ir) *S*Ir

---

Mt11 25p *cf.* EN frgm.9 (Cod. N.T. 1424[m]): Τὸ Ἰουδαϊκόν· 'εὐχαριστῶ σοι'.

cf. ETh[II] 4 (POxy 654,3): [Λέγει Ἰ(ησοῦ)ς·] οὐκ ἀποκνήσει ἄνθ[ρωπος πλήρης ἡμε]ρῶν ἐπερωτῆσε πα[ιδίον ἑπτὰ ἡμε]ρῶν περὶ τοῦ τόπου τῆ[ς ζωῆς καὶ ζήσει· εἴ]σετε ὅτι ... (*cf. ad 203.* Mt19 30)

(*transl.*): *Λέγει Ἰησοῦς· οὐκ ἀποκνήσει ὁ ἄνθρωπος ὁ παλαιὸς ἡμερῶν ἐπερωτῆσαι παιδίον μικρὸν ἑπτὰ ἡμερῶν περὶ τοῦ τόπου τῆς ζωῆς καὶ ζήσεται· ὅτι ...* (*cf. ad 203.* Mt19 30)

Mt11 27p *cf.* ETh[II] 61 (*transl.*): *... Παρεδόθη μοι ἐκ τῶν τοῦ πατρός μου ...*

(68) *80.* Heilandsruf. *Comfort for the Heavy-laden.* **Matth 11** 28-30

Jr616 [28] Δεῦτε πρός με πάντες οἱ κοπιῶντες καὶ πεφορτισμένοι, κἀγὼ ἀναπαύσω ὑμᾶς. [29] ἄρατε τὸν ζυγόν μου ἐφ' ὑμᾶς καὶ μάθετε ἀπ' ἐμοῦ, ὅτι πραΰς εἰμι καὶ ταπεινὸς τῇ καρδίᾳ, καὶ **εὑρήσετε ἀνάπαυσιν ταῖς ψυχαῖς ὑμῶν·** [30] ὁ γὰρ ζυγός μου χρηστὸς καὶ τὸ φορτίον μου ἐλαφρόν ἐστιν.

(69) *81.* Das Ährenraufen am Sabbat. *Plucking Corn on the Sabbath.*

Matth 12 1-8	**Mark 2** 23-28	**Luk 6** 1-5
[1] Ἐν ἐκείνῳ τῷ καιρῷ ἐπορεύθη ὁ Ἰησοῦς τοῖς σάββασιν διὰ τῶν σπορίμων· οἱ δὲ μαθηταὶ αὐτοῦ ἐπείνασαν, καὶ ἤρξαντο τίλλειν στάχυας καὶ ἐσθίειν.	[23] Καὶ ἐγένετο αὐτὸν ἐν τοῖς σάββασιν παραπορεύεσθαι διὰ τῶν σπορίμων, καὶ οἱ μαθηταὶ αὐτοῦ ἤρξαντο ὁδὸν ποιεῖν τίλλοντες τοὺς στάχυας.	[1] Ἐγένετο δὲ ἐν σαββάτῳ δευτεροπρώτῳ διαπορεύεσθαι αὐτὸν διὰ σπορίμων, καὶ ἔτιλλον οἱ μαθηταὶ αὐτοῦ καὶ ἤσθιον τοὺς στάχυας ψώχοντες ταῖς χερσίν.
[2] οἱ δὲ Φαρισαῖοι ἰδόντες εἶπαν αὐτῷ· ἰδοὺ οἱ μαθηταί σου ποιοῦσιν ὃ οὐκ ἔξεστιν ποιεῖν ἐν σαββάτῳ.	[24] καὶ οἱ Φαρισαῖοι ἔλεγον αὐτῷ· ἴδε τί ποιοῦσιν τοῖς σάββασιν ὃ οὐκ ἔξεστιν; [25] καὶ	[2] τινὲς δὲ τῶν Φαρισαίων εἶπον· τί ποιεῖτε ὃ οὐκ ἔξεστιν τοῖς σάββασιν; [3] καὶ ἀποκρι-
		5 10: ἔλεγον οὖν οἱ Ἰουδαῖοι τῷ τεθεραπευμένῳ· σάββατόν ἐστιν, καὶ οὐκ ἔξεστίν σοι ἆραι τὸν κράβαττον.

Mt 12,1 l. + εν‖p: W 238 | στα.] τους στα.‖p: 28-700 λ118 σ1391 D(∼ τ. στ. τιλ.) U *pc* *C*,f | *om* κ. εσθ.‖Mk: 1574 **2** ιδου ... ποι.] ιδ. ... τι ποι.‖Mk: σ — τι ... ποι.‖Lk: *S*sc | εν σαβ.] τοις σαββασιν‖p: 157 213(*om* τοις) *L*abcg^{1}hlz vg

Mk 2,24 *om* αυτω‖Lk: D *L*e[k] i | ποι. + οι μαθηται σου‖Mt: ΘΣΦ-28-565-700-1071(*om* σου) **λ φ**-*l*547 σM-115 D *al* *L*abfir^{1}t30 (∼ τ. σα. οι μ. σ.: cff^{2}g^{2}) vg^{11}(^{1}) *S*s[c]j *C*b^{1} *Arm* *Geo*^{2} *Aeth* | τοις] εν τ.‖23 Mt: *Rpl* — *txt*: ℌ⟨L-33⟩C ΘΣΦ-565-700 **λ φ** σM-179-827 A D K W Π **074** 1342 *al* | εξε. + ποιειν‖Mt: σ1675 *pc* *L*30(ποι. *prm* αυτοις) vg^{1} *C*s$^{3:4}$b$^{⟨2⟩}$ | ∼ ο ουκ εξ. τ. σα.‖Lk Mt: 28 A

Lk 6,1 εγεν.—αυτον] και εγ. αυτ. εν σα. δευ. διαπ.‖Mk: D *L*(e) a vg^{1} (*S*[sc]j^{1}) *Arm* | ● *om* δευτ.‖p: 𝔓$^{4.75v}$ ℌ⟨Δ-892⟩ 700 **λλ**⟨131-1582⟩ φ69-788 W 157 *pc* *L*(+ πρωι: e) bclqr^{1} *S*[sc]ph^{m}j *C* *Geo*(*om* -οπρωτ-) | διαπορ.] πορ.‖Mt: C*X λ1582-2193 *pc* | δια + των‖**p**: *Rpl* — *txt*: 𝔓$^{4.75v}$ ℵBLW Λ-700 λ1-131 A Δ Θ Π **047** *mu* | και^{1}—αυτου] οι δε μα. αυ. ηρξαντο τιλλειν‖p: D *L*b(και ηρξ. οι μ. αυ. τ.) | ● ∼ τους στ. κ. ησθ.‖p: *Rpl* *L*' *S*h *Aeth* — ∼ τ. στ. και ψω. τ. χ. ησθ.: D *L*e (∼ τ. χ. ψ. και: a; ∼ ψ. τ. χ. και: c)f *S*'[sc]j *C* — *txt*: 𝔓$^{4.75v}$ BC*L-579-892-1241 700 φ174 R *pc* *Aeth* | *om* και ησθ.‖Mk: 1093 | *om* τους‖Mt: ℵ*pc* **2** ειπ. + αυτοις(-τω)‖(Mk): *Rpl* (D) *L*vl' vg'(^{1}) *S*(sc],j^{abc} — *txt*: 𝔓$^{4.75v}$ ℌ⟨W-33-892⟩C*X **λ**-1582-2193 157 *pc* *L*e acr^{1} *S*j^{1} *C* | τι ποι.] ιδε τι ποιουσιν οι μαθηται σου‖p: D | ∼ τοις σα. ο ουκ εξ.‖Mk: D *L*vl⟨ff^{2}qr^{2}⟩r^{1} *Geo*^{2} | ● εξε. + ποιειν‖Mt: *Rpl* (∼ τ. σα. ποι.: L 1038) *L*q *S*[sc],j *C*b' — *txt*: 𝔓$^{4.75v}$ B 700 φ69-788 D R *L*' *C*sb^{5} *Arm* | τοις σα.] εν τ. σα.‖Mt: *Rpl* (*om* τοις: Δ Λ) *L*vg' {} — εν σαββατω‖Mt: 1241 **φ**'(εν τω: 828) Ψ *pc* *C*sb^{5} — *txt*: 𝔓$^{4.75v}$ ℌ⟨33-579⟩ 700 **λλ**⟨1278⟩ φ69-124-174-230-788-983 D R U *pc* *L*vl r^{1}30 vg^{1} {*S*[sc]h *C*b'}

Jo 5,10 κρα. + σου‖511 Mk211.9: 𝔓$^{66.75}$ ℌ⟨B-33⟩C*W^{s} NΛ-544-1071 φ13-174-230-788-826-828-983 σ1010-1293 D Θ Π **053** *mu* Chr *L*⟨e⟩ *S*'h^{+}j *C*sb^{+B}a^{5} *Geo*^{2}

---

80. cf. ETh^{II} 90 (*transl.*): *Λέγει Ἰησοῦς· δεῦτε πρός με ὅτι χρηστὸς ὁ ζυγός μου καὶ ἡ κυριότης μου πραεῖά ἐστιν, καὶ εὑρήσετε ἀνάπαυσιν ὑμῖν.*

cf. ETh^{II} 2; EH frgm.4a.b (*cf. ad 50.* Mt7$_{7f.}$)

Matth	Mark	Luk
³ ὁ δὲ εἶπεν αὐτοῖς· οὐκ ἀνέγνωτε τί ἐποίησεν Δαυιδ, ὅτε ἐπείνασεν καὶ οἱ μετ' αὐτοῦ; ⁴ πῶς εἰσῆλθεν εἰς τὸν οἶκον τοῦ θεοῦ καὶ τοὺς ἄρτους τῆς προθέσεως ἔφαγεν, ὃ οὐκ ἐξὸν ἦν αὐτῷ φαγεῖν οὐδὲ τοῖς μετ' αὐτοῦ, εἰ μὴ τοῖς ἱερεῦσιν μόνοις;	λέγει αὐτοῖς· οὐδέποτε ἀνέγνωτε τί ἐποίησεν Δαυιδ, ὅτε χρείαν ἔσχεν καὶ ἐπείνασεν αὐτὸς καὶ οἱ μετ' αὐτοῦ; ²⁶ πῶς εἰσῆλθεν εἰς τὸν οἶκον τοῦ θεοῦ ἐπὶ Αβιαθαρ ἀρχιερέως καὶ τοὺς ἄρτους τῆς προθέσεως ἔφαγεν, οὓς οὐκ ἔξεστιν φαγεῖν εἰ μὴ τοῖς ἱερεῦσιν, καὶ ἔδωκεν καὶ τοῖς σὺν αὐτῷ οὖσιν;	θεὶς πρὸς αὐτοὺς εἶπεν ὁ Ἰησοῦς· οὐδὲ τοῦτο ἀνέγνωτε ὃ ἐποίησεν Δαυιδ, ὁπότε ἐπείνασεν αὐτὸς καὶ οἱ μετ' αὐτοῦ ὄντες; ⁴ ὡς εἰσῆλθεν εἰς τὸν οἶκον τοῦ θεοῦ καὶ τοὺς ἄρτους τῆς προθέσεως λαβὼν ἔφαγεν καὶ ἔδωκεν τοῖς μετ' αὐτοῦ, οὓς οὐκ ἔξεστιν φαγεῖν εἰ μὴ μόνους τοὺς ἱερεῖς;

⁵ ἢ οὐκ ἀνέγνωτε ἐν τῷ νόμῳ ὅτι τοῖς σάββασιν οἱ ἱερεῖς ἐν τῷ ἱερῷ τὸ σάββατον βεβηλοῦσιν καὶ ἀναίτιοί εἰσιν; ⁶ λέγω δὲ ὑμῖν ὅτι τοῦ ἱεροῦ μεῖζόν ἐστιν ὧδε. ⁷ εἰ δὲ ἐγνώκειτε τί ἐστιν· **ἔλεος θέλω καὶ οὐ θυσίαν**, οὐκ ἂν κατεδικάσατε τοὺς

9 13 (65.): πορευθέντες δὲ μάθετε τί ἐστιν· ***ἔλεος θέλω καὶ οὐ θυσίαν*** *...*

Hos66

Mt 12,3 επειν. + αυτος ‖ Mk Lk: L Σ^m Φ **φ**⟨124-788⟩ σ517 Y Θ 157 *pm* *L*vl⟨k[e] lz⟩[ff²] *S*p¹h^m | **4** πως] ως ‖ Lk: W Eu (quando: *L*g²30) | θε. + επι Αβιαθαρ αρχιερεως ‖ Mk: 16 *pc* | ● εφαγον: ℵB 481 | ο] ● ους ‖ Mk Lk: *Rpl* Eu *L*' *S*h *C Geo* — *txt*: 𝔓^{70v} B **φ**⟨346⟩ D W *L*k[e] ff²qz vg¹ *S*' | εξ. ην] εξεστιν ‖ Mk Lk: C-33 28 σ1010-1675 *pc C*b¹ | μετ] συν ‖ Mk: 243 | ∼ μονοις(-ον) τ. ιερ. ‖ Lk: 544 (**σ**) Eu *L*'(k[e], *et* μον. + ποιειν ‖ 2) — *om* μον. ‖ Mk: λ1-22-1582 *pc La*

Mk 2,25 λεγ.] αποκριθεις ειπεν ‖ Lk: D (απ. + ο Ιησους: 1342) Θ *La* | αυτοις + ο Ιησους ‖ Lk: 700 **φ**124-*l*547 *L*r¹ vg¹ | ουδ.] ουδε τουτο ‖ Lk: W *L*e[k] bcff²iqt vg¹ | ανεγ. + εν ταις γραφαις ‖ 12 10 Mt 21 42: 28 | τι] ο ‖ Lk: 700 W — οτι: σ1082 | αυτου + οντες ‖ 26 Lk: D **26** *om* επι Α. αρχ. ‖ Mt Lk: D W 271 *pc L*e[k] abff²ir¹t *S*s[c] | ∼ και²—ουσ. ους—ιερ. ‖ Lk: Θ-565-700 D W *L*vl[k]⟨flqz⟩r¹ vg¹ *Arm* | τ. ιερ.] + μονοις ‖ Mt: Δ-33(αρχιερ.: 579 Φ) σ179-1391-1402 *pc l*21 *l*22 *L*δ vg² {*C*s²b'⟨1⟩}¹ — + μονον ‖ p: 1071 (∼ μ. τ. ι.: **φ**174 485) 14 {*Sj Geo*}¹ — μονοις τ. ι. ‖ p: **φ**-*l*547 *L*vl'[k]r¹g² vg⁹ Hi *Arm Aeth* — ● τους ιερεις ‖ Lk: ℵBL(τοις)-892 {}² — *txt*: *Rpl* (αρχιερ.: 28 **φ**230 σ692) *L*aff²i vg' *S* {*C*s²b³}² | *om* και³ ‖ Lk: D *L Sp*¹ | συν αυ.] μετ αυτου ‖ p 25: ΘΣ-565-700 D W *pc* | *om* ουσιν ‖ 25 Mt Lk: Θ-565-700 σ1675 W

Lk 6,3 προς—Ι.] ο Ι. ειπ. πρ. αυ. ‖ 5 31 7 40 *etc.*: C³X-579(*om* πρ. αυ.)-892-1241 544-1604 (πρ. αυ.] αυτοις: **λ**')-131-1582 **φ** σM-945-1223-(= **λ**': 1424-1606) A D(ελεγεν) K R Π *al l*33 *l*44 *l*47 *l*48 *l*183 *l*^{a1} *L*vl'(e *om* ο Ι.)r¹ *S*[sc]pj(κυριος Ι.) *C Arm*^{pc} — ● ο Ι. πρ. αυ. ειπ.: ℵLW 700 σ990-1207 Θ Ψ 157 *pc L*vg' *S*h — πρ. αυ. ο Ι. ειπ.: 33 28 111 *Arm*' — *txt*: 𝔓^{75v} *Rpl* (*om* ο: 𝔓^{4v} B) (∼ ειπ. πρ. αυ.: σ517 251) (*om* πρ. αυ.: *pc l*3) (*L*abl vg² = 517) *Arm* | ουδεποτε ‖ Mk: L D H | *om* τουτο ‖ p: L H *Arm Aeth* | ο²] τι ‖ p: **φ**1689 Ep *L*vl⟨e acq⟩r¹30 vg³ | οπ.] οτε ‖ Mt Mk: 𝔓⁴ ℌCX 544-1604 **λλ**⟨1278⟩ **φ**69-788 σ517-1424 D Δ Ψ **047** 157 *pc* | μετ αυ.] συν αυτω ‖ Mk 26: D | ● *om* οντ. ‖ Mt Mk: 𝔓⁴ ℌX 700 **λλ**⟨1278⟩ **φ**69-788 D Θ 157 *pc l*32 *S*[sc]pj^{abl⟨c⟩} **4** ως] πως ‖ p: ℵ^cLX-33-1241 544-700 **λ**-1278-1582 **φ** σ517-1424 R Θ 157 *l*5 | λαβ.] ● ελαβεν και: *Rpl L S*h {} — *om* ‖ **p**: ℵW-579-1241 544-700 **λ**-1278-1582 **φ** σ945-990-1223 D K Π **047** 157 *al l*24 *l*31 *l*44 *l*47 *l*50 *l*80 *l*150 *l*196 *l*303 *l*1627 *l*1642 *Sj*^{abc⟨1⟩} *Arm Aeth* — *txt*: 𝔓^{4v} ℌ'X Θ 251 {*S*[sc]p *C Δ*ad i^T l^{FG} md n E^{aB}} | τοις] ● και τ. ‖ Mk: *Rpl Sp*¹hj^{abl} *C*b *Geo* — *txt*: 𝔓^{4v} BLW 1604 **λ**⟨131⟩ Ψ *pc L S*[sc]p'j^c *Cs Arm Got* | αυτ. + ουσιν ‖ 3 Mk: **σ**⟨1675⟩-1188 *Sj* | εξε.] εξον ην (+ αυτω) ‖ Mt: (σM) D (*pc*) *L*e bcf(l)qr^{1.2}30 Am *S*[sc]p'(⁴)j^{acl⟨b⟩} *C*(s¹) (+ αυτοις: s⁴b) *Arm*(^{mu} + τινι) *Geo*^{⟨B⟩} *Aeth*(= *C*b) | μονοις τοις ιερευσιν ‖ p: D157 *pc* | ιερ. + Agr.↓: D

Mt12 7p *cf.* EEb frgm.6 (Ep haer. 30,16,5): ... ⁵ὡς τὸ παρ' αὐτοῖς εὐαγγέλιον καλούμενον περιέχει ὅτι 'ἦλθον καταλῦσαι τὰς θυσίας, καὶ ἐὰν μὴ παύσησθε τοῦ θύειν, οὐ παύσεταί ἀφ' ὑμῶν ἡ ὀργή'.

Matth	Mark	Luk
ἀναιτίους.	[27] καὶ ἔλεγεν αὐτοῖς·	[5] καὶ ἔλεγεν αὐτοῖς·
	τὸ σάββατον διὰ τὸν ἄνθρωπον ἐγένετο, καὶ οὐχ ὁ ἄνθρωπος διὰ τὸ σάββατον· [28] ὥστε	
[8] κύριος γάρ ἐστιν τοῦ σαββάτου ὁ υἱὸς τοῦ ἀνθρώπου.	κύριός ἐστιν ὁ υἱὸς τοῦ ἀνθρώπου καὶ τοῦ σαββάτου.	ὅτι κύριός ἐστιν ὁ υἱὸς τοῦ ἀνθρώπου καὶ τοῦ σαββάτου.

(70) *82.* Die Heilung der verdorrten Hand. *The Healing of the Man with the Withered Hand.*

Matth 12 9–14	**Mark 3** 1–6	**Luk 6** 6–11
[9] Καὶ μεταβὰς ἐκεῖθεν ἦλθεν εἰς τὴν συναγωγὴν αὐτῶν. [10] καὶ ἰδοὺ ἄνθρωπος χεῖρα ἔχων ξηράν· καὶ ἐπηρώτησαν αὐτὸν λέγοντες· εἰ ἔξεστιν τοῖς σάββασιν θεραπεύειν; ἵνα κατηγορήσωσιν αὐτοῦ.	[1] Καὶ εἰσῆλθεν πάλιν εἰς τὴν συναγωγήν. καὶ ἦν ἐκεῖ ἄνθρωπος ἐξηραμμένην ἔχων τὴν χεῖρα· [2] καὶ παρετήρουν αὐτὸν εἰ τοῖς σάββασιν θεραπεύσει αὐτόν, ἵνα κατηγορήσωσιν αὐτοῦ.	[6] Ἐγένετο δὲ ἐν ἑτέρῳ σαββάτῳ εἰσελθεῖν αὐτὸν εἰς τὴν συναγωγὴν καὶ διδάσκειν. καὶ ἦν ἄνθρωπος ἐκεῖ καὶ ἡ χεὶρ αὐτοῦ ἡ δεξιὰ ἦν ξηρά· [7] παρετηροῦντο δὲ οἱ γραμματεῖς καὶ οἱ Φαρισαῖοι εἰ ἐν τῷ σαββάτῳ θεραπεύει, ἵνα εὕρωσιν κατηγορεῖν αὐτοῦ. [8] αὐτὸς

Mt 12,8 του—αν.] ο—αν. και του σαβ. ‖ p: 33-892 Φ-1604 λ1-1582 ϕ788 σ7-349-517-945-1424 **047** 157 *al l*48 *l*49 *L*lz vg' — *txt* (*prm* και): *Rpl* (*pm*) Or *L*vl'[e](f vg^1) *S*'(h) *C*,f **10** ανθ.] α. ην εκει(*om*) ‖ p: *R* (X 28-565-700 λ118-209 ϕ174-230 G K S V Y Γ Π Ω *pl*) *al* *L*a(bc)fff^{2}g^1(^{2} vg^4)(*om* ιδου: vg^2 *S*p)h — ην εκ. α. (∼ α. ε. ‖ Lk) ‖ Mk: (Φ-1604) E (U) *pc* (*l*49) *L*k[e](*om* ην) ff^1(h)qz *Geo* — *txt*: ℵBC-892 W 372 Chr *L*l vg' *S*sc *C Aeth* | χει. εχ.] ● την χ. εχ. ‖ Mk: *Rpl* Chr^1 — εχ. την χ. ‖ Mk: ΝΣ *pc* Chr^1 *L*ff^1 Ar — *txt*: ℵBC-892 σ71-692 W | ● θεραπευσαι ‖ Lk14 3: ℵL D W 1574

Mk 2,27 και^1—^{28}ωστε] λεγω δε υμιν ‖ p: D *L*e[k] acff^{2}ir^1 **3,1** *om* παλ. ‖ Mt Lk: W *L*e[k] ci *C*s$^{2:6}$b^4 | ● *om* την^1 ‖ Mt: ℵB | εξη.] ξηραν ‖ **p** 3: D W(∼ εχ. εξ.) **2** παρετηρουντο ‖ Lk: C*Δ-579 ΘΣ-565-700 **λ** σ1149 A D W **074** 1342 *pc l*253 | τοις] ● εν τ. ‖ 2 23 Lk: ℵC Θ ϕ346-983 σM-827-1606 D H **047** 1241 | ● θεραπευει ‖ Lk: ℵΔ Σ W *pc* | *om* αυτον^2 ‖ Lk Mt: D W 1354 *L* *S*p^1 *C*b^2

Lk 6,5 ∼ 6-10.5 *cf. ad* 4: D Mcn | ● *om* οτι ‖ Mk: 𝔓^{4v} ℵ*BW-579 700 **λ**⟨118⟩-1582-2193 σ954 157 872 *l*32 *S*[sc]j *Arm Aeth* | ο—σαβ.] ● του σαβ. ο υι. τ. αν. ‖ Mt: 𝔓^4 ℵBW *S*[sc]pj *C*(*prm* και: sb')^7
6 6] και εισελθοντος αυτου παλιν εις την συναγωγην σαββατω εν η ην ανθρωπος ξηραν εχων την χειρα ‖ Mk Mt: D | εισε.] ελθειν ‖ Mt: 1093 1515 | ∼ εκει αν. ‖ Mk: *Rpl* (D) *L* *S*[sc],j — *om* εκει: *Aeth* — *txt*: 𝔓^4 𝔥 1071-1604 **λ**-1582-2193 **σ**-1188 R 157 *pc* Cr *C* **7** παρετηρουν ‖ Mk: *Rpl* (-ουν τε οι γρ. ...: λ22 H 660) — *txt*: 𝔓^4 𝔥⟨ℵW-892⟩X 700-1604 λ1-131-1582-2193 ϕ69-230-788 σM-517 A D(*om* δε) R Δ Θ Π Ψ 157 *al* Cr | παρε. δε] και π.(+ δε) ‖ p: **ϕ** 2533 (*L*vg^1) *S*[sc]p | ● δε + αυτον ‖ 14 1 Mk: 𝔓^4 𝔥X 1071-1604 **ϕ**-174-230-*l*547 σ517-1424 D 157 *pc* Cr *S*[sc],j *C*' — *txt*: *Rpl* *L*,Te *C*b^3 | *om* εν ‖ p 6 2 14 3: 544 D K Π *pm* *L*vl⟨fr^2⟩r^{1v} vg^7 | θεραπευσει ‖ Mk: 𝔓^4 *Rpl* Cr *C* — *txt*: ℵLW-579 1604 A D Π Ψ *pc* | θε. + αυτον ‖ Mk: X-33 700-1071 **ϕ**-*l*547 σM *pc* *S*[sc]p^2 *C*s$^{4:5}$b^1 | ευρ. κατ.] κατηγορησωσιν ‖ p: Ψ 472 — ● ευρ. κατηγοριαν *cf.* Mt26 20 Mk14 55 Jo18 29.38: *Rpl* (∼: 892 2533) Cr *L*f(occasionem accusandi)r^1 *S*h^m *C*b'$^{\langle 1\rangle}$ *Arm* — *txt*: 𝔓^4 ℵ*BX-1241 28-1604 **λ**-22-1278-1582-2193 ϕ124-174 D(κατηγορησαι) S Θ Ω *pc* *L*' *S*'[sc],j *C*sb^3 | αυτ.] ● κατ αυτ. ‖ 23 14: LW-33-579-892 1071 ϕ124-174-1689 σ1424 F K R Π *al* *S*[sc]h^m *Arm*

Mt12 10p *cf.* EN frgm.10 (Hi Mt *ad* 12 13): In evangelio, quo utuntur Nazareni et Ebionitae, ... homo iste, qui aridam habet manum, caementarius scribitur, istiusmodi vocibus auxilium precans: Caementarius eram manibus victum quaeritans; precor te, Jesu, ut mihi restituas sanitatem, ne turpiter mendicem cibos.

Mk2 27f.p *cf.* Agr. (Cod. Evv. D *et* *L*d: Lk6 4 +): Τῇ αὐτῇ ἡμέρᾳ θεασάμενός τινα ἐργαζόμενον τῷ σαββάτῳ εἶπεν αὐτῷ· ἄνθρωπε, εἰ μὲν οἶδας τί ποιεῖς, μακάριος εἶ, εἰ δὲ μὴ οἶδας, ἐπικατάρατος καὶ παραβάτης εἶ τοῦ νόμου.

Matthew

^{11} ὁ δὲ εἶπεν αὐτοῖς· τίς ἔσται ἐξ ὑμῶν ἄνθρωπος ὃς ἕξει πρόβατον ἕν, καὶ ἐὰν ἐμπέσῃ τοῦτο τοῖς σάββασιν εἰς βόθυνον, οὐχὶ κρατήσει αὐτὸ καὶ ἐγερεῖ; ^{12} πόσῳ οὖν διαφέρει ἄνθρωπος προβάτου. ὥστε ἔξεστιν τοῖς σάββασιν καλῶς ποιεῖν. ^{13} τότε λέγει τῷ ἀνθρώπῳ· ἔκτεινόν σου τὴν

Mark

^{3} καὶ λέγει τῷ ἀνθρώπῳ τῷ τὴν ξηρὰν χεῖρα ἔχοντι· ἔγειρε εἰς τὸ μέσον. ^{4} καὶ λέγει αὐτοῖς· ἔξεστιν τοῖς σάββασιν ἀγαθοποιῆσαι ἢ κακοποιῆσαι, ψυχὴν σῶσαι ἢ ἀποκτεῖναι; οἱ δὲ ἐσιώπων. ^{5} καὶ περιβλεψάμενος αὐτοὺς μετ' ὀργῆς, συλλυπούμενος ἐπὶ τῇ πωρώσει τῆς καρδίας αὐτῶν, λέγει τῷ ἀνθρώπῳ· ἔκτεινον τὴν

14 5 (182.): καὶ πρὸς αὐτοὺς εἶπεν· τίνος ὑμῶν υἱὸς ἢ βοῦς εἰς φρέαρ πεσεῖται, καὶ οὐκ εὐθέως ἀνασπάσει αὐτὸν ἐν ἡμέρᾳ τοῦ σαββάτου;

Luke

δὲ ᾔδει τοὺς διαλογισμοὺς αὐτῶν, εἶπεν δὲ τῷ ἀνδρὶ τῷ ξηρὰν ἔχοντι τὴν χεῖρα· ἔγειρε καὶ στῆθι εἰς τὸ μέσον· καὶ ἀναστὰς ἔστη. ^{9} εἶπεν δὲ ὁ Ἰησοῦς πρὸς αὐτούς· ἐπερωτῶ ὑμᾶς τί ἔξεστιν τῷ σαββάτῳ ἀγαθοποιῆσαι ἢ κακοποιῆσαι, ψυχὴν σῶσαι ἢ ἀπολέσαι; ^{10} καὶ περιβλεψάμενος πάντας αὐτοὺς εἶπεν αὐτῷ· ἔκτεινον τὴν

13 15 (177.): ἀπεκρίθη δὲ αὐτῷ ὁ κύριος καὶ εἶπεν· ὑποκριταί, ἕκαστος ὑμῶν τῷ σαββάτῳ οὐ λύει τὸν βοῦν αὐτοῦ ἢ τὸν ὄνον ἀπὸ τῆς φάτνης καὶ ἀπαγαγὼν ποτίζει;

14 3f. (182.): καὶ ἀποκριθεὶς ὁ Ἰησοῦς εἶπεν πρὸς τοὺς νομικοὺς καὶ Φαρισαίους λέγων· ἔξεστιν τῷ σαββάτῳ θεραπεῦσαι ἢ οὔ; ^{4} οἱ δὲ ἡσύχασαν...

Mt 12,11 εστιν ‖ 7$_9$: 33-892 544 φ828 σ349-517 D Θ 157 *pc* Chr *Lk*[e] fq — *om* ‖ Lk4.5 17$_7$: CL(*om* ανθ.)X φ124-346-788-983 σ267 *pc* *L*abcff$^{1.2}$g^{1}h *C* **12** ποσω + μαλλον (*om* ουν) ‖ Lk12$_{24}$ Mt7$_{11}$: 33 **φ** (**σ**)-659-1402 Θ *pc l*48 (*l*49 *l*184) *L*⟨k[e] ff^1⟩ *Δ*ad l | καλο ποιειν ‖ Lk9: **φ**⟨124-788⟩ σ349 *pc* **13** ∼ τ. χ. σου ‖ Lk: *Rpl* — *txt*: ℌ NΣ λ1-1582 **φ** **σ**-659 Θ 157 *pc l*49 *l*184

Mk 3,3 ξη.] ● εξηραμμενην ‖ 1: *Rpl* — *txt*: ℌ⟨579⟩C* Θ-565 σ1675 W 1342 372 | την ξ. χ. εχ.] εξηραμμενην (ξ.) εχ. τ. χ. ‖ 1Lk: *Rpl*(33 σ1675 372 1342) *S*' — ● τ. χ. εχ. ξ. (εξη.) ‖ Mt10: BL-892 (28)-565 (φ124-*l*547) *L*a *S*j — εχ. τ. χ. ξ. (εξη.): (D) W (*pc*) *L*' *S*h — *txt*: ℵCD Θ | εγει. + και(*om*) στηθι ‖ Lk: D 372 *L*(e[k] cf *Arm*) *Geo*(^{1} *om* εγ. και)$^{2.ch}$ *Aeth* **4** αυτ.] προς αυτους ‖ Lk: D *L*vl⟨e[k] g^{2}lz⟩r^1 vg^1 | αυτ. + τι ‖ Lk9: 700 **λ**-22 σ115-179-954 E *pc* — + ει ‖ Mt12$_{10}$: *L*g^{2}30 vg^5 | τοις] εν τ. ‖ Lk6f.: Θ-28-565 **φ**-*l*547 σ115-1402 A D E *pc l*253 *L*30 | αγαθ.] ● αγαθον(*prm* τι) ποι.: ℵ (D) W | κακ.] ου ‖ 12$_{14}$p Lk3: W | αποκ.] απολεσαι ‖ Lk9: LΔ-579-892 Θ-28-565-700 **λ**-22 φ124-828-*l*547 σ349-517 W **047** 1342 *al* Vic^A *L*, Au *S*s[c]pj *C*s$^{1:6}$ | *om* οι—εσιω. ‖ Lk9: 4 273 *C*s$^{1:8}$ **5** λεγ.] ειπεν ‖ Lk: 579 *L*cff^{2}q vg^2 | την χ.] ● τ. χ. σου ‖ Lk: *Rpl* {*L S*,j *C*} — σου τ. χ. ‖ Mt: φ13(+ σου)-346-828 σ1675 713 1342 {} — *txt*: B Φ-544 σM-27-1194-1424 E S U V Γ Π^c **0135**

Lk 6,8 ηδει ... δε^2] γινωσκων ‖ 5$_{22}$: D {*L*bf *S*[sc]p^3} — ειδως ‖ 9$_{47}$ Mk12$_{15}$ Mt9$_4$: σ1424 {} — ιδων: **σ**⟨517⟩ | ειπ.] λεγει ‖ Mk: D *L*e c *Arm* — ειπ. δε] και ειπ. ‖ Mk: *Rpl* Cr *L*' *S*[sc]p$^{⟨3⟩}$hj — *om* δε: D σ517 *C*b'(^{1} + ουν) — *txt*: 𝔓^4 ℌX 700-1604 **λ**-1582-2193 **φ**⟨124-346⟩ Θ 157 *pc L*a *C*sb^2 | ανδ.] ανθρωπω ‖ 6p Mt13 Mk5: *Rpl* (D *om* τω αν.) *S*h — *txt*: ℌ⟨W-892⟩ 700 **λ** *pc* Cr *S*[sc]p | ξη.] εξηραμμενην ‖ Mk1: 544 1071 φ*l*547(ξηραμμ.) σM-517-1010-1424 K Π *al l*32 — την ξη. ‖ Mk: ℵ A | και^2] ● ο δε: *Rpl S*h *C*s — *txt*: 𝔓^4 ℌX 700 **λ**-1582-2193 **σ**-1188 D Θ Ψ 157 *pc* Cr *L S*[sc]pj *C*b **9** επερωτησω ‖ Mk11$_{29}$p: *Rpl* (ερω-: **λ**⟨131⟩-2193 σ692 872) *L*vl'r^1 vg^2 *S*[sc] *C*sb^1 — *txt*: 𝔓^4 ℵBLW λ1582 *L*e flr^{2}z vg' *S*j *C*b' *Aeth* | *om* επερ. υμ. ‖ Mk: 1574 *L*vg^1 | τι] ● ει ‖ Mt12$_{10}$ 19$_3$p: 𝔓^4 ℌ⟨33⟩ D 157 Cr *L*' *S*j^1 *C* — *txt*: *Rpl L*qr^1 *S*[sc],j^{abc} | τοις σαββασιν ‖ Mt Mk: *Rpl L*afr$^{1.2}$ vg^1 Mcn *S*h *C*sb^5 — *txt*: 𝔓^4 ℌ⟨33⟩ D Cr *L*' *S*[sc]p *C*b | απολ.] αποκτειναι ‖ Mk: *Rpl* (*om* ψυ.—απολ.: 33) *L*e *S*h^t — *txt*: 𝔓^4 ℌ'X 1071-1604 **λ**-22-1278-1582 **φ** D Ψ 157 *pc L*' *S*[sc]ph^{m}j *C* | απολ. + οι δε εσιωπων ‖ 4 Mk: Λ φ124-174-230-346-*l*547 σ945-954-1010-1207-1223-1293 D *al L*vg^1 *C*b^7 **10** *om* παντ. ‖ Mk: φ983-1689 1555 | αυτους + μετ οργης ‖ Mk: **φ** 157 {} — ● + εν οργη ‖ Mk: X Λ-1071-1604 **λ**-22-1278-1582-2193 φ230-*l*547 D Θ {*L*vl'⟨e⟩(esse intra = in ira?: a)r^1 vg^1 *S*hj^{abc} *Arm Aeth*} — *txt*: 𝔓^4 *Rpl L*f vg' *S*[sc]pj^1 *C* | ειπ.] λεγει ‖ p: D | αυτω] τω ανθρωπω ‖ p: ℵL WX-33 1071-1604 **λ**-1582 **φ** D 157 *al L*(+ εκεινω: e c) *S*[sc]ph^{m}j^{a1} *C*b *Arm*^{pc}

Matth	Mark	Luk
χεῖρα. καὶ ἐξέτεινεν, καὶ ἀπεκατεστάθη ὑγιὴς ὡς ἡ ἄλλη. [14] ἐξελθόντες δὲ οἱ Φαρισαῖοι συμβούλιον ἔλαβον κατ' αὐτοῦ, ὅπως αὐτὸν ἀπολέσωσιν.	χεῖρα. καὶ ἐξέτεινεν, καὶ ἀπεκατεστάθη ἡ χεὶρ αὐτοῦ. [6] καὶ ἐξελθόντες οἱ Φαρισαῖοι εὐθὺς μετὰ τῶν Ἡρῳδιανῶν συμβούλιον ἐδίδουν κατ' αὐτοῦ, ὅπως αὐτὸν ἀπολέσωσιν.	χεῖρά σου. ὁ δὲ ἐποίησεν, καὶ ἀποκατεστάθη ἡ χεὶρ αὐτοῦ. [11] αὐτοὶ δὲ ἐπλήσθησαν ἀνοίας, καὶ διελάλουν πρὸς ἀλλήλους τί ἂν ποιήσαιεν τῷ Ἰησοῦ.

(72) *83.* Berufung der zwölf Apostel. *The Call of the Twelve.* **Luk 6** 12–16 *85.*

85.

[12] Ἐγένετο δὲ ἐν ταῖς ἡμέραις ταύταις ἐξελθεῖν αὐτὸν εἰς τὸ ὄρος προσεύξασθαι, καὶ ἦν διανυκτερεύων ἐν τῇ προσευχῇ τοῦ θεοῦ. [13] καὶ ὅτε ἐγένετο ἡμέρα, προσεφώνησεν τοὺς μαθητὰς αὐτοῦ, καὶ ἐκλεξάμενος ἀπ' αὐτῶν δώδεκα, οὓς καὶ ἀποστόλους ὠνόμασεν, [14] Σίμωνα, ὃν καὶ ὠνόμασεν Πέτρον, καὶ Ἀνδρέαν τὸν ἀδελφὸν αὐτοῦ καὶ Ἰάκωβον καὶ Ἰωάννην καὶ Φίλιππον καὶ Βαρθολομαῖον [15] καὶ Μαθθαῖον καὶ Θωμᾶν καὶ Ἰάκωβον Ἁλφαίου καὶ Σίμωνα τὸν καλούμενον ζηλωτὴν [16] καὶ Ἰούδαν Ἰακώβου καὶ Ἰούδαν Ισκαριωθ, ὅς ἐγένετο προδότης.

Mt 12,13 απεκατεστη ‖ Mk 8 25: Φ (απο-: λ1-1582) σ1424 U Π *l*48 | απεκ. + η χειρ αυτου ‖ p: **λ**⟨1⟩ ϕ983-1689 σ1293-1424 *pc l*184 | *om* ως η αλλη ‖ p: ℵ-892 | *om* υγιης ‖ p: *l*184 *L*abcff$^{1.2}$g^{1}h Hil *S*scp **14** εξε. δε] και εξε. ‖ Mk: **σ**⟨1675⟩-659 D *Lk*[e] abfff$^{1.2v}$g^{1}h *S*scp | κατ. αυτ.] *om* ‖ 22 15: 245 — κατα του Ιησου ‖ 27 1: *Lz*

Mk 3,5 απεκατεστη ‖ 8 25: C^{v} | *om* η. χ αυτ. ‖ Mt: 544 *pc Ss*[c]j | αυτου + υγιης(*om*) ως η αλλη ‖ Mt: *Rpl L*(abcg^{2})30 (*Ss*[c]j) — + ευθεως: D *L*ff^{2}ir^{1} vg^{1} — *txt*: ℌ⟨L-892⟩C* ΘΣΦ-28-565 **λ**⟨131⟩-22 A K P W Π *al L' S' C* **6** *om* ευθ. ‖ Mt: L 1604 σ267-827 D W 157 *pc L*bcff^{2}g$^{1.2}$iq30 vg^{4} *Cs*$^{1:7}$ *Geo*$^{2.ch}$ *Aeth* | εδ.] ελαβον ‖ Mt: σ267 *S*p {*Cs*} — ● εποιησαν ‖ 15 1: ℵCΔ-892^{m} Θ-1071 σ827 *pc C*b' — εποιουν ‖ ←: *Rpl* (-ντο: W; ποιουντες: D) *L S*h *Arm* — *txt*: BL 28-565-700 **ϕ** *C*b^{3} {}

Lk 6,10 ο δε] και ‖ p: W **σ**⟨954⟩-1188 D 713 *L S*[sc],j$^{abc⟨l⟩}$ | εποι.] εξετεινεν ‖ **p**: ℵWX 1071-1604 **λ**-1582-2193 **ϕ**⟨124⟩ σ517-1424 D 157 *pc l*1642 *L S*[sc]ph^{m}j^{1} *C*(+ αυτην) — + ουτως ‖ 9 15: ϕ*l*547 σ990-1207 K Π *pm l*13 *l*14 *l*17 *l*32 *l*80 *l*^{al} *S*h^{-}j^{abc} | - εσταθη] -εστη ‖ Mk 8 25: ℵ* **λ**-1582-2193 ϕ*l*547 *pc* | αυτου + υγιης ως η αλλη ‖ Mt: *Rpl* (ωσει: 28 *pc*; ∼ ως η αλ. υγ.: 892) + ως(+ και) η αλλη ‖ Mt: X 1604 (**λ**)-22-1278-(1582) **ϕ**174-788 σ990-1010-1223 A (D) K Q U Δ Θ Π Ψ **047** 157 *pc L*bc(*prm* και εγενετο)qr^{2}(fr^{1} vg^{2})^{1} *S*[sc], j — + υγιης ‖ Mt: W-579 — *txt*: 𝔓^{4} ℵBL-33 *pc L' C* | *cf. ad* 65 *init.* **11** διελ.] ελαλουν ‖ Act 26 31: 𝔓^{4} 544 σ990-1207 K U Π Ψ 157 *mu* — συνελαλουν ‖ 4 36: 33 — διελογιζοντο ‖ 20 14: D {*Cs*} | τι—l.] πως απολεσωσιν αυτον ‖ p: D | τι] το τι ‖ 19 48: Θ 157 **12** εξε. αυτ.] εξηλθεν ‖ 2 1 Mk 1 35 1 42 6 Mt 26 30: *Rpl L'*[a] *C*b — *txt* (*om* αυτ.): 𝔓$^{4.75}$ ℵBLW(X)-33-579-(1241) 1604 A D Ψ 157 (213) *pc Le* r^{1v} *Cs*$^{6:7}$ **13** προσ.] εφωνησεν ‖ Mk 9 35: **λ**-22-1582-2193 D 157 872 Eu {*Le* az vg$^{⟨3⟩}$} — εκαλεσεν ‖ Mt 4 21 p: 579 {} | δωδ.] τους δ. ‖ 9 1 p: 1047 *C*b **14** Σι. *prm* πρωτον ‖ Mt: D *Lr*^{1} | και Ια.] Ια. ‖ Mt: *Rpl* Bas^{1} Eu *L' S*h *Cs*^{3}b' — *txt*: 𝔓$^{4.75v}$ ℌ⟨892⟩ 544 **ϕ**-230 σ945-1207-1223 D K Δ Π 157 *al* Bas^{1} *L*abcr$^{1.2}$ *S' Cs*^{4}b^{1} | ∼ Ιω. ... Ια. ‖ 9 28 Act: *L*blr^{1} | Ιω. + τον αδελφον αυτου ους επωνομασεν· Βοανη Ργες ο εστιν· υιοι βροντης ‖ Mk: D — τ. αδ. αυτ. ‖ p: *L*ff^{2} *C*$^{2:7}$b^{6} — + τους υιους του Ζεβεδαιου ‖ 5 10 Mt 26 37 Mk 10 35: *Ss*[c] | και Φι.] Φι. ‖ Mt Act: *Rpl* Bas *L' S*h *Cs*$^{3(+2?)}$b' — *txt*: 𝔓$^{4.75v}$ ℌ⟨892-1241⟩ 1071 D 157 *pc* Eu *L*abcl *S' Cs*^{3}b^{3} **15** και Μα.] Μα. *cf.* Mt Act: *Rpl* (Δ *om* και^{1}—Θω.) *L' S*h *Cs*^{3}b^{3} — *txt*: 𝔓^{4} ℵBLW-1241 1071 **ϕ**⟨69-124⟩ D 161 Bas Eu *L*abcff^{2}lq *S' Cs*$^{3(+1?)}$b' | ∼ Θω. ... Μα. ‖ Mt: X 213 *Lz* vg^{5} | Θω. + τον επικαλουμενον Διδυμον ‖ Jo 11 16 *etc.*: D | και Ια.] ● Ια. ‖ Mt Act: *Rpl* Bas *L' S*h *Cs*^{3}b^{5} — *txt*: 𝔓^{4} ℵL-33-1241 700 **ϕ**⟨124⟩ D *pc L*abcff^{2}l vg^{1} *S' Cs*^{3}b' | Ια. + τον του ‖ Mk Mt: *Rpl* Bas — *txt*: 𝔓^{4} ℌ⟨892⟩ 700 **λ**-1582-2193 **ϕ**⟨124⟩ *pc Arm* | *om* καλ. ‖ Act: σ954 1093 **16** *om* και^{1} *cf.* Mt Act: *Rpl* (*om* κ. Ιου. Ια.: Λ ∩?) *Le* fqr^{2} vg' *S*h — *txt*: 𝔓$^{4.75v}$ ℌ⟨33⟩ **ϕ**-230 σ1207 D F^{W} Q *pc* Bas *L*abcff^{2}lr^{1} vg^{2} *S' C* | Ισκαριωτην ‖ Mt: *Rpl* Bas Mcn^{Ep} *S*h *C*bs^{4}(^{6} *Arm'*: Σκα-) — *txt* (Σκα-): 𝔓$^{4.75v}$ ℵ*BL-33-579 (D)Mcn^{Ep} Or (*L'*)(Scariotha: c; Inscarioth: d; *om*: abr^{1}) vg^{1} *S'*(Skarjuta) *Arm*^{pc} | ος + και ‖ Mk Mt: *Rpl* Bas Or *S*h — *txt*: 𝔓^{75v} ℌ⟨33-1241⟩ *pc* Mcn *L S' C*

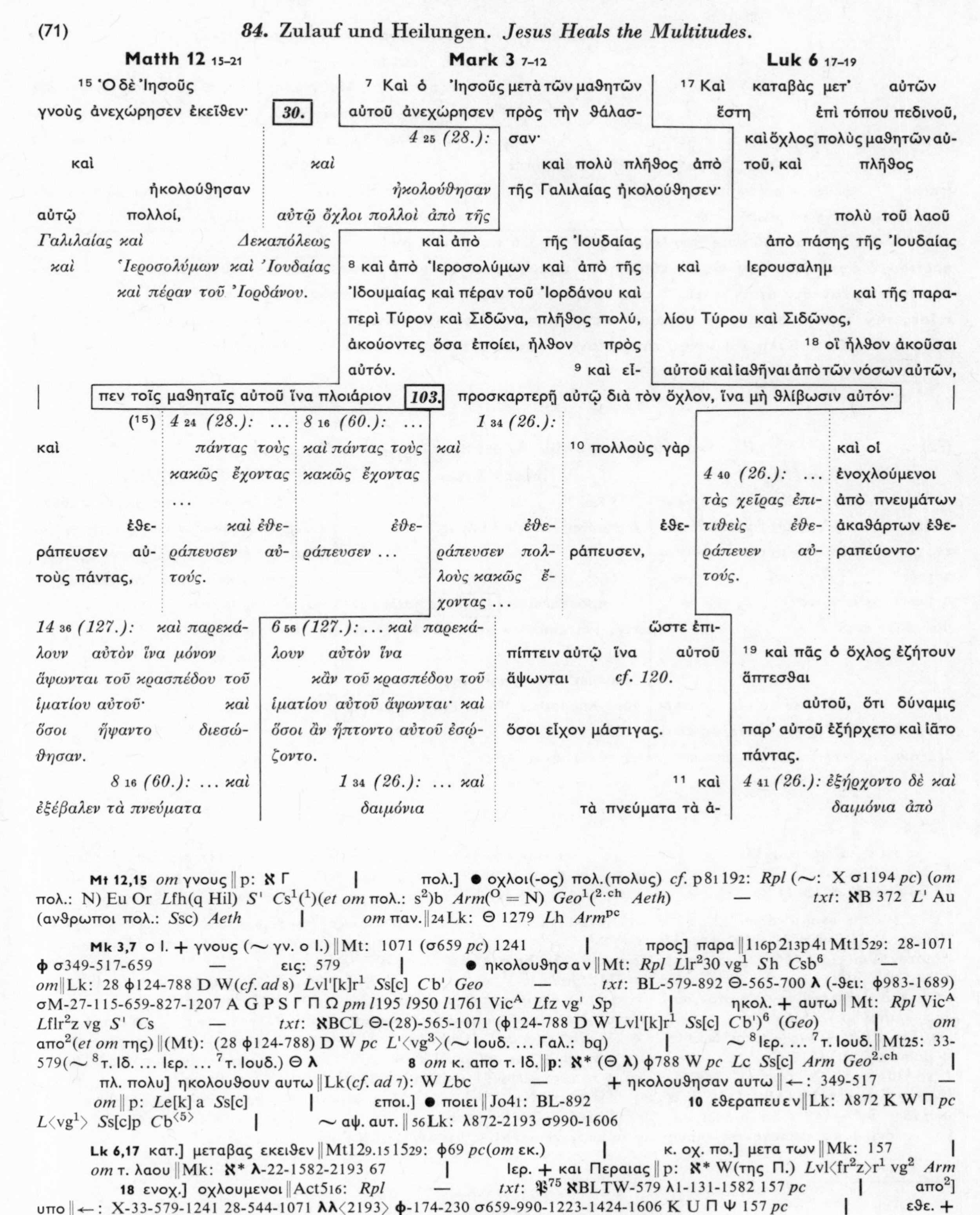

(71)

84. Zulauf und Heilungen. *Jesus Heals the Multitudes.*

Matth 12 15–21

15 Ὁ δὲ Ἰησοῦς γνοὺς ἀνεχώρησεν ἐκεῖθεν· [*30.*] καὶ ἠκολούθησαν αὐτῷ πολλοί,

4 25 (28.): καὶ ἠκολούθησαν αὐτῷ ὄχλοι πολλοὶ ἀπὸ τῆς Γαλιλαίας καὶ Δεκαπόλεως καὶ Ἱεροσολύμων καὶ Ἰουδαίας καὶ πέραν τοῦ Ἰορδάνου.

(15) καὶ ἐθεράπευσεν αὐτοὺς πάντας,

4 24 (28.): ... πάντας τοὺς κακῶς ἔχοντας ... καὶ ἐθεράπευσεν αὐτούς.

8 16 (60.): ... καὶ πάντας τοὺς κακῶς ἔχοντας ἐθεράπευσεν ...

14 36 (127.): καὶ παρεκάλουν αὐτὸν ἵνα μόνον ἅψωνται τοῦ κρασπέδου τοῦ ἱματίου αὐτοῦ· καὶ ὅσοι ἥψαντο διεσώθησαν.

8 16 (60.): ... καὶ ἐξέβαλεν τὰ πνεύματα

Mark 3 7–12

7 Καὶ ὁ Ἰησοῦς μετὰ τῶν μαθητῶν αὐτοῦ ἀνεχώρησεν πρὸς τὴν θάλασσαν· καὶ πολὺ πλῆθος ἀπὸ τῆς Γαλιλαίας ἠκολούθησεν· καὶ ἀπὸ τῆς Ἰουδαίας 8 καὶ ἀπὸ Ἱεροσολύμων καὶ ἀπὸ τῆς Ἰδουμαίας καὶ πέραν τοῦ Ἰορδάνου καὶ περὶ Τύρον καὶ Σιδῶνα, πλῆθος πολύ, ἀκούοντες ὅσα ἐποίει, ἦλθον πρὸς αὐτόν. 9 καὶ εἶπεν τοῖς μαθηταῖς αὐτοῦ ἵνα πλοιάριον [*103.*] προσκαρτερῇ αὐτῷ διὰ τὸν ὄχλον, ἵνα μὴ θλίβωσιν αὐτόν·

1 34 (26.): καὶ ἐθεράπευσεν πολλοὺς κακῶς ἔχοντας ...

10 πολλοὺς γὰρ ἐθεράπευσεν, ὥστε ἐπιπίπτειν αὐτῷ ἵνα αὐτοῦ ἅψωνται *cf. 120.* ὅσοι εἶχον μάστιγας.

6 56 (127.): ... καὶ παρεκάλουν αὐτὸν ἵνα κἂν τοῦ κρασπέδου τοῦ ἱματίου αὐτοῦ ἅψωνται· καὶ ὅσοι ἂν ἥπτοντο αὐτοῦ ἐσῴζοντο.

1 34 (26.): ... καὶ δαιμόνια

11 καὶ τὰ πνεύματα τὰ ἀ-

Luk 6 17–19

17 Καὶ καταβὰς μετ' αὐτῶν ἔστη ἐπὶ τόπου πεδινοῦ, καὶ ὄχλος πολὺς μαθητῶν αὐτοῦ, καὶ πλῆθος πολὺ τοῦ λαοῦ ἀπὸ πάσης τῆς Ἰουδαίας καὶ Ιερουσαλημ καὶ τῆς παραλίου Τύρου καὶ Σιδῶνος, 18 οἳ ἦλθον ἀκοῦσαι αὐτοῦ καὶ ἰαθῆναι ἀπὸ τῶν νόσων αὐτῶν,

4 40 (26.): ... τὰς χεῖρας ἐπιτιθεὶς ἐθεράπευεν αὐτούς.

καὶ οἱ ἐνοχλούμενοι ἀπὸ πνευμάτων ἀκαθάρτων ἐθεραπεύοντο· 19 καὶ πᾶς ὁ ὄχλος ἐζήτουν ἅπτεσθαι αὐτοῦ, ὅτι δύναμις παρ' αὐτοῦ ἐξήρχετο καὶ ἰᾶτο πάντας.

4 41 (26.): ἐξήρχοντο δὲ καὶ δαιμόνια ἀπὸ

Mt 12,15 *om* γνους ‖ p: ℵ Γ | πολ.] ● οχλοι(-ος) πολ.(πολυς) *cf.* p81 192: *Rpl* (∼: X σ1194 *pc*) (*om* πολ.: N) Eu Or *L*fh(q Hil) *S*' *C*s^1(1)(*et om* πολ.: s^2)b *Arm*(O = N) *Geo*^{1}(2.ch *Aeth*) — *txt*: ℵB 372 *L*' Au (ανθρωποι πολ.: *S*sc) *Aeth* | *om* παν. ‖ 24 Lk: Θ 1279 *L*h *Arm*^{pc}

Mk 3,7 ο Ι. + γνους (∼ γν. ο Ι.) ‖ Mt: 1071 (σ659 *pc*) 1241 | προς] παρα ‖ 1 16 p 2 13 p 4 1 Mt15 29: 28-1071 ϕ σ349-517-659 — εις: 579 | ● ηκολουθησαν ‖ Mt: *Rpl* *L*lr^{2}30 vg^1 *S*h *C*sb^6 — *om* ‖ Lk: 28 ϕ124-788 D W(*cf. ad* 8) *L*vl'[k]r^1 *S*s[c] *C*b' *Geo* — *txt*: BL-579-892 Θ-565-700 λ (-θει: ϕ983-1689) σM-27-115-659-827-1207 A G P S Γ Π Ω *pm* *l*195 *l*950 *l*1761 Vic^A *L*fz vg' *S*p | ηκολ. + αυτω ‖ Mt: *Rpl* Vic^A *L*flr^{2}z vg *S*' *C*s — *txt*: ℵBCL Θ-(28)-565-1071 (ϕ124-788 D W *L*vl'[k]r^1 *S*s[c] *C*b')^6 (*Geo*) | *om* απο^2(*et om* της) ‖ (Mt): (28 ϕ124-788) D W *pc* *L*'⟨vg^3⟩(∼ Ιουδ. ... Γαλ.: bq) | ∼ 8 Ιερ. ... 7 τ. Ιουδ. ‖ Mt25: 33-579(∼ 8 τ. Ιδ. ... Ιερ. ... 7 τ. Ιουδ.) Θ λ **8** *om* κ. απο τ. Ιδ. ‖ p: ℵ* (Θ λ) ϕ788 W *pc* *L*c *S*s[c] *Arm* *Geo*$^{2.ch}$ | πλ. πολυ] ηκολουθουν αυτω ‖ Lk(*cf. ad* 7): W *L*bc — + ηκολουθησαν αυτω ‖ ←: 349-517 — *om* ‖ p: *L*e[k]a *S*s[c] | εποι.] ● ποιει ‖ Jo4 1: BL-892 **10** εθεραπευεν ‖ Lk: λ872 K W Π *pc* *L*⟨vg^1⟩ *S*s[c]p *C*b$^{⟨5⟩}$ | ∼ αψ. αυτ. ‖ 56 Lk: λ872-2193 σ990-1606

Lk 6,17 κατ.] μεταβας εκειθεν ‖ Mt12 9.15 15 29: ϕ69 *pc*(*om* εκ.) | κ. οχ. πο.] μετα των ‖ Mk: 157 | *om* τ. λαου ‖ Mk: ℵ* λ-22-1582-2193 67 | Ιερ. + και Περαιας ‖ p: ℵ* W(της Π.) *L*vl⟨fr^{2}z⟩r^1 vg^2 *Arm* **18** ενοχ.] οχλουμενοι ‖ Act5 16: *Rpl* — *txt*: 𝔓^{75} ℵBLTW-579 λ1-131-1582 157 *pc* | απο^2] υπο ‖ ←: X-33-579-1241 28-544-1071 λλ⟨2193⟩ ϕ-174-230 σ659-990-1223-1424-1606 K U Π Ψ 157 *pc* | εθε. + απαντες ‖ 19 Mt: ϕ69 *L*l(*om* 19 πας) **19** παντας + αυτους ‖ Mt15: 579 *L*l(*om* παντ.)

Matth 12		Mark 3	
λόγῳ ...	*πολλὰ ἐξέβαλεν,*	κάθαρτα, ὅταν αὐτὸν ἐθεώρουν, προσέπιπτον αὐτῷ καὶ ἔκραζον λέγοντα ὅτι σὺ εἶ ὁ υἱὸς τοῦ θεοῦ.	*πολλῶν, κραυγάζοντα καὶ λέγοντα ὅτι σὺ εἶ ὁ υἱὸς τοῦ θεοῦ.*
[16] καὶ ἐπετίμησεν αὐτοῖς ἵνα μὴ φανερὸν αὐτὸν ποιήσωσιν· [17] ἵνα πληρωθῇ	*καὶ οὐκ ἤφιεν λαλεῖν τὰ δαιμόνια, ὅτι ᾔδεισαν αὐτόν.*	[12] καὶ πολλὰ ἐπετίμα αὐτοῖς ἵνα μὴ αὐτὸν φανερὸν ποιήσωσιν.	*καὶ ἐπιτιμῶν οὐκ εἴα αὐτὰ λαλεῖν, ὅτι ᾔδεισαν τὸν Χριστὸν αὐτὸν εἶναι.*

Is42 1–4 τὸ ῥηθὲν διὰ Ἠσαΐου τοῦ προφήτου λέγοντος· [18] **ἰδοὺ ὁ παῖς μου ὃν ᾑρέτισα, ὁ ἀγαπητός μου εἰς ὃν εὐδόκησεν ἡ ψυχή μου· θήσω τὸ πνεῦμά μου ἐπ' αὐτόν, καὶ κρίσιν τοῖς ἔθνεσιν ἀπαγγελεῖ.** [19] **οὐκ ἐρίσει οὐδὲ κραυγάσει, οὐδὲ ἀκούσει τις ἐν ταῖς πλατείαις τὴν φωνὴν αὐτοῦ.** [20] **κάλαμον συντετριμμένον οὐ κατεάξει καὶ λίνον τυφόμενον οὐ σβέσει, ἕως ἂν ἐκβάλῃ εἰς νῖκος τὴν κρίσιν.** [21] **καὶ τῷ ὀνόματι αὐτοῦ ἔθνη ἐλπιοῦσιν.**

(72) *85.* Berufung der zwölf Apostel. *The Call of the Twelve.*

10 1–4 (70.)	**Mark 3** 13–19	*6 12–16 (83.)*
5 1 (30.): Ἰδὼν δὲ τοὺς ὄχλους ἀνέβη εἰς τὸ ὄρος· καὶ καθίσαντος αὐτοῦ προσῆλθαν αὐτῷ οἱ μαθηταὶ αὐτοῦ. (10) [1] *καὶ*	[13] Καὶ ἀναβαίνει εἰς τὸ ὄρος,	[12] *Ἐγένετο δὲ ἐν ταῖς ἡμέραις ταύταις ἐξελθεῖν αὐτὸν εἰς τὸ ὄρος προσεύξασθαι, καὶ ἦν διανυκτερεύων ἐν τῇ προσευχῇ τοῦ θεοῦ.* [13] *καὶ ὅτε ἐγένετο ἡμέρα,*
προσκαλεσάμενος τοὺς δώδεκα μαθητὰς αὐτοῦ	καὶ προσκαλεῖται **122.** οὓς ἤθελεν αὐτός, καὶ ἀπῆλθον πρὸς αὐτόν. [14] καὶ ἐποίησεν δώδεκα ἵνα ὦσιν μετ' αὐτοῦ, καὶ ἵνα ἀποστέλλῃ αὐτοὺς κηρύσσειν	*προσεφώνησεν τοὺς μαθητὰς αὐτοῦ, καὶ ἐκλεξάμενος ἀπ' αὐτῶν δώδεκα, οὓς καὶ ἀποστόλους ὠνόμασεν,*
ἔδωκεν αὐτοῖς ἐξουσίαν πνευμάτων ἀκαθάρτων, ὥστε ἐκβάλλειν αὐτὰ καὶ θεραπεύειν πᾶσαν νόσον	[15] καὶ ἔχειν ἐξουσίαν ἐκβάλλειν τὰ δαιμόνια·	

Mt 12,16 επετιμα ‖Mk: Θ C^{2} ΝΣ σ517-659-1675 Chr | ∼ αυτον φαν. ‖Mk12: 892 *Lk*[e] ff^{1}h **17** δια] υπο ‖1 22 2 15 22 31: C*-33 λ1-1582 σ1424 D Eu — εν ω ‖17 5 3 17 Mk1 11: *Aeth* — εις ο: ϕ13-346-826-828 — *txt*: *Rpl* Eu **18** εις ον] ● ον: ℵ*B-892 σ115 244 Eu *Aeth* — εις ο: ϕ13-346-826-828 — *txt*: *Rpl* Eu

Mk 3,11 εκραυγαζον ‖Lk: σ27-71-349-692-1194 *pc* — ανεκραζε ‖1 23 p Lk8 28: 252 | ει + ο Χριστος ‖Lk: C Φ σM-7-1402 P *pc* *S*h^{+} *C*s$^{1:4}$b^{1} **12** 12] και επιτιμων ουκ εια αυτα λαλειν οτι ηδεισαν αυτον Χριστον ειναι ‖Lk: 565^{c} | *om* πολ. ‖Mt Lk: σ1424 W *Le*[k] bcff^{2}iqr^{1v}t vg^{1} | επετιμησεν ‖Mt: σ349-517 *C*b$^{\langle 6\rangle}$ | ∼ φαν. αυ. ‖Mt: *Rpl* — *txt*: 𝔊⟨L-579⟩C Θ-565 **λ ϕ** D W | ποιη. + οτι ηδεισαν τον Χριστον αυτον ειναι ‖Lk: C(*om* ειν.) Φ *pc* *La*(*om* τ. Χ. ... ειν.: bff^{2}g^{2}qt^{v} vg^{2}) **13** *om* και^{3}—αυτον ‖p: 255 *C*s$^{1:3}$b^{2} **14** εποι. + ους και αποστολους ωνομασεν ‖Lk: C*^{v} — ● δω. + ους—ων. ‖Lk: ℵBΔ(∼ ους—αυτου δω.) Θ-28 **ϕ** 238 *S*h^{m} (*om* και: *C*s^{2}b) *Aeth* — αυτου + ους—ων. ‖Lk: W(δω. + μαθητας ‖Mt) 1012 *Geo*^{1} — αυτους + και απ. ων. ‖Lk: Φ — *txt* (∼ ινα ωσ. δω.): *Rpl* (D *L*⟨e[k] bfq⟩) *S*' *C*s^{1} *Geo*^{2} | κη. + το ευαγγελιον ‖1 14 Mt4 23 9 35: D W *Le*[k] bfff^{2}iqr$^{1.2}$t vg^{11} **15** εχ.] εδωκεν αυτοις ‖6 6 Mt Lk9 1: D W *L*⟨e[k]aq⟩ *C*s^{2}(δωη)b^{5} | εξ. + θεραπευειν τας νοσους και ‖Mt Lk←: *Rpl* (*om* τας: Θ; ∼ εκβ. τ. δαι. κ. θε. τ. νο.: 700) *L* *S*(= 700) *C*b^{2} *Arm* — *txt*: 𝔊⟨33-579⟩C* 565 *C*' *Geo* | δαι. + και περιαγοντες κηρυσσειν το ευαγγελιον ‖Mt4 23 9 35: W *Le*[k](+ του θεου) acg^{2} vg^{5}

---

85. cf. EEb frgm.1 (*cf. ad 23.*)

καὶ πᾶσαν μαλακίαν. 2 τῶν δὲ δώδεκα ἀποστόλων τὰ ὀνόματά ἐστιν ταῦτα· πρῶτος

cf. 28.

16 καὶ ἐπέθηκεν ὄνομα τῷ

1 42: ... ὁ Ἰησοῦς εἶπεν· σὺ εἶ Σίμων ὁ υἱὸς Ἰωάννου, σὺ κληθήσῃ Κηφᾶς (ὃ ἑρμηνεύεται Πέτρος).

Matth	Mark	Luk	Act
Σίμων ὁ λεγόμενος Πέτρος καὶ	Σίμωνι Πέτρον· 17 καὶ	14 Σίμωνα, ὃν καὶ ὠνόμασεν Πέτρον, καὶ	**Act 1** 13: ... ὅ τε Πέτρος καὶ
Ἀνδρέας ὁ ἀδελφὸς αὐτοῦ,		Ἀνδρέαν τὸν ἀδελφὸν αὐτοῦ καὶ	
Ἰάκωβος ὁ τοῦ Ζεβεδαίου καὶ	Ἰάκωβον τὸν τοῦ Ζεβεδαίου καὶ	Ἰάκωβον καὶ	
Ἰωάννης ὁ ἀδελφὸς αὐτοῦ,	Ἰωάννην τὸν ἀδελφὸν τοῦ Ἰακώβου, καὶ ἐπέθηκεν αὐτοῖς ὀνόματα Βοανηργες, ὅ ἐστιν υἱοὶ βροντῆς· 18 καὶ	Ἰωάννην καὶ	Ἰωάννης καὶ Ἰάκωβος καὶ
	Ἀνδρέαν καὶ		Ἀνδρέας,
3 Φίλιππος καὶ	Φίλιππον καὶ	Φίλιππον καὶ	Φίλιππος καὶ Θωμᾶς,
Βαρθολομαῖος,	Βαρθολομαῖον καὶ	Βαρθολομαῖον 15 καὶ	Βαρθολομαῖος καὶ
Θωμᾶς καὶ			
Μαθθαῖος ὁ τελώνης,	Μαθθαῖον καὶ	Μαθθαῖον καὶ	Μαθθαῖος,
	Θωμᾶν καὶ	Θωμᾶν καὶ	
Ἰάκωβος ὁ τοῦ Ἁλφαίου καὶ	Ἰάκωβον τὸν τοῦ Ἁλφαίου καὶ	Ἰάκωβον Ἁλφαίου καὶ	Ἰάκωβος Ἁλφαίου καὶ
Θαδδαῖος,	Θαδδαῖον καὶ		
4 Σίμων ὁ Καναναῖος καὶ	Σίμωνα τὸν Καναναῖον 19 καὶ	Σίμωνα τὸν καλούμενον ζηλωτὴν 16 καὶ	Σίμων ὁ ζηλωτὴς καὶ
		Ἰούδαν Ἰακώβου καὶ	Ἰούδας Ἰακώβου.
Ἰούδας ὁ Ἰσκαριώτης ὁ καὶ παραδοὺς αὐτόν.	Ἰούδαν Ισκαριωθ, ὃς καὶ παρέδωκεν αὐτόν.	Ἰούδαν Ισκαριωθ, ὃς ἐγένετο προδότης.	

Mk 3,16 και] ● *prm* και εποιησεν τους δωδεκα ‖ 14: 𝔊⟨L-33-892⟩C* 565 1342(*om* τους) — *prm* πρωτον Σιμονα ‖ Mt: ϕ Cs^1 — *txt*: *Rpl* *L* *S* Cs^1b | ονοματα (*prm* αυτοις) ‖ 17 Mt: 892-(33-1241) Θ-(1071) *pc* (Lr^1) **17** 17-19] κοινως δε αυτους εκαλεσεν Βοανανη Ργε ο εστιν υιοι βροντης. ησαν δε ουτοι· Σιμων και Ανδρεας, Ιακωβος και Ιωαννης, Φιλιππος και Μαρθολομεος και Μαθθεος και Θωμας και Ιακωβος ο του Αλφαιου και Σιμων ο Κανανaιος και Ιουδας Ισκαριωτης ο και παραδους αυτον ‖ Mt: W (*sim.*: *Le*[k] bcq) | *om* τ. αδ. τ. Ια. ‖ Lk Act: 544 | του Ια.] αυτου ‖ Mt: 579-1241 ΘΣ-28 λ2193 ϕ69-983 σ1402 G 1342 *pc* Lg^2 vg^1 *Ss*[c] | ον.] ● ονομα ‖ 16: B 28 D *pc* $Sp^{\langle 1 \rangle}$ Cb^1 **18** Μα.] Λευιν ‖ 2 14 Lk 5 27: Or — + τον τε-λωνην ‖ Mt: Θ-565-700-1071 ϕ *pc* Sh^m | ∼ Θω. κ. Μα. ‖ Mt: 33 998 | Θα.] Λεββαιον *cf. ad* Mt 10 3: D Or $La^v(b)ff^2iqr^1$ — *om* και Θα. ‖ Lk Act: (W *Le*[k]) — Λευην: Or **19** Ισκαριωτην ‖ Mt: *Rpl* (W) (τον Ισ.: 700) (Σκα-: *Le*[k] cfr^2) *C* — *txt* (Σκα-): 𝔊C Θ-565 (D) 372 1342 Or ($L'\langle vg^2\rangle$) | παρ. αυ.] εγενετο προδοτης ‖ Lk: 76

Jo 1,42 ειπ.] περιπατουντι λεγει ‖ 1 36: 579 | Ιωαν.] Ιωνα ‖ Mt 16 17: *Rpl* Chr Cr Ep *L*cqz30 vg^9 *S*,j Cb^1 *Aeth* *Δ*a i^V p — Ιωαννα: 1241 Θ 2148 Lvg^1 *Δ*ad i^{T3} l md n' — *txt*: $𝔓^{66.75}$ 𝔊'⟨579-892⟩W^s Non *L*vl'⟨e⟩ vg^3 *C*' *Aeth* *Δ*i^{T2} me n^C

Act 1,13 ∼ Αν. ... Ια. ... Ιω. ‖ Mt Mk: E(= **08**) | ∼ Ια. ... Ιω. ‖ p: *Rpl* Chr Thy *S*hj *Arm* — *txt*: ℵABC-1175 D 61 1838 1891 1898 *pc* *L*,Au *Sp* *C* Arm^O | Φιλ.] και Φ. ‖ Mk Lk: 2138 *pc* *S*hj Cb^1 | Θω. + και ... Μα. + και ‖ Mk Lk: 2138 *S*hj Cb^1(*om* $και^2$) | Αλ.] ο του Αλ. ‖ Mt Mk: D 462 808 Sh^+

Die Feldrede. *The Sermon on the Plain.*

Luk 6 20–49

(73) *86.* Die Seligpreisungen. *The Beatitudes.* Luk 6 20–23

cf. 30.

5 3.6.4.11f. *(31.): μακάριοι οἱ πτωχοὶ τῷ πνεύματι, ὅτι αὐτῶν ἐστιν ἡ βασιλεία τῶν οὐρανῶν.* [6] *μακάριοι οἱ πεινῶντες καὶ διψῶντες τὴν δικαιοσύνην, ὅτι αὐτοὶ χορτασθήσονται.* [4] *μακάριοι οἱ* **πενθοῦντες**, *ὅτι αὐτοὶ* **παρακληθήσονται** *...* [11] *μακάριοί ἐστε ὅταν ὀνειδίσωσιν ὑμᾶς καὶ διώξωσιν καὶ εἴπωσιν πᾶν πονηρὸν καθ' ὑμῶν ἕνεκα ἐμοῦ.* [12] *χαίρετε καὶ ἀγαλλιᾶσθε, ὅτι ὁ μισθὸς ὑμῶν πολὺς ἐν τοῖς οὐρανοῖς· οὕτως γὰρ ἐδίωξαν τοὺς προφήτας τοὺς πρὸ ὑμῶν.*

Is61 2

[20] Καὶ αὐτὸς ἐπάρας τοὺς ὀφθαλμοὺς αὐτοῦ εἰς τοὺς μαθητὰς αὐτοῦ ἔλεγεν· μακάριοι οἱ πτωχοί, ὅτι ὑμετέρα ἐστὶν ἡ βασιλεία τοῦ θεοῦ. [21] μακάριοι οἱ πεινῶντες νῦν, ὅτι χορτασθήσεσθε. μακάριοι οἱ κλαίοντες νῦν, ὅτι γελάσετε. [22] μακάριοί ἐστε ὅταν μισήσωσιν ὑμᾶς οἱ ἄνθρωποι, καὶ ὅταν ἀφορίσωσιν ὑμᾶς καὶ ὀνειδίσωσιν καὶ ἐκβάλωσιν τὸ ὄνομα ὑμῶν ὡς πονηρὸν ἕνεκα τοῦ υἱοῦ τοῦ ἀνθρώπου. [23] χάρητε ἐν ἐκείνῃ τῇ ἡμέρᾳ καὶ σκιρτήσατε· ἰδοὺ γὰρ ὁ μισθὸς ὑμῶν πολὺς ἐν τῷ οὐρανῷ· κατὰ τὰ αὐτὰ γὰρ ἐποίουν τοῖς προφήταις οἱ πατέρες αὐτῶν.

16 2: ἀποσυναγώγους ποιήσουσιν ὑμᾶς·...

Lk 6,20 *om* αυτου^{1}‖Jo6 5: σ7-115-267 *L*⟨e⟩ Or | πτω. + τω(*prm* εν) πνευματι‖p: ℵ^{ca}(X)-33-579 544-1071-1604 **λ**-1582-2193 **ϕ**-174-*l*547 σ517-692-945-990-1223-1424 (Q) Θ *al* *L*acfr$^{1.2}$30 vg^{2} *S*j *C*b^{7} *Arm* | υμ.] αυτων‖**p**: W *L*ff^{2} Mcn^{Te} *S*s[c]j$^{b⟨a2.c⟩}$ *C*s^{1} | τ. θε.] των ουρανων‖**p**: X-1241 544 λ118-209-1582 ϕ69 **σ**⟨1675⟩-1188 157 *pc* *l*18 *l*19 *l*49 *L*cf vg^{1} Am Mcn$^{Te1:2}$ Or *S*s[c]j Af *C*sb^{4} **21** πειν. + και διψωντες (*et om* νυν^{1})‖**p**: 2533 *L*vl'⟨fr^{2}⟩ vg^{1}(^{1}) — + κ. διψ. την δικαιοσυνην (*et om* νυν^{1})‖p: *L*e (cl)r^{1} | χορτασθησονται (*prm* αυτοι)‖**p**: ℵ*X ϕ69 213 (237) *l*55 *L*(e bq)ff^{2}lr^{1} vg^{1} Am Mcn^{Te} *S*s[c] *C*s$^{1:6}$ *Arm*$^{⟨1⟩}$ *Aeth* | *om* μακ.^{2}—γελ.‖p: D | *om* νυν^{2}(*et* ^{1})‖p: 2145 Eu Or (*L*Mcn^{Te}) | γελασουσιν(-ονται)‖p: W (Ddy Eu Or) *L*e vg^{1} Mcn^{Te} *S*s[c] *C*s$^{2:5}$ *Arm*$^{⟨1⟩}$ *Aeth* **22** *om* οταν^{2}‖p: W *L*Cp *S*s[c]p *C* | *om* υμας^{2}‖p: 𝔓^{75v} σ267 D **23** χαρ.] χαιρετε‖p: 579(και χ.) σ517 — χαρησετε‖Jo16 22: 1071 | ημ.] ωρα‖Mt10 9: 579 *L*a *S*s[c] | ιδ. γαρ] οτι‖p: D *pc* *l*253 *L*Cp$^{1:5}$ *S*s[c]p | τοις ουρανοις‖ p: B-579 1071 **ϕ** ⟨124⟩-*l*547 σ1424 R *pc* *l*184 Bas *L*e f Cp | τα αυ.] ταυτα‖p: *Rpl* Or *L*'(ομοιως: a; ουτως: d) Mcn^{Te} *S* *C*s — *txt*: 𝔓^{75} 𝔥⟨ℵL-579⟩XΞ 1071 D Q Ψ *pc* Mcn^{Ep} *L*e c *Arm* | τους προφητας‖ p: σ517-954 243

Lk6 20p *cf.* ETh^{II} 54 (*transl.*): *Λέγει Ἰησοῦς· μακάριοι οἱ πτωχοί, ὅτι ὑμετέρα ἐστὶν ἡ βασιλεία τῶν οὐρανῶν.*

Lk6 21p *cf.* ETh^{II} 69b (*cf. ad 31.* Mt5 6)

Lk6 22f.p *cf.* ETh^{II} 69a (*cf. ad 31.* Mt5 8.10)

Lk6 22p *cf.* ETh^{II} 68 (*cf. ad 31.* Mt5 11)

(74)

87. Die Weherufe. *The Woes.* Luk 6 24–26

[24] Πλὴν οὐαὶ ὑμῖν τοῖς πλουσίοις, ὅτι ἀπέχετε τὴν παράκλησιν ὑμῶν. [25] οὐαὶ ὑμῖν, οἱ ἐμπεπλησμένοι νῦν, ὅτι πεινάσετε. οὐαί, οἱ γελῶντες νῦν, ὅτι πενθήσετε καὶ κλαύσετε. [26] οὐαὶ ὅταν καλῶς ὑμᾶς εἴπωσιν πάντες οἱ ἄνθρωποι· κατὰ τὰ αὐτὰ γὰρ ἐποίουν τοῖς ψευδοπροφήταις οἱ πατέρες αὐτῶν.

(75)

88. Von der Feindesliebe. *On Loving One's Enemies.* Luk 6 27–36

5 39 f. 42. 44–48 (38. 39.): [44] *ἐγὼ δὲ λέγω ὑμῖν, ἀγαπᾶτε τοὺς ἐχθροὺς ὑμῶν*

καὶ προσεύχεσθε ὑπὲρ τῶν διωκόντων ὑμᾶς·... [39] *... ὅστις σε ῥαπίσει εἰς τὴν δεξιάν σου σιαγόνα, στρέψον αὐτῷ καὶ τὴν ἄλλην·* [40] *καὶ τῷ θέλοντί σοι κριθῆναι καὶ τὸν χιτῶνά σου λαβεῖν, ἄφες αὐτῷ καὶ τὸ ἱμάτιον· ...* [42] *τῷ αἰτοῦντί σε δός, καὶ τὸν θέλοντα ἀπὸ σοῦ δανείσασθαι μὴ ἀποστραφῇς. 7 12 (51.): Πάντα οὖν ὅσα ἐὰν θέλητε ἵνα ποιῶσιν ὑμῖν οἱ ἄνθρωποι, οὕτως καὶ ὑμεῖς ποιεῖτε αὐτοῖς· ...*

(5) [46] *ἐὰν γὰρ ἀγαπήσητε τοὺς ἀγαπῶντας ὑμᾶς, τίνα μισθὸν ἔχετε; οὐχὶ καὶ οἱ τελῶναι τὸ αὐτὸ ποιοῦσιν;* [47] *καὶ ἐὰν ἀσπάσησθε τοὺς*

[27] Ἀλλὰ ὑμῖν λέγω τοῖς ἀκούουσιν· ἀγαπᾶτε τοὺς ἐχθροὺς ὑμῶν, καλῶς ποιεῖτε τοῖς μισοῦσιν ὑμᾶς, [28] εὐλογεῖτε τοὺς καταρωμένους ὑμᾶς, προσεύχεσθε περὶ τῶν ἐπηρεαζόντων ὑμᾶς. [29] τῷ τύπτοντί σε ἐπὶ τὴν σιαγόνα πάρεχε καὶ τὴν ἄλλην, καὶ ἀπὸ τοῦ αἴροντός σου τὸ ἱμάτιον καὶ τὸν χιτῶνα μὴ κωλύσῃς. [30] παντὶ αἰτοῦντί σε δίδου, καὶ ἀπὸ τοῦ αἴροντος τὰ σὰ μὴ ἀπαίτει. [31] καὶ καθὼς θέλετε ἵνα ποιῶσιν ὑμῖν οἱ ἄνθρωποι, ποιεῖτε αὐτοῖς ὁμοίως. [32] καὶ εἰ ἀγαπᾶτε τοὺς ἀγαπῶντας ὑμᾶς, ποία ὑμῖν χάρις ἐστίν; καὶ γὰρ οἱ ἁμαρτωλοὶ τοὺς ἀγαπῶντας αὐτοὺς ἀγαπῶσιν. [33] καὶ ἐὰν ἀγαθοποιῆτε

Lk 6,25 *om* νυν^{1}‖Mt56: *Rpl* Bas^{1} *L'* Ir Pau^{N} *Sp* — *txt*: 𝔓^{75} 𝔥TXΞ Λ-700-1071-1604 **λ**-22-1582 **φ**-230 σ517-1194-1424-1606 Q R Δ Θ 157 *al* Bas^{1} Ores *Lf* *S*(*om* ουαι^{1}—πειν.: s[c])h^{+} *C* *Arm* *Aeth* | *om* νυν^{2}‖Mt 54: 270 *Lb* Hil | *om* και κλαυ.‖←: X 213 *Lvg*^{1} — *om* πεν. και: σ1424 **26** ● ∼ καλ. ειπ. υμ.‖622Mt511: 𝔥⟨BW-1241⟩ 544-1071 φ983-1689 σ1606 A H Ψ *pc* Bas Mac *Lff*^{2}lr^{1}z30 vg^{1} Ir — ∼ υμ. καλ. ειπ.: 𝔓^{75v} B *Le* q vg^{2} Mcn^{Te} — *txt* (ουαι + υμιν *et om* υμας): *Rpl* (φ69) Chr *L*acf(b vg^{1})' | τα αυ.] ταυτα‖Mt512: *Rpl* *L'*(ομοιως: a) Ir Mcn^{Te} *S* *C*sb(γαρ + και) — *txt*: 𝔓^{75} ℵ^{a}BWXΞ-33-892-1241 σ267-517-1424 D K R Π 157(*om* τα) *pc* *Le* c | *om* οι πα. αυ.‖←: 𝔓^{75v} B-1241 700(*om* οι πατ.) *Ss*[c] *Cs* **27** ∼ λε. υμιν‖p: σ267 *pc* | υμων + και‖p: W *L*30 Mcn^{Te} *Ss*[c]p *Cb*^{5} **28** προσευ.] και πρ.‖p: 251 *pc* *Lg*^{2} Mcn^{Te} *Ss*[c]p | περι] υπερ‖**p**: *Rpl* Or — *txt*: 𝔓^{75} 𝔥⟨33-892⟩Ξ 700 | επη.] διωκοντων‖p: *C* | υμ.^{2} + και διωκοντων υμας‖p: φ⟨346⟩ **29** επι] ● εις‖p: ℵ*W-892 700 D Θ Cl Mcn Or — *txt*: 𝔓^{75} *Rpl* Bas | την^{1} + δεξιαν‖p: ℵ*-579-1241 28-1604 φ983-1689 **σ**-1188 E 106(∼ σ. δ.) *l*49 Bas Or *Lr*^{2} *Cb*^{2} | παρε.] στρεψον αυτω(*om*)‖p: **φ**'(983) {*L*vlg^{2}r^{1}30 vg^{4} *Ss*[c]p} *Cs* {*Aeth*} — + αυτω‖p: 579 28 σ1424 D *pc* *l*49 {} *L*Am *Aeth* | ∼ το ιμ. σου‖p: σ1424 *l*184 | ∼ χι. ... ιμ.‖p: Cl$^{1:3}$ *L*bdff^{2}lqr^{1} vg^{1} *Cs* | χι. + σου‖p: 700 φ124(∼ σου τ. χ.) A Γ *pc* *Ss*[c](και^{3}] η)ph *C* **30** παν. + δε τω‖p1248: *Rpl* Bas *L'*(*om* 30: q) *Sh*$^{+}$ *Cb'* — + τω‖p: L-1241 **λ** σ1424 K R Π **047** 157 *al* Brn(ℵ^{c}) CAp Cl — *txt*: 𝔓^{75v} ℵBW-579-892 *Lbff*^{2}lr^{1}z vg^{3}(+ γαρ) *S'* *Csb*^{1} | διδ.] δος‖p: 33 **31** ● ανθ.(αυτοις) + και υμεις‖p: *Rpl* *L*(b)cf vg' *S*(p)hj *C*(b)(ποι. + κ. υμ.: s *Arm*) *Geo* — + υμεις‖p: φ174 *pc* *Le* (q) — + καλως, ουτως(*om*) κ. υμ.‖p: *Lr*^{2} (vg^{2}) — *txt* (+ καλως‖27): 𝔓^{75} B-579-1241 700 Cl Ir *Lff*^{2}l(r^{1})z PsAu Ir (*Ss*[c]) *Δ*l^{F} | ∼ ομ. ποι. αυ.‖p: 892 *Lar*^{1} *Ss*[c]pj — *om* ομ.‖p: D 248 Cl *Le*(∼ αυ. ποι. Ir Mcn^{Te} *Cs* **32** ει] εαν‖p33p: 238 1047 | αμ. + τουτο ποιουσιν‖p: D (^{32}⌒^{33}αμ.: **λ**⟨131⟩ 74) **33** ● και^{1} + γαρ‖32Mt46a: 𝔓^{75} ℵ*B 700 — *txt*: *Rpl* *L* *S*,j *C* *Geo*(εαν + ουν) | εαν] ει‖32: σ945

---

88. cf. Did12-5 (*cf. ad 38.*)

Lk627f.p *cf.* Ev. apocr. (POxy 1224 fol. 2r° col. 1; *cf. ad 39.* Mt544)

Lk630.34f. *cf.* ETh^{II} 95 (*cf. ad 38.* Mt542)

ἀδελφοὺς ὑμῶν μόνον, τί περισσὸν ποιεῖτε; οὐχὶ καὶ οἱ ἐθνικοὶ οὕτως ποιοῦσιν;

τοὺς ἀγαθοποιοῦντας ὑμᾶς, ποία ὑμῖν χάρις ἐστίν; καὶ οἱ ἁμαρτωλοὶ τὸ αὐτὸ ποιοῦσιν. [34] καὶ ἐὰν δανείσητε παρ' ὧν ἐλπίζετε λαβεῖν, ποία ὑμῖν χάρις ἐστίν; καὶ ἁμαρτωλοὶ ἁμαρτωλοῖς δανείζουσιν ἵνα ἀπολάβωσιν τὰ ἴσα. [35] πλὴν ἀγαπᾶτε τοὺς ἐχθροὺς ὑμῶν καὶ ἀγαθοποιεῖτε καὶ δανείζετε μηδὲν ἀπελπίζοντες· καὶ ἔσται ὁ μισθὸς ὑμῶν πολύς, καὶ ἔσεσθε υἱοὶ ὑψίστου, ὅτι αὐτὸς χρηστός ἐστιν ἐπὶ τοὺς ἀχαρίστους καὶ πονηρούς.

... [45] ὅπως γένησθε υἱοὶ τοῦ πατρὸς ὑμῶν τοῦ ἐν οὐρανοῖς, ὅτι τὸν ἥλιον αὐτοῦ ἀνατέλλει ἐπὶ πονηροὺς καὶ ἀγαθοὺς καὶ βρέχει ἐπὶ δικαίους καὶ ἀδίκους ... [48] **ἔσεσθε** οὖν ὑμεῖς **τέλειοι** ὡς ὁ πατὴρ ὑμῶν ὁ οὐράνιος τέλειός ἐστιν.

Dt18 13

[36] γίνεσθε οἰκτίρμονες, καθὼς καὶ ὁ πατὴρ ὑμῶν οἰκτίρμων ἐστίν.

(76)

89. Vom Richten. *On Judging.* Luk 6 37–42

7 1-5 (48.): Μὴ κρίνετε, ἵνα μὴ κριθῆτε·

[2] ἐν ᾧ γὰρ κρίματι κρίνετε κριθήσεσθε, καὶ ἐν ᾧ μέτρῳ μετρεῖτε μετρηθήσεται ὑμῖν. 15 14 (128.): ἄφετε αὐτούς· τυφλοί εἰσιν ὁδηγοὶ τυφλῶν· τυφλὸς δὲ τυφλὸν ἐὰν ὁδηγῇ, ἀμφότεροι πεσοῦνται εἰς βόθυνον. 10 24 f. (71.): οὐκ ἔστιν μαθητὴς ὑπὲρ

[48.]

[37] Καὶ μὴ κρίνετε, καὶ οὐ μὴ κριθῆτε· καὶ μὴ καταδικάζετε, καὶ οὐ μὴ καταδικασθῆτε. ἀπολύετε, καὶ ἀπολυθήσεσθε· [38] δίδοτε, καὶ δοθήσεται ὑμῖν· μέτρον καλὸν πεπιεσμένον σεσαλευμένον ὑπερεκχυννόμενον δώσουσιν εἰς τὸν κόλπον ὑμῶν· τῷ γὰρ αὐτῷ μέτρῳ ᾧ μετρεῖτε ἀντιμετρηθήσεται ὑμῖν. [39] εἶπεν δὲ καὶ παραβολὴν αὐτοῖς· μήτι δύναται τυφλὸς τυφλὸν ὁδηγεῖν; οὐχὶ ἀμφότεροι εἰς βόθυνον ἐμπεσοῦνται; [40] οὐκ ἔστιν μαθητὴς ὑπὲρ

13 16: Αμην αμην λέγω ὑμῖν, οὐκ ἔστιν

15 20: ... ἐγὼ εἶπον ὑμῖν· οὐκ ἔστιν

Lk 6,33 το αυ.] τουτο‖p: D 998 (αυτο: Λ *pc*) *L*⟨e r[1]⟩ *S*s[c]pj *C*s(ουτως: b) **35** πλην + λεγω υμιν‖27p: σ1194 U *l*1231 *l*1623 *L*e(*om* υμ.) | πολ. + εν τοις(-ω) ουρανοις(-ω)‖23p: ℵ[a] 1071(*om* τοις) σ-1188 A 213 *L*(al) cr[1]z vg[1] *S*s[c] | υψ.] του υψ.‖p: λ-22-1582 φ⟨13⟩-230 *l*80 *l*333 *l*1599 *l*1634 Bas | *om* αυτ.‖p: 998 *L*vg[1] *C*b[3] **36** γιν. + ουν‖p: *Rpl* Bas *L*fr[1]z vg Cp[1] Or *S*,j — *txt*: 𝔓[45.75] ℵBLWΞ-33 700 λλ⟨22⟩ D 157 *pc* Cr Mac Or *L*vl' Cp[1] *S*s[c] *C* *Arm*(και γιν.) *Geo* | καθ. και] ως‖p: 700 Ath Chr Cl[1] {*L*cd vg[2] Mcn[Te] *S*s[c]j Ath *C*b(οτι: s)} — ● καθως‖p: 𝔓[75v] 𝔥⟨33-1241⟩Ξ 1071 λ-1582-2193 Ψ *pc* Cl[1] {} — ως και‖p: Ddy Iu Or — *txt*: *Rpl* Bas Cr *L*' Cp *S*' | υμ. + ο ουρανιος‖p: ℵ[a]-579 φ-174-*l*547 σ954 *pc* Ath[1:4] Bas[1:2] PsBas Chr[1:4] Cl Cr Iu[1:2] Mac *L*Or — + ο εν τοις ουρανοις‖Mt6 1.9 7 11 *etc.*: *l*184 Ath[1:4] Chr[1:4] *C*b[1] **37** *om* και[1]‖p: 700 λ-1582-2193 σ1194 D 157 *pc* *L* *S*s[c]p *C* | και[2] ου] ινα‖p: W Λ A D Ψ *pc* *L*e acfr[2]30 vg[2] Am Mcn[Te] *S*s[c] *C*sb[6] *Geo* *Aeth* | *om* και[3]—καταδικασθ.‖p: Γ | και[4] ου] ινα‖p: W* D Bas *L*e acff[2]r[2] vg[1] Mcn[Te] *S*s[c] *C*s *Geo* *Aeth* | *om* απολ. κ. απολ.‖**p**: σ1424-1675 *L*l **38** τω ... αυτω μετρω ω] ● ω ... με.‖p: 𝔥'(υμιν[1]∩[2]: 579)Ξ λ-1582-2193 D 872 *L*e c {} *Aeth* — τω ... με. ω‖p: X σ1223 *pc* {*C*} — *txt*: 𝔓[45.75v] *Rpl* *L*' Te *S*h *Arm* | *om* γαρ‖Mk4 24: 𝔓[45] 700 φ13-69-543-788-826-828 Θ 565 *l*34 *L*abff[2]lqr[1]z Te *S*s[c] *C*s[1:7] *Arm* *Geo*[1](2 και τω) | αντιμετρ.] μετρ.‖←: B-33 28 P *pc* *L*e bq **39** ∼ εμπ. εις βο.‖p: φ⟨124⟩ 161 *C*ETh[II]↓ *Aeth* | εμπεσ.] πεσ.‖p: *Rpl* *L*' — *om*: 𝔓[75v] — *txt*: 𝔥⟨ℵ-33⟩ 700 λ-1582 φ⟨124-828⟩ σ71-115-1424 D P R[v] Θ **047** 157 *pc* *L*a

---

Lk6 37f.p *cf.* 1Cl13 2: οὕτως γὰρ εἶπεν· ἐλεᾶτε ἵνα ἐλεηθῆτε· ἀφίετε, ἵνα ἀφεθῇ ὑμῖν· ὡς ποιεῖτε, οὕτω ποιηθήσεται ὑμῖν· ὡς δίδοτε, οὕτως δοθήσεται ὑμῖν· ὡς κρίνετε, οὕτως κριθήσεσθε· ὡς χρηστεύεσθε, οὕτως χρηστευθήσεται ὑμῖν· ᾧ μέτρῳ μετρεῖτε, ἐν αὐτῷ μετρηθήσεται ὑμῖν.

Lk6 39p *cf.* ETh[II] 34 (*transl.*): *Λέγει Ἰησοῦς· τυφλὸς ἐὰν ὁδηγῇ τυφλόν, ἀμφότεροι καταπεσοῦνται εἰς βόθυνον.*

τὸν διδάσκαλον οὐδὲ δοῦλος ὑπὲρ τὸν κύριον αὐτοῦ. 25 ἀρκετὸν τῷ μαθητῇ ἵνα γένηται ὡς ὁ διδάσκαλος αὐτοῦ, καὶ ὁ δοῦλος ὡς ὁ κύριος αὐτοῦ . . . (7) 3 τί δὲ βλέπεις τὸ κάρφος τὸ ἐν τῷ ὀφθαλμῷ τοῦ ἀδελφοῦ σου, τὴν δὲ ἐν τῷ σῷ ὀφθαλμῷ δοκὸν οὐ κατανοεῖς; 4 ἢ πῶς ἐρεῖς τῷ ἀδελφῷ σου· ἄφες ἐκβάλω τὸ κάρφος ἀπὸ τοῦ ὀφθαλμοῦ σου, καὶ ἰδοὺ ἡ δοκὸς ἐν τῷ ὀφθαλμῷ σου; 5 ὑποκριτά, ἔκβαλε πρῶτον τὴν δοκὸν ἐκ τοῦ ὀφθαλμοῦ σου, καὶ τότε διαβλέψεις ἐκβαλεῖν τὸ κάρφος ἐκ τοῦ ὀφθαλμοῦ τοῦ ἀδελφοῦ σου.

τὸν διδάσκαλον· κατηρτισμένος δὲ πᾶς ἔσται ὡς ὁ διδάσκαλος αὐτοῦ.

δοῦλος μείζων τοῦ κυρίου αὐτοῦ, οὐδὲ ἀπόστολος μείζων τοῦ πέμψαντος αὐτόν.

δοῦλος μείζων τοῦ κυρίου αὐτοῦ. εἰ ἐμὲ ἐδίωξαν, καὶ ὑμᾶς διώξουσιν· εἰ τὸν λόγον μου ἐτήρησαν, καὶ τὸν ὑμέτερον τηρήσουσιν.

41 τί δὲ βλέπεις τὸ κάρφος τὸ ἐν τῷ ὀφθαλμῷ τοῦ ἀδελφοῦ σου, τὴν δὲ δοκὸν τὴν ἐν τῷ ἰδίῳ ὀφθαλμῷ οὐ κατανοεῖς; 42 πῶς δύνασαι λέγειν τῷ ἀδελφῷ σου· ἀδελφε, ἄφες ἐκβάλω τὸ κάρφος τὸ ἐν τῷ ὀφθαλμῷ σου, αὐτὸς τὴν ἐν τῷ ὀφθαλμῷ σου δοκὸν οὐ βλέπων; ὑποκριτά, ἔκβαλε πρῶτον τὴν δοκὸν ἐκ τοῦ ὀφθαλμοῦ σου, καὶ τότε διαβλέψεις τὸ κάρφος τὸ ἐν τῷ ὀφθαλμῷ τοῦ ἀδελφοῦ σου ἐκβαλεῖν.

(77) 90. Baum und Frucht. *The Tree and Its Fruit.* Luk 6 43–46

7 18.16 (53.): 18 οὐ δύναται δένδρον ἀγαθὸν καρποὺς πονηροὺς ποιεῖν, οὐδὲ δένδρον σαπρὸν καρποὺς

12 33 (99.): ἢ ποιήσατε τὸ δένδρον καλὸν καὶ τὸν καρπὸν αὐτοῦ καλόν, ἢ ποιήσατε τὸ δένδρον σαπρὸν καὶ τὸν καρπὸν

43 Οὐ γάρ ἐστιν δένδρον καλὸν ποιοῦν καρπὸν σαπρόν, οὐδὲ πάλιν δένδρον σαπρὸν ποιοῦν καρπὸν

Lk 6,40 διδασκαλον + αυτου ‖ 40b Jo: *Rpl* Cr *S*⟨s[c]⟩ *C* — + αυτου ουδε δουλος υπερ τον κυριον αυτου ‖ p: 579(*om* αυτ.[1]) 1071(ως ο κυριος) σ1194(του κυριου) — *txt*: 𝔓75 𝔥'⟨1241⟩ΧΞ 700 **λ**-1582-2193 **ϕ**-230 D Θ *pc* Or *L*,Ir Mcn[Te] *Geo* | *om* κατη.—αυτ.(αυτου[1] ⌒ [2]?) ‖ p: Λ Γ *l*48 *S*s[c] | *om* δε ‖ p: Ξ Δ *C*sb[4] *Arm* | αυτ. + και ο δουλος ως ο κυριος αυτου ‖ p: σ1194 **41** δοκ.—οφ.[2]] εν τω σω οφ. δοκ. ‖ p: **ϕ** P 161 1047(∼ ου κατ. δοκ.) | ιδ. οφ.] σω οφ. ‖ **p**: (**ϕ**) D (P 161) *L* — σω οφ. τω ιδ. ‖ p: (1047) — ιδ. σου οφ.: 348 1279 **42** πως] ● η πως ‖ p: 𝔓75v *Rpl* *L*vl'r[1] *S*' *C*s[7]b'([1] *om* πως) — και πως: 251 *pc* *L*vg' *Aeth* — πως δε: ℵ-579-892 — *txt*: B *L*e ff[2] vg[1] *S*s[c] *C*s[1]b[1] | *om* αδελφε ‖ p: D **047** 157 *L*vl⟨f⟩r[1] *C*b[3] | το[2] εν τ. οφ. σου] εκ(απο) του οφθαλμου σ. ‖ p: (33) D 472 *L*⟨f⟩ *S*s[c]p *C* | αυτος την ... βλε.] την δε ... κατανοεις ‖ 41 p: 1241 | αυτος—βλε]. και ιδου η δοκος εν τω σω οφ. υποκειται(*om*) ‖ (p): D vl'⟨f⟩(e d) *S*s[c](p) | ∼ εκβαλειν το καρ.[2]—σου ‖ p: *Rpl* ETh[II]26↓ *S*h *C*s[1]b[2] — εκβ. το κ.[2] εκ του οφθαλμου του αδ. σου ‖ p: D *pc* *L* *S*' *C*s[7]b' ETh[II]26↓ — το κ.[2] εκβ. το εν—σου: L λ1-131-1582-2193 — *txt*: 𝔓75 𝔥'⟨ℵ-33⟩ 700 **ϕ** *pc* **43** καρπους σαπρους ... καρπους(-ον) καλους(-ον) ‖ Mt 18: D *L*'(ff[2]lr[1]z vg⟨1⟩) | *om* παλ. ‖ ←: *Rpl* *L*' *S* *C*s — *txt*: 𝔓75 𝔥⟨33⟩Ξ 1071 **λ**[118]⟨209⟩-1582-2193 **ϕ** 157 *pc* *L*bq vg[1] *C*b *Arm*

Jo 15,20 αυτ. + ουδε αποστολος μειζων του πεμψαντος αυτον ‖ 13 16: 254 *l*55 *L*a(*et* + ει ταυτα οιδατε, μακαριοι εστε εαν ποιητε αυτα. ου περι παντων υμων λεγω· εγω οιδα τινας εξελεξαμην ‖ 13 17f.) *C*p[1:4]

Lk 6 41f.p *cf.* ETh[II] 26 (*cf. ad 48.* Mt 7 3-5)

Lk 6 43p *cf.?* ETh[II] 43 (*transl.*): ... *ἀλλὰ ὑμεῖς ἐγενήθητε ὡς οἱ Ἰουδαῖοι ὅτι ἀγαπῶσιν τὸ δένδρον, μισοῦσιν (δὲ) τὸν καρπὸν αὐτοῦ· καὶ ἀγαπῶσιν τὸν καρπόν, μισοῦσιν (δὲ) τὸ δένδρον.*

καλοὺς ποιεῖν ... αὐτοῦ σαπρόν· 16 ἀπὸ τῶν καρπῶν ἐκ γὰρ τοῦ καρποῦ τὸ αὐτῶν ἐπιγνώσεσθε αὐτούς. μήτι δένδρον γινώσκεται. συλλέγουσιν ἀπὸ ἀκανθῶν σταφυλὰς ἢ ἀπὸ τριβόλων σῦκα; 12 35.34 (99.): 35 ὁ ἀγαθὸς ἄνθρωπος ἐκ τοῦ ἀγαθοῦ θησαυροῦ ἐκβάλλει ἀγαθά, καὶ ὁ πονηρὸς ἄνθρωπος ἐκ τοῦ πονηροῦ θησαυροῦ ἐκβάλλει πονηρά ... 34 ... ἐκ γὰρ τοῦ περισσεύματος τῆς καρδίας τὸ στόμα λαλεῖ. 7 21 (54.): Οὐ πᾶς ὁ λέγων μοι· κύριε κύριε, εἰσελεύσεται εἰς τὴν βασιλείαν τῶν οὐρανῶν, ἀλλ' ὁ ποιῶν τὸ θέλημα τοῦ πατρός μου τοῦ ἐν τοῖς οὐρανοῖς.

καλόν. 44 ἕκαστον γὰρ δένδρον ἐκ τοῦ ἰδίου καρποῦ γινώσκεται· οὐ γὰρ ἐξ ἀκανθῶν συλλέγουσιν σῦκα, οὐδὲ ἐκ βάτου σταφυλὴν τρυγῶσιν. 45 ὁ ἀγαθὸς ἄνθρωπος ἐκ τοῦ ἀγαθοῦ θησαυροῦ τῆς καρδίας αὐτοῦ προφέρει τὸ ἀγαθόν, καὶ ὁ πονηρὸς ἐκ τοῦ πονηροῦ προφέρει τὸ πονηρόν· ἐκ γὰρ περισσεύματος καρδίας λαλεῖ τὸ στόμα αὐτοῦ. 46 τί δέ με καλεῖτε· κύριε κύριε, καὶ οὐ ποιεῖτε ἃ λέγω;

(78)

91. Schlußgleichnisse. *Hearers and Doers of the Word.*

7 24–27 (55.):

24 Πᾶς οὖν ὅστις ἀκούει μου τοὺς λόγους τούτους καὶ ποιεῖ αὐτούς, ὁμοιωθήσεται ἀνδρὶ φρονίμῳ, ὅστις ᾠκοδόμησεν αὐτοῦ τὴν οἰκίαν ἐπὶ τὴν πέτραν. 25 καὶ κατέβη ἡ βροχὴ καὶ ἦλθαν οἱ ποταμοὶ καὶ ἔπνευσαν οἱ ἄνεμοι καὶ προσέπεσαν τῇ οἰκίᾳ ἐκείνῃ, καὶ οὐκ ἔπεσεν·

Luk 6 47–49

47 Πᾶς ὁ ἐρχόμενος πρός με καὶ ἀκούων μου τῶν λόγων καὶ ποιῶν αὐτούς, ὑποδείξω ὑμῖν τίνι ἐστὶν ὅμοιος. 48 ὅμοιός ἐστιν ἀνθρώπῳ οἰκοδομοῦντι οἰκίαν, ὃς ἔσκαψεν καὶ ἐβάθυνεν καὶ ἔθηκεν θεμέλιον ἐπὶ τὴν πέτραν· πλημύρης δὲ γενομένης προσέρρηξεν ὁ ποταμὸς τῇ οἰκίᾳ ἐκείνῃ, καὶ οὐκ ἴσχυσεν σα-

Lk 6,44 *om* ιδιου‖Mt33: σ1223 V *pc* | σταφυλας‖p: L ϕ⟨124⟩ Ψ *Le* cl(συκα] στα.: b) *S* **45** ● *om* αυτ.¹ ‖45bp: 𝔓75 ℵB-579 Ddy *Cs*¹ᵛ — *txt*: *Rpl*(∼ αυ. της κ.: D) Or *L*'(*om* της κ.: ff²) *S Cs*⁷b | το αγ.] αγαθον‖p: W D 1187 {*S C*} — αγαθα‖p: Or(τα αγ.) *Le* c vg⁵ {} | πονηρος + αθρωπος‖**p**: *Rpl L*' *S Cs*¹ — *txt*: 𝔓75 ℵ*BL-579-892 700 λ1-131-1582-2193 D Ψ 130 *L*abl vg¹ *Cs*⁷b | πονηρου + θησαυρου‖**p**: ϕ69-788 *L*bz vg' *C*' — + θησ. της καρδιας αυτου‖45a: *Rpl L*vl'g²r¹30 vg² *S C*b¹ *Geo*(*om* του πο. θη.) — *txt*: 𝔓75 ℌ⟨33⟩Ξ 700 λ1-131-1582-2193 D *L*aff²l vg⁷ *C*b⁵ *Arm* | το πον.] πονηρον‖p: W *l*184 {*S Cs*} — πονηρα‖p: 80 1038 *L*blqz30 vg⁴ {} | περισ.] του πε.‖**p**: *Rpl* — *txt*: 𝔓75v ℵBWXΞ-33 Λ-700-1604 λ22 ϕ174 σ7-267-990-1223 A D E H K S V Y Δ Π Ψ *al* | καρδ.²] της κ.‖**p**: *Rpl* (+ αυτου: 1093) — *txt*: 𝔓75v ℵBWΞ 700-1604 ϕ174 σ7-267 A D Y Ψ *pc* | ∼ το στ. αυτου(*om*) λαλ.‖p: ℵ(C-579) *L*vl'⟨e⟩(r¹z vg')³ | *om* αυτ.²‖p: C-579-892 700 λ1278 ϕ983-1689 **σ**⟨954⟩-7-267-659 Fᵂ *pc L*r¹z vg⟨³⟩ *S*s[c](τ. στο.] τα χειλη: p) *Cs*²:⁷b⁷ *Arm* (*Aeth*) **46** καλ.] λεγετε‖p: 28 D Cl Ddy *L*Gau Ir Or **47** τ. λογ.] τους λογους (+ τουτους)‖p: C(X) 1604 σM Fᵂ Ψ 157 (213) *pc* (*L*bq *S*p¹) | *om* υποδ.—ομ.‖p: 1093 | εσται‖p: 1241 1604 Δ *pc* **48** ανθ.] ανδρι φρονιμω‖p: 28 *L*r¹ — οικοδεσποτη‖Mt13 52 20 1: ϕ543 | οικιαν] την οι.‖p: **047** *C*b¹(+ αυτου) — τ. οι. αυτου επι την πετραν‖p: 157

Lk 6 44f.p *cf.* ETh^II 45 (*transl.*): *Λέγει Ἰησοῦς· οὐ τρυγῶσιν ἐξ ἀκανθῶν σταφυλὰς οὐδὲ συλλέγουσιν σῦκα ἀπὸ τριβόλων· οὐ γ[ὰρ] ποιοῦσιν καρπόν. (ὁ) ἀγαθὸς ἄνθρωπος προφέρει (τὸ) ἀγαθὸν ἐκ τοῦ θησαυροῦ αὐτοῦ (καὶ ὁ) κακὸς ἄνθρωπος προφέρει πονηρὰ ἐκ τοῦ θησαυροῦ αὐτοῦ τοῦ κακοῦ, ὅς ἐστιν ἐν τῇ καρδίᾳ αὐτοῦ, καὶ λαλεῖ πονηρά· ἐκ γὰρ τοῦ περισσεύματος τῆς καρδίας προφέρει πονηρά.*

Lk 6 46p *cf.* EN frgm. 6 (*cf. ad 54.* Mt 7 21ff.)

cf. Ev. apocr. (PEg 2 fol. 1r°): ... 13 ὁ δὲ Ἰη(σοῦς) εἰδὼς [τὴν δι]άνοιαν [αὐτ]ῶν ἐμβρειμ[ησάμενος] εἶπεν α[ὐτοῖς]· 'τί με καλεῖτ[ε τῷ στό]ματι ὑμ[ῶν δι]δάσκαλον μ[ὴ ἀκού]οντες ὃ [λ]έγω ... (*cf. ad 220.*)

τεθεμελίωτο γὰρ ἐπὶ τὴν πέτραν.	λεῦσαι αὐτὴν διὰ τὸ καλῶς ᾠκοδομῆσθαι αὐτήν.
26 καὶ πᾶς ὁ ἀκούων μου τοὺς λόγους τούτους καὶ μὴ ποιῶν αὐτοὺς ὁμοιωθήσεται ἀνδρὶ μωρῷ, ὅστις ᾠκοδόμησεν αὐτοῦ τὴν οἰκίαν ἐπὶ τὴν ἄμμον. 27 καὶ κατέβη ἡ βροχὴ καὶ ἦλθον οἱ ποταμοὶ καὶ ἔπνευσαν οἱ ἄνεμοι καὶ προσέκοψαν τῇ οἰκίᾳ ἐκείνῃ, καὶ ἔπεσεν, καὶ ἦν ἡ πτῶσις αὐτῆς μεγάλη.	49 ὁ δὲ ἀκούσας καὶ μὴ ποιήσας ὅμοιός ἐστιν ἀνθρώπῳ οἰκοδομήσαντι οἰκίαν ἐπὶ τὴν γῆν χωρὶς θεμελίου, ᾗ προσέρρηξεν ὁ ποταμός, καὶ εὐθὺς συνέπεσεν, καὶ ἐγένετο τὸ ῥῆγμα τῆς οἰκίας ἐκείνης μέγα.

(79) **92.** Der Hauptmann von Kapernaum. *The Centurion's Servant.* **Luk 7 1–10** *58.*

56. *58.*

1 Ἐπειδὴ ἐπλήρωσεν πάντα τὰ ῥήματα αὐτοῦ εἰς τὰς ἀκοὰς τοῦ λαοῦ, εἰσῆλθεν εἰς Καφαρναουμ. 2 ἑκατοντάρχου δέ τινος δοῦλος κακῶς ἔχων ἤμελλεν τελευτᾶν, ὃς ἦν αὐτῷ ἔντιμος. 3 ἀκούσας δὲ περὶ τοῦ Ἰησοῦ ἀπέστειλεν πρὸς αὐτὸν πρεσβυτέρους τῶν Ἰουδαίων, ἐρωτῶν αὐτὸν ὅπως ἐλθὼν διασώσῃ τὸν δοῦλον αὐτοῦ. 4 οἱ δὲ παραγενόμενοι πρὸς τὸν Ἰησοῦν παρεκάλουν αὐτὸν σπουδαίως, λέγοντες ὅτι ἄξιός ἐστιν ᾧ παρέξῃ τοῦτο· 5 ἀγαπᾷ γὰρ τὸ ἔθνος ἡμῶν καὶ τὴν συναγωγὴν αὐτὸς ᾠκοδόμησεν ἡμῖν. 6 ὁ δὲ Ἰησοῦς ἐπορεύετο σὺν αὐτοῖς. ἤδη δὲ αὐτοῦ οὐ μακρὰν ἀπέχοντος ἀπὸ τῆς οἰκίας, ἔπεμψεν πρὸς αὐτὸν φίλους ὁ ἑκατόνταρχος λέγων αὐτῷ· κύριε, μὴ σκύλλου· οὐ γὰρ ἱκανός εἰμι ἵνα ὑπὸ τὴν στέγην μου εἰσέλθῃς· 7 διὸ οὐδὲ ἐμαυτὸν ἠξίωσα πρὸς σὲ ἐλθεῖν· ἀλλὰ εἰπὲ λόγῳ, καὶ ἰαθήτω ὁ παῖς μου. 8 καὶ γὰρ ἐγὼ ἄνθρωπός εἰμι ὑπὸ ἐξουσίαν τασσόμενος, ἔχων ὑπ' ἐμαυτὸν στρατιώτας, καὶ λέγω τούτῳ· πορεύθητι, καὶ πορεύεται, καὶ ἄλλῳ· ἔρχου, καὶ ἔρχεται, καὶ τῷ δούλῳ μου· ποίησον τοῦτο, καὶ ποιεῖ. 9 ἀκούσας δὲ ταῦτα ὁ Ἰησοῦς ἐθαύμασεν αὐτόν, καὶ στραφεὶς τῷ ἀκολουθοῦντι αὐτῷ ὄχλῳ εἶπεν· λέγω ὑμῖν, οὐδὲ ἐν τῷ Ισραηλ τοσαύτην πίστιν εὗρον. 10 καὶ ὑποστρέψαντες εἰς τὸν οἶκον οἱ πεμφθέντες εὗρον τὸν ἀσθενοῦντα δοῦλον ὑγιαίνοντα.

Lk 6,48 διαautην] τεθεμελιωτο γαρ επι την πετραν‖**p**: *Rpl* (τη πετρα: Γ) *L S*' *C*b^{9} — *om*: 𝔓^{45v} 700 *S*s[c] — τεθ.—πετ. και καλως ωκοδομηται‖p: *Aeth* — *txt*: 𝔓^{75} 𝔊Ξ Cr *S*h^{m} *C*' **49** οικιαν] την οι. (+ αυτου)‖p: 𝔓^{75} λ118-209-1278 (σ115) U Θ *pm* (*C*s$^{2:6}$b^{3}) | *om* η (*et* ποτ. + τη οικια εκεινη)‖p: D *Le* (vl'⟨f⟩r^{1}(*et om* εκ.) vg^{1}) | η προσε.] και πρ. αυτη‖p: W *S*s[c](και + οτε: p) — ευθυς δε πρ. αυτη *et om* ευθ.^{2}: *C*s^{2}(^{1} *om* δε) | *om* ευθ.‖p: D *L*ac | συνεπ.] επ.‖**p**: *Rpl L*' — *txt*: 𝔓$^{45.75}$ 𝔊⟨W⟩Ξ 700 **λ**-1582-2193 **ϕ** σ7-267-659 D R Θ 157 *pc l*11 *l*18 *l*19 *l*49 *l*184 *Le* blq vg^{8} | μεγαλη‖p: 1047 **7,1** επειδη] και εγενετο οτε‖Mt7 28 19 1 26 1: D *L*vl'(εγ. δε οτε: ac) vg^{1} (*S*h^{m} = ac) *Arm*^{O} — οτε δε‖←: Θ *pc* {} — επει δε: *Rpl* {*Le* fr^{1} vg' *S*h^{t} *C*b'(^{1} και επει δε)} — επειδη δε: 892 σ1194-1606 K *pc* {} — *txt*: BC*WX-579 ϕ124-174 A Π *pc L*30 (*prm* και: *S*' *Arm Cs* | επλ.] ετελεσεν‖←: D {*Le* c} | πα. τα ρ. αυτ.] *om* πα.‖Mt7 28 13 53 19 1: ℵ*X-579-892 λ131 *Le Aeth* — ταυτα τ. ρ.‖←Mt26 1: D *C*b^{1} — πα. τα ρ. ταυ.‖16 5 Mt26 1: ϕ69-124 σM-1194 *pc L*q30 vg^{1} *C*b^{5} — αυτ. πα. τα ρ. ταυ.‖Mt←7 28: **ϕ**'(∼ τα ρ. ταυ. πα.: 788) Θ — πα. τα ρ.‖2 51: σ990 *L*vl'⟨fz⟩r^{1} vg^{1} *S*s[c]p *C*b^{1} | εις—λαου] λαλων‖5 4: D **4** παρεκαλεσαν‖4 38: {𝔓^{75}} A *pc C*sb^{8} — ● ηρωτων‖3 4 38 Jo: ℵ*LΞ-579 700 λ1-131-1582-2193 **ϕ**⟨124⟩ D 161 — *txt*: {} *Rpl C*b' **6** επε. ... λεγ.] πεμψας ... ελεγεν‖Mt11 2: **λ**-1582-2193 | προς—εκατ.] πρ. αυ. ο εκ. φι.: 𝔓^{45v} *Rpl* (προς] επ: A) *L*' *S* — πρ. αυ. φι.: D' — ● φι. ο εκ.: 𝔓^{75} 𝔊' *C*s^{1v}(^{7} τους φι. αυ.) — *txt*: CLW (αυτους)XΞ-33 1071 λ131 Ψ 713 *Le* c *S*j *C*b *Aeth* | ● ∼ ειμι ικ.‖p 3 16 p: *Rpl L*vl' Or *S*hj *Arm* — *txt*: 𝔓^{75} ℵBW 700 *L*bff^{2}lqr^{1} vg *S*' | ∼ μου υπο τ. στ.‖p: 𝔓^{45v} *Rpl* — *txt*: 𝔓^{75} B Λ λ22 ϕ13-346(μου υ. τ. στ. μου)-788-826-828 σ27-71-990-1010-1207-1293 A E G H K S U V Y Δ Θ Π Ω **047** 565(*om* μου) 157 *pm l*12 *l*32 *l*303 *l*333 *l*1634 *l*1642 *l*1663 *l*1963 **7** *om* διο—ελθ.‖**p**: 700 D *pc L*vl⟨fqz⟩r^{1}30 *S*s[c] | αλλα + μονον‖p: C **ϕ** Ψ *pc L*lr^{1} *S*h^{+} — λογω + μονον‖p: 579-892 *C*s$^{5:9}$ | ιαθησεται‖**p**: *Rpl L C*b' — ζησεται‖Jo Mt9 18: *Aeth* — *txt*: 𝔓^{75v} BL-1241 *C*s$^{8(+1v)}$b^{2} **8** τασσ.] ων‖p: *Cs* — *om*‖p: 33 λ2193 ϕ69 *pc l*50 *S*p^{1} | πορευου‖17 19 16 37 Jo: X 1604 λ209 σ1194 D *pc* **9** *om* ταυ.‖p: 700 *pc S*s[c]j$^{\langle 1\rangle}$ *C*b^{1} | *om* αυτον‖**p**: X 700 ϕ983-1689 D R Θ *pc l*1663 *L*⟨q⟩ *S*p^{1} | στρ.] επιστρ.‖Mk5 30 8 33: 1093 | τω^{1}—ειπεν] ειπ. τω ακ. (+ αυτω) οχ.‖p: D (*Le*) {*S*,j} (*C*b$^{\langle 3\rangle}$) | *om* αυτω‖p: W λ22 (D) *pc l*1963 | ειπ. + αμην‖**p**: X **ϕ** D Θ Ψ 472 *l*1627 *L*vl'⟨bp⟩(αμ.] αμην αμην: ff^{2}r^{1}30 vg^{1})' *C*b^{6} *Arm* | ουδε] εν ουδενι‖p: Θ *L*vl⟨e f⟩r^{1} vg^{1} Am *C*s$^{1:11}$ *Aeth* **10** ● *om* ασθ.‖p: 𝔓^{75} 𝔊⟨33⟩ 700 λ-1582 157 *pc* Cr *L*vl'r^{1} vg^{1} *S*s[c]j *C Geo Aeth Δ*md me n^{CL} p — *txt*: *Rpl* (*om* δουλ:. D) *L*f vg' *S*' *Aeth Δ*a ad i^{T} l^{FG} n'

(80)

93. Der Jüngling von Nain. *The Widow's Son at Nain.* Luk 7 11–17

11 Καὶ ἐγένετο ἐν τῷ ἑξῆς ἐπορεύθη εἰς πόλιν καλουμένην Ναιν, καὶ συνεπορεύοντο αὐτῷ οἱ μαθηταὶ αὐτοῦ ἱκανοὶ καὶ ὄχλος πολύς. 12 ὡς δὲ ἤγγισεν τῇ πύλῃ τῆς πόλεως, καὶ ἰδοὺ ἐξεκομίζετο τεθνηκὼς μονογενὴς υἱὸς τῇ μητρὶ αὐτοῦ, καὶ αὕτη ἦν χήρα, καὶ ὄχλος τῆς πόλεως ἱκανὸς ἦν σὺν αὐτῇ. 13 καὶ ἰδὼν αὐτὴν ὁ κύριος ἐσπλαγχνίσθη ἐπ' αὐτῇ καὶ εἶπεν αὐτῇ· μὴ κλαῖε. 14 καὶ προσελθὼν ἥψατο τῆς σοροῦ, οἱ δὲ βαστάζοντες ἔστησαν, καὶ εἶπεν· νεανίσκε, σοὶ λέγω, ἐγέρθητι. 15 καὶ ἀνεκάθισεν ὁ νεκρὸς καὶ ἤρξατο λαλεῖν, **καὶ ἔδωκεν αὐτὸν τῇ μητρὶ αὐτοῦ.** 16 ἔλαβεν δὲ φόβος ἅπαντας, καὶ ἐδόξαζον τὸν θεὸν λέγοντες ὅτι προφήτης μέγας ἠγέρθη ἐν ἡμῖν, καὶ ὅτι ἐπεσκέψατο ὁ θεὸς τὸν λαὸν αὐτοῦ. 17 καὶ ἐξῆλθεν ὁ λόγος οὗτος ἐν ὅλῃ τῇ Ἰουδαίᾳ περὶ αὐτοῦ καὶ πάσῃ τῇ περιχώρῳ.

1Rg17 23

(81)

94. Anfrage des Täufers. *The Baptist's Question.* Luk 7 18–23 76.

76.

18 Καὶ ἀπήγγειλαν Ἰωάννῃ οἱ μαθηταὶ αὐτοῦ περὶ πάντων τούτων. καὶ προσκαλεσάμενος δύο τινὰς τῶν μαθητῶν αὐτοῦ ὁ Ἰωάννης 19 ἔπεμψεν πρὸς τὸν κύριον λέγων· σὺ εἶ ὁ ἐρχόμενος, ἢ ἄλλον προσδοκῶμεν; 20 παραγενόμενοι δὲ πρὸς αὐτὸν οἱ ἄνδρες εἶπαν· Ἰωάννης ὁ βαπτιστὴς ἀπέστειλεν ἡμᾶς πρὸς σὲ λέγων· σὺ εἶ ὁ ἐρχόμενος, ἢ ἄλλον προσδοκῶμεν; 21 ἐν ἐκείνῃ τῇ ὥρᾳ ἐθεράπευσεν πολλοὺς ἀπὸ νόσων καὶ μαστίγων καὶ πνευμάτων πονηρῶν, καὶ τυφλοῖς πολλοῖς ἐχαρίσατο βλέπειν. 22 καὶ ἀποκριθεὶς εἶπεν αὐτοῖς· πορευθέντες ἀπαγγείλατε Ἰωάννῃ ἃ εἴδετε καὶ ἠκούσατε· ὅτι **τυφλοὶ ἀναβλέπουσιν,** χωλοὶ περιπατοῦσιν, λεπροὶ καθαρίζονται, κωφοὶ ἀκούουσιν, νεκροὶ ἐγείρονται, **πτωχοὶ εὐαγγελίζονται·** 23 καὶ μακάριός ἐστιν ὃς ἐὰν μὴ σκανδαλισθῇ ἐν ἐμοί.

Is61 1 LXX

(82)

95. Jesu Zeugnis über den Täufer. *Jesus' Testimony to the Baptist.* Luk 7 24–35 77.

77.

24 Ἀπελθόντων δὲ τῶν ἀγγέλων Ἰωάννου ἤρξατο λέγειν πρὸς τοὺς ὄχλους περὶ Ἰωάννου· τί ἐξεληλύθατε εἰς τὴν ἔρημον θεάσασθαι; κάλαμον ὑπὸ ἀνέμου σαλευόμενον; 25 ἀλλὰ τί ἐξεληλύθατε ἰδεῖν; ἄνθρωπον ἐν

Lk 7,11 *om* εν‖9 37 *cf.* Act21 1 *etc.*: W D | ● τω] τη‖←: ℵ*CW-892 28-544-1071 λ1278 ϕ124-174 σM-7-267-990-1194-1207 D K S Π 157 *pm l*12 *l*32 *l*303 *l*374 *l*1231 *l*1564 *l*1627 *l*1634 *l*1663 *l*1963 *L*e cf *S*ph *C*b *Got* | ● *om* ικα.: 𝔓75 ℌ⟨33-892⟩Ξ 1604 ϕ*l*547 D F 157 *pc l*1663 *L*' *S*'j *C Δ* — *om* οι: **λ**-1582 *pc* — *txt*: *Rpl L*bcq *S*h | ∼ και ικανος‖12 Mk10 46: 1012 **12** ● ∼ υι. μον.‖8 42 9 38: *Rpl* Bas^S *L*' *Arm Aeth*(*om* μον.) — *txt*: 𝔓75 ℌ⟨33-1241⟩XΞ Cr *L*c | *om* ην^1‖2 37: *Rpl S*h^t — *txt*: 𝔓75 ℌ⟨W-1241⟩C*Ξ 28-1071-1604 **λ**1-22-1582 ϕ69-124 S V Θ Ω *al* {*L*} *S*'h^m j **13** επ αυτην‖Mt14 14 15 32 Mk6 34 8 2: ℵX-33-1241 544-700-1071-1604 **ϕ**⟨124⟩-230-*l*547 σ7-945-1194-1223-1424 K R U Γ Π Ψ *al l*18 *l*20 *l*44 *l*47 *l*184 *l*196(?) *l*259 *l*1564 *l*1963 Bas^S1:2 — *om cf.* 10 33 15 20: Θ 476 *L*ff^2 l **16** ηγε.] εγηγερται‖Mt11 11 Mk6 14: *Rpl* — *txt*: 𝔓75 ℌ⟨W-1241⟩CΞ 700 **λ**-1582-2193 A D(εξηγε.) 157 **17** ∼ ουτ. ο λογ.‖Jo21 23: D *L*⟨ac⟩ | περιχ. + του Ιορδανου‖3 3p: 1071 **18** τουτ.] των εργων αυτου‖p: σ7-267-659 *l*13 *l*14 *l*15 *l*17 *l*18 *l*19 *l*184 | *om* τινας‖19 29p Mk14 13: σ1223 D *pc L*⟨e a⟩ *C Geo Aeth Got* **19** αλλ.] ετερον‖**p**: ℌXΞ 28-1071 λ2193 ϕ124-983 σ27-945-1424 R Ψ 157 2533 Cr **20** ● απεσταλκεν‖Jo5 33: *Rpl* (19⌒20 προσδ.: σ267-349 R) Cr — *txt*: 𝔓75 ℵBW-1241 544 ϕ124 σ1424 157 *pc* | αλλ.] ετερον‖Mt3: ℌ⟨B-892⟩XΞ 1071 **λ**-1582-2193 ϕ983-1689 D Ψ 157 *pc* **21** εκ.] αυτη‖10 21 13 31: *Rpl L*' *S*s[c]j^b *Arm* — *txt*: 𝔓75 ℌ⟨33⟩ 700-1604 **λ**[118]-1582-2193 **ϕ**-174 157 *pc l*184 Bas^S Cr *L*e cq *S*'j^ac 1 *C* | ωρα] ημερα‖Mt22 23 13 1 Mk4 35: ℵ*L ϕ69 Cr | πον.] ακαθαρτων‖6 18 Mt10 1: ℵ*-1241 *L*blz **22** αποκ. + ο Ιησους‖p: *Rpl L*cfff^2 qr^1 *S*'j(κυριος I.) *C*b^1 — *txt*: 𝔓75v ℵBWΞ-892-1241 700 D 157 *al* Cr *L*' *S*s[c] *C*' *Arm* | απαγγ.] ειπατε‖13 22 Mt28 7p: W-579-892 D *L*vg^1 *S*s[c]pj⟨1⟩ | ειδ. κ. ηκ.] ακουετε κ. βλεπετε‖p: ϕ69 1574 Ddy — ειδ. κ. ακουετε‖p: 579 28 Θ — ηκ. κ. ειδ.‖p: 130 *L*ff^2 r^1 z Am *Aeth* | ● *om* οτι‖**p**: 𝔓75 ℌ⟨33⟩ XΞ 700-1604 **λ**[118]-1582-2193 **ϕ**⟨124-346⟩ σ7-267-659-1675 Θ Ψ 157 *pc l*12 *l*18 *l*19 *l*31 *l*49 *l*184 Cr Isai Or *L*vl' vg^1 Am *S*j *C*b^2 — *txt*: *Rpl L*e fr^1 vg' *S C*' | χω.] και χ.‖p: 𝔓75* W-1241 1604 ϕ69-124-346 σ267-659-1424 Θ Ψ 157 *pc L*e z vg^2 *S*,j *C*s^1:11 | κω.] και κ.‖p: 𝔓75 ℌ⟨L-33-892⟩ Λ-1604 λ131-1278 **ϕ**⟨983⟩ σ71-692-1424 D F Γ Δ *pc* Cr *S*s[c]pj *C*s^6:9 *Arm*^pc | νεκ.] και ν.‖p: ϕ124 W Cr *S*s[c](∼ πτ. ευ. ... νε.εγ.)pj | πτ.] και πτ.‖p: ℵX-33-892-1241 1071-1604 **λλ**⟨118-209⟩ **ϕ**-174-230 σ1194-1223-1424 F Θ *pc* Cr *L*e *S*(s[c])pj
24 πρ. τ. οχ.] τοις οχλοις‖p: *Rpl* — *txt*: 𝔓75v ℵ^c BLWXΞ-13-1241 544-1071-1604 **λ**-22-1582 **ϕ**-174 σM-7-267-659-990-1207 A K S U Θ Π Ψ *al L* **24.25** ● 24 εξηλθατε *et* 25‖p: 𝔓75(24.25^v) ℌ⟨24: 33⟩Ξ λ1-131-1582-2193 **ϕ**-174 σ(25: M-692)-71-(24: 115) A D K Π Ψ 157 *al* (25: *l*48) *l*183 — *txt*: *Rpl* Or

13.

μαλακοῖς ἱματίοις ἠμφιεσμένον; ἰδοὺ οἱ ἐν ἱματισμῷ ἐνδόξῳ καὶ τρυφῇ ὑπάρχοντες ἐν τοῖς βασιλείοις εἰσίν. [26] ἀλλὰ τί ἐξεληλύθατε ἰδεῖν; προφήτην; ναὶ λέγω ὑμῖν, καὶ περισσότερον προφήτου. [27] οὗτός ἐστιν περὶ οὗ γέγραπται· **ἰδοὺ ἀποστέλλω τὸν ἄγγελόν μου πρὸ προσώπου σου, ὃς κατασκευάσει τὴν ὁδόν σου ἔμπροσθέν** σου. [28] λέγω ὑμῖν, μείζων ἐν γεννητοῖς γυναικῶν προφήτης Ἰωάννου οὐδείς ἐστιν· ὁ δὲ μικρότερος ἐν τῇ βασιλείᾳ τοῦ θεοῦ μείζων αὐτοῦ ἐστιν. [29] καὶ πᾶς ὁ λαὸς ἀκούσας καὶ οἱ τελῶναι ἐδικαίωσαν τὸν θεόν, βαπτισθέντες τὸ βάπτισμα Ἰωάννου· [30] οἱ δὲ Φαρισαῖοι καὶ οἱ νομικοὶ τὴν βουλὴν τοῦ θεοῦ ἠθέτησαν εἰς ἑαυτούς,

Ex23 20 Ml3 1

21 32 (217.): ἦλθεν γὰρ Ἰωάννης πρὸς ὑμᾶς ἐν ὁδῷ δικαιοσύνης, καὶ οὐκ ἐπιστεύσατε αὐτῷ· οἱ δὲ τελῶναι καὶ αἱ πόρναι ἐπίστευσαν αὐτῷ· ὑμεῖς δὲ ἰδόντες οὐδὲ μετεμελήθητε ὕστερον τοῦ πιστεῦσαι αὐτῷ.

77.

μὴ βαπτισθέντες ὑπ' αὐτοῦ. [31] τίνι οὖν ὁμοιώσω τοὺς ἀνθρώπους τῆς γενεᾶς ταύτης, καὶ τίνι εἰσὶν ὅμοιοι; [32] ὅμοιοί εἰσιν παιδίοις τοῖς ἐν ἀγορᾷ καθημένοις καὶ προσφωνοῦσιν ἀλλήλοις λέγοντες· ηὐλήσαμεν ὑμῖν καὶ οὐκ ὠρχήσασθε· ἐθρηνήσαμεν καὶ οὐκ ἐκλαύσατε. [33] ἐλήλυθεν γὰρ Ἰωάννης ὁ βαπτιστὴς μὴ ἄρτον ἔσθων μήτε οἶνον πίνων, καὶ λέγετε· δαιμόνιον ἔχει. [34] ἐλήλυθεν ὁ υἱὸς τοῦ ἀνθρώπου ἐσθίων καὶ πίνων, καὶ λέγετε· ἰδοὺ ἄνθρωπος φάγος καὶ οἰνοπότης, φίλος τελωνῶν καὶ ἁμαρτωλῶν. [35] καὶ ἐδικαιώθη ἡ σοφία ἀπὸ τῶν τέκνων αὐτῆς πάντων.

(83) *96.* Die große Sünderin. *The Woman Who Was a Sinner.* Luk 7 36–50

244.

[36] Ἠρώτα δέ τις αὐτὸν τῶν Φαρισαίων ἵνα φάγῃ μετ' αὐτοῦ· καὶ εἰσελθὼν εἰς τὸν οἶκον τοῦ Φαρισαίου κατεκλίθη. [37] καὶ ἰδοὺ γυνὴ ἥτις ἦν ἐν τῇ πόλει ἁμαρτωλός, καὶ ἐπιγνοῦσα ὅτι κατάκειται ἐν τῇ οἰκίᾳ τοῦ Φαρισαίου, κομίσασα ἀλάβαστρον μύρου [38] καὶ στᾶσα ὀπίσω παρὰ τοὺς πόδας αὐτοῦ κλαίουσα, τοῖς δάκρυ-

Lk 7,26 ● εξηλθατε‖p: 𝔓^{75} 𝔥⟨W-33⟩Ξ 1071 λ1-131-1582-2193 ϕ-174 σ-1188 D 157 *al l*183 Or — *txt*: *Rpl* Or | προφητου + οτι ουδεις μειζων εν γεννητοις γυναικων προφητης Ιωαννου του βαπτιστου *cf. ad* 28: D — υμιν + ουδ.—γυν. περισσοτερος(amplior) l. τ. βα. *cf.* ←: *La* **27** ουτ. + γαρ‖Mt3 3: 33-892-1241 1071-1604 **λλ**⟨1278⟩ ϕ-174 σ7-267-659-1424 U Θ Ψ *mu* *Le* b30 *Sp*^{1}hj *C*b^{10} *Arm* *Δ*i^{T} l md me n | ιδ. + εγω‖ p Mk1 2 Ml3 1: *Rpl* *L*Mcn^{Te} *S*'j — *txt*: 𝔓^{75v} ℵBLWΞ-579 **λ**-1582-2193 D *pc* Mcn^{Ep} *L* *S*s[c] *C* *Arm* | *om* εμπ. σου‖Mk ←: D 122 *L*alr^{1}z Mcn^{Te} **28** λεγ.] αμην λ.‖p: ℵLXΞ-579-892 157 213 *l*1578 Cr *S*j *Arm* *Aeth* — ● λ. γαρ *cf.* 38p Mt5 20 18 10 *etc.*: *Rpl* *L*fq vg' *S*h — λ. δε *cf.* 12 27p Mt8 11 12 6 *etc.*: W ϕ D 1279 *l*211 *L*vl'r^{1} vg^{3} — *txt*: 𝔓^{75v} B-33-1241 700-1604 σ7-267-659 Ψ *pc l*18 *l*19 *l*49 *l*184 *S*' *C* | *om* μει.^{1}—εστιν^{1} ... δε *cf. ad* 26 | ● *om* προφ.‖p: 𝔓^{75} 𝔥'XΞ 544-700-1604 **λλ**⟨118-209⟩ σM-692 K Π 157 *al* Ddy Or *L*vl' *S*h^{m}(?)j *C* *Aeth* — *txt*: *Rpl* (∼ l. πρ.: 892; *om* l.: 1241) Cl *L*fqr^{1}z vg Am PsAu Mcn^{Te} *S*' | l. + του βαπτιστου‖**p**: *Rpl* (D) *L*,Am PsAu *S*' *C*s^{1}b^{4} — *txt*: 𝔓^{75} ℵBLWΞ-579-892-1241 (*om* l.) 700 **λλ**⟨118-209⟩ Ψ *pc* Ddy Or *S*s[c]p^{3}j *C*s^{6}b' *Arm* | του θε.] των ουρανων‖p: 1241 495 *L*r^{2} *C*b$^{\langle 7\rangle}$ **30** *om* εις εαυ.‖Mk7 9: ℵ σ659 D *pc* Cr$^{1:2}$ *C*s *Aeth* **31** ουν] δε‖p: ℵ-579 — *om*: σ1194-1424 F^{W} *pc* *C*s$^{6:9}$b$^{\langle 5\rangle}$ *Aeth* **32** *om* τοις‖p: 1012 | αγ.] τη αγ.‖p: D — αγοραις‖ p: W F^{W} Δ *C*b^{2} *Geo* | ∼ καθ. εν αγ.‖p: 1574 *L*bfff^{2}qr^{1}z vg *S*s[c]p | και^{1}—λεγ.] α προσφωνουντα (+ αλληλοις) λεγουσιν‖p: 579 (*La*) | αλλ.] τοις εταιροις αυτων‖p: 998 *S*s[c]p | λεγ.] ● α λεγει (οι -ουσιν)‖p: ℵ*B (Λ)-700 λ1-22-1582-2193 697 (*pc*) — και λεγουσιν‖p: *Rpl* (-οντες: ϕ174-230) *L*fr^{2} vg *S*'(s[c] *om*) — *txt* (-ντα): (ℵ^{c})L(WΞ) ϕ D (157) *L*vl'r^{1}30 *C* | εθ. + υμιν‖32a p: *Rpl* Bas *L*' *S* *C* — *txt*: 𝔥⟨33-579⟩Ξ ϕ⟨69-124⟩ D 1038 *l*184 *L*clr^{1}z vg *Arm* | εκλαυ.] εκοψασθε‖ p: ϕ⟨124⟩ σM^{m} 161 *La* **33** μη ... μητε] μητε ... μητε‖p: *Rpl* *L*' — μη ... μηδε: ℵW 157 {} — *txt*: BΞ *L*f Oro {*C*(s μη ... μη)b} | ● ∼ εσ. αρτ. *et* ∼ πι. οιν.‖p: 𝔓^{82v} ℵBLWΞ-1241 σ990 157 *L*fr^{2}z vg *Sp* *Arm*^{1} — *om* αρτ. *et* οιν.‖**p**: 700 **λλ**⟨118-209⟩ ϕ⟨124-346⟩ D 1574(*om* οιν.) *pc l*18 Or *L*vl'(*om* αρτ.: g^{2} vg^{1}) Oro *S*sc *Arm*'(^{O}: $^{+}$) *Aeth* — *txt*: *Rpl* (∼ εσ. αρτ.: 579; ∼ πι. οιν.: 243 *l*48) *L*r^{1} *S*h | λεγουσιν‖p: Λ σ-71 *pc* **34** εληλ.] ηλθεν‖**p**: X | λεγουσιν‖p: 892 σ71 | ∼ τελ.φι.‖ p: X-1241 1071 H Ψ *pc* | ∼ τελ. κ. αμ. φι.‖p: 130 *L*bq **35** *om* παν.‖p: ℵ^{c}LX-1241 28-700-1604 **λλ** ϕ13 σM-71-692-990-1194-1223 D F^{W} Θ Ψ *pc* HM *L*vg^{1} *S*c — ● ∼ παν. τ. τεκ. αυ.: (ℵ*)BW-579-892 ϕ' *L*'⟨r^{1}⟩ *S*sp — *txt*: *Rpl* *S*h *C* | τεκ.] εργων‖p: ℵ HM *L*Am **36** φαγη + αρτον‖14 1: 1093 — αυτου + αρτ.‖←: σ659 | ανεκλιθη‖Mt8 11p 14 19 Mk6 39: *Rpl* Amph — *txt*: 𝔓^{75v} 𝔥'⟨W⟩ (ℵ* κατεκειτο)XΞ 1071 **λλ** σ990 D *pc* Mcn^{Ep} **37** ανακειται‖Mt26 7 Jo12 2 Mk14 18: *Rpl* — *txt*: 𝔓^{3} 𝔥' (κατεκλιθη: 1241)XΞ Λ σ267-990 A D(∼ εν^{2}—Φ. κατ.) *pc* Or **38** αυτου^{1}] του Ιησου‖Jo12 3: 1241 σ945-1207(*om* του)-1223 A K Y Θ Π *al* Amph *S*h *Geo*^{2} | *om* κλαι. (*et om* τ. δακρ.)‖←: F (157) *pc* *L*⟨e acf⟩ Am *Δ*i^{V} l^{AD} me

σιν ἤρξατο βρέχειν τοὺς πόδας αὐτοῦ, καὶ ταῖς θριξὶν τῆς κεφαλῆς αὐτῆς ἐξέμασσεν, καὶ κατεφίλει τοὺς πόδας αὐτοῦ καὶ ἤλειφεν τῷ μύρῳ. 39 ἰδὼν δὲ ὁ Φαρισαῖος ὁ καλέσας αὐτὸν εἶπεν ἐν ἑαυτῷ λέγων· οὗτος εἰ ἦν προφήτης, ἐγίνωσκεν ἂν τίς καὶ ποταπὴ ἡ γυνὴ ἥτις ἅπτεται αὐτοῦ, ὅτι ἁμαρτωλός ἐστιν. 40 καὶ ἀποκριθεὶς ὁ Ἰησοῦς εἶπεν πρὸς αὐτόν· Σίμων, ἔχω σοί τι εἰπεῖν. ὁ δέ· διδάσκαλε, εἰπέ, φησίν. 41 δύο χρεοφειλέται ἦσαν δανειστῇ τινι· ὁ εἷς ὤφειλεν δηνάρια πεντακόσια, ὁ δὲ ἕτερος πεντήκοντα. 42 μὴ ἐχόντων αὐτῶν ἀποδοῦναι ἀμφοτέροις ἐχαρίσατο. τίς οὖν αὐτῶν, εἰπέ, πλεῖον αὐτὸν ἀγαπήσει; 43 ἀποκριθεὶς Σίμων εἶπεν· ὑπολαμβάνω ὅτι ᾧ τὸ πλεῖον ἐχαρίσατο. ὁ δὲ εἶπεν αὐτῷ· ὀρθῶς ἔκρινας. 44 καὶ στραφεὶς πρὸς τὴν γυναῖκα τῷ Σίμωνι ἔφη· βλέπεις ταύτην τὴν γυναῖκα; εἰσῆλθόν σου εἰς τὴν οἰκίαν, ὕδωρ μοι ἐπὶ πόδας οὐκ ἔδωκας· αὕτη δὲ τοῖς δάκρυσιν ἔβρεξέν μου τοὺς πόδας καὶ ταῖς θριξὶν αὐτῆς ἐξέμαξεν. 45 φίλημά μοι οὐκ ἔδωκας· αὕτη δὲ ἀφ' ἧς εἰσῆλθον οὐ διέλειπεν καταφιλοῦσά μου τοὺς πόδας. 46 ἐλαίῳ τὴν κεφαλήν μου οὐκ ἤλειψας· αὕτη δὲ μύρῳ ἤλειψεν τοὺς πόδας μου. 47 οὗ χάριν λέγω σοι, ἀφέωνται αἱ ἁμαρτίαι αὐτῆς αἱ πολλαί, ὅτι ἠγάπησεν πολύ· ᾧ δὲ ὀλίγον ἀφίεται, ὀλίγον ἀγαπᾷ. 48 εἶπεν δὲ αὐτῇ· ἀφέωνταί σου αἱ ἁμαρτίαι. 49 καὶ ἤρξαντο οἱ συνανακείμενοι λέγειν ἐν ἑαυτοῖς· τίς οὗτός ἐστιν, ὃς καὶ ἁμαρτίας ἀφίησιν; 50 εἶπεν δὲ πρὸς τὴν γυναῖκα· ἡ πίστις σου σέσωκέν σε· **πορεύου εἰς εἰρήνην.**

1Sm1 17

(84)

97. Die dienenden Frauen. *The Ministering Women.* **Luk 8 1–3**

28. **265.**

1 Καὶ ἐγένετο ἐν τῷ καθεξῆς καὶ αὐτὸς διώδευεν κατὰ πόλιν καὶ κώμην κηρύσσων καὶ εὐαγγελιζόμενος τὴν βασιλείαν τοῦ θεοῦ, καὶ οἱ δώδεκα σὺν αὐτῷ, 2 καὶ γυναῖκές τινες αἳ ἦσαν τεθεραπευμέναι ἀπὸ πνευμάτων πονηρῶν καὶ ἀσθενειῶν, Μαρία ἡ καλουμένη Μαγδαληνή, ἀφ' ἧς δαιμόνια ἑπτὰ ἐξεληλύθει, 3 καὶ

Lk 7,38 αυτου^{2}] του l.‖←: 1241 *al* | ● εξεμαξεν‖44 Jo←: 𝔓^{3} 𝔥⟨B-892⟩X 1071-1604 σ990 A D Ψ 157 *pc* *L*r^{1} PsCp *C* **39** *om* λεγ.‖184 Mt9 3: WX ϕ69 D *pc* Amph *L*e r^{1} Or *S*h^{t}j *C*s$^{7:9}$ | προφ.] ● ο πρ.‖Mt 21 11 Jo 21.25 *etc.*: B*Ξ 482 **40** Σ. + Σιμων‖22 31: ϕ983-1689 1093 *L*Or **42** μη εχ.] + δε‖Mt18 25: 𝔓^{3} *Rpl* *L*bfqr^{1} vg^{1} Am *S*h *C*' *Δ*l^{D} — + ουν: Amph Da *Δ*me — *prm* και: *L*e c vg^{1} PsCp *S*'j *Δ*a i^{VT1} md n p — *txt*: BLΞ D P *pc* Or *L*' Au Or *C*s$^{2:9}$ *Δ*ad i$^{T'}$ l' | ● *om* ειπε‖Mt21 31: 𝔓^{3} 𝔥⟨33⟩ Ξ 1071 **λ**-1582-2193 σ115-990 D Ψ 157 *pc* *L* *S*(*et om* ουν: sc)p *C* *Δ*⟨i^{V} me⟩ — *txt*: *Rpl* (επι: A) *S*h(+ μοι^{+}) j(∼ αγ. αυ. πλ. ειπε *et* + μοι) *Arm*(∼ ειπε ουν· τις *et om* αυτων^{2}) *Geo* | ● ∼ πλ. αγ. αυ.: 𝔓^{3} 𝔥XΞ σ990 F Ψ 157 *pc* *S*' — ∼ αυ. πλ. αγ. (*et om* αυτων^{2}): (D *L*vl')e (vg')^{1} — ∼ αγ. αυ. πλ.: *S*scj — πλ. αγ.‖47: ϕ983-1689-*l*547 σ1606 Γ Δ **047** *pc* *l*54 *L*PsCp Nov — *txt* (*om* αυτων^{2}): 𝔓^{75v} *Rpl* *L*fl vg^{2} **43** αποκ.] ● απ. δε: 𝔓^{3} *Rpl* Amph^{1} Lafqr^{1} Nov *S*hj *C*s^{5}b^{4} — ο δε: W 700 **λ**-1582 **079** — *om*: *S*sc *Arm* — *txt* (*prm* και): 𝔓^{75v} BL^{c}Ξ D *l*22 Amph^{1} *L*'(z vg^{1}) *S*p *C*s^{4}b' (*Aeth*) *Δ*a l (n^{CL}) | εκρ.] απεκριθης‖10 28: 28 *l*547 **44** μοι επι πο.] επι τους πο. μου‖46 Jo13 9: *Rpl* Amph^{1}(^{1} επι] εις) {*L*' *C*b} *Δ*ad l md me n' p E^{sa} — ● μου επι τους πο.‖44b.45: 𝔓^{3v} ℵLΞ 1071(*om* τους) {} — μοι επι τους πο.: X-33-579-892 Ψ Cat^{Ox} *Δ*i n^{L} — *txt*: BW(υπο πο. μοι) D(επι πο. μοι) *L*e (aff^{2}q vg^{1} = D) *S*j *C*s(επι] του νιπτειν τους) | ∼ εξεμ. τ. θρι. αυ.‖Jo12 3: 28 | θρι. + της κεφαλης‖38: *Rpl* *L*vg^{1} *S*sc *C*s$^{1:9}$ — *txt*: 𝔥⟨33⟩XΞ 544-700-1071-1604 **λλ**⟨1582-2193⟩ σ990-1424 A D K P Θ Π Ψ **079** 157 *mu* *l*32 *L*' *S*'j *C*' **45** ∼ τους πο. μου‖46: P *pc* **46** ● ∼ μου τους πο.‖44: *Rpl* (*om* μου: 157) — *om*‖Mt7 Mk3: W D **079** *pc* *L*bcq *Arm* — *txt* (∼ τ. πο. μου ηλ.): B(LΞ)-33 700-1071 λ22 ϕ230 **σ**⟨954⟩-945-1606 A E F G H P U V Γ Θ Ω **047** *al* *l*183 (*S*sp) **47** αφιενται‖Mt9 2.5 Mk2 5.9: WF *L*acfr$^{1.2}$z30(αφεθησονται: e d vg')^{10} PsCp | ● ∼ αυτ. αι αμ.‖←48: ℵW-579-892 544-1071 ϕ69-*l*547 σ990-1207-1424 A F K Π Ψ *pc* Amph Cl — αυτη αι αμ. αυτης(*om*)‖5 20.23: P (*L*'⟨q⟩; *et* αυτη] σοι: b) Am (Au) PsCp Nov Or *S*,j *C* **48** αφιενται‖Mt← Mk←: W *L*PsCp | σου] σοι‖5 20.23: 1071 ϕ1689 σ945 P *al* *L*,PsCp Or *S*'h^{+}j *C* *Δ*⟨i^{V} me p⟩ | αμ. + σου‖←: 1071 *L*ff^{2}l 30 vg^{1} Or *S*,j *C* *Δ*⟨i^{V} me p⟩ **49** ∼ εστ. ουτ.‖5 21 9 9 Mt21 10: 1241 700-1071 **λ**⟨131⟩-1582-2193 **ϕ**⟨124⟩ D P 156 *pc* *L*(*om* ουτ.: b) PsCp **50** γυν. + γυναι‖Mt15 28: D — + θυγατερ‖8 48p: 213 | πορ.] υπαγε‖Mk5 34: 472 **8,1** καθ.] εξης‖7 11: A | δω. + αποστολοι‖9 1 Mt10 2: σ990 *pc* — + μαθηται‖Mt10 1 20 17: *L*vl⟨eff^{2}l⟩r^{1} vg^{1}(^{1} *om* δω.) *Geo* | συν] μετ *cf.* Mt26 69.71 Mk3 14 5 40 *etc.*: 544 D **2** απο + νοσων και μαστιγων και(+ απο)‖7 21: 1071 **σ**-(7)-267-659-1188 713 (60 *l*12) | πον.] ακαθαρτων‖6 18 11 24p: Θ *pc* *L*abcdfz vg^{1} PsCp | *om* καλ.‖Mt27 56.61 28 1 Mk15 40.47 16 1: σ115(*om* η κ.) *pc* *S*j | αφ] εξ‖Mk1 25f. 5 8 7 29 9 25: D {*L*e acf PsCp} | ∼ επτα δ.‖Mk16 9: W D 1555 *S*scpj | δαι.] πνευματα‖11 26p: 1555 | εξελ.] εκβεβληκει‖Mk16 9: σ1424(∼ εκβ. επ.) 1555(∼ εκβ. επ. δαι.) *S*c *C*b$^{\langle 6\rangle}$ *Δ*a^{BE} md n^{HgHrS}p E^{s}(^{a} εξεβληθη)

Ἰωάννα γυνὴ Χουζα ἐπιτρόπου Ἡρῴδου καὶ Σουσάννα καὶ ἕτεραι πολλαί, αἵτινες διηκόνουν αὐτοῖς ἐκ τῶν ὑπαρχόντων αὐταῖς.

(85)

98. „Er ist von Sinnen.“ “*He is out of His Mind.*” Mark 3 20–21

Mark: 20 Καὶ ἔρχεται εἰς οἶκον· καὶ συνέρχεται πάλιν ὁ ὄχλος, ὥστε μὴ δύνασθαι αὐτοὺς μηδὲ ἄρτον φαγεῖν. 21 καὶ ἀκούσαντες οἱ παρ᾽ αὐτοῦ ἐξῆλθον κρατῆσαι αὐτόν· ἔλεγον γὰρ ὅτι ἐξέστη.

Luk: *8 19 (117.): ... 19b καὶ οὐκ ἠδύναντο συντυχεῖν αὐτῷ διὰ τὸν ὄχλον.* *19a Παρεγένοντο δὲ πρὸς αὐτὸν ἡ μήτηρ καὶ οἱ ἀδελφοὶ αὐτοῦ ...*

(85.86)

99. Die Lästerung der Schriftgelehrten. *The Beelzebul Controversy.*

Matth 12 22–37 — Mark 3 22–30

Matth: 22 Τότε προσηνέχθη αὐτῷ δαιμονιζόμενος τυφλὸς καὶ κωφός· καὶ ἐθεράπευσεν αὐτόν, ὥστε τὸν κωφὸν λαλεῖν καὶ βλέπειν. 23 καὶ ἐξίσταντο πάντες οἱ ὄχλοι καὶ ἔλεγον· μήτι οὗτός ἐστιν ὁ υἱὸς Δαυιδ; 24 οἱ δὲ Φαρισαῖοι ἀκούσαντες εἶπον· οὗτος οὐκ ἐκβάλλει τὰ δαιμόνια εἰ μὴ ἐν τῷ Βεελ Ζεβουλ ἄρχοντι τῶν δαιμονίων. 25 εἰδὼς δὲ τὰς ἐνθυμήσεις αὐτῶν εἶπεν αὐτοῖς· πᾶσα βασιλεία μερισθεῖσα καθ᾽ ἑαυτῆς ἐρημοῦται, καὶ πᾶσα πόλις ἢ οἰκία μερισθεῖσα καθ᾽ ἑαυτῆς οὐ σταθήσεται.

Matth 9 32 (69.): ... ἰδοὺ προσήνεγκαν αὐτῷ ἄνθρωπον κωφὸν δαιμονιζόμενον. 33 καὶ ἐκβληθέντος τοῦ δαιμονίου ἐλάλησεν ὁ κωφός. καὶ ἐθαύμασαν οἱ ὄχλοι λέγοντες· οὐδέποτε ἐφάνη οὕτως ἐν τῷ Ἰσραηλ. 34 οἱ δὲ Φαρισαῖοι ἔλεγον· ἐν τῷ ἄρχοντι τῶν δαιμονίων ἐκβάλλει τὰ δαιμόνια.

Mark: 22 Καὶ οἱ γραμματεῖς οἱ ἀπὸ Ἱεροσολύμων καταβάντες ἔλεγον ὅτι Βεελ Ζεβουλ ἔχει, καὶ ὅτι ἐν τῷ ἄρχοντι τῶν δαιμονίων ἐκβάλλει τὰ δαιμόνια. 23 καὶ προσκαλεσάμενος αὐτοὺς ἐν παραβολαῖς ἔλεγεν αὐτοῖς· πῶς δύναται σατανᾶς σατανᾶν ἐκβάλλειν; 24 καὶ ἐὰν βασιλεία ἐφ᾽ ἑαυτὴν μερισθῇ, οὐ δύναται σταθῆναι ἡ βασιλεία ἐκείνη· 25 καὶ ἐὰν οἰκία ἐφ᾽ ἑαυτὴν μερισθῇ, οὐ δυνήσεται ἡ οἰκία ἐκείνη στῆναι.

Luk 11 14–23 (163.): Καὶ ἦν ἐκβάλλων δαιμόνιον, καὶ αὐτὸ ἦν κωφόν· ἐγένετο δὲ τοῦ δαιμονίου ἐξελθόντος ἐλάλησεν ὁ κωφός· καὶ ἐθαύμασαν οἱ ὄχλοι. 15 τινὲς δὲ ἐξ αὐτῶν εἶπον· ἐν Βεελ Ζεβουλ τῷ ἄρχοντι τῶν δαιμονίων ἐκβάλλει τὰ δαιμόνια· 16 ἕτεροι δὲ πειράζοντες σημεῖον ἐξ οὐρανοῦ ἐζήτουν παρ᾽ αὐτοῦ. 17 αὐτὸς δὲ εἰδὼς αὐτῶν τὰ διανοήματα εἶπεν αὐτοῖς· πᾶσα βασιλεία ἐφ᾽ ἑαυτὴν διαμερισθεῖσα ἐρημοῦται, καὶ οἶκος ἐπὶ οἶκον πίπτει.

Joh 7 31: ... ἔλεγον· ὁ Χριστός, ὅταν ἔλθῃ, μὴ πλείονα σημεῖα ποιήσει ὧν οὗτος ἐποίησεν;

Mt 12,22 ● προσηνεγκαν ... δαιμονιον -ον και -ον ‖ 8 16 9 32 14 35: B σ1424-1675 Chr *S*⟨p^{1}⟩ *Geo Aeth* **25** ειδ.] ιδων ‖ 9 2 p: 𝔓^{21} ℵ^{b}-33-892 ϕ13 D *pc* Chr *L*k[e] ff^{1} *S*sc *C*b | διαμερ.^{1} *et* ^{2} ‖ Lk: 1193 | καθ. εαυ.^{1} *et* ^{2}] εφ εαυτην ‖ p: D (^{2}: *l*49)

Mk 3,20 ● ερχονται: *Rpl* *L*flqr^{2}z vg *S*' *C*s^{1}b^{5} — *txt*: ℵ*BW σ1207-1223 Γ 1342 *pc l*80 *l*211 Vic^{A} *L*vl'(venit⌒convenit: c)r^{1} *S*s[c] *C*s^{3}b' *Aeth* | ● *om* ο: *Rpl* (οχλοι: *S*p⟨1⟩h^{t} *C*b^{1})^{5} — *txt*: ℵ^{c}B L^{c}Δ-892 Θ^{c}-544-565 A D *al l*48 **23** σα. σα.] ο σα. τον σα. ‖ Mt 26: 892(*om* ο) σ27 **24** ∼ μερ. εφ εαυ. ‖ Mt: σ945 **25** δυν. ... στη.] σταθησεται ‖ Mt: 1241

Lk 8,3 αυτοις] ● αυτω ‖ Mt 27 55 p 8 15: ℵLX-33-579-1241 544-1604 **λλ**⟨2193⟩ σM-7-267-945-990-1207-1223 A Π Ψ *pm* *L*ablqz vg^{8} Au^{1} PsAu PsCp Mcn^{Te} *S*h^{+}j^{a} *C Arm Aeth* *Δ*l^{AD} md n — *txt*: *Rpl* Or *L*'Au^{1} *S*'h^{m}j^{bc} *Δ*a (*om*: i^{V})

Matth

26 καὶ εἰ ὁ σατανᾶς τὸν σατανᾶν ἐκβάλλει, ἐφ' ἑαυτὸν ἐμερίσθη· πῶς οὖν σταθήσεται ἡ βασιλεία αὐτοῦ; 27 καὶ εἰ ἐγὼ ἐν Βεελ Ζεβουλ ἐκβάλλω τὰ δαιμόνια, οἱ υἱοὶ ὑμῶν ἐν τίνι ἐκβάλλουσιν; διὰ τοῦτο αὐτοὶ κριταὶ ἔσονται ὑμῶν. 28 εἰ δὲ ἐν πνεύματι θεοῦ ἐγὼ ἐκβάλλω τὰ δαιμόνια, ἄρα ἔφθασεν ἐφ' ὑμᾶς ἡ βασιλεία τοῦ θεοῦ. 29 ἢ πῶς δύναταί τις εἰσελθεῖν εἰς τὴν οἰκίαν τοῦ ἰσχυροῦ καὶ τὰ σκεύη αὐτοῦ ἁρπάσαι, ἐὰν μὴ πρῶτον δήσῃ τὸν ἰσχυρόν; καὶ τότε τὴν οἰκίαν αὐτοῦ διαρπάσει. 30 ὁ μὴ ὢν μετ' ἐμοῦ κατ' ἐμοῦ ἐστιν, καὶ ὁ μὴ συνάγων μετ' ἐμοῦ σκορπίζει. 31 διὰ τοῦτο λέγω ὑμῖν, πᾶσα ἁμαρτία καὶ βλασφημία ἀφεθήσεται τοῖς ἀνθρώποις,

Mark

26 καὶ εἰ ὁ σατανᾶς ἀνέστη ἐφ' ἑαυτὸν καὶ μεμέρισται, οὐ δύναται στῆναι ἀλλὰ τέλος ἔχει. 27 ἀλλ' οὐδεὶς δύναται τὰ σκεύη τοῦ ἰσχυροῦ εἰσελθὼν εἰς τὴν οἰκίαν αὐτοῦ διαρπάσαι, ἐὰν μὴ πρῶτον τὸν ἰσχυρὸν δήσῃ, καὶ τότε τὴν οἰκίαν αὐτοῦ διαρπάσει. [*144.*] 28 αμην λέγω ὑμῖν ὅτι πάντα ἀφεθήσεται τοῖς υἱοῖς τῶν ἀνθρώπων

Luk

18 εἰ δὲ καὶ ὁ σατανᾶς ἐφ' ἑαυτὸν διεμερίσθη, πῶς σταθήσεται ἡ βασιλεία αὐτοῦ; ὅτι λέγετε ἐν Βεελ Ζεβουλ ἐκβάλλειν με τὰ δαιμόνια. 19 εἰ δὲ ἐγὼ ἐν Βεελ Ζεβουλ ἐκβάλλω τὰ δαιμόνια, οἱ υἱοὶ ὑμῶν ἐν τίνι ἐκβάλλουσιν; διὰ τοῦτο αὐτοὶ κριταὶ ὑμῶν ἔσονται. 20 εἰ δὲ ἐν δακτύλῳ θεοῦ ἐκβάλλω τὰ δαιμόνια, ἄρα ἔφθασεν ἐφ' ὑμᾶς ἡ βασιλεία τοῦ θεοῦ. 21 ὅταν ὁ ἰσχυρὸς καθωπλισμένος φυλάσσῃ τὴν ἑαυτοῦ αὐλήν, ἐν εἰρήνῃ ἐστὶν τὰ ὑπάρχοντα αὐτοῦ· 22 ἐπὰν δὲ ἰσχυρότερος αὐτοῦ ἐπελθὼν νικήσῃ αὐτόν, τὴν πανοπλίαν αὐτοῦ αἴρει, ἐφ' ᾗ ἐπεποίθει, καὶ τὰ σκῦλα αὐτοῦ διαδίδωσιν. 23 ὁ μὴ ὢν μετ' ἐμοῦ κατ' ἐμοῦ ἐστιν, καὶ ὁ μὴ συνάγων μετ' ἐμοῦ σκορπίζει με.

Mt 12,26 και ει] ει δε‖Lk: D(+ και) *Ld* (δε) και: k[e], ουν: cff^{1}h, γαρ: bff^{2}g^{1}q vg^4) *Cs*$^{3:4}$(= k) | μεμερισται‖Mk: 252 1574 PsAth(*prm* και εφ εαυ. ανεστη και) **27** και ει] ει δε‖**p**: 33 λ1-1582 **σ**⟨954⟩-1391 D *l*49 *l*184 *Lk*[e] | ~ κρ. υμ. εσ.‖p: **λ**'(κρ. + και: 118)-1582 ϕ124 Θ Chr^1 *Lcg*^{2} vg^4 Am Opt *Geo*' — υμ. εσ. κρ.: *Rpl* (ημων: X 247) — υμ. κρ. εσ. L *pc* (~ υμ. αυτ.: *pc*) Chr^1 — εσ. υμ. κρ.: 1093 Cr *L*(~ κρ. υμ.: vg^2) (υμιν: *S*) *Arm* — *txt*: ℌ' σ517-659-945-1391-1424 D W(~ κρ. εσ. αυτ. υμ.) 157 *l*49 *l*184 *L*' *Geo*^{A} *Aeth* **28** ~ εγω εν πν. θε.‖27: λ1(+ εγω)-1582 σ7-71-659-1391 157 *pm* Ath^2 PsAth Bas$^{4:5}$ Eu *L*flz vg⟨2⟩ *S*c[s]p^1 PsAth(~ εκβ. τ. δ. εν πν. θε.: *C*sf) — *om* εγω‖p: ϕ983 σM-1402 **047** *pc* Ath^1 Chr$^{1:2}$ Ep *L*k[e] bcg^1 *S*h | πν.] δακτυλω‖**p**: N *S*p^1 **29** διαρπα.‖Mk: *Rpl* Eu — *txt*: BC*X-892 NΣ λ1-1582 σ7-517-659-1391 W *pc l*49 *l*184 | ~ τ. ισχ. δη.‖Mk: **ϕ**-174 Δ *pc S*c[s] **30** ο^1 + γαρ‖Mk940 Lk950: **σ**-349-659 *l*49 *l*184 | σκο. + με‖p: ℵ-33 λ1582 *L*30(a me) *S*h^m *C*b *Aeth* **31** υμ. + οτι‖**p**: 28 σ1293 *pc L*k[e] h *S*scp

Mk 3,26 αν. εφ. εαυ.] σαταναν εκβαλλει‖Mt: 544(τον σα.) D *L*vl⟨flz⟩r^1 vg^1 *Geo*^{1}(+ και εφ εαυ.) | *om* ανεστη … και^2‖Lk: W *S*s[c] | μεμ.] ● εμερισθη‖p: ℵBC*^{v}LΔ-892 W 1342 | ~ εμερ. και‖Mt: ℵ*C*^{v}Δ *L*vl'(*om* και)flz vg | ου] πως‖MtLk: σ827 | στην.] σταθηναι η βασιλεια αυτου‖p: ϕ983-1689 D W *L*(~ η β. αυ. ου δυν. στ.: e[k] cff^2)abiqr^1 vg^1 **27** αλλ—δυν.] ● αλλ ου δυν. ουδ.: ℵBC*^{v}Δ 372 (*om* αλλ) *C*b — ουδ. δυν.‖Mt624Jo644: *Rpl* (*prm spat.*: λ118) *L*' *S*' — ουδ. δε δυν.: Θ σ945 *pc L*adff^2 *C*s^2 — και ουδ. δυν.‖Jo1029: C^{2v} G *Aeth* — *txt*: L-33-579-892 28-700-1071 **λ**' **ϕ** 1342 *S*h^m *C*s^1 *Arm* | ● ~ εις την οι. τ. ισχ. εισε. τα σκ.‖Mt: ℵ(~ εισε. εις—ισχ.)BCLΔ-33-579(εισελθειν και)-892 Θ-(1071) 1342(~ εισελθειν εις—ισχ. και) *S*' *C* — *txt*: *Rpl* (*om* εισε.—αυτου^1: G; εισε.—διαρπ.] διαρπ. εισε.—οι.: W) *L S*h *Arm* | διαρπ.] αρπ.‖Mt: **ϕ**⟨124-346-543⟩ *l*48 | ~ δηση τ. ισ.‖Mt: **047** *L*g^2 vg^1 **28** τοις υ. τ. αν.] τ. ανθρωποις‖p: Δ 544 λ118-209 σ1402 157 *pc L*Cp$^{1:3}$

Mt1229p *cf.* ETh^{II} 21 (*cf. ad 172.* Lk1239)

ETh^{II} 35 (*transl.*): *Λέγει Ἰησοῦς· οὐ δύναταί τις εἰσελθεῖν εἰς τὴν οἰκίαν τοῦ ἰσχυροῦ καὶ διαρπάσαι αὐτήν, ἐὰν μὴ δήσῃ τὰς χεῖρας αὐτοῦ. τότε τὴν οἰκίαν αὐτοῦ ἀνατρέψει.*

Mt1230p *cf.* Ev. apocr. (POxy 1224 fol.2r^o col.1; *cf. ad 144.* Mk940)

Mt1231f.p *cf.* ETh^{II} 44 (*transl.*): *Λέγει Ἰησοῦς· ὃς ἂν βλασφημήσῃ τὸν πατέρα, ἀφεθήσεται αὐτῷ· καὶ ὃς ἂν βλασφημήσῃ τὸν υἱόν, ἀφεθήσεται αὐτῷ· ὃς δ' ἂν βλασφημήσῃ εἰς τὸ πνεῦμα τὸ ἅγιον, οὐκ ἀφεθήσεται αὐτῷ οὔτε ἐπὶ τῆς γῆς οὔτε ἐν τῷ οὐρανῷ.*

ἡ δὲ τοῦ πνεύματος βλασφημία οὐκ ἀφεθήσεται. 32 καὶ ὃς ἐὰν εἴπῃ λόγον κατὰ τοῦ υἱοῦ τοῦ ἀνθρώπου, ἀφεθήσεται αὐτῷ· ὃς δ' ἂν εἴπῃ κατὰ τοῦ πνεύματος τοῦ ἁγίου, οὐκ ἀφεθήσεται αὐτῷ οὔτε ἐν τούτῳ τῷ αἰῶνι οὔτε ἐν τῷ μέλλοντι. 33 ἢ ποιήσατε τὸ δένδρον καλὸν καὶ τὸν καρπὸν αὐτοῦ καλόν, ἢ ποιήσατε τὸ δένδρον σαπρὸν καὶ τὸν καρπὸν αὐτοῦ σαπρόν· ἐκ γὰρ τοῦ καρποῦ τὸ δένδρον γινώσκεται. 34 γεννήματα ἐχιδνῶν, πῶς δύνασθε ἀγαθὰ λαλεῖν πονηροὶ ὄντες; ἐκ γὰρ τοῦ περισσεύματος τῆς καρδίας τὸ στόμα λαλεῖ. 35 ὁ ἀγαθὸς ἄνθρωπος ἐκ τοῦ ἀγαθοῦ θησαυροῦ ἐκβάλλει ἀγαθά, καὶ ὁ πονηρὸς ἄνθρωπος ἐκ τοῦ πονηροῦ θησαυροῦ ἐκβάλλει πονηρά. 36 λέγω δὲ ὑμῖν ὅτι πᾶν ῥῆμα ἀργὸν ὃ ἐὰν λαλήσωσιν οἱ ἄνθρωποι, ἀποδώσουσιν περὶ αὐτοῦ λόγον ἐν ἡμέρᾳ κρίσεως· 37 ἐκ γὰρ τῶν λόγων σου δικαιωθήσῃ, καὶ ἐκ τῶν λόγων σου καταδικασθήσῃ.

τὰ ἁμαρτήματα καὶ αἱ βλασφημίαι, ὅσα ἐὰν βλασφημήσωσιν· 29 ὃς δ' ἂν βλασφημήσῃ εἰς τὸ πνεῦμα τὸ ἅγιον, οὐκ ἔχει ἄφεσιν εἰς τὸν αἰῶνα, ἀλλὰ ἔνοχός ἐστιν αἰωνίου ἁμαρτήματος. 30 ὅτι ἔλεγον· πνεῦμα ἀκάθαρτον ἔχει.

12 10 *(169.): καὶ πᾶς ὃς ἐρεῖ λόγον εἰς τὸν υἱὸν τοῦ ἀνθρώπου, ἀφεθήσεται αὐτῷ· τῷ δὲ εἰς τὸ ἅγιον πνεῦμα βλασφημήσαντι οὐκ ἀφεθήσεται.*

90.

(87) ***100.*** Die Zeichenforderung der Pharisäer. *The Pharisees Seek a Sign.* **Matth 12** 38–42

38 Τότε ἀπεκρίθησαν αὐτῷ τινες τῶν γραμματέων καὶ Φαρισαίων λέγοντες· διδάσκαλε, θέλομεν ἀπὸ σοῦ σημεῖον ἰδεῖν.	*16* 1f. 4 *(132.): Καὶ προσελθόντες οἱ Φαρισαῖοι καὶ Σαδδουκαῖοι πειράζοντες ἐπηρώτησαν αὐτὸν σημεῖον ἐκ τοῦ οὐ-*	*8* 11f. *(132.): Καὶ ἐξῆλθον οἱ Φαρισαῖοι καὶ ἤρξαντο συζητεῖν αὐτῷ, ζητοῦντες παρ' αὐτοῦ σημεῖον ἀπὸ τοῦ οὐ-*	*11* 16 *(163.): ἕτεροι δὲ* *cf. 163.* *πειράζοντες σημεῖον ἐξ οὐ-*	2 18 : ἀπεκρίθησαν οὖν οἱ Ἰουδαῖοι καὶ εἶπαν αὐτῷ· τί σημεῖον δεικνύεις ἡμῖν, ὅτι ταῦτα ποιεῖς; 6 30 : εἶπον οὖν αὐτῷ· τί οὖν ποιεῖς σὺ σημεῖον, ἵνα ἴδωμεν καὶ

Mt 12,31 *om* η—αφεθ.‖p: X *l*47 *L*ag^{1}l(30 remittetur^{1} ⌒ ^{2}) vg^{3} **35** θησ.^{1} + της καρδιας αυτου(*om*)‖Lk645: L-33 λ1-22-1582 (ϕ1689 σ517) 157 *pc* Chr$^{1:2}$ Or$^{1:2}$ *L*(f)z30 vg^{3} Au *S*scj *Arm Aeth* — + αυτου: *C* | εκβ.(^{1} *et*)^{2}] προφερει‖←: ΝΣ-1604 (1093 *L*'⟨k[e]⟩)d (vg Au) | ● αγαθα] τα αγ.‖←: ℵCL-33 ΝΣΦ-28-1604 **λ**-1582 ϕ13-346-826-828-*l*547 σ1010-1207-1293-1424 U Δ Ω *pc* Chr Or *C*s$^{2:6}$b^{1} — το αγαθον‖←: σ945 *pc C*s$^{1:6}$b' | θησ.^{2} + της καρδιας αυτου(*om*)‖Lk645a: L-33 (1604 ϕ1689) σ1424-1675 157 *pc* Chr$^{1:2}$ *L*30 vg^{2} Au$^{3:5}$ *S*scj^{ab} *Arm* — + αυτου: *C* | πονηρα] τα π.‖Lk645: L-33 ΝΣ-28-1604 **λ**⟨1⟩ ϕ13-346-826-828-1689 σ267-659-945-954-1207-1293 U Δ Chr *C*s$^{2:6}$b^{6} — το πονηρον‖←: 1579 *L*vg^{1} *C*s$^{1:6}$b'
36 ◆ *om* εαν: ℵB D 1555 *L*' — *txt* (αν): *Rpl* (L σ267) Chr Or^{1}(^{1}) *L*hz | ◆ λαλησουσιν: ℵBC-33 945-1223-1391 D(λαλουσιν) Θ 1555 *pc* — *txt*: *Rpl* Or

Mk 3,28 *om* οσα—βλα.‖**p**: W *L*vl⟨flz⟩r^{1} vg^{1} Cp **29** το πν. το αγ.] το αγ. πν.‖Lk: 28 472 | εις τ. αι.] ουτε εν τω νυν αιωνι ουτε εν τω μελλοντι‖Mt: 1579 Ath^{1} *L*30 — *om*‖Lk: Θ-28-565-700 **λ**⟨118⟩ D W Ath^{1} *L*vl⟨cflz⟩r^{1} Cp *S*s[c] Ath | ● εσται‖Mt521f.: 𝔥⟨B⟩ Σ σ945 D 1342 *pc l*10 *l*48 *l*185 *L*⟨b⟩ Au Cp$^{2:3}$ Eug *S*s[c] *C*s^{1} *Arm Geo*^{1} *Aeth*^{v} *Δ*E^{sa} | αμ.] κρισεως‖←: *Rpl* {*L*fr^{1} vg^{1} *S*' Ath *C*b^{3} *Geo*^{2}}^{1} — κολασεως‖Mt2546: 16 *pc Δ*a p — κριματος‖H62: σ517-1424 {}^{1} — αμαρτιας: C*^{v} **ϕ**'⟨124⟩ (κρισ. και αμαρτιας: 826-828) D W Ath {*L*e[k] a Cp^{2}}^{2} — *txt*: 𝔥 Θ-28-565 *pc* {*L*' Au Cp^{1}(^{1} *prm* κρισ.) Eug *S*s[c] *C*'(*om* αλλα—αμ.‖Lk: s$^{1:3}$b^{1}) *Arm Geo*^{1} *Got Δ*E^{sa}}^{2}

Mt1233-35 *cf.* ETh^{II} 45 (*cf. ad 90.* Lk644f.)
Mt1233 *cf.*? ETh^{II} 43 (*cf. ad 90.* Lk643)
Jo630 *cf.* ETh^{II} 91 (*cf. ad 132.* Mt161-3)

ρανοῦ ἐπιδεῖξαι αὐτοῖς. | ρανοῦ, πειράζοντες αὐτόν. | ρανοῦ ἐζήτουν παρ' αὐτοῦ. | πιστεύσωμέν σοι; τί ἐργάζῃ;

11 29 f. 32. 31 (166.): Τῶν δὲ ὄχλων ἐπαθροιζομένων ἤρξατο λέγειν·

[Matth] 39 ὁ δὲ ἀποκριθεὶς εἶπεν αὐτοῖς· γενεὰ πονηρὰ καὶ μοιχαλὶς σημεῖον ἐπιζητεῖ, καὶ σημεῖον οὐ δοθήσεται αὐτῇ εἰ μὴ τὸ σημεῖον Ἰωνᾶ τοῦ προφήτου. 40 ὥσπερ γὰρ **ἦν Ἰωνᾶς ἐν τῇ κοιλίᾳ τοῦ κήτους τρεῖς ἡμέρας καὶ τρεῖς νύκτας,** οὕτως ἔσται ὁ υἱὸς τοῦ ἀνθρώπου ἐν τῇ καρδίᾳ τῆς γῆς τρεῖς ἡμέρας καὶ τρεῖς νύκτας. 41 ἄνδρες Νινευῖται ἀναστήσονται ἐν τῇ κρίσει μετὰ τῆς γενεᾶς ταύτης καὶ κατακρινοῦσιν αὐτήν· ὅτι μετενόησαν εἰς τὸ κήρυγμα Ἰωνᾶ, καὶ ἰδοὺ πλεῖον Ἰωνᾶ ὧδε. 42 βασίλισσα νότου ἐγερθήσεται ἐν τῇ κρίσει μετὰ τῆς γενεᾶς ταύτης καὶ κατακρινεῖ αὐτήν· ὅτι ἦλθεν ἐκ τῶν περάτων τῆς γῆς ἀκοῦσαι τὴν σοφίαν Σολομῶνος, καὶ ἰδοὺ πλεῖον Σολομῶνος ὧδε.

Jon 2 1

[Matth 16] 2 ὁ δὲ ἀποκριθεὶς εἶπεν αὐτοῖς· ... 4 γενεὰ πονηρὰ καὶ μοιχαλὶς σημεῖον ἐπιζητεῖ, καὶ σημεῖον οὐ δοθήσεται αὐτῇ εἰ μὴ τὸ σημεῖον Ἰωνᾶ...

[Mark] 12 καὶ ἀναστενάξας τῷ πνεύματι αὐτοῦ λέγει· τί ἡ γενεὰ αὕτη ζητεῖ σημεῖον; αμην λέγω ὑμῖν, εἰ δοθήσεται τῇ γενεᾷ ταύτῃ σημεῖον.

[Luk] ἡ γενεὰ αὕτη γενεὰ πονηρά ἐστιν· σημεῖον ζητεῖ, καὶ σημεῖον οὐ δοθήσεται αὐτῇ εἰ μὴ τὸ σημεῖον Ἰωνᾶ. 30 καθὼς γὰρ ἐγένετο Ἰωνᾶς τοῖς Νινευίταις σημεῖον, οὕτως ἔσται καὶ ὁ υἱὸς τοῦ ἀνθρώπου τῇ γενεᾷ ταύτῃ ... 32 ἄνδρες Νινευῖται ἀναστήσονται ἐν τῇ κρίσει μετὰ τῆς γενεᾶς ταύτης καὶ κατακρινοῦσιν αὐτήν· ὅτι μετενόησαν εἰς τὸ κήρυγμα Ἰωνᾶ, καὶ ἰδοὺ πλεῖον Ἰωνᾶ ὧδε ... 31 βασίλισσα νότου ἐγερθήσεται ἐν τῇ κρίσει μετὰ τῶν ἀνδρῶν τῆς γενεᾶς ταύτης καὶ κατακρινεῖ αὐτούς· ὅτι ἦλθεν ἐκ τῶν περάτων τῆς γῆς ἀκοῦσαι τὴν σοφίαν Σολομῶνος, καὶ ἰδοὺ πλεῖον Σολομῶνος ὧδε.

(88)

101. Spruch vom Rückfall. *The Return of the Evil Spirit.*

Matth 12 43-45

43 Ὅταν δὲ τὸ ἀκάθαρτον πνεῦμα ἐξέλθῃ ἀπὸ τοῦ ἀνθρώπου, διέρχεται δι' ἀνύδρων τόπων ζητοῦν ἀνάπαυσιν, καὶ οὐχ εὑρίσκει. 44 τότε λέγει· εἰς τὸν οἶκόν μου ἐπιστρέψω ὅθεν ἐξῆλθον· καὶ ἐλθὸν εὑρίσκει σχολάζοντα σεσαρωμένον καὶ κεκοσμημένον. 45 τότε πορεύεται καὶ παραλαμβάνει μεθ' ἑαυτοῦ ἑπτὰ ἕτερα πνεύματα πονηρότερα ἑαυτοῦ, καὶ εἰσελθόντα κατοικεῖ ἐκεῖ· καὶ γίνεται τὰ ἔσχατα τοῦ ἀνθρώπου ἐκείνου χείρονα τῶν πρώτων. οὕτως ἔσται καὶ τῇ γενεᾷ ταύτῃ τῇ πονηρᾷ.

11 24-26 (164.)

24 Ὅταν τὸ ἀκάθαρτον πνεῦμα ἐξέλθῃ ἀπὸ τοῦ ἀνθρώπου, διέρχεται δι' ἀνύδρων τόπων ζητοῦν ἀνάπαυσιν, καὶ μὴ εὑρίσκον λέγει· ὑποστρέψω εἰς τὸν οἶκόν μου ὅθεν ἐξῆλθον· 25 καὶ ἐλθὸν εὑρίσκει σεσαρωμένον καὶ κεκοσμημένον. 26 τότε πορεύεται καὶ παραλαμβάνει ἕτερα πνεύματα πονηρότερα ἑαυτοῦ ἑπτά, καὶ εἰσελθόντα κατοικεῖ ἐκεῖ· καὶ γίνεται τὰ ἔσχατα τοῦ ἀνθρώπου ἐκείνου χείρονα τῶν πρώτων.

Mt 12,39 επιζ.] ζητει‖Mk Lk: L **40** ην] εγενετο‖p: σ-7-1391 Θ l49 l184 Eu — om: D 472 | εστ. + και‖p: L Σ σ267-692-945-1010-1293-1424-1675 D E W al l1485 Amph Ath Chr[1:2] Cr Eu PsIg Lk[e] abff[1.2]g[1]h Cp[1:2] Ir Or Sc Cb **43** om δε‖p: L 1200 Ss Cb[1] | ουχ ευρ.] μη ευρισκον (et om [44]τοτε)‖(p): (544)-700 (Chr) S(s)c **44** ∼ επιστ./υποστ. εις τ. οι. μου‖p: Rpl L,Eu Or — txt: ℵBZ-33-892 D σ-7-349 | υποστρεψω‖p: Z-892 Σ-700 λ1-1582 ϕ σ71-1391 157 pc | om σχο.‖p: 213 Lg[2] Cs[4:5] | ● σεσ. prm και: ℵC*Z[v] Φ-544 λ⟨1⟩ ϕ174 σ⟨1675⟩ pc Chr[1:2] Lacff[1]hqz30 S Geo[1.A] **45** om μεθ εαυ.‖p: 291 Lff[1]g[1] vg[1]('⟨6⟩ ∼ επ. ετ. πν. μ. εαυ.)

Mt12 40 cf. EN frgm.11 (Cod. Evv. 899): Τὸ Ἰουδαϊκὸν οὐκ ἔχει· τρεῖς ἡ[μέρας καὶ τρεῖς νύκτας].

(89)

102. Jesu wahre Verwandte. *Jesus' Real Brethren.*

Matth 12 46–50

[46] Ἔτι δὲ αὐτοῦ λαλοῦντος τοῖς ὄχλοις, ἰδοὺ ἡ μήτηρ καὶ οἱ ἀδελφοὶ αὐτοῦ εἱστήκεισαν ἔξω ζητοῦντες αὐτῷ λαλῆσαι. [47] εἶπεν δέ τις αὐτῷ· ἰδοὺ ἡ μήτηρ σου καὶ οἱ ἀδελφοί σου ἔξω ἑστήκασιν ζητοῦντές σοι λαλῆσαι. [48] ὁ δὲ ἀποκριθεὶς εἶπεν τῷ λέγοντι αὐτῷ· τίς ἐστιν ἡ μήτηρ μου, καὶ τίνες εἰσὶν οἱ ἀδελφοί μου; [49] καὶ ἐκτείνας τὴν χεῖρα αὐτοῦ ἐπὶ τοὺς μαθητὰς αὐτοῦ εἶπεν· ἰδοὺ ἡ μήτηρ μου καὶ οἱ ἀδελφοί μου.

Mark 3 31–35

[31] Καὶ ἔρχονται οἱ ἀδελφοὶ καὶ ἡ μήτηρ αὐτοῦ, **98.** καὶ ἔξω στήκοντες ἀπέστειλαν πρὸς αὐτὸν φωνοῦντες αὐτόν. [32] καὶ ἐκάθητο περὶ αὐτὸν ὄχλος, καὶ λέγουσιν αὐτῷ· ἰδοὺ ἡ μήτηρ σου καὶ οἱ ἀδελφοί σου καὶ αἱ ἀδελφαί σου ἔξω ζητοῦσίν σε. [33] καὶ ἀποκριθεὶς αὐτοῖς λέγει· τίς ἐστιν ἡ μήτηρ μου ἢ οἱ ἀδελφοί μου; [34] καὶ περιβλεψάμενος τοὺς περὶ αὐτὸν κύκλῳ καθημένους λέγει· ἴδε ἡ μήτηρ μου καὶ οἱ ἀδελφοί μου.

8 19–21 (117.)

[19] *Παρεγένοντο δὲ πρὸς αὐτὸν ἡ μήτηρ καὶ οἱ ἀδελφοὶ αὐτοῦ, καὶ οὐκ ἠδύναντο συντυχεῖν αὐτῷ διὰ τὸν ὄχλον.* [20] *ἀπηγγέλη δὲ αὐτῷ ὅτι ἡ μήτηρ σου καὶ οἱ ἀδελφοί σου ἑστήκασιν ἔξω ἰδεῖν σε θέλοντες.* [21] *ὁ δὲ ἀποκριθεὶς εἶπεν πρὸς αὐτούς· μήτηρ μου καὶ ἀδελφοί μου οὗτοί εἰσιν*

15 14: ὑμεῖς φίλοι μού ἐστε,

Mt 12,46 ετι—λαλου.] ● ετι αυ.λα.: ℵB-33 σ1424 *pc* *L*'(*prm* και: g^{2}) *C*b^{1} *Arm* — ταυτα αυ. λα.: *L*k[e] abff^{2}g^{1}hz — λα. δε(*om*) αυ.: LZ-892 D (Or) *L*(ff^{1}) Or *S*(sc)p *C*s^{5}(^{2})b'(^{1} *Aeth*) — *txt*: *Rpl* *L*q *S*h *C*b^{1} | μη. + αυτου‖Mk: ϕ1689 157 *pc* Or *L*⟨cq⟩ *S* *C* **47** ● *om* 47 (^{46}⌒^{47}λαλη.?): ℵ*BLΓ*pc* *l*12 *L*k[e] ff^{1} *S*sc *C*s | ∼ εστ. εξω‖46Lk: 33 **σ**-349-659 D 253 *l*49 Eu *L*a Or *Geo* | σοι λαλ.] σε ιδειν (*om*)‖Lk: (ℵ^{a})-892(σοι) **σ**⟨954⟩-7 *l*49 *L*a(lz vg$^{\langle 3\rangle}$) Or (*C*b) **48** *om* η‖Lk: X Ep$^{1:2}$(∼ μου εστ. μη.) | και] η‖Mk: D W Θ 248(η και) 1012 *L*k[e] aff$^{1.2}$hq vg^{1} *S*s *C*b *Arm* | τιν. εισ.] τινες: W *pc* *l*48 *l*184 Chr$^{1:3}$ — *om*‖Mk: Σ 258 Chr$^{1:3}$ *L*k[e] cff^{2}g^{1} Or *S*s

Mk 3,31 ● ερχεται: ℵ-892 Θ-565 **λ** σ115-179 D G W *pc* *L*vl'r^{1} vg^{1} — *txt*: *Rpl* *L*cflz vg' Au *S*'[sc] *C* | ∼ η μη. ... οι αδ.‖Mt: 𝔥⟨33⟩C Θ-565-1071 **λ**'(εξερ-‖21: 131) σ7-115-179-267-349-659 D G W 1241 1342 *l*2 *l*36 *l*49 *l*184 *L*,Au *S*p *C* — *txt* (αδ. + αυτου): *Rpl* (ϕ983 σM-27-1402 A K Π *al* *l*18 *l*19) *S*(s[c])h *Arm* | φων. αυ.] ● καλουντες αυ.: 𝔥'⟨33⟩C Θ-28-700 **λ** **ϕ**'(828 αυτω) W {*L*⟨ac⟩} *S*,j — λαλουντες αυ.: 565 — ζητουντες αυ.‖Mt: A — *om*: Δ(*spat.*) **32** κ. λεγ.] ειπον δε‖Mt: *Rpl* (ειποντων δε *et* αυτων: Θ-28-565-700) *S*h *C*s — *txt*: 𝔥⟨33⟩C 1071 **ϕ** D W 1342 *L*'(κ. ειπον: e[k] ac) *S*' *C*b | *om* ιδ.‖Lk: 472 569 | ● *om* κ. αι αδ. σου‖**p**33: 𝔥C ΘΣΦ-28-565-1071-1604 **λ** **ϕ**-230 σ115-179-827-1082-1402 G K W Π **074** *al* *L*e[k] lr^{1}z vg Fau^{R} Hgm *S*' *C* — *txt*: *Rpl* EEb↓ *L*vl' *S*h^{m} | ζητ.] στηκουσιν ζητουντες‖Mt: W *L*a(?)b(+ σοι λαλησαι‖Mt)fr^{1}(?) — στ.(-οντες) ζητ.(-ουσιν) σε ιδειν‖Lk: *L*e[k] (c) **33** αποκ. αυ. λεγ.] ● απεκριθη αυ. λεγων(*om*): *Rpl* *L*(a)f *C*s — ειπεν αυ.‖Mt: 33 *S*s[c] — απεκρ. και ειπεν αυ.‖Mt: W *S*p — απεκρ. αυ. και λεγει: 28-700 **λ**⟨118⟩ **ϕ**⟨124⟩ *L*b(ειπεν *et* *om* αυ.) *C*b^{1}(^{3}∼ και λε. αυ.) — αποκ. ειπ. αυ.: e[k] cff^{2}qr^{1}(?) — *txt*: 𝔥⟨33⟩C(∼ λε. αυ.) 1071-1604 *pc* *L*l(*om* αυ.)z vg'(^{2}) *S*h *C*b' | *om* η^{1}‖Lk: 700 ϕ13-346 | η^{2}] ● και‖Mt: ℵBCLΔ-892 ΘΦ-565-1071 **λ** ϕ543-983 σ27-349-517-692-1082-1194-1606 G U V W Y Ω 1342 *pm* *L*ablz vg *S*p *C*' — *txt*: *Rpl* *L*vl'[k] *S*' *C*b^{1} *Arm* | *om* οι‖Lk: 700 D *pc* | ● *om* μου^{2}: B D *Arm* **34** καθ.] *prm* μαθητας‖Mt: Θ-28-565-700 **ϕ** *C*s$^{3:5}$ *Arm* — καθ. + μαθ.: W | λεγ.] ειπεν‖p: Θ-28-565-700 **ϕ** D G 495 *L*acff^{2} | ιδου‖Mt: Δ-33 Σ-28-565-700 **λ** **ϕ** σM-1402 A D G K Y Π *pm* | μου^{2} + ουτοι εισιν‖Lk: 1071

---

102. cf. EEb frgm.5 (Ep haer. 30,14,5): ... ἀπὸ τοῦ λόγου οὗ εἴρηκεν ὁ σωτὴρ ἐν τῷ ἀναγγελῆναι αὐτῷ ὅτι· 'ἰδοὺ ἡ μήτηρ σου καὶ οἱ ἀδελφοί σου ἔξω ἑστήκασιν', ὅτι· 'τίς μού ἐστιν μήτηρ καὶ ἀδελφοί;' καὶ ἐκτείνας τὴν χεῖρα ἐπὶ τοὺς μαθητὰς ἔφη· 'οὗτοί εἰσιν οἱ ἀδελφοί μου καὶ ἡ μήτηρ καὶ ἀδελφαὶ οἱ ποιοῦντες τὰ θελήματα τοῦ πατρός μου.'

cf. ETh^{II} 99 (*transl.*): *Εἶπον οἱ μαθηταὶ αὐτῷ· οἱ ἀδελφοί σου καὶ ἡ μήτηρ σου ἑστήκασιν ἔξω. εἶπεν αὐτοῖς· οὗτοι οἱ ποιοῦντες τὸ θέλημα τοῦ πατρός μου, οὗτοί εἰσιν οἱ ἀδελφοί μου καὶ ἡ μήτηρ μου. αὐτοὶ εἰσελεύσονται εἰς τὴν βασιλείαν τοῦ πατρός μου.*

Matth	Mark		Luk
[50] ὅστις γὰρ ἂν ποιήσῃ τὸ θέλημα τοῦ πατρός μου τοῦ ἐν οὐρανοῖς, αὐτός μου ἀδελφὸς καὶ ἀδελφὴ καὶ μήτηρ ἐστίν.	[35] ὃς γὰρ ἂν ποιήσῃ τὸ θέλημα τοῦ θεοῦ, οὗτος ἀδελφός μου καὶ ἀδελφὴ καὶ μήτηρ ἐστίν.	*οἱ τὸν λόγον τοῦ θεοῦ ἀκούοντες καὶ ποιοῦντες.*	ἐὰν ποιῆτε ἃ ἐγὼ ἐντέλλομαι ὑμῖν.

(90) **103.** Das Gleichnis vom Säemann. *The Parable of the Sower.*

Matth 13 1–9	Mark 4 1–9		Luk 8 4–8
[1] Ἐν τῇ ἡμέρᾳ ἐκείνῃ ἐξελθὼν ὁ Ἰησοῦς τῆς οἰκίας ἐκάθητο παρὰ τὴν θάλασσαν· [2] καὶ συνήχθησαν πρὸς αὐτὸν ὄχλοι πολλοί, ὥστε αὐτὸν	[1] Καὶ πάλιν ἤρξατο διδάσκειν παρὰ τὴν θάλασσαν· καὶ συνάγεται πρὸς αὐτὸν ὄχλος πλεῖστος, ὥστε αὐτὸν		[4] Συνιόντος δὲ ὄχλου πολλοῦ καὶ τῶν κατὰ πόλιν ἐπιπορευομένων πρὸς αὐτὸν
εἰς πλοῖον ἐμβάντα καθῆσθαι, καὶ πᾶς ὁ ὄχλος ἐπὶ τὸν αἰγιαλὸν εἱστήκει.	εἰς πλοῖον ἐμβάντα καθῆσθαι ἐν τῇ θαλάσσῃ, καὶ πᾶς ὁ ὄχλος πρὸς τὴν θάλασσαν ἐπὶ τῆς γῆς ἦσαν.	*3 9 (84.): ... ἵνα πλοιάριον προσκαρτερῇ αὐτῷ διὰ τὸν ὄχλον, ἵνα μὴ θλίβωσιν αὐτόν· ...*	*5 3 (29.): ἐμβὰς δὲ εἰς ἓν τῶν πλοίων, ... καθίσας δὲ ἐκ τοῦ πλοίου ἐδίδασκεν τοὺς ὄχλους.*
[3] καὶ ἐλάλησεν αὐτοῖς πολλὰ ἐν παραβολαῖς λέγων·	[2] καὶ ἐδίδασκεν αὐτοὺς ἐν παραβολαῖς πολλά, καὶ ἔλεγεν αὐτοῖς ἐν τῇ διδαχῇ αὐτοῦ·		εἶπεν διὰ παραβολῆς·

Mt 12,50 οστ.] ος‖Mk: L Σ *pc* | ● ποιη‖7 24 Jo 9 31 7 17: C 700 σ1010-1194-1293 D(-ει *et om* αν) Δ *pc* — *txt*: *Rpl* Or *L*,Or | αυτ.] ουτος‖Mk: L Σ-28-700-1604 ϕ174 σ1424 Δ 157 *pc* Chr *Le*(ille)k ff[1] *S*ch[m] *C*s | εν + τοις *cf.* 5 17 6 9 7 11 *etc.*: 33-892 σ1010-1293 *pc* **13,3** ~ εν παρ. πο.‖Mk: C 157 *pc* *L*z

Mk 3,35 ● *om* γαρ: B W(και ος) *Le*[k] b(= W: ac) *C*b⟨3⟩ | ποι.] ποιη‖Jo: W *pc* | θε.] πατρος μου‖Mt: 998 1342 *C*b[2] | ουτ.] αυτος‖Mt: 256 | ~ μου αδελφος‖Mt: D W 713 1574 *L*(μοι: e[k] b)ff[2]qz vg[1] **4,1** συνηχθη(-ησαν)‖5 21(Mt): *Rpl* (565 A *pc l*8 *l*10) *L*Or — συνερχεται (-ονται)‖3 20: λ1-(131)-209 — *txt*: ℌ⟨33⟩C 28-700 ϕ | πλει.] πολυς‖5 21 Lk Mt: *Rpl* *L*Or *Geo* — *txt*: ℌ⟨Δ-33⟩C D W | εις + το‖5 18 6 45 8 10 p: *Rpl* *C*' *Δ*a — *txt*: ℌ⟨Δ⟩C ΘΣΦ-565 λ σM-115-179-517-954-1402 K Π 074 157 1342 *al* *C*b[2](εις εν των πλοιων) | εν τη θ.] παρα τον αιγιαλον‖Mt: W *Le*[k] abcff[2] *C*b[2](*prm* εν τ. θ.) | προς[2]—γης] εν τω αιγιαλω‖Mt: W *Le*[k] bcfff[2]r[1]z vg[1] **2** ~ πο. εν παρ.‖Mt: ℵ 1574 *S*s[c] *C*s[2:5]b | και[2] ελ.] λεγων‖Mt: 28 | και[2]—αυτου] λεγων‖Mt: W *Le*[k] bc Or — + λεγ.: *L*q

Lk 8,4 δια πα.] παραβολην τοιαυτην(*om*) προς αυτους‖15 3 12 16 13 6: D 39 *Le*(*om* πρ. αυ.) b(c)lqr[1] (vg[1]) Or(= e) *Δ*i[V]

Jo 15,14 ποιησητε‖Mt Mk: D *L*⟨a⟩ Cp PsCp | α] οσα‖Mt 28 20: *Rpl* Cr[1] Thd[C2] *S*' {} — ● ο: B-579 *Le* aq Cp Luc[2] *C*b[B] *Arm Aeth* — *txt*: 𝔓[66] ℵLWX 1071 λ1-1582 ϕ⟨124⟩ D 0141 565 Thd[C1] *L*' PsCp Luc[1] *S*s[c]h[m]j {*C*'a[s]} | *om* εγω‖←: Λ *pc* *Le* a vg[1] Cp PsCp *S*s[c]ph[Brs] *C*[+B]a[s]

Mt 12 50 p *cf.* 2Cl 9 11: καὶ γὰρ εἶπεν ὁ κύριος· 'ἀδελφοί μου οὗτοί εἰσιν οἱ ποιοῦντες τὸ θέλημα τοῦ πατρός μου.'

103. cf. ETh[II] 9 (*transl.*): *Λέγει Ἰησοῦς· ἰδοὺ ἐξῆλθεν ὁ σπείρων (καὶ) ἔπλησεν τὴν χεῖρα αὐτοῦ (καὶ) ἐξέβαλεν. ἃ μὲν ἔπεσεν ἐπὶ τὴν ὁδόν, (καὶ) ἦλθεν τὰ πετεινὰ (καὶ) συνέλεξεν αὐτά. ἄλλα ἔπεσεν ἐπὶ τὴν πέτραν καὶ οὐκ ἔβαλεν ῥίζαν εἰς τὴν γῆν κάτω οὐδὲ ἀνέπεμψεν στάχυν εἰς τὸν οὐρανὸν ἄνω. καὶ ἄλλα ἔπεσεν εἰς τὰς ἀκάνθας, (καὶ) ἀπέπνιξαν τὸν σπόρον καὶ ὁ σκώληξ ἔφαγεν αὐτά. καὶ ἄλλα ἔπεσεν ἐπὶ τὴν γῆν τὴν ἀγαθήν, καὶ ἔδωκεν καρπὸν ἀγαθόν. ἔφερεν ἑξήκοντα κατ' ἄρουραν καὶ ἑκατὸν εἴκοσι κατ' ἄρουραν.*

Matth	Mark	Luk
ἰδοὺ ἐξῆλθεν ὁ σπείρων τοῦ	[3] ἀκούετε. ἰδοὺ ἐξῆλθεν ὁ σπείρων	[5] ἐξῆλθεν ὁ σπείρων τοῦ
σπείρειν. [4] καὶ	σπεῖραι. [4] καὶ ἐγένετο	σπεῖραι τὸν σπόρον αὐτοῦ. καὶ
ἐν τῷ σπείρειν αὐτὸν ἃ μὲν ἔπεσεν	ἐν τῷ σπείρειν ὃ μὲν ἔπεσεν	ἐν τῷ σπείρειν αὐτὸν ὃ μὲν ἔπεσεν
παρὰ τὴν ὁδόν, καὶ	παρὰ τὴν ὁδόν, καὶ	παρὰ τὴν ὁδὸν καὶ κατεπατήθη, καὶ
ἦλθεν τὰ πετεινὰ καὶ κατέφα-	ἦλθεν τὰ πετεινὰ καὶ κατέφα-	τὰ πετεινὰ τοῦ οὐρανοῦ κατέφα-
γεν αὐτά. [5] ἄλλα δὲ ἔπεσεν ἐπὶ	γεν αὐτό. [5] καὶ ἄλλο ἔπεσεν ἐπὶ	γεν αὐτό. [6] καὶ ἕτερον κατέπεσεν ἐπὶ
τὰ πετρώδη ὅπου οὐκ εἶχεν γῆν	τὸ πετρῶδες ὅπου οὐκ εἶχεν γῆν	τὴν πέτραν,
πολλήν, καὶ εὐθέως ἐξανέτειλεν διὰ τὸ	πολλήν, καὶ εὐθὺς ἐξανέτειλεν διὰ τὸ	καὶ φυὲν
μὴ ἔχειν βάθος γῆς·	μὴ ἔχειν βάθος γῆς· [6] καὶ ὅτε ἀνέτειλεν	
[6] ἡλίου δὲ ἀνατείλαντος ἐκαυματίσθη,	ὁ ἥλιος ἐκαυματίσθη,	ἐξηράνθη
καὶ διὰ τὸ μὴ ἔχειν ῥίζαν ἐξηράνθη.	καὶ διὰ τὸ μὴ ἔχειν ῥίζαν ἐξηράνθη.	διὰ τὸ μὴ ἔχειν ἰκμάδα.
[7] ἄλλα δὲ ἔπεσεν ἐπὶ τὰς	[7] καὶ ἄλλο ἔπεσεν εἰς τὰς	[7] καὶ ἕτερον ἔπεσεν ἐν μέσῳ τῶν
ἀκάνθας, καὶ ἀνέβησαν αἱ ἄκανθαι	ἀκάνθας, καὶ ἀνέβησαν αἱ ἄκανθαι	ἀκανθῶν, καὶ συμφυεῖσαι αἱ ἄκανθαι
καὶ ἔπνιξαν αὐτά.	καὶ συνέπνιξαν αὐτό, καὶ καρπὸν οὐκ	ἀπέπνιξαν αὐτό.
[8] ἄλλα δὲ ἔπεσεν ἐπὶ	ἔδωκεν. [8] καὶ ἄλλα ἔπεσεν εἰς	[8] καὶ ἕτερον ἔπεσεν εἰς
τὴν γῆν τὴν καλὴν καὶ ἐδίδου	τὴν γῆν τὴν καλὴν καὶ ἐδίδου	τὴν γῆν τὴν ἀγαθὴν καὶ φυὲν ἐποίη-
καρπούς,	καρπὸν ἀναβαίνοντα καὶ αὐξα-	σεν καρπὸν
ὃ μὲν ἑκατόν,	νόμενα, καὶ ἔφερεν ἓν τριάκοντα	ἑκατοντα-

Mt 12,3 *om* ιδου‖Lk: 280 1396 *pc* *L*ff^1 | *om* του‖Mk: σ1424 D | σπειραι‖p: ℵLX-33-892 ΣΦ-28-544-700 **λ** **ϕ**-174-230 σM-7-71-267-659-1010-1293-1391-1424-1675 D S W Θ Ω *pc* Or | σπει. + τον σπορον αυτου(*om*)‖Lk: 28 σ71 (485 1241) *pc* *L*bff^{1}h30 (*S*s) **4** και^1 + εγενετο‖Mk: 485 *C*s^{1}b^2 | α] ο‖p: ϕ828 Δ *pc* | οδ. + και επατηθη‖Lk: ϕ346 726 | ηλθ.—και^3] ● ελθοντα τα πε.: B **ϕ**-174 (+ και) σ659-1391-1402-1424-1675 Θ *pc* — *txt*: *Rpl* (ηλθον: LZ-33 ϕ1689 D *pc*) *L* | πετ. + του ουρανου‖4 32p Lk: ΣΦ **ϕ**-174 **σ**⟨1675⟩-M-659-1010-1293-1402 E K Θ Π *al* *L*bff^{1}h vg^2 *S*ch *C*sb^2 *Arm* *Aeth* | αυτα] αυτο‖p: 1012 **5** αλλα δε] και αλλο‖p: 1012 **7** επι] εις‖Mk: **ϕ**⟨828⟩-230 D Eu | ● απεπνι.‖Lk: *Rpl* — συνεπνι.‖Mk: 1574 — *txt*: ℵ Φ **ϕ**-174 D Θ

Mk 4,3 ακουσατε‖Mt13 18: C 565 σ349-517 *pc* — *om*‖**p**: λ872 σ27-1194 *pc* *L*cq Or | *om* ιδου‖Lk: 217 *pc* *L*Or *Geo*^{2}(+ τουτο) | σπειραι] σπειρειν‖Mt: 1279 {} — του σπει.‖p: *Rpl* Hip {} — *om*: D' *C*s^{1}b' — + τον σπορον αυτου‖Lk: 1071 σ71-179-1424-1606 F **047** 157 *pc* *L*g^2 — *txt*: ℵ*B W **074** 2145 {*C*s^{3}b^8} **4** *om* εγε.‖Mt Lk: σ1082 D F W *L*⟨a vg^2⟩ *S*s[c]p *C*s | σπει. + αυτον‖Mt Lk: 1071 σ827 *pc* | ο] α‖Mt: 33 28 1241 *L*e[k] *C*s$^{4:6}$ | πετ. + του ουρανου‖4 30 Lk: 892 σM-115-179 D G *al* *l*50 *l*51 *L*ag^{2}iqr^1 vg^1 *C*s$^{1:5}$ | αυτα‖Mt: 33 Θ-28-565 *pc* *L*e[k] ff^2 *C*s **5** και αλ.] αλλο(-α) δε‖8 Mt: *Rpl* (28 **ϕ** W) *L*' *S*' *C*s^1(^{4}) — αλλο: σM-945-1223 *L*b vg^2 — και αλλο δε‖Mt: *l*49 *l*184 *l*251 *l*260 *L*a — *txt* (-α): 𝔋'(33)C Θ-(565)-1071 σM^c (D) 1342 *pc* *l*12 (*l*18 *l*19) *l*48 *L*d *S*s[c] *C*b *Arm* | τα πετρωδη‖Mt: ℵ*-33 Θ-565 **λ** σ179-517 D W 1342 *pc* *L*⟨ag^{2}i vg^1⟩ | εξαν.] ● εξεβλαστησαν‖4 27 Mt13 26: 28-700 **λ**'(131 εβλ-) **ϕ** **6** και—ηλ.] ηλιου δε ανατειλαντος‖Mt: *Rpl* *L*e[k] af — *txt*: 𝔋⟨33⟩C Θ-565-1071 σ349-517 D 372 1342 *L*'⟨bc30⟩ *C* **7** αλλα(-ο) … αυτα‖8 Mt: 33 (Θ)-28 ϕ124 W *L*e[k] (b) *C*s^4(^{1}) | εις] επι‖Mt: C-33 Θ-544-565-700 σM-1194-1402 D W *al* *l*48 *L*b *C*sb$^{\langle 4\rangle}$ | απεπν.‖Lk: 33-892 Σ-700 σ7-179-267-349-517-659-945-1194 1342 *pc* — επν.‖Mt: 21 108 | εδω.] εποιησεν‖Lk8 13 9 Mt13 26: Θ 565 σ517 **8** ● αλλο‖5.7 Lk: *Rpl* *L*' — *txt*: 𝔋⟨Δ⟩C Θ-28 ϕ124 W *L*e[k] *C* | εις] επι‖Mt: C Σ-28-544-565 **λ** ϕ124 σ349-1402 *al* *l*49 *C* | καλ.] αγαθην‖Lk: 565 | αυξανοντα‖Mt6 28p Lk13 19: *Rpl* — *txt* (-ον): ℵB(LD-892) 1071 (A D W 238) | εν … εν … εν] ● εις … εις(εν) … εις(εν): ℵ(B)C*^{v}(L) Δ 28-700

Lk 8,5 εξ.] ιδου εξ.‖p: 74 483 *L*vl⟨cf⟩g^{2}r^{1}30 *S*scj *C*b^1 | *om* του^1‖Mk: W 1604 D K Π *al* | σπειραι] σπειρειν‖Mt: W | *om* αυτον‖Mk: D | ο] α‖Mt: BW *C*s | κατεπ. + υπο των ανθρωπων‖Mt5 13: 472 | *om* του ουρ.‖p: W 544 D *L*e abff^{2}lq *S*scp | αυτο] αυτα‖Mt: 𝔓^{75} B *pc* *C*s **6-8** ετερον] αλλο‖p: D **6** κατεπ.] επεσεν‖**p**5**p**.7**p**.8**p**: *Rpl* — *txt*: 𝔓^{75}BLΞ 700 R | πετρ. + οπου ουκ ειχεν γην πολλην‖p: 1604 | ικμ.] ριζαν‖p: 579 *Aeth* **7** απε.] επνιξαν‖Mt: ℵ* | αυτα‖Mt: 𝔓^{75} 472 **8** εις] επι‖Mt: W-1241 544-700 λ1278-1582-2193 ϕ124 **σ**⟨1675⟩-945 D **047** 157 *al* *L*ac | αγ.] καλην‖8 15 Mt Mk: **σ**' 713 — αγ. και καλ.‖p 8 15: Θ σ1424 D *L*e a(∼) cr^1 *S*c(αγ. και καρποφορουσαν)p

Matth	Mark	Luk
ὃ δὲ ἑξήκοντα, ὃ δὲ τριάκοντα. 9 ὁ ἔχων ὦτα ἀκουέτω.	καὶ ἓν ἑξήκοντα καὶ ἓν ἑκατόν. 9 καὶ ἔλεγεν· ὃς ἔχει ὦτα ἀκούειν ἀκουέτω.	πλασίονα. ταῦτα λέγων ἐφώνει· ὁ ἔχων ὦτα ἀκούειν ἀκουέτω.

(91) **104.** Zweck der Gleichnisrede. *The Reason for Parables.*

Matth 13 10–15	Mark 4 10–12	Luk 8 9–10
10 Καὶ προσελθόντες οἱ μαθηταὶ εἶπαν αὐτῷ· διὰ τί ἐν παραβολαῖς λαλεῖς αὐτοῖς; 11 ὁ δὲ ἀποκριθεὶς εἶπεν αὐτοῖς· ὅτι ὑμῖν δέδοται γνῶναι τὰ μυστήρια τῆς βασιλείας τῶν οὐρανῶν, ἐκείνοις δὲ οὐ δέδοται. 12 ὅστις γὰρ ἔχει, δοθήσεται αὐτῷ καὶ περισσευθήσεται· ὅστις δὲ οὐκ ἔχει, καὶ ὃ ἔχει ἀρθήσεται ἀπ' αὐτοῦ. 13 διὰ τοῦτο ἐν παραβολαῖς αὐτοῖς λαλῶ, (Is6 9) ὅτι **βλέποντες** οὐ **βλέπουσιν** καὶ	10 Καὶ ὅτε ἐγένετο κατὰ μόνας, ἠρώτων αὐτὸν οἱ περὶ αὐτὸν σὺν τοῖς δώδεκα τὰς παραβολάς. 11 καὶ ἔλεγεν αὐτοῖς· ὑμῖν τὸ μυστήριον δέδοται τῆς βασιλείας τοῦ θεοῦ· ἐκείνοις δὲ τοῖς ἔξω [107.] ἐν παραβολαῖς τὰ πάντα γίνεται, 12 ἵνα **βλέποντες** **βλέπωσιν καὶ**	9 Ἐπηρώτων δὲ αὐτὸν οἱ μαθηταὶ αὐτοῦ τίς αὕτη εἴη ἡ παραβολή. 10 ὁ δὲ εἶπεν· ὑμῖν δέδοται γνῶναι τὰ μυστήρια τῆς βασιλείας τοῦ θεοῦ, τοῖς δὲ λοιποῖς ἐν παραβολαῖς, ἵνα **βλέποντες** μὴ **βλέπωσιν** καὶ

Mt 13,9 ωτα + ακουειν ‖ Mk Lk: *Rpl* Eu *L*' *S*'Ef *C* — *txt*: ℵ*BL 1241 *L*ek aff^{1} Te *S*s **10** μα + αυτου ‖ Lk: CX σ71-1010-1293 *pc* Eu *L*abcdfg^{1}hπ vg^{3} *S*'h^{+} *C* *Geo*^{B} **11** ● *om* αυτ. ‖ Lk: ℵCZ-892 σ1391 *pc* Eu *L*k ff^{1} *C*bf — *txt*: *Rpl* *L*' *S* *C*s | *om* οτι ‖ **p**: σM Eu *S*p^{1} *Geo*^{A} | τ. ουρ.] του θεου ‖ Mk Lk: 157 *pc* *L*ff^{1}(*om* τ. βασ.) *S*p^{1} — *om*: Eu *L*ek abff^{2}g^{1} *S*s | ου δεδ.] εν παραβολαις ‖ p: σ659-1194-1424-1675 **12** εχ.^{1}] αν εχει(-η) ‖ Lk8 18: (σ1293) Δ 2145 | εχ.^{3}] δοκει εχειν ‖ ←: 301 *pc* Chr *L*Fil **13** οτι] ινα ‖ **p**: λ1-22-1582 ϕ(οτι ινα: 13-346-543-826-828)-124-174-788-983 σ7-1424-1675 D Θ *pc* Cr^{I} Eu *L*ek abff$^{1.2}$g^{1}h Te *C*s | ου βλε. ... ουκ ακ.] μη βλεπωσιν ... μη(*om*) ακουωσιν ‖ Lk Mk: λ1-22-1582 ϕ'(983)-174 σ7-1424-1675 D(ακουσωσιν) Θ *pc* Cr^{I} Eu *L*ek acff^{1}h(∼ ακ. μ. ακ. κ. βλ. μ. βλ.) (bff^{2}g^{1}) Te *C*s

Mk 4,9 ος εχ.] ο εχων ‖ Mk Lk: *Rpl* — *txt*: ℵ*BCΔ-33 544 D **10** επηρωτων(-ησαν) ‖ Lk: Θ-565-(28-700 ϕ) σ517 D(W) *l*251 | οι—δω.] οι μαθηται αυτου ‖ Lk Mt: Θ-28-565 ϕ D W *L*vl[ek]⟨flz⟩r^{1v} vg^{1} Or(*om* αυτου) *S*s[c] — οι μα. αυ. οι—δω. ‖ Lk Mt: σ1424-1675 443 | δω.] μαθηταις αυτου ‖ Lk Mt: 700 — + φρασον ημιν ‖ Mt15 15 13 36: Φ | ● την παραβολην(+ ταυτην) ‖ 7 17(4 13 Lk12 41 20 19): *Rpl* (σ827) *L*vg^{2} (*S*p) *C*b^{1} *Arm*^{pc} — τις η παραβολη αυτη ‖ Lk: Θ-28-565 ϕ D W *pc* *L*vl'[ek] r^{1v} vg^{2} Or *Geo*^{2} — *txt* (+ ταυτας): 𝔖⟨33-579⟩C *L*z vg' (*S*s[c]) *C*' *Arm*' (*Geo*^{1}) **11** *om* αυτ. ‖ Lk: 33 | το μυ. δεδ.] δεδ. γνωναι τ. μ. ‖ Mt Lk: *Rpl* *L*' *S*' *C*b^{4} — δεδ. τ. μ. ‖ p: A K W Π 1342(+ γνωναι) *S*s[c] *C*s — *txt*: ℵBC*^{v}L-892 *C*b' | τα μυστηρια ‖ p: ΣΦ **λ** ϕ983-1689 σ115-517-1194 G *al* *l*49 *l*184 *l*251 *C*s$^{1:5}$b | τ. εξω] ου δεδοται τ. εξω αλλ ‖ Mt: ϕ346 *L*vg^{1} — *om* ‖ Lk: σ71-692 | γιν.] λεγεται ‖ Mt: ΘΣ-28-565-1071 ϕ124 σ349-517-659 D *pc* *L*vl[ek]⟨flz⟩r^{1} vg^{1} *C*s *Geo* **12** βλεπωσιν και] *prm* μη ‖ Lk Mt: Δ 28-1604 σ1082-1223 E F G H *al* Or *L*Or$^{1:2}$ *S*s[c](*om* και) — *om* ‖ Lk Mt: W | *om* και μη ειδ. ‖ Lk Mt: Δ 28 3 Or *L*vg^{1} Or$^{1:2}$ *S*s[c]

Lk 8,8 *om* ταυ.—ακου. *cf. ad* 8 15: 1071 ϕ⟨124⟩-*l*547 σ267-659 Ω *pc* *l*^{p1} **9** *om* αυτου ‖ Mt: W 700 R *pc* *L*abcff^{2}l *Arm* | τις—παρ.] τις ειη η παρ. αυ. ‖ Mk4 13: *Rpl* (*om* ειη: Γ **047** *pc*) (ειη] η: *l*32) *L*e c {} — τις ειη αυ. η παρ. ‖ 11: **λ**-1582 {} — τις αυ. η παρ.: LΞ-1241 σ1223 *pc* {} — περι της παραβολης ‖ Mk7 27 10 10: R — *txt* (*om* η): 𝔓^{75} ℵ(B)W-33-(579) 700 {*L*'Or} **10** ειπ. + αυτοις ‖ p: 1241 1071 **λλ**⟨22-1278⟩ ϕ Θ *pc* *l*32 *L*⟨a⟩ *S*s^{v}cph^{m}j *C* | του θε.] των ουρανων ‖ Mt: ϕ983-1689 *l*1627 *C*b^{2} | παρ. + λαλω ‖ Mt: Λ-1071 ϕ13-230-346-543-826-828 *pc* *L*b *C*s(b^{1} ελαλει) | μη βλε.] μη ειδωσιν(ιδ-) ‖ Mk Is6 9(*cf.* MT!): (LWΞ 700 λ1-131-1582-2193) D — βλε. και μη ιδωσιν ‖ Mk: R

Mt13 9p *cf.* ETh^{II} 24.63.65.96 (*transl.*): *ὁ ἔχων ὦτα ἀκουέτω* (*cf. ad 45.* Mt6 22; *ad 170.*; *ad 218.*; *ad 111.*)

Mt13 12 *cf.* ETh^{II} 41 (*cf. ad 107.* Mk4 25)

Mk4 9 Lk8 8 *cf.* ETh^{II} 8.21 (*transl.*): ... *ὁ ἔχων ὦτα ἀκούειν ἀκουέτω* (*cf. ad 115.*; *ad 108.* Mk4 29)

Matth 13	Mark 4	Luk 8
ἀκούοντες οὐκ **ἀκούουσιν οὐδὲ συνίουσιν.**	**μὴ εἰδῶσιν,** καὶ **ἀκούοντες ἀκούωσιν καὶ μὴ συνίωσιν, μήποτε ἐπιστρέψωσιν καὶ** ἀφεθῇ **αὐτοῖς.**	**ἀκούοντες μὴ συνίωσιν.**

Matth 13		Jo 12
14 καὶ ἀναπληροῦται αὐτοῖς ἡ προφητεία Ἠσαΐου ἡ λέγουσα· **ἀκοῇ ἀκούσετε καὶ οὐ μὴ συνῆτε, καὶ βλέποντες βλέψετε καὶ οὐ μὴ εἰδῆτε.** 15 **ἐπαχύνθη γὰρ ἡ καρδία τοῦ λαοῦ τούτου, καὶ τοῖς ὠσὶν βαρέως ἤκουσαν, καὶ τοὺς ὀφθαλμοὺς αὐτῶν ἐκάμμυσαν· μήποτε ἴδωσιν τοῖς ὀφθαλμοῖς καὶ τοῖς ὠσὶν ἀκούσωσιν καὶ τῇ καρδίᾳ συνῶσιν καὶ ἐπιστρέψωσιν, καὶ ἰάσομαι αὐτούς.**	cf. v. 12 ↑	12 39f.: διὰ τοῦτο οὐκ ἐδύναντο πιστεύειν, ὅτι πάλιν εἶπεν Ἠσαΐας· 40 **τετύφλωκεν αὐτῶν τοὺς ὀφθαλμοὺς καὶ ἐπώρωσεν αὐτῶν τὴν καρδίαν, ἵνα μὴ ἴδωσιν τοῖς ὀφθαλμοῖς καὶ νοήσωσιν τῇ καρδίᾳ καὶ στραφῶσιν, καὶ ἰάσομαι αὐτούς.** (Is69f.)

(92)

105. Selige Augenzeugen. *The Blessedness of the Disciples.*

Matth 13 16–17	*10 23–24 (156.)*
16 Ὑμῶν δὲ μακάριοι οἱ ὀφθαλμοὶ ὅτι βλέπουσιν, καὶ τὰ ὦτα ὑμῶν ὅτι ἀκούουσιν. 17 αμην γὰρ λέγω ὑμῖν ὅτι πολλοὶ προφῆται καὶ δίκαιοι ἐπεθύμησαν ἰδεῖν ἃ βλέπετε καὶ οὐκ εἶδαν, καὶ ἀκοῦσαι ἃ ἀκούετε καὶ οὐκ ἤκουσαν.	*23 Καὶ στραφεὶς πρὸς τοὺς μαθητὰς κατ' ἰδίαν εἶπεν· μακάριοι οἱ ὀφθαλμοὶ οἱ βλέποντες ἃ βλέπετε. 24 λέγω γὰρ ὑμῖν ὅτι πολλοὶ προφῆται καὶ βασιλεῖς ἠθέλησαν ἰδεῖν ἃ ὑμεῖς βλέπετε καὶ οὐκ εἶδαν, καὶ ἀκοῦσαι ἃ ἀκούετε καὶ οὐκ ἤκουσαν.*

Mt 13,13 ουκ ακ. ουδε] ου‖Lk: 544 *pc* | ουδε συνι.] και μη συνιωσιν‖p: λ1-22(κ. μη] μηδε)-1582 **ϕ**-174 σ7-(συνωσιν: 1424-1675 D) Θ *pc* l^{pl}(= 22: *l*950; = D: *l*12 *l*70 *l*80 *l*150 *l*299 *l*850 *l*1084) Cr^{I} *L*bcff$^{1.2}$h Te *Cs* — *om*: Eu *La* | συνι. + μηποτε επιστρεψωσιν(+ και ιασομαι αυτους‖15p)‖Mk: λ1-1582 **ϕ**-174 D Θ (Eu) *L*ek bcff^{2}g^{1}(h) *S*sc **15** συνιωσιν‖Mk12 Lk10: C-33 ϕ13-124-346 | επιστραφωσιν‖Jo: 700 *pc* **17** ● *om* γαρ *cf.* 62.5.16 10 15 *etc.*: ℵX Φ ϕ174-983-1689 1170 1241 *L*'(δε: q; quippe: r^{2} vg$^{\langle 4\rangle}$) Hil *S*p^{2} *C*s^{1}b' *Arm Aeth* — *txt*: *Rpl* *Lk* *S*' *C*s^{2}b^{8}f | *om* και δικ.‖p: B* Eus$^{1:5}$ *L*Cp$^{1:2}$ | βλε. *prm* υμεις‖p: 544 *pc* Eu(*et* ακουετε + υμεις) *L*cfg^{1}30 vg^{1} Cp$^{1:2}$ Ir$^{1:2}$

Mk 4,12 μη^{1}] ου μη‖Mt14 Is69 LXX: λ1278 ϕ346-828 σ179-1082-1391 **047** *pc* | ακουωσιν] ουκ ακ.‖Mt: 443 495 — μη ακ.‖Mt: Δ Or^{1} *L*Or$^{1:2}$ *C*b^{1} — ακουουσιν‖Mt: σ349 Π *pc* — ακουσωσιν‖Mt15: C-33-892 Θ **ϕ**⟨69⟩ σM-179 S *pc* Or^{1} — ακοην *et om* και^{3} *S*s[c] — *om* ακ. και‖Lk: 28 W Or$^{1:2}$ *La* | μη^{2}] ου μη‖Mt14 Is←: 565 λ1278 σ179-1082-1391 | συνωσιν‖Mt15 Is610 LXX: L-892 565-1071 **λ**⟨131⟩ σ179-1424-1606 D* W *pc* Or | αφεθησεται‖Mt15p Is←: 565 λ872 σ179-827 A K Π *al* — αφησω‖←: D^{c}(*αφεθησομαι!) *L*ff^{2}iqr^{1} vg^{1} *Aeth* | αυτ. + τα αμαρτηματα(+ αυτων)‖328: *Rpl* (Δ 700 238 1241) {*L*'(vg^{1} *S*'h αυτων^{+})} — + τα παραπτωματα (+ αυτων)‖11 25 Mt6 14f.: Σ *pc* {} — *txt*: ℵBCL-892 **λ**-1278 W Or *L*b *S*j *C* *Geo*

Lk 8,10 ακ. + ακουσωσιν(ακουωσιν) και‖Mk: (ℵ)-579 1071 **ϕ**'⟨346⟩(983) R Θ *pc* — + μη ακουσωσιν μηδε‖Mt: F^{W} *pc* *L*30 *S*h^{m} *C*b *Aeth* | συνι.] ακουωσιν‖Mt: 157 *L*dl

Jo 12,40 ∼ τους οφ. αυ.‖Mt: 1242 {*L*⟨c⟩} | τοις οφ. + και τοις ωσιν ακουσωσιν‖Mt Is610 LXX: 544 **ϕ**-*l*547$^{1:2}$ | νοησ. τ. καρ.] τ. καρ. συν(ι)ωσιν‖Mt Is←: ℵ 544 σ1223 K Π *al* (*pc*) *L*ff^{2}lqz — ακουσωσιν‖Mt: *S*s[c] | επιστρ.‖Mt Is←: *Rpl* — επεστρεψωσιν(-ουσιν)‖←: LWX (**ϕ**')-543-(*l*547$^{1:2}$) σM-1223-1293 K Π *pc* Ath Ddy Eu — *txt*: 𝔓$^{66.75}$ 𝔥'⟨892⟩ D* Ψ Or

---

105. cf. ETh^{II} 38 (POxy 655 IIa): Λέ[γει Ἰ(ησοῦ)ς· π]ο[λλάκις ἐπεθυμήσα]τα[ι ἀκοῦσαι τοὺς λό]γ[ους οὓς ὑμῖν λέγω] κα[ὶ οὐκ ἔχετε τὸ]ν [ἐροῦντα ὑμῖν] κα[ὶ ἐλεύσονται] ἡμ[έραι ὅτε ζητή]σε[τέ με καὶ οὐχ εὑρήσετέ με.]
(*transl.*): *Λέγει Ἰησοῦς· πολλάκις ἐπεθυμήσατε ἀκούειν ταῦτα τὰ ῥήματα ἃ ἐγὼ λέγω ὑμῖν καὶ οὐκ ἔ(σ?)χετε ἄλλον τινὰ τοῦ ἀκούειν αὐτὰ παρ' αὐτοῦ. ἐλεύσονται ἡμέραι, ὅτε ζητήσετέ με (καὶ) οὐχ εὑρήσετέ με.*

(93) **106.** Deutung des Gleichnisses vom Säemann. *The Interpretation of the Parable of the Sower.*

Matth 13 18–23

[18] Ὑμεῖς οὖν ἀκούσατε τὴν παραβολὴν τοῦ σπείραντος. [19] παντὸς ἀκούοντος τὸν λόγον τῆς βασιλείας καὶ μὴ συνιέντος ἔρχεται ὁ πονηρὸς καὶ ἁρπάζει τὸ ἐσπαρμένον ἐν τῇ καρδίᾳ αὐτοῦ· οὗτός ἐστιν ὁ παρὰ τὴν ὁδὸν σπαρείς. [20] ὁ δὲ ἐπὶ τὰ πετρώδη σπαρείς, οὗτός ἐστιν ὁ τὸν λόγον ἀκούων καὶ εὐθὺς μετὰ χαρᾶς λαμβάνων αὐτόν· [21] οὐκ ἔχει δὲ ῥίζαν ἐν ἑαυτῷ ἀλλὰ πρόσκαιρός ἐστιν, γενομένης δὲ θλίψεως ἢ διωγμοῦ διὰ τὸν λόγον εὐθὺς σκανδαλίζεται. [22] ὁ δὲ εἰς τὰς ἀκάνθας σπαρείς, οὗτός ἐστιν ὁ τὸν λόγον ἀκούων, καὶ ἡ

Mark 4 13–20

[13] Καὶ λέγει αὐτοῖς· οὐκ οἴδατε τὴν παραβολὴν ταύτην, καὶ πῶς πάσας τὰς παραβολὰς γνώσεσθε; [14] ὁ σπείρων τὸν λόγον σπείρει. [15] οὗτοι δέ εἰσιν οἱ παρὰ τὴν ὁδὸν ὅπου σπείρεται ὁ λόγος, καὶ ὅταν ἀκούσωσιν, εὐθὺς ἔρχεται ὁ σατανᾶς καὶ αἴρει τὸν λόγον τὸν ἐσπαρμένον εἰς αὐτούς. [16] καὶ οὗτοί εἰσιν ὁμοίως οἱ ἐπὶ τὰ πετρώδη σπειρόμενοι, οἳ ὅταν ἀκούσωσιν τὸν λόγον εὐθὺς μετὰ χαρᾶς λαμβάνουσιν αὐτόν, [17] καὶ οὐκ ἔχουσιν ῥίζαν ἐν ἑαυτοῖς ἀλλὰ πρόσκαιροί εἰσιν, εἶτα γενομένης θλίψεως ἢ διωγμοῦ διὰ τὸν λόγον εὐθὺς σκανδαλίζονται. [18] καὶ ἄλλοι εἰσὶν οἱ ἐπὶ τὰς ἀκάνθας σπειρόμενοι· οὗτοί εἰσιν οἱ τὸν λόγον ἀκούσαντες, [19] καὶ αἱ

Luk 8 11–15

[11] Ἔστιν δὲ αὕτη ἡ παραβολή. ὁ σπόρος ἐστὶν ὁ λόγος τοῦ θεοῦ. [12] οἱ δὲ παρὰ τὴν ὁδόν εἰσιν οἱ ἀκούσαντες, εἶτα ἔρχεται ὁ διάβολος καὶ αἴρει τὸν λόγον ἀπὸ τῆς καρδίας αὐτῶν, ἵνα μὴ πιστεύσαντες σωθῶσιν. [13] οἱ δὲ ἐπὶ τῆς πέτρας οἳ ὅταν ἀκούσωσιν μετὰ χαρᾶς δέχονται τὸν λόγον· καὶ οὗτοι ῥίζαν οὐκ ἔχουσιν, οἳ πρὸς καιρὸν πιστεύουσιν καὶ ἐν καιρῷ πειρασμοῦ ἀφίστανται. [14] τὸ δὲ εἰς τὰς ἀκάνθας πεσόν, οὗτοί εἰσιν οἱ ἀκούσαντες, καὶ ὑπὸ

Mt 13,18 ● σπειροντος‖13 3p: *Rpl* — *txt*: ℵ*BX-33 Φ-544-1604 ϕ13-346 σ517-1675 W *pc* Or **19** αρπ.] αιρει‖Mk Lk: σ-7 | αυτων‖Lk: D *Lq* **20** χαρ. + δεχομενος‖Lk: σ1424-1675 | λαμβανει‖Mk: λ⟨1⟩ **21** *om* δε^1‖p: L σ1675 F *pc L*(και ουκ: e hz)ff^1 vg^1 *C*b^1⟨f⟩ | *om* εν εαυ.‖Lk: σ1194 *S*c | γεν. δε] ειτα γεν.‖Mk: G(+ δε) Θ *pc* — και γεν.: *S*p | σκανδαλιζονται‖p: σ1424-1675 1574 *L*blz30 vg^2 *C*b^1⟨f⟩ **22** εις] επι‖13 7 Mk: 33 659-1424-1675 *pc C*bf | σπα.] σπειρομενος‖Mk: D *L*ek acff^{2}g^1 — πεσων‖Lk: σ990 *S*sc Eu *C*f | λογ.^{1} + μου‖Jo 5 24 Lk 10 39: W

Mk 4,15 ακ. + αυτον(-ου)‖Mt: Φ(Θ-565-700 σ⟨954⟩ *pc*) | *om* ευθ.‖**p**: λ⟨131⟩ σ827 *pc S*s[c] *Arm* | αιρ.] αρπαζει‖Mt: ℵCΔ 1342 | εις αυτ.] ● εν αυτοις‖Mt: ℌ'⟨33⟩C *L*c {} *C*s^5(^{1} εν αυτω)b'f — εν ταις(τη) καρδιαις(-ια) αυτων‖Mt: *Rpl L*[ek] afi(bg^{2}qr^{1}30 vg^6)^3 *S*(')h^t (*C*b^7; *et* αυτου: b^1) *Arm* — εις τας καρδιας αυτων‖Mt: *L*dff^{2}z vg' — απο της καρδιας αυτων‖Lk: A *Ll Aeth* — *txt*: B 28 λ⟨131⟩ ϕ⟨124-346⟩ W {*S*h^m *Geo*} **16** ● ∼ ομ. εισ.: ℌ⟨B⟩C 1071 1342 *pc l*^{pl} {} — *om* ομ.‖**p**: 579 Θ-28-565-700 λ ϕ⟨124-346⟩ D W 435 Or *L*vl'[ek]r^1 vg^1 *S*' *C*sf — *txt*: *Rpl* {*L*flz vg'} *S*h {*C*b} | τ. λογ.—αυτ.] μετα χ. δεχονται τ. λ.‖Lk: 579 | *om* ευθ.‖Lk: (579) σ7-267-349 D *L*cff^{2}iq *S*s[c] *C*b$^{⟨4⟩}$f | λαμ.] δεχονται‖Lk: (579) λ *pc* | ● *om* αυτ.: (579) Θ-28-565-700 λ ϕ⟨346⟩ Or *Arm* **17** εν εαυ.] *om*‖Lk: σ945 *Geo*$^{1.A}$ — εν αυτω (*sc.* τ. λογω): *S*s[c] | σκανδαλιζεται‖Mt: W* — -σθησονται‖Mt 24 10: D **18** και—οι^1] οι δε‖p: W *C*s^2(^{2} *om* δε)$^{:6}$ | αλλ. εισ. ... ουτ. εισ.] *om om* ... ουτ. εισ.‖**p**: 892 Θ-28-565-700 λ ϕ σ1606 W *S*[sc]p *C*s^4 — ουτ. εισ. ... *om om*‖15f.: *Rpl L*fq *S*h — ουτ. εισ. ... ουτ. εισ.(*om*): Φ (λ131) — *txt*: ℵBCLΔ D 372(*om* ουτ. εισ.) *L*'(*om* εισ.^{1}: bc) *C*s^{2}b | επι] ● εις‖4 7 Mt Lk: *Rpl C*b^2 — *txt*: ℵCΔ-579 372 *C*' | λογ. + μου‖Jo 5 24 Lk 10 39: λ⟨131⟩ | ακουοντες‖Mt: *Rpl L S*h *Arm* — *txt*: ℵ(∼ ακ. τ. λ.)BCLΔ-33-892 28-565-1071 ϕ σ27-71-1194-1207 D 1342 *S*[sc]p *C* **19** αι μερ.] η μεριμνα‖Mt: σ827 1342 *S*[sc]p *C*s$^{3:5}$b$^{⟨6⟩}$

Lk 8,12 ακουοντες‖Mt 20.22.19: *Rpl* (ακολουθουντες: D') *L S*,j *C*' — 𝔓^{75} ℵBLΞ-579-892 28 ϕ983-1689 U *C*b^2 | ακου. + τον λογον(+ του θεου)‖15 Mt 19f.22f. Mk 4 16.18.20: (X) ϕ124-174 *pc L*e (b)cr^1(*et* + εν ταις καρδιαις αυτων‖12b) *S*s^v(c)pj *C*(s$^{1:8}$)b^1 — τ. λογ. τον εσπαρμενον‖Mk Mt: 1241 713 **13** ● την πετραν‖8 6 Mt Mk: ℵ*X-1241 1071 D F^W *pc l*48 Or — *txt*: 𝔓^{75} *Rpl* Bas | πετ. + ουτοι εισιν‖14p.15p Mt Mk: 579(*om* ουτ.) *L*vl'⟨e l⟩r$^{1.2}$(*om* εισ.) *S*scp *C*s(*om* οταν)b | ∼ τ. λογ. (+ ευθεως) μ. χ. δεχ.‖Mk Mt: σ1424 Ψ 273 *L*br^1 *S*(sc)j | ουτ.] αυτοι: B*-1241 2145 *L*acr^1 {} — *om*‖Mk Mt: D *L*e r^2 {*S*scp$^{⟨1⟩}$j$^{⟨1⟩}$} *C*b^1 *Arm Aeth* **14** οι + τον λογον‖**p**: Θ λ *pc L*acfr^1 vg^1 *S*cpj$^{⟨a⟩}$ *C*sb^1 | ακουοντες‖Mt 20.22.23: 33-1241 λ1582-2193 σ1207 K Π *al l*1231 *L*abclqz *S*scpj *C*s$^{⟨5⟩}$

Matth	Mark	Luk
μέριμνα τοῦ αἰῶνος τούτου καὶ ἡ	μέριμναι τοῦ αἰῶνος καὶ ἡ	μεριμνῶν καὶ
ἀπάτη τοῦ πλούτου	ἀπάτη τοῦ πλούτου καὶ αἱ περὶ τὰ	πλούτου καὶ
	λοιπὰ ἐπιθυμίαι εἰσπορευόμεναι	ἡδονῶν τοῦ βίου πορευόμενοι
συμπνίγει τὸν λόγον, καὶ ἄκαρ-	συμπνίγουσιν τὸν λόγον, καὶ ἄκαρ-	συμπνίγονται καὶ οὐ τελε-
πος γίνεται. [23] ὁ δὲ ἐπὶ	πος γίνεται. [20] καὶ ἐκεῖνοί εἰσιν οἱ ἐπὶ	σφοροῦσιν. [15] τὸ δὲ ἐν
τὴν καλὴν γῆν σπαρείς,	τὴν γῆν τὴν καλὴν σπαρέν-	τῇ καλῇ γῇ,
οὗτός ἐστιν ὁ	τες, οἵτινες	οὗτοί εἰσιν οἵτινες ἐν καρδίᾳ καλῇ
τὸν λόγον ἀκούων καὶ	ἀκούουσιν τὸν λόγον καὶ	καὶ ἀγαθῇ ἀκούσαντες τὸν λόγον
συνίων, ὃς δὴ καρποφορεῖ καὶ	παραδέχονται καὶ καρποφοροῦσιν	κατέχουσιν καὶ καρποφοροῦσιν
ποιεῖ ὃ μὲν ἑκατόν, ὃ δὲ ἑξήκοντα,	ἓν τριάκοντα καὶ ἓν ἑξήκοντα	ἐν ὑπομονῇ.
ὃ δὲ τριάκοντα.	καὶ ἓν ἑκατόν.	

(94) ***107.*** Sprüche über das rechte Hören der Parabeln. *The Right Use of Parables.*

5 15 (32.):	**Mark 4** 21–25	**Luk 8** 16–18	*11 33 (167.):*
	[21] Καὶ ἔλεγεν αὐτοῖς·		
οὐδὲ καίουσιν λύχνον	μήτι ἔρχεται ὁ λύχνος	[16] Οὐδεὶς δὲ λύχνον	*Οὐδεὶς λύχνον*
καὶ τιθέασιν		ἅψας καλύπτει	*ἅψας εἰς κρύπτην τίθησιν*
αὐτὸν ὑπὸ τὸν μόδιον,	ἵνα ὑπὸ τὸν μόδιον τεθῇ ἢ	αὐτὸν σκεύει ἢ	*οὐδὲ ὑπὸ τὸν μόδιον,*
	ὑπὸ τὴν κλίνην; οὐχ	ὑποκάτω κλίνης τίθησιν,	

Mt 13,22 ● *om* τουτου‖Mk: ℵB D *L*ek aff^{2}g^{1}h *S*p^1 Eu | πλου. + και περι τα λοιπα επιθυμιαι εισπορευομεναι‖Mk: L^m **23** τ. καλ. γην] τ. γ. την(*om*) καλ.‖13 8 Mk: *Rpl* (ϕ13-543-826-828) — *txt*: 𝔖⟨892⟩C ΝΟΣ-700 λ1-1582 ϕ124-174-983 σ1010-1194-1293 Δ 157 *pc* | ∼ ακ. τ. λογ.‖p: 892 D *L*⟨qz vg^1⟩ | ● συνιεις‖19: ℵB-892 Φ D Θ 1555 Or | ος δη] και‖p: 700(ος δη και) *L*' *S*cp Eu *Geo*^{1} — τοτε(*prm* και): D *Le*(k) abcff^{2}hq (*S*s)

Mk 4,19 αιω.] βιου‖Lk: Θ-565-700 σ517-1675 D W *pc* *L*vl'[k] — αιω. τουτου‖Lk: *Rpl* *L*f *S*[sc] *C*s^{4}b — *txt*: ℵBCLΔ-892 28 **λ**⟨131⟩ σ1424 *L*lr^{2}z vg *Arm* *Aeth* | *om* και^3—επιθυ. (*et om* εισπορ.)‖(Mt)Lk: (Θ)-28-(565-700) **λ** D W *L*vl[k]⟨flz⟩ *Arm* — ∼ συμπνιγει τ. λογ. και^3—εισπορ.‖Mt: ℵ* **20** εκειν.] ουτοι(+ δε)‖15f Lk Mt: *Rpl*(W) *L*'(eff^2) *S*h — *om*: Θ-28-565 Or — *txt*: ℵBCLΔ-892 *S*[sc]p | τ. γην τ. καλ.] τ. καλ. γην‖p: C 28 ϕ124 235 | παραδε.] δεχονται‖Lk13: 700 **21** ● αυτ. + οτι: BL-892 | ερχ. ο λ.] απτεται ο(*om*) λ.‖Lk: D {*L*vl[k]⟨blqr^{2}z⟩r^1 vg^1} *C*s^2(^{2})$^{:5}$b^1('⟨5⟩f^v) — ο(*om*) λ. καιεται‖Mt: (ϕ')-346 W {} | *om* ο‖p: 28 λ118-209 ϕ⟨346⟩ *C*s$^{2:4}$b⟨6⟩f^v | υπο^2] υποκατω‖Lk16: 476 | *om* η—κλιν.‖Mt: 291 472 *L*ir^1 | *om* την^1‖Lk16: 476 485 *C*sf | ουχ] αλλ‖p: 544 W *Le*[k] bcq *C*f

Lk 8,14 και^2] του‖p: σ1675 {} *C*s$^{4:9}$ — και του: 1071 σ954 472 — *om*‖p: 1604 ϕ69 D 1355 {*Le* cf} **15** εν τη καλ. γη] εις την καλην γην‖p 8: D 157 Or *L* | ακουοντες‖Mt20.22.23: 1071 ϕ σ-1188 *pc* *l*44(*prm* οι) *l*47 *l*1963 *L* *S*pj *C*s$^{1:6}$b^2 | υπομ. + ταυτα λεγων εφωνει· ο εχων ωτα ακουειν ακουετω‖*cf. ad* 8 8: X-579 Λ-1071 ϕ⟨788⟩-174-230-*l*547 σM-1207-1675 E^c F^c G^c H S^m Γ *pm* *l*^{pl}; *cf.* *l*303 *l*374 *l*1642 (*l*49): ουτως μεν αναγινωσκεται και τελειται(τελειοι) εις τας εξω εκκλησιας. εις δε την μεγαλην εκκλησιαν το· ταυτα λεγων εφωνει ου λεγεται, αλλα μετα το· εν υπομονη προστιθεται ταυτα· αρχη της συνοδου (αρ. τ. συ.] οι δε αρχιερεις ...) ... Lk20 21-25 **16** *om* δε‖33: 579 ϕ346 σ692-1424 Θ *al* *Le* *S*'s^v *C*s$^{5:6}$b⟨1⟩ | καλ.] κρυπτει‖33: Bas | σκευει] εις σκευος‖←: λ1-131-1582-2193 | σκ. + η υπο τον μοδιον‖p: 472 (*om* σκ. η: *L*bc) | υπ. κλ.] υπ. της κλ.‖Mk: ϕ346 *C*b^1 — υπο τον μοδιον‖p: (*om* καλ.—η: *L*bc)(+ η την κλινην: c) *S*p^1 — + η εις κρυπτην‖33: *S*c

---

Mk4 21p *cf.* ETh^{II} 33b (*transl.*): (*cf. ad 72.* Mt10 27) ... [b] *Οὐδεὶς γὰρ λύχνον ἅψας τίθησιν ὑπὸ τὸν μόδιον οὐδὲ εἰς κρύπτην, ἀλλ' ἐπὶ τὴν λυχνίαν τίθησιν, ἵνα πάντες οἱ εἰσπορευόμενοι καὶ οἱ ἐκπορευόμενοι βλέπωσιν τὸ φῶς αὐτοῦ.*

Matth	Mark	Luk 8	Luk
ἀλλ' ἐπὶ τὴν λυχνίαν, καὶ λάμπει πᾶσιν τοῖς ἐν τῇ οἰκίᾳ. 10 26 (72.): ... οὐδὲν γάρ ἐστιν κεκαλυμμένον ὃ οὐκ ἀποκαλυφθήσεται, καὶ κρυπτὸν ὃ οὐ γνωσθήσεται.	ἵνα ἐπὶ τὴν λυχνίαν τεθῇ; [22] οὐ γάρ ἐστίν τι κρυπτὸν ὃ ἐὰν μὴ φανερωθῇ· οὐδὲ ἐγένετο ἀπόκρυφον, ἀλλ' ἵνα ἔλθῃ εἰς φανερόν. [23] εἴ τις ἔχει ὦτα ἀκούειν ἀκουέτω. [24] καὶ ἔλεγεν αὐτοῖς· βλέπετε τί ἀκούετε. ἐν ᾧ μέτρῳ μετρεῖτε μετρηθήσεται ὑμῖν, καὶ προστεθήσεται ὑμῖν	ἀλλ' ἐπὶ λυχνίας ἐπιτίθησιν, ἵνα οἱ εἰσπορευόμενοι βλέπωσιν τὸ φῶς. [17] οὐ γάρ ἐστιν κρυπτὸν ὃ οὐ φανερὸν γενήσεται, οὐδὲ ἀπόκρυφον ὃ οὐ μὴ γνωσθῇ καὶ εἰς φανερὸν ἔλθῃ. [18] βλέπετε οὖν πῶς ἀκούετε·	*ἀλλ' ἐπὶ τὴν λυχνίαν, ἵνα οἱ εἰσπορευόμενοι τὸ φέγγος βλέπωσιν. 12 2 (169.): οὐδὲν δὲ συγκεκαλυμμένον ἐστὶν ὃ οὐκ ἀποκαλυφθήσεται, καὶ κρυπτὸν ὃ οὐ γνωσθήσεται.*

Matth (48.)	Matth	Mark	Luk 8	Luk
25 29 (240.): τῷ γὰρ ἔχοντι παντὶ δοθήσεται καὶ	*13 12 (104.): ὅστις γὰρ ἔχει, δοθήσεται αὐτῷ καὶ*	τοῖς ἀκούουσιν. [25] ὃς γὰρ ἔχει, δοθήσεται αὐτῷ·	ὃς ἂν γὰρ ἔχῃ, δοθήσεται αὐτῷ·	*19 26 (209.): λέγω ὑμῖν ὅτι παντὶ τῷ ἔχοντι δοθήσεται,*

Mk 4,21 τεϑη[2]] επιτιϑη‖Lk16: *Rpl* — *txt*: 𝔊C Θ-28-565-700-1071-1604 **ϕ** σ71-179-692-827-1207-1402-1424 D W 1342 **22** ου] ουδεν‖Mt Lk2: W | ● *om* τι‖Lk17: B-579 Θ-28-565-700-1604 **λ ϕ** σM-349-1194-1207 D H K U W Y Π *pm l*184 {*L*vl'[k] g[2]} *Geo*[2] *Aeth* — *txt*: *Rpl L*cflr[2]z{} vg *S*[sc]ph *Geo*[1] | ο εαν μη] ● εαν μη ινα‖22b: ℵBΔ **047** 1241 — ει μη ινα‖←: 579 Θ-28-565-700 **λ**⟨118⟩ **ϕ**'⟨124⟩ 1342 {}[1] — αλλ ινα‖←: D W 49 {*L*vl'[k] r[1]}[1] — ο ου‖Mt Lk: σ827 *pc* {}[2] — ο ου μη‖Lk17b: λ872 (*om* ου: 220) *al* {}[2] — εαν μη: CL-33-892 Σ ϕ346 σ27-1207-1223 A K Π *al* — *txt*: *Rpl* (ος αν: U; *om* μη: *l*184) {*L*cfr[2]z vg}[2] | ελ. εις ϕ.] εις ϕ. ελ.‖Lk: *Rpl* — φανερωϑη‖22a: B — *txt*: ℵCLΔ-579 Θ-565-1071 σ7-267 D *l*49 *l*184 *l*251 **24** ω + γαρ‖Lk6 38: 235 713 *l*48 *L*b vg[1] *C*b[1] *Geo*[1.A] | αντιμετρηϑησεται‖←: 579 565-1071 σ179-1194 157 *pm* Or | *om* και[2]—ακου.‖Mt7 2 Lk←: 579 565 σ1082 D W *pc l*184 *L*e[k] blr[2]30 vg[2] Cp — ● *om* τοις ακ.‖Mt← Lk←: 𝔊'⟨33⟩C 700 *L*cff[2]ir[1]z vg *C*s[1]b' *Arm Aeth* — *txt*: *Rpl* (υμιν[1]⌒[2]: G *pc l*10 *l*12 *l*184[1] *l*1231 *l*1761) *L*f(ακου.] πιστευ.)q *S*[sc] *C*s[4]b[5] | προστεϑ.] περισσευϑησεται‖Mt13 12 25 29: Θ 433 **25** ος] οστις‖Mt12: Θ | εχ.[1]] αν εχη‖Lk18: *Rpl* — *txt* (∼ εχ. γαρ): ℵBCLΔ-892 (28)-700 (**ϕ**'⟨124⟩)-983 W | αυτω + και περισσευϑησεται‖Mt: 213 *L*g[2]

Lk 8,16 λυχνιας] την λυχνιαν‖33 Mk Mt: ℵX-1241 1071 σM-990 D K Π 157 *al l*1963 {*C*sb[6]} — λυχνιαν‖p: 579 700 ϕ346 U Θ Ψ *l*20 *l*29 *l*31 *l*32 *l*40 *l*44 *l*47 *l*48 *l*53 *l*1627 *l*1633 — της λυχνιας‖p: 245 {} | επιτ.] ● τιϑησιν‖16a Mk: 𝔓[75] 𝔊'⟨33⟩Ξ Λ-1071 **λλ**⟨22⟩ **ϕ**'⟨69-124⟩-*l*547 σ1194-1424 D(τιϑει) F Θ 157 *l*1963 Bas[1:2] — *om*‖33 Mt: 1241 ϕ983-1689 1093 *L*e cff[2]l 30 *S*j[a⟨bcl⟩] *Aeth* | *om* ινα—φως‖Mk: 𝔓[75] B 1574 | ∼ τ. φως βλε.‖33: 579-1241 λ1-131-1582-2193 ϕ174 1375 *L*l vg[1] *Geo* **17** κρυ.] τι κρυ.‖Mk: X U 1216(∼) *pc Arm* | φα. γε.] φανερωϑησεται‖p: λ1-131-1582-2193 157 *pc l*47 Cr | ο ου μη] ο ου‖17a.2 Mt: *Rpl* — αλλ ινα‖Mk: D — ει μη ινα‖Mk: 157 *L*abff[2]lq — *txt*: 𝔓[75] ℵB-33-579-1241 1071 σ1424 F Θ Ψ Cr | γνωσϑησεται‖2 Mt: *Rpl* — *txt*: 𝔓[75] 𝔊Ξ D Θ Ψ 372 157 Cr | *om* και—ελϑη‖2 Mt: σ1194 **18** *om* ουν‖Mk: 59 *pc L*vl⟨e fr[1]⟩ *S*scq *C*s[1](+ δε)[:6]b[1] | ακου. + και προστεϑησεται υμιν τοις ακουουσιν‖Mk: ϕ | ∼ γαρ αν/εαν‖9 24p.26p: *Rpl* (*om* αν‖Mk: W 28) — *txt*: 𝔓[75](οσον γαρ) ℵBLΞ-579(οσα γαρ) ϕ983(εαν) σ945 44 157 *l*46 *l*47 | αυτω + και περισσευϑησεται‖Mt: *l*44 *Sc*

Mk4 22p *cf.* ETh[II] 5 (POxy 654,4): Λέγει Ἰη(σοῦ)ς· γ[νῶθι τὸ ὂν ἔμπροσ]θεν τῆς ὄψεώς σου, καὶ [τὸ κεκαλυμμένον] ἀπὸ σοῦ ἀποκαλυφ⟨θ⟩ήσετ[αί σοι· οὐ γάρ ἐσ]τιν κρυπτὸν ὃ οὐ φανε[ρὸν γενήσεται] καὶ θεθαμμένον ὃ ο[ὐκ ἐγερθήσεται].
(*transl.*): *Λέγει Ἰησοῦς· γνῶθι τὸ ἔμπροσθεν τῆς ὄψεώς σου, καὶ τὸ κεκρυμμένον ἀπὸ σοῦ ἀποκαλυφθήσεταί σοι· οὐδὲν γάρ ἐστιν κρυπτὸν ὃ οὐ φανερὸν γενήσεται.*
cf. ETh[II] 6 (*cf. ad 40.*)

Mk4 23 *cf.* ETh[II] 8.21 (*cf. ad 103.* Mk4 9)

Mk4 25p *cf.* ETh[II] 41 (*transl.*): *Λέγει Ἰησοῦς· ὅστις ἔχει ἐν τῇ χειρὶ αὐτοῦ, δοθήσεται αὐτῷ· καὶ ὅστις οὐκ ἔχει, καὶ τὸ μικρὸν ὃ ἔχει ἀρθήσεται ἀπ' αὐτοῦ.*

περισσευθήσεται·	*περισσευθήσεται·*	καὶ	καὶ	*ἀπὸ δὲ*
τοῦ δὲ μὴ ἔχοντος	*ὅστις δὲ οὐκ ἔχει,*	ὃς οὐκ ἔχει,	ὃς ἂν μὴ ἔχῃ,	*τοῦ μὴ ἔχοντος*
καὶ ὃ ἔχει	*καὶ ὃ ἔχει*	καὶ ὃ ἔχει	καὶ ὃ δοκεῖ ἔχειν	*καὶ ὃ ἔχει*
ἀρθήσεται ἀπ᾽ αὐτοῦ.	*ἀρθήσεται ἀπ᾽ αὐτοῦ.*	ἀρθήσεται ἀπ᾽ αὐτοῦ.	ἀρθήσεται ἀπ᾽ αὐτοῦ.	*ἀρθήσεται ἀπ᾽ αὐτοῦ.*

(95) ***108.*** Das Gleichnis von der selbstwachsenden Saat. **Mark 4** 26–29
The Parable of the Seed Growing Secretly.

[26] Καὶ ἔλεγεν· οὕτως ἐστὶν ἡ βασιλεία τοῦ θεοῦ, ὡς ἄνθρωπος βάλῃ τὸν σπόρον ἐπὶ τῆς γῆς, [27] καὶ καθεύδῃ καὶ ἐγείρηται νύκτα καὶ ἡμέραν, καὶ ὁ σπόρος βλαστᾷ καὶ μηκύνηται ὡς οὐκ οἶδεν αὐτός. [28] αὐτομάτη ἡ γῆ καρποφορεῖ, πρῶτον χόρτον, εἶτεν στάχυν, εἶτεν πλήρη σῖτον ἐν τῷ στάχυϊ. [29] ὅταν δὲ παραδοῖ ὁ καρπός, εὐθὺς **ἀποστέλλει τὸ δρέπανον, ὅτι παρέστηκεν ὁ θερισμός.** Joel4 13

(96) ***109.*** Das Gleichnis vom Unkraut unter dem Weizen. *The Parable of the Tares.* **Matth 13** 24–30

[24] Ἄλλην παραβολὴν παρέθηκεν αὐτοῖς λέγων· ὡμοιώθη ἡ βασιλεία τῶν οὐρανῶν ἀνθρώπῳ σπείραντι καλὸν σπέρμα ἐν τῷ ἀγρῷ αὐτοῦ. [25] ἐν δὲ τῷ καθεύδειν τοὺς ἀνθρώπους ἦλθεν αὐτοῦ ὁ ἐχθρὸς καὶ ἐπέσπειρεν ζιζάνια ἀνὰ μέσον τοῦ σίτου καὶ ἀπῆλθεν. [26] ὅτε δὲ ἐβλάστησεν ὁ χόρτος καὶ καρπὸν ἐποίησεν, τότε ἐφάνη καὶ τὰ ζιζάνια. [27] προσελθόντες δὲ οἱ δοῦλοι τοῦ οἰκοδεσπότου εἶπον αὐτῷ· κύριε, οὐχὶ καλὸν σπέρμα ἔσπειρας ἐν τῷ σῷ ἀγρῷ; πόθεν οὖν ἔχει ζιζάνια; [28] ὁ δὲ ἔφη αὐτοῖς· ἐχθρὸς ἄνθρωπος τοῦτο ἐποίησεν. οἱ δὲ δοῦλοι αὐτῷ λέγουσιν· θέλεις οὖν ἀπελθόντες συλλέξωμεν αὐτά; [29] ὁ δέ φησιν· οὔ, μήποτε συλλέγοντες τὰ ζιζάνια ἐκριζώσητε ἅμα αὐτοῖς τὸν σῖτον. [30] ἄφετε συναυξάνεσθαι ἀμφότερα μέχρι τοῦ θερισμοῦ· καὶ ἐν καιρῷ τοῦ θερισμοῦ ἐρῶ τοῖς θερισταῖς· συλλέξατε πρῶτον τὰ ζιζάνια καὶ δήσατε αὐτὰ εἰς δέσμας πρὸς τὸ κατακαῦσαι αὐτά, τὸν δὲ σῖτον συναγάγετε εἰς τὴν ἀποθήκην μου.

Mt 13,24 ωμ.] ομοια εστιν ‖ 13 31.33.44.47: 1604 *L*vl⟨k ff[1] lr[2]⟩ vg[2] *S*scp Eu *Geo*[1] **25** τ. ανθ.] αυτον ‖ 4 27: σ-659 **30** μεχ.] ● εως: B-892 σ-659 D — αχρι: ℵL Or — *txt*: *Rpl* (μεχρις: Φ W) | ● εν + τω *cf.* 21 34: ℵ*CL 28-544 σ-659-990-1010-1293-1391-1402 E *al*

Mk 4,25 εχ.[3]] δοκει εχειν ‖ Lk 18: ϕ346 *L*Hi **26** σπο. + αυτου ‖ Lk 8 5: Σ 157 *pc* Gel *Lg*[2] *Cs*[2(+1v):5]b | την γην ‖ 4 20 Mt 13 8.23: 579 544 λ σ179 1342 *L*⟨e[k] r[1.2] 30 vg[3]⟩ **29** ● παραδω: *Rpl* — *txt*: ℵ*BΔ Θ-28-565 D | ευθ.] τοτε ‖ 13 27: λ

Lk 8,18 μη] ουκ ‖ Mt 12 Mk: Λ

Mk 4 29 *cf.* ETh[II] 21d (*transl.*) (*cf. ad 172.* Lk 12 39): ... [d] *γένοιτο ἐκ μέσου ὑμῶν ἄνθρωπος ἐπιστήμων· ὅτε παρέδωκεν ὁ καρπός, ἦλθεν ταχέως (καὶ) τὸ δρέπανον ἐν τῇ χειρὶ αὐτοῦ (καὶ) ἐθέρισεν αὐτόν. ὁ ἔχων ὦτα ἀκούειν ἀκουέτω* (*cf. ad 103.* Mk 4 9).

109. cf. ETh[II] 57 (*transl.*): *Λέγει Ἰησοῦς· ὡμοιώθη ἡ βασιλεία τοῦ πατρὸς ἀνθρώπῳ ἔχοντι [καλὸν] σπέρμα. ἦλθεν αὐτοῦ ὁ ἐχθρὸς ἐν τῇ νυκτὶ (καὶ) ἐπέσπειρεν ζιζάνιον τῷ καλῷ σπέρματι. ὁ ἄνθρωπος οὐκ εἴασεν αὐτοὺς συλλέγειν τὸ ζιζάνιον. ἔφη αὐτοῖς· μήποτε ἀπελθόντες συλλέξαι τὸ ζιζάνιον ἐκριζώσητε ἅμα αὐτῷ τὸν σῖτον. ἐν γὰρ τῇ ἡμέρᾳ τοῦ θερισμοῦ τὰ ζιζάνια φανήσεται. συλλέξουσιν αὐτὰ καὶ κατακαύσουσιν αὐτά.*

(97)

110. Das Gleichnis vom Senfkorn. *The Parable of the Mustard Seed.*

Matth 13 31–32	Mark 4 30–32	*13 18–19 (178.)*
31 Ἄλλην παραβολὴν παρέθηκεν αὐτοῖς λέγων· ὁμοία ἐστὶν ἡ βασιλεία τῶν οὐρανῶν κόκκῳ σινάπεως, ὃν λαβὼν ἄνθρωπος ἔσπειρεν ἐν τῷ ἀγρῷ αὐτοῦ· 32 ὃ μικρότερον μέν ἐστιν πάντων τῶν σπερμάτων, ὅταν δὲ αὐξηθῇ, μεῖζον τῶν λαχάνων ἐστὶν καὶ γίνεται δένδρον, ὥστε ἐλθεῖν **τὰ πετεινὰ τοῦ οὐρανοῦ** καὶ **κατασκηνοῦν ἐν τοῖς κλάδοις αὐτοῦ.**	30 Καὶ ἔλεγεν· πῶς ὁμοιώσωμεν τὴν βασιλείαν τοῦ θεοῦ, ἢ ἐν τίνι αὐτὴν παραβολῇ θῶμεν; 31 ὡς κόκκον σινάπεως, ὃς ὅταν σπαρῇ ἐπὶ τῆς γῆς, μικρότερον ὂν πάντων τῶν σπερμάτων τῶν ἐπὶ τῆς γῆς, 32 καὶ ὅταν σπαρῇ, ἀναβαίνει καὶ γίνεται μεῖζον πάντων τῶν λαχάνων, καὶ ποιεῖ κλάδους μεγάλους, ὥστε δύνασθαι **ὑπὸ τὴν σκιὰν αὐτοῦ τὰ πετεινὰ τοῦ οὐρανοῦ κατασκηνοῦν.**	*18 Ἔλεγεν οὖν· τίνι ὁμοία ἐστὶν ἡ βασιλεία τοῦ θεοῦ, καὶ τίνι ὁμοιώσω αὐτήν; 19 ὁμοία ἐστὶν κόκκῳ σινάπεως, ὃν λαβὼν ἄνθρωπος ἔβαλεν εἰς κῆπον ἑαυτοῦ, καὶ ηὔξησεν καὶ ἐγένετο εἰς δένδρον, καὶ* ***τὰ πετεινὰ τοῦ οὐρανοῦ κατεσκήνωσεν ἐν τοῖς κλάδοις αὐτοῦ.***

Dn4 12.21 LXX

(98)

111. Das Gleichnis vom Sauerteig. *The Parable of the Leaven.*

Matth 13 33	*13 20–21 (178.)*
33 Ἄλλην παραβολὴν ἐλάλησεν αὐτοῖς· ὁμοία ἐστὶν ἡ βασιλεία τῶν οὐρανῶν ζύμῃ, ἣν λαβοῦσα γυνὴ ἐνέκρυψεν εἰς ἀλεύρου σάτα τρία, ἕως οὗ ἐζυμώθη ὅλον.	*20 Καὶ πάλιν εἶπεν· τίνι ὁμοιώσω τὴν βασιλείαν τοῦ θεοῦ; 21 ὁμοία ἐστὶν ζύμῃ, ἣν λαβοῦσα γυνὴ ἔκρυψεν εἰς ἀλεύρου σάτα τρία, ἕως οὗ ἐζυμώθη ὅλον.*

Mt 13,31 παρεθ.] ελαλησεν(-λει) ‖ 13 33: L ΝΟΣ λ1582 **ϕ**-174 **σ**-349 D Θ 1574 *L*ek abcff^{2}hπ (*S*sc, *et om* λεγ.) (*Geo*) *Δ*i^{V}md n^{HgHrS} | ομ. εσ.] ωμοιωθη ‖ 13 24 **18** 23 22 2: L *pc* **32** *om* μεν ‖ Mk: λ118-209 ϕ828-983-1689 157 *pc L*l | αυξηση ‖ Lk: ℵ^b **ϕ** D 713 | μει. + παντων ‖ Mk: 28-544 σ659-1424 K Y Π 157 565 *L*, Or *S Cs*$^{1:6}$b^{4}f | *om* ελθ. … και ‖ Lk Mk: σM 299 *L*e | -σκηνωσαι ‖ 32a Lk: 1355 2145 **33** ελα.] παρεθηκεν ‖ 13 24.31: C 1604 *pc S*p^4 *Cs*$^{4:6}$f$^{1v:2}$ *Δ*a n^L p | ενεκ.] εκρυψεν ‖ Lk: *Rpl* — *txt*: ℌ⟨L⟩C-**0164** ΘΦ-565 **ϕ**⟨346-828⟩-174 σM-27-1010-1293 D E F K S U V Δ Π Ω **047 055 0106 0119 0137** *al*

Mk 4,30 πως] τινι ‖ Mt11 16 **p** Lk13 18b.20: *Rpl* Or *L*' *S*[sc] *C*⟨b^1⟩ *Geo*^{1} — *txt*: ℌC 28 **ϕ**⟨124⟩ σ7-179-267 W 1241 *l*49 *l*184 *L*e[k] *Geo*^{1} | ομοιωσω ‖ ←: 28-544 **ϕ**⟨124⟩-230 σ27-1424 K *pc Cs*^{1}b^5 *Arm*^{1} *Aeth* | του θε.] των ουρανων ‖ Mt: σ827 *S*[sc]p^1 *C*b^1 **31** ως] ομοια εστιν (+ η βασιλεια του θεου ‖ Mt) ‖ Lk: D *L*(c)g^2 vg^1 *Cs*$^{2:4}$b | ● κοκκω ‖ p: ℵBCΔ ΣΦ-565 ϕ124 σ1082-1194-1391-1402 D Π 157 *al* | την γην ‖ **4** 20 Mt13 8.23: L 28 D W *pc L*vl[k]⟨cff^{2}r^{2}z⟩ vg^3 | μικ. ον π. τ. σπ.] μικροτερον(-ος) εστιν π. τ. σπ. ‖ Mt: (ΣΦ) σM^c D *pc l*48 — μικροτερος(-ον) π. τ. σπ. εστιν ‖ Mt: *Rpl* (A ∼ των^2—γης^2 εστ.)(33-579 28-700 ϕ13 σM*-179-517 1241 1342) — *txt*: ℵBLΔ-892 Θ-1071 W | *om* των επι τ. γ. ‖ Mt: C 271 *L*e b *Cs*$^{2:4}$ **32** κ. οτ. σπ. αναβ.] αυξει ‖ Lk Mt: W *L*e b30(*om* σπ.: cqr^1) — *om*: D *L*ff^{2}i | σπ.] αυξηθη ‖ p: λ1278 σ1082-1391-1402 *al S*[sc]h^m

---

110. cf. ETh^{II} 20 (*transl.*): *Ἔλεγον οἱ μαθηταὶ τῷ Ἰησοῦ· εἰπον ἡμῖν, τίνι ὁμοία ἐστὶν ἡ βασιλεία τῶν οὐρανῶν. εἶπεν αὐτοῖς· ὁμοία ἐστὶν κόκκῳ σινάπεως, ὃ μικρότερον (μέν) ἐστιν πάντων τῶν σπερμάτων. ὅταν δὲ πέσῃ εἰς τὴν γῆν τὴν ἐργαζομένην, ποιεῖ* (sc. *ἡ γῆ*) *κλάδον μέγαν καὶ γίνεται σκέπη τοῖς πετεινοῖς τοῦ οὐρανοῦ.*

111. cf. ETh^{II} 96 (*transl.*): *[Λέγει] Ἰησοῦς· ὁμοία ἐστὶν ἡ βασιλεία τοῦ πατρὸς γυναικί [τινι]. ἔλαβεν μικρὸν ζύμης [(καὶ) ἔκρυψεν] αὐτὴν εἰς ἄλευρον (καὶ) ἐποίησεν αὐτὸ ἄρτους μεγάλους. ὁ ἔχων ὦτα ἀκουέτω* (*cf. ad 103.* Mt13 9).

(99)

112. Gebrauch der Gleichnisrede. *The Use of Parables.*

Matth 13 34–35	Mark 4 33–34		
34 Ταῦτα πάντα ἐλάλησεν ὁ Ἰησοῦς ἐν παραβολαῖς τοῖς ὄχλοις, καὶ χωρὶς παραβολῆς οὐδὲν ἐλάλει αὐτοῖς· 35 ὅπως πληρωθῇ τὸ ῥηθὲν διὰ τοῦ προφήτου λέγοντος· **ἀνοίξω ἐν παραβολαῖς τὸ στόμα μου, ἐρεύξομαι κεκρυμμένα ἀπὸ καταβολῆς.**	33 Καὶ τοιαύταις παραβολαῖς πολλαῖς ἐλάλει αὐτοῖς τὸν λόγον, καθὼς ἠδύναντο ἀκούειν· 34 χωρὶς δὲ παραβολῆς οὐκ ἐλάλει αὐτοῖς, κατ' ἰδίαν δὲ τοῖς ἰδίοις μαθηταῖς ἐπέλυεν πάντα.		Ps78 2

(100)

113. Deutung des Gleichnisses vom Unkraut. **Matth 13** 36–43
The Interpretation of the Parable of the Tares.

36 Τότε ἀφεὶς τοὺς ὄχλους ἦλθεν εἰς τὴν οἰκίαν. καὶ προσῆλθαν αὐτῷ οἱ μαθηταὶ αὐτοῦ λέγοντες· διασάφησον ἡμῖν τὴν παραβολὴν τῶν ζιζανίων τοῦ ἀγροῦ. 37 ὁ δὲ ἀποκριθεὶς εἶπεν· ὁ σπείρων τὸ καλὸν σπέρμα ἐστὶν ὁ υἱὸς τοῦ ἀνθρώπου· 38 ὁ δὲ ἀγρός ἐστιν ὁ κόσμος· τὸ δὲ καλὸν σπέρμα, οὗτοί εἰσιν οἱ υἱοὶ τῆς βασιλείας· τὰ δὲ ζιζάνιά εἰσιν οἱ υἱοὶ τοῦ πονηροῦ, 39 ὁ δὲ ἐχθρὸς ὁ σπείρας αὐτά ἐστιν ὁ διάβολος· ὁ δὲ θερισμὸς συντέλεια αἰῶνός ἐστιν, οἱ δὲ θερισταὶ ἄγγελοί εἰσιν. 40 ὥσπερ οὖν συλλέγεται τὰ ζιζάνια καὶ πυρὶ καίεται, οὕτως ἔσται ἐν τῇ συντελείᾳ τοῦ αἰῶνος. 41 ἀποστελεῖ ὁ υἱὸς τοῦ ἀνθρώπου τοὺς ἀγγέλους αὐτοῦ, καὶ συλλέξουσιν ἐκ τῆς βασιλείας αὐτοῦ πάντα **τὰ σκάνδαλα** καὶ **τοὺς ποιοῦντας τὴν ἀνομίαν,** 42 καὶ βαλοῦσιν αὐτοὺς εἰς τὴν κάμινον τοῦ πυρός· ἐκεῖ ἔσται ὁ κλαυθμὸς καὶ ὁ βρυγμὸς τῶν ὀδόντων. 43 τότε οἱ δίκαιοι ἐκλάμψουσιν ὡς ὁ ἥλιος ἐν τῇ βασιλείᾳ τοῦ πατρὸς αὐτῶν. ὁ ἔχων ὦτα ἀκουέτω.

Ps141 9

(101)

114. Die Gleichnisse vom Schatz und von der Perle. **Matth 13** 44–46
The Parables of the Hidden Treasure and of the Pearl of Great Price.

44 Ὁμοία ἐστὶν ἡ βασιλεία τῶν οὐρανῶν θησαυρῷ κεκρυμμένῳ ἐν τῷ ἀγρῷ, ὃν εὑρὼν ἄνθρωπος ἔκρυψεν, καὶ ἀπὸ τῆς χαρᾶς αὐτοῦ ὑπάγει καὶ πωλεῖ πάντα ὅσα ἔχει καὶ ἀγοράζει τὸν ἀγρὸν ἐκεῖνον.

Mt 13,34 και χω.] χω. δε‖Mk: Σ | ουδ.] ουκ‖Mk: *Rpl* Eu Or *L*'Te *S*' *C*b — *txt*: ℵ*BC ΝΟΣ-1604 **φ**⟨124⟩-174 σM-7-1010-1293 Δ *al* Chr Cl *L*f *S*h *C*sf *Arm* **35** δια] υπο‖22 31 12 22 15: O | ● κατ. + κοσμου *cf.* 25 34 Lk11 50 Jo17 24 *etc.*: *Rpl* *L*'Hil *S*' *C*,f — *txt*: ℵ^{b}B λ1-22-1582 Eu Or *L*ek *S*sc *Aeth* **36** διασ.] ● φρασον‖15 15: *Rpl* (ειπε: Eu) Or *L*e cfff^{1}r^2{} vg — *txt*: ℵ*B σ Θ Or {*L*vl'π} *C*,f **40** ● κατακαιεται‖13 30 3 12p: ℵB-892 λ1-22-1582 σ1010-1293 D(-ονται) *pl* Or *L* {} — *txt*: LCX-33 ΟΣΦ-28-700 λ118-209 **φ**-174-230 σM *R* 157 *pm* Or {*S*,j} **43** ωτα + ακουειν‖Mk4 9.23 Lk8 8 14 35: *Rpl* Eu Or *L*vl' g^{2}30 vg^{10} Au^1 Hil *S*,j *C*,f — *txt*: ℵ*B 700 Θ **0242** *L*ek ab vg' Au^1 Hil **44** ομ.] παλιν ομ.‖45 13 47: *Rpl* Or *L*fhq *S*'j^1 *C*f — *txt*: ℵB-892 D *pc* *L*' Or *S*scj^a *C* *Aeth* | ● *om* παν.‖19 21 Mk10 21: B 28 *pc* Or *C*b⟨f⟩

Mk 4,33 *om* καθ.—ακ.‖Mt: Φ *L*e **34** χω. δε] και χω.‖Mt: B Φ-700 **047** 1342 *S*[sc]p *C*s$^{3:5}$b$^{⟨7⟩}$f

---

Mt13 43b *cf.* ETh^{II} 24.63.65.96 (*cf. ad 103.* Mt13 9)

Mt13 44 *cf.* ETh^{II} 109 (*transl.*): *Λέγει Ἰησοῦς· ὁμοία ἐστὶν ἡ βασιλεία ἀνθρώπῳ ἔχοντι ἐν τῷ ἀγρῷ αὐτοῦ θησαυρὸν κεκρυμμένον ὃν οὐκ οἶδεν. καὶ ἀποθανὼν κατέλιπεν αὐτὸν τῷ υἱῷ [αὐτοῦ. οὐδὲ] ὁ υἱὸς ᾔδει. λαβὼν τὸν ἀγρὸν ἐκεῖνον ἐπώλησεν. καὶ ὁ ἀγοράσας αὐτὸν ἦλθεν (καὶ) ἀροτριῶν [εὗρεν] τὸν θησαυρόν· ἤρξατο δανείζειν χαλκὸν οἷς ἠθέλησεν.*

45 πάλιν ὁμοία ἐστὶν ἡ βασιλεία τῶν οὐρανῶν ἀνθρώπῳ ἐμπόρῳ ζητοῦντι καλοὺς μαργαρίτας· 46 εὑρὼν δὲ ἕνα πολύτιμον μαργαρίτην ἀπελθὼν πέπρακεν πάντα ὅσα εἶχεν καὶ ἠγόρασεν αὐτόν.

(102) *115.* Das Gleichnis vom Fischnetz. *The Parable of the Drag-net.* **Matth 13** 47–50

47 Πάλιν ὁμοία ἐστὶν ἡ βασιλεία τῶν οὐρανῶν σαγήνῃ βληθείσῃ εἰς τὴν θάλασσαν καὶ ἐκ παντὸς γένους συναγαγούσῃ· 48 ἣν ὅτε ἐπληρώθη ἀναβιβάσαντες ἐπὶ τὸν αἰγιαλὸν καὶ καθίσαντες συνέλεξαν τὰ καλὰ εἰς ἄγγη, τὰ δὲ σαπρὰ ἔξω ἔβαλον. 49 οὕτως ἔσται ἐν τῇ συντελείᾳ τοῦ αἰῶνος· ἐξελεύσονται οἱ ἄγγελοι καὶ ἀφοριοῦσιν τοὺς πονηροὺς ἐκ μέσου τῶν δικαίων, 50 καὶ βαλοῦσιν αὐτοὺς εἰς τὴν κάμινον τοῦ πυρός· ἐκεῖ ἔσται ὁ κλαυθμὸς καὶ ὁ βρυγμὸς τῶν ὀδόντων.

(103) *116.* Abschluß der Gleichnisrede. *The End of the Parables.* **Matth 13** 51–52

51 Συνήκατε ταῦτα πάντα; λέγουσιν αὐτῷ· ναί. 52 ὁ δὲ εἶπεν αὐτοῖς· διὰ τοῦτο πᾶς γραμματεὺς μαθητευθεὶς τῇ βασιλείᾳ τῶν οὐρανῶν ὅμοιός ἐστιν ἀνθρώπῳ οἰκοδεσπότῃ, ὅστις ἐκβάλλει ἐκ τοῦ θησαυροῦ αὐτοῦ καινὰ καὶ παλαιά.

(104) *117.* Jesu wahre Verwandte. *Jesus' Real Brethren.* **Luk 8** 19–21 *102.*

98. *102.*

19 Παρεγένοντο δὲ πρὸς αὐτὸν ἡ μήτηρ καὶ οἱ ἀδελφοὶ αὐτοῦ, καὶ οὐκ ἠδύναντο συντυχεῖν αὐτῷ διὰ τὸν ὄχλον. 20 ἀπηγγέλη δὲ αὐτῷ ὅτι ἡ μήτηρ σου καὶ οἱ ἀδελφοί σου ἑστήκασιν ἔξω ἰδεῖν σε θέλοντες. 21 ὁ δὲ ἀποκριθεὶς εἶπεν πρὸς αὐτούς· μήτηρ μου καὶ ἀδελφοί μου οὗτοί εἰσιν οἱ τὸν λόγον τοῦ θεοῦ ἀκούοντες καὶ ποιοῦντες.

Mt 13,45 ● *om* ανθ.: ℵ*B σ1424 *pc* PsAth Chr Cr *L*Am **46** ευρ. δε] ος(και) ευρ.‖44: *Rpl* *L*(d)fq (Cp^{1}; ^{1}*et* + γαρ) (*S*' *Geo* *Δ*a i md n) — *txt*: ℌ λ1-1582 ϕ788 D Θ *L*'(^{45}∩^{46}μαργ.: r^{2}) Cp^{2}(^{1} δε] γαρ) *S*pj *C*sb^{10}(') f *Δ*lp | *om* παν.‖1921 Mk1021: D *L*acff^{2}h *C*b⟨1⟩⟨f⟩ *Δ*i^{V} **52** εκβ.] προφερει‖Lk645: λ1 **σ**(φερει: 1424; προσ-: 1675) Ddy Or *L*,Ir

Lk 8,19 ● παρεγενετο: $\mathfrak{P}^{75}$ BX-579 σ71 D *pc* *L*vg^{1} | *om* προς αυ.‖p: 579 *l*1642 **20** απηγγειλαν‖p: X 1071 213 *L*vg^{1} — ειπον: *S*scp | αυτω + λεγοντων‖Mk: *Rpl* (-τες: 1071 213) Bas^{1} *L*r^{1} *S*h *Arm* — *txt*: $\mathfrak{P}^{75}$ ℌΞ **λλ**⟨1278⟩ D W Δ Θ 157 872 Bas^{1} *L*' *S*'j *C* | οτι] ιδου‖p: 998 *L*30 *C*b' — ● *om*‖p: $\mathfrak{P}^{75}$ *Rpl* Bas^{1} *L*r$^{1.2}$ vg' *S*' {} — *txt*: ℌ⟨B⟩X 1071 **λ**-1582-2193 **σ**-1188 D Θ Ψ 157 *pc* *l*184 Bas^{1} *L*vl' vg^{1} *S*hj {*C*sb^{8}} | ∼ εξω εστ.‖Mt: λ131 D *pc* Bas$^{1:2}$ *L*e c30 vg^{1} Te *Aeth* | ιδ. σε θελ.] ζητουντες σε‖p: D 1396 — θελ. ιδ. σε‖Mt: σ1675 — ● ιδ. θελ. σε: $\mathfrak{P}^{75}$ BΞ **21** προς αυ.] αυτοις‖Mk: 579 D *pc* Bas *L*e c — πρ. αυτον‖Mt: $\mathfrak{P}^{75}$ *L*b | μητ. ... αδ.] η μητ. ... οι(*om*) αδ.‖p: X-579-1241 1071 ϕ69-346 σ(1675)(*om* η: 954-1424) D Δ *pc* (*l*44 *l*104) | ποι. + αυτον‖647 Mt724.36: *Rpl* Cr *L*Mcn^{Te}(+ αυτα) *S*' {*C*} — *txt*: $\mathfrak{P}^{75}$ ℌ⟨579-1241⟩Ξ 544-700-1604 **λ**-22-1582 **σ**⟨954⟩-7-267-990-1207-1223 A D H^{c} V* W Δ Θ Π Ψ *al* Bas Ti *L* *S*shj *Arm* *Aeth*

Mt1345f. *cf.* ETh^{II} 76 (*transl.*): *Λέγει Ἰησοῦς· ὁμοία ἐστὶν ἡ βασιλεία τοῦ πατρὸς ἀνθρώπῳ ἐμπόρῳ ἔχοντι φορτία, ὃς εὗρεν μαργαρίτην. ὁ ἔμπορος ἐκεῖνος φρόνιμός ἐστιν· ἐπώλησεν τὰ φορτία (καὶ) ἠγοράσατο ἑαυτῷ τὸν μαργαρίτην ἕνα. ζητεῖτε ...* (*cf. ad 44.* Mt620)

115. cf. ETh^{II} 8 (*transl.*): *Καὶ ἔλεγεν· ὅμοιός ἐστιν ὁ ἄνθρωπος ἁλιεῖ φρονίμῳ ὅστις ἔβαλεν τὴν σαγήνην αὐτοῦ εἰς τὴν θάλασσαν (καὶ) εἵλκυσεν αὐτὴν ἐκ τῆς θαλάσσης πλήρη ἰχθύων μικρῶν. ἐν αὐτοῖς εὗρεν μέγαν ἰχθῦν καλὸν ὁ ἁλιεὺς ὁ φρόνιμος. ἐξέβαλεν πάντας τοὺς μικροὺς ἰχθύας κάτω εἰς τὴν θάλασσαν. ἐξελέξατο τὸν ἰχθῦν τὸν μέγαν χωρὶς κόπου. ὁ ἔχων ὦτα ἀκούειν ἀκουέτω* (*cf. ad 103.* Mk49).

117. cf. ETh^{II} 99 (*cf. ad 102.*)

(105)

118. Der Seesturm. *The Stilling of the Tempest.*

8 18. 23–27 (61. 62.)

18 Ἰδὼν δὲ ὁ Ἰησοῦς πολλοὺς ὄχλους περὶ αὐτὸν ἐκέλευσεν ἀπελθεῖν εἰς τὸ πέραν ... 23 Καὶ ἐμβάντι αὐτῷ εἰς πλοῖον, ἠκολούθησαν αὐτῷ οἱ μαθηταὶ αὐτοῦ. 24 καὶ ἰδοὺ σεισμὸς μέγας ἐγένετο ἐν τῇ θαλάσσῃ, ὥστε τὸ πλοῖον καλύπτεσθαι ὑπὸ τῶν κυμάτων· αὐτὸς δὲ ἐκάθευδεν. 25 καὶ προσελθόντες οἱ μαθηταὶ ἤγειραν αὐτὸν λέγοντες· κύριε, σῶσον, ἀπολλύμεθα. 26 καὶ λέγει αὐτοῖς· τί δειλοί ἐστε, ὀλιγόπιστοι; τότε ἐγερθεὶς ἐπετίμησεν τοῖς ἀνέμοις καὶ τῇ θαλάσσῃ, καὶ ἐγένετο γαλήνη μεγάλη.

Mark 4 35–41

35 Καὶ λέγει αὐτοῖς ἐν ἐκείνῃ τῇ ἡμέρᾳ ὀψίας γενομένης· διέλθωμεν εἰς τὸ πέραν. 36 καὶ ἀφέντες τὸν ὄχλον παραλαμβάνουσιν αὐτὸν ὡς ἦν ἐν τῷ πλοίῳ, καὶ ἄλλα πλοῖα ἦν μετ' αὐτοῦ. 37 καὶ γίνεται λαῖλαψ μεγάλη ἀνέμου, καὶ τὰ κύματα ἐπέβαλλεν εἰς τὸ πλοῖον, ὥστε ἤδη γεμίζεσθαι τὸ πλοῖον. 38 καὶ ἦν αὐτὸς ἐν τῇ πρύμνῃ ἐπὶ τὸ προσκεφάλαιον καθεύδων. καὶ διεγείρουσιν αὐτὸν καὶ λέγουσιν αὐτῷ· διδάσκαλε, οὐ μέλει σοι ὅτι ἀπολλύμεθα; 39 καὶ διεγερθεὶς ἐπετίμησεν τῷ ἀνέμῳ καὶ εἶπεν τῇ θαλάσσῃ· σιώπα, πεφίμωσο. καὶ ἐκόπασεν ὁ ἄνεμος, καὶ ἐγένετο γαλήνη μεγάλη. 40 καὶ εἶπεν αὐτοῖς· τί δειλοί ἐστε οὕτως; οὔπω ἔχετε πίστιν; 41 καὶ

Luk 8 22–25

22 Ἐγένετο δὲ ἐν μιᾷ τῶν ἡμερῶν καὶ αὐτὸς ἐνέβη εἰς πλοῖον καὶ οἱ μαθηταὶ αὐτοῦ, καὶ εἶπεν πρὸς αὐτούς· διέλθωμεν εἰς τὸ πέραν τῆς λίμνης· καὶ ἀνήχθησαν. 23 πλεόντων δὲ αὐτῶν ἀφύπνωσεν. καὶ κατέβη λαῖλαψ ἀνέμου εἰς τὴν λίμνην, καὶ συνεπληροῦντο καὶ ἐκινδύνευον. 24 προσελθόντες δὲ διήγειραν αὐτὸν λέγοντες· ἐπιστάτα ἐπιστάτα, ἀπολλύμεθα. ὁ δὲ διεγερθεὶς ἐπετίμησεν τῷ ἀνέμῳ καὶ τῷ κλύδωνι τοῦ ὕδατος· καὶ ἐπαύσαντο, καὶ ἐγένετο γαλήνη. 25 εἶπεν δὲ αὐτοῖς· ποῦ ἡ πίστις ὑμῶν;

Mk 4,36 πλοια] -αρια‖Jo6 23: *Rpl* — *txt*: 𝔋*C* ΘΣ-28-565-700-1071 **λ** **φ**⟨124⟩ σM-7-349-517-659-827-1194-1402 D(-αι!) K W(αλ. πλ.] αμα πολλοι) Π 157 1342 *pc l*49 *l*184 **37** γιν.] εγενετο‖Mt: D *L* | γεμ.] βιθυζεσθαι‖Lk5 7: 33 **λ** σ7-179-267-349-659 G *pc l*10 *l*12 *l*18 *l*19 *l*184 — καταποντιζεσθαι‖Mt14 30: σ27 *pc* **38** κ. ην αυ.] ● κ. αυ. ην‖5 1.17: 𝔋⟨33⟩C 1071 1342 *l*48 *L* vg^{1} *C*b *Arm* — αυ. δε ην‖Mt: *La* (δε + Ιησους: *S*p) *Cs Aeth* — ην δε αυ.: *Le*[k] b — *txt*: *Rpl L'* *S*[sc]h | διεγ.] ● εγειρ.‖Mt: ℵB*C*Δ Π *pc* — διεγειραντες(εγει-) *et om* και^{3}: Θ-28-565-700 (**φ**) D W *Lvl*⟨e[k] alz⟩ | κ. λεγ.] λεγοντες‖**p**: 472 *La Cs* | *om* αυτω‖Mt Lk: σ1402 W 472 *Le*[k] a^{v}ff^{2}q *S*[sc]p^{1} *Cs*$^{2:6}$ **39** διεγ.] εγερθεις‖Mt: 579 28-700-1604 **φ** σ954 D W *pc* | ειπ. τη θαλ.] τη θ. και(*om*) ειπ.‖p: (28)-565-700 **λ** D W (*pc*) *Lvl'*[k a]⟨flr^{2}⟩(cq) *Geo* | *om* μεγ.‖Lk: W *Le*[k] **40** ουτως] ολιγοπιστοι‖Mt: 579 σ1424 — ● *om*‖Mt: 𝔋'⟨33⟩ Θ-565-700 D 1342 *L C* — ∼ τι ου. δει. εστε: 𝔓^{45v} 28(*om* εστε) **λ**⟨118⟩ **φ**⟨124⟩ *Arm'* — *txt*: *Rpl S*[sc] *Arm*^{pc} *Aeth* | ουπω] ● πως ουκ‖Mt16 11 Lk12 56: *Rpl Lf S*[sc|p(τι ουκ)h *Geo*^{2} — *om*: W *Le*[k] q — *txt*: 𝔋⟨33⟩ Θ-28-565-700 **λ**⟨118⟩ **φ**⟨124⟩ D 1342 *L' C Arm Geo*^{1} *Aeth*

Lk 8,22 πλοι.] το πλ.‖Mk36 8 10p: 1071 **φ**-174-230 σM-71-1194 H V W **047** *pc* **23** *om* αφυ. και‖p: 1012 | αν. + πολλη‖p: D | ∼ εις τ. λι. αν.‖Mk: B-579 *La* — *om* εις τ. λι.: *Le* bff^{2}lq vg^{1} | συνεπληρουτο‖p: φ983-1689 Ψ 251 *pc* *S*cs(+ το πλοιον αυτων)p(+ τ. πλ. *et om* κ. εκινδ.) *Arm Geo*$^{+ch\,v}$ (+ το πλ.) — συνεπληρουτο υπο των κυματων το πλ.‖Mt: *Lvl'*⟨e ar^{2}⟩r^{1}30(∼ τ. πλ. υ. τ. κυ.: f) *S*c(+ αυτων) **24** πρ. δε] και πρ.‖Mt: σ990-1207 K Y Π *pm Ss*cp | διηγ.] ηγειραν‖Mt: **σ**-27-1188 *pc* | επισ. επισ.] επισ.‖p5 5: ℵ^{a} *vel*^{c} X-579 λ131 φ13-124-174 **σ**⟨954⟩ W Y Γ 157 *al l*21 *l*33 Cr *L*⟨q⟩ *Cs*$^{1(?):8}$b$^{\langle 1\rangle}$ *Arm*^{pc} *Geo Aeth* — κυριε κυριε‖Mt: D — κυριε‖Mt: *S*c | επισ.^{2} + σωσον‖Mt: φ124-174 σ115 U *pc* Cr | διεγ.] εγερθ.‖Mt: *Rpl* Mcn^{Ep} — *txt*: 𝔓^{75} 𝔋⟨579⟩ **φ**⟨69⟩ Θ 157 *pc* Cr | αν. + και τη θαλασση‖p: σ990 1047 Mcn^{Ep} — τ. υδ.] της θαλασσης‖p: *Lf Ssp*^{7} *C*b^{1} | *om* κ. επαυ.‖Mt: λ131 44 *Ssc C*b^{1} | επαυσατο‖Mk: ℵ 28-544 **λ**⟨131⟩-1582 φ230 σ267 E F G H W Θ Ψ *al* Cr *L*cff^{2}lr^{2}z vg *S*h^{m} *C*sb^{1} | γαλ. + μεγαλη‖p: 28-544-1604 **λ**-1582 φ124-174 σ1207-1223 K Δ Θ Π Ψ 157 *al L*bf g^{2}z vg^{2} *S*h^{+} *Cs*$^{2:6}$b$^{\langle 3\rangle}$ *Geo*$^{+ch\,v}$ *Aeth* **25** ειπ. δε] και ειπ.‖Mk: L-33-892 1071 σ7-267-659 *pc l*184 *Sscp C*b

Matth	Mark	Luk
[27] *οἱ δὲ ἄνθρωποι ἐθαύμασαν λέγοντες· ποταπός ἐστιν οὗτος, ὅτι καὶ οἱ ἄνεμοι καὶ ἡ θάλασσα αὐτῷ ὑπακούουσιν;*	ἐφοβήθησαν φόβον μέγαν, καὶ ἔλεγον πρὸς ἀλλήλους· τίς ἄρα οὗτός ἐστιν, ὅτι καὶ ὁ ἄνεμος καὶ ἡ θάλασσα ὑπακούει αὐτῷ;	φοβηθέντες δὲ ἐθαύμασαν, λέγοντες πρὸς ἀλλήλους· τίς ἄρα οὗτός ἐστιν, ὅτι καὶ τοῖς ἀνέμοις ἐπιτάσσει καὶ τῷ ὕδατι, καὶ ὑπακούουσιν αὐτῷ;

(106)

119. Der gerasenische Besessene. *The Gerasene Demoniac.*

8 28–34 (63.)	**Mark 5** 1–20	**Luk 8** 26–39
[28] *Καὶ ἐλθόντος αὐτοῦ εἰς τὸ πέραν εἰς τὴν χώραν τῶν Γαδαρηνῶν*	[1] Καὶ ἦλθεν εἰς τὸ πέραν τῆς θαλάσσης εἰς τὴν χώραν τῶν Γερασηνῶν. [2] καὶ	[26] Καὶ κατέπλευσαν εἰς τὴν χώραν τῶν Γεργεσηνῶν, ἥτις ἐστὶν ἀντιπέρα τῆς Γαλιλαίας.
ὑπήντησαν αὐτῷ δύο δαιμονιζόμενοι ἐκ τῶν μνημείων ἐξερχόμενοι,	ἐξελθόντος αὐτοῦ ἐκ τοῦ πλοίου, εὐθὺς ἀπήντησεν αὐτῷ ἐκ τῶν μνημείων ἄνθρωπος ἐν πνεύματι ἀκαθάρτῳ,	[27] ἐξελθόντι δὲ αὐτῷ ἐπὶ τὴν γῆν ὑπήντησεν ἀνήρ τις ἐκ τῆς πόλεως ἔχων δαιμόνια, καὶ χρόνῳ ἱκανῷ οὐκ ἐνεδύσατο ἱμάτιον,
χαλεποὶ λίαν, ὥστε μὴ ἰσχύειν τινὰ παρελθεῖν διὰ τῆς ὁδοῦ ἐκείνης.	[3] ὃς τὴν κατοίκησιν εἶχεν ἐν τοῖς μνήμασιν, καὶ οὐδὲ ἁλύσει οὐκέτι	καὶ ἐν οἰκίᾳ οὐκ ἔμενεν ἀλλ' ἐν τοῖς μνήμασιν.

οὐδεὶς ἐδύνατο αὐτὸν δῆσαι, [4] διὰ τὸ αὐτὸν πολλάκις πέδαις καὶ ἁλύσεσιν δεδέσθαι, καὶ διεσπάσθαι ὑπ' αὐτοῦ τὰς ἁλύσεις καὶ τὰς πέδας συντετρῖφθαι, καὶ οὐδεὶς ἴσχυεν αὐτὸν δαμάσαι· [5] καὶ διὰ παντὸς νυκτὸς καὶ ἡμέρας ἐν τοῖς μνήμασιν καὶ ἐν τοῖς ὄρεσιν ἦν κράζων καὶ κατακόπτων ἑαυτὸν λίθοις. (cf. v. 29↓)

Matth	Mark	Luk
[29] *καὶ ἰδοὺ ἔκραξαν*	[6] καὶ ἰδὼν τὸν Ἰησοῦν ἀπὸ μακρόθεν ἔδραμεν καὶ προσεκύνησεν αὐτόν, [7] καὶ κράξας	[28] ἰδὼν δὲ τὸν Ἰησοῦν ἀνακράξας προσέπεσεν αὐτῷ καὶ

Mk 4,41 εφο. + σφοδρα ‖ Mt27 54: 473 *pc* | ~ εστ. αρα(*om*) ουτ. ‖ (Mt): Θ-565-700 (λ22-1278 σ1082 D *pc*) | οι ανεμοι ‖ Mt Lk: ℵ^{c}-33 ΘΦ-565-700-1071 **λ** σ179-517 D E W 1342 *pc l*9 *l*48 Vic^{A} *Lvl*⟨e[k] flr^{2}⟩r^{1} vg^{3} *C*b⟨3⟩ | ● ~ αυ. υπακ. ‖ Mt: ℵ*CΔ 28 **λ** **ϕ**⟨124⟩ σ1082 Vic^{A} — υπακουουσιν αυ. ‖ Lk Mt: *Rpl* (*om* αυτω: D; ~: 1342) *L S C* — *txt*: ℵ^{c}BL-892 ϕ124-230 **5,1** ● ηλθον ‖ Lk: *Rpl L'* *S*p^{1}h^{m} *C*sb^{1} *Aeth* — *txt*: CLΔ-579-892 Θ-28-700-1604 **ϕ** σM-1207-1223-1606 G 1342 *al l*2 *l*8 *l*10 *l*13 *l*14*l*17 Ep *Lq S'* *Arm* | *om* τ. θαλ. ‖ Mt: **ϕ**⟨124-346⟩ D(+ και) *L*ff^{2}iqr^{1} *S*p^{1} *C*b^{1} | θαλ.] λιμνης ‖ Lk8 22: 700 | τ. Γερασ.] τ. Γαδαρηνων ‖ Mt: *Rpl* Or *S'* — τ. Γεργεσηνων(*cj.* -σαιων: Or) ‖ Lk: ℵ^{c}LΔ-33-579-892 Θ-28-565-700-1071 **λ**-22 σ1194 U W(Γεργυστηνων) *pc l*^{p1} Thy *S*s[c]h^{m} *C*b *Arm Aeth* — της Γεργεσθαν: Ep^{1}(^{1} της Γεργεσηνων!) — *txt*: ℵ*B D Or *L Cs* **2** εξελθοντι αυτω ‖ Lk: *Rpl L'* {} — -ντων -των: D W *L*e[k] cff^{2} *Geo*^{A} — *txt*: 𝔖C Θ-565-700 **λ**-22 **ϕ** σ7-179-267-659 *pc l*18 *l*19 *l*49 *l*184 *L*bfr^{2} {*S C Geo*^{1ch}} | ● *om* ευθ. ‖ **p**: B W 998 *L*e[k] bcff^{2}i vg^{1} *S*s[c] *Arm* | ● υπηντ. ‖ Mt Lk: ℵBCLΔ-579 Θ-28-544-565-700-1071 **λ** **ϕ**⟨124⟩ σ349-517-1207-1402 D G W 1342 *pc* — *txt*: *Rpl* Ep **6** ● αυτω ‖ 15 19 Lk Mt2 11 **14**33 28 9: *Rpl* — *txt*: BCLΔ-892 544-700-1071 σ179-659-1606 A **047** 1342 *pc l*2 *l*19 *l*48 *l*49 *l*184 **7** ανακρα. ‖ Lk: 1574

Lk 8,25 λεγ. πρ. αλλ.] ● ~ πρ. αλλ. λεγ.: LΞ-33-579-892-1241 **σ**⟨1675⟩-945-990-1223 Ψ 157 *pc L*vl'r^{1} vg^{1} *S*h — *om* πρ. αλλ.: ℵ *l*183 *C*s$^{1:8}$ — *txt*: 𝔓^{75} *Rpl L*fr^{2}z vg' *S'* | ~ εστ. ουτ. ‖ Mt: 1241 **ϕ**-174 157 1093 *L*vl⟨afr^{2}⟩r^{1} vg^{1} *Aeth* | οτι] ος ‖ 5 21 7 49: 251 *L*e acfff^{2}r^{1} *C*b^{1} *Δ*⟨l me⟩ | τ. υδ.] τη θαλασση ‖ p: σ1424 *L*⟨e a⟩ *S*scp(*prm* τω κλυδωνι και ‖ 24) *Δ*ad i l me **26** κατεπλευσεν (+ ο Ιησους) ‖ p: R W (Θ 472) 20 *L*r^{2}30(?) *C*sb^{3} | Γεργ. (*cf. ad* 37)] Γαδαρηνων ‖ Mt: *Rpl* Or *S'* — ● Γερασηνων ‖ Mk: 𝔓^{75} B D Or *L S*h^{m} *Cs* — *txt*: 𝔖'⟨892⟩XΞ 700-1604 **λλ**⟨1278⟩ σ990-1604 Θ **0267** 156 *pc* Cr Ep (*cj.* -αιων: Or) Ti *Sj Cb Arm Aeth* | αντ.] περαν (+ της θαλασσης) ‖ p: 28 σM-71-1606 S Ω (435) *al* **27** απηντ. ‖ 17 12 Mk: Γ *pc* | υπη. + αυτω ‖ p: *Rpl L* — *txt*: 𝔓^{75} ℵBΞ-33-579 700 **λ**⟨131⟩-1582-2193 E W Ψ 157 *pc* Ath | δαιμονιον ‖ Mk: 472 *pc l*1963 *L*⟨e⟩ *C*b$^{2(+1?)}$ | μνημειοις ‖ p: D *pc l*1627 | μνη. + και εν τοις ορεσιν ην κραζων και κατακοπτων εαυτον λιθοις ‖ Mk: X 1071(κατεκοπτεν) **σ**-1188 *S*c(*om* εν τ. ορ.) **28** ανακ.] κραξας ‖ Mk: R | ανακ.—μεγ.] ανακ. φω. μεγ. ‖ Mt: D — ~ προσε. αυ. κ. ανακ. φω. μεγ. ‖ Mk: *L'*(*om* αυτω: a; *om* και: vg^{1}) — αν. φω. μ. πρ. αυ. ‖ Mk: *Le*

λέγοντες· τί ἡμῖν καὶ σοί, υἱὲ τοῦ θεοῦ; ἦλθες ὧδε πρὸ καιροῦ βασανίσαι ἡμᾶς;

30 ἦν δὲ μακρὰν ἀπ' αὐτῶν ἀγέλη χοίρων πολλῶν βοσκομένη. 31 οἱ δὲ δαίμονες παρεκάλουν αὐτὸν λέγοντες· εἰ ἐκβάλλεις ἡμᾶς, ἀπόστειλον ἡμᾶς εἰς τὴν ἀγέλην τῶν χοίρων.

φωνῇ μεγάλῃ λέγει· τί ἐμοὶ καὶ σοί, Ἰησοῦ υἱὲ τοῦ θεοῦ τοῦ ὑψίστου; ὁρκίζω σε τὸν θεόν, μή με βασανίσῃς. 8 ἔλεγεν γὰρ αὐτῷ· ἔξελθε τὸ πνεῦμα τὸ ἀκάθαρτον ἐκ τοῦ ἀνθρώπου.

cf. v. 4 ↑

9 καὶ ἐπηρώτα αὐτόν· τί ὄνομά σοι; καὶ λέγει αὐτῷ· λεγιὼν ὄνομά μοι, ὅτι πολλοί ἐσμεν. 10 καὶ παρεκάλει αὐτὸν πολλὰ ἵνα μὴ αὐτοὺς ἀποστείλῃ ἔξω τῆς χώρας. 11 ἦν δὲ ἐκεῖ πρὸς τῷ ὄρει ἀγέλη χοίρων μεγάλη βοσκομένη· 12 καὶ παρεκάλεσαν αὐτὸν λέγοντες· πέμψον ἡμᾶς εἰς τοὺς χοίρους, ἵνα εἰς αὐτοὺς εἰσέλθωμεν.

φωνῇ μεγάλῃ εἶπεν· τί ἐμοὶ καὶ σοί, Ἰησοῦ υἱὲ τοῦ θεοῦ τοῦ ὑψίστου; δέομαί σου, μή με βασανίσῃς. 29 παρήγγελλεν γὰρ τῷ πνεύματι τῷ ἀκαθάρτῳ ἐξελθεῖν ἀπὸ τοῦ ἀνθρώπου. πολλοῖς γὰρ χρόνοις συνηρπάκει αὐτόν, καὶ ἐδεσμεύετο ἁλύσεσι καὶ πέδαις φυλασσόμενος, καὶ διαρρήσσων τὰ δεσμὰ ἠλαύνετο ὑπὸ τοῦ δαιμονίου εἰς τὰς ἐρήμους. 30 ἐπηρώτησεν δὲ αὐτὸν ὁ Ἰησοῦς· τί σοι ὄνομά ἐστιν; ὁ δὲ εἶπεν· λεγιών, ὅτι εἰσῆλθεν δαιμόνια πολλὰ εἰς αὐτόν. 31 καὶ παρεκάλουν αὐτὸν ἵνα μὴ ἐπιτάξῃ αὐτοῖς εἰς τὴν ἄβυσσον ἀπελθεῖν. 32 ἦν δὲ ἐκεῖ ἀγέλη χοίρων ἱκανῶν βοσκομένων ἐν τῷ ὄρει· καὶ παρεκάλεσαν αὐτὸν ἵνα ἐπιτρέψῃ αὐτοῖς εἰς ἐκείνους εἰσελθεῖν.

Mk 5,7 λεγ.] ειπεν ‖ Lk: *Rpl* {*L*vl'[k] r^1 vg^8 *C*b} — λεγων: Π 1047 *Cs* — *txt*: 𝔖C ΘΣ Φ-1071 **λ** σM-349-517-1207 A K W 1342 *al l*48 *l*49 *l*184 *L*lz30 vg' {} | εμ.] ημιν ‖ Mt: Θ 106 2145 *S*p^{1}h *Cs*$^{2:5}$ *Geo*^{B}(∼ σοι κ. ημ.) | *om* Ι. ‖ Mt: 33 Φ-700 **λ**⟨131⟩ **ϕ**983-1689 σ179-349-1082-1675 *pc* | τ. υψ.] τ. ζωντος ‖ Mt16 16: Σ A *S*h^m — *om* ‖ Mt: *Cs*$^{1:5}$b^1 **8** εκ] απο ‖ Lk: 33 565-1604 λ118 σ1194 A **047** 157 *pc* **9** επερωτησεν ‖ Lk: σ349-517-659 A 477 *Le*[k] acff^{2}iqr^1 vg^1 *S*p *Cs*$^{4:5}$b^1 *Geo*$^{ch.2}$ | ∼ σοι ον. (+ εστιν) ‖ Lk: *Rpl* (D 477)(∼ σοι εστ. ον.: σ1402) (*L*) — *txt*: 𝔖C ΘΣΦ-28 **λ** **ϕ**⟨124⟩ σM-349-517 A K W Π 1342 *al l*48 *l*49 *l*184 | λεγει αυτω] ● απεκριθη λεγων(*om*): *Rpl* (D *pc*) (+ αυτω: 998 1279) *L*(e[k] abfff^{2}iq)cz — *txt* (*om* αυτω ‖ Lk): 𝔖C ΘΣΦ-28 **λ** **ϕ**⟨124⟩ σM-349-517 A K W Π 1342 *al L*lr^2(30) vg *S Cs*b'(^{2}) | μοι + εστιν ‖ Lk30a: B **ϕ** D(∼ εστ. μ. ον. λεγιων) *pc L*vl'[a]⟨e[k]⟩(= D: qr^1)(*om* και^2—εσμεν: ff^2) | πολλα ‖ Lk: 565 **10** παρεκαλουν ‖ 12p Lk: Δ Θ-28-565 **λ**-22 **ϕ**983-1689 A **047** *pc l*48 *L*cff^{2}g^2 vg^1 *S*s[c] *Cs*$^{3:5}$b^1 *Arm Geo*^{2} | *om* πολλα ‖ Lk: L-892 λ872 σ827 1342 *pc Le*[k] vg^1 *S*s[c] | αυτους] ● αυτα ‖ Lk30: BCΔ Θ {} — αυτον: ℵL-892 σ1194-1207 K W Π 1342 *al L' S*p *C*b — *txt*: *Rpl* {*L*cff^2 vg^1 *S' Cs Arm*} **11** ∼ αγ. χ. μεγ. βοσκ. πρ. τ. ορ. ‖ Lk: Σ(∼ βο. με: **ϕ**346-543) A K Π (U **074**) 1241(πρ.] εν) *pc l*48 *l*184 *Lc S*h *C*b *Geo*^{1} — αγ. χ. μ. πρ. τ. ορ. βοσκ. ‖ Lk: **ϕ**' σM — *om* πρ. τ. ορει ‖ Mt: 33^v λ1-872 (**ϕ** 983-1689) *L*r^{2}30 *Geo*^{2} | μεγ.] *om* ‖ p: L-579-892 λ131 **ϕ**983-1689 σ71-692 D U **074** *pc l*48 *l*184 *Le*[k] bff^{2}i *Cs*$^{2:5}$ — πολλων ‖ Mt: Φ(χοι. πολ. αγ. μεγ.) *pc L*q | βοσκομενων ‖ Lk: ℵ^{c}LΔ σ1402 A *pc L*bdq vg^1 **12** παρεκαλουν ‖ Mt: 544-565 σM-827 A D K Π *al L*⟨c⟩ *S*s[c]p *C*b$^{⟨6⟩}$ | αυτον + οι δαιμονες ‖ Mt: 579 λ872 σM-27 A K Π *Lc* {*S'*}^{1} — + τα δαιμονια ‖ Mt: D *Le*[k] f{r^1}^{1} — + παντες οι δαιμονες (*et* + εκεινοι) ‖ Mt: *Rpl* {*S*h (*Geo*^{2})}^{2} — + παντα τα δαιμονια ‖ Mt: Θ-565-700 *La* {}^{2} — + τα πνευματα(+ εκεινα *L'*(b) *Aeth* — *txt*: 𝔖'⟨33⟩C 28 **λ**-22-1278 **ϕ**⟨124⟩ W 1342 *C Geo*^{1}

Lk 8,28 ειπ.] λεγει ‖ Mk: σ1675 — λεγων ‖ Mt: *Le* cr^1 vg^1 | *om* Ιησου ‖ Mt: 𝔓^{75} 579 1071 **λλ**⟨22-131⟩ σ1082 D R *al l*184 *l*374 *l*1963 *Le C*b$^{⟨7⟩}$ **29** παρη.] ελεγεν ‖ Mk: D *Le* | εξελθε ‖ Mk: D *Le* | απο τ. αν.] απ αυτου ‖ 435p: L-33 | υπο] ● απο: BΞ | τ. δαι.] τ. δαιμονος ‖ Mt31: *Rpl La* — των δαιμον(ι)ων ‖ (27) Mt31; Λ (1093 1187) *S*h^m *Cs*$^{1:6}$ — *txt*: 𝔓^{75} ℵBC*XΞ-579 D E Ψ *L'*(*om* υπ. τ. δαι.: ff^2) **30** σοι ον. εσ.] ον. σοι ‖ Mk: C* *L*vg^1(∼) *Aeth* — ον. σοι εσ. ‖ Mk: 579 — σοι εσ. ον.: *Rpl S*h — *txt*: 𝔓^{75} 𝔖'Ξ 1071 **λ**-1582-2193 σ954-990 DΨ 872 157 *L'* | ειπ. + αυτω ‖ Mk: 251 *pc S*scp | λεγ. + ονομα μοι ‖ Mk: σ990 D *Lc Sj Aeth* | οτι—αυτον] πολλα γαρ ησαν δαιμ. (+ εν αυτω) ‖ Mk: D *L*(af)cff^2 — οτι πολλοι εσμεν (+ εν αυτω) ‖ Mk: *L*bl (*S*sc) **31** παρεκαλει ‖ Mk: *Rpl* Ep *C*b^2 — *txt*: 𝔓^{75} 𝔖C 28-1071-1604 **λ**-1582 **ϕ**-*l*547 σ990-1424 D F S W(*om* και π. αυ.) Ω 157 *al l*1 *l*32 *l*1963 *l*^{4} *L*[e] *S*,j *Cs*(-εσαν)b' **32** ικ.] πολλων ‖ Mt: X σ990 *pc* — ικανη ‖ Mk: 1396 *La Sj Cs* — *om* ‖ Mk: 579 D 49 60(*et om* βοσκ.) *L*cr^1 *C*b$^{⟨6⟩}$ | ● βοσκομενη(-ην) ‖ p: 𝔓^{75} ℵB 544 **ϕ**'⟨983⟩(13-346-788-826)-*l*547 σ71-692-990 D' K U Θ Π *al l*3 *l*31 *l*1599 *l*1627 *l*^{10} Or *La Spj Cs*^{6} — *txt*: *Rpl L'*[e] *S' Cs*^{1}b | παρεκαλουν ‖ 31p Mt: *Rpl* (-λει: 565 *pc l*32 *l*50) *L*r^2 vg' *S C*b — *txt*: ℵ^{c}BC*LΞ-33-892 700 λ1-131-1582-2193 **ϕ**124 σ990 156 *pc L*vl'[e] r^1 vg^1 *Sj Cs* | αυτον + οι δαιμονες ‖ Mt: 213 *L*l(οι δε δαι. παρε. αυ.) (+ εκεινοι: *S*sc) | επιτ.—εισελ.] εις τους χοιρους εισελθωσιν ‖ Mk: D *Lc* — εις εκ.(αυτους) εισελθω. ‖ Mk: *L*(a)bff^{2}qz | εκ.] τους χοιρους ‖ Mk: (D *Lc*) *S*sp (+ εκ.: j) *C*b^1 — εκεινην αγελην των χοιρων ‖ Mt: *S*c

32 καὶ εἶπεν αὐτοῖς· ὑπάγετε. οἱ δὲ ἐξελθόντες ἀπῆλθαν εἰς τοὺς χοίρους· καὶ ἰδοὺ ὥρμησεν πᾶσα ἡ ἀγέλη κατὰ τοῦ κρημνοῦ εἰς τὴν θάλασσαν, καὶ ἀπέθανον ἐν τοῖς ὕδασιν. 33 οἱ δὲ βόσκοντες ἔφυγον, καὶ ἀπελθόντες εἰς τὴν πόλιν ἀπήγγειλαν πάντα καὶ τὰ τῶν δαιμονιζομένων. 34 καὶ ἰδοὺ πᾶσα ἡ πόλις ἐξῆλθεν εἰς συνάντησιν τῷ Ἰησοῦ, καὶ ἰδόντες αὐτὸν παρεκάλεσαν ὅπως μεταβῇ ἀπὸ τῶν ὁρίων αὐτῶν.

13 καὶ ἐπέτρεψεν αὐτοῖς. καὶ ἐξελθόντα τὰ πνεύματα τὰ ἀκάθαρτα εἰσῆλθον εἰς τοὺς χοίρους, καὶ ὥρμησεν ἡ ἀγέλη κατὰ τοῦ κρημνοῦ εἰς τὴν θάλασσαν, ὡς δισχίλιοι, καὶ ἐπνίγοντο ἐν τῇ θαλάσσῃ. 14 καὶ οἱ βόσκοντες αὐτοὺς ἔφυγον καὶ ἀνήγγειλαν εἰς τὴν πόλιν καὶ εἰς τοὺς ἀγρούς. καὶ ἦλθον ἰδεῖν τί ἐστιν τὸ γεγονός· 15 καὶ ἔρχονται πρὸς τὸν Ἰησοῦν, καὶ θεωροῦσιν τὸν δαιμονιζόμενον καθήμενον ἱματισμένον καὶ σωφρονοῦντα, τὸν ἐσχηκότα τὸν λεγιῶνα, καὶ ἐφοβήθησαν. 16 καὶ διηγήσαντο αὐτοῖς οἱ ἰδόντες πῶς ἐγένετο τῷ δαιμονιζομένῳ καὶ περὶ τῶν χοίρων. 17 καὶ ἤρξαντο παρακαλεῖν αὐτὸν ἀπελθεῖν ἀπὸ τῶν ὁρίων αὐτῶν.

καὶ ἐπέτρεψεν αὐτοῖς. 33 ἐξελθόντα δὲ τὰ δαιμόνια ἀπὸ τοῦ ἀνθρώπου εἰσῆλθον εἰς τοὺς χοίρους, καὶ ὥρμησεν ἡ ἀγέλη κατὰ τοῦ κρημνοῦ εἰς τὴν λίμνην καὶ ἀπεπνίγη. 34 ἰδόντες δὲ οἱ βόσκοντες τὸ γεγενημένον ἔφυγον καὶ ἀπήγγειλαν εἰς τὴν πόλιν καὶ εἰς τοὺς ἀγρούς. 35 ἐξῆλθον δὲ ἰδεῖν τὸ γεγονός· καὶ ἦλθαν πρὸς τὸν Ἰησοῦν, καὶ εὗραν καθήμενον τὸν ἄνθρωπον ἀφ' οὗ τὰ δαιμόνια ἐξῆλθεν ἱματισμένον καὶ σωφρονοῦντα παρὰ τοὺς πόδας τοῦ Ἰησοῦ, καὶ ἐφοβήθησαν. 36 ἀπήγγειλαν δὲ αὐτοῖς οἱ ἰδόντες πῶς ἐσώθη ὁ δαιμονισθείς. 37 καὶ ἠρώτησεν αὐτὸν ἅπαν τὸ πλῆθος τῆς περιχώρου τῶν Γεργεσηνῶν ἀπελθεῖν ἀπ' αὐτῶν, ὅτι φόβῳ

Mk 5,13 και + ο Ιησους: (565-700) *Geo*^{1} — + ευθεως κυριος I.: D *Lac*(*om* κυ.)ff^{2}i(*om* I.)q(*om* κυ. I.)r^{1} | επετ. αυτ.] επεταξεν αυτ.‖127924Lk31: *Arm Geo* — επεμψεν αυτους (+ εις τους χοιρους)‖(12): 565-700 σ71 (D) *pc* (*L*cff^{2}r^{1v}) | ● αυτ. + ευθεως ο Ιησους: *Rpl* (αυτους: σ71-349 U; επεστρ.: ϕ13; *om* ο I.: E) *L*fl(∼ ο I. ευ.)z vg *S*h — + ο I.: 579 *pc* *l*48 Da *L*q *Geo*^{B} *Aeth* — *txt*: ℌ'⟨33⟩C Θ-28 **λ** ϕ788 W 1342 *L*e[k] abi(αυτους *et* + ελθειν εις τους χοιρους) *S*' *Cs*(+ ελθειν)b *Arm Geo*' | ακαθ. + απο του ανθρωπου‖Lk: 579 238 *Cs*$^{1:6}$ | και^{3} + ιδου‖Mt: 483 484 | ωρμ. + πασα‖Mt: 349-517-945-1223 *al* *Cs*$^{3:6}$ | ως] ησαν δε ως‖89: *Rpl* *L*afg^{2}ilr^{2} vg^{4} *Geo*^{1} — ησ. γαρ ως‖Lk914: 28 *pc* Ep r^{1} vg^{1} *S*h *Geo*^{2} — *txt*: ℌ⟨33-579⟩C* 565 λ1 D W *L*' *S*' **14** *om* αυτ.‖p: 1342 *pc* | ● απηγγ.‖MtLk: ℌ⟨Δ⟩C ΘΣΦ-700 **λ** σM-517 A D K Π **074** **0107** 1342 *al* *l*48 *l*49 *l*184 | εξηλθον‖Lk Mt: *Rpl* *L*'*S*' *Cs* — *txt*: ℌ⟨ℵ*Δ⟩ℵ^{c} ΣΦ-565 λ118-209 σM A K U Π **074** **0107** 1342 *al* *l*18 *l*19 *Lvg*^{1}(?) *S*h *C*b | *om* τι εστ.‖Lk: 579 H *pc* *l*48 *C*sb^{1} — *om* εστ.‖Lk: σ827 A*^{v} *pc* **15** ερχ.] ηλθον‖Lk: σ1194 *L*bcf30 vg^{2} | θεω.] ευρισκουσιν‖Lk: W *Aeth* | καθ. + παρα τους ποδας του Ιησου‖Lk: 157 **16** εγ. τω δαιμ.] εσωθη ο δαιμονισθεις‖Lk: **λ**-22-1582 *pc* **17** ηρξ. παρ.] παρεκαλουν‖MtLk31: Θ-565-700 σ517 D *pc* *L*a^{v}

Lk 8,33 εξελ. δε] και εξ.‖Mk: 579 1047 *L*a *S*scpj | *om* απο τ. αν.‖p: 28 λ1-131 σ659 | και^{1} + ιδου‖Mt: 483 | η] πασα η‖Mt: X ϕ69 Θ *pc* *Lvg*^{1} *S*s(αγ. + εκεινη: cp)j *Geo*'(^{B} = c) | λιμ.] θαλασσαν‖MtMk: ℵ-579-1241 28 ϕ174 σ115-990-1675 *pc* *l*32 *L*acr^{1v}30 | απεπνιγησαν‖p: 579 1071 S *pc* *L*vl'[e]⟨afr^{2}⟩ *S*scpj *C*b$^{\langle 7\rangle}$ *Arm*^{1} — επνιγη‖Mk: σ1675 1038 — απεπνιγοντο‖Mk: C **34** ● γεγονος‖35p8 56 24 12: 𝔓^{75} ℌCΞ 544-1071-1604 **λ**-1582-2193 **ϕ**⟨124⟩-*l*547 σ990-1207 A D K P R U W Θ Π *al* — γενομενον‖2347: Ψ Ω *pc* *l*29 *l*184 | και^{1} + απελθοντες‖Mt: 440 472 **35** 35] παραγενομενων δε εκ της πολεως και θεωρησαντων καθημενον τον δαιμονιζομενον σωφρονουντα και ηματισμενον καθημενον παρα τους ποδας του Ιησου εφοβ.‖Mk: D | εξηλθον δε] και εξ.‖p: C* λ1-131-1582-2193 σ1194 *S*scpj | ιδ + τι εστιν‖Mk: C^{c} | ηλθ.] ερχονται‖Mk: **λ**-1582-2193 | ∼ τ. αν. καθ.‖Mk: 892 **λ**-1582-2193 ϕ124 P W 157 *pc* *L*[e]⟨a⟩ | εξηλθεν] εξεληλυθει‖38 82 Mk729f.: *Rpl* (-εν: 1241 4) (D) *L*'[e](-εσαν) vg^{1} | *txt* (-ον): 𝔓^{75} ℵ*(^{c})B σ990 716 (*L*fr^{2}z vg^{2}) *S*,j | εφο.] εξεθαμβηθησαν‖Mk915 165: 28 **36** απηγγ.] διηγησαντο‖Mk: 1574 *Lf* | δαιμονιζομενος‖Mk: **σ**-1188 **37** ηρω.] παρεκαλεσαν‖p: Θ — ● ηρωτησαν(-ωτων)‖p: *Rpl* (1038) Bas *L*'[e] (*S*'j) *C*sb'(^{2}) *Geo*^{A} — *txt* (ηρωτα): ℌ⟨L⟩CX(επηρ-) 28-544-1604 **ϕ**-174 σM-71-115-692-990-1194-1207-1223 A K P R S Π 157 *mu* *L*ar^{2} *S*h (*Geo*') | Γεργ.] Γαδαρηνων‖Mt28: *Rpl* Bas *S* — ● Γερασηνων‖Mk1: 𝔓^{75} BC*-579 D Cr *L*[e] *Cs*$^{6+1v}$ — *txt*: ℵ*$^{et\,c}$C^{c}(Γεργαρση-)LX-33-1241 700-1071-1604 **λλ**⟨1278⟩ **ϕ**'⟨124-346⟩(Γεσινων: 69)-230 P Θ 157 *pc* Ti *S*j *C*b$^{\langle 1\rangle}$ *Arm* *Geo* *Aeth* | απ] απο των οριων‖p: 700-1071 *Arm*

Matth	Mark	Luk
9 1 (64.): Καὶ ἐμβὰς εἰς πλοῖον διεπέρασεν, καὶ ἦλθεν εἰς τὴν ἰδίαν πόλιν.	18 καὶ ἐμβαίνοντος αὐτοῦ εἰς τὸ πλοῖον παρεκάλει αὐτὸν ὁ δαιμονισθεὶς ἵνα μετ' αὐτοῦ ᾖ. 19 καὶ οὐκ ἀφῆκεν αὐτόν, ἀλλὰ λέγει αὐτῷ· ὕπαγε εἰς τὸν οἶκόν σου πρὸς τοὺς σούς, καὶ ἀνάγγειλον αὐτοῖς ὅσα σοι ὁ κύριος πεποίηκεν καὶ ἠλέησέν σε. 20 καὶ ἀπῆλθεν καὶ ἤρξατο κηρύσσειν ἐν τῇ Δεκαπόλει ὅσα ἐποίησεν αὐτῷ ὁ Ἰησοῦς, καὶ πάντες ἐθαύμαζον.	μεγάλῳ συνείχοντο· αὐτὸς δὲ ἐμβὰς εἰς πλοῖον ὑπέστρεψεν. 38 ἐδεῖτο δὲ αὐτοῦ ὁ ἀνὴρ ἀφ' οὗ ἐξεληλύθει τὰ δαιμόνια εἶναι σὺν αὐτῷ. ἀπέλυσεν δὲ αὐτὸν λέγων· 39 ὑπόστρεφε εἰς τὸν οἶκόν σου, καὶ διηγοῦ ὅσα σοι ἐποίησεν ὁ θεός. καὶ ἀπῆλθεν καθ' ὅλην τὴν πόλιν κηρύσσων ὅσα ἐποίησεν αὐτῷ ὁ Ἰησοῦς.

(107)

120. Die Tochter des Jairus und das blutflüssige Weib.
Jairus' Daughter and the Woman with the Issue of Blood.

9 18–26 (67.)	Mark 5 21–43	Luk 8 40–56
18 Ταῦτα αὐτοῦ λαλοῦντος αὐτοῖς, ἰδοὺ ἄρχων εἷς ἐλθὼν προσεκύνει αὐτῷ λέγων· ἡ θυγάτηρ	21 Καὶ διαπεράσαντος τοῦ Ἰησοῦ ἐν τῷ πλοίῳ πάλιν εἰς τὸ πέραν συνήχθη ὄχλος πολὺς ἐπ' αὐτόν, καὶ ἦν παρὰ τὴν θάλασσαν. 22 καὶ ἔρχεται εἷς τῶν ἀρχισυναγώγων, ὀνόματι Ἰάϊρος, καὶ ἰδὼν αὐτὸν πίπτει πρὸς τοὺς πόδας αὐτοῦ, 23 καὶ παρακαλεῖ αὐτὸν πολλὰ λέγων ὅτι τὸ θυγάτρι-	40 Ἐν δὲ τῷ ὑποστρέφειν τὸν Ἰησοῦν ἀπεδέξατο αὐτὸν ὁ ὄχλος· ἦσαν γὰρ πάντες προσδοκῶντες αὐτόν. 41 καὶ ἰδοὺ ἦλθεν ἀνὴρ ᾧ ὄνομα Ἰάϊρος, καὶ οὗτος ἄρχων τῆς συναγωγῆς ὑπῆρχεν· καὶ πεσὼν παρὰ τοὺς πόδας Ἰησοῦ παρεκάλει αὐτὸν εἰσελθεῖν εἰς τὸν οἶκον αὐτοῦ, 42 ὅτι θυγάτηρ

Mk 5,18 εμβαντος‖p: *Rpl S Cb Geo*^{A} — *txt*: ℌ⟨579⟩C Σ λ1-131 ϕ124 σM-7-349-517 A D K W Π **074 0107**^{v} *pc l48 l49 l184 L Cs Geo*^{1} | *om* το‖41 Lk Mt: 449 1574 **19** • απαγγ.‖Mt 8 33 Lk 34: ℵBC Δ-579 ΘΣ σ827 1342 *pc* — διαγγ.‖Lk 9 60 8 39: 𝔓^{45} 28-700 **λ ϕ** D W | *om* αυτοις‖**p**: U *Aeth* | • ~ ο κυ. σοι: BCΔ Θ *Lff*^{2} | κυ.] θεος‖p: 1071(~ πεπ.—σε ο θε.) D 238 1241 | πεπ.] εποιησεν‖p: Φ-565-700 **λ** σ115-517-1606 D K *pc* | ~ πεπ.(εποι.) ο κυ.(θεος)‖p: Ω (1241) *Lar*^{1}(?) vg^{1} | *om* κ. ηλ. σε‖p: 4 273 *Le*[k] *Cb*^{1} **20** *om* και πα. εθαυ.‖**p**: 483 | εθαυμασαν‖Lk 13 6 2 18 8 25 Mt 8 27: σ1424 213 *Lbcff*^{2} *Csb*^{1} *Aeth* **21** επ] προς‖41p: 579 ΝΘΣ-28-565-700 **ϕ** σ1194 D 90 **22** και^{1} + ιδου‖Lk Mt: 𝔓^{45} *Rpl Lcf Sh Arm Geo*^{1} — *txt*: ℌ⟨579⟩ Θ D 1342 *L*' Au *S*' *C Geo*^{A} | ον.] ω ονομα‖Lk: Θ-565-700 W | *om* ον. Ι.‖Mt: D *Le*[k] aff^{2}ir^{1v} | *om* ιδ. αυ.‖**p**: D *Le*[k] | προς] παρα‖Lk: ΝΣΦ σ1082-1391 — εις‖Jo 11 32: σ517 *pc l19* | ~ αυτου πρ. τ. ποδ.‖←: λ1-131-872 σ(517)-1424 *La*(αυτω) **23** και παρεκαλει‖Lk: *Rpl L*' — παρακαλων‖1 40: D *L*(*prm* και: e[k] ff^{2})abiq — *txt*: ℵCL-33-892 28-565-1071 σ71-1606 A *pc l48* | *om* πολ.‖Lk: 1604 ϕ983-1689 D *pc l251 Lbcff*^{2}ilq *Ss*[c] | *om* οτι‖Mt: Θ **ϕ**⟨124-346-828⟩ D *Le*[k] ac30 *Ss*[c]p | το θυ.] η θυγατηρ‖Mt Lk: σ1082 448

Lk 8,37 πλοι.] το πλ.‖Mk: *Rpl* (*om* εις το πλ.: D) Bas (*Ll*) *Cs*^{3}b — *txt*: ℌCX 28-700-1604 λ1-131-1582-2193 σ954-1207-1606 R Θ Ψ 157 *pc Cs*^{3} **39** σου + προς τους σους‖p: X-579(τους σου!) *Sc* | σοι επ. ο θε.] σ. πεποιηκεν ο θε.‖p: 579 R Cr *La* vg^{12} — σ. ο κυριος πεπ.‖p: C* *Lb* — σ. ο θε. επ.‖p: D *Lf* — επ. σ. ο θε.(κυ.)‖39b(Mk): *Rpl* Bas *S*'(c)j — *txt*: 𝔓^{75} ℌ'⟨1241⟩(σου: L)X 1071 **λ**-1582-2193 P W Θ Ψ *pc* Ti Vic^{A} *L*[e]' | και^{2} + ηλεησεν σε και‖Mk: C* **λ**-2193 ϕ124 872 | ~ κη. καθ—πολιν‖Mk: 1396 *Sscp* | ~ αυτω πεποιηκεν‖Mk 19: 579 *Ldr*$^{1.2}$30 vg^{1} **40** υπεδεξ.‖19 6: X σ945 *pc* | οχ.] λαος‖1 21: **λ**⟨131⟩-1582-2193 *Ld* — + πολυς‖Mk: *Sscp* — + χαιρων‖19 6: 251 *pc* | προσδ.] προς‖Mk: 472 **41** *om* ιδ.‖Mk: σ1675 D *Lc Sscpj* | ω ον.] ονοματι‖23 50 19 2 Mk: 1071 ϕ*l*547 Θ *pc La* | ουτ.] • αυτος‖19 2 Mt 27 54 Mk 15 43: *Rpl L*'[e] *Shj*('*om*) *Arm* — *txt*: 𝔓^{75} B-579 **λ**-1582-2193 **ϕ**-174-230 σ71-692-954-1424 D R 157 *pc Lafr*^{1} *Cb*(*om*: s) *Geo Aeth* | υπηρ.] υπαρχων‖23 50: K *pc* — ην: 28 | εισελ.] ινα εισελθη‖Mk: C*^{v} 1071

Matthew

μου ἄρτι ἐτελεύτησεν· ἀλλὰ ἐλθὼν ἐπίθες τὴν χεῖρά σου ἐπ' αὐτήν, καὶ ζήσεται. 19 καὶ ἐγερθεὶς ὁ Ἰησοῦς ἠκολούθησεν αὐτῷ καὶ οἱ μαθηταὶ αὐτοῦ.

20 καὶ ἰδοὺ γυνὴ αἱμορροοῦσα δώδεκα ἔτη

προσελθοῦσα ὄπισθεν ἥψατο τοῦ κρασπέδου τοῦ ἱματίου αὐτοῦ· 21 ἔλεγεν γὰρ ἐν ἑαυτῇ· ἐὰν μόνον ἅψωμαι τοῦ ἱματίου αὐτοῦ, σωθήσομαι.

22 ὁ δὲ Ἰησοῦς στραφεὶς

Mark

όν μου ἐσχάτως ἔχει, ἵνα ἐλθὼν ἐπιθῇς τὰς χεῖρας αὐτῇ, ἵνα σωθῇ καὶ ζήσῃ. 24 καὶ ἀπῆλθεν μετ' αὐτοῦ. καὶ ἠκολούθει αὐτῷ ὄχλος πολύς, καὶ συνέθλιβον αὐτόν.

25 καὶ γυνή τις οὖσα ἐν ῥύσει αἵματος δώδεκα ἔτη, 26 καὶ πολλὰ παθοῦσα ὑπὸ πολλῶν ἰατρῶν καὶ δαπανήσασα τὰ παρ' ἑαυτῆς πάντα, καὶ μηδὲν ὠφεληθεῖσα ἀλλὰ μᾶλλον εἰς τὸ χεῖρον ἐλθοῦσα, 27 ἀκούσασα τὰ περὶ τοῦ Ἰησοῦ, ἐλθοῦσα ἐν τῷ ὄχλῳ ὄπισθεν ἥψατο τοῦ ἱματίου αὐτοῦ· 28 ἔλεγεν γὰρ ὅτι ἐὰν ἅψωμαι κἂν τῶν ἱματίων αὐτοῦ, σωθήσομαι. 29 καὶ εὐθὺς ἐξηράνθη ἡ πηγὴ τοῦ αἵματος αὐτῆς, καὶ ἔγνω τῷ σώματι ὅτι ἴαται ἀπὸ τῆς μάστιγος. 30 καὶ εὐθὺς ὁ Ἰησοῦς ἐπιγνοὺς ἐν ἑαυτῷ τὴν ἐξ αὐτοῦ δύναμιν ἐξελθοῦσαν, ἐπιστραφεὶς ἐν τῷ ὄχλῳ ἔλεγεν· τίς μου ἥψατο τῶν ἱματίων; 31 καὶ ἔλεγον αὐτῷ οἱ μαθηταὶ αὐτοῦ· βλέπεις τὸν ὄχλον συνθλίβοντά σε,

Luke

μονογενὴς ἦν αὐτῷ ὡς ἐτῶν δώδεκα καὶ αὕτη ἀπέθνῃσκεν. Ἐν δὲ τῷ ὑπάγειν αὐτὸν οἱ ὄχλοι συνέπνιγον αὐτόν.

43 καὶ γυνὴ οὖσα ἐν ῥύσει αἵματος ἀπὸ ἐτῶν δώδεκα, ἥτις ἰατροῖς προσαναλώσασα ὅλον τὸν βίον οὐκ ἴσχυσεν ὑπ' οὐδενὸς θεραπευθῆναι, 44 προσελθοῦσα ὄπισθεν ἥψατο τοῦ κρασπέδου τοῦ ἱματίου αὐτοῦ, *cf. 84.* καὶ παραχρῆμα ἔστη ἡ ῥύσις τοῦ αἵματος αὐτῆς.

45 καὶ εἶπεν ὁ Ἰησοῦς· τίς ὁ ἁψάμενός μου; ἀρνουμένων δὲ πάντων εἶπεν ὁ Πέτρος· ἐπιστάτα, οἱ ὄχλοι συνέχουσίν σε καὶ ἀποθλίβουσιν.

Mk 5,23 τας χ.] χειρα‖Mt: 28 ϕ 258 *L*cfg²z vg³ *S*s[c]p *C* *Geo*¹·ᴮ | χειρ. + σου‖Mt: Δ-892 (D) *L*bcff² g²iqr¹30 vg¹ *S* *Cs*⁷:⁸b⟨²⟩ | αυτη] επ αυτη(ν)‖Mt: (28)-565 230 (258) *L*cflr²z vg | ζησεται‖Mt: *Rpl* *L*' *S*' *Cs*⁵ — *txt*: 𝔥⟨33⟩C Θ-565-700 ϕ D *L*e[k] cr¹·²z *S*h *Cs*³b *Geo*¹ **24** απηλ.] υπηγεν‖Lk: ϕ124 D | ηκολουθησεν‖Mt: CL-892 ϕ*l*547 σMᵐ-1675 *pc* (-σαν: *l*48 *l*253) *S*j *C* **25** ● *om* τις‖p 7₂₅: 𝔥⟨579⟩C λ1-209 A W 1342 *l*32 {*L*'} Sj *Geo*ᴮ *Aeth* — *txt*: *Rpl* Laf{} *S* *Geo*' | ∼ ετη δωδ.‖Lk: *Rpl* — *txt*: 𝔥C 28 λ⟨118⟩ ϕ W 1342 **26** εαυ.] ● αυτης: *Rpl* (τα υπαρχοντα αυτης παν.: Φ) Or — *txt* (*om* παρ): ℵCΔ (Θ-565-700)-28(∼ παν. τα εαυ.)-1071 (λ) ϕ230 σ7-27(?)-179-267-349-517-659 (D W) K Π *al* **27** ● *om* τα‖7₂₅ Lk7₃ 23₈: *Rpl* — *txt*: ℵ*BC*ᵛΔ 1546 *l*33 | *om* εν τ. οχ.‖p: λ⟨131⟩-22-1278 σ1194 *pc* *L*e[k] | ηψ. + του κρασπεδου‖p 6₅₆ p: 33-579 1071 λ⟨131⟩ σM 1588 *l*48 *Aeth* **28** γαρ + εν εαυτη‖Mt: 33-579 NΘΣ-565-700-1604 λ⟨131⟩ ϕ346 σ7-267-349-659-827-1402-1606 D K Π *pm* *l*251 *L*acff²iqr¹ vg² *Cs*¹:⁷ *Geo* | *om* οτι‖Mt: 33 28-565 *pc* *L*vl[k]⟨flr²⟩r¹ *Arm* | εαν—αυτου] καν τ. ιμ. αυ. αψ.‖6₅₆: *Rpl* (*om* αυ.: *l*184) *L*' *S*[sc] *Cs*³b' — *txt*: ℵBᶜCLΔ-892 Θ σ349-659 W(∼ καν τ. ιμ. αψ.) 1241(*om* αυ.) *pc* *l*49 *L*z(*om* καν) Sj *Cs*³b¹ | αψ. καν] μονον αψ.‖Mt: 33 1588 *Cs*³b' — μον. αψ. καν‖Mt: σ1675 *Cs*³ — αψ.‖Mt: B* σ954 1342 *L*e[k] cdz vg¹ *Cs*¹b¹ | του ιματιου‖27 6₅₆ p Mt: ℵ-33-579 D *L*⟨q vg²⟩ *S*[sc]pjᶜ **30** εξ] απ‖Lk₄₆: D **047** **31** συνπνιγοντα‖Lk₄₂: 565

Lk 8,42 *om* ως‖Mk₄₂: 579 D 240 *C*b | εν—υπαγ.] και εγενετο εν τω πορευεσθαι‖17₁₁: C* 1071 D P *pc* — εγ. δε(*om*) εν τω πο.: Mcn^Ep1(¹) | αυτον¹] αυτους‖10₃₈: Ep Mcn^Ep | συνεθλιβον‖Mk: CL-33-892 28-1071 ϕ⟨124-788⟩-*l*547 U(-γον) Θ **047** 157 *pc* *l*47 *l*48 *l*49 *l*183 *l*1663 *l*1963 **43** γυνη + τις‖Mk: 1071 ϕ1689 σ⟨1675⟩-1606 *pc* *l*20 *l*1627 *L*[e]⟨a⟩ *S*scp | ητις—θερα.] ην ουδε εις ισχυεν θεραπευσαι‖Mk₅₄ Mt17₁₆: D *Cs* | ● *om* ιατ.—βιον: 𝔓⁷⁵ B(D) *S*sjᵃᵇᶜ (*Cs*) *Arm*⟨⁰⟩ | βιον + (ε)αυτης‖Mk12₄₄: (ℵ*) CX (1071) σ-1188 Ψ 157 *pc* *l*950 *L*[e] ⟨vg¹⟩ *S*scpjᵃ *C*b *Got* | ουκ] και ουκ‖p: ℵ* 157 *C*b | υπ] ● απ *cf.* 6₁₈ 7₃₅ 17₂₅: 𝔓⁷⁵ BΞ A R *pc* — παρ: ϕ69 — *txt*: *Rpl*⟨D⟩ Or **44** *om* τ. κρα.‖Mk: D *L*aff²lr¹ Mcn^Te **45** και¹—Ι.] ο δε Ι. γνους την εξελθουσαν εξ αυτου δυναμιν επηρωτα(ειπεν)‖Mk: D (*L*a) | ο αψ. μου] μ. ηψατο‖p: D 28 *L*acqz vg⁶ Mcn^Te | ● Π. + και οι συν αυτω‖9₃₂: 𝔥'CΞ 1071 λ-1582-2193 ϕ-174 σ1424 A D P R U W Θ 157 *pc* *l*12 *l*18 *l*19 *l*36 *l*48 *l*49 *l*303 *l*333 *l*374 *l*1634 {*L*[e] *S*' *C*b *Got*} — + και οι μετ αυτου‖6₃f. p Mk1₃₆: *Rpl* {} — *txt*: 𝔓⁷⁵ B 544-700 σ990-1207-1223 Π *al* *S*scj *Cs* *Geo* *Aeth* | *om* επισ.‖p: 544 482 | αποθ. + και λεγεις τις μου ηψατο‖p: 1071 D Ψ *pc* *L*[e] *S*,jᵃ — + κ. λεγ. τις ο αψαμενος μου‖p45a: *Rpl* (τι: C*) *C*b¹ — *txt*: 𝔓⁷⁵ ℵBL-1241 λλ⟨118⟩ 157 *pc* *S*jᵇᶜ *C*' *Arm*

Matth 9:

καὶ ἰδὼν αὐτὴν

εἶπεν· θάρσει, θύγατερ, ἡ πίστις σου σέσωκέν σε. καὶ ἐσώθη ἡ γυνὴ ἀπὸ τῆς ὥρας ἐκείνης.

²³ καὶ ἐλθὼν ὁ Ἰησοῦς εἰς τὴν οἰκίαν τοῦ ἄρχοντος καὶ ἰδὼν τοὺς αὐλητὰς καὶ τὸν ὄχλον θορυβούμενον

Mark 5:

καὶ λέγεις· τίς μου ἥψατο; ³² καὶ περιεβλέπετο ἰδεῖν τὴν τοῦτο ποιήσασαν. ³³ ἡ δὲ γυνὴ φοβηθεῖσα καὶ τρέμουσα, εἰδυῖα ὃ γέγονεν ἐπ' αὐτῇ, ἦλθεν καὶ προσέπεσεν αὐτῷ καὶ εἶπεν αὐτῷ πᾶσαν τὴν ἀλήθειαν. ³⁴ ὁ δὲ εἶπεν αὐτῇ· θύγατερ, ἡ πίστις σου σέσωκέν σε· **ὕπαγε εἰς εἰρήνην**, καὶ ἴσθι ὑγιὴς ἀπὸ τῆς μάστιγός σου.

³⁵ ἔτι αὐτοῦ λαλοῦντος ἔρχονται ἀπὸ τοῦ ἀρχισυναγώγου λέγοντες ὅτι ἡ θυγάτηρ σου ἀπέθανεν· τί ἔτι σκύλλεις τὸν διδάσκαλον; ³⁶ ὁ δὲ Ἰησοῦς παρακούσας τὸν λόγον λαλούμενον λέγει τῷ ἀρχισυναγώγῳ· μὴ φοβοῦ, μόνον πίστευε. ³⁷ καὶ οὐκ ἀφῆκεν οὐδένα μετ' αὐτοῦ συνακολουθῆσαι εἰ μὴ Πέτρον καὶ Ἰάκωβον καὶ Ἰωάννην τὸν ἀδελφὸν Ἰακώβου. cf.v. 40 ↓

³⁸ καὶ ἔρχονται εἰς τὸν οἶκον τοῦ ἀρχισυναγώγου, καὶ θεωρεῖ θόρυβον, καὶ κλαίοντας καὶ ἀλαλάζοντας

Luk 8:

⁴⁶ ὁ δὲ Ἰησοῦς εἶπεν· ἥψατό μού τις· ἐγὼ γὰρ ἔγνων δύναμιν ἐξελθοῦσαν ἀπ' ἐμοῦ. ⁴⁷ ἰδοῦσα δὲ ἡ γυνὴ ὅτι οὐκ ἔλαθεν, τρέμουσα ἦλθεν καὶ προσπεσοῦσα αὐτῷ δι' ἣν αἰτίαν ἥψατο αὐτοῦ ἀπήγγειλεν ἐνώπιον παντὸς τοῦ λαοῦ, καὶ ὡς ἰάθη παραχρῆμα. ⁴⁸ ὁ δὲ εἶπεν αὐτῇ· θύγατερ, ἡ πίστις σου σέσωκέν σε· **πορεύου εἰς εἰρήνην.** 1Sm1 17

⁴⁹ ἔτι αὐτοῦ λαλοῦντος ἔρχεταί τις παρὰ τοῦ ἀρχισυναγώγου λέγων ὅτι τέθνηκεν ἡ θυγάτηρ σου· μὴ σκύλλε τὸν διδάσκαλον. ⁵⁰ ὁ δὲ Ἰησοῦς ἀκούσας ἀπεκρίθη αὐτῷ· μὴ φοβοῦ· μόνον πίστευσον, καὶ σωθήσεται. ⁵¹ ἐλθὼν δὲ εἰς τὴν οἰκίαν οὐκ ἀφῆκεν εἰσελθεῖν τινα σὺν αὐτῷ εἰ μὴ Πέτρον καὶ Ἰωάννην καὶ Ἰάκωβον καὶ τὸν πατέρα τῆς παιδὸς καὶ τὴν μητέρα.

⁵² ἔκλαιον δὲ πάντες καὶ ἐκόπτοντο

Mk 5,33 ειδ.] ιδουσα‖p: 28 | επ] εν: Δ^{v} F 213 {*Lcflz vg Sh C'*} — ● *om*‖5 16 Mt18 19 Jo15 7: ℵBCL-892 544 σ1675 D 1342 *l*184 *La*(*om* επ. αυ.: ff^{2}i) *S*[sc]pj *C*b^{6} — *om* ειδ.—αυτη‖p: *Le*[k] bq — *txt*: *Rpl* (αυτην: Φ-565-1604 ϕ⟨983⟩-230-*l*547 *pc l*48) {} *Geo* | αυτω^{2} + εμπροσθεν παντων‖p Mt26 70: W ϕ⟨983⟩-*l*547 σ827 *Cs*$^{5:6(+1v)}$ | αλη.] αιτιαν αυτης(*om*)‖p: W (28 λ1-1582) ϕ⟨124-983⟩ *Cs*$^{5:6}$ (*Geo*$^{2.ch}$) **34** δε + Ιησους‖Mt: C Φ-28-565-700 **λ**⟨131⟩ ϕ⟨983⟩ σM^{m}-1082-1391 D *al l*20 *l*44 *l*47 *l*48 *l*50 *l*183 *Lvl* ⟨e[k] lz⟩r^{1} vg^{5} *S*[sc]h^{+}j$^{\langle f\rangle}$ *Arm Geo*^{1} | θυγ.] θαρσει θ.(∼)‖Mt: C^{c} σ1194 **047** (483) *l*44 *l*47 *l*48 *l*50 *pc Lq* | υπα.] πορευου‖Lk48 7 50: ΝΘΣ-565-700 σ1223 1342 *pc* | *om* και—σου‖**Lk** Mt: 565 σ1223 238 *l*47 *l*50 *l*253 *C*b^{1} **35** ερχ.—λεγ.] ερχεται τις του αρχ. λεγων‖p: 1241 — ερχεται απο τ. αρχ. λεγοντος‖p: 2(λεγων) 473 482 | λεγ. + αυτω: 33-579 D 1241 *l*48 *L*bi *S*[sc]p^{1} *Cs Aeth* | απεθ.] τεθνηκε‖**p**: σ1082 **36** ● Ι. + ευθεως: *Rpl* (ακου. + ευ.: N λ131 ϕ230-828-983-1689; λογ. + ευ.: Σ) *La*(ευ. ο Ι.) *S*h — *txt*: ℵBLΔ-892 W Θ-28(*om* Ι.)-700 **λ**⟨131⟩ ϕ788 σ517-1606 D 1342 *pc L' S*[sc]pj *C* | παρακ.] ακουσας‖p: *Rpl L' S*[sc],j *C* — *txt*: ℵ^{b}(*παρακαουσας!)BLΔ-892 W *Le*[k] **37** συνακ.] εισελθειν‖p: σ827 *Le*[k] | Π.] ● τον Π.‖14 33 Mt17 1: ℵBCΔ | Ιακωβου] αυτου‖Mt17 1 10 2: Δ Φ **λ**⟨131⟩ D G *al l*48 *l*185 *La S*[sc]h(*et* + Ιακ.$^{+}$) **38** την οικιαν‖**p**: 565-700 D

Lk 8,46 ● εξεληλυθυιαν: $\mathfrak{P}^{75}$ $\mathfrak{H}$⟨1241⟩ Cr Or {*L*[e],Or} *Aeth* EpAp — *txt*: *Rpl* Mcn^{Ep} Or {} | ∼απ εμ. εξ.‖Mk30: 440 *L*[e]⟨aff^{2}⟩ | απ] εξ‖←: 700 σ945 **47** απηγγ. + αυτω‖p: *Rpl Sh Cs* — *txt*: $\mathfrak{P}^{75}$ ℵ(διηγγ.)BC^{c}LXΞ-33-579 700 **λ**-1582-2193 ϕ⟨124-346⟩-230 A D W Θ Π Ψ 157 *al l*1663 *L*[e] *S'*j *C*b **48** αυτη + θαρσει‖Mt: *Rpl Lq S'* — *txt*: $\mathfrak{P}^{75}$ ℵBLΞ-579-892 **λ**-1582-2193 D Ψ 157 *pc L'*[e] *S*scj *C Geo* **49** ερχ. τις ... λεγ.] ερχονται ... λεγοντες‖p: D(-ονται! τις ... -ων: E) *Lc Ssc* | παρα] απο‖p: 700-1071 **λ**-1582-2193 **σ**⟨1675⟩-1188-1293 A D W Θ *pc l*1627 Da — εκ: 579 | ● λεγ. + αυτω: *Rpl* Da *L' S* — *txt*: $\mathfrak{P}^{75v}$ ℵBLXΞ-33-1241 700 **λ**-1582 σ945 157 *pc Le Sj C* | μη] ● μηκετι‖p: $\mathfrak{P}^{75}$ ℵB-579 D Ep *Sh*$^{+}$j *Cs Aeth* — *txt*: *Rpl* Da *L S' C*b *Arm* **50** ακ. + τον λογον‖p: D *L* — + οτι ουτως ελαλησαν: *Sc* | απεκ. αυ.] ειπεν αυ.‖p: {} ℵ*-579 **σ**-1188 16 *Lvl'*r^{1} vg^{1} *S' Cs*^{4}(^{1} *om* αυ.) — απεκ. αυ. λεγων‖p: *Rpl S*shj *C*b'(απεκ. ειπ. *et om* αυ.) *Arm* — *txt*: {$\mathfrak{P}^{75v}$} $\mathfrak{H}$'⟨W⟩XΞ Λ **λ**-1582-2193 **σ**⟨1675⟩-692-1293 *al Lr*^{2}z vg' *C*b^{2} | ● πιστευε‖**p**: *Rpl* (πιστευετε: 579) — *txt*: BLΞ **51** ουκ—συν] ουδενα αφηκεν συνεισελθειν‖p: ℵ | εισελ.—αυτω] εισελ. ουδενα‖p: *Rpl Ssc Arm* — εισελ. ουδ. συν αυτω‖p: {}^{1} L-892 σ1194 Θ *pc* {}^{2} — συνεισελ. αυτω ουδ.‖p: σ1604 {}^{2} — τινα συνελ. αυτω: {}^{1} ϕ'(εισελ. συν: 69) 1071(συνελ. συν α. τ.) {}^{2} — *txt*: {$\mathfrak{P}^{75v}$}^{1} BCX-33-579-1241 D(∼ σ. α. τ.) {*L'*(τινας: e) *S'*j *C*sb$^{\langle 7\rangle}$}^{2} | ● ∼Ια. ... Ιω.‖p: ℵLX-33-892-1241 Λ-700-1071 σ1194-1424-1606 A S 157 *al Lr*^{2} vg^{10} *S' Cs*^{1}b *Got* — *txt*: $\mathfrak{P}^{75}$ *Rpl L' S*hj *Cs*^{5} | τ. παι.] του κορασιου‖Mt24f. Mk41f.: D

Matth	Mark	Luk
24 *ἔλεγεν· ἀναχωρεῖτε· οὐ γὰρ ἀπέθανεν τὸ κοράσιον ἀλλὰ καθεύδει. καὶ κατεγέλων αὐτοῦ.* 25 *ὅτε δὲ ἐξεβλήθη ὁ ὄχλος,*	πολλά, 39 καὶ εἰσελθὼν λέγει αὐτοῖς· τί θορυβεῖσθε καὶ κλαίετε; τὸ παιδίον οὐκ ἀπέθανεν ἀλλὰ καθεύδει. 40 καὶ κατεγέλων αὐτοῦ.	αὐτήν. ὁ δὲ εἶπεν· μὴ κλαίετε· οὐκ ἀπέθανεν ἀλλὰ καθεύδει. 53 καὶ κατεγέλων αὐτοῦ, εἰδότες ὅτι ἀπέθανεν. cf.v. 51↑
εἰσελθὼν ἐκράτησεν τῆς χειρὸς αὐτῆς,	ὁ δὲ ἐκβαλὼν πάντας παραλαμβάνει τὸν πατέρα τοῦ παιδίου καὶ τὴν μητέρα καὶ τοὺς μετ' αὐτοῦ, καὶ εἰσπορεύεται ὅπου ἦν τὸ παιδίον ἀνακείμενον. 41 καὶ κρατήσας τῆς χειρὸς τοῦ παιδίου λέγει αὐτῇ· ταλιθα κουμ, ὅ ἐστιν μεθερμηνευόμενον· τὸ κοράσιον, σοὶ λέγω, ἔγειρε.	54 αὐτὸς δὲ κρατήσας τῆς χειρὸς αὐτῆς ἐφώνησεν λέγων· ἡ παῖς, ἔγειρε.
καὶ ἠγέρθη τὸ κοράσιον.	42 καὶ εὐθὺς ἀνέστη τὸ κοράσιον καὶ περιεπάτει· ἦν γὰρ ἐτῶν δώδεκα. cf.v. 43↓ καὶ ἐξέστησαν ἐκστάσει μεγάλῃ.	55 καὶ ἐπέστρεψεν τὸ πνεῦμα αὐτῆς, καὶ ἀνέστη παραχρῆμα, καὶ διέταξεν αὐτῇ δοθῆναι φαγεῖν. 56 καὶ ἐξέστησαν οἱ γονεῖς αὐτῆς·
26 *καὶ ἐξῆλθεν ἡ φήμη αὐτῆς εἰς ὅλην τὴν γῆν ἐκείνην.*	43 καὶ διεστείλατο αὐτοῖς πολλὰ ἵνα μηδεὶς γνοῖ τοῦτο, καὶ εἶπεν δοθῆναι αὐτῇ φαγεῖν.	ὁ δὲ παρήγγειλεν αὐτοῖς μηδενὶ εἰπεῖν τὸ γεγονός. cf.v. 55↑

(108)

121. Verwerfung in Nazareth. *The Rejection at Nazareth.*

Matth 13 53–58	Mark 6 1–6a	*4 16–30 (22.)*
53 Καὶ ἐγένετο ὅτε ἐτέλεσεν ὁ Ἰησοῦς τὰς παραβολὰς ταύτας, μετῆρεν ἐκεῖθεν.	1 Καὶ ἐξῆλθεν ἐκεῖθεν,	
54 καὶ ἐλθὼν εἰς τὴν πατρίδα αὐτοῦ	καὶ ἔρχεται εἰς τὴν πατρίδα αὐτοῦ, καὶ ἀκολουθοῦσιν αὐτῷ οἱ μαθηταὶ αὐτοῦ.	16 *Καὶ ἦλθεν εἰς Ναζαρα, οὗ ἦν τεθραμμένος, καὶ εἰσῆλθεν κατὰ τὸ εἰωθὸς αὐτῷ ἐν τῇ ἡμέρᾳ τῶν σαββάτων*
ἐδίδασκεν αὐτοὺς ἐν τῇ συναγωγῇ αὐτῶν,	2 καὶ γενομένου σαββάτου ἤρξατο ἐν τῇ συναγωγῇ διδάσκειν·	*εἰς τὴν συναγωγήν, καὶ ἀνέστη ἀναγνῶναι.* 17 *καὶ ἐπεδόθη αὐτῷ*

Mk 5,39 *om* εισελ.‖p: 565 λ1 | τι] μη‖Lk52 713 Act2010: 238 *pc* | παι.] κορασιον‖Mt: 33 | ∼ ουκ απ. το παι.‖Mt: 28 *Aeth* **40** αυτου¹ + ειδοτες οτι απεθανεν‖Lk: W **ϕ**'(ειδ.] ιδοντες: 828-983) *C*s$^{4:5}$ | ο] ● αυτος‖Lk: ℌC Θ D 1342 *l*48 *L*' *Geo*$^{2.ch}$ — *txt* (δε + Ιησους): *Rpl* (Φ **λ**⟨131⟩ ϕ124 σM-115 *pc*) *L*e[k] *S*[sc]p(h^{+}) *Geo*^{1} | παν.] τους(-ον) οχλους(-ον)‖Mt: D *L*e[k] (bcdff^{2}iqr^{1}) | κατακειμενον‖1302 4Jo56 Act933: WΘΣ-28-565-700 **λ**⟨131⟩-22 45 {} — κατακεκλιμενον: **ϕ**'⟨124⟩ {} — ● *om*: ℵBLΔ-892 ϕ983-1689 D **0153** *L*vl'[k]r^{1} *C*s^{4} — *txt*: *Rpl* {*L*cflqz vg *S*[sc] *C*s^{1}b} **41** *om* αυτη‖Lk: W 1241 **42** ευθ.] παραχρημα‖Lk: 579 | ανεσ.] ηγερθη‖Mt: 579 Θ | το κορ.‖Lk: 544 | ετων] ως ετ.‖Lk42: 33-579 565-700 **λ**⟨131⟩ ϕ788 238 {*S*[sc]p^{2} *C*s$^{5:7}$ *Arm* *Δ*a i^{T}} — ωσει ετ.‖Lk323: ℵCΔ-33 Θ-1604 λ1582 ϕ124 σ945-954 {} | ● εξεστ. + ευθυς: ℌC *C*s^{2}b' *Aeth* — + οι γονεις αυτης‖Lk: σ1402 *pc l*48 *L*vg^{1} — + παντες‖212 Lk247 Akt212: D *L*vl'g^{2}30 vg^{1} *C*s^{4}b^{1} — *txt*: 𝔓^{45} *Rpl* *L*e[k] ablz vg' *S*[sc] *C*b^{1} **43** *om* πολ.‖Lk: σ1424 D 474 *L*vl[k]⟨aflz⟩ | ∼ αυ. δοθ.‖Lk: **σ** *L*bcf **6,2** γεν. σαβ.] ημερα σαββατων‖Lk: D *L*ir^{1}(-ατου: ff^{2}q) | σαβ. + δευτεροπρωτου‖Lk61: σ945 | ● ∼ διδ. εν τη(ταις) συναγωγη(-αις)‖Mt1354(423 935 Lk415)Jo1820: ℌC (Θ)-544 D 569 1342 *L*ff^{2}r^{1} *S*[sc],j *C* *Geo*^{1} — *txt*: 𝔓^{45} *Rpl* *L*'

Lk 8,52 ουκ] ● ου γαρ‖Mt: ℌCX 1071-1604 **λ**-1582 **ϕ**-174-*l*547 σ945-1194 D F W Δ Θ Ψ **047** 157 *al l*11 *l*19 *l*31 *l*32 *l*40 *l*48 *l*303 *l*1627 *l*1634 *l*1642 Cr *L*vl'g^{2}r^{1}30 vg^{10} *S*'h^{+} *C* — *txt*: 𝔓^{75v} *Rpl* *L*e br^{2} vg' | απεθ. + το κορασιον‖Mt: LX-33-1241 1071 **λλ**⟨2193⟩ ϕ13-69-983 **σ**⟨954⟩-M F Θ *pc* Cr *L*cg^{2}r^{1}z vg^{8} Am *S*ch^{+}j *C*s$^{1:7}$b *Geo* *Aeth* **54** δε + εκβαλων εξω(*om*) παντας και‖Mk40 Act940: *Rpl* (C* ϕ788 1355) *C*sb'(^{8}) — + εκβ. πα. εξω και‖←: 33-892 1071 ϕ124-174-*l*547 **σ**⟨954⟩-115-945-1207-1606 A K R S U W Θ Π 157 *al l*32 *l*48 *l*^{a1} *L*fq *S*'j — *txt*: 𝔓^{75} ℌ'X 700 **λ**-1582 D *pc* *L*' *S*sc *Aeth* | λεγ. + αυτη‖Mk: 1355 *S*cp^{1}j^{bc} **55** ∼ δοθ. αυ.‖Mk: 33-1241 1071 **λλ**⟨22⟩ ϕ69-124-*l*547 D R W Ψ *al* *L*ar^{2} vg^{5}

Luk 4:

βιβλίον τοῦ προφήτου Ἠσαΐου, καὶ ἀναπτύξας τὸ βιβλίον εὗρεν τόπον οὗ ἦν γεγραμμένον· [18] **πνεῦμα κυρίου ἐπ' ἐμέ, οὗ εἵνεκεν ἔχρισέν με· εὐαγγελίσασθαι πτωχοῖς ἀπέσταλκέν με, κηρύξαι αἰχμαλώτοις ἄφεσιν καὶ τυφλοῖς ἀνάβλεψιν, ἀποστεῖλαι τεθραυσμένους ἐν ἀφέσει,** [19] **κηρύξαι ἐνιαυτὸν κυρίου δεκτόν.** [20] καὶ πτύξας τὸ βιβλίον ἀποδοὺς τῷ ὑπηρέτῃ ἐκάθισεν· καὶ πάντων οἱ ὀφθαλμοὶ ἐν τῇ συναγωγῇ ἦσαν ἀτενίζοντες αὐτῷ. [21] ἤρξατο δὲ λέγειν πρὸς αὐτοὺς ὅτι σήμερον πεπλήρωται ἡ γραφὴ αὕτη ἐν τοῖς ὠσὶν ὑμῶν. [22] καὶ πάντες ἐμαρτύρουν αὐτῷ καὶ ἐθαύμαζον ἐπὶ τοῖς λόγοις τῆς χάριτος τοῖς ἐκπορευομένοις ἐκ τοῦ στόματος αὐτοῦ, καὶ ἔλεγον· οὐχὶ υἱός ἐστιν Ιωσηφ οὗτος; [23] καὶ εἶπεν πρὸς αὐτούς· πάντως ἐρεῖτέ μοι τὴν παραβολὴν ταύτην· ἰατρέ, θεράπευσον σεαυτόν· ὅσα ἠκούσαμεν γενόμενα εἰς τὴν Καφαρναουμ, ποίησον καὶ ὧδε ἐν τῇ πατρίδι σου.

Is 61 1.2 586

Matth 13:

ὥστε ἐκπλήσσεσθαι αὐτοὺς καὶ λέγειν· πόθεν τούτῳ ἡ σοφία αὕτη καὶ αἱ δυνάμεις; [55] οὐχ οὗτός ἐστιν ὁ τοῦ τέκτονος υἱός; οὐχ ἡ μήτηρ αὐτοῦ λέγεται Μαριαμ καὶ οἱ ἀδελφοὶ αὐτοῦ Ἰάκωβος καὶ Ιωσηφ καὶ Σίμων καὶ Ἰούδας; [56] καὶ αἱ ἀδελφαὶ αὐτοῦ οὐχὶ πᾶσαι πρὸς ἡμᾶς εἰσιν; πόθεν οὖν τούτῳ ταῦτα πάντα; [57] καὶ ἐσκανδαλίζοντο ἐν αὐτῷ. ὁ δὲ Ἰησοῦς

Mark 6:

καὶ οἱ πολλοὶ ἀκούοντες ἐξεπλήσσοντο λέγοντες· πόθεν τούτῳ ταῦτα, καὶ τίς ἡ σοφία ἡ δοθεῖσα αὐτῷ; καὶ δυνάμεις τοιαῦται διὰ τῶν χειρῶν αὐτοῦ γίνονται; [3] οὐχ οὗτός ἐστιν ὁ τέκτων, ὁ υἱὸς τῆς Μαρίας καὶ ἀδελφὸς Ἰακώβου καὶ Ἰωσῆτος καὶ Ἰούδα καὶ Σίμωνος; καὶ οὐκ εἰσὶν αἱ ἀδελφαὶ αὐτοῦ ὧδε πρὸς ἡμᾶς; καὶ ἐσκανδαλίζοντο ἐν αὐτῷ. [4] καὶ

Joh:

7 15: ἐθαύμαζον οὖν οἱ Ἰουδαῖοι λέγοντες· πῶς οὗτος γράμματα οἶδεν μὴ μεμαθηκώς; 6 42: καὶ ἔλεγον· οὐχ οὗτός ἐστιν Ἰησοῦς ὁ υἱὸς Ιωσηφ, οὗ ἡμεῖς οἴδαμεν τὸν πατέρα καὶ τὴν μητέρα; ...

4 44: αὐτὸς γὰρ Ἰησοῦς

Mt 13,54 του. + ταυτα και τις‖Mk: W 713 **55** ουχ[2]] ουχι‖Lk: *Rpl* Eu — *txt*: ℌ⟨L-892⟩C N ΟΣ-544-700 λ22 ϕ-230 σM W Θ *al* Eu Or | Ιωσης(-η)‖Mk: *Rpl* (700-1604 λ118-209 ϕ230 σ1010 157 *pc*) *l*12 *l*69 *l*211 *l*303 *l*333 *l*850 *l*1084 *l*1579 *l*1642 *l*1761 Bas Ep[2] *Lk*[e] (*S*') *C*sb[3]([4])([2]-ητος)f *Arm*' — Ιωαννης‖4 21 10 2 *etc.*: ℵ*[v]X σ⟨954⟩-M-1207 D E F G S U V Γ Ω *pc* *l*[pl] Ep[1] Or *L*r[2]30(Ιωα. και Ιωσηφ Σιμων) vg[2]([2]) — *txt*: ℵ[a]BC-33-892 ΝΟΣ λ1-1582 Θ *l*184 *l*997 Eu Or *L*'Hi *S*sch[m]j *C*b' *Arm*[1] *Geo* *Aeth*

Mk 6,2 εξεπ. + επι τη διδαχη αυτου(*om*)‖122p 11 18 Mt22 33: 𝔓[45v] ΘΦ-565-700 σ115-1402 D *al* *l*184 *L*'⟨e[k]⟩(g[2]) *S*[sc]h *Arm* *Geo*[1] | αυτω] ● τουτω‖2a: ℌ⟨33⟩C 1342 *C*s[3]b⟨[1]⟩ *Arm* *Aeth* — *txt*: *Rpl* *L*a(' illi) vg[1] *S*[sc],j *C*s[3] | και[4]] ● κ. αι‖p: ℵB-33-892 Σ σ517 1342 *pc* {}[1] *C*s[5]b — ινα κ.: C*λ872-1278 ϕ124-346 σ827 D K Y Π *l*7 *l*68 *l*1761 *L*ff[2](∼: b *S*p[1])h — ινα: Θ-700 472 *L*iqr[1] {*S*[sc]p' *C*s[1] *Arm*}[2] — οτι και(*om*): σ954 (U *pc*) *pc* *l*299 (*Lf* {}[2] *Got*) — *txt*: *Rpl* Thy {*L*' *S*j}[1] | τοι.] αι τοι. αι: ℵ[c]Δ — τοι. αι: L | ● γινομεναι‖Mt11 21p.23: ℌ 1342 *l*31 *L*clz vg *S*j *C*s[5]b *Aeth* — *txt* (*vel* -ωνται): *Rpl* Thy *L*vl'[k]r[1] *S*[sc] *C*s[1] **3** τεκτ. ο υι.] του τεκτονος υι. και(*om*)‖(Mt): 33-579 (565)-700 ϕ69-983 (σ1194, *et om* του) *pc* *l*31 *l*48 *l*184 {Or} *L*abcir[1]z30 vg[10] — του τεκτ. ο υι. και(*om*)‖(Mt): 𝔓[45v] ϕ'⟨788⟩(543 τεκτος!)-*l*547 ({}) *L*(e[k] g[2](υι. + Ιωσηφ)(vg[1]) *C*b[3] (*Aeth*) | ουκ—αυτου] αι αδ. αυτ. ουχι‖Mt: σ1424 | και ουκ] ουχι και‖Mt: D *L*vl'⟨e[k]⟩r[1](*om* και: bg[2]z30 vg[3]) | ∼ αι αδ. αυ. ωδε πρ. ημ. εισ.‖Mt: σ827 D *L*vl'⟨e[k] bcff[2]30⟩(*om* ωδε: r[1v]) | ωδε] πασαι‖Mt: 6(+ ωδε) 475

Jo 6,42a ουχι‖Lk: 𝔓[75] BT | *om* Ιη.‖**p**: 1241 N-700 ϕ230-983 **σ**⟨1424⟩-M-267-1223 **053** Amm Ath[1:2] Chr *L*bg[2]30 vg[1] Amst *C*b[2] *Geo*[B] | ου] ουχ‖Mt: N

Mt13 57 p *cf.* ETh[II] 31 (POxy 1,6): Λέγει Ἰ(ησοῦ)ς· οὐκ ἔστιν δεκτὸς προφήτης ἐν τῇ π(ατ)ρίδι αὐτ[ο]ῦ, οὐδὲ ἰατρὸς ποιεῖ θεραπείας εἰς τοὺς γεινώσκοντας αὐτόν.

(*transl.*): *Λέγει Ἰησοῦς· οὐκ ἔστιν δεκτὸς προφήτης ἐν τῇ πατρίδι αὐτοῦ, οὐ(δὲ) ἰατρὸς θεραπεύει τοὺς γινώσκοντας αὐτόν.*

Matth	Mark	Luk	Joh
εἶπεν αὐτοῖς· οὐκ ἔστιν προφήτης ἄτιμος εἰ μὴ ἐν τῇ πατρίδι	ἔλεγεν αὐτοῖς ὁ Ἰησοῦς ὅτι οὐκ ἔστιν προφήτης ἄτιμος εἰ μὴ ἐν τῇ πατρίδι αὐτοῦ καὶ ἐν τοῖς συγγενεῦσιν αὐτοῦ	[24] *εἶπεν δέ· αμην ὑμῖν λέγω ὅτι οὐδεὶς προφήτης δεκτός ἐστιν ἐν τῇ πατρίδι αὐτοῦ.*	ἐμαρτύρησεν ὅτι προφήτης ἐν τῇ ἰδίᾳ πατρίδι τιμὴν οὐκ ἔχει.
καὶ ἐν τῇ οἰκίᾳ αὐτοῦ. [58] καὶ οὐκ ἐποίησεν ἐκεῖ δυνάμεις πολλὰς (1Rg17 9)	καὶ ἐν τῇ οἰκίᾳ αὐτοῦ. [5] καὶ οὐκ ἐδύνατο ἐκεῖ οὐδεμίαν δύναμιν ποιῆσαι, εἰ μὴ ὀλίγοις ἀρρώστοις ἐπιθεὶς τὰς χεῖρας ἐθεράπευσεν.	[25] *ἐπ' ἀληθείας δὲ λέγω ὑμῖν ὅτι πολλαὶ χῆραι ἦσαν ἐν ταῖς ἡμέραις Ἠλίου ἐν τῷ Ισραηλ, ὅτε ἐκλείσθη ὁ οὐρανὸς ἐπὶ ἔτη τρία καὶ μῆνας ἕξ, ὡς ἐγένετο λιμὸς μέγας ἐπὶ πᾶσαν τὴν γῆν,* [26] *καὶ πρὸς οὐδεμίαν αὐτῶν ἐπέμφθη Ἠλίας εἰ μὴ* ***εἰς Σαρεπτα τῆς Σιδωνίας*** *πρὸς* ***γυναῖκα χήραν.*** [27] *καὶ πολλοὶ λεπροὶ ἦσαν ἐν τῷ Ισραηλ ἐπὶ Ἐλισαίου τοῦ προφήτου, καὶ οὐδεὶς αὐτῶν ἐκαθαρίσθη εἰ μὴ Ναιμαν ὁ Σύρος.*	
διὰ τὴν ἀπιστίαν αὐτῶν.	[6a] καὶ ἐθαύμαζεν διὰ τὴν ἀπιστίαν αὐτῶν.		

[28] *καὶ ἐπλήσθησαν πάντες θυμοῦ ἐν τῇ συναγωγῇ ἀκούοντες ταῦτα,* [29] *καὶ* **22.** *ἀναστάντες ἐξέβαλον αὐτὸν ἔξω τῆς πόλεως, καὶ ἤγαγον αὐτὸν ἕως ὀφρύος τοῦ ὄρους ἐφ' οὗ ἡ πόλις ᾠκοδόμητο αὐτῶν, ὥστε κατακρημνίσαι αὐτόν·* [30] *αὐτὸς δὲ διελθὼν διὰ μέσου αὐτῶν ἐπορεύετο.*

(109)

122. Die Aussendung der Zwölf. *The Mission of the Twelve.*

Matth	Mark 3 13–15	Mark 6 6b–13	Luk 9 1–6	Luk 10 1–12
28. *10 1 (70.): καὶ προσκαλεσάμενος τοὺς*	*3 13–15 (85.): Καὶ ἀναβαίνει εἰς τὸ ὄρος, καὶ προσκαλεῖται οὓς ἤθελεν αὐτός, καὶ ἀπῆλθον πρὸς αὐτόν.* [14] *καὶ ἐποίησεν*	[6b] Καὶ περιῆγεν τὰς κώμας κύκλῳ διδάσκων. [7] καὶ προσκαλεῖται τοὺς	[1] Συγκαλεσάμενος δὲ τοὺς	*10 1–12 (153.): Μετὰ δὲ ταῦτα ἀνέδειξεν ὁ κύριος καὶ ἑτέρους*
δώδεκα μαθητὰς αὐτοῦ	*δώδεκα ἵνα ὦσιν μετ' αὐτοῦ, καὶ ἵνα ἀποστέλλῃ αὐτοὺς κηρύσσειν*	δώδεκα, καὶ ἤρξατο αὐτοὺς ἀποστέλλειν δύο δύο,	δώδεκα ἀποστόλους	*ἑβδομήκοντα δύο, καὶ ἀπέστειλεν αὐτοὺς ἀνὰ δύο πρὸ προσώπου αὐτοῦ εἰς πᾶσαν πό-*
ἔδωκεν αὐτοῖς ἐξουσίαν	[15] *καὶ ἔχειν ἐξουσίαν*	καὶ ἐδίδου αὐτοῖς ἐξουσίαν	ἔδωκεν αὐτοῖς δύναμιν καὶ ἐξουσίαν	

Mt 13,57 πατ.] ● ιδια πατ.‖Jo: ℵC(+ αυτου)Z ϕ-174 σ945-990-1223 1241(∼) Or {} (*C*sf = C) — πατ. αυτου‖Mk: *Rpl* Bas Chr Or {*L*'} *S*,j *C*b — *txt*: B-33 D Θ *L*k a vg[1] {}

Mk 6,4 *om* οτι‖Mt: Δ-579 Θ-565-700 ϕ-230-*l*547 S *al* *S*[sc]pj — τη[1] + ιδια‖Jo: ℵ[c]L-892 A 273 *C*s[5:6] **5** ∼ ποι. εκ. ουδ. δυ.‖Mt: σ1402 (*L*e bcff[2]) *S*s[v][c]pj — ● εκ. ποι. ουδ. δυ.‖Mt: ℌ⟨33-579⟩C Θ (ποι. ουδεμιν!) λ⟨118⟩ *C*b — εκ. ουδ. ποι. δυ.: W(ουδ.] ουκετι)-565-700 ϕ124 D 1342 Or *L*a — *txt*: *Rpl* *L*'(iqr[1]) *S*h **6a** ● εθαυμασεν‖Mt8 10p: ℵ*B-579 565 σ179-1402 E*[v] 569 *C*b *Aeth* **6b** περ. + ο Ιησους‖Mt4 23 9 35: ℵ 28 ϕ-*l*547 σ179-517-659 713 1342 *L*ff[2] vg[1] *Geo*[B] — + τας πολεις και‖Mt9 35: Φ | κω.] πολεις‖←: 273 | *om* κυκ.‖←: 348 *C*s[1:3] **7** -καλεσαμενος *et om* και[2]‖Mt Lk9: 565 λ D 472 *L*vl[k]⟨flz⟩r[1] | δωδ. + μαθητας αυτου(*om*)‖Mt: 1071 σ71-267-349-659-692 (D) *pc* *l*3 (*L*bff[2]g[2]iqr[1v]) *S*s[c]p(*om* μαθ.) | ηρξ.—αποστ.] απεστειλεν αυτ.‖Lk9 2p 10: 565 D *L*vl[k]⟨flqz⟩ *S*s[c] *Aeth* | δυο[1]] ανα‖Lk10: 565 D Or[1]([1]ανα δ. δ.) | εδωκεν‖Mt Lk9: W *L*f *S*p *C*

Lk 9,1 απο.] μαθητας αυτου‖Mt: C[3] 1604 ϕ1689-*l*547 E F H U 157 *pc* *l*12 *l*32 *l*303 *l*333 *l*374 *l*1599 *l*1627 *l*1634 *l*1642 *l*1663 *l*1963 Eu *L*vl'r[1] vg[1] Ad(*om* αυτ.) (*om* μηθ.: *S*' *C*s[1]) — ● *om*‖Mk: 𝔓[75] *Rpl* Ad *C*s[5] *Geo* — *txt*: ℌ⟨B⟩C*ΧΞ Λ-544-1071 ϕ-174-230 σ⟨954⟩ Θ Ψ *pc* *L*e acfr[2]z vg' *S*hj *C*b *Arm* *Aeth* | *om* δυν. και‖Mt Mk: 229 *l*1963 *L*Ad

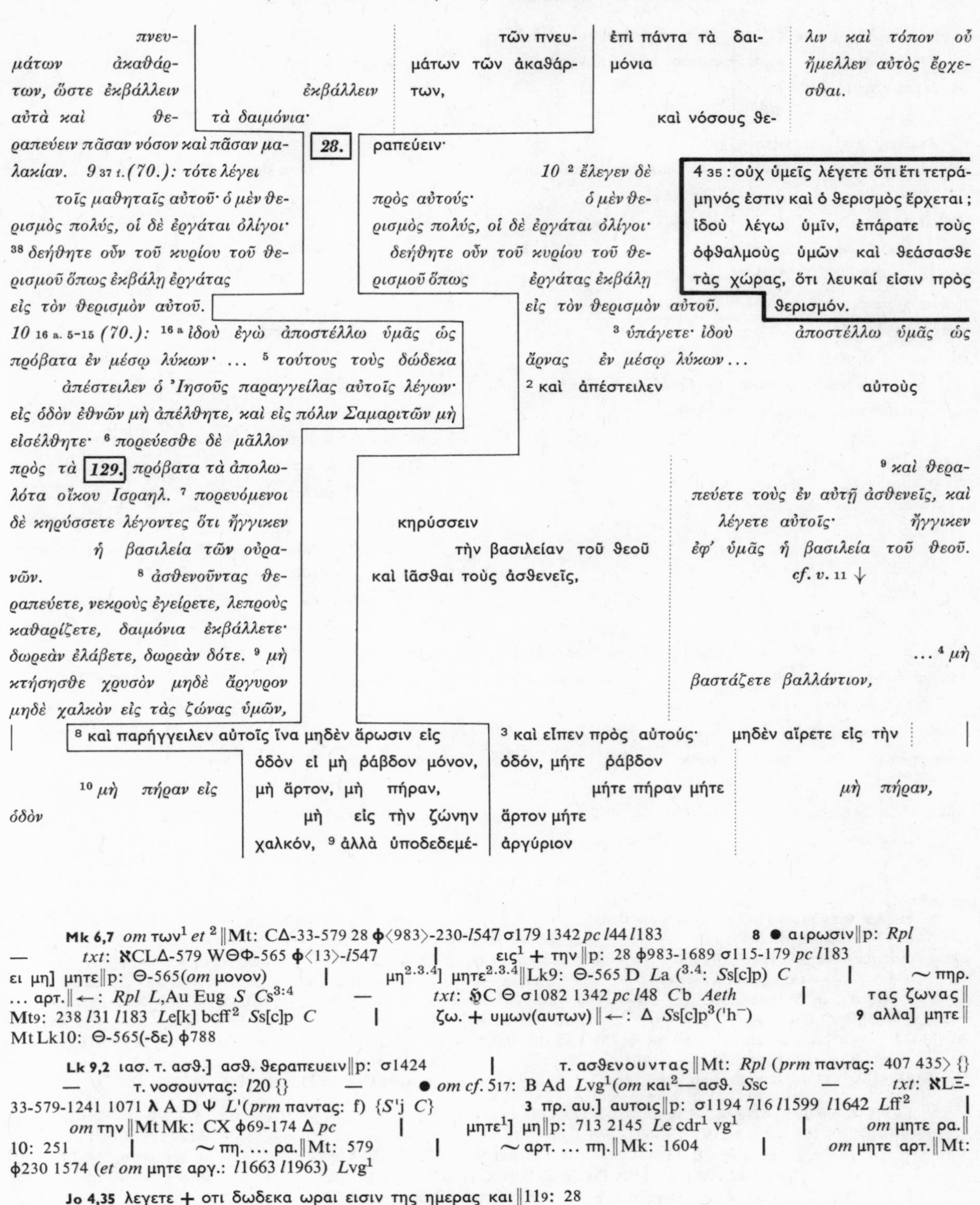

πνευμάτων ἀκαθάρτων, ὥστε ἐκβάλλειν αὐτὰ καὶ θεραπεύειν πᾶσαν νόσον καὶ πᾶσαν μαλακίαν. 9 37 f. (70.): τότε λέγει τοῖς μαθηταῖς αὐτοῦ· ὁ μὲν θερισμὸς πολύς, οἱ δὲ ἐργάται ὀλίγοι· 38 δεήθητε οὖν τοῦ κυρίου τοῦ θερισμοῦ ὅπως ἐκβάλῃ ἐργάτας εἰς τὸν θερισμὸν αὐτοῦ. 10 16 a. 5–15 (70.): 16a ἰδοὺ ἐγὼ ἀποστέλλω ὑμᾶς ὡς πρόβατα ἐν μέσῳ λύκων· ... 5 τούτους τοὺς δώδεκα ἀπέστειλεν ὁ Ἰησοῦς παραγγείλας αὐτοῖς λέγων· εἰς ὁδὸν ἐθνῶν μὴ ἀπέλθητε, καὶ εἰς πόλιν Σαμαριτῶν μὴ εἰσέλθητε· 6 πορεύεσθε δὲ μᾶλλον πρὸς τὰ **129.** *πρόβατα τὰ ἀπολωλότα οἴκου Ἰσραηλ. 7 πορευόμενοι δὲ κηρύσσετε λέγοντες ὅτι ἤγγικεν ἡ βασιλεία τῶν οὐρανῶν. 8 ἀσθενοῦντας θεραπεύετε, νεκροὺς ἐγείρετε, λεπροὺς καθαρίζετε, δαιμόνια ἐκβάλλετε· δωρεὰν ἐλάβετε, δωρεὰν δότε. 9 μὴ κτήσησθε χρυσὸν μηδὲ ἄργυρον μηδὲ χαλκὸν εἰς τὰς ζώνας ὑμῶν, 10 μὴ πήραν εἰς ὁδὸν*

ἐκβάλλειν τὰ δαιμόνια· **28.**

τῶν πνευμάτων τῶν ἀκαθάρτων,

8 καὶ παρήγγειλεν αὐτοῖς ἵνα μηδὲν ἄρωσιν εἰς ὁδὸν εἰ μὴ ῥάβδον μόνον, μὴ ἄρτον, μὴ πήραν, μὴ εἰς τὴν ζώνην χαλκόν, 9 ἀλλὰ ὑποδεδεμέ-

ἐπὶ πάντα τὰ δαιμόνια καὶ νόσους θεραπεύειν·

10 2 ἔλεγεν δὲ πρὸς αὐτούς· ὁ μὲν θερισμὸς πολύς, οἱ δὲ ἐργάται ὀλίγοι· δεήθητε οὖν τοῦ κυρίου τοῦ θερισμοῦ ὅπως ἐργάτας ἐκβάλῃ εἰς τὸν θερισμὸν αὐτοῦ. 3 ὑπάγετε· ἰδοὺ ἀποστέλλω ὑμᾶς ὡς ἄρνας ἐν μέσῳ λύκων...

2 καὶ ἀπέστειλεν αὐτοὺς κηρύσσειν τὴν βασιλείαν τοῦ θεοῦ καὶ ἰᾶσθαι τοὺς ἀσθενεῖς,

3 καὶ εἶπεν πρὸς αὐτούς· μηδὲν αἴρετε εἰς τὴν ὁδόν, μήτε ῥάβδον μήτε πήραν μήτε ἄρτον μήτε ἀργύριον

λιν καὶ τόπον οὗ ἤμελλεν αὐτὸς ἔρχεσθαι.

4 35 : οὐχ ὑμεῖς λέγετε ὅτι ἔτι τετράμηνός ἐστιν καὶ ὁ θερισμὸς ἔρχεται; ἰδοὺ λέγω ὑμῖν, ἐπάρατε τοὺς ὀφθαλμοὺς ὑμῶν καὶ θεάσασθε τὰς χώρας, ὅτι λευκαί εἰσιν πρὸς θερισμόν.

9 καὶ θεραπεύετε τοὺς ἐν αὐτῇ ἀσθενεῖς, καὶ λέγετε αὐτοῖς· ἤγγικεν ἐφ' ὑμᾶς ἡ βασιλεία τοῦ θεοῦ. cf. v. 11 ↓

... 4 μὴ βαστάζετε βαλλάντιον, μὴ πήραν,

Mk 6,7 *om* των^{1} *et* ^{2}‖Mt: CΔ-33-579 28 φ⟨983⟩-230-*l*547 σ179 1342 *pc l*44 *l*183 | **8** ● αιρωσιν‖p: *Rpl* — *txt*: ℵCLΔ-579 WΘΦ-565 φ⟨13⟩-*l*547 | εις^{1} + την‖p: 28 φ983-1689 σ115-179 *pc l*183 | ει μη] μητε‖p: Θ-565(*om* μονον) | μη$^{2.3.4}$] μητε$^{2.3.4}$‖Lk9: Θ-565 D *La* ($^{3.4}$: *S*s[c]p) *C* | ∼ πηρ. ... αρτ.‖←: *Rpl L*,Au Eug *S Cs*$^{3:4}$ — *txt*: 𝔖C Θ σ1082 1342 *pc l*48 *Cb Aeth* | τας ζωνας‖Mt9: 238 *l*31 *l*183 *Le*[k] bcff^{2} *S*s[c]p *C* | ζω. + υμων(αυτων)‖←: Δ *S*s[c]p^{3}('h^{-}) | **9** αλλα] μητε‖MtLk10: Θ-565(-δε) φ788

Lk 9,2 ιασ. τ. ασθ.] ασθ. θεραπευειν‖p: σ1424 | τ. ασθενουντας‖Mt: *Rpl* (*prm* παντας: 407 435) {} — τ. νοσουντας: *l*20 {} — ● *om cf.* 517: B Ad *L*vg^{1}(*om* και^{2}—ασθ. *S*sc — *txt*: ℵLΞ-33-579-1241 1071 λ A D Ψ *L*'(*prm* παντας: f) {*S*'j *C*} | **3** πρ. αυ.] αυτοις‖p: σ1194 716 *l*1599 *l*1642 *L*ff^{2} | *om* την‖MtMk: CX φ69-174 Δ *pc* | μητε^{1}] μη‖p: 713 2145 *L*e cdr^{1} vg^{1} | *om* μητε ρα.‖10: 251 | ∼ πη. ... ρα.‖Mt: 579 | ∼ αρτ. ... πη.‖Mk: 1604 | *om* μητε αρτ.‖Mt: φ230 1574 (*et om* μητε αργ.: *l*1663 *l*1963) *L*vg^{1}

Jo 4,35 λεγετε + οτι δωδεκα ωραι εισιν της ημερας και‖119: 28

Mt937f.p *cf.* ETh^{II} 73 (*cf. ad 70.* Mt937f.)

Matth:

μηδὲ δύο χιτῶνας μηδὲ ὑποδήματα μηδὲ ῥάβδον· ἄξιος γὰρ ὁ ἐργάτης τῆς τροφῆς αὐτοῦ. 11 εἰς ἣν δ' ἂν πόλιν ἢ κώμην εἰσέλθητε, ἐξετάσατε τίς ἐν αὐτῇ ἄξιός ἐστιν· κἀκεῖ μείνατε ἕως ἂν ἐξέλθητε. 12 εἰσερχόμενοι δὲ εἰς τὴν οἰκίαν ἀσπάσασθε αὐτήν· 13 καὶ ἐὰν μὲν ᾖ ἡ οἰκία ἀξία, ἐλθέτω ἡ εἰρήνη ὑμῶν ἐπ' αὐτήν· ἐὰν δὲ μὴ ᾖ ἀξία, ἡ εἰρήνη ὑμῶν πρὸς ὑμᾶς ἐπιστραφήτω.

cf. v. 11 ↑
cf. v. 10 ↑
cf. v. 7 ↑

14 καὶ ὃς ἂν μὴ δέξηται ὑμᾶς μηδὲ ἀκούσῃ τοὺς λόγους ὑμῶν, ἐξερχόμενοι τῆς οἰκίας ἢ τῆς πόλεως ἐκείνης ἐκτινάξατε τὸν κονιορτὸν τῶν ποδῶν ὑμῶν.

Mark:

νους σανδάλια, καὶ μὴ ἐνδύσασθαι δύο χιτῶνας. 10 καὶ ἔλεγεν αὐτοῖς· ὅπου ἐὰν εἰσέλθητε εἰς οἰκίαν, ἐκεῖ μένετε ἕως ἂν ἐξέλθητε ἐκεῖθεν.

cf. v. 10 ↑

11 καὶ ὃς ἂν τόπος μὴ δέξηται ὑμᾶς μηδὲ ἀκούσωσιν ὑμῶν, ἐκπορευόμενοι ἐκεῖθεν ἐκτινάξατε τὸν χοῦν τὸν ὑποκάτω τῶν ποδῶν ὑμῶν

Luk 9:

μήτε ἀνὰ δύο χιτῶνας ἔχειν. 4 καὶ εἰς ἣν ἂν οἰκίαν εἰσέλθητε, ἐκεῖ μένετε καὶ ἐκεῖθεν ἐξέρχεσθε.

cf. v. 4 ↑
cf. v. 2 ↑

5 καὶ ὅσοι ἂν μὴ δέχωνται ὑμᾶς, ἐξερχόμενοι ἀπὸ τῆς πόλεως ἐκείνης τὸν κονιορτὸν ἀπὸ τῶν ποδῶν ὑμῶν ἀποτινάσ-

Luk 10:

μὴ ὑποδήματα· καὶ μηδένα κατὰ τὴν ὁδὸν ἀσπάσησθε ... 7 ... ἄξιος γὰρ ὁ ἐργάτης τοῦ μισθοῦ αὐτοῦ ... 5 εἰς ἣν δ' ἂν εἰσέλθητε οἰκίαν,

cf. v. 7 ↓

πρῶτον λέγετε· εἰρήνη τῷ οἴκῳ τούτῳ. 6 καὶ ἐὰν ᾖ ἐκεῖ υἱὸς εἰρήνης, ἐπαναπαήσεται ἐπ' αὐτὸν ἡ εἰρήνη ὑμῶν· εἰ δὲ μή γε, ἐφ' ὑμᾶς ἀνακάμψει. 7 ἐν αὐτῇ δὲ τῇ οἰκίᾳ μένετε, ἔσθοντες καὶ πίνοντες τὰ παρ' αὐτῶν· ἄξιος γὰρ ὁ ἐργάτης τοῦ μισθοῦ αὐτοῦ. μὴ μεταβαίνετε ἐξ οἰκίας εἰς οἰκίαν. 8 καὶ εἰς ἣν ἂν πόλιν εἰσέρχησθε καὶ δέχωνται ὑμᾶς, ἐσθίετε τὰ παρατιθέμενα ὑμῖν, 9 καὶ θεραπεύετε τοὺς ἐν αὐτῇ ἀσθενεῖς, καὶ λέγετε αὐτοῖς· ἤγγικεν ἐφ' ὑμᾶς ἡ βασιλεία τοῦ θεοῦ. 10 εἰς ἣν δ' ἂν πόλιν εἰσέλθητε καὶ μὴ δέχωνται ὑμᾶς, ἐξελθόντες εἰς τὰς πλατείας αὐτῆς εἴπατε· 11 καὶ τὸν κονιορτὸν τὸν κολληθέντα ἡμῖν ἐκ τῆς πόλεως ὑμῶν εἰς τοὺς πόδας ἀπομασ-

Mk 6,9 ● ενδυσησθε(*vel* -θαι)‖8 Lk10 Mt: *Rpl* {} *La Cb* — ενδεδυσθαι(*vel* -θε)‖16 Mt22 11: L NΣ σ7-115-349-517 *pc l*18 *l*19 *l*48 *l*49 — ενδιδυσκεσθε‖Lk16 19: 1241 — *txt* (*vel* -θε): B-33-892 ϕ124-346(ενδησεσθε)-788 S Π Ω {**0167**(ενδυ[...]θε)} 265(-σεσθαι) *al l*51 *L*' *S Cs* **10** εως—εκ.] και εκ. εξερχεσθε‖Lk: 33 | ∼ εκ. εξελ.‖Lk: Θ 1342 **11** ος—δεξ.] οσοι αν μη δεξωνται‖Lk9: *Rpl L*'[ek] *S*' *Geo*² — ος αν. μη δεξηται‖Mt: C*ᵛ-579 **λ**⟨118⟩ *L*ff² vg² *S*s[c] — *txt*: ℵBLΔ W-28 **ϕ**⟨983⟩-*l*547 (δεξωνται: *L*vg¹) *S*hᵐ *C Geo*¹ *Aeth* | ακουση‖Mt: W **λ**⟨118*⟩ *L*vg¹ *S*s[c] | υμων¹ + του λογου‖Mt: 1342 | εκπ.] εξερχομενοι‖Mt Lk9 10: 700 ϕ230 σ27 *pc* | εκτινασσεσθε‖Lk9: 565 | χουν] κονιορτον‖**p**: 33 **λ**(∼) 1241 | τον υποκ.] απο‖Lk9: 579 *L*'[ek]⟨cq⟩ *Geo*² — *om*‖Mt Act13 51: 33 565-700 D *Lab S*s[c] *Arm* — τον κολληθεντα εκ‖Lk10: *l*184

Lk 9,3 ● *om* ανα‖Mt Mk: ℵBCLΞ-**0202**-579-1241 ϕ*l*547 F *l*48 *l*1963 — *txt*: *Rpl S*h **4** αν] δ'αν‖10 5.10 Mt: X 700 **λ**-1582-2193 σM-692-1194 Γ *pc* | οικ.] πολιν η οικ.‖8.10 Mt: λ1278 *pc L*vg¹(*om* η οικ.) *S*h | εκει] εν αυτη‖7: 1574 | μεινατε‖Mt: ℵ 1047(-ετε) **5** δεξωνται‖Mt Mk: *Rpl* — *txt*: 𝕳CΞ 1604 **λ**⟨131⟩ ϕ124-*l*547 σM-1194 K U W Θ Π Ψ 157 *pc* | απο¹] εκ‖Mt: ℵ 28 D *l*47 | της + οικιας η απο της‖Mt: **ϕ** 713 *C*b¹(∼ πολ.] κωμης ... οικ.) | πολ. + η κωμης‖Mt 11: 33 | τον] ● και τ.‖**11**: *Rpl L*'Am *S*,j — *txt*: 𝔓⁷⁵ 𝕳⟨1241⟩CXΞ **λ** ϕ124 **σ**⟨954⟩ D W Θ Ψ 213 *Lacf C Arm Aeth* | κον. + τον‖11 Mk: L-33-892 **σ**⟨1424⟩ 213 *l*1663(∼ υμων τον α. τ. ποδ.) *S*h | *om* απο²‖Mt: 28 λ22 ϕ*l*547 D U *al l*1963 *L*cr²z vg⟨1⟩ *S*sc *C* | αποτιναξατε‖Mt Mk: {} *Rpl* — εκτιναξατε‖Mt Mk: D(∼ εκτ. τ. κον.—υμ.) — *txt*: {𝔓⁷⁵} ℵB-579 **λ** 157 372

Matth	Mark	Luk
εἰς μαρτύριον αὐτοῖς.	σετε εἰς μαρτύριον ἐπ' αὐτούς.	σόμεθα ὑμῖν·
cf. v. 7 ↑	cf. v. 2 ↑	πλὴν τοῦτο γινώσκετε, ὅτι ἤγγικεν ἡ βασιλεία τοῦ θεοῦ. 12 λέγω ὑμῖν ὅτι Σοδόμοις ἐν τῇ ἡμέρᾳ ἐκείνῃ ἀνεκτότερον ἔσται ἢ τῇ πόλει ἐκείνῃ.
15 αμην λέγω ὑμῖν, ἀνεκτότερον ἔσται γῇ Σοδόμων καὶ Γομόρρων ἐν ἡμέρᾳ κρίσεως ἢ τῇ πόλει ἐκείνῃ.		
	12 καὶ ἐξελθόντες ἐκήρυξαν ἵνα μετανοῶσιν, 13 καὶ δαιμόνια πολλὰ ἐξέβαλλον, καὶ ἤλειφον ἐλαίῳ πολλοὺς ἀρρώστους καὶ ἐθεράπευον.	6 ἐξερχόμενοι δὲ διήρχοντο κατὰ τὰς κώμας εὐαγγελιζόμενοι καὶ θεραπεύοντες πανταχοῦ.

(110)

123. Urteil des Herodes über Jesus. *Herod's Opinion of Jesus.*

Matth 14 1–2	Mark 6 14–16	Luk 9 7–9
1 Ἐν ἐκείνῳ τῷ καιρῷ ἤκουσεν Ἡρῴδης ὁ τετράρχης τὴν ἀκοὴν Ἰησοῦ,	14 Καὶ ἤκουσεν ὁ βασιλεὺς Ἡρῴδης, φανερὸν γὰρ ἐγένετο τὸ ὄνομα αὐτοῦ,	7 Ἤκουσεν δὲ Ἡρῴδης ὁ τετράρχης τὰ γινόμενα πάντα, καὶ διηπόρει διὰ
16 14 (135.): οἱ δὲ εἶπαν· οἱ μὲν Ἰωάννην τὸν βαπτιστήν,	*8 28 (135.): οἱ δὲ ἀπεκρίθησαν αὐτῷ λέγοντες· Ἰωάννην τὸν βαπτιστήν,*	*9 19 (135.): οἱ δὲ ἀποκριθέντες εἶπαν· Ἰωάννην τὸν βαπτιστήν,*
2 καὶ εἶπεν τοῖς παισὶν αὐτοῦ· οὗτός ἐστιν Ἰωάννης ὁ βαπτιστής· αὐτὸς ἠγέρθη ἀπὸ τῶν νεκρῶν, καὶ διὰ τοῦτο αἱ δυ-	καὶ ἔλεγεν ὅτι Ἰωάννης ὁ βαπτίζων ἐγήγερται ἐκ νεκρῶν, καὶ διὰ τοῦτο ἐνεργοῦσιν αἱ δυ-	τὸ λέγεσθαι ὑπό τινων ὅτι Ἰωάννης ἠγέρθη ἐκ νεκρῶν,

Mt 14,2 βαπ. + ον εγω(*om*) απεκεφαλισα ‖ Mk16: Φ D *L*(a)bff¹(g²)h30 vg¹ *S*j | αυτ.] ουτος ‖ ←: C λ1 61 *Ld* | ∼ ενερ. αι δυ. ‖ p: 28 σM-1402 *pc*

Mk 6,11 αυτ.] επ αυτοις ‖ Lk9 Act ←: 700 — + αμην λεγω υμιν· ανεκτοτερον εσται Σοδομοις η Γομορροις εν ημερα κρισεως η τη πολει εκεινη ‖ Mt15 Lk12: *Rpl Lafg²q S' Cb⁸* ⟦Σοδ.] γη Σοδομων ‖ Mt: 33-579 | η] και ‖ Mt: 579 1071 σ682 472(και η) *l*48 | *om* η Γομ. ‖ Lk12: 131 | ημ. κρι.] τη ημ. εκεινη ‖ ←: *l*44 — καιρω κρι.: λ209⟧ — *txt*: ℌ'C WΘ-28-565 D *pc L'*[ek] *Ss*[c] *C' Arm* **12** ● μετανοησωσιν: *Rpl* (-ησουσιν: 579) — *txt*: BL-892 WΘ D **13** εθε. + αυτους ‖ Lk4 40 Mt4 24 15 30 21 14: W Θ-28-565 φ-*l*547 σM *C Arm* — + πολλους ‖ 1 34 3 10: σ1606 6 **14** βα.] τετραρχης ‖ MtLk: φ983-1689 | Η. + την ακοην Ιησου ‖ Mt: 892 1071 φ⟨124-788⟩-230-*l*547 σM-7-349-945-1194-1223 S *mu* — περι Ι.(αυτου): 1038 *Sp C*(s⁵ː⁶)b⁴ | ● ελεγον ‖ 15 Lk7: B W D(-οσαν) *pc Labff² vg² Au Cs¹ː⁵* — ειπεν τοις παισιν αυτου ‖ Mt: Φ | βαπτιστης ‖ Mt2: 33-579 WΘ-28-700 φ⟨124⟩ D S Ω *pc* {*Ss*[c]pj} | εγη.] ηγερθη ‖ MtLk: *Rpl* — ανεστη ‖ Lk8.19: σ27 A K Π *al* — *txt*: ℌ⟨579⟩ 565-700 D 1342 | εκ] απο (+ των) ‖ (Mt): (579) σ179-349-517-1606 (1241) *pc* | ∼ αι δυ. ενερ. ‖ Mt: Δ-33-579 NΘΣΦ-544-565 λ131-1278 φ13 σ349-517-945-1082-1402-1606 K 1342 *al l*54 *l*246 *l*253 {*L*[ek] acff²r¹·²z30 vg³ *S*phj *C Aeth*}

Lk 9,5 επ. αυ.] αυτοις ‖ 11 Mk: ℵ*-579 28-544 φ σ1424 *pc l*5 *l*40 *l*1599 *l*1627 *l*1642 *l*³ *Laf Ss*(αυ.] υμιν)c *Arm* — επ αυτοις: ℵᶜX λ2193 Ψ 2533(εν αυ.) *pc l*11 *l*32 *l*33 *l*333 *l*1634 **6** *om* τας ‖ 13 22: 579 D *pc* Ad | κω.] πολεις και κω. ‖ 8 1 13 22 Mt11: 1071 Ad Mcn *Llff²*(∼ κω. … πο.: bcq vg² *S*scp) *Cs¹ː⁶ Arm* **7** γιν. + υπ αυτου ‖ 13 17 23 8: *Rpl* Eu *Lcfr²qz vg S' Δ*a ad lᶠᴳ — + υπο του Ιησου: *l*17 *Δ*lᴬᴰ p — *txt*: 𝔓⁷⁵ ℵBC*LΞ-579-1241 φ⟨124-346⟩ D 157 161 *Lvl'r¹ Sscj C Arm* | ηγ.] εγηγερται ‖ Mk14: *Rpl* — ανεστη ‖ 8 16 31: D(∼ εκ νε. αν.) — *txt*: 𝔓⁷⁵ ℌ⟨33⟩CΞ 700-1071 λ-1582 φ σ⟨1424⟩-1188 157 *pc* | εκ] απο των ‖ Mt: 1241 φ σ954 *pc* — εκ των ‖ Mt: X σ71 *pc l*184

	νάμεις ἐνεργοῦσιν ἐν αὐτῷ.		νάμεις ἐν αὐτῷ.		
ἄλλοι δὲ *Ἠλίαν, ἕτεροι δὲ Ἰερεμίαν ἢ ἕνα τῶν προφητῶν.*	*καὶ ἄλλοι* *Ἠλίαν, ἄλλοι δὲ ὅτι εἷς τῶν προφητῶν.*	¹⁵ ἄλλοι δὲ ἔλεγον ὅτι Ἠλίας ἐστίν· ἄλλοι δὲ ἔλεγον ὅτι προφήτης ὡς εἷς τῶν προφητῶν. ¹⁶ ἀκούσας δὲ ὁ	*ἄλλοι δὲ* *Ἠλίαν, ἄλλοι δὲ ὅτι προφήτης τις τῶν ἀρχαίων ἀνέστη.*	⁸ ὑπό τινων δὲ ὅτι Ἠλίας ἐφάνη, ἄλλων δὲ ὅτι προφήτης τις τῶν ἀρχαίων ἀνέστη. ⁹ εἶπεν δὲ ὁ	**J 1** 21.25: καὶ ἠρώτησαν αὐτόν· τί οὖν; Ἠλίας εἶ σύ; καὶ λέγει· οὐκ εἰμί. ὁ προφήτης εἶ σύ; καὶ ἀπεκρίθη· οὔ ... ²⁵ ... καὶ εἶπαν αὐτῷ· τί οὖν βαπτίζεις εἰ σὺ οὐκ εἶ ὁ Χριστὸς οὐδὲ Ἠλίας οὐδὲ ὁ προφήτης;
	Ἡρῴδης ἔλεγεν· ὃν	ἐγὼ ἀπεκεφάλισα Ἰωάννην,		Ἡρῴδης· Ἰωάννην ἐγὼ ἀπεκεφάλισα· τίς δέ ἐστιν	
	οὗτος ἠγέρθη.			οὗτος περὶ οὗ ἀκούω τοιαῦτα; καὶ ἐζήτει ἰδεῖν αὐτόν.	

(111) **124.** Der Tod des Täufers. *The Death of the Baptist.*

Matth 14 ₃₋₁₂	Mark 6 ₁₇₋₂₉	*3* ₁₉₋₂₀ *(17.)*
³ Ὁ γὰρ Ἡρῴδης κρατήσας τὸν Ἰωάννην ἔδησεν αὐτὸν καὶ ἐν φυλακῇ ἀπέθετο διὰ Ἡρῳδιάδα τὴν γυναῖκα Φιλίπ-	¹⁷ Αὐτὸς γὰρ ὁ Ἡρῴδης ἀποστείλας ἐκράτησεν τὸν Ἰωάννην καὶ ἔδησεν αὐτὸν ἐν φυλακῇ διὰ Ἡρῳδιάδα τὴν γυναῖκα Φιλίπ-	¹⁹ *ὁ δὲ Ἡρῴδης ὁ τετράρχης, ἐλεγχόμενος ὑπ' αὐτοῦ περὶ Ἡρῳδιάδος τῆς γυναικὸς*

Mt 14,3 ● Ηρωδης + τοτε: B 700-1604 φ σ1010-1293 Θ 1295 *C*sf *Geo*^1.B | ● *om* αυτον: ℵ*B 700 1515 Or *L*ff^1hq *C*b^2 *Geo*^B — *txt*: *Rpl* Or *L*' *S*'(*om* εδη. αυτ.: s)j *C*'f *Geo*' | *om* και *et* απεθ.‖Mk: Z D 61 Or *L*ek a *Aeth* | ● εν + τη‖10p Lk23₁₉: ℵ^cB^3Z Φ-1604 λ1 σ517-954 D Θ 157 *pc* Or | ● *om* Φ.‖Lk: D *L*k[e] acff^1g^1l vg Au

Mk 6,15 *om* ελεγον^2‖p: ℵ Θ-28-565-700 **λ** σ827-1675 *pc* *L*[ek] abcff^2r^1 *S*p *C*s | προφητης] ο πρ.‖Jo1₂₁.₂₅ 614 740: 700 — *om* πρ. (*et om* ως)‖28 Mt: (D) *L*[ek] dir^1(bcff^2) | ως εις τ. πρ.] τις των αρχαιων ανεστη‖Lk: 33 — *om*: *L*a | προφητων + αρχ.‖Lk: 61^c 291(∼) *C*b *Geo*^2 **16** ελεγ.] ● ειπεν‖p: *Rpl* *L*[ek] acff^2z *S*,j^b *C*s — *txt*: 𝔊C Θ 1342 *L*f *S*j^ac *C*b | Ι. ουτ.] ουτ. εστιν Ιωαννης. αυτος(ουτ.)‖Mt2: Θ-565-700 λ1 *L*(aff^2iqr^1)(αυτ. ... ουτ.: b) — ∼ ουτ. Ιωαννης: ℵ*(^a + αυτος) *L*vg^1 — *om* Ι.: D *L*d(*et om* ουτ.) — Ιωαννην, ουτ. εστιν. αυτος(*om*)‖←: *Rpl* (φ13-346-828) — *txt* (αυτος): ℵ^cBLΔ-(33)-892^c W-28 φ'⟨124⟩ (σ945-1223-1402 1342) *L*'[ek](f) Hi (*C*,f) | ηγ.] ηγ. εκ (+ των) νεκρων‖14p: *Rpl* (σ71-692-1194-1402) {*L*vl'[ek] 30 *S*' (*C*b^1)} — ηγ. απο των νε.‖Mt2: C NΣ φ*l*547 σ179-349-517 *al* {} *Aeth* — εκ νε. ηγ.‖12₂₅ Lk16₃₁: Θ-28-565-700 φ D *L*ailr^1.2 vg — *txt*: 𝔊 W 1342 *S*s[c]j *C*'f *Geo* **17** αυτ. γαρ ο] ο γαρ(δε)‖Mt(Lk): ℵ^cL-892 *C*s^2(+1v):7b'(^1)f | εδη.] εθετο‖Mt: 544 σ1082 238(εθηκεν) *l*53(*om* αυτον) — εβαλεν‖Mt18₃₀: Φ *S*j^b — αυτον + και εβαλεν‖←: Θ-28-565-700 φ D *L*vl[ek]⟨clz⟩r^1(εβα. + αυτον) *C*s | εν] εν τη‖27p Lk23₁₉: Φ **λ** *pc* | εν φυ.] εις (+ την) φυλακην‖Mt18₃₀: Θ-28-(565)-700 D *L*[ek]⟨cfz⟩ | γυν.—αυτου] αυτου γυν.: 𝔓^45v | *om* Φ.‖Lk: (𝔓^45) 47

Lk 9,8 υπο τιν. δε] αλλοι δε‖19 Mt Mk15: φ69 *S*(και αλλοι‖Mk28: c; + ελεγον: scp) *C*b'(^1 *om* δε) — υπ αλλων δε‖p: *L*a *C*s — + λεγοντων‖7₂₁₅ Mk15: W 472(*om* υπο) | αλλοι δε‖19 Mk: 579 D *pc* *L*e — + ελεγον‖Mk15: *S*sc(και αλλοι)p | τις] εις‖Mk Mt: {}^1 *Rpl* *L*' {}^2.3 *C*s — *om*: φ69 D Ω 142 {}^2 *S*pj — *txt*: {𝔓^75}^1 𝔊CXΞ 1071 λ-1528 φ'⟨124⟩ σ7-267-659 Ψ 157 *pc* *l*184 {*L*e a Mcn^Te}^2 {*S*' *C*b}^3 *Arm* *Got* | ανεσ.] ηγερθη‖7: 579 **9** ● *om* ο: 𝔓^75 *Rpl* — *txt*: 𝔊⟨ℵ Δ⟩XΞ 700 **λ** φ Ψ 157 *pc* | ∼ ουτ. εστ.‖7₄₉: 579

Jo 1,21 τι ουν Ηλ. ει συ] συ τις ει Ηλ. ει‖1₁₉: 1071 — συ ει Ηλ.: *C* — συ ουν τι Ηλ. ει: B 1170(∼ τι ουν) — τι ουν (+ ει) συ Ηλ. ει: 𝔓^66(τις)^75 C-33 Ψ **Or** *L*(e) ff^2l vg^1(^1) *S*j — ● τι ουν Ηλ. ει: ℵL **0141** *pc* Cr *L*a {} — *txt* (∼ ει συ Ηλ.): *Rpl* (W^s) Chr *L*'(*om* τι ουν: br^1) {*S*c(*om* τι—ειμι)[s]p}h | ● *om* και^2: ℵ *L*abr^1 *S*j^b(και] ο δε) *C*b | *om* ο‖Mk15 Lk9.19 7₃₉: ℵ* φ69 **25** *om* ο^2‖←: σ267 Δ *C*b^3

που τοῦ ἀδελφοῦ αὐτοῦ· 4 ἔλεγεν γὰρ αὐτῷ ὁ Ἰωάννης· οὐκ ἔξεστίν σοι ἔχειν αὐτήν. 5 καὶ θέλων αὐτὸν ἀποκτεῖναι ἐφοβήθη τὸν ὄχλον, ὅτι ὡς προφήτην αὐτὸν εἶχον. 6 γενεσίων δὲ γενομένων τοῦ Ἡρῴδου ὠρχήσατο ἡ θυγάτηρ τῆς Ἡρῳδιάδος ἐν τῷ μέσῳ καὶ ἤρεσεν τῷ Ἡρῴδῃ, 7 ὅθεν μεθ' ὅρκου ὡμολόγησεν αὐτῇ δοῦναι ὃ ἐὰν αἰτήσηται. 8 ἡ δὲ προβιβασθεῖσα ὑπὸ τῆς μητρὸς αὐτῆς· δός μοι, φησίν, ὧδε ἐπὶ πίνακι τὴν κεφαλὴν Ἰωάννου τοῦ βαπτιστοῦ. 9 καὶ ἐλυπήθη ὁ βασιλεύς· διὰ δὲ τοὺς ὅρκους καὶ τοὺς συνανακειμένους ἐκέλευσεν δοθῆναι, 10 καὶ πέμψας ἀπεκεφάλισεν τὸν Ἰωάννην ἐν τῇ φυλακῇ.

που τοῦ ἀδελφοῦ αὐτοῦ, ὅτι αὐτὴν ἐγάμησεν· 18 ἔλεγεν γὰρ ὁ Ἰωάννης τῷ Ἡρῴδῃ ὅτι οὐκ ἔξεστίν σοι ἔχειν τὴν γυναῖκα τοῦ ἀδελφοῦ σου. 19 ἡ δὲ Ἡρῳδιὰς ἐνεῖχεν αὐτῷ καὶ ἤθελεν αὐτὸν ἀποκτεῖναι, καὶ οὐκ ἠδύνατο· 20 ὁ γὰρ Ἡρῴδης ἐφοβεῖτο τὸν Ἰωάννην, εἰδὼς αὐτὸν ἄνδρα δίκαιον καὶ ἅγιον, καὶ συνετήρει αὐτόν, καὶ ἀκούσας αὐτοῦ πολλὰ ἠπόρει, καὶ ἡδέως αὐτοῦ ἤκουεν. 21 καὶ γενομένης ἡμέρας εὐκαίρου ὅτε Ἡρῴδης τοῖς γενεσίοις αὐτοῦ δεῖπνον ἐποίησεν τοῖς μεγιστᾶσιν αὐτοῦ καὶ τοῖς χιλιάρχοις καὶ τοῖς πρώτοις τῆς Γαλιλαίας, 22 καὶ εἰσελθούσης τῆς θυγατρὸς αὐτῆς τῆς Ἡρῳδιάδος καὶ ὀρχησαμένης καὶ ἀρεσάσης τῷ Ἡρῴδῃ καὶ τοῖς συνανακειμένοις, εἶπεν ὁ βασιλεὺς τῷ κορασίῳ· αἴτησόν με ὃ ἐὰν θέλῃς, καὶ δώσω σοι· 23 καὶ ὤμοσεν αὐτῇ ὅτι ὃ ἐάν με αἰτήσῃς δώσω σοι **ἕως ἡμίσους τῆς βασιλείας μου.** 24 καὶ ἐξελθοῦσα εἶπεν τῇ μητρὶ αὐτῆς· τί αἰτήσωμαι; ἡ δὲ εἶπεν· τὴν κεφαλὴν Ἰωάννου τοῦ βαπτίζοντος. 25 καὶ εἰσελθοῦσα εὐθὺς μετὰ σπουδῆς πρὸς τὸν βασιλέα ᾐτήσατο λέγουσα· θέλω ἵνα ἐξαυτῆς δῷς μοι ἐπὶ πίνακι τὴν κεφαλὴν Ἰωάννου τοῦ βαπτιστοῦ. 26 καὶ περίλυπος γενόμενος ὁ βασιλεὺς διὰ τοὺς ὅρκους καὶ τοὺς ἀνακειμένους οὐκ ἠθέλησεν ἀθετῆσαι αὐτήν. 27 καὶ εὐθὺς ἀποστείλας ὁ βασιλεὺς σπεκουλάτορα ἐπέταξεν ἐνεχθῆναι τὴν κεφαλὴν αὐτοῦ. καὶ ἀπελθὼν ἀπεκεφάλισεν αὐτὸν ἐν τῇ φυλακῇ,

τοῦ ἀδελφοῦ αὐτοῦ καὶ περὶ πάντων ὧν ἐποίησεν πονηρῶν ὁ Ἡρῴδης, 20 προσέθηκεν καὶ τοῦτο ἐπὶ πᾶσιν, κατέκλεισεν τὸν Ἰωάννην ἐν φυλακῇ.

Esth5 3 7 2

Mt 14,4 ● ∼ ο Ι. αυτω ‖ Mk: ℵ^{c}BZ 251 — *txt*: *Rpl* (*om* αυτω: ℵ* 28 *pc*) Or *L* | Ι. + οτι ‖ Mk: σM *S Geo*$^{ch.2}$ **5** εφοβειτο ‖ **p**: σ954-1424 *al Sscp*$^{\langle 1\rangle}$ *Cb*^{1} *Arm Aeth* **6** ● γενεσιοις δε γενομενοις(αγομ-) ‖ p: ℵBLZ (λ1-22-1582 *pc*) D **7** ωμολ.] ωμοσεν ‖ p: Z 1604 ϕ-174 Chr *Sp* **8** δος μ. φησ.] ειπεν θελω ινα μοι δως εξαυτης(*om*) ‖ p: σ1424-(1675) **9** ελυπ.] ● λυπηθεις *et* 9b *om* δε ‖ p: B 700 λ1-1582 **ϕ** σ1424-1675 D Θ *La* {*Ssc*} *Cb*^{1}(9b: δια δε τους) *Aeth* — *om* δε ‖ p: L *Lbff*$^{1.2}$*g*^{1}*h vg*^{3} {}
10 ● *om* τον ‖ 8: ℵ*BZ λ1-1582 **0106**

Mk 6,18 ο Ι. τω Η.] αυτω ο Ι. ‖ Mt: 33 *Lc* | *om* οτι ‖ Mt: 892 28 σ179-517-659 D *pc l*47 *l*54 *l*183 *L*[ek] ⟨abq⟩ *Sj* | την—σου] αυτην ‖ Mt: 33 **19** ηθ. ... αποκ.] εζητει ... απολεσαι ‖ Lk19 47p: C* | ηθ.] εζη. ‖ ←: *Lvl*[ek]⟨flz⟩*dr*^{1} **21** εποει ‖ Lk14 16: *Rpl Geo'* — *txt*: ℵBCLΔ WΘ-28 **ϕ** D 6 *l*1596 *L*[ek] *C Geo*^{A} **22** αυτης της] ● αυτου: ℵBLΔ 565 D — της ‖ p: **λ**-22 σ827 *Lbcfz S'j C' Got* — *txt*: *Rpl* (*om* της: W 440 *l*55 *l*185) *L'*[ek] *Sh* | και αρεσ.] ● ηρεσεν *et* ειπ. ο βασ.] ο δε βασ. ειπ. ‖ p: ℵBC*LΔ-33 1342 *l*1596 *Lcff*^{2} {*Cs*}*b'*(^{4} *om* δε) — *txt*: 𝔓^{45}*(βασ.] Ηρωδης) *Rpl L'*[ek] *Sh* {}
23 ωμοσ.] ωμολογησεν ‖ p: F *Cs* | ● *om* ο: 𝔓^{45} BΔ-33* λ118 ϕ124 1342 *pc* | ● *om* με ‖ p: 𝔓^{45v} ℵL-892 1071 **ϕ**⟨124⟩ σ1424-1606 H *pc l*24 *l*44 *l*253 *L*[ek] *bclqr*^{2}*z vg Sp*$^{\langle 3\rangle}$ *Cb* **24** και] η δε ‖ p: *Rpl La bf S'j Cs*^{4}(^{2}∼ εξ. δε) *Geo*^{2} — *txt*: 𝔖 Θ 1342 *L'*[ek] *Ss*[c] *Cb Geo*^{1} | βαπτιστου ‖ 25**p**: *Rpl S'j* — *txt*: ℵBLΔ Θ-28-565 *l*1596 *Sh* **25** θελω—δως] δος ‖ p: D *Lff*^{2}(cz) — εξαυτης δος ‖ p: Θ-565 *L*[ek] *abiqr*^{1} | *om* εξ. ‖ p: 1241 *pc Lf Cs*$^{2:8}$ | επι πιν.] *prm* ωδε ‖ p: D(∼ επι π. ω.) *Lq* | βαπτιζοντος ‖ 24: L-892 700 **26** δια + δε ‖ p: 1071 σ179 *pc Lcfff*^{2}*g*^{2} *Sp Cs*$^{4(+1v):7}$*b*^{6} | ● συνανακει. ‖ **p**22: *Rpl L*[ek] *Shj Cs*$^{2:7}$*b Geo*^{2} — *txt*: BC^{2}LΔ W *pc S' Geo*^{1} **27** *om* ευθ. ‖ p: 1241 *L*[ek] *cff*^{2}*ilr*^{2}*z vg*$^{\langle 4\rangle}$ *Ss*[c] | *om* ο βασ. ‖ **p**: W-28-565-700 **λ**-22-1278 D *pc L*[ek] *Ss*[c]*j Geo*^{2} | ● ενεγκαι ‖ 28: ℵBCΔ-892 1342 *l*1596 {*S,j Cs*$^{4:7}$*b*$^{\langle 9\rangle}$} — *txt*: *Rpl* {} *Cs*$^{2:7}$ | και^{2}] ● ο δε: *Rpl Shj Cs* — *txt*: BCLΔ W-28-544 **λ**⟨118⟩ *pc l*184 *l*1596 *L*[ek] *S'* | αυτον] τον Ιωαννην ‖ p: Θ *pc Sp*

Matth 14	Mark 6
[11] καὶ ἠνέχθη ἡ κεφαλὴ αὐτοῦ ἐπὶ πίνακι καὶ ἐδόθη τῷ κορασίῳ, καὶ ἤνεγκεν τῇ μητρὶ αὐτῆς. [12] καὶ προσελθόντες οἱ μαθηταὶ αὐτοῦ ἦραν τὸ πτῶμα καὶ ἔθαψαν αὐτό, καὶ ἐλθόντες ἀπήγγειλαν τῷ Ἰησοῦ.	[28] καὶ ἤνεγκεν τὴν κεφαλὴν αὐτοῦ ἐπὶ πίνακι καὶ ἔδωκεν αὐτὴν τῷ κορασίῳ, καὶ τὸ κοράσιον ἔδωκεν αὐτὴν τῇ μητρὶ αὐτῆς. [29] καὶ ἀκούσαντες οἱ μαθηταὶ αὐτοῦ ἦλθαν καὶ ἦραν τὸ πτῶμα αὐτοῦ καὶ ἔθηκαν αὐτὸ ἐν μνημείῳ.

(112)

125. Rückkehr der Jünger und Speisung der Fünftausend.
The Return of the Twelve and the Feeding of the Five Thousand.

Matth 14 13–21	Mark 6 30–44	Luk 9 10–17	
	[30] Καὶ συνάγονται οἱ ἀπόστολοι πρὸς τὸν Ἰησοῦν, καὶ ἀπήγγειλαν	[10] Καὶ ὑποστρέψαντες οἱ ἀπόστολοι διηγήσαντο	*10 17 (154.): Ὑπέστρεψαν δὲ οἱ ἑβδομήκοντα δύο μετὰ χαρᾶς λέγοντες· κύριε, καὶ τὰ δαιμόνια ὑποτάσσεται ἡμῖν ἐν τῷ ὀνόματί σου.*
[13] Ἀκούσας δὲ ὁ Ἰησοῦς	αὐτῷ πάντα ὅσα ἐποίησαν καὶ ὅσα ἐδίδαξαν. [31] καὶ λέγει αὐτοῖς· δεῦτε ὑμεῖς αὐτοὶ	αὐτῷ ὅσα ἐποίησαν. καὶ παραλαβὼν αὐτοὺς	
	κατ' ἰδίαν εἰς ἔρημον τόπον καὶ ἀναπαύσασθε ὀλίγον. ἦσαν γὰρ οἱ ἐρχόμενοι καὶ οἱ ὑπάγοντες πολλοί,		
ἀνεχώρησεν ἐκεῖθεν ἐν πλοίῳ εἰς ἔρημον τόπον κατ' ἰδίαν·	καὶ οὐδὲ φαγεῖν εὐκαίρουν. [32] καὶ ἀπῆλθον εἰς ἔρημον τόπον τῷ πλοίῳ κατ' ἰδίαν.	ὑπεχώρησεν κατ' ἰδίαν εἰς πόλιν καλουμένην Βηθσαιδά.	
καὶ ἀκούσαντες οἱ ὄχλοι ἠκολούθησαν αὐτῷ πεζῇ ἀπὸ τῶν πόλεων.	[33] καὶ εἶδον αὐτοὺς ὑπάγοντας καὶ ἐπέγνωσαν πολλοί, καὶ πεζῇ ἀπὸ πασῶν τῶν πόλεων συνέδραμον ἐκεῖ καὶ προῆλθον αὐτούς.	[11] οἱ δὲ ὄχλοι γνόντες ἠκολούθησαν αὐτῷ· καὶ ἀποδεξάμενος αὐτοὺς ἐλάλει αὐτοῖς περὶ τῆς βασιλείας τοῦ θεοῦ,	

Matth 14	*Matth*	Mark 6	*Mark*	Joh
[14] καὶ ἐξελθὼν εἶδεν πολὺν	*9 36 (70.): ἰδὼν δὲ τοὺς*	[34] καὶ ἐξελθὼν εἶδεν πολὺν	*8 1–9 (131.): Ἐν ἐκείναις ταῖς ἡμέραις πάλιν πολλοῦ*	6 1–13: Μετὰ ταῦτα ἀπῆλθεν ὁ Ἰησοῦς πέραν τῆς θαλάσ-

Mt 14,11 επι] ● εν τω: 892 700 λ1-1582 Θ — εν: ϕ — *txt* (+ τω): *Rpl* (Z^v-33 D) *S*h | και^3 + το κορασιον‖p: **σ** *L*e bcfff^{2}h vg^2 *S*c *C*b⟨4⟩ | ηνεγκεν] εδωκεν‖p: σ1424 **0131** 299 — + αυτην‖p: σM *pc* *S*scp *C*s^{5}bf — + εδω. αυτ.‖p: *C*s^1 **12** πτω. + αυτου‖p: ℵ*L Σ-544-1604 σ954-1402 D 157 565 *al* *L*cff^{1}g^{2}hlq30 vg^{11} *S*scp *C*sf | αυτο] ● αυτον: ℵ*B **0106** *L*aff^1 **13** απο + πασων‖Mk: ΟΣ 713 1241

Mk 6,28 εδωκ.^{2}] ηνεγκεν‖p: C-33 *l*53 *S*s[c] *C*b^6 — ην. και εδωκ.‖p: *C*s^6⟨^{2}f⟩ | *om* αυτην^2‖p: 33 544 σ179-827 D *pc* *L*[ek]⟨bfq⟩ *S*p **29** εθη.] εθαψαν‖**p**: 477 | αυτο] ● αυτον: ℵ W ϕ346 σ7 *pc* *l*1596 **31** αναπαυεσθε‖14₄₁p: *Rpl* — *txt*: BCΔ-579 λ1582 **ϕ**'⟨124⟩(-σεσθε: 983) σM-267 A S Ω 1342 *al* | ολ.] λοιπον‖←: W **32** απηλθεν‖p: 700-1071 λ22 **ϕ**⟨983⟩ σ27-945-954-1675 E F G H V Y Γ Ω 157 1342 *al* | ● ~ τω πλ. εις ερ. το.‖Mt: 𝔋 Θ **ϕ 0187** 157 1342 (~ τ. πλ. απηλ.: *L*[ek]⟨b⟩) *C*b *Arm* *Aeth* | τω πλ.] εν πλ.‖Mt: ℵ 565-700 σ349-517 *pc* {}^{1} — ● εν τω πλ.‖Mt: 𝔋' N ΘΣ **ϕ** σ1194 {*S* *C*b'}^{1} — τω πλοιαριω‖Jo21₈: **λ** {}^{2} — αναβαντες εις το πλοιον‖6₅₁ Mt14₃₂: D 66^m *L*'[ek](*om*: b) *C*s^7(^{2} *om* το) — *txt*: *Rpl* {*C*b^1}^{2} **33** υπα. + οι οχλοι‖p: W **ϕ** σ349 *C*s$^{6(+1v):8}$ | επεγ.] ● εγνωσαν‖Lk: B* **λ** D | πολ.] ● αυτους πολ.‖p: 𝔋' NΣ λ1278 ϕ124 σM-7-115-267-349-517(αυτοις)-659-1082 A K U Π 1342 *al* *L*fq *S*(')h *C*(s^2)b *Geo*^{1} — αυτον πολ.: *Rpl* — αυτον‖Lk: **ϕ**' — *txt*: B WΘ-28-700 **λ** D **0187** *L*'[ek]⟨c⟩ *C*s^6 *Geo*^{2} | *om* πασ.‖Mt: 225 *L*ir^1 *C*s$^{1:5}$

Lk 9,10 οσα] παντα οσα‖Mk: 579 1071 σ659 Θ 235 *L*f vg^1 *S*,j | εποι. + και οσα εδιδαξαν‖Mk: A (788) 157 *S*c | ανερχωρησεν‖Mt: 700^c σ1194 D *l*184 | πολ. καλ. Β.] τοπον ερημον (~)‖p: ℵ* *et* ^{b}-(1241) ϕ69-(788) 157 *S*c — τοπ. ερ. (+ καλουμενον) Β.‖p: Ψ 1154 *L*'(e af) *S*p *C*b^3 — τοπ. ερ. πολεως καλουμενης Β.‖p: *Rpl* (*om* και^2—Β.: 579) *S*h *Arm* — ερ.(*om*) τοπ. πολεως καλουμενης Β.‖p: (700 **λ**) **ϕ**'⟨124⟩ A *pc* *S*s(ερ. τοπ.] πυλην)(j *Geo*) — κωμην λεγομενην Β. (+ εις ερ. τοπ.)‖(p): D (Θ *L*r^1) — *txt*: 𝔓^{75} ℵ^{a}BLXΞ-33 *C* **11** επιγνον.‖Mk: Ψ

Jo 6,1 l. + εις ερημον τοπον‖Mt₁₃ Mk₃₂: 28

[Matth 14]

ὄχλον,

καὶ ἐσπλαγχνίσθη ἐπ' αὐτοῖς

καὶ ἐθεράπευσεν τοὺς ἀρρώστους αὐτῶν.

[15] ὀψίας δὲ γενομένης προσῆλθαν αὐτῷ οἱ μαθηταὶ λέγοντες· ἔρημός ἐστιν ὁ τόπος καὶ ἡ ὥρα ἤδη παρῆλθεν· ἀπόλυσον

[Matth 15]

15 32–38 *(131.): Ὁ δὲ Ἰησοῦς προσκαλεσάμενος τοὺς μαθητὰς αὐτοῦ εἶπεν· σπλαγχνίζομαι ἐπὶ τὸν ὄχλον, ὅτι ἤδη ἡμέραι τρεῖς προσμένουσίν μοι καὶ οὐκ ἔχουσιν τί φάγωσιν· καὶ ἀπολῦσαι αὐτοὺς νήστεις οὐ θέλω, μήποτε ἐκλυθῶσιν ἐν τῇ ὁδῷ.*

[33] καὶ λέγουσιν αὐτῷ οἱ μαθηταί· πόθεν ἡμῖν ἐν ἐρημίᾳ ἄρτοι τοσοῦτοι ὥστε χορτάσαι

ὄχλους ἐσπλαγχνίσθη περὶ αὐτῶν, ὅτι ἦσαν ἐσκυλμένοι καὶ ἐρριμμένοι ***ὡσεὶ πρόβατα μὴ ἔχοντα ποιμένα.***

[Mark 6]

ὄχλον, καὶ ἐσπλαγχνίσθη ἐπ' αὐτοὺς ὅτι ἦσαν **ὡς πρόβατα μὴ ἔχοντα ποιμένα,**

καὶ ἤρξατο διδάσκειν αὐτοὺς πολλά.

[35] καὶ ἤδη ὥρας πολλῆς γενομένης προσελθόντες αὐτῷ οἱ μαθηταὶ αὐτοῦ ἔλεγον ὅτι ἔρημός ἐστιν ὁ τόπος καὶ ἤδη ὥρα πολλή· [36] ἀπόλυσον

[Mark 8]

ὄχλου ὄντος καὶ μὴ ἐχόντων τί φάγωσιν, προσκαλεσάμενος τοὺς μαθητὰς λέγει αὐτοῖς·[2] σπλαγχνίζομαι ἐπὶ τὸν ὄχλον, ὅτι ἤδη ἡμέραι τρεῖς προσμένουσίν μοι καὶ οὐκ ἔχουσιν τί φάγωσιν· [3] καὶ ἐὰν ἀπολύσω αὐτοὺς νήστεις εἰς οἶκον αὐτῶν, ἐκλυθήσονται ἐν τῇ ὁδῷ· καί τινες αὐτῶν ἀπὸ μακρόθεν ἥκασιν. [4] καὶ ἀπεκρίθησαν αὐτῷ οἱ μαθηταὶ αὐτοῦ· πόθεν τούτους δυνήσεταί τις ὧδε χορτάσαι ἄρτων ἐπ' ἐρημί-

[Luk 9]

καὶ τοὺς χρείαν ἔχοντας θεραπείας ἰᾶτο.

[12] ἡ δὲ ἡμέρα ἤρξατο κλίνειν· προσελθόντες δὲ οἱ δώδεκα εἶπον αὐτῷ· ἀπόλυσον

[Joh 6]

σης τῆς Γαλιλαίας τῆς Τιβεριάδος. [2] ἠκολούθει δὲ αὐτῷ ὄχλος πολύς, ὅτι ἑώρων τὰ σημεῖα ἃ ἐποίει ἐπὶ τῶν ἀσθενούντων. [3] ἀνῆλθεν δὲ εἰς τὸ ὄρος Ἰησοῦς, καὶ ἐκεῖ ἐκαθέζετο μετὰ τῶν μαθητῶν αὐτοῦ. [4] ἦν δὲ ἐγγὺς τὸ πασχα, ἡ ἑορτὴ τῶν Ἰουδαίων.

[5] ἐπάρας οὖν τοὺς ὀφθαλμοὺς ὁ Ἰησοῦς

Nu27 17 *etc.*

Mt 14,14 επ αυτ.] επ αυτους‖Mk34: 33-892 Φ ϕ13-983-1689 σ1424 — επ αυτον‖32 Mk2: ϕ*l*547 **067** Or — περι αυτων‖36: D **15** μαθ. + αυτου‖Mk: *Rpl* Or² *L'* *S*,j *C*,f — *txt*: 𝔥'⟨L⟩Z^v ϕ346 1555 Or² *Lek* b *Arm* | ● απολ. + ουν: ℵCZ-892 λ1-1582 *pc* Or² *S*h^m *Cs*³b'f — *txt*: *Rpl* Or¹ *L* *S*'j *Cs*³b¹

Mk 6,34 αυτ.¹] αυτοις‖Mt14: *Rpl* — *txt*: ℵB 28 σ1424-1675 D F | ησ. + εσκυλμενοι και εριμμενοι‖Mt36: 579 28 **35** προσηλθον‖Mt15: ΝΣ 213 *L*[ek]⟨q⟩ *S Cs* | ● *om* αυτω‖Lk: ℵ*-579 Θ-544-565-700-1071 σ115?-827-945-1223 A D K Π 1342 *al* *L*[ek] abff²ilr¹(τω Ιησου: r²) vg *Ss*[c] *Arm Aeth* | αυτου] *om*‖Mt: W-28-1071 **λ**⟨118⟩ **ϕ**⟨124⟩ *pc* *Lc Arm* — αυτω‖Lk Mt33: A 330 *l*51 | ελεγ.] ειπον‖Lk: Φ *S' Geo'* — λεγουσιν‖Mt33: *Rpl* Lq *Arm*^pc — λεγοντες‖Mt15: ΝΣ 213 *L*'[ek] *S*h *Cs* — *txt*: 𝔥 Θ *C*b *Arm' Geo*^B | ελεγ. /λεγ. + αυτω‖Mt33 Lk: 544-565-700-1071 **ϕ**'(∼: 69)-230 σ71-115?-179-827-945-1082-1223-1402 D K Π 157 1342 *al* Labg²q *Ss*[c]p *Cs*^7(+1v):9b⁴ | ηδη ωρα] η ω. ηδη(*om*)‖Mt15: (L) **λ** ϕ983-1689 σ179 *pc* (*pc*) *L*[ek] abcff²qz30 vg² | πολλη] παρηλθεν‖Mt15: W *L*'[ek]⟨aff²⟩(πολ. παρη.: i) *Ss*[c] *C Geo*

Lk 9,11 ● ιασατο‖9 42 14 4 22 51 Mt14: CLΞ-33-579-892-1241 28-1071 **ϕ** σ7-27-71-267-692-1194-1424 *pc* *l*303 *Cs* — *prm* παντας‖6 19 Mt8 16 12 15: D — *txt*: 𝔓^75v *Rpl L Ss*^v cph *C*b **12** η δε] ηδη‖24 29 Mk35a.b Mt15: B-579 60 *Le* — ηδη δε η‖←: σ659 *L*flr¹ | ημ.] ωρα‖Mk35a.b Mt15: ϕ983-1689

Jo 6,1 της Γ.] *om*‖21 1: N σ7-1675 G **0210** 157 *pc* *C*b¹ **2** ηκολουθησαν(-εν)‖Mt13 Lk11 Mk33: **σ**⟨1424⟩-1010-1293 (F) 348 (*pc*) *Lf S*(sc)p'(¹ *Geo*¹) | εω.] ● εθεωρουν(-ων)‖2 23 7 3: 𝔓^66c.75 BL-33-579-1241 N-1071(-ρει) (**ϕ**')-69-(230) σ1010-1293 A D Θ Ψ **053 0210** — θεωρουντες *et om* οτι‖2 23: W — εορακεν: σ1223(-ασιν: *pc*) — *txt* (-ουν): 𝔓^66* *Rpl* (ϕ1689) Chr Chrn | εω. + αυτου‖2 23: *Rpl Lvg*¹(∼) — *txt*: 𝔓^75v 𝔥 Λ-28-565-1071 **λ**-22 **ϕ**⟨124⟩-230 σ1223 A D K S Θ Π Ψ Ω **053 0210** *mu* Chr Chrn Ep *L' S*,j *C*^+B a^s **3** απηλθεν‖Mk6 46.32: ℵ* ϕ124-230 D 565 *pc* Chr *L*aff²jlz vg¹ | Ι.] ● ο Ι.: *Rpl* (∼ ο Ι. εις το ο.: 1241 U Ep) Chr Chrn {*S*h}j(κυριος Ι.) — *om*: Δ — ο κυριος: *Ss* — *txt*: 𝔓^66 ℵ*BW D {*L S' C*^+B a^s} | ∼ εκαθ. εκει‖Mt15 29: **λ** D U *pc* *C*^+B a^s | ● εκαθητο‖←: 𝔓^75 *Rpl* — *txt*: 𝔓^66 **ℵ ϕ** D Ep **4** *om* 4‖p: 472 850^c | *om* η εορ.‖2 13 11 55: ϕ543

τοὺς ὄχλους, ἵνα ἀπελθόντες εἰς τὰς κώμας ἀγοράσωσιν ἑαυτοῖς βρώματα.	*ὄχλον τοσοῦτον;*	αὐτούς, ἵνα ἀπελθόντες εἰς τοὺς κύκλῳ ἀγροὺς καὶ κώμας ἀγοράσωσιν ἑαυτοῖς τί φάγωσιν.	*ας;*	τὸν ὄχλον, ἵνα πορευθέντες εἰς τὰς κύκλῳ κώμας καὶ ἀγροὺς καταλύσωσιν καὶ εὕρωσιν ἐπισιτισμόν, ὅτι ὧδε ἐν ἐρήμῳ τόπῳ ἐσμέν.	καὶ θεασάμενος ὅτι πολὺς ὄχλος ἔρχεται πρὸς αὐτόν, λέγει πρὸς Φίλιππον· πόθεν ἀγοράσωμεν ἄρτους ἵνα φάγωσιν οὗτοι; 6 τοῦτο δὲ ἔλεγεν πειράζων αὐτόν· αὐτὸς γὰρ ᾔδει τί ἤμελλεν ποιεῖν.
16 ὁ δὲ Ἰησοῦς εἶπεν αὐτοῖς· οὐ χρείαν ἔχουσιν ἀπελθεῖν· δότε αὐτοῖς ὑμεῖς φαγεῖν.		37 ὁ δὲ ἀποκριθεὶς εἶπεν αὐτοῖς· δότε αὐτοῖς ὑμεῖς φαγεῖν.		13 εἶπεν δὲ πρὸς αὐτούς· δότε αὐτοῖς ὑμεῖς φαγεῖν.	
17 οἱ δὲ λέγουσιν αὐτῷ·		καὶ λέγουσιν αὐτῷ· ἀπελθόντες ἀγοράσωμεν δηναρίων διακοσίων ἄρτους, καὶ δώσωμεν αὐτοῖς φαγεῖν;		οἱ δὲ εἶπαν·	7 ἀποκρίνεται αὐτῷ ὁ Φίλιππος· διακοσίων δηναρίων ἄρτοι οὐκ ἀρκοῦσιν αὐτοῖς, ἵνα ἕκαστος βραχύ τι λάβῃ.
	34 καὶ λέγει αὐτοῖς ὁ Ἰησοῦς· πόσους ἄρτους ἔχετε;	38 ὁ δὲ λέγει αὐτοῖς· πόσους ἄρτους ἔχετε; ὑπάγετε ἴδετε. καὶ γνόντες λέγουσιν·	*5 καὶ ἐπηρώτα αὐτούς· πόσους ἔχετε ἄρτους;*		8 λέγει αὐτῷ εἷς ἐκ τῶν μαθητῶν αὐτοῦ, Ἀνδρέας ὁ ἀδελφὸς Σίμωνος Πέτρου·
οὐκ ἔχομεν	*οἱ δὲ εἶπον·*		*οἱ δὲ εἶπαν·*	οὐκ εἰσὶν ἡμῖν	9 ἔστιν παιδάριον

Mt 14,15 τας + κυκλω‖p: C*-33 ΟΣ-700 σ1293 Θ *pc* $Sp^{1}h^{m}$\{j\} Cs^{1}(^{1}κω. + και αγρους‖p)$^{:6}$ *Arm* **16** ● *om* Ι.‖p: ℵ* 1604 σ D *Lek Sscp* $Cs^{4:6}$f

Mk 6,36 αυτ.] τους οχλους‖p: Θ Geo^{2}(τον οχλον τουτον) — τους ανθρωπους τουτους: *S*s[c] | ∼ τας κυ. κω. κ. αγρ.‖Lk: λ1 σ945 | κω.] εις τας κω.‖Mt: D *Li* | αγο. εαυ.] καταλυσωσιν‖Lk: λ1-22 — + βρωματα‖Mt Lk13: ℵ Θ $Lclr^{2}$ vg Sp^{1} — + αρτους‖37p Jo: *Rpl* (∼ αρτ. αγ. εαυ.: 565) *L*b(-τον)f *S*' — *txt*: $\mathfrak{P}^{45}$ BLΔ-(^{36}∩^{37}αγορ.: 579)-892 W-28 λ872 φ788 D *L*vl'[ek] *S*s[c] *C* | τι] οτι ουκ εχουσιν τι‖2Mt32: 213 | τι φαγ.] τι γαρ(*om*) φαγ. ουκ εχουσιν‖←: *Rpl* (φ543 σ1675 157) *L*f(∼ τι φ. ου γαρ εχ.: bq) *S*' *Δ*a p — τι φαγειν: D' *S*s[c] — *om*: **0187**^{v} — *txt*: $\mathfrak{P}^{45}$ ℵBLΔ-892 WΘ-28 φ788 *L*'[ek] *C Geo* **37** αυτοις^{1} + ου χρειαν εχουσιν απελθειν‖Mt: σ1194 | και^{1}] οι δε‖p: 33 $Lcff^{2}$ vg^{1} Cs^{4}(ειπον δε) — *om*‖Jo: 59 *pc* *S*s[c]j $Cs^{2(+1v)}$ | *om* αυτω‖Lk: **λ**⟨118⟩ *Lc* | ∼ διακ. δην.‖Jo: 579(∼ αρ. δι. δη.) WΘΣ-565-700 σM-1207 D Γ 157 1342 *pc* Lg^{2} vg^{3} *S*s[c]p | φαγ.^{2}] ινα φαγωσιν‖Jo5: 565-700 \{*L*[ek] abq\} — ινα εκαστος (+ αυτων) βραχυ λαβη‖Jo: $\mathfrak{P}^{45}$? W **φ**'(983)-1689(βρ. + τι) $Cs^{6:7}$ **38** ο—αυτ.] και λεγ. αυτ. ο Ιησους‖Mt: σ1424 (*om* ο Ι.) D *L*b(*om* και)q vg^{1} Geo^{2}(ο δε Ι. λ. αυ.) | ● ∼ εχ. αρ.‖5: BLΔ Θ **0187** 1342 Geo^{2} *Aeth* | λεγου. + αυτω‖Mt17: 579 NWΘΣ-565-700 **φ** $σM^{m}$-827 A D *al* *L*vl'[ek]⟨c⟩$g^{2}r^{1}$30 vg^{5} *S*s[c]p $Cs^{7:9}b^{4}$

Lk 9,12 τους οχλους (+ τουτους)‖Mt15: $ℵ^{c}$ 28 σ27-1424 157 *pc* $Lcdff^{2}z$ vg (*S*sc) $Cs^{2:5}b^{\langle 4\rangle}$ | πορ.] απελθοντες‖Mt Mk: *Rpl* — *txt*: ℌCΞ 1071 **φ** **σ**⟨1424⟩-7-267-659-1391-1402-1606 A D R 157 *pc* | επισι. + εν τη οδω‖Mt32 Mk3: 1241 **13** προς αυ.] αυτοις‖p: ℵLΞ-579-1241 1071 φ124 | αυτους + ου χρειαν εχουσιν υπαγειν‖Mt: σ1424 | ● ∼ φαγ. υμ.: B *L*bl

Jo 6,5 αγορασωσιν‖Mt Mk Lk: $\mathfrak{P}^{75}$ **7** αποκ.] ● απεκριθη: $\mathfrak{P}^{66}$ *Rpl* \{*L*'(αποκριθεις: ff^{2})\} — απεκρινατο: σ1675 \{\} — *txt*: ℵ*W σ1424 D' | ● *om* ο: $\mathfrak{P}^{75}$ *Rpl* — *txt*: $\mathfrak{P}^{66}$ ℵLW-892 N-1071 λ1582-2193 213 | τριακοσ.‖12s Mk14s: **σ**⟨1424⟩

Matth 14	Matth 15	Mark 6	Mark 8	Luk 9	Joh 6
ὧδε εἰ μὴ πέντε	*ἑπτά,*	πέντε,	*ἑπτά.*	πλεῖον ἢ πέντε	ὧδε ὃς ἔχει πέντε
ἄρτους				ἄρτοι	ἄρτους κριθίνους
καὶ δύο ἰχθύας.	*καὶ ὀλίγα ἰχθύδια.*	καὶ δύο ἰχθύας.		καὶ ἰχθύες	καὶ δύο ὀψάρια·
18 ὁ δὲ εἶπεν· φέ-				δύο, εἰ μήτι πο-	ἀλλὰ ταῦτα τί
ρετέ μοι ὧδε αὐ-				ρευθέντες ἡμεῖς	ἐστιν εἰς τοσού-
τούς.				ἀγοράσωμεν εἰς	τους;
				πάντα τὸν λαὸν	
				τοῦτον βρώματα.	
				14 ἦσαν γὰρ ὡσεὶ	
cf.v. 21 ↓	*cf.v.* 38 ↓	cf.v. 44 ↓	*cf.v.* 9 ↓	ἄνδρες πεντακισ-	
19 καὶ κελεύσας	35 *καὶ παραγγεί-*	39 καὶ ἐπέταξεν	6 *καὶ παραγγέλ-*	χίλιοι. εἶπεν δὲ	10 εἶπεν ὁ
	λας		*λει*	πρὸς	Ἰησοῦς· ποιήσατε
τοὺς ὄχλους	*τῷ ὄχλῳ*	αὐτοῖς	*τῷ ὄχλῳ*	τοὺς μαθητὰς αὐ-	τοὺς ἀνθρώπους
ἀνακλιθῆναι	*ἀναπεσεῖν*	ἀνακλῖναι	*ἀναπεσεῖν*	τοῦ· κατακλίνατε	ἀναπεσεῖν.
		πάντας συμπόσια		αὐτοὺς κλισίας	
ἐπὶ τοῦ	*ἐπὶ τὴν*	συμπόσια ἐπὶ τῷ	*ἐπὶ τῆς*	ὡσεὶ ἀνὰ πεντή-	
χόρτου,	*γῆν,*	χλωρῷ χόρτῳ.	*γῆς·*	κοντα. 15 καὶ	ἦν δὲ χόρτος
		40 καὶ ἀνέπεσαν		ἐποίησαν οὕτως	πολὺς ἐν τῷ τόπῳ.
		πρασιαὶ πρασιαὶ		καὶ κατέκλιναν	ἀνέπεσαν οὖν οἱ
		κατὰ ἑκατὸν καὶ		ἅπαντας.	ἄνδρες τὸν ἀριθ-
cf.v. 21 ↓	*cf.v.* 38 ↓	κατὰ πεντήκοντα.	*cf.v.* 9 ↓		μὸν ὡς πεντακισ-
λαβὼν	36 *ἔλαβεν*	41 καὶ λαβὼν	*καὶ λαβὼν*	16 λαβὼν	χίλιοι. 11 ἔλαβεν
τοὺς πέντε	*τοὺς ἑπτὰ*	τοὺς πέντε	*τοὺς ἑπτὰ*	δὲ τοὺς πέντε	οὖν τοὺς
ἄρτους καὶ τοὺς	*ἄρτους καὶ τοὺς*	ἄρτους καὶ τοὺς	*ἄρτους,*	ἄρτους καὶ τοὺς	ἄρτους ὁ Ἰησοῦς,
δύο ἰχθύας, ἀνα-	*ἰχθύας,*	δύο ἰχθύας, ἀνα-		δύο ἰχθύας, ἀνα-	
βλέψας εἰς τὸν οὐ-		βλέψας εἰς τὸν οὐ-		βλέψας εἰς τὸν οὐ-	
ρανὸν εὐλόγησεν,	*καὶ εὐχαριστή-*	ρανὸν ηὐλόγησεν	*εὐχαριστή-*	ρανὸν ηὐλόγησεν	καὶ εὐχαριστή-

Mt 14,19 εκελευσεν‖Mk39: ℵZ *pc* *l*184 *L*e[k] ff^1 | τον οχλον‖35 Mk6: 892 D *L*⟨e[k] z⟩ *C*b^4 | ανακ.] αναπεσειν‖35 Mk6: 28 *pc* *l*184 | χορ. + και‖Mk: ℵC* σ1010-1293 W **067** *L*e[k] ff^{1}h | ελαβεν‖36: D *L*e[k]

Mk 6,38 πεν. + αρτους‖Mt17 Lk: 579 565 σ827 D *l*184 *L*vl'[ek]⟨b⟩g^{2}30 vg^4 *S*s[c]p *C*b **39** ● ανακλιθηναι‖Mt17: ℵB Θ(~ πα. αν.)Φ-28-565-700-1071 **λ ϕ**⟨124⟩ σ659-945-1010 G **047 0187** 157 1342 *pc* *l*185 Or^1 *L*vl'[ek] r^1 vg^1 *S*s[c] {*C*b} — *txt*: *Rpl* Or^1 *L*flr^2 vg' *S*' *C*s{} | παν.] αυτους‖Lk: 33 54 — *om*‖p: 𝔓^{45v} 700 σ827 *C*b$^{\langle 1\rangle}$ | *om* χλω.‖Mt19 Jo: 106 1574 *S*s[c]p **40** κατα ... κατα] ανα ... ανα(*om*)‖Lk14: *Rpl* (1342 Or) {} — ανδρες ... ανα: W — *txt*: ℵB (*om* κατα^2: ϕ983-1689) D 21 {*C*b} | *om* κατα^1—πεντ.‖6 Mt: 𝔓^{45}

Lk 9,13 η] ει μη‖Mt: N *pc* | πεντε] επτα‖Mt15 Mk8: C | ● ~ αρ. πε. *cf.* 13b ιχθ. δυο: ℵ*B-579 σ115 — *txt*: *Rpl* (C) *L* *S* | ~ δυο ιχθ.‖Mt17 Mk: LΞ-33-892-1241 N-1071 σ1424 D R Ψ *pc* *L*' *S* — *txt*: *Rpl* *L*a | *om* ημεις‖Mk37: 213 *pc* *L*q | λαον] οχλον‖12 Mt14p33: λ1-131-1582-2193 *L*⟨e ac⟩ *S*s^{v}c **14** γαρ] ● δε‖Mk9 Mt21.38: ℵ*L-892 1071 *L*e ar^{2}z vg *S*j *C*b$^{\langle 1\rangle}$ | ~ ανδ. ωσει^1‖Mt21 Jo10: **λ**-2193 D *pc* *L*e afff^2 | ωσει^1] ως‖Mk9 Jo10: ϕ1689 D 1012 — *om* Mt38 Mk44: *L*q *S*sc *C*b^1 | ανακλιν.‖Mt19 Mk39: 700 | ● *om* ωσει^2‖Mk40: *Rpl* *L*' *S* *C*b — *txt*: ℌCΞ D R 1012 Or *L*e *C*s | ανα + εκατον και ανα‖←: Θ *L*vg^1 **15** ανεκλ.‖Mt19 Mk39: *Rpl* — *txt*: ℌ⟨1241⟩Ξ 700-1071 **λ**-1582-2193 **ϕ** 157

Jo 6,10 ● ειπ. + δε: *Rpl* Bas *L*bq *S*hj — + ουν: 𝔓^{66} 33-1241 D G **0141** *L*' — *prm* και: *C*b' *Aeth* — *txt*: 𝔓$^{28v.75}$ ℵBL 397 Or *L*a *S*' *C*sb^{B1}a^s | ανεπ. ουν] και αν.‖Mk40 Lk: **047** *pc* *L*e jqr^2 vg^1 *S*cph (*om* και: *C*b^{B9} *Geo*^{2})^1 | ως] ωσει‖Mt21 Lk14: 𝔓$^{28v.66}$ *Rpl* Bas {} — *om*‖Mt38 Mk44: *S*cp *C*s^{1}b^{+B} *Geo*^{1} — *txt*: 𝔓^{75} ℌ⟨33-1241⟩ N D Ψ *pc* {*Arm* *Geo*^{2}} **11** ελ. ουν] και λαβων‖Mk41.6: **λ ϕ**-*l*543 G Θ 565 *S*cpj | τους + πεντε‖Mt19.36 Mk Lk: 1604 D' 59 | ευχ.] ● ευχαριστησεν και‖Mt19 Mk41 Lk: ℵ D *L*e abqr^1 *Aeth*

Matth		Mark		Luk	
καὶ κλάσας ἔδωκεν τοῖς μαθηταῖς τοὺς ἄρτους, οἱ δὲ μαθηταὶ τοῖς ὄχλοις.	*σας ἔκλασεν καὶ ἐδίδου τοῖς μαθηταῖς, οἱ δὲ μαθηταὶ τοῖς ὄχλοις.*	καὶ κατέκλασεν τοὺς ἄρτους, καὶ ἐδίδου τοῖς μαθηταῖς αὐτοῦ ἵνα παρατιθῶσιν αὐτοῖς, καὶ τοὺς δύο ἰχθύας ἐμέρισεν πᾶσιν.	*σας ἔκλασεν καὶ ἐδίδου τοῖς μαθηταῖς αὐτοῦ ἵνα παρατιθῶσιν, καὶ παρέθηκαν τῷ ὄχλῳ. [7] καὶ εἶχαν ἰχθύδια ὀλίγα· καὶ αὐτὰ εὐλογήσας εἶπεν παραθεῖναι.*	αὐτοὺς καὶ κατέκλασεν, καὶ ἐδίδου τοῖς μαθηταῖς παραθεῖναι τῷ ὄχλῳ.	σας διέδωκεν τοῖς ἀνακειμένοις, ὁμοίως καὶ ἐκ τῶν ὀψαρίων ὅσον ἤθελον.
[20] καὶ ἔφαγον πάντες καὶ ἐχορτάσθησαν,	[37] *καὶ ἔφαγον πάντες καὶ ἐχορτάσθησαν, καὶ*	[42] καὶ ἔφαγον πάντες καὶ ἐχορτάσθησαν,	[8] *καὶ ἔφαγον καὶ ἐχορτάσθησαν,*	[17] καὶ ἔφαγον καὶ ἐχορτάσθησαν πάντες,	[12] ὡς δὲ ἐνεπλήσθησαν, λέγει τοῖς μαθηταῖς αὐτοῦ· συναγάγετε τὰ περισσεύσαντα κλάσματα, ἵνα μή τι ἀπόληται.
καὶ ἦραν τὸ περισσεῦον τῶν κλασμάτων,	*τὸ περισσεῦον τῶν κλασμάτων*	[43] καὶ ἦραν κλασμάτων	*καὶ ἦραν περισσεύματα κλασμάτων,*	καὶ ἤρθη τὸ περισσεῦσαν αὐτοῖς κλασμάτων	[13] συνήγαγον οὖν, καὶ ἐγέμισαν
δώδεκα κοφίνους	*ἦραν, ἑπτὰ σπυρίδας*	δώδεκα κοφίνων	*ἑπτὰ σπυρίδας.*	κόφινοι δώδεκα.	δώδεκα κοφίνους

Mt 14,19 μαθηταις + αυτου ‖ Mk: 892 **φ**-174-*l*547 Θ **047** Chr *L*e[k] abcff^{2}hz30 vg^{6} *S*scp *C*sf | τ. αρτ.^{2}] *om* ‖ p: 242 Chr *L*e[k] bff^{1}h vg^{1} *S*p — αυτους: *C*s$^{2:6}$f Sch | οχλοις] ανακειμενοις ‖ Jo: 1574 **20** περισσευσαν ‖ Lk: σ1424 — περισσευμα ‖ Mk8: 1515

Mk 6,41 κατεκ. τ. αρ. και] κλασας τ. αρ. ‖ Mt19: ℵ*-(33)-892 σ517 *l*184 | κατεκ.] εκλασεν ‖ 6 14 22 p Mt: L | ~ εδωκεν τ. μαθ. τ. αρ. ‖ Mt19: 33 | εδιδ.] εδωκεν ‖ 14 22 Mt19 Lk22 19: 33 *L*[ek] *S*s[c]p *C* — διεδιδ. ‖ Jo: 21 | ● *om* αυτου ‖ Mt Lk: 𝔋 σ7-267-517-659-1391^{s} **0187**^{v} 1241 1342 *l*^{pl} *L*dg^{2} *C*s^{4}b *Arm* — *txt*: 𝔓^{45} *Rpl* *l*76 *l*184 *l*185 *l*313 *l*1761 *L*'[ek] *S* *C*s^{4} | αυτοις] τω οχλω ‖ 6 Lk Mt: σM **42** ~ και^{2} εχ. παντες(*om*) ‖ Lk: (33)-579 **λ**⟨118⟩-(872 *L*vg^{1} *Arm*$^{⟨0⟩}$) **43** κλασ.] το περισσευον των. κλ. ‖ Mt: σ1194 F U {} *Aeth* — το περισσευσαν των κλ. ‖ Lk Jo: 700 {*L*'[ek] *Geo*^{2}} — των περισσευοντων(-σαντων) κλ. ‖ p: σ179 (472) 569 {*Geo*^{1}} — περισσευματα των κλ. ‖ 8: 33(τα περ.) σ349-517-659 {} — ● κλασματα ‖ Jo: 𝔓^{45} BLΔ-892 28-1604 σ1606 1342 *pc* *S*s[c]pj *Geo*^{ch} — *txt*: *Rpl* *L*bcq *C* | κοφινους πληρεις ‖ 8 19 Mt: *Rpl* {} *L*'[ek](*om* πλ.: fiq) *S*,j *C*⟨b^{1}⟩ *Geo*$^{ch.2}$ — *txt* (κοφινους): 𝔓^{45} ℵB(LΔ-{33})-892 W **λ**⟨118⟩ **φ**

Lk 9,16 *om* αυτ. ‖ Mt19 Mk41: ℵX-1241 *S*pj | *om* και κατεκ. ‖ Jo: D *L*q | μαθ. + αυτου ‖ Mk: LΞ-33-892 1071 **φ** R *pc* *L*e clr$^{1.2}$z vg *S*s^{v}cph^{+}j *C*s$^{2:6}$b^{7} | παρατιθεναι ‖ ←: *Rpl* — *txt*: 𝔓^{75} ℵBCX-579-1241 N-700-1604 **λ**-1582-2193 φ69(-τιθηναι)-124 σ7-659 Θ Ψ *pc* | τοις οχλοις ‖ Mt19.36: D *L*'⟨ff^{2}l⟩(τω λαω: e) *C*b$^{⟨8⟩}$ **17** ~ παν. και εχο. ‖ Mt Mk42: 579 N **φ** σ115 Ψ *pc* *L*fr$^{1.2}$z vg' *S*(*om* και εχ.: s)cpj — *om* παν. ‖ Mk8: *L*abcff^{2}lq vg^{1} | ηραν ‖ **p**: 1071 **σ**⟨1424⟩ S Ψ 716 *L*f *Arm* | το περισσευμα ‖ Mk8: **φ**⟨124⟩ D W — τα περισσευματα ‖ ←: 579 — το περισσευον ‖ Mt: φ174 *pc* | αυτ.] *om* ‖ Mt Jo: ℵ D *pc* — αυτων 579 W | κλασ.] των κλ. ‖ Mt: ℵ D W 4 | ~ δωδ. κοφ. ‖ Mt20 Mk43 Jo: 28 σM-692 157 *al* *L*vg^{4} *S*,j | κοφινους ‖ Mt20 Jo: W *L*abfff^{2}q vg^{4}

Jo 6,11 διεδ.] ● εδωκεν(δεδ-) ‖ **p** Mk14 22 **p**: 𝔓$^{28.66}$ ℵ-579-1241 N-(28)-1071 φ69 σ71-1194 D Γ **047** (*pc*) Chr Or *L*e bqr^{1} — *txt*: *Rpl* Bas *L*' | διεδ. + τοις μαθηταις(+ αυτου) οι δε μαθηται ‖ Mt: *Rpl* (**σ**⟨954⟩ 270 *L*e bj^{v}) *C*b^{B1}(a^{s}) *Aeth* — + τοις μ. αυτ. ινα παρατιθωσιν ‖ Mk Lk: *S*s — *txt*: 𝔓$^{28.66.75}$ 𝔋⟨892⟩ N **λ** σ1010-1293 A Π *al* Bas Chr Non Or *L*' *S*'j *C*' *Aeth* | οψ.] ιχθυων ‖ **p**: φ124(-ιων)-*l*547 **12** περισσευματα ‖ Mk8: **σ**⟨954⟩ — περισσευοντα ‖ Mt: B σ71-1194 **0141** *pc* | κλασ.] των(*om*) κλασματων ‖ p: N **σ**(954)-71-(394)-1194 (1170) *pm* *L*d(~ τ. κλ. τα π.)jlq vg^{4}

Matth 14	Matth 15	Mark 6	Mark 8	Luk 9	Joh 6
πλήρεις. 21 οἱ δὲ ἐσθίοντες ἦσαν ἄνδρες ὡσεὶ πεντακισχίλιοι χωρὶς γυναικῶν καὶ παιδίων.	*πλήρεις.* *38 οἱ δὲ ἐσθίοντες ἦσαν τετρακισχίλιοι ἄνδρες χωρὶς γυναικῶν καὶ παιδίων.*	πληρώματα καὶ ἀπὸ τῶν ἰχθύων. 44 καὶ ἦσαν οἱ φαγόντες τοὺς ἄρτους πεντακισχίλιοι ἄνδρες.	*9 ἦσαν δὲ ὡς τετρακισχίλιοι. καὶ ἀπέλυσεν αὐτούς.*	cf. v. 14 ↑	κλασμάτων ἐκ τῶν πέντε ἄρτων τῶν κριθίνων ἃ ἐπερίσσευσαν τοῖς βεβρωκόσιν. cf. v. 10 ↑

(113) ***126.*** Das Wandeln auf dem See. ***The Walking on the Water.***

Matth 14 22–33	Mark 6 45–52		Joh 6 15–21
22 Καὶ εὐθέως ἠνάγκασεν τοὺς μαθητὰς ἐμβῆναι εἰς πλοῖον καὶ προάγειν αὐτὸν εἰς τὸ πέραν, ἕως οὗ ἀπολύσῃ τοὺς ὄχλους. 23 καὶ ἀπολύσας τοὺς ὄχλους ἀνέβη εἰς τὸ ὄρος κατ' ἰδίαν προσεύξασθαι. ὀψίας δὲ γενομένης μόνος ἦν ἐκεῖ. 24 τὸ δὲ πλοῖον ἤδη μέσον τῆς θαλάσσης ἦν,	45 Καὶ εὐθὺς ἠνάγκασεν τοὺς μαθητὰς αὐτοῦ ἐμβῆναι εἰς τὸ πλοῖον καὶ προάγειν εἰς τὸ πέραν πρὸς Βηθσαιδαν, ἕως αὐτὸς ἀπολύει τὸν ὄχλον. 46 καὶ ἀποταξάμενος αὐτοῖς ἀπῆλθεν εἰς τὸ ὄρος προσεύξασθαι. 47 καὶ ὀψίας γενομένης ἦν πάλαι τὸ πλοῖον ἐν μέσῳ τῆς θαλάσσης, καὶ αὐτὸς μόνος ἐπὶ τῆς		6 15–21: Ἰησοῦς οὖν γνοὺς ὅτι μέλλουσιν ἔρχεσθαι καὶ ἁρπάζειν αὐτὸν ἵνα ποιήσωσιν βασιλέα, ἀνεχώρησεν πάλιν εἰς τὸ ὄρος αὐτὸς μόνος. 16 ὡς δὲ ὀψία ἐγένετο, κατέβησαν οἱ μαθηταὶ αὐτοῦ ἐπὶ τὴν θάλασσαν, 17 καὶ ἐμβάντες εἰς πλοῖον ἤρχοντο πέραν τῆς θαλάσσης εἰς Καφαρναουμ. καὶ σκοτία ἤδη ἐγεγόνει καὶ οὔπω ἐληλύθει πρὸς

Mt 14,21 *om* ανδ.‖Mk9: 700 *S*s | ωσει] ως‖←: 33 1604 λ1-1582 D Δ Θ **067** 1515 — *om*‖38 Mk44: W **0106** *pc* Or *L*,Au *S C*bf **22** μα. + αυτου‖**p**: BX-892 Σ-28 **φ**-174-230-*l*547 σ71-1207 E F K P Θ Π 157 *pm* *l*^{p1} *L*vl[k] g^{2}30 vg^{12} *S*,j *C*,f | ● εις^1 + το‖p 1539p: *Rpl* Chr^1 Or *C*'f — *txt*: B-33-892 Σ-700 **λ**-1582 *pc* Chr^1 Eu *C*b^1 | *om* αυτ.‖p: D 1295 *L*e[k] abff$^{1.2}$g^{1}h Ar *Arm* | τον οχλον‖p: F 59 *C*s$^{3:8}$b^{9}f **23** *om* κατ ιδ.‖p: 245 1093 *S*j^a **24** *om* ηδη‖p: 28 D **047** 1093 *L*afff^{1}lz vg *S*c[s] | μ. τ. θαλ. ην] ην (+ εις) μ. τ. θαλ.‖p: **σ** (D) Eu(εν μεσω‖p) *L*e[k] ff^1 Ar — ● σταδιους πολλους απο της γης απειχε‖Jo19: B (Φ) **φ**'(*om* απο τ. γ.: 983-1689)-174-*l*547 *S*c[s]pj(+ μ. τ. θαλ.) *C*sb(πολ.] ως εικοσι πεντε)⟨f⟩ — απειχεν απο τ. γ. στ. ικανους‖←: 700 (∼ στ. τ. γ. απει. ικ., *om* απο) Θ

Mk 6,43 ιχθ.] δυο ιχθ.‖38 Mt17 Lk13 Jo9: ℵ **φ** *S*s[c] *Δ*a i^V **44** *om* τ. αρ.‖Mt: 𝔓^{45} ℵ WΘ-28-565-700 **λ**⟨118⟩ D Thy *L*[ek]⟨cf⟩ *S*s[c](+ εξ αυτων) *C*s *Arm* | πεν.] ωσει π.‖Mt21 Lk: 28 **λ** {} — ως π.‖9 Jo: ℵ Θ-565-700 20 {*C*s$^{1:8}$ *Arm* | *om* ανδ.‖9: 565 **45** *om* το‖p41: ℵ-33 Θ-565 λ1 253 1342 *Arm* | προαγ. + αυτον‖p: NΘΣΦ-28-565-700 **λ φ** D(αυτου) *al* Or *L*[ek] *S*s[c]pj *C*s$^{7:8}$b | προς] εις‖822: Θ-28-565-700 **λ**⟨118⟩ Or | *om* πρ. Β.‖**p**: φ983-1689 | εως + ου‖**p**: **λ**⟨1⟩-1278 σ1207-1424-1606 *pc* *l*48 | απολυση *vel* -σει‖**p**: 𝔓^{45v} *Rpl* — *txt*: ℵBLΔ λ1 D | τους οχλους‖p: 565-700-1071 λ1 φ69 *pc* **46** ανηλθεν‖p: **λ** σ1402 1038 *C*sb^1 *Geo*^{2} *Aeth* **47** και οψ.] οψ. δε‖132 Mt1424.15 816 *etc.*: NΣ φ983-1689 σ945 1396 *S*s[c]p *C*s | ● *om* παλαι‖**p**: *Rpl* *L*'[ek] *S*,j *C* *Geo*^{1}(^{2} παλιν) *Aeth* — *txt*: 𝔓^{45} 28 **λ**-22 σ1402 D *pc* *L*abff^{2}g^{2}i30 | *om* και^2—γης‖**p**: 1661 *pc* *l*48 | μον. + ην‖Mt23: σ115-1194 A U *al* *L*(c)30 *S*s[c]j *C* *Geo* — γης + ην‖←: σM *pc* *S*h

Jo 6,13 ● επερισσευσεν: *Rpl* — *txt*: 𝔓^{75} BW-**091** σ1293 D **15** μον. + κακει προσηυχετο‖p: D — + προσευξασθαι‖p: *C*s$^{1v:8}$ **17** εις^1 + το‖Mk45 Mt1339p: *Rpl* Chr *C*'a^s — *txt*: 𝔓^{75} 𝔖⟨W⟩ 544-1071 σ1207 Δ **063** *pc* *C*b^B | ηρχ. + εις το‖Mt22p: **φ**⟨124⟩ D *pc* *l*253 Chr | κ. σκ. ηδη εγεγ.] ● κατελαβεν δε αυτους η σκ.‖15 1235: ℵ D

βασανιζόμενον ὑπὸ τῶν κυμάτων, ἦν γὰρ ἐναντίος ὁ ἄνεμος. 25 τετάρτῃ δὲ φυλακῇ τῆς νυκτὸς ἦλθεν πρὸς αὐτοὺς περιπατῶν ἐπὶ τὴν θάλασσαν. 26 καὶ ἰδόντες αὐτὸν οἱ μαθηταὶ ἐπὶ τῆς θαλάσσης περιπατοῦντα ἐταράχθησαν λέγοντες ὅτι φάντασμά ἐστιν, καὶ ἀπὸ τοῦ φόβου ἔκραξαν. 27 εὐθὺς δὲ ἐλάλησεν αὐτοῖς ὁ Ἰησοῦς λέγων· θαρσεῖτε, ἐγώ εἰμι· μὴ φοβεῖσθε. 28 ἀποκριθεὶς δὲ αὐτῷ ὁ Πέτρος εἶπεν· κύριε, εἰ σὺ εἶ, κέλευσόν με ἐλθεῖν πρός σε ἐπὶ τὰ ὕδατα. 29 ὁ δὲ εἶπεν· ἐλθέ. καὶ καταβὰς ἀπὸ τοῦ πλοίου Πέτρος περιεπάτησεν ἐπὶ τὰ ὕδατα καὶ ἦλθεν πρὸς τὸν Ἰησοῦν. 30 βλέπων δὲ τὸν ἄνεμον ἰσχυρὸν ἐφοβήθη, καὶ ἀρξάμενος καταποντίζεσθαι ἔκραξεν λέγων· κύριε, σῶσόν με. 31 εὐθέως δὲ ὁ Ἰησοῦς ἐκτείνας τὴν χεῖρα ἐπελάβετο αὐτοῦ, καὶ λέγει αὐτῷ· ὀλιγόπιστε, εἰς τί ἐδίστασας; 32 καὶ ἀναβάντων αὐτῶν εἰς τὸ πλοῖον ἐκόπασεν ὁ ἄνεμος. 33 οἱ δὲ ἐν

γῆς. 48 καὶ ἰδὼν αὐτοὺς βασανιζομένους ἐν τῷ ἐλαύνειν, ἦν γὰρ ὁ ἄνεμος ἐναντίος αὐτοῖς, περὶ τετάρτην φυλακὴν τῆς νυκτὸς ἔρχεται πρὸς αὐτοὺς περιπατῶν ἐπὶ τῆς θαλάσσης· καὶ ἤθελεν παρελθεῖν αὐτούς. 49 οἱ δὲ ἰδόντες αὐτὸν ἐπὶ τῆς θαλάσσης περιπατοῦντα ἔδοξαν φάντασμα εἶναι, καὶ ἀνέκραξαν· 50 πάντες γὰρ αὐτὸν εἶδον καὶ ἐταράχθησαν. ὁ δὲ εὐθὺς ἐλάλησεν μετ' αὐτῶν, καὶ λέγει αὐτοῖς· θαρσεῖτε, ἐγώ εἰμι· μὴ φοβεῖσθε. 51 καὶ ἀνέβη πρὸς αὐτοὺς εἰς τὸ πλοῖον, καὶ ἐκόπασεν ὁ ἄνεμος· καὶ λίαν ἐκ

αὐτοὺς ὁ Ἰησοῦς, 18 ἥ τε θάλασσα ἀνέμου μεγάλου πνέοντος διηγείρετο. 19 ἐληλακότες οὖν ὡς σταδίους εἴκοσι πέντε ἢ τριάκοντα θεωροῦσιν τὸν Ἰησοῦν περιπατοῦντα ἐπὶ τῆς θαλάσσης καὶ ἐγγὺς τοῦ πλοίου γινόμενον, καὶ ἐφοβήθησαν. 20 ὁ δὲ λέγει αὐτοῖς· ἐγώ εἰμι· μὴ φοβεῖσθε. 21 ἤθελον οὖν λαβεῖν αὐτὸν εἰς τὸ πλοῖον, καὶ εὐθέως ἐγένετο τὸ πλοῖον ἐπὶ

Mt 14,24 ανεμ. + αυτοις(-ω)‖p: Φ Θ *L*abcff$^{1.2}$g^{2}hqz30 *C*s(bf) — *txt*: ℵBC^{2}-**084**-33 Σ λ1-1582 **ϕ**-174 **σ**⟨1424⟩-659-1010-1293 Θ *pc* Chr Eu Or *L S*'j *C*s^{3}bf | **25** ● απηλθεν: *Rpl L*Ar *S*h^{m} *C*s^{5} — *txt*: ℵB-**084** Φ-544-700-1604 λ1-1582 **ϕ**-174 P W Δ Θ **0106** *pc* Or | της θαλασσης‖26 Mk Jo: *Rpl* Eu — **26** και^{1}—μα.] ● οι δε μα. ιδ. αυ.‖p: ℵ^{a}B **ϕ**'(346 οι δε οι!) D *pc S*j^{ac}(και οι) *C*f(*om* μα.) *Geo* — ● ιδ. δε αυ. (+ οι μα.)‖p: ℵ* (Φ)-700 Θ Eu^{1} *L*' *C*s — ιδ.: *S*c — κ. ιδ. αυ.‖p: λ1-22-1582 1241 Eu^{1} *L*cl vg Au *C*b' — *txt* (+ αυτου): *Rpl* (Σ *S*')h *C*b^{1}(^{4}) *Arm*(*om* και) | ∼ περ. ε. τ. θα.‖25p: **084** 544-700 **ϕ**-174 σ7 Θ *pc* Chr Eu *L*g^{1} *S*,j | επι την θαλασσαν‖25: *Rpl* — εν τη θαλασση: 544 — *txt*: ℵBC-**084**-33 Σ-700 λ1-1582 **ϕ**-174 σ954-1010-1293 D Θ *pc* Chr Eu | εταρ.] εφοβηθησαν‖Jo: 1093 **27** ● ∼ ο Ι. αυ.: ℵ^{a}B *pc L*'⟨fq⟩ — ● *om* ο Ι.‖p: ℵ*-**084**^{v}-892 ϕ983 σ1010-1293 D Eu *L*ff^{1} *S*c *C*⟨f⟩ | *om* θαρ.‖Jo: ϕ983-1689 **σ** **28** ● ∼ πρ. σε ελθ.: *Rpl L*vg^{4} — *txt*: ℵBC-**073**-33 ΣΦ-544 λ1-1582 **ϕ**'(απελθ.: 346)-174 σ267-954-1402-1675 D W Θ **0106** 157 *pc* Eu Or *L*'Ar *S*,j **29** ● Π.] ο Π.‖28: *Rpl* — *txt*: ℵB D Eu **30** ● *om* ισχ.: ℵB-**073**-33 *C*,f | *om* με‖8 25: λ1-1582

Mk 6,48 ∼ εν. ο αν. αυτ.(*om*)‖(p): ℵ (**λ**⟨118⟩) σ179-517 A 1342 *al* — ο αν. αυτ. εν.: σ827 *L*b — εν. αυτ. ο αν.‖p: λ872 | *om* αυτοις‖p: 565 **λ**⟨118⟩ *L*i | περι + δε‖p: 565-700 1342 *L*b *C*s$^{6:7}$b | ∼ επι τ. θα. περ.‖49p: **λ**⟨118⟩ | *om* και^{2}—αυτους‖**p**: G 495 *L*r^{1}? **49** ∼ περ. επι τ. θα.‖48p: *Rpl L*'[ek] *S*' *C* — *txt*: ℌ Θ 1342 *pc l*48 *L*30 vg^{1} *S*s[c]j | φαν. ειν.] ● οτι φαν. εστιν‖**p**: ℌ 1342 | ανεκ.] εκραξαν‖p: 131 713 — *prm* απο του φοβου‖p: 1342 **50** εταρ.] εφοβηθησαν‖Jo: σ1424 *S*p | μετ αυ.] αυτοις‖p: 565 *L*b | κ. λεγ. αυ.] λεγων‖p: D *L*abff^{2}ir^{1} *C*s | *om* θαρ.‖Jo: G *pc* **51** *om* προς αυ.‖p: σ179(+ ευθυς) 1579 | λι. εκ περ.] περισσως‖10 26 7 37: 565-700 D' {*L*bz vg^{1} *S*p}(*om* s[c]) — εκπερισσως‖14 31 7 37: λ1 {} — εκ περισσου: WΘ-28 {} — ● λιαν: ℵBLΔ-892 1342 {}

Jo 6,17 ο Ι. + εις το πλοιον‖21p: ϕ13-543-826-828-983 σ1223 K *al* — *prm* εις τ. πλ.‖←: 544 *pc* **19** ● σταδια: ℵ*D *pc* | ∼ επι τ. θαλ. περ.‖Mt 26 p: 1241 *L*e

τῷ πλοίῳ προσεκύνησαν αὐτῷ λέγοντες· ἀληθῶς θεοῦ υἱὸς εἶ.

περισσοῦ ἐν ἑαυτοῖς ἐξίσταντο· [52] οὐ γὰρ συνῆκαν ἐπὶ τοῖς ἄρτοις, ἀλλ' ἦν αὐτῶν ἡ καρδία πεπωρωμένη.

τῆς γῆς εἰς ἣν ὑπῆγον.

(114)

127. Heilungen in Gennesaret. *Healings at Gennesaret.*

Matth 14 34–36	**Mark 6** 53–56
[34] Καὶ διαπεράσαντες ἦλθον ἐπὶ τὴν γῆν εἰς Γεννησαρετ. [35] καὶ ἐπιγνόντες αὐτὸν οἱ ἄνδρες τοῦ τόπου ἐκείνου ἀπέστειλαν εἰς ὅλην τὴν περίχωρον ἐκείνην, καὶ προσήνεγκαν αὐτῷ πάντας τοὺς κακῶς ἔχοντας,	[53] Καὶ διαπεράσαντες ἦλθον ἐπὶ τὴν γῆν Γεννησαρετ καὶ προσωρμίσθησαν. [54] καὶ ἐξελθόντων αὐτῶν ἐκ τοῦ πλοίου εὐθὺς ἐπιγνόντες αὐτὸν **26.** [55] περιέδραμον ὅλην τὴν χώραν ἐκείνην καὶ ἤρξαντο ἐπὶ τοῖς κραβάττοις τοὺς κακῶς ἔχοντας περιφέρειν, ὅπου ἤκουον ὅτι ἐστίν. [56] καὶ ὅπου ἂν εἰσεπορεύετο εἰς κώμας ἢ εἰς πόλεις ἢ εἰς ἀγρούς, ἐν ταῖς ἀγοραῖς ἐτίθεσαν τοὺς ἀσθενοῦντας,
[36] καὶ παρεκάλουν αὐτὸν ἵνα μόνον ἅψωνται τοῦ κρασπέδου τοῦ ἱματίου αὐτοῦ· καὶ ὅσοι ἥψαντο διεσώθησαν.	καὶ παρεκάλουν αὐτὸν ἵνα κἂν **84.** τοῦ κρασπέδου τοῦ ἱματίου αὐτοῦ ἅψωνται· καὶ ὅσοι ἂν ἥπτοντο αὐτοῦ ἐσῴζοντο.

(115)

128. Rein und Unrein. *Clean and Unclean.*

Matth 15 1–20	**Mark 7** 1–23
[1] Τότε προσέρχονται τῷ Ἰησοῦ ἀπὸ Ἱεροσολύμων Φαρισαῖοι καὶ γραμματεῖς	[1] Καὶ συνάγονται πρὸς αὐτὸν οἱ Φαρισαῖοι καί τινες τῶν γραμματέων ἐλθόντες ἀπὸ

Mt 14,34 επι τ. γ. εις] ● εις τ. γ.‖Jo3 22 21 9: *Rpl* Or {*L*,Hil *S*pj}^{1} *C*b'{f}^{2} — επι τ. γ.‖p: C NΣ **ϕ**-174 **σ**'-1010-1293-1402 157{}^{1} *C*sb^{1}{}^{2} — *txt*: **ℵB-084**-33-892 Φ σ1675 D W Δ Θ **0119** *S*(∼ επι τ. γ. ηλϑ.: sc)h *Arm* **36** ινα + καν (*et om* μον.‖(p): 33 Φ λ1-22-1582 **ϕ**-174 **σ**-659 Θ *pc* Or (*L*'⟨e[k] ff^{1}⟩)f Au *S*p | οσοι + αν‖p: C-33 157 *pc* {*L*} | διεσ.] εσωϑ.‖p: ℵ-892 *pc* Chr **15,1** τω I.] προς αυτον‖p: D *L*,Au {} *C*f *Aeth* — αυτω‖p: 892 λ1-1582 **σ**-349-659 Or {*S*s} | απο] οι απο‖p: *Rpl S*' — *txt*: ℵB 700 λ1-1582 ϕ124-174-346-543-788 **σ**-349-659 D Θ 157 *pc* Or *S*s *C*,f *Aeth* | ∼ Φ. κ. γρ. απο I.‖p: λ1-1582 (*L*⟨e[k] ff^{1}⟩ *S*c)p'(^{1}h) *C*sb^{1} | ● ∼ γρ. κ. Φ.: *Rpl L*'Au Hil *S*' *C*b^{1} — *txt*: ℵB-33-892 λ1-1582 **ϕ**-174 **σ**-349-659 D Θ *pc* Or *L*e[k] ff^{1} *S*p$^{\langle 1\rangle}$ *C*'f *Arm*

Mk 6,51 εξισ.] εξεπλησσοντο‖10 26 7 37: **λ** 1200 **52** ∼ η καρ. αυ.‖7 6 Mt15 8: LΔ Φ-28-544-565 **λ**-1278 ϕ69 σ71-179-692-945-1194-1223-1402-1606 D *al* **53** ηλ.—γην] ● επι τ. γ. ηλ. εις: ℵBLΔ(*om* ηλ.)-33-579-892 1342 *C*s^{6}b *Geo*^{1} — ηλ. εις τ.(*om*) γ.: X Φ (**ϕ**⟨124⟩)-230 σ1082-1194 *pc* {*L*'[ek]} — ηλ. επι τ. γ. εις‖p: WΘ-28-565-700 σ27 — *txt*: *Rpl* {*L*acff^{2}z *S*} *C*s^{1} *Geo*^{2} | *om* και προσω.‖**p**: WΘ-28-565-700 **λ**⟨118⟩ ϕ788-983-1689 D *L*vl[ek]⟨flr^{2}⟩r^{1} *S*s[c]p *C*s$^{2:7}$ **54** *om* ευϑ.‖**p**: 565-700 *L*q *C*s$^{2:7}$ | αυτον + οι ανδρες του τοπου εκεινου(*om*)‖**p**: Δ-33 (WΘΦ-28-565-700)-1071 **λ** (**ϕ** σ827) A G (1342) *pc* (*pc*) *L*cg^{2}30 vg^{1} (*S*p) *C*s$^{6:7}$ *Arm* **55** ολην] εις ολ.‖p: W **ϕ** | περιχωρον‖p: *Rpl L*bq {} *S*h *C*sb^{1} — *txt*: ℌ Θ σ517 1342 {*L*'[ek]} *S*' *C*b' | τους] παντας τ.‖p 1 32 Mt4 24 8 16: 565-700 D 472 *L*abff^{2}qr^{1} *Geo*^{2} | οπου—εστιν] *om*‖Mt: *S*s[c] — περιεφερον γαρ αυτους οπου αν ηκουσαν τον Ιησουν ειναι: D *L*'[ek]⟨cflz⟩(γαρ] δε: bff^{2}iqr^{1}; τ. I.] αυτον: i) | ηκουσϑη‖2 1: ℵ | εστιν] εκει εσ.‖Jo12 9: *Rpl S*h *Arm* — εσ. εκ.‖←: W-28-565-700 **λ**⟨118⟩ — *txt*: ℵBLΔ-892 Θ (D) *pc L*cflr^{2}z vg *S*(s[c])p **56** ∼ πο. ... κω.‖Mt9 35 Lk13 22: 892 Φ σM-1606 *pc S*s[c] *C*s$^{1:7}$ | *om* η εις αγ.‖←: L **λ** *S*p *Δ*a | καν + μονον‖p Mt9 21: σ659 | των ιματιων‖5 28: 473 485 *C*b$^{\langle 2\rangle}$ | *om* αν^{2}‖p: ℵΔ-579 **λ**⟨118⟩ D 1342 *pc* | ηπτ.] ● ηψαντο‖**p**: ℌ WΘ-28-565 **λ**⟨118⟩ **ϕ** D **0274** 1342 *pc L*aff^{2} — *txt*: *Rpl L*'[ek] *S* | *om* αυτου^{2}‖**p**: 565 *pc L*abff^{2}iq *S*s[c] | εσω.] διεσωϑησαν‖p: Δ {} — διεσωζοντο‖p: NΣ-700 **λ**⟨118⟩ **ϕ** *pc* — εσωϑησαν‖p: 33-579-892*? 565 {*L*a} **7,1** *om* οι‖p: 565-700 **λ** σ659

Jo 6,21 την γην‖Mt14 34p: ℵ*-579 28 **ϕ**⟨983⟩- *l*547 σ1424 **063** *pc* (επι] εις: 157 *pc*) Or *L*⟨ff^{2}⟩

---

128. cf. Ev. apocr. (POxy 840; *cf. ad 224.* Mt23 25f.)

Ἱεροσολύμων. ² καὶ ἰδόντες τινὰς τῶν μαθητῶν αὐτοῦ κοιναῖς χερσίν, τοῦτ' ἔστιν ἀνίπτοις, ἐσθίοντας τοὺς ἄρτους, — ³ οἱ γὰρ Φαρισαῖοι καὶ πάντες οἱ Ἰουδαῖοι ἐὰν μὴ πυγμῇ νίψωνται τὰς χεῖρας οὐκ ἐσθίουσιν, κρατοῦντες τὴν παράδοσιν τῶν πρεσβυτέρων, ⁴ καὶ ἀπ' ἀγορᾶς ἐὰν μὴ βαπτίσωνται οὐκ ἐσθίουσιν, καὶ ἄλλα πολλά ἐστιν ἃ παρέλαβον κρατεῖν, βαπτισμοὺς ποτηρίων καὶ ξεστῶν καὶ χαλκίων καὶ κλινῶν, — ⁵ καὶ

11 38 (168.): ὁ δὲ Φαρισαῖος ἰδὼν ἐθαύμασεν ὅτι οὐ πρῶτον ἐβαπτίσθη πρὸ τοῦ ἀρίστου.

	Matth	Mark / Luk
	λέγοντες·	ἐπερωτῶσιν αὐτὸν οἱ Φαρισαῖοι καὶ οἱ γραμματεῖς·
	² διὰ τί οἱ μαθηταί σου παραβαίνουσιν	διὰ τί οὐ περιπατοῦσιν οἱ μαθηταί σου
	τὴν παράδοσιν τῶν πρεσβυτέρων; οὐ γὰρ νίπτονται τὰς χεῖρας αὐτῶν ὅταν ἄρτον ἐσθίωσιν. ³ ὁ δὲ ἀποκριθεὶς εἶπεν αὐτοῖς· διὰ τί καὶ ὑμεῖς παραβαίνετε τὴν ἐντολὴν τοῦ θεοῦ διὰ τὴν παράδοσιν ὑμῶν;	κατὰ τὴν παράδοσιν τῶν πρεσβυτέρων, ἀλλὰ κοιναῖς χερσὶν ἐσθίουσιν τὸν ἄρτον; *⁹ καὶ ἔλεγεν αὐτοῖς· καλῶς ἀθετεῖτε τὴν ἐντολὴν τοῦ θεοῦ, ἵνα τὴν παράδοσιν ὑμῶν τηρήσητε.*
Ex20 12 Dt5 16 / Ex21 16 Lv20 9	⁴ ὁ γὰρ θεὸς ἐνετείλατο λέγων· **τίμα τὸν πατέρα καὶ τὴν μητέρα,** καί· **ὁ κακολογῶν πατέρα ἢ μητέρα θανάτῳ τελευτάτω.** ⁵ ὑμεῖς δὲ λέγετε· ὃς ἂν εἴπῃ τῷ πατρὶ ἢ τῇ μητρί· δῶρον ὃ ἐὰν ἐξ ἐμοῦ ὠφεληθῇς, ⁶ οὐ μὴ τιμήσει τὸν πατέρα αὐτοῦ ἢ τὴν μητέρα αὐτοῦ· καὶ ἠκυρώσατε τὸν λόγον τοῦ θεοῦ διὰ τὴν παράδοσιν ὑμῶν.	*¹⁰ Μωυσῆς γὰρ εἶπεν·* ***τίμα τὸν πατέρα σου καὶ τὴν μητέρα σου,*** *καί·* ***ὁ κακολογῶν πατέρα ἢ μητέρα θανάτῳ τελευτάτω.*** *¹¹ ὑμεῖς δὲ λέγετε· ἐὰν εἴπῃ ἄνθρωπος τῷ πατρὶ ἢ τῇ μητρί· κορβαν, ὅ ἐστιν δῶρον, ὃ ἐὰν ἐξ ἐμοῦ ὠφεληθῇς, ¹² οὐκέτι ἀφίετε αὐτὸν οὐδὲν ποιῆσαι τῷ πατρὶ ἢ τῇ μητρί, ¹³ ἀκυροῦντες τὸν λόγον τοῦ θεοῦ τῇ παραδόσει ὑμῶν ᾗ παρεδώκατε·...*
	⁷ ὑποκριταί, καλῶς ἐπροφήτευσεν περὶ ὑμῶν Ἠσαΐας λέγων·	⁶ ὁ δὲ ἀποκριθεὶς εἶπεν αὐτοῖς· καλῶς ἐπροφήτευσεν Ἠσαΐας περὶ ὑμῶν τῶν ὑποκριτῶν, ὡς γέγραπται·
Is29 13	⁸ **ὁ λαὸς οὗτος τοῖς χείλεσίν με τιμᾷ, ἡ δὲ καρδία αὐτῶν πόρρω ἀπέχει ἀπ' ἐμοῦ·** ⁹ **μάτην**	**οὗτος ὁ λαὸς τοῖς χείλεσίν με τιμᾷ, ἡ δὲ καρδία αὐτῶν πόρρω ἀπέχει ἀπ' ἐμοῦ·** ⁷ **μάτην**

Mt 15,2 ● *om* αυ.‖Mk3: ℵB-**084**-892 700 λ1-1582 σ1424 Δ *pc* Or *L*fg¹ *Arm* | αρτ.] τον α.‖p: σ945-990 *pc* **4** ενετ. λεγ.] ● ειπεν‖p: ℵᶜB-**084**-892 700 λ1-1582 ϕ124-788 D Θ Cr Ptl^Ep *L*⟨f⟩ Hi Ir *S*scp *C*,f | πα.¹ + σου‖p Mk10 19 Lk18 20 Ex20 12 Dt5 16: CᶜL-33 NΣΦ-544-1604 **ϕ**-174-230 σM-71-267-517-1424 K U W Y Θ Π 157 *pc* Or *L*abcff²g¹lq vg⁹ *S*'h⁻ *C*,f *Geo*² | μη.¹ + σου‖p Ex←Dt←MT: 892 N σ1424 W *pc* Or *L*abcff²g¹30 vg² *S*scp *C*,f *Geo*² **5** μη. + κορβαν ο εστιν‖p: Φ Γ *L*b **6** *om* αυτ.¹‖p: **λ**-1582 σ349-517-659-1402-1424 Θ *pc l*184 Chr Or *Geo*^B | ● *om* η τ. μητ. αυ.(⌒?): ℵB 544 ϕ174 D Ω *L*e[k] a *S*c *C*s^8+1v:9 *Geo*¹ | *om* αυτ.²‖p: **084**-33-892 544-700-1071 **ϕ** *al l*1761(η) και) Chr Or *L*bff²g¹l | τ. λογ.] ● τ. νομον: ℵ*C-**084** **ϕ**-174 σ1010-1293 *pc* Ptl^Ep — την(*om*) εντολην‖3p: *Rpl* (Δ) Cr Or *L*'Or *S*h^t *Arm*^pc *Geo*^A — *txt*: ℵᶜB-892 700 D Θ Eu Or *L*e[k] abff^1.2 Au Ir *S*'h^m *C*s⁸(¹ τους λογους)b *Arm*' *Geo*' **7** ∼ Η. π. υμων‖p: 33 K Π *pc L*Or

Mk 7,2 ● αυτ. + οτι *et* εσθιουσιν *cf.* 5: ℌ σ517(*om* εσθ.) **0274** {} *C*' — *txt*: *Rpl* {*L*'[ek]} a *S*'{p *C*b¹} | τους αρ.] αρτον‖Mt2: ℵ σ1207 1342 *al L*vl'[ek] r¹30 vg³ (τον α. αυτων: *C*s) *Geo*'(^B *om*) — αρτους‖←: *Rpl* (αυτ-: Y *pc*) {} — *txt*: ℌ⟨ℵ⟩ NWΘΣ-28-544-565 **ϕ** D *pc* {*L*afi vg'} *C*b **3** πυγμη] πυκνα‖Lk5 33: ℵ W *L*bflr²z(πυκ. πυγ.) vg *C*(s *om*)b *Geo*¹ *Aeth Got Δ*ad i^T l md^Z n | ουκ εσθ.] αρτον ουκ εσθ.‖Mt2: ϕ1689 {*Arm Geo*¹ *Aeth*} — ουκ εσθ. (+ τον) αρτ.‖←: 1071 σ(Mᶜ)-27-71-179-692 D *l*48² {} *L*abc ff²i *S*s[c] **4** βαπ.] ● ραντισ. *cf.* Nu19 9ff.: ℵB σ71-179-692 *pc C*s | ● *om* κ. κλιν.: 𝔓^45v ℵBLΔ 28 440 1342 *l*48 (*om* κ. χαλ. κ. κλι.: *S*s[c]) *C*s¹b — *txt*: *Rpl* Or *L*[ek] *S*' *C*s⁸ Δ⟨i^V me⟩ **5** και¹] ● επειτα: *Rpl Lf S*' *Arm* — *txt*: ℌ⟨Δ⟩ Θ-565-700 **λ** D 1342 *L*'[ek] *S*p *C*s(και] δε)b | γρ. + λεγοντες(+ αυτω)‖p: ΔWΘ-28-565-700 **ϕ** D 472 *L*[ek] a(c)ff²g²ir¹ (*S*s[c]) *C*s⁶(¹)^:9 | ∼ οι μα. σου ου περ.‖p: 𝔓^45v *Rpl L*'[ek] *S*s[c](πε. ... κατα] τηρουσιν)ph — *txt*: ℌ σ179-349-517-659 1241 1342 *l*49² *L*vg¹ | ∼ τον(*om*) αρ. εσ.‖(p) ϕ124 (*pc*) | *om* τον‖p: K Π *al* **6** ● *om* αποκ.: ℌ 372 1342 *S*' *C* — *txt*: 𝔓^45 *Rpl L*[ek] *S*h *Arm Aeth* | ∼ περι υμ. Η.‖p: 𝔓^45 892 Σ-28 σ179-517 A 1241 *L*g²r² vg¹ *S*s[c]p *C*b | ως γεγ.] λεγων‖p: 700 *L*[ek] abcdff²g²iz | ● γεγ. + οτι‖11 17 Mt4 6p: ℵBL-892 1071 **0274** 372 1342 *S*s[c]p *Geo*² | ∼ ο λα. ουτ.‖p Is29 13: B 1071 D 372 *L*vl[ek]⟨aff²g²⟩r²30 *S*s[c]p

---

Mt15 5 p *cf.* EN frgm.12 (Cod. N. T. 1424^m): Τὸ Ἰουδαϊκόν· κορβαν ὃ ὑμεῖς ὠφεληθήσεσθε ἐξ ἡμῶν.
Mt15 8 p *cf.* Ev. apocr. (PEg 2 fol.2r°; *cf. ad 220.*)

Matthew	Mark
δὲ σέβονταί με, διδάσκοντες διδασκαλίας ἐντάλματα ἀνθρώπων.	**δὲ σέβονταί με, διδάσκοντες διδασκαλίας ἐντάλματα ἀνθρώπων.** 8 ἀφέντες τὴν ἐντολὴν τοῦ θεοῦ
cf. v. 3–6 ↑	κρατεῖτε τὴν παράδοσιν τῶν ἀνθρώπων. 9 καὶ ἔλεγεν αὐτοῖς· καλῶς ἀθετεῖτε τὴν ἐντολὴν τοῦ θεοῦ, ἵνα τὴν παράδοσιν ὑμῶν τηρήσητε. 10 Μωϋσῆς γὰρ εἶπεν· **τίμα τὸν πατέρα σου καὶ τὴν μητέρα σου,** καί· **ὁ κακολογῶν πατέρα ἢ μητέρα θανάτῳ τελευτάτω.** 11 ὑμεῖς δὲ λέγετε· ἐὰν εἴπῃ ἄνθρωπος τῷ πατρὶ ἢ τῇ μητρί· κορβαν, ὅ ἐστιν δῶρον, ὃ ἐὰν ἐξ ἐμοῦ ὠφεληθῇς, 12 οὐκέτι ἀφίετε αὐτὸν οὐδὲν ποιῆσαι τῷ πατρὶ ἢ τῇ μητρί, 13 ἀκυροῦντες τὸν λόγον τοῦ θεοῦ τῇ παραδόσει ὑμῶν ᾗ παρεδώκατε· καὶ παρόμοια
10 καὶ προσκαλεσάμενος τὸν ὄχλον εἶπεν αὐτοῖς· ἀκούετε καὶ συνίετε· 11 οὐ τὸ εἰσερχόμενον εἰς τὸ στόμα κοινοῖ τὸν ἄνθρωπον, ἀλλὰ τὸ ἐκπορευόμενον ἐκ τοῦ στόματος, τοῦτο κοινοῖ τὸν ἄνθρωπον. 12 τότε προσελθόντες οἱ μαθηταὶ λέγουσιν αὐτῷ· οἶδας ὅτι οἱ Φαρισαῖοι ἀκούσαντες τὸν λόγον ἐσκανδαλίσθησαν; 13 ὁ δὲ ἀποκριθεὶς εἶπεν· πᾶσα φυτεία ἣν οὐκ ἐφύτευσεν ὁ πατήρ μου ὁ οὐράνιος ἐκριζωθήσεται. 14 ἄφετε αὐτούς· τυφλοί εἰσιν ὁδηγοὶ τυφλῶν· τυφλὸς δὲ τυφλὸν ἐὰν ὁδηγῇ, ἀμφότεροι πεσοῦνται εἰς βόθυνον.	τοιαῦτα πολλὰ ποιεῖτε. 14 καὶ προσκαλεσάμενος πάλιν τὸν ὄχλον ἔλεγεν αὐτοῖς· ἀκούσατέ μου πάντες καὶ σύνετε. 15 οὐδέν ἐστιν ἔξωθεν τοῦ ἀνθρώπου εἰσπορευόμενον εἰς αὐτὸν ὃ δύναται κοινῶσαι αὐτόν· ἀλλὰ τὰ ἐκ τοῦ ἀνθρώπου ἐκπορευόμενά ἐστιν τὰ κοινοῦντα τὸν ἄνθρωπον. 16 εἴ τις ἔχει ὦτα ἀκούειν ἀκουέτω. 17 καὶ ὅτε εἰσῆλθεν εἰς οἶκον ἀπὸ τοῦ ὄχλου,
15 ἀποκριθεὶς δὲ ὁ Πέτρος εἶπεν αὐτῷ· φράσον ἡμῖν	ἐπηρώτων αὐτὸν οἱ μαθηταὶ αὐτοῦ

Ex20₁₂ Dt5₁₆
Ex21₁₆ Lv20₉

89.

Mt 15,10 ακουσατε‖p: Θ 348 **11** εισερ.] εισπορευομενον‖17**p**: 157 238 | τουτο] εκεινο‖18p: σ1293 D *Geo*^{1} **14** ● ~ εις βο. πεσ.‖←: *Rpl* Bas Ep *L*,Cp *S* — *txt*: LZ-**0237** (700) λ1-1582 (βο.] τον β.: **ϕ**) (D) Θ (Chr^{1})^{1} *C*ETh^{II}(καταπεσ.)↓ | εμπεσουνται‖Lk6₃₉: ΟΣΦ-700 **σ**⟨954⟩-659-1010-1293-1391-1402 D F W *al* Bas Chr$^{1:2}$ Cr Ep Or

Mk 7,7 ανθ. + βαπτισμους ξεστων και ποτηριων και αλλα παρομοια τοιαυτα ποιειτε (*cf. ad* 8)‖4.13: Θ-28-565 D **0131**^{v} *pc* *L*vl[ek]⟨flr^{2}z⟩r^{1} ⟦~ ποτ. … ξε.‖4: Θ-565 *L*bcq | τοι. ποι.] α ποι. τοι. πολλα: D *L*iff^{2}q(~ πολ. τοι. α ποι.: ar^{1}) — πολλα: *pc*⟧ **8** ανθ. + βαπτισμους ποτηριων και ξεστων και χαλκιων‖4: 1342 — ● + βα. ξε. κ. ποτ. και αλλα παρομοια τοιαυτα πολλα ποιειτε‖4.13: *Rpl* (Θ-28-565 D **0131** *pc cf. ad* 7) *L*flr^{2}z vg *S*' *C*b^{1} *Arm*^{0} ⟦~ ποτ. … ξε.‖4: 483 *S*p | *om* αλλα: A *l*303 | αλλα—ποι.] πολλα: *C*b^{1} | ~ πολ. τοι.: 157 *pc* | ~ ποι. πολ.: F K Π *pc* *L*lr^{2}z vg *Arm*^{0}⟧ — *txt*: 𝔓^{45} ℵBLΔ W **λ**-1278 **0274** *pc* *l*69^{1} *l*76^{1} *l*211^{1} *l*950^{1} *l*1127^{1} *l*1761^{1} (*om* 8: *S*s[c]⌒?) *C*' *Arm*' *Geo* **9** εντ.] βουλην‖Lk7₃₀: Δ **10** ειπ.] ενετειλατο λεγων‖p: 1574 | *om* σου^{2}‖10₁₉p Ex20₁₂ LXX: Θ λ1582 **ϕ**⟨124-346-983⟩ D 1342 *pc* *Arm* **11** εαν^{1}] ος αν‖p: 33(*om* ανθ.)-579 ΣΦ(εαν) A **12** τω π. η τη μ.] τω π. αυτου η τη μ. αυτου‖p Ex21₁₆: *Rpl* *L*vg^{1} *S* *C*s^{7}(η] και: s^{1}b^{2})' — τω π. αυτου η τη μ.‖10₇ 5₄₀: λ1 56 *L*flr^{2}z vg' — τω π. η τη μ. αυτου: 565 σ267-349-517 Γ 205 — *txt*: ℵBL-892 WΘ-28-700 **ϕ**⟨124⟩ D 1342 *L*vl'[ek] r^{1} **13** τη—η] δια την παραδοσιν υμ. ην‖p: 1071 | ● ~ πολ. τοι.: ℵ-579 700 **λ**⟨118⟩ **ϕ**'⟨124⟩-230-(*om* τοι.: 983-1689) σM 157 *pc* **14** παλ.] παντα: *Rpl* (~ τ. οχ. παντα: σ517) *L*f *S*' *C*s^{4} — παλ. παντα: *S*h^{m} — *om*‖**p**: 579 565 *pc* *L*c *C*s^{2}b^{2} — *txt*: ℵBLΔ-892 D *L*'[ek] *C*s^{1}b' | ελεγ.] ειπεν‖**p**: Θ-565-700 *L*an *S*s[c]pj *C* | ακουετε‖p: *Rpl* — *txt*: BL-892 Θ-565 D H *pc* | *om* μου‖**p**: ℵΔ σ945-1082-1223 *S*s[c] *C*b^{1} | *om* παν.‖**p**: ℵLΔ-892 *pc* *C*b *Geo*^{B} | συνιετε‖**p**: *Rpl* (συνιτε: σ1606 D) — *txt*: BLΔ-892 σ349-517 H 238 **15** εστ.^{2} *prm* εκεινα‖20p Mt: *Rpl* *l*184 *L*[ek] *S*,j — *prm* αυτα: *C*s — *txt*: ℵBLΔ-579(*om* εστ.^{2}) Θ σ517 1241 *C*b^{7} | εστ.^{2} τα κοι.] κοινοι‖20p Mt: *l*184 *S*s[c]ph^{m} **16** ● *om* 16: ℵBLΔ 28 **0274** 1342 (~: *l*48 *l*49) *C*s$^{2:8}$b$^{\langle 7\rangle}$ *Geo*^{1} | ει τις εχ.] ο εχων‖Mt**11**₁₅ **13**₄₃ Lk14₃₅: 1071 *L*vg^{1} *S*s[c]pj *C*s^{6}b^{7} **17** επερωτησαν‖Mt17₁₀ Lk20₂₁ 21₇: 33-579 Θ **λ**⟨118⟩ *pc* *L*c *S*s[c]pj *C*s *Arm*^{pc}

Mt15₁₁p. Mk7₁₈f. *cf.* ETh^{II} 14 (*transl.*): (*cf. ad 153.* Lk10₈) … *οὐ γὰρ τὸ εἰσερχόμενον εἰς τὸ στόμα ὑμῶν κοινώσει ὑμᾶς, ἀλλὰ τὸ ἐκπορευόμενον ἐκ τοῦ στόματος ὑμῶν ἔσται τὸ κοινοῦν ὑμᾶς.*

Mt15₁₃ *cf.* ETh^{II} 40 (*transl.*): *Λέγει Ἰησοῦς· ἄμπελος ἐφυτεύθη ἔξω τοῦ πατρός, καὶ μὴ οὖσα ἐστηριγμένη ἐκριζωθήσεται ἅμα ταῖς ῥίζαις αὐτῆς καὶ ἀπολεῖται.*

Mt15₁₄ *cf.* ETh^{II} 34 (*cf. ad 89.*)

τὴν παραβολὴν ταύτην. [16] ὁ δὲ εἶπεν· ἀκμὴν καὶ ὑμεῖς ἀσύνετοί ἐστε; [17] οὔπω νοεῖτε ὅτι πᾶν τὸ *cf. 133.* εἰσπορευόμενον εἰς τὸ στόμα εἰς τὴν κοιλίαν χωρεῖ καὶ εἰς ἀφεδρῶνα ἐκβάλλεται; [18] τὰ δὲ ἐκπορευόμενα ἐκ τοῦ στόματος ἐκ τῆς καρδίας ἐξέρχεται, κἀκεῖνα κοινοῖ τὸν ἄνθρωπον. [19] ἐκ γὰρ τῆς καρδίας ἐξέρχονται διαλογισμοὶ πονηροί, φόνοι, μοιχεῖαι, πορνεῖαι, κλοπαί, ψευδομαρτυρίαι, βλασφημίαι. [20] ταῦτά ἐστιν τὰ κοινοῦντα τὸν ἄνθρωπον· τὸ δὲ ἀνίπτοις χερσὶν φαγεῖν οὐ κοινοῖ τὸν ἄνθρωπον.

τὴν παραβολήν. [18] καὶ λέγει αὐτοῖς· οὕτως καὶ ὑμεῖς ἀσύνετοί ἐστε; οὐ νοεῖτε ὅτι πᾶν τὸ ἔξωθεν εἰσπορευόμενον εἰς τὸν ἄνθρωπον οὐ δύναται αὐτὸν κοινῶσαι, [19] ὅτι οὐκ εἰσπορεύεται αὐτοῦ εἰς τὴν καρδίαν ἀλλ' εἰς τὴν κοιλίαν, καὶ εἰς τὸν ἀφεδρῶνα ἐκπορεύεται, καθαρίζων πάντα τὰ βρώματα; [20] ἔλεγεν δὲ ὅτι τὸ ἐκ τοῦ ἀνθρώπου ἐκπορευόμενον, ἐκεῖνο κοινοῖ τὸν ἄνθρωπον. [21] ἔσωθεν γὰρ ἐκ τῆς καρδίας τῶν ἀνθρώπων οἱ διαλογισμοὶ οἱ κακοὶ ἐκπορεύονται, μοιχεῖαι, πορνεῖαι, φόνοι, [22] κλοπαί, πλεονεξίαι, πονηρίαι, δόλος, ἀσέλγεια, ὀφθαλμὸς πονηρός, βλασφημία, ὑπερηφανία, ἀφροσύνη· [23] πάντα ταῦτα τὰ πονηρὰ ἔσωθεν ἐκπορεύεται καὶ κοινοῖ τὸν ἄνθρωπον.

(116)

129. Die Kanaanitin. *The Syro-phoenician Woman.*

Matth 15 21–28

[21] Καὶ ἐξελθὼν ἐκεῖθεν ὁ Ἰησοῦς ἀνεχώρησεν εἰς τὰ μέρη Τύρου καὶ Σιδῶνος. [22] καὶ ἰδοὺ γυνὴ Χαναναία ἀπὸ τῶν ὁρίων ἐκείνων ἐξελθοῦσα ἔκραζεν λέγουσα· ἐλέησόν με, κύριε υἱὸς Δαυιδ· ἡ θυγά-

Mark 7 24–30

[24] Καὶ ἐκεῖθεν ἀναστὰς ἀπῆλθεν εἰς τὰ μεθόρια Τύρου. καὶ εἰσελθὼν εἰς οἰκίαν οὐδένα ἤθελεν γνῶναι, καὶ οὐκ ἠδυνάσθη λαθεῖν· [25] ἀκούσασα γὰρ γυνὴ περὶ αὐτοῦ, ἧς εἶχεν τὸ θυγά-

Mt 15,15 ● *om* ταυ.‖p: ℵBZ-892 700 λ1 Or *Cs*$^{5:6}$b *pc* (*L*ff^{1}q) *S*sc(p)h$^+$ (*C*')b^1 *Geo* **16** ειπ. + αυτω(-οις)‖(**p**): ΟΣ (σ1293-1391) 157 (1241) **17** ουπω] ● ου‖p 16 11: BZ-33 ϕ124-788 565 D Θ *L*⟨f?q⟩ *S*scp *Cs* | εισπ.] εισερχομ.‖11: B Θ *pc* | αφεδ.] τον α.‖p: ℵ-892 σ1391-1675 Γ Chr *Cs*b^1('$^{\langle 1\rangle}$τους αφεδρωνας) **18** κακ.] εκεινα‖p: D *L*cff^1 *S*p^1 *Cs*$^{1:5}$b⟨f⟩ *Geo*^{1} **19** εκ γαρ] εσωθεν εκ‖p: Eu | κλο. + πλεονεξιαι‖p: 1573 **22** ● εκραξεν: ℵ*Z ϕ Or {*L*'Au$^{1:2}$ Hil *S*sh Ef *Cs*^{6}b^1}^{1} — ● εκραυγασεν: *Rpl* (+ αυτω: ϕ174-230-*l*547) Bas {}^{1} — εκραυγαζεν: σM *pc* {}^{2} — κραζουσα *vel* κραυγ.: *Cs*^{2}b^1 — *txt*: ℵ^{c}B-892 ΟΣ-700 λ1-1582 D Θ *pc* {*Lk* cff^{1}q *S*cp *C*b'}^{2} | ● υιε *cf.* **8**29 Mk5 7 **Lk**8 28: *Rpl* Or — *txt*: B 700 σ945 D W Θ **0119**

Mk 7,17 τ. παρ.] ● περι της παραβολης‖10 10 Lk9 45 *etc.*: *Rpl* *S*,j *Cs*^{1} — *txt*: 𝔥 D 1342 *L*[ek],Au *Cs*^{7}b *Aeth* **18** ου^1] ουπω‖8 17 p.21 Mt: ℵLΔ-892 700 **λ** σ71-179-659-692 U **047** 1342 *pc* *l*18 *l*19 *l*48 *l*49 *l*184 *l*^{a1} *L*f vg^1 *S*h^m *Geo* | *om* εξω.‖**p**: Δ 1342 *S*s[c] | δυν. αυτ. κοι.] κοινοι αυτ.‖p: ℵ *S*[sc] (κοινωσει: *Cs*$^{1:7}$) **19** εισπο.] εισερχεται‖Mt 11: D | *om* τον‖p: Φ-700 **λ** σ517 S 1342 *pc* | εκπο.] εκβαλλεται‖**p**: ℵ Φ σ1194-1402-1424 **047** *al* *S*s[c]p — χωρει‖p: W **20** ∼ εκπο. εκ τ. αν.‖p Mt 11: σ179-267-827-1606 *pc* *S*s[c]p | εκει.] τουτο‖←: 1574 *L*ff^2(ταυτα) — αυτο: *C*b$^{\langle 1\rangle}$ — εκεινα‖p: D *L*'[ek](αυτα: c) **21** *om* των αν.‖**p**: **λ** *S*s[c] *Cs*$^{1:8}$ | κακ.] πονηροι‖**p**: 241 1346 | ∼ ● πορ. κλο. φο. μοι.: ℵBLΔ-579-892(∼ μοι. κλο. φο.) Θ **0274** 1342 (= 892) *C* — πορ. κλεμματα μοι. φο.: D — ∼ κλο. φο.: 33 W-565-700 **λ** ϕ124 *pc* *S*p — ∼ κλο. πορ. φο.: *L*vl'[ek n]r^1 — *txt*: *Rpl* *L*fr^2 vg *S*' *Arm* *Aeth* **23** *om* παντα‖p: L-892 *L*Au | *om* τα πον.‖**p**: 565-700 **λ**⟨118⟩ | και] κακεινα‖Mt 18 p: ℵ 238 *L*ff^2(et haec) **24** και εκ.] ● εκειθεν δε(*om*): 𝔥' 1241 1342 *S*(p)h^m *C*'(b^1) — και: W *L*r^1 *S*s[c] — *txt*: *Rpl* (κακ-: 33-579) *L*[ek] *S*h^{t}j *Arm* *Geo*^{2} | ∼ ανασ. εκ.‖p: D *L*fff^{2}qr^1 vg^1 *Geo*^{1} | εξηλθεν‖p: LΔ | μεθ.] ● ορια‖10 1 **p** Mt 22: 𝔥[33] WΘ-28-565-700 **λ**⟨118⟩ **ϕ**⟨124⟩ σ1402 D 1342 *pc* Or — μερη‖**p**: σ349 | ● Τ. + και Σιδωνος‖**p**: *Rpl* *L*'[ek] *S*' *C* — *txt*: LΔ WΘ-28-565 D Or *L*abff^{2}inr^1 Amst *S*s[c]j **25** ακ. γαρ γυ.] ● αλλ ευθυς ακ. γυ.: 𝔥 1342 *L*f *S*h^{m}j(∼ περι αυ. γυ.) *Cs*b^{10} — και ευ. ακ. γυ.: *C*b^{10}(ηκουσεν: b^1 *Δ*a) — ευ. γαρ ηκουσεν γυ.: *S*p — γυ. δε(γαρ) ευθεως ως ακ.: D *L*(vl'[ek]) g^2(*om* ευ.) (vg')^2(^{1}δε + τις) — και ακ. γυ.: *L*q(∼ περι αυ. γυ.) *S*s[c] — *txt*: *Rpl* (η γυ.: **ϕ**⟨124-543-983⟩ σM) *L*an *S*h^t (ηκουσεν: *Arm* *Geo*; *om* γαρ: *Arm* *Geo*^{1}) | γυ. + τις‖5 25: 700 (*L*vg^1) *S*p

Matth:

τηρ μου κακῶς δαιμονίζεται. 23 ὁ δὲ οὐκ ἀπεκρίθη αὐτῇ λόγον. καὶ προσελθόντες οἱ μαθηταὶ αὐτοῦ ἠρώτουν αὐτὸν λέγοντες· ἀπόλυσον αὐτήν, ὅτι κράζει ὄπισθεν ἡμῶν.

24 ὁ δὲ ἀποκριθεὶς εἶπεν· οὐκ ἀπεστάλην εἰ μὴ εἰς τὰ πρόβατα τὰ ἀπολωλότα οἴκου Ισραηλ. 25 ἡ δὲ ἐλθοῦσα προσεκύνει αὐτῷ λέγουσα· κύριε, βοήθει μοι. 26 ὁ δὲ ἀποκριθεὶς εἶπεν· οὐκ ἔστιν καλὸν λαβεῖν τὸν ἄρτον τῶν τέκνων καὶ βαλεῖν τοῖς κυναρίοις. 27 ἡ δὲ εἶπεν· ναί, κύριε· καὶ γὰρ τὰ κυνάρια ἐσθίει ἀπὸ τῶν ψιχίων τῶν πιπτόντων ἀπὸ τῆς τραπέζης τῶν κυρίων αὐτῶν. 28 τότε ἀποκριθεὶς ὁ Ἰησοῦς εἶπεν αὐτῇ· ὦ γύναι, μεγάλη σου ἡ πίστις· γενηθήτω σοι ὡς θέλεις. καὶ ἰάθη ἡ θυγάτηρ αὐτῆς ἀπὸ τῆς ὥρας ἐκείνης.

10 6 (70.): πορεύεσθε δὲ μᾶλλον πρὸς τὰ πρόβατα τὰ ἀπολωλότα οἴκου Ισραηλ.

Mark:

τριον αὐτῆς πνεῦμα ἀκάθαρτον, ἐλθοῦσα προσέπεσεν πρὸς τοὺς πόδας αὐτοῦ· 26 ἡ δὲ γυνὴ ἦν Ἑλληνίς, Συροφοινίκισσα τῷ γένει· καὶ ἠρώτα αὐτὸν ἵνα τὸ δαιμόνιον ἐκβάλῃ ἐκ τῆς θυγατρὸς αὐτῆς. 27 καὶ ἔλεγεν αὐτῇ· ἄφες πρῶτον χορτασθῆναι τὰ τέκνα· οὐ γὰρ καλόν ἐστιν λαβεῖν τὸν ἄρτον τῶν τέκνων καὶ τοῖς κυναρίοις βαλεῖν. 28 ἡ δὲ ἀπεκρίθη καὶ λέγει αὐτῷ· ναί, κύριε· καὶ τὰ κυνάρια ὑποκάτω τῆς τραπέζης ἐσθίουσιν ἀπὸ τῶν ψιχίων τῶν παιδίων. 29 καὶ εἶπεν αὐτῇ· διὰ τοῦτον τὸν λόγον ὕπαγε, ἐξελήλυθεν ἐκ τῆς θυγατρός σου τὸ δαιμόνιον. 30 καὶ ἀπελθοῦσα εἰς τὸν οἶκον αὐτῆς εὗρεν τὸ παιδίον βεβλημένον ἐπὶ τὴν κλίνην καὶ τὸ δαιμόνιον ἐξεληλυθός.

130. Heilung vieler Kranker (Matth), — eines Taubstummen (Mark).

(117) ***The Healing of Many Sick Persons (Matth), — of the Deaf Mute (Mark).***

Matth 15 29–31

29 Καὶ μεταβὰς ἐκεῖθεν ὁ Ἰησοῦς ἦλθεν παρὰ τὴν θάλασσαν τῆς Γαλιλαίας, καὶ ἀναβὰς εἰς τὸ ὄρος ἐκάθητο ἐκεῖ. 30 καὶ προσῆλθον αὐτῷ ὄχλοι πολλοὶ ἔχοντες μεθ' ἑαυτῶν χωλούς, τυφλούς, κωφούς,

Mark 7 31–37

31 Καὶ πάλιν ἐξελθὼν ἐκ τῶν ὁρίων Τύρου ἦλθεν διὰ Σιδῶνος εἰς τὴν θάλασσαν τῆς Γαλιλαίας ἀνὰ μέσον τῶν ὁρίων Δεκαπόλεως. 32 καὶ φέρουσιν αὐτῷ κωφὸν

Mt 15,22 κακ.] δεινως ‖86: λ1-1582 Or *La* **26** ειπ. + αυτη‖p: 477 *pc* *L*aff^{1} *S*scp *Cs*$^{4+1v:9}$ | ∼ καλ. εστ. ‖p: 544 σ1010-1207 *al l*309 *Geo* **27** *om* γαρ: B *Le* *S*spj *C*sb^{1} | εσθιουσιν‖p: D **29** παρα] εις‖p: σ1424 **30** χω.—κυ.] ● χω. κυ. τυ. κω.: B 1355 *Cs*^{3} — χω. τυ. κυ.(*om*) κω.: ℵ 1604 (σ1207 D 472) *pc* *L*abff^{2} *S*s — τυ. χω. κω. κυ.: Or — κω. χω. τυ. κυ.(*om*): L (O)Σ σM-1402 W Δ *pc* *L*'⟨vg^{2}⟩ (mutos] multos: g^{2} vg^{1} Au^{1})^{1} *S*h — κω. τυ. χω. κυ.: 33-892 λ1582 1241 *l*184 Or *L*(*om* κυ.: ek) (ff^{1})z vg^{2} Au^{1} *C*b^{1} *Aeth* — *txt*: *Rpl* *L*f *S*cp *Cs*^{4}b'

Mk 7,25 ● εισελθ.‖24: ℵLΔ(+ και)-579-892 700 σ115 1342 *L*'[ek]⟨aq⟩ | πρ. τ. πο. αυτ.] αυτω‖p: 28 λ⟨118⟩ ϕ⟨124⟩ *S*s[c] *Arm* **27** και ελ.] ο δε Ιησους(*om*) ειπεν‖p: *Rpl* (Bas) *L*f *S*h(j^{c}) *Geo*^{2}(^{1} και ο Ι. ειπ.) — και λεγει: Θ-700 D *L*a(ειπ.: g^{2}r^{2}30) (+ ο Ι.: q *S*s[c]p, *et om* και: *S*s) — *txt*: 𝔋 1342 *L*'[ek] *S*j^{abf} *C*s(ειπ.)b | *om* αυτη‖p: 28 λ⟨118⟩ 90 Bas *L*c *C*b^{1} | ● ∼ εστ. καλ.‖p: 𝔋[33] Θ-544-700 λ⟨118⟩ ϕ124 σ517-1402 D 1342 *al l*48 *l*49 *L*[ek] *S*h | ∼ βαλ. τ. κυ.‖p: *Rpl* Bas *L*'[ek] *S*,j — *txt*: 𝔓^{45} ℵB-892 Θ-28 λ⟨118⟩ *pc* *L*q **28** *om* αυτω‖p: 𝔓^{45v} 28-565 ϕ⟨124-346⟩ *L*vg^{1} *S*j *Cs*$^{1:8}$ | και^{2} + γαρ‖p: *Rpl* *L*aflqr^{2} vg *S*h *Geo*' — αλλα και: D *L*vl'[ek] r^{1} — *txt*: 𝔓^{45} 𝔋⟨L⟩ WΘ-28-565-700 ϕ⟨124-346-543⟩ H 1201 *l*9 *l*10 *l*12 *l*49 Bas *S*'j *C* *Geo*^{A} | ∼ εσ. υποκ. τ. τρ.‖p: ℵ(*αποκατω) 1342 1547 *L*g^{2} *Cs*^{4}b — ∼ εσ.—ψιχ.(+ των) υπ. τ. τρ.‖p: *Cs*^{1}(^{2}) | εσθιει‖p: *Rpl* Bas — *txt*: 𝔋 WΘ-28-565-700-1071 λ ϕ⟨124-983⟩ σ179-517-659 D 1241 1342 *pc l*18 *l*19 *l*49 | ψιχ. + των πιπτοντων απο τ. τρ.‖p: 1071 157 *pc* *S*s[c](*om* υποκ. τ. τρ.) Ef — + των πιπτ.(+ εκ)‖p: 485(*om* τ. παι.) (1241 *Cs*$^{4:7}$) *Aeth* — + τ. τρ.‖p: ϕ1689 1012(απο τ. τρ.) **30** το παι. βεβ.] την θυγατερα(+ αυτης) βεβλημενην‖p 25.29: 𝔓^{45} *Rpl* (Θ-565-700 *L*afnq *S* *Cs*) *Arm* — *txt*: 𝔋 σ179-517-1194 1241 1342 *pc* *L*'[ek] *S*j *C*b
31 ηλ. δια Σ.] και Σ. ηλ.‖Mt15 21: 𝔓^{45} *Rpl* (*om*: 579) *L*q *S* *Cs*^{4} — *txt*: 𝔋' Θ-565-700 D 1342 *L*'[ek] *S*j *Cs*^{5}b *Aeth* | εις] παρα‖p: σ517-1194 *pc*

Matth: κυλλούς, καὶ ἑτέρους πολλούς, καὶ ἔρριψαν αὐτοὺς παρὰ τοὺς πόδας αὐτοῦ· καὶ ἐθεράπευσεν αὐτούς· [31] ὥστε τὸν ὄχλον θαυμάσαι βλέποντας κωφοὺς λαλοῦντας, κυλλοὺς ὑγιεῖς καὶ χωλοὺς περιπατοῦντας καὶ τυφλοὺς βλέποντας· καὶ ἐδόξασαν τὸν θεὸν Ἰσραηλ.

Mark: καὶ μογιλάλον, καὶ παρακαλοῦσιν αὐτὸν ἵνα ἐπιθῇ αὐτῷ τὴν χεῖρα. [33] καὶ ἀπολαβόμενος αὐτὸν ἀπὸ τοῦ ὄχλου κατ' ἰδίαν ἔβαλεν τοὺς δακτύλους αὐτοῦ εἰς τὰ ὦτα αὐτοῦ καὶ πτύσας ἥψατο τῆς γλώσσης αὐτοῦ, [34] καὶ ἀναβλέψας εἰς τὸν οὐρανὸν ἐστέναξεν, καὶ λέγει αὐτῷ· εφφαθα, ὅ ἐστιν διανοίχθητι. [35] καὶ ἠνοίχθησαν αὐτοῦ αἱ ἀκοαί, καὶ ἐλύθη ὁ δεσμὸς τῆς γλώσσης αὐτοῦ, καὶ ἐλάλει ὀρθῶς. [36] καὶ διεστείλατο αὐτοῖς ἵνα μηδενὶ λέγωσιν· ὅσον δὲ αὐτοῖς διεστέλλετο, αὐτοὶ μᾶλλον περισσότερον ἐκήρυσσον. [37] καὶ ὑπερπερισσῶς ἐξεπλήσσοντο λέγοντες· καλῶς πάντα πεποίηκεν, καὶ τοὺς κωφοὺς ποιεῖ ἀκούειν καὶ τοὺς ἀλάλους λαλεῖν.

(118) *131.* Die Speisung der Viertausend. *The Feeding of the Four Thousand.* [*125.*]

Matth 15 32–39

[32] Ὁ δὲ Ἰησοῦς προσκαλεσάμενος τοὺς μαθητὰς αὐτοῦ εἶπεν· σπλαγχνίζομαι ἐπὶ τὸν ὄχλον, ὅτι ἤδη ἡμέραι τρεῖς προσμένουσίν μοι καὶ οὐκ ἔχουσιν τί φάγωσιν· καὶ ἀπολῦσαι αὐτοὺς νήστεις οὐ θέλω, μήποτε ἐκλυθῶσιν ἐν τῇ ὁδῷ. [33] καὶ λέγουσιν αὐτῷ οἱ μαθηταί· πόθεν ἡμῖν ἐν ἐρημίᾳ ἄρτοι τοσοῦτοι ὥστε χορτάσαι ὄχλον τοσοῦτον; [34] καὶ λέγει αὐτοῖς ὁ Ἰησοῦς· πόσους

Mark 8 1–10

[1] Ἐν ἐκείναις ταῖς ἡμέραις πάλιν πολλοῦ ὄχλου ὄντος καὶ μὴ ἐχόντων τί φάγωσιν, προσκαλεσάμενος τοὺς μαθητὰς λέγει αὐτοῖς· [2] σπλαγχνίζομαι ἐπὶ τὸν ὄχλον, ὅτι ἤδη ἡμέραι τρεῖς προσμένουσίν μοι καὶ οὐκ ἔχουσιν τί φάγωσιν· [3] καὶ ἐὰν ἀπολύσω αὐτοὺς νήστεις εἰς οἶκον αὐτῶν, ἐκλυθήσονται ἐν τῇ ὁδῷ· καί τινες αὐτῶν ἀπὸ μακρόθεν ἥκασιν. [4] καὶ ἀπεκρίθησαν αὐτῷ οἱ μαθηταὶ αὐτοῦ· πόθεν τούτους δυνήσεταί τις ὧδε χορτάσαι ἄρτων ἐπ' ἐρημίας; [5] καὶ ἐπηρώτα αὐτούς· πόσους ἔχετε

Mt 15,30 αυτους^2 + παντας‖12 15 8 16: σ945 D *L*bcff^{2}g^{1}r^1 *C*s$^{3:8}$b^1 *Δ*a md me n^{HgHrs} p **31** ● τους οχλους‖30 9 33: *Rpl* Or^1 *L*' *S* *C*s^{3}b' — *txt*: ℵC-33-892 OΦ-700 λ1-1582 **φ σ**⟨954⟩-349-1010-1293 D U Δ Θ 1241 Or^1 *L*vg^1 *C*s^{6}b^6 *Arm* **32** *om* αυτου‖p: ℵ 700 W Θ *La* Hil *Geo*^{1} | ειπ. + αυτοις‖p 14 16p: ℵ^{c}C 544 σ1010-1293 K Π 157 *pc* *S*cph^{Brsm}j *C*sb⟨1⟩ **33** μα. + αυτου‖p 32 Mk6 35: *Rpl* *L*cfq *S* *C*s^3 — *txt*: ℵB-892 700 λ1582 φ124-788 σ1010-1293 *pc* *L*' *S*j *C*s^{4}b *Arm* | ερη.] ερημω τοπω‖p 14 15p: C σ1010-1293 *pc* *S*c *C*b

Mk 7,32 ● *om* και^2: 𝔓^{45} *Rpl* *S* *C* *Arm*^{pc} — *txt*: ℵBΔ WΘ-565-700 D **0131** 1574 PsAth Cat^{ox} Vic^A *L*[ek] *S*j *Arm*' *Geo*^{2} *Aeth* *Δ*⟨a⟩ | παρεκαλουν‖6 56: 33 **0131** vl'[ek]⟨al⟩ vg⟨5⟩ *S* *Arm*^{pc} | επιθη—χει.] αυτου αψηται‖8 22: 213 *Δ*me | τας χειρας‖5 23 8 23.25 Mt19 13.15p Lk13 13: ℵ*Δ-33-579 NΣ σ179-827 1342 1555 *La* *C*b^2 **33** επιλαβο.‖8 23 Lk14 4: 700 **λ**⟨1⟩ φ983-1689 σ827-1207-1402-1606 E Γ **0131** 157 *l*184 **34** ανεστε.‖8 12: Σ **φ**-*l*547 D **0131** **35** ● και^1 + ευθεως‖14 2p 5 29 10 52p *etc.*: 𝔓^{45} *Rpl* *L*'[ek] *S* *C*s^5 *Δ*' — + τοτε: *S*j — *txt*: 𝔇 D **0131 0274** 1342 *L*abff^{2}iqr^1 *C*s^{3}b *Δ*i^V | ● και^2 + ευθυς‖←: 𝔓^{45v} ℵLΔ-892 **0274** 1342 *S*j | ορθ. + ωστε παντας εξιστασθαι‖2 12: 472 1515 *La* **36** ενετειλατο‖Mt17 9: Δ-579 | μηδ. + μηδεν‖1 44: 28-565-700 D *L*q | λεγ.] ειπωσιν‖1 44p Mt16 20: *Rpl* — *txt*: 𝔓^{45} 𝔇⟨Δ⟩ WΘ-28-565 **0131** 1342 — + περι αυτου‖8 30: 892 σ517 | ενετελλετο‖Mt17 9: Δ(-ελε-) **37** ● *om* τους^2: 𝔇⟨579⟩ σ1194 *pc* — *txt*: *Rpl* (*om* τ. αλαλ.: W-28) **8,1** οντ.] συναχθεντος‖5 21 4 1 Mt13 2: **0131**^{v} 1093 | μα. + αυτου‖p: *Rpl* *L*g^{2}r^{2}30 vg^1? *S*'j *C*sb^1 — *txt*: ℵLΔ-892 NΣΦ-28 **λ**⟨118⟩ D **0131** *L*'[ek] *S*h *C*b' | λεγ.] ειπεν‖**p**: φ124 σ827-1402 1241 *La* *Aeth* | *om* αυτοις‖p: W *L*vg^2 **2** τω οχλω‖6 34 Mt14 14 Lk7 13: WΘ-565 **3** εαν—εκλυ.] απολυσαι αυτ. νηστ.(+ εις οικον) ου θελω μη εκλυθωσιν‖p: Θ-565(μη] μηποτε)-700 (D) *l*184(*prm* εαν *et* = 565) *L*[ek] b(aff^{2}iqr^{1v})z *S*j | *om* εις οικ. αυ.‖**p**: (Θ-565-700) σ1402 1515(εκλυθωσιν) (*l*184 *L*bz *S*j) *C*s$^{1:8}$ | ηκ.] ● εισιν: BLΔ-892 *C*s^2 — ησαν: *C*b — *txt*: *Rpl* (*om*: φ346) *L*[ek] *S*,j *C*s^5 **4** ● αυτου + οτι: BLΔ-579-892 σ115 1342 — *txt*: *Rpl* *L*[ek] *S*,j | τοσουτους‖p: Θ-28-565-700 *La* | *om* ωδε‖**p**: 565-1071 φ69 σ517 D H 1342 *pc* *L*vl[ek]⟨aflr^2⟩r^{1v} *C*s$^{1:7(+1v)}$ *Geo*^{B} **5** επη.] ● ηρωτα: 𝔇⟨33⟩ W(-ησεν) 1342 — *txt*: *Rpl* (-ησαν: σM 998) | ποσ. + ωδε‖Mt14 17: W — αρτ. + ωδε‖←: *C*s$^{5:9}$ | ∼ αρ. εχ.‖**p** 6 38: ℵ-33-579 WΘΦ-28-565-700 φ13-124 σ349-517-1402 D *al* *L*[ek] ἄρτους ἔχετε; οἱ δὲ εἶπον· ἑπτά, καὶ ὀλίγα ἰχθύδια. [35] καὶ παραγγείλας τῷ ὄχλῳ ἀναπεσεῖν ἐπὶ τὴν γῆν, [36] ἔλαβεν τοὺς ἑπτὰ ἄρτους καὶ τοὺς ἰχθύας, καὶ εὐχαριστήσας ἔκλασεν καὶ ἐδίδου τοῖς μαθηταῖς, οἱ δὲ μαθηταὶ τοῖς ὄχλοις.

[37] καὶ ἔφαγον πάντες καὶ ἐχορτάσθησαν, καὶ τὸ περισσεῦον τῶν κλασμάτων ἦραν, ἑπτὰ σπυρίδας πλήρεις. [38] οἱ δὲ ἐσθίοντες ἦσαν τετρακισχίλιοι ἄνδρες χωρὶς γυναικῶν καὶ παιδίων. [39] καὶ ἀπολύσας τοὺς ὄχλους ἐνέβη εἰς τὸ πλοῖον, καὶ ἦλθεν εἰς τὰ ὅρια Μαγαδαν.

ἄρτους; οἱ δὲ εἶπαν· ἑπτά. *125.*

[6] καὶ παραγγέλλει τῷ ὄχλῳ ἀναπεσεῖν ἐπὶ τῆς γῆς· καὶ λαβὼν τοὺς ἑπτὰ ἄρτους, εὐχαριστήσας ἔκλασεν καὶ ἐδίδου τοῖς μαθηταῖς αὐτοῦ ἵνα παρατιθῶσιν, καὶ παρέθηκαν τῷ ὄχλῳ. [7] καὶ εἶχαν ἰχθύδια ὀλίγα· καὶ αὐτὰ εὐλογήσας εἶπεν παραθεῖναι. [8] καὶ ἔφαγον καὶ ἐχορτάσθησαν, καὶ ἦραν περισσεύματα κλασμάτων, ἑπτὰ σπυρίδας. [9] ἦσαν δὲ ὡς τετρακισχίλιοι. καὶ ἀπέλυσεν αὐτούς. [10] καὶ εὐθὺς ἐμβὰς εἰς τὸ πλοῖον μετὰ τῶν μαθητῶν αὐτοῦ ἦλθεν εἰς τὰ μέρη Δαλμανουθα.

Mt 15,35 παραγγ. ... [36]ελαβεν] εκελευσεν ... [36]και λαβων ‖ p Mk6 39.41 Lk9 14.16: *Rpl L*' *S*h — *txt*: 𝔖⟨L⟩ 1604 λ1-1582 **ϕ**'(και ελαβ.: 346) D Θ Or *Lek* z | τοις οχλοις ‖ 14 19: *Rpl Lek* af *Cs*^{2}b' — τους οχλους ‖ ←: C 544 ϕ174 **σ**-7-267-349-1010-1207-1293 U *pc* Chr *Ld* — *txt*: 𝔖⟨L⟩ 1604 **λ**-1582 **ϕ** D Θ 157 *pc* Or *L*' *Cs*^{6}b^{5} | αναπ.] ανακλιθηναι ‖ ← Mk6 39: σ990 **36** *om* επτα ‖ Jo6 11: 892 σ659 *pc Lek* acff^{2}g^{1} *Cs*$^{1:8}$ | *om* και τ. ιχ. ‖ p Jo ←: L σ659 | τους^{2} + δυο ‖ 14 19 Mk6 41 Lk9 16: ℵ ϕ124-174-788 σ990 *pc* *L*ff^{1}q *Geo*^{B} | *om* και^{2} ‖ p: *Rpl L*ff^{1} vg^{2} *S*h — *txt*: 𝔖⟨L⟩ 700-1604 λ1-1582 **ϕ**'⟨346⟩(και ευλογησας ευχ.: 788) **σ**⟨954⟩-349-659-1010-1293 D Θ *pc L*' *S*'j | εδωκεν ‖ 14 19 Jo6 11: *Rpl L S C Arm Aeth* — *txt*: 𝔖⟨L⟩ 700-1604 λ1582 **ϕ** D Θ 157 *pc S*j *Geo* | μαθηταις + αυτου ‖ p Mk6 41: *Rpl L*' *S Cs*^{7}b^{1} *Aeth* — *txt*: 𝔖⟨L⟩ 700-1604 λ1-22-1582 **ϕ**-*l*547 D Θ *pc* Chr *L*cff^{1}g^{2} *S*j *Cs*^{1}b' *Arm* | τω οχλω ‖ p Lk9 16: *Rpl Cs*^{5} — τω λαω: *L*' — *txt*: 𝔖 700-1604 λ1-1582 **ϕ** σM-7 K Π *pc l*184 *L*e[k] fff^{1} *Cs*^{3}b **37** *om* πα. ‖ p: σ1194 | ~ ηρ. τ. περ. τ. κλ. ‖ p 14 20 p: *Rpl L*fff^{1}q *S Geo*^{2} — *txt*: B-33-892 700 λ1-1582 D Θ *L*' *S*j *Geo*^{1} *Aeth* | το—κλα.] των περισσευσαντων κλα. ‖ Jo6 12: 472 1200(-ευοντων) 1375 | περισσευσαν ‖ Lk9 17 Jo ←: 247 — -ευμα ‖ p: 1555 **38** τετ. ανδ.] ● ως(ωσει) τετ. ανδ. ‖ p (Lk9 14): B-33 λ1-22-1582 **ϕ**-230 σ1293 Θ (157 *pc*) *pc S*hj *Cs*$^{4(+1?)}$ *Arm* — ανδ. ωσει(*om*) τετ. ‖ 14 21 Lk9 14: ℵ-892(ως) 1604 σ(1010)-1402 *pc* (*pc*) *L*ff^{1} — *txt*: *Rpl L*'Au *S*s(*om* ανδ.)cp *Cs*^{1}b **39** *om* το ‖ 14 22 Mk4 1: λ1 **ϕ** σ160-945-990-1010-1207-1223-1293 *C*b^{1}

Mk 8,6 παραγγειλας ‖ p: Θ-565 | της γ.] την γην ‖ p: 33-(εις τ. γ.: 579 1342) **λ** ϕ983-1689 σ115 *pc l*260 *L*[ek] | ευχ.] και ευχ. ‖ p Mt26 27.26: C-892 **λ**⟨1⟩-1278 σM-71-692 D S V Ω *pm L*af *Aeth* | τοις μα. αυ.] αυτοις ‖ 14 22f. Mt26 27 Lk22 19: W | *om* αυτου ‖ p Mt26 26: 579 ϕ983-1689 σ1424-1675 *L*s *Cs*$^{1:7}$b$^{\langle 8\rangle}$ **7** 7] και των δυο ιχθυων εμερισεν πασιν ‖ 6 41: 1574 | αυτα ευλ.] ευλ. ‖ 14 22 Mt ←: *Rpl l*76 *l*313 *l*1642 *l*1761 — ● ευλ. αυτα ‖ Lk9 16: 𝔖⟨33-579⟩C Θ-1071 σ349 1241 1342 *S*j *C*{}^{1}b *Aeth* — ευχαριστησας ‖ 6 p Lk22 19: D *pc L*q — ταυτα ευλ.: A F K Y Π *mu Cs*^{4} {}^{2} — *txt*: NWΣΦ-28-565 **λ ϕ** σM-1402 **0131** *al l*^{pl} *L*'[ek] *S* {*Cs*^{4}}^{1} *Got* {*Δ*i^{V} l^{AD} me}^{2} | παραθ.] ● παρατιθεναι ‖ 6 6 41: ℵ^{a}BLΔ-892 σ115 D — ● παρεθηκεν *et om* ειπεν: ℵ* — παραθετε: C-33-579 1342 — παρατεθηναι ‖ 5 43: Φ ϕ124(-τεθεναι) A 472 *l*18 *l*19 — *txt*: *Rpl* | παραθ.] ● *prm* και ταυτα(αυτα): ℵ^{a}BC LΔ-(33-579)-892 σ115 A Y Π (472) 1342 *pc* (*L*q) — *prm* και αυτους εκελευσεν: D — + αυτα: 1071 ϕ346 σ27-692-1194 V 157 482 *S*p *Cs*^{4} — + και αυτα(ταυτα): *Rpl* (Φ *S*h *Cs*^{4}b) — *txt*: (ℵ*) NWΣΘ-28-565 **λ**⟨118⟩ ϕ124 σM^{m}-71 **0131** *pc l*48 *L*'[ek] *S*' | παρ./(τ)αυτα + αυτοις ‖ 6 41: NΣ *L*vg^{2} *S*s[c]j *C* *Geo*^{2} — + τω οχλω ‖ 6 Lk9 16: σM^{m} *l*48 **8** και εφ.] ● εφ. δε: *Rpl S*h *Cs* — *txt*: 𝔖C WΘ-565-700 **λ** D 1342 *L*[ek] *S*'j *C*b$^{\langle 1\rangle}$ | εφ. + παντες ‖ p 6 42 Mt14 20: ℵ-33-579 *pc L*vg^{1} *Geo*^{A} — εχορ. + παντες ‖ Lk9 17: 1071 σM K Π *pc* | περ. κλα.] τα περ.(+ των) κλα. ‖ p Lk9 16 Jo6 12: ℵC (Θ 1241) 1342 *pc* (*C*b$^{\langle 1\rangle}$) — το περισσευσαν των κλα. ‖ p Lk9 17: 700 — περισσευσαντα κλασματα ‖ Jo ←: 33 1555 *Cs*(*prm* τα) | σπυ. + πληρεις ‖ **p** 19 Mt ←: 33 W-1071 **ϕ**1342 *pc l*18 *L*ir^{1} vg^{3} Pau^{N} *Cs*$^{6:8}$b^{1} *Geo*^{1} **9** δε + οι φαγοντες ‖ p 6 44 Mt14 21: *Rpl L S*,j *Cs*^{5}b^{6} — *txt*: 𝔖 σ517 1241 1342 *l*18 *l*19 *l*49 *l*150 *Cs*^{1}b' *Δ*me | ως] ωσει ‖ Mt ← Lk9 14: **λ**⟨1⟩ σM *pc l*48 — *om* ‖ 6 14: ℵ σ827 *l*184 *Lk*[e] z *C* | τετ. + ανδρες ‖ p 6 44 Mt ← Lk ←: Δ 1071 G 253 *L*vl⟨k[e] flr^{2}⟩ vg^{2} *Cs*$^{1:4}$ **10** εμβ. ... ηλ.] ενεβη ... και ηλ. ‖ p: WΘ-565-700 D(ανε-) *Lk*[e] afq | ● *om* το ‖ 4 1 p Mt8 23 9 1 *etc.*: L-33-579 W-28-544-700 **λ ϕ** 1342 *l*184 | τα με.] τα ορια ‖ p: Σ σ517 D U *pc L*(finem: k[e]) cfz *Arm*^{0} — τα ορη ‖ 13 14 p: N-1071 {} — το ορος ‖ ←: W-28 {*S*s[c]} | Δαλ.] Μαγεδα (*vel sim.*) ‖ p: 𝔓^{45v} 28-565 D(Μελαγαδα) Eu *L*vl[e]⟨flqr^{2}⟩r^{1} Au *S*s[c] — Μαγδαλα ‖ p: Θ **λ**⟨*spat.*: 118⟩ **ϕ**⟨124⟩ *pc S*j *Geo*^{2}

(119) **132.** Die Zeichenforderung der Pharisäer. *The Pharisees Seek a Sign.* **100.**

Matth 16 1–4

1 Καὶ προσελθόντες οἱ Φαρισαῖοι καὶ Σαδδουκαῖοι πειράζοντες ἐπηρώτησαν αὐτὸν σημεῖον ἐκ τοῦ οὐρανοῦ ἐπιδεῖξαι αὐτοῖς. 2 ὁ δὲ ἀποκριθεὶς εἶπεν αὐτοῖς· ὀψίας γενομένης λέγετε· εὐδία, πυρράζει γὰρ ὁ οὐρανός· 3 καὶ πρωΐ· σήμερον χειμών, πυρράζει γὰρ στυγνάζων ὁ οὐρανός. τὸ μὲν πρόσωπον τοῦ οὐρανοῦ γινώσκετε διακρίνειν, τὰ δὲ σημεῖα τῶν καιρῶν οὐ δύνασθε; 4 γενεὰ πονηρὰ καὶ μοιχαλὶς σημεῖον ἐπιζητεῖ, καὶ σημεῖον οὐ δοθήσεται αὐτῇ εἰ μὴ τὸ σημεῖον Ἰωνᾶ. καὶ καταλιπὼν αὐτοὺς ἀπῆλθεν.

Mark 8 11–13

11 Καὶ ἐξῆλθον οἱ Φαρισαῖοι καὶ ἤρξαντο συζητεῖν αὐτῷ, ζητοῦντες παρ' αὐτοῦ σημεῖον ἀπὸ τοῦ οὐρανοῦ, πειράζοντες αὐτόν. 12 καὶ ἀναστενάξας τῷ πνεύματι αὐτοῦ λέγει·

12 54–56 (174.): … ὅταν ἴδητε νεφέλην ἀνατέλλουσαν ἐπὶ δυσμῶν, εὐθέως λέγετε ὅτι ὄμβρος ἔρχεται, καὶ γίνεται οὕτως· 55 καὶ ὅταν νότον πνέοντα, λέγετε ὅτι καύσων ἔσται, καὶ γίνεται. 56 ὑποκριταί, τὸ πρόσωπον τῆς γῆς καὶ τοῦ οὐρανοῦ οἴδατε δοκιμάζειν, τὸν δὲ καιρὸν τοῦτον πῶς οὐ δοκιμάζετε;

τί ἡ γενεὰ αὕτη **100.** ζητεῖ σημεῖον; ἀμὴν λέγω ὑμῖν, εἰ δοθήσεται τῇ γενεᾷ ταύτῃ σημεῖον. 13 καὶ ἀφεὶς αὐτοὺς πάλιν ἐμβὰς ἀπῆλθεν εἰς τὸ πέραν.

(120) **133.** Vom Sauerteig der Pharisäer. *The Leaven of the Pharisees.*

Matth 16 5–12

5 Καὶ ἐλθόντες οἱ μαθηταὶ εἰς τὸ πέραν ἐπελάθοντο ἄρτους λαβεῖν. 6 ὁ δὲ

Mark 8 14–21

14 Καὶ ἐπελάθοντο λαβεῖν ἄρτους, καὶ εἰ μὴ ἕνα ἄρτον οὐκ εἶχον μεθ' ἑαυτῶν ἐν τῷ πλοίῳ.

12 1 (169.): Ἐν οἷς ἐπισυναχθεισῶν τῶν μυριάδων τοῦ ὄχλου, ὥστε κατα-

Mt 16,1 πει. + αυτον (*et om* αυτον 1b) ‖ p 193: σ1402 (D 1396) *Lc Sscp C* **2** ● *om* οψ.—^{3}δυνασθε ‖ 1239p Mk: ℵBX ϕ⟨346-983⟩-174 σ267 V Y Γ 157 *pc* Or *L*Hi *Ssc C*' *Arm*' — *txt*: *Rpl* CAp Chr Eu Eutha Thi *L*,Hil Iuv *S*' *C*b^{11} *Arm*^{0} | ουρ. + και γινεται ουτως ‖ Lk: K **3** ουρανος + υποκριται ‖ Lk: *Rpl* (*cf. ad* 2) *L*e[k] bff$^{1.2}$g^1 vg^2 *S*p — *txt*: C*L-33-892 1604 λ1-22-1582 ϕ983-1689 **σ**-349 D W ΔΘ *pc L*' *S*h *C*b^{11} *Arm*^{0} *Aeth* | *om* μεν ‖ p: σ71-945-1194 F *pc C*b^{11} | καιρ. + πως ‖ p 1611: ΟΣ | δυν.] δοκιμαζετε ‖ p: L — δυν. δοκιμαζειν(-σαι) ‖ p: 33 ΟΣ σM G U (W) *pc* — οιδατε δοκιμαζειν ‖ p: *S*p — δυν. γνωναι: σ7 *pc l*49 *L*e[k] abcff$^{1.2}$lz vg^8 *Arm*^{0} *Geo Δ*i^V md n^{HgHvS} — συνιετε ‖ Mk817.21: 700 **λ**⟨1⟩ ϕ230 σ659-954-1293 S Ω *C*b^{11} — *txt*: *Rpl* (*cf. ad* 2) (-αται: ϕ346) *L*' *S*h **4** γεν.] *prm* ο δε αποκριθεις ειπεν αυτοις ‖ 21239: Φ *C*b^2 — *prm* και αποκ. ο Ιησους ειπ. ‖ ←: ΟΣ-(*om* ο Ι.: 700 291) — η γεν. αυτη γεν. *et* μοι. + εστιν ‖ p Lk1129: ϕ124 | *om* κ. μοι. ‖ Lk1129: D *L*e[k] aff$^{1.2}$g^1 | ση. επιζ.] ζητει ση. (∼) ‖ p (Lk1129): (Θ) D*' *L*e[k] bc | Ι. + του προφητου ‖ **12**39: *Rpl* Or *L*e[k] abcff^{2}q vg^5 Au^1 Cp *S C*b *Δ*a i^V me p — *txt*: ℵBL 565-700 D 262 *L*'Au^1 *C*s **5** *om* οι μα. ‖ p: Δ 301 | ∼ λαβ. αρ. ‖ Mk: B-892 **σ**'-349-659 K Π *pc S* — ινα τροφας αγορασωσιν ‖ Jo48: σ1675 *L*e[k](emere panem)

Mk 8,11 παρ] απ ‖ Mt1238: W | ση. + ιδειν ‖ ←: ℵ *Lc* | απο τ.] εκ τ. ‖ **p**Lk1116: 𝔓^{45} W ϕ ⟨124⟩ *pc* — απ ‖ Lk1116: 1038 | *om* πει. αυ. ‖ Mt ←: 482 **12** αναστ.] στεναξας ‖ 734: σM-517 *pc* | *om* τι ‖ p Mt1239p: σ71 16 | ∼ ση. επιζητ. ‖ ←: *Rpl* (*om* επι-: 1241 *pc*) Or *L*fg^{2}qr^1 vg^1 *S*h *Arm Geo*^{1} — ση. αιτει: 𝔓^{45} — *txt*: ℌC Θ **λ**-872(επιζ-) σ267 D *L*'[ek] *S*'j *Geo*^{2} | λε. υμ.] ● λεγω: BL-892 1342 — *om*: 𝔓^{45} W | ει] ου ‖ ←: Δ W-1071 ϕ σ1223 *pc* {*L*vg^2 *S*s[c]p} **13** αφ.] καταλιπων ‖ **p**: ΝΣ | *om* εμβ. ‖ p: σ517-1675 1241 *l*150 *l*184 **14** επελ. + οι μαθητοι αυτου(*om*) ‖ p: 𝔓^{45} WΦ-(28)-1071 ϕ-230 σ179-1194-1606 (D Y) U **0131** *pm L*(c)r^1 (vg^5) *C*s$^{5:6}$ *Geo*^{A}(^{B}) | ∼ αρ. λαβ. ‖ Mt: 33 ϕ⟨124-346⟩ σ115-1424 *pc L*qr^1(∼ αρ. οι μα. αυ. λαβ.)

Mt161-3p *cf.* ETh^{II} 91 (*transl.*): *Εἶπον αὐτῷ εἰπὲ ἡμῖν τίς εἶ ἵνα πιστεύσωμέν σοι. εἶπεν αὐτοῖς· δοκιμάζετε τὸ πρόσωπον τοῦ οὐρανοῦ καὶ τῆς γῆς, καὶ τὸν(τά?) ἐνώπιον ὑμῶν ὄντα οὐκ ἐγνώκατε καὶ τὸν καιρὸν τοῦτον οὐκ οἴδατε δοκιμάζειν.*

Mt162b-3p *cf.* EN frgm.13 (Cod. N. T. 1424^m): Τὰ σεσημειωμένα διὰ τοῦ ἀστερίσκου (*sc.* ^{2}οψ.—^{3}δυν.) ἐν ἑτέροις οὐκ ἐμφέρεται οὔτε ἐν τῷ Ἰουδαϊκῷ.

Matthew

Ἰησοῦς εἶπεν αὐτοῖς· ὁρᾶτε καὶ προσέχετε ἀπὸ τῆς ζύμης τῶν Φαρισαίων καὶ Σαδδουκαίων. [7] οἱ δὲ διελογίζοντο ἐν ἑαυτοῖς λέγοντες ὅτι ἄρτους οὐκ ἐλάβομεν. [8] γνοὺς δὲ ὁ Ἰησοῦς εἶπεν· τί διαλογίζεσθε ἐν ἑαυτοῖς, ὀλιγόπιστοι, ὅτι ἄρτους οὐκ ἐλάβετε; [9] οὔπω νοεῖτε, *cf. 128.*

οὐδὲ μνημονεύετε τοὺς πέντε ἄρτους τῶν πεντακισχιλίων καὶ πόσους κοφίνους ἐλάβετε;

[10] οὐδὲ τοὺς ἑπτὰ ἄρτους τῶν τετρακισχιλίων καὶ πόσας σφυρίδας ἐλάβετε;

[11] πῶς οὐ νοεῖτε ὅτι οὐ περὶ ἄρτων εἶπον ὑμῖν; προσέχετε δὲ ἀπὸ τῆς ζύμης τῶν Φαρισαίων καὶ Σαδδουκαίων. [12] τότε συνῆκαν ὅτι οὐκ εἶπεν προσέχειν ἀπὸ τῆς ζύμης τῶν ἄρτων, ἀλλὰ ἀπὸ τῆς διδαχῆς τῶν Φαρισαίων καὶ Σαδδουκαίων.

Mark

[15] καὶ διεστέλλετο αὐτοῖς λέγων· ὁρᾶτε, βλέπετε ἀπὸ τῆς ζύμης τῶν Φαρισαίων καὶ τῆς ζύμης Ἡρῴδου. [16] καὶ διελογίζοντο πρὸς ἀλλήλους ὅτι ἄρτους οὐκ ἔχουσιν. [17] καὶ γνοὺς ὁ Ἰησοῦς λέγει αὐτοῖς· τί διαλογίζεσθε ὅτι ἄρτους οὐκ ἔχετε; οὔπω νοεῖτε οὐδὲ συνίετε; πεπωρωμένην ἔχετε τὴν καρδίαν ὑμῶν; [18] **ὀφθαλμοὺς ἔχοντες οὐ βλέπετε, καὶ ὦτα ἔχοντες οὐκ ἀκούετε;** καὶ οὐ μνημονεύετε, [19] ὅτε τοὺς πέντε ἄρτους ἔκλασα εἰς τοὺς πεντακισχιλίους, πόσους κοφίνους κλασμάτων πλήρεις ἤρατε; λέγουσιν αὐτῷ· δώδεκα. [20] ὅτε καὶ τοὺς ἑπτὰ εἰς τοὺς τετρακισχιλίους, πόσων σπυρίδων πληρώματα κλασμάτων ἤρατε; οἱ δὲ εἶπον· ἑπτά. [21] καὶ ἔλεγεν αὐτοῖς· οὔπω συνίετε;

Jr5 21 Ez12 2

Luke

πατεῖν ἀλλήλους, ἤρξατο λέγειν πρὸς τοὺς μαθητὰς αὐτοῦ πρῶτον· προσέχετε ἑαυτοῖς ἀπὸ τῆς ζύμης τῶν Φαρισαίων, ἥτις ἐστὶν ὑπόκρισις.

cf. v. 1 ↑

Mt 16,6 *om* και¹ (*om* ορατε και) ‖ Mk(Lk): ϕ124 *Le*[k] (ab)ff¹(² *S*sc)p | *om* και Σ. ‖p: σ115 U *pc l*184 Chr¹:² *La* vg¹ Amst **7** *om* λεγ. ‖p: K *S*sc *Cs*¹:⁶b¹ **8** ειπ. + αυτοις ‖p: *Rpl L*aff¹ vg⁶ *S*cp *C* — *txt*: ℌX ΟΣ-565-700-1604 λ-1582 ϕ124-230-788 σ-M-349-659-1010 D K S W Δ Θ Π Ω 157 *al* Or *L*' *S*sh *Arm Aeth* | ελα.] ● εχετε ‖p: אB-892 700-1604 ϕ-230 D Θ *pc L*'Luc *C*b' *Arm Geo*² *Aeth* — ελαβομεν ‖ 7: 1093 *pc l*1579 *Geo*¹ — *txt*: *Rpl* Chr Eu Or *Lf S Cs*b¹? **9** ουπω] ου ‖ 11 Mk7 18: ϕ13 | ουδε + συνιετε και ‖p: 544 | μνη. + οτε ‖p: D Δ | αρτ. + εκλασα ‖p: 345 *Cs*¹(οτε εκλ. τ. π. αρτ.)˙⁵ **10** *om* αρ. ‖p: Σ σ659 *pc* Eu | εις τους τετρακισχιλιους ‖p: Σ 157 *L*cfff¹z30 vg⁵ *Arm* **11** *om* πως ‖ 9 Mk7 18: σ1424-1675 Θ *Le*[k] | ου¹] ουπω ‖ 9p15 17 Mk: 565 | νοει.] συνιετε ‖ p Mk17: 476 — + ουδε μνημονευετε ‖ 9p: 998 **12** του αρτου: *Rpl L*cfq{¹} *Cs*¹b² *Geo*ᴬ — ● των Φαρισαιων και Σαδδουκαιων (*om* κ. Σ.) ‖ 12b.11: א*-(33) σ349 *l*185¹ *L*ff¹ *S*c *Δ*iⱽ — *om*: 565 ϕ124-174-346-788 D Θ *L*abff² Luc *S*s *Arm Geo*' — *txt* (*om* τ. ζυμης): אᶜBL-892 (λ1-1582) σ'(517-1675) 157 1241 *l*48 *l*184 *l*211 (Or) *L*'(e[k]) {*S*'}¹ *Cs*⁶b' *Δ*ad l

Mk 8,15 ορ. + και ‖ Mt: 𝔓⁴⁵ C Φ ϕ σ1424 **0131** *al L*cfg²lz vg⁹ *Cs*b⁽⁶⁾ *Got* **16** και] οι δε ‖ p: 𝔓⁴⁵ W-565 | πρ. αλ.] εν εαυτοις ‖ p: 1071 *Lc* | αλ. + λεγοντες ‖ p: *Rpl L*flr²z vg *S C*b — *txt*: 𝔓⁴⁵ אB W-28-565-700 λ⟨118⟩ D 1342 *L*' *Cs Δ*md n | εχ.] ελαβομεν ‖ p: 579 σ1424 *pc* {} — ● εχομεν ‖ p: *Rpl L*flr²z vg *S*{s[c]}ph *C*b² — ειχαν ‖ p: D *L*vl'r¹ᵛ — *txt*: 𝔓⁴⁵ B W-28-565-700 λ⟨118⟩ 1302 *Lk*[e] g² *C*' **17** κ. γν.] γν. δε ‖ p: 1012 1342 *l*150(∼ ο δε Ιησους γν.) *S*s[c]p *Cs* | ● *om* ο Ι. (*et* αυτ. + ο Ι.): אᶜB(L)Δ-892 (472 482) *L*(b)iz *S*jᵛ *Cs*³b — *txt*: *Rpl L*'[ek] *S Cs*⁴ | λεγ.] ειπεν ‖ p: Θ-565-700 | διαλ. + εν εαυτοις(αὐ-) ‖ p: 𝔓⁴⁵ 579(*om* εν) W ϕ'(69-346 σM)-1402 *pc l*150 — + εν ταις καρδιαις υμων ‖ 2 8p: ΘΦ-28-565-700 ϕ13-124 σ827 D U *pc L*vl[ek]⟨flr²z⟩g² vg² *S*h⁺ *Arm Geo*² *Aeth* | οτι] *prm* ολιγοπιστοι ‖ p: 𝔓⁴⁵ WΘΦ-28-565-700 ϕ *pc l*150 *S*h⁺ *Cs*⁴:⁷ *Arm Geo*²(¹∼) | ουπω] ουτω ‖ 7 18: 700 | *om* ουδε συ. ‖ p: λ⟨118⟩ 213 *l*184 **18** ακου. + ουπω νοειτε ‖ p: 𝔓⁴⁵ Θ-565 *Arm* | και ου] ουδε ‖ p: 𝔓⁴⁵ Θ-565 D 1342 **19** ∼ τους π. αρ. οτε ‖ p: 579 | *om* οτε *et* αρ. + ους ‖ p: 28 *pc Lk*[e] bciff²r¹ᵛ (*S*s[c]) *C*b | ποσ.] ● και πο. ‖ p: אCΔ-33-579 Θ-544-565 λ⟨118⟩ σM-7-115-267-349-517-659-1223 D *pc l*18 *l*19 *l*48 *l*49 *l*150 *l*184 *l*251 *l*260 *L*fg²lr²z30 vg⁵ *S*s[c]j *Cs*⁴:⁶ *Arm Aeth* | *om* πλ. ‖ 8 Lk9 17: 579 ϕ⟨124⟩ *pc L*vl[e]⟨fg²l⟩30 vg³ *S*p¹ *C*b¹ **20** οτε και] οτε δε και: C N *Lf Cs*³:⁶ — ● οτε δε: *Rpl L*vl'(¹⁹∩²⁰dixerunt: b)30 *S*h — ● οτε: BL-579 565 σ517 1241 — ex: *Lk*[e] — και οτε: 892 *Lc S*'j *C*b(*om* οτε) *Geo*²(¹ ειτα οτε) — *txt*: אΔ *L*lr²z vg⁽⁴⁾ *Cs*³ | επτα¹ + αρτους ‖ p: 𝔓⁴⁵ᵛ אC WΦ ϕ σMᶜ-115-517-827-1082 1342 *pc l*48 *L*cfqr¹·² vg *S*j *Cs Arm Geo*¹·ᴮ *Aeth* | ποσ.—κλα.] ποσας σπυριδας κλα. πληρεις(*om*) ‖ 19 Mt15 37: Θ-565-700 (D *L*'⟨b⟩)k[e](*om* κλα.) cf *S*(s[c])ph *Cs*b⁽¹⁾ *Geo*¹(²) *Δ*a md n — και ποσους κοφινους κλα. πλη.(*om*) ‖ 19 Mt14 20: Δ (*L*g² vg¹) *S*j | οι δε ειπ.] λεγουσιν αυτω(*om*) ‖ 19: Δ-579-892 *L*(k[e]) l vg⁴ *S*s[c]p⁶(')j *Cs*b³ — ● και λεγ. αυτω(*om*) ‖ ←: (א)BCL σ115 1342 *L*vg' *C*b' *Arm Aeth* **21** ουπω] πως ου ‖ p: *Rpl L*bdq *Cs*⁴(πως ουν ου)b *Arm* — πως ουπω ‖ p: X-33 NWΘΣΦ-565-1071 σM-1606 A D U *pm l*49 *l*251 *L*' *S*'j — πως ουν ουπω ‖ p: ϕ *Lf Cs*¹ — *txt*: אCLΔ-892 1071 λ ϕ230 σ⟨954⟩-7-267-349-659-1223-1391 K Π 1342 *al l*150 *l*184 *Lk*[e] *S*s[c] *Δ*p | συν.] νοειτε ‖ 17p Mt: B σ1207 Dᶜ(*συννο.) *pc Cs*

(121) **134.** Der Blinde von Bethsaida. *The Blind Man of Bethsaida.* **Mark 8 22–26**

[22] Καὶ ἔρχονται εἰς Βηθσαιδαν. καὶ φέρουσιν αὐτῷ τυφλόν, καὶ παρακαλοῦσιν αὐτὸν ἵνα αὐτοῦ ἅψηται. [23] καὶ ἐπιλαβόμενος τῆς χειρὸς τοῦ τυφλοῦ ἐξήνεγκεν αὐτὸν ἔξω τῆς κώμης, καὶ πτύσας εἰς τὰ ὄμματα αὐτοῦ, ἐπιθεὶς τὰς χεῖρας αὐτῷ, ἐπηρώτα αὐτόν· εἴ τι βλέπεις; [24] καὶ ἀναβλέψας ἔλεγεν· βλέπω τοὺς ἀνθρώπους, ὅτι ὡς δένδρα ὁρῶ περιπατοῦντας. [25] εἶτα πάλιν ἐπέθηκεν τὰς χεῖρας ἐπὶ τοὺς ὀφθαλμοὺς αὐτοῦ, καὶ διέβλεψεν καὶ ἀποκατέστη, καὶ ἐνέβλεπεν τηλαυγῶς ἅπαντα. [26] καὶ ἀπέστειλεν αὐτὸν εἰς οἶκον αὐτοῦ λέγων· μηδὲ εἰς τὴν κώμην εἰσέλθῃς.

cf. 207.

9 1-7: Καὶ παράγων εἶδεν ἄνθρωπον τυφλὸν ἐκ γενετῆς. [2] καὶ ἠρώτησαν αὐτὸν οἱ μαθηταὶ αὐτοῦ λέγοντες· ραββι, τίς ἥμαρτεν, οὗτος ἢ οἱ γονεῖς αὐτοῦ, ἵνα τυφλὸς γεννηθῇ; [3] ἀπεκρίθη Ἰησοῦς· οὔτε οὗτος ἥμαρτεν οὔτε οἱ γονεῖς αὐτοῦ, ἀλλ' ἵνα φανερωθῇ τὰ ἔργα τοῦ θεοῦ ἐν αὐτῷ. [4] ἡμᾶς δεῖ ἐργάζεσθαι τὰ ἔργα τοῦ πέμψαντός με ἕως ἡμέρα ἐστίν· ἔρχεται νὺξ ὅτε οὐδεὶς δύναται ἐργάζεσθαι. [5] ὅταν ἐν τῷ κόσμῳ ὦ, φῶς εἰμι τοῦ κόσμου. [6] ταῦτα εἰπὼν ἔπτυσεν χαμαὶ καὶ ἐποίησεν πηλὸν ἐκ τοῦ πτύσματος, καὶ ἐπέχρισεν αὐτοῦ τὸν πηλὸν ἐπὶ τοὺς ὀφθαλμούς, [7] καὶ εἶπεν αὐτῷ· ὕπαγε νίψαι εἰς τὴν κολυμβήθραν τοῦ Σιλωαμ, ὃ ἑρμηνεύεται ἀπεσταλμένος. ἀπῆλθεν οὖν καὶ ἐνίψατο, καὶ ἦλθεν βλέπων.

(122) **135.** Das Petrusbekenntnis. *Peter's Confession.*

Matth 16 13–20	**Mark 8 27–30**	**Luk 9 18–21**
[13] Ἐλθὼν δὲ ὁ Ἰησοῦς	[27] Καὶ ἐξῆλθεν ὁ Ἰησοῦς	[18] Καὶ ἐγένετο ἐν τῷ εἶναι αὐτὸν
εἰς τὰ μέρη	καὶ οἱ μαθηταὶ αὐτοῦ εἰς τὰς κώμας	προσευχόμενον κατὰ μόνας συνῆσαν
Καισαρείας τῆς Φιλίππου	Καισαρείας τῆς Φιλίππου· καὶ ἐν τῇ	αὐτῷ οἱ μαθηταί,
ἠρώτα τοὺς μαθητὰς αὐτοῦ	ὁδῷ ἐπηρώτα τοὺς μαθητὰς αὐτοῦ	καὶ ἐπηρώτησεν αὐτοὺς

Mt 16,13 εξελθων ‖ Mk: σ349-1194 H W *pc* *Sh*^{t}

Mk 8,22 τυφ. + δαιμονιζομενον ‖ Mt12 22: Δ | ∼ αψ. αυ. ‖ Mt8 3 Lk5 13: 700 σ1606 *pc* *S* **23** ● βλεπει: *Rpl* *L* *S*p'(*om* ει)h *Arm* *Geo*^{B} *Δ*l^{AD} md n^{HgS} — *txt* (*om* ει): BCΔ-579 Θ-565 D*' 1342 *pc* (*S*s[c]p^{4}) *C* *Geo* *Aeth* *Δ*a p **25** επεθ.] ● εθηκεν ‖ 10 16: BL-892 1093 | απεκατεσταθη ‖ 3 6p: *Rpl* — *txt*: ℌ⟨33⟩C λ118 44 **26** μηδε—εισελ.] μηδε(και εαν: *Sh*^{m}) εις την κωμην εισελθης μηδε ειπης τινι(μηδε^{2}—τινι] μηδενι ειπ.: *Sh*^{m}; + των: 892) εν τη κωμη ‖ 30p 14 4p 7 36p 9 9p Lk8 56: *Rpl* (892) *S*ph^{t}(^{m}) *C*b^{9}(τη κω.] αυτη) — υπαγε εις τον οικον σου και μηδενι ειπης(-ειν: *L*c) εις την κωμην ‖ 2 11p 5 19p *etc.*: D *L*(*om* υπα.—και: k[e] c)q(∼ εις τ. κ. ειπ.) — υπαγε εις τον(*om*: Θ-28) οικον σου και εαν(κ. εαν] και μηδε: 124; μηδε: *L*a) εις την κωμην εισελθης (∼ εισελ. εις τ. κω.: 61) μηδενι(μηδε: 1071 124 *L*a; μηδεν: Φ; + μηδεν: 28 61 *Geo*^{A}) ειπης μηδε(*om*: Θ-565 ff^{2}i *Arm* *Geo*^{2}; μηδεν: 983; τινι: Φ-1071 124) εν τη κωμη ‖ 30p *etc.* 2 11p *etc.*: (ΘΦ-28-565-1071 61) **ϕ**'(124-983) *L*(*om* μηδε—κωμη: vl'a^{v} vg)(aff^{2}i) (*Arm, et prm* μη εις την κωμην εισελθης αλλ; *Geo*^{2}) (*Δ*l^{AD} = vg) — *txt* (μηδε] μη): (ℵ*)BL (W) **λ**⟨118⟩ *S*s[c] *C*sb^{2}(')f *Geo*^{1} **27** εξηλ.] ηλθεν ‖ Mt: 1574 | *om* κ. οι μα. αυ. ‖ Mt: σ115 *Aeth*

Lk 9,18 αυτον + εν τινι τοπω ‖ 11 1: ℵ^{a}(*om* τινι) 1071 *C*s | *om* προσευ. ‖ p: D(αυτον] -ους) *L*e ac *S*c | κ. μον.] κατ ιδιαν ‖ Mt14 23 17 1 Mk9 2: **σ**⟨954⟩ | συνηντησαν ‖ 9 37: B* 157 *pc* *L*f | μα. + αυτου ‖ p: 579-892 N-1071-1604 **λλ** **ϕ**-230 σM-267-659-1424 U W Θ *pc* *L*afr^{1}z30 vg^{3} *S* *C*sb^{7} *Geo*^{1}

Jo 9,1 γεν. + καθημενον ‖ 9 8 Mt20 30p: D PsAth **4** ημ.] εμε ‖ 4 34 10 16 Lk13 33: *Rpl* Chr *L* *S* *C*b^{2}a^{s} *Δ*'⟨me⟩ E$^{s.a}$ — *txt*: 𝔓$^{66.75}$ ℵ*BLW-**0124** D(∼ δει ημ.) 850 Cr Non *L*Hi *S*j *C*'$^{+B}$ *Geo* *Aeth* | με] ● ημας ‖ 4a: 𝔓$^{66.75}$ ℵ*LW 850 Cr *C*b$^{\langle 2\rangle +B}$ *Aeth* **6** επεχ.] ● επεθηκεν ‖ p 9 15: BC*^{v} 1093 *Δ*i | επι] εις ‖ Mk2 3: **053** | οφ. + αυτου ‖ p Mt9 29: 892-1241 N-544 D *pc* *L*'(αυτω: l) Au Or *C*sb^{B}a^{s} *Δ*ad l n^{L} — + του τυφλου(+ εκεινου) ‖ **11** 37 9 32: *Rpl* Amm PsAth Chr *L*e (b)f (*S*,j) Ef *C*b(+ εκ γενετης) *Arm* *Δ*'⟨me⟩ (a) — *txt* (*et om* τ. πηλ. επι): 𝔓$^{66.75}$ ℵ*BL-**0124**-33 (**λ**) Θ **0216** (565) *L*a

---

Mt16 13-16p *cf.* ETh^{II} 13 (*transl.*): *Εἶπεν ὁ Ἰησοῦς τοῖς μαθηταῖς αὐτοῦ· ὁμοιώσατέ με καὶ εἴπατέ μοι τίνι ὅμοιός εἰμι. εἶπεν αὐτῷ Σίμων Πέτρος· ὅμοιος εἶ ἀγγέλῳ δικαίῳ. εἶπεν αὐτῷ Μαθθαῖος· ὅμοιος εἶ ἀνθρώπῳ φιλοσόφῳ φρονίμῳ. εἶπεν αὐτῷ Θωμᾶς· διδάσκαλε, ὅλως τὸ στόμα μου οὐ μὴ ἀνάσχηται λέγον, τίνι ὅμοιος εἶ ...*

Matthew 16:13–16

λέγων· τίνα λέγουσιν οἱ ἄνθρωποι εἶναι τὸν υἱὸν τοῦ ἀνθρώπου; [14] οἱ δὲ εἶπαν· οἱ μὲν Ἰωάννην τὸν βαπτιστήν, ἄλλοι δὲ Ἠλίαν, ἕτεροι δὲ Ἰερεμίαν ἢ ἕνα τῶν προφητῶν. [15] λέγει αὐτοῖς· ὑμεῖς δὲ τίνα με λέγετε εἶναι; [16] ἀποκριθεὶς δὲ Σίμων Πέτρος εἶπεν· σὺ εἶ ὁ Χριστὸς ὁ υἱὸς τοῦ θεοῦ τοῦ

Mark 8:27–29

λέγων αὐτοῖς· τίνα με λέγουσιν οἱ ἄνθρωποι εἶναι; **123.** [28] οἱ δὲ ἀπεκρίθησαν αὐτῷ λέγοντες· Ἰωάννην τὸν βαπτιστήν, καὶ ἄλλοι Ἠλίαν, ἄλλοι δὲ ὅτι εἷς τῶν προφητῶν. [29] καὶ αὐτὸς ἐπηρώτα αὐτούς· ὑμεῖς δὲ τίνα με λέγετε εἶναι; ἀποκριθεὶς ὁ Πέτρος λέγει αὐτῷ· σὺ εἶ ὁ Χριστός.

Luke 9:18–20

λέγων· τίνα με οἱ ὄχλοι λέγουσιν εἶναι; [19] οἱ δὲ ἀποκριθέντες εἶπαν· Ἰωάννην τὸν βαπτιστήν, ἄλλοι δὲ Ἠλίαν, ἄλλοι δὲ ὅτι προφήτης τις τῶν ἀρχαίων ἀνέστη. [20] εἶπεν δὲ αὐτοῖς· ὑμεῖς δὲ τίνα με λέγετε εἶναι; Πέτρος δὲ ἀποκριθεὶς εἶπεν· τὸν Χριστὸν τοῦ θεοῦ.

John 6:68 f.

6 68f.: ἀπεκρίθη αὐτῷ Σίμων Πέτρος· κύριε, πρὸς τίνα ἀπελευσόμεθα; ῥήματα ζωῆς αἰωνίου ἔχεις· [69] καὶ ἡμεῖς πεπιστεύκαμεν καὶ ἐγνώκαμεν ὅτι σὺ εἶ ὁ ἅγιος τοῦ θεοῦ.

Mt 16,13 τινα + με‖p: *Rpl* Ad PsAth Cr Ep Or *L*vl'[k] g² vg⁸ Hil Ir¹ {*S*,Ef} *Aeth* — λεγ. + με‖p: C W 399 {} — *txt*: ℵB 700 λ1582 1515 *l*1353 *L*c vg¹ Am Ir¹ Or | ∼ οι αν. λεγ. ειν.‖Lk: ℵᶜ (*∼ ειν. λεγ.) 700 D *L*e[k] abg²qr¹·² | ∼ λεγ. ειν. οι αν.: λ1-1582 *L*ff¹ **14** ειπ. + αυτω‖Mk: σ-349 *S*scj | *om* οι μεν‖p: D W *L*cflq vg⟨2⟩ **15** λεγει + δε‖Lk: λ1582 K 1515 *L*ff¹ *C*s(αυτος δε λεγει)b¹ *Geo*² **16** Σ.] ο‖p: σ517-1424 | ειπ. + αυτω‖Mk: D *L*ff¹ *C*b¹ *Geo*

Mk 8,27 *om* αυτοις‖p: ℌ⟨ℵ*B⟩ σ517-1606 D *pc l*29 *L*⟨cfl⟩30 vg³ *C*s¹:⁷b³⟨f⟩ *Arm* | ειν. + τον υιον του ανθρωπου‖Mt: 1093 *l*18 *L*vg³ **28** απεκ.] ● ειπαν‖Mt: ℌ⟨33⟩C 1342 *L*k[e] *S*s[c]p *C*,f | αυ. λεγ.] λεγ.‖p: W-1071 *L*f *S*j *Arm* — αυτω: C²-33 *al l*253 *S*s[c] *C*sb¹f *Aeth* — *om*‖p: *Rpl S*' — *txt*: ℌ'⟨892⟩C* Θ-28-565 ϕ-*l*547 D **0143**ᵛ 1342 *pc L*' *C*b' *Geo* | Ι.] ● οτι Ι.‖28b: ℵ*BC* 1342 *S*(οτι οι μεν Ι.: s[c])p *Geo*² — οι μεν Ι.‖Mt: C²Δ-579 W ϕ-*l*547 σ179-349-517-827 *L*vg¹(αλλοι Ι.) *C*sb¹f — *txt*: *Rpl L*' *S*hj *C*b' *Arm Geo*¹ *Aeth* | βαπτιζοντα‖6 14.24: 28-565 | και αλ.] αλ. δε‖p: NWΘΣ-565-700 ϕ⟨124⟩-*l*547 D *pc L*k[e] afq *C*s⁵ — αλ.‖p: Δ σ71-517-692 V *pc l*253 *L*bclr¹·² vg *S*p¹ *C*s¹b⁴f | αλ. δε] η‖Mt: σ1082-1391 *Aeth* — ετεροι δε‖Mt: 472 *l*44 | οτι εις] ενα(ως ενα)‖Mt: *Rpl* (D *L*')k[e] *S*'j *Arm* — Ιερεμιαν η ενα‖Mt: **047** 472 — *txt*: ℌ⟨Δ-33⟩C* 1342 *S*s[c]p⁶ *C*,f **29** και αυτ.] *om* (*et* αυτους + ο Ιησους)‖p: WΘ-28 **λ** ϕ788 *l*17, *S*s[c](p) *C*f (*Geo*²) — και‖p: 579 544 *S*j⟨f⟩ *C*b¹ — τοτε: *L*'⟨acff²q⟩ (*et* αυτους + ο Ι.: r¹) | επη. αυ.] λεγει αυτοις‖p: *Rpl L*' *S Cf* — *txt* (-τησεν): ℌ'⟨33⟩(ηρωτησεν: 579)C* D 1342 *pc L*a(ff²q; *et* + λεγων: c) (*S*j *C*sb *Δ*me nᴸ | αποκ.] ● + δε‖p: *Rpl L*ff² *S*jᵇ *C*s² — και απο.: 33-892 NΣ σ267-349-659 A 1342 *pc L*vl'[e] r¹ *Aeth* — *txt* (*om*): BL-579 Φ *pc L*clr²z vg *S*(s[c])phjᵃᶜᶠ *C*s¹bf (*Arm*) *Δ*a iᵀ l p | *om* ο¹‖p: σ517 Ω *pc l*253 | Π.] *prm* Σιμων‖Mt: Σ *L*vg¹ *S*p⁶(' *om* Π.) | λεγ.] ειπεν‖Mt Lk: Σ-28 σ349-659-827-945-1223 1279 *L*r¹ | *om* αυτω‖p: 33 *pc* Eu *L*vg² *C*bf | Χ. + ο υιος του θεου(+ του ζωντος)‖p: ℵL (W)-544 (ϕ)-*l*547 157 *L*b(Χ. + Ιησους)r¹ *S*(p)jᵃᵇ(ᶜᶠ) *C*s⁵:⁶⟨f⟩

Lk 9,18 ∼ λεγ. οι οχ. ειν.‖p: 𝔓⁷⁵ *Rpl L*(e) acr¹·²30 (vg¹) *S* — ∼ λεγ. ειν. οι οχ.: *L*' — *txt*: ℵ*BLΞ-892 **λ** R Cr | οχ.] ανθρωποι‖p: 579-1241 λ1278 **σ**⟨954⟩-659 A **047** *pc L*e vg¹ *C*s²:⁶b⟨4⟩ **19** ειπ. + οι μεν‖Mt: λ1278 ϕ124-174 *L*vg¹ *S*h⁺ — + λεγουσιν: 579 *S*sᵛc *C*s | Η. + ετεροι (αλλοι) δε Ιερεμιαν‖Mt: (**λλ**) ϕ⟨828⟩ *L*vg¹ *S*h⁺ | αλλοι²—ανεστη] η ενα των προφητων‖Mt Mk: D *L*e | δε³ + ενα των προφ. ετεροι δε‖p: 579 | τις] εις‖Mk Mt: 148 1093 *L*⟨c⟩ **20** Π.] Σιμων Π.‖Mt Jo 6 68: N *L*⟨e a vg¹⟩ Am *S*scp(*om* Π.) | Π. δε αποκ.] αποκ. δε(*om*) ο Π.‖Mt (Mk): *Rpl* {*L*afq(vl' ⟨r²⟩ *S*')h (*Arm*)} — αποκ. δε(*om*) Π.‖p: 33 (N)Λ-1071-(1604) λ22-1278 ϕ(13)-69-(543)-788-983 σ7-267-990 E G H S V W Y Γ Δ Θ Ψ Ω **047** 157 *mu* {} — *txt* (*om* αποκ.): 𝔓⁷⁵ ℌ'CΞ λ1-(131)-1582-2193 σ115 Δ *C*s¹(⁶*om* δε)b⟨1⟩ | ειπ.² + αυτω‖Mk: 495 *S*sc *C*s¹:⁷ *Aeth* | Χ. + τον υιον‖Mt Jo 1 49: 892 28 σ1675 D(*om* τον) 213 *L*e (συ ει ο Χ. ο υιος‖p: fl)r¹ *C*b¹

Jo 6,68 Σ.] ο‖Mk Lk: σ1424 *L*Cp **69** αγ. τ. θ.] Χριστος ο (*om* Χ. ο) υιος τ. θ. του ζωντος‖p: *Rpl* (17) Bas Chr *L*fff²qr¹ Cp¹(¹) *S*'j *C*b²{fᵛ(Χ[...)} *Geo*(ᴬ)ᴮ — Χ. ο(*om* Χ. ο) υι. τ. θ.‖p: 33 **λ** σ1010-1293 Θ **0141** *pc* Cr *L*'(b) Vicᴿ *S*s(c) *Arm Geo*¹ *Aeth* — Χ. ο αγ. τ. θ.‖p: 𝔓⁶⁶ *C*s¹²b'{}aˢ — Χ.‖Mk: *L*Te — *txt*: 𝔓⁷⁵ᵛ ℵBC*LW D Co Non *C*s¹bᴮ

Mt16 16p *cf.* ETHᴵᴵ 37 (*transl.*): ... *[ὄψεσθε] τὸν υἱὸν τοῦ ζῶντος καὶ οὐ μὴ φοβηθῆτε.*

ζῶντος. 17 ἀποκριθεὶς δὲ ὁ Ἰησοῦς εἶπεν αὐτῷ· μακάριος εἶ, Σίμων Βαριωνα, ὅτι σὰρξ καὶ αἷμα οὐκ ἀπεκάλυψέν σοι

[Jo] 1 49: ἀπεκρίθη αὐτῷ Ναθαναηλ· ραββι, σὺ εἶ ὁ υἱὸς τοῦ θεοῦ, σὺ βασιλεὺς εἶ τοῦ Ισραηλ.

ἀλλ' ὁ πατήρ μου ὁ ἐν τοῖς οὐρανοῖς. 18 κἀγὼ δέ σοι λέγω ὅτι σὺ εἶ Πέτρος, καὶ ἐπὶ ταύτῃ τῇ πέτρᾳ οἰκοδομήσω μου τὴν ἐκκλησίαν, καὶ πύλαι ᾅδου οὐ κατισχύσουσιν αὐτῆς. 19 καὶ δώσω σοι τὰς κλεῖδας τῆς βασιλείας τῶν οὐρανῶν, καὶ ὃ ἐὰν δήσῃς ἐπὶ τῆς γῆς ἔσται δεδεμένον ἐν τοῖς οὐρανοῖς, καὶ ὃ ἐὰν λύσῃς ἐπὶ τῆς γῆς ἔσται λελυμένον ἐν τοῖς οὐρανοῖς. 20 τότε διεστείλατο τοῖς μαθηταῖς ἵνα μηδενὶ εἴπωσιν ὅτι αὐτός ἐστιν ὁ Χριστός. **148.**

[Mark] 30 καὶ ἐπετίμησεν αὐτοῖς ἵνα μηδενὶ λέγωσιν περὶ αὐτοῦ.

[Luk] 21 ὁ δὲ ἐπιτιμήσας αὐτοῖς παρήγγειλεν μηδενὶ λέγειν τοῦτο

(122)

136. Erste Leidensverkündigung. *The First Prediction of the Passion.*

(s. S. 132 f.)

(123)

137. Die Leidensnachfolge der Jünger. *The Conditions of Discipleship.*

Matth 16 24–28

24 Τότε ὁ Ἰησοῦς εἶπεν τοῖς μαθηταῖς αὐτοῦ· εἴ τις θέλει ὀπίσω μου

10 38 f. (74.): καὶ ὅς

Mark 8 34—9 1

34 Καὶ προσκαλεσάμενος τὸν ὄχλον σὺν τοῖς μαθηταῖς αὐτοῦ εἶπεν αὐτοῖς· ὅστις θέλει ὀπίσω μου

14 27 (185.): ὅστις

Luk 9 23–27

23 Ἔλεγεν δὲ πρὸς πάντας· εἴ τις θέλει ὀπίσω μου

12 25 f.: 26 ἐὰν ἐμοί τις διακονῇ,

Mt 16,19 κ. δω. σοι] ● δω σοι: ℵBC^2-33 λ1-1582 *L*Cp^1 *C*b' — δω. δε σοι: σ⟨954⟩ Θ *C*sb^6 — και δω. δε σοι: *S*h^{m}j — και(*om*) σοι δω.: L (D) *L*'(ff^1) Au Cp^2(^{2}) Hil (*S*') *Δ*(a) ad i^T l n^L — *txt*: *Rpl* Ddy Eu *L*aq Or Te *S*h^t *C*b^5 *Arm* **20** διεστ.] ● επετιμησεν‖Mk Lk: B* D Or *L*e[k] *S*c[s] | τ. μα.] αυτοις‖p: 1093 Chr | ουτος‖Jo 1 34 Act 9 22 17 3: D U Θ *L*q | ο X.] Ιησους ο X. (ο X. I.)‖Jo 20 31: *Rpl* (D) *L*'(c) Au *S*h *C*s^{1}b *Geo*^{1} — *txt*: ℵ*BLX Φ-28-544-700 λ1-118(^{v} ο X. ο X.)-1582 ϕ124-174-788-826 σ71-267-1194-1402-1424-1675 Γ Δ Θ Π *al* Or *L*e[k] abff$^{1.2}$g^{1}r^{2}z vg^2 *S*'j *C*s^5 *Geo*^{2}

Mk 8,30 αυτοις] αυτω‖29b Mt 17: Δ 2145 *L*cir^2 *C*f | λεγ.] ειπωσιν‖Mt: C D G 1574 | αυτου] τουτ.‖Lk: N — + οτι αυτος εστιν ο Χριστος‖Mt: 125^m *l*18 *l*49 **34** οστ.] ● ει τις‖9 35 Mt 24 Lk 23 14 26: ℌC*W-28-565-700-1071 **λ**⟨118⟩ **ϕ** σ115-827 D **0214** 1342 *l*48 *l*49^1 Or *L*,Au *S*h^m *Arm* — *txt*: *Rpl* *S*'j *Δ*a i^V md me n p

Lk 9,21 επετιμησεν *et* παρ. + δε‖Mk: **σ**-1188 1093(*et* παραγγειλας) | λεγ.] ειπειν‖Mt: *Rpl* — *txt*: 𝔓^{75} ℵBCLWΞ-33 544-700-1071 **λ**-1582 **ϕ**⟨124⟩-174-230 σM-71-990-1194-1207-1223 A D K Θ Π 157 *mu* Or

Jo 1,49 αυτω N.] αυτω(*om*) N. και ειπεν: (ℵ)X 28 ϕ124 σ1293 Ψ *pc* Ep *L*' (*S*j$^{a1.b1.c1}$) *C*b^5(^{2}) *Geo*(^{1})^A *Δ*'⟨me n^L⟩ — ● αυτω N. και λεγει: ϕ *l*547 — N. κ. λεγ.(ειπεν) αυτω: *Rpl* (Γ Δ *pc* *l*49)(αυτω N. κ. λ. αυτω: σ1223 273) Chr Cr *L*(qr^1)(*om* αυτω: c vg^1) *S*[sc],(j$^{a1.b1.c1}$ = *L*c) *C*b'(^{6} = 1223) *Geo*^{B} *Δ*a (i^V p = *L*c) — *txt*: 𝔓$^{66.75}$ ℌ'⟨892⟩W^s **0141** 249 *L*e(και N. απεκ., *om* αυτω) bz *C*s$^{12:13}$ *Aeth* | ει^1 + αληθως‖Mt 14 33 27 54 p: 𝔓^{66*} 1241 | βασ. ει] ει ο βασ.‖18 33: 𝔓^{66} *Rpl* Chr Cr Ddy Ep^1 Thd^M *L*⟨vg^1⟩ — *txt*: 𝔓^{75} BLW^s-**083**-33-579 λ1-1582 A Ψ **0141**(*om* ει) Cr Ep^1 **12,26** ∼ τις εμ. διακ.‖26b Mt 24 Lk 23: 33 **λ** **ϕ**-*l*547^1 D(μοι) Θ **053** *pc* *L* — ● ∼ διακ. τις: *Rpl* — *txt*: 𝔓$^{66.75}$ ℵBL(μοι)WX-579-1241 544-1071 σM A K U Π Ψ *al* Chr Cat

---

Mt 16 17 *cf.* EN frgm.14 (Cod. Evv. 566^m; Cod. N. T. 1424^m): τὸ Ἰουδαϊκόν (*sc.* Βαριωνα]): υἱὲ Ἰωάννου.

Mt 16 24 p *cf.* ETh^{II} 55.101 (*cf. ad 74.* Mt 10 37 f.)

Matth 16	Mt 10	Mark 8	Lk 14 / 17	Luk 9	Jo 12
ἐλθεῖν, ἀπαρνησάσθω ἑαυτὸν καὶ ἀράτω τὸν σταυρὸν αὐτοῦ, καὶ ἀκολουθείτω μοι.	*οὐ λαμβάνει τὸν σταυρὸν αὐτοῦ καὶ ἀκολουθεῖ ὀπίσω μου, οὐκ ἔστιν μου ἄξιος.*	ἀκολουθεῖν, ἀπαρνησάσθω ἑαυτὸν καὶ ἀράτω τὸν σταυρὸν αὐτοῦ, καὶ ἀκολουθείτω μοι.	*οὐ βαστάζει τὸν σταυρὸν ἑαυτοῦ καὶ ἔρχεται ὀπίσω μου, οὐ δύναται εἶναί μου μαθητής.*	ἔρχεσθαι, ἀρνησάσθω ἑαυτὸν καὶ ἀράτω τὸν σταυρὸν αὐτοῦ καθ' ἡμέραν, καὶ ἀκολουθείτω μοι.	ἐμοὶ ἀκολουθείτω ...
25 ὃς γὰρ ἐὰν θέλῃ τὴν ψυχὴν αὐτοῦ σῶσαι, ἀπολέσει αὐτήν· ὃς δ' ἂν ἀπολέσῃ τὴν ψυχὴν αὐτοῦ ἕνεκεν ἐμοῦ, εὑρήσει αὐτήν.	*39 ὁ εὑρὼν τὴν ψυχὴν αὐτοῦ ἀπολέσει αὐτήν, καὶ ὁ ἀπολέσας τὴν ψυχὴν αὐτοῦ ἕνεκεν ἐμοῦ εὑρήσει αὐτήν.*	35 ὃς γὰρ ἐὰν θέλῃ τὴν ψυχὴν αὐτοῦ σῶσαι, ἀπολέσει αὐτήν· ὃς δ' ἂν ἀπολέσῃ τὴν ἑαυτοῦ ψυχὴν ἕνεκεν ἐμοῦ καὶ τοῦ εὐαγγελίου, σώσει αὐτήν.	*17 33 (198.): ὃς ἐὰν ζητήσῃ τὴν ψυχὴν αὐτοῦ περιποιήσασθαι, ἀπολέσει αὐτήν, καὶ ὃς ἐὰν ἀπολέσῃ, ζῳογονήσει αὐτήν.*	24 ὃς γὰρ ἂν θέλῃ τὴν ψυχὴν αὐτοῦ σῶσαι, ἀπολέσει αὐτήν· ὃς δ' ἂν ἀπολέσῃ τὴν ψυχὴν αὐτοῦ ἕνεκεν ἐμοῦ, οὗτος σώσει αὐτήν.	25 ὁ φιλῶν τὴν ψυχὴν αὐτοῦ ἀπολλύει αὐτήν, καὶ ὁ μισῶν τὴν ψυχὴν αὐτοῦ ἐν τῷ κόσμῳ τούτῳ εἰς ζωὴν αἰώνιον φυλάξει αὐτήν.
26 τί γὰρ ὠφεληθήσεται ἄνθρωπος, ἐὰν		36 τί γὰρ ὠφελήσει ἄνθρωπον, ἐάν		25 τί γὰρ ὠφελεῖται ἄνθρωπος	

(Fortsetzung / *continuation* s. S. 134)

Mt 16,24 ελϑ.] ακολουϑειν‖Mk: 16 *pc* Or | **25** τ. ψυ. αυ.²] τ. εαυτου ψυ.‖Mk: 28 *l*48 *l*49 | ευρ.] ουτος σωσει‖Lk24 Mk: 33 **λ**-22-1582 1365 Or Ir¹:² | **26** ωφελειται‖Lk: *Rpl* Chr¹ Cl PsIg Iu *L'* *Sc*[s] *C*b¹ — ωφελησει (*et* ανϑρωπον)‖Mk: Φ-(1604) **σ**'(1424)-349-945 *pc* {} — *txt*: ℵBL-33 700 λ1-22-1582 **ϕ**-174 Θ 157 *pc* Chr¹ Or {*Le*[k] fqr²30 *Sp*⁶h *C'*}

Mk 8,34 ακο.] ● ελϑειν‖p: ℌ⟨Δ⟩C² Σ-544-1071 **ϕ**' σ179-827-1082-1194-1402 A K Γ Π **047** 1342 *al* *Lk*[e] clz30 vg¹ Or — *txt*: 𝔓⁴⁵ *Rpl* (ελϑ. και ακο.: Δ) Or *L'*Au | απαρ.] αρνησασϑω‖Lk: D *Cs*¹:⁷f **35** τ. ψ¹. αυ.] ● τ. εαυτου ψ.‖35b: B 28 Or | τ. εαυ. ψ.²] ● τ. ψ. αυτου‖35a Mt Lk24 Jo: 𝔓⁴⁵ᵛ ℌC* ΣΦ-565-1071 λ1-827 σ1082-1391-1402 A **0214** 1342 *pm* — αυτην: D Γ 1093 — *om*‖Lk33: Or *Lq* | *om* κ. τ. ευαγ.‖Mt25.39 Lk: 33-579 *Lff*² *Cf* | σω.] ουτος σω.‖Lk24: *Rpl Geo* — ουτ.(*om*) ευρησει‖(Mt): (33)-579 28 (*Lff*²) — *txt*: 𝔓⁴⁵ ℌ'C*X WΘΣΦ-565-1071 **λ**⟨118⟩ σM-1194-1402-1424-1675 A D K Y Π **0214** *al* Or *L'* *S*,j *C*,f **36** ωφεληϑησεται‖Mt: {}¹ 33-579 *S'*{}² — ● ωφελει‖Lk: {𝔓⁴⁵*}¹ ℵBL-892 W **0214** 1241 *pc* *Lanq* {*Sj*(-λειται)}² *C*b¹f *Arm* — *txt*: *Rpl* Or *L'* *S*h *C'* | ανϑρωπος‖p: ℌ⟨B-892⟩C³ X Σ **λ** **ϕ**⟨124⟩ σM-349 E F G H Γ *al* *Ss*[c]pj | εαν κερ. ... ζημ.] ● κερδησαι ... ζημιωϑηναι: ℵBL(κερδησας‖Lk) **σ** *Cf* — *txt* (∼ τον κο. ολ. κερ.‖Mt): 𝔓⁴⁵ *Rpl* (C-33-579; *et* ∼ ολ. κο.: σ1606) Or *L*,Au *S*(')hj *C Geo*

Lk 9,23 ερχ.] ελϑειν‖Mt: *Rpl* — *txt*: 𝔓⁷⁵ ℌC*Ξ **λ**⟨118⟩-1582-2193 **ϕ**⟨124-346⟩-*l*547 σ990 A D K W Θ Π 157 *al* *l*303 Or | απαρν.‖Mt Mk: 𝔓⁷⁵ *Rpl* — *txt*: ℵB³LΞ-33-579 A D K Θ Π 1012 Or | *om* καϑ ημ.‖1427 Mt24.38 Mk: *Rpl* Or *Lvl*'r¹ *Ssp*¹hᵐ *Cs*¹ *Geo* — *txt*: 𝔓⁷⁵ ℵ*et*ᶜBLΞ-33-892-1241 1071-1604 **λ**-22 **ϕ** σM A K R Θ Π Ψ 157 *al* *Lfr*²z vg Hi *Scp*'h⁺ *Cs*⁷b *Arm Aeth*(∼ και² καϑ ημ.) | αυτου²] εαυτ.‖Mk: K **24** ∼ αυτου ψ.²‖Mk: Fʷ | *om* ουτος‖p: 56 *L*⟨ebq vg¹⟩ Mcn^Te *Ssc* *C*⟨b²⟩ *Arm Aeth* **25** ωφελει(-ησει)‖(Mk): ℵC-579 700 D (Ψ) 1396 (-ησεται: 157) (*l*49 *C*) | αν. κερ. ... απολ. ... ζημ.] αν. εαν κερδηση ... απολεση ... ζημιωϑη‖p: Dᶜ *L'*(l) Cp¹ *Arm* — ανϑρωπον κερδησαι ... απολεσαι ... ζημιωϑηναι‖Mk: D* *La*(ζημιωϑη)c Cp¹

Jo 12,25 απολεσει‖p: *Rpl* **ϕ***l*547 *L'* Cp¹ PsCp *S* *C*'⁺ᴮaˢ — *txt*: 𝔓⁶⁶·⁷⁵ ℵBLW-33 Ψ *Lff*²z Cp⁴ *C*b¹ | μισ.] απολεσας‖p: σ659 *Lg*² vg¹

Mt16 26p *cf.* ETh^II 67 (*transl.*): *Λέγει Ἰησοῦς· ὅστις τὰ πάντα γινώσκει ὑστερούμενος ἑαυτοῦ, παντὸς τοῦ τόπου ὑστερεῖται.*

(122)

136. Erste Leidensverkündigung.

Matth 16 21–23	Mark 8 31–33	Luk 9 22	*Mt 17 22–23 (141.)*	*Mk 9 31–32 (141.)*	
21 Ἀπὸ τότε ἤρξατο	31 Καὶ ἤρξατο		*22 ... εἶπεν*	*31 ... ἔλεγεν*	
ὁ Ἰησοῦς δεικνύειν	διδάσκειν		*αὐτοῖς ὁ Ἰησοῦς·*	*αὐτοῖς*	
τοῖς μαθηταῖς αὐτοῦ ὅ-	αὐτοὺς ὅ-	... 22 εἰπὼν ὅ-		*ὅ-*	*3*
τι δεῖ αὐτὸν εἰς Ἱεροσό-	τι δεῖ τὸν υἱὸν τοῦ	τι δεῖ τὸν υἱὸν τοῦ	*μέλλει ὁ υἱὸς τοῦ*	*τι ὁ υἱὸς τοῦ*	
λυμα ἀπελθεῖν καὶ πολ-	ἀνθρώπου πολ-	ἀνθρώπου *cf. 198.* πολ-	*ἀνθρώπου παρα-*	*ἀνθρώπου παρα-*	
λὰ παθεῖν	λὰ παθεῖν καὶ ἀποδοκι-	λὰ παθεῖν καὶ ἀποδοκι-	*δίδοσθαι*	*δίδοται*	*6*
ἀπὸ τῶν πρε-	μασθῆναι ὑπὸ τῶν πρε-	μασθῆναι ἀπὸ τῶν πρε-	*εἰς χεῖρας ἀν-*	*εἰς χεῖρας ἀν-*	
σβυτέρων καὶ ἀρχ-	σβυτέρων καὶ τῶν ἀρχ-	σβυτέρων καὶ ἀρχ-	*θρώπων,*	*θρώπων,*	
ιερέων καὶ γραμ-	ιερέων καὶ τῶν γραμ-	ιερέων καὶ γραμ-			*9*
ματέων	ματέων	ματέων			
					12
					15
καὶ ἀποκτανθῆναι	καὶ ἀποκτανθῆναι	καὶ ἀποκτανθῆναι	*23 καὶ ἀποκτενοῦσιν αὐ-*	*καὶ ἀποκτενοῦσιν αὐ-*	*18*
καὶ	καὶ	καὶ	*τόν, καὶ*	*τόν, καὶ ἀποκτανθεὶς*	
τῇ τρίτῃ ἡμέρᾳ	μετὰ τρεῖς ἡμέρας	τῇ τρίτῃ ἡμέρᾳ	*τῇ τρίτῃ ἡμέρᾳ*	*μετὰ τρεῖς ἡμέρας*	
ἐγερθῆναι.	ἀναστῆναι·	ἐγερθῆναι.	*ἐγερθήσεται.*	*ἀναστήσεται.*	*21*
	32 καὶ παρρησίᾳ τὸν λόγον ἐλά-				
22 καὶ προσλαβόμενος αὐτὸν	λει. καὶ προσλαβόμενος αὐτὸν			*32 οἱ δὲ*	
ὁ Πέτρος ἤρξατο ἐπιτιμᾶν αὐτῷ	ὁ Πέτρος ἤρξατο ἐπιτιμᾶν αὐτῷ.			*ἠγνόουν*	*24*
λέγων· ἵλεώς σοι, κύριε· οὐ μὴ ἔ-				*τὸ ῥῆμα,*	
σται σοι τοῦτο. 23 ὁ δὲ στρα-	33 ὁ δὲ ἐπιστρα-				
φεὶς	φεὶς καὶ ἰδὼν τοὺς μαθητὰς ἐπ-				*27*
εἶπεν τῷ Πέτρῳ· ὕπαγε ὀ-	ετίμησεν Πέτρῳ λέγων· ὕπαγε ὀ-				
πίσω μου, σατανᾶ· σκάνδαλον	πίσω μου, σατανᾶ,		*καὶ ἐλυπήθησαν σφό-*	*καὶ ἐφοβοῦντο αὐτὸν*	
εἶ ἐμοῦ, ὅτι οὐ φρονεῖς τὰ τοῦ	ὅτι οὐ φρονεῖς τὰ τοῦ		*δρα.*	*ἐπερωτῆσαι.*	*30*
θεοῦ ἀλλὰ τὰ τῶν ἀνθρώπων.	θεοῦ ἀλλὰ τὰ τῶν ἀνθρώπων.				

Mt 16,21 ο Ι.] ● Ι. Χριστος(*om*): ℵ*B*(2 D) 1279(*prm* ο) *C*s3:5b⟨2⟩ — *om*‖Mk8: ℵa-892 1604 Chr Or *L*Ir *Geo*2 | παθ. + και αποδοκιμασθηναι‖Mk8 Lk9 22: 700(*om* πολ. παθ.)-1604 *Arm* | απο] υπο‖Mk8: σ1402 D | τη τρ. ημ.] μετα τρεις ημερας‖27 63 Mk: D *C*b — μετα την τριτην ημεραν: *L*e[k] abcff2r1.2 | εγερθ.] αναστηναι‖Mk Lk24 7.46 18: Σ-544 σ1293 D 157 *pc l*184 **23** επιστραφεις‖Mk: L Σ-544 **ϕ σ** D K Θ Π *pc* Or

Mk 8,31 και1 + απο τοτε‖Mt16: W **ϕ**-*l*547 *C*s3:6b1f | ηρξ. + ο Ιησους‖Mt16: ϕ983-1689 | υπο] απο‖←Lk9 22: *Rpl* — *txt*: 𝔖⟨Δ-579⟩C NWcΣΦ-1071 λ872 σ115-517-827-945-1223 D G K Π *al* | *om* τ. πρε. και‖10 Mt20: 238 | ∼ αρχ. ... πρε.‖←: **ϕ**-*l*547 σ945-1223 | *om* των2‖Mt16 20 Lk←: 𝔖⟨ℵB⟩-[33] NΣ-28-565-700 **λ ϕ**⟨983⟩-*l*547 σ115-945-1606 A F G K Γ Π 1342 *al* | *om* των3‖←: XΔ-33-579 NWΣΦ-544-1071 **λ** ϕ230-*l*547 σ115-179-1424 A G K Π 157 1342 *al* | μετα τρ. ημ.] τη τριτη ημερα‖Mt16 17 **20** Lk9 18 24 7.46: 33-579 W-28-565 **λ ϕ**-*l*547 1342 *l*26 *l*258 *L*dg2 vg1 *S*s[c] *C*s2(3?):6(7?)f *Arm Aeth* | αναστ.]

(Fortsetzung / *continuation* → S. 133)

(122)

136. The First Prediction of the Passion.

	Lk 9 44–45 (141.)	Lk 24 6–8 (268.)	Mt 20 17–19 (205.)	Mk 10 33–34 (205.)	Lk 18 31–34 (205.)
	44 ... τοὺς λόγους	6 ... ὡς ἐλάλησεν	17 ... εἶπεν		31 ... εἶπεν πρὸς
	τούτους·	ὑμῖν ἔτι ὢν ἐν τῇ Γαλι-	αὐτοῖς· 18 ἰδοὺ ἀναβαί-	33 ὅτι ἰδοὺ ἀναβαί-	αὐτούς· ἰδοὺ ἀναβαί-
3		λαίᾳ, 7 λέγων	νομεν εἰς Ἱεροσόλυ-	νομεν εἰς Ἱεροσόλυ-	νομεν εἰς Ἰερουσαλημ,
	ὁ γὰρ υἱὸς τοῦ	τὸν υἱὸν τοῦ	μα, καὶ ὁ υἱὸς τοῦ	μα, καὶ ὁ υἱὸς τοῦ	
	ἀνθρώπου μέλλει παρα-	ἀνθρώπου ὅτι δεῖ παρα-	ἀνθρώπου παρα-	ἀνθρώπου παρα-	
6	δίδοσθαι	δοθῆναι	δοθήσεται	δοθήσεται	καὶ τελε-
	εἰς χεῖρας ἀν-	εἰς χεῖρας ἀν-			σθήσεται πάντα τὰ γε-
	θρώπων.	θρώπων ἁμαρτωλῶν			γραμμένα διὰ τῶν προ-
9			τοῖς ἀρχ-	τοῖς ἀρχ-	φητῶν τῷ υἱῷ τοῦ ἀν-
			ιερεῦσιν καὶ γραμ-	ιερεῦσιν καὶ τοῖς γραμ-	θρώπου·
			ματεῦσιν, καὶ κατακρι-	ματεῦσιν, καὶ κατακρι-	
12			νοῦσιν αὐτὸν θανάτῳ	νοῦσιν αὐτὸν θανάτῳ	
			19 καὶ παραδώσουσιν	καὶ παραδώσουσιν	32 παραδοθήσεται
			αὐτὸν τοῖς ἔθνεσιν εἰς	αὐτὸν τοῖς ἔθνεσιν,	γὰρ τοῖς ἔθνεσιν
15			τὸ ἐμπαῖξαι	34 καὶ ἐμπαίξουσιν αὐ-	καὶ ἐμπαιχθήσεται
				τῷ καὶ	καὶ ὑβρισθήσεται καὶ
			καὶ	ἐμπτύσουσιν αὐτῷ καὶ	ἐμπτυσθήσεται, 33 καὶ
18			μαστιγῶσαι	μαστιγώσουσιν αὐτὸν	μαστιγώσαντες
		καὶ σταυρωθῆναι	καὶ σταυρῶσαι,	καὶ ἀποκτενοῦσιν,	ἀποκτενοῦσιν αὐ-
		καὶ	καὶ	καὶ	τόν, καὶ
21		τῇ τρίτῃ ἡμέρᾳ	τῇ τρίτῃ ἡμέρᾳ	μετὰ τρεῖς ἡμέρας	τῇ ἡμέρᾳ
		ἀναστῆναι.	ἐγερθήσεται.	ἀναστήσεται.	τῇ τρίτῃ ἀναστήσεται.
	45 οἱ δὲ	8 καὶ			34 καὶ αὐτοὶ οὐδὲν
24	ἠγνόουν	ἐμνήσθησαν			τούτων συνῆκαν, καὶ ἦν
	τὸ ῥῆμα	τῶν ῥημάτων αὐτοῦ, ...			τὸ ῥῆμα
	τοῦτο, καὶ ἦν παρακε-				τοῦτο κε-
27	καλυμμένον ἀπ᾽ αὐτῶν				κρυμμένον ἀπ᾽ αὐτῶν,
	ἵνα μὴ αἴσθωνται αὐτό,				καὶ οὐκ ἐγίνωσκον
	καὶ ἐφοβοῦντο				τὰ λεγόμενα.
30	ἐρωτῆσαι αὐτὸν περὶ				
	τοῦ ῥήματος τούτου.				

εγερθηναι ‖ Lk9 Mt: 579 σ517 1241 txt: *Rpl L*' *S*ph **32** ● ∼ ο Π. αυ.: BL-892 *La* — *om* αυ.: D *Geo*^{B} — σ1402 | Π.] τω Π.: *Rpl* — txt: ℵBL D 21 **33** επιστ.] στραφεις ‖ Mt16: 33 σ517-827-1402 1342 *pc* | επετ.] ειπε ‖ ←: (ϕ346) 1093 1342 *Lk*[e] ff^{2}(ειπεν) *S*' *C*b'(^{1}f) — *om* ‖ Mt16: 60 | λεγ.] ● και(*om*) λεγει: ℌ⟨33-579⟩ C — *txt*: *Rpl L*' *S*h Cs$^{5:6}$

Lk 9,22 *om* και αποδ. ‖ Mt16: 28 | απο] υπο ‖ Mk8: λ-1582-2193 D | ∼ αρχ. ... πρε. ‖ Mk 14 53 15 1p: 579 ϕ' 213 *L*ff^{2}lqr^{1} vg^{1} — ∼ αρχ. ... γρα. ... πρε. ‖ Mk11 27 14 43 *etc.*: ϕ983 | τη τρ. ημ.] μεθ ημερας τρεις ‖ Mt27 63 Mk: D Mcn^{Ep} *L*e[k] bcff^{2}lq *S*s — μετα την τριτην ημεραν: *L*ar^{1} | εγερϑ.] αναστηναι ‖ 24 7.46 18 Mk: *Rpl* (*om* και^{5}—εγερϑ.: 579 477 ∩?) GrTh — εγερθησεται ‖ Mt17 20: ϕ13-346-543 *S*h^{Brs} — *txt*: 𝔓^{75} ℌ'XΞ Λ-28-700-1071-1604 λ22 ϕ124-174-230-788-983 σ⟨954⟩-M-945-1194-1207 E F^{W} G H R S U V W Γ Δ Θ Ψ Ω *mu* Mcn^{Ep}

(*137.* s. S. 130)

(Fortsetzung von / *continued from* S. 131)

Matthew	Mark	Luke
τὸν κόσμον ὅλον κερδήσῃ, τὴν δὲ ψυχὴν αὐτοῦ ζημιωθῇ; ἢ τί δώσει ἄνθρωπος ἀντάλλαγμα τῆς ψυχῆς αὐτοῦ;	κερδήσῃ τὸν κόσμον ὅλον καὶ ζημιωθῇ τὴν ψυχὴν αὐτοῦ; 37 τί γὰρ δώσει ἄνθρωπος ἀντάλλαγμα τῆς ψυχῆς αὐτοῦ;	κερδήσας τὸν κόσμον ὅλον ἑαυτὸν δὲ ἀπολέσας ἢ ζημιωθείς;
10 33 (72.): ὅστις δ' ἂν ἀρνήσηταί με ἔμπροσθεν τῶν ἀνθρώπων, ἀρνήσομαι αὐτὸν κἀγὼ ἔμπροσθεν τοῦ πατρός μου τοῦ ἐν οὐρανοῖς.	38 ὃς γὰρ ἐὰν ἐπαισχυνθῇ με καὶ τοὺς ἐμοὺς λόγους ἐν τῇ γενεᾷ ταύτῃ τῇ μοιχαλίδι καὶ ἁμαρτωλῷ, καὶ ὁ υἱὸς τοῦ ἀνθρώπου ἐπαισχυνθήσεται αὐτόν, ὅταν ἔλθῃ ἐν τῇ δόξῃ τοῦ πατρὸς αὐτοῦ μετὰ τῶν ἀγγέλων τῶν ἁγίων.	26 ὃς γὰρ ἂν ἐπαισχυνθῇ με καὶ τοὺς ἐμοὺς λόγους, τοῦτον ὁ υἱὸς τοῦ ἀνθρώπου ἐπαισχυνθήσεται, ὅταν ἔλθῃ ἐν τῇ δόξῃ αὐτοῦ καὶ τοῦ πατρὸς καὶ τῶν ἁγίων ἀγγέλων.
27 μέλλει γὰρ ὁ υἱὸς τοῦ ἀνθρώπου ἔρχεσθαι ἐν τῇ δόξῃ τοῦ πατρὸς αὐτοῦ μετὰ τῶν ἀγγέλων αὐτοῦ, καὶ τότε **ἀποδώσει ἑκάστῳ κατὰ τὴν πρᾶξιν αὐτοῦ.** (Ps62 13 etc.)		*12 9 (169.): ὁ δὲ ἀρνησάμενός με ἐνώπιον τῶν ἀνθρώπων ἀπαρνηθήσεται ἐνώπιον τῶν ἀγγέλων τοῦ θεοῦ.*
28 αμην λέγω ὑμῖν ὅτι εἰσίν τινες τῶν ὧδε ἑστώτων οἵτινες οὐ μὴ γεύσωνται θανάτου ἕως ἂν ἴδωσιν τὸν υἱὸν τοῦ ἀνθρώπου ἐρχόμενον ἐν τῇ βασιλείᾳ αὐτοῦ.	9 1 καὶ ἔλεγεν αὐτοῖς· αμην λέγω ὑμῖν ὅτι εἰσίν τινες τῶν ὧδε ἑστηκότων οἵτινες οὐ μὴ γεύσωνται θανάτου ἕως ἂν ἴδωσιν τὴν βασιλείαν τοῦ θεοῦ ἐληλυθυῖαν ἐν δυνάμει.	*cf. 234.* 27 λέγω δὲ ὑμῖν ἀληθῶς· εἰσίν τινες τῶν αὐτοῦ ἑστηκότων οἳ οὐ μὴ γεύσωνται θανάτου ἕως ἂν ἴδωσιν τὴν βασιλείαν τοῦ θεοῦ.

Mt 16,26 την δε—ζημ.] και ζημ. τ. ψ. αυ.(*om*)‖Mk: σ945 (1093) 1574 Chr$^{1:2}$ *L*ff^2 (∼ τ. ψ. αυ. ζ.: *S*c[s]p) *C*$^{2:7}$ **27** αγγ. αυ.] αγιων αγγ. αυ.‖Lk26: D* **047** Chr$^{1:2}$ *S*p$^{\langle 2\rangle}$ — αγγ. των αγι.‖Mk: C 1365 *L*b(αγγ. + αυ.) **28** *om* οτι‖Lk: *Rpl* Or *L*' — *txt*: ℵBL 700-1604 **ϕ σ**-349-1207-1223 Θ 157 *pc* *L*e[k] bcff$^{1.2}$g^{1}r^2 Or *S* | τ. ωδε εστ.] ωδε εστωτες: X ϕ174 E F G H V W Γ Δ *pm* | εστηκοτων‖p: 544 λ118 σM-349-1391-1402-1424 K Y Π *pl* Or$^{2:4}$

Mk 8,36 ∼ τ. ψ. αυ. ζημ.‖p: 544 σ267-1082 *pc* *L*r^2 *S*s[c]pj | τ. ψ. αυ.] τ. εαυτου ψ.‖35b: W σ179 **37** τι γαρ] η τι (+ γαρ)‖**p**: *Rpl* (σ1194 D) *L*'Au *S*'j *C*s^1 *Geo*^{1} — και τι: *S*s[c] *C*s^2 *Geo*^{2} *Δ*n^L — *txt* (*om* γαρ): 𝔓^{45} 𝔥⟨33⟩ W-28-565 **0214**^{v} 1241 Or *L*q *C*s^{4+1v}bf) *Arm* (*Δ*i^V n') | δωσ.] ● δοι: 𝔓^{45} ℵB(δω: ℵ^{c}L) — *txt*: *Rpl* (*om* δωσ. αν.: Δ) Or **38** *om* ταυ.‖Mt12 39 16 4: 𝔓^{45} W Or *L*k[e] ainr^2 Or | τ. μοι.] τ. πονηρα και μοι.‖←: ΘΦ ϕ124 — *prm* τη απιστω και *et om* και αμ.‖9 19p: *C*f | *om* αυτου‖Lk26: *l*53 Or *L*k[e] 30 | μετα] και‖←: 𝔓^{45} W *S*s[c] *Arm* | αγγ. τ. αγ.] αγ. αγγ.‖Lk9: 90 *pc* Or *L*cff^{2}z | αγγ. + αυτου‖Mt: ϕ346 F Cl *L*l* vg^3 *S*pj^{abf} *C*s$^{3:5}$b$^{\langle 1\rangle}$f | *om* τ. αγιων‖Mt: **λ** F Cl *L*l*^{v} vg^2 **9,1** *om* και ελ. αυ.‖**p**: 273 | *om* οτι‖Lk: 565 **σ**⟨954⟩ *pc* *l*49 *l*54 *S*j | ● ∼ ωδε τ. εστ. (∼ ωδε τινες): BD*(+ μετ εμου) *L*(k[e])n(= D?) (*S*s[c]) — ∼ τ. εστ. ωδε: 𝔓^{45} λ1-872 Or *S*p *C*,f *Geo*^{1} — *txt* (+ μετ εμου): *Rpl* (D^1) *L*'(abff^{2}qr^1) (*prm* ωδε: c; *om* ωδε: bir^1) *S*hj *Geo*^{2} | εστωτων‖Mt: ℵ-33-579 1047 | οιτι.] οι‖Lk: 33-579

Lk 9,25 ∼ ολ. τ. κο.‖Mk14 9p: 1071 157 *pc* *L*vl'⟨ar^2⟩r^{1}30 Cp | εαυ. δε] την δε ψυχην αυτου‖p: 472 | *om* απολ. η‖**p**: σ1424 *S*c *C*s$^{1:8}$ *Aeth* | ζημ. + την ψυχην αυτου‖MkMt: 175 *L*l(η ζ.] και)r^2 *C*s$^{2:8}$ **26** *om* αυτου και‖Mt27 Mk: ϕ1689 **047**(*om* αυτου) 59 477(*om* και) *pc* *S*s(*om* αυ. και τ. πατ.)cp *C*s$^{1:8}$b^1 | πατ. + αυτου‖p: ϕ1689 D *pc* *L*30 *S*cp *C*s$^{6(+1v):8}$b | και^3] μετα‖Mt27 Mk: 1093 1574 *S*sp **27** αλη.] αλη. οτι(∼)‖p: 𝔓^{45}(^{75}) 544 ϕ346 σM-267-1194 (D) K R Y Π *al* (*pc*) *L*vg^1(*om* αλ.) *S* — *om*‖p: 213 | αυτου] ωδε‖p: *Rpl* PsCae Eu Or^1 — *txt*: 𝔓^{75} ℵBLΞ λ1-1582 Cr^I Or^1 | εστωτων‖Mt: *Rpl* Eu Or^1 — *txt*: 𝔓^{75v} 𝔥⟨33⟩XΞ 28 λ2193 R U Γ *mu* Cr^I Or^1 | οι] οιτινες‖Mt Mk: 1241 544-700 **σ**⟨1675⟩-27 A K Y Π Ψ *al* PsCae Or | τ. βασ. τ. θε.] τον υιον του ανθρωπου ερχομενον εν τη δοξη αυτου‖Mt: D Or | θε. + εληλυθυιαν εν δυναμει‖Mk: 213 *pc* *l*53 (δυν.] δοξη)

(124)

138. Die Verklärung. *The Transfiguration.*

Matth 17 1–8

[1] Καὶ μεθ' ἡμέρας ἓξ παραλαμβάνει ὁ Ἰησοῦς τὸν Πέτρον καὶ Ἰάκωβον καὶ Ἰωάννην τὸν ἀδελφὸν αὐτοῦ, καὶ ἀναφέρει αὐτοὺς εἰς ὄρος ὑψηλὸν κατ' ἰδίαν. [2] καὶ μετεμορφώθη ἔμπροσθεν αὐτῶν, καὶ ἔλαμψεν τὸ πρόσωπον αὐτοῦ ὡς ὁ ἥλιος, τὰ δὲ ἱμάτια αὐτοῦ ἐγένετο λευκὰ ὡς τὸ φῶς.

[3] καὶ ἰδοὺ ὤφθη αὐτοῖς Μωυσῆς καὶ Ἠλίας μετ' αὐτοῦ συλλαλοῦντες.

[4] ἀποκριθεὶς δὲ ὁ Πέτρος εἶπεν τῷ Ἰησοῦ· κύριε,

Mark 9 2–8

[2] Καὶ μετὰ ἡμέρας ἓξ παραλαμβάνει ὁ Ἰησοῦς τὸν Πέτρον καὶ τὸν Ἰάκωβον καὶ Ἰωάννην, καὶ ἀναφέρει αὐτοὺς εἰς ὄρος ὑψηλὸν κατ' ἰδίαν μόνους. καὶ μετεμορφώθη ἔμπροσθεν αὐτῶν,

[3] καὶ τὰ ἱμάτια αὐτοῦ ἐγένετο στίλβοντα λευκὰ λίαν, οἷα γναφεὺς ἐπὶ τῆς γῆς οὐ δύναται οὕτως λευκᾶναι. [4] καὶ ὤφθη αὐτοῖς Ἠλίας σὺν Μωυσεῖ, καὶ ἦσαν συλλαλοῦντες τῷ Ἰησοῦ.

[5] καὶ ἀποκριθεὶς ὁ Πέτρος λέγει τῷ Ἰησοῦ· ῥαββί,

Luk 9 28–36

[28] Ἐγένετο δὲ μετὰ τοὺς λόγους τούτους ὡσεὶ ἡμέραι ὀκτώ, καὶ παραλαβὼν Πέτρον καὶ Ἰωάννην καὶ Ἰάκωβον ἀνέβη εἰς τὸ ὄρος προσεύξασθαι. [29] καὶ ἐγένετο ἐν τῷ προσεύχεσθαι αὐτὸν τὸ εἶδος τοῦ προσώπου αὐτοῦ ἕτερον καὶ ὁ ἱματισμὸς αὐτοῦ λευκὸς ἐξαστράπτων.

[30] καὶ ἰδοὺ ἄνδρες δύο συνελάλουν αὐτῷ, οἵτινες ἦσαν Μωυσῆς καὶ Ἠλίας, [31] οἳ ὀφθέντες ἐν δόξῃ ἔλεγον τὴν ἔξοδον αὐτοῦ, ἣν ἤμελλεν πληροῦν ἐν Ἰερουσαλήμ. [32] ὁ δὲ Πέτρος καὶ οἱ σὺν αὐτῷ ἦσαν βεβαρημένοι ὕπνῳ· διαγρηγορήσαντες δὲ εἶδον τὴν δόξαν αὐτοῦ καὶ τοὺς δύο ἄνδρας τοὺς συνεστῶτας αὐτῷ. [33] καὶ ἐγένετο ἐν τῷ διαχωρίζεσθαι αὐτοὺς ἀπ' αὐτοῦ εἶπεν Πέτρος πρὸς τὸν Ἰησοῦν· ἐπιστάτα,

> 1 14: ... καὶ ἐθεασάμεθα τὴν δόξαν αὐτοῦ, δόξαν ὡς μονογενοῦς παρὰ πατρός, πλήρης χάριτος καὶ ἀληθείας,

---

Mt 17,1 και[2](*et*[3]) + τον‖Mk: ℵ-33-(892 D*) Θ 157 | κατ ιδ.] λιαν‖4s: D Eu **2** το φ.] χιων‖28 3: D 372 Dio[A1] Ep *L*⟨q⟩ Hil *S*c[s]p[1] Ef *C*b[2] *Geo*[2] **3** *om* ιδ.‖Mk: 28 Chr *L*vg[1] *S*c[s]pj *C*b[1] *Geo*[2]([1] ευθεως) | ● ωφθησαν: 𝔓[44v] *Rpl* Chr Or *L*ff[1]q vg[4] *S*'j *C*s[3]b — *txt*: ℵB-33 λ1582 φ⟨983⟩-*l*547 σ945 D Θ 157 *pc l*184 *L*' *S*c[s] *C*[1v] | ● ∼ συλ. μετ αυ.‖Mk: ℵB-892 λ1-1582 W Chr *L*ff[1.2]q {*C*} **4** *om* ο‖Lk: 892 σ1194 H W Θ

Mk 9,2 *om* ο Ιη.‖Lk: 348 *pc L*30 *C*b[1] | τ. Ια. κ. Ιω.] Ια. κ. (+ τ.) Ιω.‖14 33 Mt: (X)Δ Θ-544-700 λ118 (φ983-1689) σ349 Γ Ω **0131** 157 *pm* — ● τ. Ια. κ. τον Ιω.: 𝔓[45] ℵC[v]L-33-579 W-(28)-565 λ'-22 φ'-230 D K U Y Π 1342 *pm* — *txt*: *Rpl* | ∼ Ιω. ... Ια.‖Lk: 28 *pc C*s[1:6] | αναφ.] αναγει‖Lk 4 5: 565 D **0131** | υψ. + λιαν‖Mt 4 8: ℵ φ124 52 *l*18 *l*19 *C*f — altissimum: *L*bcff[2]ir[1] | *om* μον.‖Mt: 579 *pc l*32 *l*184 *C*b[1] | και[5] + εν(εγενετο εν: 565) τω προσευχεσθαι αυτον(-ους)‖Lk: (𝔓[45v] W)Θ-28-565 (φ) 472 Or *S*j | αυτων + και ελαμψεν το προσωπον αυτου ως ο ηλιος‖Mt: 1038 *l*32 *l*48 *l*49 *l*251 *S*s[c](*om* το—ηλιος) **3** *om* στιλ.‖Mt: λ⟨118⟩ φ346 *Lk*[e] l *S*s[c] *C*b[1] | *om* λιαν‖p: Δ 544 σ1424 *pc L*(*et om* λευκα: bcr[2])l 30 *S*s[c] *C*b[1]f *Geo*[2] *Aeth* | λιαν + ως(ωσει) χιων‖Mt 28 3: *Rpl* (28-1071 φ230 σ179-827 K Y Π *al l*184) *L*' *S*,j *C*b'(ως χ. και λευ. λι.) *Geo*[2] — + ως το φως‖Mt: *l*13 *l*48 *l*49 *l*251 Or — *txt*: 𝔓[45v] 𝔥⟨33-579⟩C WΘ **λ**⟨118⟩ φ1689 *Lk*[e] d vg[1] *C*sb[4](στιλ. + και)f *Arm Geo*[1] *Aeth* | *om* οια—λευ.‖p: X *L*an *S*s[c] **4** και[1] + ιδου‖Mt Lk: W-28-565-700 **φ**⟨124⟩ *S*j — + ελαμψεν το προσωπον αυτου ως ο ηλιος και‖Mt 2: *l*251 | αυτω‖Lk: 28 *L*c(συν αυτω) *Geo*[1] | συν Μ.] και Μωυσης (∼ Μ. και Η.)‖p: 544 1093 *L*(cz) vg[1] *S*s[c]p'([8] *C*s[3:6]b[1]f) | *om* και ησ.‖Mt: 544 1093 *l*48 *l*49 *L*c *S*s[c]p *C*sf | ησ. συλ.] συνελαλουν‖Lk: Θ-565-700 D **λ**⟨118⟩ *L*anq *Arm* **5** ∼ ειπεν Πε. *et om* ο‖Lk: 𝔓[45] W | *om* ο‖Lk: (𝔓[45] W) F 253 | λεγ.] ειπεν‖Mt: (𝔓[45]) 892 (W)Θ-565-700 σ945 D *L*abn[v] vg[1]

Lk 9,28 οκ.] εξ‖p: 1071 *L*l | *om* και[1] *cf.* 21.46 7 11 *etc.*: 𝔓[45] ℵ*B-579(παρ. + δε) 28 H 157 *L*vl'r[1] vg[4] Hi *S*' *C*' — *txt*: 𝔓[75v] *Rpl L*e cfqz vg' *S*scj *C*b[1] | παραλαμβανει‖p: 1093 *L*vg[1] Hi — παρελαβεν‖p: *L*'⟨a⟩ Hi *S*scpj *C*⟨b[1]⟩ | παρ. + ο Ιησους‖p: σ115 Ω (1093) *pc L*vg[1] *S*pj(ο κυριος Ι.) *C*s[3:8] | Π.] τον Π.‖**p**: 1071 φ124-174 *pc* Eu | ∼ Ια. ... Ιω.‖Mt Mk: 𝔓[45.75] C[3]LXΞ-33-892 σM-71-692-1194 D G[m] 157 *pc L*r[1.2] vg[10] Hi *S*scp *C*s[3:9]b | ανεβη] και αν.‖p: G 1093 *pc L*⟨a⟩ Hi *S*scpj | *om* προσευ.‖Mt Mk: L **29** αυτον + κατα μονας‖9 18: 1375 | τ. ειδ.] η ειδεα‖Mt 28 3: D Or **30** συνελ.] συλλαλουντες‖p: 𝔓[45] *pc S*sc **31** οφθ. + αυτω‖p: C[3] φ983-1689 σM-71-267-659-692-1194 *al l*40 *l*50 *C*s[1:9] **33** Π.] ● ο Π.‖p: 𝔓[45.75] 𝔥CXΞ N-544-1071 **λ φ** σM A D K R Δ Π 157 *pm* — *txt*: *Rpl* | πρ. τ. Ι.] τω Ιησου‖Mt Mk: D'

Matth 17

καλόν ἐστιν ἡμᾶς ὧδε εἶναι· εἰ θέλεις, ποιήσω ὧδε τρεῖς σκηνάς, σοὶ μίαν καὶ Μωυσεῖ μίαν καὶ Ἠλίᾳ μίαν.

⁵ ἔτι αὐτοῦ λαλοῦντος, ἰδοὺ νεφέλη φωτεινὴ ἐπεσκίασεν αὐτούς,

3 17 (18.):	
καὶ ἰδοὺ φωνὴ ἐκ τῶν οὐρανῶν λέγουσα· οὗτός ἐστιν ***ὁ υἱός μου ὁ ἀγαπητός, ἐν ᾧ εὐδόκησα.***	καὶ ἰδοὺ φωνὴ ἐκ τῆς νεφέλης λέγουσα· οὗτός ἐστιν **ὁ υἱός μου ὁ ἀγαπητός, ἐν ᾧ εὐδόκησα·** αὐτοῦ ἀκούετε. ⁶ καὶ ἀκούσαντες οἱ μαθηταὶ ἔπεσαν ἐπὶ πρόσωπον αὐτῶν καὶ ἐφοβήθησαν σφόδρα. ⁷ καὶ προσῆλθεν ὁ Ἰησοῦς καὶ ἁψάμενος αὐτῶν εἶπεν· ἐγέρθητε καὶ

Ps 2 7 Is 42 1 44 2

Mark 9

καλόν ἐστιν ἡμᾶς ὧδε εἶναι, καὶ ποιήσωμεν σκηνὰς τρεῖς, σοὶ μίαν καὶ Μωυσεῖ μίαν καὶ Ἠλίᾳ μίαν. ⁶ οὐ γὰρ ᾔδει τί ἀποκριθῇ· ἔκφοβοι γὰρ ἐγένοντο. ⁷ καὶ ἐγένετο νεφέλη ἐπισκιάζουσα αὐτοῖς,

1 11 (18.):	
καὶ φωνὴ ἐγένετο ἐκ τῶν οὐρανῶν· ***σὺ εἶ ὁ υἱός μου ὁ ἀγαπητός, ἐν*** *σοὶ* ***εὐδόκησα.***	καὶ ἦλθεν φωνὴ ἐκ τῆς νεφέλης· οὗτός ἐστιν **ὁ υἱός μου ὁ ἀγαπητός,** ἀκούετε αὐτοῦ.

Luk 9

καλόν ἐστιν ἡμᾶς ὧδε εἶναι, καὶ ποιήσωμεν σκηνὰς τρεῖς, μίαν σοὶ καὶ μίαν Μωυσεῖ καὶ μίαν Ἠλίᾳ, μὴ εἰδὼς ὃ λέγει. ³⁴ ταῦτα δὲ αὐτοῦ λέγοντος ἐγένετο νεφέλη καὶ ἐπεσκίαζεν αὐτούς· ἐφοβήθησαν δὲ ἐν τῷ εἰσελθεῖν αὐτοὺς

3 22 (18.):	
... καὶ φωνὴν ἐξ οὐρανοῦ γενέσθαι· ***υἱός μου εἶ σύ, ἐγὼ σήμερον γεγέννηκά σε.***	εἰς τὴν νεφέλην. ³⁵ καὶ φωνὴ ἐγένετο ἐκ τῆς νεφέλης λέγουσα· οὗτός ἐστιν **ὁ υἱός μου ὁ ἐκλελεγμένος,** αὐτοῦ ἀκούετε.

Mt 17,4 *om* ει θελ.‖p: Or *Lc Sp*^{1} *Geo*^{2} | ποιησωμεν‖p: *Rpl* Or *L*' *S*,j *C* — *txt*: ℵBC* 700 ϕ174 *L*bff$^{1.2}$ vg^{4} | *om* ωδε^{2}‖p: σ945-1223 252 Or *L*ff^{1}g^{1} vg^{3} *S*j *C*b^{2} *Arm* | ∼ σκ. τρ.‖p: B *L*e[k] | ∼ μι. σοι‖Lk: ΟΣ *L*r^{1v} vg^{1} *Sp* {*C*} *Geo*$^{2.ch}$ | ∼ μι. M.‖Lk: *Sp* {*C*} *Geo*$^{2.ch}$ | ∼ μι. H.‖Lk: *Rpl Lq Sp* {*C*} *Geo*$^{2.ch}$ — *txt*: ℌ⟨B⟩C ΟΣΦ-700 λ1-1582 ϕ⟨983⟩-174-230-*l*547 σ349-517-1010-1293-1424 D K Δ Θ Π 157 *pm L*' *S*'j{} *Geo*^{1} *Aeth* | μι.^{3} + μη ειδως τι λεγει‖Lk: 1093 **5** ετι + δε‖Lk: Θ 245 *C*b^{1} | *om* ιδου(*et*)^{2}‖(p): (1396) *L* vg^{1} *S*c[s]p *Geo*$^{2.ch}$ | επεσκιαζεν‖Lk: D*^{v} *L*ff^{2} | ● ∼ ακου. αυ.‖Mk7: ℵB-33 λ1-1582 D Hip Or *L*ff^{1}r^{2} *C Geo*^{1} — *txt*: *Rpl* Chr *L*' PsAu Cp Hil *S*,j Ef *Geo*$^{2.ch}$

Mk 9,5 και^{2}] ει θελεις‖Mt: 28 — θελ.‖Mt: Θ-565 ϕ D *L*bff^{2}i *C*f — και ει θελ.‖Mt: 700 *L*ac(ει ουν θελ.)fn^{v}q — και θελ.‖Mt: 1071 W | ποιησω‖Mt: W-1071 D *L*bff^{2}ir^{2} | ποι. + ωδε‖Mt: 𝔓^{45} C WΘ-565 1093 1342 *L*cff^{2}z vg^{1} *S*j *C*b^{2} *Geo*^{2} | ● ∼ τρεις σκ.‖Mt: 𝔓^{45} ℌC 1071 σ1082-1391-1402-1424 1342 *pc L*' *S*'j — *txt*: *Rpl L*fq *S*h *Arm* | ∼ μιαν H.‖Lk: 579 σ1082 157 1342 *pc L*k[e] *C*,f *Arm Aeth* **7** και^{1} + ιδου‖Mt: WΘ-28-565-1071 ϕ 50 | αυτοις] αυτους‖MtLk: 𝔓^{45v} W-28-1071 ϕ⟨543-983⟩ σ517-659-1675 H U *pc l*48 *l*49 *l*184 | ηλθ.] ● εγενετο‖11Lk: ℌ'⟨33⟩(∼ εκ τ. νε. εγ. φω.: ℵ) C 1342 *Sp*^{5}h^{m} *C*bf *Arm* — ιδου‖Mt: *L*cz — ιδου εγενετο‖p: 300 *L*ff^{2}(ιδ. φω. εξηλθ.) — *om*‖Mt: W **λ**⟨118⟩ σ7-267-1391 Y *L*[ek] *Sp*' — *txt*: *Rpl L*' *S*' | ∼ φωνη ηλ.‖11Lk: 28 ϕ 1093 (*L*ff^{2}) *S*s[c] *C*sb^{1}f | νεφελης + λεγουσα‖MtLk35: LΔ(λεγων)Ψ-33 WΘΦ-28-565-700-1071 **λ** ϕ-230 σM-7-71-115-179-267-692-1223-1606-1675 A D 157 *al L*⟨k[e]⟩ *Sph*$^{+}$j *C*s$^{2:6}$f *Arm*$^{\langle pc\rangle}$ | αγα. + εν ω ευδοκησα‖11Mt5.17: ℵ^{a}Δ ϕ983-1689 — + ον εξελεξαμην‖Lk35: **0131** 1093 | ∼ αυ. ακου.‖p: *Rpl L*bff^{2}q *S*,j — *txt* (-σατε): ℌ⟨Δ(*om*)⟩C WΘ-(28)-565-1071 **λ**⟨118⟩ σ179-517-(954) D **0131** 1342 *pc* Hip *L*' *C*,f *Geo*

Lk 9,33 *om* και^{2}‖Mt: 𝔓^{45} ϕ69 σM-7-1194 D U *al L*ff^{2}lr^{1}z vg^{3} *S*j *C*sb^{2} | ποι.] ει θελεις ποιησω(-σωμεν)‖Mt: D(*om* ει) (*L*ff^{2} *C*b) | ποι. + ωδε‖Mt: D 1093 *L*lr^{1} vg^{1} *S*c *C*s$^{1:7}$b^{3} *Geo*^{1} | ∼ τρεις σκ.‖Mt: LΞ-33-892 544-1071 ϕ σ1424 D F^{W}K *pc L*⟨abq vg^{1}⟩ Mcn^{Te} *S*scp | ∼ σοι μι.‖MtMk: ℵ-579 **λ**-1582-2193 Ψ *pc l*48 *L*q30 vg^{1} Ar Mcn^{Te} *S*scpj | ∼ M. μι.‖MtMk: ℵ-579 λ1278 *pc L*ff^{2} Ar Mcn^{Te} *S*scpj | ∼ H. μι.‖p: 579 700 **λ**-1582-2193 Ψ *pc l*48 *L*ff^{2} Ar Mcn^{Te} *S*scpj | ∼ H. ... M.‖Mk4: ϕ13-69 | ο] τι‖Mk: σ7-267-659-1391-1606 Or$^{1:2}$ **34** λεγ.] λαλουντος‖Mt: 1604 σ1207 K *pc L*⟨e a⟩ — + ιδου‖Mt: 700 *C*b^{1} *Geo* | *om* εγεν. ... και‖Mt: N-700(*om* εγεν.)-1604 *C*b^{1} *Geo* | νεφελη + φωτεινη‖Mt: N-1604 *Sp*^{1} *C*b^{1} | ● επεσκιασεν‖Mt: 𝔓^{45} *Rpl L*' *S*'j *C Arm* — *txt*: 𝔓^{75} ℵBL-579-1241 157 *l*47 *l*183 *L*a *Sp*^{1} *Geo* **35** φω. εγ.] ηλθεν φω.‖Mk7: D — εγ. φω.‖←Mt: **λ**-2193 *pc* — φω.‖Mt: K | *om* λεγ.‖22Mk: 𝔓^{45} 700 *pc* Ep(∼) *L*b(?)cl *S*s *C*s$^{1:5}$ | εκλ.] αγαπητος (+ εν ω ευδοκησα)‖(Mt5.17Mk11)7: *Rpl* (C^{3} 544 ϕ1689 σM-7-71-692-1194 D Ψ *al l*12^{1} *l*19 *l*31 *l*47 *l*48 *l*49 *l*69^{1} *l*183 *l*185^{1} *l*211^{1} *l*950 *l*1127^{1} *l*1642^{1} *l*1663^{1}) Cl Ep *L*' Mcn^{Te} *S*c(και ο αγαπ. μου)ph^{1}j *C*b^{1} Sch — εκλεκτος‖23 25: 700 λ1-22-2193 ϕ*l*547^{1}(ο^{1}—εκλ.] ο εκλεκ. μου υιος) Θ *pc* {} — *txt*: 𝔓$^{45.75}$ ℌ'⟨33⟩(λεγμενος(!): 579)Ξ {*L*aff^{2}lz30 vg^{3} *S*sh^{m} *C*' *Arm Aeth*} | ∼ ακου. αυ.‖Mk7: 579 D *L*ec

μὴ φοβεῖσθε. 8 ἐπάραντες δὲ τοὺς ὀφθαλμοὺς αὐτῶν οὐδένα εἶδον εἰ μὴ αὐτὸν Ἰησοῦν μόνον.	8 καὶ ἐξάπινα περιβλεψάμενοι οὐκέτι οὐδένα εἶδον ἀλλὰ τὸν Ἰησοῦν μόνον μεθ' ἑαυτῶν.	36 καὶ ἐν τῷ γενέσθαι τὴν φωνὴν εὑρέθη Ἰησοῦς μόνος. καὶ αὐτοὶ ἐσίγησαν καὶ οὐδενὶ ἀπήγγειλαν ἐν ἐκείναις ταῖς ἡμέραις οὐδὲν ὧν ἑόρακαν.

(125)

139. Das Kommen des Elias. *The Coming of Elijah.*

Matth 17 9–13	Mark 9 9–13	
9 Καὶ καταβαινόντων αὐτῶν ἐκ τοῦ ὄρους ἐνετείλατο αὐτοῖς ὁ Ἰησοῦς λέγων· μηδενὶ εἴπητε τὸ ὅραμα ἕως οὗ ὁ υἱὸς τοῦ ἀνθρώπου ἐκ νεκρῶν ἀναστῇ.	9 Καταβαινόντων δὲ αὐτῶν ἀπὸ τοῦ ὄρους διεστείλατο αὐτοῖς ἵνα μηδενὶ ἃ εἶδον διηγήσωνται, εἰ μὴ ὅταν ὁ υἱὸς τοῦ ἀνθρώπου ἐκ νεκρῶν ἀναστῇ. 10 καὶ τὸν λόγον ἐκράτησαν πρὸς ἑαυτοὺς συζητοῦντες τί ἐστιν τὸ ἐκ νεκρῶν ἀναστῆναι.	*cf.* 140.
10 καὶ ἐπηρώτησαν αὐτὸν οἱ μαθηταὶ λέγοντες· τί οὖν οἱ γραμματεῖς λέγουσιν ὅτι Ἠλίαν δεῖ ἐλθεῖν πρῶτον; 11 ὁ δὲ ἀποκριθεὶς εἶπεν· **Ἠλίας** μὲν ἔρχεται καὶ **ἀποκαταστήσει** πάντα·	11 καὶ ἐπηρώτων αὐτὸν λέγοντες· ὅ τι λέγουσιν οἱ γραμματεῖς ὅτι Ἠλίαν δεῖ ἐλθεῖν πρῶτον; 12 ὁ δὲ ἔφη αὐτοῖς· **Ἠλίας** ἐλθὼν πρῶτον **ἀποκαθιστάνει** πάντα·	Ml 3 22f.
cf. v. 12b ↓	καὶ πῶς γέγραπται ἐπὶ τὸν υἱὸν τοῦ ἀνθρώπου, ἵνα πολλὰ πάθῃ καὶ ἐξουδενηθῇ;	
12 λέγω δὲ ὑμῖν ὅτι Ἠλίας ἤδη ἦλθεν, καὶ οὐκ ἐπέγνωσαν αὐτόν, ἀλλ' ἐποίησαν	13 ἀλλὰ λέγω ὑμῖν ὅτι καὶ Ἠλίας ἐλήλυθεν, καὶ ἐποίησαν	

Mt 17,8 ουδ.] ουκετι ουδ.‖Mk: C*ΟΣ | αυτον] ● τον‖Mk: *Rpl* *L*(∼ μο. τ. Ι.: ')qr² *Sj* — *txt*: ℵ(∼ Ι. αυ.)B* 700 Θ | μο. + μεθ εαυτων‖Mk: C*-33 **9** εκ¹] απο‖pLk 9 37: ΟΣ σ-349 K *pc* | *om* ο Ι.‖p: λ⟨1⟩ *pc l*253 | αναστη] ● εγερθη *cf.* Jo 2 22 21 14 R 7 4: B 1604 D **10** τι ουν] τι(οτι)‖(p): (33) 700 *l*184(τι οτι) *Sc*[s] *C*b *Geo*² | ∼ λεγ. οι γρ.‖p: 33 *Lr*¹30 *Sc*[s]p³ **11** ειπ. + αυτοις‖p: *Rpl L*'Au¹ *Sc*[s]p⁶hj *Cs*² — *txt*: B-33 700 φ124-788 D W Θ *Le*[k] abcff²r² vg² Au¹ *Sp*' *Cs*⁷b Sch | ερχ. + πρωτον‖p: *Rpl* (-ος: ΟΣ; ∼ κ. αποκ. πρω.: L) *Lf*q *S*' — *txt*: ℵB 700 λ1-22-1582 φ788 σ-349-659-1194-1402 D W Θ Chr Iu *L*'Au *Sc*[s]j *C Arm* **12** οτι + και‖p: 473 478 *Sc* | ηδη] *om*‖p: Z σ1424 *S*scp *C*b¹ *Geo*¹ — μεν ηδη: *Lan*ᵛ

Mk 9,8 *om* ουκετι‖Mt: 𝔓⁴⁵ᵛ 565 σ267 *pc Lk*[e] *Sp C*bf *Geo*¹ᶜ·² | αλλα] ● ει μη‖Mt: ℌ⟨LΔ⟩ ΝΣ-544 σ⟨954⟩-1402 D 0131 1342 *al l*13 *l*48 *l*49 *l*251 *L Ss*[c]p⁵hj *Aeth* | *om* μεθ εαυ.‖Mt: 544 0131 *pc Lk*[e] *al* vg¹ *Ss*[c] *Cs*¹:⁶f **9** κατ. δε] ● και κατ.‖p: ℌ⟨579(*om* κατ.—απο)⟩C ΝΣ-1071 σ1223 D 0131 1342 *pc L*' *S*(*om* και: s[c])pj *C*b — *txt*: *Rpl* (*om* δε: φ828 *Lf Sh Cs*(εγενετο δε κατ.: f) | απο] ● εκ‖p: BΨ-33 D *pc* | διεστ.] ενετειλατο‖p: 1574 — + ο Ιησους‖p: 565 (∼ αυτοις ο Ι.: *pc*) *Sj*(κυριος Ι. *et* = *pc*) *Aeth* | ινα—οταν] λεγων μηδενι ειπητε εως ου‖p: 1574 — *prm* λεγων‖p: *Cf* | ει μη οτ.] εως ου‖p: 700 **11** επηρωτησαν‖p: 33-579 W-28 λ⟨118⟩ φ A *pc l*48 *Laq* vg¹ *Sj C*,f | αυτ. + οι μαθηται‖p: 1093 | ο τι] τι ουν‖p: WΘ *Lacflr*²z vg *Sp* — τι‖p: 238 *Lk*[e] qr¹ *C*sb'⁽⁴⁾ — τι οτι‖p: σ1402 *Sj* — πως ουν(*om*)‖Mt 22 43: φ *C*b¹(f *Geo*ᴮ) | ∼ οι γρ. λεγ.‖p: W D *La Sj* **12** εφη] αποκριθεις ειπεν‖p: *Rpl L S*'j *Arm* — *txt*: ℌ⟨33⟩C 1093 1342 *Sp C*,f *Δ*a iᵀ | ● Η. + μεν‖p: *Rpl Sh*ᵗ *C*,f — *txt*: LΨ-892 W-28-565 λ⟨118⟩ σ1207 D *L Ss*[c]phᵐ | *om* πρω.‖p: 700 *Cs*³:⁴ | αποκαταστησει‖p: C-579 Θ-565 1093 *L*⟨k[e] vg¹⟩ *Sh*ᵐ *C*⟨f⟩ *Arm* | επι τ. υι.] περι του υιου‖14 21 Mt 26 24: 1093 **13** *om* και¹‖p: ΝWΘΣ-28-565-700 λ φ69-346-543-788 σM-7-692-827 U Γ *al Lk*[e] alr² vg⁵ *Ss*[c]p¹ *C*b *Arm Aeth* | Η. + ηδη‖p: C ΝW(∼)Σ-700 λ⟨118⟩-1278 σ945 *pc Lf*i30 *Sj* | ελη.] ηλθεν‖p: C W-28-700 λ⟨118⟩ *pc* | εποι. + εν‖p: ℵᶜLΨ λ872 σ27-1194 K Y Π *al Ss*[c]hᵐ

Lk 9,36 ∼ουδεν απη.—ημ.‖Mk 16 8: 998 *L*bff²lq

Mt 17 12p *cf.* ETh^II 51 (*transl.*): *Εἶπον αὐτῷ οἱ μαθηταὶ αὐτοῦ· ποίᾳ ἡμέρᾳ γενήσεται ἡ ἀνάπαυσις τῶν νεκρῶν καὶ ποίᾳ ἡμέρᾳ ἔρχεται ὁ κόσμος ὁ καινός; εἶπεν αὐτοῖς· αὕτη ἣν προσδέχεσθε ἐλήλυθεν· ἀλλ' ὑμεῖς οὐ γινώσκετε αὐτήν.*

ἐν αὐτῷ ὅσα ἠθέλησαν· οὕτως καὶ ὁ υἱὸς τοῦ ἀνθρώπου μέλλει πάσχειν ὑπ' αὐτῶν. ¹³ τότε συνῆκαν οἱ μαθηταὶ ὅτι περὶ Ἰωάννου τοῦ βαπτιστοῦ εἶπεν αὐτοῖς.

11 14 (77.): καὶ εἰ θέλετε δέξασθαι, αὐτός ἐστιν Ἠλίας ὁ μέλλων ἔρχεσθαι.

αὐτῷ ὅσα ἤθελον, καθὼς γέγραπται ἐπ' αὐτόν.

cf. v. 12 b ↑

(126) ***140.*** **Heilung des epileptischen Knaben.** ***The Healing of an Epileptic Child.***

Matth 17 14–20	**Mark 9** 14–29	**Luk 9** 37–43 a
¹⁴ Καὶ ἐλθόντων αὐτῶν πρὸς τὸν ὄχλον	*cf. 139.* ¹⁴ Καὶ ἐλθὼν πρὸς τοὺς μαθητὰς εἶδεν ὄχλον πολὺν περὶ αὐτοὺς καὶ γραμματεῖς συζητοῦντας πρὸς αὐτούς. ¹⁵ καὶ εὐθὺς πᾶς ὁ ὄχλος ἰδόντες αὐτὸν ἐξεθαμβήθησαν, καὶ προστρέχοντες ἠσπάζοντο αὐτόν. ¹⁶ καὶ ἐπηρώτησεν αὐτούς· τί συζητεῖτε πρὸς αὐτούς; ¹⁷ καὶ ἀπεκρίθη αὐτῷ εἷς ἐκ τοῦ ὄχλου·	³⁷ Ἐγένετο δὲ τῇ ἑξῆς ἡμέρᾳ κατελθόντων αὐτῶν ἀπὸ τοῦ ὄρους συνήντησεν αὐτῷ ὄχλος πολύς.
προσῆλθεν αὐτῷ ἄνθρωπος γονυπετῶν αὐτὸν ¹⁵ καὶ λέγων· κύριε, ἐλέησόν μου τὸν υἱόν, ὅτι σεληνιάζεται καὶ κακῶς πάσχει· πολλάκις γὰρ πίπτει εἰς τὸ πῦρ καὶ πολλάκις εἰς τὸ ὕδωρ·	διδάσκαλε, ἤνεγκα τὸν υἱόν μου πρός σε, ἔχοντα πνεῦμα ἄλαλον· ¹⁸ καὶ ὅπου ἐὰν αὐτὸν καταλάβῃ, cf. v. 22 ↓ ῥήσσει αὐτόν, καὶ ἀφρίζει καὶ τρίζει τοὺς ὀδόντας καὶ ξηραίνεται·	³⁸ καὶ ἰδοὺ ἀνὴρ ἀπὸ τοῦ ὄχλου ἐβόησεν λέγων· διδάσκαλε, δέομαί σου ἐπιβλέψαι ἐπὶ τὸν υἱόν μου, ὅτι μονογενής μοί ἐστιν, ³⁹ καὶ ἰδοὺ πνεῦμα λαμβάνει αὐτόν, καὶ ἐξαίφνης κράζει καὶ σπαράσσει αὐτὸν μετὰ ἀφροῦ, καὶ μόγις ἀποχωρεῖ ἀπ' αὐτοῦ συντρῖβον αὐτόν·
¹⁶ καὶ προσήνεγκα αὐτὸν τοῖς μαθηταῖς σου, καὶ οὐκ ἠδυνάσθησαν αὐτὸν θεραπεῦσαι. ¹⁷ ἀποκριθεὶς δὲ ὁ Ἰησοῦς εἶπεν· ὦ γενεὰ ἄπιστος καὶ διεστραμ-	καὶ εἶπα τοῖς μαθηταῖς σου ἵνα αὐτὸ ἐκβάλωσιν, καὶ οὐκ ἴσχυσαν. ¹⁹ ὁ δὲ ἀποκριθεὶς αὐτοῖς λέγει· ὦ γενεὰ ἄπιστος,	⁴⁰ καὶ ἐδεήθην τῶν μαθητῶν σου ἵνα ἐκβάλωσιν αὐτό, καὶ οὐκ ἐδυνήθησαν. ⁴¹ ἀποκριθεὶς δὲ ὁ Ἰησοῦς εἶπεν· ὦ γενεὰ ἄπιστος καὶ διεστραμ- — 14 9: λέγει αὐτῷ ὁ Ἰησοῦς·

Mt 17,12 *om* εν ‖ p: ℵ 28-700 ϕ13-230-543-826-828 σ⟨954⟩-1010-1293-1391-1402 D F U W **047** *pc* {*L*abcff$^{1.2}$g^{1}r$^{1.2}$z} *S*h^{t}j *Cs*$^{3:8}$b *Geo* | ηθελον ‖ p: 1515 **14** ελ. αυτ.] ● ελθοντων: ℵBZ λ1-1582 ϕ124-788 — ελθων ‖ Mk: D {*L*'⟨b(cum venisse!)⟩ Au Hi Hil *S*scp^{3}j *Cs*^{1}b^{10} *Arm*^{0}} — ελθοντος αυτου ‖ Mk: 253 {} — *txt*: *Rpl* Or *L*(*om*: ff^1)q *S*' *Cs*^{6}b' *Arm*' **15** ● πασχ.] εχει *cf.* 4 24 8 16 *etc.*: ℵBLZ^v ΟΣ Θ Chr Or **17** αποκ.—Ι.] ο δε αποκρ. ‖ Mk: ℵ* | ειπ. + αυτοις(-ω) ‖ Mk: ℵ(1093) *L*e[k] (αποκ. αυτω ο Ι. ειπ.: ff^1) vg^1 *S*c

Mk 9,13 ηθελησαν ‖ p: *Rpl L S Cs* — *txt*: ℵBC*^{v}LΨ-892 D 1342 | επ. αυ.] περι αυτου ‖ 14 21 Mt 26 24: 28 ϕ *pc* **14** ● ελθοντες(-τος αυτου) ... ειδον ‖ p: ℌ⟨33-579⟩ W 1342 *L*k[e] (*S*s[c]) *Cs Arm Geo*^{1} **17** και—οχ.] τω καιρω ανθρωπος τις προσηλθεν τω Ιησου γονυπετων αυτον και λεγων ‖ Mt: G **18** ρη.] σπαρασσει ‖ Lk: *l*26 | ~ εκβ. αυ. ‖ Lk: ΘΦ-28-565 70 *L*⟨k[e] a⟩ | ισ.] εδυνηθησαν ‖ p: W-700 σ115 **19** ο δε απ. αυ.] και απ. ο Ιησους (+ αυτοις) ‖ p: ϕ (*pc*) *L*cr^{1}z *S*(*om* και: s[c]p)j (κυριος Ι.) — και(*om Geo*^{2}) απ. αυτοις(-ω) ο Ι. ‖ p: 𝔓45 WΘ-(28)-565 (*Geo*^{B}) (^{A} *om* αυτοις) | *om* αυτοις ‖ Mt Lk: C*ϕ*l*547 *pc L*k[e] 30 | λεγ.] ειπεν ‖ p: 𝔓45 Θ-565-1071(~ ει. αυ.) *pc L*vl⟨lz⟩g^{2}r^{1}30 vg^6 | απισ. + και διεστραμμενη ‖ Mt Lk: 𝔓45 W-565 ϕ-*l*547 157 *pc l*53 (*L*vg^1)

Lk 9,37 κατελ. αυ.] καταβαινοντων ‖ Mt 17 9 p: ϕ69 | απο] εκ ‖ Mt 17 9: 28 Γ **39** κ. εξ. κρα.] εξ. κ. ρησσει ‖ Mk: D(~ εξ. πνευμα κ. ρη.) *L*e aff^{2}lr^1 *S*sc(~ κ. εξ.) *Aeth* | κρα. + και ρη. (+ αυτον) ‖ Mk: ℵ-579-(892) 1604 λ-1582-2193 (ϕ230-*l*547) D Θ 157 *pc L*bcfqr^{2}z vg$^{\langle 1\rangle}$ *C*b$^{\langle 2\rangle}$ *Arm* | σπα.] ρη. ‖ Mk: X ϕ174 213 *S*(*om*: c)j | ● μολις: B 700-1071 λ σ⟨954⟩-1188 R W Θ 157 *pc* — *txt*: 𝔓75 *Rpl* **40** τοις μαθηταις ‖ p: ϕ13 237 | ~ αυ. εκβ. ‖ Mk: Ψ *pc* | εδυν.] ισχυσαν ‖ Mk: C^3 1038 **41** *om* κ. διεσ. ‖ Mk: Ep Mcn^{Ep} *L*e a Mcn^{Te}

Matth 17

μένη, ἕως πότε μεθ' ὑμῶν ἔσομαι; ἕως πότε ἀνέξομαι ὑμῶν; φέρετέ μοι αὐτὸν ὧδε.

cf. v. 15↑

[18] καὶ ἐπετίμησεν αὐτῷ ὁ Ἰησοῦς, καὶ ἐξῆλθεν ἀπ' αὐτοῦ τὸ δαιμόνιον, καὶ ἐθεραπεύθη ὁ παῖς ἀπὸ τῆς ὥρας ἐκείνης. [19] τότε προσελθόντες οἱ μαθηταὶ τῷ Ἰησοῦ κατ' ἰδίαν

Mark 9

ἕως πότε πρὸς ὑμᾶς ἔσομαι; ἕως πότε ἀνέξομαι ὑμῶν; φέρετε αὐτὸν πρός με. [20] καὶ ἤνεγκαν αὐτὸν πρὸς αὐτόν. καὶ ἰδὼν αὐτὸν τὸ πνεῦμα εὐθέως συνεσπάραξεν αὐτόν, καὶ πεσὼν ἐπὶ τῆς γῆς ἐκυλίετο ἀφρίζων. [21] καὶ ἐπηρώτησεν τὸν πατέρα αὐτοῦ· πόσος χρόνος ἐστὶν ὡς τοῦτο γέγονεν αὐτῷ; ὁ δὲ εἶπεν· ἐκ παιδιόθεν· [22] καὶ πολλάκις καὶ εἰς πῦρ αὐτὸν ἔβαλεν καὶ εἰς ὕδατα ἵνα ἀπολέσῃ αὐτόν· ἀλλ' εἴ τι δύνῃ, βοήθησον ἡμῖν σπλαγχνισθεὶς ἐφ' ἡμᾶς. [23] ὁ δὲ Ἰησοῦς εἶπεν αὐτῷ· τὸ εἰ δύνῃ, πάντα δυνατὰ τῷ πιστεύοντι. [24] εὐθέως κράξας ὁ πατὴρ τοῦ παιδίου ἔλεγεν· πιστεύω· βοήθει μου τῇ ἀπιστίᾳ. [25] ἰδὼν δὲ ὁ Ἰησοῦς ὅτι ἐπισυντρέχει ὄχλος, ἐπετίμησεν τῷ πνεύματι τῷ ἀκαθάρτῳ λέγων αὐτῷ· τὸ ἄλαλον καὶ κωφὸν πνεῦμα, ἐγώ σοι ἐπιτάσσω, ἔξελθε ἐξ αὐτοῦ καὶ μηκέτι εἰσέλθῃς εἰς αὐτόν. [26] καὶ κράξας καὶ πολλὰ σπαράξας ἐξῆλθεν· καὶ ἐγένετο ὡσεὶ νεκρός, ὥστε τοὺς πολλοὺς λέγειν ὅτι ἀπέθανεν. [27] ὁ δὲ Ἰησοῦς κρατήσας αὐτὸν τῆς χειρὸς ἤγειρεν αὐτόν, καὶ ἀνέστη. [28] καὶ εἰσελθόντος αὐτοῦ εἰς οἶκον οἱ μαθηταὶ αὐτοῦ κατ' ἰδίαν

Luk 9

μένη, ἕως πότε ἔσομαι πρὸς ὑμᾶς καὶ ἀνέξομαι ὑμῶν; προσάγαγε ὧδε τὸν υἱόν σου. [42] ἔτι δὲ προσερχομένου αὐτοῦ ἔρρηξεν αὐτὸν τὸ δαιμόνιον καὶ συνεσπάραξεν· ἐπετίμησεν δὲ ὁ Ἰησοῦς τῷ πνεύματι τῷ ἀκαθάρτῳ, καὶ ἰάσατο τὸν παῖδα καὶ ἀπέδωκεν αὐτὸν τῷ πατρὶ αὐτοῦ. [43a] ἐξεπλήσσοντο δὲ πάντες ἐπὶ τῇ μεγαλειότητι τοῦ θεοῦ.

Joh 14

τοσοῦτον χρόνον μεθ' ὑμῶν εἰμι καὶ οὐκ ἔγνωκάς με, Φίλιππε;

Mt 17,17 ∼ ανεξ. υμ. ... μεθ υμ. εσ.: φ13-346-543-826-828 *L*abcff^{2}g^{1}n | ∼ εσ. μεθ υμ.‖Lk: *Rpl L*'(a bcff^{2}g^{1}n) *S*,j — *txt*: ℌ⟨L⟩C 565-700 λ1-1582 φ'(13-346-543-826-828)-230 D Θ *pc* Or *L*ff^1(εσ.] ειμι)r^2(εως ποτε^1∩^{2}) **19** τω Ι.] αυτου (+ τω Ι.)‖Mk: σ1424 655 Chr *L*(d)z *S*s(c *C*b^1 *Aeth*)

Mk 9,19 ∼ εσ. πρ. υμ.‖Lk: σM-267 **047** 157 *pc Lc* vg^1 *S*s[c]pj *Geo*^{2} | αυ. προς με] μοι αυ.‖Mt: 330 472 *Geo*^{2}(+ ωδε) | προς με] ωδε‖p: 1012 — ωδε προς με‖p: 565 *pc Lc S*h(ωδε$^+$) *C*s$^{1:5}$(ωδε] μοι) *Aeth* **20** *om* ευθ.‖Lk: D *L*abff^{2}iqr^1 *Geo*^{B} | *om* αυτον^4‖Lk: W **21** ως] εως(+ ου): 𝔓^{45} B (713) 1342 — ● εξ ου: ℌ'⟨ℵ*⟩C* WΘ-565 σ517 *al* — αφ ου‖Lk13 7: NΣ-28 φ⟨69-788⟩-*l*547 σ945-954 40 **22** *om* και^2‖Mt15: 𝔓^{45} 579 WΘ-565 λ⟨118⟩-22 φ⟨124⟩ σ7 D **067** *pc L*vl⟨cfr^2⟩ vg^8 *S*s[c]pj *C* | πυρ] το π.‖←: Φ-700 λ118 φ124 σM-71-692 A E F G K V Γ Π^c Ω *al* | αυτον^1—υδ.] και εις υδωρ γεγονος π!‖←: **0153** | υδατα] τα υδ.‖←: 18 *pc* | δυ. + κυριε‖Mt15 15 25: **067** *S*s[c] *Geo*^{B} | ημιν + κυριε‖←: Θ-565 D G *L*abff^{2}g^{2}iq *S*j *Arm Geo*^{A} | σπλ. + κυριε‖←: 565 | ημας + κυριε‖←: Θ-1071 *pc* **23** παν. + γαρ‖10 27: 28-565 **24** παιδος‖Mt18 Lk42: λ φ1689 | πιστ. + κυριε‖Mt15 15 25: *Rpl* Bas *L*'(∼: q) Au *S*s[c]p'j^{ac} *C*b^7 *Arm*^{0} *Geo*^{B} *Δ*' — *txt*: ℌ⟨Δ-33⟩C* WΘΦ-28-565 A D *L*k[e] ilr$^{1.2}$30 vg^{10} *S*p^{7}hj^b *C*' *Arm*' *Geo*' *Aeth Δ*p | μου] μοι‖Mt15 25: φ13-543 K S 299 *l*53 *l*184 *L*g^2 **25** οχ.] ● ο οχ.‖14f.: ℌ⟨B-892⟩X WΦ-28-565-700-1071 λ1278 φ-230-*l*547 σM-349-517-945-1223 A S Y Π Ω 1342 *al C* — οχ. πολυς‖14 Lk37: λ — *txt*: *Rpl* | ● ∼ επιτ. σοι: ℌ(*om* εγω: ℵ*)C W {*L*k[e] *S*'j} — *txt*: *Rpl* Ddy^v {*L*'} *S*s[c] | εξ] απ‖Mt: C*Δ Θ-565-700 σ1424 1342 *al* **26** εξηλ. + απ αυτου‖Mt: Δ(επ αυτω) 565 σ827 D *pc L*⟨q⟩ *S*s[c]j *C*s *Geo*^{2} **27** αυτον^1 τ. χ.] ● τ. χ. αυτου‖54 1p: ℌ⟨33-579⟩ Θ-28-565 λ φ⟨124⟩ σ115 D 1342 *pc l*184 *L S*j *C Arm Geo*^{2} *Δ*a' ad i l — αυτου τ. χ.‖Mt28 9: σ827 *pc* — τ. χ.‖13 1: W *l*26 *Geo*^{1} — *txt*: *Rpl* (+ αυτου: C*) *S Δ*a^A md n | κ. ανεσ.] κ. απεδωκεν αυτον τω πατρι αυτου‖Lk: *L*vg^1 *S*s[c] — *om*‖p: 𝔓^{45v} W 63 **28** οικ. + προσηλθον αυτω‖Mt: (𝔓^{45v}) WΘ-28-565-700 φ⟨124⟩ | *om* αυτου^2‖Mt: W *Lc* vg^2 *S*j^c *C*b^2

Lk 9,41 εσ. πρ. υμ.] πρ. υμ. εσ.‖Mk: φ⟨983⟩ *pc Lc* — μεθ υμων εσ.‖Mt: ℵ 716 | και^2] εως ποτε‖p: X λ φ⟨983⟩ K Y(*prm* και) Π Ψ 157 *al l*11 *l*12 *l*19 *l*32 *l*49 *l*303 *l*333 *l*374 *l*1634 *L*e(= Y) b(+ εσομαι μεθ υμων και‖Mt) *S*p^{1v}(= Y) *C*s *Arm*^{pc} | προσα.] προσενεγκε‖p: D — προσαγαγετε‖p: φ543 — + μοι‖p: ℵ^{c}LXΞ-33-892 Ψ **0115** *pc L*r^1(προς με‖Mk) *S*ch$^+$ *C*sb$^{\langle 1\rangle}$ *Aeth* | ∼ τ. υι. σ. ωδε‖Mt: *Rpl S*ch *C* — *om* ωδε‖Mk: D *L*r^1 vg^4 — *txt*: 𝔓^{75} ℵBLXΞ-579-892 700 λ *al L*' *S*'j **42** ερρη.] ερριψεν‖4 35: 544 φ983-1689 *pc l*32 *l*1642 | δαιμ. + εις το μεσον‖←: 1574 | συνεσ. + αυτον‖Mk: 544 φ346 σ990-1010 K Π *al L*cfr^1 *S*,j *C* | ιασ.—αυτου] αφηκεν αυτον και απεδωκεν τ. παι.‖43 9p: D (*L*e) | τ. παι.] αυτον‖Mk: φ983-1689 *L*e **43a** επι^1 + τη διδαχη αυτου και‖43 2p Mt22 33 Mk11 18: 1555

Jo 14,9 ● τοσουτω χρονω: ℵ*LQW D Cr Eu Or *L*⟨ff^2⟩ Ir Te

Matth: εἶπον· διὰ τί ἡμεῖς οὐκ ἐδυνήθημεν ἐκβαλεῖν αὐτό; [20] ὁ δὲ λέγει αὐτοῖς· διὰ τὴν ὀλιγοπιστίαν ὑμῶν· ἀμὴν γὰρ λέγω ὑμῖν, ἐὰν ἔχητε πίστιν ὡς κόκκον σινάπεως, ἐρεῖτε τῷ ὄρει τούτῳ· μετάβα ἔνθεν ἐκεῖ, καὶ μεταβήσεται, καὶ οὐδὲν ἀδυνατήσει ὑμῖν. **215.**

Mark: ἐπηρώτων αὐτόν· ὅ τι ἡμεῖς οὐκ ἠδυνήθημεν ἐκβαλεῖν αὐτό; [29] καὶ εἶπεν αὐτοῖς· τοῦτο τὸ γένος ἐν οὐδενὶ δύναται ἐξελθεῖν εἰ μὴ ἐν προσευχῇ καὶ νηστείᾳ.

(127) 141. Zweite Leidensverkündigung. *The Second Prediction of the Passion.* 136.

Matth 17 22–23

[22] Συστρεφομένων δὲ αὐτῶν ἐν τῇ Γαλιλαίᾳ εἶπεν αὐτοῖς ὁ Ἰησοῦς· μέλλει ὁ υἱὸς τοῦ ἀνθρώπου παραδίδοσθαι εἰς χεῖρας ἀνθρώπων, [23] καὶ ἀποκτενοῦσιν αὐτόν, καὶ τῇ τρίτῃ ἡμέρᾳ ἐγερ-

Mark 9 30–32

[30] Κἀκεῖθεν ἐξελθόντες παρεπορεύοντο διὰ τῆς Γαλιλαίας, καὶ οὐκ ἤθελεν ἵνα τις γνοῖ· [31] ἐδίδασκεν γὰρ τοὺς μαθητὰς αὐτοῦ, καὶ ἔλεγεν αὐτοῖς **136.** ὅτι ὁ υἱὸς τοῦ ἀνθρώπου παραδίδοται εἰς χεῖρας ἀνθρώπων, καὶ ἀποκτενοῦσιν αὐτόν, καὶ ἀποκτανθεὶς μετὰ τρεῖς ἡμέρας ἀνα-

Luk 9 43b–45

[43b] Πάντων δὲ θαυμαζόντων ἐπὶ πᾶσιν οἷς ἐποίει εἶπεν πρὸς τοὺς μαθητὰς αὐτοῦ· [44] θέσθε ὑμεῖς εἰς τὰ ὦτα ὑμῶν τοὺς λόγους τούτους· ὁ γὰρ υἱὸς τοῦ ἀνθρώπου μέλλει παραδίδοσθαι εἰς χεῖρας ἀνθρώπων.

[Jo] 7 1: καὶ μετὰ ταῦτα περιεπάτει ὁ Ἰησοῦς ἐν τῇ Γαλιλαίᾳ· οὐ γὰρ ἤθελεν ἐν τῇ Ἰουδαίᾳ περιπατεῖν, ὅτι ἐζήτουν αὐτὸν οἱ Ἰουδαῖοι ἀποκτεῖναι.

Mt 17,20 ως κο. σι.] και μη διακριθητε ‖ 21 21: 1574 | ● υμιν^{2} + ^{21}τουτο δε το γενος ουκ εκπορευεται (εκβαλλεται) ει μη εν προσευχη και νηστεια ‖ Mk: *Rpl* (ℵ^{b}) (εκπο.] εξερχεται: 544 λ⟨1⟩ *pc*) Chr **Or** (*L*'Au Am Hil) *Sp* (∼ νη. ... πρ.)h *C*b^{12} *Arm Geo*^{Bc} *Aeth* (= *S*p) — *txt*: ℵ*-B-33-892 1604 φ788 Θ Eu *Le*[k] ff^{1} *S*scj *C*' *Geo*' *Aeth* **22** ● αναστρ. *cf.* 16 13: *Rpl* Chr (στρε.: Or) *L S*,j *C* — *txt*: ℵB-892 λ1-1582 | ανθρωπων + αμαρτωλων (*et om* ανθρ.) ‖ (26 45p) Lk 24 7: 544 157 (1579) *l*47 *pc* Chr$^{2:4}$ (*L*ff^{1} *C*s^{1})$^{1:9}$ **23** τη τρ. ημ.] μετα τρεις ημερας ‖ p 27 63 Mk 8 31 10 34: D *Le*[k] PsCp *S*s *C*b — μετα την τριτην ημεραν: *L*abcnqr$^{1v.2}$ | εγερ.] αναστησεται ‖ p Mk 10 34 8 31 Lk 18 33 24 7.46: B-892 544 λ⟨1⟩ φ σ1424 **047** *pc* Chr Or

Mk 9,28 ∼ επηρ. αυ. (∼ επ. αυτον οι μ. αυτου) κατ ιδ. ‖ 13 3: *Rpl* (+ λεγοντες: *pc*) *L*(c)z *S*(s[c]pj)h *C* — κατ ιδ. και επηρ.(ηρωτ.) αυτον λεγ.: WΘ-(28)-565(-των)-700 φ⟨124⟩ — και ηρωτησαν αυτον: 𝔓^{45v} — *txt* (ηρωτων): 𝔥'(∼ κατ ιδ. εις—αυτου^{2}: Ψ)C 1071 (λ⟨118⟩) σ517 (D) 1342 *pc* *L*'(+ λεγ.: bcfir^{1} vg^{1}) *Arm Geo*^{1} (^{2}-ησαν) | ο τι] δια τι ‖ Mt: 33 Φ-1071 λ872 σ115-827-945-1223-1606 A D K Y Π *al L S*phj^{bl} {} — οτι δια τι ‖ Mt: U 131 *pc l*15 *l*49 *S*s[c] {*C*} — τι οτι: 38 *pc S*j^{c} **29** εν—εξε.] ουκ εκπορευεται ‖ Mt 17 21 (*cf. ad* 20): 33-579 σ7-1391 1574 *l*7 *l*184 *Arm* | εν ουδ.] ου ‖ ←: C* Bas(ουκ) | δυν. εξε.] εξερχεται ‖ ←: σ827 1342 *pc* Bas *S*s[c] *Geo*^{1} | ∼ νη. ... πρ. ‖ ←: *S*s[c]pj *C*b^{1} *Δ*a i^{T} md n p — ● *om* και νη. *cf.* 2 19p: ℵ*B **0274** Cl *Lk*[e] *Geo*^{1} **31** παραδοθησεται ‖ p 10 33 Mt 20 18 Lk 18 32: Θ-28-565-700 φ⟨124⟩ σ115-827 *L*⟨k[e] vg^{1}⟩ *C Geo Aeth* | ανθ.] ανομων ‖ Act 2 23: Ψ — ανθ. αμαρτωλων ‖ 14 41p Lk 24 7: 700 157 258 | *om* αποκτανθ. ‖ p 10 34 Lk 18 33: D *l*183 *l*184 *Lk*[e] acz vg^{1} *C*b *Aeth* | μετα τρ. ημ.] τη τριτη ημερα ‖ p Mt 16 21 **20** 19 Lk 9 22 18 33 24 7.46: *Rpl L*' *S*' — μετα την τριτην ημεραν: *Lk*[e]aq *S*h^{m} — *txt*: 𝔥⟨33-1241⟩C* D 1342 *L*bcff^{2v}i *S*j *C* | ανασ.] εγερθησεται ‖ p Mt 20 19 16 21 Lk 9 22: λ1 φ⟨124⟩ 474 *l*26 *l*184 — εγειρεται ‖ 31a Mt 27 63: W-28 1542 *Arm*$^{\langle 0\rangle}$

Lk 9,43b εποιησεν ‖ Mt 21 15: *Rpl* — *txt*: 𝔓^{75} 𝔥CΞ 700-1071 λ-1582-2193 φ⟨788⟩ A D Θ **0115** *L*⟨vg^{2}⟩ *C*s(ποιει)b | εποι. + ο Ιησους(θεος) ‖ 8 39: *Rpl* (16) *L*fqr^{1} *S*' *C*b^{1} — *txt*: 𝔓^{75} 𝔥⟨33-892⟩Ξ 700 λ⟨118⟩-1582-2193 D Θ *pc L*' *S*sc *C*' *Arm* **44** θεσ. + ουν ‖ 21 14: 716 | *om* υμεις ‖ ←: 1241 *L*bq vg^{1} *C*sb^{1} *Geo*^{1} | τ. ωτα] τας καρδιας ‖ ← 1 66: 544 661 *L*(τ. ωτα υμων και εν τη καρδια: r^{1})r^{2} vg | παραδοθηναι ‖ 24 7: 544(∼ εις χ. αν. αμ. παρ.)-700 | ανθ.] ανθ. αμαρτωλων ‖ ←: 1241 544 λ1278 *pc S*h — αμ. ‖ Mt 26 45p: V

Jo 7,1 ● *om* και ‖ 3 22 5 1.14 6 1 21 1: 𝔓^{66} ℵC^{2}-892 σ1010-1293 D **0141** *L*⟨q⟩ *S*scp *C*sb^{B}f^{v}a^{s}

Mt 17 20 *cf.* ETh^{II} 48.106 (*cf. ad 215.* Mt 21 21p)

Matth	Mark	Luk	
ϑήσεται. καὶ ἐλυπήϑησαν σφόδρα.	στήσεται. 32 οἱ δὲ ἠγνόουν τὸ ῥῆμα, καὶ ἐφοβοῦντο αὐτὸν ἐπερωτῆσαι.	45 οἱ δὲ ἠγνόουν τὸ ῥῆμα τοῦτο, καὶ ἦν παρακεκαλυμμένον ἀπ' αὐτῶν ἵνα μὴ αἴσθωνται αὐτό, καὶ ἐφοβοῦντο ἐρωτῆσαι αὐτὸν περὶ τοῦ ῥήματος τούτου.	16 6: ἀλλ' ὅτι ταῦτα λελάληκα ὑμῖν, ἡ λύπη πεπλήρωκεν ὑμῶν τὴν καρδίαν.

(128) **142.** Die Tempelsteuer. *The Temple Tax.* Matth 17 24–27

24 Ἐλϑόντων δὲ αὐτῶν εἰς Καφαρναουμ προσῆλϑον οἱ τὰ δίδραχμα λαμβάνοντες τῷ Πέτρῳ καὶ εἶπαν· ὁ διδάσκαλος ὑμῶν οὐ τελεῖ τὰ δίδραχμα; 25 λέγει· ναί. καὶ ἐλϑόντα εἰς τὴν οἰκίαν προέφϑασεν αὐτὸν ὁ Ἰησοῦς λέγων· τί σοι δοκεῖ, Σίμων; οἱ βασιλεῖς τῆς γῆς ἀπὸ τίνων λαμβάνουσιν τέλη ἢ κῆνσον; ἀπὸ τῶν υἱῶν αὐτῶν ἢ ἀπὸ τῶν ἀλλοτρίων; 26 εἰπόντος δέ· ἀπὸ τῶν ἀλλοτρίων, ἔφη αὐτῷ ὁ Ἰησοῦς· ἄρα γε ἐλεύϑεροί εἰσιν οἱ υἱοί. 27 ἵνα δὲ μὴ σκανδαλίσωμεν αὐτούς, πορευϑεὶς εἰς ϑάλασσαν βάλε ἄγκιστρον καὶ τὸν ἀναβάντα πρῶτον ἰχϑὺν ἆρον, καὶ ἀνοίξας τὸ στόμα αὐτοῦ εὑρήσεις στατῆρα· ἐκεῖνον λαβὼν δὸς αὐτοῖς ἀντὶ ἐμοῦ καὶ σοῦ.

cf. 143.

(129) **143.** Der Rangstreit. *The Dispute about Greatness.*

Matth 18 1–5	Mark 9 33–37	Luk 9 46–48
cf. 142.	33 Καὶ ἦλϑεν εἰς Καφαρναουμ. καὶ ἐν τῇ οἰκίᾳ γενόμενος ἐπηρώτα	
1 Ἐν ἐκείνῃ τῇ ὥρᾳ προσῆλϑον οἱ μαϑηταὶ τῷ Ἰησοῦ λέγοντες· τίς ἄρα μείζων ἐστὶν ἐν τῇ βασιλείᾳ τῶν οὐρανῶν;	αὐτούς· τί ἐν τῇ ὁδῷ διελογίζεσϑε; 34 οἱ δὲ ἐσιώπων· πρὸς ἀλλήλους γὰρ διελέχϑησαν ἐν τῇ ὁδῷ τίς μείζων.	46 Εἰσῆλϑεν δὲ διαλογισμὸς ἐν αὐτοῖς, *cf. 250.* τὸ τίς ἂν εἴη μείζων αὐτῶν. 47 ὁ δὲ Ἰησοῦς εἰδὼς τὸν διαλογισμὸν τῆς καρδίας αὐτῶν,

Mt 17,24 τα²] το (*et* τα¹] το): (W) 245 1093 — ● *om*: ℵ* σ1010 D *C*b **25** τ. γης] των εϑνων‖Lk22 25: 700 *Arm*⟨0⟩

Mk 9,32 επερ.] ερωτησαι‖Lk: W-565 **λ**⟨118⟩ **ϕ**⟨124-788⟩ σ179-1424 *pc l*251 — ∼ ερωτ. αυτον‖579(επε-) 565 1375 *l*251 *L*c30 **33** εισηλϑεν: 700 ϕ13-69-543 235 — ● ηλϑον‖Mt17 24: ℵB W-565 **λ** σ1424 D (-οσαν) **0274** *al l*251 *L*⟨fq⟩ *S*p⟨1⟩j *C*s | διελ.] προς εαυτους διελ.‖34 11 31: *Rpl* (*om* προς: Ωᵛ) *S*h — διελ. πρ. εαυ.‖←: WΘ-28-565-1071 **λ**⟨118⟩ **ϕ**'⟨124⟩(ελογ.: 828) *pc S*p(∼ διελ. εν τ. οδ.) *Geo*' *Aeth* — διελ. πρ. αλληλους‖34 Lk20 14: σ1424 *L*f *S*s[c]j *C*s — *txt*: ℌ⟨1241⟩C σ827-1223 D 1342 *L*' *C*b *Geo*ᴬ **34** μειζ.] μ. εστιν‖Mt: ℵ *Geo*¹(² εσται) — αυτων μ. ειη(γενηται)‖Lk: W-(Θ-565) **ϕ**⟨124-983⟩ *pc L*' — μ. γενηται αυτων‖Lk: D *L*ir² *S*p(*om* γεν.) — ειη(η) μ.‖Lk: (1071) 435 *S*'j

Lk 9,45 ∼ αυτ. ερ.‖Mk: 565-1071 **ϕ**⟨13⟩ σ954 1574 *pc* | επερωτ.‖20 40p Mk: C (1071) σM-27-692-990-1194-1207-1223 D K Π (1574) *al* **46** *om* το‖Mk: 28(*et* ∼ τις μ. αυ. αν ειη) **λ**-1582-2193 *pc* | *om* ειη‖Mk: 245 2533 *S*p **47** ο—αυτων] και(*om*)‖p: ϕ(983, ⁴⁶∩⁴⁷αυτων?)-1689 | ειδως] ● ιδων‖5 20p: {}¹ *Rpl* Or *L C*b *Δ*me — γνους‖Mt16 8p: **λλ**' 1365 {}² — *txt*: {𝔓⁷⁵ᵛ}¹ ℵB Λ-700-1604 λ1278 ϕ124-174 σ990-1207-1424 F K Π *al l*76 *S C*s {*Δ*a md n}² | τους διαλογισμους‖5 22 6 8: 565 **047** *pc L*⟨a⟩ *C*s¹:⁴ | *om* της καρ.‖←: 28-544 σ1223 Γ *pc L*l *S*c *C*s¹:⁴

Mt18 1p *cf.* ETh^II 12 (*transl.*): *Εἶπον οἱ μαϑηταὶ τῷ Ἰησοῦ· οἴδαμεν ὅτι ὑπάγεις ἀφ' ἡμῶν. τίς ἔσται ὁ μέγας ἐφ' ἡμᾶς; λέγει Ἰησοῦς αὐτοῖς· ἐν ᾧ προσήλϑατε τόπῳ ἐλεύσεσϑε πρὸς τὸν Ἰάκωβον τὸν δίκαιον, δι' ὃν ὁ οὐρανὸς καὶ ἡ γῆ ἐγένοντο.*

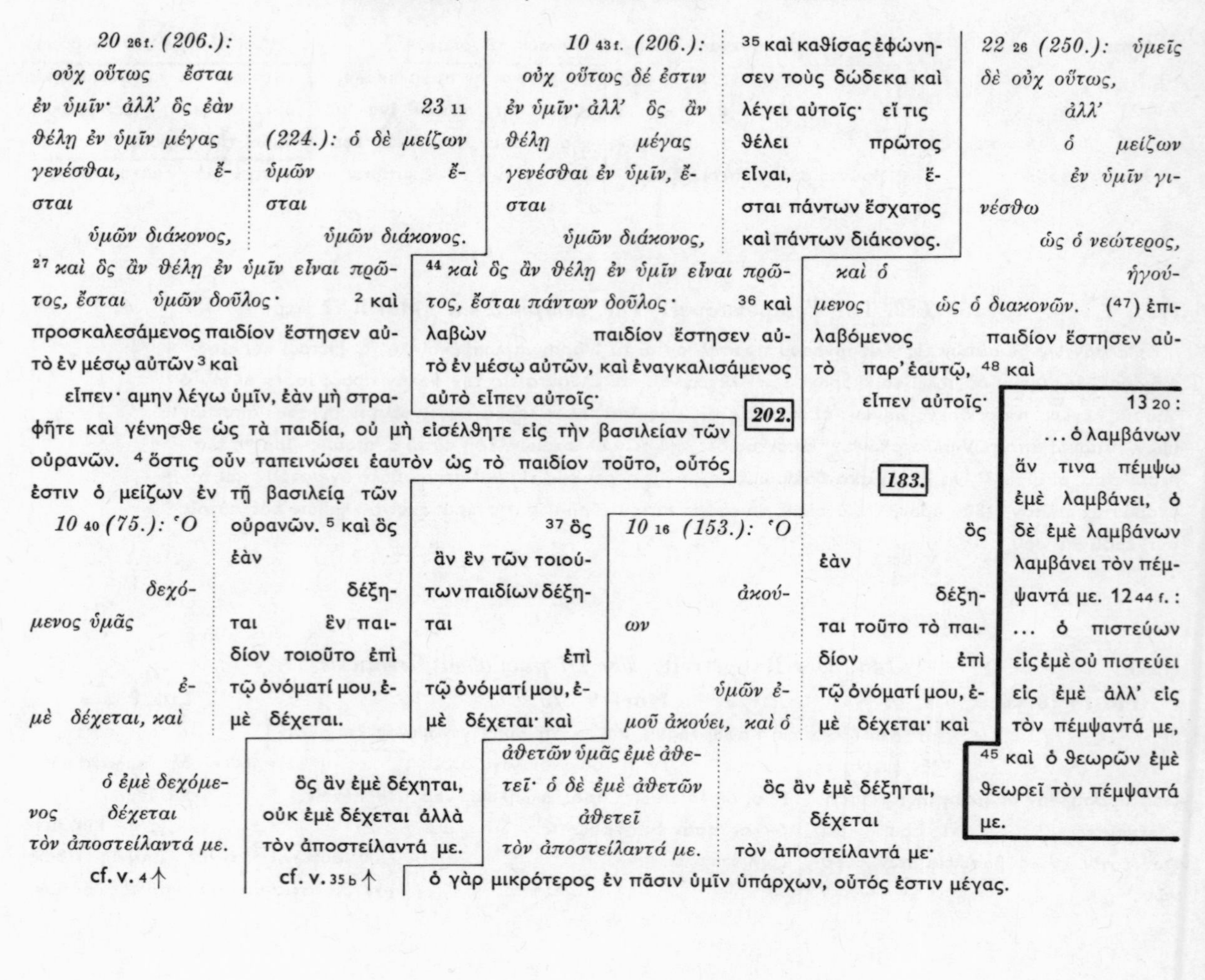

20 26f. (206.): οὐχ οὕτως ἔσται ἐν ὑμῖν· ἀλλ' ὃς ἐὰν θέλῃ ἐν ὑμῖν μέγας γενέσθαι, ἔσται ὑμῶν διάκονος, ²⁷ καὶ ὃς ἂν θέλῃ ἐν ὑμῖν εἶναι πρῶτος, ἔσται ὑμῶν δοῦλος·

23 11 (224.): ὁ δὲ μείζων ὑμῶν ἔσται ὑμῶν διάκονος.

² καὶ προσκαλεσάμενος παιδίον ἔστησεν αὐτὸ ἐν μέσῳ αὐτῶν ³ καὶ εἶπεν· αμην λέγω ὑμῖν, ἐὰν μὴ στραφῆτε καὶ γένησθε ὡς τὰ παιδία, οὐ μὴ εἰσέλθητε εἰς τὴν βασιλείαν τῶν οὐρανῶν. **202.** ⁴ ὅστις οὖν ταπεινώσει ἑαυτὸν ὡς τὸ παιδίον τοῦτο, οὗτός ἐστιν ὁ μείζων ἐν τῇ βασιλείᾳ τῶν οὐρανῶν. ⁵ καὶ ὃς ἐὰν δέξηται ἓν παιδίον τοιοῦτο ἐπὶ τῷ ὀνόματί μου, ἐμὲ δέχεται.

10 43f. (206.): οὐχ οὕτως δέ ἐστιν ἐν ὑμῖν· ἀλλ' ὃς ἂν θέλῃ μέγας γενέσθαι ἐν ὑμῖν, ἔσται ὑμῶν διάκονος, ⁴⁴ καὶ ὃς ἂν θέλῃ ἐν ὑμῖν εἶναι πρῶτος, ἔσται πάντων δοῦλος·

³⁵ καὶ καθίσας ἐφώνησεν τοὺς δώδεκα καὶ λέγει αὐτοῖς· εἴ τις θέλει πρῶτος εἶναι, ἔσται πάντων ἔσχατος καὶ πάντων διάκονος. ³⁶ καὶ λαβὼν παιδίον ἔστησεν αὐτὸ ἐν μέσῳ αὐτῶν, καὶ ἐναγκαλισάμενος αὐτὸ εἶπεν αὐτοῖς· ³⁷ ὃς ἂν ἓν τῶν τοιούτων παιδίων δέξηται ἐπὶ τῷ ὀνόματί μου, ἐμὲ δέχεται· καὶ ὃς ἂν ἐμὲ δέχηται, οὐκ ἐμὲ δέχεται ἀλλὰ τὸν ἀποστείλαντά με. cf. v. 35b ↑

22 26 (250.): ὑμεῖς δὲ οὐχ οὕτως, ἀλλ' ὁ μείζων ἐν ὑμῖν γινέσθω ὡς ὁ νεώτερος, καὶ ὁ ἡγούμενος ὡς ὁ διακονῶν.

(⁴⁷) ἐπιλαβόμενος παιδίον ἔστησεν αὐτὸ παρ' ἑαυτῷ, ⁴⁸ καὶ εἶπεν αὐτοῖς· **183.** ὃς ἐὰν δέξηται τοῦτο τὸ παιδίον ἐπὶ τῷ ὀνόματί μου, ἐμὲ δέχεται· καὶ ὃς ἂν ἐμὲ δέξηται, δέχεται τὸν ἀποστείλαντά με· ὁ γὰρ μικρότερος ἐν πᾶσιν ὑμῖν ὑπάρχων, οὗτός ἐστιν μέγας.

13 20: ... ὁ λαμβάνων ἄν τινα πέμψω ἐμὲ λαμβάνει, ὁ δὲ ἐμὲ λαμβάνων λαμβάνει τὸν πέμψαντά με. 12 44f.: ... ὁ πιστεύων εἰς ἐμὲ οὐ πιστεύει εἰς ἐμὲ ἀλλ' εἰς τὸν πέμψαντά με, ⁴⁵ καὶ ὁ θεωρῶν ἐμὲ θεωρεῖ τὸν πέμψαντά με.

10 40 (75.): Ὁ δεχόμενος ὑμᾶς ἐμὲ δέχεται, καὶ ὁ ἐμὲ δεχόμενος δέχεται τὸν ἀποστείλαντά με. cf. v. 4 ↑

10 16 (153.): Ὁ ἀκούων ὑμῶν ἐμοῦ ἀκούει, καὶ ὁ ἀθετῶν ὑμᾶς ἐμὲ ἀθετεῖ· ὁ δὲ ἐμὲ ἀθετῶν ἀθετεῖ τὸν ἀποστείλαντά με.

Mt 18,5 εν παι. τοι.] το παι. τουτο‖Lk: O

Mk 9,35 ειν. + εν υμιν‖44 Mt27: 700 *Lb Csb*^{1} | διακ.] δουλος‖←: σM-71-692-1194 *pc*
36 *om* αυτοις‖Mt: 566 *pc* **37** τοι. παι.] ● παι. τουτων‖Mt18 6 Lk17 1: ℵCΔ σ179 **047** 1342 *pc* Or *Cs*$^{2:3}$f | δεχηται] δεξηται‖37a Mt5 Lk48: *Rpl* — *txt* (-εται): (ℵ)BLΨ(*)^{c}-892 σ179 *pc* | και—αλλα] ο εμε δοχομενος δεχεται‖Mt Jo20: i241 | *om* ουκ εμε ... αλλα‖Mt Lk: 579 **0274** *Lf Cf Geo*^{1} | αποσ.] πεμψαντα‖Jo44f.20: 28

Lk 9,47 ● παιδιου‖20 20.26 *etc.*: *Rpl* — *txt*: 𝔓^{75} BC-579 28-565 λ2193 φ983-1689 D *pc* Cr | εστ. + εν μεσω (+ αυτων)‖p: 1574 (*Cb*^{1} *Arm*) *Aeth* | *om* παρ εαυ.‖p: 1047 *Cb*^{2} *Aeth* **48** *om* αυτ.‖Mt: 𝔓^{45} D 157 *Lvl*⟨fz⟩r^{1} vg^{1} *Ssc Geo*^{2} | ∼ το παι. του.‖Mt4: 𝔓^{75} 579 **λ**-1582-2193 σ692-990-1207 D *pc* Cr *L*'(του. το] τοιουτο *et* ∼ ος^{2}—δεξ.^{2} ουκ εμε δεχεται αλλα τ. απ. με και ος^{1}—δεχ.^{1}: l) *Sscp*^{5}h | δεχ.^{2}] ουκ εμε δεχ. αλλα‖Mk: 1579 *L*⟨e fz⟩r^{1v} vg^{1} | *om* πασ.‖Mt26f. p.11: E *Lr*^{1} vg^{3} *Cp*$^{3:5}$ *Ssc Cs*$^{1:4+1}$ | εσται‖← Mk35 10 43f.: *Rpl* Cr **Or** *Le* q *Cp S*'j — *txt*: 𝔓$^{45.75}$ 𝔥⟨892⟩CXΞ 700-1071 **λ**-1582-2193 σ7-267-659-1402-1606 *pc* **Or** *L*' *Ssc C Geo*

Jo 12,44 πεμ.] αποστειλ.‖←: 892 σ954 **45** πεμ.] αποστειλ.‖←: φ-*l*547 **13,20** ο δε] και ο‖Mk37 Lk48: 33 λ2193 D *pc* Chr *Le* br^{1} *Ss*[c]p *Geo*^{2} | πεμψα.] αποστειλαντα‖Mt40 Mk Lk48.16: X-892 544 **λ** Cr

---

Mt18 3 *cf.* ETh^{II} 22 (*cf. ad 202.*)

(130)

144. Der fremde Exorzist. *The Strange Exorcist.*

Mark 9 38–41

38 Ἔφη αὐτῷ ὁ Ἰωάννης· διδάσκαλε, εἴδομέν τινα ἐν τῷ ὀνόματί σου ἐκβάλλοντα δαιμόνια, ὃς οὐκ ἀκολουθεῖ ἡμῖν, καὶ ἐκωλύομεν αὐτόν. 39 ὁ δὲ εἶπεν· μὴ κωλύετε αὐτόν· οὐδεὶς γάρ ἐστιν ὃς ποιήσει δύναμιν ἐπὶ τῷ ὀνόματί μου καὶ δυνήσεται ταχὺ κακολογῆσαί με· 40 ὃς γὰρ οὐκ ἔστιν καθ' ἡμῶν, ὑπὲρ ἡμῶν ἐστιν. 41 ὃς γὰρ ἂν ποτίσῃ ὑμᾶς ποτήριον ὕδατος ἐν ὀνόματι, ὅτι Χριστοῦ ἐστε, αμην λέγω ὑμῖν ὅτι οὐ μὴ ἀπολέσῃ τὸν μισθὸν αὐτοῦ.

12 30 (99.): ὁ μὴ ὢν μετ' ἐμοῦ κατ' ἐμοῦ ἐστιν, καὶ ὁ μὴ συνάγων μετ' ἐμοῦ σκορπίζει. **75.**

Luk 9 49–50

49 Ἀποκριθεὶς δὲ Ἰωάννης εἶπεν· ἐπιστάτα, εἴδομέν τινα ἐπὶ τῷ ὀνόματί σου ἐκβάλλοντα δαιμόνια, καὶ ἐκωλύομεν αὐτόν, ὅτι οὐκ ἀκολουθεῖ μεθ' ἡμῶν. 50 εἶπεν δὲ πρὸς αὐτὸν ὁ Ἰησοῦς· μὴ κωλύετε· ὃς γὰρ οὐκ ἔστιν καθ' ὑμῶν, ὑπὲρ ὑμῶν ἐστιν.

11 23 (163.): ὁ μὴ ὢν μετ' ἐμοῦ κατ' ἐμοῦ ἐστιν, καὶ ὁ μὴ συνάγων μετ' ἐμοῦ σκορπίζει με.

(131)

145. Vom Ärgernis. *About Offences.*

Matth 18 6–9

6 Ὃς δ' ἂν σκανδαλίσῃ ἕνα τῶν μικρῶν τούτων τῶν πιστευόντων εἰς

Mark 9 42–48

42 Καὶ ὃς ἂν σκανδαλίσῃ ἕνα τῶν μικρῶν τῶν πιστευόντων,

17 1–2 (192.)

2b ... ἢ ἵνα σκανδαλίσῃ ἕνα τῶν μικρῶν τούτων.

Mk 9,38 εφη] αποκριθεις δε εφη(*om*)‖p: C 157 (*La*) — και(*om*) αποκ.‖p: W-565-700 ϕ⟨124⟩ (*Ld* vg¹ *Aeth*) — απεκριθη‖p: σ⟨1424⟩-179 D *l*47 *l*184 *L'* *S*,j¹(*prm* και: j^abc) *C*b¹ — απεκ. δε‖p: *Rpl* *L*cfff²qr¹ — *txt*: ℌ Θ-1071 1342 *S*p *C'*f | *om* αυτω‖p: 2 *pc* *l*47 *L*acq *S*s[c]j | *om* ο‖p: *R pm* — *txt*: ℌCXΘΣΦ λ118 σM-7-945-1424-1675 Ω 1342 *pm* | I. + και(*om*) ειπεν‖(p): (W ϕ⟨124⟩) σ1402 (∼ και ει I.) D *L*(ad)ff² (+ αυτω: c *S*s[c]j) (*C*b¹) — + και(*om*) λεγει‖p: 28-(565-700) λ⟨118⟩ *L*b(+ αυτω)ir¹ — λεγων‖p: *Rpl* *L'* — *txt*: ℌ⟨L⟩C Θ 1342 1537 *L*k[e] vg¹ *S*p *C'*f | εν] επι‖p: σ115-1402 U 1342 *pc* — *om*‖Mt7 22: *Rpl* — *txt*: ℌ⟨Ψ⟩C NWΘΣΦ-565-700-1071 λ ϕ⟨69-788⟩ σ827-1082 D 157 *pc* | ● *om* ος—ημ.‖**p**: ℌC Θ-1071 σ115-1194 **0274** 1342 *pc* *l*44 *L*fz *S*s[c]pj *C*,f *Δ*⟨i^V l^FG me⟩ | ημ.] μεθ ημων‖p: D 90 1342 *L*k[e] a *Δ*l^FG | ● αυτον + οτι ουκ ακολουθει(ηκο.) ημιν‖p: *Rpl* (אBΔ Θ *l*44¹) (ημιν] μεθ ημων: L Φ 1342 *pc*) *L*fz *S*s[c]ph⁺j *C*(sf = L)b (οτι] ος: *Δ*ad l^AD — *txt*: X W-28-565-700 λ⟨118⟩-1278 ϕ σ349-1402-1424 D *al* *L'* *Arm* *Δ*i^V l^FG me

39 ● δε + Ιησους‖p: *Rpl* *L'* *S'*j(κυριος I.) *C*,f — *txt*: W-28-565 λ ϕ⟨124⟩ D *L*k[e] abff²ir^1v *S*s[c] *Arm* | *om* αυτ.‖p: σ115 D *L*air¹

40 ημ. ... ημ.] υμ. ... υμ.‖Lk50: *Rpl* *L'* *S'* *C*b¹ — υμ. ... ημ.‖←: X λ118 σ115 U *pc* *l*24 *l*31 — ημ. ... υμ.‖←: L — *txt*: ℌ'CWΘ-28-565-1071 λ⟨118⟩ ϕ⟨124⟩ σ267-1402 1342 *pc* *L*k[e] *S*s[c]h^mj *C'* *Arm*

41 ος γαρ] και ος‖Mt10 42: Θ-565-700 *L*k[e] *Arm* *Aeth* | υδ.] ψυχρου υδ.(∼)‖←: σ115 (*L*bfg²30) vg³ | *om* οτι²‖←: *Rpl* Or *L'* *Geo* *Δ'* — *txt*: ℌ⟨Ψ-579⟩C* WΘ-565-1071 σ115-1194-1207 D *al* *L*k[e] bff²lq30 vg² *S*,j *Δ*i p

42 σκανδαλιζη‖43.45.47Mt8f.29f.: D' | τ. μικ.] ● τ. μ. τουτων‖MtLk: ℌ⟨Ψ-892⟩C NΘΦ-28-565-700-1071 λ ϕ124 σ⟨954⟩-M^c-267-349-659-827-945-1402 A D 1342 *al* *L*ciq *S*h {*Geo*^B} — τουτων τ. μ.‖p: ϕ983-1689 *pc* *l*18 *l*19 *L'* *S'* {*C*,f} — τ. μ. μου: W — τ. μ. υμων: *L*k[e] a — *txt*: *Rpl* *L*vg¹ *Arm* *Geo'* *Δ*me^v | πισ.] π. εις εμε‖Mt: *Rpl* *L'* *S* *C'*f^v — πιστιν εχοντων: D *L*a — *txt*: אC*^vΔ *L*k[e] bff²i *C*b⁶

Lk 9,49 I.] ● ο I.‖p: *Rpl* — *txt*: 𝔓^45.75 ℌ⟨אL-33⟩C*(?) 28 ϕ⟨124-983⟩ D W Y *pc* | επισ.] διδασκαλε‖p: 𝔓^45 CLΞ-892 157 *pc* {*L*e adr¹} *S*h^m | επι] ● εν‖p: 𝔓^45.75 ℌ⟨W⟩XΞ 700-1071 λ-1582-2193 ϕ σ7-267 Y Δ Ψ *pc* *l*18 *l*19 *l*49 — *txt*: *Rpl* | ∼ δαι. εκβ.‖Mk1 39: σ-115-1188 409 | δαι.] τα δαι.‖←: 565 H 476 | μεθ ημ.] ημιν‖p: 1241 28 ϕ69 F *pc* *l*184 *S*j *C*b¹

50 ● *om* ο: א*B | κω. + αυτον(-ους)‖p: CL(X) 1071 σ⟨1424⟩-M-71-692-1188-1194 (213) D F *pc* *l*48 *L*vg¹ *S*j *C*b⁹(¹) *Arm* *Geo*¹ *Aeth* | ος] ● ου γαρ εστιν καθ υμων(ημων) ος‖(p): LΞΨ-33-892 σ(7-267-659-1391-1402-1606)-1194 *pc* *S*h⁺ | ος—εστιν²] ου γαρ εστιν καθ ημων ουδε υπερ υμων: 𝔓^45 | υμ. ... υμ.] ημ. ... ημ.‖p: *Rpl* *S*j *Geo* — υμ. ... ημ.‖p: {} א*XΔ λ22 ϕ69(καθ υμ. μεθ ημ. υπερ ημ.) A *pc* — ημ. ... υμ.‖p: Θ 1355 — *txt*: {𝔓^75(υμων υπ[...]μων)} ℌ'א^cCΞ 565-700-1071 λ1278 ϕ124 σM-76-692-945-1194-1424 D K W Π Ψ *al* *l*36 *l*49 *l*184 *L* *S* *C*

Mk9 40p *cf.* Ev. apocr. (POxy 1224 fol.2r° col. 1): (*cf. ad 39.* Mt5 44) ... Ὁ γὰρ μὴ ὢν [κατὰ ὑμ]ῶν ὑπὲρ ὑμῶν ἐστιν. [ὁ σήμερον ὢ]ν μακρὰν αὔριον [ἐγγὺς ὑμῶν γ]ενήσεται ...

Matth 18	Mark 9 / (Matth 5)	(Luk 17) / Mark 9
ἐμέ, συμφέρει αὐτῷ ἵνα κρεμασθῇ μύλος ὀνικὸς εἰς τὸν τράχηλον αὐτοῦ καὶ καταποντισθῇ ἐν τῷ πελάγει τῆς θαλάσσης.	καλόν ἐστιν αὐτῷ μᾶλλον εἰ περίκειται μύλος ὀνικὸς περὶ τὸν τράχηλον αὐτοῦ καὶ βέβληται εἰς τὴν θάλασσαν.	*2a λυσιτελεῖ αὐτῷ εἰ λίθος μυλικὸς περίκειται περὶ τὸν τράχηλον αὐτοῦ καὶ ἔρριπται εἰς τὴν θάλασσαν ...*
7 οὐαὶ τῷ κόσμῳ ἀπὸ τῶν σκανδάλων· ἀνάγκη γὰρ ἐλθεῖν τὰ σκάνδαλα, πλὴν οὐαὶ τῷ ἀνθρώπῳ δι' οὗ τὸ σκάνδαλον ἔρχεται.		*1 Εἶπεν δὲ πρὸς τοὺς μαθητὰς αὐτοῦ· ἀνένδεκτόν ἐστιν τοῦ τὰ σκάνδαλα μὴ ἐλθεῖν, οὐαὶ δὲ δι' οὗ ἔρχεται·*
8 εἰ δὲ ἡ χείρ σου ἢ ὁ πούς σου σκανδαλίζει σε, ἔκκοψον αὐτὸν καὶ βάλε ἀπὸ σοῦ· καλόν σοί ἐστιν εἰσελθεῖν εἰς τὴν ζωὴν κυλλὸν ἢ χωλόν, ἢ δύο χεῖρας ἢ δύο πόδας ἔχοντα βληθῆναι εἰς τὸ πῦρ τὸ αἰώνιον.	*5 29f. (35.): 30 καὶ εἰ ἡ δεξιά σου χεὶρ σκανδαλίζει σε, ἔκκοψον αὐτὴν καὶ βάλε ἀπὸ σοῦ· συμφέρει γάρ σοι ἵνα ἀπόληται ἓν τῶν μελῶν σου καὶ μὴ ὅλον τὸ σῶμά σου εἰς γέενναν ἀπέλθῃ.*	43 καὶ ἐὰν σκανδαλίζῃ σε ἡ χείρ σου, ἀπόκοψον αὐτήν· καλόν ἐστίν σε κυλλὸν εἰσελθεῖν εἰς τὴν ζωήν, ἢ τὰς δύο χεῖρας ἔχοντα ἀπελθεῖν εἰς τὴν γέενναν, εἰς τὸ πῦρ τὸ ἄσβεστον.
		45 καὶ ἐὰν ὁ πούς σου σκανδαλίζῃ σε, ἀπόκοψον αὐτόν· καλόν ἐστίν σε εἰσελθεῖν εἰς τὴν ζωὴν χωλόν, ἢ τοὺς δύο πόδας ἔχοντα βληθῆναι εἰς τὴν γέενναν.
9 καὶ εἰ ὁ ὀφθαλμός σου σκανδαλίζει σε, ἔξελε	*29 εἰ δὲ ὁ ὀφθαλμός σου ὁ δεξιὸς σκανδαλίζει σε, ἔξελε*	47 καὶ ἐὰν ὁ ὀφθαλμός σου σκανδαλίζῃ σε, ἔκβαλε

Mt 18,6 μυ. ον.] λιθος μυ.‖Lk: L *l*184 | εις^{2}] ● περι‖MkLk: 𝔥 ΟΣ-28-544 σ1391 157 *pc* — επι *cf.* Act15 10: ΝΦ φ230 σ517-1424 D U *pc* {} — *txt*: *Rpl* Or {*L*,Hil *C*b(*om* τ. τραχ.)}s | εν—θα.] εις την θαλασσαν‖p: **σ** *L*⟨cz⟩ *C*b | θα. + η ινα σκανδαλιση ενα των μικρων τουτων‖Lk: 477 *pc* *C*b^{5} **7** ∼ τα σκ. ελθ.‖Lk: 443 2145 | ανθ. + εκεινω (∼)‖Mt26 24p: *Rpl* (W) Bas Cl Cr Da *L*vl'(e[k] ff^{1})g^{2}32 vg^{5} Au^{2} Cp Hil Luc *C*s^{9} *Arm* (*Geo*) *Δ*a' i$^{T4.V}$(*om* ανθ.) — *txt*: ℵL-892 λ1-22-1582 D F *l*184 Or *L*g^{1}r^{2}z vg' Au^{1} *S* *C*s^{1v}b *Δ*a^{A} ad i^{T1} l n | το σκ.] τα σκανδαλα‖7a Lk: 700 **φ** σ71 *pc* Chr *S*' — *om*‖Lk: Θ *S*s **8** ∼ σκα. σε η—σου^{2}‖Mk: σ1010-1293 | *om* και—σου^{3}‖Mk: 1093 | *om* η δ. ποδ.‖Mk: **σ** | το—αιων.] την γεενναν του πυρος (τ. πυ.] αιων.)‖p9p5 22 Mk45: λ1-1582 *L*(e[k] c)ff^{2} *S*c(p^{1} *C*s$^{1:8}$) **9** σου^{1} + δεξιος‖29: Chr *C*s$^{2:8}$b

Mk 9,42 μυ. ον.] λιθος μυλικος‖Lk: *Rpl* (∼: 28 *pc*) *L*q *S*h *Geo*^{1} — μυλωνικος λι.‖Lk: Θ-565 **φ**⟨124⟩ 258(∼) — *txt*: 𝔥C W(-ον -ον) **λ** σ1402 D 1342 *pc* *L*'(*om* ον.: d) *S*'j *Geo*^{2} **43** ● σκανδαλιση‖42p: 𝔥 W-28 H 1342 *pc* *L*k[e] aflz vg | εκκοψον‖p: φ230 125 *l*184 | εστ. σε] σοι εστ. (∼)‖Mt8f.: *Rpl* (φ230-543-983 D *L*')(*om* εστ.: g^{2}) — εστ.: 579 φ69 1342 *pc* — *txt*: 𝔥C Θ-28-565-700 **φ**'⟨124⟩ **σ** *L*a | ∼ εις τ. ζ. εισελ. κυλ.‖←: W 472 — κυλ. εις τ. ζ. εισελ.‖←: *Rpl* *S*h *Arm*' *Geo*^{1ch} — *txt*: 𝔥C Θ-565-700 σ115-517 A D 1342(+ σε) *pc* *L* *S*' *Arm*^{pc} *Geo*^{2} | *om* τας‖Mt8: Ψ 1071 D 440 *l*185 | απελ.] βληθηναι‖45.47 Mt8.9.29: D *al* *L*k[e] af30 *C*b^{1}f | *om* εις τ. γε. (εις^{2}⌒^{3})‖Mt8: W-28 **λ** φ788 435 *S*s[c] *Geo*^{1} | *om* την^{2}‖Mt29f.: 259 *pc* | εις^{3}—ασ.] του πυρος (+ του ασβεστου)‖Mt9: F (1515 *L*q30 vg^{1} *S*h *C*s$^{2:3}$b^{4}) — οπου εστιν το^{1}—ασβ.‖48: D *L*k[e] bcff^{2}ir^{1} — *om*‖45.47 Mt29f.: ℵ^{ca}LΔΨ-892 544-700 **0274** *pc* *l*1642 *S*p | ασ. + ^{44}οπου ο σκωληξ αυτων ου τελευτα και το πυρ(+ αυτων) ου σβεννυται‖48: *Rpl* (*pc*) *L*'(bcr^{1})(*om* αυτ.^{1}: r^{2}; *om* και—σβ.: f) Au (*S*ph) *Arm*^{0} *Aeth*(∼ το—σβ. και ο—τελ.) — *txt*: 𝔥⟨579⟩C W-28-544-565 **λ**-22-1278 **0274** *pc* *l*260 *L*k[e] *S*s[c] *C*,f *Arm*' **45** σκανδαλιση‖42p: L-892 W 90 *L*g^{2} vg^{1} | εκκοψον‖Mt8.30: 565-1071 *pc* | αυτ. + βαλε(*om*) απο σου‖Mt8f.29f.: 1396 (*L*c) *S*s[c] (h *C*s)b$^{\langle 3\rangle}$(*om* απο σου) | καλ. + γαρ‖Mt29f.: 1071 λ872 φ230 σ945-1207 A K Π *al* *L*c *S*s[c] *C*s$^{1:3}$b^{5} | εστ. σε] σοι εστ.‖Mt8f.: WΣ λ1278 φ124 σM^{c}-7-115-349-659-827 D S 157 *mu* *l*184 *L*bz vg^{5} — εστ. σοι‖←: *Rpl* *L*' — *txt*: 𝔥CX ΘΦ-28(∼ εισελ. σε)-565-700 **λ**-22 **φ**'⟨983⟩ σ517 A E F G H K V Y Π Ω 1342 *al* | ∼ εις τ. ζ. εισελ. χω.‖Mt9: ℵ λ22-1278 σ27-71-349-659-692-945-1194-1223 F Γ — ∼ χω. εισελ. εις τ. ζ.‖←: 565-700 D *L* *S*s[c] *Arm* *Aeth* | χωλον] κυλλον η χ.‖Mt8: ℵ | *om* τους‖←: σ349-517-1082-1675 1396 *l*48 *l*49 *l*184 *l*251 *l*260 | βλη.] απελθειν‖43 Mt30: W-28 **λ** *pc* *S*s[c] | *om* την^{2}‖Mt29f.: XΨ N-28 **φ**⟨124-346⟩ σM *pc* | γεεν. + του πυρος(+ του ασβεστου)‖Mt9: σ827 F *pc* *l*70 (*L*')(του πυ. ασβεστον: l) (*S*h) — + οπου(+ εστιν) το πυρ το ασβ.‖48: *L*(ar^{1})ff^{2}i — + εις το πυρ το ασβ.‖43 Mt8: *Rpl* (*om* εις τ. γε.: 700; *om* την^{2}: X) *L*fq *Arm*^{0} — *txt*: 𝔥⟨579-892⟩C W-28(*om* την^{2})-544 **λ**-22 1342 *pc* *l*260 *L*k[e] b *S*' *Arm*' *C*,f | γεεν. + ^{46}οπου ο σκωληξ αυτων ου τελευτα και το πυρ(+ αυτων) ου σβεννυται‖48: *Rpl* (*pc*) *L*'(abcr^{1} vg^{1}) Au *S*' *C*' *Arm*^{0} *Aeth* — *txt*: 𝔥⟨579⟩C W-28-544-565 **λ**-22-1278 **0274** *pc* *l*19 *L*k[e] *S*s[c] *C*,f *Arm*' **47** σου + ο δεξιος‖Mt29f.: *l*184 *C*s$^{1:3}$ | σκανδαλιση‖42p: W *L*k[e] | εκβ. αυ.] εκβ.(εξελε) αυ. και βαλε απο σου‖(p) Mt8.30: (579) Φ σ179-(827) *C*sf — εκβ. αυ. απο σου‖p: *L*c *S*s[c] *C*sb^{1}

αὐτὸν καὶ βάλε ἀπὸ σοῦ· καλόν σοί ἐστιν μονόφθαλμον εἰς τὴν ζωὴν εἰσελθεῖν, ἢ δύο ὀφθαλμοὺς ἔχοντα βληθῆναι εἰς τὴν γέενναν τοῦ πυρός.

αὐτὸν καὶ βάλε ἀπὸ σοῦ· συμφέρει γάρ σοι ἵνα ἀπόληται ἓν τῶν μελῶν σου καὶ μὴ ὅλον τὸ σῶμά σου βληθῇ εἰς γέενναν.

αὐτόν· καλόν σέ ἐστιν μονόφθαλμον εἰσελθεῖν εἰς τὴν βασιλείαν τοῦ θεοῦ, ἢ δύο ὀφθαλμοὺς ἔχοντα βληθῆναι εἰς τὴν γέενναν, 48 ὅπου **ὁ σκώληξ αὐτῶν οὐ τελευτᾷ καὶ τὸ πῦρ οὐ σβέννυται.** Is66 24

(132)

146. Vom Salz. *About Salt.* **Mark 9** 49–50

32.

49 Πᾶς γὰρ πυρὶ ἁλισθήσεται.
50 καλὸν τὸ ἅλας· ἐὰν δὲ τὸ ἅλας ἄναλον γένηται, ἐν τίνι αὐτὸ ἀρτύσετε; ἔχετε ἐν ἑαυτοῖς ἅλα καὶ εἰρηνεύετε ἐν ἀλλήλοις.

32.

(133)

147. Das Gleichnis vom verlorenen Schaf. *The Lost Sheep.*

Matth 18 10–14

10 Ὁρᾶτε μὴ καταφρονήσητε ἑνὸς τῶν μικρῶν τούτων· λέγω γὰρ ὑμῖν ὅτι οἱ ἄγγελοι αὐτῶν ἐν οὐρανοῖς διὰ παντὸς βλέπουσιν τὸ πρόσωπον τοῦ πατρός μου τοῦ ἐν οὐρανοῖς. 12 τί ὑμῖν δοκεῖ; ἐὰν γένηταί τινι ἀνθρώπῳ ἑκατὸν πρόβατα καὶ πλανηθῇ ἓν ἐξ αὐτῶν, οὐχὶ ἀφήσει τὰ ἐνενήκοντα ἐννέα ἐπὶ τὰ ὄρη καὶ πορευθεὶς ζητεῖ τὸ πλανώμενον;

15 3–7 *(186.)*

3 εἶπεν δὲ πρὸς αὐτοὺς τὴν παραβολὴν ταύτην λέγων· 4 τίς ἄνθρωπος ἐξ ὑμῶν ἔχων ἑκατὸν πρόβατα καὶ ἀπολέσας ἐξ αὐτῶν ἓν οὐ καταλείπει τὰ ἐνενήκοντα ἐννέα ἐν τῇ ἐρήμῳ καὶ πορεύεται ἐπὶ τὸ ἀπολωλὸς ἕως εὕρῃ αὐτό;

Mt 18,9 την²—πυρος] το σκοτος το εξωτερον‖8 12 22 13 25 30: σ1675 | *om* του πυ.‖p Mk4 5: D
10 τουτ. + των πιστευοντων εις εμε‖18 6 Mk9 42: Φ D(∼ τουτ. τ. μικ. *L*bcff¹·²(*om* τουτ.: g¹·²)r¹·²32 *S*cj *C*s⁵:⁹ *Δ*a | ● ουρ.² + ¹¹ηλθεν γαρ ο υιος του ανθρωπου σωσαι το απολωλος‖Lk19 10 *Rpl* Chr *L'*Au Hi Hil *S'*j¹ *C*b⁴ *Geo'* *Aeth* *Δ*<me> [[ηλθ.] και (+ οτι) η.: *l*10 *l*12 *l*69 *l*70 *l*80 *l*185¹ *l*211 *l*299 *l*303 *l*374 *l*1642 (*S*c) | γαρ] δε: *L*aln *S*j¹ — *om*: *L*br²32 Hi *Δ*a ad i^T *l*^FG p | *om* ο: Δ | τ. ανθρ.] της παρθενου: *Δ*i^T | σωσ.] ζητησαι και σ.‖Lk19 10: L^c(*om* και)-892^m 1604 ϕ346 σ990-1010-1402 G *al* *l*10 *l*12 *l*69 *l*70 *l*80 *l*185¹ *l*211 *l*299 *l*303 *l*374 *l*950 *l*1536 *l*1642 *L*Au *S*p²h *C*b⁴ *Aeth* — σ. και ζητ.: *L*c]] — *txt*: ℌ λ1-1582 **ϕ**<124-346>-230 Θ CAp Eu Or *L*e[k] ff¹ Hi Hil Iuv *S*sj^abc *C'* *Geo*^A *Aeth* **12** ● αφεις *et om* και²: *Rpl* *L*q *S*h — *txt*: BL-892 ϕ-*l*547 D(αφιησιν) Θ 157 *pc* *L'*(= D: ff¹ vg²)

Mk 9,47 σε εστ.] σοι εστ. (∼)‖Mt9.8: *Rpl* (579 σM) (*om* σοι: 892 W) (*L'*)vg²(¹ *om* εστ.) *Geo*¹(= W) — εστ.(*om*) σε‖43.45: LΔ Θ-(28)-700 (ϕ<124>) — *txt*: ℵBΨ 565(*om* εστ.) 1342 *L*vg¹(*om* σε) | ∼ εστ.(*om*) μονο. εισελ. σε: ϕ'<124>(69) | ∼ εστ. μονο. σε: 28 | ∼ εις τ. βα. τ. θε. εισελ.‖Mt9: Φ-544 (ϕ124) A *pc* | εις¹] εις την ζωην και εις‖43.45 Mt9: ϕ124 | βα. τ. θε.] ζωην‖43.45 Mt9.8: 544 σ517 | βλη.] απηλθειν‖43 Mt30: **λ** σ7-179-517(επ-)-1082-1391-1424-1606-1675 D *pc* *l*18 *l*19 *l*184 *L*ci *S*s[c] *Geo*¹ *Aeth* | ● *om* την²‖Mt29f.: BLΨ 28 | γεεν. + του πυρος(+ του ασβεστου)‖Mt9: *Rpl* *L'*(g²) *S'* *C*b¹ — εις το πυρ το ασβεστον‖43 Mt8: F(*om* εις τ. γε.) 4 273 — *txt*: ℌ W-28-565-700 **λ** D 1342 **0274** *pc* *l*260 *L*k[e] abcff²r¹ *S*s[c] *C'*f *Arm* **48** *om* v. *cf. ad* 43.45: *C*b **49** πυρι] εν π.‖50 Mt5 13: ℵC 1342 **50** αναλ. γεν.] μωρανθη‖Mt5 13 Lk14 34: 579 W | *om* αυτο‖Mt5 13 Lk14 34: **λ**<118> **σ**<1675>-M Γ *pc* *L*f | αρτ.] αρτυθησεται‖Lk←: **λ** K *pc* *L*df30 *C*b² *Arm* — αρτυεται‖←: σ517-1424(-τε) *C*b'f — αλισθησεται‖Mt5 13: (salietis: *L*q) *S*p

---

Mt18 12-14p *cf.* ETh^II 107 (*transl.*): *Λέγει Ἰησοῦς· ἡ βασιλεία ὁμοία ἐστὶν ἀνθρώπῳ ποιμένι ἔχοντι ἑκατὸν πρόβατα. ἓν ἐξ αὐτῶν, τὸ μέγιστον, ἐπλανήθη. κατέλιπεν (τὰ) ἐνενήκοντα ἐννέα (καὶ) ἐζήτησεν τὸ ἕν, ἕως εὗρεν αὐτό. κοπιάσας εἶπεν τῷ προβάτῳ· ἐπιποθῶ σε παρὰ (τὰ) ἐνενήκοντα ἐννέα.*

13 καὶ ἐὰν γένηται εὑρεῖν αὐτό, αμην λέγω ὑμῖν ὅτι χαίρει ἐπ' αὐτῷ μᾶλλον ἢ ἐπὶ τοῖς ἐνενήκοντα ἐννέα τοῖς μὴ πεπλανημένοις.

14 οὕτως οὐκ ἔστιν θέλημα ἔμπροσθεν τοῦ πατρὸς ὑμῶν τοῦ ἐν οὐρανοῖς ἵνα ἀπόληται ἓν τῶν μικρῶν τούτων.

5 καὶ εὑρὼν ἐπιτίθησιν ἐπὶ τοὺς ὤμους αὐτοῦ χαίρων, 6 καὶ ἐλθὼν εἰς τὸν οἶκον συγκαλεῖ τοὺς φίλους καὶ τοὺς γείτονας, λέγων αὐτοῖς· συγχάρητέ μοι, ὅτι εὗρον τὸ πρόβατόν μου τὸ ἀπολωλός. 7 λέγω ὑμῖν ὅτι οὕτως χαρὰ ἐν τῷ οὐρανῷ ἔσται ἐπὶ ἑνὶ ἁμαρτωλῷ μετανοοῦντι ἢ ἐπὶ ἐνενήκοντα ἐννέα δικαίοις οἵτινες οὐ χρείαν ἔχουσιν μετανοίας.

(134)

148. Vom Mahnen und Beten unter Brüdern. Matth 18 15–20
On Reproving One's Brother.

15 Ἐὰν δὲ ἁμαρτήσῃ εἰς σὲ ὁ ἀδελφός σου, ὕπαγε ἔλεγξον αὐτὸν μεταξὺ σοῦ καὶ αὐτοῦ μόνου. ἐάν σου ἀκούσῃ, ἐκέρδησας τὸν ἀδελφόν σου· 16 ἐὰν δὲ μὴ ἀκούσῃ, παράλαβε μετὰ σεαυτοῦ ἔτι ἕνα ἢ δύο, ἵνα **ἐπὶ στόματος δύο μαρτύρων ἢ τριῶν σταθῇ πᾶν ῥῆμα·** 17 ἐὰν δὲ παρακούσῃ αὐτῶν, εἰπὲ τῇ ἐκκλησίᾳ· ἐὰν δὲ καὶ τῆς ἐκκλησίας παρακούσῃ, ἔστω σοι ὥσπερ ὁ ἐθνικὸς καὶ ὁ τελώνης. 18 αμην λέγω ὑμῖν, ὅσα ἐὰν δήσητε ἐπὶ τῆς γῆς ἔσται δεδεμένα ἐν τῷ οὐρανῷ, καὶ ὅσα ἐὰν λύσητε ἐπὶ τῆς γῆς ἔσται λελυμένα ἐν τῷ οὐρανῷ. 19 πάλιν αμην λέγω ὑμῖν ὅτι ἐὰν δύο συμφωνήσωσιν ἐξ ὑμῶν ἐπὶ τῆς γῆς περὶ παντὸς πράγματος οὗ ἐὰν αἰτήσωνται, γενήσεται αὐτοῖς παρὰ τοῦ πατρός μου τοῦ ἐν οὐρανοῖς. 20 οὗ γάρ εἰσιν δύο ἢ τρεῖς συνηγμένοι εἰς τὸ ἐμὸν ὄνομα, ἐκεῖ εἰμι ἐν μέσῳ αὐτῶν.

Dt19 15 17 6

17 3 (193.): Προσέχετε ἑαυτοῖς. ἐὰν ἁμάρτῃ ὁ ἀδελφός σου, ἐπιτίμησον αὐτῷ, καὶ ἐὰν μετανοήσῃ, ἄφες αὐτῷ.

16 19 (135.): ... καὶ ὃ ἐὰν δήσῃς ἐπὶ τῆς γῆς ἔσται δεδεμένον ἐν τοῖς οὐρανοῖς, καὶ ὃ ἐὰν λύσῃς ἐπὶ τῆς γῆς ἔσται λελυμένον ἐν τοῖς οὐρανοῖς.

20 22 f.: ... καὶ λέγει αὐτοῖς· λάβετε πνεῦμα ἅγιον. 23 ἄν τινων ἀφῆτε τὰς ἁμαρτίας, ἀφέωνται αὐτοῖς· ἄν τινων κρατῆτε, κεκράτηνται.

215.

Mt 18,14 ουρ.] τοις ου. *cf.* 5 17 6 9 7 11 *etc.*: 892 **σ**⟨1424⟩ D E V 157 *pc* — *txt*: 𝔋 NΣ-1604 σM^{m}-1010-1293 D 157 *pc* *L*e[k] vg^{1} | εν^{2}] ● εις ‖18 6 10 42: *Rpl* Or *L*' Geo(+ ουν) | **15** *om* δε ‖p: **ϕ**⟨346⟩ Θ *pc* *Cs*$^{4:10}$b^{3} *Arm* | ● *om* εις σε ‖p: ℵB 544 λ1-22-1582 Bas^{3} Cr Or *Cs*^{8}b^{7} EpAp *Aeth*EpAp — *txt*: *Rpl* Bas^{2} *L*,PsCp Hil Luc *S*,j *Cs*^{2}b' PS **16** σεαυτου] ● σου: *Rpl* — *txt*: 𝔋⟨B⟩ NΣ-28 λ1-1582 **ϕ**'(σου αυτου: 346) σM-659-1675 K Θ 157 *al* Or **18** τω ου.^{1}] τοις ουρανοις ‖Mt16: ℵL-33-892 1604 D **078**^{v} *pc* *L*cfr^{1} vg^{2} *C* — ● *om* τω ‖6 10.20: B ϕ124-174 Θ Or {*L*' Or} — *txt*: *Rpl* {} | τω ου.^{2}] τοις ουρανοις ‖Mt16: L-33 1604 σM D **078**^{v} 157 *pc* *L*cd(γης^{1}∩^{2})f vg^{3} *C* — ● *om* τω ‖6 10.20: ℵB ϕ124-788 Θ Or {*L*'(γης^{1}∩^{2}: g^{2}n) Or} — *txt*: *Rpl* (ου.^{1}∩^{2}: ϕ*l*547) {} **19** γεν.] δοθησεται ‖7 7p: 33 DAp

Jo 20,23 *cf. ad 273.*

Mt18 19 *cf.* ETh^{II} 48 (*cf. ad 215.* Mt21 21)

Mt18 20 *cf.* ETh^{II} 30 (POxy 1,5): [Λέγε]ι ['I(ησοῦ)ς· ὅ]που ἐὰν ὦσιν [γ' θε]ο[ί,] ε[ἰσὶ]ν θεοί· καὶ [ὅ]π[ου] ε[ἷς] ἐστιν μόνος [αὐ]τῷ, ἐγώ εἰμι μετ' αὐτ[οῦ].

(*transl.*): *Λέγει Ἰησοῦς· ὅπου ἐὰν ὦσιν τρεῖς θεοί, θεοί εἰσιν· οὐ εἰσιν δύο ἢ εἷς, ἐγώ εἰμι μετ' αὐτοῦ.*

(135) ## *149.* Von der Versöhnlichkeit. *On Reconciliation.* **Matth 18** 21–22

[21] Τότε προσελθὼν αὐτῷ ὁ Πέτρος εἶπεν· κύριε, ποσάκις ἁμαρτήσει εἰς ἐμὲ ὁ ἀδελφός μου καὶ ἀφήσω αὐτῷ; ἕως ἑπτάκις; [22] λέγει αὐτῷ ὁ Ἰησοῦς· οὐ λέγω σοι ἕως ἑπτάκις, ἀλλ' ἕως ἑβδομηκοντάκις ἑπτά.

17 4 (193.): καὶ ἐὰν ἑπτάκις τῆς ἡμέρας ἁμαρτήσῃ εἰς σὲ καὶ ἑπτάκις ἐπιστρέψῃ πρός σε λέγων· μετανοῶ, ἀφήσεις αὐτῷ.

(136) ## *150.* Das Gleichnis vom Schalksknecht. **Matth 18** 23–35
The Parable of the Unmerciful Servant.

[23] Διὰ τοῦτο ὡμοιώθη ἡ βασιλεία τῶν οὐρανῶν ἀνθρώπῳ βασιλεῖ, ὃς ἠθέλησεν συνᾶραι λόγον μετὰ τῶν δούλων αὐτοῦ. [24] ἀρξαμένου δὲ αὐτοῦ συναίρειν, προσηνέχθη αὐτῷ εἷς ὀφειλέτης μυρίων ταλάντων. [25] μὴ ἔχοντος δὲ αὐτοῦ ἀποδοῦναι, ἐκέλευσεν αὐτὸν ὁ κύριος πραθῆναι καὶ τὴν γυναῖκα καὶ τὰ τέκνα καὶ πάντα ὅσα εἶχεν, καὶ ἀποδοθῆναι. [26] πεσὼν οὖν ὁ δοῦλος προσεκύνει αὐτῷ λέγων· μακροθύμησον ἐπ' ἐμοί, καὶ πάντα ἀποδώσω σοι. [27] σπλαγχνισθεὶς δὲ ὁ κύριος τοῦ δούλου ἐκείνου ἀπέλυσεν αὐτόν, καὶ τὸ δάνειον ἀφῆκεν αὐτῷ. [28] ἐξελθὼν δὲ ὁ δοῦλος ἐκεῖνος εὗρεν ἕνα τῶν συνδούλων αὐτοῦ, ὃς ὤφειλεν αὐτῷ ἑκατὸν δηνάρια, καὶ κρατήσας αὐτὸν ἔπνιγεν λέγων· ἀπόδος εἴ τι ὀφείλεις. [29] πεσὼν οὖν ὁ σύνδουλος αὐτοῦ παρεκάλει αὐτὸν λέγων· μακροθύμησον ἐπ' ἐμοί, καὶ ἀποδώσω σοι. [30] ὁ δὲ οὐκ ἤθελεν, ἀλλὰ ἀπελθὼν ἔβαλεν αὐτὸν εἰς φυλακὴν ἕως οὗ ἀποδῷ τὸ ὀφειλόμενον. [31] ἰδόντες οὖν οἱ σύνδουλοι αὐτοῦ τὰ γινόμενα ἐλυπήθησαν σφόδρα, καὶ ἐλθόντες διεσάφησαν τῷ κυρίῳ ἑαυτῶν πάντα τὰ γενόμενα. [32] τότε προσκαλεσάμενος αὐτὸν ὁ κύριος αὐτοῦ λέγει αὐτῷ· δοῦλε πονηρέ, πᾶσαν τὴν ὀφειλὴν ἐκείνην ἀφῆκά σοι, ἐπεὶ παρεκάλεσάς με· [33] οὐκ ἔδει καὶ σὲ ἐλεῆσαι τὸν σύνδουλόν σου, ὡς κἀγὼ σὲ ἠλέησα; [34] καὶ ὀργισθεὶς ὁ κύριος αὐτοῦ παρέδωκεν αὐτὸν τοῖς βασανισταῖς ἕως οὗ ἀποδῷ πᾶν τὸ ὀφειλόμενον αὐτῷ. [35] οὕτως καὶ ὁ πατήρ μου ὁ οὐράνιος ποιήσει ὑμῖν, ἐὰν μὴ ἀφῆτε ἕκαστος τῷ ἀδελφῷ αὐτοῦ ἀπὸ τῶν καρδιῶν ὑμῶν.

42.

Mt 18,21 ● ∼ ο Π. ειπ. αυτω(*om*): (א*)B-892 1604 σ D(*om* ο) *pc* l^{pl} (Da) Or (*S*s) — αυτω ο Π. ειπ. αυτω: *L*vl' Luc *S*c *C* *Geo*^{B}(αυτω] τω Ιησου) *Aeth* — ο Π. αυτω ειπ.: *L*l vg Luc — *txt*: *Rpl* *l*76 *l*333 *l*850 Chr *L*e[k] g^{2}qz Au *S*' *Geo*' | ● ∼ ο αδ. μ. εις εμε‖Lk17 3: B ϕ Θ 1241 — *txt*: *Rpl* {*L*,Au} **24** ● προσηχθη *cf.* Lk9 41 Act16 20: B D 1579 Or | ● ∼ εις αυτω: א*B **25** ειχ.] ● εχει‖13 44: B λ1-1582 ϕ124 Θ *pc* Or *Δ*p **26** προσε. *prm* προς τους ποδας του κυριου αυτου: *L*ah — αυτω] τω κυριω αυτου: *L*e[k] cf *S*sc *Δ*n^{L}(*om* αυτου: i^{V} md n' p) | ● λεγ. + κυριε: *Rpl* Da *L*fff^{2}g^{1}qz vg^{1} Or *S*'j *C* *Δ*a md n^{LHr} p — εμ. + κυ.: *L*hr$^{1.2}$30 vg^{4} Or *Geo*^{Bc} — *txt*: B 700 D Θ *pc* *l*47 *l*76 *l*184 Chr Or *L*'Hi$^{1:2}$ Luc *S*sc *Arm* *Geo*' *Δ*ad i l n' | ● ∼ σοι αποδ.: *Rpl* *L*fq — *om* σοι: 700 D *L*e[k](*om* παντα σοι) bff$^{1.2}$r^{2} *S*s — *txt*: ℌ ΟΣ ϕ⟨346⟩ σ 157 *pc* Or *L*'Hi$^{1:2}$ Luc *S*'j *C* **30** ● *om* ου‖5 26p: אBCL-892 **31** ιδ. ουν] ● ιδ. δε: *Rpl* *L*'Hi$^{1:2}$ Luc Or *S*,j^{abc} *C* *Geo*^{A} *Δ*l — και ιδ.: *Aeth* *Δ*' — ιδ.: *L*r^{2v} *Arm* *Geo*^{B} *Δ*i n^{L} p — *txt*: א*B-33-892 D 21 *L*e[k] *S*j^{1} *Geo*^{1} **34** *om* ου‖←: B-892 σ990 **35** απο—υμων + τα παραπτωματα αυτων(-ου)‖6 14: *Rpl* (σ945-990-1223) *L*fh *S*(p)hj^{1} *Arm* *Δ*(a' n^{L})(το παραπτωμα αυτου: a^{A}) — *prm* τα π. αυτων *et* απο + ολων: *S*j^{b} — *om*: *S*j^{ac} — *txt*: אBL-892 700 λ1-22-1582 D Θ 251 Or *L*'Au PsAu Luc *S*sc *C*sb(' αφ ολης της καρδιας αυτου; b^{1} απο τ. κ. αυτου) *Geo* *Aeth*

---

149. cf. EN frgm.15 (Codd. Evv. 566^{m} 899^{m}): Τὸ Ἰουδαϊκὸν ἑξῆς ἔχει μετὰ τὸ ἑβδομηκοντάκις ἑπτά· καὶ γὰρ ἐν τοῖς προφήταις μετὰ τὸ χρισθῆναι αὐτοὺς ἐν πνεύματι ἁγίῳ εὑρίσκετο ἐν αὐτοῖς λόγος ἁμαρτίας.

(Hi Pel. 3,2): 'Si peccaverit', inquit, 'frater tuus in verbo, et satis tibi fecerit, septies in die suscipe eum'. Dixit illi Simon discipulus eius: 'Septies in die?' respondit dominus, et dixit ei: 'Etiam ego dico tibi, usque septuagies septies. Etenim in prophetis quoque postquam uncti sunt spiritu sancto, inventus est sermo peccati'.

II. Der lukanische Reisebericht. *The Lucan Travel Narrative.*

Luk 951 —**18**14

(137)

151. Die Samariterherberge. *The Samaritan Villages.* Luk 9 51–56

[51] Ἐγένετο δὲ ἐν τῷ συμπληροῦσθαι τὰς ἡμέρας τῆς ἀναλήμψεως αὐτοῦ καὶ αὐτὸς τὸ πρόσωπον ἐστήρισεν τοῦ πορεύεσθαι εἰς Ἰερουσαλημ, [52] καὶ ἀπέστειλεν ἀγγέλους πρὸ προσώπου αὐτοῦ. καὶ πορευθέντες εἰσῆλθον εἰς κώμην Σαμαριτῶν, ὥστε ἑτοιμάσαι αὐτῷ· [53] καὶ οὐκ ἐδέξαντο αὐτόν, ὅτι τὸ πρόσωπον αὐτοῦ ἦν πορευόμενον εἰς Ἰερουσαλημ. [54] ἰδόντες δὲ οἱ μαθηταὶ Ἰάκωβος καὶ Ἰωάννης εἶπαν· κύριε, θέλεις εἴπωμεν **πῦρ καταβῆναι ἀπὸ τοῦ οὐρανοῦ καὶ ἀναλῶσαι** αὐτούς; [55] στραφεὶς δὲ ἐπετίμησεν αὐτοῖς. [56] καὶ ἐπορεύθησαν εἰς ἑτέραν κώμην.

!Rg1 10.12

(138)

152. Verschiedene Nachfolger. *Claimants to Discipleship.* Luk 9 57–62 *61.*

61.

[57] Καὶ πορευομένων αὐτῶν ἐν τῇ ὁδῷ εἶπέν τις πρὸς αὐτόν· ἀκολουθήσω σοι ὅπου ἐὰν ἀπέρχῃ. [58] καὶ εἶπεν αὐτῷ ὁ Ἰησοῦς· αἱ ἀλώπεκες φωλεοὺς ἔχουσιν καὶ τὰ πετεινὰ τοῦ οὐρανοῦ κατασκηνώσεις, ὁ δὲ υἱὸς τοῦ ἀνθρώπου οὐκ ἔχει ποῦ τὴν κεφαλὴν κλίνῃ.

[59] εἶπεν δὲ πρὸς ἕτερον· ἀκολούθει μοι. ὁ δὲ εἶπεν· ἐπίτρεψόν μοι ἀπελθόντι πρῶτον θάψαι τὸν πατέρα μου. [60] εἶπεν δὲ αὐτῷ· ἄφες τοὺς νεκροὺς θάψαι τοὺς ἑαυτῶν νεκρούς, σὺ δὲ ἀπελθὼν διάγγελλε τὴν βασιλείαν τοῦ θεοῦ.

[61] εἶπεν δὲ καὶ ἕτερος· ἀκολουθήσω σοι, κύριε· πρῶτον δὲ ἐπίτρεψόν μοι ἀποτάξασθαι τοῖς εἰς τὸν οἶκόν μου. [62] εἶπεν δὲ πρὸς αὐτὸν ὁ Ἰησοῦς· οὐδεὶς ἐπιβαλὼν τὴν χεῖρα αὐτοῦ ἐπ' ἄροτρον καὶ βλέπων εἰς τὰ ὀπίσω εὔθετός ἐστιν τῇ βασιλείᾳ τοῦ θεοῦ.

Lk 9,52 κωμ.] πολιν ‖ Mt10 5: ℵ* Λ-28-544 λ1278-2193 **φ** Γ Ψ *al* AnMt *L*⟨e c⟩ Te$^{1:3}$ *S*p^{1} *C*b^{1} **54** κυ.] ει ‖ Mt17 4: 1241 — κυ. ει: *L*vg^{1} *S*j | απο του] απ(απο) ‖ 17 19 21 11: LΞ-579-892-1241 544-1071-1604 1396 (716) — *om*: 1241 **55** αυτοις + και ειπεν· ουκ οιδατε οιου πνευματος εστε υμεις; [56] ο γαρ υιος του ανθρωπου ουκ ηλθεν ψυχας ανθρωπων απολεσαι αλλα σωσαι (*om* ο—σωσαι) ‖ 19 10 69: *Rpl* (D *l*1127^{1}) *l*12^{1} *l*69^{1} *l*76 *l*185^{1} *l*331 *l*854 *l*950 *l*1579 *l*1642 *l*1761 AnMt Ant (Chr) (Ddy *et* εσ. υμ.] εστιν ο υιος του ανθρωπου) Dio^{Ar} (Ep^{1}) (^{1} = Ddy) *L*'(g^{2}) Am Cp *S*'j *C*b^{8} *Geo Aeth Got Δ*' ⟦οιου] ποιου: 579(*cf. ad* 9 57) 700-1604 **λλ**⟨131-2193⟩ σ267-659-945 D *al* *l*12^{1} *l*69^{1} Ant Chr | *om* υμ.: 579(9 57) Λ-700 **φ**⟨346⟩-174-230 σ7-954 D F^{W} U Γ Θ *al* Ant Chr$^{1:2}$ Ep {*L*⟨lr^{2} vg^{6}⟩} *Geo*^{2} *Got Δ*a^{A} | ο γαρ] ο: 579(9 57) Λ-544-700-1604 **λ**-22-1582 **φ**⟨346⟩-174-230 σ945-954-1223 U Γ Θ *al* *l*69^{1} Ant *L*e ab(οτι ο)r^{1}z vg$^{⟨6⟩}$ *S*h *C*b^{8}(και ο) *Δ*a^{BE} i^{T} l^{AD} md n p | ψυχην ‖ 69: Γ | *om* ανθρωπων ‖ 69: *L*e cz vg$^{⟨10⟩}$ *S*cp *Got Δ*a i^{T} l^{AD} md n p | απολ.] αποκτειναι ‖ Mk3 4: 700 φ124-174 σ115-954 U Γ *pc*⟧ — *txt*: 𝔓$^{45.75}$ 𝔋'(579 *cf. ad* 9 57; *om* 56: 579-1241)CXΞ 28-1071 **σ**⟨954⟩-71-990-1010 A E G H S V W Δ Ψ Ω **047** Bas Cat^{Ox} Cr^{I} *L*lr^{2}30 vg^{6} Hi *S*s *C*' *Aeth Δ*ad i^{V} l^{FG} **57** προς αυ.] αυτω ‖ Mt8 19: 251 716 — + ουκ οιδατε—σωσαι (*cf. ad* 55): 579 | απερ.] υπαγης ‖ Jo13 36: 𝔓^{45} D 157 **59** ● ειπ.^{2} + κυριε ‖ **p** 61: 𝔓$^{45.75}$ *Rpl* Bas *L*' *S*'j *C* — *txt*: B* D V *pc* Thd^{C} *L*g^{2} *S*s | απελ. πρω.] πρω. απελθειν (+ και) ‖ (**p**): 579 544-1071-1604 **λ**-1582 **φ**⟨124-828⟩(*om* πρω.: 69) **σ**-990 (A K Π) *pc* (*pc*) *l*184 *L*cg^{2}l(vl'r^{1} vg')^{10} {*S*'j^{ac} *Geo*^{1}} — απελθειν πρω. ‖ ←: *l*19 *l*32 *l*1963 *l*^{13} *Arm* — ● πρω. απελθοντι ‖ ←: ℵB-33-892 28 D(-οντα) *pc* *l*80 {} — απελθοντι: W Thd^{C} *S*j^{b} *Δ*i^{V} — *txt* (*om* απελ.): 𝔓$^{45.75}$ *Rpl* (-οντα: Θ) (1241) Bas *S*h (*Geo*^{2} *Δ*i$^{T1:10}$ n^{Hr}) **60** αυτω + ο Ιησους(κυριος) ‖ p: *Rpl* (Bas) *L*' *S*'j(κυ. Ι.) — *txt*: 𝔓$^{45.75}$ 𝔋Ξ σ990 D(ο δε ειπεν) **0181** 1574 *L*a *S*s *C* | αφες] ακολουθει μοι και αφ. ‖ p: 1574 *L*l | απελ.] πορευθεις ‖ 7 22p Mt 28 7.19: D Ep Ir **62** ● *om* αυτου ‖ 20 19 Mt26 50 Mk14 46 Jo7 30.44: 𝔓^{75} B **λ**⟨118⟩-1582-2193 **0181** *pc* PsBas Cr Ddy Ep Or Val^{Ir} *L*ablq Cp$^{2:5}$ Te *Arm*

(139)

153. Die Aussendung der Zweiundsiebzig. Luk 10 1–16 [*122.*]
The Mission of the Seventy Two.

[*122.*] [*78.*]

1 Μετὰ δὲ ταῦτα ἀνέδειξεν ὁ κύριος καὶ ἑτέρους ἑβδομήκοντα δύο, καὶ ἀπέστειλεν αὐτοὺς ἀνὰ δύο πρὸ προσώπου αὐτοῦ εἰς πᾶσαν πόλιν καὶ τόπον οὗ ἤμελλεν αὐτὸς ἔρχεσθαι. 2 ἔλεγεν δὲ πρὸς αὐτούς· ὁ μὲν θερισμὸς πολύς, οἱ δὲ ἐργάται ὀλίγοι· δεήθητε οὖν τοῦ κυρίου τοῦ θερισμοῦ ὅπως ἐργάτας ἐκβάλῃ εἰς τὸν θερισμὸν αὐτοῦ. 3 ὑπάγετε· ἰδοὺ ἀποστέλλω ὑμᾶς ὡς ἄρνας ἐν μέσῳ λύκων. 4 μὴ βαστάζετε βαλλάντιον, μὴ πήραν, μὴ ὑποδήματα· καὶ μηδένα κατὰ τὴν ὁδὸν ἀσπάσησθε. 5 εἰς ἣν δ' ἂν εἰσέλθητε οἰκίαν, πρῶτον λέγετε· εἰρήνη τῷ οἴκῳ τούτῳ. 6 καὶ ἐὰν ᾖ ἐκεῖ υἱὸς εἰρήνης, ἐπαναπαήσεται ἐπ' αὐτὸν ἡ εἰρήνη ὑμῶν· εἰ δὲ μή γε, ἐφ' ὑμᾶς ἀνακάμψει. 7 ἐν αὐτῇ δὲ τῇ οἰκίᾳ μένετε, ἔσθοντες καὶ πίνοντες τὰ παρ' αὐτῶν· ἄξιος γὰρ ὁ ἐργάτης τοῦ μισθοῦ αὐτοῦ. μὴ μεταβαίνετε ἐξ οἰκίας εἰς οἰκίαν. 8 καὶ εἰς ἣν ἂν πόλιν εἰσέρχησθε καὶ δέχωνται ὑμᾶς, ἐσθίετε τὰ παρατιθέμενα ὑμῖν, 9 καὶ θεραπεύετε τοὺς ἐν αὐτῇ ἀσθενεῖς, καὶ λέγετε αὐτοῖς· ἤγγικεν ἐφ' ὑμᾶς ἡ βασιλεία τοῦ θεοῦ. 10 εἰς ἣν δ' ἂν πόλιν εἰσέλθητε καὶ μὴ δέχωνται ὑμᾶς, ἐξελθόντες εἰς τὰς πλατείας αὐτῆς εἴπατε· 11 καὶ τὸν κονιορτὸν τὸν κολληθέντα ἡμῖν ἐκ τῆς πόλεως ὑμῶν εἰς τοὺς πόδας ἀπομασσόμεθα ὑμῖν· πλὴν τοῦτο γινώσκετε, ὅτι ἤγγικεν ἡ βασιλεία τοῦ θεοῦ. 12 λέγω ὑμῖν ὅτι Σοδόμοις ἐν τῇ ἡμέρᾳ ἐκείνῃ ἀνεκτότερον ἔσται ἢ τῇ πόλει ἐκείνῃ.

13 Οὐαί σοι, Χοραζιν, οὐαί σοι, Βηθσαιδα· ὅτι εἰ ἐν Τύρῳ καὶ Σιδῶνι ἐγενήθησαν αἱ δυνάμεις αἱ γενόμεναι ἐν ὑμῖν, πάλαι ἂν ἐν σάκκῳ καὶ σποδῷ καθήμενοι μετενόησαν. 14 πλὴν Τύρῳ καὶ Σιδῶνι ἀνεκτότερον ἔσται

Lk 10,1 ● *om* και^{1}: 𝔓^{75} BLΞ-579-892 1071 **0181** *pc* Cr *Lr*^{1} *S*sp *Δ*⟨l^{DFG}⟩ | ● *om* δυο^{1}: *Rpl* Ad^{2} ATh Bas Chr Cl Cr Eu Or Ti *L*qr^{1}? Ad^{1} Am Hi Ir Mcn^{Te} Or Te *S*'j *C*b' — *txt*: 𝔓^{75} B 1604 σM D R$^{cap.}$ **0181** *pc* Ad^{3} PsCl Ep Or *L*' Ad^{2} Amst Au DAp *S*sc ATh DAp Ef HIo Is^{M} *C*sb^{1} *Arm* | δυο^{2} + δυο‖Mk7: B **ϕ**⟨124-983⟩ σ71-990 K Y Θ Π Eu$^{2:4}$ *S*h^{+} Eu | διερχ.‖194: **ϕ**⟨124⟩ σ71-1194 *pc* **2** ● ∼ εκβ. εργ.‖**p**: *Rpl* Bas *L*' — *txt*: B 700 D **0181** *L*e | θερισμον] αμπελωνα‖Mt20 1f.: 477 **3** ιδου + εγω‖p Mt11 10 Mk1 2: *Rpl* *L*' *S*' *C*s^{3}b — *txt*: 𝔓^{75} ℵB-579 A *pc* *L*e abr^{1} *S*cj *C*s^{1} | αρν.] προβατα‖**p**: 28-1604 (πρ. + αρν.) σM-27-71-692-1223 A *al* **4** μη^{2}] μητε‖9 3: σM-71-692 *pc* *L*⟨e ac⟩ Am *S*scpj *Arm*^{pc} | μη^{3}] μηδε‖Mt: *Rpl* Cl {} — μητε‖9 3: **ϕ** σM-71-692-1194 *pc* {*L*' Am} *S*'j — *txt*: 𝔓^{75} 𝔥Ξ 700-1071 **λλ**⟨22⟩ σ945 D **0181** *pm* *L*e c *S*h *Arm* **5** ∼ οικ. εισ.‖9 4 Mt: *Rpl* *L*' *S*,j — πολιν εισ. η οικιαν‖←: **ϕ**'(εισερχ.: 124)-*l*547 — *txt*: 𝔓^{75} ℵB-579-1241 D **0181** *L*e Mcn | εισελ.] εισερχησθε‖8: *Rpl* CAp *S* — *txt*: 𝔓^{75} 𝔥CXΞ 700-1071 **λ**-1278 **ϕ**⟨124⟩ D Γ **0181** *pc* *L* *S*j | οικ. πρω.] οικ.‖p: 579 D^{c} CAp *L*dr^{1} vg^{1} Mcn Or — πρω. οικ.: D* *L*ac *S*sc **6** εαν + μεν‖p: 1604 *pm* Eu Or | ● ∼ εκει η: 𝔓^{75} B **0181**(εκ. ην) *pc* Or *L*⟨e c⟩(*om* ^{5}λεγ.—^{11}*fin.*: r^{2}) | μηγε + η ειρηνη υμων‖p: 1604 R Or *S*p^{5}j *C*b *Aeth* (∼ αν. η ει. υ.) | εφ] προς‖p: **ϕ**⟨124⟩-*l*547 **σ** {(ad: *L*e cfz vg)} | ανακ.] επιστρεψει η ειρηνη υμων‖p: D *C*b **7** τ. μισ. της τροφης‖p: 348 *L*vg^{1} *S*c *C*b⟨^{6}⟩ **8** εισελθησθε‖5 p10: λ2193 | δεξωνται‖Mt14 Mk11: **σ**-1188 59 — δεχεται‖←: ϕ983-1689 **9** ασθενουντας‖Mt8: D 565 *L*e c — αρρωστους‖Mt14 14: 472 | *om* αυτοις‖Mt: σ1424 *L*l *S*sc | ηγγ.] οτι η.‖11 Mt: 1241 ϕ124-174-*l*547 σ115-954 *l*184 *L*l *S*scp^{2} | *om* εφ υμ.‖p Mt4 17 **p**: Γ *pc* *L*e(+ η παρουσια *et* της βασιλειας) *C*b⟨^{6}⟩ **10** δεξωνται‖Mt Mk: D 713 Bas *L* *S*scpj **11** κον. + των ποδων(+ ημων)‖Mt: (28) ϕ124-983 σ267-990-1207 | *om* τ. κολλ.‖p: 𝔓^{45} | *om* εκ τ. πο. υμ.‖p: 2533 *S*sc | εις τ. ποδ.] *om*: *Rpl* Bas *L*z vg' — ● + ημων (*et om* ημιν)‖p: 𝔥'CXΞ 1071 **λλ**⟨2193⟩ **ϕ**⟨124-346-788⟩ σM-115 A G K U W Θ Π Ψ *al* *L*f {*S*,j} *C*⟨b^{1}⟩ *Δ*a — *txt*: 𝔓$^{45.75}$ ℵB-1241 D R 157 *pc* *L*vl'r^{1} vg^{3} {} | απομ.] αποτινασσομεθα‖p: 579 28 57 | *om* υμιν‖Mt: 𝔓^{45} *S*sc | ηγγ. + εφ υμας‖9: *Rpl* Bas *L*fl vg^{1} *S*h {} *Arm*^{pc} *Geo*^{B} *Aeth* — θε. + εφ υμας‖←: λ118-209 {*C*cb^{1}} — *txt*: 𝔥Ξ **λλ**'⟨22-1278⟩ **σ**-1188 D **0181** 157 *pc* *l*184 *L*'Mcn^{Te} *S*',j *C*b' *Arm*' *Geo*' **12** ημ. εκ.] ημ. κρισεως‖p Mt11 22 p: σ1424 157 *L*lr^{2}30 *S*scp^{5} *C*s$^{1:5}$ *Δ*a — βασιλεια του θεου: D *L*e (*om* τ. θε.: ab) | ∼ αν. εστ. εν τ. ημ. εκ.‖p Mt11 24: **ϕ** (σ1424) A (D) *pc* (∼ αν. εστ. Σο.: 157 *L*e) lqr^{2} vg^{2} *S*scp **13** εγενοντο‖Mt11 21: *Rpl* Or — *txt*: 𝔓$^{45.75}$ 𝔥Ξ 700-1071 **ϕ** **σ**⟨954⟩ D Θ 126 157 | *om* καθ.‖←: 68 108 *L*e qr^{1} vg^{1} *S*scp

---

Lk10 2 *cf.* ET^{II} 73 (*cf. ad 70.* Mt9 37f.)

Lk10 3 *cf.* 2Cl5 2 *et* PsTt 492f. (*cf. ad 70.* Mt10 16a)

Lk10 8 *cf.* ETh^{II} 14 (*transl.*): (*cf. ad 40.*) ... *καὶ εἰς ἣν ἂν γῆν εἰσέρχησθε καὶ περιπατῆτε ἐν ταῖς χώραις καὶ παραδέχωνται ὑμᾶς, ἐσθίετε τὰ παρατιθέμενα ὑμῖν (καὶ) θεραπεύετε τοὺς ἐν αὐτοῖς(αὐταῖς?) ἀσθενεῖς· οὐ γὰρ* ... (*cf. ad 128.* Mt15 11)

Lk10 13 *cf.* NE frgm.27 (*cf. ad 78.* Mt11 20f.)

Is14₁₃.₁₅

ἐν τῇ κρίσει ἢ ὑμῖν. 15 καὶ σύ, Καφαρναουμ, μὴ **ἕως τοῦ οὐρανοῦ ὑψωθήσῃ; ἕως ᾅδου καταβιβασθήσῃ.**

[143.] 16 Ὁ ἀκούων ὑμῶν ἐμοῦ ἀκούει, καὶ ὁ ἀθετῶν ὑμᾶς ἐμὲ ἀθετεῖ· ὁ δὲ ἐμὲ ἀθετῶν ἀθετεῖ τὸν ἀποστείλαντά με.

> 5 23 : ... ὁ μὴ τιμῶν τὸν υἱὸν οὐ τιμᾷ τὸν πατέρα τὸν πέμψαντα αὐτόν. 15 23 : ὁ ἐμὲ μισῶν καὶ τὸν πατέρα μου μισεῖ.

(140) **154.** Die Rückkehr der Zweiundsiebzig. *The Return of the Seventy Two.* **Luk 10 17–20**

[125.] 17 Ὑπέστρεψαν δὲ οἱ ἑβδομήκοντα δύο μετὰ χαρᾶς λέγοντες· κύριε, καὶ τὰ δαιμόνια ὑποτάσσεται ἡμῖν ἐν τῷ ὀνόματί σου. 18 εἶπεν δὲ αὐτοῖς· ἐθεώρουν τὸν σατανᾶν ὡς ἀστραπὴν ἐκ τοῦ οὐρανοῦ πεσόντα.

> 12 31 : νῦν κρίσις ἐστὶν τοῦ κόσμου τούτου· νῦν ὁ ἄρχων τοῦ κόσμου τούτου ἐκβληθήσεται ἔξω.

Ps91₁₃

19 ἰδοὺ δέδωκα ὑμῖν τὴν ἐξουσίαν τοῦ **πατεῖν ἐπάνω ὄφεων** καὶ σκορπίων, καὶ ἐπὶ πᾶσαν τὴν δύναμιν τοῦ ἐχθροῦ, καὶ οὐδὲν ὑμᾶς οὐ μὴ ἀδικήσει. 20 πλὴν ἐν τούτῳ μὴ χαίρετε ὅτι τὰ πνεύματα ὑμῖν ὑποτάσσεται, χαίρετε δὲ ὅτι τὰ ὀνόματα ὑμῶν ἐγγέγραπται ἐν τοῖς οὐρανοῖς.

(141) **155.** Jubelruf. *Jesus' Gratitude to His Father.* **Luk 10 21–22** [79.]

[79.] 21 Ἐν αὐτῇ τῇ ὥρᾳ ἠγαλλιάσατο τῷ πνεύματι τῷ ἁγίῳ καὶ εἶπεν· ἐξομολογοῦμαί σοι, πάτερ, κύριε τοῦ οὐρανοῦ καὶ τῆς γῆς, ὅτι ἀπέκρυψας ταῦτα ἀπὸ σοφῶν καὶ συνετῶν, καὶ ἀπεκάλυψας αὐτὰ νηπίοις· ναί, ὁ πατήρ, ὅτι οὕτως ἐγένετο εὐδοκία ἔμπροσθέν σου. 22 πάντα μοι παρεδόθη ὑπὸ τοῦ πατρός μου, καὶ οὐδεὶς γινώσκει τίς ἐστιν ὁ υἱὸς εἰ μὴ ὁ πατήρ, καὶ τίς ἐστιν ὁ πατὴρ εἰ μὴ ὁ υἱὸς καὶ ᾧ ἐὰν βούληται ὁ υἱὸς ἀποκαλύψαι.

(142) **156.** Selige Augenzeugen. *The Blessedness of the Disciples.* **Luk 10 23–24** [105.]

[105.] 23 Καὶ στραφεὶς πρὸς τοὺς μαθητὰς κατ' ἰδίαν εἶπεν· μακάριοι οἱ ὀφθαλμοὶ οἱ βλέποντες ἃ βλέπετε. 24 λέγω γὰρ ὑμῖν ὅτι πολλοὶ προφῆται καὶ βασιλεῖς ἠθέλησαν ἰδεῖν ἃ ὑμεῖς βλέπετε καὶ οὐκ εἶδαν, καὶ ἀκοῦσαι ἃ ἀκούετε καὶ οὐκ ἤκουσαν.

Lk 10,14 τ. κρ.] ημερα κρισεως‖Mt11₂₂.₂₄: φ'⟨124⟩(η ημ. κρ.: 346) σ'(τη ημ.: 1424)-1188 *pc* *L*cfr^1.2 *S*cp^4 *C*'s^2:8 *Arm*^mu *Aeth* — ημ. εκεινη‖12: Ψ 1574 *S*s **15** ● *om* του‖Mt11₂₃: 𝔓^45.75 ℵBC* σ990-1207 D *pc* — *txt*: *Rpl* | αδ.] ● του αδ.: 𝔓^75 BL **0115** 157 *pc* *l*36 *l*88 — *txt*: 𝔓^45 *Rpl* | ● καταβηση‖Is14₁₅LXX: 𝔓^75 B-579 D *L*d(-εται)r^2 *S*scp^1 *Arm* *Aeth* **16** ο δε] και ο‖9₄₈p: LΞ-892 1071 λ1582 φ983 CAp *L*cf(*om* δε: i)r^1 *S*p^1 **17** ● *om* δυο (*cf. ad* 10₁): *Rpl* *L*fiq *S*'j *C*b' *Δ*a l^A — *txt* (*cf. ad* 1): 𝔓^45.75 B 1604 D *L*' *S*h^m *C*sb^1 *Arm* *Δ*'⟨me⟩ | χα. + μεγαλης‖24₅₂ Mt28₈: φ13 Ψ *pc* *L*f *S*p *Δ*a i^V md me n^L **21** ηγ. + ο Ιησους‖p: LX-33-579 N-1071 φ⟨69-124-983⟩-*l*547^1 Θ *pc* *L*e cff^2r^1.2 vg^4 *S*pj(κυριος I.) *C*b^6 — και^1 *prm* ο Ιησους‖p: 𝔓^45v *Rpl* Bas *L*fq *S*h — *txt*: 𝔓^75 ℵBΞ-1241 D 157 *L*' *S*sc *C*' | τω^1] ● εν τω‖Mk12₃₆: 𝔓^45 𝔥⟨B-579⟩XΞ σ1194 D F^w **0115** *pc* *L* vl' vg^2 — *txt*: 𝔓^75 *Rpl* Bas *L*fr^1z vg' | *om* τ. αγιω‖Mk2₈ 8₁₂ Jo11₃₃ 13₄: 𝔓^45 *Rpl* Bas *L*fq *S*j^c1 *Δ*i^T2V E^a(εν τω πν. αυτου) — *txt*: 𝔓^75 𝔥⟨892⟩CXΞ 700-1071-1604 λ1-2193 φ*l*547^1 σ1010-1207-1223 D K Θ Π *al* *L*' *S*,j^abc1 *C* *Δ*'⟨p⟩ | εξομ.] ευχαριστω‖Jo11₄₁: Mcn^Ep — ευχαρ. και εξομ.‖←: *L* Men^Te | ● ∼ευδ. εγ.‖p: 𝔓^75 BC*LXΞ-**0124**-33-579 λ1 *L*e bcff^2lqr^1 Ir — *txt*: 𝔓^45 *Rpl* Bas *L*i30 vg^1 **22** παρεδ.] παραδεδοται‖46: K Π *pc* Hip | γιν.] επιγ.‖p: C-**0124**-33-578 544-700-1071-1604 λ131 φ124-983 σ115-1194-1424 F^W H Δ *al* *l*19 *l*184 | τις^1—υι.] τον υιον‖p: 544-1604 | πατ.^2 + ουδεις γινωσκει‖p: φ69 **23** βλεπετε + και ακουοντες α ακουετε‖p: D — και τα ωτα α ακουουσιν‖p: *L*e cf **24** κ. βα.] κ. δικαιοι κ. βα.‖p: σ1424 — *om*‖p: D *L*e aff^2il vg^1 Mcn^Te — κ. δικ.‖p: *L*bqr^1 vg^1 | ηϑ.] επεϑυμησαν‖p: 579 *L*30 *C*s^1:5 | *om* υμεις‖p23: 1241 *L*vg^1 *C*

Jo 12,31 εκβλ. εξω] βληϑ. κατω(εξω)‖p15₆: (𝔓^66 D) Θ (∼: 1093 *l*22 Chr^1)^2 Ep *L*e bff^2lr^1 Amst Qu *S*s[c] *C*s *Geo*^2

Lk10₂₂ *cf.* ETh^II 61 (*cf. ad 79.* Mt11₂₇)

(143) *157.* Die Frage nach dem großen Gebot. *The Great Commandment.* **Luk 10** 25–28 [*222.*]

[*203.*] [*222.*]

25 Καὶ ἰδοὺ νομικός τις ἀνέστη ἐκπειράζων αὐτὸν λέγων· διδάσκαλε, τί ποιήσας ζωὴν αἰώνιον κληρονομήσω; 26 ὁ δὲ εἶπεν πρὸς αὐτόν· ἐν τῷ νόμῳ τί γέγραπται; πῶς ἀναγινώσκεις; 27 ὁ δὲ ἀποκριθεὶς εἶπεν· **ἀγαπήσεις κύριον τὸν θεόν σου ἐξ ὅλης τῆς καρδίας σου καὶ ἐν ὅλῃ τῇ ψυχῇ σου καὶ ἐν ὅλῃ τῇ ἰσχύϊ σου** καὶ ἐν ὅλῃ τῇ διανοίᾳ σου, καὶ **τὸν πλησίον σου ὡς σεαυτόν.** 28 εἶπεν δὲ αὐτῷ· ὀρθῶς ἀπεκρίθης· **τοῦτο ποίει καὶ ζήσῃ.**

Dt 6 5 Lv 19 18

Gn 42 18

(144) *158.* Der barmherzige Samariter. *The Good Samaritan.* **Luk 10** 29–37

29 Ὁ δὲ θέλων δικαιῶσαι ἑαυτὸν εἶπεν πρὸς τὸν Ἰησοῦν· καὶ τίς ἐστίν μου πλησίον; 30 ὑπολαβὼν δὲ ὁ Ἰησοῦς εἶπεν· ἄνθρωπός τις κατέβαινεν ἀπὸ Ἰερουσαλημ εἰς Ἰεριχω, καὶ λῃσταῖς περιέπεσεν, οἳ καὶ ἐκδύσαντες αὐτὸν καὶ πληγὰς ἐπιθέντες ἀπῆλθαν ἀφέντες ἡμιθανῆ. 31 κατὰ συγκυρίαν δὲ ἱερεύς τις κατέβαινεν ἐν τῇ ὁδῷ ἐκείνῃ, καὶ ἰδὼν αὐτὸν ἀντιπαρῆλθεν. 32 ὁμοίως δὲ καὶ Λευίτης κατὰ τὸν τόπον ἐλθὼν καὶ ἰδὼν ἀντιπαρῆλθεν. 33 Σαμαρίτης δέ τις ὁδεύων ἦλθεν κατ' αὐτὸν καὶ ἰδὼν ἐσπλαγχνίσθη, 34 καὶ προσελθὼν κατέδησεν τὰ τραύματα αὐτοῦ ἐπιχέων ἔλαιον καὶ οἶνον, ἐπιβιβάσας δὲ αὐτὸν ἐπὶ τὸ ἴδιον κτῆνος ἤγαγεν αὐτὸν εἰς πανδοχεῖον καὶ ἐπεμελήθη αὐτοῦ. 35 καὶ ἐπὶ τὴν αὔριον ἐκβαλὼν δύο δηνάρια ἔδωκεν τῷ πανδοχεῖ καὶ εἶπεν· ἐπιμελήθητι αὐτοῦ, καὶ ὅ τι ἂν προσδαπανήσῃς ἐγὼ ἐν τῷ ἐπανέρχεσθαί με ἀποδώσω σοι. 36 τίς τούτων τῶν τριῶν πλησίον δοκεῖ σοι γεγονέναι τοῦ ἐμπεσόντος εἰς τοὺς λῃστάς; 37 ὁ δὲ εἶπεν· ὁ ποιήσας τὸ ἔλεος μετ' αὐτοῦ. εἶπεν δὲ αὐτῷ ὁ Ἰησοῦς· πορεύου καὶ σὺ ποίει ὁμοίως.

(145) *159.* Martha und Maria. *Martha and Mary.* **Luk 10** 38–42

38 Ἐν δὲ τῷ πορεύεσθαι αὐτοὺς αὐτὸς εἰσῆλθεν εἰς κώμην τινά· γυνὴ δέ τις ὀνόματι Μάρθα ὑπεδέξατο αὐτὸν εἰς τὸν οἶκον αὐτῆς. 39 καὶ τῇδε ἦν ἀδελφὴ καλουμένη Μαριαμ, ἣ καὶ παρακαθεσθεῖσα πρὸς τοὺς

Lk 10,25 ανεσ.] προσηλθεν (+ τω Ιησου)‖Mk Mt19 16: (C^{3})-33 (1093) *l*12 *l*21(+ αυτω) *l*32 *l*303 *l*374 *l*1599 *l*1627 *l*1634 *l*1642 *l*1663 *l*1963 *S*sc | εκπ.] πειραζων‖11 16 Mt**22**35 16 1p 19 3p: 28-1604 φ*l*547 *pc l*5 *l*12 *l*13 *l*14 *l*15 *l*16 *l*17 *l*21 *l*28 *l*32 *l*77 *l*108 *l*130 *l*251 *l*258 *l*259 *l*303 *l*333 *l*374 *l*1599 *l*1627 *l*1634 *l*1642 *l*1663 *l*1963 | διδ.] *om*‖Mk: D — + αγαθε‖18 18 Mk10 17: σM-692-1194 472^{c} 484^{c} | ποιησας] + ινα(!)‖Mk10 17 Mt19 16: ℵ* λ131 — ποιησω ινα‖←: *L*fr^{2} *S*,j — ποιων: 700 157 **26** προς αυ.] αυτω‖Mt22 37: 472 **27** εξ ολ. τ. καρ.] εν ολη τη(*om*) καρδια‖←: (λ1-131-209-1582-2193) D 157 *L*vl⟨e fr^{2}z⟩ vg^{1} *C*s — *om*: 544 *S*j^{bc} *C*b^{1} | εν ολη $τη^{1.2.3}$] εξ ολης $της^{1.2.3}$ *et* ψυχης … ισχυος … διανοιας‖Mk12 30 Dt6 5: *Rpl* (εξ ολ. $της^{2}$ *et* ισχυι(!) … διανοιας(!): **0124**) Or *L*e fz(1°: c; 2°: a) vg Mcn^{Tel} *C*b^{3}(1° 2°: b^{4}; 1°: b^{3}) — *om* $και^{1}$—ψυ. σου: λ132 157 1047 — *om* $και^{2}$—ισ. σου‖Mt22 37: 1241 U Ω *pc l*1663 *l*1963 Bas *C*b^{1} *Geo*^{2} — *om* $και^{3}$—διαν. σου: D Γ *L*bff^{2}ilr^{1} Mcn^{Tel}(∼ ισ. … ψυ.) — *txt*: $𝔓^{45.75}$ ℵBLΞ-579 1071(*om* $τη^{1.2}$: **λ**'⟨118⟩-1582-2193) *L*q(*om* $εν^{3}$) *C*' *Geo*^{1} **28** απεκ.] εκρινας‖7 43: L σ1675 *pc* **30** ● *om* δε(*et om* υπολ.): $𝔓^{75}$ ℵ*BC^{*v} (*S*'j) *C*$s^{2}b^{3}$ *Geo* (*Δ*a) — *txt*: $𝔓^{45v}$ *Rpl L S*h *C*s^{3}b' *Δ*ad(thô)1 **31** *om* αυτ.‖32f.: **λ**⟨131⟩-1582 **32** Λευ. … ελθ.] ● Λ. γενομενος … ελθ.: *Rpl L*q *S*' — Λ. γεν. … *om* ελθ.: $𝔓^{45}$ σ990 D Π *pc l*32 *L*' — *om* κατα—$και^{2}$: *L*e Ar — *txt*: $𝔓^{75}$ ℵ(* *om* 32)^{c}BLXΞ-**0190**-33-892-1241 700 **λ**-1582-2193 *pc* (∼ ελθ. κατα τ. τοπ.: *L*acf *S*scj) *C* | ιδ. + αυτον‖31 7 13 13 12 Mt9 36: 1071 φ*l*547 **σ**⟨1424⟩-990 A D Γ Δ 157 *al l*21 *l*32 *l*1642 *L*vl⟨c⟩r^{2} vg Ar *C* *Δ*⟨i^{V} md me n^{L}⟩ **33** ιδ. + αυτον‖←: *Rpl L*'Ar {*S*,j} *C*s^{2}b' — *txt*: $𝔓^{45.75}$ 𝔥⟨579⟩Ξ-**0190** 700 **λ**-1582-2193 Ψ *pc L*bcilqr^{2} vg^{1} {} *C*s^{1}(*om* ιδ.)b^{5} **36** τις + ουν‖7 42: *Rpl L*ec *S*'j *C*b' *Geo*^{2} — *txt*: $𝔓^{45.75}$ ℵBLΞ-**0190**-892 **λ**⟨131⟩-1582-2193 Ψ 872 *L*'Or *S*sc *C*sb^{3} *Geo*^{1} *Δ*'⟨me⟩(και τις: i^{V}) E^{sa} | τουτ.] εκ τ.‖Mt21 31: 1574 *L*e **37** ομ.] ουτως‖12 43p: X — + και εξεις ζωην αιωνιον‖10 25 Mt19 16p: 1093 — + και ζηση‖10 28: $Θ^{c}$ 1012 *L*c *S*p^{1c} **38** εν δε] ● (και) εγενετο δε(*om*) εν *cf.* 18 35 1 8 26 *etc.*: *Rpl* (243) *L S*h(pj) — *txt*: $𝔓^{45.75}$ 𝔥Ξ-**0190** *pc S*sc *C Geo*(και εν) *Aeth* | αυτους] αυτον‖18 35: **λ**-1582-2193 D 157 *pc L*r^{2} vg^{4} *S*j *C*s *Arm*^{pc} | αυτος] ● και αυ.‖5 1 9 51 17 11: *Rpl L*' *S*hj *Arm* — *om*: D *S*' *C*b' — *txt*: $𝔓^{45}$(∼ εισηλ. αυτος)^{75} 𝔥⟨579⟩Ξ-**0190** φ69-788 *pc L*a *C*sb^{4} | εις τ. οικ. αυτ.] ● εις την οικιαν (+ αυτης)‖9 4 10 5 Mk6 10: $𝔓^{3}$ ℵ*(^{a})^{c}C*(^{2})LΞ-33-579 — *om*: $𝔓^{45.75}$ B *L*l(υπεδ.—^{39}καλ.] και) *C*s — *txt*: *Rpl* Bas *L*' *S*,j *C*b

---

Lk10 27 *cf.* Did1 2 (*cf. ad 38.*)

Lk10 27b *cf.* Brn 19,5 *et* ETh^{II} 25 (*cf. ad 222.* Mt22 39)

πόδας τοῦ κυρίου ἤκουεν τὸν λόγον αὐτοῦ. 40 ἡ δὲ Μάρθα περιεσπᾶτο περὶ πολλὴν διακονίαν·

> 12 2: ἐποίησαν οὖν αὐτῷ δεῖπνον ἐκεῖ, καὶ ἡ Μάρθα διηκόνει ...

ἐπιστᾶσα δὲ εἶπεν· κύριε, οὐ μέλει σοι ὅτι ἡ ἀδελφή μου μόνην με κατέλειπεν διακονεῖν; εἰπὲ οὖν αὐτῇ ἵνα μοι συναντιλάβηται. 41 ἀποκριθεὶς δὲ εἶπεν αὐτῇ ὁ κύριος· Μάρθα Μάρθα, μεριμνᾷς καὶ θορυβάζῃ περὶ πολλά, 42 ὀλίγων δέ ἐστιν χρεία ἢ ἑνός· Μαριαμ γὰρ τὴν ἀγαθὴν μερίδα ἐξελέξατο, ἥτις οὐκ ἀφαιρεθήσεται αὐτῆς.

(146)

160. Das Unser-Vater. *The Lord's Prayer.* Luk 11 1–4 [*42.*]

[*42.*]

1 Καὶ ἐγένετο ἐν τῷ εἶναι αὐτὸν ἐν τόπῳ τινὶ προσευχόμενον, ὡς ἐπαύσατο, εἶπέν τις τῶν μαθητῶν αὐτοῦ πρὸς αὐτόν· κύριε, δίδαξον ἡμᾶς προσεύχεσθαι, καθὼς καὶ Ἰωάννης ἐδίδαξεν τοὺς μαθητὰς αὐτοῦ. 2 εἶπεν δὲ αὐτοῖς· ὅταν προσεύχησθε, λέγετε·

Πάτερ,
ἁγιασθήτω τὸ ὄνομά σου·
ἐλθέτω ἡ βασιλεία σου·
3 τὸν ἄρτον ἡμῶν τὸν ἐπιούσιον δίδου ἡμῖν τὸ καθ' ἡμέραν·
4 καὶ ἄφες ἡμῖν τὰς ἁμαρτίας ἡμῶν, καὶ γὰρ αὐτοὶ ἀφίομεν παντὶ ὀφείλοντι ἡμῖν·
καὶ μὴ εἰσενέγκῃς ἡμᾶς εἰς πειρασμόν.

(147)

161. Gleichnis vom bittenden Freund. *The Friend at Midnight.* Luk 11 5–8

5 Καὶ εἶπεν πρὸς αὐτούς· τίς ἐξ ὑμῶν ἕξει φίλον, καὶ πορεύσεται πρὸς αὐτὸν μεσονυκτίου καὶ εἴπῃ αὐτῷ· φίλε, χρῆσόν μοι τρεῖς ἄρτους, 6 ἐπειδὴ φίλος μου παρεγένετο ἐξ ὁδοῦ πρός με καὶ οὐκ ἔχω ὃ παραθήσω αὐτῷ· 7 κἀκεῖνος ἔσωθεν ἀποκριθεὶς εἴπῃ· μή μοι κόπους πάρεχε· ἤδη ἡ θύρα κέκλεισται, καὶ τὰ παιδία μου μετ' ἐμοῦ εἰς τὴν κοίτην εἰσίν· οὐ δύναμαι ἀναστὰς δοῦναί σοι. 8 λέγω ὑμῖν, εἰ καὶ οὐ δώσει αὐτῷ ἀναστὰς διὰ τὸ εἶναι φίλον αὐτοῦ, διά γε τὴν ἀναίδειαν αὐτοῦ ἐγερθεὶς δώσει αὐτῷ ὅσων χρῄζει.

Lk 10,39 τους λογους‖Mt7 24.26: 34 *pc* *L*e vg^{3} *S*cph | *om* αυτ.‖8 15p: D **41** μερ.—^{42}γαρ] θορυβαζη. Μαρια: D — Μαρια: *L*e abff^{2}ilr^{1} Am Pos *S*s | μερ.] μη μερ.‖12 22p Mt6 34: 660 | *om* μερ. κ. θορ.: Bas^{cat} *L*Au(*om* μερ. και) **42** ολ.—ενος] ● ολ. δε εστ. χρ.: 38 Or^{1} *S*j(και ολ. ε. χ.) *C*b$^{1+1?}$ — αλλα(*om*) ωδε ολ. εστ. χρ.: *Arm* (*Geo*) — ● ενος δε εστ. χρ.: 𝔓$^{45.75}$ *Rpl* Ant Bas^{1} Da Mac^{M} *L*fqr^{2}(εν δε] αλλα εν.: z vg Au) *S*' *C*s *Δ* — *om* (*cf. ad* 41): D *L*e abcff^{2}ilr^{1} Am Pos *S*s — *txt*: 𝔓^{3} ℵ(* *om* χρ.)^{c}B(∼ χρ. εστ.)C^{2}L-33-579 λ1-2193 Bas^{2} Cr Ol **Or**^{1} *L*Hi *S*h^{m} *C*b' *Aeth* | γαρ] δε: *Rpl* Bas PsBas Mac^{M} *L*fqr^{2} *S*'j *C*b'⟨1⟩ — *om* (*cf. ad* 41): D *pc* *L*' Am Au Hi *S*sc *Arm* *Aeth*(και Μ.) *Δ*⟨p⟩ — *txt*: 𝔓$^{3.75}$ ℵBLX^{cmt}-33-1241 Λ-1071 λ1-1582-2193 φ69 **σ**⟨954⟩ 157 *pc* *l*37 Ant Bas Cat^{Ox} Da *C*sb^{4}

11,2 προσευ. + μη βαττολογειτε ως οι λοιποι· δοκουσιν γαρ τινες οτι εν τη πολυλογια αυτων εισακουσθησονται. αλλα προσευχομενοι‖Mt7: D | λεγ. + ουτως(∼)‖p: ℵ* (*S*p) *C*b^{1} | πατ. + ημων ο εν τοις ουρανοις‖p: *Rpl* (*om* ημ.: 33^{v}) Or *L*vl'(ημ.] αγιε: acff^{2}ir^{1} vg^{1}; ημ. + αγιε: r^{2}) *S*' *C* — + ημων‖p: L 443 470 *L*30 *Arm* — + αγιε: *L*vg^{1} — *txt*: 𝔓^{75} ℵB 700 λ1-22-1582 Cr **Or** *L*z vg' Mcn^{Te} *S*s | αγ.—σου^{1}] ελθετω το αγιον πνευμα σου εφ ημας και καθαρισατω ημας: Mcn^{Te} | σου^{1} + εφ ημας‖11 20p 10 9: D(∼ σου η βα.) | *om* ελθ.—σου^{2}: *Geo*^{2} | η βα. σου] ● το αγ. πν. σου εφ ημ. και καθ. ημ.: 700(τ. πν. σου τ. αγ.) 162(σου τ. πν. τ. αγ. *et om* εφ ημ.) Gr^{Ny} Max^{C}(= 162) | σου^{2} + γενηθητω το θελημα σου ως εν ουρανω και επι της(*om*) γης‖p: *Rpl* (ℵ*C-892 φ69 σM-179-954-1207 A D P W Δ Θ *pc* *l*48) (*om* σου: 565) Ti *L*vl'(*om* ως: e bl; *om* ως—γης: a vg^{2})r^{1} vg^{11} *S*' *C*(= *L*a: sb^{2})' *Geo*(= *L*a) — *txt*: 𝔓^{75} BL λ1-1582-2193 *pc* Cr **Or** *L*30 vg' Au Mcn^{Te} *S*sc *Arm* **3** διδ.] δος‖**p**: ℵ 28-1071 σ71-115-1675 D *al* Cr Or$^{1:5}$ | το καθ ημ.] σημερον‖p: 28-1071 σ71-692 D *pc* *L*vl⟨q⟩r^{1} vg^{11} Hil *S*h^{t} *C*b^{2} *Aeth* **4** τας αμ.] τα οφειληματα‖p: λ131 D *L*e(+ και τας αμ.) bcff^{2}r^{2} vg^{3} *S*p^{1} — τα αμαρτηματα‖p Mk3 28: **λ**' — τα παραπτωματα‖Mt6 14f. Mk11 25: 50 | και γαρ] ως και‖**p**: ℵ* D *L*vl[e]⟨r^{2}z⟩r^{1} vg^{1} (*om* ως: *S*sc) *Aeth* | αυτοι] ημεις‖**p**: D Cl *L*vl[e]⟨aiqr^{2}z⟩r^{1} vg^{1} | αφηκαμεν‖p: Or^{1} | πα. οφ. ημ.] τοις οφειλεταις ημων‖**p**: D *L*bcf(*prm* πασιν)ff^{2}lr^{1} *C*b^{7} *Geo*(= f) | ημιν^{2}] ημων‖p: φ69 | πειρ. + αλλα ρυσαι ημας απο του πονηρου‖**p**: *Rpl* *L*vl[e]r^{1} vg^{5} *S*' *C*b^{9} *Aeth*(του] παντος) — *txt*: 𝔓^{75} ℵ*BL 700 λ1-22-131-1582-2193 *pc* Cr **Or** *L*vg' Au Mcn^{Te} Te *S*s *C*' *Arm* **6** εξ οδ.] απ αγρου‖23 26 Mk15 21: D *Aeth* **7** παρεχετε‖Mt26 10 Mk14 16: 579 59 Or

---

160. cf. Did 82f. *et* EN frgm.5 (*cf. ad 42.* Mt6 9-13.11)

(148)

162. Von der Gebetserhörung. *The Answer to Prayer.* Luk 11 9–13 [*50.*]

[*50.*]

[9] Κἀγὼ ὑμῖν λέγω, αἰτεῖτε, καὶ δοθήσεται ὑμῖν· ζητεῖτε, καὶ εὑρήσετε· κρούετε, καὶ ἀνοιγήσεται ὑμῖν. [10] πᾶς γὰρ ὁ αἰτῶν λαμβάνει, καὶ ὁ ζητῶν εὑρίσκει, καὶ τῷ κρούοντι ἀνοιγήσεται. [11] τίνα δὲ ἐξ ὑμῶν τὸν πατέρα αἰτήσει ὁ υἱὸς ἰχθῦν, μὴ ἀντὶ ἰχθύος ὄφιν αὐτῷ ἐπιδώσει; [12] ἢ καὶ αἰτήσει ᾠόν, μὴ ἐπιδώσει αὐτῷ σκορπίον; [13] εἰ οὖν ὑμεῖς πονηροὶ ὑπάρχοντες οἴδατε δόματα ἀγαθὰ διδόναι τοῖς τέκνοις ὑμῶν, πόσῳ μᾶλλον ὁ πατὴρ ὁ ἐξ οὐρανοῦ δώσει πνεῦμα ἅγιον τοῖς αἰτοῦσιν αὐτόν.

(149)

163. Gegen den Vorwurf des Teufelsbündnisses. Luk 11 14–23 [*99.*] *The Beelzebul Controversy.*

[*99.*] [*100.*]

[14] Καὶ ἦν ἐκβάλλων δαιμόνιον, καὶ αὐτὸ ἦν κωφόν· ἐγένετο δὲ τοῦ δαιμονίου ἐξελθόντος ἐλάλησεν ὁ κωφός· καὶ ἐθαύμασαν οἱ ὄχλοι.

[15] τινὲς δὲ ἐξ αὐτῶν εἶπον· ἐν Βεελ Ζεβουλ τῷ ἄρχοντι τῶν δαιμονίων ἐκβάλλει τὰ δαιμόνια· [16] ἕτεροι δὲ πειράζοντες σημεῖον ἐξ οὐρανοῦ ἐζήτουν παρ' αὐτοῦ. [17] αὐτὸς δὲ εἰδὼς αὐτῶν τὰ διανοήματα εἶπεν αὐτοῖς· πᾶσα βασιλεία ἐφ' ἑαυτὴν διαμερισθεῖσα ἐρημοῦται, καὶ οἶκος ἐπὶ οἶκον πίπτει. [18] εἰ δὲ καὶ ὁ σατανᾶς ἐφ' ἑαυτὸν διεμερίσθη, πῶς σταθήσεται ἡ βασιλεία αὐτοῦ; ὅτι λέγετε ἐν Βεελ Ζεβουλ ἐκβάλλειν με τὰ δαιμόνια.

Lk 11,11 τινα] ● τις‖p: ℵLX-33-892-1241 D 157 *pc* Cat^{Ox} Or *L*cr^{2}z vg *S* — *txt*: 𝔓$^{45.75}$ *Rpl* Ep Mcn^{Ep} *L*vl'[e]r^1 Mcn^{Te} | ∼ αιτ. τον(*om*) πατ.: (𝔓^{75}) B 1241 | τ. πατ.] *om*‖p: *l*48^1 *L*b — ον: *S*sc — πατηρ ον: *S*' — υιος ος: *S*h^m | αιτ. ο υι.] αιτ. ο(*om*) υι. αυτου‖**p**: λ(1-118)-131-(209-1582-2193) ϕ124 σ267-659 *pc* *l*48 *l*49 *L*bfff^{2}q30 vg^1 *S*' — ● αιτ.: ℵL-892-1241 *L*cr^{2}z vg' *S*h^m(+ τ. πατερα αυτου) — ο(*om*) υι. αιτ.: 700-1071 D W *pc* Ep (Mcn^{Ep} Or) *C*s^2(^{2} υι. + αυτου)b — *txt*: 𝔓^{45} (*om* ο)(^{75}) *Rpl* (∼ αρτον ο υι.: 544) *L*vl'[e]r^1 | ιχθυν] ● *prm* αρτον μη λιθον επιδωσει αυτω; η και(*om*)‖p: *Rpl* (ℵL-33-892 28-700 157 *pc*) *L*(vl'[e]r^1)q vg *S*(c)ph *C*b (*Geo*) — *txt*: 𝔓$^{(45)75}$ B-579-1241 440 Ep Mcn^{Ep} *L*ff^2 ilr^2 Mcn^{Te} *S*s *C*s *Arm* | *om* ιχθυν—^{12}αιτησει‖p: ϕ174-788 565 | ιχθυν + αιτησει‖p: ϕ124 D *L*vl'[e]⟨ff^{2}ilqr^2⟩r^1 vg^1 *S*cp *C*b — *prm* εαν αιτ.‖p: 1241 *L*ac(+ ο υι. σου) | *om* αντι ιχθ.‖**p**: 1093 *C*s$^{1:4}$b^2 | ∼ επιδ. αυ.‖**p**: 𝔓^{45} *Rpl* Mcn^{Ep} Or *L*'[e] *S*'(s *om* αυ.) — *txt*: 𝔓^{75} BL-892 700 D Ep *L*aa^{2}c **12** *om* 12‖p: 544 157 *l*31 | ∼ ωον αιτ.‖p: σ115(+ αυτον) D R U *pc* *L*c *S*scp | ωον] αρτον‖p: 𝔓^{45} | ● *om* μη: 𝔓$^{45.75}$ BL-892 *C*s$^{3:4}$ | ∼ σκ. επιδ. αυ.‖p11: 579 1604 D(∼ αυ. επιδ.) *L*bc(*om* αυ.)lr^1 *S*scp **13** υπαρ.] οντες‖p: ℵX λ2193 **σ**⟨954⟩-M-27-71-692-1010-1194 D K Π 157 *al* Cr Ep — *om*: Mcn^{Ep} | πα. + υμων‖p: 𝔓^{45} C 1071 λ1278 ϕ346 σ7-267-1424 U 157 *al* *l*18 *l*49 *l*185 *l*1127^1 Cr Ep *L*[e]⟨a^{2}f⟩ *S*p *C*s | ο εξ ουρ.] ● εξ ουρ.: 𝔓^{75} ℵLX-33-892 700-1071 Ψ 157 *pc* *l*1127 *L*'[e]⟨i(*om*)⟩ *S*cp *C*' *Geo*^{2}(^{1} ∼ δω. εξ ου.) — ο εν τοις ουρανοις‖p: *l*48 *S*s *C*b^6(∼ δω. πν. αγ. εν τω ουρανω) — ο ουρανιος‖Mt5 48 6 14 *etc.*: 𝔓^{45} 579 σ1424 Cr Ep(επουρ.) *L*l | πν. αγ.] αγαθα‖p: *L*vg^1 *S*s *Arm* — πν. αγαθον‖p: 𝔓45 L σ7-267-659 1093 *pc* *l*4 *l*12 *l*15 *l*19 *l*69 *l*70^1 *l*185 *l*211 *l*1127 *L*r^{2}z vg' *S*h^m — αγαθον δομα‖p: D *L*vl'[e]r^1 Am *Aeth*(+ πνευματος αγιου) — δοματα αγαθα(∼)‖p: Θ 106 2533 *l*32^1 *l*1599^1 (*L*a^2)

14 14] ταυτα δε ειποντος αυτου προσφερετε αυτω δαιμονιζομενος κωφος· και εκβαλοντος αυτου παντες εθαυμαζον‖Mt 32f. 12 22f.: D (*L*a^{2c}cf) | ● και αυ. ην *cf.* Mk9 17.25: 𝔓$^{45.75}$ 𝔥⟨579⟩ **λ**-22-1582 ϕ788 A* (D) 157 *pc* *S*sc *C* *Arm* *Aeth* — *txt*: *Rpl* *L*[e] *S*' *Δ*a | εξελ.] εκβληθεντος‖Mt9: CLX-33-892-1241 1071-1604 **ϕ** A *pc* Ddy^1(^{1} εκβαντος) *L*[e]⟨q⟩ *C*b^5 **15** ειπ. + οτι‖Mk: 157 1574 | *om* τω‖Mt24: *Rpl* Or — *txt*: 𝔓$^{45.75}$ 𝔥C 700-1071 **ϕ** σM-71-692-1010-1194 A K W Θ Π Ψ 157 *mu* Ddy | δαιμονια + ο δε (ο δε] και) αποκριθεις ειπεν· πως δυναται σατανας σαταναν εκβαλλειν;‖Mk23: X-579 544-1071(δε + Ιησους)-1604 (ϕ346) σM-71-692-1194-(990-1207) A D W (K Π) 157 (2533, *et* σατ.^{1} + τον) *mu* *L*a^{2c}(r^1, *et* αποκ. + αυτοις ο Ι.) *S*h *Aeth* **16** εκ πειρ.‖10 25: 1241 157 — + αυτον‖Mk8 11 10 2p: λ131 *pc* *S*scp *C*s *Δ*a p | επεζη.‖Mt12 39 16 4: σM-71-692-1194 **17** ∼ τα διαν. αυτων‖Mt: 𝔓^{45} σ990 A K Π *al* *L*[e] | ● ∼ διαμερ. εφ εαυ.‖Mt: (𝔓^{45}) ℵL-33-892 (ϕ124) A D W (Ψ) *l*184 *L*a^2 *S*sp | εφ] καθ‖Mt: Ψ | διαμερ.] μερ.‖←: 𝔓^{45} CX-579-1241 N-700-1604 ϕ124 σM-71-115-692-1194-1223-1424 F W Γ Θ Ψ 157 *al* | ερημωθησεται‖Mt25b: **σ**-1188 *L*a^2 cdlr^{2}z vg$^{⟨10⟩}$ *S*s^{v}cp | πιπ.] πεσειται‖←: D *L*a^{2}fff^{2}iqr^{2}z vg *S*scp **18** διεμ.] εμερισθη(μερ-)‖Mt: (𝔓^{45}) ℵC-579-1241 Λ-28-544 ϕ124 σ945 W (Γ *pc*) *al* | πως] ου‖Mk: D — + ουν‖Mt: Cr *C*b$^{⟨1⟩}$

| 99. | 144. |

19 εἰ δὲ ἐγὼ ἐν Βεελ Ζεβουλ ἐκβάλλω τὰ δαιμόνια, οἱ υἱοὶ ὑμῶν ἐν τίνι ἐκβάλλουσιν; διὰ τοῦτο αὐτοὶ κριταὶ ὑμῶν ἔσονται. 20 εἰ δὲ ἐν δακτύλῳ θεοῦ ἐκβάλλω τὰ δαιμόνια, ἄρα ἔφθασεν ἐφ' ὑμᾶς ἡ βασιλεία τοῦ θεοῦ. 21 ὅταν ὁ ἰσχυρὸς καθωπλισμένος φυλάσσῃ τὴν ἑαυτοῦ αὐλήν, ἐν εἰρήνῃ ἐστὶν τὰ ὑπάρχοντα αὐτοῦ· 22 ἐπὰν δὲ ἰσχυρότερος αὐτοῦ ἐπελθὼν νικήσῃ αὐτόν, τὴν πανοπλίαν αὐτοῦ αἴρει, ἐφ' ᾗ ἐπεποίθει, καὶ τὰ σκῦλα αὐτοῦ διαδίδωσιν. 23 ὁ μὴ ὢν μετ' ἐμοῦ κατ' ἐμοῦ ἐστιν, καὶ ὁ μὴ συνάγων μετ' ἐμοῦ σκορπίζει με.

(150) *164.* Spruch vom Rückfall. *The Return of the Evil Spirit.* Luk 11 24–26 | 101. |

| 101. |

24 Ὅταν τὸ ἀκάθαρτον πνεῦμα ἐξέλθῃ ἀπὸ τοῦ ἀνθρώπου, διέρχεται δι' ἀνύδρων τόπων ζητοῦν ἀνάπαυσιν, καὶ μὴ εὑρίσκον λέγει· ὑποστρέψω εἰς τὸν οἶκόν μου ὅθεν ἐξῆλθον· 25 καὶ ἐλθὸν εὑρίσκει σεσαρωμένον καὶ κεκοσμημένον. 26 τότε πορεύεται καὶ παραλαμβάνει ἕτερα πνεύματα πονηρότερα ἑαυτοῦ ἑπτά, καὶ εἰσελθόντα κατοικεῖ ἐκεῖ· καὶ γίνεται τὰ ἔσχατα τοῦ ἀνθρώπου ἐκείνου χείρονα τῶν πρώτων.

(151) *165.* Seligpreisung der Mutter Jesu. *The Blessedness of Jesus' Mother.* Luk 11 27–28

27 Ἐγένετο δὲ ἐν τῷ λέγειν αὐτὸν ταῦτα ἐπάρασά τις φωνὴν γυνὴ ἐκ τοῦ ὄχλου εἶπεν αὐτῷ· μακαρία ἡ κοιλία ἡ βαστάσασά σε καὶ μαστοὶ οὓς ἐθήλασας. 28 αὐτὸς δὲ εἶπεν· μενοῦν μακάριοι οἱ ἀκούοντες τὸν λόγον τοῦ θεοῦ καὶ φυλάσσοντες.

Lk 11,19 αυ. κρ. υμ. εσ.] ● αυ. κρ. εσ. υμ.‖p: ℵ σ267(*om* αυ.) *L*vl'[e]r^{1}30 vg^{2} — αυ. εσ. υμ.(∼ υμ. εσ.) κρ.: 𝔓^{45} (N)-1604 σ1194 (474) 477 — κρ. υμ. αυ. εσ.: *Rpl* (∼ αυ. υμ.: *pm*) — ● αυ. υμ. κρ. εσ.: 𝔓^{75} B-579 700 D *pc* *L*a^{2}c(υμιν) — *txt*: ℌ'C 1071 λ1-131-1582-2193 ϕ σM-71-692 A K U W Θ Π Ψ 157 *mu* *L*r^{2}z vg' **20** δε + εγω‖19p: N D *pc* *l*49 Bas^{1} HM *L*c Mcn^{Te} *C* *Aeth* | ● θε. + εγω‖p: 𝔓^{75} ℵ^{a}BCL-33-579-892 1071-1604 ϕ R 157 *pc* *l*184 Bas^{1} *L*ff^{2}lqr^{1} Au *S*h^{+} **22** ισχ.] ο ισχ.‖316Mk17: 𝔓^{45} *Rpl* *C*s — *txt*: 𝔓^{75} ℵBL-1241 700-1071 D W Γ Θ *pc* *C*b *Arm* | *om* επελθ.‖p: 579 | σκυ.] σκευη‖←: σ945-990-1010-1223-1293 F K Π *al* *S*h^{t} | διαδωσει‖←: **λλ**⟨131-1278⟩ *pc* *l*184 *L*[e]⟨a^{2}l vg^{7}⟩d Or *C*s **23** ● *om* με‖p: 𝔓$^{45.75}$ *Rpl* *L*'[e] *S*' *C*sb^{1} — *txt*: ℵ$^{*et\,cb}$C^{2}L-33-579-892 1071 Θ Ψ *L*30(a me) *S*s^{v} *C*b' *Aeth* **24** οταν + δε‖p: 𝔓$^{45.75}$ X-1241 1604 λ1278-2193 ϕ983-1689 D U W 157 *pc* *L*br^{2}z *S*h *C*sb^{5} | ● ευρ. + τοτε‖p: 𝔓^{75} ℵ^{c}B^{v}LXΞ-**0124** 1071-1604 Θ 157 *L*bl Or *S*h *C* *Aeth* — *txt*: 𝔓^{45} *Rpl* *L*'[e] *S*' **25** σεσ.] σχολαζοντα σεσ.(∼)‖p: ℵ^{c}BCLΞ-33-579-892 544-1604 **λ**-22-1582 **ϕ**'(13-69-124-174-346)-230 R Γ Ψ *pc* *L*flr^{1} Or *S*h^{+}(σχ. + και) *C*b *Aeth* — *txt*: 𝔓^{75} *Rpl* *L*'⟨r^{2}⟩ *S*' *C*s *Geo*^{1} **26** παραλ. + μεθ εαυτου‖p: ℵ^{*2v} CX-33-1241 1071 ϕ69 Ψ 213 *L*g^{2}lr^{1} vg^{1} *S*j | ∼ επ. ετ. πν. πο. εαυτ.‖p: *Rpl* (∼ πν. ετ.: Δ) *L*'(*om* επ.: r^{2}; *om* ετ.: l; *om* εαυτ.: ff^{2}) *S*(*om* πν.: s; ∼ πν. ετ.: cp)h *Arm* — ∼ ετ. επ. πν. πο. εαυτ.‖p: 28(∼ πν. επ.) D (ετ.] αλλα) G *pc* *L*e aa^{2}c(∼ πο. πν.) *Geo* — *txt*: 𝔓^{75} ℵBLΞ-1241 **ϕ**-174-230 157(∼ πο. αυτ. πν.) *S*j **27** ∼ γυ. τις επα. φω. εκ τ. οχ.: D *L*e *C* — γυ. τις εκ τ. οχ. επα. φω.: *L*c *S*(επ. φω.] φωνη μεγαλη: sc) — ● επα. τις γυ. φω. εκ τ. οχ. (∼ εκ τ. οχ. φω.): *Rpl* (579 λ1 σ990 K Π *pc*) *S*'j — *txt*: 𝔓^{75} ℵBL *l*1043 *l*1749 *L*'(*om* εκ τ. οχ.: aa^{2}bl) **28** φυλ.] ποιουντες‖**8**21 647p 49p: 2145 *L*q Mcn^{Te} *S*p^{1}h^{+} *Arm*⟨pc⟩

Lk11 21f. *cf.* ETh^{II} 21 (*cf. ad 172.* Lk12 39)

Lk11 23 *cf.* Ev. apocr. (POxy 1224 (fol.2r° col. 1; *cf. ad 144.* Mk9 40)

165. cf. ETh^{II} 79 (*transl.*): *Εἶπεν αὐτῷ τις γυνὴ ἐκ τοῦ ὄχλου· μακαρία ἡ κοιλία ἡ βαστάσασά σε καὶ οἱ μαστοὶ οἱ θρέψαντές σε. Εἶπεν αὐτῇ· μακάριοι οἱ ἀκούσαντες τὸν λόγον τοῦ πατρὸς (καὶ) φυλάξαντες αὐτὸν ἐπ' ἀληθείας. ἡμέραι* ... (*cf. ad 263.* Lk23 29)

(152) ***166.*** Das Zeichen für dieses Geschlecht. *The Sign for this Generation.* **Luk 11** 29–32 **[100.]**

[100.]

29 Τῶν δὲ ὄχλων ἐπαθροιζομένων ἤρξατο λέγειν· ἡ γενεὰ αὕτη γενεὰ πονηρά ἐστιν· σημεῖον ζητεῖ, καὶ σημεῖον οὐ δοθήσεται αὐτῇ εἰ μὴ τὸ σημεῖον Ἰωνᾶ. 30 καθὼς γὰρ ἐγένετο Ἰωνᾶς τοῖς Νινευίταις σημεῖον, οὕτως ἔσται καὶ ὁ υἱὸς τοῦ ἀνθρώπου τῇ γενεᾷ ταύτῃ. 31 βασίλισσα νότου ἐγερθήσεται ἐν τῇ κρίσει μετὰ τῶν ἀνδρῶν τῆς γενεᾶς ταύτης καὶ κατακρινεῖ αὐτούς· ὅτι ἦλθεν ἐκ τῶν περάτων τῆς γῆς ἀκοῦσαι τὴν σοφίαν Σολομῶνος, καὶ ἰδοὺ πλεῖον Σολομῶνος ὧδε. 32 ἄνδρες Νινευῖται ἀναστήσονται ἐν τῇ κρίσει μετὰ τῆς γενεᾶς ταύτης καὶ κατακρινοῦσιν αὐτήν· ὅτι μετενόησαν εἰς τὸ κήρυγμα Ἰωνᾶ, καὶ ἰδοὺ πλεῖον Ἰωνᾶ ὧδε.

(153) ***167.*** Vom Licht. *About Light.* **Luk 11** 33–36

[107.] **[45.]**

33 Οὐδεὶς λύχνον ἅψας εἰς κρύπτην τίθησιν οὐδὲ ὑπὸ τὸν μόδιον, ἀλλ' ἐπὶ τὴν λυχνίαν, ἵνα οἱ εἰσπορευόμενοι τὸ φέγγος βλέπωσιν. 34 ὁ λύχνος τοῦ σώματός ἐστιν ὁ ὀφθαλμός σου. ὅταν ὁ ὀφθαλμός σου ἁπλοῦς ᾖ, καὶ ὅλον τὸ σῶμά σου φωτεινόν ἐστιν· ἐπὰν δὲ πονηρὸς ᾖ, καὶ τὸ σῶμά σου σκοτεινόν. 35 σκόπει οὖν μὴ τὸ φῶς τὸ ἐν σοὶ σκότος ἐστίν. 36 εἰ οὖν τὸ σῶμά σου ὅλον φωτεινόν, μὴ ἔχον μέρος τι σκοτεινόν, ἔσται φωτεινὸν ὅλον ὡς ὅταν ὁ λύχνος τῇ ἀστραπῇ φωτίζῃ σε.

Lk 11,29 *om* γεν.^{2}‖Mt: *Rpl* *S*pj^{1v} — *txt*: 𝔓^{75} ℌ⟨579⟩XΞ-**0124** 700-1071 **λλ φ** A D Θ Ψ 157 *pc* Amph *L* *S*sch^{+}j^{a} *C* *Arm* | επιζη.‖Mt39.4: *Rpl* — αιτει: *cf.* 1K122: Ep — *txt*: 𝔓$^{45.75}$ ℵBLΞ 700-1071 σ7-267-1391-1606 A **047** *pc* *l*2 *l*18 *l*19 *l*49 | I. + του προφητου‖Mt39: *Rpl* (*om* του: Δ) *Le* fqr^{1} vg^{2} *S*' *C*' *Arm*^{pc} *Geo*^{1} — *txt*: 𝔓$^{45.75}$ ℵBLΞ-892-1241 700 D *L*' *S*(*om* το σ. I. *et om* ^{30}γαρ: c)j *C*sb^{2} *Arm*' *Geo*^{2} **30** 30] ωσπερ—γης (= Mt1240) *cf. ad* 30b: *Le* | καθ.] ωσπερ‖p: 998 | *om* και‖p1724: 𝔓^{45} Ψ 16 *L*c *S*j *C*s | τ. γεν. ταυ.] εν τη καρδια της γης‖p: *L*i — + και καθως Ιωνας εν τη κοιλια του κητου εγενετο τρεις ημερας και τρεις νυκτας ουτως και ο υιος του ανθρωπου εν τη γη‖p *cf. ad* 30a: D *L*aff^{2}r^{1} ⟦*om* τρ. ημ. και τρ. νυ. *cf.* EN↓: aff^{2} | ουτως + εσται‖p: ar^{1} | *om* και‖p1724: r^{1} | γη] καρδια της γης‖p: ff^{2}⟧ **31** *om* τ. ανδ.‖32 **p**: C 28(*om* μετα—ταυτης) σ1424 *L*vg^{1} *S*sc *C*b^{1} | αυτην‖p32: 𝔓^{45} *L*d vg^{1} **32** μετα + των ανδρων‖31: ϕ230 σM-1194 U 1093 *L*i *C*b^{1} **33** ουδεις + δε‖816: *Rpl* *L*bfff^{2}q *S*h *C*b^{7} — *txt*: 𝔓$^{45.75}$ ℵBC-33-579-1241 700 ϕ174 σ945-1424 D U Γ *pc* *L*' *S*'j *C*' | ουδε] η‖←Mk421: **σ**⟨1424⟩ *al* *L*Ar *S*c(∼ υπο τ. μ. … εις κρ.)p *C*b^{3} | ινα—βλεπ.] και λαμπει πασιν τοις εν τη οικια‖Mt515: 579 | φεγγ.] φως (∼ βλεπ. τ. φ.)‖816: 𝔓^{75} ℌ⟨L-579⟩C(X)-**0124** 1071 **λ**'(118-209 **ϕ**) **σ**⟨954⟩-1194 D W Θ 157 *mu* (*pc*) — *txt*: 𝔓^{45} *Rpl* **34** *om* σου^{1}‖Mt622: *Rpl* *S*sc *C*sb^{1} *Arm* — *txt*: 𝔓$^{45.75}$ ℵ*BC-1241 ϕ13-346-788-826 σM A D W *L* *S*' *C*b' | οταν + ουν‖←: *Rpl* *S*,j *Geo*^{1} — *txt*: 𝔓$^{45.75}$ ℌ⟨33-892⟩-**0124** Λ ϕ174 D W *pc* *L* *C*s$^{4:6}$b$^{\langle 3\rangle}$ *Arm* *Geo*^{2} *Aeth* | ∼ η ο οφθ. σ. απλ.‖←: D *Le* bff^{2}qr^{1} | *om* και^{1}‖←: C-1241 **ϕ**⟨13⟩ **σ**⟨954⟩ D Γ Ψ *pm* *L*⟨e⟩ *C*b *Arm* *Aeth* | εστιν^{2}] εσται‖←: 𝔓^{45} LX-33-579-1241 28 **λ** ϕ124-983 **σ**⟨954⟩-M-7-990-1194-1207-1223 K Π 157 *mu* *Le* bflqr$^{1.2}$z vg *S*p *C*b$^{\langle 6\rangle}$ | πον. η] *prm* ο οφθαλμος σου‖Mt623: X *L*a vg^{1} *S*scp^{4} *C*sb^{1} *Arm*(*om* σου) *Geo*^{2}(^{1} *om* επαν—σκ.) *Aeth* — πον. ο οφ.‖Mt623: **0124** | και^{2}] ολον‖←: 28 348 *L*fr^{1} *C* *Aeth* — κ. ολ.‖←34a: ℵ^{c}X **λ** *pc* *S*c | σκο. + εσται‖Mt622: 𝔓^{45} X-1241 1604 **ϕ**⟨69-788⟩ σM-1194 K U Θ Π *mu* *L*' *S*ph^{+} *C*s — + εστιν‖←34a: **0124** 1071 D^{c}(* ∼ εσ. σκ.) Ω *al* (∼ *pc*) *Le* *S*j *Aeth* **35** 35] ει ουν το φως το εν σοι σκοτος εστιν(*om*) το σκοτος ποσον‖Mt623: 1241 (D) *Le* abff^{2}ir^{1v} — *om*‖←: 579 *pc* *L*g^{2} **36** 36] και ει το φως—ποσον (*cf. ad* 35)‖←: *S*c — *om*‖←: D *Le* abff^{2}g^{2}ir^{1}

Lk1130 *cf.* EN frgm.11 (*cf. ad 100.* Mt1240)

Lk1133 *cf.* ETh^{II} 33b (*cf. ad 107.* Mk421)

Lk1134-36 *cf.* ETh^{II} 24 (*cf. ad 45.*)

(154)

168. Rede gegen Pharisäer und Schriftgelehrte. Luk 11 37–54 224.
Discourse against the Scribes and Pharisees.

128.

[37] Ἐν δὲ τῷ λαλῆσαι ἐρωτᾷ αὐτὸν Φαρισαῖος ὅπως ἀριστήσῃ παρ᾿ αὐτῷ· εἰσελθὼν δὲ ἀνέπεσεν. [38] ὁ δὲ Φαρισαῖος ἰδὼν ἐθαύμασεν ὅτι οὐ πρῶτον ἐβαπτίσθη πρὸ τοῦ ἀρίστου. [39] εἶπεν δὲ ὁ κύριος πρὸς αὐτόν· νῦν ὑμεῖς οἱ Φαρισαῖοι τὸ ἔξωθεν τοῦ ποτηρίου καὶ τοῦ πίνακος καθαρίζετε, τὸ δὲ ἔσωθεν ὑμῶν γέμει ἁρπαγῆς καὶ πονηρίας. [40] ἄφρονες, οὐχ ὁ ποιήσας τὸ ἔξωθεν καὶ τὸ ἔσωθεν ἐποίησεν; [41] πλὴν τὰ ἐνόντα δότε ἐλεημοσύνην, καὶ ἰδοὺ πάντα καθαρὰ ὑμῖν ἐστιν. [42] ἀλλὰ οὐαὶ ὑμῖν τοῖς Φαρισαίοις, ὅτι ἀποδεκατοῦτε τὸ ἡδύοσμον καὶ τὸ πήγανον καὶ πᾶν λάχανον, καὶ παρέρχεσθε τὴν κρίσιν καὶ τὴν ἀγάπην τοῦ θεοῦ· ταῦτα ἔδει ποιῆσαι κἀκεῖνα μὴ παρεῖναι. [43] οὐαὶ ὑμῖν τοῖς Φαρισαίοις, ὅτι ἀγαπᾶτε τὴν πρωτοκαθεδρίαν ἐν ταῖς συναγωγαῖς καὶ τοὺς ἀσπασμοὺς ἐν ταῖς ἀγοραῖς.

224.

[44] οὐαὶ ὑμῖν, ὅτι ἐστὲ ὡς τὰ μνημεῖα τὰ ἄδηλα, καὶ οἱ ἄνθρωποι οἱ περιπατοῦντες ἐπάνω οὐκ οἴδασιν. [45] ἀποκριθεὶς δέ τις τῶν νομικῶν λέγει αὐτῷ· διδάσκαλε, ταῦτα λέγων καὶ ἡμᾶς ὑβρίζεις. [46] ὁ δὲ εἶπεν· καὶ ὑμῖν τοῖς νομικοῖς οὐαί, ὅτι φορτίζετε τοὺς ἀνθρώπους φορτία δυσβάστακτα, καὶ αὐτοὶ ἑνὶ τῶν δακτύλων ὑμῶν οὐ προσψαύετε τοῖς φορτίοις. [47] οὐαὶ ὑμῖν, ὅτι οἰκοδομεῖτε τὰ μνημεῖα τῶν προφητῶν, οἱ δὲ πατέρες ὑμῶν ἀπέκτειναν αὐτούς. [48] ἄρα μάρτυρές ἐστε καὶ συνευδοκεῖτε τοῖς ἔργοις τῶν πατέρων ὑμῶν, ὅτι αὐτοὶ μὲν ἀπέκτειναν αὐτούς, ὑμεῖς δὲ οἰκοδομεῖτε.

[49] διὰ τοῦτο καὶ ἡ σοφία τοῦ θεοῦ εἶπεν· ἀποστελῶ εἰς αὐτοὺς προφήτας καὶ ἀποστόλους, καὶ ἐξ αὐτῶν ἀποκτενοῦσιν καὶ ἐκδιώξουσιν, [50] ἵνα ἐκζητηθῇ τὸ αἷμα πάντων τῶν προφητῶν τὸ ἐκκεχυμένον ἀπὸ καταβολῆς κόσμου ἀπὸ τῆς γενεᾶς ταύτης, [51] ἀπὸ αἵματος Ἀβελ ἕως αἵματος Ζαχαρίου τοῦ ἀπολομένου μεταξὺ τοῦ θυσιαστηρίου καὶ τοῦ οἴκου· ναὶ λέγω ὑμῖν, ἐκζητηθήσεται ἀπὸ τῆς γενεᾶς ταύτης.

Lk 11,37 εν—ερωτα ... οπως] εδεηθη δε ... ινα‖512: D *S*sc *Δ*ad i^{T} l^{FG} me n⟨L⟩ | ηρωτα‖736: *Rpl* *L*' (-ησεν) — *txt*: 𝔓$^{45.75}$ **ℵB-0124 ϕ**⟨13-124-983⟩-174 σM-71-1194-1675 A W Θ Ψ *pc* *L*e | Φ.] Φ. τις(∼)‖736: *Rpl* (X D) *L* *S*,j{} — των Φαρισαιων τις‖←: 213 1555 *Δ*a — *txt*: 𝔓$^{45.75}$ **ℵBL-0124**-579-1241 **λ ϕ**⟨124⟩-174-230 {*Δ*'} | παρ αυ.] μετ αυτου‖←: D *L*abff^{2}iq *Aeth* | εισ. δε ανεπ.] και εισ. εις την οικιαν του Φαρισαιου ανεκλιθη‖←: **ϕ** (*om* του Φ.: *L*z vg^{1}) — και εισ. ανεκ.‖←: *L*'⟨ar^{1}⟩ *S*s^{v}cp *Arm*(και + αυτος) **38** ιδ. εθ.] ηρξατο διακρινομενος εν εαυτω λεγειν‖749 521: D *pc* *L*⟨f⟩ *S*c(*om* διακ.) | οτι] δια τι‖Mt152p: D *L*⟨af⟩ Mcn^{Te} *S*sc **39** Φ. + υποκριται‖p: D *L*b | *om* υμων‖p: σ1424 *C*s **42** *om* αλλα‖p: 579 σ1194 *C*b^{1} | πηγ.] ανηθον‖p: 𝔓^{45} 157 *L*e — αν. και το πηγ.‖p: **ϕ** 1573 | παρερ. + τα βαρυτερα του νομου‖p: 1241 | *om* του θε.‖p: B* | ● ταυ. + δε: 𝔓$^{45.75}$ BC LX-**0124**-33-579-892 1071 **ϕ** σM-7-1194 K Θ Π Ψ **0108** *pc* *L*cz vg' *S*cph^{+} *C*' — + γαρ: *L*e bfqr$^{1.2}$ vg^{1} — *txt*: *Rpl* (*om* ταυ.—παρ.: D) *L*aff^{2}i30 Mcn^{Te} *S*s *C*b^{3} *Arm* | παρει.] αφιεναι(-ειναι)‖p: (𝔓^{45}) *Rpl* (ℵ*-892 σ945 440 *l*184) *L*a — *txt*: 𝔓^{75} ℵ^{c}B*L-1241(*om* μη) 700-1071 **ϕ**⟨69-124⟩-174-230 A(παραφ-) 1355 *L*' **43** τοις Φ.] Φαρισαιοι‖Mt13 *etc.*: ℵ D *L*vl⟨f⟩ vg^{5} — γραμματεις και Φαρισαιοι‖←: *S*c *Aeth*(+ υποκριται) | συναγ. + και την πρωτοκλισιαν εν τοις δειπνοις‖p: **ϕ** — αγορ. + και τας πρωτοκλισιας εν τ. δει.‖p: C 1071 D(*om* τας) *pc* *L*blqr^{1} vg^{1} *Aeth* **44** υμιν + γραμματεις και Φαρισαιοι υποκριται(*om*)‖p: *Rpl* (D) Cr *L*vl'(ir$^{1.2}$) vg^{1} (Luc) *S*' *C*b^{7} — *txt*: 𝔓$^{45.75}$ 𝔋⟨579⟩C **λ** *L*e acff^{2}lz vg' *S*sc *C*' *Arm* **46** δυσβ.] βαρεα‖p: *L*ec *S*sc(+ και επιτιθετε επι τους ωμους των ανθρωπων)p *C*s — βαρ. και(*om*) δυσβ.‖p: CX 28 Ψ *al* Bas$^{1:2}$ (*S*h^{m}) | τω δακτυλω‖p: X(*om* ενι) 1071 σM-71 G *pc* *L*⟨e a⟩ *Arm* **48** μ. εστε] μαρτυρειτε‖p: 𝔓^{75} *Rpl* Chr *L*⟨e⟩ *C*⟨b^{3}⟩ — *txt*: ℵBL-892-1241 Or *Aeth* | και] οτι‖p: **ϕ**⟨983⟩ *pc* *L*r$^{1.2}$z vg⟨3⟩ *Arm* | οικ. + (*prm*) τους ταφους αυτων‖47p: **λ** (**ϕ**-174-230) 157 *L*'(*om* αυτ.: vg^{1}) Luc *S*ph {*C*b^{8}} (*Arm*) — + αυτων τα μνημεια‖←: *Rpl* (∼ τα μν. αυ.: *pc* *l*184 Chr) *L*fq Luc {} — *txt*: 𝔓^{75} ℵBL-579-1241 D *L*e abilr^{1} *S*s *C*' **49** *om* και^{1}—ειπ.‖p: D *L*b Luc | *om* του θε.‖735p: 472 | αποστελλω‖p: 579-1241 σ1424 D Θ *pc* *L*bqr^{1} Luc | αυτ.] υμας‖p: ϕ124 *L*c *C*b^{5} | *om* και^{3}‖p: 579 λ1 **ϕ**⟨346⟩ σ990-1223 A K U W Π 157 *al* *L*d *S* | αποκτενειτε *et* εκδιωξετε‖p: ϕ124 *L*c | εκδ.] ● διωξ.‖p: 𝔋⟨892⟩CX 1071 λ1-131 σM-1194 Θ *pc* — *txt*: 𝔓^{75} *Rpl* (-κουσιν: ϕ69) **50** εκκεχ.] ● εκχυννομενον‖p: 𝔓^{75} *Rpl* — *txt*: 𝔓^{45} B-33-1241 **ϕ**⟨124-983⟩ **51** αιμ.^{1}] του αιμ.‖p: *Rpl* — *txt*: 𝔓$^{45.75}$ 𝔋CX λ1-131 σ1194 D 213 | Α. + του δικαιου‖p: 1604 ϕ124-346-983 σM-990-1194-1675 K Π 157 *mu* *L*e cir$^{1.2}$z vg^{1} *S*h^{+} *C*s$^{1v:8}$b^{3} | αιμ.^{2}] του αιμ.‖p: *Rpl* — *txt*: 𝔓$^{45.75}$ 𝔋X **λ** D Ψ | Ζ. + υιου Βαραχιου‖p: D *pc* *S*c *C*s$^{1:8}$b⟨5⟩ | του απολ. μετ.] ον εφονευσαν ανα μεσον‖p: D *L*ar^{2} *Aeth* | οικ.] ναου‖p: D σ659 *L*e r^{2} *S*scp(∼ ναου ... θυσ.) *Arm* *Aeth*

224.

[52] οὐαὶ ὑμῖν τοῖς νομικοῖς, ὅτι ἤρατε τὴν κλεῖδα τῆς γνώσεως· αὐτοὶ οὐκ εἰσήλθατε καὶ τοὺς εἰσερχομένους ἐκωλύσατε.

[53] λέγοντος δὲ αὐτοῦ ταῦτα πρὸς αὐτοὺς ἤρξαντο οἱ γραμματεῖς καὶ οἱ Φαρισαῖοι δεινῶς ἐνέχειν καὶ ἀποστοματίζειν αὐτὸν περὶ πλειόνων, [54] ἐνεδρεύοντες αὐτὸν θηρεῦσαί τι ἐκ τοῦ στόματος αὐτοῦ, ἵνα κατηγορήσωσιν αὐτοῦ.

(155)

169. Aufforderung zum furchtlosen Bekenntnis. Luk 12 1–12 **72.**
Exhortation to Fearless Confession.

72. **133.** **107.**

[1] Ἐν οἷς ἐπισυναχθεισῶν τῶν μυριάδων τοῦ ὄχλου, ὥστε καταπατεῖν ἀλλήλους, ἤρξατο λέγειν πρὸς τοὺς μαθητὰς αὐτοῦ πρῶτον· προσέχετε ἑαυτοῖς ἀπὸ τῆς ζύμης τῶν Φαρισαίων, ἥτις ἐστὶν ὑπόκρισις.

[2] οὐδὲν δὲ συγκεκαλυμμένον ἐστὶν ὃ οὐκ ἀποκαλυφθήσεται, καὶ κρυπτὸν ὃ οὐ γνωσθήσεται. [3] ἀνθ' ὧν ὅσα ἐν τῇ σκοτίᾳ εἴπατε, ἐν τῷ φωτὶ ἀκουσθήσεται· καὶ ὃ πρὸς τὸ οὖς ἐλαλήσατε ἐν τοῖς ταμιείοις, κηρυχθήσεται ἐπὶ τῶν δωμάτων. [4] λέγω δὲ ὑμῖν τοῖς φίλοις μου, μὴ φοβηθῆτε ἀπὸ τῶν ἀποκτεινόντων τὸ σῶμα καὶ μετὰ ταῦτα μὴ ἐχόντων περισσότερόν τι ποιῆσαι. [5] ὑποδείξω δὲ ὑμῖν τίνα φοβηθῆτε· φοβήθητε τὸν μετὰ τὸ ἀποκτεῖναι ἔχοντα ἐξουσίαν ἐμβαλεῖν εἰς τὴν γέενναν. ναὶ λέγω ὑμῖν, τοῦτον φοβήθητε. [6] οὐχὶ πέντε στρουθία πωλοῦνται ἀσσαρίων δύο; καὶ ἓν ἐξ αὐτῶν οὐκ ἔστιν ἐπιλελησμένον ἐνώπιον τοῦ θεοῦ. [7] ἀλλὰ καὶ αἱ τρίχες τῆς κεφαλῆς ὑμῶν πᾶσαι ἠρίθμηνται. μὴ φοβεῖσθε· πολλῶν στρουθίων διαφέρετε. [8] λέγω δὲ ὑμῖν,

Lk 11,52 ηρ.] εκρυψατε‖Mt25 18.25: D 157 *L*(κρυπτετε: e q)abc *Ssc Arm Δ*a E^{a} — εκρ. και ηρ.‖←: Θ *Aeth*(∼ ηρ. … εκρ.) | αυτ. + γαρ‖p: σM-1194 1047 *pc* | εκω.] κωλυετε‖p: G *Lc Sh*^{Brst} *C*b⟨7⟩ *Arm Aeth* — ουκ αφιετε εισελθειν‖p: Ep **53** λεγ.—αυτους] ● κακειθεν εξελθοντος αυτου (+ ειπεν ταυτα προς αυτους ενωπιον παντος του λαου και κατησχυνοντο‖13 17) και: 𝔥⟨892⟩C (*om*: ϕ69)-788 (*Sh*^{m}) *C*' — *txt*: *Rpl* (αυτου] του Ιησου: 1071 *l*48, *om*: λ118-131 D *pc*; ∼ πρ. αυ. ταυ.: σ267-659; ταυ. + παντα: ϕ13; εαυτους: ϕ124) *Le* ac('*om* δε) *S*' *C*b^{1}(*om* πρ. αυ.) *Arm*(= ϕ13) *Δ*a l^{AD} p | αυτους + ενωπιον παντος του λαου (οχλου)‖13 17: (X) 1604 D 157 (213) *pc Lvl*⟨z⟩r^{1} *Ssc Geo* — + ενω. τ. λα. κατισχυνονται(< -ησχυ-?) και‖←: Θ 254(-ησχυνθησαν) *Sh*^{m} *Arm*(τ.] παντος τ.) | γρ.] νομικοι‖7 30 14 3: **λ** (D) 239 *Li Sh*^{m} | γρ. … Φ.] Φ. … νομ.‖7 30: D *L*⟨ai⟩ | Φ. + και οι νομ.‖←: Θ **54** ενεδ. αυ. θηρ.] ζητουντες θηρ.‖19 47 p 20 19 p: D *Lvl*'r^{1} *S*' *Arm*(ζη.] και ζητησαι) *Δ*a — ενεδ. αυ. ζητ. θηρ.‖←: *Rpl* (*om* αυ.: XΘΨ 213; ∼ τι θηρ.: **σ**⟨1424⟩-990 K Θ Π *al*) *Lf Sp* — ενεδ. αυ. και ζητ. θηρ.‖←: σ1207 *L*30(*om* αυ.: z vg) *Sh Δ*l^{AD} — ενεδ. αυ. θηρ. και ζητ.‖←: 1071 — *txt* (*om* αυ.): 𝔓$^{45.75}$ (ℵ)BL-579-1241 **λ** 239 *Csb*^{1}(' *Geo*) *Aeth* | ● *om* ινα—αυτου^{2}(∩?): 𝔓$^{45.75}$ 𝔥⟨33⟩ 477 *Ss C Aeth* — ινα] πως‖22 2 Mk14 1: *Ll* — κατ.] ευρωσιν κατηγορησαι‖6 7: D *Lf S*' — *txt*: *Rpl L*' *Sh Arm Δ*l^{AD} **12,1** κατ. αλ.] αλ. συνπνιγειν‖8 42: D | *om* εαυ.‖Mt16 6: Θ *pc* Ep *Lailqz* vg Te | ● ∼ ητ. εσ. υπ. Φ.: 𝔓^{75} BL-1241 *Le Cs* — *txt*: 𝔓^{45} *Rpl* Ep *L*' Luc Mcn^{Te} Te *S Cb*(+ αυτων) *Δ*a **2** δε] γαρ‖p: D *La*30 vg^{3} *Ssch*^{m} *Arm* | ∼ εστ. συγκ.‖p 8 17 p: (C*) *pc Lr*^{1} | συγκ.] κεκαλ.‖p: 𝔓^{45} ℵC*-1241 | ουκ αποκ.] ου φανερωθησεται‖8 17 Mk4 22: D' **3** προς] εις‖p: 700 | *om* εν τ. ταμ.‖**p**: 28 σ1424 *Lbq* **4** φοβ.] πτοηθητε‖21 9: 𝔓^{45} 700 | και—μη^{2}] την δε ψυχην μη δυναμενων αποκτειναι‖p: D(+ μηδε) 157(*om* εχ.—ποι.) | μη εχ. περ. τι] ● μη εχ. τι περ. (περισσον): LX-(33)-892-1241 1071 **ϕ**⟨124⟩-*l*547 σ1424 (Θ Ψ) *pc* — περ. μη εχ. τι: 700 **λ**-1582 *Lir*^{1} — *txt* (περισσον): 𝔓^{75} *Rpl* (σ1194 A D K R Π *al*) Or *L*'(*om* περ.: *Ssc Aeth*) **5** ∼ εξ. εχ.‖5 24 p Jo19 10: 𝔓^{45} *Rpl* (*om*: 477) Mcn^{Te} — *txt*: 𝔓^{45} 𝔥X-**0191** 700-1071 **λ**-1582 **ϕ** σ7-267 A D K R W Θ Π Ψ 157 *al l*32 *l*48 *l*49 *l*184 Mcn^{Ep} Or | *om* την‖p Mt5 29f.: 700 D R Ψ 157 Iu Mcn^{Ep} Or Thdt^{A} | γεεν. + του πυρος‖Mt5 22 18 9: σ1424 **6** πωλειται‖p: 𝔓^{45} *Rpl* (∼ δυο ασ.: W) Cr Ep^{1} Or — *txt*: 𝔓^{75} ℵB-892-1241 1071 **ϕ**⟨124-983⟩-*l*547 Θ Ψ 1355 Ep^{1} | ∼ ασ. δυο πωλ.‖p: 1047 Ep Or(∼ δυο ασ.) — ∼ ασ. πωλ. δυο‖p: 579 **7** ηρι.] ηριθμημεναι εισιν(*om*)‖p: (𝔓^{45}) 579 1071-1604 ϕ124 D Θ *pc* (Cl) | μη + ουν‖p: *Rpl* Or *L*' *S Cb*^{1} — *txt*: 𝔓$^{45.75}$ BL-**0191**-579-1241 R 157 *Labff*^{2}il Am *Sj C*' *Arm* | διαφ. + υμεις‖**p**: 33 1071-1604 **ϕ**-174-230-*l*547 σM-71-692-1207 D F G K Y Θ Π *pm l*183 *l*184 *Le* a(∼ υμ. στ. διαφ.) 30 vg^{1} *Sj*^{b} *Arm Aeth*

Lk12 2 *cf.* ETh^{II} 5f. (*cf. ad 107.* Mk4 22; *ad 40.*)

72. | **137.** **99.** **229.**

πᾶς ὃς ἂν ὁμολογήσῃ ἐν ἐμοὶ ἔμπροσθεν τῶν ἀνθρώπων, καὶ ὁ υἱὸς τοῦ ἀνθρώπου ὁμολογήσει ἐν αὐτῷ ἔμπροσθεν τῶν ἀγγέλων τοῦ θεοῦ· 9 ὁ δὲ ἀρνησάμενός με ἐνώπιον τῶν ἀνθρώπων ἀπαρνηθήσεται ἐνώπιον τῶν ἀγγέλων τοῦ θεοῦ. 10 καὶ πᾶς ὃς ἐρεῖ λόγον εἰς τὸν υἱὸν τοῦ ἀνθρώπου, ἀφεθήσεται αὐτῷ· τῷ δὲ εἰς τὸ ἅγιον πνεῦμα βλασφημήσαντι οὐκ ἀφεθήσεται.

11 ὅταν δὲ εἰσφέρωσιν ὑμᾶς ἐπὶ τὰς συναγωγὰς καὶ τὰς ἀρχὰς καὶ τὰς ἐξουσίας, μὴ μεριμνήσητε πῶς ἢ τί ἀπολογήσησθε ἢ τί εἴπητε· 12 τὸ γὰρ ἅγιον πνεῦμα διδάξει ὑμᾶς ἐν αὐτῇ τῇ ὥρᾳ ἃ δεῖ εἰπεῖν.

(156)

170. Der törichte Reiche. *The Rich Fool.* Luk 12 13–21

13 Εἶπεν δέ τις ἐκ τοῦ ὄχλου αὐτῷ· διδάσκαλε, εἰπὲ τῷ ἀδελφῷ μου μερίσασθαι μετ' ἐμοῦ τὴν κληρονομίαν. 14 ὁ δὲ εἶπεν αὐτῷ· ἄνθρωπε, τίς με κατέστησεν κριτὴν ἢ μεριστὴν ἐφ' ὑμᾶς; 15 εἶπεν δὲ πρὸς αὐτούς· ὁρᾶτε καὶ φυλάσσεσθε ἀπὸ πάσης πλεονεξίας, ὅτι οὐκ ἐν τῷ περισσεύειν τινὶ ἡ ζωὴ αὐτοῦ ἐστιν ἐκ τῶν ὑπαρχόντων αὐτῷ. 16 εἶπεν δὲ παραβολὴν πρὸς αὐτοὺς λέγων· ἀνθρώπου τινὸς πλουσίου εὐφόρησεν ἡ χώρα. 17 καὶ διελογίζετο ἐν ἑαυτῷ λέγων· τί ποιήσω, ὅτι οὐκ ἔχω ποῦ συνάξω τοὺς καρπούς μου; 18 καὶ εἶπεν· τοῦτο ποιήσω· καθελῶ μου τὰς ἀποθήκας καὶ μείζονας οἰκοδομήσω, καὶ συνάξω ἐκεῖ πάντα τὰ γενήματά μου, 19 καὶ ἐρῶ τῇ ψυχῇ μου· ψυχή, ἔχεις πολλὰ ἀγαθὰ κείμενα εἰς ἔτη πολλά· ἀναπαύου, φάγε, πίε, εὐφραίνου. 20 εἶπεν δὲ αὐτῷ ὁ θεός· ἄφρων, ταύτῃ τῇ νυκτὶ τὴν ψυχήν σου ἀπαιτοῦσιν ἀπὸ σοῦ· ἃ δὲ ἡτοίμασας, τίνι ἔσται; 21 οὕτως ὁ θησαυρίζων ἑαυτῷ καὶ μὴ εἰς θεὸν πλουτῶν.

Lk 12,8 *om* πας‖926 Mk838: 21 *Li* *Sj*^{b} | *om* αν‖10: 655 1573 | ∼ ομ. ο υι. τ. αν.‖p: σ1424 | *om* τ. αγγ.‖**p**: ℵ* 259 Mcn^{Ep} *L*Mcn^{Te} **9** ενωπ.^{1}] εμπροσθεν‖**p8p**: **0191**-892 1604 ϕ983-1689 A D K Q Θ Π **047** *al* | απαρνηθησεται] αρν.‖p9a: σ115 D *pc* — απαρνησομαι καγω(*om*) αυτον: X 213 (Cl) *L*b Cp *Sj* *Geo*^{1} *Aeth* — αρνησεται αυτον‖p: 4 | ενωπ.^{2}] εμπροσθεν‖**p8p**: D *pc* Cl | αγγ.] αγιων αγγ.‖926 Mk838: 251 **10** ος + αν‖8 Mt1232a.bp: σ115 D *pc* | ∼ βλα.(ειποντι) εις το αγ. πν.‖Mk329p: 225 245 *L*(e r^{1})al Luc (Mcn^{Te}) *Sj* *Aeth* | αγ. πν.] πν. το αγ.‖←: **ϕ**-174-*l*547 D *pc* *l*47 *l*53 | αφεθ.^{2} + αυτω‖Mt1232: Λ G 157 *pc* *L*vl'⟨fz⟩ff^{2}(αυτοις) vg^{4} Mcn^{Te} *S*scpj — + αυτω ουτε εν τω αιωνι τουτω ουτε εν τω μελλοντι‖←: D *L*e c (Luc) *Aeth* **11** επι] εις‖2112 Mk139: ℵ-579-1241 λ1-131-1582 **ϕ** D R Θ *pc* Cl | μεριμνατε‖Mt625p Mk1311: {𝔓^{45}} *Rpl* Bas — προμεριμνατε‖Mk ←: {} D Cl — *txt* (-ησετε): 𝔓^{75} 𝔥X-**0191** 700-1071 (**λ**-1582) **ϕ**⟨124⟩-174-230-*l*547 σ1194 Q R Θ Ψ *pc* *l*20 Cr^{I} Or | απολ.] λαλησητε‖Mt1019 Mk←: 579 28(*et* ειπ.] απολ.) *pc* *Aeth* | *om* η τι ειπ.‖←: 21 *pc* *l*19 *C*b^{2} *Aeth* **12** *om* εν—ωρα‖Jo1426: 33 Or | αυτη] εκεινη‖←: 700 67 *L*cff^{2} *S*s^{v}cp *C*⟨b^{1}⟩ **16** δε + και‖536 639 189: 1604 **λ**-1582 σ27 Θ 157 *pc* *L*vg^{1} PsAu | ∼ πρ. αυ. παραβ.‖153 189: 579 D 1093 *L*Ar *S*s *C*s *Δ*a i^{T} md n$^{⟨L⟩}$ **18** παντα—μου] τους καρπους μου‖17: *l*39 *l*184 (*prm* παντας: *L*e acd{}^{1} *Geo*{}^{2}) — παντα τα αγαθα μου‖19: 1537 — ● πα. τα γεν. και τα αγ. μου: *Rpl* (∼ αγ. ... γεν.: Π *pc*; *om* μου: σ1675) Bas *L*'{}^{3} *S*' *Δ*ad i^{V}(= Π) l md n$^{⟨L⟩}$ — ● πα.(*om* ℵ^{a}) τον σιτον (+ μου) και τα αγ. μου‖317p Mt1330: 𝔓$^{45.75}$(*)^{c} (σιτ. + μου: ℵ^{a} *et* ^{c})BL(X)-**070**(*om* τα)-(33)-579-892-1241 **λ**-1582 (**ϕ**')(σιτ. + μου τα γεν. μου: ϕ346) (W *Sj* *C*) *Arm*(∼ τον σ. κ. πα.) *Aeth*(*om* πα.) (*Δ*a me) — *txt*: ℵ* D *L*bff^{2}ilqr^{1}{32}^{3} Am Ar {PsAu}^{1} (*om* πα.: *S*sc) *Δ*{i^{T}}^{2}p **20** θε.] κυριος‖168 186: A Cp$^{2:5}$ | απαιτ.] αιτ.‖1248: 𝔓^{75} BL-**070**-33-579 Q

Lk1210 *cf.* ETh^{II} 44 (*cf. ad 99.* Mt1231f.)

Lk1213-15 *cf.* ETh^{II} 72 (*transl.*): *[Εἶπεν ἄνθρωπός τις] αὐτῷ· εἰπὲ τοῖς ἀδελφοῖς μου μερίσασθαι μετ' ἐμοῦ τὰ σκεύη τοῦ πατρός μου. εἶπεν αὐτῷ· ὦ ἄνθρωπε, τίς με κατέστησεν μεριστήν; (καὶ) στραφεὶς πρὸς τοὺς μαθητὰς αὐτοῦ εἶπεν· μήτι εἰμὶ μεριστής;*

Lk1216-21 *cf.* ETh^{II} 63 (*transl.*): *Λέγει Ἰησοῦς· ἄνθρωπός τις ἦν, ὃς εἶχεν πολλὰ χρήματα. εἶπεν· τοῖς ἐμοῖς χρήμασιν χρήσομαι σπείρων (καὶ) θερίζων (καὶ) φυτεύων (καὶ) πληρῶν τὰς ἀποθήκας μου καρπῶν, ἵνα μηδενὸς ὑστερήσω. ταῦτα ἐφρόνει ἐν τῇ καρδίᾳ αὐτοῦ. καὶ ἐν ἐκείνῃ τῇ νυκτὶ ἀπέθανεν. ὁ ἔχων ὦτα ἀκουέτω* (*cf. ad 103.* Mt139)

(157)

171. Vom Sorgen und Schätzesammeln. *On Earthly Cares.* Luk 12 22–34 [47.]

[47.]

[44.]

^{22} Εἶπεν δὲ πρὸς τοὺς μαθητὰς αὐτοῦ· διὰ τοῦτο λέγω ὑμῖν, μὴ μεριμνᾶτε τῇ ψυχῇ τί φάγητε, μηδὲ τῷ σώματι τί ἐνδύσησθε. ^{23} ἡ γὰρ ψυχὴ πλεῖόν ἐστιν τῆς τροφῆς καὶ τὸ σῶμα τοῦ ἐνδύματος. ^{24} κατανοήσατε τοὺς κόρακας, ὅτι οὔτε σπείρουσιν οὔτε θερίζουσιν, οἷς οὐκ ἔστιν ταμιεῖον οὐδὲ ἀποθήκη, καὶ ὁ θεὸς τρέφει αὐτούς· πόσῳ μᾶλλον ὑμεῖς διαφέρετε τῶν πετεινῶν. ^{25} τίς δὲ ἐξ ὑμῶν μεριμνῶν δύναται προσθεῖναι ἐπὶ τὴν ἡλικίαν αὐτοῦ πῆχυν; ^{26} εἰ οὖν οὐδὲ ἐλάχιστον δύνασθε, τί περὶ τῶν λοιπῶν μεριμνᾶτε; ^{27} κατανοήσατε τὰ κρίνα, πῶς αὐξάνει· οὐ κοπιᾷ οὐδὲ νήθει· λέγω δὲ ὑμῖν, οὐδὲ Σολομὼν ἐν πάσῃ τῇ δόξῃ αὐτοῦ περιεβάλετο ὡς ἓν τούτων. ^{28} εἰ δὲ ἐν ἀγρῷ τὸν χόρτον ὄντα σήμερον καὶ αὔριον εἰς κλίβανον βαλλόμενον ὁ θεὸς οὕτως ἀμφιέζει, πόσῳ μᾶλλον ὑμᾶς, ὀλιγόπιστοι. ^{29} καὶ ὑμεῖς μὴ ζητεῖτε τί φάγητε καὶ τί πίητε, καὶ μὴ μετεωρίζεσθε· ^{30} ταῦτα γὰρ πάντα τὰ ἔθνη τοῦ κόσμου ἐπιζητοῦσιν· ὑμῶν δὲ ὁ πατὴρ οἶδεν ὅτι χρῄζετε τούτων· ^{31} πλὴν ζητεῖτε τὴν βασιλείαν αὐτοῦ, καὶ ταῦτα προστεθήσεται ὑμῖν. ^{32} μὴ φοβοῦ, τὸ μικρὸν ποίμνιον· ὅτι εὐδόκησεν ὁ πατὴρ ὑμῶν δοῦναι ὑμῖν τὴν βασιλείαν.

^{33} πωλήσατε τὰ ὑπάρχοντα ὑμῶν καὶ δότε ἐλεημοσύνην· ποιήσατε ἑαυτοῖς βαλλάντια μὴ παλαιούμενα, θησαυρὸν ἀνέκλειπτον ἐν τοῖς οὐρανοῖς, ὅπου κλέπτης οὐκ ἐγγίζει οὐδὲ σὴς διαφθείρει· ^{34} ὅπου γάρ ἐστιν ὁ θησαυρὸς ὑμῶν, ἐκεῖ καὶ ἡ καρδία ὑμῶν ἔσται.

Lk 12,22 *om* ειπ.—αυτ.‖p: 245 | ψυ. + υμων‖p: 𝔓^{45} *Rpl* Eu *Le* a30 vg^{2} *S*' *C* — *txt*: 𝔓^{75} ℵBL-892 700-1071 λ1 A D Q W Θ 157 *al* *l*48 *L*' *S*sh *Arm* | φαρ. + η τι πιητε‖29p: 59 | σω. + υμων‖p: B-**070**-33 28 λ22-1278-1582 **ϕ** **σ**⟨1424⟩-945 *al* *L*a vg^{2} *S*p *C* **23** η γαρ] ουχι η‖p: **070** ϕ230 **σ**⟨1424⟩-7-945-990 **047** *pc* *L*l vg^{1} *S*h^{Brsm} **24** τ. κορ.] τα πετεινα του ουρανου‖**p**: 𝔓^{45}(τα πε. τ. ου. και τ. κορ.) D *Le* lr^{1}(*om* τ. ου.: f vg^{1})^{1} | ουτε ... ουτε] ● ου ... ουδε‖p: 𝔓$^{45.75}$ *Rpl* (ου ... ου: σM *l*48; ου ... ουγε: **070**) Cl *L*'Te *C*s^{2}(^{4} = M)b *Aeth* — *txt*: ℵL-579-892 1071 D Q 157 *Le* | θερ. + ουδε συναγουσιν εις αποθηκας‖p: 157 | αυτα‖p: 𝔓^{45} ϕ⟨124⟩-174-230 D 253 *L*fl(illas)r^{1} vg^{1} | ποσω + ουν‖Mt12$_{12}$: ϕ124 1093 *S*scp (υμεις + ουν: *C*s$^{3:5}$ | π. μαλ.] ουχι‖p: D Cl(ουχ) *Le* cff^{2}il(∼ ουχι υμ. μαλ.)r^{1} vg^{1} — *om*‖Lk12$_{6}$p: *C*s **25** ● επι τ. ηλ. αυ. προσ.: 𝔓^{75} B-579 | πηχ. + ενα‖**p**: *Rpl* Eu *L*' *S* — *txt*: 𝔓$^{45.75}$ ℵ*B D *L*ff^{2}il *C* **26** ει—λοι.] και περι τ. λοι. τι‖p: D *Le*(*om* τι) abcff^{2}ilr^{1} **27** κρι. + του αγρου‖**p**: X σ1424 *pc* *Le* abcir^{1} vg^{4} *S*c | αυξ.—νηθ.] ● ουτε νηθει ουτε υφαινει (∼ υφ. ... νη.): D Cl *L*(a Mcn^{Te}) Te *S*sc — + ουτε υφ.: *L*bc(*om* κοπ. ουδε)ff^{2}(ουδε] ου)ilr^{1} — αυξανουσιν ... κοπιωσιν ... νηθουσιν‖p: 579 F — *txt*: 𝔓$^{45.75}$ *Rpl* *Le*(ου] et florescunt neque) fq(ουδε] ου: z vg) *S*p(αυξ. + α)h *C*,a^{v} *Arm* | ● υμ. + οτι‖p: ℵLX-33-892 1071-1604 **λ**-1278-1582 **ϕ** σM-27-71-1194-1424 A D Ψ **047** *al* Cl *L*vl'r^{1} vg^{10} *S* {*C*s^{2}b} — *txt*: 𝔓$^{45.75}$ *Rpl* *L*a vg' *C*s^{2} *Arm* **28** εν—σημ.] τ. χο. του αγρου ση. ον.‖p: X 28 λ22-(ση. + εν τω αγρω: 118-209 ϕ69)-346(*om* τω) **σ**-7-267-349-1188-1223 D H *Le* *S*c(= 118) *C*a — τ. χο. εν τ. αγ. ση. ον.‖p: *Rpl* *C*s^{1} — τ. χο. ση. εν (+ τω) αγ. ον.‖p: **070**-33 Λ(∼ εν αγ. ον. ση.)-1071-(1604 λ1-131-1582) **ϕ**'⟨124⟩ σM-27-71-692-(990-1194-1207) A Q U W Θ (K Π Ψ) *pc* (*mu*) Cl *L*' *S*' (*C*s^{4}b) — εν αγ. ση. τ. χο. ον.: 𝔓^{45} 700 157 — *txt*: (∼ ση. ον.): 𝔓^{75} ℵBL-579(*om* χο.)-892-(1241 713 1012) | αμφιεννυσιν‖**p**: *Rpl* Cl — *txt*: 𝔓$^{45.75}$ B(-αζει)L-**070** D | ποσω] ου(*om*) πολλω‖p: (579) 1555 (2533) *S*p^{1} — + ουν‖Mt12$_{12}$: 𝔓^{45} *S*c *Aeth* **29** *om* και τι πι.‖22p: σ1424 | και^{2}] η‖p: 𝔓^{75} *Rpl* Ath Cl *L*' *S*h *C*sb^{7}a *Arm* — *txt*: 𝔓^{45} 𝔋⟨892⟩-**070** 1071 σ7-71-267-659-1391-1402-1606 Q 157 *pc* *l*18 *l*19 *l*49 Bas *Le* *S*' *C*b' **30** ∼ πα. γ. ταυ.‖p: 700 **λ** *pc* *l*184 | *om* τ. κοσ.‖p: 579 N W* Ψ *al* *L*l | υμ.—οιδ.] οιδ. γαρ(δε) ο πα. υμ.‖p: D (Cl) *Le* a b[γαρ]cl(fff^{2}iqr^{1} vg^{1} Mcn^{Te} Te) *C*s$^{1:5}$ *Aeth* | τουτ. + απαντων(παν-)‖p: X-(579)-1241 N-28 λ131 **ϕ** Θ 157 (226) *pc* Ath Cl *L*abf vg^{1} *C*b^{1} *Arm* *Aeth* **31** πλ. ζη.] ζη. δε‖p: D Mcn^{Ep} *L*a — ζη. δε πρωτον‖p: 1241 28 λ131 **ϕ** Ath *L*i vg^{2} Mcn$^{Te1:2}$ *C*a *Arm*^{pc} | αυτ.] του θεου‖p: 𝔓^{45} *Rpl* Cl Ep Mcn^{Ep} *L*' Mcn^{Te} Te *S* — *om*: 𝔓^{75} — *txt*: ℵBL-579-892 D*' Ψ Ath *L*ac *C* *Aeth* | αυτ. / θε. + και την δικαιοσυνην αυτου‖p: ϕ983-1689 *S*p^{2} *C*a *Arm*^{pc} *Aeth* | ταυ. + παντα‖p: *Rpl* Ath Ep Mcn^{Ep} *L*'Am *S*ph^{+} *C*s^{2}ba *Arm*^{pc} — *txt*: 𝔓$^{45.75}$ ℵBL-892 Λ λ22-131-1582 ϕ174 σ7-115-954 E H Q S V W Δ Ω **047** *al* *l*18 *l*19 *Le* a Mcn^{Te} *S*sc *C*s^{4} *Arm*' **32** οτι] + εν αυτω‖Mt3$_{17}$ 17$_{5}$ Mk1$_{11}$: D — εν ω‖←: *Le* **33** κλεπται ... εγγιζουσιν(κλεπτουσιν)‖Mt6$_{20}$: 716 (*S*cj) **34** ∼ εσται κ. η κα. υμ.‖Mt6$_{21}$: σ1675(*om* και) D(η μων) 1093 *L*(υμ.$^{1.2}$] σου$^{1.2}$: e l)abfff^{2}r^{1} Au PsAu *S*pj

---

Lk12$_{22\text{-}28}$ *cf.* ETh^{II} 36 (*cf. ad 47.* Mt6$_{25\text{-}30}$ 6$_{25}$)

Lk12$_{31}$ *cf.* Agr (Cl strom.; Eu Ps; Or orat.) (*cf. ad 47.* Mt6$_{33}$)

Lk12$_{33}$ *cf.* ETh^{II} 76 (*cf. ad 44.* Mt6$_{20}$)

(158) **172. Von der Wachsamkeit und Treue.** *Watchfulness and Faithfulness.* **Luk 12 35–46**

239.

[35] Ἔστωσαν ὑμῶν αἱ ὀσφύες περιεζωσμέναι καὶ οἱ λύχνοι καιόμενοι· [36] καὶ ὑμεῖς ὅμοιοι ἀνθρώποις προσδεχομένοις τὸν κύριον ἑαυτῶν, πότε ἀναλύσῃ ἐκ τῶν γάμων, ἵνα ἐλθόντος καὶ κρούσαντος εὐθέως ἀνοίξωσιν αὐτῷ. [37] μακάριοι οἱ δοῦλοι ἐκεῖνοι, οὓς ἐλθὼν ὁ κύριος εὑρήσει γρηγοροῦντας· αμην λέγω ὑμῖν ὅτι περιζώσεται καὶ ἀνακλινεῖ αὐτοὺς καὶ παρελθὼν διακονήσει αὐτοῖς. [38] κἂν ἐν τῇ δευτέρᾳ κἂν ἐν τῇ τρίτῃ φυλακῇ ἔλθῃ καὶ εὕρῃ οὕτως, μακάριοί εἰσιν ἐκεῖνοι. [39] τοῦτο δὲ γινώσκετε, ὅτι εἰ ᾔδει ὁ οἰκοδεσπότης ποίᾳ ὥρᾳ ὁ κλέπτης ἔρχεται, οὐκ ἂν ἀφῆκεν διορυχθῆναι τὸν οἶκον αὐτοῦ. [40] καὶ ὑμεῖς γίνεσθε ἕτοιμοι, ὅτι ᾗ ὥρᾳ οὐ δοκεῖτε ὁ υἱὸς τοῦ ἀνθρώπου ἔρχεται. [41] εἶπεν δὲ ὁ Πέτρος· κύριε, πρὸς ἡμᾶς τὴν παραβολὴν ταύτην λέγεις ἢ καὶ πρὸς πάντας; [42] καὶ εἶπεν ὁ κύριος· τίς ἄρα ἐστὶν ὁ πιστὸς οἰκονόμος ὁ φρόνιμος, ὃν καταστήσει ὁ κύριος ἐπὶ τῆς θεραπείας αὐτοῦ τοῦ διδόναι ἐν καιρῷ τὸ σιτομέτρι-

13 4f.: ... ἐγείρεται ἐκ τοῦ δείπνου καὶ τίθησιν τὰ ἱμάτια, καὶ λαβὼν λέντιον διέζωσεν ἑαυτόν· [5] εἶτα βάλλει ὕδωρ εἰς τὸν νιπτῆρα, καὶ ἤρξατο νίπτειν τοὺς πόδας τῶν μαθητῶν καὶ ἐκμάσσειν τῷ λεντίῳ ᾧ ἦν διεζωσμένος.

cf. v. 46 ↓

236.

24 43–51 (237. 238.): Ἐκεῖνο δὲ γινώσκετε, ὅτι εἰ ᾔδει ὁ οἰκοδεσπότης ποίᾳ φυλακῇ ὁ κλέπτης ἔρχεται, ἐγρηγόρησεν ἂν καὶ οὐκ ἂν εἴασεν διορυγῆναι τὴν οἰκίαν αὐτοῦ. [44] διὰ τοῦτο καὶ ὑμεῖς γίνεσθε ἕτοιμοι, ὅτι ᾗ οὐ δοκεῖτε ὥρᾳ ὁ υἱὸς τοῦ ἀνθρώπου ἔρχεται.

[45] Τίς ἄρα ἐστὶν ὁ πιστὸς δοῦλος καὶ φρόνιμος, ὃν κατέστησεν ὁ κύριος ἐπὶ τῆς οἰκετείας αὐτοῦ τοῦ δοῦναι αὐτοῖς τὴν τροφὴν

cf. 236.

Lk 12,37 αυτοις + και εαν ελθη τη εσπερινη φυλακη και ευρη ουτως ποιουντας, μακαριοι εισιν, οτι ανακλινει αυτους και διακονησει αυτοις‖37a.38 2227: **λ**⟨131⟩-1582 872 D *Le* bcff²ilr¹ vg¹ Ir *Sc* ⟦εσπ.] πρωτη: *Sc* | ευρησει: D | ουτ. ποι.] ουτ.‖38: *L*bff²il vg¹ Ir — ουτ. ποιησει: D *Le* — γρηγορουντας‖37a: *Sc* | *om* μακ.—αυτοις: D *Lc* | μακ. εισ.] *om Le* — + οι δουλοι εκεινοι‖37a: *L*vg¹ | διακ.] παρελθων δ.‖37a: *L*ff²il vg¹ | *om* αυτοις: *Le* [b] *Sc*⟧ **38** *om* 38 *cf. ad* 37: *L*b | *om* ελθη—ουτ. *cf. ad* 37: D *Le* cff²il Ir(*om* φυ.—ουτ.) | ελθη και] ελθων‖43p.37 Mk1336: σ1207(∼ ελθ. εν τ. τρ. φυ.)-1223 *pc* — και ελθων‖←: σ990 A K Π — *om*: *L*vl⟨fqz30⟩r¹ vg¹ | ευρησει‖37.43 Mt2446: 33 σ71-692-1194 P Δ Ω *pc* | ουτ.] ουτ. ποιουντας‖43 Mt←: 213(-ντα) Cr *Lc* (γρηγορουντας: *Sc*) *C*,a | εκει.] οι δουλοι εκ.‖←37: *Rpl* Bas¹(¹ *om* εκ.) Da *L*cfqz vg *S*'j *C*sb⁹a *Δ*'⟨me⟩ — ● *om*: ℵ* *L*vl' Ir — *txt*: 𝔓⁷⁵ ℵᵃBL D 440(ουτοι) Cr *Le Ssc Cb' Geo Δ*a^BE **39** ωρα] φυλακη‖p: 68 *pc Sph Cs*^1:6 | ουκ αν] εγρηγορησεν αν και ουκ αν‖p: *Rpl* Bas Da {*L*' *S*'j *Cs*¹b *Arm*⁰} — ● εγρη. αν και ουκ‖p: ℵᵃB L-579-892-1241 28-1071 **λ**-1278-1582 **φ**⟨124⟩-174-230 σ71-990-1207-1223-1675 K P S W Π Ω 157(*om* αν) *mu* {} — *txt*: 𝔓⁷⁵ ℵ* D(*om* αφη.—αυτου) *Le* i *Ssc Cs*⁵a *Arm* | αφη.] ειασεν‖p: 998 *l*21 | την οικιαν‖p: 892 λ1278 **σ**⟨1424⟩-71-692-1194 Ψ **047** 157 *al l*1642 **40** *om* 40: **λ**'-1582-2193 | υμ. + ουν(δε)‖p Mk 1335p: *Rpl* (D) Bas Da *Ld S*' — *txt*: 𝔓⁷⁵ ℵBL-**070**-579 28 λ131 Q Θ Ψ 157 242 *l*63 *l*1963 *L*' *Ssc C*,a *Arm Aeth* | ωρα] + η‖46p: L D — ημερα η‖←: *Lc* | δοκ.] προσδοκατε‖←: σ954 *Lc Sj* — οιδατε‖Mt2442p: *Ssc Csb*⁹ **41** ∼ λεγ. τ. παρ. ταυ.‖181.9 2019: D *L S*⟨h⟩ (∼ λεγ. πρ. ημ.: *C*,a) *Geo*² *Aeth* **42** οικ.] δουλος‖p: ℵ* 1573 *Lc*(δου. πισ. οικ.) | ο³] και‖p: *Rpl* Eu *L*' *S*(*om* ο φρ.: s) cpht(ᵐ και αυτος) *Cb* — *txt*: 𝔓⁷⁵ **B-070** NΛ-28 σ1424 D E G H K P Q S V W Δ Θ(και ο) Ψ Ω *pc Le* c *Cs* *Aeth* | φρο. + και αγαθος‖1917 Mt2521.23: D(και] ο) 157 *l*60 *l*63 *Le* c *Sc* Ef *Aeth*(∼ αγ. ... πισ. ... φρο.) | κατεστησεν‖p: ℵ*-**070** **φ**124 σ115-990 Ef *Le* bclq vg⟨10⟩ Or *Sp*¹ | θερ.] οικετειας‖p: λ1-131 (οικιας)-1582-2193 **φ**124 *L*(familia), Or | διδ.] δουναι‖p: 1241 N-28-700 σ1424 W Θ Ψ *pc* — διαδουναι: 𝔓⁷⁵(διαδιδοναι) ℵ* λ118(διαδοναι) *Le* — + αυτοις‖p: 28 **φ**⟨983⟩ R 161 *L*' *Ssc C Aeth* — + τοις συνδουλοις‖Mt49: Eu *Le*(+ αυτου)

Lk1235.39p *cf.* ETh^II 103 (*transl.*): *Λέγει Ἰησοῦς· μακάριος ἀνήρ, ὃς οἶδεν ποίῳ μέρει (τῆς νυκτὸς) οἱ λησταὶ εἰσέρχονται, ἵνα ἀναστὰς συναγάγῃ τὴν [...] αὐτοῦ καὶ περιζώσηται τὰς ὀσφύας αὐτοῦ πρὶν ἢ εἰσελθεῖν αὐτούς.*

Lk1239p *cf.* ETh^II 21b.c (*transl.*): ... ᵇ*διὰ τοῦτο λέγω· εἰ οἶδεν ὁ οἰκοδεσπότης ὅτι ἔρχεται ὁ κλέπτης γρηγορήσει πρὶν ἐλθεῖν αὐτὸν καὶ οὐκ ἀφήσει αὐτὸν διορύσσειν τὴν οἰκίαν αὐτοῦ τῆς βασιλείας αὐτοῦ, ἵνα ἄρῃ τὰ σκεύη αὐτοῦ.* ᶜ*ὑμεῖς δὲ γρηγορεῖτε ἐνώπιον τοῦ κόσμου· περιζώσασθε τὰς ὀσφύας ὑμῶν ἐν δυνάμει μεγάλῃ, ἵνα μὴ εὕρωσιν οἱ λησταί, ποίας εἰσέλθωσιν εἰς ὑμᾶς.* ᵈ*γένοιτο* ... (*cf. ad 108.*)

Jo135 *cf.* EN frgm.31 (*cf. ad 250.* Jo135)

ἐν καιρῷ; ⁴⁶ μακάριος ὁ δοῦλος ἐκεῖνος, ὃν ἐλθὼν ὁ κύριος αὐτοῦ εὑρήσει οὕτως ποιοῦντα. ⁴⁷ αμην λέγω ὑμῖν ὅτι ἐπὶ πᾶσιν τοῖς ὑπάρχουσιν αὐτοῦ καταστήσει αὐτόν. ⁴⁸ ἐὰν δὲ εἴπῃ ὁ κακὸς δοῦλος ἐκεῖνος ἐν τῇ καρδίᾳ αὐτοῦ· χρονίζει μου ὁ κύριος ἐλθεῖν, ⁴⁹ καὶ ἄρξηται τύπτειν τοὺς συνδούλους αὐτοῦ, ἐσθίῃ δὲ καὶ πίνῃ μετὰ τῶν μεθυόντων, ⁵⁰ ἥξει ὁ κύριος τοῦ δούλου ἐκείνου ἐν ἡμέρᾳ ᾗ οὐ προσδοκᾷ καὶ ἐν ὥρᾳ ᾗ οὐ γινώσκει, ⁵¹ καὶ διχοτομήσει αὐτόν, καὶ τὸ μέρος αὐτοῦ μετὰ τῶν ὑποκριτῶν θήσει· ἐκεῖ ἔσται ὁ κλαυθμὸς καὶ ὁ βρυγμὸς τῶν ὀδόντων.

³⁷ μακάριοι οἱ δοῦλοι ἐκεῖνοι, οὓς ἐλθὼν ὁ κύριος εὑρήσει γρηγοροῦντας· αμην λέγω ὑμῖν ὅτι ...

ον; ⁴³ μακάριος ὁ δοῦλος ἐκεῖνος, ὃν ἐλθὼν ὁ κύριος αὐτοῦ εὑρήσει ποιοῦντα οὕτως. ⁴⁴ ἀληθῶς λέγω ὑμῖν ὅτι ἐπὶ πᾶσιν τοῖς ὑπάρχουσιν αὐτοῦ καταστήσει αὐτόν. ⁴⁵ ἐὰν δὲ εἴπῃ ὁ δοῦλος ἐκεῖνος ἐν τῇ καρδίᾳ αὐτοῦ· χρονίζει ὁ κύριός μου ἔρχεσθαι, καὶ ἄρξηται τύπτειν τοὺς παῖδας καὶ τὰς παιδίσκας, ἐσθίειν τε καὶ πίνειν καὶ μεθύσκεσθαι, ⁴⁶ ἥξει ὁ κύριος τοῦ δούλου ἐκείνου ἐν ἡμέρᾳ ᾗ οὐ προσδοκᾷ καὶ ἐν ὥρᾳ ᾗ οὐ γινώσκει, καὶ διχοτομήσει αὐτόν, καὶ τὸ μέρος αὐτοῦ μετὰ τῶν ἀπίστων θήσει.

(159)

173. Vom Knechtslohn. *The Servant's Wages.* Luk 12 47–48

⁴⁷ Ἐκεῖνος δὲ ὁ δοῦλος ὁ γνοὺς τὸ θέλημα τοῦ κυρίου αὐτοῦ καὶ μὴ ἑτοιμάσας ἢ ποιήσας πρὸς τὸ θέλημα αὐτοῦ δαρήσεται πολλάς· ⁴⁸ ὁ δὲ μὴ γνούς, ποιήσας δὲ ἄξια πληγῶν, δαρήσεται ὀλίγας. παντὶ δὲ ᾧ ἐδόθη πολύ, πολὺ ζητηθήσεται παρ' αὐτοῦ, καὶ ᾧ παρέθεντο πολύ, περισσότερον αἰτήσουσιν αὐτόν.

(160)

174. Vom Ernst der Zeit. *Signs for this Age.* Luk 12 49–56

206. *73.*

⁴⁹ Πῦρ ἦλθον βαλεῖν ἐπὶ τὴν γῆν, καὶ τί θέλω εἰ ἤδη ἀνήφθη. ⁵⁰ βάπτισμα δὲ ἔχω βαπτισθῆναι, καὶ πῶς συνέχομαι ἕως ὅτου τελεσθῇ. ⁵¹ δοκεῖτε ὅτι εἰρήνην παρεγενόμην δοῦναι ἐν τῇ γῇ; οὐχί, λέγω ὑμῖν, ἀλλ' ἢ διαμερισμόν. ⁵² ἔσονται γὰρ ἀπὸ τοῦ νῦν πέντε ἐν ἑνὶ οἴκῳ διαμεμερισμένοι, τρεῖς ἐπὶ δυσὶν καὶ δύο ἐπὶ τρισὶν ⁵³ διαμερισθήσονται, πατὴρ ἐπὶ υἱῷ καὶ **υἱὸς** ἐπὶ **πατρί,** μήτηρ ἐπὶ θυγατέρα καὶ **θυγάτηρ ἐπὶ τὴν μητέρα,** πενθερὰ ἐπὶ τὴν νύμφην αὐτῆς καὶ **νύμφη ἐπὶ τὴν πενθεράν.** Mch7₆

Lk 12,43 *om* ο δου.‖38: σ1675 *Ss* | *om* αυτ.‖37: 280 *Le* cfff^{2}lz vg⟨1⟩ | ∼ ουτ. ποι.‖p: 𝔓$^{45.75}$ ℌ⟨B⟩X-070 **ϕ**⟨124⟩ σ7-267-659-1391-1402-1606 Ψ 157 *pc l*18 *l*49 *l*184 *l*185 Ir *L Aeth* — *txt*: *Rpl* Eu *S C*,a^{v} **44** αλη.] αμην‖**p**: D *pc Lc Geo* **45** ο^{1} + κακος‖p: X-579-1241 1071 **ϕ** σM-1194 *pc Sp*^{1}h^{Brs} *C*b⟨3⟩ *Aeth* | ∼ μου ο κυ.‖p: ℵ* *et* ^{cb}-579 σ1207 K Π Ψ *al* | ερχ.] ελθειν‖p: ϕ983-1689 σM-27-71-652-1194-1207 K Y Π *al* | παιδ.—παιδισ.] συνδουλους‖**p**: σ692-1194 *pc* | τε] δε‖p: 1071 λ22 σ945 *pc Ld C*b^{5} | και μεθ.] μετα των μεθυοντων‖p: 472 1028 **46** απισ.] υποκριτων‖p: X-579 **λλ**⟨1278⟩ **σ**⟨954⟩ *pc L*30 vg^{1} **47** *om* προς‖Mt7₂₁ 12₅₀ Mk3₃₅: 245 *pc C*p$^{1:3}$ **48** παρ] απ‖8₁₈p 19₂₆p: 579 700 **λ**-22 D R *pc* Cr | απαιτησ.‖6₃₀ 12₂₀: 28 ϕ346 σ945-954 D U *mu* Ant Bas$^{4:5}$ PsBas CAp Ep Iu Mac^{S} **51** δου.] βαλειν‖49 Mt10₃₄: σ1424 1093 *l*49 *l*63 *L*blqr$^{1.2}$30 Mcn^{Te} Te *S*sp Eu *C*s$^{1:6}$b PS *Aeth* | εν τη γη] επι την γην‖←: 𝔓^{45}(της γης) σ1424 157 1093 Or^{1}(^{1} επι γης) *L*'(*om*: e) *S*h^{m} *C*s$^{1:6}$b^{6} | αλλ η] αλλα‖←: 𝔓^{45} 579 700 ϕ69 σ71-692 D Θ *pc* **53** διαμ. + γαρ‖Mt10₃₅: σ945-1223 *pc Sp* | πατρι + αυτου‖←: D *L*⟨b⟩ *S*scp *C*s | πενθεραν + αυτης‖←: *Rpl L S C*sb^{8} *Geo*^{1} — *txt*: 𝔓$^{45.75}$ ℵ*BL-579-892 D 157 Eu *L*Mcn^{Te} *S*Eu *C*b' *Geo*^{2}

Lk12₄₅p *cf.* EN frgm.18 (*cf. ad 240.*)

Lk12₄₉ *cf.* ETh^{II} 10 (*transl.*): *Λέγει Ἰησοῦς· πῦρ ἔβαλον εἰς τὸν κόσμον. καὶ ἰδοὺ τηρῶ αὐτό(ν?), ἕως ἂν ἀνακάιηται.*

Lk12₅₁₋₅₃ *cf.* Agr. Iu. dial 35,3 *et* ETh^{II} 16 (*cf. ad 73.*)

132.

[54] ἔλεγεν δὲ καὶ τοῖς ὄχλοις· ὅταν ἴδητε νεφέλην ἀνατέλλουσαν ἐπὶ δυσμῶν, εὐθέως λέγετε ὅτι ὄμβρος ἔρχεται, καὶ γίνεται οὕτως· [55] καὶ ὅταν νότον πνέοντα, λέγετε ὅτι καύσων ἔσται, καὶ γίνεται. [56] ὑποκριταί, τὸ πρόσωπον τῆς γῆς καὶ τοῦ οὐρανοῦ οἴδατε δοκιμάζειν, τὸν δὲ καιρὸν τοῦτον πῶς οὐ δοκιμάζετε;

(161)

175. Empfehlung rechtzeitigen Ausgleichs. **Luk 12** 57–59 *34.*
Agreement with One's Adversary.

34.

[57] Τί δὲ καὶ ἀφ' ἑαυτῶν οὐ κρίνετε τὸ δίκαιον; [58] ὡς γὰρ ὑπάγεις μετὰ τοῦ ἀντιδίκου σου ἐπ' ἄρχοντα, ἐν τῇ ὁδῷ δὸς ἐργασίαν ἀπηλλάχθαι ἀπ' αὐτοῦ, μήποτε κατασύρῃ σε πρὸς τὸν κριτήν, καὶ ὁ κριτής σε παραδώσει τῷ πράκτορι, καὶ ὁ πράκτωρ σε βαλεῖ εἰς φυλακήν. [59] λέγω σοι, οὐ μὴ ἐξέλθῃς ἐκεῖθεν ἕως καὶ τὸ ἔσχατον λεπτὸν ἀποδῷς.

(162)

176. Bußruf. *The Call to Repentance.* **Luk 13** 1–9

[1] Παρῆσαν δέ τινες ἐν αὐτῷ τῷ καιρῷ ἀπαγγέλλοντες αὐτῷ περὶ τῶν Γαλιλαίων ὧν τὸ αἷμα Πιλᾶτος ἔμιξεν μετὰ τῶν θυσιῶν αὐτῶν. [2] καὶ ἀποκριθεὶς εἶπεν αὐτοῖς· δοκεῖτε ὅτι οἱ Γαλιλαῖοι οὗτοι ἁμαρτωλοὶ παρὰ πάντας τοὺς Γαλιλαίους ἐγένοντο, ὅτι ταῦτα πεπόνθασιν; [3] οὐχί, λέγω ὑμῖν, ἀλλ' ἐὰν μὴ μετανοῆτε, πάντες ὁμοίως ἀπολεῖσθε. [4] ἢ ἐκεῖνοι οἱ δεκαοκτὼ ἐφ' οὓς ἔπεσεν ὁ πύργος ἐν τῷ Σιλωαμ καὶ ἀπέκτεινεν αὐτούς, δοκεῖτε ὅτι αὐτοὶ ὀφειλέται ἐγένοντο παρὰ πάντας τοὺς ἀνθρώπους τοὺς κατοικοῦντας Ιερουσαλημ; [5] οὐχί, λέγω ὑμῖν, ἀλλ' ἐὰν μὴ μετανοήσητε, πάντες ὡσαύτως ἀπολεῖσθε.

[6] ἔλεγεν δὲ ταύτην τὴν παραβολήν. συκῆν εἶχέν τις πεφυτευμένην ἐν τῷ ἀμπελῶνι αὐτοῦ, καὶ ἦλθεν ζητῶν καρπὸν ἐν αὐτῇ καὶ οὐχ εὗρεν. [7] εἶπεν δὲ πρὸς τὸν ἀμπελουργόν· ἰδοὺ τρία ἔτη ἀφ' οὗ ἔρχομαι ζητῶν καρπὸν ἐν τῇ συκῇ ταύτῃ καὶ οὐχ εὑρίσκω· ἔκκοψον αὐτήν· ἱνατί καὶ τὴν γῆν καταργεῖ; [8] ὁ δὲ ἀποκριθεὶς λέγει αὐτῷ· κύριε, ἄφες αὐτὴν καὶ τοῦτο τὸ ἔτος, ἕως ὅτου σκάψω περὶ αὐτὴν καὶ βάλω κόπρια, [9] κἂν μὲν ποιήσῃ καρπὸν εἰς τὸ μέλλον· εἰ δὲ μή γε, ἐκκόψεις αὐτήν.

Lk 12,54 *om* οτι‖Mt16 2f.: *Rpl L*' *S*p' — *txt*: 𝔓$^{45.75}$ ℵBLX-33-579 N-1071 ϕ σ71-659-990-1194-1207 A K U Θ Π Ψ *al* Bas *Le S*scp^{2}h *Arm Aeth* **55** ● *om* οτι‖←: 𝔓^{45} ℵ*L-579-892 1071 D 157 *l*48 *l*63 *L*r^{1} vg^{1} *S*p *Aeth Δ*p — *txt*: 𝔓^{75} *Rpl* Bas *L*' *S*' *Δ*a **56** το + μεν‖Mt16 3: 1604 ϕ983-1689 D 51 *l*184 *L*bq *C*b^{1} | ∼ τ. ουρ. κ. τ. γης‖21 33p Mt5 18: 𝔓$^{45.75}$ ℵ^{c}LX-**070**-33-1241 N-28-1071-1604 λ1278 ϕ174 σ7-1010 D K Π Ψ 157 *pm L*vlr^{1}30 vg^{12} Mcn^{Te} *S*scp^{5} *C Arm Aeth Δ*a l^{AD} — *om* τ. γης κ.‖Mt16 3: ϕ983 **σ**⟨954⟩ — *txt*: *Rpl* Bas *L*vg' *S*' | τον δε κ.] ● τ. κ. δε: 𝔓^{75} B — πλην τ. κ.: 𝔓^{45} D 157 — και τ. κ.: 1038 — τ. κ.: *L S*sc *C*s$^{1:5}$ | *om* τουτ.‖Mt16 3: **047** *C*s$^{1:6}$ | *om* πως‖←: D 1573 *L*vl⟨fqz⟩ *S*sc *C*s$^{1:6}$b^{2} | ου δοκ.] ου δυνασθε δοκιμαζειν‖←: 1573 *L*ff^{2}l *S*s(ου θελετε δ.) — ουκ οιδατε δοκ.‖← 56a: 𝔓^{75} ℵBL-(*om* τον—δοκ.∩?: X)-**070**(δοκιμαζεται! = -ετε)-33-892 Θ *pc L*Mcn^{Te} *S*h^{m} *C*'(b^{3} = X) — *txt*: 𝔓^{45} *Rpl* Bas *L*' *S*' **58** κατασ.] παρασυρη‖p: 1241 348 — παραδω‖p: *Le* cfz30 vg^{10} Or | παραδωσει] παραδω‖p: *Rpl* — *txt* (∼ παρ. σε): 𝔓$^{(45)75}$ ℵB-**070**-(1241 1071) ϕ A (D) Θ (157 Mcn^{Ep}) **59** λεγ.] αμην λ.‖**p**: L 1579 *pc l*62 *L*Or *S*p^{5} | εως] εως αν‖p: **070** Θ — εως ου‖Mt18 30.34: *Rpl* (εως του: σ1194 A) — *txt*: 𝔓$^{45.75}$ ℵBL-892-1241 λ1-131-1582-2193 ϕ124 1038 | *om* και‖**p**: D *pc Le* fff^{2}i vg^{1} Or *S*scp *C* | ∼ αποδ. και—λεπ.‖p: X **σ**⟨1424⟩ D 213 *Le* bc30 vg^{1} *S*scp | το ... λεπ.] τον ... κοδραντην‖**p**: D *L*vlr^{1}30 vg^{2} Mcn^{Te} **13,1** αυτω^{1}] εκεινω *cf.* Mt11 25 12 1 14 1: 579(αυ. τω κ. εκει.) σ1223 *pc Le S C* **6** δε + παλιν‖Mt22 1: ϕ983-1689 — + και‖5 36 6 39: 157 | ∼ τ. παρ. ταυ.‖4 23 15 3 *etc.*: K Y Π *pc S*scp **7** ευρ. + φερε την αξινην‖3 9p: D | ● εκκο. + ουν: 𝔓^{75} LX-**070**-33-579-892 1071-1604 ϕ A Θ Ψ *al L*' *S*h *C Arm Aeth Δ*'⟨me⟩ — *txt*: *Rpl* Bas PsBas Cr Or Pt^{A} *Le S*'(ει μη εκκ. *cf.* 9: s) *Δ*a p **9** αυτην + ταυτα λεγων εφωνει ο εχων ωτα ακουειν ακουετω *cf.* 8 8 *etc.*: Γ *al l*7 *l*13 *l*17 *l*55

Lk12 54-56 *cf.* EN frgm.13 *et* ETh^{II} 91 (*cf. ad 132.* Mt16 2b-3 *et* 1-3)

(163)

177. Heilung der verkrümmten Frau. Luk 13 10–17
The Healing of the Woman with a Spirit of Infirmity.

82.

[10] Ἦν δὲ διδάσκων ἐν μιᾷ τῶν συναγωγῶν ἐν τοῖς σάββασιν. [11] καὶ ἰδοὺ γυνὴ πνεῦμα ἔχουσα ἀσθενείας ἔτη δεκαοκτώ, καὶ ἦν συγκύπτουσα καὶ μὴ δυναμένη ἀνακύψαι εἰς τὸ παντελές. [12] ἰδὼν δὲ αὐτὴν ὁ Ἰησοῦς προσεφώνησεν καὶ εἶπεν αὐτῇ· γύναι, ἀπολέλυσαι τῆς ἀσθενείας σου, [13] καὶ ἐπέθηκεν αὐτῇ τὰς χεῖρας· καὶ παραχρῆμα ἀνωρθώθη, καὶ ἐδόξαζεν τὸν θεόν. [14] ἀποκριθεὶς δὲ ὁ ἀρχισυνάγωγος, ἀγανακτῶν ὅτι τῷ σαββάτῳ ἐθεράπευσεν ὁ Ἰησοῦς, ἔλεγεν τῷ ὄχλῳ ὅτι ἓξ ἡμέραι εἰσὶν ἐν αἷς δεῖ ἐργάζεσθαι· ἐν αὐταῖς οὖν ἐρχόμενοι θεραπεύεσθε καὶ μὴ τῇ ἡμέρᾳ τοῦ σαββάτου. [15] ἀπεκρίθη δὲ αὐτῷ ὁ κύριος καὶ εἶπεν· ὑποκριταί, ἕκαστος ὑμῶν τῷ σαββάτῳ οὐ λύει τὸν βοῦν αὐτοῦ ἢ τὸν ὄνον ἀπὸ τῆς φάτνης καὶ ἀπαγαγὼν ποτίζει; [16] ταύτην δὲ θυγατέρα Αβρααμ οὖσαν, ἣν ἔδησεν ὁ σατανᾶς ἰδοὺ δέκα καὶ ὀκτὼ ἔτη, οὐκ ἔδει λυθῆναι ἀπὸ τοῦ δεσμοῦ τούτου τῇ ἡμέρᾳ τοῦ σαββάτου; [17] καὶ ταῦτα λέγοντος αὐτοῦ κατῃσχύνοντο πάντες οἱ ἀντικείμενοι αὐτῷ, καὶ πᾶς ὁ ὄχλος ἔχαιρεν ἐπὶ πᾶσιν τοῖς ἐνδόξοις τοῖς γινομένοις ὑπ' αὐτοῦ.

(164)

178. Gleichnisse vom Senfkorn und Sauerteig. Luk 13 18–21
The Parables of the Mustard Seed and Leaven.

111. 110.

[18] Ἔλεγεν οὖν· τίνι ὁμοία ἐστὶν ἡ βασιλεία τοῦ θεοῦ, καὶ τίνι ὁμοιώσω αὐτήν; [19] ὁμοία ἐστὶν κόκκῳ σινάπεως, ὃν λαβὼν ἄνθρωπος ἔβαλεν εἰς κῆπον ἑαυτοῦ, καὶ ηὔξησεν καὶ ἐγένετο εἰς δένδρον, καὶ **τὰ πετεινὰ τοῦ οὐρανοῦ κατεσκήνωσεν ἐν τοῖς κλάδοις αὐτοῦ.** Dn 4 12.21 LXX

[20] Καὶ πάλιν εἶπεν· τίνι ὁμοιώσω τὴν βασιλείαν τοῦ θεοῦ; [21] ὁμοία ἐστὶν ζύμῃ, ἣν λαβοῦσα γυνὴ ἔκρυψεν εἰς ἀλεύρου σάτα τρία, ἕως οὗ ἐζυμώθη ὅλον.

Lk 13,10 συν.] ημερων‖8 22: 579 H — ημ. και των συν.: ϕ13-346-543-826 **11** ιδου] ην (+ εκει)‖66 Mk 3 1: W 700 238 *S*s(cp)j | γυνη] γ. ην‖14 2 7 37: *Rpl* (γ. εν ασθενεια ην πνευματος: D) *L*e — γ. τις ην(*om*)‖←: Or (*S*scj) *Aeth* — *txt*: 𝔓45.75 ℵBLX-**070**-579-1241 N-1071 157 *L*' *S*' *C* | ∼ εχ. πν.‖4 33 Mk 9 17: 579 1071 *L*⟨e ar¹⟩ **13** εδο.] εδωκεν δοξαν‖17 18: 1038 **15** υπ.] υποκριτα‖6 42p: 𝔓45 X-579 N-544-1071 **λλ**⟨1278-2193⟩ σ7-267-1207-1223 D V W Ω *al* *l*12 *l*32 *l*80 *l*303 *l*333 *l*1599 *L*fl *S*scp *Geo*² *Δ*a^BE i md n⟨L⟩ p | ∼ ονον … βουν‖14 5: ϕ69 *L*Mcn^Te | την ον.‖Mt 21 7: A V Ψ 86 **17** οχ.] λαος‖7 29 18 43: L-579 G Ψ *pc* *L* *S*s^v cp *C*b *Δ*'⟨p⟩ **18** ομοια—αυτ.] ομοιωσω την βασιλειαν τ. θε.‖20 Mk 4 30: 579 | τ. θε.] των ουρανων‖Mt 13 31: N U *pc* | και] η‖Mk 4 30: N *L*vg¹ *C*s^1:8 | ομοιωσωμεν‖←: σ267-659 60 **19** εις¹ + τον‖Mt 13 31: ℵ^a-579 700 ϕ124-174 D *pc* *C* | *om* εις²‖Mt 13 22: λ1-131-1582-2193 D *L*vl⟨e r²z⟩r¹ Am *S*scp *C*s | ● δεν. + μεγα‖← Mk 4 32: 𝔓45 *Rpl* *L*' *S*' *C*b⁵ — *txt*: 𝔓75 ℵBL-**070**-892-1241 σ990 D *pc* *L*e aa²bff²ilr¹ Am *S*scj *C*' *Arm* | εν τ. κλ.] υπο τους κλαδους‖Mk ←: D *L*ir¹ *C*s^2:9 **20** 20] η τινι ομοια εστιν η βασιλεια του θε. και τινι ομοιωσω αυτην‖18: D 61 *L*a (*om* η¹ *et* αυτην)a²(*om* η¹) | ομ.—θε.] ομοιωθησεται η βασ. τ. θε.‖Mt 25 1 7 24.26: *L*b(?)ff² | θε. + και τινι ομοιωσω αυτην‖18 Mk 4 30: *L*r¹ **21** ● ενεκρυ.‖Mt 13 33: 𝔓75 *Rpl* Ath — *txt*: 𝔓45 BL N-1071 **λ**⟨1⟩-22 ϕ124 σ71-692-954 K U Π **047** 157 *pm* *l*12 *l*18 *l*22 *l*24 *l*32 *l*33 *l*36 *l*44 *l*47 *l*50 *l*303 *l*333 *l*1634 *l*1642 *al*¹⁶ | ολ. + ταυτα παντα ελαλησεν ο Ιησους εν παραβολαις· χωρις παραβολης ουδεν ελαλει αυτοις‖Mt 13 34: 1574

Lk 13 18f. *cf.* ETh^II 20 (*cf. ad 110.*)

Lk 13 20f. *cf.* ETh^II 96 (*cf. ad 111.*)

(165)

179. Ausschließung aus dem Reiche Gottes. **Luk 13** 22–30
Exclusion from the Kingdom of God.

52. 54. 58. 203.

Ps69 Ps1073

22 Καὶ διεπορεύετο κατὰ πόλεις καὶ κώμας διδάσκων καὶ πορείαν ποιούμενος εἰς Ἱεροσόλυμα. 23 Εἶπεν δέ τις αὐτῷ· κύριε, εἰ ὀλίγοι οἱ σῳζόμενοι; ὁ δὲ εἶπεν πρὸς αὐτούς· 24 ἀγωνίζεσθε εἰσελθεῖν διὰ τῆς στενῆς θύρας, ὅτι πολλοί, λέγω ὑμῖν, ζητήσουσιν εἰσελθεῖν καὶ οὐκ ἰσχύσουσιν. 25 ἀφ᾽ οὗ ἂν ἐγερθῇ ὁ οἰκοδεσπότης καὶ ἀποκλείσῃ τὴν θύραν, καὶ ἄρξησθε ἔξω ἑστάναι καὶ κρούειν τὴν θύραν λέγοντες· κύριε, ἄνοιξον ἡμῖν, καὶ ἀποκριθεὶς ἐρεῖ ὑμῖν· οὐκ οἶδα ὑμᾶς πόθεν ἐστέ. 26 τότε ἄρξεσθε λέγειν· ἐφάγομεν ἐνώπιόν σου καὶ ἐπίομεν, καὶ ἐν ταῖς πλατείαις ἡμῶν ἐδίδαξας· 27 καὶ ἐρεῖ· λέγω ὑμῖν, οὐκ οἶδα πόθεν ἐστέ· **ἀπόστητε ἀπ᾽ ἐμοῦ πάντες ἐργάται ἀδικίας.** 28 ἐκεῖ ἔσται ὁ κλαυθμὸς καὶ ὁ βρυγμὸς τῶν ὀδόντων, ὅταν ὄψησθε Αβρααμ καὶ Ισαακ καὶ Ιακωβ καὶ πάντας τοὺς προφήτας ἐν τῇ βασιλείᾳ τοῦ θεοῦ, ὑμᾶς δὲ ἐκβαλλομένους ἔξω. 29 καὶ ἥξουσιν **ἀπὸ ἀνατολῶν καὶ δυσμῶν καὶ** ἀπὸ **βορρᾶ** καὶ νότου, καὶ ἀνακλιθήσονται ἐν τῇ βασιλείᾳ τοῦ θεοῦ. 30 καὶ ἰδοὺ εἰσὶν ἔσχατοι οἳ ἔσονται πρῶτοι, καὶ εἰσὶν πρῶτοι οἳ ἔσονται ἔσχατοι.

25 10–12 (239.): ... καὶ ἐκλείσθη ἡ θύρα. 11 ὕστερον δὲ ἔρχονται καὶ αἱ λοιπαὶ παρθένοι λέγουσαι· κύριε κύριε, ἄνοιξον ἡμῖν. 12 ὁ δὲ ἀποκριθεὶς εἶπεν· αμην λέγω ὑμῖν, οὐκ οἶδα ὑμᾶς.

(166)

180. Abschied von Galiläa. *The Departure from Galilee.* **Luk 13** 31–33

31 Ἐν αὐτῇ τῇ ὥρᾳ προσῆλθάν τινες Φαρισαῖοι λέγοντες αὐτῷ· ἔξελθε καὶ πορεύου ἐντεῦθεν, ὅτι Ἡρῴδης θέλει σε ἀποκτεῖναι. 32 καὶ εἶπεν αὐτοῖς· πορευθέντες εἴπατε τῇ ἀλώπεκι ταύτῃ· ἰδοὺ ἐκβάλλω δαιμόνια καὶ ἰάσεις ἀποτελῶ σήμερον καὶ αὔριον, καὶ τῇ τρίτῃ τελειοῦμαι. 33 πλὴν δεῖ με σήμερον καὶ αὔριον καὶ τῇ ἐχομένῃ πορεύεσθαι, ὅτι οὐκ ἐνδέχεται προφήτην ἀπολέσθαι ἔξω Ιερουσαλημ.

Lk 13,22 κατα + τας‖96: LX-**070** 544-1071 Θ 157 *pc l*1963 *Cs*$^{1:11}$ | πολιν ... κωμην‖81: **λ**-1582-2193 | ∼ κω. ... πολ.‖Mk656: 544 ϕ69 *pc Sscp Δa* **24** θυ.] πυλης‖Mt713: *Rpl* (θυ. στηνης πυλ.: **070**) Bas Mac^{S1} Or^{2} *L*bcfz vg *Cs* — *txt*: 𝔓$^{45.75}$ ℵBL-1241 **λ**⟨1⟩-1582 σ990 D Θ Mac^{S1} Or^{1} *L*vl'r^{1} Luc *C*b | *om* λεγω υμ.‖Mt713: W 213 *S*j *C*b^{1} | ουκ ισ.] ουχ ευρησουσιν‖Mt714: D 1093 **25** εγ.] εισελθη(ελθη)‖Mt2510: **ϕ**'⟨124⟩(69-983) D(∼ ο οικ. εισελ.) PsBas *L*⟨e bq⟩ Am FauM^{Au} *Arm Δ*⟨a me p⟩ | κυ. + κυριε‖p: *Rpl* Bas PsBas *L*vl' Luc *S*'j *C*b^{5} *Δ*a^{BE}p — *txt*: 𝔓^{75} ℵBL-892 157 *L*e aa^{2}clr^{2} vg *Ss C*' *Δ*'⟨me n^{Hr}⟩ | υμ. + οτι‖Mt723: U *S*p **26** λεγ. + κυριε‖25Mt722: 1604 D **27** ● λεγων: 𝔓$^{75c(1?)}$ B-892 σ115-1424 — *om*‖Mt723: ℵ-579 σ1010 *pc L Sp C* | ουκ οιδ.] ουδεποτε ειδον υμης‖←: D *L*e(∼ υμ. ει.) | ● οιδα + υμας‖←25Mt2512: *Rpl* Cr Or *L*'(^{25}∩^{27}εστε: r^{2}) *S*,j *C Aeth* — *txt*: 𝔓^{75} BL-**070**-1241 ϕ346 R 157 *L*bff^{2}il vg^{1} Luc | *om* ποθ. εστε‖Mt723 2512: σ7-692 D *pc* Cr *L*e | αποσ.] αποχωρειτε‖Mt723: σM-71 *pc* | *om* παν.‖Mt723: **047** HM *L*z vg^{1} *S*p | παν. + οι‖←: *Rpl* Cs^{2}b *Arm* — *txt*: 𝔓^{75} ℵBLX-**070**^{v}-892 NΛ-28-1604 σ7-115-267 D E G H R S V W Δ Ψ Cat Cr *Cs*^{7} | εργ. αδ.] εργαζομενοι την ανομιαν(αδικιαν)‖←: 122 (1573) 2533 Or *L*fir$^{1.2}$ *C*PS | αδ.] της αδ.‖←: *Rpl* Cr *C*' — ανομιας(της αν.)‖←: D *l*183 (Ep *C*b^{2}) — *txt*: 𝔓^{75} ℵBL-892 R 21 **29** ηξ. + πολλοι‖Mt811: **λλ**⟨1278⟩ 872 (∼: 251 697) **30** ∼ πρ. ... εσχ. ... εσχ. ... πρ.‖Mt1930 Mk1031: X 213 | εισ.^{1} + οι‖Mt2016: 𝔓^{75} 579 *pc Cs*$^{2:9}$ | *om* οι εσον.^{1}‖Mt1930: 68 1375 *L*l **31** ωρα] ημερα‖2312 2413: *Rpl L S*(εν εκειναις ταις ημεραις: sc)ph^{t} *Cs*^{1}b *Δ*a ad i^{V} l n^{HgHr}(= *S*s)^{s} p — *txt*: 𝔓^{75} ℵB*LX-579-892 700-1071 **λ**-1582 **ϕ** A D R 157 *pc S*h^{m} *Cs*^{6} | θελ.] ζητει‖Jo719f. 837: N D *pc S*sc *Cs*$^{1:6}$ *Geo Δ*a **32** ειπατε] απαγγειλατε‖Mt114p: ϕ124 *L*aa^{2}

Lk1326f. *cf.* EN frgm.6 (*cf. ad 54.* Mt721ff.)

Lk1330 *cf.* ETh^{II} 4 (*cf. ad 203.* Mt1930)

(167)

181. Weissagung über Jerusalem. *The Lament over Jerusalem.*

23 37-39 (225.)

[37] *Ιερουσαλημ Ιερουσαλημ, ἡ ἀποκτείνουσα τοὺς προφήτας καὶ λιθοβολοῦσα τοὺς ἀπεσταλμένους πρὸς αὐτήν, ποσάκις ἠθέλησα ἐπισυναγαγεῖν τὰ τέκνα σου, ὃν τρόπον ὄρνις ἐπισυνάγει τὰ νοσσία αὐτῆς ὑπὸ τὰς πτέρυγας, καὶ οὐκ ἠθελήσατε.* [38] *ἰδοὺ ἀφίεται ὑμῖν ὁ οἶκος ὑμῶν ἔρημος.* [39] *λέγω γὰρ ὑμῖν, οὐ μή με ἴδητε ἀπ' ἄρτι ἕως ἂν εἴπητε·* ***εὐλογημένος ὁ ἐρχόμενος ἐν ὀνόματι κυρίου.***

Luk 13 34-35

[34] Ιερουσαλημ Ιερουσαλημ, ἡ ἀποκτείνουσα τοὺς προφήτας καὶ λιθοβολοῦσα τοὺς ἀπεσταλμένους πρὸς αὐτήν, ποσάκις ἠθέλησα ἐπισυνάξαι τὰ τέκνα σου ὃν τρόπον ὄρνις τὴν ἑαυτῆς νοσσιὰν ὑπὸ τὰς πτέρυγας, καὶ οὐκ ἠθελήσατε. [35] ἰδοὺ ἀφίεται ὑμῖν ὁ οἶκος ὑμῶν. λέγω δὲ ὑμῖν, οὐ μὴ ἴδητέ με ἕως ἥξει ὅτε εἴπητε· **εὐλογημένος ὁ ἐρχόμενος ἐν ὀνόματι κυρίου.**

Ps118 26

(168)

182. Heilung eines Wassersüchtigen. *Healing of a Man with the Dropsy.* Luk 14 1-6

82.

[1] Καὶ ἐγένετο ἐν τῷ ἐλθεῖν αὐτὸν εἰς οἶκόν τινος τῶν ἀρχόντων τῶν Φαρισαίων σαββάτῳ φαγεῖν ἄρτον, καὶ αὐτοὶ ἦσαν παρατηρούμενοι αὐτόν. [2] καὶ ἰδοὺ ἄνθρωπός τις ἦν ὑδρωπικὸς ἔμπροσθεν αὐτοῦ. [3] καὶ ἀποκριθεὶς ὁ Ἰησοῦς εἶπεν πρὸς τοὺς νομικοὺς καὶ Φαρισαίους λέγων· ἔξεστιν τῷ σαββάτῳ θεραπεῦσαι ἢ οὔ; [4] οἱ δὲ ἡσύχασαν. καὶ ἐπιλαβόμενος ἰάσατο αὐτὸν καὶ ἀπέλυσεν. [5] καὶ πρὸς αὐτοὺς εἶπεν· τίνος ὑμῶν υἱὸς ἢ βοῦς εἰς φρέαρ πεσεῖται, καὶ οὐκ εὐθέως ἀνασπάσει αὐτὸν ἐν ἡμέρᾳ τοῦ σαββάτου; [6] καὶ οὐκ ἴσχυσαν ἀνταποκριθῆναι πρὸς ταῦτα.

Lk 13,34 επισυναγαγειν ‖p: 579-892 28-544 λ118(-αξγαγειν!) σ⟨1424⟩-71-692-1194 *pc l*183 | ορν.] επισυναγει ο.‖p: 1579 *S*h(∼) — ο. η επισ.‖p: 998 *Ss*ᵛcp *Cs* | τα ... νοσσια‖p: 1241 Λ λ'(τ. ν. αυτης: 131) σM-71-692 A D(= 131) K Π 157 *al Lvl*⟨abz⟩r¹ *S Cs* **35** υμων + ερημος‖p: *Rpl* Ep¹ *Lvl*'r¹30 vg⁹ *S*' *C*b⁶ — *txt*: 𝔓45.75 ℵBL-579 Λ λ1-118ˢ-209-1582 ϕ69-124-174-230-788 σ71-990-1207-1223 A K R S V W Y Γ Π Ω **047** Ep² *Le* ff²iz vg' *Ss C*' *Arm* | δε] γαρ‖p: 1604 *pc Le* a *Sp Δ*l^FG md me n — ● *om*: 𝔓45 ℵ*L 1071 *pc L*bcff²il *Ss*(και λεγω)c *C*sb⁴ | ● υμιν² + οτι: *Rpl L*afr²z vg' *S* — *txt*: 𝔓45.75 ℵBL **λ**-1582-2193 D H R W Θ *pc Lvl*'r¹30 vg¹ | ∼ με ιδ.‖p: 𝔓45.75 *Rpl* Eu *Le* bcqr¹·² vg² — *txt*: ℵB 1071 **ϕ**⟨124-346⟩ σM-692-990 A K R W Θ Π *mu* Ep *L*' | ιδ. / με + απ αρτι‖p: 1241 Δ Θ *pc Sp*¹ *Cs*³:⁶b⟨³⟩ *Geo Aeth* | εως + αν‖p: 𝔓45 *Rpl* — *txt*: 𝔓75 BL-892 λ2193 D K R Π Mcn | ηξει οτε] *om*‖p: 𝔓45.75 ℵBLX-892-1241 1071-1604 **ϕ**⟨124-346⟩ σM-1010 R Θ 157 *pc Le* i vg¹ *Sp C*,f — οτε‖p: K Π *al Aeth* — ηξει η ημερα οτε: *L*abf *Sch*⁻ — *txt*: *Rpl* (οταν: 579 251; οτι: H *l*211) Mcn *L*' *Ss* **14,2** *om* τις‖Mt12 10: **λ**-1582 ϕ124-983 D 472(∼ ην αν.) *L*bcff²ilq30 vg¹ *Ss Δ*a | *om* ην‖← 13 11: Λ *pc Sj* **3** *om* λεγ.‖69: D *l*15 *Le* a[b]fqr¹ *S*scpj *Cs*²:¹⁰ *Δ*a i md n⟨L⟩p | εξ.] ει εξ.‖Mt←: 𝔓45 *Rpl L*' *Cs*¹⁰b⁴ *Arm Δ*l {me} — *txt*: 𝔓75 ℵBL-892-1241 D Θ Ψ 157 *pc l*15 Cat^Ox *Lf* vg² *Sj Cs*¹b' *Aeth Δ*'{} | τω σα.] εν τ. σ.‖67: λ2193 *pc Lr*² — τοις(εν τ.) σαββασιν‖4 31 13 10 Mt← Mk3 2 23: **λ**-1582-(2193 872) *pc l*48 *l*49 *La* vg³ *C*b¹ | θεραπευειν‖Mt←: *Rpl* Cr — *txt*: 𝔓45.75 𝔥⟨33⟩ 1604 **λλ**⟨22-1278⟩ ϕ124 D W Θ 157 *pc* Cat^Ox | *om* η ου‖Mt←: 𝔓45 *Rpl L*' *Ssp Δ*⟨me⟩ — *txt*: 𝔓75 𝔥[33] 1071 **λλ**⟨22-1278⟩ **ϕ**-*l*547 D Θ *pc* Cat^Ox Cr *Le* bfqr¹·² vg⁴ *Sch*⁺j *C*,f *Aeth* **5** ● και¹ + αποκριθεις(+ ο Ιησους)‖3 13 15: *Rpl* (X λ1278 W) *Lf*z vg *S*hj *Δ*⟨me⟩ — *txt*: 𝔓45.75 ℵ^ca BL-892-1241 544-1604 **λλ**'⟨2193⟩ ϕ69-124-788-*l*547 D K Y Π *al Lvl*'r¹ *S*' *C*,f *Δ*a i^V n^Hr p | τινος + εξ‖Mt12 11: D | υι.] προβατον‖←: D — ● ονος(∼ βους η ον.)‖13 15: 𝔥'[33]⟨B⟩(ορος!: 892)X 1071-1604 **λ**-1582 **ϕ**-174-*l*547 K Y Π Ψ 157 *mu l*333 *L*' *S*(s)j *C*bf *Arm Aeth Δ*'(i^V me) — ον. υι.‖←: Θ — *txt*: 𝔓45(η υι.)75 *Rpl* (ο υι.: 700 A S U; ∼ βους η υι.: 544; + υμων: 1344 *l*184 *l*1579; + η ον.: 477 2174) Cat^Ox Cr *Le* fq *Sc* (= 477)ph *Cs Δ*a p(= 544) | εμπεσ.‖Mt←: *Rpl* (-σει: Θ 213) — *txt*: 𝔓45.75 𝔥[33]⟨1241⟩ **λλ**⟨22-2193⟩-118ˢ ϕ-*l*547 σ990-1207 A W Π 157 *al* | και²—σα.] τη ημ. τ. σα. και²—αυτον‖←: D (*Le* a) *S*scp | *om* και²‖←: **ϕ**⟨124⟩-*l*547 *Le* a *Geo*¹ | αυτον] αυτο‖←: A | εν] τη‖13 14.16: LX-892-1241 **ϕ** σ267-990-1207 A (D) K Δ Θ Π *al L*'(*om* εν—σαβ.: i) — εν τη‖4 16: *Rpl* {} — *txt*: 𝔓45.75 ℵB λ131-1582 {*Le* afqr¹}

(169)

183. Gastmahlsreden. *Teaching on Humility.* Luk 14 7–14

[7] Ἔλεγεν δὲ πρὸς τοὺς κεκλημένους παραβολήν, ἐπέχων πῶς τὰς πρωτοκλισίας ἐξελέγοντο, λέγων πρὸς αὐτούς· [8] ὅταν κληθῇς ὑπό τινος εἰς γάμους, μὴ κατακλιθῇς εἰς τὴν πρωτοκλισίαν, μήποτε ἐντιμότερός σου ᾖ κεκλημένος ὑπ' αὐτοῦ, [9] καὶ ἐλθὼν ὁ σὲ καὶ αὐτὸν καλέσας ἐρεῖ σοι· δὸς τούτῳ τόπον, καὶ τότε ἄρξῃ μετὰ αἰσχύνης τὸν ἔσχατον τόπον κατέχειν. [10] ἀλλ' ὅταν κληθῇς, πορευθεὶς ἀνάπεσε εἰς τὸν ἔσχατον τόπον, ἵνα ὅταν ἔλθῃ ὁ κεκληκώς σε ἐρεῖ σοι· φίλε, προσανάβηθι ἀνώτερον· τότε ἔσται σοι δόξα ἐνώπιον πάντων τῶν συνανακειμένων σοι. [11] ὅτι πᾶς ὁ ὑψῶν ἑαυτὸν ταπεινωθήσεται, καὶ ὁ ταπεινῶν ἑαυτὸν ὑψωθήσεται.

18 4 (143.): ὅστις οὖν ταπεινώσει ἑαυτὸν ὡς τὸ παιδίον τοῦτο, οὗτός ἐστιν ὁ μείζων ἐν τῇ βασιλείᾳ τῶν οὐρανῶν.

23 12 (224.): ὅστις δὲ ὑψώσει ἑαυτὸν ταπεινωθήσεται, καὶ ὅστις ταπεινώσει ἑαυτὸν ὑψωθήσεται.

18 14 (200.): ... ὅτι πᾶς ὁ ὑψῶν ἑαυτὸν ταπεινωθήσεται, ὁ δὲ ταπεινῶν ἑαυτὸν ὑψωθήσεται.

[12] ἔλεγεν δὲ καὶ τῷ κεκληκότι αὐτόν· ὅταν ποιῇς ἄριστον ἢ δεῖπνον, μὴ φώνει τοὺς φίλους σου μηδὲ τοὺς ἀδελφούς σου μηδὲ τοὺς συγγενεῖς σου μηδὲ γείτονας πλουσίους, μήποτε καὶ αὐτοὶ ἀντικαλέσωσίν σε καὶ γένηται ἀνταπόδομά σοι. [13] ἀλλ' ὅταν δοχὴν ποιῇς, κάλει πτωχούς, ἀναπήρους, χωλούς, τυφλούς· [14] καὶ μακάριος ἔσῃ, ὅτι οὐκ ἔχουσιν ἀνταποδοῦναί σοι· ἀνταποδοθήσεται γάρ σοι ἐν τῇ ἀναστάσει τῶν δικαίων.

(170)

184. Das Gleichnis vom Abendmahl. *The Parable of the Great Supper.*

22 1–10 (219.)

[1] Καὶ ἀποκριθεὶς ὁ Ἰησοῦς πάλιν εἶπεν ἐν παραβολαῖς αὐτοῖς λέγων· [2] ὡμοιώθη ἡ βασιλεία τῶν οὐρανῶν ἀνθρώπῳ βασιλεῖ, ὅστις ἐποίησεν γάμους τῷ υἱῷ αὐτοῦ. [3] καὶ ἀπέ-

Luk 14 15–24

[15] Ἀκούσας δέ τις τῶν συνανακειμένων ταῦτα εἶπεν αὐτῷ· μακάριος ὅστις φάγεται ἄρτον ἐν τῇ βασιλείᾳ τοῦ θεοῦ. [16] ὁ δὲ εἶπεν αὐτῷ· ἄνθρωπός τις ἐποίει δεῖπνον μέγα, καὶ ἐκάλεσεν πολλούς, [17] καὶ ἀπέ-

Lk 14,7 δε + και‖5 36 6 39: D 660 Laff^{2}r$^{1.2}$z vg⟨9⟩ *Arm*(*om* δε) | πρωτοκαδεδριας‖20 46p: **047** 1093 **8** γαμον‖Jo2 2: 1604 D *l*17 *C*f | η—αυτου] ηξει *cf. ad 206.* Mt20 28: D *S*j(+ κεκ. υπ αυ.) **11** και ο] ο δε‖Mt4: X-579 1604 λ118^{s} ϕ69-*l*547 Θ *pc l*32 *l*183 *l*184 *l*1642 *C*s$^{2:12}$ **13** ∼ τυφ. χω.‖14 21: 1071 *L*e i vg^{3} Cp (∼ τυφ. χω. αν.: *S*sc) **15** οστις] ος‖7 23p: *Rpl* PsBas Cl Ep Eu^{2} — *txt*: 𝔓^{75} ℵ^{a}BLX-579 1071-1604 λ-1582 ϕ P R *pc l*48 Cat^{Ox} Eu^{5} | αρτ.] ● αριστον‖14 12 Mt4: *Rpl* PsBas^{1} Cat^{Ox} Cr Or^{1} *S*sc *Arm* — *txt*: 𝔓^{75} 𝔋[33]X NΛ-1071-1604 λ ϕ174 A D E G H K P R Δ Θ Ψ 157 *pc* PsBas^{1} Cl Ep Eu *L*,Or *S*' *C* *Δ*⟨me⟩ | τ. θ.] των ουρανων‖Mt8 11: 579 ϕ69-788 *pc* Cat^{Ox} Ep Eu — *om*: *L*r^{1v} **16** αυτοις‖p: U *L*c *C*b^{1} | *om* τις‖20 9 Mk12 1 Mt21 28: P *S*j | εποιησεν‖pJo12 2 Mk6 21: *Rpl* PsBas Cl Eu Or^{1} *L*⟨vg^{1}⟩ Mcn^{Te} Te *S*'j — *txt*: 𝔓^{75} ℵB λ⟨131⟩-1582-2193 R *S*sc Or^{1}

184. cf. ETh^{II} 64 (*transl.*): *Λέγει Ἰησοῦς· ἀνθρώπῳ τινὶ ξένοι ἦσαν· καὶ ἑτοιμάσας τὸ δεῖπνον ἀπέστειλεν τὸν δοῦλον αὐτοῦ ἵνα καλέσῃ τοὺς ξένους. ἐλθὼν πρὸς τὸν πρῶτον εἶπεν αὐτῷ· ὁ κύριός μου καλεῖ σε. εἶπεν· ἀργύρια ἐδάνεισα ἐμπόροις, οἳ ἐλεύσονται τῆς ἑσπέρας· πορεύομαι ἐπιτάσσειν αὐτοῖς, παραιτοῦμαι περὶ τοῦ δείπνου. ἐλθὼν πρὸς ἕτερον εἶπεν αὐτῷ· ὁ κύριός μου ἐκάλεσέν σε. εἶπεν αὐτῷ· οἰκίαν ἠγόρασα καὶ αἰτοῦσίν με (ἐλθεῖν) ἐν μιᾷ τῶν ἡμερῶν· οὐκ εὐκαιρῶ. ἐρχόμενος πρὸς ἕτερον εἶπεν αὐτῷ· ὁ κύριός μου καλεῖ σε. εἶπεν αὐτῷ· ὁ φίλος μου γαμήσει καὶ ἐγὼ δεῖπνον ποιήσω· οὐ δυνήσομαι ἐλθεῖν, παραιτοῦμαι περὶ τοῦ δείπνου. ἐλθὼν πρὸς ἕτερον εἶπεν αὐτῷ· ὁ κύριός μου καλεῖ σε. εἶπεν αὐτῷ· χωρίον ἠγόρασα (καὶ) πορεύομαι λαβεῖν τὸν μισθόν· οὐ δυνήσομαι ἐλθεῖν, παραιτοῦμαι. παραγενόμενος ὁ δοῦλος ἀπήγγειλεν τῷ κυρίῳ αὐτοῦ· οὓς ἐκάλεσας εἰς τὸ δεῖπνον παρῃτήσαντο. εἶπεν ὁ κύριος τῷ δούλῳ αὐτοῦ· ἔξελθε εἰς τὰς ὁδοὺς (καὶ) ὅσους ἐὰν εὕρῃς εἰσάγαγε ἵνα δειπνήσωσιν. οἱ ἀγοράζοντες καὶ οἱ ἔμποροι οὐ μὴ [εἰσέλθωσιν] εἰς τοὺς τόπους τοῦ πατρός μου.*

στειλεν τοὺς δούλους αὐτοῦ καλέσαι τοὺς κεκλημένους εἰς τοὺς γάμους, καὶ οὐκ ἤθελον ἐλθεῖν. [4] πάλιν ἀπέστειλεν ἄλλους δούλους λέγων· εἴπατε τοῖς κεκλημένοις· ἰδοὺ τὸ ἄριστόν μου ἡτοίμακα, οἱ ταῦροί μου καὶ τὰ σιτιστὰ τεθυμένα, καὶ πάντα ἕτοιμα· δεῦτε εἰς τοὺς γάμους. [5] οἱ δὲ ἀμελήσαντες ἀπῆλθον, ὃς μὲν εἰς τὸν ἴδιον ἀγρόν,

ὃς δὲ ἐπὶ τὴν ἐμπορίαν αὐτοῦ·

[6] οἱ δὲ λοιποὶ κρατήσαντες τοὺς δούλους αὐτοῦ ὕβρισαν καὶ ἀπέκτειναν.

[7] ὁ δὲ βασιλεὺς ὠργίσθη, καὶ πέμψας τὰ στρατεύματα αὐτοῦ ἀπώλεσεν τοὺς φονεῖς ἐκείνους καὶ τὴν πόλιν αὐτῶν ἐνέπρησεν. [8] τότε λέγει τοῖς δούλοις αὐτοῦ· ὁ μὲν γάμος ἕτοιμός ἐστιν, οἱ δὲ κεκλημένοι οὐκ ἦσαν ἄξιοι· [9] πορεύεσθε οὖν ἐπὶ τὰς διεξόδους τῶν ὁδῶν, καὶ ὅσους ἐὰν εὕρητε καλέσατε εἰς τοὺς γάμους.

[10] καὶ ἐξελθόντες οἱ δοῦλοι ἐκεῖνοι εἰς τὰς ὁδοὺς συνήγαγον πάντας οὓς εὗρον, πονηρούς τε καὶ ἀγαθούς· καὶ ἐπλήσθη ὁ νυμφὼν ἀνακειμένων.

στειλεν τὸν δοῦλον αὐτοῦ τῇ ὥρᾳ τοῦ δείπνου εἰπεῖν τοῖς κεκλημένοις· ἔρχεσθε,

ὅτι ἤδη ἕτοιμά εἰσιν. [18] καὶ ἤρξαντο ἀπὸ μιᾶς πάντες παραιτεῖσθαι. ὁ πρῶτος εἶπεν αὐτῷ· ἀγρὸν ἠγόρασα, καὶ ἔχω ἀνάγκην ἐξελθὼν ἰδεῖν αὐτόν· ἐρωτῶ σε, ἔχε με παρῃτημένον. [19] καὶ ἕτερος εἶπεν· ζεύγη βοῶν ἠγόρασα πέντε, καὶ πορεύομαι δοκιμάσαι αὐτά· ἐρωτῶ σε, ἔχε με παρῃτημένον. [20] καὶ ἕτερος εἶπεν· γυναῖκα ἔγημα, καὶ διὰ τοῦτο οὐ δύναμαι ἐλθεῖν.

[21] καὶ παραγενόμενος ὁ δοῦλος ἀπήγγειλεν τῷ κυρίῳ αὐτοῦ ταῦτα. τότε ὀργισθεὶς ὁ οἰκοδεσπότης

εἶπεν τῷ δούλῳ αὐτοῦ·

ἔξελθε ταχέως εἰς τὰς πλατείας καὶ ῥύμας τῆς πόλεως, καὶ τοὺς πτωχοὺς καὶ ἀναπήρους καὶ τυφλοὺς καὶ χωλοὺς εἰσάγαγε ὧδε. [22] καὶ εἶπεν ὁ δοῦλος· κύριε, γέγονεν ὃ ἐπέταξας, καὶ ἔτι τόπος ἐστίν. [23] καὶ εἶπεν ὁ κύριος πρὸς τὸν δοῦλον· ἔξελθε

εἰς τὰς ὁδοὺς καὶ φραγμοὺς καὶ ἀνάγκασον εἰσελθεῖν, ἵνα γεμισθῇ μου ὁ οἶκος· [24] λέγω γὰρ ὑμῖν ὅτι οὐδεὶς τῶν ἀνδρῶν ἐκείνων τῶν κεκλημένων γεύσεταί μου τοῦ δείπνου.

(171) | **74.** |

185. Bedingungen der Jüngerschaft. *The Cost of Discipleship.* Luk 14 25–35

[25] Συνεπορεύοντο δὲ αὐτῷ ὄχλοι πολλοί, καὶ στραφεὶς εἶπεν πρὸς αὐτούς· [26] εἴ τις ἔρχεται πρός με καὶ οὐ μισεῖ τὸν πατέρα αὐτοῦ καὶ τὴν μητέρα καὶ τὴν γυναῖκα καὶ τὰ τέκνα καὶ τοὺς ἀδελφοὺς καὶ τὰς ἀδελφάς,

Lk 14,17 τους δουλους ‖ p: P 472 *C*b^{1} *Arm*⟨pc⟩ | ετ. εισ.] παντα ετ. εστιν ‖ p: D' *Le* a *S*scp(+ υμιν)j *C* — ετ. εστ. πα. ‖ p: *Rpl* (εισιν: ℵ^{a} σ1223) PsBas *L*' *S*h *Arm* — ετ. εστ.: 𝔓^{45} B {} — *txt*: 𝔓^{75} ℵ**et*^{c}L-579 R Θ {*L*bcff^{2}ilq} **21** ∼ χω. κ. τυ. ‖ 14 13: *Rpl* *Le* 30 *S*(∼ χω. κ. αναπ. κ. τυ.: sc)p *Δ*a p — τους τυ.: **φ**' A *S*j *C*b^{1} *Δ*n^{L} — *txt*: 𝔓$^{45.75}$ 𝔥 1071-1604 λ1278 φ124-346(*prm* τους) σM-71-115-692-990-1207 D F K P U W Θ Π 157 *pm* *l*32 PsBas Eu *L*'Au *S*h *C*' *Geo* *Aeth* *Δ*'⟨i^{V} me⟩ **22** o^{2}] ως ‖ Mt 1242 16: *Rpl* (καθως: Λ) PsBas *L*' *S*'j^{a} — *txt*: 𝔓$^{45.75}$ ℵBL-579 **λ**-1582-2193 D R Θ Ψ *Le* *S*sch^{m}j^{bc} *C* *Arm* | προσεταξας ‖ ← 5 14p: 579 28-544 **λ** **φ**-*l*547 *pc* **24** 24 + πολλοι γαρ εισιν κλητοι ολιγοι δε εκλεκτοι ‖ Mt 22 14: *Rpl* (γαρ εισ.] δε εσονται: X 213; ολ. δε] ολ. γαρ: 579 — και ολ.: 28) *S*j^{a} *Geo* *Aeth* — *txt*: 𝔓$^{45.75}$ ℵBL N-1604 **λ**-22 σM-71-659-692-990-1207-1223-1675 A D E F K P R S U V W Δ Θ Π Ψ **047** 157 *mu* *L* *S*,j^{bc} *C* *Aeth* **26** *om* αυτ. ‖ Mt 10 37: 579 Cl Or *Le* Or | *om* και^{3}—αδελφας ‖ ←: 477

Lk 14 26f. *cf.* ETh^{II} 55. 101 (*cf.* *ad 74.* Mt 10 37f.)

137.		ἔτι δὲ καὶ τὴν ἑαυτοῦ ψυχήν, οὐ δύναται εἶναί μου μαθητής. [27] ὅστις οὐ βαστάζει τὸν σταυρὸν ἑαυτοῦ καὶ ἔρχεται ὀπίσω μου, οὐ δύναται εἶναί μου μαθητής. [28] τίς γὰρ ἐξ ὑμῶν θέλων πύργον οἰκοδομῆσαι οὐχὶ πρῶτον καθίσας ψηφίζει τὴν δαπάνην, εἰ ἔχει εἰς ἀπαρτισμόν; [29] ἵνα μήποτε θέντος αὐτοῦ θεμέλιον καὶ μὴ ἰσχύοντος ἐκτελέσαι πάντες οἱ θεωροῦντες ἄρξωνται αὐτῷ ἐμπαίζειν [30] λέγοντες ὅτι οὗτος ὁ ἄνθρωπος ἤρξατο οἰκοδομεῖν καὶ οὐκ ἴσχυσεν ἐκτελέσαι. [31] ἢ τίς βασιλεὺς πορευόμενος ἑτέρῳ βασιλεῖ συμβαλεῖν εἰς πόλεμον οὐχὶ καθίσας πρῶτον βουλεύσεται εἰ δυνατός ἐστιν ἐν δέκα χιλιάσιν ὑπαντῆσαι τῷ μετὰ εἴκοσι χιλιάδων ἐρχομένῳ ἐπ' αὐτόν; [32] εἰ δὲ μή γε, ἔτι αὐτοῦ πόρρω ὄντος πρεσβείαν ἀποστείλας ἐρωτᾷ τὰ πρὸς εἰρήνην. [33] οὕτως οὖν πᾶς ἐξ ὑμῶν ὃς οὐκ ἀποτάσσεται πᾶσι τοῖς ἑαυτοῦ ὑπάρχουσιν οὐ δύναται εἶναί
32.		μου μαθητής. [34] καλὸν οὖν τὸ ἅλας· ἐὰν δὲ καὶ τὸ ἅλας μωρανθῇ, ἐν τίνι ἀρτυθήσεται; [35] οὔτε εἰς γῆν οὔτε εἰς κοπρίαν εὔθετόν ἐστιν· ἔξω βάλλουσιν αὐτό. ὁ ἔχων ὦτα ἀκούειν ἀκουέτω.

(172) *186.* Die Gleichnisse vom verlorenen Schaf und vom verlorenen Groschen. Luk 15 1–10 [147.]
The Lost Sheep and the Lost Coin.

65.	147.	[1] Ἦσαν δὲ αὐτῷ ἐγγίζοντες πάντες οἱ τελῶναι καὶ οἱ ἁμαρτωλοὶ ἀκούειν αὐτοῦ. [2] καὶ διεγόγγυζον οἵ τε Φαρισαῖοι καὶ οἱ γραμματεῖς λέγοντες· ὅ τι οὗτος ἁμαρτωλοὺς προσδέχεται καὶ συνεσθίει αὐτοῖς; [3] εἶπεν δὲ πρὸς αὐτοὺς τὴν παραβολὴν ταύτην λέγων· [4] τίς ἄνθρωπος ἐξ ὑμῶν ἔχων ἑκατὸν πρόβατα καὶ ἀπολέσας ἐξ αὐτῶν ἓν οὐ καταλείπει τὰ ἐνενήκοντα ἐννέα ἐν τῇ ἐρήμῳ καὶ πορεύεται ἐπὶ τὸ ἀπολωλὸς ἕως εὕρῃ αὐτό; [5] καὶ εὑρὼν ἐπιτίθησιν ἐπὶ τοὺς ὤμους αὐτοῦ χαίρων, [6] καὶ ἐλθὼν εἰς τὸν οἶκον συγκαλεῖ τοὺς φίλους καὶ τοὺς γείτονας, λέγων αὐτοῖς· συγχάρητέ μοι, ὅτι εὗρον τὸ πρόβατόν μου τὸ ἀπολωλός. [7] λέγω ὑμῖν ὅτι

Lk 14,26 ● ~ ψυ. εαυτ.(αυτ.)‖(9$_{24}$ 17$_{33}$ Mt10$_{39}$ 16$_{25}$): 𝔓^{75} ℵB-579-(1241) ϕ69-788 — *txt*: 𝔓^{45} *Rpl* Bas PsBas Ddy Or **27** οστ.] και ος‖Mt10$_{38}$: D 716 — και οστ.‖←: *Rpl* (*om* 27⌒: 544 ϕ69-788 σM-71-659-692 R Γ *pc*) *L*'(και ει: e; και ει τις: r^{1} vg^{1}; = 544: vg^{1}) Hil(= e) *S*(s = 544)cph *C*s — οστ. γαρ: 1604 157 *Arm* — ος‖←: 713 Ep Ir — *txt*: 𝔓$^{45.75}$ ℵ*B*(ου] ουν, ^{c}ουν ου)-579 σ1675(ει τις) *C*b'(^{1} = 544) *Aeth* | βαστ.] λαμβανει‖Mt←: 270 *pc* HM | ερχ.] ακολουθει‖←9$_{23}$p: σ71-990-1207 K Π *al* PsBas Ir(οπ. μου] μοι) *L*vg^{1} *C* **34** *om* καλ.—αλας‖Mt5$_{13}$: Γ | *om* ουν‖Mk9$_{50}$: *Rpl* *L* *S* *C*s$^{5:6}$ b^{4} — *txt*: 𝔓^{75} ℌ[33]X 1604 **ϕ** Θ 161 Cat^{Ox} *C*b' *Geo* | *om* και‖Mt← Mk←: 𝔓^{75} *Rpl* *L*efff^{2}ir^{1} vg^{2} *S*'p^{1} *C*s$^{5:6}$ PS(*om* δε και) *Arm* — *txt*: ℵBLX-579-1241 N-1604 D Θ Ψ 157 *pc* *L*' *S*p' | τινι + αυτου(< αυτο?)‖Mk←: Θ | αρτ.] αρτυσεται(= -τε)‖←: Θ 4 — αλισθησεται‖Mt← Mk9$_{49}$: 33 **λ**-2193 *pc* *L*d *S*scp *C* **15,1** *om* οι^{2}‖5$_{30}$p: λ131 σ7-115-990 D U *al* *l*12 *l*18 *l*49 *l*80 *l*184 *l*303 *l*333 *l*1599 **2** διεγ.] εγογγ.‖5$_{30}$: λ1582-2193 Ψ | *om* τε‖←: *Rpl* Bas — *txt*: 𝔓^{75} ℵBL-892-1241 D Θ *pc* | ~ γρα. ... Φ. *cf.* Mt23$_{2.13}$ *etc.* Mk2$_{16}$: 1071 **ϕ**⟨983⟩-230 σ115 A Ψ *pc* Bas *L*vg^{1} *S*scp *Δ*a p | ο τι] δια τι‖←Mk9$_{10}$: 1071 *L*ar^{1} *Arm* | *om* ουτος‖Mk2$_{16}$: ℵ* ϕ983-1689 **3** *om* λεγ.‖18$_{9}$ 20$_{9}$: 28 **ϕ**⟨124-346-983⟩ σ1194 D Θ *pc* *L*e b *S*scp *Δ*a i md n^{HgS} **4** ~ ανθ. τις *cf.* 10$_{30}$ 14$_{16}$ *etc.*: 1200 *L*δ(*om* τις) | ~ εξ υμ. αν.‖Mt7$_{9}$ 12$_{11}$: 579-892 *pc* Meth *L*⟨e⟩ *S*p | *om* ανθ.‖11$_{5}$ 12$_{25}$p 14$_{28}$ 17$_{7}$: 348 *pc* *S*sc *Geo*^{A} | εχων] ος εξει(εχει)‖11$_{5}$ Mt12$_{11}$: D (Meth *L*⟨e⟩; *et om* ος: c vg^{1}) | και απολ.] καν πλανηθη(απολεση)‖p (Mt12$_{11}$): (Meth) *L*vl'(e ac) | ~ εν εξ αυ.‖**p**: *Rpl* Meth *L*'(*om*: i) PsCp — *txt*: 𝔓^{75} ℵB-579 **λ**-1582-2193 **ϕ**⟨124-983⟩ D' W 157 *pc* *L*e | ουχι‖**p**8: L **ϕ**-230 *L*⟨e bqr^{1}⟩ | ου κατ.] ουκ αφιησι‖p: D Meth | εν τ. ερ.] επι τοις ορεσιν‖p: Meth *L*(+ εν τ. ερ.: cff^{2})l | πορ.—απολ.] απελθων το απολ. ζητει‖p: D Meth(πορευθεις επι το απ. ζη.) *L*e af PsCp *S*scp *C*sb$^{\langle 4\rangle}$ | *om* εως—αυτο‖**p**: 1574 *L*PsCp | ● εως + ου‖8: ℵ-579 NΛ-1071-1604 **λλ**⟨2193⟩ **ϕ**-174-230 σM-990-1223 A U Y Δ Ψ *pm* *l*12 *l*48 *l*49 *l*80 *l*303 *l*333 *l*1599 *l*1634 Bas — + αν: 1093 — *txt*: 𝔓^{75} *Rpl* Meth **5** ευρ. + αυτο‖p: 157 *L*⟨e ac⟩ *S*scp *C* **7** οτι + χαιρει επι(επ) αυτω μαλλον(+ η επι τοις ενενηκοντα εννεα τοις μη πεπλανωμενοις)‖p: (544) 157 *pc* *S*h

---

Lk14$_{35}$ *cf.* ETh^{II} 93 (*cf. ad 49.* Mt7$_{6}$)
cf. ETh^{II} 8.21 (*cf. ad 103.* Mk4$_{9}$)

Lk15$_{2}$ *cf.* Ev. apocr. (POxy 1224 fol.2v° col.2; *cf. ad 65.* Mt9$_{11f.}$)

οὕτως χαρὰ ἐν τῷ οὐρανῷ ἔσται ἐπὶ ἑνὶ ἁμαρτωλῷ μετανοοῦντι ἢ ἐπὶ ἐνενήκοντα ἐννέα δικαίοις οἵτινες οὐ χρείαν ἔχουσιν μετανοίας. [8] ἢ τίς γυνὴ δραχμὰς ἔχουσα δέκα, ἐὰν ἀπολέσῃ δραχμὴν μίαν, οὐχὶ ἅπτει λύχνον καὶ σαροῖ τὴν οἰκίαν καὶ ζητεῖ ἐπιμελῶς ἕως οὗ εὕρῃ; [9] καὶ εὑροῦσα συγκαλεῖ τὰς φίλας καὶ γείτονας λέγουσα· συγχάρητέ μοι, ὅτι εὗρον τὴν δραχμὴν ἣν ἀπώλεσα. [10] οὕτως, λέγω ὑμῖν, γίνεται χαρὰ ἐνώπιον τῶν ἀγγέλων τοῦ θεοῦ ἐπὶ ἑνὶ ἁμαρτωλῷ μετανοοῦντι.

(173)

187. Das Gleichnis vom verlorenen Sohn. *The Prodigal Son.* **Luk 15** 11–32

[11] Εἶπεν δέ· ἄνθρωπός τις εἶχεν δύο υἱούς. [12] καὶ εἶπεν ὁ νεώτερος αὐτῶν τῷ πατρί· πάτερ, δός μοι τὸ ἐπιβάλλον μέρος τῆς οὐσίας. ὁ δὲ διεῖλεν αὐτοῖς τὸν βίον. [13] καὶ μετ᾽ οὐ πολλὰς ἡμέρας συναγαγὼν ἅπαντα ὁ νεώτερος υἱὸς ἀπεδήμησεν εἰς χώραν μακράν, καὶ ἐκεῖ διεσκόρπισεν τὴν οὐσίαν αὐτοῦ ζῶν ἀσώτως. [14] δαπανήσαντος δὲ αὐτοῦ πάντα ἐγένετο λιμὸς ἰσχυρὰ κατὰ τὴν χώραν ἐκείνην, καὶ αὐτὸς ἤρξατο ὑστερεῖσθαι. [15] καὶ πορευθεὶς ἐκολλήθη ἑνὶ τῶν πολιτῶν τῆς χώρας ἐκείνης, καὶ ἔπεμψεν αὐτὸν εἰς τοὺς ἀγροὺς αὐτοῦ βόσκειν χοίρους· [16] καὶ ἐπεθύμει γεμίσαι τὴν κοιλίαν αὐτοῦ ἀπὸ τῶν κερατίων ὧν ἤσθιον οἱ χοῖροι, καὶ οὐδεὶς ἐδίδου αὐτῷ. [17] εἰς ἑαυτὸν δὲ ἐλθὼν ἔφη· πόσοι μίσθιοι τοῦ πατρός μου περισσεύονται ἄρτων, ἐγὼ δὲ λιμῷ ὧδε ἀπόλλυμαι. [18] ἀναστὰς πορεύσομαι πρὸς τὸν πατέρα μου καὶ ἐρῶ αὐτῷ· πάτερ, ἥμαρτον εἰς τὸν οὐρανὸν καὶ ἐνώπιόν σου, [19] οὐκέτι εἰμὶ ἄξιος κληθῆναι υἱός σου· ποίησόν με ὡς ἕνα τῶν μισθίων σου. [20] καὶ ἀναστὰς ἦλθεν πρὸς τὸν πατέρα ἑαυτοῦ. ἔτι δὲ αὐτοῦ μακρὰν ἀπέχοντος εἶδεν αὐτὸν ὁ πατὴρ αὐτοῦ καὶ ἐσπλαγχνίσθη, καὶ δραμὼν ἐπέπεσεν ἐπὶ τὸν τράχηλον αὐτοῦ καὶ κατεφίλησεν αὐτόν. [21] εἶπεν δὲ αὐτῷ ὁ υἱός· πάτερ, ἥμαρτον εἰς τὸν οὐρανὸν καὶ ἐνώπιόν σου, οὐκέτι εἰμὶ ἄξιος κληθῆναι υἱός σου. [22] εἶπεν δὲ ὁ πατὴρ πρὸς τοὺς δούλους αὐτοῦ· ταχὺ ἐξενέγκατε στολὴν τὴν πρώτην καὶ ἐνδύσατε αὐτόν, καὶ δότε δακτύλιον εἰς τὴν χεῖρα αὐτοῦ καὶ ὑποδήματα εἰς τοὺς πόδας, [23] καὶ φέρετε τὸν μόσχον τὸν σιτευτόν, θύσατε, καὶ φαγόντες εὐφρανθῶμεν, [24] ὅτι οὗτος ὁ υἱός μου νεκρὸς ἦν καὶ ἀνέζησεν, ἦν ἀπολωλὼς καὶ εὑρέθη. καὶ ἤρξαντο εὐφραίνεσθαι. [25] ἦν δὲ ὁ υἱὸς αὐτοῦ ὁ πρεσβύτερος ἐν ἀγρῷ· καὶ ὡς ἐρχόμενος ἤγγισεν τῇ οἰκίᾳ, ἤκουσεν συμφωνίας καὶ χορῶν, [26] καὶ προσκαλεσάμενος ἕνα τῶν παίδων ἐπυνθάνετο τί εἴη ταῦτα. [27] ὁ δὲ εἶπεν αὐτῷ ὅτι ὁ ἀδελφός σου ἥκει, καὶ ἔθυσεν ὁ πατήρ σου τὸν μόσχον τὸν σιτευτόν, ὅτι ὑγιαίνοντα αὐτὸν ἀπέλαβεν. [28] ὠργίσθη δὲ καὶ οὐκ ἤθελεν εἰσελθεῖν· ὁ δὲ πατὴρ αὐτοῦ ἐξελθὼν παρεκάλει αὐτόν. [29] ὁ δὲ ἀποκριθεὶς εἶπεν τῷ πατρί· ἰδοὺ τοσαῦτα ἔτη δουλεύω σοι καὶ οὐδέποτε ἐντολήν σου παρῆλθον, καὶ ἐμοὶ οὐδέποτε ἔδωκας ἔριφον ἵνα μετὰ τῶν φίλων μου εὐφρανθῶ· [30] ὅτε δὲ ὁ υἱός σου οὗτος ὁ καταφαγών σου τὸν βίον μετὰ πορνῶν ἦλθεν, ἔθυσας αὐτῷ τὸν σιτευτὸν μόσχον. [31] ὁ δὲ εἶπεν αὐτῷ· τέκνον, σὺ πάντοτε μετ᾽ ἐμοῦ εἶ, καὶ πάντα τὰ ἐμὰ σά ἐστιν· [32] εὐφρανθῆναι δὲ καὶ χαρῆναι ἔδει, ὅτι ὁ ἀδελφός σου οὗτος νεκρὸς ἦν καὶ ἔζησεν, καὶ ἀπολωλὼς καὶ εὑρέθη.

17 10: καὶ τὰ ἐμὰ πάντα σά ἐστιν καὶ τὰ σὰ ἐμά ...

Lk 15,7 δικ. + τοις μη πεπλανωμενοις‖p: 544 **8** *om* ου‖4: 892 φ69 D 716 **13** απα.] ● παντα: 𝔓75 B-1241 D P *pc* **14** ισχ.] μεγαλη‖425: *L*dr1(*om*: bff2il) Ar *Sp C* — μεγας ισχυρος‖←: 716 **16** γεμ.—απο] χορτασθηναι εκ(απο)‖1621: 𝔓75 ℵBL-579-(1241) 1604 λ1-131-1582-2193 **φ**'(69)-*l*547 D R *pc* CatOx *L*e a(+ τ. κοιλ. αυ.)f *S*cj *C*s *Geo*2(+ τ. κ.) *Aeth Got* — γεμ. τ. κοιλ. και χορτ. απο‖←: W — *txt*: *Rpl* Hi *L*'Ar *S*' *C*b *Geo*1 **17** ● περισσευουσιν *cf.* 1K88 *etc.*: *Rpl* — *txt*: 𝔓75 B-579-1241 1604 **λλ**⟨131-1278⟩ A P *pc l*1663 **21** ● ∼ ο υι. αυτω(αυτου): 𝔓75 BL-(579) **λ**-1582-2193 157 *pc* (*L*d) **26** τι] ● τι αν‖946Act1017524: 𝔓75v BX-33-579 N-1604 **λ**-1582 **φ**' σ1223-1424 P Q R Ψ *pc l*44 *l*1963 *L*e afr1.2v Ar Hi — τινα (+ αν): L Λ φ124-174-230-*l*547 *L*'(b vg1) Au — *txt*: *Rpl* | ειη ταυ.] ειη τουτο‖1836: 1604 σM-990-1223 K Π Ψ *al L*f — θελει του. ειναι‖Act212: D *l*42 **28** παρεκ.] ηρξατο παρακαλειν‖Mk57: D'(*om* παρ.) *L*⟨e⟩ Ar Hi **32** χαρ.] αγαλλιαθηναι‖Act← *cf.* Ps169Mt512: K Π *pc*

Lk1513.30 *cf.* EN frgm.18 (*cf. ad 240.*)

Lk1525-32 *cf.* EH frgm.5 (*cf. ad 34.* Mt523)

(174) **188. Das Gleichnis vom ungerechten Haushalter. *The Unjust Steward.*** **Luk 16 1–13**

[1] Ἔλεγεν δὲ καὶ πρὸς τοὺς μαθητάς· ἄνθρωπός τις ἦν πλούσιος ὃς εἶχεν οἰκονόμον, καὶ οὗτος διεβλήθη αὐτῷ ὡς διασκορπίζων τὰ ὑπάρχοντα αὐτοῦ. [2] καὶ φωνήσας αὐτὸν εἶπεν αὐτῷ· τί τοῦτο ἀκούω περὶ σοῦ; ἀπόδος τὸν λόγον τῆς οἰκονομίας σου· οὐ γὰρ δύνῃ ἔτι οἰκονομεῖν. [3] εἶπεν δὲ ἐν ἑαυτῷ ὁ οἰκονόμος· τί ποιήσω, ὅτι ὁ κύριός μου ἀφαιρεῖται τὴν οἰκονομίαν ἀπ' ἐμοῦ; σκάπτειν οὐκ ἰσχύω, ἐπαιτεῖν αἰσχύνομαι. [4] ἔγνων τί ποιήσω, ἵνα ὅταν μετασταθῶ ἐκ τῆς οἰκονομίας δέξωνταί με εἰς τοὺς οἴκους ἑαυτῶν. [5] καὶ προσκαλεσάμενος ἕνα ἕκαστον τῶν χρεοφειλετῶν τοῦ κυρίου ἑαυτοῦ ἔλεγεν τῷ πρώτῳ· πόσον ὀφείλεις τῷ κυρίῳ μου; [6] ὁ δὲ εἶπεν· ἑκατὸν βάτους ἐλαίου. ὁ δὲ εἶπεν αὐτῷ· δέξαι σου τὰ γράμματα καὶ καθίσας ταχέως γράψον πεντήκοντα. [7] ἔπειτα ἑτέρῳ εἶπεν· σὺ δὲ πόσον ὀφείλεις; ὁ δὲ εἶπεν· ἑκατὸν κόρους σίτου. λέγει αὐτῷ· δέξαι σου τὰ γράμματα καὶ γράψον ὀγδοήκοντα. [8] καὶ ἐπῄνεσεν ὁ κύριος τὸν οἰκονόμον τῆς ἀδικίας ὅτι φρονίμως ἐποίησεν· ὅτι οἱ υἱοὶ τοῦ αἰῶνος τούτου φρονιμώτεροι ὑπὲρ τοὺς υἱοὺς τοῦ φωτὸς εἰς τὴν γενεὰν τὴν ἑαυτῶν εἰσιν. [9] καὶ ἐγὼ ὑμῖν λέγω, ἑαυτοῖς ποιήσατε φίλους ἐκ τοῦ μαμωνᾶ τῆς ἀδικίας, ἵνα ὅταν ἐκλίπῃ δέξωνται ὑμᾶς εἰς τὰς αἰωνίους σκηνάς. [10] ὁ πιστὸς ἐν ἐλαχίστῳ καὶ ἐν πολλῷ πιστός ἐστιν, καὶ ὁ ἐν ἐλαχίστῳ ἄδικος καὶ ἐν πολλῷ ἄδικός ἐστιν. [11] εἰ οὖν ἐν τῷ ἀδίκῳ μαμωνᾷ πιστοὶ οὐκ ἐγένεσθε, τὸ ἀληθινὸν τίς ὑμῖν πιστεύσει; [12] καὶ εἰ ἐν τῷ ἀλλοτρίῳ πιστοὶ οὐκ ἐγένεσθε, τὸ ὑμέτερον τίς δώσει ὑμῖν; [13] οὐδεὶς οἰκέτης δύναται δυσὶ κυρίοις δουλεύειν· ἢ γὰρ τὸν ἕνα μισήσει καὶ τὸν ἕτερον ἀγαπήσει, ἢ ἑνὸς ἀνθέξεται καὶ τοῦ ἑτέρου καταφρονήσει. οὐ δύνασθε θεῷ δουλεύειν καὶ μαμωνᾷ.

46.

(175) **189. Verurteilung des pharisäischen Hochmuts.** **Luk 16 14–15**
The Hypocrisy of the Pharisees.

[14] Ἤκουον δὲ ταῦτα πάντα οἱ Φαρισαῖοι φιλάργυροι ὑπάρχοντες, καὶ ἐξεμυκτήριζον αὐτόν. [15] καὶ εἶπεν αὐτοῖς· ὑμεῖς ἐστε οἱ δικαιοῦντες ἑαυτοὺς ἐνώπιον τῶν ἀνθρώπων, ὁ δὲ θεὸς γινώσκει τὰς καρδίας ὑμῶν· ὅτι τὸ ἐν ἀνθρώποις ὑψηλὸν βδέλυγμα ἐνώπιον τοῦ θεοῦ.

(176) **190. Vom Gesetz und von der Ehescheidung.** **Luk 16 16–18**
About the Law and about Divorce.

77. *234.*

[16] Ὁ νόμος καὶ οἱ προφῆται μέχρι Ἰωάννου· ἀπὸ τότε ἡ βασιλεία τοῦ θεοῦ εὐαγγελίζεται καὶ πᾶς εἰς αὐτὴν βιάζεται. [17] εὐκοπώτερον δέ ἐστιν τὸν οὐρανὸν καὶ τὴν γῆν παρελθεῖν ἢ τοῦ νόμου μίαν κεραίαν πεσεῖν.

Lk 16,1 μαθ. + παραβολην *cf.* 14 7 *etc.*: 579 **7** λεγει] ● και λ.: *Rpl* *L*(~: blq)30 vg[2] *S*h *C*b[1] *Arm* *Δ*i[V] ad md[T] n[L] — λ. δε: ℵ-892 ϕ'⟨13⟩(ο δε λ.: 828 D) 157 *L*a(+ και) *C*b[4] — *txt*: 𝔓[75] BL-579-1241 1071-1604 ϕ69-124 σ71-692 R *pc* *L*' *S*cp *C*' *Δ*a i[T] l md' n' p **9** ~ ποι. εαυ.‖12 33: *Rpl* (~ ποι. φιλ. εαυ.: 579) PsBas Cl Meth *L*,Or — *txt*: 𝔓[75] ℵ*BL R **10** ελαχ.[1]] ολιγω‖Mt25 21.23: *L*e df30 vg[2] Hi *S*scp Ef *Δ*a i n[L] p | ελαχ.[2]] ολιγω‖←: **λλ**⟨22-1278⟩ D 872 *L*⟨a⟩ *S*scp *Δ*⟨me n[Hr]⟩ **12** ● ημετερον: BL *pc* *l*21 Or *C*b[1?] — εμον: 157 *L*e il Mcn[Te] — αληθινον‖11: 2145 **14** οι] ● και οι: *Rpl* *S*h *Geo*[1] — *txt*: 𝔓[75] ℵ[a](**om* οι Φ.)BL-579-1241 D R Ψ 157 *pc* *l*150 Or *L*,Cp Hi *S*s[c]p *C* *Geo*[2] *Δ*⟨me⟩ **15** ενω. τ. θε.] παρα τω θεω‖18 27p: 579 243 CAp PsIg(*om* τω) *L* **16** μεχρι] εως‖Mt11 13: *Rpl* Ep Mcn[Ep] Or — *txt* (-ις): 𝔓[75] ℵBLX-579-(891-1241) 1604 (**λλ**⟨22-1278⟩) ϕ R *pc* Cl (Eu) Or | l. + επροφητευσαν(προεφ-)‖←: (σ1675) D (Θ 1579) *l*13 *l*17 *L*vg[1] **17** δε] γαρ‖18 25: *L*l 30 — *om*‖Mt 19 24 Mk10 25: 1241 ϕ⟨124⟩ *pc* *L*vg[1] *S*p[1] *Geo*[2] | πεσ.] παρελθειν‖Mt5 18: W 472 *L*a30 *S*s[c]p

---

Lk16 10-12 *cf.* 2Cl 8,5: Λέγει γὰρ ὁ κύριος ἐν τῷ εὐαγγελίῳ(EAe?)· εἰ τὸ μικρὸν οὐκ ἐτηρήσατε, τὸ μέγα τίς ὑμῖν δώσει; λέγω γὰρ ὑμῖν ὅτι ὁ πιστὸς ἐν ἐλαχίστῳ καὶ ἐν πολλῷ πιστός ἐστιν.

cf. Ir haer. II 56,1 (PsHil ap. 1): Si in modico fideles non fuistis, quod magnum(maius) est quis dabit vobis?

Lk16 13 *cf.* ETh[II] 47 (*cf. ad 46.*)

Lk16 17 *cf.* ETh[II] 11 (*cf. ad 234.* Mt24 35)

201. [18] πᾶς ὁ ἀπολύων τὴν γυναῖκα αὐτοῦ καὶ γαμῶν ἑτέραν μοιχεύει, καὶ ὁ ἀπολελυμένην ἀπὸ ἀνδρὸς γαμῶν μοιχεύει.

(177)

191. Vom reichen Mann und armen Lazarus. *Dives and Lazarus.* Luk 16 19–31

[19] Ἄνθρωπος δέ τις ἦν πλούσιος, καὶ ἐνεδιδύσκετο πορφύραν καὶ βύσσον εὐφραινόμενος καθ' ἡμέραν λαμπρῶς. [20] πτωχὸς δέ τις ὀνόματι Λάζαρος ἐβέβλητο πρὸς τὸν πυλῶνα αὐτοῦ εἱλκωμένος [21] καὶ ἐπιθυμῶν χορτασθῆναι ἀπὸ τῶν πιπτόντων ἀπὸ τῆς τραπέζης τοῦ πλουσίου· ἀλλὰ καὶ οἱ κύνες ἐρχόμενοι ἐπέλειχον τὰ ἕλκη αὐτοῦ. [22] ἐγένετο δὲ ἀποθανεῖν τὸν πτωχὸν καὶ ἀπενεχθῆναι αὐτὸν ὑπὸ τῶν ἀγγέλων εἰς τὸν κόλπον Αβρααμ· ἀπέθανεν δὲ καὶ ὁ πλούσιος καὶ ἐτάφη. [23] καὶ ἐν τῷ ᾅδῃ ἐπάρας τοὺς ὀφθαλμοὺς αὐτοῦ, ὑπάρχων ἐν βασάνοις, ὁρᾷ Αβρααμ ἀπὸ μακρόθεν καὶ Λάζαρον ἐν τοῖς κόλποις αὐτοῦ. [24] καὶ αὐτὸς φωνήσας εἶπεν· πάτερ Αβρααμ, ἐλέησόν με καὶ πέμψον Λάζαρον ἵνα βάψῃ τὸ ἄκρον τοῦ δακτύλου αὐτοῦ ὕδατος καὶ καταψύξῃ τὴν γλῶσσάν μου, ὅτι ὀδυνῶμαι ἐν τῇ φλογὶ ταύτῃ. [25] εἶπεν δὲ Αβρααμ· τέκνον, μνήσθητι ὅτι ἀπέλαβες τὰ ἀγαθά σου ἐν τῇ ζωῇ σου, καὶ Λάζαρος ὁμοίως τὰ κακά· νῦν δὲ ὧδε παρακαλεῖται, σὺ δὲ ὀδυνᾶσαι. [26] καὶ ἐν πᾶσι τούτοις μεταξὺ ἡμῶν καὶ ὑμῶν χάσμα μέγα ἐστήρικται, ὅπως οἱ θέλοντες διαβῆναι ἔνθεν πρὸς ὑμᾶς μὴ δύνωνται, μηδὲ ἐκεῖθεν πρὸς ἡμᾶς διαπερῶσιν. [27] εἶπεν δέ· ἐρωτῶ οὖν σε, πάτερ, ἵνα πέμψῃς αὐτὸν εἰς τὸν οἶκον τοῦ πατρός μου· [28] ἔχω γὰρ πέντε ἀδελφούς· ὅπως διαμαρτύρηται αὐτοῖς, ἵνα μὴ καὶ αὐτοὶ ἔλθωσιν εἰς τὸν τόπον τοῦτον τῆς βασάνου. [29] λέγει δὲ Αβρααμ· ἔχουσι Μωυσέα καὶ τοὺς προφήτας· ἀκουσάτωσαν αὐτῶν. [30] ὁ δὲ εἶπεν· οὐχί, πάτερ Αβρααμ, ἀλλ' ἐάν τις ἀπὸ νεκρῶν πορευθῇ πρὸς αὐτούς, μετανοήσουσιν. [31] εἶπεν δὲ αὐτῷ· εἰ Μωυσέως | 5 46 : εἰ γὰρ ἐπιστεύετε Μωυσεῖ, ἐπιστεύετε ἂν ἐμοί ... | καὶ τῶν προφητῶν οὐκ ἀκούουσιν, οὐδὲ ἐάν τις ἐκ νεκρῶν ἀναστῇ πεισθήσονται.

(178)

192. Vom Ärgernis. *On Offences.* Luk 17 1–2 **145.**

145. [1] Εἶπεν δὲ πρὸς τοὺς μαθητὰς αὐτοῦ· ἀνένδεκτόν ἐστιν τοῦ τὰ σκάνδαλα μὴ ἐλθεῖν, οὐαὶ δὲ δι' οὗ ἔρχεται· [2] λυσιτελεῖ αὐτῷ εἰ λίθος μυλικὸς περίκειται περὶ τὸν τράχηλον αὐτοῦ καὶ ἔρριπται εἰς τὴν θάλασσαν, ἢ ἵνα σκανδαλίσῃ ἕνα τῶν μικρῶν τούτων.

Lk 16,18 ετ.] αλλην‖Mt19,9 Mk10,11: 28 | μοιχαται^{1}‖Mt5,32 19,9 Mk←: X σM-27-71-692-990 K Π *al* *l*13 *l*17 | *om* απο ανδ.‖Mt5,32: 28 D 64 *L*PsAu *S*s[c]p *C*b^{1} *Geo*^{1} | μοιχαται^{2}‖Mt←19,9 Mk←: σ71-692-1194 U Iu **19** *om* δε *cf.* 15,11 16,1 *etc.*: X-579 1604 σ267 D Δ Θ 238 *l*12 *l*32 *l*80 *l*303 *l*333 *l*1627 *l*1634 *l*1642 *l*1663 *l*1963 *l*^{56} Or *L*e fqz vg$^{\langle 1\rangle}$ *S*s[c] *C*s$^{1:9}$b^{2} *Arm* *Aeth* **20** τις + ην *et* Λ. + ος(και)‖16,1 14,2: *Rpl* *L*' *S*h('j) *C*s *Δ*'(a) (*om* ος: p) — *txt* (Λ. + ος): 𝔓75 ℵBL-33^{v}-579-1241 1604 (ϕ*l*547) D (P) Ψ 157 *pc* (*l*$^{3+1?}$) Ad Cl *L*e a(f) *C*b^{7}(') *Arm* *Aeth* **21** απο^{1} + των ψιχιων‖Mt15,27p: *Rpl* (-χων: D) Cl Or *L*afz vg$^{\langle 1\rangle}$ Ad *S*' Ef *C*s^{1}b^{4} *Δ* — πιπτ. + ψιχ.‖←: λ⟨131⟩-1582-2193 872 — *txt*: 𝔓75 ℵ*BL Ad Cl *L*vl'r^{1} Am Gau *S*s[c]j *C*s^{6}b' | πλου. + και ουδεις εδιδου αυτω‖15,16: 1071 ϕ-174-*l*547 *pc* *L*l vg^{3} *S*j Af *Δ*i l^{AD} md me n **27** ● ∼ σε ουν: B ϕ⟨124-983⟩ A D *pc* *l*^{2} *L*vg^{1} *S*h *C*s^{1} — *om* ουν: 579 W *L*e fl(*om* ουν σε)r^{1} *S*j *C*b' *Aeth* — *txt*: 𝔓75 *Rpl* Ad Or *L*'(*om* σε: i vg^{3}) *S*Ef *C*s^{4}b^{1} *Arm* **30** απο] εκ‖3,1 9,7 Mk6,14: 28-1604 λλ⟨1278⟩ D F 157 *pc* *l*^{3} Ef | νεκ.] των ν.‖Mt14,2 27,64 28,7: Λ ϕ174-230-543-826-828 σ27-71-692-1194 *pc* | πορ.] εγερθη (*et om* προς αυ.)‖3,1 9,7 Mt14,2: 𝔓75 {(*L*vl⟨e fz⟩r^{1})} — αναστη‖31: ℵ-579 {} — αναστη και πορ.‖←: ϕ69 *L*PsAu Ir *S*Ef **31** εκ] απο των‖Mt←27,64 28,7: ϕ V(εκ τ. ν.) (*om* των: 478 *l*^{2}) | αναστη] εγερθη‖9,7p: 𝔓75 579 **17,1** ● ∼ μη ελθ. τ. σκ.‖p: *Rpl* Chr Da Or *L*' *S* (*Aeth*) — *txt*: 𝔓75 ℌ[33]X *L*e *C*s | το σκανδαλον‖Mt7b: 1071 | ουαι δε] πλην ουαι (+ δε)‖p: 𝔓75 ℌ'[33](579) λ ϕ'(346) D Ψ 998 *L*vl'r^{1v} *S*s[c]h^{m} (^{Brs}) *C* *Arm* — *txt*: *Rpl* Da *L*flz vg *S*' (*Aeth*) **2** λυσ.] συμφερει‖Mt: D | ει] ινα‖Mt: 28 *L*vl⟨fz⟩ | λιθ. μυ.] μυλος ονικος‖p: *Rpl* Da *S* *C*b^{3} — λιθ. ον.‖p: W 157 — *txt*: 𝔓75 ℌ[33] 1071 λ-22 ϕ'⟨13-124⟩ D Θ *pc* *L*, Mcn^{Te} *C*' *Arm* | περικ.] περιτεθη‖Mt: σ1194 | εν τη θαλασση‖←: N | ● ∼ τ. μι. του. ενα‖15,4: ℌ[33]⟨1241⟩ Ψ — *txt*: *Rpl* *L*

Jo 5,46 επιστευσατε^{1} *et* ^{2} (-ετε ... -σατε)‖Mt21,25**p**: Λ λ2193 (ϕ174 *pc*) *l*184 Eu (PsIg) *L*e (-σατε ... -ετε: q *C*p^{1})^{1}

(179)

193. Von der Versöhnlichkeit. *On Forgiveness.* Luk 17 3–4

[148.] [149.]

3 Προσέχετε ἑαυτοῖς. ἐὰν ἁμάρτῃ ὁ ἀδελφός σου, ἐπιτίμησον αὐτῷ, καὶ ἐὰν μετανοήσῃ, ἄφες αὐτῷ. 4 καὶ ἐὰν ἑπτάκις τῆς ἡμέρας ἁμαρτήσῃ εἰς σὲ καὶ ἑπτάκις ἐπιστρέψῃ πρός σε λέγων· μετανοῶ, ἀφήσεις αὐτῷ.

(180)

194. Vom Glauben. *On Faith.* Luk 17 5–6 [215.]

[215.]

5 Καὶ εἶπαν οἱ ἀπόστολοι τῷ κυρίῳ· πρόσθες ἡμῖν πίστιν. 6 εἶπεν δὲ ὁ κύριος· εἰ ἔχετε πίστιν ὡς κόκκον σινάπεως, ἐλέγετε ἂν τῇ συκαμίνῳ· ἐκριζώθητι καὶ φυτεύθητι ἐν τῇ θαλάσσῃ· καὶ ὑπήκουσεν ἂν ὑμῖν.

(181)

195. Vom Knechtslohn. *The Servant's Wages.* Luk 17 7–10

7 Τίς δὲ ἐξ ὑμῶν δοῦλον ἔχων ἀροτριῶντα ἢ ποιμαίνοντα, ὃς εἰσελθόντι ἐκ τοῦ ἀγροῦ ἐρεῖ αὐτῷ· εὐθέως παρελθὼν ἀνάπεσε, 8 ἀλλ' οὐχὶ ἐρεῖ αὐτῷ· ἑτοίμασον τί δειπνήσω, καὶ περιζωσάμενος διακόνει μοι ἕως φάγω καὶ πίω, καὶ μετὰ ταῦτα φάγεσαι καὶ πίεσαι σύ ; 9 μὴ ἔχει χάριν τῷ δούλῳ ὅτι ἐποίησεν τὰ διαταχθέντα ; 10 οὕτως καὶ ὑμεῖς, ὅταν ποιήσητε πάντα τὰ διαταχθέντα ὑμῖν, λέγετε ὅτι δοῦλοι ἀχρεῖοί ἐσμεν, ὃ ὠφείλομεν ποιῆσαι πεποιήκαμεν.

(182)

196. Heilung von zehn Aussätzigen. *The Healing of Ten Lepers.* Luk 17 11–19

11 Καὶ ἐγένετο ἐν τῷ πορεύεσθαι αὐτὸν εἰς Ιερουσαλημ, καὶ αὐτὸς διήρχετο διὰ μέσον Σαμαρείας καὶ Γαλιλαίας. 12 καὶ εἰσερχομένου αὐτοῦ εἴς τινα κώμην ἀπήντησαν δέκα λεπροὶ ἄνδρες, οἳ ἔστησαν πόρρωθεν, 13 καὶ αὐτοὶ ἦραν φωνὴν λέγοντες· Ἰησοῦ ἐπιστάτα, ἐλέησον ἡμᾶς. 14 καὶ ἰδὼν εἶπεν αὐτοῖς· πορευ-

Lk 17,3 εαν^{1} + δε‖Mt18 15: *Rpl* Eu *L*qr^{1} *S*h — *txt*: 𝔥'(+ αν: L)X N-1604 σ1675 D Θ Ψ *pc* *L*' *S*'j *C* | αμ. + εις σε‖4 Mt18 15.21: *Rpl* Ant Eu *Le* cqr^{1} vg^{4} *S*h^{Brs} *C*b^{3} *Arm*^{O} *Geo*^{2} — *txt*: 𝔥[33]⟨579⟩ 1071 **λ**⟨118⟩ A W Θ *pc* Cl Da *L*'Mcn^{Te} *S*'j *C*' *Arm* *Geo*^{1} **4** *om* εις σε‖3: 28 σ1675 *S*s *C*b^{1} **6** ει εχ.] εαν εχητε‖Mt: σM *pc* | αν^{1} + τω ορει τουτω μεταβα εντευθεν εκει και μετεβαινεν και‖p: D (*om* και τη συκ.— υμιν: HM *L*Ar) *S*c(μεταβα] ινα μεταβη) | συκ.] συκη‖Mt21: 579 | ● συκ. + ταυτη‖p: *Rpl* *L*' *S*'j *C*s — *txt*: 𝔓^{75} ℵLX-579 1071 D 213 *L*s *S*c *C*b | μεταφυθ.‖Mt17 20: D G *L*'⟨e a⟩(*om* και φυ.: s) | εις την θαλασσαν‖p: σ954 D *L*'⟨e vg^{2}⟩(*om*: s) **7** *om* εξ‖14 5: 𝔓^{75} L-1241 D' 1012 | ~ εχ. δου.‖15 4: 1579 *pc* *L*,Cp | εκ] απο‖23 26 Mk15 21: σ1675 | ερει] μη ερ.‖11 11p: D *Le* lr$^{1.2}$s *S*scj *C*b **8** ετ. + μοι‖Mt26 17: ℵ *L*abdfqr$^{1.2}$ vg^{1} *S*scp$^{⟨1⟩}$h^{+} *C*s$^{1:7}$(ετ.] δος μοι)b^{6} *Aeth* *Δ*a n^{L} p **9** δου. + εκεινω‖12 43p 45f.p Mt18 27f.: *Rpl* (~ εκ. τ. δ.: σ990 K Π *pc*) Ant *Le* fr^{2} vg Au Cp *S* *Aeth*(~) — *txt*: 𝔓^{75} 𝔥[33]⟨ℵ*(*om* τ. δου.)⟩X σ1207 A D Ψ *pc* *L*vl'r^{1} Am *S*j(τ. δου.] αυτω) *C* | διατ.] διατεταγμενα‖3 13 Act 23 31: λ 2193 *pc* **10** ~ αχρ. δου.‖Mt25 30: 892-1241 1071 ϕ13-69-543 σ990(~ εσμ. α. δ.) U *pc* *l*32 *l*80 *l*1642 Ant Bas$^{1:2}$ Ep **11** αυτον] ● *om*: 𝔓^{75} ℵBL-579 — τον Ιησουν: *S*p *Δ*'⟨me⟩ — *txt*: *Rpl* *Δ*ad i^{V} l$^{⟨A⟩}$ | διηρ. + την Ιεριχω και‖19 1: 28 | δια] ανα‖Mk7 31: **λ ϕ** — *om*: D **12** απηντ.] ● υπηντ.‖8 27 Jo4 51 Mt8 28: 𝔥[33]⟨B⟩ N-544-1071-1604 **λ ϕ**⟨124⟩ σ71 Θ Ψ 157 *pc* *l*32 Bas Da {} — οπου ησαν: D *Le* — και ιδου: *L*vl' *S*sc — *txt*: 𝔓^{75} *Rpl* {*L*fr^{1}(*prm* και)r^{2}z vg *S*'j *C*} | ● δεκα *prm* αυτω *cf.* 8 27p Jo4 51 *etc.*: *Rpl* *L*fr$^{1.2}$z vg *S*phj *C*' — *txt*: 𝔓^{75} BL D Θ 157 *C*b^{1} **13** ηρ. φω.] εκραξαν φωνη μεγαλη‖4 33 8 28 Mk5 7: D *Le* **14** ιδ.] + αυτους *cf.* 18 24 *etc.*: 1241 1604 ϕ-*l*547 D Θ *l*44 *L* *S*scp *C*s — + αυτους ο Ιησους εσπλαγχνισθη και‖7 13 10 33 *etc.*: 1071 — + την πιστιν αυτων‖5 20p: *l*1663 | αυτοις + θελω καθαρισθητε και ευθεως εκαθαρισθησαν‖5 13p: 𝔓^{75m} | πορ.] υπαγετε‖14b Mt8 4 Mk1 44: 157

Lk17 4 *cf.* EN frgm.15 (*cf. ad 149.*)

196. cf. Ev. apocr. (PEg 2 fol.1r°; *cf. ad 57.*)

ϑέντες ἐπιδείξατε ἑαυτοὺς τοῖς ἱερεῦσιν. καὶ ἐγένετο ἐν τῷ ὑπάγειν αὐτοὺς ἐκαθαρίσθησαν. [15] εἷς δὲ ἐξ αὐτῶν, ἰδὼν ὅτι ἰάθη, ὑπέστρεψεν μετὰ φωνῆς μεγάλης δοξάζων τὸν ϑεόν, [16] καὶ ἔπεσεν ἐπὶ πρόσωπον παρὰ τοὺς πόδας αὐτοῦ εὐχαριστῶν αὐτῷ· καὶ αὐτὸς ἦν Σαμαρίτης. [17] ἀποκριθεὶς δὲ ὁ Ἰησοῦς εἶπεν· οὐχ οἱ δέκα ἐκαθαρίσθησαν; οἱ δὲ ἐννέα ποῦ; [18] οὐχ εὑρέθησαν ὑποστρέψαντες δοῦναι δόξαν τῷ ϑεῷ εἰ μὴ ὁ ἀλλογενὴς οὗτος; [19] καὶ εἶπεν αὐτῷ· ἀναστὰς πορεύου· ἡ πίστις σου σέσωκέν σε.

(183) ***197.*** Vom Reiche Gottes. *On the Kingdom of God.* **Luk 17** 20–21

cf. 231.

[20] Ἐπερωτηθεὶς δὲ ὑπὸ τῶν Φαρισαίων πότε ἔρχεται ἡ βασιλεία τοῦ ϑεοῦ, ἀπεκρίθη αὐτοῖς καὶ εἶπεν· οὐκ ἔρχεται ἡ βασιλεία τοῦ ϑεοῦ μετὰ παρατηρήσεως, [21] οὐδὲ ἐροῦσιν· ἰδοὺ ὧδε, ἤ· ἐκεῖ. ἰδοὺ γὰρ ἡ βασιλεία τοῦ ϑεοῦ ἐντὸς ὑμῶν ἐστιν.

(184) ***198.*** Der Tag des Menschensohns. *The Day of the Son of Man.* **Luk 17** 22–37

24 26–27 (231.): ἐὰν οὖν εἴπωσιν ὑμῖν· ἰδοὺ ἐν τῇ ἐρήμῳ ἐστίν, μὴ ἐξέλθητε· ἰδοὺ ἐν τοῖς ταμιείοις, μὴ πιστεύσητε· [27] ὥσπερ γὰρ ἡ ἀστραπὴ ἐξέρχεται ἀπὸ ἀνατολῶν καὶ φαίνεται ἕως δυσμῶν,

231.

[22] Εἶπεν δὲ πρὸς τοὺς μαθητάς· ἐλεύσονται ἡμέραι ὅτε ἐπιθυμήσετε μίαν τῶν ἡμερῶν τοῦ υἱοῦ τοῦ ἀνθρώπου ἰδεῖν καὶ οὐκ ὄψεσθε. [23] καὶ ἐροῦσιν ὑμῖν· ἰδοὺ ἐκεῖ, ἰδοὺ ὧδε· μὴ ἀπέλθητε μηδὲ διώξητε. [24] ὥσπερ γὰρ ἡ ἀστραπὴ ἀστράπτουσα ἐκ τῆς ὑπὸ τὸν οὐρανὸν εἰς τὴν ὑπ' οὐρανὸν

Lk 17,16 προσω. + αυτου ‖ Mt17 6 26 39: 28 213 *Lcf S*,j *C Δ*a ad n⟨L⟩ p | παρα] προς ‖ Mk5 22 7 25: D *Le* aff^2 **19** σε + πορευου εις ειρηνην ‖ 7 50 8 48 Mk5 34: X **21** εκει] ιδου εκ. ‖ 17 23 Mk13 21: *Rpl* Or *L'* Or *S' Δ*a n — *txt* (*om* ιδου 21a): 𝔓^{75} ℵBL-1241 Θ 157 1354 *l*14 *Le* ff^{2}g^{2}ils Or (*S*s) *C*s^{10}(^{1}b) *Arm* | εκει + μη πιστευσητε ‖ Mt24 23.26 Mk←: D **23** και] κ. εαν ‖ p Mt24 23p: σ659 Γ(καν) *pc S'*h$^-$ | *om* υμ. ‖ 17 21: ϕ983-1689 *Ll* | ιδ.^{1}—διωξ.] ιδ. ωδε μη διωξ. η(*om*) ιδ. εκει ο Χριστος μη πιστευσητε (διωξ.) ‖ Mt←: λ'(131) | εκει ... ωδε] ωδε ... εκ. ‖ ←Mk13 21: *Rpl* Eu *L S*phj *C*sb^3 — ωδε ... ωδε ‖ Mt24 23: B* — *txt*: 𝔓^{75} ℵB^{3}L-579 *S*sc *C*b' | ● εκει + η ‖ 17 21: 𝔓^{75} *Rpl* Eu *L*acdg^{2}l 30 vg^2 *S*h *C Arm Geo*^{1} — + και: ℵ σM *pc L*vl'r^1 vg^6 *S' Geo*^{2} — *txt*: LX-33 28 λ22-131 ϕ69-983 σ71-267-1223 D K W Π *mu Le* qr^2 vg' | *om* ιδ.^{2} ‖ ←Mt24 23: ϕ⟨69-124-983⟩ *pc Ll C Arm Geo*^{1} | μη] *prm* ο Χριστος ‖ Mt24 23p: N-1604 ϕ346 σM-990-1207 K W^c Π *al S*h$^+$ | μη + πιστευσητε μηδε ‖ ←: N *S*h^m(*om* απελ. μηδε)

---

197. cf. ETh^{II} 3 (POxy 654,2): Λέγει Ἰ[η(σοῦ)ς· ἐὰν] οἱ ἕλκοντες ἡμᾶς [εἴπωσιν ὑμῖν· ἰδοὺ] ἡ βασιλεία ἐν οὐρα-[νῷ, ὑμᾶς φθήσεται] τὰ πετεινὰ τοῦ οὐρ[ανοῦ· ἐὰν δὲ εἴπωσιν ὅ]τι ὑπὸ τὴν γῆν ἐστ[ιν, εἰσελεύσονται] οἱ ἰχθύες τῆς θα-λά[σσης φθάσαν]τες ὑμᾶς καὶ ἡ βασ[ιλεία τοῦ ϑεοῦ] ἐντὸς ὑμῶν [ἐ]στι [κἀκτός. ὃς ἂν ἑαυτὸν] γνῷ, ταύτην εὑρή[σει καὶ ὅτε ὑμεῖς] ἑαυτοὺς γνώσεσθαι, [εἰδήσετε ὅτι υἱοί] ἐστε ὑμεῖς τοῦ πατρὸς τοῦ ζ[ῶντος· εἰ δὲ μὴ] γνώσ⟨εσ⟩θε ἑαυτούς, ἐν [τῇ πτωχείᾳ ἐστὲ] καὶ ὑμεῖς ἐστε ἡ πτω[χεία.]

(*transl.*): *Λέγει Ἰησοῦς· ἐὰν οἱ ἕλκοντες ὑμᾶς εἴπωσιν ὑμῖν· ἰδοὺ ἡ βασιλεία ἐν τῷ οὐρανῷ ἐστιν, ἄρα τὰ πετεινὰ φθήσεται ὑμᾶς τοῦ οὐρανοῦ. ἐὰν (δὲ) εἴπωσιν ὑμῖν· ἐν τῇ θαλάσσῃ ἐστίν, ἄρα οἱ ἰχθύες φθήσονται ὑμᾶς. ἀλλὰ ἡ βασιλεία ἐντὸς ὑμῶν ἐστιν καὶ ἐκτὸς ὑμῶν. ὅταν γνῶτε ἑαυτούς, τότε γνωσθήσεσθε καὶ εἰδήσετε ὅτι ὑμεῖς ἐστε οἱ υἱοὶ τοῦ πατρὸς τοῦ ζῶντος. ἐὰν δὲ μὴ γνῶτε ἑαυτούς, ἄρα ἐστὲ ἐν πτωχείᾳ καὶ ὑμεῖς ἐστε ἡ πτωχεία.*

cf. ETh^{II} 113 (*transl.*): *Εἶπον αὐτῷ οἱ μαθηταὶ αὐτοῦ· ποίᾳ ἡμέρᾳ ἔρχεται ἡ βασιλεία; (εἶπεν αὐτοῖς·) οὐκ ἔρχεται μετὰ ἀποκαραδοκίας οὐ(δὲ) ἐροῦσιν· ἰδοὺ ὧδε ἢ ἰδοὺ ἐκεῖ. ἀλλὰ ἡ βασιλεία τοῦ πατρὸς ἐστρωμένη (ἠνοιγμένη?) ἐστὶν ἐπὶ τῆς γῆς καὶ οἱ ἄνθρωποι οὐ βλέπουσιν αὐτήν.*

Lk17 22 *cf.* ETh^{II} 38 (*cf. ad 105.*)

Lk17 23p *cf.* ETh^{II} 113 (*cf. ad 197.*)

Matth:

οὕτως ἔσται ἡ παρουσία τοῦ υἱοῦ τοῦ ἀνθρώπου· ...

24 37–41 (235.): *Ὥσπερ γὰρ αἱ ἡμέραι τοῦ Νωε, οὕτως ἔσται ἡ παρουσία τοῦ υἱοῦ τοῦ ἀνθρώπου. ³⁸ ὡς γὰρ ἦσαν ἐν ταῖς ἡμέραις ταῖς πρὸ τοῦ κατακλυσμοῦ τρώγοντες καὶ πίνοντες, γαμοῦντες καὶ ἐκγαμίζοντες,* Gn7₇ *ἄχρι ἧς ἡμέρας* ***εἰσῆλθεν Νωε εἰς τὴν κιβωτόν,*** *³⁹ καὶ οὐκ ἔγνωσαν ἕως ἦλθεν ὁ κατακλυσμὸς καὶ ἦρεν ἅπαντας, οὕτως ἔσται καὶ ἡ παρουσία τοῦ υἱοῦ τοῦ ἀνθρώπου.*

⁴⁰ τότε δύο ἔσονται ἐν τῷ ἀγρῷ, εἷς παραλαμβάνεται καὶ εἷς ἀφίεται· ⁴¹ δύο ἀλήθουσαι ἐν τῷ μύλῳ, μία παραλαμβάνεται καὶ μία ἀφίεται.

cf. 136.

Luk:

λάμπει, οὕτως ἔσται ὁ υἱὸς τοῦ ἀνθρώπου ἐν τῇ ἡμέρᾳ αὐτοῦ. ²⁵ πρῶτον δὲ δεῖ αὐτὸν πολλὰ παθεῖν καὶ ἀποδοκιμασθῆναι ἀπὸ τῆς γενεᾶς ταύτης. ²⁶ καὶ καθὼς ἐγένετο ἐν ταῖς ἡμέραις Νωε, οὕτως ἔσται καὶ ἐν ταῖς ἡμέραις τοῦ υἱοῦ τοῦ ἀνθρώπου·

²⁷ ἤσθιον, ἔπινον, ἐγάμουν, ἐγαμίζοντο, ἄχρι ἧς ἡμέρας **εἰσῆλθεν Νωε εἰς τὴν κιβωτόν,** καὶ ἦλθεν ὁ κατακλυσμὸς καὶ ἀπώλεσεν πάντας. ²⁸ ὁμοίως καθὼς ἐγένετο ἐν ταῖς ἡμέραις Λωτ· ἤσθιον, ἔπινον, ἠγόραζον, ἐπώλουν, ἐφύτευον, ᾠκοδόμουν· ²⁹ ᾗ δὲ ἡμέρᾳ ἐξῆλθεν Λωτ ἀπὸ

Gn19₂₄ Σοδόμων, **ἔβρεξεν πῦρ καὶ θεῖον ἀπ' οὐρανοῦ** καὶ ἀπώλεσεν πάντας. ³⁰ κατὰ τὰ αὐτὰ ἔσται ᾗ ἡμέρᾳ

230. ὁ υἱὸς τοῦ ἀνθρώπου ἀποκαλύπτεται. ³¹ ἐν ἐκείνῃ τῇ ἡμέρᾳ ὃς ἔσται ἐπὶ τοῦ δώματος καὶ τὰ σκεύη

Gn19₁₇ αὐτοῦ ἐν τῇ οἰκίᾳ, μὴ καταβάτω ἆραι αὐτά, καὶ ὁ ἐν ἀγρῷ ὁμοίως **μὴ ἐπιστρεψάτω εἰς τὰ ὀπίσω.**

137. ³² μνημονεύετε τῆς γυναικὸς Λωτ. ³³ ὃς ἐὰν ζητήσῃ τὴν ψυχὴν αὐτοῦ περιποιήσασθαι, ἀπολέσει αὐτήν, καὶ ὃς ἐὰν ἀπολέσῃ, ζῳογονήσει αὐτήν. ³⁴ λέγω ὑμῖν, ταύτῃ τῇ νυκτὶ ἔσονται δύο ἐπὶ κλίνης μιᾶς, ὁ εἷς παραλημφθήσεται καὶ ὁ ἕτερος ἀφεθήσεται· ³⁵ ἔσονται δύο ἀλήθουσαι ἐπὶ τὸ αὐτό, ἡ μία παραλημφθήσεται ἡ δὲ ἑτέρα ἀφεθήσεται. ³⁷ καὶ ἀποκριθέντες λέγουσιν αὐτῷ·

Lk 17,24 εστ. + και‖26 11 30 Mt24 39: N σ71 D 157 *al* *L*e bcis *Arm Aeth* | *om* εν—αυτ.‖p: 𝔓^{75} B D 220 *L*vl⟨flqz⟩ *C*s | ημ.] παρουσια‖p: 248 *L*l **26** N.] του N.‖**p**: 892 **λ**⟨131⟩ Eu | *om* και^{2}‖p: 579 **ϕ**⟨124⟩ Γ 245 *L*bilr$^{1.2}$s vg^{3} *S*scp *C* | εν τη ημ.^{2}] η παρουσια‖**p**: 213 *L*30 *S*h^{m}(εν τη π.)^{Brs} **27** ησθ.] *prm* εν(ως) γαρ (+ εγενετο εν) ταις ημεραις ταις προ του κατακλυσμου‖p: 33 (*C*s$^{8:9}$) — + και‖**p**: 251 *L*⟨e ais⟩ *S* *C*b^{3} | εγαμουν + και‖**p**: 251 *pc* *L*⟨e abff^{2}ils⟩ *S* *C*b^{1} | απωλ.] ηρεν‖**p**: ℵ *pc* *S*sc **28** ησθ. + και‖Mt23: 1573 *L*⟨e ails⟩ *S*scp | ηγο. + και‖←: *L*⟨e aff^{2}ilqs⟩ *Aeth* | εφυ. + και‖←: *L*cfr^{2} vg$^{⟨12⟩}$ *S*(*om* εφυ. ωκ.: s)cp *Aeth* **30** η—αποκ.] και η παρουσια του υιου τ. ανθ.‖Mt39.27: 28 | αποκ.] ερχεται‖21 27p: 1573 *L*e **31** αγρω] τω α.‖Mt24 18 Mk13 16: *Rpl* {*C*} — *txt*: 𝔓^{75} ℵBL-579 **ϕ**⟨124⟩ 157 | καταβαινετω‖Mt24 17: σM-71 2145 | εις τα] ομοιως: ϕ69 — *om*‖Mt24 18: R* **047** **33** ζητ.] θελησῃ‖**9** 24 Mt16 25 Mk8 35: D *S*scp | περιπ.] σωσαι‖←: *Rpl* *L*' *S* — ζωογονησαι‖33b: D(∼ ζ. τ. ψ. αυ.) *Aeth* — *txt*: 𝔓^{75} BL-579 (liberare: *L*bciq) | και ος εαν] ος δ αν‖**9** 24 Mt← Mk←: 𝔓^{75} ℵBL-579 28-1071 ϕ69-788 Ψ 245 *C*b^{3} *Aeth* — και ος δ αν‖9 24 Mt← Mk←: **ϕ**'⟨124⟩ — *txt*: *Rpl* (*om* και—αυτην: X; και ος αν: D) *L*'(ος γαρ εαν: l) *S* *C*s^{1}(*om* και: s^{7} b')^{6}a^{v} | απολεση + ενεκεν εμου‖9 24p: Λ ϕ230(+ αυτην ενε. εμ.) *L*vl⟨a⟩r^{1}30 vg^{3} *C*s$^{1:8}$ | ζωογ.] σωσει‖**9** 24 Mk←: **λ** ϕ69-788 475 *L*vl'⟨e r^{2}z⟩r^{1} vg^{1} — ευρησει‖Mt←10 39: *L*l *S*c **34** *om* ο^{1}‖p: *Rpl* Bas Cr *C*sa — *txt*: 𝔓^{75} ℵB-579-892 1071 **λ**-22 **ϕ** Θ 157 *C*b | παραλαμβανεται‖p: σ990 D' G K Π *al* — παρακληθησ.‖16 25 Mt5 4: ϕ13 | και ο ετ.] η δε ετερα‖35: ϕ983-1689 | αφιεται‖p: D K 116 *L*z *Got* **35** *om* 35(∩?): ℵ* λ209 *pc* *L*l vg^{1} | *om* εσον.‖p: 476 Bas *L*e bcff^{2}i (∼ 36.35)q Am *C*a^{v} | επι το αυ.] εν τω(ενι) μυλωνι‖p: K *L*Max^{T} (*S*s) *C*b^{1}(*om* τω) — εν ενι μυλ. επι το αυ.‖p: *S*c | *om* η^{1}‖p: *Rpl* Bas *C*'a — *txt*: 𝔓^{75} ℵ^{a}B-579 **λ** **ϕ**-174-230 D R Θ Ω *C*b^{5} | η δε] και η‖p34: *Rpl* Bas *L*, Max^{T} *S* *C*' — η: 1241 *S* *C*b^{6}a — *txt*: 𝔓^{75} ℵ^{a}B L-892 **ϕ**⟨124⟩-174 R | αφεθ. + ^{36}δυο εσονται εν τω αγρω εις παραλημφθησεται και ο ετερος αφεθησεται‖Mt40: 579 Λ-700-1071 **ϕ**⟨69-788⟩-174-230 σ1194 D U *al* *l*^{p1} *L*'⟨vg^{1}⟩(∼ 36.35: i) Am Au *S* ⟦*om* εσον.‖Mt41: 579^{v}-1241 700-1071 ϕ230 D *al* *l*185 *l*1579 *L*⟨vg^{1}⟩ Am Au | *om* τω‖31 15 25: 1241 700-1071 D *l*185 *l*1579 | εις] ο εις‖34: Λ σ1194 *pc* | και ο ετ.] και ο εις‖Mt40: σ267-659 *L*vl⟨afqr^{1}z⟩ vg^{1} *S*sc — η δε ετερα‖35: ϕ13-346-543-826-828⟧ — *txt*: 𝔓^{75} *Rpl* *l*184 *l*950 Bas *L*PsChr Max^{T} *C*,a *Geo*

Lk17 34p *cf.* ETh^{II} 61 (*transl.*): *Λέγει Ἰησοῦς· δύο ἐπὶ κλίνης ἀναπαύσονται, ὁ εἷς ἀποθανεῖται, ὁ εἷς ζήσεται ...*

ἐκεῖ 24 28 (231.): ὅπου ἐὰν ᾖ τὸ πτῶμα, συναχθήσονται οἱ ἀετοί.

ποῦ, κύριε; ὁ δὲ εἶπεν αὐτοῖς· ὅπου τὸ σῶμα, ἐκεῖ καὶ οἱ ἀετοὶ ἐπισυναχθήσονται.

(185) *199.* Das Gleichnis vom gottlosen Richter. *The Parable of the Unjust Judge.* Luk 18 1–8

[1] Ἔλεγεν δὲ καὶ παραβολὴν αὐτοῖς πρὸς τὸ δεῖν πάντοτε προσεύχεσθαι αὐτοὺς καὶ μὴ ἐγκακεῖν, [2] λέγων· κριτής τις ἦν ἔν τινι πόλει τὸν θεὸν μὴ φοβούμενος καὶ ἄνθρωπον μὴ ἐντρεπόμενος. [3] χήρα δὲ ἦν ἐν τῇ πόλει ἐκείνῃ, καὶ ἤρχετο πρὸς αὐτὸν λέγουσα· ἐκδίκησόν με ἀπὸ τοῦ ἀντιδίκου μου. [4] καὶ οὐκ ἤθελεν ἐπὶ χρόνον· μετὰ ταῦτα δὲ εἶπεν ἐν ἑαυτῷ· εἰ καὶ τὸν θεὸν οὐ φοβοῦμαι οὐδὲ ἄνθρωπον ἐντρέπομαι, [5] διά γε τὸ παρέχειν μοι κόπον τὴν χήραν ταύτην ἐκδικήσω αὐτήν, ἵνα μὴ εἰς τέλος ἐρχομένη ὑπωπιάζῃ με. [6] Εἶπεν δὲ ὁ κύριος· ἀκούσατε τί ὁ κριτὴς τῆς ἀδικίας λέγει· [7] ὁ δὲ θεὸς οὐ μὴ ποιήσῃ τὴν ἐκδίκησιν τῶν ἐκλεκτῶν αὐτοῦ τῶν βοώντων αὐτῷ ἡμέρας καὶ νυκτός, καὶ μακροθυμεῖ ἐπ' αὐτοῖς; [8] λέγω ὑμῖν ὅτι ποιήσει τὴν ἐκδίκησιν αὐτῶν ἐν τάχει. πλὴν ὁ υἱὸς τοῦ ἀνθρώπου ἐλθὼν ἆρα εὑρήσει τὴν πίστιν ἐπὶ τῆς γῆς;

(186) *200.* Pharisäer und Zöllner. *The Pharisee and the Publican.* Luk 18 9–14

[9] Εἶπεν δὲ καὶ πρός τινας τοὺς πεποιθότας ἐφ' ἑαυτοῖς ὅτι εἰσὶν δίκαιοι καὶ ἐξουθενοῦντας τοὺς λοιποὺς τὴν παραβολὴν ταύτην· [10] ἄνθρωποι δύο ἀνέβησαν εἰς τὸ ἱερὸν προσεύξασθαι, ὁ εἷς Φαρισαῖος καὶ ὁ ἕτερος τελώνης. [11] ὁ Φαρισαῖος σταθεὶς ταῦτα πρὸς ἑαυτὸν προσηύχετο· ὁ θεός, εὐχαριστῶ σοι ὅτι οὐκ εἰμὶ ὥσπερ οἱ λοιποὶ τῶν ἀνθρώπων, ἅρπαγες, ἄδικοι, μοιχοί, ἢ καὶ ὡς οὗτος ὁ τελώνης· [12] νηστεύω δὶς τοῦ σαββάτου, ἀποδεκατῶ πάντα ὅσα κτῶμαι. [13] ὁ δὲ τελώνης μακρόθεν ἑστὼς οὐκ ἤθελεν οὐδὲ τοὺς ὀφθαλμοὺς ἐπᾶραι εἰς τὸν οὐρανόν, ἀλλὰ ἔτυπτεν τὸ στῆθος αὐτοῦ λέγων· ὁ θεός, ἱλάσθητί μοι τῷ ἁμαρτωλῷ. [14] λέγω ὑμῖν, κατέβη οὗτος δεδικαιωμένος εἰς τὸν οἶκον αὐτοῦ παρ' ἐκεῖνον· ὅτι πᾶς ὁ ὑψῶν ἑαυτὸν ταπεινωθήσεται, ὁ δὲ ταπεινῶν ἑαυτὸν ὑψωθήσεται.

183.

Lk 17,37 οπου + αν γενηται ‖p: Θ *L*' — εσται ‖p: 1093 *C*sa — εστιν *Le*(∼ σω. εστ.) | σω.] πτωμα ‖p: 579-1241 28-544 ϕ σ659-1223 E G H Θ *al* Bas *Le Sh*[m] | *om* και[2] ‖p: *Rpl* Cr *L*' *S*' *C*sb[4] — *txt*: ℌ[33] Λ-1071 ϕ69-346-983 σ954-1223 U 1279 *pm* Bas Eu *L*dz vg[2] Am *S*h *C*b'a | ∼ επισυν. οι αετ. ‖p: *Rpl* Cr *L*' *S*' *C*s[1]b[4] — ∼ συναχ. και οι αετ. ‖p: σ1223 1279 Bas Eu *L*dz vg[2] Am *S*h *C*b' — *txt* (συναχ.): ℵBL-(579)-892-(1241) 1071 (ϕ⟨124⟩ 300) *l*184 *C*s[5]a *Arm* | επι-συν.] συναχ. ‖p: *Rpl* (*om*: Λ; αχθ.: Ω) Bas — *txt*: ℵBL 1071 σ7-659 Q *pc l*19 **18,1** ● *om* και[1] ‖ 12 16 13 6 14 7: ℌ[33] 1071 ϕ σM *pc* Bas Or *L*abcq vg[2] *S*h[Brs] *C*,a *Aeth*(και ελ. πα.) *Δ*'⟨me⟩ — *txt* (*om* δε): *Rpl* (σ71 29) Ant *L*'(il vg[1]) *S* (*Geo*) *Δ*a i[T] l p **4** ● ∼ δε ταυ. ‖10 1 Jo19 38 [Mk16 12]: *Rpl* Bas *S*h — *om* δε: *L*bcdl *S*s(και μετα: cj[ac]; κ. μ. ταυ. δε: j[b]) *Arm* — *txt*: BL-**0139**-579-892 Q *L*' *S*p | ειπ. εν εαυ.] ηλθεν εις εαυτον και λεγει ‖15 17: D *L*PsVig **5** κοπουϛ ‖11 7 Mt26 10 p: ℵ* N-1071 λ ϕ⟨346⟩-*l*547 σ1194 E G R Θ Ω *al l*184 **7** ∼ νυκ. ... ημ. ‖2 37 Mk5 5: 1241 σ-1194 D 472 Ant Mac[S] *Δ*a me p | και[2]] ναι λεγω *et om* [8]λεγω υμ. οτι ‖11 51 12 5 Mt11 9 p: ϕ69 **8** λεγω] ναι λ. ‖←: N-28-1071 λ1278 ϕ⟨69⟩-*l*547 σM-71-692 G R Θ Ψ *pc* Ant Mac[S] *L*Ir *S*j *C*b[⟨4⟩] *Arm*, Ir | *om* οτι ‖←: ϕ(69)-983-1689 D G *pc* Mac[S] *L*bcff[2]ilr[1] vg[1] Ir *Δ*md p **9** *om* και[1] ‖12 16 13 6 14 7: *Rpl L*vl'r[1]30 vg[2] *S*(∼ και ειπ. τ. πα. ταυ. προς—λοιπ.: scp)hj *C*,a *Δ*'⟨me⟩ — *txt*: 𝔓[75] ℌ[33]X-**0139** N λ-1582 ϕ124 σM-1223 D Q R Δ Θ Ψ Ω 157 *al L*afff[2]iz vg' *S*h[Brs] *Arm*(*om* δε) **10** ο εις ... ο ετε.] εις ... εις ‖Mt24 40: D *L*Cp[1:2] Opt[1] — εις ... ο ετε. ‖←: BX σ71 R 213 *L*Opt[1] *C*s[5:9]([2:9] *om* ο)a **11** προσηυξατο ‖Mt26 42 p.44: 1241 1071 λ-1582(ηυξ-: 2193) A Π *pc L*r[2] — ειπεν προσευχομενος: *C*sa **13** μακ.] απο μ. ‖16 23 Mt15 40 27 55: 700 ϕ124-*l*547 σ27 G Θ 157 *pc* **14** ο δε] και(+ πας) ο ‖14 11 Mt23 12: 579 λ A Ψ *pc* (Or) *L*'⟨i vg[1]⟩(br[1]) Cp *S*s(cp)j *C*s[2:9]b[1] *Arm Aeth*

III. Die judäische Periode. *The Judean Period.*

Matth 19—27 = Mark 10—15 = Luk 1815**—23**

1. Der Zug nach Jerusalem. *The Journey to Jerusalem.*

Matth 19—20 = Mark 10 = Luk 1815**—19**27

(187) *201.* Verbot der Ehescheidung. *The Forbidding of Divorce.*

	Matth 19 1–12	Mark 10 1–12
	1 Καὶ ἐγένετο ὅτε ἐτέλεσεν ὁ Ἰησοῦς τοὺς λόγους τούτους, μετῆρεν ἀπὸ τῆς Γαλιλαίας καὶ ἦλθεν εἰς τὰ ὅρια τῆς Ἰουδαίας πέραν τοῦ Ἰορδάνου. 2 καὶ ἠκολούθησαν αὐτῷ ὄχλοι πολλοί, καὶ ἐθεράπευσεν αὐτοὺς ἐκεῖ. 3 καὶ προσῆλθον αὐτῷ Φαρισαῖοι πειράζοντες αὐτὸν καὶ λέγοντες· εἰ ἔξεστιν ἀπολῦσαι τὴν γυναῖκα αὐτοῦ κατὰ πᾶσαν αἰτίαν;	1 Καὶ ἐκεῖθεν ἀναστὰς ἔρχεται εἰς τὰ ὅρια τῆς Ἰουδαίας καὶ πέραν τοῦ Ἰορδάνου, καὶ συμπορεύονται πάλιν ὄχλοι πρὸς αὐτόν, καὶ ὡς εἰώθει πάλιν ἐδίδασκεν αὐτούς. 2 καὶ προσελθόντες Φαρισαῖοι ἐπηρώτων αὐτὸν εἰ ἔξεστιν ἀνδρὶ γυναῖκα ἀπολῦσαι, πειράζοντες αὐτόν. 3 ὁ δὲ ἀποκριθεὶς εἶπεν αὐτοῖς· τί ὑμῖν ἐνετείλατο Μωυσῆς;
Dt 24 1	*7 λέγουσιν αὐτῷ· τί οὖν Μωυσῆς ἐνετείλατο* ***δοῦναι βιβλίον ἀποστασίου καὶ ἀπολῦσαι αὐτήν;*** *8 λέγει αὐτοῖς· ὅτι Μωυσῆς πρὸς τὴν σκληροκαρδίαν ὑμῶν ἐπέτρεψεν ὑμῖν ἀπολῦσαι τὰς γυναῖκας ὑμῶν· ἀπ' ἀρχῆς δὲ οὐ γέγονεν οὕτως.* 4 ὁ δὲ ἀποκριθεὶς εἶπεν· οὐκ ἀνέγνωτε ὅτι ὁ	4 οἱ δὲ εἶπαν· ἐπέτρεψεν Μωυσῆς **βιβλίον ἀποστασίου γράψαι καὶ ἀπολῦσαι.** 5 ὁ δὲ Ἰησοῦς εἶπεν αὐτοῖς· πρὸς τὴν σκληροκαρδίαν ὑμῶν ἔγραψεν ὑμῖν τὴν ἐντολὴν ταύτην. 6 ἀπὸ δὲ ἀρχῆς
Gn 1 27	κτίσας ἀπ' ἀρχῆς **ἄρσεν καὶ θῆλυ ἐποίησεν αὐτούς;**	κτίσεως **ἄρσεν καὶ θῆλυ ἐποίησεν αὐτοὺς**
Gn 2 24	5 καὶ εἶπεν· **ἕνεκα τούτου καταλείψει ἄνθρωπος τὸν πατέρα καὶ τὴν μητέρα καὶ κολληθή-**	ὁ θεός· 7 **ἕνεκεν τούτου καταλείψει ἄνθρωπος τὸν πατέρα αὐτοῦ καὶ τὴν μητέρα καὶ προσκολληθή-**

Mt 19,1 Ιου. + και ‖ p: ϕ174 *L*acff^{1}h37. 38 vg^{2} Hi Or *L*Hil *S*'j *C* {*Geo*^{2} *Aeth*} — + ανδρι ‖ p: σ1424 *pc* *L* *S*sc{} — + τινι ‖ p: 700 *Geo*^{1} — *txt*: ℵ*BL 28 σ517 Γ *pc* *L*Au *Aeth* | **3** ● εξ. + ανθρωπω(+ τινι) ‖ p: *Rpl* (565) Da Gr^{Na} **4** ειπ. + αυτοις ‖ 3.5: *Rpl* *L*' *S*,j *Arm*(∼) *Δ*' — *txt*: ℵB L-892 700 D 1574 Or *L*e[k] acff$^{1.2}$h37. 38 Hi *C* *Δ*i^{T1V} | αυτους + ο θεος ‖ p: Σ *L*Au$^{2:3}$(*om* ο κτι.) — + ο κυριος: *Aeth*(*om* ο κτι.) **5** πα. + αυτου ‖ p: C-33 ΟΣΦ-28-1604 λ1-22-1582 **ϕ**-174-*l*547 σ517-945-990-1010-1194-1293-1391-1402-1424 E U Y Δ **078** 157 *pm* Ath Ep^{2} *L*Or *S*,Ath *C* *Arm* *Geo*^{2} — *txt*: *Rpl* Ath Ep^{2} Or *L*,Au Hil *Arm* *Geo*^{1} | προσκολλ. ‖ **p**Gn2 24 LXX: *Rpl* Ath Chr Ep — *txt*: B 28 λ22 **ϕ**⟨124-983⟩ σ7-659-954-1391-1402 D E F G H S U V W Θ Ω **078** 157 *pc* Ep Or

Mk 10,1 και^{2}] ● δια του: *Rpl* (και δια του: 1071) *S*h *Aeth* — *om*: C^{2}Δ-579 WΘ-28-565 **λ**-22-1278 **ϕ** σ115-349-517-659-954-1082-1194 D G 1342 *pc* *l*^{p1} *L*,Au *S*s[c]p *Got* — *txt*: 𝔋'C* *C* | *om* παλ.^{1} ‖ p: 892 W **ϕ** *pc* *l*260 *L*bcff^{2}ir^{1} *S*p *Geo*$^{\langle ch\rangle}$ | οχ. + πολλοι (οχλος πολυς) ‖ p: 579 (**λ**) ϕ124 *pc* (*pc*) *S*p (*Geo*^{1}) **4** ∼ Μω. επετ. ‖ Mt7f.: *Rpl* *L*'Au *S* *C*sf — *txt*: 𝔋C σ7-179-1082-1391 D 1342 *pc* *l*18 *l*48 *l*184 *l*185 *L*k[e] *C*b *Aeth* | επετ.] ενετειλατο ‖ 3p: **λ** *pc* *L*k[e] q *C*b'(^{1} + ημιν)f *Geo* | γρα.] δουναι ‖ **p**: 61 998(∼) *L*br^{1v} *C*sf *Geo*^{2} — δου. γραψαι ‖ p: D (dare scriptum: *L*cdff^{2}q) — ∼ γρα. βιβ. αποσ. + και δου. ‖ p: *S*s[c] | απολ. + αυτην ‖ pDt24 1: N *S*s[c] *C*(αυτας: s)f **5** αυτ. + Μωυσης ‖ p: σ945 *pc* *S*s[c]p^{8} | εγρα.] επετρεψεν ‖ p: 579 ΝΣΦ ϕ124 238 *S*s[c] — + M. ‖ p: D *L*k[e] cg^{2} *C*(∼: sf)b^{1} *Geo*^{2} | υμιν + M. ‖ p: Ψ-579 1342 *pc* *L*b(*om* υμ. *et* ∼ τ. εντ. ταυ. M.)f vg^{1} **6** απο δε αρχ.] απ αρχ. δε ‖ p: 237 *pc* | *om* κτι. ‖ **p**: D 255 *l*36 *L*bff^{2}q vg^{1} *S*s[c]p | ● *om* ο θε. ‖ p: 𝔋⟨Ψ-892⟩C λ872 1342 Cat *L*c *C*,f *Geo*^{2ch} | θε. + και ειπεν(*om*) ‖ p: NWΘΣ-28-565-700-1071 **ϕ** σ7 D *al* *l*7 *L*(k[e]) bcff^{2}g^{2}qr^{1}30(λεγων) vg^{9} *Arm* (*Aeth*) **7** *om* αυτου^{1} ‖ pMt15 4: N-565 σM D **047** 1093 *L*30 vg^{3} | ● μη. + αυτου ‖ Mt15 6 Gn2 24: ℵΨ-579 σM D(εαυ-) *pc* *l*48 *l*185 *L*abcfff^{2} vg^{3} *S*s[c]p *C*,f *Geo*^{1ch}

σεται τῇ γυναικὶ αὐτοῦ, **καὶ ἔσονται οἱ δύο εἰς σάρκα μίαν·** 6 ὥστε οὐκέτι εἰσὶν δύο ἀλλὰ σὰρξ μία. ὃ οὖν ὁ θεὸς συνέζευξεν, ἄνθρωπος μὴ χωριζέτω. 7 λέγουσιν αὐτῷ· τί οὖν Μωυσῆς ἐνετείλατο **δοῦναι βιβλίον ἀποστασίου καὶ ἀπολῦσαι αὐτήν;** 8 λέγει αὐτοῖς· ὅτι Μωυσῆς πρὸς τὴν σκληροκαρδίαν ὑμῶν ἐπέτρεψεν ὑμῖν ἀπολῦσαι τὰς γυναῖκας ὑμῶν· ἀπ' ἀρχῆς δὲ οὐ γέγονεν οὕτως. 9 λέγω δὲ ὑμῖν ὅτι ὃς ἂν ἀπολύσῃ τὴν γυναῖκα αὐτοῦ μὴ ἐπὶ πορνείᾳ καὶ γαμήσῃ ἄλλην, μοιχᾶται· καὶ ὁ ἀπολελυμένην γαμήσας μοιχᾶται. 10 λέγουσιν αὐτῷ οἱ μαθηταί· εἰ οὕτως ἐστὶν ἡ αἰτία τοῦ ἀνθρώπου μετὰ τῆς γυναικός, οὐ συμφέρει γαμῆσαι. 11 ὁ δὲ εἶπεν αὐτοῖς· οὐ πάντες χωροῦσιν τὸν λόγον τοῦτον, ἀλλ' οἷς δέδοται. 12 εἰσὶν γὰρ εὐνοῦχοι οἵτινες ἐκ κοιλίας μητρὸς ἐγεννήθησαν οὕτως, καὶ εἰσὶν εὐνοῦχοι οἵτινες εὐνουχίσθησαν ὑπὸ τῶν ἀνθρώπων, καὶ εἰσὶν εὐνοῦχοι οἵτινες εὐνούχισαν ἑαυτοὺς διὰ τὴν βασιλείαν τῶν οὐρανῶν. ὁ δυνάμενος χωρεῖν χωρείτω.

5 32 (36.): ἐγὼ δὲ λέγω ὑμῖν ὅτι πᾶς ὁ ἀπολύων τὴν γυναῖκα αὐτοῦ παρεκτὸς λόγου πορνείας ποιεῖ αὐτὴν μοιχευθῆναι, καὶ ὃς ἐὰν ἀπολελυμένην γαμήσῃ, μοιχᾶται.

σεται **πρὸς τὴν γυναῖκα αὐτοῦ,** 8 **καὶ ἔσονται οἱ δύο εἰς σάρκα μίαν·** ὥστε οὐκέτι εἰσὶν δύο ἀλλὰ μία σάρξ. 9 ὃ οὖν ὁ θεὸς συνέζευξεν, ἄνθρωπος μὴ χωριζέτω.

cf. v. 3–5 ↑

10 καὶ εἰς τὴν οἰκίαν πάλιν οἱ μαθηταὶ περὶ τούτου ἐπηρώτων αὐτόν. 11 καὶ λέγει αὐτοῖς· ὃς ἂν ἀπολύσῃ τὴν γυναῖκα αὐτοῦ καὶ γαμήσῃ ἄλλην, μοιχᾶται ἐπ' αὐτήν· 12 καὶ ἐὰν γυνὴ ἀπολύσῃ τὸν ἄνδρα αὐτῆς καὶ γαμήσῃ ἄλλον, μοιχᾶται.

16 18 (190.): πᾶς ὁ ἀπολύων τὴν γυναῖκα αὐτοῦ καὶ γαμῶν ἑτέραν μοιχεύει, καὶ ὁ ἀπολελυμένην ἀπὸ ἀνδρὸς γαμῶν μοιχεύει.

Dt 24₁

Mt 19,5 τη γυ.] προς την γυναικα ‖ p Gn 2₂₄: 1200 *al* Chr — **6** ~ μια σαρξ ‖ p: ℵ D Or {*L*⟨q⟩ Au} *Arm Aeth* — **7** ενετ.] εγραψεν ‖ Mk₅: 28 — + ημιν ‖ Mk₃: NOΣ-700 *Cs Arm* | αυτην] την γυναικα (+ αυτου) ‖ ₃: *l*5ᵐ *L*bcff² vg² Am Ir (*S*sc) — αυτας: *C*sb⟨1⟩ — ● *om* ‖ Mk₄: ℵLZ 700 λ1-22-1582 D Θ 1295 Or *L*'⟨fq⟩ Au PsChr *S*j *Arm Aeth* — **8** *om* οτι ‖ **p**: **λ**⟨1⟩ *L*e[k] f30 *S*scp | επετ.] εγραψεν ‖ p: σ1424 Eu — **9** *om* οτι ‖ Mk: BZ σ517-1424 D 440 *L*e[k] abcff¹·²g²hr¹ | μη επι πο.] παρεκτος λογου πο. ‖ ₃₂: 𝔓²⁵ᵛ B-33 Φ(λο. + επι) λ1-1582 **ϕ**-*l*547 D *pc* Chr Cr Or *L*vl⟨l⟩r¹30 vg³ Au *S*cj Eu *C Geo Aeth* — *om* ‖ Mk Lk: 1574 Athg | *om* και γαμ. αλ. ‖ ₃₂: B-33 NO λ1-1582 *pc* Or *L*ff¹ *C*b | μοιχ.¹] ποιει αυτην μοιχευθηναι ‖ ←: 𝔓²⁵ᵛ B C*-33 NO λ1-1582 ϕ*l*547 σ1402(-ασθαι) Cr Or *L*ff¹ Au *S*j *C*b | ● *om* και²—μοιχ.²(∩?): ℵC³L λ209 ϕ69-828 σ7-990-1223 D S *pc l*305 *l*845 Chr **Or** *L*vl'[k] vg¹ PsAu¹ *S*sc *C*sb¹ — *txt*: 𝔓²⁵(και *prm* ωσαυτως *et* ~ γαμ. απολ.) *Rpl* Bas Da **Or** *L*cfqz vg' Au PsAu¹ *S*'j *C*b' | γαμησας] ● γαμων ‖ Lk: 𝔓²⁵ C* NOΣΦ-1604 λ1-1582 **ϕ**⟨69-828-983⟩-174-*l*547 **σ**-659-1010-1293 W Y Δ Θ Π **078** *pc S*h

Mk 10,7 ● *om* και προσκ.—αυτου²: ℵBΨ-892 *l*48 *S*s[c] *Got* — πρ. την γυ.] τη γυναικι ‖ p: CLΔ-579 NΣ **λ** σ827-1194 A 1342 *pc l*12 — *txt*: *Rpl L*'(*om* αυτ.²: k[e] vg¹) *S*' C,f — **8** ~ σαρξ μια ‖ p ₈ₐ Gn 2₂₄ LXX: ℵC-579-892 WΘΦ-544-565-700-1071 **λ ϕ** σMᶜ-349-1082 A F K U Y Γ Π 1342 *pm L*vg¹ *Arm* — *txt*: *Rpl L*'Au *S* — **11** ¹¹ος—¹²μοιχ.] ¹²εαν απολ. γυνη τον—μοιχ. και εαν ανηρ ¹¹απολ.—μοιχ.: W(*om* ¹²αυτου—αλλην) λ1-209(*om* κ. εαν αν. ¹¹απολ.—μοιχ.)-872 *S*s[c] *Geo*¹ — *om* επ αυτ. ‖ Mt₉ Lk: WΘ-28-544-565 **λ**⟨118⟩-872 *S*s[c]ph *Geo* — **12** εαν—ανδρσ] ● εαν αυτη απολυσασα τ. αν.: ℌC 1342 *C* — γυνη εαν εξελθη απο (+ του: 28 D) ανδρος: Θ-(28)-565-700 **ϕ** D(~ εαν γυ.) *L*vl'[e] *Arm Geo*²ᶜʰ — *txt* (~ *cf. ad* ₁₁): *Rpl* (W λ1-872) *L*flr² vg Au *S*(s[c]ph (*Geo*¹) | ● *om* και²: ℌ⟨Δ⟩C 1342 | ● γαμηθη αλλω: *Rpl* — *txt*: ℌ⟨579⟩C* WΘ-28-565 **λ**⟨118⟩ **ϕ** σ 179 D(~) 1342

Mt 19₁₂ *cf.* EAe frgm.b (*cf. ad 33.* Mt 5₁₇)

(188)

202. Segnung der Kinder. "*Suffer Little Children.*"

Matth 19 13–15

[13] Τότε προσηνέχθησαν αὐτῷ παιδία, ἵνα τὰς χεῖρας ἐπιθῇ αὐτοῖς καὶ προσεύξηται· οἱ δὲ μαθηταὶ ἐπετίμησαν αὐτοῖς.
[14] ὁ δὲ Ἰησοῦς εἶπεν· ἄφετε τὰ παιδία καὶ μὴ κωλύετε αὐτὰ ἐλθεῖν πρός με· τῶν γὰρ τοιούτων ἐστὶν ἡ βασιλεία τῶν οὐρανῶν. *18* 3 *(143.): … αμην λέγω ὑμῖν, ἐὰν μὴ στραφῆτε καὶ γένησθε ὡς τὰ παιδία, οὐ μὴ εἰσέλθητε εἰς τὴν βασιλείαν τῶν οὐρανῶν.* [15] καὶ ἐπιθεὶς τὰς χεῖρας

Mark 10 13–16

[13] Καὶ προσέφερον αὐτῷ παιδία ἵνα ἅψηται αὐτῶν· οἱ δὲ μαθηταὶ ἐπετίμων τοῖς προσφέρουσιν. [14] ἰδὼν δὲ ὁ Ἰησοῦς ἠγανάκτησεν καὶ εἶπεν αὐτοῖς· ἄφετε τὰ παιδία ἔρχεσθαι πρός με, μὴ κωλύετε αὐτά· τῶν γὰρ τοιούτων ἐστὶν ἡ βασιλεία τοῦ θεοῦ. [15] αμην λέγω ὑμῖν, ὃς ἂν μὴ δέξηται τὴν βασιλείαν τοῦ θεοῦ ὡς παιδίον, οὐ μὴ εἰσέλθῃ εἰς αὐτήν. [16] καὶ ἐναγκαλισάμενος αὐτὰ κατευλόγει τιθεὶς τὰς χεῖρας ἐπ' αὐτά.

(Matth:) αὐτοῖς ἐπορεύθη ἐκεῖθεν.

Luk 18 15–17

[15] Προσέφερον δὲ αὐτῷ καὶ τὰ βρέφη ἵνα αὐτῶν ἅπτηται· ἰδόντες δὲ οἱ μαθηταὶ ἐπετίμων αὐτοῖς.
[16] ὁ δὲ Ἰησοῦς προσεκαλέσατο αὐτὰ λέγων· ἄφετε τὰ παιδία ἔρχεσθαι πρός με καὶ μὴ κωλύετε αὐτά· τῶν γὰρ τοιούτων ἐστὶν ἡ βασιλεία τοῦ θεοῦ. [17] αμην λέγω ὑμῖν, ὃς ἂν μὴ δέξηται τὴν βασιλείαν τοῦ θεοῦ ὡς παιδίον, οὐ μὴ εἰσέλθῃ εἰς αὐτήν.

Jo 3 3.5: … αμην αμην λέγω σοι, ἐὰν μή τις γεννηθῇ ἄνωθεν … [5] … οὐ δύναται εἰσελθεῖν εἰς τὴν βασιλείαν τοῦ θεοῦ.

Mt 19,13 επετιμων(εκωλυον) ‖ p: C 66 *L*vl(')e[k] g^{1}l vg Or (*Aeth*) **14** ● ειπ. + αυτοις ‖ Mk: ℵCL-892 1604 ϕ788-983 σM-659 D W *pc* *L*fg^{1}hlz vg *S*'h$^+$ *C*s$^{1:10}$b | ∼ ελθ. πρ. με και—αυτα ‖ p: ϕ983-1689 (σ1424 157) *L*e[k] 30 vg^5 *S*sc(+ ελθ. πρ. με)p | *om* και ‖ Mk: **λ**-22-1582 *C*b | ελθ.] ερχεσθαι ‖ **p**: 28(*om* και—αυτα) σ945-1424 157 713 Chr **15** αυτοις + ευλογησεν αυτα και ‖ Mk: 713

Mk 10,13 παι.] βρεφη ‖ Lk: Or | ● ∼ αυ. αψ. ‖ Lk: 𝔋C Θ-544 ϕ124 σ517 1342(-ωνται) *pc* *l*49 *l*184 Bas *L*fr^2 — επιθη την χειρα αυτου(*om*) αυτοις ‖ Mt: *S*s[c] *C*s (*Arm*) — *txt*: *Rpl* Or *L*' *S*' *C*b | ● επετιμησαν ‖ Mt: 𝔋C 1342 *S*s[c] *C* | τ. προσφ.] ● αυτοις ‖ p: 𝔋C 1342 *L*k[e] c *C*s$^{3:4}$b **14** ∼ μη—αυτα ερχ.—με ‖ Mt: 1555 | μη] και μη ‖ p: ℵCL-892 ΘΦ-28-544-565-1071-1604 **λ**-1278 ϕ983-1689 σM^c A D 1342 *pm* Bas *L*,Au *S* | τ. θε.] των ουρανων ‖ Mt: 579 W σ179-517-945-1194-1293 157 *al* *l*49 Bas *L*30 vg^1 *C*b^1 *Geo*^{2ch} **16** εναγκ.] προσκαλεσαμενος ‖ Lk16 Mt18 2: D *L*cfff^{2}qr^1 *S*s[c] | κατευ.—αυτα^2] τιθ.—αυτα ευλογει αυτα ‖ p: *Rpl* *L*flr^2 vg'(^{2} την χειρα) ⟦*prm* και ‖ p: **λ** *L*lr^{2}z vg | τιθων 28 λ1 **ϕ** — επιθεις ‖ p: 565-700 *l*251 | κατευλ.: ΝΣ*^{v} | ευλογησεν: F G K *pc* | *om* ευλ. αυτα: ϕ346 410⟧ — ετιθει τας χ. επ αυτα και ευλ. αυτα: W(επετι. ‖ Mt) D *L*'(την χειρα: bc; *om* κ. ευλ. αυ.: r^1) *S*[c](εθηκεν: sp; ευλογησεν: p)h ετ.—επ. αυ.$^+$ — *txt*: 𝔋'C Θ **σ**'(επ αυ.] αυτοις: 517)-7-115-179-1082-1391-1606 1342(κατευ. + αυτα) *pc* *l*12 *l*18 *l*19 *l*36 *l*49 *l*184 *C*(-λογησεν εθηκεν) *Aeth*

Lk 18,15 *om* και ‖ **p**: σ267-659-1391-1402 D *L*ablr^{2}30.31 *S*p^2 *C*s$^{4:7}$b *Arm*^{pc} *Aeth* | *om* τα ‖ **p**: **λ**-1582-2193 **ϕ**⟨124-346⟩ D *pc* Or *C* *Arm* | βρε.] παιδια ‖ Mt Mk: D 660 | ∼ απτ. αυ. ‖ Mk: (X) **078** *pc* *S*p | απτ.] αψηται ‖ p: X σ115 P 1093 | επετιμησαν ‖ Mt: *Rpl* *L*e *S*sp *C*s — *txt*: 𝔋[33] 1071 **λ**-1582-2193 **ϕ**⟨124⟩ D G *pc* *L*'(εκωλυον: r$^{1.2}$) *S*ch *C*b **16** προσεκ. αυ. λεγ.] ειπεν αυτοις ‖ Mk Mt: *S*s(ο—λεγ.] ει. αυ. ο Ι.)c — προσκαλεσαμενος αυτα ειπ. ‖ p: *Rpl* *L*'(αυ.] τους υιους: 31) *S*{}h(+ αυτοις$^+$) *C*b^1 *Arm*' — προσκαλ. αυτα ελεγεν(λεγει) ‖ p: **ϕ**'⟨124⟩(69 157) — *txt* (-καλειτο): 𝔓^{75}(*om* αυ.) 𝔋'[33](B = 𝔓^{75}) (1071 **λ**-1582-2193 D G) *L*a(εκελευσεν αυτοις)r^1(λεγ.] ειπεν: r^2) {*S*p(+ αυτοις)} *C*' *Arm*^{pc}(= r^2) *Aeth* | τ. θε.] των ουρανων ‖ Mt: 579-1241 Λ-1604 ϕ983-1689 157 *pc* *L*abc31 vg^1 *S*scp *C*b^2 **17** παι.] το παι. (+ τουτο) ‖ Mt18 4.3: σ267-659 *pc* (*L*il *S*c *C*b^5) | αυτ.] την βασιλειαν του θεου ‖ Mt: ϕ124

Jo 3,3 *om* αμην^2 ‖ Mt Mk Lk: Θ *L*bl | σοι] υμιν ‖ **p**: 𝔓$^{66.75}$ 579 713 **5** εισελ. εις] ιδειν ‖ 3 Mt 16 28 **p**: ℵ*-1241 σM 1093 *L*z *C*b^1 | τ. θε.] ● των ουρανων ‖ Mt: ℵ* **0141** *pc* CAp Chr^3 PsCl Eu Ir Iu *L*e PsAu Cp^1 PsCp Or^2 Te^1 — *txt*: 𝔓$^{66.75}$ *Rpl* Chr^3 Cr Gr^{Ny} *L*'Cp^4 Or^3 Te^1 *S*,j *C*,fa^s

---

202. cf. ETh^{II} 22 (*transl.*): *Εἶδεν ὁ Ἰησοῦς παιδία θηλάζοντα (καὶ) εἶπεν τοῖς μαθηταῖς αὐτοῦ· ταῦτα τὰ παιδία τὰ θηλάζοντα ὅμοιά ἐστιν τοῖς εἰσερχομένοις εἰς τὴν βασιλείαν. εἶπον αὐτῷ· ἄρα παιδία γενόμενοι εἰσελευσόμεθα εἰς τὴν βασιλείαν; εἶπεν Ἰησοῦς αὐτοῖς· ὅταν ποιήσητε τὰ δύο εἰς ἓν καὶ ποιήσητε τὰ ἔσω ὡς τὰ ἔξω καὶ τὰ ἔξω ὡς τὰ ἔσω καὶ τὰ ἄνω ὡς τὰ κάτω … τότε εἰσελεύσεσθε εἰς [τὴν βασιλείαν].*

(189)

203. Von der Gefahr des Reichtums. *The Rich Young Man.*

Matth 19 16–30

^{16} Καὶ ἰδοὺ εἷς προσελθὼν αὐτῷ εἶπεν· διδάσκαλε, τί ἀγαθὸν ποιήσω ἵνα σχῶ ζωὴν αἰώνιον; ^{17} ὁ δὲ εἶπεν αὐτῷ· τί με ἐρωτᾷς περὶ τοῦ ἀγαθοῦ; εἷς ἐστιν ὁ ἀγαθός. εἰ δὲ θέλεις εἰς τὴν ζωὴν εἰσελθεῖν, τήρησον τὰς ἐντολάς. ^{18} λέγει αὐτῷ· ποίας; ὁ δὲ Ἰησοῦς εἶπεν· τὸ **οὐ φονεύσεις, οὐ μοιχεύσεις, οὐ κλέψεις, οὐ ψευδομαρτυρήσεις,** ^{19} **τίμα τὸν πατέρα** **καὶ τὴν**

Mark 10 17–31

^{17} Καὶ ἐκπορευομένου αὐτοῦ εἰς ὁδὸν προσδραμὼν εἷς καὶ γονυπετήσας αὐτὸν ἐπηρώτα αὐτόν· διδάσκαλε ἀγαθέ, τί ποιήσω ἵνα ζωὴν αἰώνιον κληρονομήσω; ^{18} ὁ δὲ Ἰησοῦς εἶπεν αὐτῷ· τί με λέγεις ἀγαθόν; οὐδεὶς ἀγαθὸς εἰ μὴ εἷς ὁ θεός. ^{19} τὰς ἐντολὰς οἶδας· **μὴ φονεύσῃς, μὴ μοιχεύσῃς, μὴ κλέψῃς, μὴ ψευδομαρτυρήσῃς,** μὴ ἀποστερήσῃς, **τίμα τὸν πατέρα σου καὶ τὴν**

Luk 18 18–30

^{18} Καὶ ἐπηρώτησέν τις αὐτὸν ἄρχων λέγων· διδάσκαλε ἀγαθέ, τί *cf. 157.* ποιήσας ζωὴν αἰώνιον κληρονομήσω; ^{19} εἶπεν δὲ αὐτῷ ὁ Ἰησοῦς· τί με λέγεις ἀγαθόν; οὐδεὶς ἀγαθὸς εἰ μὴ εἷς ὁ θεός. ^{20} τὰς ἐντολὰς οἶδας· **μὴ μοιχεύσῃς, μὴ φονεύσῃς, μὴ κλέψῃς, μὴ ψευδομαρτυρήσῃς, τίμα τὸν πατέρα σου καὶ τὴν**

Ex 20 12–16 Dt 5 16–20

Mt 19,16 διδ. + αγαθε ‖ Mk Lk: *Rpl* Bas Chr Cr^{I} Ir Or *L*Iuv **Or** *S* *C*sb^{10} — *txt*: ℌ⟨33-579⟩ λ1-22-1582 σ1010-1293 D *pc l*5 **Or** *L*e[k] aff^{1} Hil **Or** *C*b' *Aeth* | *om* αγ. ‖ Mk Lk: Σ *pc* *L*ff^{2} *S*cj^{b} *C*sb^{4} | ποι. ινα] ποιησας ‖ Lk: ℵL-33-892 28 157 *pc* Chr | σχω ζ. αι.] ζ. αι. κληρονομησω ‖ p: ℵL-33-892 28 σ945-990-1010-1207-1223-1293 157 *pc* Or *L*e[k] *S*sch^{m}j *C*s$^{1:9}$b *Aeth* **17** ο δε + Ιησους ‖ Mk: 33 544 σM E *pc* *L*abc ff$^{1.2}$hr^{1} *S*c *Geo*^{2} *Aeth* | ερω. π. τ. αγ.] λεγεις αγαθον ‖ Mk Lk: *Rpl* Chr *L*fq Hil *S*' *C*sb^{1} *Geo*$^{A\,c}$ — *txt*: ℵBL-892 Θ-700 λ1-22-1582 D(*om* του) 660 Ant Cl PsCl Dio^{A1} Eu Mcn **Or** *L*Au Hi Iuv Mcn Nov **Or** *S*sch^{m}j *C*b' *Arm* *Geo*' *Aeth* | εις—αγ.] ουδεις αγ. ει μη εις ο θεος ‖ p: *Rpl* (ουδ. + εστιν: 892; *om* ο: U) *L*fg^{1} hq Au^{6} PsAu *S*' *C*s *Geo*$^{A\,c}$ — αγ. + ο θ. ‖ p: Ep(ο αγ.] αγ.) *L*'(∼ ο θ. ο αγ.: ff^{1} Nov *S*j^{b})c *C*b *Geo*^{A*}(+ μονος ο θ.)^{B} — αγ. + ο πατηρ (+ μου ο εν τοις ουρανοις) ‖ 548 Lk 6 36: Cl PsCl(ο γαρ αγ. εις εστ. *et om* μου) (Hip Ir) Iu (Marcos, *et om* μου ο) *L*e[k] Au^{1} Iuv Or — *txt* (*om* ο): ℵB(* *om* εις)L (Θ-700 λ1-22)-1582 (D) 660 Iu **Or** *L*a **Or** *S*sj^{ac1} *Arm* *Geo*^{1} | ● τηρει 𝔓^{71v} B D 565 **18** ειπ.] ● εφη: 𝔓^{71} B ϕ⟨69⟩ | *om* το ‖ p: σM D W *l*184 *Geo*^{1} **19** πα. + σου ‖ p Mk 7 10: C^{2}-33-1241 544-700-1604 ϕ-230-*l*547 σ659-945-990-1010-1293-1391 W *pl* *L*abfff$^{1.2}$hr^{1} vg^{11} *S*,j *C*

Mk 10,17 εις] τις ‖ Lk: λ1278 *mu* Cl *L*⟨aq⟩ | γονυπετων ‖ 140 Mt 17 14: 28 ϕ D *L*k[e] bcff^{2}qr^{1} | επηρ. αυ.] ειπεν ‖ Mt: *L*ff^{2}(ελεγεν: c) — + λεγων ‖ Lk: WΘ-565-700 ϕ D *pc* Cl *L*'⟨r^{2} vg^{10}⟩ *S*p *C*s | ποι. ινα] ποιησας(-σω) ‖ Lk: Ψ-(579 ϕ543 245) (+ ινα: 238) *pc* (*l*184) | ζ. αι. κληρ.] εχω ζ. αι. ‖ Mt: *l*36 **18** *om* I. ‖ Mt: Δ **19** *om* μη αποστ. ‖ p Ex 20 16 Dt 5 20: B*ΔΨ-579 WΣ-28-544-700 **λ** ϕ69-788-983 σ179-267-1010 K Π *al* *l*10 *l*950 *l*1642 *l*1761 Cl Ir *L*vg^{1} *S*s[c]p^{1} *Arm* | *om* σου ‖ Mt 15 4 19 19: 579 D *L*ff^{2}q

Lk 18,18 επηρ.—αρχ.] ανθρωπος τις ‖ Mt: ϕ*l*547 | αρχ.] των αρχοντων (+ των Φαρισαιων) ‖ (14 1): 157 *pc* PsCl *S*s(cp^{6})' *C*b^{1} — *om* ‖ p: Mcn^{Ep} *L*vl⟨cfz⟩r^{1} — + προσελθων τω Ιησου πειραζων αυτον και ‖ p 10 25 Mt 22 35: ϕ*l*547(-ηλθεν) 1093 (*om* πει.—και: *pc*) | *om* λεγ. ‖ p: D *L*vg^{1} | τι + αγαθον ‖ Mt: *l*183 | ποιη.] ποιησω ινα ‖ p: 245 1012 *L*e g^{2} vg^{1} *C* **19** ειπ.—I.] ο δε ειπ. αυ. ‖ Mt: D G | ● *om* ο^{2}: ℵ*B* **20** οιδ. + ο δε(*om* ο δε: *L*e a) ειπεν (+ αυτω: *L*e) ποιας; ειπεν δε ο Ιησους(*om* ειπ.—I.: *L*a)· το ‖ Mt: D (*L*e a) | μη … -ης$^{1.2.3.4}$] ου … -εις$^{1.2.3.4}$ ‖ Mt Ex 20 13ff. LXX Dt 5 17ff. LXX: D *L*vl⟨e⟩ r^{1}30 | ∼ φον. … μοι. ‖ p: 1012 *pc* Ad *L*'(*om* μη φον.: e) *S*scp *C*b^{1} | *om* σου ‖ Mt: 245 1012 *L*vg^{1}

Mt 19 16-24 p *cf.* EN frgm.16 (Hi Mt 19 16ff.): Dixit, inquit (sc. evangelium quod dicitur secundum Hebraeos), ad eum alter divitum: 'magister, quid bonum faciens vivam?' dixit ei: 'homo, legem et prophetas fac.' respondit ad eum: 'feci.' dixit ei: 'vade, vende omnia quae possides et divide pauperibus et veni sequere me.' coepit autem dives scalpere caput suum et non placuit ei. et dixit ad eum dominus: 'quomodo dicis: feci legem et prophetas? quoniam scriptum est in lege: diliges proximum tuum sicut te ipsum, et ecce multi fratres tui filii Abrahae amicti sunt stercore, morientes prae fame, et domus tua plena est multis bonis et non egreditur omnino aliquid ex ea ad eos.' et conversus dixit Simoni discipulo suo sedenti apud se: 'Simon, fili Jonae, facilius est camelum intrare per foramen acus, quam divitem in regnum coelorum.'

Matth	Mark	Luk
Lv19₁₈ **μητέρα,** καὶ **ἀγαπήσεις τὸν πλησίον σου ὡς σεαυτόν.** 20 λέγει αὐτῷ ὁ νεανίσκος· πάντα ταῦτα ἐφύλαξα· τί ἔτι ὑστερῶ;	**μητέρα.** *cf. 222.* 20 ὁ δὲ ἀποκριθεὶς εἶπεν αὐτῷ· διδάσκαλε, ταῦτα πάντα ἐφυλαξάμην ἐκ νεότητός μου.	**μητέρα.** 21 ὁ δὲ εἶπεν· ταῦτα πάντα ἐφύλαξα ἐκ νεότητός μου.
21 ἔφη αὐτῷ ὁ Ἰησοῦς· εἰ θέλεις τέλειος εἶναι, ὕπαγε πώλησόν σου τὰ ὑπάρχοντα καὶ δὸς πτωχοῖς, καὶ ἕξεις θησαυρὸν ἐν οὐρανῷ, καὶ δεῦρο ἀκολούθει μοι.	21 ὁ δὲ Ἰησοῦς ἐμβλέψας αὐτῷ ἠγάπησεν αὐτὸν καὶ εἶπεν αὐτῷ· ἕν σε ὑστερεῖ· ὕπαγε, ὅσα ἔχεις πώλησον καὶ δὸς τοῖς πτωχοῖς, καὶ ἕξεις θησαυρὸν ἐν οὐρανῷ, καὶ δεῦρο ἀκολούθει μοι ἄρας τὸν σταυρόν.	22 ἀκούσας δὲ ὁ Ἰησοῦς εἶπεν αὐτῷ· ἔτι ἕν σοι λείπει· πάντα ὅσα ἔχεις πώλησον καὶ διάδος πτωχοῖς, καὶ ἕξεις θησαυρὸν ἐν οὐρανοῖς, καὶ δεῦρο ἀκολούθει μοι.
22 ἀκούσας δὲ ὁ νεανίσκος τὸν λόγον ἀπῆλθεν λυπούμενος· ἦν γὰρ ἔχων κτήματα πολλά.	22 ὁ δὲ στυγνάσας ἐπὶ τῷ λόγῳ ἀπῆλθεν λυπούμενος, ἦν γὰρ ἔχων κτήματα πολλά.	23 ὁ δὲ ἀκούσας ταῦτα περίλυπος ἐγενήθη, ἦν γὰρ πλούσιος σφόδρα.
23 ὁ δὲ Ἰησοῦς εἶπεν τοῖς μαθηταῖς	23 καὶ περιβλεψάμενος ὁ Ἰησοῦς λέγει τοῖς μαθηταῖς	24 ἰδὼν δὲ αὐτὸν ὁ Ἰησοῦς εἶπεν·

Mt 19,19 μη. + σου‖Mk←: 1241 σ1391-1424 *pc* *L*abff$^{1.2}$ vg^{2} *S*scpj *C* *Geo*^{2} **20** ● ∼ ταυ. παν.‖p: B O ΣΦ-1604 λ1-1582 **φ**-*l*547 **σ**⟨954⟩-M-659-1207-1293-1402 D H K *pc* Chr Or *L*ff^{1}r^{1v} vg^{1} *S* *Geo*^{B} — *txt*: *Rpl* *L*' *S*j *Geo*' | εφυ.] εφυλαξαμην εκ νεοτητος μου‖p: *Rpl* (-ξα *et om* μου: D) Chr Or *L*vl'[k]30 vg^{5} Hil *S*,j *C* — *txt*: ℵBL Θ-700 λ1-22-1582 *L*ff^{1}g^{1}lz vg' Cp **21** *om* υπαγε‖Lk: 1093 PsAth$^{1:3}$ Ep *L*Cp$^{1:4}$ Or | σου τα υπ.] παντα(*om*) οσα εχεις‖(Mk)Lk: PsAth *L*ff^{1}g^{2}(^{1}lz vg')^{5} Cp$^{3:5}$ Ir *S*s(h) | πτω.] ● τοις π.‖Mk: B D Θ *C* | ● ουρανοις‖Lk18₂₂12₃₃: BC φ230-828 σ1194-1391-1402 D Γ *pc* Ep *L*e[k] g^{1} Cp^{2} *C*sb^{1} — *txt*: *Rpl* PsAth Or *L*'Cp^{2} *C*b' | ουρ. + και λαβων τον σταυρον σου‖10₃₈Mk: Ath PsAth Ep *S*c Af **22** ● λογ. + τουτον‖Lk: B-892^{m} *pc* *l*5 *l*51 *L*abcff^{1}n vg^{2} *S*scp *C*b^{2} *Geo*^{1} — ● *om* τ. λογ.: ℵLZ *l*950 *L*e[k] fh Chr$^{1:2}$ *Geo*^{2}

Mk 10,19 ● μητ. + σου‖7₁₀Dt5₁₆: ℵ*C NWΘΣ-28-565-1071 φ124 σ179-827 F *al* *l*18 *L*abcfr$^{1.2}$30 vg3 *S*s[c]p *C* **20** αποκ. ειπ.] ● εφη(*cf. ad* 29): ℌ **0274** 1342 *C* *Geo*^{B} | *om* αυτω‖Lk: K Y Π *al* *L*k[e] cqr^{2}z vg⟨8⟩ | *om* διδ.‖p: **λ** σ1194-1223 K Π 1342 *al* *l*185 Cl | ∼ παν. ταυ.‖Mt: Θ D Cl Or *L*k[e] bqr^{2} vg⟨9⟩ | εφυλαξα‖p: 892 28 A D Cl Or | *om* εκ νεο. μ.‖Mt: Cl^{1m} | μου + τι ετι υστερω‖Mt: NW(τι υσ. ετι)ΘΣ-28-565-1071 λ872 **φ** σM-1391 K Y Π *al* Lac *S*h^{+} *C*s$^{1:4}$ *Arm* **21** *om* ηγ. αυ. και … αυτω‖p: 579 — *om* ηγ. αυ. και‖p: 11 15 *L*vg^{3} | εν—υστ.] *prm* ει θελεις τελειος ειναι‖Mt: NWΘΣΦ(*om* τελ. ει.)-28-565-1071 λ872 **φ** σM K Y Π *al* *l*184 *S*hει—ειναι^{+} *C*s$^{3:4}$b^{9} *Aeth* — + ει θελ. τελ. ει.‖Mt: σ7-517-659-1082-1391 1241 *pc* *l*18 *l*19 *l*36 *l*49 *l*251 *l*260 Cl *Arm* — *om*‖Mt: φ230* 1542 *C*b' | εν^{1}] ετι εν‖Lk: ℵ λ118 *pc* *C* | σε] σοι‖Lk: *Rpl* (*om* 1241) Cl Or — *txt*: ℌ⟨Ψ⟩C WΘ-28-1071 σM-179-1675 Π 114 *l*18 *l*19 *l*48 *l*49 *l*184 | *om* υπαγε‖Lk: Cl | ∼ πω. οσα εχ.‖Mt: σ267 1093 Cl *L*cff^{2}30 | διαδος‖Lk: **φ**⟨124⟩ Cl *L*k[e] a | *om* τοις‖p: *Rpl* Cl — *txt*: ℵC-892 ΘΦ-28-565 **λ** φ788 σ71 D **0274** *C* | ουρανοις‖Lk12₃₃18₂₂: W σ349 E *pc* *L*c | ∼ αρ. τ. στ. δευρο(*om*) ακ. μοι‖8₃₄p: W-(28) **λ φ** G *pc* *L*a (*S*s[c]p *C*s^{2})^{1} (*Arm*) *Geo*^{1} *Aeth* — ● *om* αρ. τ. σταυ.‖MtLk: ℌC Θ-565 D **0274** 1342 *pc* Cl *L*' *C*s^{1}b' *Geo*^{2ch} — *txt*: *Rpl* *L*q *S*h *C*b^{4} | σταυ. + σου‖8₃₄p: W-1071 **φ** σ7-517-659-1606 E *l*184 *S*s[c]p^{7} *C*s **22** τω] τουτω τω‖Lk: Θ-28-565 **φ**⟨983⟩ D *L*vl[e]⟨lr^{2}⟩ vg^{1} *S*s[c]p *C*b^{1} **23** λεγ.] ειπεν‖p: Δ σ27-71-692 *L*k[e] q

Lk 18,20 ● μητ. + σου‖Mk7₁₀Ex20₁₂MT Dt5₁₆: *Rpl* Ad *L*abcr^{2} vg^{2} *S*'j *C* — *txt*: ℌ[33]⟨ℵ-579(*om* κ. τ. μη.)⟩X 1071-1604 **λ**⟨131⟩-1582-2193 φ788 σM-71-692-1207 A D K P W Θ Π Ψ **078** 157 *mu* *L*' *S*h *Arm* | μητ./σου + και τον πλησιον ως σεαυτον‖20₂₇Mt: *l*36 *S*j^{am} **21** ειπ. + αυτω‖p: G 157 *L*cff^{2}il *S*cpj *C*s$^{5:8}$b^{1} | ∼ παν. ταυ.‖Mt: N σ1207 A K Θ Π **078** *al* *l*32 *L*e ff^{2}(∼ παν. εφω. ταυ.) vg^{1} *S*h | εφυλαξαμην‖Mk: *Rpl* — *txt*: ℵBL-579 **λ**⟨131⟩-1582 A Θ *pc* Ad | ● *om* μου *cf.* Act26₄: B D Ad *L*l | μου + τι ετι υστερω‖Mt: 1574 **22** ετι] οτι‖Mk: ℵ* 700 F H V *al* *l*32 *l*50 *Aeth* — *om*: *L*Mcn^{Te} *S*p | λει.] υστερει‖MkMt: 382 1093 — + υπαγε‖p: φ346 σ27-1207 *pc* *S*p⟨2⟩ | διαδ.] δος‖MtMk: ℵL-33-1241 N-1071 **λλ**⟨22-1278⟩ σM-71-692 A D R Δ Ω **078** 157 *al* *l*1642 Ad *L* | πτω.] τοις π.‖Mk: φ124-*l*547 D Θ *C* | εν ουρ.] ● εν τοις ουρανοις‖12₃₃: B D {} *C* — εν ουρανω‖p: *Rpl* (εξ ουρανου: 1604) Ad Bas^{1} *L*' — *txt*: ℵL-892 1071 φ230 A R *al* Bas^{1} {*L*e a} **23** περιλ. εγ.] απηλθεν λυπουμενος‖MtLk: 213 | ● εγενετο *cf.* 23₁₂Mk9₆ *etc.*: *Rpl* Cr — *txt*: ℵBL-579 | πλ. σφο.] εχων κτηματα πολλα‖p: 1574

Mt19₁₉b *cf.* ETh^{II} 25 (*cf. ad 222.* Mt22₃₉)

αὐτοῦ· αμην λέγω ὑμῖν ὅτι πλούσιος δυσκόλως εἰσελεύσεται εἰς τὴν βασιλείαν τῶν οὐρανῶν.

[24] πάλιν δὲ λέγω ὑμῖν,

εὐκοπώτερόν ἐστιν κάμηλον διὰ τρυπήματος ῥαφίδος εἰσελθεῖν ἢ πλούσιον εἰς τὴν βασιλείαν τοῦ θεοῦ. [25] ἀκούσαντες δὲ οἱ μαθηταὶ ἐξεπλήσσοντο σφόδρα λέγοντες· τίς ἄρα δύναται σωθῆναι; [26] ἐμβλέψας δὲ ὁ Ἰησοῦς εἶπεν αὐτοῖς· παρὰ ἀνθρώποις

αὐτοῦ· πῶς δυσκόλως οἱ τὰ χρήματα ἔχοντες εἰς τὴν βασιλείαν τοῦ θεοῦ εἰσελεύσονται. [24] οἱ δὲ μαθηταὶ ἐθαμβοῦντο ἐπὶ τοῖς λόγοις αὐτοῦ. ὁ δὲ Ἰησοῦς πάλιν ἀποκριθεὶς λέγει αὐτοῖς· τέκνα, πῶς δύσκολόν ἐστιν τοὺς πεποιθότας ἐπὶ χρήμασιν εἰς τὴν βασιλείαν τοῦ θεοῦ εἰσελθεῖν· [25] εὐκοπώτερόν ἐστιν κάμηλον διὰ τῆς τρυμαλιᾶς τῆς ῥαφίδος διελθεῖν ἢ πλούσιον εἰς τὴν βασιλείαν τοῦ θεοῦ εἰσελθεῖν. [26] οἱ δὲ περισσῶς ἐξεπλήσσοντο λέγοντες πρὸς ἑαυτούς· καὶ τίς δύναται σωθῆναι; [27] ἐμβλέψας αὐτοῖς ὁ Ἰησοῦς λέγει· παρὰ ἀνθρώποις

πῶς δυσκόλως οἱ τὰ χρήματα ἔχοντες εἰς τὴν βασιλείαν τοῦ θεοῦ εἰσπορεύονται·

[25] εὐκοπώτερον γάρ ἐστιν κάμηλον διὰ τρήματος βελόνης εἰσελθεῖν ἢ πλούσιον εἰς τὴν βασιλείαν τοῦ θεοῦ εἰσελθεῖν. [26] εἶπον δὲ οἱ ἀκούσαντες· καὶ τίς δύναται σωθῆναι; [27] ὁ δὲ εἶπεν· τὰ ἀδύνατα παρὰ ἀνθρώποις

Mt 19,23 ∼ δυσκ. πλου. ‖ p: *Rpl* Or *Le*[k] fff^{2}hqr^1 vg^2 Ar *S,j*^{1} — *txt*: ℌC 700 λ1-1582 **ϕ** D Θ 157 Or *L*'(^{23}∩^{24} υμιν: l) *Sj*^{abc} *Geo* | ∼ εις—ουρ. εισελ. ‖p: Σ *pc* **24** τρυπ.] ● τρηματος ‖ Lk: ℵB — τρυμαλιας ‖ Mk: C ΣΦ-544-700 ϕ124-*l*547 σM-945-1223 K U Θ *al* Or — *txt*: *Rpl* Or(τρυπης) | διελθειν ‖ Mk: *Rpl* Or *L*,Ar Hil *Sc Cs*^{4} — *txt*: ℌ⟨B⟩C ΟΣΦ-28-544 **λ**-1582 **ϕ**⟨124⟩-174-230-*l*547 σM-71-517-692-990-1010-1207-1293-1424 E F H K U W Δ 157 *pc* Or *Sj Cs*^{7}b | πλου. + εισελ. ‖ p: B 700 ϕ124 D Θ Or *L*' *Cs*$^{7+1?}$b *Geo* — θε. + εισελθειν ‖ p: *Rpl LHil Sp*$^{\langle 1\rangle}$h *Cs*$^{1?}$ *Arm* — *txt*: ℌ' **λ**-1582 157 *pc* Chr Or *Lff*^{1} vg^1 Ar *Sscj* **25** τις] και τ. ‖ p: 33 *Lff*^{2} **26** ειπ.] λεγει ‖ Mk: K Y 565 *pc Lvg*^{1}

Mk 10,23 οι—εχον.] πλουσιος *et* ελευσεται ‖ Mt: 1047 | ∼ εισελ. εις τ. β. τ. θε. ‖ Mt: Ψ 544 ϕ983-1689 σ827 482 Cl | εισελ. + 25 ‖ p: 235 **24** ∼ 25.24 ‖ p: D *Labff*^{2} — *om* 24 ‖ p: *Lr*$^{1.2}$ | τ. πεπ. επι χρ.] πλουσιον ‖ Mt23: W(∼ εις—εισελ. πλου.) *Lc* — ● *om*: ℵBΔΨ *Lk*[e] *Csb*^{6} *Aeth* — οι τα χρηματα εχοντες *et om* εστιν ‖ 23 Lk18 24: 1241 — *txt* (επι + τοις): *Rpl* (ΘΦ-28-565 **λ**⟨118⟩ **ϕ** D *pc*) Cl *L*'(τους τ. χρ. εχοντας η π. επ αυτοις: a) *S C*b'(^{3}) **25** ευκοπ.] + γαρ ‖ Lk: 131 *al l*10 *Lg*^{2} *Ss*[c] *Cs*$^{2:3}$ — ταχιον *et om* εστιν: D *La* | ● *om* της^1 ‖ p: ℌ⟨B⟩C NWΘΣ-28-544-565-700-1071 **λ ϕ** σM-349-517-692 A D F K U Γ Π 1342 157 *pm* | τρυμ.] τρυπηματος ‖ Mt: **ϕ** — τηματος(< τρη-?) ‖ Lk: ℵ* | ● *om* της^2 ‖ MtLk: ℌ⟨B⟩C NWΘΣ-544-700-1071 **λ ϕ** σM-349-517 A D G K U Π 1342 *al C* | ραφ.] βελονης ‖ Lk: **ϕ** Cl | διελθ.] εισελθ. ‖ p25b: *Rpl* Cl *Lk*[e] a(intravit = -bit) vg^1 *Ss*[c]ph^m *Cs* — *txt*: BC-892 700-1071 **λ ϕ**⟨69⟩ σ517-954-1194-1402-1606 D(-ελευσεται) K Π *L*' *S*h^t *C*b *Arm Aeth* | τ. θε.] των ουρανων ‖ Mt23: 579 *Lg*^{2} Pau^N *Ss*[c] | *om* εισελ. ‖ Mt: 579 Θ D 1241 Cl *Lk*[e] aff^2 vg^1 *Ss*[c] **26** πρ. εαυ.] ● πρ. αυτον: ℌ⟨579⟩C 1555 *C*' — *om* ‖ MtLk: σ179 *pc* Cl *Cb*^{1} — πρ. αλληλους: σM *Lk*[e] acz *Sp* — *txt*: *Rpl* (εαυτον: ϕ788) *L*'Au *S*' | τις + αρα ‖ Mt: 2145 *pc* (*et om* και: *Ss*[c]h) **27** εμβ.] εμβ. δε ‖ Mt: *Rpl Lk*[e] *S*' *Cs* — αποκριθεις δε: Θ-565-700 406 — *prm* ο δε *et om* ο Ι. ‖ Lk: Cl — *txt* (και εμβ.): ℵBC*ΔΨ λ1 *l*18 *l*19 *l*49^2 *l*150^1 *L*(vl'r^1)a30 *Ss*[c] *C*b *Arm* | ∼ ο Ι. λεγ. αυ. ‖ Mt: 892 Θ-565-700 **047** *pc* | ∼ ο Ι. αυ. ‖ Mt: Γ *Lvg*^{1} | λεγ.] ειπεν ‖ p: ℵ* **σ**⟨954⟩ Γ *pc* Cl *Lk*[e] aq | λεγ. + αυτοις ‖ Mt: ϕ230 *Ss*[c]p *Cs*

Lk 18,24 ∼ εισπορ./εισελ. εις τ. β. τ. θε. ‖ Mt: *Rpl Lfl* — *txt*: ℌ[33] ϕ124-*l*547 D R Ψ 157 *pc L*' | τ. θε.] των ουρανων ‖ Mt: σM-27-71-692 K Y Π *al* | εισελευσονται ‖ p: *Rpl L*' — *txt*: BL-892 *Lr*^{2} *C Aeth* **25** *om* γαρ ‖ p: 579-1241 N-1071(+ δε) ϕ69 Π *pc l*36 *l*1663 *l*1963 *Lb*(+ δε: dir^1) vg^2 *Sp Cp*^{2} | τρημ.] τρυμαλιας ‖ Mk: *Rpl* — τρυπηματος ‖ Mt: L-1241 λ22^c R Θ 157 242 *l*31 *l*32 *l*150 — *txt*: ℵB D 49 | βελ.] ραφιδος ‖ MtMk: *Rpl* — *txt*: ℵBL-579-1241 **λλ**⟨131-1278⟩ **ϕ**-*l*547 D Θ(+ μαλιας ραφιδος!) 157 *pc* | εισελ.^{1}] διελθειν ‖ Mk: 1071 **λ**⟨131⟩-1582 ϕ⟨96-983⟩-*l*547 σM-692-954 A D P Θ *pc L*'⟨e⟩(*om* 25: l) Ar *Ssch*^{t} *Csb*$^{\langle 4\rangle}$ *Arm Aeth* | *om* εισελ.^{2} ‖ Mt: 579 Ψ *Le* aff^2 g^{2}ir^2 Ar *Ssp* **26** ακουσ.] μηθηται ‖ Mt: σ1194 248(+ αυτου) | δυν.] αρατε (< αρα δυναται?) ‖ Mt: 1574 **27** ∼ π. ανθ. αδυ. ‖ p: ϕ69 Ad Thi *Sscp*

Matth 19

τοῦτο ἀδύνατόν ἐστιν, παρὰ δὲ θεῷ πάντα δυνατά.
27 τότε ἀποκριθεὶς ὁ Πέτρος εἶπεν αὐτῷ· ἰδοὺ ἡμεῖς ἀφήκαμεν πάντα καὶ ἠκολουθήσαμέν σοι· τί ἄρα ἔσται ἡμῖν; 28 ὁ δὲ Ἰησοῦς εἶπεν αὐτοῖς· αμην λέγω ὑμῖν ὅτι ὑμεῖς οἱ ἀκολουθήσαντές μοι,

ἐν τῇ παλιγγενεσίᾳ, ὅταν καθίσῃ ὁ υἱὸς τοῦ ἀνθρώπου ἐπὶ θρόνου δόξης αὐτοῦ, καθήσεσθε καὶ αὐτοὶ ἐπὶ δώδεκα θρόνους κρίνοντες τὰς δώδεκα φυλὰς τοῦ Ισραηλ. 29 καὶ πᾶς ὅστις ἀφῆκεν οἰκίας ἢ ἀδελφοὺς ἢ ἀδελφὰς ἢ πατέρα ἢ μητέρα ἢ γυναῖκα ἢ τέκνα ἢ ἀγροὺς ἕνεκεν τοῦ

Mark 10

ἀδύνατον, ἀλλ' οὐ παρὰ θεῷ· πάντα γὰρ δυνατὰ παρὰ τῷ θεῷ.
28 ἤρξατο λέγειν ὁ Πέτρος αὐτῷ· ἰδοὺ ἡμεῖς ἀφήκαμεν πάντα καὶ ἠκολουθήκαμέν σοι. 29 ἀποκριθεὶς ὁ Ἰησοῦς εἶπεν· αμην λέγω ὑμῖν,

οὐδείς ἐστιν ὃς ἀφῆκεν οἰκίαν ἢ ἀδελφοὺς ἢ ἀδελφὰς ἢ μητέρα ἢ πατέρα ἢ τέκνα ἢ ἀγροὺς ἕνεκεν

Luk 18

δυνατὰ παρὰ τῷ θεῷ ἐστιν.
28 εἶπεν δὲ Πέτρος· ἰδοὺ ἡμεῖς ἀφέντες τὰ ἴδια ἠκολουθήσαμέν σοι.
29 ὁ δὲ εἶπεν αὐτοῖς· αμην λέγω ὑμῖν ὅτι ... *22 28–30 (250.): ὑμεῖς δέ ἐστε οἱ διαμεμενηκότες μετ' ἐμοῦ ἐν τοῖς πειρασμοῖς μου· 29 κἀγὼ διατίθεμαι ὑμῖν καθὼς διέθετό μοι ὁ πατήρ μου βασιλείαν, 30 ἵνα ἔσθητε καὶ πίνητε ἐπὶ τῆς τραπέζης μου ἐν τῇ βασιλείᾳ μου, καὶ καθήσεσθε ἐπὶ θρόνων τὰς δώδεκα φυλὰς κρίνοντες τοῦ Ισραηλ.* (29) οὐδείς ἐστιν ὃς ἀφῆκεν οἰκίαν ἢ γυναῖκα ἢ ἀδελφοὺς ἢ γονεῖς ἢ τέκνα εἵνεκεν τῆς

Mt 19,26 *om* εστ.‖Mk: 238 1515 | δε^2 + τω‖Mk27b Lk27b: 28 **λ**⟨1⟩ σM D *pc* | ● ∼ δυν. παν.‖Lk: ℵLZ σ1010-1293 | δυν. + εισιν(εστιν)‖Lk: C^3 Φ ϕ174-230-*l*547 σM-27-71-517-659-692-945-1010-1194-1293-1424 D E F G V^c Ω (157) *al* **27** αφηκ. ... και] αφεντες‖Lk: Θ | ηκολουθηκαμεν‖Mk: D* **28** θρονων‖Lk22 30: Σ Bas$^{1:5}$ Ddy **29** οστις] ος‖p: *Rpl* Chr^1 — *txt*: 𝔖C ΣΦ-544-700-1604 λ1-1582 **ϕ**-174-*l*547 D E K W Y Δ Θ 157 *al* Bas Chr^6 Cr Or | ● ∼ αδελφους—αγρ. η οικιας(-αν): ℵ^{a}C*L-892 λ1-1582 1295 (Chr$^{1:7}$) Or *Sj* *C*b$^{⟨1⟩}$ *Aeth* | οικιαν‖p: 33 544-700 σ71-692-1391-1402 K Y Θ *pc* Chr$^{2:7}$ *L*⟨e[k] q⟩ Or *Geo* | *om* η αδελφας‖Lk: 2145 Chr$^{4:7}$ | πα. η μη.] γονεις‖Lk: λ1-1582 Or *L*e[k](∼ τεκ. η γον.) — μη. η πα.‖Mk: Φ 1646 | ● *om* η γυν.‖Mk: B 1604 λ1-1582 D Chr$^{6:7}$ Or *L*e[k] abff$^{1.2}$nr^2 *S*sj | τ. ον. μου] ● τ. εμου ον.: ℵB ϕ124 Θ — εμου‖Mk: 1295

Mk 10,27 αδυν.] τουτο αδ.‖Mt: C^2 NWΘΣ-28-700-1071 **ϕ** σ349-517 D *L*bg^2(∼ του. π. ανθ. αδυν.: c30) vg^2 *S*s[c]p (∼ αδ. του.: *C*s *Geo*^{2ch} *Aeth*) | αδυνατα‖Lk: Γ *L*g^2 | αδυ. + εστιν‖Mt: 28-700-1071 σ115-349-517 D 157 *pc* *L*⟨g^2(videntur)⟩ | αλλ—θεω^2] παρα δε(*om* k) τω θεω δυνατον (+ εστιν)‖p: D 157(*om* τω) Cl (*om* δε τω) *L*(k[e] af)ff^2 | θεω^1] τω θ.‖27b Lk: WΦ-28 λ118-872 ϕ13 σ659-827-945 A K Π *al* | δυν. + εστιν‖Lk: *Rpl* (*L*k[e] abcfr$^{1.2}$z)g^{2}30 — + εστιν τω πιστευοντι‖9 23: 90 483 — *txt* (θεω^1∩^{2}): 𝔖'(ΔΨ)C WΘ-28-565-700 (**λ**⟨118⟩ ϕ69)-124 **σ**⟨1424⟩-7-659-(1082 157) 1342 *pc* (*al l*184) Cl *L*(l)q vg'(^{1}) | *om* τω‖27a Mt: B-892 Θ-28-1071-1604 λ1278 ϕ124 σ349-517 **28** ηρξ.] τοτε ηρξ.‖Mt: ϕ983-1689 *L*vg^1 *S*h^m — ηρξ. δε‖Lk: NΣ-28-700-1071 λ872 ϕ124-230-346 σ349-945-954-1223-1606-1675 K Π *mu* *L*f *C*sb^{10} | ● ηκολουθησαμεν‖p: *Rpl* Cl — *txt*: BC W D 1216 | σοι + τι αρα(*om*) εσται ημιν‖Mt: ℵ 51 *l*20 *L*(b)30 (vg^1) **29** αποκ. ... ειπ.] ● εφη ... *om* (*cf. ad* 20): 𝔖⟨Ψ⟩ 1342(και εφη) *pc* *C*s$^{3:4}$b | αποκ. + δε‖p: 28-1071 λ872-2193 D(*om* ειπ.) K Γ(*om* ο I.) Π 157 *pm* Cl^1(^{1} = D) *L*k[e] cff^{2}q (ο + δε: *C*sb^1) | αποκ. / εφη + αυτω‖p: ℵ 1342 *pc* *Geo*^{1} — + αυτοις (ειπ. + αυτοις)‖p: Ψ(*om* ο I.)-579 (*L*cf *C*s^1)^3(b^1 *Geo*^{2ch}) | υμ. + οτι‖Mt Lk: A* *pc* *S* | οικιας‖Mt: Ψ 700 σM F *pc* *S*p | ∼ πα. η μη.‖Mt Ex20 12 Dt5 16: *Rpl* Bas *L*vl' vg^7 Au^1 *S*p$^{⟨4⟩}$h *C*s^2 *Arm* *Geo*^{1} *Aeth* — *om* η πα.: D *L*k[e] aff^{2}30 vg^1 — *txt*: BCΔ WΘΦ-565-700 σ115 *pc* *L*cfq vg' Au^1 *S*s[c] *C*s^{3}b *Geo*^{2ch} | τεκ.] γυναικα η τεκ.‖p: *Rpl* Bas$^{1:2}$ *L*fq *S*' *C*b^1 *Geo*^{2ch} — *txt*: ℵBΔ-892 WΘ-565 **λ**⟨118⟩ D *pc* Cl *L*'Au *S*s[c] *C*' *Arm* *Geo*^{1} | *om* η αγρ.‖Lk: Ψ Cl *L*k[e] b *C*b^1

Lk 18,27 π. τ. θεω εστ.] εστ. π. τ. θεω‖Mk: *Rpl* (σ1223 P Ω 475) *L*'⟨vg^1⟩(αδυνατα∩δυνατα: ff^2) Eu Ir *C* — π. τ. θεω‖Mk: 1071 *pc* Ad(∼ π. τ. θεω δυν.) *L*Ir Te *S*h — *txt*: 𝔖[33] 28-1071-1604 **λ**-1582-2193 **σ**⟨1675⟩-267-659-1194 (D W 157) Ψ 248 *L*e a Hi | *om* τω‖Mk: σ1223 D P W Ω 157 475 Iu Thi **28** Π.] ● ο Π.‖**p**: 𝔖X N-700-1071 **λ**-22-1582 **ϕ**-174-230 σ1194 D R U Θ Ψ 157 *al* | αφ. ... ηκ.] αφηκαμεν ... και ηκ.‖Mt Mk: *Rpl* *L*e dfz vg Am Au {*C*} — *txt* (και ηκ.): ℵ^{c}BL-892 **λ**-1582-2193 (**ϕ**'⟨13-124⟩ 69-788) D Θ *L*vl'r^1 | τα ιδ.] παντα‖**p**: *Rpl* *L*fz vg Am Au *S*' — παντα τα ιδ.‖p: **λ**-1582-2193 **ϕ** *L*e aclq *S*sc *C*s^1 *Arm* — *txt*: ℵ^{c}BL-892 Θ D *L*bff^{2}ir$^{1.2}$(retibus < rebus) *S*h^m *C*s^{9}b | ηκολουθηκαμεν‖Mk: R | σοι + τι αρα εσται ημιν‖Mt: ℵ^{c}X *pc* *L*lr$^{1.2}$ vg^1(*om* αρα) **29** ● *om* οτι‖Mk: ℵ* λ131 D Δ *L*⟨f⟩ Cp Hi | οικιας‖Mt: ϕ69 D H 157 *pc l*49 *S*p | *om* η γυν.‖Mk: 1241 vg^1 *S*h^{Brs} | αδ.] αδελφας‖p: 579 1071 — + η αδελφας‖p: X-1241 σ115 D Δ Ψ *pc l*18 *l*19 *L*vg^1 *C*p$^{1:5}$ *S*p^{1}h^{Brs} *C*s$^{1:9}$ | γον.] αγρους‖p: 251 *pc*

Matth	Mark	Luk
ὀνόματός μου,	ἐμοῦ καὶ ἕνεκεν τοῦ εὐαγγελίου,	βασιλείας τοῦ θεοῦ,
ἑκατονταπλασίονα	³⁰ ἐὰν μὴ λάβῃ ἑκατονταπλασίονα	³⁰ ὃς οὐχὶ μὴ ἀπολάβῃ πολλαπλασίονα
λήμψεται	νῦν ἐν τῷ καιρῷ τούτῳ οἰκίας καὶ	ἐν τῷ καιρῷ τούτῳ
	ἀδελφοὺς καὶ ἀδελφὰς καὶ μητέρας καὶ τέκνα καὶ ἀγροὺς μετὰ διωγμῶν,	
καὶ ζωὴν αἰώνιον κληρονομήσει.	καὶ ἐν τῷ αἰῶνι τῷ ἐρχομένῳ ζωὴν αἰώνιον.	καὶ ἐν τῷ αἰῶνι τῷ ἐρχομένῳ ζωὴν αἰώνιον.
³⁰ πολλοὶ δὲ ἔσονται πρῶτοι ἔσχατοι καὶ ἔσχατοι πρῶτοι.	³¹ πολλοὶ δὲ ἔσονται πρῶτοι ἔσχατοι καὶ οἱ ἔσχατοι πρῶτοι.	
20 16 (204.): οὕτως ἔσονται οἱ ἔσχατοι πρῶτοι καὶ οἱ πρῶτοι ἔσχατοι.		*13 30 (179.): καὶ ἰδοὺ εἰσὶν ἔσχατοι οἳ ἔσονται πρῶτοι, καὶ εἰσὶν πρῶτοι οἳ ἔσονται ἔσχατοι.*

(190)

204. Das Gleichnis von den Arbeitern im Weinberg. **Matth 20 ₁₋₁₆**
The Parable of the Labourers in the Vineyard.

¹ Ὁμοία γάρ ἐστιν ἡ βασιλεία τῶν οὐρανῶν ἀνθρώπῳ οἰκοδεσπότῃ, ὅστις ἐξῆλθεν ἅμα πρωῒ μισθώσασθαι ἐργάτας εἰς τὸν ἀμπελῶνα αὐτοῦ. ² συμφωνήσας δὲ μετὰ τῶν ἐργατῶν ἐκ δηναρίου τὴν ἡμέραν ἀπέστειλεν αὐτοὺς εἰς τὸν ἀμπελῶνα αὐτοῦ. ³ καὶ ἐξελθὼν περὶ τρίτην ὥραν εἶδεν ἄλλους ἑστῶτας ἐν τῇ ἀγορᾷ ἀργούς, ⁴ καὶ ἐκείνοις εἶπεν· ὑπάγετε καὶ ὑμεῖς εἰς τὸν ἀμπελῶνα, καὶ ὃ ἐὰν ᾖ δίκαιον δώσω ὑμῖν. ⁵ οἱ δὲ ἀπῆλθον. πάλιν ἐξελθὼν περὶ ἕκτην καὶ ἐνάτην ὥραν ἐποίησεν ὡσαύτως. ⁶ περὶ δὲ τὴν ἑνδεκάτην ἐξελθὼν εὗρεν ἄλλους ἑστῶτας, καὶ λέγει αὐτοῖς· τί ὧδε ἑστήκατε ὅλην τὴν ἡμέραν ἀργοί; ⁷ λέγουσιν αὐτῷ· ὅτι οὐδεὶς ἡμᾶς ἐμισθώσατο. λέγει αὐτοῖς· ὑπάγετε καὶ ὑμεῖς εἰς τὸν ἀμπελῶνα. ⁸ ὀψίας δὲ γενομένης λέγει ὁ κύριος τοῦ ἀμπελῶνος τῷ ἐπιτρόπῳ αὐτοῦ· κάλεσον τοὺς ἐργάτας καὶ ἀπόδος αὐτοῖς τὸν μισθόν, ἀρξάμενος

Mt 19,29 ● πολλαπλασιονα‖Lk: BL σ945-990-1010-1207-1223-1293 Cr Or *Sj Cs Aeth* — *prm* και νυν‖Mk: *Le*[k] vg^{1}(*om* και) | λημψ. + εν τω καιρω τουτω‖p: Chr$^{5:6}$ *Lr*^{2}(και.] αιωνι) **30** ∼ εσχ. πρ. και πρ. (+ οι) εσχ.‖20₁₆ Lk: ℵL-892 (21) 157 *Aeth* | και + οι‖20₁₆ Mk: C-892 Σ λ22 **φ**⟨124-788⟩-174-*l*547 σM-1010 *pc* **20,3** ειδ.] ευρεν‖6: λ1582 σ1424 D 245 *L*abcff$^{1.2}$g^{2}hnr^{1}30.32 **4** ● αμπ. + μου‖1f.: ℵC-33 Σ-28 **φ**⟨983⟩ Θ Π Or *L*' *S*h^{Brs} *Cs Arm Aeth Δ*'⟨me⟩ — *txt*: *Rpl L*blq vg^{10} Or *S*'j *C*b *Δ*l^{FG} p*^{v} **5** παλ.] ● παλ. δε: ℵCL-892 544-1604 D *L*cg^{1}lz vg$^{\langle 1\rangle}$ *S*h^{+}j *Cs* — και παλ.(*om*): (Ω) 4 273 *L*f *S*' *Geo*^{2} | *om* ωρ.‖6: λ22 *pc* **6** ενδ. + ωραν‖3.5.9: *Rpl* Chr *Le*[k] cfff^{2}g^{2}q30.32 vg^{1} Ar Hil {*S*,j *C*} — *txt*: ℵBL-**085**-892 D Θ *pc* Cr Or *L*' *Aeth* | ευρ.] ειδεν‖3: Chr *Ss Cs* | εστω. + αργους‖3.6b: *Rpl* Chr *L*hq *S*' *Δ*a p — + εν τη αγορα αργους‖3: Φ *pc L*f — *txt*: ℵBL-**085**-892 D Θ 565 Cr Or *L*' Ar *Ssc C Aeth Δ*'⟨i^{V} me⟩ **7** αμπ. + μου‖1f.: Z-**085** Σ φ174-230-346-828-*l*547 σ71-1010-1207 D Π *al* Chr^{1} Cr *L*vl[k]⟨cff^{1}lq⟩g^{2}30.32 PsChr *Ss Cs*$^{7:8}$ *Geo Aeth* | αμπ./μου + και ο εαν η δικαιον λημψεσθε(δωσω υμιν)‖(4): *Rpl* (440) Chr^{1} *L*fg^{2}hqr^{2}30.32 (vg^{1}) PsChr^{1} *S*'(c)j^{a} (*C*b^{4}) *Geo*^{Bc} (*Aeth*) — *txt*: 𝕳⟨33⟩-**085** λ1-1582 D Θ Or *L*' PsChr^{1} *S*sj^{bc} *C*' *Geo*' **8** ● *om* αυτοις: ℵCLZ-**085** Or *Geo*' — *txt*: *Rpl* Chr Cr *L*,Ar Or *S*,j *C Geo*^{A}

Mk 10,29 *om* ενεκ.^{2}‖8₃₅: B* 544-700 **σ**⟨954⟩-7-659-1606 A S 1342 *al* Bas *Lk*[e] cz **30** εαν] ος ου‖Lk: Θ-28-565-700 D(ος αν) Bas *L*' *S*h — και: *Lk*[e] *S*p | απολαβη‖Lk: ℵ **λ**⟨118⟩ *pc* Cl | *om* νυν‖Lk: 544 D' *pc* Bas *L*aq *Ss*[c] *Geo*^{B} | τεκ.] γυναικα(-ας) και τεκ.‖Mt₂₉ Lk₂₉: Ψ^{c} (φ124 σ349)-517-659-1606 *pc* | αιωνιον + λημψεται‖Mt₂₉a: D *L*vl'⟨fqr^{2}z⟩ vg^{1} *C*b^{1} — + κληρονομησει‖Mt: 1071 472 *Lk*[e] *Ss*[c] **31** *om* οι‖Mt₃₀: *Rpl C*b — *txt*: BCX-892 NΣΦ-1604 λ118 **φ**⟨124⟩-230 σ115-1082-1207-1606 E F G H S U Y Γ Ω **047** *al* Cl *Cs*

Lk 18,30 ος ουχι] εαν‖Mk: D *Le* bcil *Arm* | απολ.] ● λαβη‖Mk: B 1071 σM-1223 D *pc l*48 *La* | εκατονταπλασ.‖MtMk: 1241 *Ssc* — επταπλ.: D *L*vl⟨fz⟩r^{1} Am Au Cp Hi | εν^{1}] νυν εν‖Mk: X σ1194 213 244(∼ εν τω νυν) | ζω. αι. + κληρονομησει‖Mt: N Θ *L*vl⟨fqz⟩g^{2}r^{1}30 vg^{4} *Ssc Arm*

Mt19₃₀p *cf.* ETh^{II} 4 (POxy 654,3): (*cf. ad 79.* Mt11₂₅) ... εἴ]σετε ὅτι πολλοὶ ἔσονται π[ρῶτοι ἔσχατοι καὶ] οἱ ἔσχατοι πρῶτοι καὶ [ζωὴν αἰώνιον ἔξου]σιν.

(*transl.*): (*cf. ad 79.* Mt11₂₅) ... *ὅτι πολλοὶ ἔσονται πρῶτοι ἔσχατοι καὶ γενήσονται εἷς μόνος.*

ἀπὸ τῶν ἐσχάτων ἕως τῶν πρώτων. 9 ἐλθόντες οὖν οἱ περὶ τὴν ἑνδεκάτην ὥραν ἔλαβον ἀνὰ δηνάριον. 10 καὶ ἐλθόντες οἱ πρῶτοι ἐνόμισαν ὅτι πλεῖον λήμψονται· καὶ ἔλαβον τὸ ἀνὰ δηνάριον καὶ αὐτοί. 11 λαβόντες δὲ ἐγόγγυζον κατὰ τοῦ οἰκοδεσπότου 12 λέγοντες· οὗτοι οἱ ἔσχατοι μίαν ὥραν ἐποίησαν, καὶ ἴσους αὐτοὺς ἡμῖν ἐποίησας τοῖς βαστάσασι τὸ βάρος τῆς ἡμέρας καὶ τὸν καύσωνα. 13 ὁ δὲ ἀποκριθεὶς ἑνὶ αὐτῶν εἶπεν· ἑταῖρε, οὐκ ἀδικῶ σε· οὐχὶ δηναρίου συνεφώνησάς μοι; 14 ἆρον τὸ σὸν καὶ ὕπαγε· θέλω δὲ τούτῳ τῷ ἐσχάτῳ δοῦναι ὡς καὶ σοί· 15 οὐκ ἔξεστίν μοι ὃ θέλω ποιῆσαι ἐν τοῖς ἐμοῖς; ἢ ὁ ὀφθαλμός σου πονηρός ἐστιν ὅτι ἐγὼ ἀγαθός εἰμι; 16 οὕτως ἔσονται οἱ ἔσχατοι πρῶτοι καὶ οἱ πρῶτοι ἔσχατοι.

203.

(191) *205.* Dritte Leidensverkündigung. *The Third Prediction of the Passion.* 136.

Matth 20 17–19 — **Mark 10** 32–34 — **Luk 18** 31–34

Matth 20 17–19	Mark 10 32–34	Luk 18 31–34
17 Καὶ ἀναβαίνων ὁ Ἰησοῦς εἰς Ἱεροσόλυμα	32 Ἦσαν δὲ ἐν τῇ ὁδῷ ἀναβαίνοντες εἰς Ἱεροσόλυμα,	
	καὶ ἦν προάγων αὐτοὺς ὁ Ἰησοῦς, καὶ ἐθαμβοῦντο, οἱ δὲ ἀκολουθοῦντες ἐφοβοῦντο.	
παρέλαβεν τοὺς δώδεκα μαθητὰς κατ' ἰδίαν, καὶ ἐν τῇ ὁδῷ εἶπεν αὐτοῖς·	καὶ παραλαβὼν πάλιν τοὺς δώδεκα ἤρξατο αὐτοῖς λέγειν τὰ μέλλοντα αὐτῷ συμβαίνειν, 33 ὅτι	31 Παραλαβὼν δὲ τοὺς δώδεκα εἶπεν πρὸς αὐτούς·
18 ἰδοὺ ἀναβαίνομεν εἰς Ἱεροσόλυμα, καὶ ὁ υἱὸς τοῦ ἀνθρώπου παραδοθήσεται τοῖς ἀρχιερεῦσιν καὶ γραμματεῦσιν, καὶ κατακρινοῦσιν αὐτὸν θανάτῳ 19 καὶ παραδώσουσιν αὐτὸν τοῖς ἔθνεσιν εἰς τὸ ἐμπαῖξαι	ἰδοὺ ἀναβαίνομεν εἰς Ἱεροσόλυμα, καὶ ὁ υἱὸς τοῦ ἀνθρώπου παραδοθήσεται τοῖς ἀρχιερεῦσιν καὶ τοῖς γραμματεῦσιν, καὶ κατακρινοῦσιν αὐτὸν θανάτῳ καὶ παραδώσουσιν αὐτὸν τοῖς ἔθνεσιν, 34 καὶ ἐμπαίξουσιν αὐτῷ	ἰδοὺ ἀναβαίνομεν εἰς Ἰερουσαλημ, καὶ τελεσθήσεται πάντα τὰ γεγραμμένα διὰ τῶν προφητῶν τῷ υἱῷ τοῦ ἀνθρώπου· 32 παραδοθήσεται γὰρ τοῖς ἔθνεσιν καὶ ἐμπαιχθήσεται καὶ ὑβρι-

Mt 20,9 ελθ. ουν] ● ελθ. δε] B *L*r^2 vg^2 *S*cj *C*s^{5}b^2 — ● και(*om*) ελθ.: *Rpl* Chr *S*' *C*b' (*Arm Geo*^{2}) — *txt*: 33 ϕ'(*prm* και: 124)-*l*547 D Θ *L*'Ar Or *C*s^1 *Geo*^{1} | *om* ωρ.‖6: 713 *L*e[k] ff^{1}q Ar **10** *om* το‖9: *Rpl* Chr — *txt*: ℵCLZ-**085**-33 NOΣ Θ Or **11** διεγο.‖Lk15 2 19 7: 1604 σ945-1010-1293 *pc* **12** ● ∼ ημ. αυτους: *Rpl* Chr^1 Or *L*c vg^1 *S*h (*Arm*) — *txt*: ℵLZ-**085**-892 ϕ'(*om* αυτ.: 543)-174-*l*547 σ1391 D *pc* Chr^2 *L*'(30) Ar Or *S*' **15** ουκ] ● η ουκ: *Rpl* Chr *L*'Or *S*'j *C* — *txt*: BLZ D Θ 700 *L*r^2 *S*sc *Aeth* **16** *om* οι$^{1.2}$‖19 30: L 566 | ∼ πρω. εσχ. … εσχ. πρω.‖←: 28 ϕ788-*l*547 σ1606 1295 Chr$^{1:2}$ Or *L*fq *C*s *Δ*i^V l^A p | εσχ.^{2} + πολλοι γαρ(δε) εισιν κλητοι ολιγοι δε εκλεκτοι‖22 14: *Rpl* (γαρ εισ.] δε: σ954; *om* γαρ: 251; οι κλητοι: Θ) Brn Chr Or *L*'(lq37. 38) (*om* δε: c vg^1) Au Hi *S*(scp)h (*om* γαρ: j^b Af *C*b^5)^1 *Arm* *Δ*⟨me⟩(*om* γαρ: a ad i^V) — *txt*: ℵBLZ-**085** *pc* *C*' *Aeth* **17** και^1—Ιη.] ● μελλων δε ο Ι. αναβαινειν: B(∼ αν. Ι. *et om* ο) λ1-1582 Or$^{2:3}$ *S*p$^{\langle 1\rangle}$ *C*s(b = B) | μαθ. + αυτου: ϕ'⟨69-124-983⟩ σ659-1010 *pc* (∼: *l*184) *l*^{p1} *L*e[k] acff^{1}g$^{1.2}$nr^{2}z vg^8 *S*p *C*s^6 *Aeth* — ● *om*‖p: ℵLZ-892 λ1-1582 ϕ788 D Θ Or *L*Hil *C*b *Arm Geo*^{1} *Aeth* — αυτου: *S*sc *Δ*p — *txt*: *Rpl* Chr *L*' *S*h *C*s^2 *Geo*^{2} | *om* κατ ιδ.‖**p**: σ945-990-1010-1207-1223-1293 *L*bff$^{1.2}$r^2 **18** θαν.] ● εις θανατον *cf.* 10 21 Mk13 12: ℵ — *om*: B *Aeth*

Mk 10,32 *om* παλ.‖**p**: σ267 *pc* *L*br^1 *S*s[c]pj *C*s$^{1:5}$ | δωδ. + μαθητας(+ αυτου)‖Mt: (ϕ124-*l*547 σ267 *pc* *l*49 *l*54) 1241 **33** παραδιδοται‖9 31: Ψ-892 K *L*vg^1 | *om* τοις^2(*om* και τ. γρα.)‖Mt**20** 18 16 21: *Rpl* (ℵ* 700 ϕ983-1689 259 *C*s^1) — *txt*: ℌ' ΘΣΦ-28 **λ**⟨118⟩ ϕ'⟨124⟩ σ71-267-692-945-1223-1606 A H Y *mu* *C*s^{4}b

Lk 18,31 δωδ. + μαθητας(+ αυτου)‖Mt: E *L*a(b)cfff^{2}ir$^{1.2}$ — + αυτου: *S*sc *Δ*p | προς αυ.] αυτοις‖Mt Mk: σ115 D 1574 *L*⟨e abqr^1⟩ | τελειωθησ.‖Jo19 28: 579 σ267-659 *pc* *l*2 *l*18 *l*19 *l*38 *l*49 *l*184 *l*185 Or | τω υι.] περι(*om*) του υιου‖Mt26 24 Mk14 21: (1071) ϕ D (Δ) Θ(περι τω υιω) *pc* Ep *L* *S* *C*s$^{2:8}$b *Δ*⟨me p⟩ **32** ∼ εμπτυ. … υβρ.‖Mk: 892 *pc* (*L*c vg^1) | κ. υβρ.] *om*‖p:L-1241 700 ϕ828-1689 D' *pc* *l*48 *l*184 *L*e abff^{2}il(*om* γαρ—εμπτυ. ∩ ?)qr^1 *S*h$^+$ *Arm*$^{\langle pc\rangle}$ — κ. μαστιγωθησεται‖p: *L*(c)fr^{2}z vg'(^{1})

Mt20 16 *cf.* ETh^{II} 4 (*cf. ad 203.* Mt19 30)

καὶ μαστιγῶσαι καὶ σταυρῶσαι, καὶ τῇ τρίτῃ ἡμέρᾳ ἐγερθήσεται.

καὶ ἐμπτύσουσιν αὐτῷ καὶ μαστιγώσουσιν αὐτὸν καὶ ἀποκτενοῦσιν, καὶ μετὰ τρεῖς ἡμέρας ἀναστήσεται.

σθήσεται καὶ ἐμπτυσθήσεται, 33 καὶ μαστιγώσαντες ἀποκτενοῦσιν αὐτόν, καὶ τῇ ἡμέρᾳ τῇ τρίτῃ ἀναστήσεται. 34 καὶ αὐτοὶ οὐδὲν τούτων συνῆκαν, καὶ ἦν τὸ ῥῆμα τοῦτο κεκρυμμένον ἀπ' αὐτῶν, καὶ οὐκ ἐγίνωσκον τὰ λεγόμενα.

(192) **206.** Jesus und die Zebedaiden. *Jesus and the Sons of Zebedee.*

Matth 20 20–28

20 Τότε προσῆλθεν αὐτῷ ἡ μήτηρ τῶν υἱῶν Ζεβεδαίου μετὰ τῶν υἱῶν αὐτῆς προσκυνοῦσα καὶ αἰτοῦσά τι παρ' αὐτοῦ. 21 ὁ δὲ εἶπεν αὐτῇ· τί θέλεις; λέγει αὐτῷ· εἰπὲ ἵνα καθίσωσιν οὗτοι οἱ δύο υἱοί μου εἷς ἐκ δεξιῶν σου καὶ εἷς ἐξ εὐωνύμων σου ἐν τῇ βασιλείᾳ σου. 22 ἀποκριθεὶς δὲ ὁ Ἰησοῦς εἶπεν· οὐκ οἴδατε τί αἰτεῖσθε. δύνασθε πιεῖν τὸ ποτήριον ὃ ἐγὼ μέλλω πίνειν;

Mark 10 35–45

35 Καὶ προσπορεύονται αὐτῷ Ἰάκωβος καὶ Ἰωάννης οἱ υἱοὶ Ζεβεδαίου λέγοντες αὐτῷ· διδάσκαλε, θέλομεν ἵνα ὃ ἐὰν αἰτήσωμέν σε ποιήσῃς ἡμῖν. 36 ὁ δὲ εἶπεν αὐτοῖς· τί θέλετε ποιῆσαί με ὑμῖν; 37 οἱ δὲ εἶπαν αὐτῷ· δὸς ἡμῖν ἵνα εἷς σου ἐκ δεξιῶν καὶ εἷς ἐξ ἀριστερῶν καθίσωμεν ἐν τῇ δόξῃ σου. 38 ὁ δὲ Ἰησοῦς εἶπεν αὐτοῖς· οὐκ οἴδατε τί αἰτεῖσθε. δύνασθε πιεῖν τὸ ποτήριον ὃ ἐγὼ πίνω, ἢ τὸ βάπτισμα ὃ ἐγὼ βαπτί-

12 50 (174.): βάπτισμα δὲ ἔχω βαπτι-

Mt 20,19 εγερ.] αναστησεται ‖ p Mk9 31 8 31 Lk24 7.46: *Rpl* Or¹ — *txt*: ℵC*LZ-892NOΣ-1604 *pc* Or¹ **20** παρ] ● απ: B D 700 *pc* **21** ● *om* σου¹ *cf.* 27.38 Lk23 33: ℵB **22** μελ. πιν.] πινω ‖ p: **λ**⟨1⟩ *pc* | πιν. + η(και) το βαπτισμα ο εγω βαπτιζομαι βαπτισθηναι ‖ Mk: *Rpl* (892 700 **λ**⟨1⟩ σ71-659-1207-1402 S *pc* Chr) *L*fhq Or *S'* *C*b⁹ (*Geo*¹)² — *txt*: ℵBLZ-**085** λ1-22-1582 ϕ230-788 D Θ Or *L'* *S*sc *C'* *Aeth*

Mk 10,34 ∼ μασ. αυ. και εμπτ. αυτω ‖ Mt: *Rpl* *S* *Cs*¹ — *om* κ. εμπτ. αυ.(αυτω¹ ⌒ ² ?) ‖ Mt: 28 λ872-2193 ϕ346 σ115-692-827 157 *al l*44 *L*e[k] — *om* κ. μασ. αυ.: σ115 D *pc* *L*e[k] ff²g²r² — *txt*: ℌC Θ-565-1071 1342 *pc* *S*j *Cs*³b *Aeth* | κ. αποκ.] + αυτον ‖ 9 31 p Lk: *Rpl* *L'* *S*,j *C* — *om*(αυτον ⌒ ?) ‖ Mt: D 157 *pc l*44 *L*g² — *txt*: ℌ⟨Ψ-579⟩ Θ-565 **λ**⟨118⟩ *l*13 *L*bc *Arm* | με. τρ. ημ.] τη τριτη ημερα ‖ Mt20 19 16 21 17 23 Lk9 22 24 7.46 18 33: *Rpl* Or *L'* *S'*j — μετα την τριτην ημεραν: *L*acq *S*hᵐ — *txt*: ℌC D 1342 *L*bff²ir¹ *C* | αναστ.] εγερθησεται ‖ Mt17 23 20 19 16 21 Lk9 22: σ517-1675 1241 **35** προσπο.] προσηλθον ‖ p: Wᶜ(* -ελθοντες) *L*vl'⟨k[e] l⟩r¹ — προσερχονται ‖ p: 273 | ● οι + δυο ‖ Mt21 26 37: BC-579 1342 *L*Au *C* *Aeth* — *om* οι: X NΘΣ-28-544-565-700 λ872-2193 ϕ828 σM-71-349-517-692-1207-1223-1675 A K U Y Π 157 *al* Or | διδ. + αγαθε ‖ 10 17 Lk18 18: σ1424 **36** ποι. με] ● ποιησω ‖ 10 51 Mt20 32 Lk18 41: C Θ-565 **λ** **ϕ**⟨124⟩ σ827-1082(-σωμαι)-1675 D(*om* τι θελ.) *al l*27 *l*184(-σομαι) *L*(*om* 36: k[e]; *om*. θελ.: abir¹)q *S*p *Geo*²(και ποι.) — με ποιησαι: ℵᶜᵇᵛL-579 Wᶜ 1342 *pc* — ● με ποιησω ‖ ←: ℵᶜBΨ *Arm* — ποιησαι: Δ W* *pc l*29 — ινα ποιησω: λ1278 σ1402 *pc* *L'* — *txt*: *Rpl* **37** ● ∼ εκ δεξ. σου ‖ p: *Rpl* — *txt*: ℌ⟨579⟩C* 1241 1342 | εξ αρ.] εξ ευωνυμων ‖ **p**: 579 WΘ-565-1604 λ1 σ1424 D 72 {}¹ — εξ ευων. σου ‖ p: *Rpl* {*L*aflr²z vg' *S*,j *C* *Geo*²}² — σου εξ ευων. ‖ p: ℵ-892 1241 1342 {}² — ● σου εξ αρ.: LΨ {}² — *txt*: BΔ {*L*vl'[e] g² vg² Au *Arm* *Geo*¹}¹ | δοξη] βασιλεια της δοξης ‖ p: W(*om* σου) **ϕ**-*l*547 *Cs*⁴:⁵(δοξη τ. βασιλειας) **38** l. + αποκριθεις ‖ p: WΘ-28-565 **λ**⟨118⟩ **ϕ**-*l*547 D *pc* *L*k[e] abff²iq *S*s[c]j *Cs*²:⁵ *Arm*

Lk 18,32 *om* κ. εμπτυ. ‖ Mt: λ2193 P R *pc* *L*(l)r¹ *Arm* **33** ∼ αυ. αποκ. ‖ Mk: 485 | τη ημ. τη τρ.] τη τρ. ημ. ‖ 24 7 9 22 Mt17 23 20 19 16 21: X-892 544-1071 **λ**-1582 **ϕ** σ954 Δ Ψ *mu* Ep *L*vl⟨e ar²z⟩r¹30 vg⁵ *Arm* — μετα τρεις ημερας ‖ p Mt27 63 Mk9 31 8 31: *L*l | αναστ.] εγερθησεται ‖ 9 22 Mt17 23 20 19 16 21: L-892 *pc l*184 Ep¹:² *C*b¹ **34** *om* τουτο ‖ Mk9 32: **λ**-1582-2193 D 157 *pc* *L*vl⟨fz⟩r¹30 *S*sc *Cs*¹:⁹b⟨5⟩ *Arm* | κεκρ.] κεκαλυμμενον ‖ 9 45 Mt10 6p: G Γ *pc l*2

Mt20 22f.p *cf.* EAe(?) (Hip ref. V 8,11): τοῦτο, φησίν, ἐστὶ τὸ εἰρημένον ὑπὸ τοῦ σωτῆρος· '... ἀλλὰ κἂν πίητε', φησί, 'τὸ ποτήριον ὃ ἐγὼ πίνω, ὅπου ἐγὼ ὑπάγω, ἐκεῖ ὑμεῖς εἰσελθεῖν οὐ δύνασθε' (*cf.* Jo8 21 13 33).

λέγουσιν αὐτῷ· δυνάμεθα. 23 λέγει αὐτοῖς· τὸ μὲν ποτήριόν μου πίεσθε, τὸ δὲ καθίσαι ἐκ δεξιῶν μου καὶ ἐξ εὐωνύμων οὐκ ἔστιν ἐμὸν τοῦτο δοῦναι, ἀλλ' οἷς ἡτοίμασται ὑπὸ τοῦ πατρός μου. 24 ἀκούσαντες δὲ οἱ δέκα ἠγανάκτησαν περὶ τῶν δύο ἀδελφῶν. 25 ὁ δὲ Ἰησοῦς προσκαλεσάμενος αὐτοὺς εἶπεν· οἴδατε ὅτι οἱ ἄρχοντες τῶν ἐθνῶν κατακυριεύουσιν αὐτῶν καὶ οἱ μεγάλοι κατεξουσιάζουσιν αὐτῶν. 26 οὐχ οὕτως ἔσται ἐν ὑμῖν· ἀλλ' ὃς ἐὰν θέλῃ ἐν ὑμῖν μέγας γενέσθαι, ἔσται ὑμῶν διάκονος, 27 καὶ ὃς ἂν θέλῃ ἐν ὑμῖν εἶναι πρῶτος, ἔσται ὑμῶν δοῦλος· 28 ὥσπερ ὁ υἱὸς τοῦ ἀνθρώπου οὐκ ἦλθεν

ζομαι βαπτισθῆναι; 39 οἱ δὲ εἶπαν αὐτῷ· δυνάμεθα. ὁ δὲ Ἰησοῦς εἶπεν αὐτοῖς· τὸ μὲν ποτήριον ὃ ἐγὼ πίνω πίεσθε, καὶ τὸ βάπτισμα ὃ ἐγὼ βαπτίζομαι βαπτισθήσεσθε· 40 τὸ δὲ καθίσαι ἐκ δεξιῶν μου ἢ ἐξ εὐωνύμων οὐκ ἔστιν ἐμὸν δοῦναι, ἀλλ' οἷς ἡτοίμασται. 41 καὶ ἀκούσαντες οἱ δέκα ἤρξαντο ἀγανακτεῖν περὶ Ἰακώβου καὶ Ἰωάννου. 42 καὶ προσκαλεσάμενος αὐτοὺς ὁ Ἰησοῦς λέγει αὐτοῖς· οἴδατε ὅτι οἱ δοκοῦντες ἄρχειν τῶν ἐθνῶν κατακυριεύουσιν αὐτῶν καὶ οἱ μεγάλοι αὐτῶν κατεξουσιάζουσιν αὐτῶν. **143.** 43 οὐχ οὕτως δέ ἐστιν ἐν ὑμῖν· ἀλλ' ὃς ἂν θέλῃ μέγας γενέσθαι ἐν ὑμῖν, ἔσται ὑμῶν διάκονος, 44 καὶ ὃς ἂν θέλῃ ἐν ὑμῖν εἶναι πρῶτος, ἔσται πάντων δοῦλος· 45 καὶ γὰρ ὁ υἱὸς τοῦ ἀνθρώπου οὐκ ἦλθεν

σθῆναι, καὶ πῶς συνέχομαι ἕως ὅτου τελεσθῇ.

22 25–27 (250.): ὁ δὲ εἶπεν αὐτοῖς· οἱ βασιλεῖς τῶν ἐθνῶν κυριεύουσιν αὐτῶν, καὶ οἱ ἐξουσιάζοντες αὐτῶν εὐεργέται καλοῦνται. 26 ὑμεῖς δὲ οὐχ οὕτως, ἀλλ' ὁ μείζων ἐν ὑμῖν γινέσθω ὡς ὁ νεώτερος, καὶ ὁ ἡγούμενος ὡς ὁ διακονῶν. 27 τίς γὰρ μείζων, ὁ ἀνακείμενος ἢ ὁ δια-

Mt 20,23 μου[1]] ο εγω πινω‖p22: σ1293-1424 1574 | πιεσ. + και το βαπτ.—βαπτισθηναι (*cf. ad* 22)‖p: *Rpl* Chr *L*fhq Or *S*' *C*b[6] — *txt*: ℵBLZ-**085** λ1-22-1582 ϕ788 D Θ Ep Or *L*' *S*sc *C*' *Aeth* | και] ● η‖p: BL-33 λ1 Θ Ep[1:2] Or *L*vl[k]⟨ff[1]g[1]lq⟩ vg[9] *C*sb[9] | ● *om* τουτο‖p: *Rpl* Ep Or *L*' Or *S*p *C* — *txt* (∼ δου. του.): C-**085**-33 Φ-1604 ϕ(174)-346-(1689) σ1010-1194(∼ του. ουκ—δου.) D U(= 1194) V W Δ (Π *pc*) *pc* Chr *L*q *S*(= 1194: sc)h *Aeth* **24** ακ. δε] ● και ακ.‖p: *Rpl* *L*' *S*ch *Arm* *Geo*[1] — *txt* (*om* δε): ℵ[c]LZ-33-892 **ϕ**⟨346⟩ **σ**⟨517⟩-349 Θ Or *L*z vg[1] *S*(s)p *C*'(b[1] *Geo*[2]) | ηγαν.] ηρξαντο αγανακτειν‖p: ℵ σ1207 *pc* | τ. δυο αδ.] Ιακοβου και Ιωαννου‖p: Γ **25** ειπ. + αυτοις‖Mk Lk: D W *L*e[k] r[2] vg[2] *S*c[s]p *C* | αρχ.] δοκουντες αρχειν‖Mk: 473 | μεγ. + αυτων‖Mk: σ1424 348 *L*r[2]? *S* *C*b **26** ουτ. + δε‖Mk: CX-**085**-33-892 Φ-28-700 ϕ174-346 σM Γ *pl* *L*cff[2] *S*c[s]p[8]h *C*b⟨5⟩ | εσται[1]] ● εστιν: BZ D 1242 Chr *L*r[2] *C*s *Geo*[1] *Aeth* | εν[2]—γεν.] ∼ μ. εν υμ. γ.‖Mk: B σ1675 *pc* — ∼ μ. γ. εν υμ.‖Mk: C σ1402 *L*ff[1] | εσται[2]] εστω‖Lk: ℵ[c]L-892 28-544-700 λ22 ϕ828-1689 σM-27-267-659-1391-1606 H S **047** 157 *mu* Chr *L*fg[1]lz30 vg *C*s[1:7] *Geo*[1] **27** εστω‖Lk: *Rpl* {} *Geo*[1] — *txt*: 𝔓[45] 𝔥⟨B-892⟩C-**085** NOΣΦ-700-1604 **λ**-22-1582 **ϕ**-174-230 σM-71-267-1194-1207-1606 D K U W Δ Θ Π 157 *pm* Or *L* *C*s{b} *Geo*[2] | υμων] παντων‖Mk10 44 9 35: σM *pc*

Mk 10,39 οι δε ειπ.] λεγουσιν‖p: Ψ(οι δε λεγ.)-579 213 *S*s[c]p | ο δε Ι. ειπ. αυ.] λεγει αυ. ο Ι.‖p: Ψ (*om* αυ. ο. Ι.) 213 *L*bcff[2](και λεγ.)i(*om* ο Ι.)q *S*s[c]p | ● *om* μεν: ℵBC*LΔ *L*r[2]30 vg[2] *S*s[c]p *C*b' *Geo*[1] — *txt*: *Rpl* *L*' *S*hj *C*sb[1] *Geo*[2] | ο εγω πι.] μου‖p: σ349 1342 **40** η] και‖p: *Rpl* *L*k[e] *S*'j — *txt*: 𝔥⟨579⟩ W D *pc* *l*72 *L*' *S*s[c] *C* | ητοι. + υπο(παρα) του πατρος μου‖p: ℵ**et*[b] (Θ)Φ **λ**-(22-1278) σ(7)-1606 1241 1342 (1365) *pc* (*l*60, *et om* μου) *L*ar[1v] *S*h[m] *C*b[2] **41** ηρξ. αγ.] ηγανακτησαν‖p: 579 **λ** A *pc* *L*g[2]q vg[1] | Ια. κ. Ιω.] των δυο αδελφων‖p: A *pc* *Aeth* **42** κ. προσκ. αυ. ο Ι.] ο δε Ι.(*om*) πρ. αυ.‖p: *Rpl* (W 238) (*om* αυ.: **λ**⟨118⟩ *pc*) *L*flqr[2] vg *S*h *C*s[4] (*Geo*[1])[2] — *txt*: ℵ(* *om* ο)BCLΔΨ(*om* αυ.: 579-892) Θ-565-700 D 1342 *pc* *L*vl'[e]r[1] *S*s[c](*om* ο Ι.)pj(κυριος Ι.) *C*s[1]b | μεγ.] βασιλεις‖Lk: ℵC*[v] | *om* αυτων[2]‖Mt: ℵC*[v] NΣ-28 **λ σ**⟨954⟩-71-179-692-1194-1402 **047** 1342 *L*k[e] **43** *om* δε‖Mt: WΘ-565 D 229 *l*251 *L*abfff[2]iqr[1.2]z vg[9] *S*s[c]j *C*s[2:5]b[1] *Arm* | εστιν] εσται‖Mt: *Rpl* *L*q *S*,j *C*b[1] — *txt*: ℵBC*LΔ Ψ WΘ-700 D *pc* *L*' *C*' *Aeth* | μ. γεν. εν υμ.] εν υμ. μ. γεν.(ειναι)‖Mt: W-28-565 *pc* *l*251 (*L*abi) *Arm* (*Geo*[2]) — ἐν υμ. ειν. μεγας(πρωτος)‖Mt: (Θ)-700 *L*k[e] c *S*s[c]p'(∼ ειν. εν υμ.: p[4]j) — μ. εν υμ. ειν.: D *pc* — γεν.(ειν.) μ. εν υμ.: *Rpl* *S*h *C* (*Geo*[1]) — γεν.(ειν.) μ.: *L*l(43 ∩ 44 ος αν: r[2])(z) vg — *txt* (γεν.] ειν.): 𝔥C* 1071 **λ**⟨118⟩ **ϕ**-*l*547 σ349-517-1606 1342 *pc* (*L*fff[2]q) | εσται] εστω‖Lk: ℵCXΔ 565 λ2193 ϕ69 σ71-349 **047** *pc* *Geo*[1] **44** εν υμ. ειν. πρω.] ● υμων γενεσθαι(ειν.) πρω.: *Rpl* (W-565 **λ** D) (∼ υμ. θελη: *S*s[c]p) *Arm*(∼ υμ. πρω.) — γεν. υμων πρω.: Σ ϕ*l*547 *pc* *S*hj — *txt*: ℵBC*LΔ(∼ εν υμ. πρω. ειν.)Ψ(∼ ειν. πρω. εν υμ.)-579-892 Θ(πρω.] μεγας‖43p)-28-700 σ517 1342 *pc* *L*'(∼ πρω. ειν.: r[1.2]; *om* ειν.: 30) | εστω‖Lk: **047** *pc* *Geo*[1] | παντ.] υμων‖Mt: 565-700 D 1342 *pc* *L*ag[2] *S*j[c] *Geo*[2] *Aeth* — υμ. παντ.‖Mt: W 238(∼) *S*hj[ab] *C* *Arm*⟨mu⟩

διακονηθῆναι, ἀλλὰ διακονῆσαι καὶ	διακονηθῆναι ἀλλὰ διακονῆσαι καὶ	*κονῶν; οὐχὶ ὁ ἀνακείμενος; ἐγὼ δὲ ἐν*
δοῦναι τὴν ψυχὴν αὐτοῦ λύτρον ἀντὶ	δοῦναι τὴν ψυχὴν αὐτοῦ λύτρον ἀντὶ	*μέσῳ ὑμῶν εἰμι ὡς ὁ διακονῶν.*
πολλῶν.	πολλῶν.	

(193) ***207.*** Die Heilung des Bartimäus. *The Healing of Bartimaeus.*

Matth 20 29–34		Mark 10 46–52	Luk 18 35–43
[29] Καὶ		[46] Καὶ ἔρ-	[35] Ἐγένετο δὲ ἐν τῷ ἐγ-
	9 27–30 (68.):	χονται εἰς Ιεριχω. καὶ	γίζειν αὐτὸν εἰς Ιεριχω
ἐκπορευομένων αὐτῶν ἀπὸ	*Καὶ παράγοντι ἐκεῖθεν τῷ*	ἐκπορευομένου αὐτοῦ ἀπὸ	
Ιεριχω ἠκολούθησεν αὐτῷ	*Ἰησοῦ ἠκολούθησαν αὐτῷ*	Ιεριχω καὶ τῶν μαθητῶν αὐ-	
ὄχλος πολύς.		τοῦ καὶ ὄχλου ἱκανοῦ ὁ υἱὸς	
[30] καὶ ἰδοὺ δύο τυφλοὶ	*δύο τυφλοὶ*	Τιμαίου, Βαρτιμαῖος ὁ τυφλός,	τυφλός
καθήμενοι παρὰ τὴν ὁ-		ἐκάθητο παρὰ τὴν ὁ-	τις ἐκάθητο παρὰ τὴν ὁ-
δόν, ἀκού-		δὸν προσαιτῶν. [47] καὶ ἀκού-	δὸν ἐπαιτῶν. [36] ἀκού-
σαντες		σας	σας δὲ ὄχλου διαπορευομέ-
			νου ἐπυνθάνετο τί εἴη τοῦτο.
ὅτι		ὅτι	[37] ἀπήγγειλαν δὲ αὐτῷ ὅτι
Ἰησοῦς παρ-		Ἰησοῦς ὁ Ναζαρηνός ἐστιν,	Ἰησοῦς ὁ Ναζωραῖος παρ-
άγει, ἔκραξαν	*κράζοντες*	ἤρξατο κράζειν	έρχεται. [38] καὶ ἐβόησεν
λέγοντες· κύριε,	*καὶ λέγοντες·*	καὶ λέγειν· υἱὲ Δαυιδ	λέγων· Ἰησοῦ υἱὲ Δαυιδ,
ἐλέησον ἡμᾶς, υἱὸς	*ἐλέησον ἡμᾶς, υἱὲ*	Ἰησοῦ, ἐλέησόν με.	ἐλέησόν με.

Mt 20,28 πολλων + υμεις δε ζητειτε εκ μικρου αυξησαι και εκ μειζονος ελαττων ειναι. εισερχομενοι δε και παρακληθεντες δειπνησαι μη ανακλινεσθε(*om*: Φ) εις τους εξεχοντας τοπους (+ ανακλινεσθε: Φ) μηποτε ενδοξοτερος σου επελθη και προσελθων ο δειπνοκλητωρ ειπη σοι ετι κατω χωρει και καταισχυνθηση. εαν δε αναπεσης εις τον ηττονα τοπον και(*om* Φ) επελθη σου ηττων ερει σοι ο δειπνοκλητωρ συναγε(αγε: Φ) ετι ανω και εσται σοι τουτο χρησιμον(-ωτερον: Φ)‖Lk14 8-10: Φ D(*sim*: *L*vl'[k] $g^2r^1$37. 38 vg^2 Hi *Sc*) — *txt*: *Rpl* *L*flq vg' *S*s^vph *C* **29** εκπορευομενου αυτου(του Ιησου)‖Mk: (C^3)-33 σ7-1194 F H (G Γ) Δ *pc* Bas^S *L*(e[k]) f(32 *Sp*) *Cs*$^{2:9}b^{10}$ *Arm*^{pc} **30** ακου.] και ακ.‖Mk: 700 *Sc*[s]pj *Geo*^{2} *Aeth* | ∼ ελε. ημ. κυ.: $\mathfrak{P}^{45}$? *Rpl* Da Or *L*fq PsChr *S*ph *Cs*^{2} *Geo*^{Ach} *Aeth*^{pp} — ● *om* κυ.‖p: ℵ 700 **λ**⟨1⟩ **ϕ**⟨124⟩ D Θ 157 *pc* *l*76^v *L*vl'[k] *Sc*[s]j^b *Arm* *Geo*' *Aeth*^{ms} — *txt*: BLZ-**085**-892 1254 *L*g^1lr^1z vg *S*j^{acl} *Cs*^{8}b *Aeth*^{ro} | υι.] ● υιε‖p: $\mathfrak{P}^{45}$? C Φ-544 λ1 ϕ13-174-230-346-*l*547 σ1010-1293-1391-1402 D E F Π *pm* Chr^1 Eu Or {} — Ιησου υιε‖Lk Mk: ℵL-892 ΝΟΘΣ-700 **ϕ**'-1689 1365 *L*e[k] chn *S*j *Cs*^{3}b' *Geo*' — *txt*: *Rpl* Chr^1 Or {*L*' PsChr *S* *Cs*$^5b^1$ *Geo*^{Ac}}

Mk 10,46 *om* κ. ερχ. εις Ι.‖Mt: B* 63 *Cs*$^{1:4}$ | εκπορ.—αυτ.^{2}] εκπορευομενων αυτων απο Ι.‖Mt20: 472 *L*c(-ου -ου)z | απο Ι.] εκειθεν‖Mt9: D Or *L*abfff^{2}iqr^{1v} — *om et* αυτ.^{2} + εκειθεν: Θ-565-700 | ικ.] πολλου‖Mt20: 551 — + ιδου‖←: 28-700 **ϕ** *pc* Or *L*cflz | ● *om* ο^2‖Lk: ℌ W ϕ124 σ⟨954⟩-1391 D *pl* *l*18 *l*36 *l*49 *l*184 Or *L*cfz *C* | ● ∼ προσαιτης εκα. π. τ. οδ.‖Jo9 8a: ℵ(*prm* και)BLΔ Ψ-892 1342 *L*k[e] *C*b$^{\langle 2\rangle}$ *Arm*(∼ εκα. προσαι.) — εκα. π. τ. οδ. επαιτων‖Lk: Θ-565 D Or {} — εκα. π. τ. οδ.‖Mt20: C*-579 — *txt*: *Rpl* {*L*' *S*,j *Cs* *Geo*'(^{A}∼ προσ. π. τ. οδ.)} **47** Ναζωραιος(-ζα-)‖Lk: *Rpl* (4 38) *L*ff^{2}q*(cr^2z vg^2) *Cs*$^1b^2$ — *txt* (-ζω-): BLΔΨ-892 WΘ-(28) **λ** (D) Or *L*'(lq^c) *Cs*^{7}b' | εστ.] παραγει‖Mt20: 1396 1654 — παρερχεται‖Lk: 348 *pc* *L*c vg^1 | κ. λεγ.] λεγων‖Mt20Lk: 1542 1654 *Cs*$^{6:7}$b | υι. Δ. Ι.] υιος Δ. Ι.(*om*)‖Mt←: σ349 D K *pc* (Or) {} — κυριε υιος Δ.‖←: 28 — ● ο υιος Δ. Ι.(*om*)‖←: *Rpl* (σ267-827 *pc*) {} — Ι.(+ ο) υιος Δ.‖←Lk: 565 **ϕ**⟨124⟩ *pc* (*pc*) *L*ac(∼ ελ. με Ι. υιος Δ.)ff^2 vg^1 *S*h *Cs*^{7}b — *txt* (*om* Ι.): ℵBC(L)Δ(Ψ-579)-892 ΘΣ σM^m-7-517-659-1082-1391 1241(^{47}∩^{48}υι.) 1342 (*l*18 *l*19) *l*48 *l*49 (*l*184) {*L*k[e](∼ υι. Δ. ελ. με Ι.) b(i)lqr^2(z) vg' (*S*' *Cs*^{1})}

Lk 18,35 προσαιτ.‖MkJo9 8b: *Rpl* — *txt*: ℵBL-579 D 157 Ad Or **36** ● τι + αν‖9 46 Act10 17 5 24: LX-579-892-1241 1071-1604 **λλ**⟨1278⟩ **ϕ**-*l*547 σM-692 D K Q R Θ Π Ψ *mu* *l*32 *l*1963 Ad Or *L*a — *txt*: *Rpl* *L*' Ad | του.] ταυτα‖15 26: ϕ69-983 σ267 474 *l*12 *l*80 *l*184 *l*303 *l*333 *l*382 *l*1634 *l*1663 **37** ο Ναζαρηνος(-ζω-)‖Mk: **λλ**⟨1278⟩ D 697 Or *L*'(e il){} — *om*‖Mt: Ad — *txt* (-ζα-): *Rpl* (σM) *L*b(c)dfff^{2}qr^1{(^{2} Naza[...)} *C*'(b^1) **38** εβο.] εκραξεν‖p: P | *om* Ι.‖39 Mt: 579 σ1223 A E K Π **063** *al* *l*1642 Or

Δαυιδ. 31 ὁ δὲ ὄχλος ἐπετίμησεν αὐτοῖς ἵνα σιωπήσωσιν· οἱ δὲ μεῖζον ἔκραξαν λέγοντες· κύριε, ἐλέησον ἡμᾶς, υἱὸς Δαυιδ. 32 καὶ στὰς ὁ Ἰησοῦς ἐφώνησεν αὐτοὺς καὶ εἶπεν· τί θέλετε ποιήσω ὑμῖν; 33 λέγουσιν αὐτῷ· κύριε, ἵνα ἀνοιγῶσιν οἱ ὀφθαλμοὶ ἡμῶν. 34 σπλαγχνισθεὶς δὲ ὁ Ἰησοῦς ἥψατο τῶν ὀμμάτων αὐτῶν, καὶ εὐθέως ἀνέβλεψαν καὶ ἠκολούθησαν αὐτῷ.

Δαυιδ. ... *28 ἐλθόντι δὲ εἰς τὴν οἰκίαν προσῆλθαν αὐτῷ οἱ τυφλοί, καὶ λέγει αὐτοῖς ὁ Ἰησοῦς· πιστεύετε ὅτι δύναμαι τοῦτο ποιῆσαι; λέγουσιν αὐτῷ· ναί, κύριε. 29 τότε ἥψατο τῶν ὀφθαλμῶν αὐτῶν λέγων· κατὰ τὴν πίστιν ὑμῶν γενηθήτω ὑμῖν. 30 καὶ ἠνεῴχθησαν αὐτῶν οἱ ὀφθαλμοί...*

48 καὶ ἐπετίμων αὐτῷ πολλοὶ ἵνα σιωπήσῃ· ὁ δὲ πολλῷ μᾶλλον ἔκραζεν· υἱὲ Δαυιδ, ἐλέησόν με. 49 καὶ στὰς ὁ Ἰησοῦς εἶπεν· φωνήσατε αὐτόν. καὶ φωνοῦσιν τὸν τυφλὸν λέγοντες αὐτῷ· θάρσει, ἔγειρε, φωνεῖ σε. 50 ὁ δὲ ἀποβαλὼν τὸ ἱμάτιον αὐτοῦ ἀναπηδήσας ἦλθεν πρὸς τὸν Ἰησοῦν. 51 καὶ ἀποκριθεὶς αὐτῷ ὁ Ἰησοῦς εἶπεν· τί σοι θέλεις ποιήσω; ὁ δὲ τυφλὸς εἶπεν αὐτῷ· ραββουνι, ἵνα ἀναβλέψω. 52 ὁ δὲ Ἰησοῦς εἶπεν αὐτῷ· ὕπαγε, ἡ πίστις σου σέσωκέν σε. καὶ εὐθὺς ἀνέβλεψεν, καὶ ἠκολούθει τῷ Ἰησοῦ ἐν τῇ ὁδῷ. *cf. 134.*

39 καὶ οἱ προάγοντες ἐπετίμων αὐτῷ ἵνα σιγήσῃ· αὐτὸς δὲ πολλῷ μᾶλλον ἔκραζεν· υἱὲ Δαυιδ, ἐλέησόν με. 40 σταθεὶς δὲ ὁ Ἰησοῦς ἐκέλευσεν αὐτὸν ἀχθῆναι πρὸς αὐτόν. ἐγγίσαντος δὲ αὐτοῦ ἐπηρώτησεν αὐτόν· 41 τί σοι θέλεις ποιήσω; ὁ δὲ εἶπεν· κύριε, ἵνα ἀναβλέψω. 42 καὶ ὁ Ἰησοῦς εἶπεν αὐτῷ· ἀνάβλεψον, ἡ πίστις σου σέσωκέν σε. 43 καὶ παραχρῆμα ἀνέβλεψεν, καὶ ἠκολούθει αὐτῷ δοξάζων τὸν θεόν. καὶ πᾶς ὁ λαὸς ἰδὼν ἔδωκεν αἶνον τῷ θεῷ.

Mt 20,31 μειζ.] πολλω μαλλον‖Mk Lk: ℵ | εκραζον(εκραυγαζον)‖p: *Rpl* (Φ ϕ⟨983⟩ Θ) *L S*hj *C*b^{5} — *txt*: 𝔓^{45}(-αυγασαν) ℌ⟨33⟩ 700 D Π *S*' *C*' | *om* κυ.‖9 27 Mk Lk: 700 λ⟨1⟩ σ1675 *L*e[k](ημ. + Ιησου) vg^{1} *S*pj^{ac} | υι.] ● υιε‖p: ℌ⟨BZ⟩C NOΣΦ-1604 ϕ230-*l*547 σ659-990-1010-1293-1402-1606 D *pc* Eu Or **32** θελεις‖20 21 Mk Lk: C | ποι.] ποιησαι με‖Mk10 36: 28 — ινα ποιησω: ℵ^{c}LZ-892 σ1010-1223-1293-1391 *pc* Ath Cr Or *L*Hi **33** ∼ ημ. οι οφ.‖9 30 Jo9 10: *Rpl* (υμων: Δ) — *txt*: ℌ⟨ℵ* (υμων)⟩ σ990-1010-1223-1293 D 1295 Or **34** ανεβλ.] ανεωχθησαν αυτων οι οφθαλμοι‖9 30: 1170 *S*p· *C*s^{1} — ανεβλ. αυ. οι οφ.‖←: *Rpl L*q *S*h^{t} — *txt*: ℌ'Z^{v} 28-700-1604 λ1-22-1582 ϕ124-788 σ990-1010-1207-1293 D Θ *L*' *S*c[s]h^{m}j *C*s^{7}b

Mk 10,48 πολλα‖3 12: 892 ϕ346 473 *l*48 | ο] αυτος‖Lk: 1071 | εκραξεν‖Mt: D' *L*vg^{2} *C*s | υι.] υιος‖Mt: D F 2145 Or$^{1:2}$ {} — ο υιος‖Mt: 1071 λ {} — κυριε υιος‖Mt: 28 ϕ124 108 — κυ. υιε‖Mt: 1606 *pc* — Ιησου υιε‖47 Lk38: ϕ'⟨788⟩ 1342 — *txt*: *Rpl* {*L S C*} **49** σταθεις‖Lk: σ517 67 1241 | ειπ.] εκελευσεν‖Lk: 472 *l*48 *L*'⟨k[e]⟩(κελευει: r^{2} vg^{4}) *S*p *C*s | φω. αυ.] αυ. φωνηθηναι(∼)‖Lk: *Rpl* (Σ λ σ1606 *l*48 *l*49) Or *L*' *S*(αυ. αχθηναι‖Lk: s[c])ph^{t}j — *txt*: ℌC σ7-517-1082-1391 1342 *pc l*18 *l*19 *l*184^{1} *L*k[e] *S*h^{m} **51** ∼ θελ. ποι. σοι‖Mt20: *Rpl* (ποιησαι‖10 36: Γ) *L*abcfff^{2}z — *txt*: ℌ⟨579⟩C Θ-565-1071 σ7-349-517-659-1082-1223-1391 K Y Π 1342 *pc l*18 *l*19 *l*48 *l*49 *l*184 *L*' | *om* αυτω^{2}‖Lk: 28 *L*c | ρα.] κυριε ραββει‖p: D 409(*om* ρα.) *L*a^{v}bff^{2}i (*om* κυ.: k[e] q) *C*b^{6}(^{1}*om* ρα.) **52** ο δε] ● και ο‖Lk: ℌ⟨ℵ*⟩ σ7-517-659-1082-1391 1342 *pc l*48 *l*49 *l*184^{1} *L*q *S*p *C*s$^{1:7}$b^{7} | υπα.] αναβλεψον‖Lk: 61 *S*p$^{⟨7⟩}$ | σε + πορευου(+ εις ειρηνην)‖(5 34 Lk7 50 8 48): 579 (1515) | ηκολουθησεν‖Mt20: 544 ϕ346 σ71-179-692-954 *pm l*184 *L*q *C*s | τω Ι.] ● αυτω‖Mt ← Lk: ℌC W-28-565-700-1071 λ⟨118⟩ ϕ σM^{m}-349-517-1606 A D 1342(-ον) *pc* Or^{1} *L S*s[c](*om*: p)h^{m} *C Arm Aeth* — *txt*: *Rpl* Or^{1} *S*h^{t} | *om* εν τη οδω‖Mt20 Lk: 544 ϕ788 *Geo*$^{⟨B⟩}$

Lk 18,39 παραγον.‖37 Mt20 30: A K Π *al* (παραπορευομενοι: *l*32) | σιγ.] σιωπηση‖Mk Mt: *Rpl* Or^{1} — *txt*: BLX D P W Ψ *pc* Or^{1} | αυτος] ο‖p: ℵ | *om* πολλω‖Mt: D *L*cr^{2}(*om* πο. μαλ.) vg^{1} *S*scpj *C*s | εκραξεν‖Mt: 245 251 Or *L*vg^{3} *C*s | εκρ. + λεγων‖Mt: σM-71-692 E G H *al l*20 *l*47 *l*148 *S*s *C*s$^{6:7}$ *Aeth* | υιε] Ιησου υιε‖38 Mk47: ℵ λ1-1582 ϕ-*l*547 U **063** *pc* — υιος‖Mt: D *pc* **40** στα. δε] και στας‖p: ϕ124-*l*547 *S*scp | αυτον^{3} + ο Ιησους‖Mk: X ϕ-*l*547 σ267-659-1606 Q *pc l*12 *l*18 *l*19 *l*49 *l*80 *l*303 *l*333 *l*1642 **41** ειπ. + αυτω‖p: R *S*sch^{m}j^{ab} *C*s$^{3:8}$b^{10} *Aeth* **43** ηκολουθησεν‖Mt20: W* 565 *pc l*48 *l*49 *L*30 *C*sb$^{⟨6⟩}$ | αυτω] τω Ιησου‖Mk: 251 *pc* | λαος] οχλος *cf.* 13 17 Mk9 15 *etc.*: Λ σ7-115-659 Q *al l*12 *l*18 *l*19 *l*20 *l*32 *l*47 *l*49 *l*50 *l*303 *l*333 *l*1634 *l*1663 *l*1963 | αιν.] δοξαν‖17 18 Jo9 24: D

(194)

208. Zakchäus. *Zacchaeus.* Luk 19 1–10

[1] Καὶ εἰσελθὼν διήρχετο τὴν Ιεριχω. [2] καὶ ἰδοὺ ἀνὴρ ὀνόματι καλούμενος Ζακχαῖος, καὶ αὐτὸς ἦν ἀρχιτελώνης, καὶ αὐτὸς πλούσιος· [3] καὶ ἐζήτει ἰδεῖν τὸν Ἰησοῦν τίς ἐστιν, καὶ οὐκ ἐδύνατο ἀπὸ τοῦ ὄχλου, ὅτι τῇ ἡλικίᾳ μικρὸς ἦν. [4] καὶ προδραμὼν εἰς τὸ ἔμπροσθεν ἀνέβη ἐπὶ συκομορέαν, ἵνα ἴδῃ αὐτόν, ὅτι ἐκείνης ἤμελλεν διέρχεσθαι. [5] καὶ ὡς ἦλθεν ἐπὶ τὸν τόπον, ἀναβλέψας ὁ Ἰησοῦς εἶπεν πρὸς αὐτόν· Ζακχαῖε, σπεύσας κατάβηθι· σήμερον γὰρ ἐν τῷ οἴκῳ σου δεῖ με μεῖναι. [6] καὶ σπεύσας κατέβη, καὶ ὑπεδέξατο αὐτὸν χαίρων. [7] καὶ ἰδόντες πάντες διεγόγγυζον λέγοντες ὅτι παρὰ ἁμαρτωλῷ ἀνδρὶ εἰσῆλθεν καταλῦσαι. [8] σταθεὶς δὲ Ζακχαῖος εἶπεν πρὸς τὸν κύριον· ἰδοὺ τὰ ἡμίση μου τῶν ὑπαρχόντων, κύριε, τοῖς πτωχοῖς δίδωμι, καὶ εἴ τινός τι ἐσυκοφάντησα, ἀποδίδωμι τετραπλοῦν. [9] εἶπεν δὲ πρὸς αὐτὸν ὁ Ἰησοῦς ὅτι σήμερον σωτηρία τῷ οἴκῳ τούτῳ ἐγένετο, καθότι καὶ αὐτὸς υἱὸς Αβρααμ ἐστίν· [10] ἦλθεν γὰρ ὁ υἱὸς τοῦ ἀνθρώπου **ζητῆσαι** καὶ σῶσαι **τὸ ἀπολωλός.**

(195)

209. Das Gleichnis von den Minen. *The Parable of the Pounds.*

25 14–30 (240.)

[14] Ὥσπερ γὰρ ἄνθρωπος ἀποδημῶν ἐκάλεσεν τοὺς ἰδίους δούλους καὶ παρέδωκεν αὐτοῖς τὰ ὑπάρχοντα αὐτοῦ, [15] καὶ ᾧ μὲν ἔδωκεν πέντε τάλαντα, ᾧ δὲ δύο, ᾧ δὲ ἕν, ἑκάστῳ κατὰ τὴν ἰδίαν δύναμιν, καὶ ἀπεδήμησεν. εὐθέως [16] πορευθεὶς ὁ τὰ πέντε τάλαντα λαβὼν ἠργάσατο ἐν αὐτοῖς καὶ ἐποίησεν ἄλλα πέντε· [17] ὡσαύτως ὁ τὰ δύο ἐκέρδησεν καὶ

Luk 19 11–27

[11] Ἀκουόντων δὲ αὐτῶν ταῦτα προσθεὶς εἶπεν παραβολήν, διὰ τὸ ἐγγὺς εἶναι Ιερουσαλημ αὐτὸν καὶ δοκεῖν αὐτοὺς ὅτι παραχρῆμα μέλλει ἡ βασιλεία τοῦ θεοῦ ἀναφαίνεσθαι· [12] εἶπεν οὖν· ἄνθρωπός τις εὐγενὴς ἐπορεύθη εἰς χώραν μακρὰν λαβεῖν ἑαυτῷ βασιλείαν καὶ ὑποστρέψαι. [13] καλέσας δὲ δέκα δούλους ἑαυτοῦ ἔδωκεν αὐτοῖς δέκα μνᾶς, καὶ εἶπεν πρὸς αὐτούς· πραγματεύσασθε ἐν ᾧ ἔρχομαι.

Lk 19,1 την] εις‖1835: σ71-659 1579 — εις την‖←: σM *pc* **2** *om* καλ. *cf.* 2350 15: 892-1241 D G *pc l*17 *l*22 *l*26 *L*<e r^2> Ar *S*scp *C*s$^{1:7}$(*om* ου. καλ.)b^7 *Δ*<me> | αυτ.^{1}] ουτος‖841: 579 1071 **φ**<13-124> D 475 *L* *C*b — *om*: *L*Ar *S*scp(∼ πλου. ... αρχ.) | ην—πλου.] αρχων της συναγωγης υπηρχεν‖←: Ψ *l*47 | αυτ.^{2}] ουτος ην‖←: *Rpl* (*om* και^3: W 157; *om* ην: λ22 *pc*) *L*f *S*h(^{t} = W)^m — ● ην (*et om* και): ℵL-(892)-1241 (245 1012) *S*sc(p)j *C*b — *om* (*et om* και): (D *L*e) ls *C*s *Aeth* — αυτ. ην: Θ(ο αυτ.)-1071 U *L*acff^{2}r^1 vg^4 *Arm*^{pc} — *txt*: **B-0139**-579 **λ**<209> **φ**<124> K Π *pc* *L*'Ar *Arm*' **4** προσδραμων‖Mk10 17: L Λ-544-1604 φ346-828-983 σ115-267-1223 E F G H V W Γ Π Ψ **063** *pm l*2 *l*16 *l*17 *l*19 *l*32 *l*33 *l*36 *l*47 *l*52 *l*55 *l*183 *l*1627 *l*1692 *l*1663 — αποδρ.: 42 — δραμων: 579 φ69 σ945-1424 *pm l*16 *l*17 *l*184 *L*q(*om* εις—εμπρ.) — *txt*: *Rpl* (προλαβων: D 1093) *L*' *Geo* **5** Ι. + ειδεν αυτον και‖21 1 Mt4 18p.21 Mk1 19: *Rpl* (αν.] ειδ. αυτ.· αναβλ. δε: 157) *L*'(∼ ο Ι. ει. αυ. αν.: abcff^{2}il) *S*hj *Δ*' — αν. ο Ι.] ειδ. (*prm* ο Ι.) αυτ. και‖←: D(*om* αυ.) *S*(*om* και: sc)(p{}) *Δ*ap — + και ιδων αυτ.‖←: Ψ — *txt*: ℵBL-**0139**-579-1241 Θ-1071 **λ**-1582 1093 *C*s{b} *Aeth* *Δ*md n **7** παν.] οι Φαρισαιοι‖15 2: **φ**<124> | διεγ.] διελογιζοντο‖←Mk2 6: 4 | ∼ ανδ. αμαρ.‖5 8 ℵ *L* | ανδ.] ανθρωπω‖24 7 Jo9 16: L *L*<as> **8** *om* τοις‖18 22 Mt19 21 26 9 Jo12 5: B σ71-692-1194 **12** τις + ην *et* ευγ. + και(*om*)‖14 2 16 1: W (1573) *L*(e* b)cf(ilqr^1 *C*b) (και] ος: *Δ*i^V md n) **13** εν ω] εως‖Jo21 22f.: *Rpl* (ως: φ69; + αν: *pc*) *L*a Or *S*,j *C*sb(εν τουτοις εως) — εως εν ω‖←: λ2193 *pc* — *txt*: ℵBL-1241 1604 **λλ**'<1278> A D K R W Π Ψ 157 *al* Or *L*'Ar

---

L19 8–10 *cf.* TMti (Cl strom. IV 6,35,2): Ζακχαῖον τοίνυν, οἱ δὲ Ματθίαν φασίν, ἀρχιτελώνην, ἀκηκοότα τοῦ κυρίου καταξιώσαντος πρὸς αὐτὸν γενέσθαι· ἰδοὺ τὰ ἡμίση τῶν ὑπαρχόντων μου δίδωμι ἐλεημοσύνην, φάναι, κύριε, καὶ εἴ τινός τι ἐσυκοφάντησα, τετραπλοῦν ἀποδίδωμι. ἐφ' οὗ καὶ ὁ σωτὴρ εἶπεν· ὁ υἱὸς τοῦ ἀνθρώπου ἐλθὼν σήμερον τὸ ἀπολωλὸς εὗρεν.

αὐτὸς ἄλλα δύο. 18 *ὁ δὲ τὸ ἓν λαβὼν ἀπελθὼν ὤρυξεν γῆν καὶ ἀπέκρυψεν τὸ ἀργύριον τοῦ κυρίου αὐτοῦ.*

14 οἱ δὲ πολῖται αὐτοῦ ἐμίσουν αὐτόν, καὶ ἀπέστειλαν πρεσβείαν ὀπίσω αὐτοῦ λέγοντες· οὐ θέλομεν τοῦτον βασιλεῦσαι ἐφ' ἡμᾶς.

19 *μετὰ δὲ πολὺν χρόνον ἔρχεται ὁ κύριος τῶν δούλων ἐκείνων καὶ συναίρει λόγον μετ' αὐτῶν.* 20 *καὶ προσελθὼν ὁ τὰ πέντε τάλαντα λαβὼν προσήνεγκεν ἄλλα πέντε τάλαντα λέγων· κύριε, πέντε τάλαντά μοι παρέδωκας· ἴδε ἄλλα πέντε τάλαντα ἐκέρδησα.* 21 *ἔφη αὐτῷ ὁ κύριος αὐτοῦ· εὖ, δοῦλε ἀγαθὲ καὶ πιστέ, ἐπὶ ὀλίγα ἦς πιστός, ἐπὶ πολλῶν σε καταστήσω· εἴσελθε εἰς τὴν χαρὰν τοῦ κυρίου σου.* 22 *προσελθὼν δὲ καὶ ὁ τὰ δύο τάλαντα εἶπεν· κύριε, δύο τάλαντά μοι παρέδωκας· ἴδε ἄλλα δύο τάλαντα ἐκέρδησα.* 23 *ἔφη αὐτῷ ὁ κύριος αὐτοῦ· εὖ, δοῦλε ἀγαθὲ καὶ πιστέ, ἐπὶ ὀλίγα ἦς πιστός, ἐπὶ πολλῶν σε καταστήσω· εἴσελθε εἰς τὴν χαρὰν τοῦ κυρίου σου.* 24 *προσελθὼν δὲ καὶ ὁ τὸ ἓν τάλαντον εἰληφὼς εἶπεν· κύριε, ἔγνων σε ὅτι σκληρὸς εἶ ἄνθρωπος, θερίζων ὅπου οὐκ ἔσπειρας, καὶ συνάγων ὅθεν οὐ διεσκόρπισας·* 25 *καὶ φοβηθεὶς ἀπελθὼν ἔκρυψα τὸ τάλαντόν σου ἐν τῇ γῇ· ἴδε ἔχεις τὸ σόν.* 26 *ἀποκριθεὶς δὲ ὁ κύριος αὐτοῦ εἶπεν αὐτῷ· πονηρὲ δοῦλε καὶ ὀκνηρέ, ᾔδεις ὅτι θερίζω ὅπου οὐκ ἔσπειρα, καὶ συνάγω ὅθεν οὐ διεσκόρπισα.* 27 *ἔδει σε οὖν βαλεῖν τὸ ἀργύριόν μου τοῖς*

15 καὶ ἐγένετο ἐν τῷ ἐπανελθεῖν αὐτὸν λαβόντα τὴν βασιλείαν καὶ εἶπεν φωνηθῆναι αὐτῷ τοὺς δούλους τούτους οἷς δεδώκει τὸ ἀργύριον, ἵνα γνοῖ τίς τί διεπραγματεύσατο. 16 παρεγένετο δὲ ὁ πρῶτος λέγων· κύριε, ἡ μνᾶ σου δέκα προσηργάσατο μνᾶς. 17 καὶ εἶπεν αὐτῷ· εὖγε, ἀγαθὲ δοῦλε, ὅτι ἐν ἐλαχίστῳ πιστὸς ἐγένου, ἴσθι ἐξουσίαν ἔχων ἐπάνω δέκα πόλεων. 18 καὶ ἦλθεν ὁ δεύτερος λέγων· ἡ μνᾶ σου, κύριε, ἐποίησεν πέντε μνᾶς. 19 εἶπεν δὲ καὶ τούτῳ· καὶ σὺ ἐπάνω γίνου πέντε πόλεων. 20 καὶ ὁ ἕτερος ἦλθεν λέγων· κύριε, ἰδοὺ ἡ μνᾶ σου, ἣν εἶχον ἀποκειμένην ἐν σουδαρίῳ· 21 ἐφοβούμην γάρ σε, ὅτι ἄνθρωπος αὐστηρὸς εἶ, αἴρεις ὃ οὐκ ἔθηκας, καὶ θερίζεις ὃ οὐκ ἔσπειρας. 22 λέγει αὐτῷ· ἐκ τοῦ στόματός σου κρινῶ σε, πονηρὲ δοῦλε. ᾔδεις ὅτι ἐγὼ ἄνθρωπος αὐστηρός εἰμι, αἴρων ὃ οὐκ ἔθηκα, καὶ θερίζων ὃ οὐκ ἔσπειρα. 23 καὶ διὰ τί οὐκ ἔδωκάς μου τὸ ἀργύριον ἐπὶ

Lk 19,15 τουτ.] εκεινους‖p: 477 *Lf Sscpj* | τις τι] ● τι: ℵBL-579 D Ψ **047** 157 *pc* Or *Le* (πως: r^{1v}) *Ssc* (ποσον: *Aeth*) — *txt*: *Rpl* (*om* τι: 1241) *L*'Luc *S*' | διεπ.] επραγμ.‖13: 1071 σ1675 W (πρα-: Δ!) *pc* | ● -ματευσαντο: ℵBL-579 D R Ψ 157 1296 Or *Le Sscp*^{2}h *Geo Aeth* — *txt*: *Rpl L*'Luc *Sp*' **16** κυ. + ιδου‖p: 477 **17** ευγε] ευ‖p: *Rpl* — *txt*: B-892 D *pc* Or (euge: *L*⟨a (tanto melior)⟩ Luc) | ∼ δου. αγ.‖p: ℵ-579 544 **λλ**⟨22-1278⟩ **ϕ**-*l*547 σM-71-692 157 *pc* Eu *L*cfff^{2}ilr^{1}30 vg^2 Or *Arm* | δου./αγ. + και πιστε‖p: 1241 Eu *Lf Arm Aeth* | *om* οτι‖**p**: ϕ69-788 *Ls Geo*^{1} | πιστος εγ.] ης π.‖**p**: 1375 *Le* i vg^1 **18** ∼ κυ. η μνα σ.‖p16: *Rpl* (κυριος: σ1424) *L*' *S C* — *om* κυριε: 716 *L*ff^2 *Arm* — *txt*: ℵBL-579-892 *L*Luc | πεντε] αλλας π.‖Mt20.22: 1071 *La* **20** *om* ιδου‖p18: λ131 σ1194 44 157 *l*238 *L*r^1 vg^1 **21** αιρων ... θεριζων(-εις)‖p22: **063** 157 (*L*ff^2 vg^1) | o^2] οπου‖p: 579 *L*30 vg^1 | εσπ. + και συναγεις οθεν ου διεσκορπισας‖p: NΛ-1071 **ϕ**-174-230-*l*547 σ7 U Θ **063** *Aeth* — + και φοβηθεις απεκρυψα το αργυριον σου εν τη γη ιδε εχεις το σον‖p: 90 **22** αυτω + ο κυριος αυτου‖**p**: **ϕ**-174 **047** *L*Luc(*om* αυτου) *Sc Aeth* | *om* εγω‖p: L-1241 Θ *L*cff^{2}r^{1}30 vg^1 | αιρω ... θεριζω‖ p: 579-892 (-ρων: ϕ1689 *pc*) D (-ζων: F **063** 1579) *L*vl⟨fz⟩r^1 Luc *Sscp* | εσπ. + και συναγων οθεν(ο) ου διεσκορπισα‖p: 1241(*om* και θερ.—εσπ.) NΛ-1071 (**ϕ**-*l*547) U(-αγω) Θ **063** *al l*19 *l*36(= 1241) *l*49 (*Aeth*) **23** κ. δια τι] δια τι ουν‖p: D *Le* r^1 | εξεδω.‖209p: λ2193 | ∼ το αρ. μου‖p: *Rpl* — *txt*: 𝔥[33] A W Θ Ψ **0182** 157 *pc l*48

Lk1916p.18p *cf.* 2Cl (EAe?); Ir haer. II 56,1; PsHil ap. 1 (*cf. ad 188.* Lk1610-12)

Matth		Luk
τραπεζίταις, καὶ ἐλθὼν ἐγὼ ἐκομισάμην ἂν τὸ ἐμὸν σὺν τόκῳ. ²⁸ ἄρατε οὖν ἀπ' αὐτοῦ τὸ τάλαντον καὶ δότε τῷ ἔχοντι τὰ δέκα τάλαντα· ²⁹ τῷ γὰρ ἔχοντι παντὶ δοθήσεται καὶ περισσευθήσεται· τοῦ δὲ μὴ ἔχοντος καὶ ὃ ἔχει ἀρθήσεται ἀπ' αὐτοῦ. ³⁰ καὶ τὸν ἀχρεῖον δοῦλον ἐκβάλετε εἰς τὸ σκότος τὸ ἐξώτερον· ἐκεῖ ἔσται ὁ κλαυθμὸς καὶ ὁ βρυγμὸς τῶν ὀδόντων.	107.	τράπεζαν; κἀγὼ ἐλθὼν σὺν τόκῳ ἂν αὐτὸ ἔπραξα. ²⁴ καὶ τοῖς παρεστῶσιν εἶπεν· ἄρατε ἀπ' αὐτοῦ τὴν μνᾶν καὶ δότε τῷ τὰς δέκα μνᾶς ἔχοντι. ²⁵ καὶ εἶπαν αὐτῷ· κύριε, ἔχει δέκα μνᾶς. ²⁶ λέγω ὑμῖν ὅτι παντὶ τῷ ἔχοντι δοθήσεται, ἀπὸ δὲ τοῦ μὴ ἔχοντος καὶ ὃ ἔχει ἀρθήσεται ἀπ' αὐτοῦ. ²⁷ πλὴν τοὺς ἐχθρούς μου τούτους τοὺς μὴ θελήσαντάς με βασιλεῦσαι ἐπ' αὐτοὺς ἀγάγετε ὧδε καὶ κατασφάξατε αὐτοὺς ἔμπροσθέν μου.

2. Die jerusalemischen Tage. *The Days in Jerusalem.*
Matth 21—25 = Mark 11—13 = Luk 19₂₈—21.

(196)

210. Der Einzug in Jerusalem. *The Entry into Jerusalem.*

Matth 21 ₁₋₉	Mark 11 ₁₋₁₀	Luk 19 ₂₈₋₃₈
		²⁸ Καὶ εἰπὼν ταῦτα ἐπορεύετο ἔμπροσθεν ἀναβαίνων εἰς Ἱεροσόλυμα.
¹ Καὶ ὅτε ἤγγισαν εἰς Ἱεροσόλυμα καὶ ἦλθον εἰς Βηθφαγη εἰς τὸ ὄρος τῶν ἐλαιῶν, τότε Ἰησοῦς ἀπέστειλεν δύο	¹ Καὶ ὅτε ἐγγίζουσιν εἰς Ἱεροσόλυμα εἰς Βηθφαγη καὶ Βηθανίαν πρὸς τὸ ὄρος τῶν ἐλαιῶν, ἀποστέλλει δύο	²⁹ καὶ ἐγένετο ὡς ἤγγισεν εἰς Βηθφαγη καὶ Βηθανίαν πρὸς τὸ ὄρος τὸ καλούμενον ἐλαιών, ἀπέστειλεν δύο

Mt 21,1 ηγγισεν ‖ Lk: C³-892 544-1604 φ983-1689-*l*547(+ ο Ιησους) S Vᵐ *pc* *Le*[k] bff²30 vg⁴ *S*,jᵃᵇ *C*b⁴ | *om* κ. ηλθ. ‖ p: 1295 | ηλθεν ‖ Lk: ℵ*C³-892 28-544-1604 φ983-1689-*l*547 E S U Vᵐ W Δ 157 *pc* Or *Le*[k] ff²q vg¹ *Sc*[s]pjᵃᵇ *Cs*¹:¹⁰ *Geo*¹ | Βηθφ. + και Βηθανιαν ‖ Mk Lk: C²-33 Φ **φ**⟨124-788-983⟩-174-*l*547(*om* Βηθφ. και) σ990-1010-1223-1293 *Sj* | εις³] ● προς ‖ Mk Lk: *Rpl* Or *L*' *Sc*[s]p{h}j — *txt*: BC²-33 σ71 Or *Le*[k] abcff¹·²hnqr¹·² {} | Ιη.] ● ο Ιη.: *Rpl* Or¹ — *om* ‖ p: φ*l*547 Ω *pc* *Lr*² *Sp*¹ — *txt*: B 700 λ22 D E H V 157 *pc* Or¹ | αποστελλει ‖ Mk: σ1194

Mk 11,1 εγγ.] ηγγισαν(-ζον) ‖ Mt: (Σ) **φ**' σM (713) *pc* *l*48 *La* *Cs*⁶b' — ηγγισεν(-ζεν) ‖ Lk: φ13-983-*l*547 (D *l*7 *l*12 *l*13 *l*14 *l*49 *l*251) *l*184 *Lk*[e] bcfilq *Sp* *Cs*²b¹ | I. + και ηλθον(-εν) ‖ Mt: 892 (1071) σ⟨954⟩-349 *pc* (*l*49 *l*251) *Cb*²('⟨1⟩) | *om* κ. Βηθα. ‖ Mt: Ψ *l*184 *Cs*¹:⁹ | των¹] το (+ καλουμενον) ‖ Lk: B (Σ) *Lk*[e] | απεστειλεν ‖ p: **λ**⟨118⟩ σ1207 F H *pc* *l*184 *L*abcfg²z — επεμψεν: C

Lk 19,23 ∼ και ελθ. εγω ‖ p: 1241 544 λ1278 **φ**⟨124⟩-*l*547 *pc* | συν—επρ.] εκομισαμην αν το εμον σ. τοκω ‖ p: G 475(∼ σ. τοκω εκο.—εμ.) | επρ.] εκομισ. ‖ **p**: 1604 **24** ∼ εχ. τ. δεκα μν. ‖ p: **λλ**⟨22-1278⟩ **φ**⟨124⟩ Or *L*cff²g²iq30 vg² Or **25** *om* 25 ‖ **p**: φ69 σ1675 D W **047** *pc* *l*ᵖˡ *Le* bff²g² Luc *Ssc* Crᶜᵐᵗ *Cb*¹ **26** λεγω + γαρ ‖ 818p: *Rpl* *S*' — + δε: *L*'Luc *Geo*' — *txt*: 𝔥[33] 1604 **λλ**⟨22-1278⟩ φ788 *pc* *Las*? *Sp* *C* *Geo*ᶜʰ | δοθ.] προστιθεται ‖ Mt633p Mk424: D *Ss* — + και περισσευθησεται ‖ p Mt1312: 579 544 **φ**-*l*547 *pc* Cr *L*30 vg³ *Sc* *Geo*² *Aeth* | εχει] δοκει εχειν ‖ 818: λ2193 φ69-346 Θ *pc* Cr *L*Mcnᵀᵉ *Sch*⁺ | ● *om* απ. αυτου: ℵ*BL *pc* *Li*30 Luc Mcnᵀᵉ — *txt*: *Rpl* Cr *L*' *S*,Ef **27** τουτ.] εκεινους ‖ Mt227: *Rpl* (∼ εκ. τ. εχθ. μ.: D) Eu Or *L* *S* *Cb*¹ — *om*: σ1207 *pc* — *txt*: ℵ BL-1241 σM-71-692 K Π *pc* Ddy *C*' | μου² + και τον αχρειον δουλον εκβαλετε εις το σκοτος το εξωτερον εκει εσται ο κλαυθμος και ο βρυγμος των οδοντων ‖ p: D **29** το καλ. ελ.] των ελ. ‖ Mt Mk: 28 φ69 σ659 K Π *pc* *Le* *Ssj* *Arm* — των ελ. καλ. ‖ p: D — το καλ. των ελ. ‖ p: σ1223 *S*' *C*⟨b¹(*om*)⟩

Lk1926p *cf.* ETh^II 41 (*cf. ad 107.* Mk425)

Matthew

μαθητὰς ² λέγων αὐτοῖς· πορεύθητε εἰς τὴν κώμην τὴν ἀπέναντι ὑμῶν, καὶ εὐθέως εὑρήσετε ὄνον δεδεμένην καὶ πῶλον μετ' αὐτῆς· λύσαντες ἀγάγετέ μοι. ³ καὶ ἐάν τις ὑμῖν εἴπῃ τι, ἐρεῖτε ὅτι ὁ κύριος αὐτῶν χρείαν ἔχει· εὐθὺς δὲ ἀποστελεῖ αὐτούς. ⁴ τοῦτο δὲ γέγονεν ἵνα πληρωθῇ τὸ ῥηθὲν διὰ τοῦ προφήτου λέγοντος· ⁵ **εἴπατε τῇ θυγατρὶ Σιων· ἰδοὺ ὁ βασιλεύς σου ἔρχεταί σοι πραῢς καὶ ἐπιβεβηκὼς ἐπὶ ὄνον καὶ ἐπὶ πῶλον υἱὸν ὑποζυγίου.**

Is40 9 62 11 Zch9 9

Mark

τῶν μαθητῶν αὐτοῦ ² καὶ λέγει αὐτοῖς· ὑπάγετε εἰς τὴν κώμην τὴν κατέναντι ὑμῶν, καὶ εὐθὺς εἰσπορευόμενοι εἰς αὐτὴν εὑρήσετε πῶλον δεδεμένον ἐφ' ὃν οὐδεὶς οὔπω ἀνθρώπων κεκάθικεν· λύσατε αὐτὸν καὶ φέρετε. ³ καὶ ἐάν τις ὑμῖν εἴπῃ· τί ποιεῖτε τοῦτο; εἴπατε ὅτι ὁ κύριος αὐτοῦ χρείαν ἔχει καὶ εὐθὺς αὐτὸν ἀποστέλλει πάλιν ὧδε.

Luke

τῶν μαθητῶν ³⁰ εἰπών· ὑπάγετε εἰς τὴν κατέναντι κώμην, ἐν ᾗ εἰσπορευόμενοι εὑρήσετε πῶλον δεδεμένον, ἐφ' ὃν οὐδεὶς πώποτε ἀνθρώπων ἐκάθισεν, καὶ λύσαντες αὐτὸν ἀγάγετε. ³¹ καὶ ἐάν τις ὑμᾶς ἐρωτᾷ· διὰ τί λύετε; οὕτως ἐρεῖτε· ὅτι ὁ κύριος αὐτοῦ χρείαν ἔχει.

John

12 14f.: εὑρὼν δὲ ὁ Ἰησοῦς ὀνάριον ἐκάθισεν ἐπ' αὐτό, καθώς ἐστιν γεγραμμένον· ¹⁵ **μὴ φοβοῦ, θυγάτηρ Σιων· ἰδοὺ ὁ βασιλεύς σου ἔρχεται, καθήμενος ἐπὶ πῶλον ὄνου.**

Mt 21,1 μα.] των μαθητων αυτου‖p: 33 28 φ-l547 Θ (εκ των: 157 pc) pc Lhr[1](om αυ.)r[2] Hil Sc[s]pj[ab](c = r[1]) — + αυτου‖Mk Lk: 245 1555 Le[k] bcdfff[1.2]g[1]lnq30 vg[4] Cb[3] Aeth **2** om αυτοις‖Lk: σ517-692-1675 157 1012 Chr Le[k] bdff[1.2]r[2] vg[1] Hil Cb[1] | ● πορευεσθε‖p: ℌ 1604 φ σ⟨954⟩-990-1010-1293-1606 D S[v] Θ 157 pc Ath[1] Chr Eu[1] Or — υπαγετε‖p: l184 — txt: Rpl Ath[2] Eu[2](-θεντες et om και[1]) | ∼ εις τ. απε. κω. et om υμ.‖Lk: 16 Ath[1:3] PsAth Eu[2]([1]κατεναντι + υμων) | ● κατεναντι‖p: ℌC Φ-28-700-1604 φ-l547 σ160-267-945-990-1010-1207-1223-1293 D Θ 157 pc Ath Chr Eu[2] Or — txt: Rpl PsAth Eu[1] | om ευθ.‖Lk: 544 482 Ath[1:3] PsAth Chr Labcff[1]hn Cb | ευθ. + εισπορευομενοι‖p: Φ | δεδεμενον‖p: σ517(∼ ον. κ. πω. δεδ.) 1574 Eu[2:3](om μετ αυ.) Lf Sj[bc] | αυτης] αυτου‖p: 1574 Lf Sj[bc] **3** τι + ποιειτε(+ ουτως)‖Mk (Lk): D (157) Or[1:2] | αυτων] αυτου‖p: ℵ 544 φl547 σ1194 Θ pc | ευθ. δε] και ευθεως‖Mk: 33 σ1010 D 1396 Chr L⟨q⟩ S,j Cb[3] | αποστελλει‖Mk: Rpl Chr Or Ldh vg[1] — απεστειλεν‖1: σ349-1293-1424-1675 — txt: ℵB λ1582 φ69 σM-517-945 D H Ω 157 pc Or L'[n] C | αυτου + ωδε‖Mk: Φ Sp **4** δε + ολον‖1 22 26 56: Rpl Chr[1] Lg[2]q30 vg[4] Sp[6]hj Csb[1] Arm Geo[1]([2] om δε) Δl[AD](τουτο δε] και τ.: i[V]; om δε: a md n) — txt: ℌ⟨B⟩C* D Θ pc Chr[1] Or L' Sc[s]p' Cb[1] Aeth Δ'⟨me p⟩ | δια] ● υπο‖2 23 1 22 2 15: LZ-892 544-700 φ-l547 Θ pc — txt: Rpl Chr Or **5** om σοι‖Jo Is40 9 62 11 MT: Φ Or Cb[1]

Mk 11,2 κ. λεγ.] λεγων‖p: WΘ-28-700 λ1 φ⟨124⟩ pc La Cs | om αυτοις‖Lk: 28 λ⟨118⟩ pc Ss[c] | την[1]—υμ.] την κατε. κω.‖Lk: W Lk[e] | κωμ.] πολιν‖14 13 p: σ27[c]-1223 al l13 l15 l184 | απεναντι‖Mt: 544 σM-1082-1606 pc l48 | δεδμενην‖Mt: 1375 | ουπω] πωποτε‖Lk: A 1342 pc l36 | κεκ.] ● εκαθισεν‖Lk: ℌC Θ-565-700 σ7-517 1342 pc l36 Or | λυσ. αυ. και] και λυσαντες αυ.‖Lk: 28 φ⟨124⟩ — λυσαντες αυ.(om)‖p: Rpl (544 σ517-1424 472) — txt (λυσαντες): ℌ'⟨892⟩ (L)C (D*') 1342 Or L | φερ.] αγαγετε (+ μοι)‖p: Rpl (544-1071-1604 σ115 pc) (απαγ.: 565) (L32[v] Geo) — txt: ℌ⟨L⟩C 1342 Or **3** ποι. του.] λυετε τον πωλον‖Lk: Θ-28-565-700-1071 φ-l547 D Or Labf ff[2]ir[1] Sp — om‖Mt: W λ pc Ss[c] Geo | ● om οτι‖Lk34 Mt26 18: BΔ φ788 pc Lk[e] abcff[2]i | αυ. αποστ. παλ.] παλ. αποστ. αυ.‖Mt: Θ Aeth — αποστ. παλ. αυ.‖Mt: B 372 Lc — αποστ. αυ.‖Mt Φ φ1689 σ179-827-1402 pc Lff[2]g[2]l Arm Geo[2]([1] prm μοι) | αυτον] αυτους‖Mt: σ827 258 l48 l184[1] | αποστελει‖Mt: Ψ WΦ-700-1071 λ1-22-209 σ27-71-115-179-1194 G U Π al Or Ladfff[2]iqr[1v.2] vg⟨2⟩ C Arm | om παλιν‖Mt: Rpl Or[2] L' S,j Cs[6]b — txt: ℌ'⟨Ψ⟩(om αυτον: Δ)C*[v](∼ παλ. απ.) Θ σ7-659 D pc l[pl] Or[1]([1] = Δ) Lacq Cs[3] Aeth | om ωδε‖Mt: σ827 l184 Or Lk[e] cz vg[1]

Lk 19,29 μαθ. + αυτου‖Mk: Rpl Eul L S C — txt: ℵBL-579 157 pc Or Le lqr[1]s Am **30** ειπ.] ● λεγων‖Mt Mk: ℌ[33]⟨579⟩ φ⟨124⟩ 157 D Θ Eul Or | ειπ. + αυτοις‖p: 245 Sscpj Cs[1:7] | κατ. κω.] κω. την κατ. υμων‖p: 1071 213 Lg[2]qr[1]z30 vg[10] | απεναντι‖Mt: 579 φ69 565 pc | κω.] πολιν‖20 10 p: σ71 | εν η] και‖p: D Eul Sscp | om εισπο.‖Mt: **063** | πω. + και ονον‖Mt: 1241 Eul(ον. κ. πω. νεον) La(∼ ον. κ. πω.) — + ονου‖Mt: L'⟨s vg[1]⟩ | εκα.] κεκαθικεν‖Mk: λλ 157 pc | om και‖p: Rpl Or L S,j C' — txt: BL-892 D 74[c] 157 Cb[5] | om αυτ.‖Mt: L-1241 φ230 D al | αγ. + μοι‖Mt: 1241 σ1194 G pc Eul Lvg[1] Geo Aeth **31** υμ. ερ.] υμιν ειπη‖p: 472 Eul Ld — υμιν ερ.‖p: σ1675 **063** pc Lvg[3] | om δια τι λυ.‖Mt: D Le cff[2]ls — om δια‖33 Mk: σ1675 Or Liq | om ουτως‖p: Eul Or Lacff[2]l Or Sc Cs | om οτι‖34 22 11 Mt26 18: σ659 Sscp⟨5⟩

6 πορευθέντες δὲ οἱ μαθηταὶ
καὶ ποιήσαντες
καθὼς προσέταξεν
αὐτοῖς ὁ Ἰησοῦς
7 ἤγαγον τὴν ὄνον καὶ τὸν πῶλον,
καὶ ἐπέθηκαν ἐπ'
αὐτῶν τὰ ἱμάτια,
καὶ ἐπεκάθισεν ἐπάνω αὐτῶν.
8 ὁ δὲ πλεῖστος ὄχλος
ἔστρωσαν ἑαυτῶν τὰ ἱμάτια
ἐν τῇ ὁδῷ, ἄλλοι δὲ
ἔκοπτον κλάδους

4 καὶ ἀπῆλθον καὶ
εὗρον πῶλον δεδεμένον πρὸς θύραν
ἔξω ἐπὶ τοῦ ἀμφόδου, καὶ λύουσιν
αὐτόν. 5 καί τινες τῶν ἐκεῖ
ἑστηκότων ἔλεγον
αὐτοῖς· τί ποιεῖτε λύοντες τὸν πῶλον;
6 οἱ δὲ εἶπον αὐτοῖς καθὼς εἶπεν
ὁ Ἰησοῦς· καὶ ἀφῆκαν αὐτούς.
7 καὶ φέρουσιν τὸν πῶλον
πρὸς τὸν Ἰησοῦν, καὶ ἐπιβάλλουσιν
αὐτῷ τὰ ἱμάτια αὐτῶν,
καὶ ἐκάθισεν ἐπ' αὐτόν.
8 καὶ πολλοὶ τὰ ἱμάτια αὐτῶν
ἔστρωσαν
εἰς τὴν ὁδόν, ἄλλοι δὲ
στιβάδας, κό-

32 ἀπελθόντες δὲ οἱ ἀπεσταλμένοι
εὗρον καθὼς εἶπεν αὐτοῖς.
33 λυόντων δὲ
αὐτῶν τὸν πῶλον
εἶπαν οἱ κύριοι αὐτοῦ πρὸς
αὐτούς· τί λύετε τὸν πῶλον;
34 οἱ δὲ εἶπαν· ὁ κύριος αὐτοῦ χρείαν
ἔχει.
35 καὶ ἤγαγον αὐτὸν
πρὸς τὸν Ἰησοῦν, καὶ ἐπιρρίψαντες
αὐτῶν τὰ ἱμάτια ἐπὶ τὸν πῶλον ἐπεβίβασαν τὸν Ἰησοῦν.
36 πορευομένου δὲ αὐτοῦ ὑπεστρώννυον τὰ ἱμάτια
ἑαυτῶν ἐν τῇ ὁδῷ.
37 ἐγ-

cf. v. 14 ↑ 12 12f.: τῇ ἐπαύριον ὄχλος πολὺς ὁ ἐλθὼν εἰς τὴν ἑορτήν, ἀκούσαντες ὅτι ἔρχεται Ἰησοῦς εἰς Ἱεροσόλυμα, 13 ἔλαβον τὰ βάϊα

Mt 21,6 ● συνεταξ.‖26 19 27 10: BC-33 700-1604 D 372 *l*48 — *txt*: *Rpl* Eu Or **7** επ αυτων] επ(*om*) αυτω‖p: 33 Φ(-τον) (φ')-69-788-983-(*l*547) D(= Φ) Θ *Le*[k] abfff$^{1.2}$g^{2}hqr^{2}30 vg^6 Ar *S*(*om*: c[s])p | ● ιμ. + αυτων‖p: *Rpl* Or(εαυ-) *L*' *S*,j *C Arm*^{pc} — *txt*: ℵ*B D Θ 1295 Or *Le*[k] bff$^{1.2}$g^{2}r^2 *Arm*' | επεκαθ.] εκαθισεν(-αν)‖Mk (Lk): (ℵL-892) NΣ σ71-1194-1223-1402-1424 K W Y Θ Π *pc* (*pc Lg*^{1}lz vg *Cs*$^{3:8}$b) | αυτων^2] αυτου‖Mk: D Θ *l*27 *Lvl*'g^2 *Spj* — αυτον‖Lk: ℵ^c-892 *Lg*^{1}lz vg **8** εστρωσαν] -ωννυον‖8b Lk: σ-349 *Lh* | ~ τα ιμ. αυτων‖p: Φ φ13 σ-349-945-990-1223-1402 *pc*

Mt 11,4 απηλ. και] απελθοντες‖p: Θ-565-700 D Or *L*⟨k[e] c⟩ *Geo*^{1} | πωλον] ● τον π.: ℵCΔ Θ-28-544-1071 λ22 σM-7-179-267-945-954-1082-1223-1391 1342 *pm* Or *Csb*^{1} — *txt*: 𝔥⟨ℵ-579⟩ WΘ-565 φ788 1093 Or^2 *C*' *Arm* | ● προς + την‖13 32 2: *Rpl* (τη θυρα: φ230) Or^1 *Cb*^{2} — *txt*: 𝔥⟨ℵ-579⟩ WΘ-565 φ788 1093 Or^2 *C*' *Arm* | *Lk*[e] bcff^{2}ir^2 vg^1 | ειπ.] ειρηκει‖Lk22 13: 579(-κεν) D *Lvl*'⟨k[e]⟩ — **6** *om* αυτοις‖Lk: D 1574 *l*48 vg | ειπ. + αυτοις‖14 15p Mt: 579 WΘΦ-28-544-565-700-1071-1604 λ-22 φ13-69-124-788-983 σM-7-267-827-1424 D *al l*48 *l*184 *L Ss*[c]p *Csb*⟨5⟩ — προσεταξεν‖Mt: *L*adflr^{2}z **7** φερ.] ηγαγον‖p: *Rpl Lcdflqr*^{2}z vg — αγουσιν‖p: ℵ*C WΘ-28 λ⟨118⟩ φ-*l*547 1342 *pc* — *txt*: 𝔥'⟨579⟩ ℵ^c 1071 Or | επιβ.] επεθηκαν‖Mt: 544 472 {} — επεβαλον(-λλον)‖Mt: *Rpl* (157 *pc*) {*Lk*[e] acfg^{2}q30 vg^3} — *txt*: 𝔥C WΘ-28-565-700 λ⟨118⟩ D 1342 *pc* Or *L*'⟨vg^6⟩ | ~ αυτων ... αυτω‖Lk: ℵ* 565(*om* αυτω) *Lc* | εκαθισαν‖Lk: ℵ*? 471 *l*184 *Aeth* | επανω αυτου‖Mt: 544 φ*l*547 **8** και πο.] πο. δε‖p: *Rpl L*' *S*' *Cs*^{9} — *txt*: 𝔥C 1071 *pc Lk*[e] q *Ss*[c] *Cs*^{1}b *Arm* | εστρωννυον‖Lk Mt8b: WΘ(-υαν)-28-565-700 λ⟨118⟩ D *al Lvl*[e]⟨flr^2⟩r^1 *Ss*[c]p | εις τ. οδ.] εν τη οδω‖p: NΣ-28-700 λ872-2193 φ69 σM-517-659-945-1028-1223-1391-1402 A K Y Π *al L*⟨bff^{2}i⟩ | *om* αλλ.—αγρ.‖Lk: W *Li Ss*[c] | κοψ.] εκοπτον(-ψαν)‖Mt: *Rpl L*'⟨i vg^1⟩(r^2) *Sp*(~ εκο. στι.)h (*C*) — *txt*: 𝔥⟨579⟩ 1342 Or *Ll*

Lk 19,32 οι απεστ.] οι μαθηται‖Mt: Or — *om*‖Mk: 713 *Le Sc* | αυτ. + εστωτα τον πωλον‖Mk: 1071 σ7-267-659-1391-1402 U(*om* εστ.) 157(*om* τον) *pc l*18 *l*19 *l*49 *l*185 Or$^{1:3}$ *L*(*om* τ. πω.: e ilqr^{1}s^v; τ. π.] την ονον: a; ~ τ. π. εστ.: cff^2)fz30 vg'(^{2} = c) *Shj*^{b}(c + δεδεμενον‖Mk) *Arm Aeth* **34** ● ειπ. + οτι‖31p: 𝔥[33] ⟨892⟩ N-1071 λ-1582 φ-230 σM-1194-1207-1223 A D K W Θ Π Ψ 157 *mu* Or *Lafqz* vg *S*'j — *txt*: *Rpl Lvl*'r^1 *Ss Arm* **35** αυτον] τον πωλον‖Mk Mt: D *Le* 30 *Sscp*^{1} | *om* πρ. τ. Ι.‖Mt: D *Le* | επιρ. ... επεβι.] επερριψαν ... και επεβι.‖p: λ-1582-2193 D *Lvl*⟨asz⟩r^1 | ~ τα ιμ. αυ.‖Mk: φ*l*547 D *pc* | *om* αυτων‖Mt: 579 *Ls* | επι τ. πω.] επ αυτον‖p: D *Le* cq vg^3 *Ssc* **36** υπεστ.] εστρωννυον‖p: 251 | τ. ιμ. εαυ.] ● τ. ιμ. αυτων‖Mk: *Rpl* Or {} — αυ. τ. ιμ.‖Mt: 1071 251 {} — τ. ιμ.‖Mt7: 1241 *pc* — *txt*: B N-1604 λ1582 φ124-*l*547 σ1207-1223 A K R U W Θ Π Ψ *al* {*L S C*}

Jo 12,12 οχ. πο. ο] ● ο οχ. πο. ο: 𝔓^{66*} BL φ *pc Ss*[c] *Cb*'a — ο οχ. ο πο. ο‖12 17.29: 𝔓^{66c} Θ — οχ. πο.: ℵ*-892-1241 Δ *pc Lff*^{2} — *txt*: 𝔓^{2v} *Rpl* Or *S*'j *Csb*^{B}a^s | ~ Ιη. ερχ.‖11 20: LX-33-1241 544 φ*l*547 σ1223 A **0141** 157 *pc* Cat Or *Le* acff^{2}z vg^1 *Ss*[c]pj(Ιη.] κυριος Ιη.) *C*$^{+B}$aa^s | Ιη.] ● ο Ιη.: 𝔓$^{66.75}$ B-579 λ22 φ-230 σ1293 Γ Θ Ω **053** *pm* Cr {} — *om*: 28 **047** 565 *Ll* — *txt*: *Rpl* Or {*L*' *C*$^{+B}$aa^s}

	Matth	Mark	Luk	Jo
	ἀπὸ τῶν δένδρων καὶ ἐστρώννυον ἐν τῇ ὁδῷ. 9 οἱ δὲ ὄχλοι οἱ προάγοντες αὐτὸν καὶ οἱ ἀκολουθοῦντες ἔκραζον	ψαντες ἐκ τῶν ἀγρῶν. 9 καὶ οἱ προάγοντες καὶ οἱ ἀκολουθοῦντες ἔκραζον·	γίζοντος δὲ αὐτοῦ ἤδη πρὸς τῇ καταβάσει τοῦ ὄρους τῶν ἐλαιῶν ἤρξαντο ἅπαν τὸ πλῆθος τῶν μαθητῶν χαίροντες αἰνεῖν τὸν θεὸν φωνῇ μεγάλῃ περὶ πασῶν ὧν εἶδον δυνάμεων, 38 λέγοντες·	τῶν φοινίκων καὶ ἐξῆλθον εἰς ὑπάντησιν αὐτῷ, καὶ ἐκραύγαζον·
Ps118 25f.	λέγοντες· **ωσαννα** τῷ υἱῷ Δαυιδ· **εὐλογημένος ὁ ἐρχόμενος ἐν ὀνόματι κυρίου·**	**ωσαννα· εὐλογημένος ὁ ἐρχόμενος ἐν ὀνόματι κυρίου·** 10 εὐλογημένη ἡ ἐρχομένη βασιλεία τοῦ πατρὸς ἡμῶν Δαυιδ·	**εὐλογημένος ὁ ἐρχόμενος** βασιλεὺς **ἐν ὀνόματι κυρίου·**	**ωσαννα· εὐλογημένος ὁ ἐρχόμενος ἐν ὀνόματι κυρίου,** ὁ βασιλεὺς τοῦ Ισραηλ.
	ωσαννα ἐν τοῖς ὑψίστοις.	**ωσαννα** ἐν τοῖς ὑψίστοις.	ἐν οὐρανῷ εἰρήνη καὶ δόξα ἐν ὑψίστοις.	

(197) 211. Weissagung von der Zerstörung Jerusalems. *Prediction of the Destruction of Jerusalem.*

Luk 19 39–44

Hab 2 11 — *cf.* 212.

39 Καί τινες τῶν Φαρισαίων ἀπὸ τοῦ ὄχλου εἶπαν πρὸς αὐτόν· διδάσκαλε, ἐπιτίμησον τοῖς μαθηταῖς σου. 40 καὶ ἀποκριθεὶς εἶπεν αὐτοῖς· λέγω ὑμῖν ὅτι ἐὰν οὗτοι σιωπήσουσιν, **οἱ λίθοι κράξουσιν.** 41 καὶ ὡς ἤγγισεν, ἰδὼν τὴν πόλιν ἔκλαυσεν ἐπ' αὐτήν, 42 λέγων ὅτι εἰ ἔγνως καὶ σὺ ἐν τῇ ἡμέρᾳ ταύτῃ τὰ πρὸς εἰρή-

Mt 21,8 εστρωννυον] -ωσαν‖8a Mk: ℵ* D Δ^v *L*e[k] cff^{2}q *C*b **9** *om* αυτον‖Mk: *Rpl L*' *Arm* — *txt*: 𝔥C λ1-1582 ϕ⟨13-346-983⟩ σ1010-1293 D 157 Eu Or *L*ff^1 Ar *S*,j *C* | υψ. + απηντων δε αυτω πολλοι χαιροντες και δοξαζοντες τον θεον περι παντων ων ειδον‖Lk37: Φ *S*c[s]

Mk 11,8 εκ] απο‖Mt: σ954-1606 *pc l*36 | αγρ.] δενδρων‖Mt: *Rpl L S*ph$^+$ *C*b' — *txt*: 𝔥C 1342 Or *S*h *C*sb^3 | αγρ./δεν. + και εστρωννυον εις(εν) την(τη) οδον(οδω)‖Mt: *Rpl* (579 ΝΘΣ-700 λ872 σM-827-945-1082-1223 K Y Π; *et om* εν: 565) (*om* και: 1342 Or; *om* εις: D) Or(εστρωσαν) *L*k[e](*om* εις τ. οδ.) (abcf)ff^{2}l (*om* και)(qr$^{1v.2}$ vg) *S*ph *C*b' — *txt*: 𝔥⟨579⟩C *C*sb^3 **9** εκρ.] + λεγοντες‖p: *Rpl* (ελεγον κραζοντες: Φ) *L*'Hi *S C*s^{4}b^2 — ελεγον: Ψ 495 — *txt*: 𝔥'⟨579⟩C σ115 1342 *pc l*20 Or *L*k[e] cff^2 *C*s^{6}b' | *om* ωσα.‖Lk: W D *L*bff^{2}r^1 | κυ. + ωσαννα εν τοις υψιστοις‖Mt: λ872-2193 **10** ωσα.] ειρηνη‖Lk: W-28-700 Or *S*s[c] — ειρ. εν ουρανω και δοξα (+ ωσα.)‖Lk19 38 2 14: Θ λ22*(^{c}-1278 *pc*) *Arm* | ωσα.—υψ. + (*prm*) ειρ. εν ουρ. και δοξα εν υψ.‖←: **λ** (*S*h$^+$)

Lk 19,37 φω. μεγ.] μετα φωνης μεγαλης‖17 35: 1038 **38** λεγ. + ωσαννα‖p: 1071 | ο ερχ. βασ.] ο ερχ.‖Mt Mk: 579 Λ ϕ*l*547 (D) W *pc l*18 *l*48 *l*76 Eul Meth Ti *L*acff^{2}ir$^{1.2}$s vg^3 *C*b^1 *Aeth* — ● ο(*om*) βασ.: ℵ* (H **063** *l*950^1 *l*1127^1) Or (*om* εν ον. κυ.: *L*e l) — *txt*: *Rpl* (ερχ. + ο: B) *L*' *S*,j *C*' | κυ. + ευλογημενος ο(*om* 157) βασιλευς(+ του Ισραηλ)‖Mk: D (157) *L*acff^{2}is(r^1 *S*h$^+$) | εν υψ.] επι γης‖2 14: 235(ε. της γ.) 473 *L*vg^1 **39** των Φ.] Φαρισαιοι‖13 31: W **40** ● *om* αυτ.: ℵBL-1241 Or *C*' *Arm Δ*n — *txt*: *Rpl L S*,j *C*b^1 *Δ*'(τουτοις τοις Φαρισαιοις: i^V) E^{sa} | ● *om* οτι: B* 1604 λ1278 ϕ69-788 W Θ *al L*vl⟨fqz⟩r^{1}30 vg^1 *Δ*⟨me⟩ | ● σιωπησωσιν: *Rpl* (σιωπωσιν: 157) Cr Or *L*' — *txt*: ℵBL-579 N ϕ788 A D(σιγησ.) R Δ *pc L*e i vg^1 **42** ● εν—ταυ. και συ: 𝔥[33] 1012 Or *S*j *Aeth* — *om* και συ: *S*scp(∼ τα—ειρ. εν—ταυ.) Eu *Δ*a(= *S*p) ad — *txt* (*om* και): *Rpl* Bas Eu Ir *L*'(e aff^{2}ilr^{1}s) Or *S*h Ef *C Arm* (*Geo*) *Δ*i^{V}l E^{sa} | εν τ. ημ. ταυ.] ● καιγε εν τ. ημ. σου(*om*) ταυ.: *Rpl* (**λ**-1582 ϕ124 σ71 A Ψ *pc l*10 *l*184 Bas)(∼ σου εν τ. ημ.: ϕ346) *L*' *S*(sc)ph Ef (Eu) *Δ*ad l E^{saA1}(^{1B}) — *txt* (ημ. + σου): ℵBL-579-892 (σ1194) D Θ 1012 Or *L*e fqs Or *C Arm Aeth Δ*(a i^T)^{V}n | τα] ηρωτησας αν τα‖14 32: 157

Jo 12,13 απαντ.‖Mt25 1.6 1Th4 17: 28 ϕ*l*547 σ71-1194 A K U V^s Π *pm* Or — συναντ.‖Mt8 34: LX-1241 1071 ϕ⟨124⟩ σ954 D G **050 0141** *pc* Cat — *txt*: 𝔓$^{66.75}$ *Rpl* | αυτου‖Mt25 6: σ954 D V^s Γ *pc* | εκρ.] εκραζον‖Mt Mk: *Rpl* Or — *txt* (-ασαν): 𝔓^2(^{66})^{75} ℵ(B*)LQW-579 σ1188-1293 D Ω 157 (*C*sb^1) | εκρ. + λεγοντες‖Mt Mk: 𝔓^{66} ℵQX 544-1071 **λ**-22 ϕ⟨69-124-788⟩ σ1188-1293 A D Π **053** 157 *mu L*aff^2 vg^1 *S*'h^{Brs}j^b *C*b' — *txt*: 𝔓^{2v75} *Rpl* Or *L*' *S*hj^{ac} *C*sb^{B}aa^s | *om* ο βασ. τ. Ισ.‖Mt: σ1207 | ο βασ.] βασ.: *Rpl* {} — ● και ο βασ.: 𝔓^{75v} 𝔥'⟨1241⟩Q λ209? Ψ Or^1 *C*b' *Geo*^{1} *Aeth* — *txt*: 𝔓^{66} LX 1071 **λ**'-22 ϕ346 D K Θ Π *pc* Or^1 {*L S*,j *C*sb^{B2}a^s *Geo*^{2}} | Ισ. + ωσαννα εν τοις υψιστοις‖Mt Mk: **0141**

νην σου· νῦν δὲ ἐκρύβη ἀπὸ ὀφθαλμῶν σου. 43 ὅτι ἥξουσιν ἡμέραι ἐπὶ σὲ καὶ παρεμβαλοῦσιν οἱ ἐχθροί σου χάρακά σοι καὶ περικυκλώσουσίν σε καὶ συνέξουσίν σε πάντοθεν, 44 καὶ **ἐδαφιοῦσίν** σε καὶ **τὰ τέκνα σου** ἐν σοί, καὶ οὐκ ἀφήσουσιν λίθον ἐπὶ λίθον ἐν σοί, ἀνθ' ὧν οὐκ ἔγνως τὸν καιρὸν τῆς ἐπισκοπῆς σου. — Ps137₉

(198) ***212.*** Jesus im Tempel; (Tempelreinigung); Rückkehr nach Bethanien.
Jesus in the Temple; (the Cleansing of It); Return to Bethany.

Matth 21 10–17	**Mark 11** 11	
10 Καὶ εἰσελθόντος αὐτοῦ εἰς Ἱεροσόλυμα ἐσείσθη πᾶσα ἡ πόλις λέγουσα· τίς ἐστιν οὗτος; 11 οἱ δὲ ὄχλοι ἔλεγον· οὗτός ἐστιν ὁ προφήτης Ἰησοῦς ὁ ἀπὸ Ναζαρεθ τῆς Γαλιλαίας. 12 καὶ εἰσῆλθεν Ἰησοῦς εἰς τὸ ἱερὸν τοῦ θεοῦ καὶ ἐξέβαλεν πάντας τοὺς πωλοῦντας καὶ ἀγοράζοντας ἐν τῷ ἱερῷ, καὶ τὰς τραπέζας τῶν κολλυβιστῶν κατέστρεψεν καὶ τὰς καθέδρας τῶν πωλούντων τὰς περιστεράς, 13 καὶ λέγει αὐτοῖς· γέγραπται· **ὁ οἶκός μου οἶκος προσευχῆς κληθήσεται,** ὑμεῖς δὲ αὐτὸν ποιεῖτε **σπήλαιον λῃστῶν.** 14 καὶ προσῆλθον αὐτῷ τυφλοὶ καὶ χωλοὶ ἐν τῷ ἱερῷ, καὶ ἐθεράπευσεν αὐτούς. 15 ἰδόντες δὲ οἱ ἀρχιερεῖς καὶ οἱ γραμματεῖς τὰ θαυμάσια ἃ ἐποίησεν καὶ τοὺς παῖδας τοὺς κράζοντας ἐν τῷ ἱερῷ καὶ λέγοντας· ωσαννα τῷ υἱῷ Δαυιδ, ἠγανάκτησαν, 16 καὶ εἶπον αὐτῷ· ἀκούεις τί οὗτοι λέγουσιν; ὁ δὲ Ἰησοῦς λέγει αὐτοῖς· ναί· οὐδέποτε ἀνέγνωτε ὅτι **ἐκ στόματος νηπίων καὶ θηλαζόντων κατηρτίσω αἶνον;** 17 καὶ καταλιπὼν αὐτοὺς ἐξῆλθεν ἔξω τῆς πόλεως εἰς Βηθανίαν, καὶ ηὐλίσθη ἐκεῖ.	11 Καὶ εἰσῆλθεν εἰς Ἱεροσόλυμα εἰς τὸ ἱερόν· [*214.*] καὶ περιβλεψάμενος πάντα, ὀψὲ ἤδη οὔσης τῆς ὥρας, ἐξῆλθεν εἰς Βηθανίαν μετὰ τῶν δώδεκα.	*cf. 211. cf. 242.*

Is56₇Jr7₁₁ — Ps8₃

(199) ***213.*** Die Verfluchung des Feigenbaums. *The Cursing of the Fig Tree.*

Matth 21 18–19	**Mark 11** 12–14
18 Πρωῒας δὲ ἐπανάγων εἰς τὴν πόλιν ἐπείνασεν. 19 καὶ ἰδὼν συκῆν μίαν ἐπὶ τῆς ὁδοῦ ἦλθεν ἐπ'	12 Καὶ τῇ ἐπαύριον ἐξελθόντων αὐτῶν ἀπὸ Βηθανίας ἐπείνασεν. 13 καὶ ἰδὼν συκῆν ἀπὸ μακρόθεν ἔχουσαν φύλλα ἦλθεν εἰ ἄρα τι εὑρήσει ἐν αὐτῇ, καὶ ἐλθὼν ἐπ'

Mt 21,12 ● *om* του θε.‖pMk11₁₅p: ℵBL-892 700 ϕ13-543-788-826-828 **σ**-945-954-1010-1207-1223-1293 Θ *pc* Or *Lb* Hil *Sj C Arm Geo*⟨A⟩ *Aeth* ¦ αγ.] τους αγ.‖Mk11₁₅: σ1606 *pc* ¦ ∼ και τ. καθ.—περιστ. κατεστρ.‖←: **σ**-349 *L'*⟨fq⟩ (και τας περιστ. κατεστρ. και τας καθ. των καθημενων (sedebant < vendebant?): e) *Cs*⟨7:12⟩ **13** γεγ. + οτι‖Mk11₁₇: Σ σ1402 2145 *Lvg*¹(+ γαρ οτι) *S,j* ¦ κλη.] εστιν‖Lk19₄₆: 1093 — γενησεται‖←: **λ**⟨1⟩ ¦ ποι.] εποιησατε (∼ επ. αυτον‖←p(Mk←): *Rpl* (NO-700 ϕ174-1689 σ349-659-1402-1606) (αυτ. επ. αυτ.: 28) {(*L*) Hi Hil (Ir) Or *S,j Cs*} — πεποιηκατε: λ1 Or {} — *txt*: ℵBL-892 ϕ124 σ1010-1293 Θ Eu Or *Cb Aeth* **16** ακου.] ουκ ακ.‖27₁₃: 28-544-1604 ϕ230-346 σ1424-1675 F H 157 Chr *Sc Cb*⟨1⟩ *Geo*ᶜʰ **18** πρωιας] ● πρωι‖Mk11₂₀15₁: ℵ*B D Θ *l*183 ¦ δε + γενομενης‖27₁: 544 σ1424 *pc La Cb*⟨1⟩ ¦ ● επαναγαγων: ℵ*B*L 565 1295 **19** *om* μιαν‖p: 477 *pc* Chr *Le*[k] ff¹h

Mk 11,13 συκην + μιαν‖p: ℵ ϕ230 σM K Y Π *al* (∼: *pc*) *Sp* ¦ *om* εχ. φυλ.‖**p**: **0188** ¦ και²—ευρ.] ελ. δε ουδ. ευρ. εν αυτη‖p: **0188** ¦ *om* ελ. επ αυ.‖p: 579-892 700(*om* και²) D 1093 *Lk*[e] bcff²ir¹ᵛ ¦ επ αυ.] εν αυτη‖p: σ827 1574

Lk 19,42 ● *om* σου¹‖←: ℵBL-579 σ71 Θ *pc* Ir Or *L*Ir *Csb*¹ *Δi*ᵛ Eᵃᴬ¹ ᴮ¹:² — *txt* (σου] σοι): *Rpl* (ϕ⟨124-346-828⟩ D 1365) Bas Cr(∼) Eu²(³) *La*(') Eu Or *S,j Cb' Δa* (ad iᵀ l) n p Eᵃᴬ¹ **44** ∼ εν σοι² λ. επι λ.‖Mt24₂: *Rpl* (+ εν ολη σοι: Θ) *L' S* — *txt* (εν + ολη): 𝔥[33] (**λ**'-1582-2193)(*om* εν *et* σοι + ος(!)‖21₆p: 131) σ1424 (D) 157 Or *L*(*et* σοι] terra: e) alq(cff²is) *Sj C* (*Arm*) *Aeth* ¦ επι λιθω‖21₆: *Rpl* (επανω λιθου: 579) — *txt*: 𝔥' Λ-1071-1604 **λ**-1582 ϕ124 σ115-267 D R S Γ Θ Π Ψ *al l*48 *l*184 Or

---

Mt21₁₂ *cf.* EN fragm.25 (*cf. ad 214.* Mk11₁₅)

Matth	Mark
αὐτήν, καὶ οὐδὲν εὗρεν ἐν αὐτῇ εἰ μὴ φύλλα μόνον,	αὐτὴν οὐδὲν εὗρεν εἰ μὴ φύλλα· ὁ γὰρ
καὶ λέγει αὐτῇ·	καιρὸς οὐκ ἦν σύκων. [14] καὶ ἀποκριθεὶς εἶπεν αὐτῇ·
μηκέτι ἐκ σοῦ καρπὸς γένηται	μηκέτι εἰς τὸν αἰῶνα ἐκ σοῦ μηδεὶς καρπὸν φάγοι.
εἰς τὸν αἰῶνα. καὶ ἐξηράνθη παραχρῆμα ἡ συκῆ.	καὶ ἤκουον οἱ μαθηταὶ αὐτοῦ.

(200)

214. Die Tempelreinigung. *The Cleansing of the Temple.*

21 12–13 (212.)	**Mark 11** 15–19	**Luk 19** 45–48	
	[15] Καὶ ἔρχονται εἰς		2 13–16 : ... καὶ ἀνέβη εἰς
[12] *καὶ*	Ἱεροσόλυμα. καὶ	[45] Καὶ	Ἱεροσόλυμα ὁ Ἰησοῦς. [14] καὶ
εἰσῆλθεν Ἰησοῦς εἰς τὸ ἱερὸν	εἰσελθὼν εἰς τὸ ἱερὸν	εἰσελθὼν εἰς τὸ ἱερὸν	εὗρεν ἐν τῷ ἱερῷ
τοῦ θεοῦ	ἤρξατο	ἤρξατο	τοὺς πωλοῦντας βόας καὶ
			πρόβατα καὶ περιστερὰς καὶ
			τοὺς κερματιστὰς καθημέ-
			νους, [15] καὶ ποιήσας φραγέλ-
καὶ			λιον ἐκ σχοινίων πάντας
ἐξέβαλεν πάντας τοὺς πω-	ἐκβάλλειν τοὺς πω-	ἐκβάλλειν τοὺς πω-	ἐξέβαλεν ἐκ τοῦ ἱεροῦ, τά τε
λοῦντας καὶ ἀγοράζον-	λοῦντας καὶ τοὺς ἀγοράζον-	λοῦντας,	πρόβατα καὶ τοὺς βόας,
τας ἐν τῷ ἱερῷ, καὶ τὰς τραπέζας	τας ἐν τῷ ἱερῷ, καὶ τὰς τραπέζας		καὶ
τῶν κολλυβιστῶν	τῶν κολλυβιστῶν		τῶν κολλυβιστῶν ἐξέχεεν τὸ κέρμα
κατέστρεψεν			καὶ τὰς τραπέζας ἀνέστρεψεν,
καὶ τὰς καθέδρας τῶν πωλούν-	καὶ τὰς καθέδρας τῶν πωλούν-		[16] καὶ

Mt 21,19 *om* εν αυτη ‖ p: σ945-990-1424 Chr *L*ff^{1} | μηκετι] ● ου μ.: BL O | γενοιτο ‖ p: ℵ Θ Or

Mk 11,13 ευρ. + εν αυτη ‖ p: 579 (**0188**) *L*cfg^{2}q *S*p *C*s | φυ^{2} + μονον ‖ p: C^{2}-33-579 NWΣΦ-565-700-1071 **ϕ** σ1606 *pc* Or *L*bcqr^{1} *C*s *Arm Aeth* **14** εις—φαγ.] εκ σου εις τ. αιω. μηδ.—φ. ‖ p: *Rpl* (∼ καρ. εις τ. αιω.: σM) *S*h — εκ σου καρπος εις τ. αιω. γενηται ‖ p: 1515 (*pc*) — μηδ. απο σου καρπον φ. εις τ. αιω. ‖ p: **0188** — εις—σου καρπον μηδ. φ. ‖ p: W-1071 **λ** 299 — *txt*: ℵBCLΔΨ-892 Θ-28-565 D 1342 *pc* Or *L*(∼ μηδ. καρ. εκ σου: k[e] abcilq; *om* εις τ. αιω.: c; ∼ μηδ. εκ—καρ.: fff^{2}r^{1}?; ∼ καρ. μηδ.: vg) (= *L*f: *S*s[c]p) *Arm* **15** ερχεται ‖ p: 700 *L*bir^{1}z *S*s[c] *C*s$^{4:8}$b^{4} *Geo* — + παλιν ‖ 11 27: 892 NΣ σ517-659-1082-1391 713 *l*18 *l*19 *l*184 *L*a(∼ εις l. παλ.)bfff^{2}ir^{1} vg^{3} | *om* τους^{2} ‖ Mt: *Rpl* Or — *txt*: ℵBCL-892 NΣ-1071 σM-7-517-1082-1207-1391 A K U Π 1342 *al* | κολ. + εξεχεεν ‖ Jo: NWΘΣ(-χεσεν)-28-565-700 **ϕ** *Arm* | ∼ κατεστρ. και τ. καθ.—περιστ. ‖ Mt: ℵ**pc* Or *L*c(∼ κατ. τ. τρα. τ. κολ. και ηρξατο—αγο. και τ. καθ.—περ.) *C*s

Lk 19,45 πωλ. + εν αυτω και αγοραζοντας ‖ p: *Rpl* (*om* και αγ.: σ7 4) (∼ κ. αγ. εν αυ.: 2533) *L*'(αυ.] τω ιερω: vg^{1}; = 2533: 30 vg^{1}) *S*(= σ7: sc)ph — + τας περιστερας κ. αγορ. εν τω ιερω ‖ p: 28(*om* τ. περ.) *Arm*(*om* εν—ιε.) — + και αγορ. ‖ p: C(και + τους) N **ϕ**⟨124⟩ Ψ 213 *Le* s — *txt*: ℵBL-579-1241 **λλ**⟨118-131-1278⟩ **ϕ**230 Or *L*l vg^{1} *S*j *C* | 45 + και τας τραπεζας των κολλυβιστων εξεχεεν και τας καθεδρας των πωλουντων τας περιστερας(+ κατεστρεψεν) ‖ p: (Λ 262^{v}) D *pc* *L*e (κολ. + και: ad; *om* εξε. *et* πωλ. + και: i)g^{2}lr^{1}s(cff^{2}qr^{2} vg^{1})^{1} *S*h^{+} *Arm*(*om* και τ. καθ.—περιστ.) (*Aeth*)

Jo 2,13 ∼ ο Ιη. εις Ιε. ‖ p 51: 𝔓$^{66.75}$ L-1241 1071-1604 σM-1010-1293 A(Ιε. + Ιησους!) G U 713 Chrn Eu *L*br^{1} *S*[sc]j (κυριος Ιη.) *C*,a^{s} *Arm* **15** ● τα κερματα: 𝔓$^{66c\,75}$ BLW^{s}X-**083-0162**-33-579 **0141** 213 Eu Or *L*bq *S*[sc]j *C*,a^{s} — *txt*: 𝔓^{66*v} *Rpl* Cr(*om* εξε. τ. κε. και) Non *L*'(e = Cr) | κατεστρεψεν ‖ p: 𝔓^{59} ℵ **ϕ**⟨69*⟩ 157 *pc*

Mk11 15p *cf.* EN frgm.25 (Pt^{R} aur.^{sch}): In libris evangeliorum, quibus utuntur Nazareni, legitur quod: radii prodierunt ex oculis eius, quibus territi fugabantur (*sc.* e templo vendentes, ementes, nummularii).

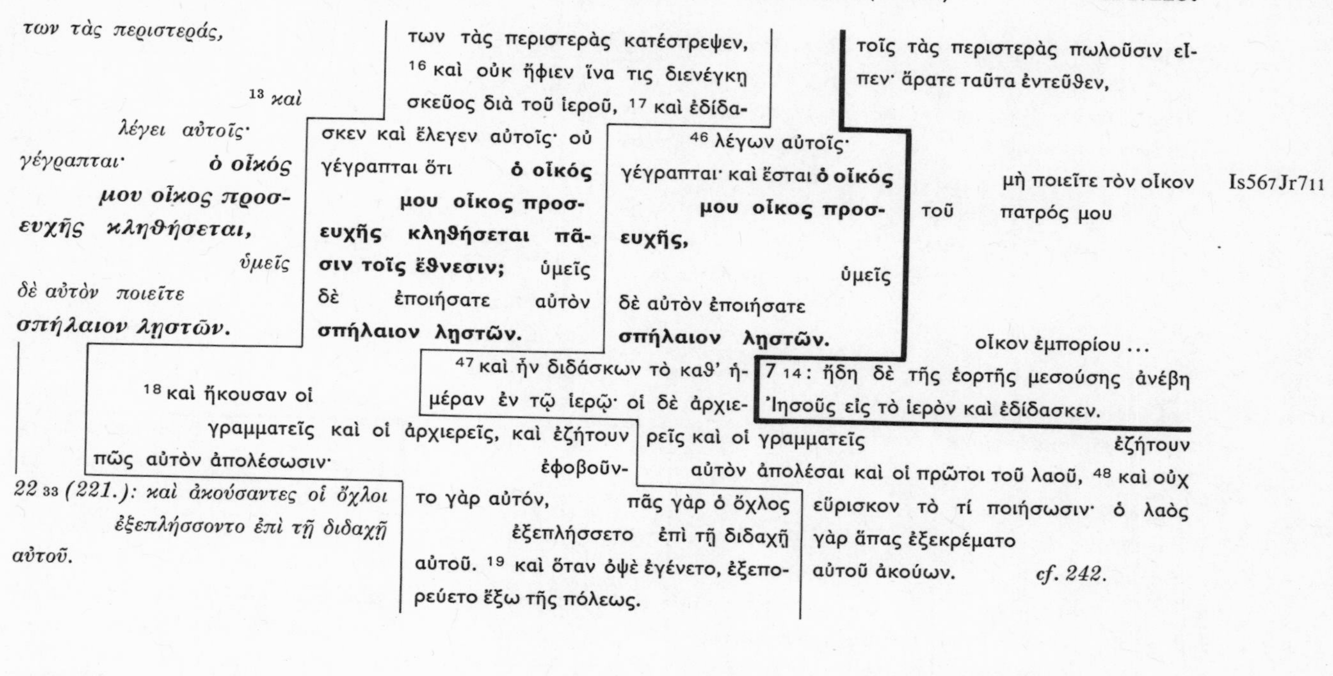

των τὰς περιστεράς, [13] *καὶ λέγει αὐτοῖς· γέγραπται·* ***ὁ οἶκός μου οἶκος προσευχῆς κληθήσεται,*** *ὑμεῖς δὲ αὐτὸν ποιεῖτε* ***σπήλαιον λῃστῶν.***

22 33 (221.): καὶ ἀκούσαντες οἱ ὄχλοι ἐξεπλήσσοντο ἐπὶ τῇ διδαχῇ αὐτοῦ.

των τὰς περιστερὰς κατέστρεψεν, [16] καὶ οὐκ ἤφιεν ἵνα τις διενέγκῃ σκεῦος διὰ τοῦ ἱεροῦ, [17] καὶ ἐδίδασκεν καὶ ἔλεγεν αὐτοῖς· οὐ γέγραπται ὅτι **ὁ οἶκός μου οἶκος προσευχῆς κληθήσεται πᾶσιν τοῖς ἔθνεσιν;** ὑμεῖς δὲ ἐποιήσατε αὐτὸν **σπήλαιον λῃστῶν.** [18] καὶ ἤκουσαν οἱ γραμματεῖς καὶ οἱ ἀρχιερεῖς, καὶ ἐζήτουν πῶς αὐτὸν ἀπολέσωσιν· ἐφοβοῦντο γὰρ αὐτόν, πᾶς γὰρ ὁ ὄχλος ἐξεπλήσσετο ἐπὶ τῇ διδαχῇ αὐτοῦ. [19] καὶ ὅταν ὀψὲ ἐγένετο, ἐξεπορεύετο ἔξω τῆς πόλεως.

[46] λέγων αὐτοῖς· γέγραπται· καὶ ἔσται **ὁ οἶκός μου οἶκος προσευχῆς,** ὑμεῖς δὲ αὐτὸν ἐποιήσατε **σπήλαιον λῃστῶν.** [47] καὶ ἦν διδάσκων τὸ καθ' ἡμέραν ἐν τῷ ἱερῷ· οἱ δὲ ἀρχιερεῖς καὶ οἱ γραμματεῖς ἐζήτουν αὐτὸν ἀπολέσαι καὶ οἱ πρῶτοι τοῦ λαοῦ, [48] καὶ οὐχ εὕρισκον τὸ τί ποιήσωσιν· ὁ λαὸς γὰρ ἅπας ἐξεκρέματο αὐτοῦ ἀκούων. *cf. 242.*

τοῖς τὰς περιστερὰς πωλοῦσιν εἶπεν· ἄρατε ταῦτα ἐντεῦθεν, μὴ ποιεῖτε τὸν οἶκον τοῦ πατρός μου οἶκον ἐμπορίου ... 7 14: ἤδη δὲ τῆς ἑορτῆς μεσούσης ἀνέβη Ἰησοῦς εἰς τὸ ἱερὸν καὶ ἐδίδασκεν.

Is567 Jr711

(201)

215. Von der Kraft des Glaubens. *The Power of Faith.*

Matth 21 20–22

[20] Καὶ ἰδόντες οἱ μαθηταὶ ἐθαύμασαν λέγοντες· πῶς παραχρῆμα

Mark 11 20–25

[20] Καὶ παραπορευόμενοι πρωῒ εἶδον τὴν συκῆν ἐξηραμμένην ἐκ ῥιζῶν. [21] καὶ ἀναμνησθεὶς ὁ Πέτρος λέγει αὐτῷ· ῥαββι, ἴδε ἡ συκῆ ἣν κατηράσω

Mt 21,20 μαθ. + αυτου‖Mk11₁₄: 1604 238 *l*48 *l*49 *Sc* *Cs*$^{7:9}$

Mk 11,15 ανεστρ.‖Jo: **0188** **17** *om* και εδι.‖p: **0188** | και ελ.] λεγων‖Lk: *Rpl* *L'* *S*h *Cs* — *txt*: 𝔥⟨33-579⟩C ϕ⟨124-788⟩ **0188** 1342 *pc* Or *Lk*[e] *S'* *C*b | *om* ου‖p: 579 Θ-28-565-700 λ ϕ69(ου] οτι) D **0188** *pc* *Lk*[e] bcff^{2}i Hi *Cs*$^{7:8}$b *Arm* | *om* οτι‖←: CΨ-579 ϕ69 D **0188** *al* *Lk*[e] abcff^{2}iq *Geo*^{2} | οικ.^{1} + του πατρος‖Jo: σ179 569 *L*Hi | *om* πα. τ. εθ.‖p: 28 213 *Lk*[e] | ∼ αυ. εποι.‖Lk Mt: 33-579 Θ-565-700 **λ**⟨118⟩ σ7-115-517-659-827-1082-1391 A Π *al* *l*184 *La* | ● πεποιηκατε: BLΨ-892 Λ 1342 Or **18** γρ.—αρχ.] ● αρχ. κ. οι γρ.‖10₃₃ 14₁ Mt24 20₁₈ Lk19₄₇ 22₂.₆: 𝔥C WΘ-28-544-565-700-1071 **λ**⟨118⟩ ϕ124 σ115-827-1194-1223 A D K Π 1342^{m}(^{1}*om* οι αρχ. και) *al* Or *L* *S'* *C* — γρ. και οι Φαρισαιοι (+ και οι αρχ.): σM^{m}-517-(7-659-1082-1391 *pc*) *pc* *l*48 (*l*18 *l*19 *l*34 *l*49 *l*184 *l*251 *l*260) — *txt*: *Rpl* *S*hj^{v} | οχλ.] λαος‖Lk: Θ-700 Or *Lk*[e] f *Ss*[c]p | ● εξεπλησσοντο‖12₂p Mt22₂₃: ℵΔ-579-892 λ1278 σM-267-945-1424 *al* *Lc*30 *Ss*[c]p **19** ● εξεπορευοντο‖11₂₀: BΔΨ (∼ εξω τ. π. εξεπ.: W-28)-565-700-1071 λ872 ϕ124 σM-115-945-1606 A K Π *al* *L*cdr^{1}z *S*ph^{m} *C*b^{1} *Geo*^{1} — *txt*: *Rpl* (εξω τ. π. εξεπ.: **λ**) (*om*: L) *L'* *S'*j *C'* *Geo*^{2} **20** παρεπορευετο‖11₁₉: ℵ* *L*ff^{2}iqr^{1} vg^{3} | ειδ.] ιδοντες‖p: Δ — και ιδων‖p11₁₉: ℵ*

Lk 19,46 και—προσ.] οτι(*om*) ο οι. μ. οι. πρ. κληθησεται‖p: C^{c}-(1241 28)-1071 (σ1675) 251 (*pc* Ep *L*e r^{1})^{2}30 vg^{1} *S*p^{1} *C*b^{2} *Aeth* — οτι ο οι. μ. οι. πρ. εστιν‖p: C*-33 N σM-1223 A D K W Π Ψ *al* *L*fs(*om* οι. μου)z vg' *S'* — ο οι. μ. οι. πρ. εστιν‖p: *Rpl* (*om* εστ.: ℵ*-579; *prm* και: 262) *L*aff^{2}iq — *txt* (*om* και): 𝔥' **λλ**⟨22-1278⟩ **ϕ** R Θ(+ εστ.) 157 (213) Or *L*c(l *Sj* *C'*) | οικ.^{1} + του πατρος‖Jo: 2145 | αυ. εποι.] αυ. ποιειτε‖Mt: L Ep(∼) *Cs*$^{5:9}$ *Aeth* — εποι. αυ.‖Mk: 565 D *pc* *l*184 Or *L*⟨a⟩ **47** *om* το‖22₅₃p: L-579 N ϕ69-124-983 σ71 *pc* | ∼ γρ. ... αρχ.‖Mk: σ267 | απολ.] αποκτειναι *cf.* Jo5₁₈ 7₁ *etc.*: 892 **σ**⟨517⟩ *Cs* | πρω.] πρεσβυτεροι‖Mt21₂₃ 26₃.₄₇ 27₁: 1071 157 1012(*om* τ. λα.) (∼ και οι πρε. τ. λα. εζητ.—απολ.: **Or** *L*fr^{1} *S*ph^{t}) **48** ο—απας] απ. γ. ο λα.‖Mk: 477 *pc* *L*⟨e ar^{1}⟩ *S*scp | ακουειν‖21₃₈: 1604 ϕ69-174-230 σM D *pc* *C*b^{5} | ∼ ακ. αυ.‖←: 1241 D *l*184 *L* *Sj*

Jo 2,16 ∼ πωλ. τας περ.‖MtMk: W^{s} *L*abff^{2}r^{1}32 vg {*C*,a^{s}} | *om* αρατε—εντ.‖**p**: 1216 1279

ἐξηράνθη ἡ συκῆ; [21] ἀποκριθεὶς δὲ ὁ Ἰησοῦς εἶπεν		ἐξήρανται. [22] καὶ ἀποκριθεὶς ὁ Ἰησοῦς λέγει	
17 20 (140.): ... αμην γὰρ	αὐτοῖς· αμην	αὐτοῖς·	*17 6 (194.):*
λέγω ὑμῖν, ἐὰν ἔχητε πίστιν	λέγω ὑμῖν, ἐὰν ἔχητε πίστιν	ἔχετε πίστιν	*... εἰ ἔχετε πίστιν*
ὡς κόκκον σινάπεως,	καὶ μὴ διακριθῆτε, οὐ	θεοῦ.	*ὡς κόκκον σινάπεως,*
	μόνον τὸ τῆς συκῆς ποιήσε-	[23] αμην γὰρ λέγω ὑμῖν ὅτι ὃς	
ἐρεῖτε τῷ ὄρει τούτῳ·	τε, ἀλλὰ κἂν τῷ ὄρει τούτῳ	ἂν εἴπῃ τῷ ὄρει τούτῳ·	*ἐλέγετε ἂν τῇ συκαμίνῳ·*
μετάβα ἔνθεν ἐκεῖ,	εἴπητε· ἄρθητι καὶ βλή-	ἄρθητι καὶ βλή-	*ἐκριζώθητι καὶ φυ-*
	θητι εἰς τὴν θάλασσαν,	θητι εἰς τὴν θάλασσαν,	*τεύθητι ἐν τῇ θαλάσσῃ·*
		καὶ μὴ διακριθῇ ἐν τῇ καρδίᾳ	
		αὐτοῦ ἀλλὰ πιστεύῃ ὅτι ὃ	
καὶ μεταβήσεται,	γενήσεται·	λαλεῖ γίνεται, ἔσται	*καὶ ὑπήκουσεν ἂν*
καὶ οὐδὲν ἀδυνατήσει ὑμῖν.		αὐτῷ.	*ὑμῖν.*
18 19 (148.): πάλιν αμην			**14 13 f.:** καὶ ὅ τι ἂν αἰτήσητε ἐν τῷ
λέγω ὑμῖν ὅτι ἐὰν δύο			ὀνόματί μου, τοῦτο ποιήσω, ἵνα δοξα-
συμφωνήσωσιν ἐξ ὑμῶν		[24] διὰ	σθῇ ὁ πατὴρ ἐν τῷ υἱῷ. [14] ἐάν τι αἰτή-
ἐπὶ τῆς γῆς περὶ παντὸς	[22] καὶ πάντα	τοῦτο λέγω ὑμῖν, πάντα	σητέ με ἐν τῷ ὀνόματί μου, ἐγὼ ποιήσω.
πράγματος οὗ ἐὰν	ὅσα ἂν	ὅσα προσεύ-	**15 7:** ... ὃ ἐὰν θέλητε αἰτήσασθε, καὶ
αἰτήσωνται,	αἰτήσητε ἐν τῇ	χεσθε καὶ αἰτεῖσθε,	γενήσεται ὑμῖν. **16 23:** ... αμην αμην
	προσευχῇ πιστεύοντες	πιστεύετε ὅτι	λέγω ὑμῖν, ἄν τι αἰτήσητε τὸν πατέρα
γενήσεται	λήμψεσθε.	ἐλάβετε, καὶ ἔσται	δώσει ὑμῖν ἐν τῷ ὀνόματί μου.

Mt 21,21 πιστ. + ως κοκκον σιναπεως ‖17 Lk: Φ 474 | ειπ.] ερειτε ‖17: 245 | γεν.] και γ. ‖17 Lk Mk24: 566 2145 *l*48 *Lh Ssp*[3]h *C*b[2]

Mk 11,21 εξηρανθη ‖ p: LΔΨ-33-579 ΝΘΣ-565-700 **λ**-22[c] σ179-349-517-1223 D 1342 *pc* Or **22** λεγ.] ειπεν ‖ p: Θ-565-700 σ517 *pc Lk*[e] | εχ.] ει εχ. ‖p: ℵ-33[c] Θ-28-565-700-1071 **ϕ** σ1194-1223 D 61 *L*abir[1] *S*s[c]j[a] Ef *Arm* | *om* θε. ‖p: 28 *Lk*[e] acr[1.2] *C*b[1] **23** ● *om* γαρ ‖Mt21: ℵBΨ-579 ΝΘ-28-544-565-700 **λ**-1278 **ϕ**124-788-983 σ827-1194 D 157 *pc L*' *S*s[c]p[2] *C*sb[2] *Arm* — *txt*: *Rpl Lq S*p'h[+]j *C*b' *Aeth* | *om* οτι[1] ‖Mt: ℵ W-33 565 σ115 D *pc Lk*[e] g[2] vg[8] *Arm Aeth* | ος αν ειπη] εαν ειπητε ‖ p: 33 *Lc* (εαν εχητε πιστιν ως κοκκον σιναπεως ερειτε ‖Mt17 Lk) *S*s[c] *Aeth* | ∼ εσται γενησεται ‖Mt21; 18 Jo15: Θ-565(γενηται)-700(οτι[2]—εστ.] το μελλον ο αν ειπη γενησ.: D) *L*' (= D *et* γεν.] εσται: d) — γενησ. γενησ.: *L*fl vg **24** οσα + αν(εαν) ‖Mt21;(18 Jo15;)14: *Rpl* (ΝΣ λ872 *al*) — *txt*: ℵBCLΔΨ-892 W-1071 D 61 157 1342 | αιτησητε(-σησθε) ‖p: (Θ)-565-700 *pc* | ελαβ.] λημψεσθε ‖Mt21: Θ-544-565-700 **λ** D Or *L*,Cp *C*s[3] *Arm*[pc] *Geo* — λαμβανετε: *Rpl* Or *S*,j *C*s[1+1?]{} *Arm*' — *txt*: ℵBCLΔΨ-892 W 1342 *C*s[1]b[1]{'}

Jo 14,13 αιτ. + τον πατερα ‖15 16; 16 23: 33 544 998 Non *L*32 — *prm* απ αυτου(εκεινου) ‖←: *L*b(c) r[1v] Am **14** με] τον πατερα ‖←: 249 *pc L*ff[2] *Aeth* — *om* ‖p13: *Rpl* Cr *L*vl'g[2]r[1]30 vg[5] Au Vic[R] *S*(*om* 14: sc)p[1] *C*,fa[s] — *txt* (μοι): 𝔓[66] ℌ⟨L-1241⟩-**060** 28-700 **ϕ**'⟨69⟩(124-346)-230-*l*547 σ1194 E H S U Γ Δ Θ Ω *mu l*64 *l*184[1] *l*219 *l*1231 *L*cf32 vg' Fu *S*p'h *Got* **15,7** ο] οσα ‖11 22 Mt21 Lk: ℵ | αιτησεσθε ‖ 16 26: *Rpl* Chr Cr *L*vg' *Sh Arm Δ*l[ADGV](F αιτεισθε) — -σασθαι *et om* και: *L*acf *S*' *Δ*a — -σησθε: 579 (∼ και αιτ.: *L*vg[6] *Δ*p) — *txt*: BLX λ1 **ϕ**⟨69(*om*)⟩-230 σM A D Γ Θ **0141** Chr *L*vl'(*om*: r[1]z) *S*j *C*sb[+B]a[s] *Aeth Δ*ad i[T] md n | γεν.] δοθησεται ‖Mt7 7 Lk11 9: **λ**⟨1⟩ 251 *S*j[b1] | *om* υμιν ‖Mt21 21: 𝔓[66] D* *Le Δ*i **16,23** αν τι] οσα αν(*om*) ‖ Mt21: *Rpl* (**047** 213) Chr Non *S*'j {*Δ*a p} — ο αν ‖ 15 7: 𝔓[22]([ο]τι? αν) ℵX-33-1241 N-544 λ2193 Θ Π *pc Sh C*[+B]a[s] *Arm* {*Geo*[1] *Δ*md n[L]} — αν: W A *pc* — *txt*: 𝔓[5] ℵBCL-**054**-33 544(εαν) D Y Ψ **0141** *al* Ath(εαν) Cr Or *L Geo*[2] | τ. πα. δωσ.] δωσω ‖14 13 f.: 713 | ∼ εν τ. ον. μ. δω. υμ. ‖15 16 14 13: 𝔓[22v] *Rpl* (*om* εν—μου: **λ**⟨1⟩ 1546) Chr Cr *L S*,j *C*b[+B] *Δ*'⟨me⟩(i[T1] = 1546) — *txt*: 𝔓[5v] ℵBC*LXΔ-**054** Y *pc* Cr Non Or *C*sa[s] *Δ*p(*et prm* εν τ. ον. μ.)

Mt21 21p *cf.* ETh[II] 48. 106 (*transl.*): *Λέγει Ἰησοῦς· ἐὰν δύο εἰρηνεύσωσιν ἐν ἀλλήλοις ἐν ταύτῃ τῇ οἰκίᾳ μιᾷ, ἐροῦσιν τῷ ὄρει· μετάβα, καὶ μεταβήσεται. ...* [106]*Λέγει Ἰησοῦς· ὅταν ποιήσητε τοὺς δύο ἕν, υἱοὶ τοῦ ἀνθρώπου γενήσεσθε. καὶ ἐὰν εἴπητε· τὸ ὄρος, μετάβα, μεταβήσεται.*

αὐτοῖς παρὰ τοῦ πατρός μου τοῦ ἐν οὐρανοῖς. [34.] [42.]

ὑμῖν. 25 καὶ ὅταν στήκετε προσευχόμενοι, ἀφίετε εἴ τι ἔχετε κατά τινος, ἵνα καὶ ὁ πατὴρ ὑμῶν ὁ ἐν τοῖς οὐρανοῖς ἀφῇ ὑμῖν τὰ παραπτώματα ὑμῶν.

(202)

216. Die Vollmachtsfrage. The Question about Authority.

Matth 21 23–27

23 Καὶ ἐλθόντος αὐτοῦ εἰς τὸ ἱερόν, προσῆλθον αὐτῷ διδάσκοντι οἱ ἀρχιερεῖς καὶ οἱ πρεσβύτεροι τοῦ λαοῦ λέγοντες· ἐν ποίᾳ ἐξουσίᾳ ταῦτα ποιεῖς; καὶ τίς σοι ἔδωκεν τὴν ἐξουσίαν ταύτην; 24 ἀπο-

Mark 11 27–33

27 Καὶ ἔρχονται πάλιν εἰς Ἱεροσόλυμα. καὶ ἐν τῷ ἱερῷ περιπατοῦντος αὐτοῦ ἔρχονται πρὸς αὐτὸν οἱ ἀρχιερεῖς καὶ οἱ γραμματεῖς καὶ οἱ πρεσβύτεροι, 28 καὶ ἔλεγον αὐτῷ· ἐν ποίᾳ ἐξουσίᾳ ταῦτα ποιεῖς; ἢ τίς σοι ἔδωκεν τὴν ἐξουσίαν ταύτην ἵνα ταῦτα ποι-

Luk 20 1–8

1 Καὶ ἐγένετο ἐν μιᾷ τῶν ἡμερῶν διδάσκοντος αὐτοῦ τὸν λαὸν ἐν τῷ ἱερῷ καὶ εὐαγγελιζομένου ἐπέστησαν οἱ ἱερεῖς καὶ οἱ γραμματεῖς σὺν τοῖς πρεσβυτέροις, 2 καὶ εἶπαν λέγοντες πρὸς αὐτόν· εἰπὸν ἡμῖν ἐν ποίᾳ ἐξουσίᾳ ταῦτα ποιεῖς; ἢ τίς ἐστιν ὁ δούς σοι τὴν ἐξουσίαν ταύτην; 3 ἀπο-

[Joh] 2 18: ἀπεκρίθησαν οὖν οἱ Ἰουδαῖοι καὶ εἶπαν αὐτῷ· τί σημεῖον δεικνύεις ἡμῖν, ὅτι ταῦτα ποιεῖς;

Mt 21,23 *om* διδ.‖Mk: σ7 *l*44 *L*e[k] abcff¹g²hlr¹·² vg² *S*sc | αρχ. + και οι γραμματεις‖p: 1574 | και³] η‖p: C Φ 440 *L*ff¹g² vg¹

Mk 11,25 εν τ. ου.] ουρανιος‖Mt6₁₄: σ1402 1342 *pc l*48 *l*184 | αφησει‖←: Θ-565-700-1604 ϕ346 D 157 *pc l*184 | *om* υμιν‖Mt6₁₅: Θ-700 157 *pc* *L*k[e] aff²i | 25 + ²⁶ει δε υμεις ουκ αφιετε ουδε ο πατηρ υμων ο εν τοις ουρανοις αφησει τα παραπτωματα υμων‖Mt6₁₅: *Rpl L*,Au PsAu Cp *S*p'h *C*b⁸ *Δ*a ⟦αφιετε + τοις ανθρωποις τα παραπτωματα αυτων‖Mt6₁₄ | υμων¹] υμιν‖25: *l*313 *l*1579 | ο εν τοις ου.] ο ουρανιος‖Mt6₁₄: 273 *pc* — *om*‖Mt6₁₅: 33-579 σ7-517-659-1391 *al l*10 *l*12¹ *l*18 *l*19 *l*32² *l*48 *l*49 *l*69 *l*70 *l*80 *l*184 *l*303 *l*333 *l*374 *Δ*a — ο εν ουρανοις: C λ⟨118⟩ ϕ69-124-543-828 σM-827 D K Π 1079 *l*1627¹ — ο εν ουρανω: ΝΣ | αφησει] αφη‖25: σ945 *pc* — + υμιν‖25: 33 ϕ⟨124-346-788⟩ σ945-1402 D *pc L*abcff²qz Au Cp *S*hp *C*b² | *om* τα παρ. υμ.‖Mt←: σ1402 | υμων² + λεγω δε υμιν αιτειτε και δοθησεται υμιν ζητειτε και ευρησετε(*om* ζητ. κ. ευ.) κρουετε και ανοιγησεται υμιν πας γαρ ο αιτων λαμβανει και ο ζητων ευρισκει και τω κρουοντι ανοιγησεται‖Mt7₇f.p: (579 ϕ230)-346 σM-827-1207 *al l*24 *l*31 *l*32² *l*33 *l*46⟧ — *txt* (²⁵⌒²⁶παρ.): ℵBLΔΨ-892 W-565-700 σ27ᶜ-179-1606 S 157 *al L*k[e] g²lr²30 vg¹ *S*s[c]p¹j *C*' *Arm*

27 ερχεται (+ ο Ιησους)‖Mt: X 544-565 D *pc* (*l*251 *l*260) *L*k[e](εξηλθεν) bcff²iqr²z *C*b¹ | *om* παλιν‖Mt: Φ-544 F 1574 | ερχ.² πρ. αυ.] προσηλθον αυτω‖Mt: Ψ | ∼ πρεσ. … γρ.‖14₄₃.₅₃ 15₁: σ⟨1424⟩ *L*ir² vg² *C*s³:⁷ | *om* οι γρ. και‖Mt: 713 1038 *C*b¹ | πρεσ. + του λαου‖Mt: 892 D

28 η] και‖Mt: *Rpl* (*om* η—ποι.: D *L*k[e])' *S*'j *C*b¹ — *txt*: 𝔋⟨33-579⟩[C] Θ-1071 σ7-517-659-1082-1391-1402 1342 *pc l*12 *l*36 *l*184 *S*hᵐ *C*'⟨b²⟩ | *om* ινα—ποι.‖p: WΘ-28-565 *pc L*abff²ir¹ᵛz *S*s[c] *Arm*

Lk 20,1 *om* τ. λα.‖Mt: Mcn^Ep *C*b⟨8⟩ | επεστ. + αυτω‖p: σ1604(αυτων) *pc S C*s | ∼ γρ. … αρχ.‖Mk11₁₈: ϕ | ● αρχιερεις‖Mt Mk: 𝔋C N-1071-1604 λ ϕ σM-7-27-267-1194-1324 D Q R Θ Ψ 157 *pc L S*,j *C*

2 κ. ειπ. λεγ.] κ. ελεγον‖Mk: 1241(*et* πρ. αυ.] αυτω) — λεγοντες‖Mt: λ-1582-2193 *L*a(*om* πρ. αυ.)30 vg² {} *S*j^fv — κ. ειπ.‖Mk: *C* 1071 D *pc L*e fq {*S*scpj^abc} *C*s(*om* και)b⟨1⟩ | *om* ειπ. ημ.‖Mt Mk: ℵ*C 4 *S*s | η] και‖Mt: 579 D *L*e a30 vg² *S*p | εστ.—σοι] σοι εδωκεν‖p: 1241 1075 σ1424 Ψ 1555 *L*e *S*sc *Geo*

Mk11₂₇f.p *cf.* Ev. apocr. (POxy 840 lin. 7-21): Καὶ παραλαβὼν αὐτοὺς εἰσήγαγεν εἰς αὐτὸ τὸ ἁγνευτήριον καὶ περιεπάτει ἐν τῷ ἱερῷ. καὶ προσε[λ](10)θὼν Φαρισαῖός τις ἀρχιερεὺς Λευ[εἰς] τὸ ὄνομα συνέτυχεν αὐτοῖς καὶ ε[ἶπεν] τῷ σωτῆρι· ʻτίς ἐπέτρεψέν σοι πατ[εῖν] τοῦτο τὸ ἁγνευτήριον καὶ ἰδεῖν [ταῦ]τα τὰ ἅγια σκεύη μήτε λουσα[μ]έν[ῳ] μ[ή](15)τε μὴν τῶν μαθητῶν σου τοὺς π[όδας βα]πτισθέντων; ἀλλὰ μεμολυ[μμένος] ἐπάτησας τοῦτο τὸ ἱερόν, τ[όπον ὄν]τα καθαρόν, ὃν οὐδεὶς ἄ[λλος εἰ μὴ] λουσάμενος καὶ ἀλλά[ξας τὰ ἐνδύ](20)ματα πατεῖ, οὐδὲ ὁ[ρᾶν τολμᾷ ταῦτα] τὰ ἅγια σκεύη. καὶ σ[ταθεὶς … (*cf. ad 224.* Mt23₂₅f.)

κριθεὶς δὲ ὁ Ἰησοῦς εἶπεν αὐτοῖς· ἐρωτήσω ὑμᾶς κἀγὼ λόγον ἕνα, ὃν ἐὰν εἴπητέ μοι, κἀγὼ ὑμῖν ἐρῶ ἐν ποίᾳ ἐξουσίᾳ ταῦτα ποιῶ. [25] τὸ βάπτισμα τὸ Ἰωάννου πόθεν ἦν; ἐξ οὐρανοῦ ἢ ἐξ ἀνθρώπων; οἱ δὲ διελογίζοντο παρ' ἑαυτοῖς λέγοντες· ἐὰν εἴπωμεν· ἐξ οὐρανοῦ, ἐρεῖ ἡμῖν· διὰ τί οὖν οὐκ ἐπιστεύσατε αὐτῷ; [26] ἐὰν δὲ εἴπωμεν· ἐξ ἀνθρώπων, φοβούμεθα τὸν ὄχλον· πάντες γὰρ ὡς προφήτην ἔχουσιν τὸν

ῆς; [29] ὁ δὲ Ἰησοῦς εἶπεν αὐτοῖς· ἐπερωτήσω ὑμᾶς καγὼ ἕνα λόγον, καὶ ἀποκρίθητέ μοι, καὶ ἐρῶ ὑμῖν ἐν ποίᾳ ἐξουσίᾳ ταῦτα ποιῶ. [30] τὸ βάπτισμα τὸ Ἰωάννου ἐξ οὐρανοῦ ἦν ἢ ἐξ ἀνθρώπων; ἀποκρίθητέ μοι. [31] καὶ ἐλογίζοντο πρὸς ἑαυτοὺς λέγοντες· ἐὰν εἴπωμεν· ἐξ οὐρανοῦ, ἐρεῖ· διὰ τί οὖν οὐκ ἐπιστεύσατε αὐτῷ; [32] ἀλλὰ εἴπωμεν· ἐξ ἀνθρώπων; — ἐφοβοῦντο τὸν λαόν· ἅπαντες γὰρ εἶχον τὸν

κριθεὶς δὲ εἶπεν πρὸς αὐτούς· ἐρωτήσω ὑμᾶς κἀγὼ λόγον, καὶ εἴπατέ μοι· [4] τὸ βάπτισμα Ἰωάννου ἐξ οὐρανοῦ ἦν ἢ ἐξ ἀνθρώπων; [5] οἱ δὲ συνελογίσαντο πρὸς ἑαυτοὺς λέγοντες ὅτι ἐὰν εἴπωμεν· ἐξ οὐρανοῦ, ἐρεῖ· διὰ τί οὐκ ἐπιστεύσατε αὐτῷ; [6] ἐὰν δὲ εἴπωμεν· ἐξ ἀνθρώπων, ὁ λαὸς ἅπας καταλιθάσει ἡμᾶς· πεπεισμένος γάρ ἐστιν

Mt 21,24 επερωτησω‖Mk: D *pc* | ∼ ενα λογ.‖Mk: C ΟΣΦ-28-1604 **λ**⟨1⟩ σ1391-1424 D F 157 Or *L*⟨q⟩ | ∼ ερω υμ.‖Mk: 33 **σ**-349-659 *pc* *L*vg^{1} *S*scpj **25** *om* το^{2}‖Lk: *Rpl* — *txt*: ℵB CZ-33 λ22-1582 157 *pc* *l*48 Or | *om* ποθ. ην‖p: 998 1012 | ουρ. + ην‖p: 157 *pc* *L*vg^{1} *S*p *Geo*$^{\langle B\rangle}$ | διελογ.] ελογ.‖Mk: 472 1093 | παρ εαυ.] ● εν εαυ.‖16 7.8 Mk 2 8 Lk 12 17: BL(αυτ-)Z-33-892 σM^{m}-1402 157 *pc* *l*184^{1} *l*185 — προς εαυτους‖p: 443 2145 | λεγ. + οτι‖Lk: **σ**-349 *S*scp | *om* ημ.‖p: σ692 *l*183 | *om* ουν‖Lk: L 28-544-700 ϕ828 σ945-990-1675 D Ω *pc* Or *L*e[k] abff^{2}qr^{1}37.38 vg^{1} Hi *S*(και δια τι: scpj^{k})^{abc} *C*s$^{1:8}$b *Geo*$^{\langle A\rangle}$ **26** οχ.] λαον‖p: λ1582^{m} *L*r^{1} | εχ.] ειχον‖21 46 Mk: λ1-22-1582 372 *L*acfff^{1}g^{2}hlqr^{2}z30.37.38 vg^{12} Hi *S*scph^{Brs}j^{1} *Arm*^{mu}

Mk 11,29 l. + αποκριθεις‖p: *Rpl* *L*' *S*'j *C*s^{2} — *txt*: 𝔓^{45v} ℌC *L*k[e] vg^{1} *S*p *C*s^{5}b | επερ.] ερωτ.‖p: 579 ϕ230 61 1342 | ∼ καγω υμας: 565 **σ**'-1606 A K Y Π *pc* *S*s[c] *Arm* *Geo*^{1}(∼ κα. επερ.) *Aeth* — ● *om* καγω: BCLΔΨ σ1675 *pc* *L*k[e] *C*s^{1}b' — *txt*: *Rpl* *L*' *S*'j *C*s^{7}b^{1} *Geo*^{2} | ∼ λογ. ενα‖Mt: Θ-28 **λ**⟨118⟩ ϕ124 σ827-1082-1391 *pc* *L*q *S* — *om* ενα‖Lk: 1542 *C*s$^{6:7}$b^{3} | αποκ. μ. και] εαν αποκ. μ.‖Mt: 472 1515 | και ερω υμ.] καγω υμ. ερω (∼ ερω υμ.)‖Mt: (ℵ^{c})LΔΨ-33-892 1071 σ517-659-1606 (D, *et* ερω] λεγω) *L*c(ff^{2}) *C*⟨b^{1}⟩ **30** *om* το^{2}‖Lk: *Rpl* — *txt*: ℵBCL Δ-33-(του: 579) Θ A D | εξ ου. ην] ποθεν ην(εστιν); εξ ου.‖Mt: ℵC-33-579 Φ-1071 (**σ**-349-1606)-827 1342 *pc* (*pc*) *L*k[e] r^{2} *S*p *C*s | *om* ην‖Mt: L 1515 | *om* αποκ. μ.‖p: 544 λ1278 *pm* **31** ● διελογ.‖Mt: ℌ'⟨579⟩ℵ^{c}C WΘ-28-544-565-1071 **λ** **ϕ** σM-27-517-954 D G K Π — προσελ.: ℵ* | προς εαυ.] εν εαυτοις‖2 8 Mt 16 7f. Lk 12 17: 33-579 σ1082-1391-1402 *L*k[e] f *S*p | λεγ. + τι(+ αυτω) ειπωμεν‖Lk←16 3: ΘΦ-28-565-700 **ϕ** D *L*(k[e]) a(bcff^{2}ir^{1}) *S*j — + οτι‖Lk: W *S*s[c]p$^{\langle 1\rangle}$ | ερει + ημιν(υμ-)‖Mt: WΘ-565-700(*)^{2} **λ** **ϕ**'(346) σM D *pc* *L*⟨k[e] lr^{2} vg^{10}⟩ *S*s[c]pj *C*sb^{7} | δ. τι ουν] και δ. τι: 1241 *S*p *Geo*^{2} — ● *om* ουν‖Lk: C*LXΔΨ-892 W-28-544-565-1071 λ872-2193 ϕ346 σM-179-517-1402-1675 A S *al* *L*vl[e]⟨flz⟩r^{1v} vg^{2} *S*s[c] *C*s$^{1:7}$b *Arm* *Geo*^{1} *Aeth* **32** αλλα] εαν (+ δε)‖(p): (565)-700-1604 **λ**⟨1⟩ σ71-179-267-945-1223 D (998) *pc* *L*(bcfff^{2})g^{2}qr^{2}z(quod si: a; και εαν: ir^{1} *S*s[cjp) (*C*b^{1}) — αλλ/αλλα εαν‖p: WΘ-28 **ϕ** σ1207 *pc* *L*l *S*h *Arm* *Aeth* | εφο.] φοβουμεθα‖Mt: Ψ^{v} NWΘΣ-28-565-700 **ϕ** D(-μεν) *al* *L*vl⟨k[e] l⟩ vg^{7} *S*h *C*s$^{5:8}$b *Arm* *Aeth* | λα.] ● οχλον‖Mt: ℵBC-33-579 ΝΣΦ σ517 106 1342 *S*h^{m} *C*s^{1}(^{1} + και τον λα.)b' — *txt*: *Rpl* *L* *S*' *C*s^{6}b^{1} | απ.] παντες‖Mt: ℵ*C-33 NWΘΣ-28-565-700 **λ** ϕ788 σ1402 D 1342 *pc* | ειχ.] εχουσιν‖Mt: Σ *C*s$^{4:7}$ — ηδεισαν: WΘ-565 D *L*vl[e]⟨lr^{2}⟩g^{2}30 *Arm* *Geo*^{2} — οιδασι‖Mt: 700

Lk 20,3 δε + ο Ιησους‖Mt: C N σ115 130 *L*ff^{2}ilq vg^{3} *S*p(*om* δε) | πρ. αυ.] αυτοις‖Mt Mk: 472 | επερω.‖Mk: 1604 D Y *pc* *l*48 | λογ.] ενα λ.‖Mk: *Rpl* *L*' *S*j^{abc} — λ. ενα‖Mt: 28 σM-71-115-692-1207-1223 A K S U Π Ω *al* *L*vg^{1} *S*h^{+} *Arm* — *om*: *L*e aff^{2}i *S*c — *txt*: ℵBL-33 **λ**-1582-2193 ϕ69-788 σ1424 R W 157 *pc* *L*cq vg^{7} *S*spj^{f} *C* | και] ον‖Mt: D 565 *Aeth* **4** ● βαπτ. + το‖p: ℵL N D R | εξ ου. ην] ποθεν ην; εξ ου.‖Mt: 1241 N *L*30 vg^{1} *S*j$^{abc\langle f\rangle}$ *C*s$^{6:9}$ *Aeth* **5** διελογ.‖Mt: 1241 N **λ**-1582-2193 *pc* *l*184 | -λογιζοντο‖Mt Mk: ℵC-1241 N(-σοντο) D W Θ 157 *pc* | εαυ.] αλληλους‖20 14 Mk 8 16: N *L*⟨e ar^{2} vg^{3}⟩ *C* | *om* οτι‖p: C-1241 N *pc* *L*e ff^{2}ilqr^{1} *S*cj$^{abc\langle f\rangle}$ *Arm* | ερει + ημιν‖Mt: C*-1241 N 716 *L*acg^{2}lqr$^{1.2}$z30 vg^{6} *S*scpj *C*s$^{8:9}$b$^{\langle 6\rangle}$ | τι + ουν‖p: C-33 N-1604 **λ**-1582-2193 ϕ346 σM-692-1207-1223 A D K Q Π 157 *pc* *L*e afqz vg$^{\langle 4\rangle}$ *S*hj^{f} *C*s$^{7:9}$ *Arm* **6** ανθρ. + φοβουμεθα μη‖p: 1573 *L*l(φοβ. τον λαον και απας ο οχλος κατ. ημ.) | ο λα. απ.] πας ο λα. *cf.* 7 29 *etc.*: *Rpl* λα.] οχλος‖p: σ1424; απας: R) *L*a(l) *S*s(∼ κατ. ημ.· πας γαρ ο λα. πεπ.)chj^{b} *Arm* — *txt*: ℌ **λ**-1582-2193 ϕ174 D(∼) 213 *L*'(*om* απ.: e) *S*pj^{acf} | πεπεισμενοι ... εισιν‖p: D' 472 *L*vl'⟨ff^{2}⟩r^{1} vg$^{\langle 1\rangle}$ *S*scp

Matth	Mark	Luk
Ἰωάννην.	Ἰωάννην ὄντως ὅτι προφήτης ἦν.	Ἰωάννην προφήτην εἶναι.
27 καὶ ἀποκριθέντες τῷ	33 καὶ ἀποκριθέντες λέγουσιν τῷ	7 καὶ ἀπεκρίθησαν
Ἰησοῦ εἶπον· οὐκ οἴδαμεν.	Ἰησοῦ· οὐκ οἴδαμεν. καὶ	μὴ εἰδέναι πόθεν. 8 καὶ
ἔφη αὐτοῖς καὶ	ἀποκριθεὶς ὁ Ἰησοῦς λέγει αὐτοῖς·	ὁ Ἰησοῦς εἶπεν αὐτοῖς·
αὐτός· οὐδὲ ἐγὼ λέγω ὑμῖν ἐν ποίᾳ	οὐδὲ ἐγὼ λέγω ὑμῖν ἐν ποίᾳ	οὐδὲ ἐγὼ λέγω ὑμῖν ἐν ποίᾳ
ἐξουσίᾳ ταῦτα ποιῶ.	ἐξουσίᾳ ταῦτα ποιῶ.	ἐξουσίᾳ ταῦτα ποιῶ.

(203) **217.** Das Gleichnis von den ungleichen Söhnen. **Matth 21 28–32**

The Parable of the Two Sons.

28 Τί δὲ ὑμῖν δοκεῖ; ἄνθρωπος εἶχεν τέκνα δύο· προσελθὼν τῷ πρώτῳ εἶπεν· τέκνον, ὕπαγε σήμερον ἐργάζου ἐν τῷ ἀμπελῶνι. 29 ὁ δὲ ἀποκριθεὶς εἶπεν· οὐ θέλω, ὕστερον δὲ μεταμεληθεὶς ἀπῆλθεν. 30 προσελθὼν δὲ τῷ δευτέρῳ εἶπεν ὡσαύτως. ὁ δὲ ἀποκριθεὶς εἶπεν· ἐγὼ κύριε, καὶ οὐκ ἀπῆλθεν. 31 τίς ἐκ τῶν δύο ἐποίησεν τὸ θέλημα τοῦ πατρός; λέγουσιν· ὁ πρῶτος. λέγει αὐτοῖς ὁ Ἰησοῦς· αμην λέγω ὑμῖν ὅτι οἱ τελῶναι καὶ αἱ πόρναι προάγουσιν ὑμᾶς εἰς τὴν βασιλείαν τοῦ θεοῦ. 32 ἦλθεν γὰρ Ἰωάννης πρὸς ὑμᾶς ἐν ὁδῷ δικαιοσύνης, καὶ οὐκ ἐπιστεύσατε αὐτῷ· οἱ δὲ τελῶναι καὶ αἱ πόρναι ἐπίστευσαν αὐτῷ· ὑμεῖς δὲ ἰδόντες οὐδὲ μετεμελήθητε ὕστερον τοῦ πιστεῦσαι αὐτῷ.

95.

Mt 21,27 ∼ ειπ. τω Ι.‖Mk: 440 1574(τω Ι.] αυτω) | κ. αυτος] ο Ιησους‖p: ℵ 485 (ο Ι. κ. αυ.: 1093) *Le*[k] (*prm* και: acff²)¹hr² *S*cp⟨1⟩ (κ. αυ. ο κυριος Ι.: j^abc; ο κυ. Ι.: j^k) — *om*‖p: 700 *Ll* **28** ανθ. + τις‖Lk15 11: C-33 ΟΣΦ-544-1604 λ1-22-1582 **φ**-*l*547 σM-349-517-945-1010-1293-1424 E U Δ Θ **047** 157 *al l*184 Eu Or *L*⟨g²z vg¹¹⟩ *S*,j^abc(^k∼) *Δ*ad i^T l^AD | ∼ δυο τε.‖←: B 544 σ692-1402-1424-1606 *pc* {*L*} *S*Ef | προσελ.] ● και πρ.: *Rpl* Cr Eu *L*'*S*' *Δ*⟨me p⟩ — *om*: *S*sc *Aeth* — *txt*: ℵ*LZ Or *Le*[k] ff¹ *C* | εις τον αμπελωνα‖20 1.4.7: D(το) Chr *L*vl[k]⟨lr²⟩30 vg¹² **29.30** ● ∼ ³⁰εγω κυ. και ουκ … ²⁹ου θε.— μεταμ.: B 700 **φ**-*l*547 Θ *pc* PsAth Isd *Lr*² vg¹ *S*j^abc Ef *C*s³b *Arm Aeth*^ms *Δ*me E^a — *txt*: *Rpl* Chr Cr Eu Ir Or *L*'Hil *S*,j^k *C*s^5+1? *Aeth*^edd *Δ*' **29** υστ. δε] ● υστ.: ℵ*B σ1010 H *pc* PsAth Isd *Le*[k] bhg² *S*Ef *C*s^6:7 *Aeth*^ms *Δ*ad l^A md p — και υστ.: *L*aff¹r² vg¹ *S*s *Δ*a | απηλ. + εις τον αμπελωνα‖20 2: D *Le*[k] abc ff^1.2hr^1v2 vg¹ *S*scj^abc *Δ*n^L **30** εγω κυ.] υπαγω κυ. (∼): 700 *pc L Geo Δ*ad l (md n^HgS)(^Hr*om* κυ.) — εγω κυ. υπα.: D 372 *S*j^abc *Δ*E^a **31** τις + ουν‖Lk7 42: ΟΣ σ1424 **0138** *l*80 *l*184¹ *l*1127 Chr^1:2 *L*ff¹hr^1.2 vg² *C*s^1:9b⁴ | πρω.] ● εσχατος: 700 **φ**-*l*547 D Θ *pc* PsAth *L*vl'[k]⟨cfq⟩r¹37.38 vg¹⁴ Hi {*S*j^abc} *C*s^4:10b *Arm Geo*⟨A⟩ *Δ*l^FG — υστερος: B 565 {} *Aeth*^ms *Δ*ad — δευτερος: 4 273 *Δ*E^a **32** Ι. πρ. υμ.] Ι.‖11 18 Lk7 33: σ1424 *S*p¹ *Arm*' *Δ*i^V — πρ. υμ. Ι.: *Rpl L*' *S*' *Arm*^pc *Δ*a ad l E^a — *txt*: ℌC λ118-209 σ349-517-1010-1194-1293-1675 157 *pc* Chr Or *L*cr^1.2 vg⁴ *S*j

Mk 11,32 οντως] *om*‖MtLk: ℵ*-579 ΝΘΣ-28-544-565-700 **λ**-22 φ124-788 σ7-517-659-1391 *al l*184 *Lk*[e] cr¹ *S*s[c] *Arm Geo*² — αληθως‖Jo6 14 7 40: D | οτι πρ. ην] ως προφητην‖Mt: Δ ΝΣ-544 *pc* — πρ. ειναι‖Lk: *L*bcff²ir¹ **33** ● ∼ τω Ι. λεγ.‖Mt: 𝔓^45v ℌC NWΘΣ-28-1071 **φ** σ954 *L*a(απεκριθησαν τω Ι. λεγοντες: ff² vg¹) | λεγου.] ειπον‖Mt: σ827-954 *L*⟨q vg⁹⟩ | *om* και²‖Mt: D 273 *L*clr²z vg⟨5⟩ *S*s[c]p *C*sb³ *Geo*^B | αποκ. ο Ι.] ο (+ δε) Ι. αποκ.‖Lk: {} *Rpl* (*om* ο Ι.: φ230) (*C*s³) *Arm Geo*^A(^B) — ● ο (+ δε) Ι.‖p: ℌC ΝΣ σ71-659-954-1293-1391 Γ 1342 *pc Lk*[e] af(λεγει αυτοις και ο Ι.: c) (*C*s⁵b³)' — *om*‖Mt: σ659 *pc S*p — *txt*: {𝔓^45v} Φ-1071 **λ**⟨118⟩ **φ**⟨124⟩ σM-115-827 A D K Y Π *al L*'(∼ λεγ. αυ. ο Ι.: b; απεκριθη: ff²) *S*' *Geo*¹ | λεγει] ειπεν‖Lk: σ115-517-659 *Lk*[e] af

Lk 20,7 και απεκ.] κ. αποκριθεντες ειπον‖p: 213 *Ll C*b⁴ — απεκ. δε λεγοντες‖Mk: *L*c(κ. απεκ. λεγ.) *C*s^7:8 | *om* ποθ.‖p: Λ φ174 σ1194 E K *pc L*cf **8** ο Ι.] αποκριθεις‖Mk: ℵ* 213 — *om*‖Mt: φ983-1689 *C*s^1:8

(204) *218.* Das Gleichnis von den bösen Winzern. *The Parable of the Wicked Husbandmen.*

Matth 21 33–46	**Mark 12** 1–12	**Luk 20** 9–19
	1 Καὶ ἤρξατο αὐτοῖς	9 Ἤρξατο δὲ πρὸς τὸν λαὸν λέ-
33 Ἄλλην παραβολὴν ἀκούσατε.	ἐν παραβολαῖς λαλεῖν. **ἀμ-**	γειν τὴν παραβολὴν ταύτην.
ἄνθρωπος ἦν οἰκοδεσπότης	**πελῶνα** ἄνθρωπος	ἄνθρωπος
Is52 ὅστις **ἐφύτευσεν ἀμπελῶνα, καὶ**	**ἐφύτευσεν, καὶ**	**ἐφύτευσεν ἀμπελῶνα,**
φραγμὸν αὐτῷ περιέθηκεν	**περιέθηκεν φραγ-**	
καὶ ὤρυξεν ἐν αὐτῷ ληνὸν	**μὸν καὶ ὤρυξεν ὑπολήνιον**	
καὶ ᾠκοδόμησεν πύργον, καὶ ἐξέδο-	**καὶ ᾠκοδόμησεν πύργον,** καὶ ἐξέδο-	καὶ ἐξέδο-
το αὐτὸν γεωργοῖς, καὶ ἀπεδήμησεν.	το αὐτὸν γεωργοῖς, καὶ ἀπεδήμησεν.	το αὐτὸν γεωργοῖς, καὶ ἀπεδήμησεν
34 ὅτε δὲ ἤγγισεν ὁ καιρὸς τῶν	2 καὶ	χρόνους ἱκανούς. 10 καὶ καιρῷ
καρπῶν, ἀπέστειλεν	ἀπέστειλεν πρὸς τοὺς γεωρ-	ἀπέστειλεν πρὸς τοὺς γεωρ-
τοὺς δούλους αὐτοῦ πρὸς	γοὺς τῷ καιρῷ δοῦλον, ἵνα παρὰ	γοὺς δοῦλον, ἵνα
τοὺς γεωργοὺς λαβεῖν τοὺς καρ-	τῶν γεωργῶν λάβῃ ἀπὸ τῶν καρ-	ἀπὸ τοῦ καρ-
ποὺς αὐτοῦ. 35 καὶ λαβόν-	πῶν τοῦ ἀμπελῶνος· 3 καὶ λαβόν-	ποῦ τοῦ ἀμπελῶνος δώσουσιν αὐτῷ·
τες οἱ γεωργοὶ τοὺς δούλους	τες	οἱ δὲ γεωργοὶ δείραντες
αὐτοῦ ὃν μὲν ἔδειραν, ὃν δὲ ἀπέκτει-	αὐτὸν ἔδειραν καὶ ἀπέστειλαν	αὐτὸν ἐξαπέστειλαν
ναν, ὃν δὲ ἐλιθοβόλησαν. 36 πάλιν	κενόν. 4 καὶ πάλιν	κενόν. 11 καὶ προσ-
ἀπέστειλεν	ἀπέστειλεν πρὸς αὐτοὺς	έθετο ἕτερον πέμψαι

Mt 21,33 *om* αυτω^1‖Mk: 566 *Ld* | *om* εν αυ.‖Mk: Chr *Le*[k](*om* ωρ.—αυτω^2) *C*b^1 **36** παλ.] και π.‖Mk: ℵ* *L*vg^1 *S*p$^{⟨1⟩}$j$^{a2.b1.c1.12.⟨k⟩}$

Mk 12,1 λαλ.] λεγειν‖Lk: *Rpl* (λεγων: Γ) *L*k[e] *S*h^t *C*s^5 — *txt*: 𝕳⟨33-579⟩ W-28 **λ ϕ** G 1342 *pc* *L*'[a] *S*'h^m *C*s^{4}b | ∼ αμπ. εφυ. αν.: *Rpl* *L*' *S*h *Geo*^{1} — αν. (+ τις) εφυ. αμπ.‖p: N(WΘ)Σ-(565 **ϕ**⟨124⟩) 433 (Or *L*cz)r^2 *S*s[c](p) *C* *Aeth* — *txt* (εφυ.] εποιησεν): 𝕳'(L-892)C Φ-1071 σ517 1342 *pc* *l*48 | περ. + αυτω‖Mt: C^{2}Ψ-892 NWΘΣ-28-565 σ827 *pc* Or *L*r^2 vg^1 *S*'h$^-$ *C* | ωκ. + εν(*om*) αυτω‖Mt: (1071) *S*s[c]p *C*b$^{⟨1⟩}$ **2** δου. + αυτου‖Mt: σ827 *S* | *om* παρα—λαβη *et* αμπ. + δωσουσιν αυτω‖Lk: D *L*vl'[e]⟨lr^2⟩r^1 *S*s[c](∼ δω. αυ. απο—αμπ.) *Aeth* | *om* παρα τ. γεω.‖Mt: Ψ 1342 *S*p | απο του καρπου‖Lk: *Rpl* (*om* τ. κα.: Γ) (D *L*vl'[a]r^1)lr^2 vg *C*s^{7}b — τους καρπους‖Mt: 579 Θ (*L*k[e]) *Geo* (-ον -ον) — *txt*: 𝕳'C N-1071 σ349-517 1342 *pc* *l*48 *l*49 (*L*df) *C*s$^{1+1?}$ **3** και^1] οι δε‖Lk: *Rpl* *S*' *C*s^4 — *txt*: 𝕳 σ7-349-517-659-1082-1391 D 1342 *l*9 *l*10 *l*12 *l*19 *l*48 *l*49 *l*184 *L*k[e] abff^{2}iqr$^{1.2}$30 *S*s[c] *C*s^{5}b *Aeth* | εδει. + και απεκτειναν‖Mt: W ϕ346 **4** *om* και^1‖Mt: 28 697 *L*cz *C*s *Geo*^{2} | *om* πρ. αυ.‖MtLk: 565 **λ**⟨118⟩ *l*48 *C*b^1 *Arm*$^{⟨pc⟩}$

Lk 20,9 ηρξ.—λεγ.] ελεγεν δε *cf.* 136536 *etc.*: D *Le*(+ και) | ∼ λεγ. πρ. τ. λα. *cf.* 421 Mt117p *etc.*: (ϕ983-1689) **σ**⟨1675⟩ Q *L*⟨e a⟩ *C* | τ. λα.] τ. οχλον‖Mt117p: L-892-1241 1071 213 — αυτους‖421 Mk: ϕ983-1689 *S*sc | ∼ αμπ. αν. εφυ.‖Mk: C — αμπ. εφυ. αν.‖Mk: D *L*vl⟨fr^{2}z⟩r^1 Am | ανθ. + τις *cf.* 1416 1511 *etc.*: 1241 544-1071-1604 **ϕ**-230 A W Θ 157 *pc* Thd^C *L*r^1 vg^2 *S*'h$^+$ **10** και + εν‖1242p Mt41 1330: *Rpl* {}^{1} — + εν τω‖←: C N Q Θ *pc* *l*49 {*Le* flr^{2}z30 vg}^{1} — + τω‖Mk: **λ**-1582-2193 {}^{2} — *txt*: 𝕳⟨892⟩ D(καιρω + δε) 38 {*L*vl'r^1}^{2} | απο—αυτω] λαβη απο—αμπ.‖p: σ1194 | απο των καρπων‖Mk: *Le* afl vg^1 *C*s$^{6:9}$ — απο τους καρπους(!)‖Mt: Λ *l*184 *C*s$^{1:9}$ (*om* απο) | ● ∼ εξαπ. αυ. δει.: ℵBL-579-(1241) — *txt*: *Rpl* (*om* οι γεω. *et* ∼ δει. δε: D) *L* *C* | εξαπ.] απεστ.‖Mk: 1241 1071 K Π *pc* **11** προσε. ετ. πεμ.] επεμψεν ετ.‖p: D *Le* | προσε. + αυτοις‖Mk: 892-1241 λ2193 Q 713 *l*19 | ∼ πεμ. ετ.‖p: *Rpl* (D *Le*) — *txt*: 𝕳⟨33⟩ A U Ψ *L*' | πεμ. + αυτοις‖Mk: C* σ267-659-1391-1402 213 *S*h *C*b

---

Mt2133-39p *cf.* ETh^{II} 65 (*transl.*): *Λέγει· ἄνθρωπος χρηστὸς ἀμπελῶνα εἶχεν. ἐξέδοτο αὐτὸν γεωργοῖς, ἵνα ἐργάσωνται ἐν αὐτῷ καὶ λάβῃ τὸν καρπὸν αὐτοῦ ἀπ' αὐτῶν. ἀπέστειλεν τὸν δοῦλον αὐτοῦ, ἵνα δῶσιν οἱ γεωργοὶ αὐτῷ τὸν καρπὸν τοῦ ἀμπελῶνος. κρατήσαντες τὸν δοῦλον αὐτοῦ ἔδειραν (καὶ) παρὰ μικρὸν ἀπέκτειναν αὐτόν. ὁ δοῦλος ἐλθὼν ἀπήγγειλεν τῷ κυρίῳ αὐτοῦ. εἶπεν ὁ κύριος αὐτοῦ· ἴσως οὐκ ἔγνω αὐτούς· (καὶ) ἀπέστειλεν ἕτερον δοῦλον. οἱ γεωργοὶ ἔδειραν καὶ τὸν ἕτερον. τότε ὁ κύριος ἀπέστειλεν τὸν υἱὸν αὐτοῦ λέγων· ἴσως ἐντραπήσονται τὸν υἱόν μου. ἐκεῖνοι (δὲ) οἱ γεωργοὶ εἰδότες, ὅτι αὐτὸς ἦν ὁ κληρονόμος τοῦ ἀμπελῶνος, συλλαβόντες ἀπέκτειναν αὐτόν. ὁ ἔχων ὦτα ἀκουέτω* (*cf. ad 103.* Mt139)

Matthew

ἄλλους δούλους πλείονας τῶν πρώτων, καὶ ἐποίησαν αὐτοῖς ὡσαύτως.

[37] ὕστερον δὲ ἀπέστειλεν πρὸς αὐτοὺς τὸν υἱὸν αὐτοῦ λέγων· ἐντραπήσονται τὸν υἱόν μου. [38] οἱ δὲ γεωργοὶ ἰδόντες τὸν υἱὸν εἶπον ἐν ἑαυτοῖς· οὗτός ἐστιν ὁ κληρονόμος· δεῦτε ἀποκτείνωμεν αὐτὸν καὶ σχῶμεν τὴν κληρονομίαν αὐτοῦ· [39] καὶ λαβόντες αὐτὸν ἐξέβαλον ἔξω τοῦ ἀμπελῶνος καὶ ἀπέκτειναν. [40] ὅταν οὖν ἔλθῃ ὁ κύριος τοῦ ἀμπελῶνος, τί

Mark

ἄλλον δοῦλον· κἀκεῖνον ἐκεφαλαίωσαν καὶ ἠτίμασαν. [5] καὶ ἄλλον ἀπέστειλεν· κἀκεῖνον ἀπέκτειναν, καὶ πολλοὺς ἄλλους, οὓς μὲν δέροντες, οὓς δὲ ἀποκτέννυντες.

[6] ἔτι ἕνα εἶχεν, υἱὸν ἀγαπητόν· ἀπέστειλεν αὐτὸν ἔσχατον πρὸς αὐτοὺς λέγων ὅτι ἐντραπήσονται τὸν υἱόν μου. [7] ἐκεῖνοι δὲ οἱ γεωργοὶ πρὸς ἑαυτοὺς εἶπαν ὅτι οὗτός ἐστιν ὁ κληρονόμος· δεῦτε ἀποκτείνωμεν αὐτόν, καὶ ἡμῶν ἔσται ἡ κληρονομία. [8] καὶ λαβόντες ἀπέκτειναν αὐτόν, καὶ ἐξέβαλαν αὐτὸν ἔξω τοῦ ἀμπελῶνος. [9] τί οὖν

Luke

δοῦλον· οἱ δὲ κἀκεῖνον δείραντες καὶ ἀτιμάσαντες ἐξαπέστειλαν κενόν. [12] καὶ προσέθετο τρίτον πέμψαι· οἱ δὲ καὶ τοῦτον τραυματίσαντες ἐξέβαλον. [13] εἶπεν δὲ ὁ κύριος τοῦ ἀμπελῶνος· τί ποιήσω; πέμψω τὸν υἱόν μου τὸν ἀγαπητόν· ἴσως τοῦτον ἐντραπήσονται. [14] ἰδόντες δὲ αὐτὸν οἱ γεωργοὶ διελογίζοντο πρὸς ἀλλήλους λέγοντες· οὗτός ἐστιν ὁ κληρονόμος· ἀποκτείνωμεν αὐτόν, ἵνα ἡμῶν γένηται ἡ κληρονομία. [15] καὶ ἐκβαλόντες αὐτὸν ἔξω τοῦ ἀμπελῶνος ἀπέκτειναν. τί οὖν

Mt 21,37 εντρ.] ισως ε.‖Lk: 16 *pc* ϕ*l*547^{1} Chr Eu *L*e[k] bcff^{2}h vg^{2} Ar Ir *S*scp *C*b^{1} — ε. ισως: *L*ff^{1} vg^{1} *S*scj$^{abc⟨k⟩1}$ Ef Eu | **38** εν εαυ.] προς εαυτους‖p: Σ | σχ. τ. κλη.] ημιν εσται η κληρονομια‖p: Φ Chr$^{1:2}$ *L*e[k] vg^{1} **39** ~ απεκτ. και εξεβ.—αμπ.‖Mk: D Θ(~ απ. αυτον) *L*e[k] abcff^{2}hr$^{1.2}$32 Iuv Luc *Geo*'(^{A} = Θ) | εξεβ. + αυτον‖p: **047** *pc* *L*e[k] cff^{2} vg^{1} Ir *S*ch^{-}j^{b}(*et om* αυτον^{1}: j^{ackl}) *C*

Mk 12,4 κακ.] οι δε κακ.‖Lk: 700 σ517-659-1606 *pc* | κακ. + λιθοβολησαντες‖Mt35: *Rpl* *S*(^{4}∩^{5}κακ.: s[c])ph — *txt*: 𝕳⟨892⟩ W-28-565-700 **λ** D 1342 *pc* *L* *C* *Arm* | ητιμ.] απεστειλαν ητιμωμενον‖Lk: *Rpl* {*S*ph *C*s^{5}} — απε. ητιμασμενον‖Lk: W-28-565-(εξαπε.)-700 **λ** 91 {} — *txt*: 𝕳 D 1342 *L*'(*om*: k[e]) *C*s^{1}(^{1}~ ητ. ... εκεφ.)b **5** απεστ. + οι δε‖Lk: 700 **6** ετι] υστερον δε (+ ετι)‖Mt: W Θ-565-(28-700 ϕ *pc*) *S*p *C*s^{6}(^{2})$^{:9}$ | αγ.] αγ. αυτου(εαυ-)‖p: *Rpl* (σ517-659-945 *l*48) {} — τον αγ. αυτου‖Lk: W **λ**⟨118⟩ ϕ⟨788⟩ {*L*cz} *S*h {*C*s^{1}} *Aeth* — *txt*: 𝕳⟨33-579⟩C Θ-565-700 σ1402 D 1342 *L*'(*om* ετι—αγ.: k[e]) *S*' *C*s^{7}b$^{⟨1⟩}$ | *om* εσχ.‖Lk: 544 ϕ788 σ1606 *L*b *S*s[c] | οτι] *om*‖Mt: LΔ-33-892 NWΣ λ1 ϕ788-826 σ1207-1606-1675 *pc* *L*k[e] cz *Geo*^{B} — ισως‖Lk: *L*abq(utique) *S*s[c]p — οτι ισως‖Lk: *L*ff^{2} vg^{1} | ~ τ. υι. μ. εντρ.‖Lk: 565-700 D *L*abff^{2}iqr^{1} **7** εκ. δε οι] οι δε‖p: D *L*'⟨cg^{2} q⟩ *C*s$^{1:9}$ *Arm* *Aeth* | γεω. + ιδοντες αυτον‖Lk Mt: ΝΣ-544 σ267 *pc* *L*c *S*p^{1} — + θεασαμενοι αυτον ερχομενον: Θ-28-565-700-1071 ϕ σ7-349-517-659-1082-1391-1606 *pc* (*om* ερχ.: *l*24 *l*31) *l*36 *l*48 *l*49 *l*184 *l*251 *l*260 *S*h^{+} *Arm* *Geo* | ~ ειπ. πρ. εαυ.‖p: *Rpl* *L* *S* *Geo*^{A}(^{B} *prm* πρ. αυτους) — *txt* (αυ-): 𝕳'(Δ)C W-(28)-1071 λ1-(209 ϕ) σ'(517-1675)-7-(349-659-1082-1391-1606 (1200 1342) *pc* *l*18 (*l*36 *l*48 *l*49) *l*184 (*l*251 *l*260 *Geo*^{1}) | *om* οτι‖Mt: ΝΘΣ-28-544-565-700 **λ**⟨118⟩ D *pc* *L* *S*p | ημ.—κληρ.] κατασχωμεν αυτου την κληρονομιαν‖Mt: 157 *pc* **8** 8] και εκβαλοντες αυτον^{2}—αμπ. απεκτ.‖Lk: 127 131 *C*b^{1} | ~ αυ. απεκτ.‖Mt: *Rpl* — *txt*: ℵBCLΔΨ-892 σ7-517-659-1082-1391-1675 1093 *l*18 *l*19 *l*31 *l*184 *l*251 *l*260 *L*k[e] ff^{2}iq | απεκτ.—αμπ.] αυ. εξεβ. εξω τ. αμπ. και(*om*) απεκτ.‖p: ϕ'(*om* τ. αμπ.: 983) σ1424-1606 (218) 1047 (*l*12) **9** ● *om* ουν‖Mt: BL-892 1342 *L*g^{2} *S*s[c] *C*s$^{4:6}$b$^{⟨1⟩}$

Lk 20,11 κακ.] και τουτον‖12: 1241 *L*⟨e a⟩ *S*cj(κ. αυτον) *C*s$^{1:9}$b^{1} | εξαπ.] απεστ.‖Mk3: σ1223 **12** προσε. τρ. πεμ.] τρ. επεμψεν‖Mk: D *L*e *S*s *Aeth* | *om* οι δε‖Mk: 1071 D *L*vl⟨fqz⟩30 *S*s *C*s$^{1:9}$ | κ. του.] κακεινον‖11 Mk: σ267-659-1207-1223 A K Π *al* *L*⟨q⟩ *S*sph^{m} **13** τ. αγαπ.] τ. μονογενη‖Jo3 16: 716 *L*e — *om*‖Mt: 4 *L*lr^{2} **14** διελογισαντο‖20 5: σ1223 A K Π *al* *L*⟨e⟩ *C*s — ειπον‖p: 1241(*om* λεγ.) N | πρ. αλλ.] πρ. εαυτους‖Mk: *Rpl* {} — εν εαυτοις‖Mt: Γ {*L*e ff^{2}q vg^{8}} *S*' *Arm*^{1} — *om*: *S*sc *Aeth* — *txt*: 𝕳 1071 **λ**-1582 ϕ124 D R 157 475 *L*'*S*h^{m} *C* *Arm*' | λεγ. + οτι‖20 5 Mk: 579 | κληρονομος + δευτε‖Mt Mk: *Rpl* Or *L*e vg^{2} *S*'h^{+} *C*s^{1}b — *txt*: B N **λλ**⟨22-1278⟩ σM-1194-1223 A K Q W Π Ψ *al* *L*' *C*s^{8} *Arm* | ινα—κλη.] και κατασχωμεν την κληρονομιαν αυτου‖Mt: 1093 | ινα] και‖p: C **λλ**⟨22-1872⟩ 4 18 *L*e cff^{2}ilqr^{1} vg^{6} *S*scp$^{⟨2⟩}$ | γεν.] εσται‖Mk: C **λλ**⟨22-1278⟩ 1555 *L*clqr^{1} **15** εκβ. αυ.] λαβοντες αυ. εξεβαλον(*om*) *et* αμπ.^{1} + και(*om*)‖p: C(L)

Matth	Mark	Luk	Jo
ποιήσει τοῖς γεωργοῖς ἐκείνοις; ⁴¹ λέγουσιν αὐτῷ· κακοὺς κακῶς ἀπολέσει αὐτούς, καὶ τὸν ἀμπελῶνα ἐκδώσεται ἄλλοις γεωργοῖς, οἵτινες ἀποδώσουσιν αὐτῷ τοὺς καρποὺς ἐν τοῖς καιροῖς αὐτῶν.	ποιήσει ὁ κύριος τοῦ ἀμπελῶνος; ἐλεύσεται καὶ ἀπολέσει τοὺς γεωργούς, καὶ δώσει τὸν ἀμπελῶνα ἄλλοις.	ποιήσει αὐτοῖς ὁ κύριος τοῦ ἀμπελῶνος; ¹⁶ ἐλεύσεται καὶ ἀπολέσει τοὺς γεωργοὺς τούτους, καὶ δώσει τὸν ἀμπελῶνα ἄλλοις. ἀκούσαντες δὲ εἶπαν· μὴ γένοιτο. ¹⁷ ὁ δὲ ἐμβλέψας αὐτοῖς εἶπεν·	
⁴² λέγει αὐτοῖς ὁ Ἰησοῦς· οὐδέποτε ἀνέγνωτε ἐν ταῖς γραφαῖς·	¹⁰ οὐδὲ τὴν γραφὴν ταύτην ἀνέγνωτε·	τί οὖν ἐστιν τὸ γεγραμμένον τοῦτο·	
(Ps118 22f.) **λίθον ὃν ἀπεδοκίμασαν οἱ οἰκοδομοῦντες, οὗτος ἐγενήθη εἰς κεφαλὴν γωνίας·**	**λίθον ὃν ἀπεδοκίμασαν οἱ οἰκοδομοῦντες, οὗτος ἐγενήθη εἰς κεφαλὴν γωνίας·**	**λίθον ὃν ἀπεδοκίμασαν οἱ οἰκοδομοῦντες, οὗτος ἐγενήθη εἰς κεφαλὴν γωνίας;**	
παρὰ κυρίου ἐγένετο αὕτη, καὶ ἔστιν θαυμαστὴ ἐν ὀφθαλμοῖς ἡμῶν;	¹¹ **παρὰ κυρίου ἐγένετο αὕτη, καὶ ἔστιν θαυμαστὴ ἐν ὀφθαλμοῖς ἡμῶν;**		
⁴³ διὰ τοῦτο λέγω ὑμῖν ὅτι ἀρθήσεται ἀφ' ὑμῶν ἡ βασιλεία τοῦ θεοῦ καὶ δοθήσεται ἔθνει ποιοῦντι τοὺς καρποὺς αὐτῆς. ⁴⁵ καὶ ἀκούσαντες οἱ ἀρχιερεῖς καὶ οἱ Φαρισαῖοι τὰς παραβολὰς αὐτοῦ ἔγνωσαν ὅτι περὶ αὐτῶν λέγει·	cf. v. 12b ↓	¹⁸ πᾶς ὁ πεσὼν ἐπ' ἐκεῖνον τὸν λίθον συνθλασθήσεται· ἐφ' ὃν δ' ἂν πέσῃ λικμήσει αὐτόν. cf. v. 19b ↓	
⁴⁶ καὶ ζητοῦντες αὐτὸν κρατῆσαι ἐφοβήθησαν τοὺς ὄχλους, ἐπεὶ εἰς προφήτην αὐτὸν εἶχον.	¹² καὶ ἐζήτουν αὐτὸν κρατῆσαι, καὶ ἐφοβήθησαν τὸν ὄχλον· ἔγνωσαν γὰρ ὅτι πρὸς αὐτοὺς	¹⁹ καὶ ἐζήτησαν οἱ γραμματεῖς καὶ οἱ ἀρχιερεῖς ἐπιβαλεῖν ἐπ' αὐτὸν τὰς χεῖρας ἐν αὐτῇ τῇ ὥρᾳ, καὶ ἐφοβήθησαν τὸν λαόν· ἔγνωσαν γὰρ ὅτι πρὸς αὐτοὺς	7 30: ἐζήτουν οὖν αὐτὸν πιάσαι, καὶ οὐδεὶς ἐπέβαλεν ἐπ' αὐτὸν τὴν χεῖρα, ὅτι οὔπω ἐληλύθει ἡ ὥ-

Mt 21,41 *om* λεγ. αυ.‖p: ϕ69 122 | εκδωσει‖p: C ΟΣ Chr$^{1:3}$ **42** *om* εν τ. γρ.‖19 42 21 16 Mk 2 25: 6 *pc* Chr Ep Or *Le*[k] g^1 Ir *S* Ef **43** ● 43 + ^{44}και(*om*) ο πεσων επι τον λιθον τουτον συνθλασθησεται εφ ον δ αν πεση λικμησει αυτον‖Lk: *Rpl* (ϕ124 Θ *pc*) Chr(και] και πας: ^{1}, πας: ^{1}) *L*'(q vg^1) Au PsChr *S*(και πας: ch)p Af Ef *C* — *txt*: 33 D Chr^3 **Or** *Le*[k] a^{v}bff$^{1.2}$r$^{1.2}$ *S*s Eu **45** και ακ.] ● ακ. δε: ℌ⟨B⟩ 59 *Lz* vg^1 *S*sc *C* | την παραβολην‖p: Δ 157 243 Cat *Arm* *Geo*^{2}(+ ταυτην‖Lk: *Geo*^{A}; ^{B} + εκεινην) **46** ζητ. … εφο.] εζητουν … και εφο.‖p: 157 *S*scp Eu {*C*b^4} | κρα.] πιασαι‖Jo 7 30: ϕ13-346-543-826-828 998 | τον οχλον‖Mk: ℵ*C *pc* *L*b *C*b — τον λαον‖Lk: *L*ff^2 *S*sc Eu

Mk 12,9 αμπελωνος + τοις γεωργοις εκεινοις; λεγουσιν αυτω‖Mt: 472 | γεω. + τουτους‖Lk: C^2-33-579 σ7-659-1082-1391 *l*18 *l*19 *l*49 *l*184 *l*251 — + εκεινους‖Mt 40: ΝΣ **λ** σ517-827-1606 G *al* *L*cz *S*ph *C*b^3 **10** ουδε] και λεγει αυτοις ο Ιησους· ουδε‖Mt: 472 **12** εζητησαν‖Lk: 565 *C*s

Lk 20,15 αυτοις] τους γεωργους‖Mt *cf.* 27 22p: 33 *C*s$^{1:9}$(+ εκεινους) — *om*‖Mk: N-1071 σ7-71-692 D *pc* *l*18 *Le* acq vg^3 *C*b^1 | ∼ ο κυ. τ. αμπ. αυτοις‖Mk: 21 *C*s **16** τ. γεω. του.] τ. γεω.‖Mk: D *Le* *C*s^{8}b' — τ. γεω. εκεινους‖Mt 40: 28 **λλ**⟨22-1278⟩ ϕ69 157 *L*cfl vg^1 *S*cp *C*b^2 — αυτους‖Mt: σ1194 *S*s(+ τ. γ.) *C*s^1 — τουτους: ℵ* | ∼ τ. αμπ. εκδωσει‖Mt: N | αλλ. + γεωργοις‖Mt: N σ1675 **19** εζητουν‖MkJo: C 1071 σ267 D *al* *L*⟨e a⟩ *C*b | γρ. … αρχ.] αρχ. … γρ. *cf.* 19 47 22 2 Mt 45: *Rpl* *L*' *S*' *C*s — Φαρισαιοι … γρ. *cf.* 5 30 15 2 Mt 15 1p *etc.*: C 716(Φ. + συν τοις αρχιερευσιν) — αρχ. και οι πρεσβυτεροι … γρ.‖Mk 14 53 15 1: ϕ69 — *txt*: ℌ⟨ℵ-892-1241⟩ **λλ**⟨22-1278⟩ **ϕ** σM-71-692-1223 A K U W Θ Π *al* *Le* *S*h *C*b *Arm* *Aeth* | την χειρα‖Jo: A Π *al* *C*b^1(*om* την) | *om* εν—ωρα‖p: 47 Mcn^{Ep} *Le* | τ. λα.] τ. οχλον‖Mk Mt: N λ22-1278 σ1604(*om* τον) W Ψ **0117** *pc* *S*h — *om cf.* 8 35 9 34: *Rpl* — *txt*: ℌC 1071 **λλ**' **ϕ** σM-1207 A D E H K R U Δ Θ Π Ψ 157 *mu* *L* *S*'h^{Brs} *C*

Jo 7,30 *cf. ad* 22.

Mt 21 42p *cf.* ETh^{II} 66 (*transl.*): *Λέγει Ἰησοῦς· δείξατέ μοι τὸν λίθον, ὃν ἀπεδοκίμασαν οἱ οἰκοδομοῦντες. αὐτός ἐστιν ὁ λίθος ὁ ἀκρογωνιαῖος.*

cf. v. 45 ↑ 22 22 (220.): ... *καὶ ἀφέντες αὐτὸν ἀπῆλθαν.*	τὴν παραβολὴν εἶπεν. καὶ ἀφέντες αὐτὸν ἀπῆλθον.	εἶπεν τὴν παραβολὴν ταύτην.	ρα αὐτοῦ.

(205)

219. Das Gleichnis vom Hochzeitsmahl. Matth 22 1–14 [184.]

The Parable of the Marriage Feast.

[1] Καὶ ἀποκριθεὶς ὁ Ἰησοῦς πάλιν εἶπεν ἐν παραβολαῖς αὐτοῖς λέγων· [2] ὡμοιώθη ἡ βασιλεία τῶν οὐρανῶν ἀνθρώπῳ βασιλεῖ, ὅστις ἐποίησεν γάμους τῷ υἱῷ αὐτοῦ. [3] καὶ ἀπέστειλεν τοὺς δούλους αὐτοῦ καλέσαι τοὺς κεκλημένους εἰς τοὺς γάμους, καὶ οὐκ ἤθελον ἐλθεῖν. [4] πάλιν ἀπέστειλεν ἄλλους δούλους λέγων· εἴπατε τοῖς κεκλημένοις· ἰδοὺ τὸ ἄριστόν μου ἡτοίμακα, οἱ ταῦροί μου καὶ τὰ σιτιστὰ τεθυμένα, καὶ πάντα ἕτοιμα· δεῦτε εἰς τοὺς γάμους. [5] οἱ δὲ ἀμελήσαντες ἀπῆλθον, ὃς μὲν εἰς τὸν ἴδιον ἀγρόν, ὃς δὲ ἐπὶ τὴν ἐμπορίαν αὐτοῦ· [6] οἱ δὲ λοιποὶ κρατήσαντες τοὺς δούλους αὐτοῦ ὕβρισαν καὶ ἀπέκτειναν. [7] ὁ δὲ βασιλεὺς ὠργίσθη, καὶ πέμψας τὰ στρατεύματα αὐτοῦ ἀπώλεσεν τοὺς φονεῖς ἐκείνους καὶ τὴν πόλιν αὐτῶν ἐνέπρησεν. [8] τότε λέγει τοῖς δούλοις αὐτοῦ· ὁ μὲν γάμος ἕτοιμός ἐστιν, οἱ δὲ κεκλημένοι οὐκ ἦσαν ἄξιοι· [9] πορεύεσθε οὖν ἐπὶ τὰς διεξόδους τῶν ὁδῶν, καὶ ὅσους ἐὰν εὕρητε καλέσατε εἰς τοὺς γάμους. [10] καὶ ἐξελθόντες οἱ δοῦλοι ἐκεῖνοι εἰς τὰς ὁδοὺς συνήγαγον πάντας οὓς εὗρον, πονηρούς τε καὶ ἀγαθούς· καὶ ἐπλήσθη ὁ νυμφὼν ἀνακειμένων. [11] εἰσελθὼν δὲ ὁ βασιλεὺς θεάσασθαι τοὺς ἀνακειμένους εἶδεν ἐκεῖ ἄνθρωπον οὐκ ἐνδεδυμένον ἔνδυμα γάμου· [12] καὶ λέγει αὐτῷ· ἑταῖρε, πῶς εἰσῆλθες ὧδε μὴ ἔχων ἔνδυμα γάμου; ὁ δὲ ἐφιμώθη. [13] τότε ὁ βασιλεὺς εἶπεν τοῖς διακόνοις· δήσαντες αὐτοῦ πόδας καὶ χεῖρας ἐκβάλετε αὐτὸν εἰς τὸ σκότος τὸ ἐξώτερον· ἐκεῖ ἔσται ὁ κλαυθμὸς καὶ ὁ βρυγμὸς τῶν ὀδόντων. [14] πολλοὶ γάρ εἰσιν κλητοί, ὀλίγοι δὲ ἐκλεκτοί.

[184.]

(206)

220. Die Pharisäerfrage. *The Question concerning Tribute to Caesar.*

Matth 22 15–22	Mark 12 13–17	Luk 20 20–26
[15] Τότε πορευθέντες οἱ	[13] Καὶ ἀποστέλλουσιν πρὸς αὐτόν τινας τῶν	[20] Καὶ παρατηρήσαντες ἀπέστειλαν ἐγκαθέτους ὑπο-

Mt 22,3 καλ. τ. κεκ.] ειπειν τοις κεκλημενοις‖Lk: Φ **9** διεξ. τ. οδ.] οδους‖10p: 1555 **10** ους] ● οσους‖9: *Rpl* {*L*'}e abcff$^{1.2}$hqr$^{1.2}$ vg^{4} *Arm*' — *txt*: ℵB* ϕ124-788 D *pc* Or {} *Arm*^{pc} *Aeth* **13** δησ. —χει.] ● αρατε αυτον ποδων και χειρων(∼ χ. κ. π.) και: D (Or, *et prm* δησ.) *L*e abff^{1}qr^{1}32(cff^{2}hr^{2}) Ir Luc (*S*sc) — δησ. αυτου χειρας και ποδας αρ. αυτον και *cf.* 188Lk2439: Φ-544 ϕ174-230-*l*547 σM-267-659-1194-1293-1424 **047** *pm* *L*Amst Vic^{T} *S*h — + αρ. αυτ. και: *Rpl Lf* — *txt* (∼ χ. κ. π.): 𝔥⟨33⟩ 700-1604 **λ**'(δας και χειρας] *spat.*: 118)-22-1582 **ϕ**'⟨346⟩(828) σ1675 Θ Eu Or *L*'(vg^{5} Au Or *S*pj Ef Eu) *Cs*^{1}(^{7}b Sch) *Δ*'⟨me⟩(a i$^{T5:8}$ l^{D} md n p) | εκβ.] βαλετε(-ατε)‖1348.50 513p: 28-(544) **ϕ**'-230 σ(71-692)-954-1194-1402 D H *pm* *Cs*^{3}b Sch^{1} — εμβαλετε(-ατε): ϕ174-346 (258) (εισβ.: 1515) — *txt*: *Rpl* (-ατε: Σ Δ; -λλ-: X F **0138**) Eu Or *Cs*^{5} *Sch*^{1} | *om* αυτον‖2139: *Rpl* *L*bf *S*h^{-} — *txt*: 𝔥⟨33⟩ 700-1604 **λ**-1582 σ1675 D Θ Or *L*'Au Ir *S*'j *C*

Mk 12,12 ∼ ειπ. τ. παρ.‖Lk: σ945 1093 *L*cff^{2}z *S*s[c]p | παρ. + ταυτην‖Lk: 1071 σ115-1606 *al* *L*k[e] blr^{2}z vg *S*s[c]p *C* | *om* και^{3}—απηλ.‖**p**: W **13** απεστειλαν‖Lk: 1279 *L*k[e] ac | πρ. αυ.] αυτω‖Mt16: 213 — *om*‖Lk: D *L*k[e] acff^{2}iq *Cs*$^{1:9}$

Lk 20,19 ∼ τ. παρ. ταυ. ειπ.‖Mk: *Rpl* (*om* ταυ.: 579 σ115 **0117**; ταυ. + προς αυτους: σ1604) *S*h — *txt*: ℵBL-892 **ϕ** D(ειρηκεν) G 157 *pc* *L* *S*p *Cs*^{8}(+ προς αυτους: s^{1}b) | τ. παρ. ταυ.] τ. παρ.‖Mk: 579 — τας παραβολας‖Mt45: σ7-267

Mt221-10 *cf.* ETh^{II} 64 (*cf. ad 184.*)

220. cf. ETh^{II} 100 (*transl.*): *Ἐπέδειξαν τῷ Ἰησοῦ χρυσίον καὶ εἶπον αὐτῷ· οἱ τοῦ Καίσαρος ἀπαιτοῦσιν ἀφ' ἡμῶν τοὺς φόρους. εἶπεν αὐτοῖς· ἀπόδοτε τὰ Καίσαρος Καίσαρι. ἀπόδοτε τὰ τοῦ θεοῦ τῷ θεῷ, καὶ τὰ ἐμὰ ἀπόδοτε ἐμοί.*

cf. Ev. apocr. (PEg 2 fol. 2r° 11-14): ... [Παραγε]νόμενοι πρὸς αὐτὸν ἐξ[ετασ]τικῶς ἐπείραζον αὐτὸν λ[έγοντες]· 'διδάσκαλε Ἰη(σοῦ) οἴδαμεν ὅτι [ἀπὸ θ(εο)ῦ] ἐλήλυθας· ἃ γὰρ ποιεῖς μα[ρτυρεῖ] ὑπὲρ το[ὺ]ς προφ(ήτ)ας πάντας. [12][εἰπὲ οὖν] ἡμεῖν· ἐξὸν τοῖς βα(σι)λεῦσ[ιν ἀποδοῦ]ναι τὰ ἀν[ή]κοντα τῇ ἀρχῇ; ἀπ[οδῶμεν αὐ]τοῖς ἢ μ[ή];' [13]ὁ δὲ Ἰη(σοῦς) εἰδὼς [τὴν δι]άνοιαν [αὐτ]ῶν ἐμβριμ[ησάμενος] εἶπεν α[ὐτοῖς]· 'τί με καλεῖτ[ε τῷ στό]ματι ὑμ[ῶν δι]δάσκαλον μ[ὴ ἀκού]οντες ὃ [λ]έγω; [14]καλῶς Ἠ[σ(αΐ)ας περὶ ὑ]μῶν ἐπ[ρο]φ(ήτευ)σεν εἰπών· ὁ [λαὸς οὗ]τος τοῖς [χείλ]εσιν αὐτ[ῶν τιμῶσίν] με ἡ [δὲ καρδί]α αὐτῶ[ν πόρρω ἀπέ]χει ἀπ' ἐ[μοῦ· μ]άτη[ν μέ σέβονται] ἐντάλ[ματα ...

Matth	Mark	Luk	Jo
Φαρισαῖοι συμβούλιον ἔλαβον	Φαρισαίων καὶ τῶν Ἡρῳδιανῶν	κρινομένους ἑαυτοὺς δικαίους εἶναι,	
ὅπως αὐτὸν παγιδεύσωσιν ἐν λόγῳ.	ἵνα αὐτὸν ἀγρεύσωσιν λόγῳ.	ἵνα ἐπιλάβωνται αὐτοῦ λόγου,	
16 καὶ		ὥστε παραδοῦναι αὐτὸν τῇ ἀρχῇ καὶ	
ἀποστέλλουσιν αὐτῷ τοὺς μαθητὰς		τῇ ἐξουσίᾳ τοῦ ἡγεμόνος.	
αὐτῶν μετὰ τῶν Ἡρῳδια-	14 καὶ ἐλθόντες	21 καὶ ἐπηρώ-	3 2: ... καὶ
νῶν λέγοντες·	λέγουσιν αὐτῷ·	τησαν αὐτὸν λέγοντες·	εἶπεν αὐτῷ·
διδάσκαλε, οἴδαμεν ὅτι ἀλη-	διδάσκαλε, οἴδαμεν ὅτι ἀλη-	διδάσκαλε, οἴδαμεν ὅτι ὀρ-	ῥαββι, οἴδαμεν ὅτι ἀπὸ
θὴς εἶ καὶ τὴν ὁδὸν τοῦ θεοῦ	θὴς εἶ	θῶς λέγεις καὶ διδάσκεις	θεοῦ ἐλήλυθας διδάσκαλος
ἐν ἀληθείᾳ διδάσκεις, καὶ οὐ μέλει σοι	καὶ οὐ μέλει σοι		...
περὶ οὐδενός, οὐ γὰρ βλέπεις εἰς	περὶ οὐδενός· οὐ γὰρ βλέπεις εἰς	καὶ οὐ λαμβάνεις	
πρόσωπον ἀνθρώπων·	πρόσωπον ἀνθρώπων, ἀλλ' ἐπ' ἀληθείας	πρόσωπον, ἀλλ' ἐπ' ἀληθείας	
17 εἰπὲ οὖν ἡμῖν, τί σοι δοκεῖ; ἔξεστιν	τὴν ὁδὸν τοῦ θεοῦ διδάσκεις· ἔξεστιν	τὴν ὁδὸν τοῦ θεοῦ διδάσκεις· 22 ἔξεστιν	
δοῦναι κῆνσον Καίσαρι	κῆνσον Καίσαρι	ἡμᾶς Καίσαρι φόρον δοῦναι	
ἢ οὔ;	δοῦναι ἢ οὔ; δῶμεν ἢ μὴ δῶμεν;	ἢ οὔ;	
18 γνοὺς δὲ ὁ Ἰησοῦς τὴν	15 ὁ δὲ εἰδὼς αὐτῶν τὴν	23 κατανοήσας δὲ αὐτῶν τὴν	
πονηρίαν αὐτῶν εἶπεν· τί	ὑπόκρισιν εἶπεν αὐτοῖς· τί	πανουργίαν εἶπεν πρὸς αὐτούς·	
με πειράζετε, ὑποκριταί; 19 ἐπιδείξατέ	με πειράζετε; φέρετέ	24 δείξατε	

Mt 22,15 ελαβ. + κατ αυτου‖12 14 27 1: C^2-33 Σ λ Δ Θ Or Sj$^{a1.b1.c2}$ Cb Arm — + κατα του Ιησου‖←: C^3 φ*l*547 σM 1093 *pc* Sj$^{a1.b1}$ | *om* εν‖Mk: σ517-1424 **16** αυτω] προς αυτον‖Mk: D 372 Lacff^2(αυτους) — *om*‖Lk: σ1402 Le[k] bff^{1}qr^2 Or | ● λεγοντας ℵBL-085 700 σ27 — *txt*: *Rpl S* **17** *om* ειπε—ημ. (*et om* τισ. δοκ.)‖(p): D (σ1424 1093) Le[k] abff$^{1.2}$qr$^{1.2}$ Ss | εξ. + ημιν‖Lk: λ-1582 1187(εξ. + σοι) Ss | ∼ κη. δου.‖Lk Mk: W Θ 566 L⟨e[k] r$^{1.2}$ vg^1⟩ Or **18** πον.] πανουργιαν‖Lk: 700 Or | ειπ. + αυτοις‖Mk Lk: LZ-33 Le[k] Sscp^{1}j^{b1} Csb^1

Mk 12,13 αγρ.] παγιδευσωσιν‖Mt: Θ-565-700 D 1093 | λογ.] εν λ.‖Mt: 33 σ827 *pc* Lbcff^{2}lr^{2}z vg **14** και^1] ● οι δε: *Rpl* S' Cs^2 — *txt*: ℌC 1071 D 1342 *pc* L Ss[c] Cs^{6}b Arm(+ αυτοι) Aeth | *om* ελ.‖p: D Lk[e] Ss[c]p^1 | λεγ. αυ.] ● ηρξαντο ερωταν αυτον εν δολω λεγοντες(*om*): (W)-28 λ-(22-1278) φ'(επηρωτον!: 983) G (251) *pc* (Ss[c], *et* ερ.] λεγειν) Cs$^{3:8}$ Geo^1 — επηρωτων αυτον εν δο. λε.: Θ-565-700(-ωτησαν) (*om* εν δο.: 472 1515) *pc* Lbc(=472) (ff^{2}iqr^1; q=700) Arm Geo^A(B ∼ εν δο. επ. αυ.) — επηρ. αυ.: D(+ οι Φαρισαιοι) Lk[e](+ οι Φ. λε.) ad(∼ οι Φ. αυ.) Sp(-ωτησαν) | διδασκεις + ειπε(-ον) ουν ημιν‖Mt: C(*om* ουν) N(WΘ)ΣΦ-28-544-(565-700)-1071-1604 (φ124 σM)-7-267-349-517-659-827-1391-(1424-1675) D *pc* *l*18 *l*19(= C) (*l*49) *l*124 Lvl'(k[e] = C)g^{2}r^{1}30 vg^4 Sh$^+$ Arm Geo^1(2 = C) — *txt*: 𝔓^{45v} *Rpl* Llr^2 vg' S' C | εξ.] τι σοι δοκει; εξ.‖Mt: 544-1604 330 Lk[e] — ει εξ.‖10 2 Mt 12 10 19 3: C* D *pc* *l*18 Lbcff^{2}iqr^1 Sp^1 Geo^1 | εξ. + ημας‖Lk: D Cs$^{2:7}$ | ● ∼ δου. κη.(επικεφαλαιον) Και.‖Mt: ℌC W^c(* *om* κη.)(Θ-565) σ115-517-659-827 (D) 1342 *pc* *l*18 *l*19 *l*49 L'(k[e])(∼ K. κη.: vg^1 S')h Geo^2 — ∼ K. κη. δου.‖Lk: σ7-1082-1391 — *txt* (∼ δου. K.): *Rpl* (28 Lcff^{2}qr^{1}z30 vg^1) Geo^1 | *om* δωμ.—δωμ.‖p: D 1346 Lvl'r^1 vg^2 Sp^1 — *om* η(1)^2—δωμ.(1)^2: σ517 (Lr^2 vg' Ss[c]) Arm^{pc} (Geo') — *om* η ου: Σ Lk[e](*et om* δωμ.^{2}) q Geo^{Ac} **15** δε + Ιησους‖Mt: Θ-28-565-700 λ φ D G *pc* Lvl⟨k[e] lr^2⟩r^1 Sp^{1}j | ο δε ειδ.] ειδ. δε‖p: Σ (Laff^2) | ειδ.] ιδων‖9 25 10 15: ℵ* 28-565 φ⟨124⟩ D 1342 Lbcff^{2}iqr^{1}z | ∼ τ. υποκ. αυ.‖Mt: 544 *pc* Lvl'⟨k[e]⟩ r^1 30 | πειρ. + υποκριται‖Mt: 𝔓^{45} 33-579 NWΘΣ-28-565 λ φ F G *pc* Lq vg^2 Sh$^+$j Cs$^{6:8}$ Arm

Lk 20,21 ορ.] αληθως‖p: φ1689(*et* διδασκεις^1 *prm* ορ.) *pc* La | ου] ουδενος‖p: D 60 LAu Qu Ssc | προσ. + ανθρωπου‖p: N 998 (-ων: Laf) Ssc **22** εξ. *prm* ειπε ουν ημιν‖Mt: N | ημας] ημιν‖Jo 18 31: *Rpl* Bas^1 L — *om*‖p: 892 N Bas^1 Cb^6 Geo — *txt*: ℵBL-33-1241 φ⟨124⟩ A 157 *pc* | ∼ δου. φο. K.‖Mt: σ659 130 (∼ φ. δ.: λ1278 D *pc*) Lcfff^{2}lr^1 vg$^{⟨7⟩}$ S C | φορους‖23 2: Λ φ124-174-230 σ267-659-1391-1402 K *pc* Bas$^{1:2}$ | δου]. διδοναι‖←: λ1278 σM-692-1194 D **0117** Bas$^{1:2}$ **23** καταν.] επιγνους‖5 22 Mk 2 8 Mt: D Le Sscpj | παν.] πονηριαν‖Mt: C* σ267-659-1391-1402 D *pc* Le alr^1 Ssch^m — υποκρισιν‖Mk: 713 *l*48 Sh^m | πρ. αυ.] αυτοις‖Mk: N Δ(-ους) 1574 Lff^2 — *om*‖Mt: 998 Lf30 Cb$^{⟨7⟩}$ | 23 + τι με πειραζετε(+ υποκριται)‖(Mt) Mk: *Rpl* (C *pc*) (∼ υπ. τι μ. π.: 1071) Bas L'(l) S — *txt*: ℌ⟨33⟩ λλ⟨22-1278⟩ φ230 σ1424 **0266**^{v} 116 157 Le C Arm **24** επιδει.‖Mt: *Rpl* — *txt*: ℌ 1071 φ⟨124-346-983⟩ σM-71-692 A D P W Θ 157 *pc* Bas

Jo 3,2 εληλ.] εξηλθες και εληλ.‖16 27 f. 30 17 8: 28 — απεσταλης: Ss[c]p

Matth	Mark	Luk
μοι τὸ νόμισμα τοῦ κήνσου. οἱ δὲ προσήνεγκαν αὐτῷ δηνάριον. [20] καὶ λέγει αὐτοῖς· τίνος ἡ εἰκὼν αὕτη καὶ ἡ ἐπιγραφή;	μοι δηνάριον ἵνα ἴδω. [16] οἱ δὲ ἤνεγκαν. καὶ λέγει αὐτοῖς· τίνος ἡ εἰκὼν αὕτη καὶ ἡ ἐπιγραφή;	μοι δηνάριον· τίνος ἔχει εἰκόνα καὶ ἐπιγραφήν;
[21] λέγουσιν αὐτῷ· Καίσαρος. τότε λέγει αὐτοῖς· ἀπόδοτε οὖν τὰ Καίσαρος Καίσαρι καὶ τὰ τοῦ θεοῦ τῷ θεῷ.	οἱ δὲ εἶπον αὐτῷ· Καίσαρος. [17] καὶ ἀποκριθεὶς ὁ Ἰησοῦς εἶπεν αὐτοῖς· τὰ Καίσαρος ἀπόδοτε Καίσαρι καὶ τὰ τοῦ θεοῦ τῷ θεῷ.	ἀποκριθέντες δὲ εἶπαν· Καίσαρος. [25] ὁ δὲ εἶπεν πρὸς αὐτούς· τοίνυν ἀπόδοτε τὰ Καίσαρος Καίσαρι καὶ τὰ τοῦ θεοῦ τῷ θεῷ. [26] καὶ οὐκ ἴσχυσαν ἐπιλαβέσθαι τοῦ ῥήματος ἐναντίον τοῦ λαοῦ,
[22] καὶ ἀκούσαντες ἐθαύμασαν, καὶ ἀφέντες αὐτὸν ἀπῆλθαν.	καὶ ἐθαύμαζον ἐπ' αὐτῷ. **218.**	καὶ θαυμάσαντες ἐπὶ τῇ ἀποκρίσει αὐτοῦ ἐσίγησαν.

(207)

221. Die Sadduzäerfrage. *The Question concerning the Resurrection.*

Matth 22 23–33	**Mark 12** 18–27	**Luk 20** 27–40
[23] Ἐν ἐκείνῃ τῇ ἡμέρᾳ προσῆλθον αὐτῷ Σαδδουκαῖοι, λέγοντες μὴ εἶναι ἀνάστασιν,	[18] Καὶ ἔρχονται Σαδδουκαῖοι πρὸς αὐτόν, οἵτινες λέγουσιν ἀνάστασιν	[27] Προσελθόντες δέ τινες τῶν Σαδδουκαίων, οἱ ἀντιλέγοντες ἀνάστασιν

Mt 22,19 *om* του κη.‖Lk: 1295 *L*e[k] *pc* *L*⟨f⟩ Or *S*scp⟨1⟩j(κυριος l.) *C*b *Arm*^{pc} *Geo* *Aeth* *Δ*⟨p⟩ | **21** λεγ.] οι δε ειπον‖p: 1604 *L*f(*om* οι δε) *S*p^1 | + ο Ιησους‖Mk: Φ 481 *l*49 *l*183 *L*abcfff^{1}g^{2}hlr^2 vg^3 *Geo*^{2} | *om* ουν‖Mk: σ945-990 D 157 478 Chr Or *L*e[k] ab cff^{2}r^1 *S*scj$^{a1.b1}$ *C*b *Geo*^{2} *Aeth* **23** λεγ.] οι λ.‖Lk: *Rpl* (οι Σ.: ϕ'⟨543⟩-*l*547) *L*'Hil *S*hj *C*s(= ϕ)b *Arm* *Geo*^{1} *Aeth* *Δ*' — *txt*: 𝔥⟨L⟩ 28-544-700(οι Σ.) **λ**-1582 ϕ788(= 700) σM-349-517-659-692-1010-1675 D S W Y Π Ω **0138** 157 *mu* *l*10 *l*185^1 *l*303 *l*861 *l*950 *l*1642 Meth Or *L*ff^1 *S*' *Geo*^{2} *Δ*a l^{ms} me n^{Hg} E^a

20 ● αυτοις + ο Ιησους: LZ-33-892 ϕ-*l*547^1 σ1010-1293 D Θ 157 | *om* η^2‖Lk: ϕ⟨788-828-983⟩-174-230 *pc* | ● *om* αυτω‖Lk: ℵB 1604 *L*g^2 *S*p *C*PS | αυτοις

Mk 12,16 ην. + αυτω‖Mt: *l*48 *L*k[e] z vg⟨8⟩ *S*s[c]p *C*s$^{5:8}$b^2 | οι δε ειπ.] λεγουσιν‖Mt: 579 A 1342 *L*bdilqr$^{1.2}$z vg⟨1⟩ *S*s[c] *Aeth* — ειπαν: D 566 *L*a | *om* αυτω‖Lk: 𝔓^{45v} W-28-700 **λ** ϕ⟨124⟩ σ7-517-659-1223-1391 *pc* *l*9 *l*12 *l*49 *l*184 *L*k[e] acff^2 *S*p *C*b^5 **17** και^1—l.] ● ο δε l.(*om*)‖p: 𝔥C 1093 (1342) *L*c(∼ ειπ. αυ. και ο l.) *S*p(*om* δε) *C*s^6(^{2} δε] ουν)b^2(') — αποκ. δε ο l. (*om* ο l.)‖(p): *Rpl* (Θ-565)-700 D *L*'(vg^1) Au — *om*: *L*k[e] r^{1v} — *txt* (*om* ο l.): 𝔓^{45}? *Rpl* (W σ517-1606 238) (*om* αποκ.: σ1424) (*om* και: *L*30 *S*s[c])h *Arm*(*om* και) *Geo*'(^{A}, *et om* κ.) | ειπ.] λεγει‖Mt: 28 σ1424 *L*k[e] cdr^1 | ∼ αποδ. (+ ουν) τα Καισαρος‖p: *Rpl* (579 544 λ1278 ϕ σM-267-827-1402 *al* *l*184 *L*')k[e] i vg^1 (Au) *S*s[c](h) *C*s^1(^{6})(^{1} ∼ τα K. ουν) *Arm* — *txt* (K. + ουν): 𝔥'⟨33⟩C W(Θ)-28-(565-700) σ517 1093 *S*p *C*b | εθαυμασαν‖Mt Lk: *Rpl* *L*k[e] *S*' *C*s — ● εξεθαυ.: ℵBΨ 1342 *L*b(admirabantur vehementer) {} — *txt*: LΔ-892 Θ-565-1071 D^c(*-οντο) *pc* {*L*' *S*p^1 *C*b} **18** ∼ πρ. αυ. Σ.‖Mt: Ψ 28 D *pc* *L*bff^{2}ilqr$^{1v.2}$z vg *S*s[c]p^1 | ∼ μη ει. αν.‖Mt: λ1278 σ827-1402 **047** *pc* *l*184 *L*abff^{2}z vg^1 *S*s[c]

Lk 20,24 δη.] το νομισμα‖Mt: D — figuram: *L*d — + οι δε εδειξαν· και ειπεν‖p: 𝔥⟨B⟩C 1071-1604 **λλ** ϕ-1689 σ71-692-1207-1223 W **0266**^{v} 157 *al* *l*184 *L*c *S*(επιγρ. + και εδει. αυτω: sc)h *C* *Arm* *Aeth* ⟦οι δε] και: *L*c — *om*: λ1582-2193 | εδει.] επεδ.‖Mt: 1241 — ηνεγκαν‖Mk: 579 — προσην.‖Mt: ϕ1689 — + αυτω‖Mt: ℵ *C* — + προς αυτον‖Mt: 579 716 | και] δηναριον κ.‖Mt: 579 *L*c — *om*: *C*s^8(^{1} ο δε) | ειπ. + προς αυτους‖p25: 579 — + αυτοις‖Mt Mk: *L*c *C*b⟧ — *txt*: *Rpl* Bas *L*' *S*p | επιγρ.] την ε. ‖p: D | αποκ. δε] ● οι δε(+ αποκ.)‖p: 𝔥 N **0266**^{v} 157 213 *S*p(h^m) *C* *Geo*(^{1})^2 — και αποκ. G 475 — και: *S*sc — *txt* (*om* δε): *Rpl* (**λλ**⟨22-1278⟩ D W Γ Θ *pc*) Bas *L*(')f *S*h^t *Arm* *Aeth* **25** ο δε] και αποκριθεις ο Ιησους‖Mk: N | πρ. αυ.] αυτοις‖Mt Mk: *Rpl* Bas *L*'⟨a(*om*)⟩ — *txt*: 𝔥⟨33⟩ 1071 **λλ**⟨22-1278⟩ ϕ⟨124⟩ 157 *L*e | τοι. αποδ.] απ. ουν‖Mt: 544-1604 λ2193 Γ *pc* Bas {} — απ. τοι.‖Mt: *Rpl* {*L*' *S*' *C*s} — απ.‖Mk: D 2145 *L*e aff^{2}ilq *S*sc *Aeth* — *txt*: 𝔥⟨33⟩ ϕ⟨69-124-346⟩-230 1012 *C*b {*Arm*} **26** του ρη.] ● αυτου ρηματος‖20: *Rpl* (ρημα: λ131 D; -ατι: 238 254) *L*vg^1(+ αυτου) *S*ph^t (-ατων: *Arm*) — *txt* (+ αυτου): ℵBL-(579)-892-1241 (Θ)433 (*L*' *S*sc)h^m Cr | εναν.] ενωπιον‖847 Act6s: 1071 — + παντος‖←: 1241 ϕ124 **27** οι αντ.] ● οι λεγοντες‖p: 𝔥C NΘ-1071 **λλ** σ267-659-1391-1402 D *pc* *l*^{p1} {*S*' *C* *Got*} — οιτινες λεγουσιν‖p: Ψ 713 *l*48 {*L*e dr^1} — *txt*: *Rpl* *L*' *S*h *Arm* | ∼ μη ει. αν.‖Mt: N σ267-659 *pc* *l*49 *L* *S*sc

Matthew

καὶ ἐπηρώτησαν αὐτὸν [24] λέγοντες· διδάσκαλε, Μωυσῆς εἶπεν· (Dt25 5f.) **ἐάν τις ἀποθάνῃ μὴ ἔχων τέκνα, ἐπιγαμβρεύσει ὁ ἀδελφὸς αὐτοῦ τὴν γυναῖκα αὐτοῦ καὶ ἀναστήσει σπέρμα τῷ ἀδελφῷ αὐτοῦ.** [25] ἦσαν δὲ παρ' ἡμῖν ἑπτὰ ἀδελφοί· καὶ ὁ πρῶτος γήμας ἐτελεύτησεν, καὶ μὴ ἔχων σπέρμα ἀφῆκεν τὴν γυναῖκα αὐτοῦ τῷ ἀδελφῷ αὐτοῦ· [26] ὁμοίως καὶ ὁ δεύτερος καὶ ὁ τρίτος, ἕως τῶν ἑπτά. [27] ὕστερον δὲ πάντων

Mark

μὴ εἶναι, καὶ ἐπηρώτων αὐτὸν λέγοντες· [19] διδάσκαλε, Μωυσῆς ἔγραψεν ἡμῖν ὅτι **ἐάν** τινος ἀδελφὸς **ἀποθάνῃ** καὶ καταλίπῃ γυναῖκα **καὶ τέκνον μὴ ἀφῇ,** ἵνα **λάβῃ ὁ ἀδελφὸς αὐτοῦ τὴν γυναῖκα καὶ ἐξαναστήσῃ σπέρμα τῷ ἀδελφῷ αὐτοῦ.** [20] ἑπτὰ ἀδελφοὶ ἦσαν· καὶ ὁ πρῶτος ἔλαβεν γυναῖκα, καὶ ἀποθνῄσκων οὐκ ἀφῆκεν σπέρμα· [21] καὶ ὁ δεύτερος ἔλαβεν αὐτήν, καὶ ἀπέθανεν μὴ καταλιπὼν σπέρμα· καὶ ὁ τρίτος ὡσαύτως· [22] καὶ οἱ ἑπτὰ οὐκ ἀφῆκαν σπέρμα. ἔσχατον πάντων

Luke

μὴ εἶναι, ἐπηρώτησαν αὐτὸν [28] λέγοντες· διδάσκαλε, Μωυσῆς ἔγραψεν ἡμῖν, **ἐάν** τινος ἀδελφὸς **ἀποθάνῃ** ἔχων γυναῖκα, **καὶ οὗτος ἄτεκνος ᾖ,** ἵνα **λάβῃ ὁ ἀδελφὸς αὐτοῦ τὴν γυναῖκα καὶ ἐξαναστήσῃ σπέρμα τῷ ἀδελφῷ αὐτοῦ.** [29] ἑπτὰ οὖν ἀδελφοὶ ἦσαν· καὶ ὁ πρῶτος λαβὼν γυναῖκα ἀπέθανεν ἄτεκνος· [30] καὶ ὁ δεύτερος [31] καὶ ὁ τρίτος ἔλαβεν αὐτήν, ὡσαύτως δὲ καὶ οἱ ἑπτὰ οὐ κατέλιπον τέκνα καὶ ἀπέθαναν. [32] ὕστερον

Mt 22,23 επηρωτων‖M:k σ348 *Ss* **24** επ.] εγραψεν (+ ημιν)‖Mk Lk: 1295 (*Le*[k]) — ενετειλατο ημ.‖19 7p: *L*vg^{1} — + ημ.‖p: *L*vg^{1v} *S*scp *C*b | εξαναστ.‖p: Σ-1604 σM-1194-1424 F H Θ *pc* **26** ομοι. + δε‖Lk 31: U **0138** 348 *Lf Sj* **27** *om* παν.‖Lk: Δ *Le*[k] *S*p^{1}

Mk 12,18 επηρωτησαν‖p: *Rpl L*clz vg^{2} *S*hj *C*s *Geo*^{1} *Aeth* — *txt*: ℌC Θ-565-700-1071 σ7-517 D 1342 *pc l*18 *l*19 *L*' *S*' *C*b *Geo*^{2} **19** *om* οτι‖p: ϕ69 σ115 D *pc Geo* | κ. καταλ.] κ. εχη‖Lk: WΘ(σχη)-28 D *L*⟨lr^{2}z⟩ *Ss*[c] *Geo* — εχων‖Lk: 700 | τεκνα‖Mt: *Rpl L*' *S*'phj — σπερμα‖19b p.20ff. Mt25: *Ss*[c] — *txt*: ℵ^{ca}BLΔΨ-579-892 WΘ-565-700 **λ** 1342 *pc L*k[e] acff^{2} *Geo* | ● ∼ μη αφη τε.‖Mt: ℌC 1342 *L*ff^{2} *Ss*[c] *C Aeth* — *txt*: *Rpl* (αφη) εχων: F) *L*' *S*'j | γυν.^{2} + αυτου‖Mt: *Rpl L*' {} *S*phj *Cs Geo*' — *txt*: ℌ⟨33-579⟩C WΘ-544-565-700 **λ**⟨118⟩ 1342 *al* [*L*k[e]} *C*b *Geo*^{B} | εξαν.] αναστ.‖Mt: Γ 998 **20** επ.—ησ.] ησ. ουν παρ ημιν επ. αδ.‖p: D 1093(*om* π. ημ.) *L*a(ουν] δε)bff^{2}iq(*om* ουν)r^{1} | επ. + ουν‖Lk: C^{2}-33 Σ-1071 σM-7-349-517-659-1082-1391 (D 1093) *al l*48 *l*49 *l*184 *l*251 *L*(bff^{2}ir^{1})clr^{2}z vg *Arm Geo*^{2} *Aeth* — + δε‖Mt: 892 *pc l*14 *La S*hj^{v} *C* | ησ. + παρ ημιν‖Mt: ℵ^{a} Θ-28-565-700 **ϕ** σ267 (D) *al L*(abff^{2}iqr^{1})cz30 vg^{4} *S*h^{m}j^{v} *C*b *Arm Geo*^{2} | ελα. … και] λαβων‖Lk Mt: σ179 *La* | αποθν.] απεθανεν και‖p: WΘ-28-565-700-1071 (αποθν. απεθ. και) **λ** D *pc L*k[e] aff^{2}ir^{1}(απεθ. μη αφεις σπ.: *L*') *C*s$^{6:9}$b^{1} **21** ελα. … και] λαβων‖Lk 29: σ179 | μη κατ.] ● και ουδε αυτος(ουτ.) αφηκεν‖20: *Rpl* (X Θ-28 σ692 *pc*) (αυ. + ουκ: D *l*36) *L*(al)g^{2}qr^{2}(*om* αυ.)z vg^{2}(') *S Cs*^{5} — *om* μη—σπ.: *L*k[e] — *txt*: ℌ⟨Δ⟩C 1071 1342 *pc L*c(και ου κατελιπεν: bff^{2}r^{1v} vg^{1}) *C*s^{4}b'(^{2} *prm* και αυ.) | τρι. + ελαβεν αυτην(+ και ουκ αφηκεν σπ.)‖Lk: 700 **λ**⟨118⟩ ϕ1689 (91 299) — ωσ. + ελ αυ.‖Lk: Θ-565(∼ ωσ. κ. ο τρ. ελ. αυ.) | ωσ.—^{22}σπ.] εως των επτα‖Mt: σ1675 **22** εσχ. + δε‖Mt: 33 ΘΣ-28-544-565-700-1604 **λ**⟨118⟩ **ϕ**⟨124⟩ σM-1194 G U *al L*bq *S*h *C*s$^{7:8}$b

Lk 20,27 επηρωτων(-ουν!)‖Mk: B-579 1071 (**ϕ**')-124 157 *La S*h **28** εχ.—η] μη εχ. τεκνα‖Mt: 1241 — μη εχ. τ. και καταλιπη γ.‖Mk: *S*sc | γυν.^{2} + αυτου‖Mt: 700 σ1194-1424 *Ld S*(∼ τ. γυ. … ο αδ.: sc)ph^{+} *C*⟨b^{6}⟩ **29** ουν] δε‖Mt: *Le* ff^{2} *Sp Cs* — *om*‖Mk: D *L*aiq *Ssc Geo* | ησ. + παρ ημιν‖Mt: ℵ^{a} σM-71-692 D(∼ ησ. π. ημ. επ. αδ.) *pc L*cff^{2}lqr^{2} vg^{1} *Ss Geo Aeth*(= D, *et* ησ. + ουν) **30** 30] και ελαβεν ο δευ. την γυναικα και ουτος απεθανεν ατεκνος‖Mk: *Rpl L*' *S C*b^{1} *Arm* [[*om* και^{1}: ϕ69 *Arm* | ∼ ο δευ. ελ.‖29 Mk: 579 Θ *l*184 *L*' | τ. γυ.] αυτην‖Mk: 255(∼ αυ. ο δ.) *L*' *Arm* | ουτ.] αυτος: 235 697 *L*'⟨e lq⟩ | ∼ ατ. απεθ.: 579 σ1675 U]] — *om* (^{29}∩^{30}ατεκ.?): 218 *pc L*ff^{2} — *txt*: ℵBL-892-1241 D **0266** 157 *pc Le*(*prm* ομοιως‖Mt) g^{2}(+ ελ. αυτην) *S*Cr *C*sb'(= g^{2}) *Geo Aeth*(= g^{2}) **31** *om* ελ. αυ.‖p: D *Le* a *C*b | αυ. + ωσαυτως‖Mk: *Rpl S*h — *txt*: ℌ⟨579⟩ 544-1071 **λ** **ϕ**⟨124-983⟩ σM-27-945-1207-1223-1424 D G P S U W Δ Ψ 157 *pm L*⟨c⟩ *S*' *C* | ωσ.—οι] εως των‖Mt: 1241 *Le C*b (ωσ. δε εως τ.) | *om* δε‖Mk: σ1223 D(*et om* και^{2}) Ψ *L*⟨a⟩ *C*s$^{1:11}$b^{3} | ου κατ.] ουκ αφηκαν‖Mk: D P*? | τεκ.] σπερμα‖Mk: 1071-1604 P* *pc L*fr^{2}z vg | *om* κ. απεθ.‖p: **λλ**⟨22⟩ *pc L*cff^{2}il *S*scp **32** υσ. + δε‖Mt: *Rpl* (+ ουν: σ1194) *L*vl'⟨e(*om* 32)⟩ vg^{2} *S*h^{+} *C*s^{9}b' — *om* υσ.: *L*aciz30 *Ssc Arm*' — *txt*: ℵ*B-579 Λ-700 **ϕ**⟨346⟩-174-230 σ1675 D E H S Δ Ω **047** *pm L*vg' (*S*p) *C*s^{1}b^{2} *Arm*^{pc} *Aeth* | υσ./δε + παντων‖p: *Rpl L*fqr^{2}z vg *S*h *C*s^{5} *Geo*(πα.] αυτων) *Arm*^{pc} *Aeth* — *txt*: ℵBL-579-892 **λ**-1582 σM-1194 D E H S U V Y 157 *al L*vl'r^{1} (*S*p) *C*s^{5}b *Arm*'

ἀπέθανεν ἡ γυνή.
[28] ἐν τῇ ἀναστάσει οὖν
τίνος τῶν ἑπτὰ ἔσται γυνή; πάντες
γὰρ ἔσχον αὐτήν. [29] ἀποκριθεὶς δὲ ὁ Ἰησοῦς εἶπεν αὐτοῖς·
πλανᾶσθε μὴ εἰδότες τὰς γραφὰς μηδὲ
τὴν δύναμιν τοῦ θεοῦ.
[30] ἐν γὰρ τῇ ἀναστάσει
οὔτε γαμοῦσιν οὔτε
γαμίζονται, ἀλλ'
ὡς ἄγγελοι
θεοῦ ἐν τῷ οὐρανῷ εἰσιν.
[31] περὶ δὲ τῆς ἀναστάσεως τῶν νεκρῶν
οὐκ ἀνέγνωτε τὸ
ῥηθὲν ὑμῖν

καὶ ἡ γυνὴ ἀπέθανεν.
[23] ἐν τῇ ἀναστάσει, ὅταν ἀναστῶσιν,
τίνος αὐτῶν ἔσται γυνή; οἱ
γὰρ ἑπτὰ ἔσχον αὐτὴν γυναῖκα.
[24] ἔφη αὐτοῖς ὁ Ἰησοῦς· οὐ διὰ τοῦτο
πλανᾶσθε μὴ εἰδότες τὰς γραφὰς μηδὲ
τὴν δύναμιν τοῦ θεοῦ;
[25] ὅταν γὰρ ἐκ νεκρῶν ἀναστῶσιν,
οὔτε γαμοῦσιν οὔτε
γαμίζονται, ἀλλ'
εἰσὶν ὡς ἄγγελοι
ἐν τοῖς οὐρανοῖς.
[26] περὶ δὲ τῶν νεκρῶν
ὅτι ἐγείρονται, οὐκ ἀνέγνωτε ἐν τῇ
βίβλῳ Μωυσέως ἐπὶ τοῦ βάτου

καὶ ἡ γυνὴ ἀπέθανεν. [33] ἡ γυνὴ
οὖν ἐν τῇ ἀναστάσει
τίνος αὐτῶν γίνεται γυνή; οἱ
γὰρ ἑπτὰ ἔσχον αὐτὴν γυναῖκα. [34] καὶ
εἶπεν αὐτοῖς ὁ Ἰησοῦς· οἱ υἱοὶ τοῦ
αἰῶνος τούτου γαμοῦσιν καὶ γαμίσκονται, [35] οἱ δὲ καταξιωθέντες τοῦ αἰῶνος
ἐκείνου τυχεῖν καὶ τῆς ἀναστάσεως
τῆς ἐκ νεκρῶν οὔτε γαμοῦσιν οὔτε
γαμίζονται· [36] οὐδὲ γὰρ ἀποθανεῖν ἔτι
δύνανται, ἰσάγγελοι γάρ εἰσιν, καὶ υἱοί
εἰσιν θεοῦ τῆς ἀναστάσεως υἱοὶ ὄντες.
[37] ὅτι δὲ
ἐγείρονται οἱ νεκροί,
καὶ Μωυσῆς ἐμήνυσεν ἐπὶ τῆς βάτου,

Mt 22,27 η] και η ‖ Mk Lk: *Rpl L*'Ar *S*'j Cs^{3}b' *Geo*^{2} — *txt*: ℵBL **λ**-22-1582 σ71 U W Y Δ Π *Le*[k] *S*sc *Cs*^{3}b^{2} *Geo*^{1} **28** ουν + οταν αναστωσιν ‖ Mk: Σ | παν. γαρ] οι γαρ επτα ‖ p: σ267 *Le*[k] b Ar *Sc* | αυτ. + γυναικα ‖ p: 33 28 σM^{m} G *pc L*Ar *S*hAf Ef *Arm* **30** γαμισκονται(εγγα-) ‖ Lk34: 33 700 φ(69)-*l*547 σ267 W Θ 157 *pc* Chr Ep^{1}(^{2}) Meth Or | ∼ εισ. ως—ουρ. ‖ Mk: **λ**-1582 **σ**-349 Ath(*om* εν τ. ουρ.) PsAth(εισ.] εσονται *et* = Ath) Chr(*om* τω) Or *L* {*C*} *Arm* — ∼ εισ. θε.—ουρ. ‖ Lk: φ983-1689 — ∼ εισ. εν τ. ουρ. ‖ Lk: **φ**'-*l*547 *pc* Cr *Sc*(εν τ. ουρ.] του ουρανου)j *Geo*(εσονται) | θε.] του θε. ‖ Lk12 8f. 15 10 Jo15 1: *Rpl l*12 *l*76 *l*80 *l*184 *l*185^{1} *l*299 *l*303 *l*950^{1} *l*997 *l*1127 Or {} — ● *om* (*et* οι αγγ.) ‖ Mk: B 700 (**λ**-22) D (Θ) **0197** Ath PsAth Co^{1} Ep Meth (Or) *Le*[k] abcfff^{2}hqr^{1} vg^{2} Am *Sc Cs Arm* — *txt*: 𝔊' Σ-28-1071-1604 **φ**-*l*547 σ7-954-1424-1606 157 *pc l*^{pl} Chr Co^{2} Ep {*L*' *S*'j *C*b}

Mk 12,22 ∼ απεθ. και η γυ. ‖ Mt: *Rpl L*lg^{2}qr^{2}z30 vg^{10}('*om* και) *S* — *txt* (*om* και): 𝔊'(579)C (W)Θ-28-565-1071 **λ**⟨118⟩ **φ**⟨124⟩ D 1342 *pc l*184 *L*vl'⟨k[e](*om* εσχ.—απεθ.)⟩ *S*j^{v} **23** αναστασει] αν. ουν ‖ p: 892 WΘΣ-28-565-700-1071 **λ** D G *pc* {*L*⟨k[e] cq⟩ *S*'houv^{+} *Cs*$^{6:8}$b^{2}} — ουν αν. ‖ p: C^{c}-33-579 544 φ124 σM-7-71-115-659-945-954-1082-1223-1391-1424 A K Π *mu l*^{pl} {} | ● *om* οτ. αν. ‖ Mt Lk: 𝔊C W-544 D 1342 *pc l*13 *l*18 *l*76 *l*211 *L*k[e] cr^{1} *S*p *C*' — *txt*: *Rpl L*' *S*'j *C*b^{1}(εν εκειναις ταις ημεραις οτ. αν.) *Arm* | αυτων] των επτα ‖ Mt: **λ**⟨118⟩ *pc* | εστ.] γινεται ‖ Lk: Θ 1342 | οι γ. επ.] παντες γ. ‖ Mt: **λ**⟨118⟩ *pc* *L*(k[e]) r^{1} | *om* γυναικα ‖ Mt: 106 1574 (*L*k[e] c) *S*s[c]p **24** εφη—Ι.] αποκριθεις δε(*om*) ο Ι. ειπεν αυ. ‖ Mt: WΘ-28-565-700 **λ**⟨118⟩ **φ** 299 D *La* (*S*s[c]) *Cs*^{5} (*Geo*) — και αποκ. ο Ι. ειπ.(λεγει) αυ. ‖ Mt: *Rpl* *L*'(blqr^{2}z30)r^{1}(*om* αυ.) *S*hj^{v} — *txt*: 𝔊C 1342 *pc Sp Cs*^{5}(εφη δε αυ. ο Ι.)b | *om* ου ‖ Mt: Δ 495 1342 *L*k[e] ir^{1} *S*s[c] *Cs*$^{2:10}$ *Geo*^{2} — *om* ου δ. τουτο ‖ Mt: 544 *Lc* **25** γαμισκονται(εκγα-) ‖ Lk34: *Rpl* (σ827 A F H *al*) Cl Or — *txt* (-ζουσιν): ℵBCLΔΨ-892 Θ-(565)-1071 **λ**⟨118⟩ φ124 σ7-517-659-1391-1675 (D) G U 1342 *pc l*49 — εκγαμιζ.: 544 *pc* | ως] εισ (= ισαγγ.) ‖ Lk: Δ | αγγ. + θεου(του θε.) ‖ Mt: (33) 544-1071 **φ**⟨124-788⟩ *pc l*260 *L*l *C*b^{1} | τοις ου.] ουρανω(τω ου.) ‖ Mt: 544 1342 *pc* (*pc l*260) *L*g^{2}ilr^{1} vg^{2} (*Cs*$^{1:10}$) **26** δε + της αναστασεως ‖ Mt: 33 **φ** *Arm* | του] της ‖ Lk: Ψ-33-597 WΘΣ-565-700 φ124-983 σM-71-115-1194-1391-1606-1675 D 175(τη βατω) 1342 *al* Or

Lk 20,32 ∼ απεθ. και η γ. ‖ Mt: *Rpl L S*scp(και απεθ. υσ. κ. η γ.)h *Cs*^{1}(^{9} *om* και)b *Geo* — *txt*: 𝔊⟨892⟩ 1071 λ1-131-1582-2193 σ267-659-1391-1402-1606 D 157 *pc* **33** η—αναστ.] εν τη ουν αν. ‖ p: *Rpl* {*L*' *S*ph^{t} *Cs*^{7}b *Aeth*} — εν τη αν. ουν ‖ p: **λλ**⟨22-1278⟩ *l*49 {} — εν τη αν. (+ δε) ‖ Mk Mt: ℵ* 157 *Le* a(c)ff^{2}il *S*sc (*Cs*^{3}) — *txt*: 𝔊'⟨33⟩ *S*h^{m} | αυτων] των επτα ‖ Mt: 245 | γιν.] εσται ‖ p: ℵL-33-892 1071 **λλ**⟨1278⟩ **σ**⟨954⟩-71-692 D G Θ Ψ 157 *pc L* | οι γ. επ.] παντες γ. ‖ Mt: 1241 *Ll* vg^{1} *Cs*$^{1:10}$(+ οι επ.) | *om* γυναικα ‖ Mt: **047** *L*vg^{1} *S*cp **34** ειπ.] αποκριθεις ειπ. ‖ Mt: *Rpl* (∼ ο Ι. ειπ.: 33 λ1278 φ983-1689 *pc*) Bas(αποκ. ο Ι. ει. αυ.) *Lq S*sh *Arm* — *txt* (+ δε): 𝔊' φ124 D 157 *L*' *S*cp *Cs*^{10}(^{1})b | γαμισκ.] εκγα-: *Rpl* (εγγα-: φ983-1689 *pc*; εισγα-: 713) Bas — *txt*: 𝔊 1071 **λλ**⟨22-1278⟩ **φ**'⟨124⟩ D F 157 *l*13 *l*14 *l*15 *l*17 *l*184 *al* | -ισκονται] -ιζονται ‖ p35: 1071-1604 **λλ**⟨22⟩ **φ**⟨124⟩-1689 σM-7-115-267-692-1207-1223 A K P U W Γ Δ Θ Π **047** *al l*18 *l*49 Bas — *txt*: *Rpl* (γαμουνται: D) Eu **35** της εκ] των ‖ Mt31: φ1689 σ267-659 W* *pc Lc* Eu | γαμιζ.] εκγα-: *Rpl* Bas — *txt*: 𝔊 **λλ**⟨22-1278⟩ φ124 σ267 D Q R Γ Δ Ψ 157 *al l*49 *l*184 Cl Ep | -ιζονται] -ισκονται ‖ 34: B-1241 700 λ1278 φ124 σ71-659-1424 Ψ Ω *al l*184 Cl^{1} Ep^{1} — *txt*: *Rpl* Bas Cl^{1} Ep^{1} **36** ισαγγ. γαρ] αλλ ως αγγ. ‖ p: 157 *L*PsCp — ως αγγ. γ. ‖ p: 579 σ1675 | *om* κ. υι. εισ. ‖ p: D(θε.] τω θεω) 157 1573 Iu$^{1:2}$ *L*vl⟨fqr^{2}z⟩ vg^{1} Cp$^{1:3}$ PsCp Mcn^{Te} *S*s(*om* θε.)

Matth 22	Mark 12	Luk 20
Ex36 ὑπὸ τοῦ θεοῦ λέγοντος· 32 **ἐγώ εἰμι ὁ θεὸς Αβρααμ καὶ ὁ θεὸς Ισαακ καὶ ὁ θεὸς Ιακωβ;**	πῶς εἶπεν αὐτῷ ὁ θεὸς λέγων· **ἐγὼ ὁ θεὸς Αβρααμ καὶ ὁ θεὸς Ισαακ καὶ ὁ θεὸς Ιακωβ;**	ὡς λέγει κύριον **τὸν θεὸν Αβρααμ καὶ θεὸν Ισαακ καὶ θεὸν Ιακωβ·** 38 θεὸς δὲ
οὐκ ἔστιν ὁ θεὸς θεὸς νεκρῶν ἀλλὰ ζώντων.	27 οὐκ ἔστιν θεὸς νεκρῶν ἀλλὰ ζώντων. πολὺ πλανᾶσθε.	οὐκ ἔστιν νεκρῶν ἀλλὰ ζώντων· πάντες γὰρ αὐτῷ ζῶσιν.
33 καὶ ἀκούσαντες οἱ ὄχλοι ἐξεπλήσσοντο ἐπὶ τῇ διδαχῇ αὐτοῦ. *22 46 (223.): … οὐδὲ ἐτόλμησέν τις ἀπ' ἐκείνης τῆς ἡμέρας ἐπερωτῆσαι αὐτὸν οὐκέτι.*	**214.** *cf. 222.* *12 34 (222.): … καὶ οὐδεὶς οὐκέτι ἐτόλμα αὐτὸν ἐπερωτῆσαι.*	39 ἀποκριθέντες δέ τινες τῶν γραμματέων εἶπαν· διδάσκαλε, καλῶς εἶπας. 40 οὐκέτι γὰρ ἐτόλμων ἐπερωτᾶν αὐτὸν οὐδέν.

(208)

222. Die Frage nach dem großen Gebot. *The Great Commandment.*

Matth 22 34–40	Mark 12 28–34	*10 25–28 (157.)*
34 Οἱ δὲ Φαρισαῖοι ἀκούσαντες ὅτι ἐφίμωσεν τοὺς Σαδδουκαίους, συνήχθησαν ἐπὶ τὸ αὐτό,	28 Καὶ προσελθὼν εἷς τῶν γραμματέων, ἀκούσας αὐτῶν συζητούντων, εἰδὼς ὅτι καλῶς ἀπεκρίθη αὐτοῖς,	*25 Καὶ ἰδοὺ*
35 καὶ ἐπηρώτησεν εἷς ἐξ αὐτῶν νομικὸς πειράζων αὐτόν·	ἐπηρώτησεν αὐτόν·	*νομικός τις ἀνέστη ἐκπειράζων αὐτὸν λέγων·*
36 διδάσκαλε, ποία ἐντολὴ μεγάλη ἐν τῷ νόμῳ; 37 ὁ δὲ ἔφη αὐτῷ·	ποία ἐστὶν ἐντολὴ πρώτη πάντων; 29 ἀπεκρίθη ὁ Ἰησοῦς ὅτι πρώ-	*διδάσκαλε, τί ποιήσας ζωὴν αἰώνιον κληρονομήσω; 26 ὁ δὲ εἶπεν πρὸς αὐτόν·*

Mt 22,32 εστ. + δε ‖ Lk: ϕ-*l*547 Θ | ο θε.^{4} θε.^{5}] ● ο θε. ‖ p: BL-33 λ-1582 σ1194 Δ 157 *pc l*184 {*L*Cp Hil *S*'j *C* *Geo*^{2}} — ● θε. ‖ Mk: ℵ 28 D W *pc* Chr Eu Ir Or {} — *txt* (*om* ο): *Rpl* (544 H *pc l*1127) Chr Or *L*vg^{1} *S*h *Arm Geo*^{1} **35** επη. + αυτον(τον Ιησουν) ‖ Mk: (ϕ174) (∼: 348) *L*⟨e[k] g^{1}⟩ Hil *S*cph^{Brs}j *C* | νομ.] + τις (*et om* εις) ‖ Lk: F G H *pc* (*l*^{P1}) — ● *om*: λ-1582 Or *L*e[k] Or *S*s *Arm* | αυτον + και λεγων ‖ 19 3 Lk: *Rpl L*bcfff^{2}hqr^{2}30 vg^{1}(^{1}) *S*'j *C*s^{2} *Arm* — *txt*: 𝕳 372 *L*'Or *S*p *C*s^{3}b **36** διδ.] *om* ‖ Mk: 474 *C*s$^{1:5}$ — + αγαθε ‖ Mk10 17 Lk18 18: σ1424 | μεγ.] πρωτη ‖ Mk: 1093 — μεγ. και πρ. ‖ 38: *L*30(∼ πρ. εντ. και μεγ.) vg^{1} *S*c **37** δε + Ιησους ‖ Mk: *Rpl L*q vg *S*'j(κυριος Ι.) *C*b^{1} — ο—αυ.] εφη αυ. Ι.: D *L*vl'[k] r^{2}(*prm* και) *S*sc *Geo*^{2} *Aeth* — *txt*: 𝕳 1093 1355 *L*Or *C*' *Geo*^{1} | εφη] ειπεν ‖ Lk: 700 ϕ-*l*547^{1} W Θ

Mk 12,26 πως] ως ‖ Lk: *Rpl* Or — *txt*: ℵBCLΔΨ-892 σ7-115-659-954-1082-131-11675 U 1342 *al* | εγω + ειμι ‖ Mt Ex36: Δ-28-1071 σM-115-827 U 1342 *pc l*184 *L*'(θε.^{1}∩^{2}: b) | *om* ο$^{2.3.4}$ ‖ Ex36: W D Or — ● *om* ο$^{3.4}$ ‖ ←: B — *om* ο^{2}: 579 ϕ983-1689 157 482 — *txt*: 𝔓^{45v} *Rpl* **27** ● εστ. + ο ‖ Mt: *Rpl* Or — *txt*: BLXD-579-892 WΦ-28-1071 λ872 σM^{m}-115-692-1207-1606 D K Y Π *al* | θε. + θε. ‖ Mt: 33 Θ-544 λ2193 ϕ 1342 *al S*s[c]j | ● αλλα + θεος: *Rpl L*q vg^{1} *S*h *Aeth* — *txt*: 𝕳CX WΘΣ-28-565-700-1071 λ ϕ σM^{m}-517-692 A D F K U Π 157 1342 *mu l*49 Or *L*' *S*' *C* | ● ζω. + υμεις ουν(δε): *Rpl* (565-700 λ G *pc*) *L*'(cff^{2}r^{2} *S*s[c])ph *Geo*^{1}(^{2} *Aeth*) — *txt*: ℵBCLΔΨ-892 W *pc Lk*[e] *C* | *om* πολ. πλα. ‖ p: 1093 **28** αυτον + λεγων διδασκαλε(*om*) ‖ p: D (235 1396) *Lk*[e] bcff^{2}g^{2}i30(*om* λεγ.) vg^{1}(^{1}) *C*s$^{1:9}$ | ∼ εντ. εστ. ‖ Mt: 700 σ349-517-659(∼ εν. πρω. εστ.) — *om* εστ. ‖ Mt: 1346 | *om* παν. ‖ Mt36.38: WΘ-28-565-700 λ⟨118⟩ ϕ⟨124⟩ D *pc L*vl'[e]⟨lz⟩g^{2}r^{1} *S*s[c] *C*s$^{4:9}$b^{1} *Arm* **29** απεκ. ο Ι.] ο δε Ι. απεκ. αυτω ‖ p: *Rpl L*'(*om* δε: vg^{1}) Au *S*hj(κυριος Ι.) *C*s^{1}(∼ απ. δε ο Ι.) — ο δε Ι.(*om*) ειπεν αυτω ‖ Lk Mt: (W)Θ (λ⟨118⟩) ϕ⟨124⟩ (19) *pc l*184 *Lk*[e] (a) *Arm* — ειπ. αυ. ο Ι. ‖ p: *S*p — αποκριθεις δε ο Ι. ειπ. αυ. ‖ p: 700(∼ ο δε Ι. απ.) D 1573(= 700) *L*bc(απεκ. … λεγων) ff^{2}iqr^{1v} *C*s^{1}(∼ αυ. ο Ι. ειπ.) — + και ειπ. ‖ Lk: 579 *S*s[c] — + λεγων: *C*s^{6} — *txt*: 𝕳'(*om* ο: Ψ) 1342 *C*b | *om* οτι ‖ Mt Lk: WΘ-28-565-700 λ⟨118⟩ ϕ788 D *pc L*vl[e]⟨lr^{2}z⟩ *S*s[c]pj | *om* πρ. εστ. ‖ Mt: 229 *Lk*[e] *C*s$^{2:8}$

Lk 20,37 *om* κυ. ‖ p: 213 Ep$^{1:2}$ *L*al | θε.$^{2.3}$] τον θε.$^{2.3}$ ‖ p: *Rpl* (*om* θε.^{2}: ϕ69 σ1675) — *txt*: 𝕳⟨1241⟩ 1071 D R *pc* Ep^{1}(^{1} *om*) Or **38** θε.—εστ.] ουκ εστ. ο θε. ‖ Mk Mt: Or *L*a Cp$^{1:2}$ | *om* δε ‖ p: D(∼ νεκ. ουκ εστ.) σ1223 157 *C*s$^{5:11}$b$^{\langle 7\rangle}$ **40** ∼ αυ. επερ. ‖ Mk: 477 1574 *l*184 *L*⟨e ar$^{1.2}$⟩ | επερωτησαι ‖ Mt Mk: 579(ερω-)-892 λλ⟨22-1278⟩ σ267-659-945-1675 477 1574

---

222. cf. Did12 (*cf. ad 38.*)

Matth	Mark	Luk	
ἀγαπήσεις κύριον τὸν θεόν σου ἐν ὅλῃ τῇ καρδίᾳ σου καὶ ἐν ὅλῃ τῇ ψυχῇ σου καὶ ἐν ὅλῃ τῇ διανοίᾳ σου. 38 αὕτη ἐστὶν ἡ μεγάλη καὶ πρώτη ἐντολή. 39 δευτέρα δὲ ὁμοία αὐτῇ· ἀγαπήσεις τὸν πλησίον σου ὡς σεαυτόν. 40 ἐν ταύταις ταῖς δυσὶν ἐντολαῖς ὅλος ὁ νόμος κρέμαται καὶ οἱ προφῆται.	τη ἐστίν· ἄκουε, Ισραηλ, κύριος ὁ θεὸς ἡμῶν κύριος εἷς ἐστιν, 30 καὶ ἀγαπήσεις κύριον τὸν θεόν σου ἐξ ὅλης τῆς καρδίας σου καὶ ἐξ ὅλης τῆς ψυχῆς σου καὶ ἐξ ὅλης τῆς διανοίας σου καὶ ἐξ ὅλης τῆς ἰσχύος σου. 31 δευτέρα αὕτη· ἀγαπήσεις τὸν πλησίον σου ὡς σεαυτόν. μείζων τούτων ἄλλη ἐντολὴ οὐκ ἔστιν. 32 καὶ εἶπεν αὐτῷ ὁ γραμματεύς· καλῶς, διδάσκαλε,	ἐν τῷ νόμῳ τί γέγραπται; πῶς ἀναγινώσκεις; 27 ὁ δὲ ἀποκριθεὶς εἶπεν· ἀγαπήσεις κύριον τὸν θεόν σου ἐξ ὅλης τῆς καρδίας σου καὶ ἐν ὅλῃ τῇ ψυχῇ σου καὶ ἐν ὅλῃ τῇ ἰσχύϊ σου καὶ ἐν ὅλῃ τῇ διανοίᾳ σου, *cf. 203.* καὶ τὸν πλησίον σου ὡς σεαυτόν. 28 εἶπεν δὲ αὐτῷ· ὀρθῶς ἀπεκρίθης· τοῦτο ποίει καὶ ζήσῃ. *cf. 221.*	Dt6 4 4 35 Dt6 5 Lv19 18
7 12 (51.): ... οὗτος γάρ ἐστιν ὁ νόμος καὶ οἱ προφῆται.			

ἐπ' ἀληθείας εἶπας ὅτι εἷς ἐστιν καὶ οὐκ ἔστιν ἄλλος πλὴν αὐτοῦ· 33 καὶ τὸ ἀγαπᾶν αὐτὸν ἐξ ὅλης τῆς καρδίας καὶ ἐξ ὅλης τῆς συνέσεως καὶ ἐξ ὅλης τῆς ἰσχύος, καὶ τὸ ἀγαπᾶν τὸν πλησίον ὡς ἑαυτὸν περισσότερόν ἐστιν πάντων τῶν ὁλοκαυτωμάτων καὶ θυσιῶν. 34 καὶ ὁ Ἰησοῦς, ἰδὼν αὐτὸν ὅτι νουνεχῶς ἀπεκρίθη, εἶπεν αὐτῷ· οὐ μακρὰν εἶ ἀπὸ τῆς βασιλείας τοῦ θεοῦ. καὶ οὐδεὶς οὐκέτι ἐτόλμα αὐτὸν ἐπερωτῆσαι. (Dt6 4 4 35 6 5; Lv19 18) *221.*

(209)

223. Der Davidssohn. *About David's Son.*

Matth 22 41–46	Mark 12 35–37a	Luk 20 41–44
41 Συνηγμένων δὲ τῶν Φαρισαίων ἐπηρώτησεν αὐτοὺς ὁ Ἰησοῦς 42 λέ-	35 Καὶ ἀποκριθεὶς ὁ Ἰησοῦς ἔλεγεν διδάσκων ἐν τῷ ἱερῷ·	41 Εἶπεν δὲ πρὸς αὐτούς·
		7 42: οὐχὶ ἡ γραφὴ εἶπεν ὅτι

Mt 22,37 σου³ + και εν ολη τη ισχυι σου‖Lk: 33(*om* και¹—ψ. σου) ΟΣ φ-*l*547¹ Θ 0107 *L*e[k](ισ.] δικαιοσυνη) c(*om* και³—διαν. σου)30(et in totis viribus tuis) Cp(= c) *S*(= *L*c: sc)pj[ab1c1](∼ ισ. ... ψ.: j[b1c1]) *C*b⁴ | σου⁴ + και εν ο. τη ισ. σου (*cf. ad* σου³)‖Mk: σ1391 **39** δευ. δε] ● δευ.‖Mk: ℵ*B 157 *pc* *L*Or *C*s[1:6]b'{²} — και δευ.‖Lk: *L*Cp *S*scpj

Mk 12,30 ∼ ισ. ... διαν.‖Lk: σ267-1606 *S*p¹ *Geo*¹ | σου⁵ + αυτη(+ εστιν η) πρωτη εντολη‖Mt: *Rpl* (1071 *pc*) *l*183(πρ. + μεγαλη) (*L*')i (Au) Hil *S*,j — + αυτη πρω. παντων εντ.‖28 Mt: 33-579 Φ λ872 σ517(∼ εντ. πα.) K U Π *mu* — + αυτη πρωτη‖←: WΘ-28-565 Marcl[Eu] *L*k[e] Cp — *txt*: ℵBL ΔΨ E 1342 *L*a *C* **31** δευ.] δευ. δε‖Mt: 33-579-892 Θ-544-565-700 σ827-954 D *pc* *l*15 *l*17 *l*183 *L*ff²ilr[1.2]z vg Au *C*sb⁴ — και δευ.: *Rpl* (κ. δευ. δε: Γ *pc*) Marcl[Eu] *L*k[e](deinde secunda) cq Cp *S*,j — *txt*: ℵBLΔΨ σ1675 1342 *pc* *L*b Hil *C*b' | αυτη] ομοια αυτη(ταυ.)‖Mt: *Rpl* (φ69-346-788-828-983 D) (ομοιως: W; αυτης: 1071 σ517-1424 A*ᵛ 1515) (Marcl[Eu]) *L*'(k[e] cff²iqr²z30)(*om* δευ.—αγα.‖Lk: a) (Au) Cp Hil *S*,j — *txt*: ℌ'(+ εστιν: ℵ 1342) *C* | τουτ. + των εντολων‖Mt: σ7-659-1391 *L*cdff² **32** ∼ διδ. επ αλ. κα.‖Lk20 39: D *L*Hil *Aeth* — διδ. κα. επ αλ.‖←: *S*s[c] — *om* επ αλ.‖Lk: 892 *L*a **33** συνε. + και εξ ολης της ψυχης (∼ ψ. ... συνε. ... ισ.)‖30p: *Rpl* (*et* + σου: φ346) (σ349-517) *L*(³²αλλ.—³³πλη.] εντολη: k[e]) lz vg Au(συνε.] διανοιας: *S*ph) *C*s¹(b⁴ *Aeth*) — συνε.] ισ. *et* ισ.] ψ. (+ αυτου)‖←: *L*b(i) Hil *S*s[c](∼ ψ. ... ισ.) — συνε.] δυναμεως (*et* ισ.] ψ.‖←): Θ-565 (D, *et* ψ. + αυτου) *L*(acff²)qr[1v] (∼ ψ. ... δυν.: cff²; ισ. + κ. εξ ολ. τ. ψ. αυτου: qr[1v]) — *om* και¹—συνε. *et* ισ. + κ. εξ ολ. τ. διανοιας κ. εξ ολ. τ. ψ.‖←: 33 — *txt* (∼ ισ. ... συνε.): ℌ'(*om* και²—συνε.‖←: 579) W-28 (λ) σ179 (= 579) 1342 *L*g²(*om* εξ¹—καρδ. και) *C*s⁹b²(')(*om* και³—ισ.: s¹b¹) (*Arm*) | θυσ.] ● των θ.: ℌ⟨B-1241⟩ 544-565-1071 λ φ⟨124-788⟩ σM-71-115-349-1391-1402-1606 1342 *mu* **34** ∼ επερ. αυ.‖Mt22 46 Lk20 40: ℵ*-579 σ349-517-827-1606 *L*cz vg¹ | επερωταν‖Lk20 40: WΘ-700 φ⟨124⟩ 1542 — *prm* τι‖←: 28

Mt22 39p *cf.* ETh[II] 25 (*transl.*): *Λέγει Ἰησοῦς· ἀγαπήσεις τὸν ἀδελφόν σου ὡς τὴν ψυχήν σου· τηρήσεις αὐτὸν ὡς τὴν κόρην τοῦ ὀφθαλμοῦ σου.*

cf. Brn19 5: ἀγαπήσεις τὸν πλησίον σου ὑπὲρ τὴν ψυχήν σου.

Mk12 34 *cf.* ETh[II] 82 (*transl.*): *Λέγει Ἰησοῦς· ὅστις ἐγγύς ἐστιν ἐμοῦ, ἐγγύς ἐστιν τοῦ πυρός· καὶ ὅστις μακράν ἐστιν ἀπ' ἐμοῦ, μακράν ἐστιν ἀπὸ τῆς βασιλείας.*

223. cf. EAr 50 (*cf. ad 12.*)

2Sm7 12 Mch5 1 Ps89 4f.

γων· τί ὑμῖν δοκεῖ περὶ τοῦ Χριστοῦ; τίνος υἱός ἐστιν; λέγουσιν αὐτῷ· τοῦ Δαυιδ. [43] λέγει αὐτοῖς· πῶς οὖν Δαυιδ ἐν πνεύματι καλεῖ αὐτὸν κύριον λέγων· [44] **εἶπεν ὁ κύριος τῷ κυρίῳ μου· κάθου ἐκ δεξιῶν μου ἕως ἂν θῶ τοὺς ἐχθρούς σου ὑποκάτω τῶν ποδῶν σου;** [45] εἰ οὖν Δαυιδ καλεῖ αὐτὸν κύριον, πῶς υἱὸς αὐτοῦ ἐστιν; [46] καὶ οὐδεὶς ἐδύνατο ἀποκριθῆναι αὐτῷ λόγον, οὐδὲ ἐτόλμησέν τις ἀπ' ἐκείνης τῆς ἡμέρας ἐπερωτῆσαι αὐτὸν οὐκέτι.

Ps110 1

πῶς λέγουσιν οἱ γραμματεῖς ὅτι ὁ Χριστὸς υἱὸς Δαυιδ ἐστιν; [36] αὐτὸς Δαυιδ εἶπεν ἐν τῷ πνεύματι τῷ ἁγίῳ· **εἶπεν ὁ κύριος τῷ κυρίῳ μου· κάθου ἐκ δεξιῶν μου ἕως ἂν θῶ τοὺς ἐχθρούς σου ὑποκάτω τῶν ποδῶν σου.** [37 a] αὐτὸς Δαυιδ λέγει αὐτὸν κύριον, καὶ πόθεν αὐτοῦ ἐστιν υἱός; **221.**

πῶς λέγουσιν τὸν Χριστὸν υἱὸν Δαυιδ εἶναι; [42] αὐτὸς γὰρ Δαυιδ λέγει ἐν βίβλῳ ψαλμῶν· **εἶπεν ὁ κύριος τῷ κυρίῳ μου· κάθου ἐκ δεξιῶν μου** [43] **ἕως ἂν θῶ τοὺς ἐχθρούς σου ὑποπόδιον τῶν ποδῶν σου.** [44] Δαυιδ οὖν αὐτὸν κύριον καλεῖ, καὶ πῶς αὐτοῦ υἱός ἐστιν;

ἐκ **τοῦ σπέρματος Δαυιδ**, καὶ **ἀπὸ Βηθλεεμ** τῆς κώμης ὅπου ἦν Δαυιδ, ὁ Χριστὸς **ἔρχεται**;

Mt 22,43 πν. + αγιω‖Mk: 61 1579 Ddy *Sc Geo*^A *Aeth* | ● ~ κυ. αυ. καλ.: *Rpl* (κυ. καλ. αυ.: ϕ69 σ954) Ad Ddy Eu *Le*[k] q Or *S*h(= 69) *Geo*'(*om* αυ.) — ● ~ καλ. κυ. αυ.: ℵLZ-892 — *txt*: B-33 D Θ 1093 Cr Ddy *L*' *Ss*^v cp *Geo*^2 *Arab*EAr↓ **44** ● *om* ο *cf.* LXX Ps2 7 Is29 13 54 1 56 8 *etc.*: ℵBZ D | υποποδιον‖Lk Ps109 1 LXX: *Rpl L*'Au^1 Hil Or *S*hj *Arm Aeth* — *txt*: 𝔥⟨33⟩ λ22 ϕ⟨13-983⟩-*l*547^1 D G U Γ Θ **047** *pc Le*[k] bhqr^1 Au^5 *S*' *C* **45** Δ.(αυτον) + εν πνευματι‖43 Mk36: 565 ϕ σM-7-71-659-954-(1010-1293)-1424 D K Y Δ Θ Π (238) *mu* Ad Ddy^1(^1 πν. + αγιω) Eu Gr^Ny Thd^C *L*(ab)cfff^2hlr^1.2 Cp Hil *S*h^+j *C*b^6(^1) | ~ αυ. κυ. καλ.‖Lk: *Lz* vg^1 *Arm* — ~ αυ. καλ. κυ.‖Lk: *Lab* — ~ κυ. καλ. αυ.‖Lk: 251 {*S*sc} *Geo* — κυ. αυ. λεγει(καλ.)‖Mk: (ϕ1689 σ1606 660) 1012 Ad Ddy^1(^1λε.] ειπεν) Ep *L*Or {}

Mk 12,35 ● ~ εστ. Δ.: *Rpl* Brn *L*'Hil *Geo*^A — *txt*: 𝔥 Θ-544-565-1071 **λ** ϕ⟨124⟩ σM^c-7-115-517-659-1082-1391 D U **092**b *al l*48 *l*49 *l*1353 *Lk*[e] (~ εστ. υι. Δ.: br^2) *C Arm Geo*^B | Δ.] του Δ.‖Mt: Σ λ22 σ179-1194 1342 *al* **36** αυτ.] αυτ. γαρ(δε)‖Lk: *Rpl L*'(cff^2z vg^1) *S*'j (*Cs*^2:11b^1) *Geo*^1 — και αυτ.(ουτ.): 579 (D) *Ld Ss*[c] (*Arm*) — *txt*: ℵBLΔΨ W-28-565 ϕ⟨124-346⟩ 1342 *pc l*1353 *Lk*[e] a *Cs*^8:11b' *Geo*^2 | ~ εν—αγ. ειπ./λεγ.‖Mt: X σ1402 *Labiq Arm* | ειπ.^1] λεγει‖37 Lk: (X) 544 σ115-267-(1402)-1606 **092**b *L*'⟨d(*om*)q vg^1⟩ *Cs*^8:9b^1 (*Arm*) *Geo*^2 | *om* τω^1.2‖Mt: *Rpl* — *txt* (*om* εν): 𝔥'(B) ΘΦ (*om* τω^2)-565 σ7-115-349-692 D U (1342) *pc l*1353(*om* τω^1) | ● *om* ο *cf. ad* Mt: BΨ-579 D 472 | ● υποποδιον‖Lk Ps109 1 LXX: *Rpl L*,Hil *S*'j — *txt*: B W-28 D' 1542 *l*1353 *Ss*[c] *C Geo* **37** αυτος] αυ. ουν‖p: *Rpl L*' *S*phουν^+ *C*b^1 — ει ουν‖Mt: Σ *L*bc(*om* ουν)ff^2(ουν] αυ.) *S*(*prm* και: s[c])j *Arm* (+ αυ.) — *txt*: ℵBLΔΨ WΘ-28-565 λ1278 D 1342 *pc l*1353 *Lk*[e] aiqr^1 Hil *Cs*^9(+ δε: s^1b')^8 *Geo* | Δ. + εν πνευματι‖36 Mt43: Ψ | λεγ.] καλει‖p: Ψ-33-579 Φ-565 σM^c-349-517 U *al l*34 *l*48 *Lc* vg^1 *Ss*[c]pj *C*b^3 | ποθ.] πως‖p: ℵ*Ψ-33-579 WΘΣ-28-565-1071 **λ** ϕ⟨124⟩ σM-115 *pc l*13 *Lb Ss*[c]j *Csb*^1 | ● ~ υι. αυ. εσ.‖Mt: *Rpl Lb*30 *Arm*^pc — ~ εσ. υι. αυ.: D *L*'⟨vg^1⟩ Hil *Arm*' — ~ αυ. υι. εσ.‖Lk: σ179 569 — *txt* (~ εσ. αυ.): BL(Δ)-892 Θ-565 1342 *pc* (*Lk*[e])

Lk 20,41 πως—^42γαρ] τι υμιν δοκει περι του Χριστου; τινος υιος εστιν; λεγουσιν αυτω· του Δαυιδ. ειπεν δε προς αυτους· πως‖Mt: *Le* | λεγ. + οι γραμματεις‖Mk: ϕ 1093(~ τ. Χ. οι γρ.) *pc Sscp* | τ. Χ.—ειν.] οτι ο Χριστος υιος Δ. εστιν‖Mk: ϕ — ~ ειναι υιον Δ.: 1241 G 157 *L*30 vg^2(~ υι. ει.) — ● ~ ει. Δ. υι.: ℵBL-579 Cr(~ Δ. υι.) — *txt*: *Rpl* (*om* ει.: D) *L*'⟨e⟩ **42** αυ. γαρ] ● και αυ.‖Mk: *Rpl L*' *S*⟨p^1⟩ *Arm*' — πως‖Mt: *Le* — *txt*: 𝔥 1071 **λλ**⟨22-1278⟩ ϕ124 Q (*prm* και) R Θ 157 1012 Cr *Ll C*⟨b^1⟩ *Arm*^mu | βιβ.] τη β.‖Mk12 26: D | ● *om* ο *cf. ad* Mt: B-579 D **43** υποκατω‖p: D 145 *Lvl*⟨fr^2z⟩r^1 *Scp C*b **44** Δ. ουν] ει ουν Δ.‖Mt: σ1604 157 1093 *Lqr*^2(~ ει Δ. καλ. ουν αυ. κυ.) *Ssp* — ει Δ.‖Mt: *Le* cff^2 — Δ.‖Mk: D 471 Cr *Lail*(+ γαρ) *Cs*^1:9 | ~ καλ. αυ. κυ.‖p: σ659 R (*Lr*^2) *Sp*^4 *Aeth* — ● ~κυ. αυ. καλ.(λεγει)‖(Mk): *Rpl* (D') *L*' — *txt*: BL-33-1241(~ καλ. κυ.) ϕ983-1689 σM-71-115^v-1194 A K Q U Π 713 *al Lf* | κυ.] εν πνευματι κυ.‖Mt43 Mk36: 713 | *om* και‖Mt: D *Le* cff^2ilq *Sscp Cs*^4:9b^2 *Aeth*(πως + ουν) | ● ~ υι. αυ.‖Mt: *Rpl* — *txt*: B **λ**⟨131⟩-2193 σM A K Θ Π *al*

Jo 7,42 ● ~ ερχ. ο Χ.: 𝔓^75 BLTW-33 1071 Ψ Cr Or *Lg*^2 vg' *Sc*(Δ.^1 + εσται *et* οπ. ην] του)pj^ab — *txt*: 𝔓^66 *Rpl* (~ ο Χ. ερχ. οπ. ην Δ.: D 1355 Chr) *Lvl*⟨e(οπ.—Χ.] του Δ.)⟩r^1 30 vg^2 *Ss*(Δ.^1 + εσται ο Χ. *et* οπ.—Χ.] του Δ.)hj^c

(210)

224. Rede gegen Pharisäer und Schriftgelehrte.
Discourse against the Scribes and Pharisees.

Matth 23 1–36

[1] Τότε ὁ Ἰησοῦς ἐλάλησεν τοῖς ὄχλοις καὶ τοῖς μαθηταῖς αὐτοῦ [2] λέγων· ἐπὶ τῆς Μωυσέως καθέδρας ἐκάθισαν οἱ γραμματεῖς καὶ οἱ Φαρισαῖοι. [3] πάντα οὖν ὅσα ἐὰν εἴπωσιν ὑμῖν ποιήσατε καὶ τηρεῖτε, κατὰ δὲ τὰ ἔργα αὐτῶν μὴ ποιεῖτε· λέγουσιν γὰρ καὶ οὐ ποιοῦσιν. [4] δεσμεύουσιν δὲ φορτία βαρέα καὶ ἐπιτιθέασιν ἐπὶ τοὺς ὤμους τῶν ἀνθρώπων, τῷ δὲ δακτύλῳ αὐτῶν οὐ θέλουσιν κινῆσαι αὐτά. [5] πάντα δὲ τὰ ἔργα αὐτῶν ποιοῦσιν πρὸς τὸ θεαθῆναι τοῖς ἀνθρώποις· πλατύνουσιν γὰρ τὰ φυλακτήρια αὐτῶν καὶ μεγαλύνουσιν τὰ κράσπεδα, [6] φιλοῦσιν δὲ τὴν πρωτοκλισίαν ἐν τοῖς δείπνοις καὶ τὰς πρωτοκαθεδρίας ἐν ταῖς συναγωγαῖς [7] καὶ τοὺς ἀσπασμοὺς ἐν ταῖς ἀγοραῖς καὶ καλεῖσθαι ὑπὸ τῶν ἀνθρώπων ραββι, ραββι. [8] ὑμεῖς δὲ μὴ κληθῆτε ραββι· εἷς γάρ ἐστιν ὑμῶν ὁ διδάσκαλος, πάντες δὲ ὑμεῖς ἀδελφοί ἐστε. [9] καὶ πατέρα μὴ καλέσητε ὑμῶν ἐπὶ τῆς γῆς· εἷς γάρ ἐστιν ὑμῶν ὁ πατὴρ ὁ οὐράνιος. [10] μηδὲ κληθῆτε καθηγηταί, ὅτι καθηγητὴς ὑμῶν ἐστιν εἷς ὁ Χριστός. [11] ὁ δὲ μείζων ὑμῶν ἔσται ὑμῶν διάκονος. [12] ὅστις δὲ ὑψώσει

Mark 12 37b–40

[37 b] Καὶ ὁ πολὺς ὄχλος ἤκουεν αὐτοῦ ἡδέως. [38] καὶ ἐν τῇ διδαχῇ αὐτοῦ ἔλεγεν· βλέπετε ἀπὸ τῶν γραμματέων τῶν θελόντων ἐν στολαῖς περιπατεῖν καὶ ἀσπασμοὺς ἐν ταῖς ἀγοραῖς [39] καὶ πρωτοκαθεδρίας ἐν ταῖς συναγωγαῖς καὶ πρωτοκλισίας ἐν τοῖς δείπνοις·

Luk 20 45–47

[45] Ἀκούοντος δὲ παντὸς τοῦ λαοῦ εἶπεν τοῖς μαθηταῖς· [46] προσέχετε ἀπὸ τῶν γραμματέων τῶν θελόντων περιπατεῖν ἐν στολαῖς καὶ φιλούντων ἀσπασμοὺς ἐν ταῖς ἀγοραῖς καὶ πρωτοκαθεδρίας ἐν ταῖς συναγωγαῖς καὶ πρωτοκλισίας ἐν τοῖς δείπνοις,

11 39–44. 46–52 (168.): [46] *ὁ δὲ εἶπεν· καὶ ὑμῖν τοῖς νομικοῖς οὐαί, ὅτι φορτίζετε τοὺς ἀνθρώπους φορτία δυσβάστακτα, καὶ αὐτοὶ ἑνὶ τῶν δακτύλων ὑμῶν οὐ προσψαύετε τοῖς φορτίοις ...*

[43] *οὐαὶ ὑμῖν τοῖς Φαρισαίοις, ὅτι ἀγαπᾶτε τὴν πρωτοκαθεδρίαν ἐν ταῖς συναγωγαῖς καὶ τοὺς ἀσπασμοὺς ἐν ταῖς ἀγοραῖς ...*

13 13: ὑμεῖς φωνεῖτέ με· ὁ διδάσκαλος καὶ ὁ κύριος, καὶ καλῶς λέγετε· εἰμὶ γάρ.

143.

Mt 23,4 βαρ.] δυσβαστακτα‖p: X^cmt 544-700 σ1010-1293 — ● βαρ. και δυσβ.‖p: *Rpl* (αδυσβ.: D*) Chr Cl Da *L'*Or *S*hj *Cs Arm* — *txt*: ℵ(μεγαλα βαρ.)LX^cmt-892 **λ**-1582 *Le*[k] abff²hr¹? Ir Or *S' C*b *Aeth* (μεγ. και βαρ.) | τω δε δα.] ● αυτοι δε τω δα.‖p: 𝔥 σ1010-1293 D 157 *L*Ir Or *S*pj^abc *C*b'(²τοις -οις) *Geo*('δε + και)^B — αυ. δε ενι των δακτυλων‖p: 1093 *S*c(*om* δε)j^k *Cs* — αυ. δε *et om* αυτων‖p: *S*s — *txt* (τοις δε -οις): *Rpl L'*(*om* δε: r²) *S*h *Arm* (*Aeth*) | θελ. κιν.] προσψαυουσιν‖p: *S*sc — θελ. προσψαυειν‖p: *S*p **5** κρα. + ιματιων αυτων(*om*)‖920 1436p Lk844: *Rpl* (LΔ) (εαυ.: 700) *L*f ff²hq vg¹ Or *S*,j^abc *C*b *Δ*a (i^T) — *txt* (+ αυτων): ℵB **λ**-22 D Θ *L'*(bc vg² *S*j^k *Cs Aeth*) *Δ'*<me>
6 τας πρωτοκλισιας‖Mk Lk20: ℵ^cL-33-892 **λ**-1582 157 713 *L*<e[k] bff²q> Hil Or *C Aeth* **7** ● *om* ραβ.²‖8 *cf.* 915 1121 Jo138 *etc*: 𝔥 ΟΣ-544 **λ**-22-1582 **ϕ**13-174-*l*547¹ σ692-1010-1293 Δ Θ **0107**^c **0138** *pc l*184 Bas¹ Chr *L*,Cp Hil Or *S*pj^k *Cs*⁷b *Geo' Δ*<me> — *txt*: *Rpl* Bas¹ Iu *L*Cp *S'*j^abc *Cs*^1v *Arm Geo*^B **8** ραβ.] διδασκαλον(καθηγητην) επι της γης‖9: Chr Cl Eu (Gr^Ny) Or Pho Pld Procp Ti *S*Ef — *prm* επι τ. γης‖←: Pho | διδ. + εν τοις(*om*) ουρανοις‖←: (Cl) Eu(*prm* ο) Or(διδ.] πατηρ ο) Procp Ti *Lg' Δ*p **9** ουρ. + παντες δε υμεις αδελφοι εστε‖8: σ517-659 U *pc* Cl *L*Cp Cr Procp(*om* δε) **11** υμ.¹] εν υμιν‖2026p.27 Mk1044 Lk2226: Θ *al Lc* Or *S*pj^abc *Δ*a md n p | εστω‖Lk←: 1604 **ϕ***l*547¹ σ692-1391 G *al Lr*¹ Or *Geo*^1.B **12** δε] ουν‖184: **λ**-1582 *L*Or

Mk 12,38 και² + φιλουντων‖Lk20 Mt: **ϕ**346 σ115-1082-1606 *al S*s[c]p *Cs* | ασπ.] τους ασπ.‖Mt Lk11: σ827 *Cs*⁹(²τον -ον) **39** ∼ τ. δειπ. ... τ. συνα.‖Mt: σ1606

Lk 20,45 λαου] οχλου‖p: S *pc* | ● τ. μαθ.] + αυτου‖Mt: *Rpl L' S C* — τ. εαυτου μ.: Γ 235 *l*^pl — προς αυτους: Q — *txt*: B D *Ll Arm* **46** ∼ εν στο. περιπ.‖Mk: 𝔥<BW> 1071 **λλ**<22-1278> **ϕ**<124> σ115-1424 A G R Ψ *pc* Sp¹ *Arm* | ασπ.] τους ασπ.‖Mt Lk: 157 *C*

183.

ἑαυτὸν ταπεινωθήσεται, καὶ ὅστις ταπεινώσει ἑαυτὸν ὑψωθήσεται.

[13] Οὐαὶ δὲ ὑμῖν, γραμματεῖς καὶ Φαρισαῖοι ὑποκριταί, ὅτι κλείετε τὴν βασιλείαν τῶν οὐρανῶν ἔμπροσθεν τῶν ἀνθρώπων· ὑμεῖς γὰρ οὐκ εἰσέρχεσθε, οὐδὲ τοὺς εἰσερχομένους ἀφίετε εἰσελθεῖν.

[52] οὐαὶ ὑμῖν τοῖς νομικοῖς, ὅτι ἤρατε τὴν κλεῖδα τῆς γνώσεως· αὐτοὶ οὐκ εἰσήλθατε καὶ τοὺς εἰσερχομένους ἐκωλύσατε ...

[40] οἱ κατεσθίοντες τὰς οἰκίας τῶν χηρῶν καὶ προφάσει μακρὰ προσευχόμενοι, οὗτοι λήψονται περισσότερον κρίμα.

[47] οἳ κατεσθίουσιν τὰς οἰκίας τῶν χηρῶν καὶ προφάσει μακρὰ προσεύχονται· οὗτοι λήψονται περισσότερον κρίμα.

[15] Οὐαὶ ὑμῖν, γραμματεῖς καὶ Φαρισαῖοι ὑποκριταί, ὅτι περιάγετε τὴν θάλασσαν καὶ τὴν ξηρὰν ποιῆσαι ἕνα προσήλυτον, καὶ ὅταν γένηται, ποιεῖτε αὐτὸν υἱὸν γεέννης διπλότερον ὑμῶν.

[16] Οὐαὶ ὑμῖν, ὁδηγοὶ τυφλοὶ οἱ λέγοντες· ὃς ἂν ὀμόσῃ ἐν τῷ ναῷ, οὐδέν ἐστιν· ὃς δ' ἂν ὀμόσῃ ἐν τῷ χρυσῷ τοῦ ναοῦ, ὀφείλει. [17] μωροὶ καὶ τυφλοί, τίς γὰρ μείζων ἐστίν, ὁ χρυσὸς ἢ ὁ ναὸς ὁ ἁγιάσας τὸν χρυσόν; [18] καί· ὃς ἂν ὀμόσῃ ἐν τῷ θυσιαστηρίῳ, οὐδέν ἐστιν· ὃς δ' ἂν ὀμόσῃ ἐν τῷ δώρῳ τῷ ἐπάνω αὐτοῦ, ὀφείλει. [19] τυφλοί, τί γὰρ μεῖζον, τὸ δῶρον ἢ τὸ θυσιαστήριον τὸ ἁγιάζον τὸ δῶρον; [20] ὁ οὖν ὀμόσας ἐν τῷ θυσιαστηρίῳ ὀμνύει ἐν αὐτῷ καὶ ἐν πᾶσι τοῖς ἐπάνω αὐτοῦ· [21] καὶ ὁ ὀμόσας ἐν τῷ ναῷ ὀμνύει ἐν αὐτῷ καὶ ἐν τῷ κατοικοῦντι αὐτόν· [22] καὶ ὁ ὀμόσας ἐν τῷ οὐρανῷ ὀμνύει ἐν τῷ θρόνῳ τοῦ θεοῦ καὶ ἐν τῷ καθημένῳ ἐπάνω αὐτοῦ. 37.

[23] Οὐαὶ ὑμῖν, γραμματεῖς καὶ Φαρισαῖοι ὑποκριταί, ὅτι ἀποδεκατοῦτε τὸ ἡδύοσμον καὶ τὸ ἄνηθον καὶ τὸ κύμινον, καὶ ἀφήκατε τὰ βαρύτερα τοῦ νόμου, τὴν κρίσιν καὶ τὸ ἔλεος καὶ τὴν πίστιν· ταῦτα ἔδει ποιῆσαι κἀκεῖνα μὴ ἀφιέναι. [24] ὁδηγοὶ τυφλοί, οἱ διυλίζοντες τὸν κώνωπα, τὴν δὲ κάμηλον καταπίνοντες.

[42] ἀλλὰ οὐαὶ ὑμῖν τοῖς Φαρισαίοις, ὅτι ἀποδεκατοῦτε τὸ ἡδύοσμον καὶ τὸ πήγανον καὶ πᾶν λάχανον, καὶ παρέρχεσθε τὴν κρίσιν καὶ τὴν ἀγάπην τοῦ θεοῦ· ταῦτα ἔδει ποιῆσαι κἀκεῖνα μὴ παρεῖναι ...

Mt 23,12 υψωθ. + [14]ουαι δε υμιν, γραμματεις και Φαρισαιοι υποκριται, οτι κατεσθιετε τας οικιας των χηρων και προφασει μακρα προσευχομενοι· δια τουτο λημψεσθε περισσοτερον κριμα‖p: *Rpl* Chr PsChr Da *Lf* Hil *S'* *C*b[11] *Geo*[2] *Δ*a p ⟦*om* δε‖15.16: 544-700 ϕ124 σ954 *pc* *L*bcff[2]hlr[2] *S*cphj[a.1] *C*b[13] *Geo*[2] *Δ*'⟨me⟩ | *om* υποκ.: Δ | οτι] οι‖Lk47p: *L*fhr[2] vg[2] *Geo*[2] *Δ*'⟨me⟩ | *om* και[2]: σ692 *pc* *L*bcff[2]hlr[1.2] vg[4] *Δ*'⟨me⟩ | μακραν: σ1293 K — μικρα: ϕ13 Δ 1009 *l*76⟧ — 13 + [14]ουαι—κριμα (*cf. ad* υψωθ. *et* ⟦ ⟧)‖←: ϕ'⟨124⟩-*l*547 *pc* Chr Or *L*bcff[2]hlr[1.2] vg[4] Hil *S*cj[a.1] *C*b[3] *Arm*[O] *Δ*'⟨me⟩ — *txt* (*om* = 14): ℵBL-33-892 λ-1582 D Θ *pc* Eu Or *L*e[k] aff[1]g[1]z vg' Chri[St] Hi Or *S*sj[k] *C*sb[9] *Arm* *Geo*[1] *Δ*i[V] l[AD] **13** 13 + 14 *cf. ad* 12

21 ● κατοικησαντι: *Rpl* — *txt*: ℵB Φ-1604 λ-1582 ϕ-174-*l*547 σ-659-1402 H S Θ Ω *al* *L*⟨q(*om* 13-28)⟩ Or *S*,j *C*

23 κυμ. + και παν λαχανον‖p: 998 | ● ταυ. + δε: ℌ⟨ℵ⟩C ΟΣΦ σ-M-27-71-692-1010-1293-1402 K W Y Δ Π **0138** 157 *pc* *L*adr[2] Or *S* *C*s[5] — *txt*: *Rpl* *L*'⟨q⟩ Or *S*j *C*s[1]b *Arm* | ● αφειναι‖p: ℌ⟨33⟩ 28-565 569

Mk 12,40 κατεσθιουσιν‖Lk: λ ϕ983-1689 σ827 D *pc*

Lk 20,47 κατεσθιοντες‖Mk: X D(-εσθοντ.) P *pc* *l*1663 | προσευχομενοι (*et om* και)‖Mk: 579 ϕ-230 (D) P R Θ (L'; *et* ∼ προφ. μα. προσ. κατ.—χηρ.: cff[2]ilq)

Mt23 13p *cf.* ETh[II] 39 (POxy 655 II b): [Λέγει Ἰ(ησοῦ)ς· οἱ Φαρισαῖοι καὶ οἱ γραμματεῖς ἀπ]έλ[αβον τὰς κλεῖδας] τῆς [γνώσεως καὶ ἀπέ]κρυψ[αν αὐτάς· οὔτε] εἰσῆλ[θον καὶ τοῖς] εἰσερ[χομένοις οὐ]κ ἀν[εῖσαν· ὑμεῖς] δὲ ... (*cf. ad 70.* Mt10 16b)

(*transl.*): *Λέγει Ἰησοῦς· οἱ Φαρισαῖοι καὶ οἱ γραμματεῖς ἔλαβον τὰς κλεῖδας τῆς γνώσεως. ἔκρυψαν αὐτὰς οὐδὲ εἰσῆλθον. καὶ τοὺς θέλοντας εἰσελθεῖν ἐκώλυσαν. ὑμεῖς ...* (*cf. ad 70.* Mt10 16b)

cf. ETh[II] 102 (*transl.*): *Λέγει Ἰησοῦς· οὐαὶ αὐτοῖς τοῖς Φαρισαίοις ὅτι παρομοιάζουσιν κυνὶ καθεύδοντι ἐπὶ φάτνῃ βοῶν· οὔτε ἐσθίει οὔτε τοὺς βόας ἀφίησιν ἐσθίειν.*

25 Οὐαὶ ὑμῖν, γραμματεῖς καὶ Φαρισαῖοι ὑποκριταί, ὅτι καθαρίζετε τὸ ἔξωθεν τοῦ ποτηρίου καὶ τῆς παροψίδος, ἔσωθεν δὲ γέμουσιν ἐξ ἁρπαγῆς καὶ ἀκρασίας. 26 Φαρισαῖε τυφλέ, καθάρισον πρῶτον τὸ ἐντὸς τοῦ ποτηρίου ἵνα γένηται καὶ τὸ ἐκτὸς αὐτοῦ καθαρόν.

27 Οὐαὶ ὑμῖν, γραμματεῖς καὶ Φαρισαῖοι ὑποκριταί, ὅτι παρομοιάζετε τάφοις κεκονιαμένοις, οἵτινες ἔξωθεν μὲν φαίνονται ὡραῖοι, ἔσωθεν δὲ γέμουσιν ὀστέων νεκρῶν καὶ πάσης ἀκαθαρσίας. 28 οὕτως καὶ ὑμεῖς ἔξωθεν μὲν φαίνεσθε τοῖς ἀνθρώποις δίκαιοι, ἔσωθεν δέ ἐστε μεστοὶ ὑποκρίσεως καὶ ἀνομίας.

29 Οὐαὶ ὑμῖν, γραμματεῖς καὶ Φαρισαῖοι ὑποκριταί, ὅτι οἰκοδομεῖτε τοὺς τάφους τῶν προφητῶν καὶ κοσμεῖτε τὰ μνημεῖα τῶν δικαίων, 30 καὶ λέγετε· εἰ ἤμεθα ἐν ταῖς ἡμέραις τῶν πατέρων ἡμῶν, οὐκ ἂν ἤμεθα αὐτῶν κοινωνοὶ ἐν τῷ αἵματι τῶν προφητῶν. 31 ὥστε μαρτυρεῖτε ἑαυτοῖς ὅτι υἱοί ἐστε τῶν φονευσάντων τοὺς προφήτας.

32 Καὶ ὑμεῖς πληρώσατε τὸ μέτρον τῶν πατέρων ὑμῶν. 33 ὄφεις, γεννήματα ἐχιδνῶν, πῶς φύγητε ἀπὸ τῆς κρίσεως τῆς γεέννης; 34 διὰ τοῦτο ἰδοὺ ἐγὼ ἀποστέλλω πρὸς ὑμᾶς προφήτας καὶ σο-

39 ... νῦν ὑμεῖς οἱ Φαρισαῖοι τὸ ἔξωθεν τοῦ ποτηρίου καὶ τοῦ πίνακος καθαρίζετε, τὸ δὲ ἔσωθεν ὑμῶν γέμει ἁρπαγῆς καὶ πονηρίας. 40 ἄφρονες, οὐχ ὁ ποιήσας τὸ ἔξωθεν καὶ τὸ ἔσωθεν ἐποίησεν; 41 πλὴν τὰ ἐνόντα δότε ἐλεημοσύνην, καὶ ἰδοὺ πάντα καθαρὰ ὑμῖν ἐστιν ...

44 οὐαὶ ὑμῖν, ὅτι ἐστὲ ὡς τὰ μνημεῖα τὰ ἄδηλα, καὶ οἱ ἄνθρωποι οἱ περιπατοῦντες ἐπάνω οὐκ οἴδασιν ...

47 οὐαὶ ὑμῖν, ὅτι οἰκοδομεῖτε τὰ μνημεῖα τῶν προφητῶν, οἱ δὲ πατέρες ὑμῶν ἀπέκτειναν αὐτούς. 48 ἄρα μάρτυρές ἐστε καὶ συνευδοκεῖτε τοῖς ἔργοις τῶν πατέρων ὑμῶν, ὅτι αὐτοὶ μὲν ἀπέκτειναν αὐτούς, ὑμεῖς δὲ οἰκοδομεῖτε.

14.

49 διὰ τοῦτο καὶ ἡ σοφία τοῦ θεοῦ εἶπεν· ἀποστελῶ εἰς αὐτοὺς προφήτας καὶ ἀπο-

Mt 23,25 της παρ.] του πινακος‖p: *S*sc Af *C*s — + του(και του) πιν.‖p: ϕ(124)-230-346^{v} σM-1010-1293 Y *al* *L*Hgm(∼ πιν. ... παρ.) *S*h^{+}j^{1v} | γεμει‖p: 157 Chr PsCl | *om* εξ‖p: C 1604 D **0138** *pc* | ακρ.] αδικιας: *Rpl* Euthy Thy *L*f *S*p *Δ*a — πλεονεξιας: σM 1093 — πονηριας‖p: 998 *L*r^{2}(iniquitate) *Aeth*(+ και πλεον.) — ακαθαρσιας‖27: ΟΣ σ71 *pc* Cl Hgm PsMac^{S} *L*'⟨q⟩ *S*s[c] (*prm* πασης)j *C* *Geo* *Δ*'⟨l^{D}(*om*) me⟩ — *txt*: 𝔥 Φ **λ**-22-1582 **ϕ**-174-*l*547 **σ**⟨954⟩-1010-1293-1402 D W(+ αδικιας) Δ Θ Π *al* *L*e[k] acff^{2}hr^{1} *S*h(+ και αδικιας^{-}) *Arm* **26** ● ποτ. + και της παροψιδος‖25: *Rpl* PsAth Bas PsBas^{1} Euthy Thy *L*'⟨q⟩ Or *S*ph(*et* + και του πινακος)j *C* *Δ*a ad i l — *txt*: 700 **λ**-1582 D Θ Ant PsBas^{1} Chr Cl Cr^{I} PsMac^{S} *L*e[k] aff^{2}r$^{1.2}$ Ir *S*s[c] *Δ*md n'(^{C} *om* τ. ποτ.) p | ● αυτων: *Rpl* Bas^{1} PsCl Cr Euthy Thy *S*'j *C* — *om*: σ659 53 *l*2 PsAth Chr Cl PsMac^{S} *L*'⟨q⟩ Ir Or *Geo*^{B} — *txt*: B* 28-700 **λ** **ϕ**-*l*547 **σ**-659-1194-1606 D' E Θ 157 *pc* *l*12 *l*69 *l*70 *l*80 *l*184^{1} *l*303 *l*333 *l*374 *l*850 *l*950^{1} *l*1127 *l*1579 Bas^{1} PsBas Da *L*e[k] a *S*s[c] *Geo*' *Aeth* **28** ανομ.] πονηριας‖Lk39: 348 1279 **30** αυ. κοι.] ● κοι. αυ.: 𝔓^{77} *Rpl* Chr^{2} *L*' Or — κοι.: ΟΣ Θ *L*g^{1} *Arm* — *txt*: B 700-1604 **λ**-1582 **ϕ**⟨983⟩-*l*547 D 1295 Chr^{3} **33** κρισ. + μελλουσης‖37Lk37: σ1391 *S*h^{m} *Δ*md n **34** *om* ιδου‖p: 544 λ22 **ϕ**⟨69-983⟩-*l*547 σ1424-1675 E *L*vg^{1} | *om* εγω‖p: ϕ13-124-788-*l*547 D Or *L*vg^{4} Ir$^{1:2}$ Luc *Geo* | αποστελω‖p: 33 σ1207 D' *pc* *l*183^{1} Or *C*sb$^{⟨4⟩}$

Mt23 25f.p *cf.* ETh^{II} 89 (*transl.*): *Λέγει Ἰησοῦς· διὰ τί νίπτετε τὸ ἔξωθεν τοῦ ποτηρίου; οὐ νοεῖτε ὅτι ὁ ποιήσας τὸ ἔσωθεν οὗτος καὶ τὸ ἔξωθεν ἐποίησεν;*

cf. Ev. apocr. (POxy 840 lin. 21-45): (*cf. ad 216.* Mk11 27f.) ... καὶ σ[ταθεὶς εὐθὺς ὁ σωτὴρ] σ[ὺν τ]οῖς μαθηταῖ[ς αὐτοῦ ἀπεκρίθη·] 'σὺ οὖν ἐνταῦθα ὢν ἐν τῷ ἱερῷ καθαρεύεις;' λέγει αὐτῷ ἐκεῖνος· 'καθαρεύω· ἐλουσά(25)μην γὰρ ἐν τῇ λίμνῃ τοῦ Δαυειδ καὶ δι' ἑτέρας κλίμακος κατελθὼν δι' ἑτέρας ἀ[ν]ῆλθον, καὶ λευκὰ ἐνδύματα ἐνεδυσάμην καὶ καθαρά, καὶ τότε ἦλθον καὶ προσέβλεψα τούτοις τοῖς ἁγίοις (30) σκεύεσιν'. ὁ σωτὴρ πρὸς αὐτὸν ἀπο[κρι]θεὶς εἶπεν· 'οὐαὶ τυφλοὶ μὴ ὁρῶντ[ε]ς· σὺ ἐλούσω τούτοις τοῖς χεομένοις ὕ[δ]ασι(ν), ἐν οἷς κύνες καὶ χοῖροι βέβλην[ται] (*cf.* Mt7 6) νυκτὸς καὶ ἡμέρας, καὶ νιψάμε(35)[ν]ος τὸ ἐκτὸς δέρμα ἐσμήξω, ὅπερ [κα]ὶ αἱ πόρναι καὶ α[ἱ] αὐλητρίδες μυρί[ζ]ου[σαι κ]αὶ λούουσιν καὶ σμήχουσι [καὶ κ]αλλωπίζουσιν πρὸς ἐπιθυμί[αν τ]ῶν ἀνθρώπων, ἔνδοθεν δὲ ἐκεῖ(40)[ναι πεπλ]ήρω(ν)ται σκορπίων καὶ [πάσης ἀδι]κίας. ἐγὼ δὲ καὶ οἱ [μαθηταί μου,] οὓς λέγεις μὴ βεβα[μμένους, βεβά]μμεθα ἐν ὕδασι ζω[ῆς αἰω]νίου τοῖς κα]τελθοῦσιν ἀπὸ [τοῦ (45) θεοῦ ἐκ τοῦ οὐρανοῦ. ἀλ]λὰ οὐαὶ [τ]οῖς ...

φοὺς καὶ γραμματεῖς· ἐξ αὐτῶν ἀποκτενεῖτε καὶ σταυρώσετε, καὶ ἐξ αὐτῶν μαστιγώσετε ἐν ταῖς συναγωγαῖς ὑμῶν καὶ διώξετε ἀπὸ πόλεως εἰς πόλιν· 35 ὅπως ἔλθῃ ἐφ' ὑμᾶς πᾶν αἷμα δίκαιον ἐκχυννόμενον ἐπὶ τῆς γῆς ἀπὸ τοῦ αἵματος Αβελ τοῦ δικαίου ἕως τοῦ αἵματος Ζαχαρίου υἱοῦ Βαραχίου, ὃν ἐφονεύσατε μεταξὺ τοῦ ναοῦ καὶ τοῦ θυσιαστηρίου· 36 αμην λέγω ὑμῖν, ἥξει πάντα ταῦτα ἐπὶ τὴν γενεὰν ταύτην.

στόλους, καὶ ἐξ αὐτῶν ἀποκτενοῦσιν καὶ ἐκδιώξουσιν, 50 *ἵνα ἐκζητηθῇ τὸ αἷμα πάντων τῶν προφητῶν τὸ ἐκκεχυμένον ἀπὸ καταβολῆς κόσμου ἀπὸ τῆς γενεᾶς ταύτης,* 51 *ἀπὸ αἵματος Αβελ ἕως αἵματος Ζαχαρίου τοῦ ἀπολομένου μεταξὺ τοῦ θυσιαστηρίου καὶ τοῦ οἴκου· ναὶ λέγω ὑμῖν, ἐκζητηθήσεται ἀπὸ τῆς γενεᾶς ταύτης.*

(211) 225. Weissagung über Jerusalem. *The Lament over Jerusalem.* Matth 23 37–39 181.

37 Ιερουσαλημ Ιερουσαλημ, ἡ ἀποκτείνουσα τοὺς προφήτας καὶ λιθοβολοῦσα τοὺς ἀπεσταλμένους πρὸς αὐτήν, ποσάκις ἠθέλησα ἐπισυναγαγεῖν τὰ τέκνα σου, ὃν τρόπον ὄρνις ἐπισυνάγει τὰ νοσσία αὐτῆς ὑπὸ τὰς πτέρυγας, καὶ οὐκ ἠθελήσατε. 38 ἰδοὺ ἀφίεται ὑμῖν ὁ οἶκος ὑμῶν ἔρημος. 39 λέγω γὰρ ὑμῖν, οὐ μή με ἴδητε ἀπ' ἄρτι ἕως ἂν εἴπητε· **εὐλογημένος ὁ ἐρχόμενος ἐν ὀνόματι κυρίου.** (Ps118 26)

181.

(212) 226. Die Scherflein der Witwe. *The Widow's Mites.*

Mark 12 41–44

41 Καὶ καθίσας κατέναντι τοῦ γαζοφυλακείου ἐθεώρει πῶς ὁ ὄχλος βάλλει χαλκὸν εἰς τὸ γαζοφυλακεῖον· καὶ πολλοὶ πλούσιοι ἔβαλλον πολλά. 42 καὶ ἐλθοῦσα μία χήρα πτωχὴ ἔβαλεν λεπτὰ δύο, ὅ ἐστιν

Luk 21 1–4

1 Ἀναβλέψας δὲ εἶδεν τοὺς βάλλοντας εἰς τὸ γαζοφυλακεῖον τὰ δῶρα αὐτῶν πλουσίους. 2 εἶδεν δέ τινα χήραν πενιχρὰν βάλλουσαν ἐκεῖ λεπτὰ δύο,

Mt 23,34 εξ^{1}] και εξ ‖ p: *Rpl* Ddy Or *L'* Ir Or *S*h$^{Brsjab.1}$ *C*b *Arm*^{pc} *Aeth* — *txt*: ℵB-33 ΟΣΦ **λ**-22-1582 **φ**⟨983⟩-174 σM-517-1675 W Δ Θ Π **0138**^{v} 157 *pc* *L*e[k] q vg^{3} Or *S'*j^{c} Eu *Arm'* **35** *om* του^{1} ‖ p: L-33-892 D 157 713 *l*184 | *om* του^{3} ‖ p: 33-892 **λ**⟨1⟩-1582 D Θ | *om* υι. Β. ‖ p: ℵ* *l*6 *l*13 **36** ● ∼ ταυ. παν.: ℵCL Φ-28-544 **φ**-230 σM-1010-1424 D S Θ *pm* *l*1635 Chr^{3} *L'*Or *S'*j Eu — *om* ταυ.: *L*e[k] — *txt*: *Rpl* Chr^{1} *L*Ir *S*p^{3} **37** την νοσσιαν ‖ p: Γ 1216 — τας -ιας ‖ p: 440 | εαυτης (∼ εαυ. νο.) ‖ p: *Rpl* (1295) Cr Or Thd^{C2} {} — *om*: B 700 Cr Or^{2}(^{1}πτε. + αυτης) *L*Cp Ir *Geo*^{1} — *txt*: ℵ*B^{m}-33-892 ΣΦ-544 σM-1424 D WΔ **0138** *pc* Cr Or Thd^{C1} {*L S C Geo*^{2}} **38** ● *om* ερημος ‖ p: BL *l*184 Cr Or *L*ff^{2} *S*s *C*⟨b^{7}⟩ **39** γαρ] δε ‖ p: **σ 0138** 157 713 *L*abcff^{2}hr$^{1.2}$30 vg^{3} *C*s$^{2:7}$ | *om* απ αρτι ‖ p: *l*1635 Chr *L*e[k] r^{1}

Mk 12,42 *om* ο εστ. κο. ‖ p: 1574 *Geo*^{A}

Lk 21,1 ∼ τα δω. αυ.(*om*) εις το γαζ. ‖ p: *Rpl* (Θ) Bas *L'*(a vg^{1}; *om* τ. δω.: s; ∼ εις το γαζ. αυ.: qs) *S'* *Arm* — *txt*: ℌX 1604 **λλ**⟨22-1278⟩ **φ**-*l*547 D Ψ 157 *pc* Or *L*e *S*pj **2** *om* εκει ‖ p: λ2193 D 44 Or *L*⟨fq⟩ *S*scp | ● ∼ δυο λεπ. *cf.* 1035 *etc.*: *Rpl* Bas *L*e a vg^{1} *S*hj *Arm* — *txt*: ℌX Q Θ Ψ 157 Or *L'* *S'* | λεπ. + ο εστιν κοδραντης ‖ p: D

Mt23 35p *cf.* EIc 24,(1-2 *cf. ad 6.* Lk12 1)3: καὶ τολμήσαντες εἰσῆλθαν καὶ εἶδαν τὸ γεγονός. καὶ τὰ παθνώματα τοῦ ναοῦ ὠλόλυξαν, καὶ αὐτοὶ περιεσχίσαντο ἐπάνωθεν ἕως κάτω. καὶ τὸ πτῶμα αὐτοῦ οὐχ εὕρωσαν, ἀλλ' εὗρον τὸ αἷμα αὐτοῦ λίθον γεγενημένον. καὶ φοβηθέντες ἐξῆλθαν καὶ ἀνήγγειλαν ὅτι Ζαχαρίας πεφόνευται. καὶ ἤκουσαν πᾶσαι αἱ φυλαὶ τοῦ λαοῦ καὶ ἐπένθησαν αὐτὸν καὶ ἐκόψαντο τρεῖς ἡμέρας καὶ τρεῖς νύκτας. ^{4}μετὰ δὲ ... (*cf. ad 11.* Lk2 26)

cf. EN frgm.17 (Hi Mt *ad* 23 35): In evangelio, quo utuntur Nazareni, pro filio Barachiae *filium Joiadae* scriptum repperimus.

cf. Pt^{L} (Heinrici V 267): Ζαχαρίαν δὲ τὸν Ιωδαε [Ιωδανε] λέγει· διώνυμος γὰρ ἦν.

κοδράντης. 43 καὶ προσκαλεσάμενος τοὺς μαθητὰς αὐτοῦ εἶπεν αὐτοῖς· αμην λέγω ὑμῖν ὅτι ἡ χήρα αὕτη ἡ πτωχὴ πλεῖον πάντων βέβληκεν τῶν βαλλόντων εἰς τὸ γαζοφυλακεῖον· 44 πάντες γὰρ ἐκ τοῦ περισσεύοντος αὐτοῖς ἔβαλον, αὕτη δὲ ἐκ τῆς ὑστερήσεως αὐτῆς πάντα ὅσα εἶχεν ἔβαλεν, ὅλον τὸν βίον αὐτῆς.

3 καὶ εἶπεν· ἀληθῶς λέγω ὑμῖν ὅτι ἡ χήρα ἡ πτωχὴ αὕτη πλεῖον πάντων ἔβαλεν· 4 ἅπαντες γὰρ οὗτοι ἐκ τοῦ περισσεύοντος αὐτοῖς ἔβαλον εἰς τὰ δῶρα τοῦ θεοῦ, αὕτη δὲ ἐκ τοῦ ὑστερήματος αὐτῆς ἅπαντα τὸν βίον ὃν εἶχεν ἔβαλεν.

Die synoptische Apokalypse. *The Synoptic Apocalypse.*

Matth 24 1–36 = Mark 13 = Luk 21 5–38

(213)

227. Einleitung. Die Zerstörung des Tempels. *Introduction. The Destruction of the Temple.*

Matth 24 1–3

1 Καὶ ἐξελθὼν ὁ Ἰησοῦς ἀπὸ τοῦ ἱεροῦ ἐπορεύετο, καὶ προσῆλθον οἱ μαθηταὶ αὐτοῦ ἐπιδεῖξαι αὐτῷ τὰς οἰκοδομὰς τοῦ ἱεροῦ. 2 ὁ δὲ ἀποκριθεὶς εἶπεν αὐτοῖς· οὐ βλέπετε ταῦτα πάντα; αμην λέγω

Mark 13 1–4

1 Καὶ ἐκπορευομένου αὐτοῦ ἐκ τοῦ ἱεροῦ λέγει αὐτῷ εἷς τῶν μαθητῶν αὐτοῦ· διδάσκαλε, ἴδε ποταποὶ λίθοι καὶ ποταπαὶ οἰκοδομαί. 2 καὶ ὁ Ἰησοῦς ἀποκριθεὶς εἶπεν αὐτῷ· βλέπεις ταύτας τὰς μεγάλας οἰκοδο-

Luk 21 5–7

5 Καί τινων λεγόντων περὶ τοῦ ἱεροῦ, ὅτι λίθοις καλοῖς καὶ ἀναθήμασιν κεκόσμηται, εἶπεν· 6 ταῦτα ἃ θεωρεῖτε, ἐλεύσονται

Mt 24,1 απο] εκ‖Mk: B 1604 *pc* **2** αποκ.] Ιησους‖Mk: *Rpl Lf S*h — Ι. αποκ.‖Mk: 28 ϕ174-346 *pc Laq* Or — *om*‖Lk: 892 H *pc Ll Sp C*b^1 — *txt*: ℵBL 700-1604 **λ**-1582 **ϕ**⟨346⟩ σ1194 D Θ *pc L*'Au *S*s[c]j *C*' | *om* ου^1‖Mk: LX-33-892 700 σ659-954 D *L*⟨q⟩ Or *S*s[c] *C*s$^{1:7}$b | *om* αμ. λε. υμ.‖p: σ1424

Mk 12,43 *om* αυτοις‖p: σ1424 *l*184 | ∼ αυ. η χη.: 28 — ∼ η πτω. αυ.‖p: WΘΣΦ-565-700 σ7-517-659 D 1574 *l*49 *l*184 *l*251 Or *L*abiq | βεβ.] ● εβαλεν‖**p**: $\mathfrak{H}$'(ℵ* -λλ-)^c ΘΣ-565 ϕ13 σ7-115-517-659-827-1082-1402 A D 1342 *al l*18 *l*19 *l*49 Or | *om* των βαλ.‖**p**: W-28 **λ** ϕ13-788 *pc L*bcff^{2}g^{2}iqz *S*s[c] *Geo* | γαζ. + τα δωρα‖Lk 1.4: 700 — + δωρον‖←: *L*bff^2 **44** γαρ + ουτοι‖p: 33-579 **λ** D *pc Cs Geo*^{1} | περισσευματος αυτων(*om*)‖Lk 645 p 2K 8 13f.: ΔW σ7-349-517-659-827-1082-1391 U Γ(-τοις) *pc* (*pc l*49) *l*124 *l*251 *Geo*^{2} | υστερηματος‖p 2K ←: 1241 | *om* πα. οσα ει.‖p: W | εβαλεν + εις τα δωρα‖p: σ827 **13,1** εκ] απο‖Mt: Ψ | οικ. + του ιερου‖Mt: D *L*vl⟨air^{2}z⟩g^{2}r^{1}30 vg^9 **2** ο—αποκ.] ● *om* αποκ.‖Lk: $\mathfrak{H}$' σ115 1342 *pc S*s[c](*om* και *et* ∼ ειπ. αυ. ο Ιησους)p(και ο] ο δε) *C*s^{2}b — *om* ο Ι.‖p: WΘ-565-700 *Le*? abi — ∼ αποκ. ο Ι.: ΔWΘΣ-28-544-1071 **λ ϕ** σ1606 A D(∼ ειπ. αυ. ο Ι.) K Y Π *pm L*' *S*h *Arm*(∼ αυ. ο Ι. ει.) *Geo*^{1}(^{2}*om* και) — *txt* (και ο] ο δε): *Rpl* (240 244) *Lq Cs*(^{4})^2(*om* και) | αυτοις‖Mt: (D) 299 *L*ek abff^{2}g^{2}iqr^1 *C*s$^{1:9}$ | βλεπετε‖Mt: σM^m-659 D 713 *l*48 *L*vl'⟨lr^2⟩g^2 vg^2 *C*b^1 *Geo*' — ου βλεπετε‖Mt: Θ-565 *Lk* bcff^{2}ir^1 vg^4 *C*s$^{5:9}$ *Geo*^{B} | οικ. + αμην λεγω υμιν (+ οτι)‖Mt: **λ**(*om* αμ.) (D) *L*vl'⟨r^2⟩g^{2}r^1; *et* αμ. + αμ.: e) aq *C*b^1(= **λ**) (*Arm*, *et* = e) *Geo*^{B} — + αμην λεγω σοι‖Mt: Θ Σ-28-565-700 **ϕ** σ115-267 G *Ll*(+ οτι) *Geo*^{A}

Lk 21,3 ● αυ. η πτω.‖p: $\mathfrak{H}$⟨892⟩ **ϕ**-*l*547 D Q 157 Bas *L*'⟨e(*om* η πτω.)⟩ *Aeth* — *txt*: *Rpl* Or *Las S*h *Arm* **4** απαντες] ● παντες‖**p**: ℵB-579 ϕ230 D Δ Or | *om* ουτ.‖p: σ659 Θ *L*ff^{2}r$^{1.2}$ | περισσευματος αυτων(-τοις)‖645 p 2K 8 13f.: L-33-1241 544-1071 λ(1)-118(αυτο + *spat.*)-209^v-1582-2193 **ϕ**-*l*547 σ71 *pc l*1663 *L*ds(qr^{2}30 vg')^1 *Geo*^{2} | *om* εις τα δω.‖p: 544 | του θε.] ● *om*‖1: ℵBLX-579-1241 **λλ**⟨22-1278⟩ *l*1579 *S*scj *C*r (*et om* εις: *C*b') — αυτων *et om* εις: *C*sb^4 — *txt*: *Rpl* (*prm* αυτων: *l*1663) Bas Or *L*,*C*p *S*' | της υστερησεως‖p: 1047 | απαντα] ● παντα‖p: $\mathfrak{H}$⟨892⟩X 1071 **ϕ**⟨13-124⟩ D Q 157 *l*1963 Or — *txt*: *Rpl* (απαν: V) Bas | βιον + αυτης‖**p**: **ϕ**⟨13-69⟩ *L*⟨e s⟩ *C*b **5** ειπ. + αυτοις‖Mt Mk: 251 *pc S*sp *C*b^1 **6** *om* α‖p: L D Ψ* *L*vl⟨fg^{2}r^{2}z⟩ vg^1 *S*sc *Geo*

Matth	Mark	Luk
ὑμῖν, οὐ μὴ ἀφεθῇ ὧδε λίθος ἐπὶ λίθον ὃς οὐ καταλυθήσεται. [3] καθημένου δὲ αὐτοῦ ἐπὶ τοῦ ὄρους τῶν ἐλαιῶν προσ-ῆλθον αὐτῷ οἱ μαθηταὶ κατ' ἰδίαν λέγοντες· εἰπὲ ἡμῖν, πότε ταῦτα ἔσται, καὶ τί τὸ σημεῖον τῆς σῆς παρουσίας καὶ συντελείας τοῦ αἰῶ-νος;	μάς; οὐ μὴ ἀφεθῇ λίθος ἐπὶ λίθον ὃς οὐ μὴ καταλυθῇ. [3] καὶ καθημένου αὐτοῦ εἰς τὸ ὄρος τῶν ἐλαιῶν κατέναντι τοῦ ἱεροῦ, ἐπη-ρώτα αὐτὸν κατ' ἰδίαν Πέτρος καὶ Ἰάκωβος καὶ Ἰωάννης καὶ Ἀνδρέας· [4] εἶπον ἡμῖν, πότε ταῦτα ἔσται, καὶ τί τὸ σημεῖον ὅταν μέλλῃ ταῦτα συντελεῖσθαι πάντα;	ἡμέραι ἐν αἷς οὐκ ἀφεθήσεται λίθος ἐπὶ λίθῳ ὃς οὐ καταλυθήσεται. [7] ἐπη-ρώτησαν δὲ αὐτὸν λέγοντες· διδάσκαλε, πότε οὖν ταῦτα ἔσται, καὶ τί τὸ σημεῖον ὅταν μέλλῃ ταῦτα γίνεσθαι;

(214)

228. Der Anfang der Wehen. *The Beginning of Woes.*

Matth 24 ₄₋₈	Mark 13 ₅₋₈	Luk 21 ₈₋₁₁
[4] Καὶ ἀποκριθεὶς ὁ Ἰησοῦς εἶπεν αὐτοῖς· βλέπετε μή τις ὑμᾶς πλανήσῃ. [5] πολλοὶ γὰρ ἐλεύσον-ται ἐπὶ τῷ ὀνόματί μου λέγοντες· ἐγώ εἰμι ὁ Χριστός, *cf. 229.* καὶ	[5] Ὁ δὲ Ἰησοῦς ἀποκριθεὶς ἤρξατο λέγειν αὐτοῖς· βλέπετε μή τις ὑμᾶς πλανήσῃ. [6] πολλοὶ ἐλεύσον-ται ἐπὶ τῷ ὀνόματί μου λέγοντες ὅτι ἐγώ εἰμι, *cf. 231.* καὶ	[8] Ὁ δὲ εἶπεν· βλέπετε μὴ πλανηθῆτε. πολλοὶ γὰρ ἐλεύσον-ται ἐπὶ τῷ ὀνόματί μου λέγοντες ὅτι ἐγώ εἰμι, καί· ὁ καιρὸς ἤγγικεν· μὴ

Mt 24,2 *om* ωδε‖p: W* Lg^{1}r^1 | λιθον] λιθω‖Lk: 1093 | ου^3 + μη‖Mk: 33 Φ-1604 **λ**-1582 ϕ174-230-346-*l*547 **σ**-659 G K U Y Π *mu* **3** ελ. + κατεναντι του ιερου‖Mk: C **5** λεγ. + οτι‖p: C* Φ-1604 *pc l*49 *l*184 *L*f Or$^{1:2}$ *S*,Eu *Geo*^{2} | *om* ο Χ.‖p: σ1194

Mk 13,2 ● αφεθη + ωδε‖Mt: ℌ WΘΣ-28-565-700-1071 **λ** **ϕ**⟨69⟩ σM^c-517-827-1082-1391-1606 D G U 1342 *pm l*^{p1} *L*abg^{2}q *S*s[c]ph$^+$ *C*sb(∼ λιθος επι λιθον ωδε) — + εν(+ τουτω) τω ιερω: *L*ek (c) *C*p^1 — *txt*: *Rpl L*'Cp^1 | επι λιθω‖Lk: *Rpl L*Cp — *txt*: ℌX WΘ-28-544-700-1071 **λ** **ϕ** σM-945 G U Γ Π *mu l*^{p1} | *om* μη^2‖MtLk: ℵ*L Θ ϕ983-1689 157 1342 *pc* | καταλυθησεται‖←: ℵ*L^v Θ **ϕ**⟨124-788⟩ σ827 1342 *pc* — + και δια τριων ημερων αλλος αναστησεται ανευ χειρων‖14₅₈p: D W *L*vl'⟨lqr^{2}z⟩ (*om* αυ. χ. *et* αλ. αν.] αναστησω αυτον: c) Cp **3** και καθ.] καθ. δε(*om*)‖Mt: (L)-579 W σ115-1606 1555 *C*s$^{4:9}$b^2 | *om* κατ. τ. ιερ.‖Mt: 255 *Geo*^{1} | επηρωτων(-ησαν)‖p: *Rpl L*' ({*S*'})h^t (*C*s^{2}b') — *txt* (-ησεν): ℌ⟨Δ⟩ W-28 **ϕ**⟨124-983⟩ (713) *pc* *L*r^2 *S*h^m({} *C*s^{7}b^5) | Π.] ● ο Π.‖14₃₃ Mt17₁: ℵ Θ-565 σ115 (ο τε Π.)-827 D 1342 *pc* | ∼ Ιω. κ. Ια.‖Lk8₅₁ 9₂₈: 28 **ϕ** U *pc* **4** ειπε‖Mt: *Rpl* — *txt*: ℵBLΨ-33 WΘ-28-565-700 λ1 **ϕ**⟨124⟩ D 1342 | *om* παντα‖Lk: Δ-579 WΘ-544-565 λ209 ϕ13 σ267-517(∼ ταυ. με. συν.) *pc l*184 *L*k[e] *S*s[c] *Geo*^{2} **5** ο—αποκ.] και αποκ. (+ αυτοις) ο Ι.‖Mt: (W)Θ-28-544-565-700 **λ**'(1) **ϕ** D (G 299) *L*'(*om* και: cr^2 vg^1; κ. απ.] απ. δε: ff^2; *om* ο Ι.: k[e] an)(r^1?) *Arm*(*om* και) (*Geo*^{1} *et om* ο Ι.) — ● *om* αποκ.‖Lk: ℌ'⟨Δ⟩(*et om* Ι.: 579) σ115-267 1342 *pc* *S*p *C*s^{6}b — ειπεν αυ. ο Ι.: *S*s[c] — *txt*: *Rpl* *S*h(+ αυτοις) *C*s^3 *Geo*^{2}(*om* ο δε Ι.) | ηρξ. λε.] ειπεν(λεγει)‖MtLk: (579) Θ-565-700 σ349-517-1606 D *pc l*18 *l*19 *L*k[e] (an) *S*s[c](∼) *Arm* *Geo*^{2} | *om* αυτοις‖Lk: 544 *pc* *S*h *C*b | τις υμ. πλ.] πλανη-θητε‖Lk: σ827 *l*184 **6** πολλοι + γαρ‖MtLk: *Rpl L*⟨ff^2⟩ *S C* — *txt*: ℵBLΨ W | *om* οτι‖Mt: 33 Θ-544-700 D *l*13 *l*15 *l*17 *L*k[e] bcff^{2}q | ειμι + ο Χριστος‖Mt: 579 WΘ-28-565-700-1071 **ϕ** σ115-267 *pc* *L*bcg^{2}l30 vg^5 *C*s$^{8:10}$b *Arm*

Lk 21,6 λιθος—λιθω] *prm* ωδε‖Mt: X-33-579-1241 **λ**-22-1582 *l*950 *L*e s(+ εν τοιχω) *S*c — ● + ωδε‖Mt: ℵBL-892 **ϕ**-174-230 Ψ *pc* (*et* + εν τοιχω: *L*cff^{2}iqr$^{1.2}$ vg^2) *C*s^{8}b' — λιθος—λιθω εν τοιχω ωδε‖Mt: D *L*al(*om* ωδε) — *txt*: *Rpl L*' *S*s(*prm* εν αυτω)p(*prm* εν αυταις)h *C*s^{1}b^1 | επι λιθον‖p19₄₄: ℌ⟨ℵ*B⟩ ℵ^{c}X 1071 **λλ**⟨22-1278⟩ ϕ69-124 **σ**⟨954⟩-160-659 W Ψ Ω 157 *al l*950 | ου + μη‖Mk: ϕ124 G Ψ | καταλυθη‖Mk: Ψ 1012 **7** αυτ. + οι μαθηται(*et* + αυτου)‖Mt: D (122) 252^m (*L*vg^1) | *om* ουν‖**p**: 579-1241 544-1071 **λλ**⟨22-1278⟩ ϕ13 σ267-659-1675 D *pc* *L*⟨s⟩ *S*scp *C*s$^{7:9}$b | οταν—γιν.] της σης ελευσεως‖Mt: D *L*l | γιν.] συντελεισθαι‖MkMt: σ659 **8** δε + Ιησους‖p: 1071 | ειπ. + αυτοις‖p: 1071 472 *L*c *S*scp *C*s$^{1:9}$b^1 | πλα.] τις υμας πλανηση‖p: 1071 — + προσ-εχετε δε απο των ανθρωπων‖Mt10₁₇: 485 *pc l*13 *l*14 | ● *om* οτι‖Mt: ℵBLX-579-1241 544 *pc l*50 *L*cr^1 Mcn^{Te} *S*j *Aeth* — *txt*: *Rpl L*' *S* | ειμι + ο Χριστος‖Mt: 157 *L*vl⟨af⟩g^{2}r^{1}30 vg^4 Am Mcn^{Te} *S*p | μη^2 + ουν *cf.* Mt6₈.₃₁.₃₄ 10₂₆.₃₁: *Rpl* *L*fqr$^{1.2}$ vg *S*h *Δ*{a}n⟨^{L}⟩ — *txt*: ℵBLX-1241 D Ψ 157 *L*vl' *S*scp(+ δε)j *C* *Arm* *Aeth* *Δ*p

Matth 24	Mark 13	Luk 21	
πολλοὺς πλανήσουσιν. 6 μελλήσετε δὲ ἀκούειν πολέμους καὶ ἀκοὰς πολέμων· ὁρᾶτε μὴ θροεῖσθε· **δεῖ** γὰρ πάντα **γενέσθαι,** ἀλλ' οὔπω ἐστὶν τὸ τέλος.	πολλοὺς πλανήσουσιν. 7 ὅταν δὲ ἀκούσητε πολέμους καὶ ἀκοὰς πολέμων, μὴ θροεῖσθε· **δεῖ** **γενέσθαι,** ἀλλ' οὔπω τὸ τέλος.	πορευθῆτε ὀπίσω αὐτῶν. 9 ὅταν δὲ ἀκούσητε πολέμους καὶ ἀκαταστασίας, μὴ πτοηθῆτε· **δεῖ** γὰρ ταῦτα **γενέσθαι** πρῶτον, ἀλλ' οὐκ εὐθέως τὸ τέλος. 10 τότε ἔλεγεν αὐτοῖς·	Dn2 28
7 **ἐγερθήσεται** γὰρ **ἔθνος ἐπ' ἔθνος** καὶ βασιλεία ἐπὶ βασιλείαν, καὶ ἔσονται λιμοὶ καὶ σεισμοὶ κατὰ τόπους·	8 **ἐγερθήσεται** γὰρ **ἔθνος ἐπ' ἔθνος** καὶ βασιλεία ἐπὶ βασιλείαν. ἔσονται σεισμοὶ κατὰ τόπους, καὶ ἔσονται λιμοί·	**ἐγερθήσεται** **ἔθνος ἐπ' ἔθνος** καὶ βασιλεία ἐπὶ βασιλείαν, 11 σεισμοί τε μεγάλοι κατὰ τόπους καὶ λιμοὶ καὶ λοιμοὶ ἔσονται, φόβητρά τε καὶ σημεῖα ἀπ' οὐρανοῦ μεγάλα ἔσται.	Is19 2 2Chr15 6
8 πάντα δὲ ταῦτα ἀρχὴ ὠδίνων.	ἀρχαὶ ὠδίνων ταῦτα.		

(215)

229. Die Verfolgung der Jünger. *The Persecution of the Disciples.*

	Matth 24 9–14	Mark 13 9–13	Luk 21 12–19
10 17–22 (71.): Προσέχετε δὲ ἀπὸ τῶν ἀνθρώπων·	9 Τότε	9 Βλέπετε δὲ ὑμεῖς ἑαυτούς·	12 Πρὸ δὲ τούτων πάντων ἐπιβαλοῦσιν ἐφ' ὑμᾶς τὰς χεῖρας αὐτῶν καὶ διώξουσιν,

Mt 24,6 πολεμου + και αναστασιας ‖Lk: 1279 | ακο.] αναστασιας ‖Lk: σ517-1675 *l*183^1 | παν.] ταυτα ‖Lk: Y^m *pc l*47 *l*211 PsAth *L*'(∼ γεν. ταυ.: ab) Cp^1 Or^1 *S*s^v[c]j Af *Geo*^{B} *Aeth*^{ms} — παν. ταυ.(∼)‖Lk: (544) *pc* (*l*950 *l*1761 *L*f Or^1 *Arm Geo*' — ● *om* ‖Mk: 𝔖 1604 λ-1582 D Θ PsAth *L*g^2 Cp^1 *S*Eu *C Aeth*^{edd} — *txt*: *Rpl* (∼ γεν. παν.: ΟΣ) Chr *S*' | ουπω] ουκ ευθεως ‖Lk: U *L*vg^1(ουκ] ουπω) *Aeth* | *om* εστ. ‖Mk Lk: 33 σ1424 U *pc* PsAth *L*vg^1 *S*s[c]p **7** λι.] λοιμοι και λι. ‖Lk: L-33 W *L*' *S*j — ● λι. και λοι. ‖Lk: *Rpl* PsAth *L*hq Cp(∼ σει. ... λοι.) Or *S*'Eu *C*b(∼ σει. ... λι. ... λοι.) *Aeth* — *txt* (∼ σει. ... λι. ‖p): (ℵ)B-892 ϕ*l*547^1 D E 414 *l*13 *L*e[k] abff^{2}r$^{1.2}$ Ar Hil *S*s[c] *C*s **8** αρχαι ‖Mk: Σ ϕ543 *pc*

Mk 13,7 ακοας πολ.] αποκαταστασιας ‖Lk: λ⟨1⟩ 245 *l*184 — αποκατ. και ακ. πολ. ‖Lk: σ827 1279 | μη] ορατε μη ‖Mt: ℵ* 700 *pc* | θρο.] πτοεισθε ‖Lk: σ827-1675 245(-ηθητε) | ● δει + γαρ ‖p: *Rpl L*'(γαρ] δε: 30) *S*s[c]p^{4}h *C*s^{7}b^2 *Arm* — *txt*: ℵ*BΨ W *S*p' *C*s^{2}b' | γεν.] ταυτα γ. ‖Lk: σ115 1342 *pc L*bff^{2}z30 vg^1 | ουπω + εστιν ‖Mt: σ827 1342 *L*abcdnr^{2}30 **8** γαρ] *om* ‖Lk: W *pc l*184 *C*s^{4}b^1 *Geo*^{1} — δε: *L*k[e] bilq vg$^{\langle 5\rangle}$ | εσ.^{1}] και εσ. ‖Mt: *Rpl* Hip *L S C*s^1(εσ.^{1}∩^{2}) — *txt*: ℵBLΨ W-28 D 299 *C*s^{8}b | και εσ.^{2}] ● *om* και: ℵ^c(*om* κατα—λιμ.: ℵ* **047**∩ ?)BLΨ-892 28 *C*s^{1}b — *om* εσ. ‖p: W(*et om* και)Θ-565-700 σ1402 D *pc* Hip *L*' (= W: *S*s[c]p^1) *C*s^7 *Arm Geo*^{B} — *txt*: *Rpl L*q Or *S*p'h *C*s^2 *Geo*^{1}(εσται λιμος)^A | λι.] λι.(λοιμοι) και ταραχαι (< αρχαι?): *Rpl* (Θ σ827) (*om* και: W) *L*q Or *S C*s^8 *Δ*i^V — λι. κ. λοι. κ. ταρ.(*om* κ. ταρ.) ‖Lk: Σ 1342 (1542) *pc* (Hip) *Arm Δ*a p — *txt*: ℵ^{c}BLΨ-579 D *L*' *C*s^{2}b *Aeth* | αρ.—ταυτα] ταυ. δε παντα αρ. ωδινων ‖Mt: Θ-28-565 ϕ *pc L*g^2(∼ παν. ταυ. *et om* δε) *C*s^2 *Arm* — ταυ. (+ δε) αρ. ωδ. ‖Mt: 433 (*L*z) *S*p (*C*s^6)(^{1}ταυ. + γαρ) — αρ.—ταυ. παν. ‖Mt: 1071 *pc L*(∼ παν. ταυ.: abn)30 — αρ. δε ωδ. ταυ. ‖Mt: 1396 *C*b^2 — *om* ‖Lk: WΦ *L*c | ● αρχη ‖Mt: 𝔖 Θ-28-565-1071 ϕ σ349-517 D E^v K S U Π 1342 *mu l*48 *l*49 *L*' — *txt*: *Rpl L*bl **9** βλε.—υμας] ειτα υμας αυτους παραδ. ‖Mt9: Θ(ει.] ετι δε)-565(+ δε)-700 D *L*k[e](*prm* βλεπετε) abff^{2}inr^1 | *om* βλε.—εαυ. ‖←Lk: W-28 λ1 ϕ124 91 *S*s[c] *Arm*

Lk 21,8 πορ.] πλανηθητε ‖p: *l*5 *l*12 *l*19 *l*26 *l*44 *l*48 *l*49 *l*50 *l*80 *l*183 *l*303 *l*333 *l*1634 *l*1642 *l*1693 **9** πτο.] φοβηθητε ‖Mt10 28p: D *L*q {*S*scp} | *om* πρω. ‖**p**: 348 *C*b^1(^{3}*om* δει—πρω.) **10** τοτε—εγ.] εγ. γαρ (*om*) ‖p: ϕ983-1689 D (1574) *L*e aff^{2}ilr^1 *S*scp (*C*b^1) — τοτε—εγ. γαρ ‖p: ϕ346 *l*7 *l*13 *l*14 *l*18 *l*19 *l*184^1 *L*c **11** *om* μεγ. ‖p: σ1223 716 *S*p^1 | ● ∼ και κ. τοπ.: ℵBL-33-579 1071 *C*s^{5}b *Arm Aeth* — *om* και ‖p: 892-1241 *pc C*s^1 — *txt*: *Rpl L S*,j *C*s^1 | λι. κ. λοι.] λι. ‖p: X *pc l*184 *Aeth* — λοι. ‖p: ϕ69 — λι. κ. σεισμοι ‖Mt: ϕ983 — ● λοι. κ. λι.: B-579-1241 130 157 *L*' Mcn^{Te} *S*s(λοι. + κ. τοπ.)c — *txt*: *Rpl L*e *S*'j *C* | και^3—μεγ.] ● κ. ση. μεγ. απ ουρ.: 𝔖' 1071 ϕ σ659 Ω(∼ εστ. απ ουρ.) {} — ● κ. απ ουρ. ση. μεγ.: B λ1 — απ ουρ. κ. ση. μεγ.: D *L*,Or (και + ωφθησεται *et om* εστ.: *S*sc) *Geo*(^{1}*om* και)^2 — *txt*: *Rpl L*Te {*S*'j *C*} *Aeth*(*om* απ ουρ.) | απ] απο του *cf.* 9 54 Mt24 29 Mk8 11: 716 1574 ϕ*l*547 1093 *l*12 — + γαρ ‖←: σ267 Γ *pc* **12** επιβ.] προσεχετε απο των ανθρωπων· επιβ. γαρ ‖Mt17: 1241

(Matth 10 17–22)

παραδώσουσιν γὰρ ὑμᾶς εἰς συνέδρια, καὶ ἐν ταῖς συναγωγαῖς αὐτῶν μαστιγώσουσιν ὑμᾶς· [18] καὶ ἐπὶ ἡγεμόνας δὲ καὶ βασιλεῖς ἀχθήσεσθε ἕνεκεν ἐμοῦ, cf. v. 14 ↓ *εἰς μαρτύριον αὐτοῖς καὶ τοῖς ἔθνεσιν.*

[19] ὅταν δὲ παραδῶσιν ὑμᾶς, μὴ μεριμνήσητε πῶς ἢ τί λαλήσητε· δοθήσεται γὰρ ὑμῖν ἐν ἐκείνῃ τῇ ὥρᾳ τί λαλήσητε· [20] οὐ γὰρ ὑμεῖς ἐστε οἱ λαλοῦντες, ἀλλὰ τὸ πνεῦμα τοῦ πατρὸς ὑμῶν τὸ λαλοῦν ἐν ὑμῖν. [21] παραδώσει δὲ ἀδελφὸς ἀδελφὸν εἰς θάνατον καὶ πατὴρ τέκνον, καὶ **ἐπαναστήσονται** *τέκνα ἐπὶ γονεῖς* (Mch 7 6) *καὶ θανατώσουσιν αὐτούς. [22] καὶ*

(Matth 24 9)

παραδώσουσιν ὑμᾶς εἰς θλῖψιν ... (9) καὶ ἀποκτενοῦσιν ὑμᾶς, καὶ

(Mark 13 9–13)

παραδώσουσιν ὑμᾶς εἰς συνέδρια καὶ εἰς συναγωγὰς δαρήσεσθε καὶ ἐπὶ ἡγεμόνων καὶ βασιλέων σταθήσεσθε ἕνεκα ἐμοῦ, εἰς μαρτύριον αὐτοῖς. [10] καὶ εἰς πάντα τὰ ἔθνη πρῶτον δεῖ κηρυχθῆναι τὸ εὐαγγέλιον. [11] καὶ ὅταν ἄγωσιν ὑμᾶς παραδιδόντες, μὴ προμεριμνᾶτε τί λαλήσητε, ἀλλ' ὃ ἐὰν δοθῇ ὑμῖν ἐν ἐκείνῃ τῇ ὥρᾳ, τοῦτο λαλεῖτε· οὐ γάρ ἐστε ὑμεῖς οἱ λαλοῦντες ἀλλὰ τὸ πνεῦμα τὸ ἅγιον. [12] καὶ παραδώσει ἀδελφὸς ἀδελφὸν εἰς θάνατον καὶ πατὴρ τέκνον, καὶ **ἐπαναστήσονται** τέκνα ἐπὶ γονεῖς καὶ θανατώσουσιν αὐτούς. [13] καὶ

(Luk 12 11 f.)

12 11 f. (169.): ὅταν δὲ εἰσφέρωσιν ὑμᾶς ἐπὶ τὰς συναγωγὰς καὶ τὰς ἀρχὰς καὶ τὰς ἐξουσίας, μὴ μεριμνήσητε πῶς ἢ τί ἀπολογήσησθε ἢ τί εἴπητε· [12] τὸ γὰρ ἅγιον πνεῦμα διδάξει ὑμᾶς ἐν αὐτῇ τῇ ὥρᾳ ἃ δεῖ εἰπεῖν.

(Luk 21 12–17)

παραδιδόντες εἰς συναγωγὰς καὶ φυλακάς, ἀπαγομένους ἐπὶ βασιλεῖς καὶ ἡγεμόνας ἕνεκεν τοῦ ὀνόματός μου· [13] ἀποβήσεται δὲ ὑμῖν εἰς μαρτύριον. [14] θέτε οὖν ἐν ταῖς καρδίαις ὑμῶν μὴ προμελετᾶν ἀπολογηθῆναι· [15] ἐγὼ γὰρ δώσω ὑμῖν στόμα καὶ σοφίαν, ᾗ οὐ δυνήσονται ἀντιστῆναι ἢ ἀντειπεῖν ἅπαντες οἱ ἀντικείμενοι ὑμῖν. [16] παραδοθήσεσθε δὲ καὶ ὑπὸ γονέων καὶ ἀδελφῶν καὶ συγγενῶν καὶ φίλων, καὶ θανατώσουσιν ἐξ ὑμῶν, [17] καὶ

(Joh)

14 26: ὁ δὲ παράκλητος, τὸ πνεῦμα τὸ ἅγιον ὃ πέμψει ὁ πατὴρ ἐν τῷ ὀνόματί μου, ἐκεῖνος ὑμᾶς διδάξει πάντα καὶ ὑπομνήσει ὑμᾶς πάντα ἃ εἶπον ὑμῖν.

16 2: ... ἀλλ' ἔρχεται ὥρα ἵνα πᾶς ὁ ἀποκτείνας ὑμᾶς δόξῃ λατρείαν

Mk 13,9 παρ.] παρ. γαρ‖Mt17: *Rpl* *L*clqr^2 vg' *S*' *C*s^7 — και παρ.: W-28 λ1 ϕ124 299 *S*s[c] *Arm Aeth* — παρ. δε: 544 *L*vg^1 — *txt*: BLΨ (Θ-565-700 D *L*vl'r^1) *C*s^{2}b | εις συναγ.] εν ταις συναγωγαις (+ αυτων)‖Mt: σ659-(1391 *l*18 *l*19 *l*49 *l*183) *L*'‹b›(g^{2}30 vg^1 *S*p) | ηγεμονας ... βασιλεις‖p: 1071 1342^v | ηγ. + δε‖Mt: λ872 σ115 A K Γ Π *al* | στα.] αχθησεσθε‖p: 33-579 **λ**-1278^c **σ**‹954›-945-1606 G U *pm Cs* — στα. και αχ.‖p: σ115 **10** *om* και—εθ.‖Mt14: *S*p *C*s$^{2:10}$ | πρω. + δε‖Mt: WΘ-565 ϕ124 σ115 131 *L*bcdff^{2}g^{2}ir^1 vg^1 *S*p *C*s$^{9:10}$ *Arm Geo*^{1} — + γαρ‖Mt: σ1606 (∼ δει γ. πρω.) Hip *L*k[e] *S*s[c] *Geo*^{2} | ευαγ. + εν πασιν τοις εθνεσιν‖Mt14: D *L*ff^{2}g^2 *S*p(εν *prm* μου) *C*s$^{8:10}$ — + εις μαρτυριον αυτοις‖9 Mt18.14: σ1402 — + τουτο‖Mt14 26 13: *L*c *S*s[c] **11** κ. οτ.] οτ. δε‖MtLk: *Rpl* Or *L*ff^{2}q *S* *C*s^7 — *txt*: ℌ‹Δ› D 1342 *L*'[b] *C*s^{1}b *Geo Aeth* | προμεριμνησητε‖MtLk11: Θ-565-1071 | προμ.] μεριμνατε‖←: 33-892 544 λ1278 σM-7-71-267-349-692-827-945-954-1082-1207-1223-1391-1424 Γ *mu* *L*[b]‹r^2› *S*s[c] *C*{s}b^4 — προσμελετατε‖Lk14: Ψ **047** | τι λαλ.] μηδε προμελετατε(μελ.) τι λαλ.‖Lk14: Θ-(28)-565-700 (*pc l*251 *l*260 Or) *L*an (*Arm*) — τι λαλ. μηδε μελετατε(προμελ.)‖←: *Rpl* (38) *S*' — *txt*: ℌ‹Δ› WΣ **λ**‹118› ϕ69 σ1424 D 157 1342 *pc l*32 *L*' *S*s[c] *C* *Geo Aeth* | τι] πως η τι‖MtLk11: **ϕ** σ827 | ∼ υμεις εστε‖Mt: 579 ΣΦ-700 λ1278 σM-115-349-517-659-945-954-1194-1402-1606 U 1342 *pc l*183 *L*acff^{2}nr^{1v}30 vg^6 **12** κ. παρ.] παρ. δε(*om*)‖p: *Rpl* (ϕ230-543 σ517 V 481) Or *L*' *S*s[c](δε] γαρ)ph *C*s^6 (*Arm*) *Geo*^{1}(^{2} = *S*s) — *txt*: ℵBLΨ D 1342 *L*k[e] acn *C*s^{2}b

Lk 21,12 συναγ.] ● τας σ.‖11 44p Mt: ℵB ϕ828 D 157 473 *C*sb^1 — + αυτων‖Mt17 9 35: 579 *L*30 | απαγ.] αγομενους‖Mt: *Rpl* *L*' — *txt*: ℵBL-579 **λλ**‹22-1278› D Θ Ψ 157 *L*e **13** δε] ● *om*: ℵ*B-579 D 348 *L*a *C*s^3(^{1}*om* απ.—υμ.‖p)b^1 — γαρ: *L*cff^{2}ilr^1 — *txt*: *Rpl* (*om* υμ.: *l*184^1) *L*' *S*,j *C*s^{5}b' **14** θεσθε‖94 41 66: *Rpl* Cr Or — *txt*: ℵB*LX-33 σM A D R W Y Π Ψ *al* | εις τας καρδιας‖94 4: *Rpl* (*om* εις: σ1194-1207 Π *pc*) Or^1 — *txt*: ℵBLX-33-579 1071 **λ**-1582 A D Ψ 157 *pc* Cr Or^1 (τη καρδια: *S*p *C*sb^5) *Aeth* **15** στο.] πνευμα‖p: 1241

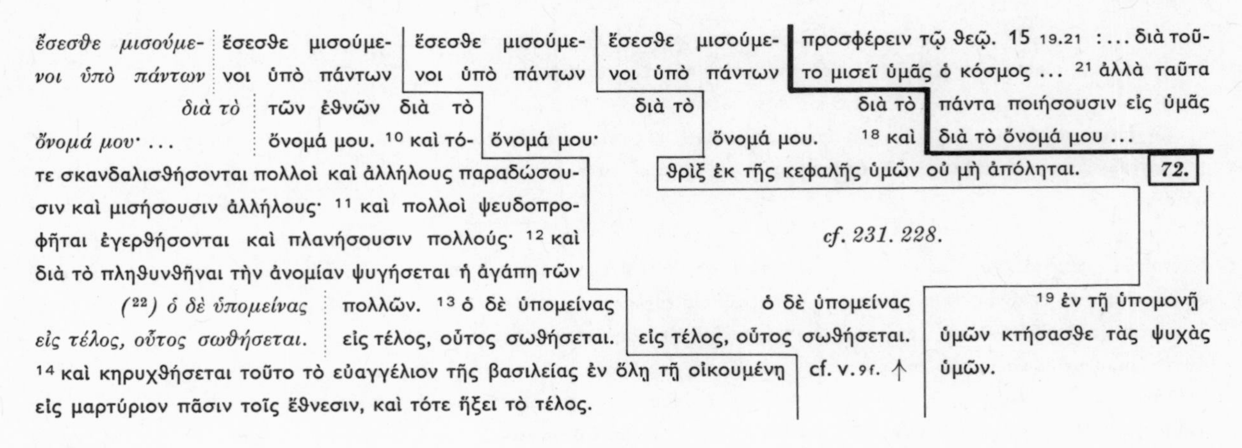

Matth (10,22)	Matth 24	Mark 13	Luk 21	Joh
ἔσεσθε μισούμενοι ὑπὸ πάντων διὰ τὸ ὄνομά μου· ...	ἔσεσθε μισούμενοι ὑπὸ πάντων τῶν ἐθνῶν διὰ τὸ ὄνομά μου. [10] καὶ τότε σκανδαλισθήσονται πολλοὶ καὶ ἀλλήλους παραδώσουσιν καὶ μισήσουσιν ἀλλήλους· [11] καὶ πολλοὶ ψευδοπροφῆται ἐγερθήσονται καὶ πλανήσουσιν πολλούς· [12] καὶ διὰ τὸ πληθυνθῆναι τὴν ἀνομίαν ψυγήσεται ἡ ἀγάπη τῶν πολλῶν.	ἔσεσθε μισούμενοι ὑπὸ πάντων διὰ τὸ ὄνομά μου·	ἔσεσθε μισούμενοι ὑπὸ πάντων διὰ τὸ ὄνομά μου. [18] καὶ θρὶξ ἐκ τῆς κεφαλῆς ὑμῶν οὐ μὴ ἀπόληται.	προσφέρειν τῷ θεῷ. 15 19.21 : ... διὰ τοῦτο μισεῖ ὑμᾶς ὁ κόσμος ... [21] ἀλλὰ ταῦτα πάντα ποιήσουσιν εἰς ὑμᾶς διὰ τὸ ὄνομά μου ... **72.**
(22) ὁ δὲ ὑπομείνας εἰς τέλος, οὗτος σωθήσεται.	[13] ὁ δὲ ὑπομείνας εἰς τέλος, οὗτος σωθήσεται.	ὁ δὲ ὑπομείνας εἰς τέλος, οὗτος σωθήσεται.	[19] ἐν τῇ ὑπομονῇ ὑμῶν κτήσασθε τὰς ψυχὰς ὑμῶν.	*cf. 231. 228.*
	[14] καὶ κηρυχθήσεται τοῦτο τὸ εὐαγγέλιον τῆς βασιλείας ἐν ὅλῃ τῇ οἰκουμένῃ εἰς μαρτύριον πᾶσιν τοῖς ἔθνεσιν, καὶ τότε ἥξει τὸ τέλος.	cf. v. 9f. ↑		

(216) ## *230.* Die Bedrängnis in Judäa. *The Abomination of Desolation.*

Matth 24 15–22	Mark 13 14–20	Luk 21 20–24	
[15] Ὅταν οὖν ἴδητε **τὸ βδέλυγμα τῆς ἐρημώσεως** τὸ ῥηθὲν διὰ Δανιηλ τοῦ προφήτου ἑστὸς **ἐν τόπῳ ἁγίῳ,** ὁ ἀναγινώσκων νοείτω, [16] τότε οἱ ἐν τῇ Ἰουδαίᾳ	[14] Ὅταν δὲ ἴδητε **τὸ βδέλυγμα τῆς ἐρημώσεως** ἑστηκότα ὅπου οὐ δεῖ, ὁ ἀναγινώσκων νοείτω, τότε οἱ ἐν τῇ Ἰουδαίᾳ	[20] Ὅταν δὲ ἴδητε κυκλουμένην ὑπὸ στρατοπέδων Ἰερουσαλημ, τότε γνῶτε ὅτι ἤγγικεν ἡ ἐρήμωσις αὐτῆς. [21] τότε οἱ ἐν τῇ Ἰουδαίᾳ φευγέτωσαν	Dn12₁₁ 11₃₁ 9₂₇
φευγέτωσαν ἐπὶ τὰ ὄρη,	φευγέτωσαν εἰς τὰ ὄρη,	εἰς τὰ ὄρη, καὶ οἱ ἐν μέσῳ αὐτῆς	
[17] ὁ ἐπὶ τοῦ δώματος μὴ καταβαινέτω	[15] ὁ δὲ ἐπὶ τοῦ δώματος μὴ καταβάτω εἰς	*17₃₁ (198.): ἐν ἐκείνῃ τῇ ἡμέρᾳ ὃς ἔσται ἐπὶ τοῦ δώματος καὶ τὰ σκεύη αὐτοῦ ἐν*	

Mt 24,9 *om* τ. εθν.‖22 Mk Lk: C OΣ **λ**-1582 **φ**828 σ1194-1391-1424-1606-1675 *pc* PsAth *Ll Ss*[c]h^{+} | μου + ο δε υπομεινας εις το τελος ουτος σωθησεται‖13.22 Mk: C^{c} σM^{m} Γ **094** 713 **10** παρ. + εις θανατον‖21 Mk12: Φ **φ**124 *pc LAr* **11** ~ πολ. πλα.‖**24**5 Mk136: ℵL-33-892 157 *pc Lhr*$^{1.2}$ *Sj Δi*^{T} {md n'(πολ.] τους ανθρωπους: n^{Hr})} **14** κ. κηρ.] δει γαρ κηρυχθηναι‖246p Mk: Ddy(*om* γαρ) Eu | ~ το ευ. του.‖2613: σ1223 D 478 Chr^{2} Cr Ddy Eu Or *L*Cp *Geo* — *om* τουτο‖423 935 Mk10 149: Φ λ22 σ692-1194-1402 Γ **047** *pc l*47 *l*48 Chr^{2} Eu *La S*Eu *Cs*$^{2:7}$ | τ. βασ.] *om*‖2613 Mk149: σ1424 Chr$^{4:5}$ Cr Eu Or *Lg*^{1}*r*^{1} *Cp*$^{1:2}$ — μου: *Ll S*Eu | πασ.] αυτοις και‖**10**18 84 Mk144 Lk514: Γ Or **15** ουν] δε‖p: ℵ^{c}L-892 157 *pc l*48 *l*49 Chr *Ll* Cp$^{1:2}$ Ir$^{1:2}$ *Ss*[c]p *Cs*$^{6:8}$b *Geo*^{1} | δια] υπο‖2231 122 215: σ1402 2145 *L*'⟨e[k] hqr^{2}⟩(in: vg^{2}) *S*h **16** επι] ● εις‖p: B-892 Σ-28-700-1604 **λ**-1582 **φ**124 **σ**-M-1194-1402 D E F G H K S U V Δ Θ **094** *pc l*48 Eu **17** ο + δε‖Mk: 33 D *Le*[k] | ● καταβατω‖Mk Lk31: ℌ Σ-700-1604 **φ**124-*l*547 **σ**-945-1402 D Θ **094** 157 *pc* Or^{1} — *txt*: *Rpl* Hip Or^{1}

Mk 13,13 παν. + των εθνων‖Mt9: 477 *Lr*^{1} vg^{1} **14** δε] ουν‖Mt: 1574 | εργ. + το ρηθεν υπο(δια) Δανιηλ του προφητου‖Mt: *Rpl* (579 Φ-28 **λ** σ1424 *pc*)(*l*184, *et* ~ το δια—πρ. ρη.) *Lk*^{c}(* υπο Δ.] ante)[e] (cq)l n^{c}z vg^{2} (*S*') *Cb*^{7} — *txt*: ℵBLΨ-892 W-565-700 D 1542 Hip *L*'Au *Ss*[c] *C*' *Arm* | εστος‖Mt: *Rpl* (εστηκος Ψ-579 D) — στηκον: W-28 **λ** **φ**⟨124⟩-1689 — στηκοντα: 892 — *txt*: ℵBL | οπ. ου δει] εν τοπω αγιω‖Mt: 544(αγνω) U^{v} *pc* vg^{1} *Aeth* — εν τοπ. οπου ου δει‖Mt: Θ(οπου] ου)-1071 σ517-659-1082 238(οπου] ω) *pc Arm* | εις] επι‖Mt: 565-700 U *pc* **15** ο δε] ● ο‖Mt: B σ827-1424 F H 1342 *pc Lc C* — και ο‖Lk21: *L*' *Ss*[c]p | καταβαινετω‖Mt: σM 473 | ● *om* εις τ. οι.‖Mt: ℵBLΨ-892 544 σ1082 *al* Hip *Lk*[e] c Au *Sp C* — *txt*: *Rpl L*' *S*' *Arm*

Lk 21,18 *om* 18‖p: Mcn^{Ep} *Sc* **19** ● κτησεσθε‖p: B-33 λ1582 **φ**⟨69⟩-174 A Θ Ω *pc l*150 Mac^{M} Or^{1} *L*⟨e q⟩ (σωσετε: Mcn^{Te}) *S*,j *Csb*^{7}(' κτασθε) — *txt*: *Rpl* Bas CAp Cr Mac^{M} Or^{1} *Li* **20** γνωσεσθε‖Jo 828.32: X 1071 σ1675 D *pc* Eu$^{1:6}$ Or$^{1:2}$ Or^{Eu} *Le* s *Arm* — γινωσκετε‖2131p. 30p: **λλ**⟨22-1278⟩ R W Eu$^{1:6}$ *Cb*^{1}(*om* τοτε) **21** εις] επι‖Mt: H 713 *l*49 *Cb*

Matthew

ἆραι τὰ ἐκ τῆς οἰκίας αὐτοῦ, [18] καὶ ὁ ἐν τῷ ἀγρῷ **μὴ ἐπιστρεψάτω ὀπίσω** ἆραι τὸ ἱμάτιον αὐτοῦ. [19] οὐαὶ δὲ ταῖς ἐν γαστρὶ ἐχούσαις καὶ ταῖς θηλαζούσαις ἐν ἐκείναις ταῖς ἡμέραις. [20] προσεύχεσθε δὲ ἵνα μὴ γένηται ἡ φυγὴ ὑμῶν χειμῶνος μηδὲ σαββάτῳ· [21] ἔσται γὰρ τότε **θλῖψις** μεγάλη, **οἵα οὐ γέγονεν** ἀπ' ἀρχῆς κόσμου **ἕως τοῦ νῦν** οὐδ' οὐ μὴ γένηται. [22] καὶ εἰ μὴ ἐκολοβώθησαν αἱ ἡμέραι ἐκεῖναι, οὐκ ἂν ἐσώθη πᾶσα σάρξ· διὰ δὲ τοὺς ἐκλεκτοὺς κολοβωθήσονται αἱ ἡμέραι ἐκεῖναι.

Gn19,17 Dt32,35 Hos9,7 Dn12,1 Zch12,3

Mark

τὴν οἰκίαν μηδὲ εἰσελθάτω τι ἆραι ἐκ τῆς οἰκίας αὐτοῦ, [16] καὶ ὁ εἰς τὸν ἀγρὸν **μὴ ἐπιστρεψάτω εἰς τὰ ὀπίσω** ἆραι τὸ ἱμάτιον αὐτοῦ. [17] οὐαὶ δὲ ταῖς ἐν γαστρὶ ἐχούσαις καὶ ταῖς θηλαζούσαις ἐν ἐκείναις ταῖς ἡμέραις. [18] προσεύχεσθε δὲ ἵνα μὴ γένηται χειμῶνος· [19] ἔσονται γὰρ αἱ ἡμέραι ἐκεῖναι **θλῖψις, οἵα οὐ γέγονεν** τοιαύτη ἀπ' ἀρχῆς κτίσεως ἣν ἔκτισεν ὁ θεὸς **ἕως τοῦ νῦν** καὶ οὐ μὴ γένηται. [20] καὶ εἰ μὴ ἐκολόβωσεν κύριος τὰς ἡμέρας, οὐκ ἂν ἐσώθη πᾶσα σάρξ· ἀλλὰ διὰ τοὺς ἐκλεκτοὺς οὓς ἐξελέξατο ἐκολόβωσεν τὰς ἡμέρας.

*τῇ οἰκίᾳ, μὴ καταβάτω ἆραι αὐτά, καὶ ὁ ἐν ἀγρῷ ὁμοίως **μὴ ἐπιστρεψάτω εἰς τὰ ὀπίσω.*** (Lk17,31)

Luke

ἐκχωρείτωσαν, καὶ οἱ ἐν ταῖς χώραις μὴ εἰσερχέσθωσαν εἰς αὐτήν, [22] ὅτι **ἡμέραι ἐκδικήσεως** αὗταί εἰσιν τοῦ πλησθῆναι πάντα τὰ γεγραμμένα. [23] οὐαὶ ταῖς ἐν γαστρὶ ἐχούσαις καὶ ταῖς θηλαζούσαις ἐν ἐκείναις ταῖς ἡμέραις· ἔσται γὰρ ἀνάγκη μεγάλη ἐπὶ τῆς γῆς καὶ ὀργὴ τῷ λαῷ τούτῳ, [24] καὶ πεσοῦνται στόματι μαχαίρης καὶ αἰχμαλωτισθήσονται εἰς τὰ ἔθνη πάντα, καὶ **Ιερουσαλημ** ἔσται **πατουμένη ὑπὸ ἐθνῶν,** ἄχρι οὗ πληρωθῶσιν καιροὶ ἐθνῶν.

Mt 24,17 τα] τι ‖ Mk: 33 28-700 **λ**-1582 σ945-1293-1402 D Θ *pc* Hip *L*,Cp Ir Or *S*(*om*: s[c])j *Arm* **18** αγρω + ομοιως ‖ Lk31: Σ σ1010-1293 | οπισω] εις τα οπ. ‖ ← Mk: 33 ΣΦ-700-1604 ϕ983 **σ**⟨1424⟩-1194 *pc* *l*48 *l*49 Chr Hip | ● τα ιματια: *Rpl* Chr *L*fr² *Arm* — *txt*: ℌ Σ-700-1604 **λ**-1582 **ϕ**-*l*547 σ71-517-659-1424 D K Y Θ Π **094** 157 *pm* Hip *L*'Ar Cp Hil Or *S*s[c]pj *C* **21** *om* τοτε ‖ p: K *pc* *l*183¹ *L*bff²g¹r^{1.2} vg² *S*j | κοσ.] κτισεως ‖ Mk: Cr^I — *om* ‖ 194.8: *L*l | ουδ] και ‖ Mk: 1574

Mk 13,15 *om* μηδε εισελ. ‖ Mt: 1071 σ1082 *pc* *L*k[e] c | ● ∼ αραι τι ‖ Mt Lk31: *Rpl* (∼ αρ. εκ—αυ. τι: W) Hip *L*,Au — *txt*: BLΨ-892 K Π *al* **16** *om* εις τα ‖ Mt: ℵ-579 D *pc* **17** *om* δε ‖ Lk: D' *C*s^{1:8} **18** γεν. + η φυγη υμων ‖ Mt: *Rpl* Hip *L*k[e] g²r²30 vg⁵ *S*' *C*' — + ταυτα (∼ χει. ταυ. γεν.) ‖ Lk21,9.28: (L Θ)-28-565 **ϕ**⟨124-346⟩ *pc* *L*abnq vg⁴ (*Arm*) — *txt*: ℵ*B W D(∼ χ. γεν.) 566 *L*'Au *S*s[c] *C*b¹ | χει. + μηδε(+ εν) σαββατω ‖ Mt: σ827-1402-(1675) *al* {*C*b¹} — + μηδε σαββατου (-ων) ‖ Mt: Σ-1071 σ276 1342 (*pc*) {} — + η(+ εν) σαββατου(-ω) ‖ Mt: L-(892 ϕ346 σ517-1606 *al*) 235 *L*k[e] g² n^c30 *C*s^{1:8} **19** εσ.—εκει.] εσται(-ονται) εν ταις ημεραις εκειναις ‖ p: Γ (1012 *L*k[e] abdnqr^{1.2}30) *S*s[c](∼ θλ. εν—εκει.)p: *C*s^{3:8}b³ | *om* τοιαυτη ‖ Mt: Ψ-892 *pc* | κτι.] κοσμου ‖ Mt: 1093 — + κοσμου ‖ Mt: 1071 | *om* ην—θε. ‖ Mt: Θ-565 σ27-1207 D *pc* *L*acff²inr¹ *Arm* | και] ουδ ‖ Mt: ΘΣ-544-565 **λ** **ϕ**⟨124⟩ D(*om* ου) F G 157 *pc* **20** εκολ.¹—ημ.¹] εκολοβωθησαν αι ημεραι εκειναι(*om*) ‖ Mt: 544 (1241) 1342 *l*184 *S*s[c]j^v | ημ.¹ + εκεινας ‖ Mt: ΔΨ-579 ΘΣ-28-1071 **λ** **ϕ** σM-517-1402-1606 E F G *L*cg² vg⁵ Au *S* *C*s^{7:8}bf | αλλα δια] δια δε ‖ Mt: 28 **λ** **ϕ**⟨124⟩ | εκολ.²-ημ.²] κολοβωθησονται αι ημεραι εκειναι(*om*) ‖ Mt: *L*b(g² *S*s[c]) — εκολοβωθησαν αι ημ. ‖ Mt22a: *S*j | ημ.² + εκεινας Mt: ΘΣ σ517-1606 1588 *L*k[e](*om* ημ.²) *S*ph⁻ *C*s^{2:7}b⁸

Lk 21,21 εκχ.] μη εκχ. ‖ p: D *L*r² vg² **22** πληρωθηναι ‖ 24,44 Mt26,56 Mk14,49: CX-33-892-1241 544-700-1071 **λλ**⟨1278⟩ **ϕ**-174-230 σ160-1675 Θ 157 *pm* — *txt*: *R* (*om* του—γεγρ. *cf.* p: Γ) *pm* Eu **23** ουαι + δε ‖ Mt Mk: *Rpl* Eu *L*fr² vg' *S* *C*s³b' — *txt*: BL λ1278 D 660 *L*vl'r¹30 vg¹ *C*s⁵b⁶ *Δ*a ad p | γαρ + τοτε ‖ Mt: **λλ** σ659-1391-1402 *pc* *l*49 *Geo*¹(∼ αν. με. το.)² — + εν εκειναις ταις ημεραις ‖ Mk: ℵ* **24** ∼ παν. τα εθ. ‖ Mk13,10 Mt28,19: *Rpl* Eu *L*' *S*(παν. τοπον: sp)ch *Arm* *Aeth* — *txt*: ℵBLΨ-579-892 1071 ϕ124 R *L*a

---

Mt24,19p *cf.* ETh^{II} 79 (*cf. ad 263.* Lk23,29)

(217. 218)

231. Warnung vor falschen Messias- und Prophetengestalten.
Against False Messiahs and False Prophets.

Matth 24 23–28

[23] Τότε ἐάν τις ὑμῖν εἴπῃ· ἰδοὺ ὧδε ὁ Χριστός, ἤ· ὧδε, μὴ πιστεύσητε· [24] **ἐγερθήσονται** γὰρ ψευδόχριστοι καὶ ψευδο**προφῆται** καὶ **δώσουσιν σημεῖα** μεγάλα καὶ **τέρατα,** ὥστε πλανῆσαι, εἰ δυνατόν, καὶ τοὺς ἐκλεκτούς. *cf. 229.* [25] ἰδοὺ προείρηκα ὑμῖν. [26] ἐὰν οὖν εἴπωσιν ὑμῖν· ἰδοὺ ἐν τῇ ἐρήμῳ ἐστίν, μὴ ἐξέλθητε· ἰδοὺ ἐν τοῖς ταμιείοις, μὴ πιστεύσητε· [27] ὥσπερ γὰρ ἡ ἀστραπὴ ἐξέρχεται ἀπὸ ἀνατολῶν καὶ φαίνεται ἕως δυσμῶν, οὕτως ἔσται ἡ παρουσία τοῦ υἱοῦ τοῦ ἀνθρώπου· [28] ὅπου ἐὰν ᾖ τὸ πτῶμα, ἐκεῖ συναχθήσονται οἱ ἀετοί.

cf. v. 21 ↑ **[198.]**

Mark 13 21–23

[21] Καὶ τότε ἐάν τις ὑμῖν εἴπῃ· ἴδε ὧδε ὁ Χριστός, ἴδε ἐκεῖ, μὴ πιστεύετε· [22] **ἐγερθήσονται** γὰρ ψευδόχριστοι καὶ ψευδο**προφῆται** καὶ **ποιήσουσιν σημεῖα** καὶ **τέρατα** πρὸς τὸ ἀποπλανᾶν, εἰ δυνατόν, τοὺς ἐκλεκτούς. *cf. 228.* [23] ὑμεῖς δὲ βλέπετε· προείρηκα ὑμῖν πάντα.

*17*23 *(198.): καὶ ἐροῦσιν ὑμῖν· ἰδοὺ ἐκεῖ, ἰδοὺ ὧδε· μὴ ἀπέλθητε μηδὲ διώξητε. cf. 197.*

Dt13₂

13 19 : ἀπ' ἄρτι λέγω ὑμῖν πρὸ τοῦ γενέσθαι, ἵνα πιστεύσητε ὅταν γένηται ὅτι ἐγώ εἰμι. 14 29 : καὶ νῦν εἴρηκα ὑμῖν πρὶν γενέσθαι, ἵνα ὅταν γένηται πιστεύσητε. 16 4 : ἀλλὰ ταῦτα λελάληκα ὑμῖν ἵνα ὅταν ἔλθῃ ἡ ὥρα αὐτῶν μνημονεύητε αὐτῶν, ὅτι ἐγὼ εἶπον ὑμῖν.

Mt 24,23 τοτε] και τ.‖24₁₄Mk: σ1391 *L*d* | η ωδε] ιδου εκει‖Mk Lk17₂₁.₂₃: 157 *pc* *L*e[k] bqr^{2} Or *S*s[c] — η (+ ιδου) εκει‖←: σ1010-1293 D *l*16 *L*'(acg^{1}hr^{1}z30 vg^{1}) Au (*S*j$^{ab1c.1v}$) *C*s$^{2:9}$b *Arm* | πιστευετε‖Mk: B* 262 Or **24** γαρ + εθνος επι εθνος και αναστησονται‖24₇p: 1515 | ~ και τερ. μεγ.‖Mk: 28 **σ**-1293 1241 Or — *om* μεγ.‖Mk: ℵ W* 273 Hip *L*ff^{2}r^{1} vg^{1} *C*s^{1v}b^{1} | ● πλανασθαι (-ηθηναι)‖Lk21₈: (ℵ)LZ-33 **λ**-22-1582 (D) Θ 157 Ath$^{1:2}$ Cr^{I} Or *L*⟨cff^{1}h⟩ PsCp — αποπλανησαι‖Mk: 213 713 *l*48 **25** υμ. + παντα‖Mk: 348 *L*Cp **27** εξερ.] αστραπτει‖Lk: Hip *S*s[c] Eu | εσται + και‖24₃₉ Lk17₂₆: *Rpl* Cr^{I} *L*' Ad Cp^{1} *S*hj^{abc} — *txt*: ℌX Σ-700 λ1-22-1582 σ71-692 D E F G H K S U V Y Γ Π *al* Ad Or *L*aff^{1}hqr^{1} vg$^{6(7?)}$ Cp^{1} *S*'j^{1} Eu *C* | η^{2}] εν τη‖←: σ1293 **28** ● οπου + γαρ: *Rpl* *L*cff^{2} q Or *S*h *C*s$^{1:6(7?)}$ *Arm* — *txt*: ℌ'(οπ.] που: ℵ*) 700 **λ**-1582 ϕ788 D Θ *pc* Hip *L*' *S*s[c]p'(^{7} + δε)j *C* *Aeth* | πτω.] σωμα‖Lk17₃₇: ℵ* *L*Hil *S*s[c]p | οι] και οι‖←: 1604 σ517-1402-1675 565 *l*54 *l*184 *L*l vg^{4} Ir Or *Arm*^{pc} | ~ οι αε. συνα.‖←: 1093 *l*184^{1}

Mk 13,21 *om* και‖Mt: ΘΣ-565 **λ**-1278 **σ**⟨1424⟩-115-659 U *L*c(τοτε + ουν) *S*p *C*s$^{1:8}$ | ιδε^{1}] ιδου‖Mt23.26 Lk17₂₁.₂₃: *Rpl* — *txt*: ℵBLΨ-892 1342 | Χ. + η‖Mt Lk17₂₁: *Rpl* Cat *L*vl'g^{2}30 vg^{1} *S*p^{1}hj *C*s^{5}bf *Arm* — + και: B *L*r^{1} vg^{1} *S*p' *C*s^{2} — *txt*: ℌ'⟨Δ⟩ W-565-700-1071 **ϕ**⟨124⟩-230 σ7-71-349-517-692-1223-1391 U 157 *pm* *L*k[e] lr^{2}z vg' *S*s[c] | ιδε^{2}] ιδου‖p Mt₂₆ Lk←: *Rpl* — *om*‖Mt Lk←: C 273 *L*ff^{2} *C*bf^{v} — *txt*: ℵBLΨ-892 28 D 1342 | πιστευσητε‖Mt: *Rpl* — *txt*: ℵBCLΔΨ W λ22 **ϕ**⟨124⟩ σ71-692 A D E F H V Y Ω 157 *pm* **22** γαρ] ● δε: ℵC — *om*: 1355 *Δ*ad p | ποι.] ● δωσουσιν‖Mt: *Rpl* *L*' *S*,j^{fv} *C*,f^{v} *Geo* — *txt*: Θ-28-565 **ϕ** D Cat Vic^{A} *La* *S*j^{1} *Geo*^{B} *Aeth* | σημ. + μεγαλα‖Mt: 579 | αποπ.] πλαναν‖Mt: W-28(-ησαι) ϕ124 *pc* — αποπλανησαι‖Mt: **σ**⟨954⟩ *pc* | ● *om* και^{4}: ℵBΨ(*om* τους) D' *C*s$^{1:8}$ **23** ● βλε. + ιδου‖Mt: *Rpl* *L*' *S*,j *C*b^{1} — *txt*: BLΨ W-28 1342 *L*ar^{1}(+ εγω) Cp *C*'

Jo 13,19 ~ οτ. γεν. πισ.‖14₂₉: *Rpl* Or^{2} Thd^{C} *L*cfqr^{1}z *S*,j *C*b^{+B}a^{s} *Δ*a i^{T} l^{FG} md n' — *txt*: 𝔓^{66} ℵBL-**068**-579(οτ.] εαν) 213 Cr Or^{3} *L*' *C*s *Aeth* *Δ*ad l^{AD} n^{L} | ειμι] ειπον υμιν‖16₄: **ϕ**⟨69-124-788⟩ σ2193 **14,29** πριν] προ του‖13₁₉: **ϕ**-*l*547 **16,4** ● *om* αυτ.^{1}(*et om* αυτ.^{2})‖17₁ 12₂₃: *Rpl* (ℵ* ϕ788 D 2148 *l*64 *l*69 *l*76 *l*184 *l*185 *l*1127 Chr(αυτ.^{2}] τουτ.) (Cr^{I}) *L*(a)ff^{2} *S*(s[c])j (*C*s)b'(^{B7} a^{s} *Arm*) *Geo* (*Δ*i^{V} {n^{L}}) — *txt* (*et om* αυτ.^{2}): 𝔓^{66v} (ℵ^{a})B(L)-33 1071 **λ**⟨1⟩-2193 (**ϕ**'-*l*547; *et* αυτ.^{1}] αυτου: 346)-124 σ1188-1207 A Θ Π*(^{c}) *al* (*l*^{pl}) Cat (*L*'Cp) *S*ph (*C*b^{1}) *Got* *Δ*a (ad i$^{T⟨1⟩}$ l md^{1})' (n'{})

Mt24₂₃p.₂₆ *cf.* ETh^{II} 113 (*cf. ad 197.*)

(219) ***232.*** Die Parusie des Menschensohns. *The Parousia of the Son of Man.*

Matth 24 29–31

Ps65 9 · Is13 10 · Is34 4 · Ps65 8 Is24 19 · Is13 11 · Zch12 12 · Dn7 13f. · Is27 13 · Zch2 10 · Dt30 4

29 Εὐθέως δὲ μετὰ τὴν θλῖψιν τῶν ἡμερῶν ἐκείνων **ὁ ἥλιος σκοτισθήσεται, καὶ ἡ σελήνη οὐ δώσει τὸ φέγγος αὐτῆς, καὶ οἱ ἀστέρες πεσοῦνται** ἀπὸ τοῦ οὐρανοῦ, **καὶ αἱ δυνάμεις τῶν οὐρανῶν** σαλευθήσονται. 30 καὶ τότε φανήσεται τὸ σημεῖον τοῦ υἱοῦ τοῦ ἀνθρώπου ἐν τῷ οὐρανῷ, καὶ **κόψονται** τότε **πᾶσαι αἱ φυλαὶ τῆς γῆς** καὶ ὄψονται **τὸν υἱὸν τοῦ ἀνθρώπου ἐρχόμενον ἐπὶ τῶν νεφελῶν τοῦ οὐρανοῦ** μετὰ δυνάμεως καὶ δόξης πολλῆς. 31 καὶ ἀποστελεῖ τοὺς ἀγγέλους αὐτοῦ μετὰ **σάλπιγγος μεγάλης,** καὶ **ἐπισυνάξουσιν** τοὺς ἐκλεκτοὺς αὐτοῦ **ἐκ τῶν τεσσάρων ἀνέμων ἀπ᾿ ἄκρων οὐρανῶν**

Mark 13 24–27

24 Ἀλλ᾿ ἐν ἐκείναις ταῖς ἡμέραις μετὰ τὴν θλῖψιν ἐκείνην **ὁ ἥλιος σκοτισθήσεται, καὶ ἡ σελήνη οὐ δώσει τὸ φέγγος αὐτῆς,** 25 **καὶ οἱ ἀστέρες** **ἔσονται** ἐκ τοῦ οὐρανοῦ **ἐκπίπτοντες,** **καὶ αἱ δυνάμεις αἱ ἐν τοῖς οὐρανοῖς** σαλευθήσονται. 26 καὶ τότε ὄψονται **τὸν υἱὸν τοῦ ἀνθρώπου ἐρχόμενον ἐν νεφέλαις** *cf. 256.* μετὰ δυνάμεως πολλῆς καὶ δόξης. 27 καὶ τότε ἀποστελεῖ τοὺς ἀγγέλους καὶ **ἐπισυνάξει** τοὺς ἐκλεκτοὺς **ἐκ τῶν τεσσάρων ἀνέμων ἀπ᾿ ἄκρου** γῆς

Luk 21 25–28

25 Καὶ ἔσονται **σημεῖα** ἐν ἡλίῳ καὶ σελήνῃ καὶ ἄστροις, καὶ ἐπὶ τῆς **γῆς** συνοχὴ **ἐθνῶν** ἐν **ἀπορίᾳ** **ἤχους θαλάσσης** καὶ **σάλου,** 26 ἀποψυχόντων ἀνθρώπων ἀπὸ **φόβου** καὶ προσδοκίας τῶν ἐπερχομένων τῇ **οἰκουμένῃ· αἱ** γὰρ **δυνάμεις τῶν οὐρανῶν** σαλευθήσονται. 27 καὶ τότε ὄψονται **τὸν υἱὸν τοῦ ἀνθρώπου ἐρχόμενον ἐν νεφέλῃ** μετὰ δυνάμεως καὶ δόξης πολλῆς.

Mt 24,29 απο] ● εκ‖Mk: ℵ D *pc l*184[1] Eu Hip **30** ● *om* τω‖6 10.20 Mk10 21: ℵBL 700 Θ | ● ∼ τοτε[2] κο.‖30ap 24 10.14: *Rpl L*,Au PsAu Or *S*(*om* και[2]—γης: s[c])'j — ● *om* τοτε[2]: ℵ* 1604 ϕ13 *Le*[k] r[2] Cp — *txt*: 892 700 **λ**⟨118⟩-1582 **ϕ**'-*l*547 D Θ *La* | επι] μετα‖Mk14 62: 700 1579 *Geo*[A.ch] — εν‖p: *L*,Cp *Aeth* | ∼ πολ. κ. δοξ.‖Mk: σ115 D *L*⟨fq⟩ Cp *Ss*[c] **31** και[1] + τοτε‖p 30p: W Hip *Lvg*[1] *Sj*[ab1c] | ● σαλπ.] + φωνης(και φωνης) *cf.* 1Th4 16 H12 19 Ap1 10 *etc.*: *Rpl* (544 ϕ1689 σ1010-1293 D) Da (*L*'Cp[1]) Hil (∼: *Sh*[+]j) *Cs*(∼ μεγ. φω. σα.) *Aeth*(∼) (*Δ*'⟨i[V] p⟩) — φωνης *cf.*←: *Lr*[2] *Cf* (*prm* μεγ.) — *txt*: ℵLX[cmt]-892 **λ**-872 **σ**-349 W Δ Θ 2145 *l*184 Chr Cr[I] Eu Thd[C] *Le*[k] Cp[1] Or *Ss*[c]ph[Brs] *Cb* *Δ*a | επισυναξει‖p: ℵ* 1604 1375 Hip *L*Hil *Ss*[c] *Cb*[2] | *om* αυτου[2]‖p: σ990-1223 Θ 565 Chr *Sj*[bc] | ακρ.[1]] ακρου‖p: 569 1579(ουρ.] του ουρανου) *Lad*

Mk 13,24 εκεινην] των ημερων εκεινων‖Mt: Σ-1071 ϕ69-346 σ27[c]-827 *pc Lvg*[1] *Arm*[1] *Geo*[B](εκεινην τ. ημ. ενεινων) **25** εσ. εκ τ. ουρ.] εκ(οι εκ) τ. ουρ. εσ.: W-28 **ϕ** σ115-827 (D) *pc l*18 *l*19 *Le* (bcff[2]q)i Qu *S*h[m] (*Cs*[1]) *Arm* — τ. ουρ. εσ.‖Ap6 13: *Rpl Ll*(∼ εσ. οι ασ. τ. ουρ.: z vg')[10] *Sh*[t] *Cs*[3] — *txt*: ℵBCΨ-579(*om* εσ.)-892 Θ-700 σ517-945-1082-1223-1391 A U Π *pc l*184 *La* | εκπ.] ● πιπτοντες‖Mt Lk10 18 Ap8 10 9 1: ℵBCLΨ-(579)-892 Θ σ7-115-659-827-945-1082-1223-1391 D Π *pc l*49 Hip *Lvl*' {} — πεσουνται (∼ πεσ. εκ τ. ουρ.) *et om* εσ.‖Mt: (W-565-700) 131 258 (1342, *et* εκ] απο) *Le* bg[2] vg[1] *Ss*[c](∼ πεσ. οι ασ. εκ τ. ουρ.)(p) *Csf*[v] *Arm* — *txt*: *Rpl L*lqz vg' Qu {*Cb*} | αι[2]—ουρ.] των ουρανων‖Mt Lk Is34 4 MT: σ115-1424 D K 1093 *L*acff[2]ir[2] (-ιων: dz) vg[1] *Ss*[c]pj *Cs*[4:7]bf **26** εν νε.] επι των νεφελων (+ του ουρανου)‖Mt: D (*Lc* vg[2]) *Cs*[7:8](b[1])f | νεφελη‖Lk: WΘ-28-565 **λ** **ϕ**⟨346⟩ 1542 *Lk Cs*[1:8] | ∼ κ. δοξης πο.‖p: Δ-892 28-700-1071 λ118 **ϕ** σM-115-349-517-827-945-1223-1606 A K Π **0104** 157 1342 *mu S*hj[fv] *Cs*[1:8](μεγαλης κ. δο. πο.) *Arm Aeth* **27** *om* τοτε‖p: Σ *Lr*[2] *Cf* | αγγ. + αυτου(+ μετα σαλπιγγος φωνης μεγαλης)‖p: *Rpl* (579 544 *pc*) Hip *L*'Or *S*,j *C*'f — *txt*: BL W D 1216 *Lek* abff[2]iq vg[1] *Cb*[4] | επισυναξουσιν‖p: L σM F *pc l*9 *l*12 *l*19 *l*251 *Le* g[2] vg[1] Or *Arm*[pc] *Aeth* — επιστρεψουσιν‖Lk1 16f.: W-28(επισυστρ.) | ● εκλ. + αυτου‖p: *Rpl* Hip *L*' *S*,j *C*,f *Geo*[B] — *txt*: LΨ-892 W-28-565 **λ**⟨118⟩ D 1342 *pc Lek* aff[2]i Or | ακρ.[1]] ακρων‖p: 565 λ22 σ827 D' *pc* La *Aeth* | γης—ουρ.] ουρ. εως ακρων αυτων‖p: 1375 *Lr*[1]? *Sj*[fv]

Lk 21,25 εσ.] ● εσται‖21 11: *Rpl* Eu — *txt*: ℵB D Ψ 229[c] 1355 **26** δυν. + αι‖Mk: L D[c](*η) *L*acff[2] Am | τ. ουρ.] εν τω ουρανω‖Mk: D *Lvl*'⟨fqr[2]⟩ Am **27** εν νε.] επι των νεφελων του ουρανου‖Mt30 26 64: N 475 *l*44 *Ll* — εν νεφελαις‖Mk: C-579-892-1241 σ945-1424 157 *pc Lvl*'⟨a⟩ vg[4] Am Te *Sj* *Cb*[2](εν ταις ν.) — εν νεφελη του ουρ.: *Aeth* — εκ των ουρανων: *L*Mcn[Te] — *om*: *l*53 *Lr*[2] | ∼ πολ. κ. δοξ.‖Mk: D Ψ *pc L*⟨l⟩ Te *S*scp(+ μεγαλης) *Aeth*

Matth	Mark	Luk
ἕως τῶν ἄκρων αὐτῶν.	**ἕως ἄκρου οὐρανοῦ.**	
		28 ἀρχομένων δὲ τούτων γίνεσθαι ἀνακύψατε καὶ ἐπάρατε τὰς κεφαλὰς ὑμῶν, διότι ἐγγίζει ἡ ἀπολύτρωσις ὑμῶν.

(220) **233.** Das Gleichnis vom Feigenbaum. *The Parable of the Fig Tree.*

Matth 24 32–33	**Mark 13** 28–29	**Luk 21** 29–31
32 Ἀπὸ δὲ τῆς συκῆς μάθετε τὴν παραβολήν· ὅταν ἤδη ὁ κλάδος αὐτῆς γένηται ἁπαλὸς καὶ τὰ φύλλα ἐκφύῃ, γινώσκετε ὅτι ἐγγὺς τὸ θέρος· 33 οὕτως καὶ ὑμεῖς, ὅταν ἴδητε ταῦτα πάντα, γινώσκετε ὅτι ἐγγύς ἐστιν ἐπὶ θύραις.	28 Ἀπὸ δὲ τῆς συκῆς μάθετε τὴν παραβολήν. ὅταν αὐτῆς ἤδη ὁ κλάδος ἁπαλὸς γένηται καὶ ἐκφύῃ τὰ φύλλα, γινώσκετε ὅτι ἐγγὺς τὸ θέρος ἐστίν· 29 οὕτως καὶ ὑμεῖς, ὅταν ταῦτα ἴδητε γινόμενα, γινώσκετε ὅτι ἐγγύς ἐστιν ἐπὶ θύραις.	29 Καὶ εἶπεν παραβολὴν αὐτοῖς· ἴδετε τὴν συκῆν καὶ πάντα τὰ δένδρα· 30 ὅταν προβάλωσιν ἤδη, βλέποντες ἀφ' ἑαυτῶν γινώσκετε ὅτι ἤδη ἐγγὺς τὸ θέρος ἐστίν· 31 οὕτως καὶ ὑμεῖς, ὅταν ἴδητε ταῦτα γινόμενα, γινώσκετε ὅτι ἐγγύς ἐστιν ἡ βασιλεία τοῦ θεοῦ.

(221) **234.** Das „Wann" der Parusie. *The Time of the Parousia.*

Matth 24 34–36	**Mark 13** 30–32	**Luk 21** 32–33
34 Αμην λέγω ὑμῖν ὅτι οὐ μὴ παρέλθῃ	30 Αμην λέγω ὑμῖν ὅτι οὐ μὴ παρέλθῃ	32 Αμην λέγω ὑμῖν ὅτι οὐ μὴ παρέλθῃ
5 18 (33.): αμην γὰρ λέγω ὑμῖν, ἕως ἂν ἡ γενεὰ αὕτη ἕως ἂν πάντα ταῦτα	ἡ γενεὰ αὕτη μέχρις οὗ ταῦτα πάντα *cf. 137. 16 17 (190.): εὐκοπώτερον*	ἡ γενεὰ αὕτη ἕως ἂν πάντα

Mt 24,31 ακρ.^{2}] ακρου‖p: Γ 569 *L*e[k] abdz | αυτων + αρχομενων δε τουτων γινεσθαι αναβλεψατε και επαρατε τας κεφαλας υμων, διοτι εγγιζει η απολυτρωσις υμων‖Lk: D 1093(ανακυψατε) *L*bh(την κεφαλην: qr^{1}; *om* υμ.^{1}: cqr^{1}) **32** ~ απα. γεν.‖Mk: **σ** *L*⟨e[k] ff^{1}h⟩ *S*h | το θε.] + εστιν‖p: 33 σ1010-1293 1093 — *prm* εστιν‖p: 544 D 482 **33** ταυ. πα.] ● πα. ταυ.: *Rpl* *L*e[k] q *S*{}h — ταυτα‖p: 1093 (~ ταυ. ιδ.) — παντα: 1375 1579 — τα πα.: 1515 — *txt*: ℵ-33-892 ΣΦ-28-700 **λ**-1582 **ϕ**-*l*547 σ517-692 D H K U V W *mu* Hip *L*'⟨ff^{1}(^{32}∩^{33}γιν.)⟩ Or *S*j{s[c]pj *C*} | πα./ταυ. + γινομενα‖p: 33 *pc* Hip *L*abcfh30(~) vg^{3} *C*b^{1} *Arm*^{pc} **34** ● *om* οτι *cf.* 5 26 10 23 24 2 *etc.*: *Rpl* Chr *L*Or — *txt*: BL-892 700 **λ**⟨118⟩-1582 **ϕ**-*l*547^{1} **σ**-1010-1293 D F G *pc* *L* *S*,j | αν] ου‖Mk: **λ**⟨1⟩ ϕ*l*547 157 | ~ ταυ. πα.‖Mk: L 544 **ϕ**-*l*547 σ1606 D H Θ Ω 157 *pc* Chr *L*e[k] aff^{2}g^{2}hl.30 vg^{1} Or {*S*s[c]pj} — *om* ταυ.‖Lk: 544 **σ**-990-1223 *pc* *L*bfff^{1}z vg^{3} Or — *txt*: *Rpl* *L*cq vg' Or *S*{}hj

Mk 13,27 ακρ.^{2} ουρ.] ακρων ουρανων(-ου)‖p: W **λ**-(22) 1200 (*pc*) (ακρου: *L*k cdff^{2}iz) **28** αυτ.—κλ.] ● ηδη ο κλ. αυτ.‖Mt: ℌ'C ΘΣ-544(ηδη] ουν)-1071 **ϕ**⟨124⟩ σ115-179-827-945-1402 A D Π 1342 *pm* *L* *Arm* — ο κλ. αυτ. ηδη‖Mt: Φ (~ ηδη αυτ.: 11 *pc*) (*om* ηδη: 259 472) — ηδη αυτ. ο κλ.‖Mt: σM-954-1082-1391 *pc* — αυτ. ο κλ. (+ ηδη)‖(Mt): W σ349-517-659 U (S Ω 44 *pc*) *pc* (*l*49 *l*251) — *txt*: *Rpl* (*om* ο: Δ) | ~ γεν. απ.‖Mt: 579 Σ-28 349-517-659 *pc* *l*49 *l*184 *l*251 | ~ τα φυ. εκφ.‖Mt: Ψ 700 λ1-872 σ115-517-1606 U *pc* *L*aff^{2}30 vg^{2} | οτι + ηδη‖Lk: D' 280 | *om* εστιν‖Mt: σ827-945-1223 Y 1342 *al* **29** ● ~ ιδ. ταυ.‖Mt Lk: ℌ⟨Δ⟩C Θ-565-1071 **λ ϕ** σ7-115-517-659-827-945-1082-1223 A (D) U Π 1342 *mu* *L*'⟨r^{2}(^{28}∩^{29}γινω.)⟩ *S*,j — *txt*: *Rpl* *L*a | ταυ.] παντα ταυ.‖Mt: D *L*i {} — ταυ. πα.‖Mt: 579 213 *L*cff^{2} qr^{1} vg^{2} *S*p^{2} {*C*sb^{3}f} *Arm* *Arth* — παντα‖Mt: 544 *pc* | *om* γινομ.‖Mt: 38 *pc* *L*a *Geo*^{2} **30** μεχρι] εως‖**p**: WΘ-28-565 **λ ϕ** σ827-1402 D *pc* | ου^{2}] αν‖p: 28 **λ ϕ** σ827 *al* | ~ πα. ταυ.‖Mt34: *Rpl* *L*'(~ πα. γεν. ταυ.: i) *S*h{} *Geo*^{1} — *om* ταυ.‖Lk32: 579 1071 **σ**' *L*k[e] ac(~ γεν. πα.) vg^{1} — *txt*: ℌ'C Θ-565-700 **ϕ**⟨124⟩ σ71-115-179-267-954-1402-1606 *al* *l*184 *L*d *S*s[c]p$^{⟨1⟩}$j {*C*} *Geo*^{2}

Lk 21,28 τ. κεφ.] τους οφθαλμους‖Jo4 35: 579 | εγγ.] ηγγικεν‖21 20: **λ** Hip(-σεν) *L*lr^{1} vg^{2} Mcn^{Te} Te *C*s *Aeth* **30** *om* βλ. αφ εαυ.‖**p**: D *pc* *L*e if *S*scj *Aeth* — *om* βλ.‖*p*: *L*' *S*p *Geo*^{2}[^{1}] *om* αφ εαυ.‖p: *C*s$^{3:7}$ | *om* ηδη^{2}‖Mt Mk: X-579 544-1604 σ659-1194 K Π Ψ *mu* *L*⟨e bq⟩ *S*scp *C* **31** ταυ. + (*prm*) παντα‖Mt: Δ **ϕ**⟨13⟩ (1216) *pc* *L*(e) r^{1}30 vg^{1} Cp (Mcn^{Te} Te) *C*b^{1} *Arm* | *om* γινομ.‖Mt: D *L*a | *om* εστιν‖Mt32: Δ **32** παντα] πα. ταυτα‖Mt34: **0179** 1071 Ψ *pc* *S*p^{5} {} *Arm*' — ταυ. πα.‖Mk: 579 **ϕ**⟨346⟩ D *pc* *L*l *S*scp' {*C*b} *Arm*^{mu}

Matth 5,18	Matth 24	Mark 13	*Luk 16,17*	Luk 21
παρέλθῃ ὁ οὐρανὸς καὶ ἡ γῆ, ἰῶτα ἓν ἢ μία κεραία οὐ μὴ παρέλθῃ ἀπὸ τοῦ νόμου, ἕως ἂν πάντα γένηται.	γένηται. 35 ὁ οὐρανὸς καὶ ἡ γῆ παρελεύσονται, οἱ δὲ λόγοι μου οὐ μὴ παρέλθωσιν. 36 περὶ δὲ τῆς ἡμέρας ἐκείνης καὶ ὥρας οὐδεὶς οἶδεν, οὐδὲ οἱ ἄγγελοι τῶν οὐρανῶν οὐδὲ ὁ υἱός, εἰ μὴ ὁ πατὴρ μόνος.	γένηται. 31 ὁ οὐρανὸς καὶ ἡ γῆ παρελεύσονται, οἱ δὲ λόγοι μου οὐ μὴ παρελεύσονται. 32 περὶ δὲ τῆς ἡμέρας ἐκείνης ἢ τῆς ὥρας οὐδεὶς οἶδεν, οὐδὲ οἱ ἄγγελοι ἐν οὐρανῷ οὐδὲ ὁ υἱός, εἰ μὴ ὁ πατήρ.	*δέ ἐστιν τὸν οὐρανὸν καὶ τὴν γῆν παρελθεῖν ἢ τοῦ νόμου μίαν κεραίαν πεσεῖν.*	γένηται. 33 ὁ οὐρανὸς καὶ ἡ γῆ παρελεύσονται, οἱ δὲ λόγοι μου οὐ μὴ παρελεύσονται.

(224) ***235.*** **Unverhofft kommt das Gericht.** ***The Unexpected Judgement.*** **Matth 24** 37–41 *198.*

37 Ὥσπερ γὰρ αἱ ἡμέραι τοῦ Νωε, οὕτως ἔσται ἡ παρουσία τοῦ υἱοῦ τοῦ ἀνθρώπου. 38 ὡς γὰρ ἦσαν ἐν ταῖς ἡμέραις ταῖς πρὸ τοῦ κατακλυσμοῦ τρώγοντες καὶ πίνοντες, γαμοῦντες καὶ ἐκγαμίζοντες, ἄχρι ἧς ἡμέρας **εἰσῆλθεν Νωε εἰς τὴν κιβωτόν,** 39 καὶ οὐκ ἔγνωσαν ἕως ἦλθεν ὁ κατακλυσμὸς καὶ ἦρεν ἅπαντας, οὕτως ἔσται καὶ ἡ παρουσία τοῦ υἱοῦ τοῦ ἀνθρώπου. (Gn7 7) *198.*

40 τότε δύο ἔσονται ἐν τῷ ἀγρῷ, εἷς παραλαμβάνεται καὶ εἷς ἀφίεται· 41 δύο ἀλήθουσαι ἐν τῷ μύλῳ, μία παραλαμβάνεται καὶ μία ἀφίεται.

Mt 24,35 παρελευσεται ‖18 Ap20 11: 𝔋⟨א⟩ 544 ϕ*l*547^{1} **σ**⟨1424⟩-1010-1606 D *al* Chr Eu *L*e[k] — *txt*: *Rpl* Cr^{I} Or *L*'Hi Or *C*b^{6} **36** και] η της ‖Mk: 33 Σ 2145 Ddy {} — η ‖Mk: σ1010-1293-1424 {*L*br^{2}30 *S*h j$^{a\,b1\,c}$} — και της ‖Mk: Φ **λ**-1582 ϕ*l*547^{1} σ517-1606 Θ Chr | ● *om* ουδε ο υι.: *Rpl* Ad Hi PsAth Bas Da Ddy Euthy Pie *L*g^{1}l vg' Am Hi Hil Opt Pau^{N} Phoe *S C Geo*^{A} — *txt*: א*B Φ-28-1604 **ϕ**⟨69-983⟩-174-*l*547^{1} σ691-1194 D Θ *pc l*490 *l*823 Chr **Or** *L*vl'[k] vg^{4} Am PsChr Hi Hil Ir Or *S*j *C*f *Arm Geo' Aeth* | ● πατ. + μου: *Rpl L*f — *txt*: 𝔋 Σ-28-700-1604 **λ**-1582 **ϕ** ⟨124⟩-*l*547 σ27-71-692-1010-1293-1424 D Y Δ Θ Π **047** 157 *al* Bas Chr Ep *L*' Ir Or *S*,j *C* **37** ● γαρ] δε(*om*): *Rpl* (565) Or *L*' *S*'(j^{bc1} *C*b^{1}) — *txt*: B D **067** Ddy *L*e[k] δr$^{1.2}$z vg^{5} Or *S*s[c]h^{m}j^{ac1} *C*' | εσται + και ‖39p: *Rpl L*' Or *S*hj$^{a\,b1\,c}$ — *txt*: 𝔋 700 σ517-1010-1675 U Γ *pc* Ddy Or *L*cdff^{1}hlqr$^{1.2}$ vg^{5} *S*s[c]pj^{b1} *C* **38** ● ημεραις + εκειναις ‖ 24 19.22.29 *etc.*: B D(*om* ταις^{2}) *pc L*bcfff^{2}hr$^{1*.2}$z vg^{2} *S*j *C*s — *txt*: *Rpl* Ddy *L*' Or *S*h *C*b *Arm* | εκγαμ.] ● γαμιζοντες(γαμισκ.) ‖p: א(B)-33 (**σ**'⟨954⟩) D *pc* — εγγαμ.: 892 Σ **ϕ**⟨69-346⟩-174-*l*547 **047** *pc* — *txt* (-ισκ-): *Rpl* (σ517 W) Ddy **39** απ.] παντ. ‖p: 700 D **067** 440 | ● *om* και^{3} ‖24 37.27: B-892 σ692 D *L*abff^{1}g^{2}hqr^{2} *S*s[c]p *C Δ*a ad i^{T} md n **40** ∼ εσ. δυο ‖Lk 34f.: א*B-892 σ1606 *pc L*hlr$^{1.2}$ | εις^{1} … εις^{2}] ο εις … ο εις ‖ p: *Rpl* (εις … ο εις: Δ; ο εις … εις: σ990){} — εις … ο ετερος(αλλος) ‖ p: Σ (1093) *L*ff$^{1.}$(^{2})hr$^{1.}$(^{2}) vg^{2} Or *S*h *Arm Aeth* — *txt*: 𝔋 **λ**-1582 ϕ124 **σ**⟨954⟩ D Θ **067**(^{1}[^{2}]) {*L*' *S*'h^{Brs}j *C*} | παραλημφθησεται ‖p: 2145 | ^{40}*et* ^{41}παραλημφθησεται … ^{40}*et* ^{41}αφεθησεται ‖p: Σ *L*'(*et* ^{41b}: abcf hq) *S*s[c]pj *C* **41** *cf. ad* 40 | *om* 41: *L*ff$^{1.2}$ | αφι. + ^{41b}δυο επι κλινης μιας(*om*), εις παραλαμβανεται και εις αφιεται ‖p: **ϕ**⟨124-788⟩ D *L*e[k](∼ 41b.a) f(abchq vg^{8}) **Or** *Aeth*

Mk 13,31 παρελευσεται^{1} ‖Mt 18 Ap20 11: *Rpl L*k[e] a — *txt*: אBCΨ-892 Θ-28-565-700-1071 **λ ϕ** σ945-1223 D K U Γ Π *pm L*' | ● *om* μη: B D* | παρελ.^{2}] παρελθωσιν ‖Mt 35.18: *Rpl* — *txt*: אBL-892 σ7-1194-1391 1342 *pc* **32** η] και ‖Mt 36: א WΘ-28-565-700 **λ ϕ** σ7-115-267-349-1082 D F S 157 *al* Bas^{1} *L*k[e] aiqr$^{1.2}$ Hil *S*'j *C*s^{7}b' — *txt*: *Rpl* Bas^{1} *L*' *S*h *C*s^{2}b^{6} | *om* της^{2} ‖p: *Rpl* Bas — *txt*: 𝔋C WΘ-565-1071 **λ** ϕ983 **σ**-M-827-1082-1391-1606 D K U Y Γ Π 1342 *mu l*49 | εν + τω ‖Mt22 30: Ψ 565 λ1278 σ71-179-267-349-945-954-1223-1606 D *pm* | εν. ουρ.] των ουρανων ‖p: Σ-28-1071 ϕ983-1689 σ115-517-827 U *mu l*15 *l*36 *l*360 *L*a vg^{1} *S*p$^{\langle 3\rangle}$j | *om* ουδε ο υι. *cf. ad* Mt: X ϕ983-1689 *L*vg^{1} | πατ. + μονος (∼ μον. ο πατ.) ‖**p**: (Δ) ΘΦ-565-1071 **ϕ**⟨69⟩ σ1606 *L*k[e] a(c) vg^{1} Hil *C*sb^{1} *Arm*^{pc}(') *Aeth*

Lk 21,33 παρελευσεται^{1} ‖Mt 18 Ap20 11: C-579-892-1241 **λλ**⟨22-1278⟩ σ1223 K W Θ Π *pm l*13 *l*1627 *l*1642 *L*e aqr$^{1.2}$ | παρελ.^{2}] παρελθωσιν ‖Mt: *Rpl* — *txt*: א**BL-0139-0179**-33-892 D W 157

Mt24 35p *cf.* ETh^{II} 11 (*transl.*): *Λέγει Ἰησοῦς· ὁ οὐρανὸς οὗτος παρελεύσεται καὶ (ὁ οὐρανὸς) ὁ ἐπάνω αὐτοῦ παρελεύσεται …*

Mt24 40f. *cf.* ETh^{II} 61 (*cf. ad 198.* Lk17 34)

(222) ***236.*** Das Gleichnis vom verreisten Hausherrn. *Watch and Pray.*

Matth 24 42

25 13–15 (239. 240.): γρηγορεῖτε οὖν, ὅτι οὐκ οἴδατε τὴν ἡμέραν οὐδὲ τὴν ὥραν. 14 Ὥσπερ γὰρ ἄνθρωπος ἀποδημῶν ἐκάλεσεν τοὺς ἰδίους δούλους καὶ παρέδωκεν αὐτοῖς τὰ ὑπάρχοντα αὐτοῦ, 15 ... ἑκάστῳ κατὰ τὴν ἰδίαν δύναμιν, καὶ ἀπεδήμησεν.

42 γρηγορεῖτε οὖν, ὅτι οὐκ οἴδατε ποίᾳ ἡμέρᾳ ὁ κύριος ὑμῶν ἔρχεται.

Mark 13 33–37

33 Βλέπετε, ἀγρυπνεῖτε καὶ προσεύχεσθε· οὐκ οἴδατε γὰρ πότε ὁ καιρός ἐστιν. *cf. 172.* 34 ὡς ἄνθρωπος ἀπόδημος ἀφεὶς τὴν οἰκίαν αὐτοῦ καὶ δοὺς τοῖς δούλοις αὐτοῦ τὴν ἐξουσίαν, ἑκάστῳ τὸ ἔργον αὐτοῦ, καὶ τῷ θυρωρῷ ἐνετείλατο ἵνα γρηγορῇ. 35 γρηγορεῖτε οὖν· οὐκ οἴδατε γὰρ πότε ὁ κύριος τῆς οἰκίας ἔρχεται, ἢ ὀψὲ ἢ μεσονύκτιον ἢ ἀλεκτοροφωνίας ἢ πρωΐ· 36 μὴ ἐλθὼν ἐξαίφνης εὕρῃ ὑμᾶς καθεύδοντας. 37 ὃ δὲ ὑμῖν λέγω, πᾶσιν λέγω, γρηγορεῖτε.

12 38 (172.): κἂν ἐν τῇ δευτέρᾳ κἂν ἐν τῇ τρίτῃ φυλακῇ ἔλθῃ καὶ εὕρῃ οὕτως, μακάριοί εἰσιν ἐκεῖνοι.

(225) ***237.*** Das Gleichnis vom wachenden Hausherrn. **Matth 24 43–44** [172.]

The Watchful Householder.

43 Ἐκεῖνο δὲ γινώσκετε, ὅτι εἰ ᾔδει ὁ οἰκοδεσπότης ποίᾳ φυλακῇ ὁ κλέπτης ἔρχεται, ἐγρηγόρησεν ἂν καὶ οὐκ ἂν εἴασεν διορυγῆναι τὴν οἰκίαν αὐτοῦ. 44 διὰ τοῦτο καὶ ὑμεῖς γίνεσθε ἕτοιμοι, ὅτι ᾗ οὐ δοκεῖτε ὥρᾳ ὁ υἱὸς τοῦ ἀνθρώπου ἔρχεται.

[172.]

(226) ***238.*** Der treue und kluge Knecht. *The Faithful and Wise Servant.* **Matth 24 45–51** [172.]

45 Τίς ἄρα ἐστὶν ὁ πιστὸς δοῦλος καὶ φρόνιμος, ὃν κατέστησεν ὁ κύριος ἐπὶ τῆς οἰκετείας αὐτοῦ τοῦ δοῦναι αὐτοῖς τὴν τροφὴν ἐν καιρῷ; 46 μακάριος ὁ δοῦλος ἐκεῖνος, ὃν ἐλθὼν ὁ κύριος αὐτοῦ εὑρήσει οὕτως·

[172.]

Mt 24,42 οτι ουκ οιδ.] ουκ οιδ. γαρ‖Mk33.35: 1295 | ημ.] ωρα‖**24**44 Lk1239: *Rpl* Ath^2 Chr Cr Thd^C *L*' Or *S*s[c]p *C*s^{2}b' *Arm* *Δ*a l^{AD} (p) — ημ. η ωρα (ωρα η ημ.)‖Mk1332 Lk←: Hip *L*(e[k] 30)r$^{1.2}$ vg^4 — ημ. και ωρα‖2436 2513 Lk←: Eu^1 *Δ*i^V — φυλακη‖2443 Lk38: Eu^1 — *txt*: 𝔥⟨L⟩ Σ **λ**1-1582 **φ**⟨346⟩-*l*547^1 **σ**⟨954⟩ D W Δ Θ **067** 157 *pc* Ath^2 *L*ff^2 Hil Ir *S*hj *C*s^{8}b^7 *Geo* **43** φυλ.] ωρα‖p: 33 **φ** σM Θ 1515 *L* *S*j$^{a\,b1\,c1}$ *C*b$^{\langle 1?\rangle}$ PS *Geo* | ειασ.] αφηκεν‖p: 1295 | τον οικον‖p: L-892 W **44** ∼ η ωρα (+ η) ου δοκ.‖p: *Rpl* (L) {*L*e[k] q Or *Δ*i^V} — η ωρα ου γινωσκετε‖50p: **λ**⟨118⟩-1582 157 *L*fg^{1}30 vg^2 *C*b *Δ*ad i^T l^{FG} p — ου γιν. ποια ωρα‖Mt2442: *L*vl'g^{2}r^1 vg^{10} Hil *Δ*l^{AD} md n — *txt* (δοκ.] γιν.): ℵB-892 700 D Θ **067** {(*L*vg') *S*'j *C*s *Δ*a} **45** φρο. + οικονομος‖p: ϕ174 | καταστησει‖p: ℵ Σ **σ**-M-349 Chr *L*vg^2 *C*b | τ. οικ.] τ. θεραπειας‖p: *Rpl* *L*e[k](+ των ε-) — τ. οικιας: ℵ-892 ϕ69-828 σ71 157(τη οικια) *al* *l*48 Bas Chr *L*q Or *Aeth* *Δ*p — *txt*: BL-33 Σ **φ**'⟨124⟩-*l*547 σ1010-1293 W Y Δ Θ Π **067** *pc* *L*'(familiam) Or *S*'(τους συνδουλους‖49: s[c]j *Δ*'⟨l^{AD} me⟩ | διδοναι‖p: *Rpl* — *txt*: 𝔥C Σ-700 **λ**-22 **φ**-*l*547 **σ**-7-1293-1606 D U Δ Θ **067** 157 *pc* Chr | *om* αυτοις‖p: W | ∼ εν καιρω την τρ.‖p: 28 157 *L*Or **46** ∼ ποι. ουτ.‖p: *Rpl* Chr *L*fq Or *S*,j^b {*C*} — γρηγορουντα‖1237: 1555 1573 Hip — *txt*: 𝔥C **λ**⟨118⟩-1582 **φ**-*l*547 σ1010-1293 D Θ **067** 157 *pc* *L*' *S*j^{ack1v} {} *Geo* *Aeth*

Mk 13,33 ● *om* κ. προσευ.‖p35p: B D 122 *L*k[e] ac vg^1 *C*f^v | ουκ] οτι ουκ (*et om* γαρ)‖**p** Mt42: ϕ346 (*L*cz) **34** ως] ωσπερ γαρ(*om*)‖p: WΘΣ-28-(565)-1071(ως γαρ) (**λ**) **φ** *pc* *L*c vg^2 *S*s[c]p *C*s$^{5:6}$b^{1}f | αποδημων‖p: X Θ-28-565 **λ** σ349-517 D 1342 *pc* **35** ουκ οιδ. γαρ] οτι ουκ οιδ. (+ γαρ)‖p Mt13: 3 *pc* *L*k vg' Au^1 *C*s$^{1:8}$(^{1}b^7)f — ουκ οιδ.‖p: 59 1038 *l*184 *L*vg^2 *C*s$^{2:9}$b^3 **36** ευρησει‖Mt2446: 579 1071 *pc* Or

---

Mt2442p *cf.* Did161: Γρηγορεῖτε ὑπὲρ τῆς ζωῆς ὑμῶν· οἱ λύχνοι ὑμῶν μὴ σβεσθήτωσαν, καὶ αἱ ὀσφύες ὑμῶν μὴ ἐκλυέσθωσαν, ἀλλὰ γίνεσθε ἕτοιμοι· οὐ γὰρ οἴδατε τὴν ὥραν, ἐν ᾗ ὁ κύριος ἡμῶν ἔρχεται.

ποιοῦντα. [47] αμην λέγω ὑμῖν ὅτι ἐπὶ πᾶσιν τοῖς ὑπάρχουσιν αὐτοῦ καταστήσει αὐτόν. [48] ἐὰν δὲ εἴπῃ ὁ κακὸς δοῦλος ἐκεῖνος ἐν τῇ καρδίᾳ αὐτοῦ· χρονίζει μου ὁ κύριος ἐλθεῖν, [49] καὶ ἄρξηται τύπτειν τοὺς συνδούλους αὐτοῦ, ἐσθίῃ δὲ καὶ πίνῃ μετὰ τῶν μεθυόντων, [50] ἥξει ὁ κύριος τοῦ δούλου ἐκείνου ἐν ἡμέρᾳ ᾗ οὐ προσδοκᾷ καὶ ἐν ὥρᾳ ᾗ οὐ γινώσκει, [51] καὶ διχοτομήσει αὐτόν, καὶ τὸ μέρος αὐτοῦ μετὰ τῶν ὑποκριτῶν θήσει· ἐκεῖ ἔσται ὁ κλαυθμὸς καὶ ὁ βρυγμὸς τῶν ὀδόντων.

172.

(227) **239.** Das Gleichnis von den zehn Jungfrauen. *The Parable of the Ten Virgins.* **Matth 25 1–13**

[1] Τότε ὁμοιωθήσεται ἡ βασιλεία τῶν οὐρανῶν δέκα παρθένοις, αἵτινες λαβοῦσαι τὰς λαμπάδας αὐτῶν ἐξῆλθον εἰς ἀπάντησιν τοῦ νυμφίου. [2] πέντε δὲ ἐξ αὐτῶν ἦσαν μωραὶ καὶ πέντε φρόνιμοι. [3] αἱ γὰρ μωραὶ λαβοῦσαι τὰς λαμπάδας οὐκ ἔλαβον μεθ' ἑαυτῶν ἔλαιον. [4] αἱ δὲ φρόνιμοι ἔλαβον ἔλαιον ἐν τοῖς ἀγγείοις μετὰ τῶν λαμπάδων αὐτῶν. [5] χρονίζοντος δὲ τοῦ νυμφίου ἐνύσταξαν πᾶσαι καὶ ἐκάθευδον. [6] μέσης δὲ νυκτὸς κραυγὴ γέγονεν· ἰδοὺ ὁ νυμφίος, ἐξέρχεσθε εἰς ἀπάντησιν αὐτοῦ. [7] τότε ἠγέρθησαν πᾶσαι αἱ παρθένοι ἐκεῖναι καὶ ἐκόσμησαν τὰς λαμπάδας αὐτῶν. [8] αἱ δὲ μωραὶ ταῖς φρονίμοις εἶπαν· δότε ἡμῖν ἐκ τοῦ ἐλαίου ὑμῶν, ὅτι αἱ λαμπάδες ἡμῶν σβέννυνται. [9] ἀπεκρίθησαν δὲ αἱ φρόνιμοι λέγουσαι· μήποτε οὐ μὴ ἀρκέσῃ ἡμῖν καὶ ὑμῖν· πορεύεσθε μᾶλλον πρὸς τοὺς πωλοῦντας καὶ ἀγοράσατε ἑαυταῖς. [10] ἀπερχομένων δὲ αὐτῶν ἀγοράσαι ἦλθεν ὁ νυμφίος, καὶ αἱ ἕτοιμοι εἰσῆλθον μετ' αὐτοῦ εἰς τοὺς γάμους, καὶ ἐκλείσθη ἡ θύρα. [11] ὕστερον δὲ ἔρχονται καὶ αἱ λοιπαὶ παρθένοι λέγουσαι· κύριε κύριε, ἄνοιξον ἡμῖν. [12] ὁ δὲ ἀποκριθεὶς εἶπεν· αμην λέγω ὑμῖν, οὐκ οἶδα ὑμᾶς. [13] γρηγορεῖτε οὖν, ὅτι οὐκ οἴδατε τὴν ἡμέραν οὐδὲ τὴν ὥραν.

236.

12 35 f. (172.): Ἔστωσαν ὑμῶν αἱ ὀσφύες περιεζωσμέναι καὶ οἱ λύχνοι καιόμενοι· [36] καὶ ὑμεῖς ὅμοιοι ἀνθρώποις προσδεχομένοις τὸν κύριον ἑαυτῶν, πότε ἀναλύσῃ ἐκ τῶν γάμων, ἵνα ἐλθόντος καὶ 179. *κρούσαντος εὐθέως ἀνοίξωσιν αὐτῷ.*

Mt 24,48 *om* κακ.‖p: λ118 *L*ff[2] vg[1] | ● *om* εκει.: ℵ* ϕ983-1689 σ692 Γ Θ *pc* *l*184 Chr[1:2] Hip *L*Au[1:2] *S*s[c] *C*s *Arm* *Δ*i[T] md n p | ∼ ο κυ. μου‖p: *Rpl* (*om* μου: ϕ 124) Chr *L*'(=124: vg[1]) — *txt*: 𝔥C 700 **σ**-1010-1293 D Θ **067** 157 *pc* Chr | ελθ.] ερχεσθαι‖p: ΣΦ **λ**-1582 157 {} — ● *om*‖25 5: 𝔥⟨L⟩ 700 6 *C*⟨b[1]⟩ — *txt*: *Rpl* {*L* *S*,j} **49** *om* αυτ.‖p: *Rpl* Bas — *txt*: 𝔥'(εαυ.: ℵ)C Φ-544-700 **λ**-22-1582 **ϕ**⟨346-983⟩-174-230-*l*547 **σ**-7-160-659-1010-1402 D Θ **067** 157 *al* Chr PsCl *L* *S*,j *C* *Δ*ad i[V](συνδ.] δου.) *l*[FG] md n | εσθιειν … πινειν‖p: Σ-28-700 ϕ174-828(εσθιη)-983-1689 G W Π* Ω *pl* Da Hip *L*a *S*j[bckl] — *txt*: 𝔥C Φ **λ**-22-1582 σM-7-1402-1606 D E F H K S U V Y Γ Δ Θ Π[c] **047 067** *al* Bas Chr *L*' *S*,j[a] | δε] τε‖p: C-33-892 700 **λ**-1582 σ692-1293 W *mu* Hip *S*s[c]pj {*C*} **51** υποκ.] απιστων‖p: 1092 1295 *L*r[1] — τελωνων: *L*ff[1] **25,1** αυτων] ● εαυ.: BL ϕ124 D Θ 713 Meth | ● υπαντ.‖Jo 12 13: 𝔥⟨L-33⟩C Σ λ1-1582 Ψ 157 Meth[1] — *txt*: *Rpl* Meth[1] **4** αυτων] ● εαυ.: ℵB σ659 *pc* **6** υπαντ.‖←: Z Σ Θ 157 Ddy — συναντ.‖Mt 8 34: C — *txt*: *Rpl* Meth | ● *om* αυτ.: ℵBZ Σ-700 Cr **7** αυτων] ● εαυ.: 𝔥⟨33⟩ Σ A 713 *l*48 **11** *om* κυ.[2]‖Lk 13 25: 213 713 *L*ff[1] *S*j[1] *C*s[4:12] *Δ*i[T1] n[C] p **12** *om* αμ. λε. υμ.‖←: **λ**-1582 1012 **13** ωρ. + εν η ο υιος του ανθρωπου ερχεται‖24 42 p. 44: *Rpl* *L*vg[2] *S*j[a1] *C*s[1] — *txt*: 𝔓[35] 𝔥⟨L⟩C*X ΣΦ-1604 **λ**⟨118⟩-22-1582 ϕ174 σ71-990-1223-1424 A D W Y Δ Θ Π **047 0136** *al* PsBas *L*'[ek] Hil Or *S*,j[a1 bckl] *C*s[9]b *Δ*⟨me p⟩

Mt 24 49 *cf.* EN frgm. 18 (*cf. ad 240.*)

Mt 25 13 *cf.* Did 16 1 (*cf. ad 236.* Mt 24 42)
cf. ETh[II] 21 (*cf. ad 172.* Lk 12 39)

(228) ***240.*** Das Gleichnis von den Talenten. *The Parable of the Talents.* **Matth 25** 14–30 [209.]

[236.]

14 Ὥσπερ γὰρ ἄνθρωπος ἀποδημῶν ἐκάλεσεν τοὺς ἰδίους δούλους καὶ παρέδωκεν αὐτοῖς τὰ ὑπάρχοντα αὐτοῦ, 15 καὶ ᾧ μὲν ἔδωκεν πέντε τάλαντα, ᾧ δὲ δύο, ᾧ δὲ ἕν, ἑκάστῳ κατὰ τὴν ἰδίαν δύναμιν, καὶ ἀπεδήμησεν. εὐθέως 16 πορευθεὶς ὁ τὰ πέντε τάλαντα λαβὼν ἠργάσατο ἐν αὐτοῖς καὶ ἐποίησεν ἄλλα πέντε· 17 ὡσαύτως ὁ τὰ δύο ἐκέρδησεν καὶ αὐτὸς ἄλλα δύο. 18 ὁ δὲ τὸ ἓν λαβὼν ἀπελθὼν ὤρυξεν γῆν καὶ ἀπέκρυψεν τὸ ἀργύριον τοῦ κυρίου αὐτοῦ.

19 μετὰ δὲ πολὺν χρόνον ἔρχεται ὁ κύριος τῶν δούλων ἐκείνων καὶ συναίρει λόγον μετ' αὐτῶν. 20 καὶ προσελθὼν ὁ τὰ πέντε τάλαντα λαβὼν προσήνεγκεν ἄλλα πέντε τάλαντα λέγων· κύριε, πέντε τάλαντά μοι παρέδωκας· ἴδε ἄλλα πέντε τάλαντα ἐκέρδησα. 21 ἔφη αὐτῷ ὁ κύριος αὐτοῦ· εὖ, δοῦλε ἀγαθὲ καὶ πιστέ, ἐπὶ ὀλίγα ἧς πιστός, ἐπὶ πολλῶν σε καταστήσω· εἴσελθε εἰς τὴν χαρὰν τοῦ κυρίου σου. 22 προσελθὼν δὲ καὶ ὁ τὰ δύο τάλαντα εἶπεν· κύριε, δύο τάλαντά μοι παρέδωκας· ἴδε ἄλλα δύο τάλαντα ἐκέρδησα. 23 ἔφη αὐτῷ ὁ κύριος αὐτοῦ· εὖ, δοῦλε ἀγαθὲ καὶ πιστέ, ἐπὶ ὀλίγα ἧς πιστός, ἐπὶ πολλῶν σε καταστήσω· εἴσελθε εἰς τὴν χαρὰν τοῦ κυρίου σου. 24 προσελθὼν δὲ καὶ ὁ τὸ ἓν τάλαντον εἰληφὼς εἶπεν· κύριε, ἔγνων σε ὅτι σκληρὸς εἶ ἄνθρωπος, θερίζων ὅπου οὐκ ἔσπειρας, καὶ συνάγων ὅθεν οὐ διεσκόρπισας· 25 καὶ φοβηθεὶς ἀπελθὼν ἔκρυψα τὸ τάλαντόν σου ἐν τῇ γῇ· ἴδε ἔχεις τὸ σόν. 26 ἀποκριθεὶς δὲ ὁ κύριος αὐτοῦ εἶπεν αὐτῷ· πονηρὲ δοῦλε καὶ ὀκνηρέ, ᾔδεις ὅτι θερίζω ὅπου οὐκ ἔσπειρα, καὶ συνάγω ὅθεν οὐ διεσκόρπισα. 27 ἔδει σε οὖν βαλεῖν τὸ ἀργύριόν μου τοῖς τραπεζίταις, καὶ ἐλθὼν ἐγὼ ἐκομισάμην ἂν τὸ ἐμὸν σὺν τόκῳ. 28 ἄρατε οὖν ἀπ' αὐτοῦ τὸ τάλαντον καὶ δότε τῷ ἔχοντι τὰ δέκα τάλαντα· 29 τῷ γὰρ ἔχοντι παντὶ δοθήσεται καὶ περισσευθήσεται· τοῦ δὲ μὴ ἔχοντος καὶ ὃ ἔχει ἀρθήσεται ἀπ' αὐτοῦ. 30 καὶ τὸν ἀχρεῖον δοῦλον ἐκβάλετε εἰς τὸ σκότος τὸ ἐξώτερον· ἐκεῖ ἔσται ὁ κλαυθμὸς καὶ ὁ βρυγμὸς τῶν ὀδόντων.

[209.]

[107.]

Mt 25,14 *om* γαρ‖Mk13 34: D W *L*vg² *C*b¹ *Arm* | ανθ. + τις‖Lk19 12 *cf.* 10 30 *etc.*: C³ φ230-*l*547¹ σM-27-692 F *pc L*vg¹ Or *Arm* **16** κ. εποι.] ● κ. εκερδησεν‖17: 𝔊⟨ℵ*⟩ℵᶜC Σ λ-1582 φ⟨13-346-828⟩-*l*547 σ-1010-1293 Aᶜ D Θ **074** *L*'[ek]⟨q⟩ *S*[sc]phᵐj *Cs* {*Δ*'⟨me⟩}l — *om*: *L*bff² **17** και αυτ.] ● *om*: 𝔊C* σ⟨954⟩-1010-1293 59 Bas *L*'[ek] *S*'j^{a1 c1 1}(^{a2 c2} *et om* εκερ. ... δυο²) *Cs*²b¹ — και: *Cs*^{8+1?}b' — εν αυτοις‖16: *L*abcff^{1.2}qr^{1v}(*prm* και) Or *S*j^{b1}(ηργασατο εν αυ. και εκερ.) — *txt* (∼ και αυ. εκερ.): *Rpl* (D 1515) *L*(*om* αυτ.: f vg^{1v})h *S*hj^{b1}(δυο² + εν αυτοις) **18** απεκρ.] ● εκρ.‖25 13 44: 𝔊C 700 σ1010-1293 A D *pc* **21** ● εφη + δε: *Rpl S*hj^{a1 b1 1} *C*b — και εφη: *L*ff¹32 vg² *Aeth* — *txt*: 𝔓³⁵ 𝔊C Σ-544-700-1071 φ124 σM-27-692-1010-1194-1293-1391 D E K U Γ Θ **074** *al* Ath PsAth *L*'[ek] *S*[sc]pj^{a1 b1 c} *Cs* | ευ] ευγε‖p: A*ᵛ PsAth *L*'[ek] Ir Or | ∼ αγ. δου.‖p: *L*abhz32 vg⟨8⟩ *Geo* | *om* και πιστε‖p: σ1293 | επι¹] επει επ‖p: D *L*[ek]⟨ff²⟩ Ir Luc Or *C Arm* **22** ● *om* δε: 𝔓^{35v} ℵB 1573 *S*[sc]pj^{b1} *Cs* **23** ευ] ευγε‖Lk17: A*ᵛ *L*[ek] Ir Or | ∼ αγ. δου.‖←: *L*hlr¹32 vg⁴ *Geo* | επι¹] επει επ‖←: D 1574 *L*[ek] Ir Luc Or *Arm Δ*'⟨me n^{L*} p⟩ **24** σκλ.] αυστηρος‖p: ℵ(∼ ανθ. αυσ. ει) λ⟨118⟩ *L*b *Cs*^{1:11} **26** ∼ δου. πον.‖18 32: X σ1010-1293 A Ddy(ανθρωπε δου. πον.) *L*'[ek]⟨q⟩(nequam serve male: c) Or *S*,j | οτι + εγω ανθρωπος αυστηρος ειμι‖p: W *S*p¹j¹ *Cs*^{1:11} | συναγων‖p 24: φ174-543-788-826-*l*547¹ Θ(-αγαγων) 697 **27** ● τα αργυρια *cf.* 27 5f.: ℵ*B 700 W Θ Or *Cs*^{2:11} | ∼ και εγω (κ. ε.] καγω) ελ.‖p: σ1391-(1424) A (713) *pc L*ff^{1.2}g²hlr^{1.2} vg² Or *S*[sc]j **29** του δε] απο δε του‖p: *Rpl* Chr **Or** *L*q *S*h — *txt*: ℵBL λ⟨118⟩-1582 φ124 D Θ *L*'[ek] *S*[sc]pj *C* | εχει] δοκει εχειν‖Lk8 18: L-33-892 Φ φ69-983-1689 σ692ᶜ-945-1010-1293-1391 Δ *pm l*184 Cr^I**Or** *L*fg¹lz vg⟨1⟩ **Or** *S*[sc]h | αυτου + ταυτα λεγων εφωνει· ο εχων ωτα ακουειν ακουετω *cf.* Lk8 8 14 35 Mk4 9 Mt11 15 13 9 *etc.*: C³-892ᵐ(ταυ. λε.] και λεγει ταυ.) σMᵐ Fᶜ Gᶜ H Vᶜ **30** οδοντ. + ταυτα—ακουετω (*cf. ad* 29): φ⟨788⟩-*l*547 Ω^{mv} *pc l*184 *l*185 (*om* ταυ.—εφω.: Γ *pc*)

---

240. cf. EN frgm.18 (Eu theoph. 22): Ἐπεὶ δὲ τὸ εἰς ἡμᾶς ἧκον Ἑβραϊκοῖς χαρακτῆρσιν εὐαγγέλιον τὴν ἀπειλὴν οὐ κατὰ τοῦ ἀποκρύψαντος ἐπῆγεν, ἀλλὰ κατὰ τοῦ ἀσώτως ἐζηκότος· τρεῖς γὰρ δούλους περιεῖχε, τὸν μὲν καταφαγόντα τὴν ὕπαρξιν τοῦ δεσπότου μετὰ πορνῶν καὶ αὐλητρίδων, τὸν δὲ πολλαπλασιάσαντα τὴν ἐργασίαν, τὸν δὲ κατακρύψαντα τὸ τάλαντον· εἶτα τὸν μὲν ἀποδεχθῆναι, τὸν δὲ μεμφθῆναι μόνον, τὸν δὲ συγκλεισθῆναι δεσμωτηρίῳ· ἐφίστημι, μήποτε κατὰ τὸν Ματθαῖον, μετὰ τὴν συμπλήρωσιν τοῦ λόγου τοῦ κατὰ τοῦ μηδὲν ἐργασαμένου, ἡ ἑξῆς ἐπιλεγομένη ἀπειλή, οὐ περὶ αὐτοῦ ἀλλὰ περὶ τοῦ προτέρου κατ' ἐπανάληψιν λέλεκται τοῦ ἐσθίοντος καὶ πίνοντος μετὰ τῶν μεθυόντων.

Mt25 29 *cf.* ETh^{II} 41 (*cf. ad 107.* Mk4 25)

(229) **241.** Die große Scheidung. *The Sheep and the Goats.* **Matth 25** 31–46

Zch14 5

[31] Ὅταν δὲ **ἔλθῃ** ὁ υἱὸς τοῦ ἀνθρώπου ἐν τῇ δόξῃ αὐτοῦ **καὶ πάντες οἱ** ἄγγελοι **μετ' αὐτοῦ,** τότε καθίσει ἐπὶ θρόνου δόξης αὐτοῦ· [32] καὶ συναχθήσονται ἔμπροσθεν αὐτοῦ πάντα τὰ ἔθνη, καὶ ἀφορίσει αὐτοὺς ἀπ' ἀλλήλων, ὥσπερ ὁ ποιμὴν ἀφορίζει τὰ πρόβατα ἀπὸ τῶν ἐρίφων, [33] καὶ στήσει τὰ μὲν πρόβατα ἐκ δεξιῶν αὐτοῦ, τὰ δὲ ἐρίφια ἐξ εὐωνύμων. [34] τότε ἐρεῖ ὁ βασιλεὺς τοῖς ἐκ δεξιῶν αὐτοῦ· δεῦτε οἱ εὐλογημένοι τοῦ πατρός μου, κληρονομήσατε τὴν ἡτοιμασμένην ὑμῖν βασιλείαν ἀπὸ καταβολῆς κόσμου. [35] ἐπείνασα γὰρ καὶ ἐδώκατέ μοι φαγεῖν, ἐδίψησα καὶ ἐποτίσατέ με, ξένος ἤμην καὶ συνηγάγετέ με, [36] γυμνὸς καὶ περιεβάλετέ με, ἠσθένησα καὶ ἐπεσκέψασθέ με, ἐν φυλακῇ ἤμην καὶ ἤλθατε πρός με. [37] τότε ἀποκριθήσονται αὐτῷ οἱ δίκαιοι λέγοντες· κύριε, πότε σε εἴδαμεν πεινῶντα καὶ ἐθρέψαμεν, ἢ διψῶντα καὶ ἐποτίσαμεν; [38] πότε δέ σε εἴδομεν ξένον καὶ συνηγάγομεν, ἢ γυμνὸν καὶ περιεβάλομεν; [39] πότε δέ σε εἴδομεν ἀσθενῆ ἢ ἐν φυλακῇ καὶ ἤλθομεν πρός σε; [40] καὶ ἀποκριθεὶς ὁ βασιλεὺς ἐρεῖ αὐτοῖς· αμην λέγω ὑμῖν, ἐφ' ὅσον ἐποιήσατε ἑνὶ τούτων τῶν ἀδελφῶν μου τῶν ἐλαχίστων, ἐμοὶ ἐποιήσατε. [41] τότε ἐρεῖ καὶ τοῖς ἐξ εὐωνύμων· πορεύεσθε ἀπ' ἐμοῦ οἱ κατηραμένοι εἰς τὸ πῦρ τὸ αἰώνιον τὸ ἡτοιμασμένον τῷ διαβόλῳ καὶ τοῖς ἀγγέλοις αὐτοῦ. [42] ἐπείνασα γὰρ καὶ οὐκ ἐδώκατέ μοι φαγεῖν, ἐδίψησα καὶ οὐκ ἐποτίσατέ με, [43] ξένος ἤμην καὶ οὐ συνηγάγετέ με, γυμνὸς καὶ οὐ περιεβάλετέ με, ἀσθενὴς καὶ ἐν φυλακῇ καὶ οὐκ ἐπεσκέψασθέ με. [44] τότε ἀποκριθήσονται καὶ αὐτοὶ λέγοντες· κύριε, πότε σε εἴδομεν πεινῶντα ἢ διψῶντα ἢ ξένον ἢ γυμνὸν ἢ ἀσθενῆ ἢ ἐν φυλακῇ καὶ οὐ διηκονήσαμέν σοι; [45] τότε ἀποκριθήσεται αὐτοῖς λέγων· αμην λέγω ὑμῖν, ἐφ' ὅσον οὐκ ἐποιήσατε ἑνὶ τούτων τῶν ἐλαχίστων, οὐδὲ ἐμοὶ ἐποιήσατε. [46] καὶ ἀπελεύσονται **οὗτοι εἰς** κόλασιν **αἰώνιον, οἱ δὲ** δίκαιοι **εἰς ζωὴν αἰώνιον.**

Dn12 2

5 29: καὶ ἐκπορεύσονται οἱ τὰ ἀγαθὰ ποιήσαντες εἰς ἀνάστασιν ζωῆς, οἱ δὲ τὰ φαῦλα πράξαντες εἰς ἀνάστασιν κρίσεως.

(223. 230) **242.** Schluß der Rede nach Lukas. **Luk 21** 34–38

The Lucan Ending to the Discourse.

[34] Προσέχετε δὲ ἑαυτοῖς μήποτε βαρηθῶσιν ὑμῶν αἱ καρδίαι ἐν κραιπάλῃ καὶ μέθῃ καὶ μερίμναις βιωτικαῖς, καὶ ἐπιστῇ ἐφ' ὑμᾶς αἰφνίδιος ἡ ἡμέρα ἐκείνη [35] ὡς **παγίς·** ἐπεισελεύσεται γὰρ **ἐπὶ** πάντας **τοὺς καθημένους ἐπὶ** πρόσωπον πάσης **τῆς γῆς.** [36] ἀγρυπνεῖτε δὲ ἐν παντὶ καιρῷ δεόμενοι ἵνα κατισχύσητε ἐκφυγεῖν ταῦτα πάντα τὰ μέλλοντα γίνεσθαι, καὶ σταθῆναι ἔμπροσθεν τοῦ υἱοῦ τοῦ ἀνθρώπου.

Matth 25,31 δοξη + του πατρος‖16 27 Mk8 38 Lk9 26: 1295 | αγγ.] αγιοι αγγ.‖Mk← Lk←: *Rpl* Ddy[1] Or *Lf S*[sc] *C*b[5] *Δ*a — *txt* (+ αυτου): 𝔖⟨892⟩ **λ**-1582 **ϕ**124 D Θ Π **074** 157 *pc l*1963 Cr Cr[I] Ddy[1]([1]) Eu PsHip Or *L*'[ek] Cp Hil *S*j *C*' *Arm Geo*'([A]) *Aeth* **39** ● ασθενουντα *cf.* 36: B **ϕ**124 D Θ 237 259 Cl *L*Cp[3:6] **40** τουτ. + των μικρων‖10 42 18 6.10.14 *etc.*: Σ **067** | *om* των αδ. μου‖45: B σ1424 16 *l*1963 *L*ff[1.2] **41** οι] ● *om*: 𝔓[45v] 𝔖⟨892⟩-**0128 0135** 1355 Hip{} — *prm* παντες‖Lk13 27: 1295 — *txt*: *Rpl* Bas Cr Eu Hip Or {*L*Cp} | το ητοιμ.] ● ο ητοιμασεν ο πατηρ μου‖20 33: **λ**-1582 D PsCl Hip Iu↓ *L*abcff[1.2] g[1]hr[1.2] vg[1] Au[2] Cp[3] Hil Ir Or Peti[Au] Te[1] — ο ητ. ο κυριος: Cl *L*Or Te[1] — *txt*: 𝔓[45v] *Rpl* Bas CAp Cl Cr Ddy Eu Hip Or *L*'[ek] Au[54] Cp[1] Hil Or Ru Te[1] **45** ελαχ.] μικρων‖10 42 18 6.10.14 *etc.*: 700 {*C*s} — αδελφων μου των ελ.‖40: **ϕ**124-174 σ954-1010-1293 Γ 157 *pc l*1663 *l*1963 Chr[1:3](~ ενι των ελ. του. τ. αδ. μου) *L*vg[1] *S*p[1]j *C*b[3] — αδελ. ελ.(!): E* *L*Cp[1:4]

Lk 21,34 *om* δε‖12 1 17 3: ℵ-1241 **λλ**⟨22-1278⟩ **ϕ**⟨124-983⟩ D *pc L*l Ir *C*s[3:7] *Arm Aeth Δ*a ad i | ~ αι καρ. υμ.‖16 15 Mk8 17: BX-**0139**-579 λ22 **ϕ**⟨346⟩ A W *pc* **36** δε] ουν‖Mt24 42p 25 13: *Rpl* Eu *L*'⟨vg[1]⟩ Te *S C*s[1]b' *Δ*'⟨me p⟩ — γρηγορειτε‖←: 157 — *om*: *S*j[a1 b1] *Δ*a — *txt*: ℵB D *L*e a *S*j[a1 b1] *C*s[6]b[1] | κατισ.] καταξιωθητε‖20 35: *Rpl L*,Te *S Δ*⟨p⟩ — *txt*: 𝔖'X-**0113-0179**(-σετε) **λλ**⟨22-1278⟩ W(-σατε) Ψ 157 *pc S*j[c] *C Aeth* | ~ παν. ταυ.‖Mt24 34: C*-**0179** N σM A W Ψ *pc L*e air[1]30 vg[2] Te *S*hj' {} *Aeth Δ*i{md n'([L]πασας τας θλιψεις ταυτας)} — παντα‖21 32: *Rpl L*vg[1] *Δ*a[BE]([A] *om*) — ταυτα‖←Mk13 29: 157 *S*'j[b1] — *txt*: 𝔖⟨ℵ*-892⟩ℵ[c]X-**0113 λ ϕ**⟨124⟩ D *L*' {*Arm*} *Δ*ad l {} E[a]

Jo 5,29 ● οι: 𝔓[66] B *L*e aff[2] Au[6] Te *C*sa[s] — οι δε] και οι: 𝔓[66*] W *L*PsAu[1] Ir *S*'j *C*b' *Geo*[1] — *txt*: 𝔓[75] *Rpl* Ddy *L*'Au[5] PsAu[1] *S*h *C*b[B3]([3] *prm* και) *Geo*[2]

Mt25 41 *cf.* Iu dial. 76,5: ὑπάγετε εἰς τὸ σκότος τὸ ἐξώτερον, ὃ ἡτοίμασεν ὁ πατὴρ τῷ σατανᾷ καὶ τοῖς ἀγγέλοις αὐτοῦ.

cf. *253.* *212.* *214.*

37 ἦν δὲ τὰς ἡμέρας ἐν τῷ ἱερῷ διδάσκων, τὰς δὲ νύκτας ἐξερχόμενος ηὐλίζετο εἰς τὸ ὄρος τὸ καλούμενον ἐλαιών. 38 καὶ πᾶς ὁ λαὸς ὤρθριζεν πρὸς αὐτὸν ἐν τῷ ἱερῷ ἀκούειν αὐτοῦ.

[8 1 f.: Ἰησοῦς δὲ ἐπορεύθη εἰς τὸ ὄρος τῶν ἐλαιῶν. 2 ὄρθρου δὲ πάλιν παρεγένετο εἰς τὸ ἱερόν, καὶ πᾶς ὁ λαὸς ἤρχετο πρὸς αὐτόν, καὶ καθίσας ἐδίδασκεν αὐτούς.]

3. Die Leidensgeschichte. *The Passion Narrative.*

Matth 26—27 = Mark 14—15 = Luk 22—23

(231)

243. Der Todesanschlag. *The Conspiracy of the Jews.*

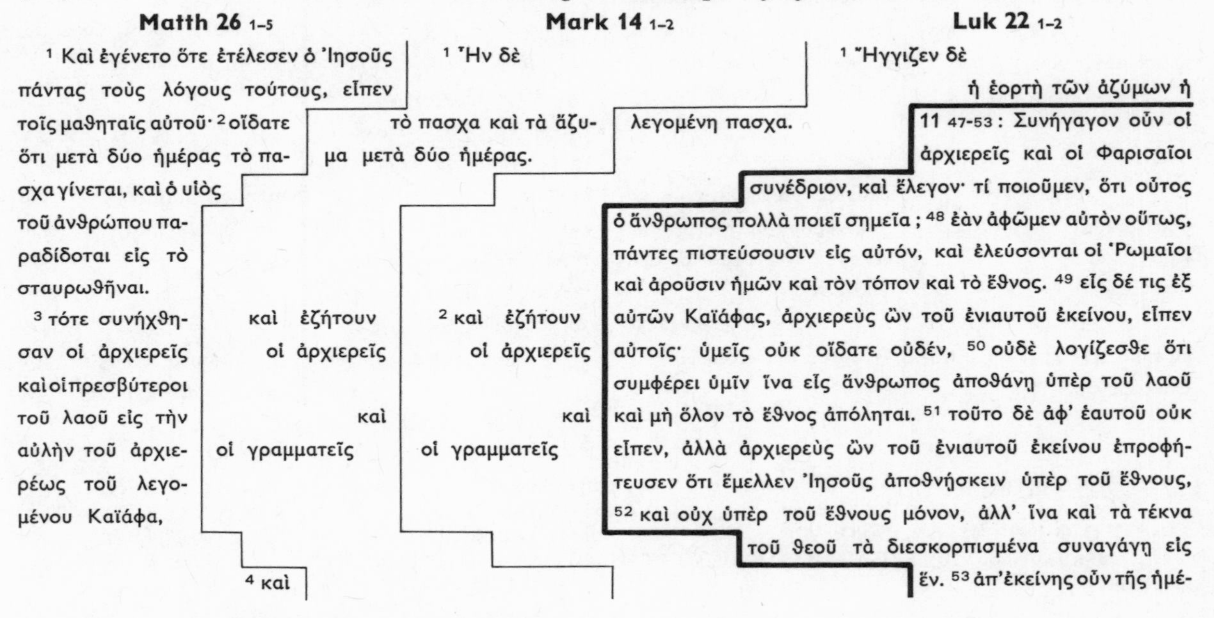

Matth 26 1–5

1 Καὶ ἐγένετο ὅτε ἐτέλεσεν ὁ Ἰησοῦς πάντας τοὺς λόγους τούτους, εἶπεν τοῖς μαθηταῖς αὐτοῦ· 2 οἴδατε ὅτι μετὰ δύο ἡμέρας τὸ πασχα γίνεται, καὶ ὁ υἱὸς τοῦ ἀνθρώπου παραδίδοται εἰς τὸ σταυρωθῆναι.
3 τότε συνήχθησαν οἱ ἀρχιερεῖς καὶ οἱ πρεσβύτεροι τοῦ λαοῦ εἰς τὴν αὐλὴν τοῦ ἀρχιερέως τοῦ λεγομένου Καϊάφα, 4 καὶ

Mark 14 1–2

1 Ἦν δὲ τὸ πασχα καὶ τὰ ἄζυμα μετὰ δύο ἡμέρας. καὶ ἐζήτουν οἱ ἀρχιερεῖς καὶ οἱ γραμματεῖς

Luk 22 1–2

1 Ἤγγιζεν δὲ ἡ ἑορτὴ τῶν ἀζύμων ἡ λεγομένη πασχα. 2 καὶ ἐζήτουν οἱ ἀρχιερεῖς καὶ οἱ γραμματεῖς

11 47–53: Συνήγαγον οὖν οἱ ἀρχιερεῖς καὶ οἱ Φαρισαῖοι συνέδριον, καὶ ἔλεγον· τί ποιοῦμεν, ὅτι οὗτος ὁ ἄνθρωπος πολλὰ ποιεῖ σημεῖα; 48 ἐὰν ἀφῶμεν αὐτὸν οὕτως, πάντες πιστεύσουσιν εἰς αὐτόν, καὶ ἐλεύσονται οἱ Ῥωμαῖοι καὶ ἀροῦσιν ἡμῶν καὶ τὸν τόπον καὶ τὸ ἔθνος. 49 εἷς δέ τις ἐξ αὐτῶν Καϊάφας, ἀρχιερεὺς ὢν τοῦ ἐνιαυτοῦ ἐκείνου, εἶπεν αὐτοῖς· ὑμεῖς οὐκ οἴδατε οὐδέν, 50 οὐδὲ λογίζεσθε ὅτι συμφέρει ὑμῖν ἵνα εἷς ἄνθρωπος ἀποθάνῃ ὑπὲρ τοῦ λαοῦ καὶ μὴ ὅλον τὸ ἔθνος ἀπόληται. 51 τοῦτο δὲ ἀφ᾽ ἑαυτοῦ οὐκ εἶπεν, ἀλλὰ ἀρχιερεὺς ὢν τοῦ ἐνιαυτοῦ ἐκείνου ἐπροφήτευσεν ὅτι ἔμελλεν Ἰησοῦς ἀποθνήσκειν ὑπὲρ τοῦ ἔθνους, 52 καὶ οὐχ ὑπὲρ τοῦ ἔθνους μόνον, ἀλλ᾽ ἵνα καὶ τὰ τέκνα τοῦ θεοῦ τὰ διεσκορπισμένα συναγάγῃ εἰς ἕν. 53 ἀπ᾽ ἐκείνης οὖν τῆς ἡμέ-

Mt 26,2 παραδοθησεται‖2018p Lk944: 700 σ1207-1223 Θ 483 *L*[ek]⟨bff^{1}⟩ Au$^{3:5}$ Or *C* | **3** οι αρχ. + και οι (*om*) γραμματεις‖p: *Rpl* (σ1223 S Δ Ω) *L*cff^{2}g^{2}hqr^{1}30 Or *S*p$^{⟨1⟩}$h *Arm* — *txt*: 𝔓^{45v} 𝔥 700 **λ**-1582 **ϕ**⟨346-983⟩ **σ**⟨1675⟩ A D Θ **089** *pc* *L*'[ek] *S*s[c]j *C*s(∼ πρεσ. … αρχ.)b *Geo* *Aeth* | πρε. + και οι γρα.‖p: σ1010-1293 *S*p^{1}

Mk 14,1 *om* κ. τ. αζ.‖Mt: D *L*aff^{2} *Geo*^{1}

Lk 21,37 ∼ διδ. τας—ιερω‖Mk1235: **0179** *C*s — ∼ διδ. εν τω ιε.‖← Jo820: **B-0139** λ2193 K *L* *S*scp *C*b$^{⟨1⟩}$ | το καλ.] των‖2239p[Jo81]: X **λλ**⟨22-1278⟩ Γ 1574 *L*e lr^{1} *Δ*i^{T} md me n p **38** λαος] οχλος‖Mt132p Mk213: 472 *C*s | **38** + [Jo753—811] (*cf. ad* [Jo81f.]): **ϕ** **22,1** *om* η λεγ. πασ.‖227: 440 **2** εζη. + αυτον‖Mk1212 Mt2146: **047**

[Jo 8,1f. ● *om* 753—811: 𝔓$^{66.75}$ 𝔥⟨579⟩C^{v}TX N-1071 λ22-209*-2193 ϕ*l*547 **σ**⟨954⟩-349 A^{v} Δ Θ Ψ **053 0141 0211** *pm* *l*^{pl} Chr Cl^{v} Co Cr Non Or Thy^{cmt} *L*aflq Cp Te *S*' *C*'$^{+B}$a^{s} *Δ*a l^{F} — 2125 + 753—811: **λ**' *Arm*' — Lk2138 + Jo753—811: **ϕ** — 752 + 753—811: *Rpl* CAp DAp *L*'Am Amst Au Hil *S*h$^{Brs\,m}$j *C*b^{11} *Arm*^{pc} **1** επορευετο‖p Mk1119: *S* *pc* | ελαι. + μονος‖615 Mt1423: 272 475 **2** παλ. + βαθεως‖Lk241: U *pm* *C*b^{1} | λαος] οχλος‖Mk213 Mt132p: Λ-28-700 G S U *mu* *C*b$^{⟨1⟩}$] **11,47** Φ.] πρεσβυτεροι‖Mt3: ϕ69 | συνε. + κατα του Ιησου‖Mt271: 700 **ϕ**-*l*547 *pc* *Δ*i^{T} md n$^{⟨L⟩}$ | πολ.] τοιαυτα‖916: D *L*e bcff^{2}z **52** ● εθν. + δε: ℵ^{ca}X-33 ϕ*l*547 Ψ 213 *L*g^{2}(sed et non) — *txt*: 𝔓$^{45v.66.75}$ *Rpl* Or *L*' *C*$^{+B}$a^{s} *Δ*{a} ad i l md n^{Hg} p

Matth	Mark	Luk	Jo
συνεβουλεύσαντο ἵνα τὸν Ἰησοῦν δόλῳ κρατήσωσιν καὶ ἀποκτείνωσιν·	πῶς αὐτὸν ἐν δόλῳ κρατήσαντες ἀποκτείνωσιν·	τὸ πῶς ἀνέλωσιν αὐτόν·	ρας ἐβουλεύσαντο ἵνα ἀποκτείνωσιν αὐτόν.
5 ἔλεγον δέ· μὴ ἐν τῇ ἑορτῇ, ἵνα μὴ θόρυβος γένηται ἐν τῷ λαῷ.	2 ἔλεγον γάρ· μὴ ἐν τῇ ἑορτῇ, μήποτε ἔσται θόρυβος τοῦ λαοῦ.	ἐφοβοῦντο γὰρ τὸν λαόν.	

(232) **244.** Die Salbung in Bethanien. *The Anointing at Bethany.*

Matth 26 6–13	Mark 14 3–9		
6 Τοῦ δὲ Ἰησοῦ γενομένου ἐν Βηθανίᾳ ἐν οἰκίᾳ Σίμωνος τοῦ λεπροῦ,	3 Καὶ ὄντος αὐτοῦ ἐν Βηθανίᾳ ἐν τῇ οἰκίᾳ Σίμωνος τοῦ λεπροῦ, κατακειμένου αὐτοῦ		12 1–8: Ὁ οὖν Ἰησοῦς ... ἦλθεν εἰς Βηθανίαν, ὅπου ἦν Λάζαρος ... 2 ... εἷς ἦν ἐκ τῶν ἀνακειμένων σὺν αὐτῷ·
7 προσῆλθεν αὐτῷ γυνὴ	ἦλθεν γυνὴ	*7 37 f. (96.): καὶ ἰδοὺ γυνὴ ἥτις ἦν ἐν τῇ πόλει ἁμαρτωλός, καὶ ἐπιγνοῦσα ὅτι κατάκειται ἐν τῇ οἰκίᾳ τοῦ Φαρισαίου,*	3 ἡ οὖν Μαρία
ἀλάβαστρον μύρου ἔχουσα βαρυτίμου καὶ	ἔχουσα ἀλάβαστρον μύρου νάρδου πιστικῆς πολυτελοῦς συντρίψασα τὸν ἀλάβαστρον	*κομίσασα ἀλάβαστρον μύρου*	λαβοῦσα λίτραν μύρου νάρδου πιστικῆς πολυτίμου
κατέχεεν ἐπὶ τῆς κεφαλῆς αὐτοῦ ἀνακειμένου.	κατέχεεν αὐτοῦ τῆς κεφαλῆς.	*38 καὶ στᾶσα ὀπίσω παρὰ τοὺς πόδας αὐτοῦ κλαίουσα, τοῖς δάκρυσιν ἤρξατο βρέχειν τοὺς πόδας αὐτοῦ, καὶ ταῖς*	ἤλειψεν τοὺς πόδας τοῦ Ἰησοῦ καὶ ἐξέμαξεν ταῖς

Mt 26,5 ινα μη] μηποτε‖Mk: 𝔓45v(*om* ποτε) L 700 *L*acfff1g1lz vg | ∼ γεν. θο.‖Mk: Θ *S*s[c]pj | εν τ. λαω] του λαου‖Mk: 1200 *S*p1 **6** εν2 + τη‖Mk: 472 **7** ● ∼ εχ. αλ. μυ.‖p: 𝔋 700 ϕ-174-*l*547 D Θ **089** 1295 *l*48 *L*[ek],Or *S*,j — αλ. εχ. μυ.: 𝔓45 157 — *txt*: *Rpl* Bas | ● πολυτιμου‖Jo: 𝔋⟨B⟩ 544 ϕ230 σ-M-7-71-659-1010-1293 A D Θ Π 157 *pc* *S*phm | ∼ αυ. της κεφ.‖Mk: 1355

Mk 14,1 πως] το π.‖Lk: Σ 1200 | *om* εν‖Mt: Δ WΣ-28-544 λ ϕ⟨124⟩-*l*547 | δολω] λογω‖12 13: U | κρα.] κρατησωσιν και‖Mt: 1241 28-544 σ827 (*om* και: 330) *L* **2** γαρ] δε‖Mt: *Rpl* *S*h *C*s *Arm* — *txt*: ℵBC*LΨ-892 D 1342 *L*,Au *S*s[c]hm *C*b⟨2⟩ | μηπ.] ινα μη(μηπ.)‖Mt: 579 σ517 (998) *pc* | ∼ θορ. εστ.‖Mt: *Rpl* (εστ.] οντος!: Δ) *L*a {Au} — θ. γενηται‖Mt: 579 28 σM-115(∼)-517 *L*'{} — *txt*: 𝔋'⟨1241⟩C Θ-565-700 D' *L*k(εστ.] γεν.) | τ. λαου] εν τω λαω‖Mt: 579 σ1424 1342 *pc* *L*cfir1.2?30 vg8 *S*p⟨2⟩h *C*,f **3** *om* τη‖Mt: ℵ* ΘΦ-544-565-700 λ1278 ϕ828-983-1689 σ945-1402-1606 1342 *pm* | ανακει.‖Mt Jo: Σ *pc* | ηλ.] προσηλ. αυτω‖Mt: ϕ-*l*547 | ∼ αλ. εχ.‖Mt: 565-700 σ1424 | ∼ αλ. μυ. εχ.‖Mt: σ1402 *pc* | *om* ναρ. πι. πολ.‖Lk: D' — *om* ναρ. πι.‖Mt: 248 *S*p1 — *om* ναρ.‖p: 348 | πολυτιμου‖Jo: WΘ-28-565-1071 λ-22 ϕ⟨828⟩-*l*547 σMm-179-827 A G 1342 *al* *l*49 | τον] το: WΘΦ σM G **0103** *pl* — ● την: 𝔋'ℵc C 1342 — *txt*: ℵ*X-892 Σ-544-565-1071 λ872 ϕ124 σ7-115-267-517-659-827-1424 *R mu* | αυ. της κεφ.] επι της κεφ. αυ.‖Mt: D *l*20 — αυ. κατα της κεφ.‖Mt: *Rpl* — *txt*: ℵBCLΔΨ(τη -η)-892 W-28 λ1-22

Lk 21,2 το πως] πως‖Mk: ϕ543 D *pc* — οπως‖Mt12 14 Mk3 6: 1241 | ανελ.] απολεσωσιν‖←19 47 Mk11 18: D | ∼ αυ. αν.‖Mk3 6 11 18: λ1278 ϕ174 *pc* *L*'⟨a⟩(αυ.] τον Ιησουν: l vg1) | γαρ] δε‖Mt: ϕ124 D *L*bcff2qz vg *Arm* | *om* εφ.—λαον‖p: G 1574

Jo 11,53 ● συνεβουλ.‖Mt: *Rpl* Or — *txt*: 𝔓45.66.75 ℵBW ϕ D Θ *pc* Ath Chr **12,3** *om* ναρ.‖Mt Lk: 𝔓66* σ1194 D *L*e bcff2r1 | πολυτελους‖Mk: ϕ1689 | ηλειφε‖Lk: σ954 | του I.] αυτου‖Lk: X | ∼ τ. θρι. αυ. εξε.‖Lk7 44: 1241 λ ϕ69(τ. θρ. εξε. ταις εμαυτης!)-543-788-826-828 Θ *pc* *Arm*

Matth	Mark	Joh
	ϑριξὶν τῆς κεφαλῆς αὐτῆς ἐξέμασσεν, καὶ κατεφίλει τοὺς πόδας αὐτοῦ καὶ ἤλειφεν τῷ μύρῳ ...	ϑριξὶν αὐτῆς τοὺς πόδας αὐτοῦ· ἡ δὲ οἰκία ἐπληρώϑη ἐκ τῆς ὀσμῆς τοῦ μύρου.
[8] ἰδόντες δὲ οἱ μαϑηταὶ ἠγανάκτησαν λέγοντες· εἰς τί ἡ ἀπώλεια αὕτη;	[4] ἦσαν δέ τινες ἀγανακτοῦντες πρὸς ἑαυτοὺς καὶ λέγοντες· εἰς τί ἡ ἀπώλεια αὕτη τοῦ μύρου γέγονεν;	[4] λέγει οὖν εἷς ἐκ τῶν μαϑητῶν αὐτοῦ Ἰούδας ὁ Ἰσκαριώτης, ὁ μέλλων αὐτὸν παραδιδόναι· [5] διὰ τί
[9] ἐδύνατο γὰρ τοῦτο πραϑῆναι πολλοῦ καὶ δοϑῆναι πτωχοῖς.	[5] ἠδύνατο γὰρ τοῦτο τὸ μύρον πραϑῆναι ἐπάνω δηναρίων τριακοσίων καὶ δοϑῆναι τοῖς πτωχοῖς· καὶ ἐνεβριμῶντο αὐτῇ.	τοῦτο τὸ μύρον οὐκ ἐπράϑη τριακοσίων δηναρίων καὶ ἐδόϑη πτωχοῖς; [6] εἶπεν δὲ τοῦτο οὐχ ὅτι περὶ τῶν πτωχῶν ἔμελεν αὐτῷ, ἀλλ' ὅτι κλέπτης ἦν καὶ τὸ γλωσσόκομον ἔχων τὰ βαλλόμενα ἐβάσταζεν.
[10] γνοὺς δὲ ὁ Ἰησοῦς εἶπεν αὐτοῖς· τί	[6] ὁ δὲ Ἰησοῦς εἶπεν· ἄφετε αὐτήν· τί αὐτῇ	[7] εἶπεν οὖν ὁ Ἰησοῦς· ἄφες αὐτήν, ἵνα εἰς

Mt 26,8 μαϑ. + αυτου‖Jo: *Rpl* Bas *L*cfq vg^{1} Or *S*,j^{ab} *C*s^{1} — *txt*: 𝔓$^{45v.64}$ 𝔥⟨892⟩ 700 ϕ69-124-788-826-983-*l*547 σ1293 D Θ **089** *L*'[ek] *S*j^{c} *C*s^{9}b *Arm* | αυτη + του μυρου‖Mk: ΣΦ σ71 157 *pc* Bas *L*ab(+ τουτου) *S*j *Arm* *Geo*(=b) *Aeth* **9** τουτο] του. το μυρον‖Mk: *Rpl* *L*cq Or *S*j — *om*: Θ 157 Amph *Geo*^{1} — *txt*: 𝔓^{45v} 𝔥⟨33⟩ ΣΦ **λ**-1582 σ71-517-1010-1675 A D E W Δ Π **089** *al* Bas *L*'[ek] *S* *C* *Geo*^{2} | πτω.] τοις πτ.‖Mk: *Rpl* *C* — *txt*: 𝔓^{45v} 𝔥⟨33⟩ **λ**-22-1582 **ϕ**⟨124⟩ σM-517 F G U Y Θ **089** *pm* Amph Bas **10** *om* αυτ.‖p: 1279

Mk 14,4 τινες + των μαϑητων(+ αυτου)‖p: W **ϕ**'⟨828⟩(983-1689)-*l*547 *S*p'(^{1}) | ησ.—αγαν.] οι δε μαϑηται αυτου διεπονουντο‖p: Θ-565 D *L*aff^{2}ir^{1} *Arm*(και οι μα., *om* αυ.) | πρ. εαυ. κ. λεγ.] ● πρ. εαυ.: ℵ(αυ.) BC*LΨ-892 1342 *C*b^{5} — κ. ελεγον: Θ-565 D *L*(*om*: i)r^{1} *Geo*^{2} — λεγ.‖**p**: *L*k[e](και λεγ.) cff^{2} — *om* και‖p: 28 σ7-517 *pc* *l*^{pl} *L*ar^{2} vg^{4} *C*s^{4}b' — κ. λεγ. πρ. εαυ.: **λ** *C*s^{2}(*om* και) *Geo*^{1} *Δ*md n — πρ. εαυ. ελεγον(ειπον): *C*s^{2}(ειπ. πρ. ε. κ. ελεγ.)b^{3}(^{1}) *Δ*a(ελ.] και ειπ.) — *txt*: *Rpl* *l*10 *l*185 *l*299 *L*' *S*' *C*s^{1} *Δ*ad i l^{FG} | *om* του μυ.‖p: W-544 **λ** *pc* *L*ac(+ η ανωφελης)l *S*s[c] *Geo*^{1} | *om* γεγ.‖p: 544 D 64 *L*aff^{2}ir^{1} *S*s[c] **5** τουτο—μυ.] τουτο‖p: *Rpl* *L*c(∼ του. γαρ εδ. πρ.) *C*b — *om*‖p: *L*k[e] *S*' *C*s^{1} *Geo*^{2} — το μ. του. (∼ πραϑ. το μ. του.): 28-565-(700 **ϕ**⟨828⟩-*l*547) σ1606 (D) *L*(fff^{2}iqr^{1}z)lr^{2} vg — το μ.: ℵ W(∼ πραϑ. το μ.) — *txt*: 𝔥'C Θ(∼ πραϑ. του. το μ.)-544-1071 **λ**-1278 **σ**-7-827-945-1082-1223-1391 A K U Π **0103** 1342 *mu* *L*a *S*h *C*s^{7} *Arm* *Geo*^{1} *Aeth* | *om* επανω‖Jo: σ⟨1424⟩ Or *L*k[e] c *S*s[c] *Geo* | ∼ τρι. δην.‖Jo: *Rpl* *L*' *S* — *txt*: ℵCLΨ-579 WΘ-565 D *L*acff^{2}ilr^{1} vg^{1} | *om* τοις‖p: 579 σ267 **047** *al* *l*184 Or **6** ειπ. + αυτοις‖p: WΘ-565 D 238 *L*vl⟨lr^{2}z⟩g^{2} vg^{2} *S*s[c] *C*s$^{7:8}$b$^{⟨4+1v⟩}$ *Arm* *Aeth* | ∼ κοπ. παρ. αυτη‖p: 544 ϕ13

Jo 12,3 ϑρι. + της κεφαλης‖**L**k: X-**065** 213 *l*251 *L*Or *S*j *C*$^{⟨B⟩}$a^{s} | τ. ποδ.^{2} αυ.] *om*‖**L**k: **λ** *pc* *L*vg^{1} Or *S*s[c] *Aeth* — αυτους: *S*j *C*$^{+B}$a^{s} **4** ουν] ● δε‖p: 𝔓$^{66.75v}$ ℵBW-579 *S*j *C*b' — *om*: L-33-1241 *pc* *L*e ar^{1} *S*'(και λε.) *C*sb^{B3}a^{s} *Arm* — *txt*: *Rpl* *L*fz vg *S*h | ● ∼ Ιου. ο Ισ. εις—αυτου‖Mk14 43p Lk22 3: 𝔓$^{66.75}$ 𝔥-**0124** 1071 **0141** **0217** 157 *pc* *S*'j *C*sa^{s} — *txt*: *Rpl* Cr Non *L*,Au *S*h *C*b$^{⟨B⟩}$a *Arm* | ● *om* εκ‖Mt26 14.47 Mk14 10.43 Lk22 47: 𝔓$^{66.75}$ 𝔥⟨ℵ-1241⟩Q **0141** *al* *Δ*a i md^{M} p | Ιου. + Σιμωνος (Σιμων)‖13 2.26 6 71: *Rpl* (F G H U *pc* *l*211 *l*1127) *L*f(bcff^{2}r^{1}z) *S*h (*C*b^{4}) *Geo*^{2} — *prm* Σιμων: *L*e a *C*b^{3} — *txt*: 𝔓$^{66.75}$ 𝔥Q-**0124** **λ** **0217**^{v} *pc* *l*185^{v} *l*251^{1} *l*253 Cr Non *L*vg Au *S*'j *C*sb'^{B}a^{v}a^{s} *Geo*^{1} | *om* ο^{1}‖Mt26 14 Mk3 19 Lk6 16: *Rpl* (απο Καρυωτου: D) — *txt*: 𝔓$^{66.75}$ 𝔥Q-**0124** 1071 **λ** σ659 F G H U **0217** *pc* *l*185^{v} *l*211 *l*1127 *C*$^{+B}$a^{s} | ο μελ.] ος ημελλεν‖6 71: D *L* | ∼ παραδουναι αυτον‖←Lk 22 6 20 20: D *L*fz vg^{1} **5** επρ. + επανω‖Mk: X-1241 213 | ∼ δην. τρι.‖Mk: Θ *L*vl⟨f⟩r^{1} | διακοσ.‖6 71 Mk6 37: L-579 **λ**⟨1⟩ **ϕ**⟨828⟩-*l*547 **053** *pc* | πτω.] τοις πτ.‖Mk: 33 1071 σ1293 D Θ Ψ **053** *pc* *C*$^{+B}$a^{sv} **6** εχ.] ειχεν και‖13 29: 𝔓^{66} *Rpl* *L*vlr^{1} vg^{2} *Δ*i — *txt* (+ και): 𝔓^{75} 𝔥⟨1241⟩Q-**0124** (**λ**) D Θ **0217**^{v} Or *L*vg' *C*s^{6}(^{1})b^{+B}a^{v}a^{s} *Δ*ad **7** αφετε‖Mk: 713 Chr *L*aδ vg^{5} Am *S*p^{2}j^{abd} *C*s *Arm*$^{⟨pc⟩}$ *Geo*^{2} *Aeth* | ινα] οτι‖Mt: ϕ13-543-826-828 Chr(∼ εις γαρ την ημ.—μου τουτο εποιησεν) {} — *om*, *et* τετηρηκεν‖Mk: *Rpl* *L*f *S*' *Δ*a p — *txt*: 𝔓$^{66.75}$ 𝔥QX-**0124** D K Θ Π Ψ **053** **0217**^{v} *pc* Non *L*' *S*h^{m}j *C*$^{+B}$a^{s} *Arm* *Aeth* *Δ*i^{V}{E^{a}}

Matth 26	Mark 14	Jo 12
κόπους παρέχετε τῇ γυναικί; ἔργον γὰρ καλὸν ἠργάσατο εἰς ἐμέ· 11 πάντοτε γὰρ τοὺς πτωχοὺς ἔχετε μεθ' ἑαυτῶν, ἐμὲ δὲ οὐ πάντοτε ἔχετε. 12 βαλοῦσα γὰρ αὕτη τὸ μύρον τοῦτο ἐπὶ τοῦ σώματός μου πρὸς τὸ ἐνταφιάσαι με ἐποίησεν. 13 αμην λέγω ὑμῖν, ὅπου ἐὰν κηρυχθῇ τὸ εὐαγγέλιον τοῦτο ἐν ὅλῳ τῷ κόσμῳ, λαληθήσεται καὶ ὃ ἐποίησεν αὕτη εἰς μνημόσυνον αὐτῆς.	κόπους παρέχετε; καλὸν ἔργον ἠργάσατο ἐν ἐμοί· 7 πάντοτε γὰρ τοὺς πτωχοὺς ἔχετε μεθ' ἑαυτῶν, καὶ ὅταν θέλητε δύνασθε αὐτοῖς εὖ ποιῆσαι, ἐμὲ δὲ οὐ πάντοτε ἔχετε. 8 ὃ ἔσχεν ἐποίησεν· προέλαβεν μυρίσαι μου τὸ σῶμα εἰς τὸν ἐνταφιασμόν. 9 αμην δὲ λέγω ὑμῖν, ὅπου ἐὰν κηρυχθῇ τὸ εὐαγγέλιον εἰς ὅλον τὸν κόσμον, καὶ ὃ ἐποίησεν αὕτη λαληθήσεται εἰς μνημόσυνον αὐτῆς.	τὴν ἡμέραν τοῦ ἐνταφιασμοῦ μου τηρήσῃ αὐτό· 8 τοὺς πτωχοὺς γὰρ πάντοτε ἔχετε μεθ' ἑαυτῶν, ἐμὲ δὲ οὐ πάντοτε ἔχετε. cf. v. 7b ↑

(233) **245.** Der Verrat des Judas. *The Betrayal by Judas.*

Matth 26 14–16	Mark 14 10–11	Luk 22 3–6	
			13 27: καὶ μετὰ τὸ ψωμίον
14 Τότε πορευθεὶς εἷς τῶν δώδεκα, ὁ λεγόμενος Ἰούδας Ἰσκαριώτης,	10 Καὶ Ἰούδας ὁ Ισκαριωθ, ὁ εἷς	3 Εἰσῆλθεν δὲ σατανᾶς εἰς Ἰούδαν τὸν καλούμενον Ἰσκαριώτην, ὄντα ἐκ	τότε εἰσῆλθεν εἰς ἐκεῖνον ὁ σατανᾶς... 6 71: ἔλεγεν δὲ τὸν Ἰούδαν Σίμωνος Ἰσκαριώτου ... εἷς ὢν ἐκ

Mt 26,10 *om* γαρ‖Mk: ℵ^{ca} λ1-22-1582 ϕ543 1573 *L*[ek] acff^{1}g^{1}lr$^{1.2}$z vg$^{\langle 1\rangle}$ *S*s[c]pj$^{a1\,c1}$ *C*s$^{6:9}$b$^{\langle 6\rangle}$ | εις εμε] εν εμοι‖Mk: σM **11** ∼ τ. πτ. γαρ πα.‖Jo: *Rpl* Amph *L*ff^2 *S*s[c] *C*s^{1}b *Geo* — *txt*: ℌ ΣΦ **λ**⟨118⟩-22-1582 **ϕ**⟨69-983⟩ σ71-1010-1194 A D G K S U V W Y Δ Θ Π Ω **092a** *L*'[ek] *S*'j *C*s^8 **13** αμην + δε‖Mk: B^2 Δ *L*q *Arm Geo*^{1} | *om* τουτο‖p Mk13 10: ϕ69(*et om* λαλ.) *L*vg^1 **14** ∼ Ιου. ο λεγ.‖Lk: ϕ983 σ1402 — *om* ο λεγ.‖Mk: σ692-1194 | Ισ.] ο Ισ.‖10 4 Mk: **λ**⟨1⟩ ϕ174 2145

Mk 14,6 καλ. ερ.] ερ. γαρ καλ.‖p: 579 1396 *S*s[c]p^{1}hγαρ$^+$ *C*s$^{3:9}$b$^{\langle 5+1v\rangle}$ *Arm* — καλ. γαρ ερ.‖p: ℵ W-28-565 **ϕ**⟨828⟩-*l*547 G *pc L*c | εν εμοι] εις εμε‖p: 579 544 **σ**-349-1606 *pc l*251^1 — επ εμοι: 330 *pc* **7** ∼ τ. πτ. γαρ παν.‖Jo: 157 1396 | *om* και—ποιη.‖**p**Jo: 4 273 *C*s$^{1:7}$ | ευ] ● παντοτε ευ: ℵ^{c}BLΨ(∼ παν. δυν. αυτ. ευ)-892 1071 *C* **8** εσχ. + αυτη‖p: *Rpl* (∼ εποι. αυ.: Δ) *L*' *S*s[c](αυτη γαρ ο εποιησεν, *om* εσχ.)p'h(+ τουτο) *Arm* — *txt*: ℵBLΨ-579 WΘ-28-565 **λ**⟨118⟩ **ϕ**⟨124-828⟩-*l*547 1342 *pc L*a(+ τουτο: l vg^2) *S*p^1 *C* | προελ. + γαρ‖p: 157 *L*f (*S*s[c]) *C*s$^{1:8}$b$^{\langle 8\rangle}$ | ● ∼ το σω. μου‖**14** 22 Mt 26 12.26 Lk22 19: ℌ⟨Δ⟩ ΘΣ-565-1071 σM^c-115-517 D *pc l*49 *L*'(το σω.] την κεφαλην: g^2) — *txt*: *Rpl L*k[e] | εις] προς‖p: **λ**-22 *pc* | εντ. + μου‖Jo: 28 *C* **9** δε] *om*‖p: *Rpl L*' *S*s[c](αμ. *prm* και: p')^{6}h *C*s^{5}b *Arm Geo*^{B} — γαρ: 28 *pc C*s^2 — *txt*: ℵBLΔ Φ λ22 ϕ828 σ71-692 D E G K S V Y Γ Π Ω **0116** *pm L*a *Geo*' | ευαγ. + τουτο‖p Mt24 14: *Rpl L*' *S*p(του.] μου τουτο)h *C*s^{6}b *Arm* — *txt*: ℵBL W-28-565 **ϕ**⟨124-828⟩-*l*547 D *L*k[e] aff$^{2\prime}$ *S*s[c](+ μου) | εν ολω τω κοσμω‖p: Θ σ827 *pc L*ar^{2}z vg$^{\langle 7\rangle}$ | ∼ λαλ. και—αυτη‖p: 579 σ659 *pc* **10** Ιου. ο] ● Ιου.‖3 19 Mt Lk6 16: ℵ*BC*^{v}-892 28-1071 **ϕ**'(ο Ιου.: 828)-230-*l*547 σ517*-1606-1675 D 1342 *al* Or — ● ο Ιου. ο: *Rpl* — *txt*: ℵ^{c}LΔ Ψ ΘΣΦ-565-700 **λ**-1278 ϕ124 σM-71-517^c A E Y Γ Π 157 *pm* Eu | Ισκαριωτης‖p: *Rpl* Eu Or *L*' *C* — *txt*: ℵBC*^{v}LΨ-892 Θ-565 1342 *L*aff^{2}iz Au *Δ*ad i$^{T\langle 3mss\rangle}$ md$^{\langle M\rangle}$ n | ο εις] εις εκ‖Lk: 565 D(*om* εις) 1542 — εις‖14 43 Mt26 14.27 Lk22 47: *Rpl* (*om* ο εις τ. δωδ.: A) Eu Or — *txt*: ℵ^{c}BC*^{v}LΨ-892 σM-1606

Lk 22,3 τ. καλ.] τ. επικ. *cf.* Act11 13 *etc*: *Rpl* Eu Or(*om* τον) *L*' {}^{1} — τ. λεγομενον‖Mt: σ1194 *pc* {}^{2} *S*h^{t}j^{ac} — *om*‖Mk: G *S*j^b — *txt*: ℌ⟨892⟩X 1071 λ1278 ϕ69 σ115 D W *pc* {*L*vg^7}^{2} {*S*'h^m *C*}^{1} | Ισκαριωθ‖Mk: D(-ωδ) Or *L*'⟨e⟩(-otha: cl)

Jo 6,71 Ισκαριωτην‖12 4 Mt Lk Mk: *Rpl* Cr *L*l(*om* Σιμ.)q *C*s^{1}b^{+B}{} *Geo*^{1}(Σκα.)^2 — απο Καριωτου (Σκα.): ℵ*(-ρυω-) **ϕ**'(13-983) Θ *S*h^m — Σκαριωθ: D *L*e(Καρ.) abff^{2}r^{1}z — *txt*: 𝔓$^{66.75}$ ℌ'⟨579⟩ℵ^{c}C 1071 ϕ1689 σ1010-1293 G Ψ **0141** 1344 *L*cf vg' {*C*s$^{10+1?}$fa^s} | ● *om* ων‖14 26 47p Mk: BC*L 544 ϕ230 D *pc S*scp *C*b^1 | *om* εκ‖←: 579 28 *pc* **13,27** *om* μετα τ. ψ.‖Lk: D *L*e 30 *C*b^1 *Δ*me p(*et om* και) | *om* τοτε‖Lk: ℵL-579 D **0141** *pc* Cr *L*abcff^{2}lr^1 vg^1 Or$^{3:7}$ *S*s[c]h^{Brs}j *C*sb^{B9}fa^s *Geo Δ*a

Matth	Mark	Luk	Jo
	cf. 247. τῶν δώδεκα,	τοῦ ἀριθμοῦ τῶν δώδεκα·	τῶν δώδεκα.
πρὸς	ἀπῆλθεν πρὸς	4 καὶ ἀπελθὼν συνελάλησεν	13 2: ...
τοὺς ἀρχιερεῖς 15 εἶπεν· τί	τοὺς ἀρχιερεῖς	τοῖς ἀρχιερεῦσιν καὶ στρα-	τοῦ διαβόλου ἤδη βεβλη-
θέλετέ μοι δοῦναι, κἀγὼ ὑμῖν	ἵνα	τηγοῖς τὸ πῶς αὐτοῖς	κότος εἰς τὴν καρδίαν ἵνα
παραδώσω αὐτόν;	παραδοῖ αὐτὸν αὐτοῖς.	παραδῷ αὐτόν.	παραδῷ αὐτὸν ...
οἱ δὲ	11 οἱ δὲ ἀκούσαντες ἐχάρησαν καὶ	5 καὶ ἐχάρησαν καὶ	Zch11 12
ἔστησαν αὐτῷ **τριάκοντα ἀργύ-**	ἐπηγγείλαντο αὐτῷ ἀργύ-	συνέθεντο αὐτῷ ἀργύ-	
ρια. 16 καὶ ἀπὸ τότε	ριον δοῦναι. καὶ	ριον δοῦναι. 6 καὶ ἐξωμολόγησεν, καὶ	
ἐζήτει εὐκαιρίαν ἵνα αὐτὸν	ἐζήτει πῶς αὐτὸν εὐκαίρως	ἐζήτει εὐκαιρίαν τοῦ	
παραδῷ.	παραδοῖ.	παραδοῦναι αὐτὸν αὐτοῖς ἄτερ ὄχλου.	

Die letzte Mahlzeit. *The Last Supper.*

Matth 26 17–29 = Mark 14 12–25 = Luk 22 7–38

(234)

246. Zurüstung zum Passamahl. *Preparation for the Passover.*

Matth 26 17–19	Mark 14 12–16	Luk 22 7–13
17 Τῇ δὲ πρώτῃ τῶν ἀζύ-	12 Καὶ τῇ πρώτῃ ἡμέρᾳ τῶν ἀζύ-	7 Ἦλθεν δὲ ἡ ἡμέρα τῶν ἀζύ-
μων	μων, ὅτε τὸ πασχα ἔθυον,	μων, ᾗ ἔδει θύεσθαι τὸ πασχα· 8 καὶ
προσῆλθον οἱ μαθηταὶ τῷ Ἰησοῦ	λέγουσιν αὐτῷ οἱ μαθηταὶ αὐτοῦ·	ἀπέστειλεν Πέτρον καὶ Ἰωάννην εἰπών·
	cf. v. 13 ↓	πορευθέντες ἑτοιμάσατε ἡμῖν τὸ πασχα,

Mt 26,15 ∼ αυ. παρ. υμ.: Ep (∼ υμ. παρ.: *L*q30) — ∼ αυ. παρ.‖16 Mk11: 157 *L*'[ek]⟨vg^{1}⟩(^{1} *om* αυ.) Or **16** παρ. + αυτοις‖Mk10 Lk: 892 D Θ Eu *L*bchqr^{2}z30 vg^{1} Or *S*p^{1} *C*s$^{1:9}$b *Arm Aeth* **17** οι — Ι.] αυτω οι μα. αυτου‖Mk: 28 σM^{m} | ∼ λεγ. τω Ι.: Σ **λ**⟨118⟩-1582 W — + αυτω‖p: *Rpl L*fq Or *S*'j^{b} — *txt*: 𝕳 Φ-700 ϕ69-788-826-983-*l*547 σ1207-1402 D K Δ Θ Π **074** *al L*'[ek] *S*hj^{ac} *C Arm*

Mk 14,10 παραδ. αυτον αυτοις] ● αυτον π. αυτοις‖11 Mt16: 𝕳C ϕ⟨124-828⟩ σ827 1342 Eu^{1} *L*fq {} — π. αυτον(∼)‖←: WΘ-28-565 (ϕ*l*547) D(προδ.) 1542 Or *L*(k[e]) acff^{2}ir^{1} *S*s[c] *Geo*^{1} — αυτοις π. αυτον‖p: **0116** — *txt*: *Rpl* Eu^{1} *L*'r^{2}? (30) {*S*p(αυτον) τον Ιησουν)h *C*} *Arm Geo*^{2} **11** οι δε] και‖Lk: A *pc* *L*lr^{2}z vg *S*s[c](+ αυτοι) *Aeth* | *om* ακου.‖Lk Mt: D Eu$^{1:2}$ *L*k[e] acff^{2}i *Geo*^{1} | επηγ.] συνεθεντο *et* ∼ αργ. αυ.‖Lk: **λ** | αργυρια‖Mt: Σ-544-1071 σ7-71-349-517-659-1082-1391-1402 A K U Y Γ Π 1342 *pm* Eu$^{1:2}$ *C*^{s} | πως] το π.‖Lk4: L | παρ. + αυτοις‖10 Lk: Δ σ517-827-1424(∼) 330 1342 *C*s$^{8:9}$ *Aeth* **12** *om* ημ.‖Mt: 157 *pc C*b^{1} | το πα. εθ.] εδει θυεσθαι το πα.‖Lk: 1047 | *om* αυτου‖Mt: D 1542 *L*acff^{2}lr^{2}z vg *Arm*

Lk 22,4 αρχ. + και τοις(*om*) γραμματευσιν‖22 2: C (N-700-1071) σ115 (P) *pc l*18 *l*19 (Eu) *L*vl⟨fz⟩ *S* | *om* κ. στρ.‖p: D *l*31 *L*vl⟨fz⟩ *S*s[c] *Aeth* | το πως] πως‖Mk11: D — οπως‖Mt12 14 Mk10 36: 1071 ϕ Eu^{1}(^{1} ινα) Or *Arm* | ∼ αυτον π. αυτοις(*om*)‖(MtJo): *Rpl* Ep Eu Mcn^{Ep} Or *L*'(e bff^{2}il) — π. αυτον‖←: {} D 471 *L*ar$^{1v.2}$(*om* αυ.) — *txt*: {𝔓^{75v}} ℵBCL σ1207-1223 GKΠ *al* | παραδοι‖Mk: D 471 **5** *om* κ. εχαρ.‖Mt: **λλ**⟨22-1278⟩ 348 *L*bff^{2}ilq | αργυρια‖Mt: CX 544-1071-1604 ϕ⟨124⟩-230 σ71-692-1223 A K U Y^{c} Θ Π *pm* Eu$^{1:2}$ *C*s *Aeth*(τριακοντα αργ.) **6** *om* κ. εξω.‖p: ℵ*C N *l*31 *l*48^{1} Eu *L*vl⟨efr^{2}z⟩ *S*s | και^{2} + απο τοτε‖Mt: N *L* f(∼ εζ. απο τ.) | του παρ.] ινα παραδω‖Mt: P *l*36(∼) | ● ∼ ατ. οχ. αυτοις: 𝔓^{75} 𝕳C A Ψ 157 *L*bil {} — *om* ατ. οχ.‖p: ϕ⟨124-346⟩ σ71-1194 *pc C*s^{1} — *om* αυτοις‖p: D σ7 *pc l*36 *L*' — *txt*: *Rpl* Eu *L*cff^{2}qr^{1} Or {*S*,j *C*s^{5}b} **7** ηλθ.] ην‖Mk14 1: 157 | *om* η^{2}—θυεσ.‖1 Mt: λ1278 *pc L*a(*et om* το πα.) Ar **8** ∼ ινα φ. το πα.‖p: ϕ Mcn^{Ep} *S*j

Jo 13,2 ∼ αυ. παρ.‖12 4 Mt16 Mk11: *Rpl L*e afq — *txt*: 𝔓^{66} 𝕳⟨892⟩X-**0124** 1071 σM (D) Ψ *pc* Cr Or *L*'

Mt26 17p *cf.* EEb frgm.7 (*cf. ad 248.* Lk22 15)

Matth 26

λέγοντες· ποῦ θέλεις ἑτοιμάσωμέν σοι φαγεῖν τὸ πασχα; 18 ὁ δὲ εἶπεν· ὑπάγετε εἰς τὴν πόλιν πρὸς τὸν δεῖνα καὶ εἴπατε αὐτῷ· ὁ διδάσκαλος λέγει· ὁ καιρός μου ἐγγύς ἐστιν· πρὸς σὲ ποιῶ τὸ πασχα μετὰ τῶν μαθητῶν μου. 19 καὶ ἐποίησαν οἱ μαθηταὶ ὡς συνέταξεν αὐτοῖς ὁ Ἰησοῦς, καὶ ἡτοίμασαν τὸ πασχα.

Mark 14

ποῦ θέλεις ἀπελθόντες ἑτοιμάσωμεν ἵνα φάγῃς τὸ πασχα; 13 καὶ ἀποστέλλει δύο τῶν μαθητῶν αὐτοῦ καὶ λέγει αὐτοῖς· ὑπάγετε εἰς τὴν πόλιν, καὶ ἀπαντήσει ὑμῖν ἄνθρωπος κεράμιον ὕδατος βαστάζων· ἀκολουθήσατε αὐτῷ, 14 καὶ ὅπου ἐὰν εἰσέλθῃ εἴπατε τῷ οἰκοδεσπότῃ ὅτι ὁ διδάσκαλος λέγει· ποῦ ἐστιν τὸ κατάλυμά μου, ὅπου τὸ πασχα μετὰ τῶν μαθητῶν μου φάγω; 15 καὶ αὐτὸς ὑμῖν δείξει ἀνάγαιον μέγα ἐστρωμένον ἕτοιμον· καὶ ἐκεῖ ἑτοιμάσατε ἡμῖν. 16 καὶ ἐξῆλθον οἱ μαθηταὶ αὐτοῦ καὶ ἦλθον εἰς τὴν πόλιν καὶ εὗρον καθὼς εἶπεν αὐτοῖς, καὶ ἡτοίμασαν τὸ πασχα.

Luk 22

ἵνα φάγωμεν. 9 οἱ δὲ εἶπαν αὐτῷ· ποῦ θέλεις ἑτοιμάσωμεν; cf. v. 8 ↑ 10 ὁ δὲ εἶπεν αὐτοῖς· ἰδοὺ εἰσελθόντων ὑμῶν εἰς τὴν πόλιν συναντήσει ὑμῖν ἄνθρωπος κεράμιον ὕδατος βαστάζων· ἀκολουθήσατε αὐτῷ εἰς τὴν οἰκίαν οὗ εἰσπορεύεται· 11 καὶ ἐρεῖτε τῷ οἰκοδεσπότῃ τῆς οἰκίας· λέγει σοι ὁ διδάσκαλος· ποῦ ἐστιν τὸ κατάλυμα, ὅπου τὸ πασχα μετὰ τῶν μαθητῶν μου φάγω; 12 κἀκεῖνος ὑμῖν δείξει ἀνάγαιον μέγα ἐστρωμένον· ἐκεῖ ἑτοιμάσατε. 13 ἀπελθόντες δὲ εὗρον καθὼς εἰρήκει αὐτοῖς, καὶ ἡτοίμασαν τὸ πασχα.

Mt 26,17 ετοι.] απελθοντες ετ.‖Mk: ϕ13-346-543-826-828 W *Arm*^{1} **18** ειπεν + αυτοις‖p: ΣΦ **ϕ**-*l*547 **σ**-M K Γ Θ *pc l*183 *l*184 *L*[ek] abcdr^{2}30 vg^{1} *S*s[c]pj *C*⟨b^{1}⟩ | την + απεναντι‖21₂p: σ692 247 *C*b^{1} **19** ως] καθως‖p21₆: 1295 | προσεταξεν‖21₆1₂₄: ϕ983-1689 σM-1010-1293 U *pc* | *om* ο I.‖p: **074**

Mk 14,12 *om* απελ.‖MtLk: σ179-659 476 *Lk*[e] *Cs*$^{1:9}$ | ετοι. + σοι‖Mt: ΔΨ-579 Θ-544-565 ϕ983-1689 σ517 D *pc L*⟨a⟩ Or *Sp Cs* | ινα φ.] φαγειν‖Mt: 579 544 σ517 *Lr*^{1} **13** κ. λεγ. αυτ.] λεγων (+ αυτοις)‖(Mt21₂)Lk19₃₀: Θ-565-700-(1071) D *L*aff^{2}iqr^{1} Or (*Cs*) | πολ. + την απεναντι υμων‖11₂p: 238 | και^{3} + εισελθοντων υμων εις την πολιν (*om* εις τ. π.)‖Lk: (W)ΘΣ-28-565 **ϕ**⟨828⟩-*l*547(εις τ. π.] εν αυτη) *pc* (*L*Or *Cs*$^{8:9}$) | αυτω + εις την οικιαν‖Lk: 579 **14** *om* και‖Lk: 579 W | εαν—ειπ.] εισπορευεται και ειπ.‖Lk: 579 | οικοδ. + της οικιας‖Lk: σ827 *Li*(τ. οικ.] loci illius)r^{1} | *om* οτι‖p: 579 Σ-700 σ115-517-1402 U *al Lv*l[e]⟨lqr^{2}z⟩ Or *S*'h^{+} | *om* μου^{1}‖Lk: *Rpl Lk*[e] cff^{2}i *S*' *C*b' — *txt*: ℵBCLΔ WΣΦ-28-1071 λ1-22 **ϕ**⟨124-828⟩-*l*547 σ7 D *pc l*12 *l*18 *l*19 *l*49 *L*'Or *S*s[c]h^{m} *C*sb^{3} *Geo* **15** κ. αυτ.] κακεινος‖Lk: **λ** σ827 | *om* ετοιμον‖Lk: Δ 565 σM A *al L*alr^{2}z vg *S*h^{t} *Geo*^{B} | *om* και^{2}‖Lk: *Rpl Lv*l'[e]r^{1} Or *S Cs*b^{5} *Geo*^{B} — *txt* (κακει): (ℵ)BCLΨ-892 Θ-1071 ϕ346 (D) 273 1342 *L*flr^{2}z vg *C*b' *Geo*' *Aeth* **16** απηλθον‖Lk: 1574 *Lv*l⟨k[e] ai⟩30[r^{2}] *S*s[c] | αυτου] ● *om*‖Mt: $\mathfrak{H}$ **λ** σ349-517 *pc l*63 *L*vg^{1} *C*s^{1}b' *Geo* — αυτω: ϕ124-*l*547 — *txt*: *Rpl L*' *S Cs*^{7}b^{2} | κ. ευρ.] κ. εποιησαν‖Mt: D *L*(*om*: k[e]) acff^{2}iq *Arm*^{1}

Lk 22,9 ετοι. + σοι(+ φαγειν το πασχα)‖Mt: (B) 1071 D P *pc Le* cff^{2}(+ το πασχα) (*S*h^{Brs}) *Cs*(b^{1}) *Geo Aeth* **10** *om* αυτοις‖Mt: D *Le* | απαντησει‖Mk: ϕ124 σ71-692-1194 D — υπαντησει‖827Mt8₂₈ *etc.*: CLX-892-1241 1071 **063** | ου] ● εις ην: 𝔓^{75v} $\mathfrak{H}$C Ψ *pc l*185^{1} *Lv*l^{1} g^{2} r^{1} vg^{11} *S*hj *C Arm* — εν η: X 213 *L*blqz vg' Ar — ου εαν(αν)‖Mk: N-1604 ϕ346-983 σM-1207-1424 A K P R Y Π *al* (*pc*) *l*183^{1} — οπου‖Mk: 157 — *txt*: *Rpl L*a *S*sc **11** λεγ.—διδ.] ο διδ. λεγ. σοι‖p: 892 *L*q *S*scp — *om* σοι‖p: X-579-1241 N D U **063** *pc l*15 *l*31 *l*44 *l*48 *l*49 | καταλ. + μου‖Mk: ℵC ϕ124 *L*Ar *C*sb^{5} *Arm* **12** κακ.] και αυτος‖Mk: 544 *L*fr$^{1.2}$z vg | εστρ. + ετοιμον‖Mk: X **ϕ**⟨13⟩ *pc* | εκει] κακει‖Mk: ℵLX N Ψ 213 *L*fr^{2}z vg *S*j *Arm*$^{\langle pc \rangle}$ *Aeth* **13** ειρ.] ειπεν‖Mk: X σ71-692-1194 157 *pc l*183 — ειρηκεν‖Jo12₅₀: *Rpl L*' — *txt*: 𝔓^{75} $\mathfrak{H}$C ϕ69 D 713 *L*ar^{2} Ar | αυτ. + ο Ιησους‖Mt: 477 *Lr*^{2} *S*j(κυριος I.)

(235)

247. Ankündigung des Verrats. *The Foretelling of the Betrayal.*

Matth 26 20–25

[20] Ὀψίας δὲ γενομένης ἀνέκειτο μετὰ τῶν δώδεκα μαθητῶν. [21] καὶ ἐσθιόντων αὐτῶν εἶπεν· αμην λέγω ὑμῖν ὅτι εἷς ἐξ ὑμῶν παραδώσει με.

[22] καὶ λυπούμενοι σφόδρα ἤρξαντο λέγειν αὐτῷ εἷς ἕκαστος αὐτῶν· μήτι ἐγώ εἰμι, κύριε;

[23] ὁ δὲ ἀποκριθεὶς εἶπεν·

Mark 14 17–21

[17] Καὶ ὀψίας γενομένης ἔρχεται μετὰ τῶν δώδεκα. [18] καὶ ἀνακειμένων αὐτῶν καὶ ἐσθιόντων ὁ Ἰησοῦς εἶπεν· αμην λέγω ὑμῖν ὅτι εἷς ἐξ ὑμῶν παραδώσει με, **ὁ ἐσθίων μετ' ἐμοῦ.** [19] ἤρξαντο λυπεῖσθαι καὶ λέγειν αὐτῷ εἷς κατὰ εἷς· μήτι ἐγώ; καὶ ἄλλος· μήτι ἐγώ;

[20] ὁ δὲ εἶπεν αὐτοῖς· εἷς ἐκ τῶν δώδεκα,

Luk 22 14

[14] Καὶ ὅτε ἐγένετο ἡ ὥρα, ἀνέπεσεν, καὶ οἱ ἀπόστολοι σὺν αὐτῷ.

22 21–23 (249.): *Πλὴν ἰδοὺ ἡ χεὶρ τοῦ παραδιδόντος με …* [23] *καὶ αὐτοὶ ἤρξαντο συζητεῖν πρὸς ἑαυτοὺς τὸ τίς ἄρα εἴη ἐξ αὐτῶν ὁ τοῦτο μέλλων πράσσειν …*

cf. 245.

Jo

6 70: … ἐξ ὑμῶν εἷς διάβολός ἐστιν. 13 18: … **ὁ τρώγων μετ' ἐμοῦ τὸν ἄρτον ἐπῆρεν ἐπ' ἐμὲ τὴν πτέρναν** αὐτοῦ.

13 21–26: … αμην αμην λέγω ὑμῖν ὅτι εἷς ἐξ ὑμῶν παραδώσει με. [22] ἔβλεπον οὖν εἰς ἀλλήλους οἱ μαθηταὶ ἀπορούμενοι περὶ τίνος λέγει. [23] ἦν δὲ ἀνακείμενος εἷς ἐκ τῶν μαθητῶν αὐτοῦ ἐν τῷ κόλπῳ τοῦ Ἰησοῦ, ὃν ἠγάπα ὁ Ἰησοῦς· [24] νεύει οὖν τούτῳ Σίμων Πέτρος καὶ λέγει αὐτῷ· εἰπὲ τίς ἐστιν περὶ οὗ λέγει. [25] ἐπιπεσὼν οὖν ἐκεῖνος οὕτως ἐπὶ τὸ στῆθος τοῦ Ἰησοῦ λέγει αὐτῷ· κύριε, τίς ἐστιν; [26] ἀποκρίνεται ὁ Ἰησοῦς· ἐκεῖνός

Ps 42 10

Mt 26,20 ● *om* μαθ.‖Mk: 𝔓37v.45v *Rpl* Chr¹ Eu *L*Au¹ *S*s[c] *C*s² *Geo*² *Δ*l^AD — *txt*: 𝔥⟨B⟩ ΣΦ-1071 ϕ174 σ-M-71 A W Y^m Δ Θ Π **074** 157 *al* Chr¹ *L*[ek],Au Or *S*'j^abc(¹*om* δωδ.) *C*s^10b *Geo*¹ *Δ*'⟨a p⟩ 𝔓37v.45 700-1604 **ϕ**-174 **σ** D Θ *l*49 Eu Or *L*[ek] *S*s[c]p¹ *C*b *Geo Aeth Δ*ad l me p | **22** ● *om* αυτω‖Lk: 𝔥C 372 *L*[ek] *S*j *C*s *Aeth Δ*ad l n — *om* εις: 𝔓37{}¹ *Rpl* Eu *S*h^t {}² *Arm* — εις εκ. αυτ.] ● *om* αυτ.: αυτ.(*om*)‖Mk: ϕ1689-(*l*547) — *txt* (*om* εκ.): 𝔓45{64v?}¹ **ϕ**'⟨828⟩-174 σM-517-(1424)-1675 D Θ 157 (1200) *pc* *S*'h^m {*C*b}² *Δ*a — εις καθεις εκ. | *om* ειμι‖Mk: σ954 Chr

Mk 14,17 μετα + των μαθητων(+ αυτου)‖Mt: ϕ983-1689 (*Lg*²30) *C*(s^3:8, *et om* τ. δωδ.) **18** *om* ο Ι.‖Mt Lk22 15: 544-700 *pc* *L*acff² **19** ηρξ.] και ηρξ.‖p: C-892 238 1342 *C*s⁵ — οι δε ηρξ.: *Rpl* (δε + και: 579) *L S* — *txt* (+ δε): ℵBLΨ *C*(s⁴b²)' | λυπ. + και αδημονειν‖14 33p: 1071 1093 | κατα εις] εκαστος‖Mt: C | εγω¹ + ειμι κυριε‖Mt: 892 σ517-1606 713 *L*vg¹ — + ειμι(+ ραββι)‖Mt24.(25): Σ-28-544-1071 **ϕ**⟨828⟩-*l*547 σ(267-659)-827 (A) *pc* *L*fg²30 vg⁵ | κ. αλ. μητι εγω] ● *om*‖Mt: 𝔥'⟨892⟩C W ϕ828 σ1082-1606 P *pc* *l*7 *l*9 *l*10 *l*12 *l*14 *l*17 *l*36 *L*lr²z vg *S*' *C* — κ. ο αλ.: 579 — η αλ.: *L*c — *txt*: *Rpl* Or *L*vl'(*om* και: k[e]) *S*h^m *Arm* | εγω² + ειμι‖Mt: Σ ϕ346 *pc* **20** ο δε + αποκριθεις‖Mt: *Rpl* *L*k[e] *S*h *Arm* — *txt*: 𝔥⟨Δ⟩C D 1342 *L*' *S*' *C* | *om* αυτ.‖Mt: 1574 | *om* εις¹—δωδ.‖Mt: 544 σM *L*k[e] | ● *om* εκ‖14 10.43p Mt26 14: ℵBCLΨ-892 W Θ σ115-954-1402-1424 1342 *C*' — *txt*: *Rpl* *C*b¹

Lk 22,14 απ.] δωδεκα‖Mk: ℵ^ca LX-1241 1071 σ1223 *pc* *l*6 *C*s³ — δωδ. απ.‖p: *Rpl* Mcn^Ep *L*fqr²z vg *S*'j *C*b — *txt*: 𝔓75 ℵ*B D 157 *L*vl'r¹ Ar *S*s(απ.] μαθηται αυτου‖Mt)c *C*s⁶ *Δ*a p

Jo 6,70 ∼ εις εξ υμ.‖13 21 Mt Mk: ℵ^c(**om* εις) D Chr Ep *L*e(∼ εστιν εξ υμ. δια.) b(εις + μεντοι)cff²(g²)qr¹z **13,18** ● *om* μετ‖6 56.58 Ps41 10: BCL-892 1071 λ2193 *pc* Cr Or³ *L*vg^1(+1?) *C*s *Aeth* *Δ*l^AD n^L — *txt* (*et* αρτ. + μου): 𝔓66 *Rpl* (E) Chr Cr Ep Eu Or¹ Thd^C *L*'(q) Te *S C*b'^+B(⁴a^s) | *om* τ. αρτ.‖Mk: **λ** **21** *om* αμην²‖p: λ2193 *L*30 *S*s[c] **22** ουν] δε: 1093 *pm* *L*a vg¹ *S*' *C*s¹ — ● *om*: ℵ^cBCL Ψ *pc* Or *L*e *C*s¹b^B(και εβλ.) *Arm Δ*p — *txt*: 𝔓66 *Rpl* *L*' *S*h *C*s⁹b'a^s *Δ*l **23** ην δε] ην ουν: *L*'⟨vg¹⟩ — και ην: *L*e *Aeth Geo* — ● ην: BC*L-892 σ1188 Ψ *pc* Or *S*s[c] — *txt*: 𝔓66 *Rpl* *L*acff²qr¹ *S*ph δε⁺ *C*^+Ba^sv | *om* εκ‖Mt26 14.47 Mk14 43 Lk22 47: *Rpl* *C*b^B — *txt*: 𝔥CX-**068** 544-1071 λ1582-2193 **ϕ** σM-945-1010-1188-1293 A D K Δ Π Ψ **0141** *mu* Cr Or *L* *C*'⟨b¹⟩a^s **25** ● αναπεσων‖13 12 21 20 Lk: ℵ^cBC^cX 1071 σ1223 K Δ Π **0141** *al* Or | επιπ. ουν] ● επ. δε: *Rpl* Cr *L*ff²q *S*h^t *C*b^B11(¹+ ουν) *Geo*^B — και επ.: *S*p *Geo*¹ *Δ*a me n — ● επ.: BC Or *L*e *S*s^v[c] *Geo*^A *Δ*i p — *txt*: 𝔓66 𝔥'X1071 **λ ϕ**⟨124⟩ σM D Δ **0141** *L*' *S*h^m *C*'a^s *Δ*ad l *pc* Cr Or *L*a *S*h^m — *txt*: 𝔓66 *Rpl* *L*' *S*' *C*^+Ba^s **26** ● αποκ. + ουν: ℵ^cBC*LX-892 1071 **0141**

Matth: ὁ ἐμβάψας μετ' ἐμοῦ τὴν χεῖρα ἐν τῷ τρυβλίῳ, οὗτός με παραδώσει. ²⁴ ὁ μὲν υἱὸς τοῦ ἀνθρώπου ὑπάγει καθὼς γέγραπται περὶ αὐτοῦ, οὐαὶ δὲ τῷ ἀνθρώπῳ ἐκείνῳ δι' οὗ ὁ υἱὸς τοῦ ἀνθρώπου παραδίδοται· καλὸν ἦν αὐτῷ εἰ οὐκ ἐγεννήθη ὁ ἄνθρωπος ἐκεῖνος. ²⁵ ἀποκριθεὶς δὲ Ἰούδας ὁ παραδιδοὺς αὐτὸν εἶπεν· μήτι ἐγώ εἰμι, ραββι; λέγει αὐτῷ· σὺ εἶπας.

Mark: ὁ ἐμβαπτόμενος μετ' ἐμοῦ εἰς τὸ τρύβλιον. ²¹ ὅτι ὁ μὲν υἱὸς τοῦ ἀνθρώπου ὑπάγει καθὼς γέγραπται περὶ αὐτοῦ· οὐαὶ δὲ τῷ ἀνθρώπῳ ἐκείνῳ δι' οὗ ὁ υἱὸς τοῦ ἀνθρώπου παραδίδοται· καλὸν αὐτῷ εἰ οὐκ ἐγεννήθη ὁ ἄνθρωπος ἐκεῖνος.

Luk: ²¹ ᵇ *μετ' ἐμοῦ ἐπὶ τῆς τραπέζης.* ²² *ὅτι ὁ υἱὸς μὲν τοῦ ἀνθρώπου κατὰ τὸ ὡρισμένον πορεύεται, πλὴν οὐαὶ τῷ ἀνθρώπῳ ἐκείνῳ δι' οὗ παραδίδοται.*

Joh: ἐστιν ᾧ ἐγὼ βάψας τὸ ψωμίον ἐπιδώσω αὐτῷ ...

13 26 f. 30: ... καὶ ἐμβάψας τὸ ψωμίον λαμβάνει καὶ δίδωσιν Ἰούδᾳ Σίμωνος Ἰσκαριώτου. ²⁷ καὶ μετὰ τὸ ψωμίον τότε εἰσῆλθεν εἰς ἐκεῖνον ὁ σατανᾶς. λέγει οὖν αὐτῷ Ἰησοῦς· ὃ ποιεῖς ποίησον τάχιον... ³⁰ λαβὼν οὖν τὸ ψωμίον ἐκεῖνος ἐξῆλθεν εὐθύς· ἦν δὲ νύξ.

(236) *248.* Die Stiftung des Herrnmahls. *The Institution of the Lord's Supper.*

Matth 26 26–29 — Mark 14 22–25 — Luk 22 15–20

Matth	Mark	Luk
cf. v. 29 ↓	cf. v. 25 ↓	¹⁵ Καὶ εἶπεν πρὸς αὐτούς· ἐπιθυμίᾳ ἐπεθύμησα τοῦτο τὸ πασχα φαγεῖν μεθ' ὑμῶν πρὸ τοῦ με παθεῖν· ¹⁶ λέγω γὰρ ὑμῖν ὅτι οὐκέτι οὐ μὴ φάγω αὐτὸ ἕως ὅτου πληρωθῇ ἐν τῇ βασιλείᾳ τοῦ θεοῦ. ¹⁷ καὶ

Mt 26,23 εμβαπτομενος ... εις το τρυβλιον ‖ Mk: D *L*Or **24** *om* ο υι. τ. ανθ.^{2} ‖ Lk: 28 *S*s[c](*et* παραδιδομαι)

Mk 14,20 εμβαψας ‖ Mt: Σ σ954-1424 1542 *L*vg^4 | εμ. + την χειρα ‖ Mt: 579 A *L*acff^{2}qz30 vg^{10} *S*s[c] *C* | εν τω τρυβλιω ‖ Mt: σ179-1424 **047** 131 CAp *L*⟨a⟩ | ● το + ἕν: BC*^{v} Θ-565 — *txt*: *Rpl* Or *L S C* | τρυ. + αυτος με παραδωσει ‖ Mt: ϕ346 σ517-1606 *pc Lc* **21** οτι] *om* ‖ Mt: *Rpl La C*s^{1}b^1 — και ‖ Mt20 18 p 26 2.45: 544 σ827 1342 *pc L*'⟨f⟩ *S Δ*a i^V p — *txt*: ℌ⟨Δ⟩ *C*s^{10}b' | υπα.—αυτου] κατα το ωρισμενον πορευεται ‖ Lk: 579 | γεγρ.] εστιν γεγραμμενον ‖ Jo12 14 6 31: D | *om* ο υι. τ. ανθ.^{2} ‖ Lk: 700 D | ● καλον + ην(εστιν) ‖ (942) Mt: *Rpl L*k[e] af(r^2 vg^9)' *S* — *txt*: BL-892 W *L*vl'30 vg^4

Lk 22,16 *om* οτι ‖ Mt: C*X N D *pc* Ep *L*lr^1 | ουκ. ου μη] ● ου μη ‖ 18 Mt29: 𝔓^{75v} ℌ⟨892⟩C* λ1 A H Θ *pc* Ep *La C* — ουκ. μη: D {} — *txt*: *Rpl L*'Or {*S*,j} | αυτο] εξ αυτου ‖ 18 p: *Rpl* {*L*f *S*h^{t}j *Arm*} — απ αυτου ‖ 18: ϕ-230 D {} — *txt*: 𝔓^{75v} ℌC* 1071 **λλ**⟨1278⟩ Ψ 239 Ep (+ απ αρτι ‖ Mt29) *L*' Or *S*'h^m *C* | πλη.] τελεσθη ‖ 12 50: 1241 ϕ983-1689 — καινον βρωθη ‖ Mt29 Mk25: D **17** ∼ 19.17.18 ‖ p: *Le* b *S*sc | *om* 17.18 ‖ p: *l*32 *S*p *C*b^1(*om* 16.17.18) | και^1 + μετα το δειπνησαι ‖ 20 1K25: *S*s

Jo 13,26 βαψ. το ψ.^{1}] ● βαψω το ψ. και: BCLX(*om* και)-1241 1071 *pc* Cr Or^2(^{1}*om* και επιδ.) — εμβαψας το ψ. ‖ 26b MtMk: W(∼ δωσω εμ. τ. ψ.) 544 **λ ϕ**⟨69-124-788⟩ σ954-1188 A D K Π **053** *al* Thd^C{} — *txt*: 𝔓^{66} *Rpl* CAp Chr Cr {*L*} | επιδ.] ● δωσω (δω): BC(L)W(∼)X-1241 (544)-1071 λ2193 σM-1010 157 *pc* Cr Or | κ. εμβ.] ● βαψας ουν ‖ 26a: ℌ⟨W-579(ψ.^{1}∩^{2})⟩CX-**068** 1071 Π^c **0141** *pc* Cr Or *La*r^1 *Aeth* — και βαψ. ‖ ←: ϕ69-788 D *pc* {} — εμβ. δε: *C*s$^{5(+1?)}$ — *txt*: 𝔓^{66c}(*om εμβα!) *Rpl* {*L*' *S*,j *C*s^{5}b(^{B}*om* και)fa^s} | Σ. Ισκαριωτη ‖ 12 4 Mt26 14 Mk14 10 Lk22 3: 𝔓^{66} *Rpl* Cr Or *L*{}^{1} vg^2 {}^{2} — Σ. απο Καρυωτου: D — Σιμωνι (*om*) τω Ισ.(-oth: *Le* ar^{1}z; -otis: 30 vg^{10}) ‖ ←: **ϕ**⟨124⟩ (69-788) *L*(e a)bcfl(r^{1}z 30) vg^2(^{10}) *C*b'(^{2} *Arm*) — *txt*: **ℵBCLX-068**-33 1071 σM-1010 Θ Π^c Ψ **0141** 157 *pc* Or *L*ff^2(Scarioth)g^2{q}^{1} vg' {*S*j *C*sb^{B}fa^s}^{2} **27** *cf. ad 245.*

Lk22 15 *cf.* EEb frgm.7 (Ep haer. 30,22,4f.): Αὐτοὶ δὲ ἀφανίσαντες ἀφ' ἑαυτῶν τὴν τῆς ἀληθείας ἀκολουθίαν ἤλλαξαν τὸ ῥητόν, ὅπερ ἐστὶ πᾶσι φανερὸν ἐκ τῶν συνεζευγμένων λέξεων, καὶ ἐποίησαν τοὺς μαθητὰς μὲν λέγοντας· 'ποῦ θέλεις ἑτοιμάσωμέν σοι τὸ πασχα φαγεῖν'; καὶ αὐτὸν δῆθεν λέγοντα· 'μὴ ἐπιθυμίᾳ ἐπεθύμησα κρέας τοῦτο τὸ πάσχα φαγεῖν μεθ' ὑμῶν;' ⁵πόθεν δὲ οὐ φωραθήσεται ἡ αὐτῶν ῥᾳδιουργία, τῆς ἀκολουθίας κραζούσης ὅτι τὸ μῦ καὶ τὸ ἦτά ἐστι πρόσθετα; ἀντὶ τοῦ γὰρ εἰπεῖν 'ἐπιθυμίᾳ ἐπεθύμησα' αὐτοὶ προσέθεντο τὸ 'μὴ' ἐπίρρημα. αὐτὸς δὲ ἀληθῶς ἔλεγεν· 'ἐπιθυμίᾳ ἐπεθύμησα τοῦτο τὸ πασχα φαγεῖν μεθ' ὑμῶν·' αὐτοὶ δὲ ἐπιγράψαντες τὸ 'κρέας' ἑαυτοὺς ἐπλάνησαν, ῥᾳδιουργήσαντες καὶ εἰπόντες· 'μὴ ἐπιθυμίᾳ ἐπεθύμησα τοῦτο τὸ πασχα κρέας φαγεῖν μεθ' ὑμῶν;'

δεξάμενος ποτήριον εὐχαριστήσας εἶπεν· λάβετε τοῦτο καὶ διαμερίσατε εἰς ἑαυτούς· 18 λέγω γὰρ

Mt	Mk	Lk	1 Kor	Jo
		ὑμῖν ὅτι οὐ μὴ πίω	**1 Kor 11** 23–25:	6 51. 53–58: Ἐγώ εἰμι ὁ ἄρτος ὁ ζῶν
cf. v. 29 ↓	cf. v. 25 ↓	ἀπὸ τοῦ νῦν ἀπὸ		ὁ ἐκ τοῦ οὐρανοῦ καταβάς· ἐάν τις
		τοῦ γενήματος τῆς		φάγῃ ἐκ τούτου τοῦ ἄρτου, ζήσει εἰς τὸν
		ἀμπέλου ἕως οὗ ἡ		αἰῶνα· καὶ ὁ ἄρτος δὲ ὃν ἐγὼ δώσω ἡ
		βασιλεία τοῦ θεοῦ	*... ὁ*	σάρξ μού ἐστιν ὑπὲρ τῆς τοῦ κόσμου
	22 Καὶ	ἔλθῃ. 19 καὶ	*κύριος Ἰησοῦς ἐν*	ζωῆς. 53 ... αμην αμην λέγω ὑμῖν,
26 Ἐσθιόντων δὲ	ἐσθιόντων		*τῇ νυκτὶ ᾗ παρε-*	ἐὰν μὴ φάγητε τὴν σάρκα τοῦ υἱοῦ τοῦ
αὐτῶν λαβὼν ὁ	αὐτῶν λαβὼν	λαβὼν	*δίδετο ἔλαβεν*	ἀνθρώπου καὶ πίητε αὐτοῦ τὸ αἷμα, οὐκ
Ἰησοῦς ἄρτον	ἄρτον	ἄρτον	*ἄρτον*	ἔχετε ζωὴν ἐν ἑαυτοῖς. 54 ὁ τρώγων μου
καὶ εὐλογήσας	εὐλογήσας	εὐχαριστή-	*24 καὶ εὐχαριστή-*	τὴν σάρκα καὶ πίνων μου τὸ αἷμα ἔχει
ἔκλασεν καὶ	ἔκλασεν καὶ	σας ἔκλασεν καὶ	*σας ἔκλασεν καὶ*	ζωὴν αἰώνιον, κἀγὼ ἀναστήσω αὐτὸν
δοὺς τοῖς μαθη-	ἔδωκεν αὐτοῖς	ἔδωκεν αὐτοῖς		τῇ ἐσχάτῃ ἡμέρᾳ. 55 ἡ γὰρ σάρξ μου
ταῖς εἶπεν· λάβετε	καὶ εἶπεν· λάβετε·	λέγων·	*εἶπεν·*	ἀληθής ἐστιν βρῶσις, καὶ τὸ αἷμά μου
φάγετε· τοῦτό	τοῦτό	τοῦτό	*τοῦτό μού*	ἀληθής ἐστιν πόσις. 56 ὁ τρώγων μου
ἐστιν τὸ σῶμά	ἐστιν τὸ σῶμά	ἐστιν τὸ σῶμά	*ἐστιν τὸ σῶμα*	τὴν σάρκα καὶ πίνων μου τὸ αἷμα ἐν
μου.	μου.	μου τὸ ὑπὲρ ὑμῶν	*τὸ ὑπὲρ ὑμῶν·*	ἐμοὶ μένει κἀγὼ ἐν αὐτῷ. 57 καθὼς

Mt 26,26 εσθ. δε] και εσθ.‖Mk: 243 *Ss*[c] | *om* ο Ι.‖MtLk: Δ 1375 | αρτ.] ● τον αρτ.‖Lk24 30 Jo21 13: *Rpl* Bas — *txt*: 𝔓^{45v} ℌC 544-700 **λ**-1582 **ϕ***l*547 σ27-517-1010-1194-1293-1424 D G Θ **074** 157 *pc C* | *om* και^{1}‖Mk: σ1010 *pc Lg*^{2} vg^{1} *C*b^{1} *Geo*^{B} | ευχαριστησας‖Lk1K: *Rpl* Bas *L*Or *S*h^{t} *Geo*^{A} — *txt*: 𝔓$^{37v.45}$ ℌC Φ-700 σ1402-1675 D G Θ **074 0160** 157 *pm L*[ek] *S*'h^{m}j Af *C Geo*' | δους τ. μ.] εδιδου τ. μ. και‖p14 19p: *Rpl* (*om* και: ℵ*) Bas — *txt*: 𝔓$^{37.45v}$ ℌ⟨ℵ*⟩ℵ$^{a?}$ 700 **λ**-1582 **ϕ**⟨124-346⟩-174(+ και)-*l*547 D Θ **0160** | ειπ.] λεγων‖Lk: 697

Mk 14,22 ● λαβων + ο Ιησους‖Mt1K: *Rpl L*' *S*' *C*b *Geo*^{A} — *txt*: ℵ^{a}B W-565 ϕ788-*l*547 D *pc Lk*[e] aff^{2}ir^{2} *Ss*[c](*om* λαβ.) *Cs Geo*' | αρτ.] τον αρτ.‖Lk24 30 Jo21 13: Σ λ22 ϕ69-983 σM-1223-1402 *al* | ευλ.] και ευλ.‖Mt1K: 892 Σ-1071 λ1278^{c} **ϕ**⟨124-828⟩-*l*547 σ827-954-1194-1606 157 1342 *pm L*vl'r^{1}30 vg^{1} — ευχαριστησας‖Lk1K: 579 1012 — και ευχ.‖Lk1K: U — και ευχ. ευλ.‖Lk1K: σ'⟨954⟩(*om* και: 1424) *pc* — ευλογησεν και‖641p: D *Lk*[e](*prm* και) a(∼: l) vg^{1}(^{1} = k) | εδω.] εδιδου‖641 86 Mt15 36 Lk9 16: W **λ** **ϕ**⟨828⟩-*l*547 *pc Geo*^{2} | αυτοις] τοις μαθηταις αυτου‖641p: ϕ69(*om* αυτ.) 235 *Ss*[c] | λαβ.] λ. φαγετε‖Mt: *Rpl Lff*^{2} *C*b^{1} — φαγ.: Δ 213 — *om*‖Lk1K: *Lk*[e] *Cs*^{1}?b^{3} — *txt*: ℵBCLΨ-892 WΘΦ-565-700 **λ**⟨118⟩ ϕ230-788-*l*547 σM-115-517 A D K P U Π *al l*9 *l*18 *l*19 *l*36 *L*' *S Cs*^{9}b'

Lk 22,17 ποτ.] το π.‖←: 𝔓^{75} 1604 σM-71-945-1207 A D K U W Θ Π **0135**? 157 *mu l*48 *l*49 | ευχ.] και ευχ.‖Mt27: 726 1375 | τουτο] *om*‖Mt26: ℵ* — το ποτηριον: 579 | *om* και^{2}‖←: D' *Le Sscj Cb*$^{\langle 1 \rangle}$ | εαυτ. + τουτο εστιν το αιμα μου, διαθηκη καινη‖20p: *Ss* **18** ● *om* οτι‖Mt: 𝔓^{75v} BCL **λλ**⟨22-1278⟩ D G *Le* vg^{1} *Aeth* — *txt*: *Rpl L*' *S*schj *Arm* | ∼ απο τ. νυν ου μη πιω‖Mk: **λ**-1582 D G 157 {} *Lr*$^{1.2}$ *Ssc Arm* — ου μη πιω‖Mk: *Rpl L*' *S*h^{t} — ου μη πιω απ αρτι‖Mt: 225 — *txt*: 𝔓^{75v} ℌ 1071 ϕ788 σM-71-1207 K W(*om* απο του^{2}) Π *al* {*Le*} *S*h^{m}j *C Aeth* | απο^{2}] εκ‖p: N *pc* | αμπ. + ταυτης‖Mt: 157 1093 *L*bf30 vg^{1} *Cs*$^{3:9}$b **19** αρτ.] τον αρτ.‖24 30 Jo21 13: 472 | λεγ. + λαβετε‖p: A | *om* το υπερ—^{20}εκχυν.‖p: D *Le* abff^{2}il

Jo 6,51 εστιν + ην εγω δωσω‖Lk19: *Rpl* Chr Cl^{1} Cr^{1} Or^{2} *L*fq *S*'j PsAth *C*b' — *txt*: 𝔓$^{66.75}$ ℵ(∼ υπερ—ζωης η σ. μ. εστ.)BCLTW-33-579 1071 D Ψ *pc* PsAth Cl^{3} Cr^{1} Or^{2} Thd^{C} *L*'Am Cp *Ssc Cs*b^{B}fa^{s} *Aeth* **53** φαγ.] λαβητε‖Mk22 Mt26: D *La* Vic^{P} **54** τη] ● εν τη: *Rpl* PsBas Chr Cr Eu Or^{2} *L*' — *txt*: 𝔓$^{66.75}$ ℵBLW-579 **λ** ϕ230 σ7-945-1010-1207 D E G H U Γ Θ Ψ **047** *pm* Or^{1} *Le* a vg^{1} **56** αυτω + καθως εν εμοι ο πατηρ καγω εν τω πατρι. αμην αμην λεγω υμιν, εαν μη λαβητε το σωμα του υιου του ανθρωπου ως τον αρτον της ζωης, ουκ εχετε ζωην εν αυτω‖53 10 38 14 10f.20 17 21: D — + εαν λαβη ανθρωπος το σωμα—ζωης, εξει ζωην εν αυτω‖←: *L*aff^{2}

1K 11,23 αρτ.] τον αρτ.‖Lk24 30 Jo21 13: D(= 06) F(= 010) G(= 012) **24** ειπ. + λαβετε φαγετε‖MtMk: *Rpl* Bas Chr Cr^{I} Da Eutha Oec Thd^{C} Thy *L*vg' Amst *Sph Arm*^{0} — *txt*: 𝔓^{46} ℵ*ABC* D(= 06)$^{+abs1}$ F(= 010) G(= 012) *al* Ath^{ThdC} PsBas Chr Cr Da Eutha *L*76.77.78 vg^{2} Cp *Sj C Arm*' | ● υμ. + κλωμενον‖Lk: *Rpl* Bas PsBas Chr Da Eutha Thd^{C} *L*75.76.77 Amst *Sph* — + διδομενον‖Lk: Eutha *L*56.59.61.65.78 vg *C Arm*^{0} *Aeth* — + θρυπτομενον‖Lk: D(= 06)* *L*75 — *txt*: 𝔓^{46} ℵ*BAC*-33-1739 Ath^{ThdC} Cr Or *L*Cp Fu Pel *Sj Arm*' Ath

Matth	Mark	Luk	1 Ko	Jo
		διδόμενον· τοῦτο ποιεῖτε εἰς τὴν ἐμὴν ἀνάμνησιν.	*τοῦτο ποιεῖτε εἰς τὴν ἐμὴν ἀνάμνησιν.*	ἀπέστειλέν με ὁ ζῶν πατὴρ κἀγὼ ζῶ διὰ τὸν πατέρα, καὶ ὁ τρώγων με κἀκεῖνος ζήσει δι' ἐμέ. 58 οὗτός ἐστιν ὁ ἄρτος ὁ ἐκ τοῦ οὐρανοῦ καταβάς, οὐ καθὼς ἔφαγον οἱ πατέρες ὑμῶν καὶ ἀπέθανον· ὁ τρώγων τοῦτον τὸν ἄρτον ζήσει εἰς τὸν αἰῶνα.
27 καὶ λαβὼν ποτήριον καὶ εὐχαριστήσας ἔδωκεν αὐτοῖς λέγων· πίετε ἐξ αὐτοῦ πάντες·	23 καὶ λαβὼν ποτήριον εὐχαριστήσας ἔδωκεν αὐτοῖς, καὶ ἔπιον ἐξ αὐτοῦ πάντες.	20 καὶ τὸ ποτήριον ὡσαύτως	*25 ὡσαύτως καὶ τὸ ποτήριον*	
28 τοῦτο γάρ ἐστιν **τὸ αἷμά** μου **τῆς διαθήκης** τὸ περὶ πολλῶν ἐκχυννόμενον εἰς ἄφεσιν ἁμαρτιῶν. (Jr31 31)	24 καὶ εἶπεν αὐτοῖς· τοῦτό ἐστιν **τὸ αἷμά** μου **τῆς διαθήκης** τὸ ἐκχυννόμενον ὑπὲρ πολλῶν.	μετὰ τὸ δειπνῆσαι, λέγων· τοῦτο τὸ ποτήριον **ἡ καινὴ διαθήκη ἐν τῷ αἵματί** μου, τὸ ὑπὲρ ὑμῶν ἐκχυννόμενον.	*μετὰ τὸ δειπνῆσαι, λέγων· τοῦτο τὸ ποτήριον **ἡ καινὴ διαθήκη** ἐστὶν **ἐν τῷ** ἐμῷ **αἵματι·** τοῦτο ποιεῖτε, ὁσάκις ἐὰν πίνητε, εἰς τὴν ἐμὴν ἀνάμνησιν.*	
29 λέγω δὲ ὑμῖν, οὐ μὴ πίω ἀπ' ἄρτι ἐκ τούτου τοῦ γενήματος τῆς ἀμπέλου	25 αμην λέγω ὑμῖν ὅτι οὐκέτι οὐ μὴ πίω ἐκ τοῦ γενήματος τῆς ἀμπέλου	*18 λέγω γὰρ ὑμῖν ὅτι ἀπὸ*	*οὐ μὴ πίω ἀπὸ τοῦ νῦν τοῦ γενήματος τῆς ἀμπέλου*	

Mt 26,27 ποτ.] το π.‖Lk1K: 𝔓^{45} *Rpl* — *txt*: ℌ Σ-28-544-700 **λ**-1582 **ϕ**13-124-346-*l*547 σ7-659-1402 E F G W Δ Θ **074** *pc* *l*185 *l*299 *l*1634 Chr *C*,PS | *om* και^{2}‖Mk23.22 Lk17.19: ℌ⟨ℵB⟩C Σ **λ**-1582 σ1194 Δ *pc* Bas *L*q | λεγ. + λαβετε(+ και)‖26 Mk22: Cl Cr Or (*L*Am) **28** *om* γαρ‖p1K: 𝔓^{45v} C^{c} **λ**-1582 σ7-659-990-1223-1391 *pc* Chr$^{1:3}$ Cl *L*ac vg^{1} Ir *S*s[c]p *C*Sch *Geo*^{2} | ∼ μου εστ. τ. αι.‖1K24: PsBas$^{3:5}$ | ● μου + το: *Rpl* PsBas — *txt*: 𝔓$^{37.45v}$ ℌ⟨892⟩ 544 D Θ | τ. διαθ.] ● τ. καινης δ.‖Lk1K: *Rpl* PsBas Chr Or *L*,Cp^{1} Ir Or *S*p'j^{ackv} *C*' *Arm* *Geo*^{2} — η καινη διαθηκη‖←: *S*s[c]p^{1}hj^{b} — *txt*: 𝔓$^{37.45v}$ ℌ⟨892⟩ 544 Θ Cr *L*Cp^{1} *S*j^{1} *C*b^{1} PS Sch *Geo*^{1} | περι] υπερ‖p: Φ D Chr Cr^{I} **29** δε] γαρ‖Lk: 238 *pc* *L*vg^{1} *S*s[c]p^{1} | υμιν + οτι‖p: *Rpl* *L*ff^{2}g^{2}r^{1}30 vg^{5} Or *S*,j^{abc}(^{k}*om* υμιν)l *Geo*^{A} — *txt*: 𝔓^{45} ℌ⟨L⟩ Σ **λ**-1582 **ϕ**⟨124-346⟩-*l*547 σ945 990 1223 D Θ *pc* Chr Cr *L*'[ek] Cp Ir *Geo*' | ∼ απ αρ. ου μη πιω‖Mk: 476 *L*h Ir Or — *om* απ αρ.‖Mk: Chr *La* vg^{1} | *om* τουτ.‖p: 892 Φ ϕ983-1689 σ659-1010 Δ 157 *pc* Chr(*et* αμπ. + ταυτης) *L*Ir *S*s[c] *C*s$^{2:9}$b^{1}

Mk 14,23 ποτ.] το π.‖Lk1K: *Rpl* — *txt*: ℵBCLXΔΨ-892 ΘΣ-28-544-700 **λ**-22 **ϕ**⟨69-346⟩-*l*547 σ7-71-267-517-659-1082-1194-1391-1424-1606 D Y **0116** 1342 *mu* *C* *Arm* | ευχ.] και ευχ.‖Mt: 247 *pc* — *om*‖Lk1K: 713 | αυτοις] τοις μαθηταις‖641p: W **24** *om* αυτοις‖Lk1K: B | της] τ. καινης‖Lk1K: X-892 *pc* *L*'(*om* τ. διαθ.: ff^{2}) *S* *C*s^{9}b^{6} — το της καιν.: *Rpl* *L*bir^{1} — το της: W D* — *txt*: ℵBCLΨ Θ-565 D^{c} *L*k[e] *C*s^{2}b' | ∼ υπερ/περι πολ. εκχ.‖p: *Rpl* *L*'(πολ.] υμων‖Lk: r^{2}) *S* — *txt*: ℵBCLΨ-892 1342 *Aeth* | υπερ] περι‖Mt: *Rpl* — *txt*: ℌC WΘ-544-565 **ϕ**⟨828⟩-*l*547 D 1342 *pc* *l*18 | εκχ. + εις αφεσιν αμαρτιων(+ αυτων)‖Mt: W-1071 **ϕ**⟨828⟩-*l*547 *pc* *l*13 *L*ag^{2} vg^{1} *C*(s$^{6:11}$b')^{2} **25** αμην + δε‖Mt: Δ-892 28 λ118-872 ϕ346 σ71-179-349(∼ λεγω δε)-659-945-1223 F S V Γ Π^{c} Ω *pm* *C*s$^{1:11}$ — + γαρ‖Lk: 1579 *pc* | *om* ουκετι‖p: ℵCLΨ-892 W D 1342 *pc* *l*211 *l*950 *L*k[e] acf vg^{1} *C*b *Aeth* | πιω + απ αρτι‖Mt: 474

Lk 22,19 διδ.] κλωμενον *cf. ad* 1K24: 1071 *C*b^{5} — *om*‖1K: *S*c **20** 20] 17.18: *S*sc | ∼ ωσ. και το πο.‖1K: *Rpl* Bas *L*cfqr^{2}z vg *S*p$^{\langle 2\rangle}$h *C*b^{1} — *txt*: 𝔓^{75} ℵBL-579-1241(ποτηρ.^{1}∩^{2}) *L*r^{1} *S*j *C*' | διαθ. + εστιν‖p1K: U *l*183 Bas *L*f | αιμ. μου] εμω αιμ.‖1K: **ϕ** *L*r^{1} | *om* το υπ. υμ. εκχ.‖1K: **063**

Jo 6,57 απεσταλκεν‖536 2021: 𝔓^{66} 579-1241 1071 **ϕ**-*l*547 σ267-954-1675 D *pc* | τρω.] λαμβανων‖Mk22 Mt26: D Vic^{P} **58** υμ.] ημων: ϕ69 Γ *pc* — ● *om*: 𝔓$^{66.75}$ ℵBCLTW Λ *pc* *l*251 Or *L*vg^{1} *C*b' — *txt*: *Rpl* Chr Cr Non *L*' *S*,j *C*sb^{B2}a^{s} *Δ*⟨me⟩

1Ko 11,25 εμω αιμ.] αιμ. μου‖Lk: 𝔓^{46} AC P(= **025**) *al* Eutha | αιμ. + το υπερ υμων εκχυννομενον‖Lk Mk Mt: 1610 1831 | *om* οσ. εαν πιν.‖24p: 81 al PsBas Da Eutha *S*j

---

Mt26 27f.p *cf.* Iu apol I 66,3: Οἱ γὰρ ἀπόστολοι ἐν τοῖς γενομένοις ὑπ' αὐτῶν ἀπομνημονεύμασιν, ἃ καλεῖται εὐαγγέλια, οὕτως παρέδωκαν ἐντετάλθαι αὐτοῖς· τὸν Ἰησοῦν λαβόντα ἄρτον εὐχαριστήσαντα εἰπεῖν· τοῦτο ποιεῖτε εἰς τὴν ἀνάμνησίν μου, τοῦτ' ἐστι τὸ σῶμά μου· καὶ τὸ ποτήριον ὁμοίως λαβόντα καὶ εὐχαριστήσαντα εἰπεῖν· τοῦτό ἐστι τὸ αἷμά μου.

Matth	Mark	Luk
ἕως τῆς ἡμέρας ἐκείνης ὅταν αὐτὸ πίνω μεθ' ὑμῶν καινὸν ἐν τῇ βασιλείᾳ τοῦ πατρός μου.	ἕως τῆς ἡμέρας ἐκείνης ὅταν αὐτὸ πίνω καινὸν ἐν τῇ βασιλείᾳ τοῦ θεοῦ.	*ἕως οὗ ἡ βασιλεία τοῦ θεοῦ ἔλθῃ.*

(237 a) ***249.*** Ankündigung des Verrats. *The Foretelling of the Betrayal.* **Luk 22** 21–23 ***247.***

247.

[21] Πλὴν ἰδοὺ ἡ χεὶρ τοῦ παραδιδόντος με μετ' ἐμοῦ ἐπὶ τῆς τραπέζης. [22] ὅτι ὁ υἱὸς μὲν τοῦ ἀνθρώπου κατὰ τὸ ὡρισμένον πορεύεται, πλὴν οὐαὶ τῷ ἀνθρώπῳ ἐκείνῳ δι' οὗ παραδίδοται. [23] καὶ αὐτοὶ ἤρξαντο συζητεῖν πρὸς ἑαυτοὺς τὸ τίς ἄρα εἴη ἐξ αὐτῶν ὁ τοῦτο μέλλων πράσσειν.

(237 b) ***250.*** Die Rangordnung im Reiche Gottes. **Luk 22** 24–30
Greatness in the Kingdom of God.

cf. 143. ***206.*** ***143.***

[24] Ἐγένετο δὲ καὶ φιλονικία ἐν αὐτοῖς, τὸ τίς αὐτῶν δοκεῖ εἶναι μείζων. [25] ὁ δὲ εἶπεν αὐτοῖς· οἱ βασιλεῖς τῶν ἐθνῶν κυριεύουσιν αὐτῶν, καὶ οἱ ἐξουσιάζοντες αὐτῶν εὐεργέται καλοῦνται. [26] ὑμεῖς δὲ οὐχ οὕτως, ἀλλ' ὁ μείζων ἐν ὑμῖν γινέσθω ὡς ὁ νεώτερος, καὶ ὁ ἡγούμενος ὡς ὁ διακονῶν. [27] τίς γὰρ μείζων, ὁ ἀνακείμενος ἢ ὁ διακονῶν; οὐχὶ ὁ ἀνακείμενος; ἐγὼ δὲ ἐν μέσῳ ὑμῶν εἰμι ὡς ὁ διακονῶν. [28] ὑμεῖς δέ ἐστε οἱ διαμεμενηκότες μετ' ἐμοῦ ἐν τοῖς πειρασμοῖς μου· [29] κἀγὼ διατίθεμαι

13 4f. 12–14: ... ἐγείρεται ἐκ τοῦ δείπνου καὶ τίθησιν τὰ ἱμάτια, καὶ λαβὼν λέντιον διέζωσεν ἑαυτόν· [5] εἶτα βάλλει ὕδωρ εἰς τὸν νιπτῆρα, καὶ ἤρξατο νίπτειν τοὺς πόδας τῶν μαθητῶν καὶ ἐκμάσσειν τῷ λεντίῳ ᾧ ἦν διεζωσμένος ... [12] ὅτε οὖν ἔνιψεν τοὺς πόδας αὐτῶν καὶ ἔλαβεν τὰ ἱμάτια αὐτοῦ καὶ ἀνέπεσεν πάλιν, εἶπεν αὐτοῖς· γινώσκετε τί πεποίηκα ὑμῖν; [13] ὑμεῖς φωνεῖτέ με· ὁ διδάσκαλος καὶ ὁ κύριος,

Mt 26,29 ● ~ καιν. μεθ υμ.‖Mk: CLZ-33 28 **λ**-1582 σ1010-1293 *pc* Chr Cr Eu *S*j *Arm*Ir *Geo*^{B} *Aeth* — *om* μεθ υμ.‖Mk: σ1402 *L*c

Mk 14,25 πινω + μεθ υμων‖Mt: σ115 1574 *L*30 vg^{1}(ημων) *S*s[c] *C*s$^{1:10}$b^{1} | θε.] πατρος μου‖Mt: 1574

Lk 22,22 οτι] και‖Mt20 18p 26 2.45: *Rpl* *L*' *S*,j — *om*‖Mt: Or *L*ad — *txt*: 𝔓^{75} 𝔇⟨892⟩ T D 158 *l*185^{1} *C* | ~ μεν υι.‖p: *Rpl* (~ μεν ο υι.: D; ο μεν ο υι.: 1241 ϕ346) Or *L*' — *txt* (*om* μεν): 𝔓^{75} ℵ^{c}(*)BT *L*e acdr$^{1.2}$ (*S*,j) *C*s^{7}(^{1}b^{3})' | ~ πορ. κατα τ. ωρ.‖p: *Rpl* *L*fr^{1}(πορ.] παραδιδοται‖22b) *S* *C* — *txt*: 𝔓^{75} 𝔇T ϕ D G Ψ 157 *pc* *l*48^{1} Or *L*' *S*j *Arm* | ωρ.] γεγραμμενον‖p Jo12 14 6 31: 472 *L*vl⟨az⟩r^{1} vg^{1} *S*h$^{Brs\,m}$ *C*s$^{2:9}$ | ωρ./γεγ. + περι αυτου‖p: 348 *pc* *L*l *S*c *C*s^{1} *Aeth* — + αυτου‖p: ϕ1689 — + αυτω‖p: Or *S*j *C*s^{8} | πλ. ουαι] ουαι δε‖Mt Mk: 1375 | *om* εκει.‖Mt18 7: 1375 | ου + ο υιος του ανθρωπου‖p: ϕ124-174 *l*6 *L*b Te **23** *om* αυτοι‖p: W *L*c vg^{1} *S*scp | ειη] εστιν‖Jo: **λλ**⟨22-1278⟩ 157 475 | *om* εξ αυτ.‖←: D **047** 142 *L*vl⟨cfr^{2}z⟩ *S*sc | πρα.] ποιειν‖Jo 27: 579 **24** *om* και‖9 46: ℵ σ692 *pc* Or *L*vl⟨efz⟩r^{1}30 vg^{5} *S*sc *C*s$^{5:9}$ | τις + αν‖←: D 1574 {*L*e abq} — + αρα‖Mt18 1: 579 {} | *om* αυτων‖← Mk9 34: D *L*al | δοκ. ειν.] ειη‖9 46: D Or *L*afq *S*scp *C* **25** δε + Ιησους‖Mt20 25p: Λ-1071 σ267-659 *pc* *l*19 *l*44 *l*48 *l*49 Bas Da (~ ειπ. δε αυ. ο Ι.: *L*cff^{2}lz) *S*p | κατακυρ.‖Mt20 25p: X N-1071-1604 ϕ⟨983⟩ σ1194 U Θ *pc* Da | οι εξ.] εξουσιαζουσιν‖Mt20 25p: W | εξ.—καλ.] μεγαλοι κατεξουσιαζουσιν αυτων‖←: 1241 | εξ. αυτων] αρχοντες των(< αυτων?) εξουσιαζουσιν αυτων και‖←: ℵ* **26** νεωτ.] μικροτερος‖9 48: D *L*acff^{2}il *S*scpj *C*s | διακονος‖p: D *L*cfff^{2}ilr$^{1.2}$z vg **27** μειζ. + εστιν‖Mt18 1 23 17: L-579-892-1241 (~) ϕ F230 *L*⟨ff^{2}⟩ *S*h^{m} *Aeth* | ειμι] ηλθον‖Mt20 18p: D'

Jo13 5 *cf.* EN frgm.31 (HPass fol.25^{v}) ... et extersit pedes eorum. Et, sicut dicitur in evangelio Nazareorum, singulorum pedes osculatus fuit.

203.

ὑμῖν καθὼς διέθετό μοι ὁ πατήρ μου βασιλείαν, 30 ἵνα ἔσθητε καὶ πίνητε ἐπὶ τῆς τραπέζης μου ἐν τῇ βασιλείᾳ μου, καὶ καθήσεσθε ἐπὶ θρόνων τὰς δώδεκα φυλὰς κρίνοντες τοῦ Ισραηλ.

καὶ καλῶς λέγετε· εἰμὶ γάρ. 14 εἰ οὖν ἐγὼ ἔνιψα ὑμῶν τοὺς πόδας ὁ κύριος καὶ ὁ διδάσκαλος, καὶ ὑμεῖς ὀφείλετε ἀλλήλων νίπτειν τοὺς πόδας...

(237 c)

251. Vorhersage der Verleugnung des Petrus. Luk 22 31–34 253.
The Prophecy of Peter's Denial.

253.

31 Σίμων Σίμων, ἰδοὺ ὁ σατανᾶς ἐξῃτήσατο ὑμᾶς τοῦ σινιάσαι ὡς τὸν σῖτον· 32 ἐγὼ δὲ ἐδεήθην περὶ σοῦ ἵνα μὴ ἐκλίπῃ ἡ πίστις σου· καὶ σύ ποτε ἐπιστρέψας στήρισον τοὺς ἀδελφούς σου. 33 ὁ δὲ εἶπεν αὐτῷ· κύριε, μετὰ σοῦ ἕτοιμός εἰμι καὶ εἰς φυλακὴν καὶ εἰς θάνατον πορεύεσθαι. 34 ὁ δὲ εἶπεν· λέγω σοι, Πέτρε, οὐ φωνήσει σήμερον ἀλέκτωρ ἕως τρίς με ἀπαρνήσῃ εἰδέναι.

(237 d)

252. Rückblick und Ausblick. *The Two Swords.* Luk 22 35–38

35 Καὶ εἶπεν αὐτοῖς· ὅτε ἀπέστειλα ὑμᾶς ἄτερ βαλλαντίου καὶ πήρας καὶ ὑποδημάτων, μή τινος ὑστερήσατε; οἱ δὲ εἶπαν· οὐθενός. 36 εἶπεν δὲ αὐτοῖς· ἀλλὰ νῦν ὁ ἔχων βαλλάντιον ἀράτω, ὁμοίως καὶ πήραν, καὶ ὁ μὴ ἔχων πωλησάτω τὸ ἱμάτιον αὐτοῦ καὶ ἀγορασάτω μάχαιραν. 37 λέγω γὰρ ὑμῖν ὅτι τοῦτο τὸ γεγραμμένον δεῖ τελεσθῆναι ἐν ἐμοί, τό· **καὶ μετὰ ἀνόμων ἐλογίσθη·** καὶ γὰρ τὸ περὶ ἐμοῦ τέλος ἔχει. 38 οἱ δὲ εἶπαν· κύριε, ἰδοὺ μάχαιραι ὧδε δύο. ὁ δὲ εἶπεν αὐτοῖς· ἱκανόν ἐστιν.

Is53 12

Lk 22,30 πιν. + μετ εμου‖22 21: N ϕ *S*sc *C*s$^{1:7}$b^{9} | θρον.] δωδεκα θρ. ‖ Mt19 28: ℵ^{c}X-579 1071 λ1278 σ71 D 157 *al* *L*vl'⟨e i⟩r^{1} *S*sch δωδ.$^{+}$ *C*b^{1} PS — θρ. δωδ. ‖ ←: ϕ-174 *L*cr^{2}z vg^{1} | θρονους ‖ ←: 1241(-νου!) 1071 ϕ D | ∼ κρι. τας δωδ. φυ. ‖ ←: *Rpl* (*et om* τας: D) *L*' — *txt*: 𝔓^{75} BT-892 *L*i **34** ειπ. + αυτω‖p: σ71-692-1194 Θ *pc* *L*e(ειπ.] λεγει) ff^{2} *S*scpj *C*s$^{7:9}$b | *om* Π.‖**p**: 579 *S*s | ου + μη‖Jo: *Rpl* — *txt*: 𝔓^{75} ℌTX σ276-659-1391-1402 Q Θ Ψ 213 *l*40 *l*44 *l*48 | εως] πριν η‖p: *Rpl* (*om* η‖Mt: Q 713) *S*h^{t} — εως ου ‖Jo: X-1241 ϕ1689 σM-1207-1223 D(ου] οτου) K Π *al* *l*22 *l*183 — *txt*: 𝔓^{75v} ℌ'T ϕ Θ 157 *pc* *L*⟨e⟩ *S*p$^{⟨1⟩}$h^{m}j *C* | ∼ απαρ. με τρις‖Jo: 1241 *C*s^{3}(+ οτι ουκ οιδα αυτον‖22 57: s^{5}; *et om* με: s^{3}) | με απαρ. ειδ.] *om* ειδ.‖p: (1241) *L*e a(∼ τρ. με)bff^{2}(∼ απ. με) (*C*s^{3}) — απαρ. με ειδ.‖Mt: **λλ**'⟨22-1278⟩(με] μ + *spat.*: 118) Q Ψ 157 2533 *L*f30 vg^{1} *Arm*(ειδ. *prm* μη) — απαρ. ειδ. με: X σM Π *pc* *L*'(*prm* με: r^{2} vg^{1}) — ● απαρ. (+ με) μη ειδ. με: *Rpl* (απ. + του: H) *S*(cp^{5})'h(j) — ● με απαρ. μη ειδ. (+ με): (1071) λ131 ϕ⟨346⟩ (D *Δ*a p) — *txt*: ℵBLT-579 Θ *L*cl vg^{1} *S*s(+ με) *C*b **35** *om* και υποδ.‖9 3: Γ σ71-692 *pc* *Aeth* **37** τελ.] πληρωθηναι‖24 44: Λ ϕ124-174-230 W *pc* *L*⟨r^{1}⟩ | το^{3}] τα‖24 27.19: *Rpl* *L*' *S*h^{m} — *txt*: ℵBLT **λλ**⟨22-1278⟩ D Q W 157 *L*b *S*h^{t} *C* | εχ. + ιδου ειπον‖Mt28 7 24 25 (< οι δε ειπον 22 38?): **047**

---

251. *cf.* Ev. apocr. (PFaj; *cf. ad 253.*)

(238) ***253.*** **Auf dem Wege nach Gethsemane; Vorhersage der Verleugnung des Petrus.**
On the Way to Gethsemane; Prophecy of Peter's Denial.

Matth 26 30–35

30 Καὶ ὑμνήσαντες ἐξῆλθον εἰς τὸ ὄρος τῶν ἐλαιῶν. 31 τότε λέγει αὐτοῖς ὁ Ἰησοῦς· πάντες ὑμεῖς σκανδαλισθήσεσθε ἐν ἐμοὶ ἐν τῇ νυκτὶ ταύτῃ· γέγραπται γάρ· **πατάξω τὸν ποιμένα, καὶ διασκορπισθήσονται τὰ πρόβατα** τῆς ποίμνης. 32 μετὰ δὲ τὸ ἐγερθῆναί με προάξω ὑμᾶς εἰς τὴν Γαλιλαίαν. 33 ἀποκριθεὶς δὲ ὁ Πέτρος εἶπεν αὐτῷ· εἰ πάντες σκανδαλισθή-

Mark 14 26–31

26 Καὶ ὑμνήσαντες ἐξῆλθον εἰς τὸ ὄρος τῶν ἐλαιῶν. 27 καὶ λέγει αὐτοῖς ὁ Ἰησοῦς ὅτι πάντες σκανδαλισθήσεσθε, ὅτι γέγραπται· **πατάξω τὸν ποιμένα, καὶ τὰ πρόβατα διασκορπισθήσονται.** 28 ἀλλὰ μετὰ τὸ ἐγερθῆναί με προάξω ὑμᾶς εἰς τὴν Γαλιλαίαν. 29 ὁ δὲ Πέτρος ἔφη αὐτῷ· εἰ καὶ πάντες σκανδαλισθή-

Luk 22 39

39 Καὶ *cf. 242.* ἐξελθὼν ἐπορεύθη κατὰ τὸ ἔθος εἰς τὸ ὄρος τῶν ἐλαιῶν· ἠκολούθησαν δὲ αὐτῷ καὶ οἱ μαθηταί.

22 31–34 (251.): Σίμων Σίμων, ἰδοὺ ὁ σατανᾶς ἐξῃτήσατο ὑμᾶς τοῦ σινιάσαι ὡς τὸν σῖτον· 32 ἐγὼ δὲ ἐδεήθην περὶ σοῦ ἵνα μὴ ἐκλίπῃ ἡ πίστις σου· καὶ σύ ποτε ἐπιστρέψας στήρισον τοὺς ἀδελφούς σου. 33 ὁ δὲ εἶπεν αὐτῷ· κύριε, μετὰ σοῦ ἕτοιμός εἰμι

18 1: ταῦτα εἰπὼν ὁ Ἰησοῦς ἐξῆλθεν σὺν τοῖς μαθηταῖς αὐτοῦ πέραν τοῦ χειμάρρου τοῦ Κεδρων ...

16 32: ἰδοὺ ἔρχεται ὥρα καὶ ἐλήλυθεν ἵνα σκορπισθῆτε ἕκαστος εἰς τὰ ἴδια κἀμὲ μόνον ἀφῆτε ...

13 36–38: λέγει αὐτῷ Σίμων Πέτρος· κύριε, ποῦ ὑπάγεις; ἀπεκρίθη Ἰησοῦς· ὅπου ὑπάγω οὐ δύνασαί μοι νῦν ἀκολουθῆσαι, ἀκολουθήσεις δὲ ὕστερον. 37 λέγει αὐτῷ Πέτρος· κύριε, διὰ τί οὐ

Zch13 7

Mt 26,31 *om* εν εμ. ‖ p: ϕ69 *pc* Or **32** Γ. + κακει με οψεσθε ‖ 287 Mk16 7: 565 *La* vg^{1} **33** ει + και(∼) ‖ Mk: ℵ^{c}(* *om* ει) 700 ϕ174 σ-71-517-1010-1293-1402-(1424) F K W Y Π *pm* Bas^{1}(^{1}) *L*[ek]fff^{1}g^{1}hlz32 vg Au *S*phj⟨1⟩

Mk 14,27 και^{1}] τοτε ‖ Mt: D *L*bcff^{2}z | *om* οτι ‖ Mt: Θ-565-700 131 *L*⟨k[e] fiq⟩ *S*p^{3} | παντ. + υμεις ‖ Mt: 579 544 **ϕ**⟨828⟩ D 1342 *pc L*vl'⟨f⟩(∼: k[e])r^{1}30 vg^{1} *Aeth* | σκα. + εν εμοι εν τη νυκτι ταυτη ‖ p: *Rpl* (*om* εν^{2}: **ϕ**'⟨124⟩) *L*cg^{2}r^{2}30 vg^{7}(' *om* εν εμοι) *S*' *C*s^{8}b^{2}(^{2} = vg') — + εν εμοι ‖ p Mt16 p: Ψ^{c} 28 ϕ828 G 157 *pc L*k[e] afilz *S*s[c] *C*s^{2}b^{1} — *txt*: ℵBC*LXΔΨ* λ872 σ27-71-179-692-827-1194 D H S V Γ Π^{c} Ω **0116** 1342 *pm L*bff^{2}q *C*s^{2}b' | οτι γεγ.] γεγ. γαρ ‖ p: ΝΣ 1542 *L*k[e] z *S*s[c]p | ∼ διασκ. τ. πρ. ‖ p: *Rpl L*' *S C*s^{2}b — *txt*: ℵBCL-892 WΘ-565 **ϕ**⟨124⟩ σ115-517-659-1424-1606 D *pc L*k[e] iq *C*s^{9} *Arm* | προβ. + της ποιμνης ‖ p: 579 1071 ϕ230-1689(∼ της ποι. και τα πρ.) σM-1606 E F K Y Π 1342 *mu L*ab(= 1689)cz vg^{1}(^{1} *et* + μου) *C*s$^{1:10}$ **28** αλλα μετα] μ. δε ‖ p: σ827 *pm C*s **29** εφη] αποκριθεις λεγει(εφη) ‖ Mt Jo: WΘ-565-700 **λ** **ϕ**⟨828⟩ *L*(k[e] a)z *S*s[c] (*C*s$^{7:11}$) *Geo* — ειπεν ‖ p: 579 280 *L*ff^{2} — λεγει ‖ Jo: Ψ D *L*' | *om* και ‖ Mt: 472 *S*s[c]p *C*s | σκα. + εν σοι ‖ Mt: **λ** ϕ983-1689 σ517 E G U *al L*b *C*s$^{1:11}$ *Geo*^{B} *Aeth*

Lk 22,39 εθος] ειωθος ‖ 4 16: 579 F 713 | των] τον καλουμενον ‖ 19 29 21 37: 477 *S*sc | μαθ. + αυτου ‖ Mt8 23 Mk6 1: *Rpl L*vl'r^{1} vg^{1} *S*'j *C*s^{9}b$^{1(+2?)}$ — *txt*: 𝔓^{75} ℵBLT Δ^{c}Ψ-892 **λλ**⟨22-1278⟩ **ϕ**⟨346-983⟩-174 σM^{c} A D W Θ *L*q vg' *S*h *C*s^{1}b' *Arm*

Jo 13,36 *om* Σ. ‖ Mt Mk Mt26 37 p: 2145 *C*b^{2} | απεκ. + ο: 1071 *pc* {}^{1} — ● + αυτω: 𝔓^{66} 579 λ22 A Θ *pc S*s[c](*om* I.) {}^{2} — ● + αυτω ο: *Rpl* Chr Cr {*L*qr^{1}30 vg^{2} *S*h *C*s^{6}b^{2}a^{s} *Arm*^{pc} *Geo*^{2} *Δ*i^{T5} *l*^{AD} md n' p}^{2} — *txt*: BC*L 1093 {*L*' *S*p *C*s^{1}b'$^{+B}$ *Arm*' *Geo*^{1} *Δ*a ad i^{T1V} l^{FG} n^{L}}^{1} | ● οπου + εγω ‖ 33: ℵX-33-1241 544-700-1071 **λ**⟨1⟩ **ϕ**-*l*547 σ7-71-659-954-1188-1223-1293 A D K S^{m} U Π Ψ **053 0141** 157 *pm* Chr$^{2\,cmt}$($^{1\,1m}$ ∼ υπαγω εγω) Cr Or *L Sj C*$^{+B}$a^{s} *Arm* — *txt*: 𝔓^{66} *Rpl S*,Eu **37** Π.] ● ο Π.: 𝔓^{66} 𝔥⟨ℵ-892⟩ 28 λ1 **ϕ**⟨13⟩-230-*l*547 σM-954 **0141** *al* Cr {} — Σιμων Π. ‖ 36: 1071 1321 *S*p — *om*: λ22 D 660 *L*r^{1v} *C*a^{s} — *txt*: *Rpl* {*C*$^{+B}$ *Arm*} **16,32** ελη.] νυν ελη. ‖ 4 23 5 25: *Rpl* Bas Cr Ddy *L*,Hil *S*' *C*b^{B} *Δ*ad(+ υμιν) l md n p — *txt*: 𝔓$^{22v.60v.66}$ ℵBC*LWX-**0109**-33 A D* 213 CAp *S*s[c]j *C*'a^{sv} *Arm Δ*i^{T}

---

253. cf. Ev. apocr. (PFaj): [ἐν δὲ τῷ ἐ]ξάγειν ὡς ε[ἶ]πε[ν] ὅτι 'ἅ[παντες ἐν ταύτῃ] τῇ νυκτὶ σκανδαλισ[θήσεσθε κατὰ] τὸ γραφέν· πατάξω τὸν [ποιμένα καὶ τὰ] πρόβατα διασκορπισθήσ[εται'. εἰπόντος το]ῦ Πέτ(ρου)· 'καὶ εἰ πάντες ο[ὐκ ἐγώ', λέγει Ἰ(ησοῦ)ς· 'πρὶ]ν ἀλεκτρυὼν δὶς κοκ[κύσει τρὶς σὺ σήμερόν με ἀ]π[αρνήσῃ.'

σονται ἐν σοί, ἐγὼ οὐδέποτε σκανδαλισθήσομαι. 34 ἔφη αὐτῷ ὁ Ἰησοῦς· αμην λέγω σοι ὅτι ἐν ταύτῃ τῇ νυκτὶ πρὶν ἀλέκτορα φωνῆσαι τρὶς ἀπαρνήσῃ με. 35 λέγει αὐτῷ ὁ Πέτρος· κἂν δέῃ με σὺν σοὶ ἀποθανεῖν, οὐ μή σε ἀπαρνήσομαι. ὁμοίως καὶ πάντες οἱ μαθηταὶ εἶπον.

σονται, ἀλλ' οὐκ ἐγώ. 30 καὶ λέγει αὐτῷ ὁ Ἰησοῦς· αμην λέγω σοι ὅτι σὺ σήμερον ταύτῃ τῇ νυκτὶ πρὶν ἢ δὶς ἀλέκτορα φωνῆσαι τρίς με ἀπαρνήσῃ. 31 ὁ δὲ ἐκπερισσῶς ἐλάλει· ἐὰν με δέῃ συναποθανεῖν σοι, οὐ μή σε ἀπαρνήσομαι. ὡσαύτως δὲ καὶ πάντες ἔλεγον.

καὶ εἰς φυλακὴν καὶ εἰς θάνατον πορεύεσθαι. 34 ὁ δὲ εἶπεν· λέγω σοι, Πέτρε, οὐ φωνήσει σήμερον ἀλέκτωρ ἕως τρίς με ἀπαρνήσῃ εἰδέναι.

δύναμαί σοι ἀκολουθῆσαι ἄρτι; τὴν ψυχήν μου ὑπὲρ σοῦ θήσω. 38 ἀποκρίνεται Ἰησοῦς· τὴν ψυχήν σου ὑπὲρ ἐμοῦ θήσεις; αμην αμην λέγω σοι, οὐ μὴ ἀλέκτωρ φωνήσῃ ἕως οὗ ἀρνήσῃ με τρίς.

11 16: εἶπεν οὖν Θωμᾶς ὁ λεγόμενος Δίδυμος τοῖς συμμαθηταῖς· ἄγωμεν καὶ ἡμεῖς, ἵνα ἀποθάνωμεν μετ' αὐτοῦ.

(239)

254. Jesus in Gethsemane. *Jesus in Gethsemane.*

Matth 26 36–46

36 Τότε ἔρχεται μετ' αὐτῶν ὁ Ἰησοῦς εἰς χωρίον λεγόμενον Γεθσημανι, καὶ λέγει τοῖς μαθηταῖς· καθίσατε αὐτοῦ ἕως οὗ ἀπελ-

Mark 14 32–42

32 Καὶ ἔρχονται εἰς χωρίον οὗ τὸ ὄνομα Γεθσημανι, καὶ λέγει τοῖς μαθηταῖς αὐτοῦ· καθίσατε ὧδε ἕως

Luk 22 40–46

40 Γενόμενος δὲ ἐπὶ τοῦ τόπου εἶπεν αὐτοῖς· προσεύχεσθε μὴ εἰσελθεῖν εἰς

18 1: ταῦτα εἰπὼν ὁ Ἰησοῦς ἐξῆλθεν σὺν τοῖς μαθηταῖς αὐτοῦ πέραν τοῦ χειμάρρου τοῦ Κεδρων, ὅπου ἦν κῆπος, εἰς ὃν εἰσῆλθεν αὐτὸς καὶ

Mt 26,33 εγω] αλλ εγω ‖ Mk: σ1293 — εγω δε ‖ ←: *La* $Cs^{8:9(+1v)}$b **34** *om* οτι ‖ Lk Jo: σ1402 1555 | *om* εν ‖ Mk: $𝔓^{37}$ D *L*[ek] abcff^{2}hqr^{1} vg^{2} | αλ. φω.] αλεκτοροφωνιας ‖ Mk13 35: $𝔓^{45}$ L(*prm* η ‖ Mk) **λ**⟨118⟩-1582 *La* | ∼ με απαρ. ‖ p: ℵ*-33 **074** 157 *L*[ek],Au Hil Or — ∼ απαρ. με τρις ‖ Jo: A **35** καν] εαν ‖ Mk: ϕ543 **074** *S*s[c]pj^{1} | ∼ συναποθ. σε ‖ Mk: 1200 | ομοιως + δε (*et om* και) ‖ Mk: *Rpl* (ϕ69) *L*q *S*h^{Brs}j^{acl} *C*^{4}(^{5}b')^{6} — *txt*: ℵBCL-33 700 λ22 ϕ346-828 σ990 D S Y **067** *pc* *L*'[ek] Or *S*'j^{b} *C*b^{2}f | *om* οι μαθ. ‖ Mk: 1579 **36** τοις μα.] αυτοις ‖ Lk: **ϕ**-*l*547 σ954 Θ 1574 *Arm Geo*^{2} | μα. + αυτου ‖ Mk: $𝔓^{53v}$ ℵC Σ-544-700 **λ**-1582 **σ**⟨954⟩-7-659-1391 A D W *al* *l*36 *l*44 *L*[ek]⟨vg^{2}⟩ Hil *S* $Cs^{1:8}$bf *Geo*^{1} | αυτου] ωδε ‖ Mk: 33 700 | *om* ου ‖ Mk: ℵC-33-892 28-700 λ22 **σ**-M 1200

Mk 14,29 ουκ εγω] εγω ου(+ ποτε) σκανδαλισθησομαι ‖ (Mt): D *L*ff^{2}qr^{1}(bz) vg^{1} ($Cs^{1:11}$ *Geo*^{2}) **30** αμ. + αμην ‖ Jo: Θ *S*s[c] *C*b^{1} | *om* συ ‖ Mt: ℵCΔ Φ-544 ϕ1689 σ7-115-659-827-954-1391-1675 D *al* *L*vl⟨k[e] cr^{2}z⟩r^{1v} $Cs^{1:10}$ *Geo*^{1} | *om* σημ. ‖ Mt: Θ-544-565-700 ϕ788 D S *L*abfff^{2}iq $Cs^{1:10}$ *Arm* | ταυ. τη νυ.] εν τη νυ. ταυ. ‖ Mt: *Rpl* (∼ εν ταυ. τη νυ.: 579; *om* σημ.—νυ.: S) *L*clr^{2}z30(∼) vg — *txt* (∼ τη νυ. ταυ.): 𝔥'⟨Δ⟩ C-**0112**(*om* τη) (W)Θ-565-700 (**λ** **ϕ**⟨124-828⟩) σ115-827-945-1223 D 1342 *L*vl'r^{1v} | *om* η ‖ Mt: ℵ-579 WΘ-544-565-700 λ209^{m} **ϕ**⟨124-828⟩ σ659 D *pc* *l*76 *l*150 *l*950 | ∼ αλ. φω. δις (∼ φω. αλ. δις) ‖ 14 72 Mt: C^{c} λ209^{c} *L*vg^{1} (*S*s[c]p) $Cs^{8:10}$b — αλ. δις φω. ‖ Mt: Θ-565-700 **ϕ**⟨124-828⟩ *pc* *L*lr^{2} vg^{1} — *om* δις ‖ **p**Jo: ℵC*-579 W ϕ983-1689 D *pc* *l*76 *l*150-*l*950 *L*k[e] abcff^{2}i $Cs^{1:10}$ *Arm Aeth* | ∼ απαρ. με ‖ Mt Jo: *Rpl* (*om* με: L Θ ϕ69) — *txt*: ℵBCΔ-**0112**-579 W(αρν. ‖ Jo) **ϕ**⟨124-828⟩ D 1342 *L* **31** ελαλ.] ελεγεν ‖ p: *Rpl* *La* vg^{1} *S* — *txt*: 𝔥⟨Δ⟩-**0112** D 1342 *L*' *C* | ● ∼ δεη με ‖ Mt: 𝔥⟨ℵ*Δ⟩ℵ^{c}-**0112** NΣ-700-1071 **λ**-1278 **ϕ**⟨828⟩σ267-349-517-1207-1402-1424-1606 A D^{c} **0116** 1342 *al* *L* — *txt*: *Rpl* (με] μη: 565 D*; *om*: ϕ230 σ27-179 *pc*) | ∼ συν σοι αποθ. ‖ Mt: L-**0112** 544-565-1071 **λ** ϕ1689 σ115-349-517-1606 1342 *pc* | ωσ.] ομοιως ‖ Mt: ℵ* *pc* | ● *om* δε^{2} ‖ Mt: B-579 544 **λ** *pc* *L*k[e] acff^{2} (*et* ∼ και ωσ.: *S*s[c]p) $Cs^{2:8}$b *Arm* **32** ερχεται ‖ Mt: Θ-565 λ118^{c}-209 | *om* αυτου ‖ Mt: Φ A $Cs^{1:10}$ *Arm* | ωδε] αυτου ‖ Mt: **λ** | εως + ου απελθων ‖ Mt: 472 1515 {*Geo*^{B} *Aeth*} — + αν(*om*) απελ. ‖ Mt: 579-892 (N)Σ-28-(544 λ118) **ϕ**⟨124-788-828⟩ σ(M)-115-517-1606 U *pc* (*al*){}

Lk 22,40 εισελθητε ‖ 46p: D *l*17(-θετε) *l*184 | εισελ.] εμπεσειν *cf.* 1T6 9: λ2193 **ϕ** *Δ*md me n

Jo 11,16 συναποθ. ‖ Mk: ϕ13-230-346-543-826-828 G Or | μετ. αυτ.] συν αυτω ‖ Mt: 544 σ1223 K Π *al* Or(*om* συν) **13,38** *om* αμ.^{2} ‖ Mt Mk: λ1582-2193 *L*e vg^{2} *S*s[c]j | σοι + οτι ‖ ←: D *L*cr^{1} *S*,j | ∼ τρ. απ. με ‖ Mt: 28 **ϕ**⟨124⟩-*l*547 *L*vg^{1} *S*s[c]j — τρ. με απ. ‖ Mk Lk: *L*e cg^{2}qr^{1}(*prm* συ)30 vg^{3} — με(συ με) τρ. απ. ‖ p: *L*(abff^{2})fz vg' — με απ. τρ. ‖ Mk Lk: W(*prm* συ)-579 | απαρνηση ‖ Mt Mk: *Rpl* Cr Cs^{4} — *txt*: $𝔓^{66}$ BLX 565 λ1-22-1582 D *pc* Or Cs^{2}fa^{s}

Matth 26

θὼν ἐκεῖ προσεύξωμαι. 37 καὶ παραλαβὼν τὸν Πέτρον καὶ τοὺς δύο υἱοὺς Ζεβεδαίου ἤρξατο λυπεῖσθαι καὶ ἀδημονεῖν. 38 τότε λέγει αὐτοῖς· **περίλυπός ἐστιν ἡ ψυχή μου ἕως θανάτου**· μείνατε ὧδε καὶ γρηγορεῖτε μετ' ἐμοῦ. 39 καὶ προελθὼν μικρὸν ἔπεσεν ἐπὶ πρόσωπον αὐτοῦ προσευχόμενος καὶ λέγων· πάτερ μου, εἰ δυνατόν ἐστιν, παρελθέτω ἀπ' ἐμοῦ τὸ ποτήριον τοῦτο· πλὴν οὐχ ὡς ἐγὼ θέλω ἀλλ' ὡς σύ.

Mark 14

προσεύξωμαι. 33 καὶ παραλαμβάνει τὸν Πέτρον καὶ Ἰάκωβον καὶ Ἰωάννην μετ' αὐτοῦ, καὶ ἤρξατο ἐκθαμβεῖσθαι καὶ ἀδημονεῖν, 34 καὶ λέγει αὐτοῖς· **περίλυπός ἐστιν ἡ ψυχή μου ἕως θανάτου**· μείνατε ὧδε καὶ γρηγορεῖτε. 35 καὶ προελθὼν μικρὸν ἔπιπτεν ἐπὶ τῆς γῆς, καὶ προσηύχετο ἵνα εἰ δυνατόν ἐστιν παρέλθῃ ἀπ' αὐτοῦ ἡ ὥρα, 36 καὶ ἔλεγεν· αββα ὁ πατήρ, πάντα δυνατά σοι· παρένεγκε τὸ ποτήριον τοῦτο ἀπ' ἐμοῦ· ἀλλ' οὐ τί ἐγὼ θέλω ἀλλὰ τί σύ.

Luk 22

πειρασμόν. 41 καὶ αὐτὸς ἀπεσπάσθη ἀπ' αὐτῶν ὡσεὶ λίθου βολήν, καὶ θεὶς τὰ γόνατα προσηύχετο 42 λέγων· πάτερ, εἰ βούλει παρένεγκε τοῦτο τὸ ποτήριον ἀπ' ἐμοῦ· πλὴν μὴ τὸ θέλημά μου ἀλλὰ τὸ σὸν γινέσθω. 43 ὤφθη δὲ αὐτῷ ἄγγελος ἀπ' οὐρανοῦ ἐνισχύων αὐτόν. 44 καὶ γενόμενος ἐν ἀγωνίᾳ ἐκτενέστερον προσηύχετο· καὶ ἐγένετο ὁ ἱδρὼς αὐτοῦ ὡσεὶ θρόμβοι αἵματος καταβαίνοντες ἐπὶ τὴν

Joh

οἱ μαθηταὶ αὐτοῦ.

12 27: νῦν ἡ ψυχή μου τετάρακται, καὶ τί εἴπω; πάτερ, σῶσόν με ἐκ τῆς ὥρας ταύτης; ἀλλὰ διὰ τοῦτο ἦλθον εἰς τὴν ὥραν ταύτην.

18 11: ... τὸ ποτήριον ὃ δέδωκέν μοι ὁ πατήρ, οὐ μὴ πίω αὐτό;

Ps42 6 Jon4 9

Mt 26,36 *om* εκει‖Mk: 565 4 *Ss*[c]p **39** ● προσελθων: 𝔓^{53} *Rpl S*hj^{abc11} — *txt*: 𝔓^{37} B-892 Σ^{c}Φ λ22 ϕ346-*l*547 σM-71-517-945-990-1194-1391-1675 Π Ω *pm* Chr$^{1:2}$ *L*[ek],Au Hil Or *S*'j^{11} *C* | ● *om* μου‖p: 𝔓^{53*} L-892 Σ **λ**-1582 Δ Chr Eu Ir Marcl^{Eu} Or *La*(+ παντα δυνατα σοι‖Mk) vg^{6} Au$^{14:15}$ Cp Hil Ir *S*j *Geo*^{B} | συ + Lk43.44: C^{m} **ϕ**-*l*547 348 713 *l*^{pm} ⟦απ] απο του (*cf. ad* Lk43): ϕ346-543-826-828-983 | και εγενετο] εγ. δε: **ϕ**' — εγ.: ϕ124-788-*l*547⟧ — + υπαγε εις Λουκ. κεφ. σπγ' ωφθη δε αυτω: M^{m}

Mk 14,32 προσευξ. + εκει‖Mt: 28 **33** τ. Π. κ. Ια. κ. Ιω.] Π. κ. Ια. κ. Ιω.‖5 37 13 3 Lk8 51 9 28: ℵ* σ27-71(Ιω. *prm* τον)-179 — τ. Π. κ. τον Ια. κ. Ιω.‖9 2: L **λ**-22 σ71 *pc* — ● τ. Π. κ. τ. Ια. κ. τον Ιω.: BΨ W-1071 λ872 **ϕ**'⟨828⟩(*om* τον^{2}: 983) A K Π *al* | ∼ Ιω. ... Ια.‖Lk9 28: ϕ230 *pc* | εκθ.] λυπεισθαι‖**p**: **λ** σ115 **34** και^{1}] τοτε‖Mt: Θ-565-700 **ϕ**⟨828⟩ D *Lab Arm* | γρη. + μετ εμου‖**p**: **0112** 28-544 **λ** σ115-945 G *al Lg*^{2}qr^{1}30 *Cs*$^{8:10}$ **35** επεσεν‖Mt: *Rpl L S C*sb^{1} — *txt*: 𝔥⟨Δ-579⟩-**0112**(επιπιπτεν!) *C*b' | επιπ. + επι προσωπον(+ αυτου)‖(Mt): ΘΣ-(28)-700-565 **λ**-22 **ϕ**⟨828⟩ σ7-517-659-692-1082-1391 D G *pc L*vl'[e]⟨fr^{2}z⟩ g^{2}(∼ επι πρ. επιπ.)r^{1}30 vg^{1}(= g^{2}) *Ss*[c] | *om* επι τ. γης‖Mt: 28 *Lc Geo*^{L} | παρελθετω‖Mt: 579 | ωρα + αυτη‖Jo27: D *L*vl⟨k[e] alr^{2}z⟩r^{1} Au *Δ*a i^{V} p **36** πατ. + μου‖Mt: W **ϕ**⟨828⟩ *pc Ss*[c](*om* αββα)p *Geo*^{2L} | ∼ απ εμ. το ποτ. τουτ.‖Mt: σM-1223-1391 K Y Π 1342(ποτ. + απ εμου!) *al L*(c)ff^{2} vg^{1} *S* | ∼ του. το ποτ.‖Lk: Ψ N **λ** D *L*abcqr^{1} Hil | αλλ] πλην αλλ‖p: NΣ | ου τι] ουχ ως‖Mt: Θ-565 **ϕ**⟨124-828⟩ D(ως] ο) *pc L*cff^{2} *C*⟨b^{1}⟩ *Arm Geo*^{L} | τι^{2}] ως‖Mt: Θ-565 **ϕ**⟨124-828⟩ *pc L*bcff^{2} *C Arm*

Lk 22,41 προσηυξατο‖22 39 Mt42.44: 𝔓^{75} ℵT-579-892-1241 1071 ϕ124 Γ 11 Bas Da *Cs*^{5}(^{3} *om*)b$^{\langle 1\rangle}$ **42** πατ. + εμου: 11 *S*ch *C* | *om* ει βου.‖p: **λλ** 660 *La* | ● παρενεγκειν *Rpl* Bas Dio^{A1} — ● παρενεγκαι(= -κε): ℵL-892 1071 **ϕ** σM K R Π *al L*d — παρελθατω‖Mt: *L*l *S*' *C* — *txt*: 𝔓^{75} BT-579-1241 **λλ**⟨2193⟩ σ1207-1223 D Θ *al* Bas CAp Da Dio^{A1} Or *L*⟨e(transfert)(-fers: ar^{1})⟩ *S*h *Arm Aeth* | ∼ το ποτ. του.‖Mt Mk: *Rpl* (∼ απ εμ. το ποτ. του.‖Mt: 1093) Bas Or *L*' *S* — *txt*: 𝔓^{75} ℵ^{a}(* + τουτο!)BLT-892 D Q Θ 157 *pc l*48 *l*49 *L*ff^{2} **43.44** *om* (*cf. ad* Mt39)‖p: 𝔓^{69v}(^{41}προσηυχ.⌒^{45}προσευχης?)^{75} ℵ^{a}BT-579 N-1071 **ϕ**'⟨13^{c}-346^{m}-828-983⟩157^{c} 713 A R W Ath^{v} PsAth^{v} Cl Cr Da Ep Mcn Or *L*f Am Hi Hil *Ss C*' *Arm*^{pc}(^{pc} *om* 44) — *txt* (*vel sim.*): *Rpl* ($^{+}$ *vel* $^{-}$: 892^{c} E S V Δ^{c} Π^{c} *pc*; 42.43] ωφθη: ϕ788^{m}-826; 42.43] ωφ. δε: 13*) *l*184 *l*211 Arius^{Ep} PsCae Chr Co Dio^{A1} Dio^{Ar} Ep Eu^{can} Gr^{Na} Hip Ir Iu Leont Thd^{C} *L*'Au EN↓ Fac Hi Hil *S*'j LG *C*b^{9} *Arm*' **43** απ] απο του *cf.* 9 54 Mt24 29 Mk8 11p 13 25: 892-1241 1604(*om* του) ϕ983-1689 D Q U Θ Ψ *pc l*253 — εξ *cf.* 3 22 Mt28 2 Jo1 32: 1038 *l*184 **44** και εγ.] ● εγ. δε: *Rpl S*h — *txt*: ℵX **λλ**⟨22-1278⟩ V Ψ 157 *pc* Arius^{Ep} PsCae Co *L*⟨f⟩ *S*cpj *C*b^{6}

Lk22 43f. *cf.* EN frgm.32 (HPass fol.32r°): Apparuit autem ei angelus de celo confortans eum. qualiter autem angelus Christum in agonia sue oracionis confortaverit, dicitur in Evangelio Nazareorum — et idem ponit Anselmus in planctu suo: 'Constans esto, domine; modo enim venit tempus quo per tuam passionem redimendum est genus humanum in Adam venditum.'

Matthew

40 καὶ ἔρχεται πρὸς τοὺς μαθητὰς καὶ εὑρίσκει αὐτοὺς καθεύδοντας, καὶ λέγει τῷ Πέτρῳ· οὕτως οὐκ ἰσχύσατε μίαν ὥραν γρηγορῆσαι μετ' ἐμοῦ; 41 γρηγορεῖτε καὶ προσεύχεσθε, ἵνα μὴ εἰσέλθητε εἰς πειρασμόν· τὸ μὲν πνεῦμα πρόθυμον, ἡ δὲ σὰρξ ἀσθενής. 42 πάλιν ἐκ δευτέρου ἀπελθὼν προσηύξατο λέγων· πάτερ μου, εἰ οὐ δύναται τοῦτο παρελθεῖν ἐὰν μὴ αὐτὸ πίω, γενηθήτω τὸ θέλημά σου. 43 καὶ ἐλθὼν πάλιν εὗρεν αὐτοὺς καθεύδοντας, ἦσαν γὰρ αὐτῶν οἱ ὀφθαλμοὶ βεβαρημένοι. 44 καὶ ἀφεὶς αὐτοὺς πάλιν ἀπελθὼν προσηύξατο ἐκ τρίτου, τὸν αὐτὸν λόγον εἰπὼν πάλιν. 45 τότε ἔρχεται πρὸς τοὺς μαθητὰς καὶ λέγει αὐτοῖς· καθεύδετε τὸ λοιπὸν καὶ ἀναπαύεσθε· ἰδοὺ ἤγγικεν ἡ ὥρα καὶ ὁ υἱὸς τοῦ ἀνθρώπου παραδίδοται εἰς χεῖρας ἁμαρτωλῶν. 46 ἐγείρεσθε, ἄγωμεν· ἰδοὺ ἤγγικεν ὁ παραδιδούς με.

Mark

37 καὶ ἔρχεται καὶ εὑρίσκει αὐτοὺς καθεύδοντας, καὶ λέγει τῷ Πέτρῳ· Σίμων, καθεύδεις; οὐκ ἴσχυσας μίαν ὥραν γρηγορῆσαι; 38 γρηγορεῖτε καὶ προσεύχεσθε, ἵνα μὴ ἔλθητε εἰς πειρασμόν· τὸ μὲν πνεῦμα πρόθυμον, ἡ δὲ σὰρξ ἀσθενής. 39 καὶ πάλιν ἀπελθὼν προσηύξατο τὸν αὐτὸν λόγον εἰπών.

40 καὶ ὑποστρέψας εὗρεν αὐτοὺς πάλιν καθεύδοντας, ἦσαν γὰρ αὐτῶν οἱ ὀφθαλμοὶ καταβαρυνόμενοι, καὶ οὐκ ᾔδεισαν τί ἀποκριθῶσιν αὐτῷ.

41 καὶ ἔρχεται τὸ τρίτον καὶ λέγει αὐτοῖς· καθεύδετε τὸ λοιπὸν καὶ ἀναπαύεσθε· ἀπέχει· ἦλθεν ἡ ὥρα, ἰδοὺ παραδίδοται ὁ υἱὸς τοῦ ἀνθρώπου εἰς τὰς χεῖρας τῶν ἁμαρτωλῶν. 42 ἐγείρεσθε, ἄγωμεν· ἰδοὺ ὁ παραδιδούς με ἤγγικεν.

cf. *268.*

14 31: ... ἐγείρεσθε, ἄγωμεν ἐντεῦθεν.

Luke

γῆν. 45 καὶ ἀναστὰς ἀπὸ τῆς προσευχῆς, ἐλθὼν πρὸς τοὺς μαθητὰς εὗρεν κοιμωμένους αὐτοὺς ἀπὸ τῆς λύπης, 46 καὶ εἶπεν αὐτοῖς· τί καθεύδετε; ἀναστάντες προσεύχεσθε, ἵνα μὴ εἰσέλθητε εἰς πειρασμόν.

Mt 26,40 και^{1} + αναστας απο της προσευχης‖Lk: C^{m} 700 σM^{m}-945-990-1223 Γ *al l*^{pm} | ∼ καθ. αυ.‖Lk: L | τω Π.] αυτοις‖Lk: 1604 ϕ⟨124⟩-230-*l*547 σM E K Π Y *al S*h^{m} | ισχυσας‖Mk: A 1396 *L*ff^{2}g^{2} 30 vg^{2} *S*h^{m} *C*b^{1} *Arm*^{pc} **41** εισελ.] ελθητε‖Mk: 𝔓^{37} *L*bff^{2} Cp **42** *om* μου‖Lk42 Mk36: 𝔓^{37} σ1402 1295 *l*48 Chr Eu *L*ach^{c} Hil *S*j^{1} | τουτο] του. το ποτηριον‖Lk42: *Rpl* (∼ παρελ. απ εμου το ποτ.: Δ 157) Chr *L*'[ek] *S*p'j^{klv} {*C*b} — το ποτ. του.‖39 Mk36: ϕ D *pc* Or *L*g^{1}l 32 vg^{1} *S*s[c]p^{3} {} *Arm* — το ποτ.: V 248 1216 — *txt*: 𝔓^{37} ℵBCL-33 λ⟨118⟩-1582 ϕ174 σ71-1010-1293 A W Δ^{c} Π **067** *al* Eu Or *L*bff^{2}q vg^{1} *S*h *C*s^{8}(^{1}*om*) *Aeth* | παρελ. + απ εμου‖39: *Rpl L*ff^{2}q vg^{3} Or *S*hj^{kl} *C Arm Δ*i^{V} p — *txt*: 𝔓^{37} ℌ 700 λ⟨118⟩-1582 ϕ69-788-*l*547 σ1424 D Θ Eu Or *L*'[ek] *S*' *Δ*'⟨me⟩ **44** *om* εκ τρι.‖Mk39: 𝔓^{37} Φ λ⟨118⟩-1582 σ71-1424 A D K Π 157 *pc L*[ek]abff^{2}r^{1} | ειπ. + Lk43: 1241(απ] απο του) | *om* παλιν^{2}‖←: *Rpl L*'[ek] *S*'j *C*s *Δ*' *Geo*^{2ch} — *txt*: 𝔓^{37} ℵBL ϕ124-*l*547 Θ *La*(ειπ. παλ.] iterato) *S*s[c] *C*b *Geo*^{1} **45** ● *om* το: ℌ⟨ℵ⟩C ϕ543 σ659-1207 W *pc* Or | παραδοθησεται‖20 18 Mk10 33 Lk9 44: 700 *L*[ek]⟨bff^{2}hl vg^{2}⟩ Or *Geo*^{A} *Aeth*(τον υιον ... παραδωσουσιν) | αμ.] ανθρωπων αμ.‖17 22p Lk24 7: ϕ230-346-543-826-828 **σ**-659 157 *al l*184 **46** αγ. + εντευθεν‖Jo14 31: λ1278 G *pc l*184 *La S*s[c]j^{c} *Arm* | ∼ ο παρ. με ηγ.‖Mk: 998 2145 *S*h

Mk 14,37 ερχ. + προς τους μαθητας‖p: 1071 *L*c(+ αυτου)z — + πρ. αυτους‖p: *L*30 vg^{1} *Geo*^{L} | ισχυσατε‖Mt: Θ-565 λ ϕ⟨828⟩ σ7-1082-1391 D 59 *l*19 *l*49 *l*251 *l*260 *l*^{a1} *Lk*[e] bff^{2}g^{2}r^{2} vg^{1} | γρη. + μετ εμου‖Mt: 579 700 F *pc L*q 30 *C*s$^{1:7}$b *Geo*^{2} **38** γρη. + ουν‖13 35p: 1071 *C*s$^{1:8}$b | εισελθ.‖Mt Lk 46.40: *Rpl L*abflr^{2}z vg — *txt*: ℵB ϕ13-346-543-788-826 *L*q **40** υποστ.—παλ.] ● παλ. ελθων ευ. αυ.‖p: ℌ⟨Δ-579⟩-**0112**^{v} 1342 *C* — ελθων (+ προς τους μαθητας) ευ. αυ.‖Mt40: D *Lk*[e] abcff^{2}q (*S*s[c]) — υποστ. παλ.(*om*) ευ. αυ.‖p: Θ-565 σ827 *pc L*flr^{2}z vg *S*p'(^{1}) *Arm* — *txt*: *Rpl* (∼ καθ. παλ.: X N; *om* παλ.: Σ 90 *l*6) *S*h | καταβαρ.] καταβαρουμενοι: W D *pc* — βαρυνομενοι‖p Lk9 32: 892 **σ**'-M *pc* — βεβαρημενοι‖←: *Rpl* (καταβε.: ℵ* 1515) — *txt*: ℌ' ℵ^{c} NΣ λ⟨118⟩-22-1278 ϕ⟨828⟩ σ7-115-1082-1223-1391-1424 A K U Y Π *mu* | καταβ. + υπνω‖Lk←: 713 *pc L*dq30 vg^{1} *S*s[c] *Geo*^{2} **41** ● *om* το^{2}: *Rpl* — *txt*: ℵBΔ-579 NΘΣΦ-565-1071 λ-22 ϕ⟨13-828⟩-230 σM-71-115-945-1223-1402-1424-1606-1675 G H K U V Y Γ Π 157 *mu* | απεχ.] + το τελος‖Lk22 37: WΘΦ-565-1071 ϕ⟨828⟩ σ1082 D *al L*abcff^{2}qr^{1} *S*(∼ τ. τελ. απ.: s[c]p)h *Δ*a — *om*‖p: Ψ *pc Lk*[e] *C*b^{1} | ∼ ιδου ηλ. η ωρα *et* + και‖p: W | ιδου] και‖p: σ827 *C*s$^{1:8}$f | *om* τας‖**p**: 579 NΘΣ-565-700 λ ϕ69-983 σ179-827-945-1223-1424-1606 A F K U Π **0116** 1342 *mu* | *om* των‖p: 579-700 ϕ⟨124-983⟩ 435 **42** ∼ ηγ. ο παρ. με‖p: 565 σ517-827 D(-διδων) *pc L*ab^{v}cfff^{2}qr$^{1v.2}$ *S*s[c]p | ● ηγγισεν‖Lk22 47: ℵC

Lk 22,45 ∼ αυ. κοιμ.‖p: *Rpl L*'(*om* αυ.: c vg^{1}) — *txt*: 𝔓^{75} ℵBLT ϕ D Ψ **0153 0171** 157 *pc* **46** ειπ.] λεγει‖p: λ1278 σ71-692 *pc L*⟨ac⟩ | *om* τι‖Mk: D (*om* τι καθ.: *L*30 vg^{2}) *C*s$^{1:9}$ | καθ. + το λοιπον‖Mt45p: 475 | *om* ανασ.‖p: 280

255. Die Gefangenennahme Jesu. *Jesus Taken Captive.*

Matth 26 47–56

47 Καὶ ἔτι αὐτοῦ λαλοῦντος, ἰδοὺ Ἰούδας εἷς τῶν δώδεκα ἦλθεν, καὶ μετ᾽ αὐτοῦ ὄχλος πολὺς μετὰ μαχαιρῶν καὶ ξύλων ἀπὸ τῶν ἀρχιερέων καὶ πρεσβυτέρων τοῦ λαοῦ. 48 ὁ δὲ παραδιδοὺς αὐτὸν ἔδωκεν αὐτοῖς σημεῖον λέγων· ὃν ἂν φιλήσω αὐτός ἐστιν· κρατήσατε αὐτόν. 49 καὶ εὐθέως προσελθὼν τῷ Ἰησοῦ εἶπεν· χαῖρε, ραββι, καὶ κατεφίλησεν αὐτόν. 50 ὁ δὲ Ἰησοῦς εἶπεν αὐτῷ· ἑταῖρε, ἐφ᾽ ὃ πάρει. τότε προσελθόντες

Mark 14 43–52

43 Καὶ εὐθὺς ἔτι αὐτοῦ λαλοῦντος παραγίνεται Ἰούδας ὁ Ἰσκαριώτης εἷς τῶν δώδεκα, καὶ μετ᾽ αὐτοῦ ὄχλος μετὰ μαχαιρῶν καὶ ξύλων παρὰ τῶν ἀρχιερέων καὶ τῶν γραμματέων καὶ τῶν πρεσβυτέρων. 44 δεδώκει δὲ ὁ παραδιδοὺς αὐτὸν σύσσημον αὐτοῖς λέγων· ὃν ἂν φιλήσω αὐτός ἐστιν· κρατήσατε αὐτὸν καὶ ἀπάγετε ἀσφαλῶς. 45 καὶ ἐλθὼν εὐθὺς προσελθὼν αὐτῷ λέγει· ραββι, ραββι, καὶ κατεφίλησεν αὐτόν. 46 οἱ δὲ

Luk 22 47–53

47 Ἔτι αὐτοῦ λαλοῦντος ἰδοὺ ὄχλος, καὶ ὁ λεγόμενος Ἰούδας εἷς τῶν δώδεκα προήρχετο αὐτούς, καὶ ἤγγισεν τῷ Ἰησοῦ φιλῆσαι αὐτόν. 48 Ἰησοῦς δὲ εἶπεν αὐτῷ· Ἰούδα, φιλήματι τὸν υἱὸν τοῦ ἀνθρώ-

Jo 18 2–11. 20

18 2–11. 20: ᾔδει δὲ καὶ Ἰούδας ὁ παραδιδοὺς αὐτὸν τὸν τόπον, ὅτι πολλάκις συνήχθη Ἰησοῦς ἐκεῖ μετὰ τῶν μαθητῶν αὐτοῦ. 3 ὁ οὖν Ἰούδας λαβὼν τὴν σπεῖραν καὶ ἐκ τῶν ἀρχιερέων καὶ Φαρισαίων ὑπηρέτας ἔρχεται ἐκεῖ μετὰ φανῶν καὶ λαμπάδων καὶ ὅπλων. 4 Ἰησοῦς οὖν εἰδὼς πάντα τὰ ἐρχόμενα ἐπ᾽ αὐτὸν ἐξῆλθεν καὶ λέγει αὐτοῖς· τίνα ζητεῖτε; 5 ἀπεκρίθησαν αὐτῷ· Ἰησοῦν τὸν Ναζωραῖον. λέγει αὐτοῖς ὁ Ἰησοῦς· ἐγώ εἰμι. εἱστήκει δὲ καὶ Ἰούδας ὁ παραδιδοὺς αὐτὸν μετ᾽ αὐτῶν. 6 ὡς οὖν εἶπεν αὐτοῖς· ἐγώ εἰμι, ἀπῆλθαν εἰς τὰ ὀπίσω καὶ ἔπεσαν χαμαί. 7 πάλιν οὖν αὐτοὺς ἐπηρώτησεν· τίνα ζητεῖτε; οἱ δὲ εἶπαν· Ἰησοῦν τὸν Ναζωραῖον. 8 ἀπεκρίθη Ἰησοῦς· εἶπον ὑμῖν ὅτι ἐγώ εἰμι· εἰ οὖν ἐμὲ ζητεῖτε, ἄφετε τούτους ὑπάγειν· 9 ἵνα πληρωθῇ ὁ λόγος ὃν εἶπεν, ὅτι οὓς δέδωκάς μοι, οὐκ ἀπώλεσα ἐξ αὐτῶν οὐδένα.

Mt 26,47 *om* και^1‖Lk: 28 σ1293 *L*[ek]⟨fqz vg^3⟩ Luc *Ss*[c] *Cs*$^{3:9}$b^1

Mk 14,43 *om* ευϑ.‖**p**: WΘΣ-565-700 **λ** **ϕ**⟨124⟩ D *L*⟨f⟩ *Ss*[c]p *C*b^1 | Ιου. ο Ισκ.] ● Ιου.‖Mt Lk Jo2.3: *Rpl* (ο Ιου.: B λ22) *Ss*[c] *C*'f *Geo*^{1} — ο Ιου. ο Ισκ.: σ1402 A {} — Ιου. Ισκ.‖3 19 Mt26 14 Lk6 16: 565 ϕ124-346 D(Σκαρ.) 1574 Or {} — *txt*: 579 ΘΦ-565-700^m-1071 λ872-1278 ϕ230-983 σM-517-659-1606 K U Y Π **0116** *mu* {*L* *S*' *C*b^1 *Geo*^{2}} | εις + ων‖Jo6 71: *Rpl* *S*h — + εκ‖←: Δ *pc* *Cs*^{7}b {*Arm*} — *txt*: 𝔥'C-**0112** NWΘΣΦ-565-700-1071 ϕ13-124-230-788-983 σ179-517-827-1207-1223-1606 A D K S U Π **0116** 1342 *mu* *l*18 *l*19 *l*49 *l*184 Or *Cs*^{2} {} *Aeth* | οχ. + πολυς‖Mt: *Rpl* Or *Lk*[e] clr^2 vg' *Ss*[c]p(οχ.] λαος) — *txt*: ℵBLΨ-**0112** Θ-565 **ϕ**⟨124-346⟩ 1342 *pc* *Lvl*'[b] vg^6 *S*h *C* *Arm* | παρα] απο‖**p**: B | ∼ πρε. … γρα.‖14 53 15 1: 700 ϕ124 *pc* *Lc* *Cs*$^{1:11}$b | *om* κ. τ. γρα.‖p: 485 *Sp*^{1} *Cs*$^{1:11}$ — *om* κ. τ. γρα. κ. τ. πρε.: *L*bff^2 | των^3] απο τ.‖p: D *L*flr^2 vg$^{\langle 10\rangle}$ **44** ∼ ο δε πα. αυ. δεδ.‖p: 1574 | δεδ.] εδωκεν‖p: D' *Lk*[e] acr^1 vg^1 *Cs*b$^{\langle 9\rangle}$ | ∼ αυτοις συσ.‖p: σ827-1424 *pc* *Lf*(∼ αυτοις ο πα.—συσ.)r^1(*om* αυτον^1)30 vg^1(= f; ^{1} = r^1) | συσ.] σημειον‖**p**: Θ-565 σ1424-1675 D 1342 *al* Cat$^{\mathrm{Ox\,Mo}}$ 348 *pc* *S*h — *om* ελ.‖Mt: Θ-544-565-700 **λ**-22-1278 ϕ230 σ517-1675 D **047**(∼ προσ. ευϑ.) 157 *al* (*om* ελ. ευϑ.: *Lvl*[e]⟨flr^{2}z⟩) *S*' | *om* προσ.‖Mt: 281 1588 | αυτω] τω Ιησου‖p: NΣ-28 *pc* | ραβ.^{1}] χαιρε‖Mt: C^c-892 WΦ-565 **λ**-22(+ ραβ.^{1}) **ϕ** σ7-517-827 251(=22) *al* *l*7 *l*10 *l*12 *l*17 *l*18 *l*19 *l*36 *l*184 *l*251 *l*260 *L*ab?cg^{2}z 30 vg^3 *S*h^m *Csf* *Geo*^{2} — ● *om*‖Mt: 𝔥'C* Θ σM-1207 D 1342 *pc* *L*' *Ss*[c] *C*b *Geo*^{1} — *txt*: *Rpl* *S*' **45** ∼ ευϑ. ελ.‖Mt:

Lk 22,47 οχ. + πολυς‖Mt: 544 D 50 *Ssc* | λεγ.] καλουμενος‖22 3: **λλ**⟨22-1278⟩ D **0171** 157(∼ Ιου. ο καλ. *et* + Ισκαριωτης) 239 *L*⟨l⟩ *Sscp* | Ιου. + Ισκαριωϑ‖←6 16 Mk: D **0171**^{v} (157) *Ll* | εις + ων‖22 3 Jo6 71: σ267 60 *Cs*$^{8:11}$ | ηγγ.—αυ.] εγγισας (+ τω Ι.) εφιλησεν τον Ιησουν(τον Ι.] αυτον)‖p: 𝔓^{69v} σ267 D *Lvl*'⟨fz⟩(qr^1) *Ssc*(p *Cs*$^{2:11}$b$^{\langle 6\rangle}$) *Aeth* | 47 + τουτο γαρ σημειον δεδωκει αυτοις· ον αν φιλησω αυτος εστιν‖p: X(+ κρατησατε αυτον) 700-1071 (δεδωκεν: **ϕ**')983-1689 σ7-267-1194 D E H(= **ϕ**') Θ 213(= X) *pm* (*sim. et* = X: *L*bcr^{1}z) *S*ph *Arm*(= X) *Geo* *Aeth* **48** Ιη. δε] ο δε Ιη.‖Mt: *Rpl* (*om* Ιη.: 544 348 *S*h Ιη.$^+$ — *txt*: 𝔓^{75} ℵBLTX-579(*om* δε)-892

Jo 18,3 Φ.] ● εκ των Φ.: ℵ* *et* ^{b} L-579 D Cr *Laz* vg^2 — των Φ.‖Mk: B **0141** — *txt*: *Rpl* Chr Cr Or *L*' *S*,j | *om* εκει‖p: ℵ* *Lr*^{1} | οπλ.] οχλων‖p: 700 (*sim.*: *Ss*[c]) **4** επερχ.‖Lk21 26: 1071 ϕ1689 σ954 Δ *pc* **5** ο Ι.] ● *om*: 𝔓^{60} D *pc* *l*150 *l*253 Or *Le* br^{1}30 Or *Ss*[c]j^c — ● Ι.: ℵB(∼ εγω ειμι Ι.) *La*(= B *et* ∼ειστ. δε) — *txt*: *Rpl* *L*' *S*'j^{ab} *C*$^{\langle B\rangle}$a^s **7** ● ∼ επη. αυ.‖9 15 Mk15 14: 𝔓$^{60v\,66v}$ BCLWX-**054**-33 1071 **ϕ**-1689-*l*547 A U Ψ **0141** *al* Chr Cr Or *Le* fg^{2}qr^{1}30 vg^4 **9** αυτου‖6 39: A

Matthew

ἐπέβαλον τὰς χεῖρας ἐπὶ τὸν Ἰησοῦν καὶ ἐκράτησαν αὐτόν.

51 καὶ ἰδοὺ εἷς τῶν μετὰ Ἰησοῦ ἐκτείνας τὴν χεῖρα ἀπέσπασεν τὴν μάχαιραν αὐτοῦ, καὶ πατάξας τὸν δοῦλον τοῦ ἀρχιερέως ἀφεῖλεν αὐτοῦ τὸ ὠτίον.

52 τότε λέγει αὐτῷ ὁ Ἰησοῦς· ἀπόστρεψον τὴν μάχαιράν σου εἰς τὸν τόπον αὐτῆς· πάντες γὰρ οἱ λαβόντες μάχαιραν ἐν μαχαίρῃ ἀπολοῦνται. 53 ἢ δοκεῖς ὅτι οὐ δύναμαι παρακαλέσαι τὸν πατέρα μου, καὶ παραστήσει μοι ἄρτι πλείους δώδεκα λεγιῶνας ἀγγέλων; 54 πῶς οὖν πληρωθῶσιν αἱ γραφαὶ ὅτι οὕτως δεῖ γενέσθαι; 55 ἐν ἐκείνῃ τῇ ὥρᾳ εἶπεν ὁ Ἰησοῦς τοῖς ὄχλοις·

ὡς ἐπὶ λῃστὴν ἐξήλθατε μετὰ

Mark

ἐπέβαλαν τὰς χεῖρας αὐτῷ καὶ ἐκράτησαν αὐτόν.

47 εἷς δέ τις τῶν παρεστηκότων σπασάμενος τὴν μάχαιραν ἔπαισεν τὸν δοῦλον τοῦ ἀρχιερέως καὶ ἀφεῖλεν αὐτοῦ τὸ ὠτάριον.

48 καὶ ἀποκριθεὶς ὁ Ἰησοῦς εἶπεν αὐτοῖς·

ὡς ἐπὶ λῃστὴν ἐξήλθατε μετὰ

Luke

που παραδίδως; 49 ἰδόντες δὲ οἱ περὶ αὐτὸν τὸ ἐσόμενον εἶπαν· κύριε, εἰ πατάξομεν ἐν μαχαίρῃ;

50 καὶ ἐπάταξεν εἷς τις ἐξ αὐτῶν τοῦ ἀρχιερέως τὸν δοῦλον καὶ ἀφεῖλεν τὸ οὖς αὐτοῦ τὸ δεξιόν. 51 ἀποκριθεὶς δὲ ὁ Ἰησοῦς εἶπεν· ἐᾶτε ἕως τούτου· καὶ ἁψάμενος τοῦ ὠτίου ἰάσατο αὐτόν.

52 εἶπεν δὲ Ἰησοῦς πρὸς τοὺς παραγενομένους ἐπ' αὐτὸν ἀρχιερεῖς καὶ στρατηγοὺς τοῦ ἱεροῦ καὶ πρεσβυτέρους· ὡς ἐπὶ λῃστὴν ἐξήλθατε μετὰ

John

10 Σίμων οὖν Πέτρος ἔχων μάχαιραν εἵλκυσεν αὐτὴν καὶ ἔπαισεν τὸν τοῦ ἀρχιερέως δοῦλον καὶ ἀπέκοψεν αὐτοῦ τὸ ὠτάριον τὸ δεξιόν. ἦν δὲ ὄνομα τῷ δούλῳ Μάλχος. 11 εἶπεν οὖν ὁ Ἰησοῦς τῷ Πέτρῳ· βάλε τὴν μάχαιραν εἰς τὴν θήκην· τὸ ποτήριον ὃ δέδωκέν μοι ὁ πατήρ, οὐ μὴ πίω αὐτό;

Mt 26,50 επι τ. Ι.] επ αυτον ‖ Mk: σ517-1424 *S*s[c](∼ επ αυ. τας χ.) | **51** πατα. ... αφει.] επαταξεν ... και αφ. ‖ Lk MkJo: D {*L*[ek]⟨ff^{1}z⟩} | ωτ. + το δεξιον ‖ Lk Jo: σ1424 1355 *L*g^2 vg^1 *S*j^1 *C*b **52** *om* σου ‖ Jo: 33 700 ϕ230 σ71-659 K U Θ Π *al* Chr *S*s[c]pj *C*b | τ. τοπ.] την θηκην ‖ Jo: 700 σ 487 Chr *C*s
53 ● πλειω: ℵ*B D — πλειον: σ1424 — *txt*: *Rpl* Or | ● πλει. + η: *Rpl* Or *L*'[ek] — *txt*: ℵBL 700 D Θ *L*b | ● λεγιωνων: ℵ*CL-33 ΣΦ-700 λ1582 ϕ13-174-543-788-826-828-*l*547 A K Δ Θ Π *pc* — *txt*: *Rpl* Or

Mk 14,46 ∼ τας χ. επεβ.: *L*vl⟨k[e] acdff^2⟩r^1 | τ. χ. αυτω] τ. χ. αυτων(*om*) επ αυτον ‖ Mt: (Ψ) λ872 (σ517-1223) A K Y Π (επ αυτω: **047** 348) *pc* (*L*cflr$^{1v.2}$ vg) *C*,f^v *Aeth* — επ αυτον τ. χ. αυτων(*om*) ‖ Mt: *Rpl* (28 σM S *pc l*36) *S* — αυτω τ. χ. αυτων(*om*) ‖ Mt: ΝΣ (*L*k[e] a *Geo*^{A}) — τ. χ. αυτων: ℵ*CΔ-892 W *Geo*^{1} — *txt* (χ. + επ): ℵ^{c}BL Θ-565-700-1071 λ1-118*^{v}-209-(872) ϕ13-69-346-543-(1689 σ1424-1675) D 11 1342 *L*(∼ αυ. τ. χ.: k[e] a)ff^2(*om* αυ.)q *Geo*^{B} **47** *om* τις ‖ Mt: ℵL-579 700 σM-692-827 A *al* *L*k[e] cfff^{2}qr^{1}z *Aeth* | *om* την ‖ Jo: W-565 **λ** ϕ124 σ349-827-1082-1381 D 1342 *pc l*150 *l*184 | ∼ τον του αρ. δου. ‖ Jo: 1241 1574 | ∼ το ωτ. αυ. ‖ Lk: σ267 | ωτα.] ωτιον ‖ MtLk: *Rpl* — + το δεξιον ‖ Lk Jo: 1579 *L*f *Got* — *txt*: ℵBΨ **λ** D 1342

Lk 22,50 *om* τις ‖ Mt: ϕ69-788 σ71-692 Γ *pc* *L*'⟨a⟩(*om* εις: δ) | ∼ τ. δου. του αρ. ‖ **p**: 𝔓^{75} *Rpl L* — *txt*: ℌ⟨579⟩T **ϕ**⟨124⟩ **0153**(τον του αρ. δ.) | ∼ αυ. το ους ‖ p: *Rpl* — *txt*: 𝔓^{75} ℌ⟨1241⟩T 1071 **ϕ**'⟨983⟩(*om* αυ.: 124) **0153 0171** *L* | ους] ωτιον ‖ Mt: D K *pc* **51** ειπ. + αυτω ‖ Mt: Γ *L*(*om* αποκ. *et* ∼ ειπ. δε αυτω ο Ι.: ai)30 vg^1(^{3} αυτοις) *C*s$^{2:11}$ | αψ.—αυ.] εκτεινας την χειρα ηψατο αυτου και απεσταθη το ους αυτου ‖ 513p 610p: D *L*(*sim.*: e afff^{2}il)r^1 (∼ 52.53. ^{51}αψ.—αυ.: il) (*sim.*: *Δ*md n {p}) **52** Ι.] ο Ι. ‖ p: *Rpl* Or {} — *om*: **λλ**⟨22-1278⟩ D 472 *L*e bil vg^1 *S*sc *Arm* — *txt*: 𝔓^{75} ℵBT A Θ **0171**^{v}(*om* 51) {*L*' *S*' *C*}

Jo 18,10 ∼ δου. του αρ. ‖ MtMk: 𝔓^{66v} ℵ σ D *L*e abcfr^1 Ar | ωτιον ‖ 1826 MtLk51: 𝔓^{66v} *Rpl* — *txt*: 𝔓^{60} ℵBC*LWX 1187 **11** μαχ. + σου ‖ Mt: *Rpl* Cr *L*e 30 vg^2 Hil *S*s[c] *C*sa^s — *txt*: 𝔓$^{60v\,66}$ ℌ⟨579⟩CX-**054** Λ-28-544-1071 λ22 ϕ230 σM-945-1194-1207-1223 A D E K S U V^s Y Γ Δ Θ Π Ψ Ω **047 0141** *pm* Non *L*' *S*'j *C*b^{+B} | τ. θηκ.] τον τοπον ‖ Mt: ϕ1689 *S*s[c]j | θηκ. + αυτης ‖ Mt: X **ϕ**-1689-*l*547 **053** *pc* *l*49 *l*184 *l*185 *L*vl vg^3 Or *S*,j *C*$^{+B}$a^s — + παντες—απολουνται (= Mt52b): Θ *pc*

Matth	Mark	Luk	Jo
μαχαιρῶν καὶ ξύλων συλλαβεῖν με· καθ' ἡμέραν ἐν τῷ ἱερῷ ἐκαθεζόμην διδάσκων, καὶ οὐκ ἐκρατήσατέ με. 56 τοῦτο δὲ ὅλον γέγονεν ἵνα πληρωθῶσιν αἱ γραφαὶ τῶν προφητῶν. τότε οἱ μαθηταὶ πάντες ἀφέντες αὐτὸν ἔφυγον.	μαχαιρῶν καὶ ξύλων συλλαβεῖν με· 49 καθ' ἡμέραν ἤμην πρὸς ὑμᾶς ἐν τῷ ἱερῷ διδάσκων, καὶ οὐκ ἐκρατήσατέ με· ἀλλ' ἵνα πληρωθῶσιν αἱ γραφαί. 50 καὶ ἀφέντες αὐτὸν ἔφυγον πάντες. 51 καὶ νεανίσκος τις συνηκολούθει αὐτῷ περιβεβλημένος σινδόνα ἐπὶ γυμνοῦ, καὶ κρατοῦσιν αὐτόν· 52 ὁ δὲ καταλιπὼν τὴν σινδόνα γυμνὸς ἔφυγεν ἀπ' αὐτῶν.	μαχαιρῶν καὶ ξύλων· 53 καθ' ἡμέραν ὄντος μου μεθ' ὑμῶν ἐν τῷ ἱερῷ οὐκ ἐξετείνατε τὰς χεῖρας ἐπ' ἐμέ· ἀλλὰ αὕτη ἐστὶν ὑμῶν ἡ ὥρα καὶ ἡ ἐξουσία τοῦ σκότους.	20 ... ἐγὼ πάντοτε ἐδίδαξα ἐν συναγωγῇ καὶ ἐν τῷ ἱερῷ, ὅπου πάντες οἱ Ἰουδαῖοι συνέρχονται, καὶ ἐν κρυπτῷ ἐλάλησα οὐδέν.

(241)

256. Jesus vor dem Hohen Rat. Die Verleugnung des Petrus.
Jesus before the Sanhedrin. Peter's Denial.

Matth 26 57–75	**Mark 14** 53–72	**Luk 22** 54–71	Jo
57 Οἱ δὲ κρατήσαντες τὸν Ἰησοῦν ἀπήγαγον πρὸς Καϊάφαν τὸν ἀρχιερέα, ὅπου οἱ γραμματεῖς καὶ οἱ	53 Καὶ ἀπήγαγον τὸν Ἰησοῦν πρὸς τὸν ἀρχιερέα, καὶ συνέρχονται αὐτῷ πάντες οἱ ἀρχιερεῖς καὶ οἱ	54 Συλλαβόντες δὲ αὐτὸν ἤγαγον καὶ εἰσήγαγον εἰς τὴν οἰκίαν τοῦ ἀρχιερέως.	18 12-16. 18: Ἡ οὖν σπεῖρα καὶ ὁ χιλίαρχος καὶ οἱ ὑπηρέται τῶν Ἰουδαίων συνέλαβον τὸν Ἰησοῦν καὶ ἔδησαν αὐτόν, 13 καὶ ἤγαγον πρὸς Ἅνναν πρῶτον· ἦν γὰρ πενθερὸς τοῦ Καϊάφα, ὃς ἦν ἀρχιερεὺς τοῦ ἐνιαυτοῦ ἐκείνου· 14 ἦν δὲ Καϊάφας ὁ συμβουλεύσας τοῖς Ἰουδαίοις ὅτι συμφέρει ἕνα ἄνθρωπον

Mt 26,55 εν τ. ι. εκαθ.] *prm* προς υμας‖p: *Rpl* Eu *L*[ek],Or *S*'j *Geo*^{2} — + πρ. υμ.: A 1355 *Geo*^{1} *Aeth* — *txt*: ℌ 700 σ1424 Chr Cr *S*s[c] *C* | ∼ εκαθ. διδ. εν τ. ι.‖Mk12 35 Jo8 20 Lk19 47 20 1: *Rpl L*'[ek] *S*h — εκαθ. εν τ. ι. διδ.‖Mk: C σ71-1293 D(εκαθημην) K Y Π **047** 157 *mu* Eu *L*abcff^{2}g^{2}hq30(εκαθεζ.] ημην: r$^{1.2}$) vg^{2} (∼ εκαθ. καθ ημε.: *C*) *Aeth* — εν τ. ι. εκαθ.: **λ**-1582 σ1207 273 — *txt*: ℌ 700 ϕ124-*l*547 Θ *pc* Chr Cr *L*Or *S*'j **56** *om* ολον‖21 4 Jo19 36: Chr *L*vg^{1} *S*p **57** τον Ι.] αυτον‖Lk: 157 *pc S*s[c]

Mk 14,49 ∼ διδ. εν τ. ιε.‖12 35 Jo8 20 Lk19 47 20 1: ϕ983-1689 P *al L*dfq vg^{1} *S*p *C*s$^{1:13}$bf | αλλ] τουτο δε ολον γεγονεν‖Mt: 1574 *S*p(αλλ—γρα. γεγ. του.) | γρα. + των προφητων‖Mt: NWΘΦ-565 **λ** σ115 *S*h^{+} *C*s$^{4:10}$ *Arm* **50** και] τοτε οι μαθηται (+ αυτου)‖p: N(W)ΘΣ(οτε)-565 **ϕ** *pc L*(clz vg)r^{2} *S*p(*om* οι μ.)h *C*s$^{7:10}$ (*Geo*^{2}) | ∼ παντ. αφ. αυ. εφυ.‖p: 443 1574 *L*r^{2}(εφυ.] εσταυρωσαν)30 vg^{1} *Geo*^{2} | αυ. + οι μα.(+ αυτου)‖p: 1071 (161) *pc* (*S*p) *Arm* — παντ. + οι μα. αυτου‖p: *S*s[c] *Aeth*(∼) **51** συνηκ.] ηκολουθησεν‖14 54p: *Rpl* {*S*h *C*s^{1}f^{v}}^{1} — ηκολουθει‖←: WΘΦ-565-700 **λ** D *l*47 *l*48 {}^{2} — συνηκολουθησεν‖14 54: Δ-579 {}^{1} — *txt*: ℌ'⟨1241⟩C **0116**^{v} 1342 {*L S*' *C*s^{5}(^{4} ακολουθει)b}^{2} | κ. κρα. αυ.] οι δε νεανισκοι κρα. (εκρατησαν) αυ.: (W)Θ-565-700 **λ**-872(και οι νε.) (**ϕ**) 1542 *S*s[c](και ελθοντες πολλοι εκρ. αυ.) (*C*s^{5} *et* νε.] υπηρεται) — ● + οι νε.: *Rpl* (*om* οι: 1342) *L*q(εκρ.) *S*h *Arm* — *txt*: ℌ ⟨579-1241⟩C*^{v} 544 λ872 D *S*p *C*s^{5}bf **52** γυ.—αυ.] ● γυ. εφ.: ℵBC {*C*,f *Aeth*} — εφ. γυ.: LΨ-892 *L*k[e] cz *S*p {} — εφ. γυ. απ αυ.: Δ 1071 1342 *l*184 *L*dfff^{2} *Arm* — εφ. απ αυ. γυ.: 237 *L*q *S*s[c] — *txt*: *Rpl L*ab^{v}flr^{1}?r^{2} Au *S*h *Geo*^{1} **53** απηγ.] ηγαγον‖Lk: 565 1342 *L*a | τ. αρχ.] τ. α. Καιαφαν(∼ Κ. τ. α.)‖Mt: 892^{m} WΘ-565-700-1071 **λ**⟨1⟩ **ϕ**⟨828-983⟩ σM-1223 A K Y Π *mu* (Or) *S*(p)h *C*s$^{4:10}$ b^{2} *Arm* — Ανναν τ. αρχ.‖Jo: 1082 | αυτω] αυτου‖Mt: 1071 λ1-22 — προς αυτον: C *pc* — ● *om*: ℵLΔ-892 WΘ-565-700 **ϕ** D 1342 1542 Or *L*'(*om* συνερ.—και^{3}: k[e], και^{2}∩^{3}?) *C*b'(=k) — συν αυτω: 495 — *txt*: *Rpl* (αυτων: N) *S*,j *C*sb^{2}f

Lk 22,52 ξυλ. + συλλαβειν με‖**p**: X-579 1071 ϕ828 *pc L*l vg^{1} *S*ph^{+} **53** *om* μεθ υμ.‖Mt: 579 **0171** *pc C*s$^{2:10}$ | ουκ] και ουκ‖p: U 435 *l*183 *l*184 *L*r^{1}30 *S*p *C*b^{1} **54** *om* και εισηγ.(∩?)‖p: 579 **λ**⟨131⟩ σ71-692 D G Θ **063** *al L*⟨c⟩ *S*scp *C*s^{1}(^{1}*om* ηγ. και)$^{:10}$

Jo 18,13 απηγαγον‖Mt Mk: 𝔓^{60v} *Rpl* Or — *txt*: 𝔓^{66} ℵ*BW-579 ϕ69-788 D *pc l*251 *L*[e] | εκεινου(πρωτον) + 24‖p: (225) 1195 Cr *S*s[c]h^{m}j^{a}

πρεσβύτεροι συνήχθησαν. [58] ὁ δὲ Πέτρος ἠκολούθει αὐτῷ ἀπὸ μακρόθεν ἕως τῆς αὐλῆς τοῦ ἀρχιερέως, καὶ εἰσελθὼν ἔσω ἐκάθητο μετὰ τῶν ὑπηρετῶν ἰδεῖν τὸ τέλος.

cf. v. 69–75 ↓

πρεσβύτεροι καὶ οἱ γραμματεῖς. [54] καὶ ὁ Πέτρος ἀπὸ μακρόθεν ἠκολούθησεν αὐτῷ ἕως ἔσω εἰς τὴν αὐλὴν τοῦ ἀρχιερέως, καὶ ἦν συγκαθήμενος μετὰ τῶν ὑπηρετῶν καὶ θερμαινόμενος πρὸς τὸ φῶς.

cf. v. 66–72 ↓

ὁ δὲ Πέτρος ἠκολούθει μακρόθεν. [55] περιαψάντων δὲ πῦρ ἐν μέσῳ τῆς αὐλῆς καὶ συγκαθισάντων ἐκάθητο ὁ Πέτρος μέσος αὐτῶν. [56] ἰδοῦσα δὲ αὐτὸν παιδίσκη τις καθήμενον πρὸς τὸ φῶς καὶ ἀτενίσασα αὐτῷ εἶπεν· καὶ οὗτος σὺν αὐτῷ ἦν. [57] ὁ δὲ ἠρνήσατο αὐτὸν λέγων· οὐκ οἶδα αὐτόν, γύναι. [58] καὶ μετὰ βραχὺ ἕτερος ἰδὼν αὐτὸν ἔφη· καὶ σὺ ἐξ αὐτῶν εἶ. ὁ δὲ Πέτρος ἔφη· ἄνθρωπε, οὐκ εἰμί. [59] καὶ διαστάσης ὡσεὶ ὥρας μιᾶς ἄλλος τις διϊσχυρίζετο λέγων· ἐπ' ἀληθείας καὶ οὗτος μετ' αὐτοῦ ἦν, καὶ γὰρ Γαλιλαῖός ἐστιν. [60] εἶπεν δὲ ὁ Πέτρος· ἄνθρωπε, οὐκ οἶδα ὃ λέγεις. καὶ παραχρῆμα ἔτι λαλοῦντος αὐτοῦ ἐφώνησεν ἀλέκτωρ. [61] καὶ στραφεὶς ὁ κύριος ἐνέβλεψεν τῷ Πέτρῳ, καὶ ὑπεμνήσθη ὁ Πέτρος τοῦ λόγου τοῦ κυρίου, ὡς εἶπεν αὐτῷ ὅτι πρὶν ἀλέκτορα φωνῆσαι σήμερον ἀπαρνήσῃ με τρίς. [62] καὶ ἐξελ-

ἀποθανεῖν ὑπὲρ τοῦ λαοῦ. [15] ἠκολούθει δὲ τῷ Ἰησοῦ Σίμων Πέτρος καὶ ἄλλος μαθητής. ὁ δὲ μαθητὴς ἐκεῖνος ἦν γνωστὸς τῷ ἀρχιερεῖ, καὶ συνεισῆλθεν τῷ Ἰησοῦ εἰς τὴν αὐλὴν τοῦ ἀρχιερέως, [16] ὁ δὲ Πέτρος εἱστήκει πρὸς τῇ θύρᾳ ἔξω. ἐξῆλθεν οὖν ὁ μαθητὴς ὁ ἄλλος ὁ γνωστὸς τοῦ ἀρχιερέως καὶ εἶπεν τῇ θυρωρῷ, καὶ εἰσήγαγεν τὸν Πέτρον ... [18] εἱστήκεισαν δὲ οἱ δοῦλοι καὶ οἱ ὑπηρέται ἀνθρακιὰν πεποιηκότες, ὅτι ψῦχος ἦν, καὶ ἐθερμαίνοντο· ἦν δὲ καὶ ὁ Πέτρος μετ' αὐτῶν ἑστὼς καὶ θερμαινόμενος.

Mt 26,58 *om* αυτω ‖Lk: 28 σ692-945-1402 *l*49 *L*g^{2} *S*h^{Bd1} | ● *om* απο ‖Lk: ℵCL-33 28 **λ**-22-1582 F S Δ Π Ω *al*

Mk 14,53 ∼ γρα. ... πρε. ‖1127 1443 Mt57 2741: 892 565-700 σ945-1223 A D K Π *mu* Or *L Sp C*s^{1}(^{1} ∼ γρα. ... αρχ. ... πρε. *Geo*^{2} | πρε. + του λαου ‖Mt263.47 271 Lk2216: 495 **54** *om* απο ‖Lk: L^{v}ΔΨ-892 | ηκολουθει ‖**p**Jo: Ψ WΘ-565-700 **λ ϕ** σ827 G *pc l*13 *l*17 *L*k[e] cdff^{2}qr^{1}?z *S*s[c]p *C*,f | *om* εσω ‖Mt: 544 **λ** ϕ13 D *pc l*184 *L*k[e] alr^{2}30 vg^{12} *S*s[c] | εις τ. αυ.] της αυλης ‖1516 Mt: 544 **λ** σ827 *pc l*184 *S*p | συγκ.] καθ. ‖p: D | *om* πρ. τ. φως ‖Jo: **λ**-22-1278 *S*s[c]

Lk 22,54 ηκολ. + αυτω ‖p: **0124 ϕ** σ71-692 D **063** 157 *pc L*⟨ac⟩ vg^{1} *S*'h^{+} *C*s^{5}(^{2} αυτοις)b | μακρ.] απο μ. ‖p: 579 Λ-544 **ϕ**⟨124⟩-174-230 σ71-692 D **047 063 0171** 157 *pc* **55** μεσος] εν μεσω ‖246 Mt182 Mk936: *Rpl* — μετ ‖p: D — *txt*: 𝔓^{75} BLT-**0124**-892 **λ**⟨131⟩-1582-2193 **0153 0171**^{v} | αυτ. + θερμαινομενος ‖Mk Jo18.25: D **56** *om* καθ.—φως ‖p: 234 235 *L*a | ειπ. ... συν αυτω] λεγει ... μετ αυτου ‖p: 1241 **57** ● *om* αυτ.^{1} ‖Mt Mk: 𝔓^{75} ℌ'TX-**0124 λ**-22 σM-1194-1223 D^{2} K S Π Ω *mu L*abcflr^{1} *S*' *C* — *txt*: *Rpl* (αυτην: 1241) Eu *L*' *S*h | *om* γυν. ‖**p**: **0124** D **58** βρα. + παλιν ‖Mk: ℵ^{a} *L*r^{1}30? | *om* Π. ‖p: 𝔓^{69v} D *L*abff^{2}ilq *S*s | εφη^{2}] ειπεν ‖Jo: 𝔓^{69} *Rpl* — *txt*: 𝔓^{75} ℵBLT-**0124**-1241 **ϕ** σM-1207-1223 K Π *al* **59** αυτων ‖p: σ659 472 **60** ο^{2}] τι ‖Mt70p: ℵ D 157 *pc L*⟨ff^{2} vg^{4}⟩ *C*s | ∼ αυ. λαλ. ‖2247p: 𝔓^{69} 579 1604 **λ** ϕ124 U Ψ *pc L*⟨ac⟩ **61** υπεμν.] εμν. ‖Mt: 579 544 2533 | λογ.] ρηματος ‖Mt Mk: 𝔓$^{69.75}$ ℌTX-**0124** ϕ124 *pc* | κυριου] Ιησου ‖p: N-1071 ϕ13-346-543-826-828 472 *L*32 *S*sp^{1} | ως] ον ‖Mk: 157 *L*32 *S*scp *C*s$^{4:9}$ | πριν + η ‖Mk1430: B 1071 Ψ | *om* σημ. ‖Mt Mk: *Rpl L*' *S*s(+ δις)p *C*s^{2} — *txt*: 𝔓$^{69v.75}$ ℌTX-**0124** Λ **ϕ**(∼ σημ. φω.) σM-27-1194-1207 K Π 157 *al* (∼ τρ. με απαρ. σημ.: *L*bff^{2}l) *S*sh^{+} *C*s^{6}b *Aeth*(= ff^{2}) | ∼ τρ. απαρ. με ‖p: D *L*(τρ. με απ.) *S*sc | 61 + μη ειδεναι(+ με) ‖2234: 1604 σ71 (D) *L*abl (*Arm*) **62** *om* 62 ‖Jo: **0171** *L*e abff^{2}ilr^{1}

Jo 18,14 αποθ.] ● απολεσθαι *cf.* 1150: *Rpl S*h^{t} — *txt*: 𝔓^{66v} ℌ⟨1242⟩C*X 1071 **λ**⟨118⟩-22 **ϕ** D^{s} Θ **0141** *al* Chr Chrn Cr Non *L*[e]⟨vg^{1}⟩ *S*'h^{m}j *C*$^{+B}$a^{s} *Δ*⟨me⟩ | λαου + και μη ολον το εθνος αποληται ‖**11**50: λ22 *L*a *C*b^{2} **15** ηκολουθησαν ‖Mk: Θ | τω I.^{1}] αυτω ‖Mt Mk: 440 — αυτοις: C* | αλλ.] ο αλλ. ‖**20**2: *Rpl C*s^{6}a^{s} — *txt*: 𝔓$^{60v.66}$ ℵ*BW A D^{s} Ψ *pc C*s^{5}b^{+B} | τ. αυλ.] το πραιτωριον ‖1828.33: 28 **16** ∼ 19-23.16-18 *et om* ^{25}ην—θερμ. ‖Mt Mk: *S*s[c]

Jo1815f. *cf.* EN fragm.33 (HPass fol.35r^{o}): In evangelio Nazareorum poniter causa unde Johannes notus fuerit pontifici. quia cum fuerit filius pauperis piscatoris Zebedei, sepe portaverat pisces ad curias pontificum Anne et Cayphe. Exivit autem Johannes ad ancillam hostiariam et ab ea impetravit quod Petrus socius suus qui ante ianuam stetit plorans fuit intromissus.

cf. v. 67 f. ↓ | cf. v. 65 ↓

θὼν ἔξω ἔκλαυσεν πικρῶς. [63] καὶ οἱ ἄνδρες οἱ συνέχοντες αὐτὸν ἐνέπαιζον αὐτῷ δέροντες, [64] καὶ περικαλύψαντες αὐτὸν ἐπηρώτων λέγοντες· προφήτευσον, τίς ἐστιν ὁ παίσας σε; [65] καὶ ἕτερα πολλὰ βλασφημοῦντες ἔλεγον εἰς αὐτόν. [66] καὶ ὡς ἐγένετο ἡμέρα, συνήχθη τὸ πρεσβυτέριον τοῦ λαοῦ, ἀρχιερεῖς τε καὶ

257. γραμματεῖς, καὶ ἀπήγαγον αὐτὸν εἰς τὸ συνέδριον αὐτῶν,

[59] οἱ δὲ ἀρχιερεῖς καὶ τὸ συνέδριον ὅλον ἐζήτουν ψευδομαρτυρίαν κατὰ τοῦ Ἰησοῦ ὅπως αὐτὸν θανατώσωσιν, [60] καὶ οὐχ εὗρον πολλῶν προσελθόντων ψευδομαρτύρων. ὕστερον δὲ προσελθόντες δύο [61] εἶπον· οὗτος ἔφη· δύναμαι καταλῦσαι τὸν ναὸν τοῦ θεοῦ καὶ διὰ τριῶν ἡμερῶν

[55] οἱ δὲ ἀρχιερεῖς καὶ ὅλον τὸ συνέδριον ἐζήτουν κατὰ τοῦ Ἰησοῦ μαρτυρίαν εἰς τὸ θανατῶσαι αὐτόν, καὶ οὐχ ηὕρισκον· [56] πολλοὶ γὰρ ἐψευδομαρτύρουν κατ' αὐτοῦ, καὶ ἴσαι αἱ μαρτυρίαι οὐκ ἦσαν. [57] καί τινες ἀναστάντες ἐψευδομαρτύρουν κατ' αὐτοῦ λέγοντες [58] ὅτι ἡμεῖς ἠκούσαμεν αὐτοῦ λέγοντος ὅτι ἐγὼ καταλύσω τὸν ναὸν τοῦτον τὸν χειροποίητον καὶ διὰ τριῶν ἡμερῶν ἄλλον ἀχειροποίητον

18 19–21: ὁ οὖν ἀρχιερεὺς ἠρώτησεν τὸν Ἰησοῦν περὶ τῶν μαθητῶν αὐτοῦ καὶ περὶ τῆς διδαχῆς αὐτοῦ. [20] ἀπεκρίθη αὐτῷ Ἰησοῦς· ἐγὼ παρρησίᾳ λελάληκα τῷ κόσμῳ· ἐγὼ πάντοτε ἐδίδαξα ἐν συναγωγῇ καὶ ἐν τῷ ἱερῷ, ὅπου πάντες οἱ Ἰουδαῖοι συνέρχονται, καὶ ἐν κρυπτῷ ἐλάλησα οὐδέν. [21] τί με ἐπερωτᾷς; ἐρώτησον τοὺς ἀκηκοότας τί ἐλάλησα αὐτοῖς· ἴδε οὗτοι οἴδασιν ἃ εἶπον ἐγώ.

2 19: ... εἶπεν αὐτοῖς· λύσατε τὸν ναὸν τοῦτον, καὶ ἐν τρισὶν ἡμέραις

Mt 26,59 ~ ολ. το συν.‖**p**Mk15ι: ΝΣ-28-1604 ϕ*l*547[1] σ659-945 *al l*48 *l*49 *l*53 *l*181[1] *L*[ek] | ~ θαν. αυ.‖27ι Mk: *Rpl* (*om* αυ.: Θ) Eu Or *Ld* — *txt*: 𝔖C ΝΣΦ-700 **λ**-1582 **ϕ**-230-*l*547[1] σ1194 D **090** 157 *pc L*'[ek] Or **60** ηυρισκον‖p: ϕ124-*l*547[1] Θ | ~ προσ. πολ. ψ.: **λ** *S*' — ● πολ. ψ. προσ.: *Rpl L*[ek] ⟨r[1.2]⟩ Or *S*hj — *txt*: ℵBL-33 ϕ124-*l*547[1] A D(-οι -ηλθον -ες) Θ **090** 301 Or | δυο + ψευδομαρτυρες(τινες ψ.)‖p: *Rpl* (ΝΣ W 157 *pc*) *L*[ek] Or *S*' *Arm* — *txt*: ℵBL **λ**-1582 ϕ124-*l*547[1] Θ Or *S*pj *C Geo*[A] ('+ τινες) **61** ουτ. εφη] τουτον ηκουσαμεν λεγοντα‖p: D *L*[ek] bcfff[2]hr[1.2] | τον ν. τ. θε.] τ. ν. τουτον‖pJo2ι9: C[c] *L*r[1] Or *S*s[c] *C*s[3:8] — τ. ν. τουτον τ. θε.‖pJo2ι9: σ1424 *L*[ek]bcff[2]hr[2](~)z vg[4]

Mk 14,55 ψευδομαρ. (~ ψ. κατα τ. Ι.)‖(**p**): (544) A S *pc* (*pc*) *L*k[e](testimonia facta < t. falsa?) *C*s[6:10]b[4]f | εις το θα.] ινα θανατωσουσιν‖p: Θ-565(-ωσιν)-1071(~ αυ. θα.) σ517-1424 D | ηυρ.] ευρον‖p: 28 *pc La* Or *S*p *C*sf **58** οτι[1]—λεγ.] οτι(ουτος) ειπεν‖p: ℵ (*L*k[e] c) | τουτον] *om*‖p: D' *S*s[c] — του θεου‖p: *L*bff[2] | *om* αχει.‖**p**: σ827 *C*f

Lk 22,64 *om* κ. περικ. αυ.‖Mt: *L*e br[2] *S*p — περικ.] δησατες‖Mt272 Mk15ι: *L*cl | αυτ.] αυτου το προσωπον‖Mk: **λ** σ1223 Δ(*om* αυ.) *L*r[1](+ ενεπαιζον αυτω και) *S*sc *C*s — αυτου το πρ. ετυπτον αυτον και‖Mk Mt2730p: λ131 D *La*(*om* αυτον)q *Arm*(= a) *Aeth* — αυτον ετυ. αυτου το πρ. και‖←: *Rpl L*fr[2](*om* αυτον)z vg *S*p⟨1⟩(αυτον] και)h — αυτον ετυ. αυτον και‖←: *L*ff[2](+ ενεπαιζον αυτω και)il — *txt*: 𝔓[75] ℵ(~ επηρ. αυ.)BLT-**0124**-1241 σM K Π *C*b | επη. λεγ.] ελεγον‖p: D *S*(+ αυτω: sc)p — λεγ.: *L*bq — ● επη. αυτον λεγ.: *Rpl* (ηρω-: ϕ69-788; -ησαν: 1071) *L*'(*om* λεγ.: c) *S*h *C* ⟨b[1]⟩ *Arm* — *txt*: 𝔓[75] ℵ(~ επηρ. αυ.)BLTX-**0124** σM K Π *pc* | προφ. + ημιν Χριστε‖Mt: X-1241 1071 λ131 *pc* Cr *L*g[2]lr[2] vg[1] *C*s[4] — + ημιν‖Mt: 472 *pc L*bci vg[1] *C*s[4]b *Aeth* **66** ημ.] πρωι‖Mt27ιp: ϕ543-983 — πρωι ημ.‖←: **ϕ**'⟨124⟩ | πρε.] συνεδριον‖Mt59p: 157

Jo 18,20 αυτω Ι.] ● αυτω ο Ι.: {} *Rpl* — ο Ι.: C-579 *L*ab vg[3] *C*s[1]b[2] — *txt*: {𝔓[60v]}[66] ℵ* (~)BL D[s] Θ Ω **0153** 440 *L*'[e](αυτοις: vg[2]) *C*s[9]b'[+B]a[s] **21** επερ. ερ.] επερ. επερ.: *Rpl* — ερ. επερ.‖19: 1071 A Y Θ *pc l*20 — ● ερ. ερ.‖19: {} 𝔖'⟨1241⟩C*X-**054** **σ**⟨1675⟩ Δ Π[c] 1321 Chr[1] Cr — *txt*: {𝔓[66]} 579 **λ**⟨118⟩ **ϕ**⟨828⟩-230 **0141** *al* Chr[1]

Mt2661p *cf.* ETh[II] 71 (*transl.*): *Λέγει Ἰησοῦς· καταλ[ύσω ταύτην τὴν] οἰκίαν καὶ οὐδεὶς δυνήσεται [πάλιν] οἰκοδομῆσαι αὐτήν.*

οἰκοδομῆσαι.

62 καὶ ἀναστὰς ὁ ἀρχιερεὺς εἶπεν αὐτῷ· οὐδὲν ἀποκρίνῃ, τί οὗτοί σου καταμαρτυροῦσιν; 63 ὁ δὲ Ἰησοῦς ἐσιώπα. καὶ ὁ ἀρχιερεὺς εἶπεν αὐτῷ· ἐξορκίζω σε κατὰ τοῦ θεοῦ τοῦ ζῶντος ἵνα ἡμῖν εἴπῃς εἰ σὺ εἶ ὁ Χριστὸς ὁ υἱὸς τοῦ θεοῦ. 64 λέγει αὐτῷ ὁ Ἰησοῦς· σὺ εἶπας· πλὴν λέγω ὑμῖν, ἀπ' ἄρτι ὄψεσθε **τὸν υἱὸν τοῦ ἀνθρώπου καθήμενον ἐκ δεξιῶν** τῆς δυνάμεως καὶ **ἐρχόμενον ἐπὶ τῶν νεφελῶν τοῦ οὐρανοῦ.**

Ps110 1 (Mt 26,64) — Dn7 13 (Mt 26,64)

cf. v. 63 f. ↑

65 τότε ὁ ἀρχιερεὺς διέρρηξεν τὰ ἱμάτια αὐτοῦ λέγων· ἐβλασφήμησεν· τί ἔτι χρείαν ἔχομεν μαρτύρων;

οἰκοδομήσω. 59 καὶ οὐδὲ οὕτως ἴση ἦν ἡ μαρτυρία αὐτῶν.

60 καὶ ἀναστὰς ὁ ἀρχιερεὺς εἰς μέσον ἐπηρώτησεν τὸν Ἰησοῦν λέγων· οὐκ ἀποκρίνῃ οὐδέν, τί οὗτοί σου καταμαρτυροῦσιν; 61 ὁ δὲ ἐσιώπα καὶ οὐκ ἀπεκρίνατο οὐδέν. πάλιν ὁ ἀρχιερεὺς ἐπηρώτα αὐτὸν καὶ λέγει αὐτῷ· σὺ εἶ ὁ Χριστὸς ὁ υἱὸς τοῦ εὐλογητοῦ; 62 ὁ δὲ Ἰησοῦς εἶπεν· ἐγώ εἰμι, καὶ ὄψεσθε **τὸν υἱὸν τοῦ ἀνθρώπου ἐκ δεξιῶν καθήμενον** τῆς δυνάμεως καὶ **ἐρχόμενον μετὰ τῶν νεφελῶν τοῦ οὐρανοῦ.**

cf. v. 61 f. ↑

63 ὁ δὲ ἀρχιερεὺς διαρρήξας τοὺς χιτῶνας αὐτοῦ λέγει· τί ἔτι χρείαν ἔχομεν μαρτύρων;

ἐγερῶ αὐτόν.

67 λέγοντες· εἰ σὺ εἶ ὁ Χριστός, εἰπὸν ἡμῖν. εἶπεν δὲ αὐτοῖς· ἐὰν ὑμῖν εἴπω, οὐ μὴ πιστεύσητε· 68 ἐὰν δὲ ἐρωτήσω, οὐ μὴ ἀποκριθῆτε.

cf. v. 70 ↓

69 ἀπὸ τοῦ νῦν δὲ ἔσται **ὁ υἱὸς τοῦ ἀνθρώπου καθήμενος ἐκ δεξιῶν** τῆς δυνάμεως τοῦ θεοῦ. *cf. 232.*

70 εἶπαν δὲ πάντες· σὺ οὖν εἶ ὁ υἱὸς τοῦ θεοῦ; ὁ δὲ πρὸς αὐτοὺς ἔφη· ὑμεῖς λέγετε ὅτι ἐγώ εἰμι. 71 οἱ δὲ εἶπαν· τί ἔτι ἔχομεν μαρτυρίας χρείαν; αὐτοὶ γὰρ

---

10 24 f.: … εἰ σὺ εἶ ὁ Χριστός, εἰπὲ ἡμῖν παρρησίᾳ. 25 ἀπεκρίθη αὐτοῖς ὁ Ἰησοῦς· εἶπον ὑμῖν, καὶ οὐ πιστεύετε …

Mt 26,61 οικ.] οικ. αυτον(-ω) ‖ Jo2 19: *Rpl* (φ346) *L*'[ek] Or[1] *S*,j — οικοδομησω αυτον ‖ p: 245 *pc* *L*q(∼) vg[1] — ● αυτον(αλλον) οικοδομησαι ‖ (Mk)Jo2 19: ℌ'C **047 090** Or *L*b(c)ff[2]hr[1] Or[1] — *txt*: B 700 **λ**⟨118⟩-1582 φ69-788-983 Θ Or *Arm* *Aeth* **62** καταμ.] καταγωρουσιν! ‖ Mk15 4: Θ **63** *om* Ι. ‖ p: σ692 E F *pc* *L*z | θε.[2] + του ζωντος ‖ 63a 16 16: C* ΝΣΦ λ209 σ1293 W Δ Θ **090** 157 *al* *l*6 *l*44 *l*184[1] *L*ff[2]r[2]30 vg[5] *S*hj[c] *C*s[4:8]b *Aeth* *Δ*a[BE](A *et* + του ευλογητου ‖ Mk) i[T1](= a[A])[V] n[Hg] **64** ειπ. + οτι εγω ειμι ‖ Lk Mk: Φ Δ *l*22 | επι] μετα ‖ Mk: 700 *L*[ek]abcff[2]30 *Geo* **65** μαρτυριων ‖ Lk: ℵ

Mk 14,60 ουκ—ουδ.] ουδ. αποκ. ‖ p: 579 28 Or *L*k[e] a **61** ο δε + Ιησους ‖ p: ℵ-579(και ο Ι.) 565 λ1278 σ1402 A Or *S*p[5] | και[1]—ουδ.] ● και(*om*) ουδ. απεκ. ‖ p 15 5 Mt27 12 Lk23 9: *Rpl* (579) *L*'(dq) Or[1] — *om* ‖ p: *L*k[e] az *C*b[1] — *txt*: ℌ'⟨Δ⟩C 544(*om* ουδ.)-1071 1342 Or[1] *C*s[9]([1] *om* και)b' *Aeth* | απεκριθη ‖ 15 5 Mt27 14: D | παλ.—αυτω] και λεγ. αυτω ο αρχ. ‖ Mt: D *L*a(*om* ο αρχ.)q | *om* αυτω ‖ Lk: 892 ΘΦ-565-700 *pc* *l*184 Or *L*cff[2]z *S*p *C*s[3:11] *Geo*[1.A] | συ] ει συ ‖ p: 440 1542 | υι. + του θεου ‖ Mt: φ346 σ827 A K Y Π 1342[c] *al* *L*30 vg[9] *Arm*⟨pc⟩ | ευλο.] θεου ‖ Mt: ℵ*-579 566[c] *Aeth* — ζωντος ‖ Mt63a: 38 1355 — ευλογημενου: Ψ W-28 *pc* **62** ειπ.] λεγει ‖ Mt: WΘ-565 D Or *L*cff[2]z *Aeth* | ειπ./λε. + αυτω ‖ Mt: WΘ-565-1071 **λ φ** D G *pc* *l*184 Or *L*⟨k[e]⟩ *S* *C*s[5:10]b[8] *Geo*[1.A] | εγω] συ ειπας οτι εγω ‖ p: Θ-565-700-1071 **φ** *pc* Or *Arm* | ∼ καθ. εκ δε. ‖ Mt Lk: 33-579 1071 λ1-872 σ945-1223 A **067** *pc* Or[1:2] *L*k[e] cfff[2]r[2]z30 *S* | δυν. + του θεου ‖ Lk: 157 *L*vg[1] *C*s[1:9] *Arm*[0] | μετα] επι ‖ Mt64 24 30: 33-579 28 **λ**-22 σ7-349-517-659-1082 G *pc* *l*18 *l*19 *l*49 *L*ar[2] *S*s[c]p *C*s **63** διαρ. … λεγ.] διερρηξεν … λεγων ‖ Mt: 579(λεγει) 565(διαρρηξας) σ517-659-1606 *L*a *C*s | τ. χιτ.] τα ιματια ‖ Mt: 579 1342 *L* *C*

Lk 22,67 ∼ ειπ. ημ. ει συ ει ο Χριστος ‖ Mt: 472 | *om* ει[1] ‖ Mk: L σ1223 D *pc* | *om*: ειπ. ημ. ‖ Mk: D 61 **69** εστ.—καθ.] οψεσθε τον υιον του αν. καθημενον ‖ p: 579 157 *C*b[1] | *om* τ. θε. ‖ p: 64 *L*e l vg[2] Or — ∼ τ. θε. της δυν.: φ69 **70** δε[1] + αυτω ‖ p: φ983-1689 *pc* *L*a *S*p[1](*om* δε) | *om* ουν ‖ Mk: Λ λ209 φ69-124-174-*l*547 D K *pc* *L*e a vg[1] *C*s[4:10]b[2] | πρ. αυ. εφη] ειπεν αυτοις (*om*) ‖ Mk Mt: D *L*'(z vg⟨1⟩) **71** ∼ χρ. εχ. μαρ. ‖ p: *Rpl* *L* — *txt*: 𝔓[75] BLT-579-1241 | μαρτυρων ‖ Mt Mk: 28-1071-1604 λ118 φ69-983 σ659 D Ψ *pc* *S*p *C*sb[5] | αυ. γαρ ηκ.] ηκ. γαρ ‖ p: D *L*e abil — ιδου γαρ ηκ.: *S*sc

Matth	Mark	Luk	Jo
ἴδε νῦν ἠκούσατε τὴν βλασφημίαν· 66 τί ὑμῖν δοκεῖ; οἱ δὲ ἀποκριθέντες εἶπον· ἔνοχος θανάτου ἐστίν.	64 ἠκούσατε τῆς βλασφημίας· τί ὑμῖν φαίνεται; οἱ δὲ πάντες κατέκριναν αὐτὸν εἶναι ἔνοχον θανάτου.	ἠκούσαμεν ἀπὸ τοῦ στόματος αὐτοῦ.	
67 τότε ἐνέπτυσαν εἰς τὸ πρόσωπον αὐτοῦ καὶ ἐκολάφισαν αὐτόν, οἱ δὲ ἐρράπισαν 68 λέγοντες· προφήτευσον ἡμῖν, Χριστέ, τίς ἐστιν ὁ παίσας σε;	65 καὶ ἤρξαντό τινες ἐμπτύειν αὐτῷ καὶ περικαλύπτειν αὐτοῦ τὸ πρόσωπον καὶ κολαφίζειν αὐτὸν καὶ λέγειν αὐτῷ· προφήτευσον, καὶ οἱ ὑπηρέται ῥαπίσμασιν αὐτὸν ἔλαβον.	*63 καὶ οἱ ἄνδρες οἱ συνέχοντες αὐτὸν ἐνέπαιζον αὐτῷ δέροντες, 64 καὶ περικαλύψαντες αὐτὸν ἐπηρώτων λέγοντες· προφήτευσον, τίς ἐστιν ὁ παίσας σε; 65 καὶ ἕτερα πολλὰ βλασφημοῦντες ἔλεγον εἰς αὐτόν ...*	18 17. 22-27: 22 ταῦτα δὲ αὐτοῦ εἰπόντος εἷς παρεστηκὼς τῶν ὑπηρετῶν ἔδωκεν ῥάπισμα τῷ Ἰησοῦ εἰπών· οὕτως ἀποκρίνῃ τῷ ἀρχιερεῖ; 23 ἀπεκρίθη αὐτῷ Ἰησοῦς· εἰ κακῶς ἐλάλησα, μαρτύρησον περὶ τοῦ κακοῦ· εἰ δὲ καλῶς, τί με δέρεις; 24 ἀπέστειλεν οὖν αὐτὸν ὁ Ἅννας δεδεμένον πρὸς Καϊάφαν τὸν ἀρχιερέα ...
69 ὁ δὲ Πέτρος ἐκάθητο ἔξω ἐν τῇ αὐλῇ· καὶ προσῆλθεν αὐτῷ μία παιδίσκη λέγουσα· καὶ σὺ ἦσθα μετὰ Ἰησοῦ τοῦ Γαλιλαίου.	66 καὶ ὄντος τοῦ Πέτρου κάτω ἐν τῇ αὐλῇ ἔρχεται μία τῶν παιδισκῶν τοῦ ἀρχιερέως, 67 καὶ ἰδοῦσα τὸν Πέτρον θερμαινόμενον ἐμβλέψασα αὐτῷ λέγει· καὶ σὺ μετὰ τοῦ Ναζαρηνοῦ Ἰησοῦ ἦσθα.	*56 ἰδοῦσα δὲ αὐτὸν παιδίσκη τις καθήμενον πρὸς τὸ φῶς καὶ ἀτενίσασα αὐτῷ εἶπεν· καὶ οὗτος σὺν αὐτῷ ἦν.*	17 λέγει οὖν τῷ Πέτρῳ ἡ παιδίσκη ἡ θυρωρός· μὴ καὶ σὺ ἐκ τῶν μαθητῶν εἶ τοῦ ἀνθρώπου τού-

Mt 26,65 της βλασφημιας‖Mk: **090** 157 | βλασ. +(*prm*) εκ του στοματος αυτου‖Lk: Φ (*S*s[c]) — ● + αυτου: *Rpl* Or *L*bff^{2}g^{2}qr^{2}30 vg^4 *S*'j^{ab} — *txt*: ℵBLZ 700 D *L*'[ek] Au *S*p^{1}j^c *C* **66** αποκ.] απεκριθησαν παντες και‖Mk: D *L*[ek]abch(r^2)30 vg^1 *S*s[c] *C*b^1 **67** *om* αυτον—ερρα.(^{67a}⌒^{67b} -ισαν?)‖p: 1241 *L*[ek]abff^{2}r^2 **69** Γ.] Ναζωραιου‖71 Mk: C **047** *pc* *S*pj^{c1}

Mk 14,64 ηκου.] ιδε νυν ηκ.‖Mt: ℵ — ιδου ηκ.‖Mt: 122 252 *S*s[c](ιδ. + γαρ)p | την βλασφημιαν‖Mt: WΘ-565 λ1 **φ** σ1194 A D G **067** *al l*13 *l*17 | βλα. + αυτου: NΣ-1071 **λ**-22 σ115-179-827 D G **067** *al L*qr^{2}30 vg^3 *S*s[c] *C*s^3 *Geo*^{1} *Aeth* — + του(εκ του) στοματος αυτου‖Lk: WΘ(αυτος) **φ**'-230-1689 *S*p(∼ εκ τ. στ. αυ. ηκ. τ. βλ.)h^m *C*s^5 *Arm* (*Geo*^{2}) — + αυτου εκ τ. στ. αυ.‖Lk: 565 **φ**124 *C*s^1 | φαι.] δοκει‖Mt: NΘΣ-28-565 D 1542 *l*13 *l*14 *l*17 | ● ∼ ενοχ. ειν.‖Mt: ℌC 1071(∼ θαν. ειν.) σ945 1342 *L*lq vg^1 — *om* ειν.: D *L*ff^2 *Geo*^{2} — *txt*: *Rpl L*' **65** εμπτ.] εμπαιζειν‖Lk: 108 *L*c vg^1 | αυτω^1] τω προσωπω αυτου‖Mt: D *L*af *S*p — αυτω τω πρ.‖Mt: Θ-565-700 | *om* και^2—προσ.‖Mt: D *L*af *S*s[c] *C*b^2 | ∼ το προσ. αυτου‖Mt: *Rpl* — *txt*: ℌC 1071(αυτω) **φ**788 σ517 U 1342 *pc* | κολ.] εκολαφιζον‖Mt: D *L*k[e]ac vg^1 *C*s$^{1:9}$ | *om* αυτω^2‖MtLk: W **λ**⟨118⟩ **φ** **067** *L*ff^2 vg^2 *S*s[c]p *C*s$^{1:10}$ | προφ. + ημιν Χριστε(*om*)‖Mt: XΔ(Ψ)-33-579-892 NΘΣ-700-1071(πρ. + νυν ημ. X.) σ(7)-71-115-179-349-517-692-1391-1606 (F^W) U *al* (*l*^{p1} *L*k[e] cfz Au) *S*h ημιν$^+$ *C*s^7(^{3})(^{1}πρ. + ημ. νυν X.)(b$^{\langle 5\rangle}$) *Arm Aeth* — + νυν X.(*om*): W **λ**-22 **φ**'(νυν] ουν: 346) G 495 — + ημιν νυν: *S*s[c] | και^5 *prm* τις εστιν ο παισας σε‖MtLk: XΔ(πεμψας)-33-579-892 NWΘΣ-565-700-1071 **φ** σ-7-115-349-517-1391-1606 U **067** *al l*^{p1} *L*30 Au *C*s$^{8:11}$b'(σε + νυν X.)(σε + X.: b^1) *Arm Aeth* **66** *om* κατω‖p: Ψ 565 **φ**69 **D 067** *pc* Eu *L*acff^{2}q *S*s^v[c] Eu *C*s$^{1:10}$ *Geo* | τ. παι.] παιδισκη‖MtLk: ℵC 1342 *S*s[c](∼)p *C*s$^{1:10}$b^1 | *om* τ. αρχ.‖**p**: 1047 **67** τ. Π.] αυτον‖Lk: 565-700 **λ φ**⟨124⟩ 1542 Eu *L*c *S*s[c](∼)p Eu | *om* θερ.‖Mt: σ517 | μετα—ησθα] με. τ. Ι. ησ. του N.‖Mt70f.: ℵ *S*s[c]p Eu — με. του(*om*) Ι. τ. N. ησ.‖←: Δ-(579 σ7-179-1082-1391) D 44 (*al l*14 *l*17 *l*36 *l*251) *l*49 Eu (ησ.] ης) *L Arm Aeth* — ησ. με. Ι. τ. N.‖←: 33 *C*,f^v *Geo*^{2} — ● με. τ. N. ησ. τ. Ι.: ℌ'C Θ 1342(*om* του^2) — *txt*: *Rpl* (*om* Ι.: 54 *pc l*19; ησ.] ης: 565-700 **λ**⟨118⟩ **φ**⟨124⟩) *Geo*^{1} | Ναζωραιου‖Mt71: Δ Θ σ179-827-1082 *pc l*14 *l*17 *l*36 *l*251 Eu *L*ff^2 vg^1 *C*s$^{7:9}$b *Geo*^{1} — Ναζωρηνου: D(-ζο-) σ115-1424 *pc L*k[e] lq

Lk 22,71 απο] εκ‖11 54 19 22: **λ** σ954 241

Jo 18,23 Ι.] ● ο Ι.: *Rpl* (ο δε Ι. ειπεν αυτω *et om* απεκ.: ℵW-579 **φ**-*l*547 *pc*) — *txt*: BC*L-1241 Θ *pc*

[70] ὁ δὲ ἠρνήσατο ἔμπροσθεν πάντων λέγων· οὐκ οἶδα τί λέγεις. [71] ἐξελθόντα δὲ αὐτὸν εἰς τὸν πυλῶνα εἶδεν αὐτὸν ἄλλη καὶ λέγει τοῖς ἐκεῖ· οὗτος ἦν μετὰ Ἰησοῦ τοῦ Ναζωραίου. [72] καὶ πάλιν ἠρνήσατο μετὰ ὅρκου ὅτι οὐκ οἶδα τὸν ἄνθρωπον. [73] μετὰ μικρὸν δὲ προσελθόντες οἱ ἑστῶτες εἶπον τῷ Πέτρῳ· ἀληθῶς καὶ σὺ ἐξ αὐτῶν εἶ, καὶ γὰρ ἡ λαλιά σου δῆλόν σε ποιεῖ. [74] τότε

[68] ὁ δὲ ἠρνήσατο λέγων· οὔτε οἶδα οὔτε ἐπίσταμαι σὺ τί λέγεις. καὶ ἐξῆλθεν ἔξω εἰς τὸ προαύλιον· καὶ ἀλέκτωρ ἐφώνησεν. [69] καὶ ἡ παιδίσκη ἰδοῦσα αὐτὸν ἤρξατο πάλιν λέγειν τοῖς παρεστῶσιν ὅτι οὗτος ἐξ αὐτῶν ἐστιν. [70] ὁ δὲ πάλιν ἠρνεῖτο. καὶ μετὰ μικρὸν πάλιν οἱ παρεστῶτες ἔλεγον τῷ Πέτρῳ· ἀληθῶς ἐξ αὐτῶν εἶ· καὶ γὰρ Γαλιλαῖος εἶ. [71] ὁ δὲ

[57] ὁ δὲ ἠρνήσατο αὐτὸν λέγων· οὐκ οἶδα αὐτόν, γύναι. *[58] καὶ μετὰ βραχὺ ἕτερος ἰδὼν αὐτὸν ἔφη· καὶ σὺ ἐξ αὐτῶν εἶ. ὁ δὲ Πέτρος ἔφη· ἄνθρωπε, οὐκ εἰμί.* *[59] καὶ διαστάσης ὡσεὶ ὥρας μιᾶς ἄλλος τις διϊσχυρίζετο λέγων· ἐπ' ἀληθείας καὶ οὗτος μετ' αὐτοῦ ἦν, καὶ γὰρ Γαλιλαῖός ἐστιν.* *[60] εἶπεν δὲ ὁ Πέ-*

του; λέγει ἐκεῖνος· οὐκ εἰμί ... [25] ἦν δὲ Σίμων Πέτρος ἑστὼς καὶ θερμαινόμενος. εἶπαν οὖν αὐτῷ· μὴ καὶ σὺ ἐκ τῶν μαθητῶν αὐτοῦ εἶ; ἠρνήσατο ἐκεῖνος καὶ εἶπεν· οὐκ εἰμί. [26] λέγει εἷς ἐκ τῶν δούλων τοῦ ἀρχιερέως, συγγενὴς ὢν οὗ ἀπέκοψεν Πέτρος τὸ ὠτίον· οὐκ ἐγώ σε εἶδον ἐν τῷ κήπῳ μετ' αὐτοῦ; [27] πάλιν οὖν ἠρνήσατο Πέ-

Mt 26,70 τι λεγ.] τον ανθρωπον ‖ 72.74 Mk71 Lk57: **σ** | λεγεις + ουδε επισταμαι ‖ Mk: **λ**-1582 D Δ(ουτε) **090** *L*[ek]abnr[1.2]30.32 Cp(επ.] οιδα σε) *S*s[c]j **71** εξελθοντα ... αυτον ... αυτον] -ντος ... -ου ... -ον: Φ D *l*17 *L*'[ek](exeunte ... illum ... eum!: ff[2]) — -ντων ... -ων(*om*) ... -ον: σ659-(1010-1293) *pc* — ● *om* αυτον[1]: 𝔥 ϕ13 *pc* *L*(egressus ... *om* ... illum!: an) — *om* αυτον[2]: **λ**⟨118⟩ Θ 1012 — *txt*: *Rpl* *L*b g[1](exeuntem illo ... eum)r[1] {*S*,j *C*} | τοις] ● αυτοις: *Rpl* *L*q(eis ibi) Or(αυτω) *S*(*om* εκει: s[c])p — *txt*: ℵB Φ ϕ⟨124-346⟩-174-230-*l*547[1] σ1010 D E[c] G K S W Θ Π Ω *al* *L*'[ek] *S*hj | ουτ. *prm* και ‖ LkJo: *Rpl* Chr *L*[ek],Or *S*'j *C*b(αυτος) *Geo*[A] — *txt*: ℵB D 1355 *S*s[c] *Cs* *Geo*' | Ναζαρηνου ‖ Mk67: **λ**⟨118(Ναζ *et spat.*)⟩-1582 *L*'[ek]⟨ff[2]l vg[1]⟩(-ωρην-: qr[1] vg[1]) Or *Aeth* — Γαλιλαιου ‖ 69: **047** 1093 *l*183[1] *Lr*[2] **72** *om* με. ορκ. ‖ MkLk: *l*184 **73** δε + παλιν ‖ Mk: **λ**-1582 **σ** 157 | ειπ.] ελεγον ‖ Mk: Σ | *om* και συ (*et* ει + συ) ‖ Mk: λ1-1582 D Θ *L*(vl[ek]⟨fff[2]g[1]z⟩r[1]32)30 Or[1](1) | γαρ + Γαλιλαιος ει και ‖ p: C*Σ *S*h[+] **74** τοτε—ομν.] και ηρνησατο και ωμοσεν και κατηρασατο ‖ 70p.72 Mk70 Jo27: 4 273 EN↓

Mk 14,68 ηρν. + αυτον ‖ Lk: λ872 σM Y *al* | ουτε ... ουτε] ουκ ... ουδε(ουκ) ‖ p: *Rpl* **(067)** *La* vg[2] *S*' — ουκ ... ουτε ‖ p: CΔ 28-544 λ1-22 ϕ'⟨828⟩ σ115-692-1082-1194-1402-1606 E G H S V 157 *pm* — *om* ουτε επ. ‖ p: *Lk*[e] vg[1] *S*p — *txt*: ℵBLΨ-892 WΘ-565-700-1071 **λ**'-1582 ϕ124 D 1342 Eu *L*' *C* *Geo*[1] | οιδα + αυτον ‖ Lk: 42 *Cs* | ● ∼ τι συ ‖ Mt: *Rpl* Eu — *om* συ ‖ Mt: 544 D *pc* — *txt*: 𝔥C NWΣ-565-1071 **λ** σ115-517 U *pc* | ● *om* και[2]—εφω. ‖ p: 𝔥⟨Δ-33⟩ W *l*17 *l*76 *Lc* *S*s[c] *Cs*[5]b' *Geo*[1] — και[2] + ευθεως ‖ Mt74 Jo27: σ517-1606 *pc* *C*b[1] *Geo*[B] — *txt*: Eu *L*' *S*'Eu *Cs*[6](∼ κ.[2] αλ. εφω. και[1]—προαυ.) *Geo*[A] **69** οτι] και ‖ Lk56: 579 σ115 1574 *S*s[c] — οτι και ‖ ←: Θ-565-700 **ϕ** σ349-1424 D' *al* *L*acff[2]z vg[1] *S*p *Geo*[2] — *om* ‖ Mt: Eu | εξ αυ. εστ.] μετ αυτου ην ‖ MtLk59: 579 **70** ηρνησατο ‖ Mt: XΔ-579 NWΣ-565-700 **λ** **ϕ** σM-179-827-945 D G 1342 *al* *l*7 *l*13 *l*17 *l*49 Eu *L*'(*om* ο—ηρν.: d) Au *S*s[c]p *Cs*b⟨3⟩ | *om* παλ.[2] ‖ Mt: Ψ *L*Au *Cs*[11:12] *Geo* | περιερτωτες(-ηκοτες): (W) λ1 G 495 *La* *Arm* — εστωτες ‖ Mt: 1574 *Lk*[e] dq — *txt* (-ηκοτες): *Rpl* (ϕ124 D) Eu *L*'Au | ελ.] ειπον ‖ Mt: L 17 *L*cff[2]qz *S*s[c]p *Cs* | αλη. + και συ ‖ p: σM *La*(*om* αλ.) vg[2](*om* και) | και[2]—ει] και γαρ η λαλια σου δηλον σε ποιει ‖ Mt: 579 — κ. η λαλ. σε ομοιαζει ‖ Mt: ϕ543 σ1675 *pc* — ● + κ. η λαλ. σε ομοι.(δηλοι) ‖ Mt: *Rpl* (NΣ) (*om* η: Δ; δηλον σε ομοι.!: 33) *Lq* *S*' *C*b[2](4 *om* και) — *om* ‖ Mt: W *pc* *La* *Cs*[1] — *txt*: 𝔥'⟨892⟩C 565-700 **λ** D 1342 Eu *L*' *S*s[c] Eu *Cs*[11]b' *Geo*

Jo 18,25 *cf. ad* 16 | *om* Σ. ‖ Mt69 Mk66 Lk55: X *pc* Chr | ειπαν] ειπεν ‖ Lk56: Λ 1187 *Lg*[2] *Cs*[1:11] **26** ωταριον ‖ 18: 579 **27** Π.] ● ο Π.: 𝔓[60v?] *Rpl* {} — *om*: 565 *L*e ab *Ca*[s] — *txt*: 𝔥⟨ℵ-33⟩C*-**054** Λ-700 λ1-22 σ7-945-1010-1194-1424 A D[s] E G K Y Γ Λ Π Ψ *al* Cr *L*' {*C*[+B]}

Mt2674p *cf.* EN frgm.19 (Codd. Evv. 566[m] 899[m] 1424[m]): Τὸ Ἰουδαϊκόν· καὶ ἠρνήσατο καὶ ὤμοσεν καὶ κατηράσατο.

Matth	Mark	Luk	Jo
ἤρξατο καταθεματίζειν καὶ ὀμνύειν ὅτι οὐκ οἶδα τὸν ἄνθρωπον. καὶ εὐθὺς ἀλέκτωρ ἐφώνησεν.	ἤρξατο ἀναθεματίζειν καὶ ὀμνύναι ὅτι οὐκ οἶδα τὸν ἄνθρωπον τοῦτον ὃν λέγετε. [72] καὶ ἐκ δευτέρου ἀλέκτωρ ἐφώνησεν.	*τρος· ἄνθρωπε, οὐκ οἶδα ὃ λέγεις. καὶ παραχρῆμα ἔτι λαλοῦντος αὐτοῦ ἐφώνησεν*	τρος, καὶ εὐθὺς ἀλέκτωρ ἐφώνησεν.
[75] καὶ ἐμνήσθη ὁ Πέτρος τοῦ ῥήματος Ἰησοῦ εἰρηκότος ὅτι πρὶν ἀλέκτορα φωνῆσαι τρὶς ἀπαρνήσῃ με· καὶ ἐξελθὼν ἔξω ἔκλαυσεν πικρῶς.	καὶ ἀνεμνήσθη ὁ Πέτρος τὸ ῥῆμα ὃ εἶπεν αὐτῷ ὁ Ἰησοῦς ὅτι πρὶν ἀλέκτορα φωνῆσαι δὶς τρίς με ἀπαρνήσῃ· καὶ ἐπιβαλὼν ἔκλαιεν.	*ἀλέκτωρ. [61] καὶ στραφεὶς ὁ κύριος ἐνέβλεψεν τῷ Πέτρῳ, καὶ ὑπεμνήσθη ὁ Πέτρος τοῦ λόγου τοῦ κυρίου, ὡς εἶπεν αὐτῷ ὅτι πρὶν ἀλέκτορα φωνῆσαι σήμερον ἀπαρνήσῃ με τρίς. [62] καὶ ἐξελθὼν ἔξω ἔκλαυσεν πικρῶς.*	

(242) ***257.*** **Übergabe des Verurteilten an Pilatus.** ***Jesus Delivered to Pilate.***

Matth 27 ₁₋₂	Mark 15 ₁	Luk 23 ₁₋₂	Jo
[1] Πρωΐας δὲ γενομένης συμβούλιον ἔλαβον πάντες οἱ ἀρχιερεῖς καὶ οἱ πρεσβύτεροι τοῦ λαοῦ κατὰ τοῦ	[1] Καὶ εὐθὺς πρωῒ συμβούλιον ποιήσαντες οἱ ἀρχιερεῖς μετὰ τῶν πρεσβυτέρων	*22 66 (256.): καὶ ὡς ἐγένετο ἡμέρα, συνήχθη τὸ πρεσβυτέριον τοῦ λαοῦ, ἀρχιερεῖς τε*	18 ₂₈₋₃₂: Ἄγουσιν οὖν τὸν Ἰησοῦν ἀπὸ τοῦ Καϊάφα εἰς τὸ πραιτώριον· ἦν δὲ πρωΐ· καὶ αὐτοὶ οὐκ εἰσῆλθον εἰς τὸ πραιτώριον, ἵνα μὴ μιανθῶσιν ἀλλὰ φάγωσιν τὸ πασχα. [29] ἐξῆλθεν οὖν ὁ Πιλᾶτος ἔξω πρὸς αὐτοὺς καὶ φησίν· τίνα κατηγορίαν φέρετε κατὰ τοῦ ἀνθρώπου τούτου; [30] ἀπεκρίθησαν καὶ εἶπαν

Mt 26,74 καταναθεμ.‖Mk: Φ *pc* **75** ειρ. + αυτω‖p: *Rpl* (αυτου: ϕ*l*547¹) *L*bfq Or *S*,j *Cs*¹b *Geo*² — *txt*: ℌ D *pc L*'[ek a] *Cs*⁶⁺¹ᵛ *Arm Geo*¹ | πριν + η‖Mk14₃₀: A *pc* | αλ. φω.] αλεκτοροφωνιας‖Mk13₃₅: λ⟨118⟩-1582 | ∼ απαρ. με τρ.‖Lk: ϕ69 *Arm* **27,1** δε + ηδη‖Jo21₄: 348 *l*183¹ *L*vg¹ | *om* τ. λαου‖Mk: 241 *al l*54 *Cs*¹:⁸b¹ | *om* κατα τ. l.‖22₁₅Mk: Φ ϕ*l*547¹ σ1424 *l*47 *Cs*¹:⁷b *Aeth*

Mk 14,71 καταθεμ.‖Mt: 565 σ1223-1402 *pc* | ● ομνυειν‖Mt: ℌ⟨BL-892⟩C NWΘΣ-28-565-1071 λ-22 ϕ-230 σM-267-349-517-827-1606 A G K Π 157 1342 *mu* Eu | *om* του. ον λεγ.‖Mt: ℵ 544 1588 *Lk*[e](*om* ον λεγ.) — *om* του.‖Lk: ΝΣ λ⟨1⟩ σ27-1207 D' K *pc Lr*² *Sp*¹ *Cs*²:⁹⁺¹? **72** εκ δευ.] ευθυς(-εως)‖p: ℵ (C*ᵛ)L-(579) *Lc* vg¹ — ● ευθεως(-υς) εκ δευ.‖Mt: (B) WΘ-(565)-700 ϕ σ1606 D G 1342(εκ δ.] δις) *pc* Eu *L*'Au *Sp* Eu *Cs*¹b¹ — *txt*: *Rpl S*' *Cs*¹⁰b' | ανεμ.] εμνησθη‖Mt: 579 544-565 σ349-659-1424 *al l*251 | του ρηματος‖MtLk: 579 W-28-700 λ ϕ σM-659-954 | ο²—l.] ● ως ειπ. αυ. ο(*om*) l.‖Lk: ℌ'(Ψ)C 1071 σ1223 A 1342 *al Cs*⁵b — του Ιησου ο ειπ. αυ.‖p: 28(*om* του) σ1424 *Lvg*¹ *Sp Cs*¹ *Arm*ᵖᶜ(*om* αυ.) — του Ιησου ειποντος‖Mt: 579(*om* ειπ.) λ *Sh*ᵗ(ειποντος αυτω τ. l.) — ου ειπεν αυ. ο l.: W-700 ϕ-230 σM-954 1542 {} — *txt*: *Rpl* (*om* αυ.: D Θ; *om* ο³: σ1606) {*L*'Au *Ss*[c]hᵐ *Cs*⁴ *Arm*' *Geo*²[¹]} | ● ∼ δις φω.: B Θ-565-700 1342 1542 *Lk*[e] *Arm*⟨ᵖᶜ⟩ | *om* δις‖**p**: ℵC*ᵛ Δ-579 WΣ 251 *L*cff²lq vg¹ Au *Cs*²:¹⁰b¹ *Geo Aeth* | ∼ απαρ. με τρ.‖Lk: *Rpl Sh C* — τρ. απαρ. με‖Mt: 579 1342 {} *Geo*ᴬ(ᴮ *om* τρ.)[¹] — *txt*: ℌ'⟨33⟩C W *L*⟨a⟩ Au {*Ss*[c]p *Aeth*} | επιβ. εκλ.] εξελθων εξω εκλ. πικρως‖p: 579 *Sj*ᶠᵛ | εκλαυσεν‖**p**: ℵ*C-579 1342(εκλασεν) *S*ᶠ *C*⟨b¹⟩ **15,1** ευθ.] ευθ. εγενετο‖p: σ1424(συμβ. + δε) *C*b¹fᵛ — εγενετο‖p: *L*cz *Cs* — *om*‖p: *Ss*[c] | πρωι] ● επι το(τω) πρ.: *Rpl* (700-1071 ϕ346-543-828 σ659-1402 E S Ω *al*) (εν τω πρ.: **047**) — *txt*: ℵBCLΨ-892 Θ-565 σ267(το πρ.)-1424 D 1342 *pc* Or | ποι.] ● ετοιμασ.: ℵCL-892 1342 — λαβοντες‖Mt: *l*13 (ελαβον: *Ss*[c]) — εποιησαν‖p: Θ-565 σ827 D **047** *pc l*ᵖᵐ Or {*Lvl*'[e] *S*'j} — *txt*: *Rpl Llr*² vg Au {} | ∼ γρα. ... πρε.‖11₂₇14₄₃Mt27₄₁: C 1342(και οι γραμματεις μετα των πρε.) *l*47 *Lz Sp*¹ *Cs*¹fᵛ | πρε. + και των αρχιερεων‖8₃₁pLk: σ1082

Jo 18,28 πρωια‖Mt: **054** N-28 λ2193 ϕ124-230 σ-7-349-1010-1223 E G H K S Y Γ Θ Π Ω **047** *pm* Chr **29** ● *om* κατα‖Lk2: ℵB-579 *Le* q

Matth	Mark	Luk	Jo
Ἰησοῦ ὥστε θανατῶσαι αὐτόν· 2 καὶ δήσαντες αὐτὸν ἀπήγαγον καὶ παρέδωκαν Ποντίῳ Πιλάτῳ τῷ ἡγεμόνι.	καὶ γραμματέων καὶ ὅλον τὸ συνέδριον, δήσαντες τὸν Ἰησοῦν ἀπήνεγκαν καὶ παρέδωκαν Πιλάτῳ.	*καὶ γραμματεῖς, καὶ ἀπήγαγον αὐτὸν εἰς τὸ συνέδριον αὐτῶν, ...* 1 καὶ ἀναστὰν ἅπαν τὸ πλῆθος αὐτῶν ἤγαγον αὐτὸν ἐπὶ τὸν Πιλᾶτον. 2 ἤρξαντο δὲ κατηγορεῖν αὐτοῦ λέγοντες· τοῦτον εὕρομεν διαστρέφοντα τὸ ἔθνος ἡμῶν καὶ κωλύοντα φόρους Καίσαρι διδόναι, καὶ λέγοντα ἑαυτὸν Χριστὸν βασιλέα εἶναι.	αὐτῷ· εἰ μὴ ἦν οὗτος κακοποιός, οὐκ ἄν σοι παρεδώκαμεν αὐτόν. 31 εἶπεν οὖν αὐτοῖς ὁ Πιλᾶτος· λάβετε αὐτὸν ὑμεῖς, καὶ κατὰ τὸν νόμον ὑμῶν κρίνατε. εἶπον οὖν αὐτῷ οἱ Ἰουδαῖοι· ἡμῖν οὐκ ἔξεστιν ἀποκτεῖναι οὐδένα· 32 ἵνα ὁ λόγος τοῦ Ἰησοῦ πληρωθῇ ὃν εἶπεν σημαίνων ποίῳ θανάτῳ ἤμελλεν ἀποθνῄσκειν.

(243) **258.** Das Ende des Judas. *The Death of Judas.* **Matth 27** 3–10

3 Τότε ἰδὼν Ἰούδας ὁ παραδιδοὺς αὐτὸν ὅτι κατεκρίθη, μεταμεληθεὶς ἀπέστρεψεν τὰ τριάκοντα ἀργύρια τοῖς ἀρχιερεῦσιν καὶ πρεσβυτέροις 4 λέγων· ἥμαρτον παραδοὺς αἷμα ἀθῷον. οἱ δὲ εἶπον· τί πρὸς ἡμᾶς; σὺ ὄψῃ. 5 καὶ **ῥίψας τὰ ἀργύρια εἰς τὸν ναὸν** ἀνεχώρησεν, καὶ ἀπελθὼν ἀπήγξατο. 6 οἱ δὲ ἀρχιερεῖς λαβόντες τὰ ἀργύρια εἶπαν· οὐκ ἔξεστιν βαλεῖν αὐτὰ **εἰς τὸν κορβανᾶν,** ἐπεὶ τιμὴ αἵματός ἐστιν. 7 συμβούλιον δὲ λαβόντες ἠγόρασαν ἐξ αὐτῶν τὸν ἀγρὸν τοῦ κεραμέως εἰς ταφὴν τοῖς ξένοις. 8 διὸ ἐκλήθη ὁ ἀγρὸς ἐκεῖνος ἀγρὸς αἵματος ἕως τῆς σήμερον. 9 τότε ἐπληρώθη τὸ ῥηθὲν διὰ Ἰερεμίου τοῦ προφήτου λέγοντος· **καὶ ἔλαβον τὰ τριάκοντα ἀργύρια, τὴν τιμὴν τοῦ τετιμημένου ὃν ἐτιμήσαντο ἀπὸ** υἱῶν Ισραηλ, 10 **καὶ ἔδωκαν αὐτὰ εἰς** τὸν ἀγρὸν τοῦ **κεραμέως,** καθὰ **συνέταξέν μοι κύριος.**

(Zch11 13; Zch11 13)

Mt 27,1 ωστε] οπως‖26 59: S | ωστε θα.] ινα θανατωσωσιν‖←: D | ∼ αυ. θαν.‖←: ϕ69 1279 *L*[ek]⟨hr^1? vg^1⟩ Or **2** ● παρεδ. + αυτον: *Rpl* *L*vg^3 Or *S*'h$^-$j *C* *Geo*^{2} — *txt*: ℵBC*L-33 Σ-1604 **λ**⟨1⟩ ϕ983-1689 σ1194-1402 K *al l*184 Eu Or *L*'[ek] *Arm* *Geo*^{1} | ● *om* Πο.] Mk Lk: ℵBL-33 Σ Eu Or Pt^A *S*'j^{c1} *C* — *txt*: *Rpl* *L*[ek],Au Diod Or *S*hj^{abc1} *Arm* *Aeth*(∼ Πι. Πο.) **3** ● παραδους: BL-33 259 *C* | απεστ.] ● εστρεψεν: ℵBL 544 1375 *l*184^1 Or — *txt*: *Rpl* Ep Eu **8** εκειν. + Ακελδαμαχ, τουτ εστιν‖Act1 19: *L*'[ek]⟨f⟩d(*om* τουτ εσ.: vg^5) Or *S*j^1 | εως] μεχρι‖28 15: 348

Mk 15,1 γρα. + του λαου‖p: 579 | δησ. τ. Ι.] και δ. τ. Ι.‖Mt: Θ-565 D **0250** *pc l*^{pm} Or {*L*vl'[e]⟨lr^2⟩ *S*s[c]p *C*s$^{11:12}$ *Aeth*} — κατα του Ιησου και δ. αυτον‖Mt: 1579 *l*7 *l*9 *l*12 *l*14 | απην.] απηγαγον‖p: C-892 NWΘΣ-565-700 **λ** ϕ124-*l*547 σ179-517-1675 D G *pc l*13 *l*17 Or | Π.] τω Π.‖Lk: *Rpl* {} — Ποντιω Π.‖Mt: 495 1047 *L*vg^1 — *txt*: ℵBCLΔΨ-892 Θ-565-700 **λ σ**⟨954⟩-179 D 1342 *pc* Or {*L*' *S*,j}

Lk 23,1 αν.—αυτων] ανασταντες‖p: D *pc* | απαν] ολον‖Mk: L *La* **2** *om* ημ.‖23 5.14: *Rpl* (*om* το εθ. ημ.: λ1) Cr Eu Mcn^{Ep} Thd^C *La*r^1 — *txt*: 𝔓^{75} 𝔋T-**0124** N-1071-1604 **λ**'⟨209⟩-2193 **ϕ**-174-230-*l*547 σM D H K R Y Π Ψ *mu* *L*' *S* *C* | ημ. + και καταλυοντα τον νομον ημων(*om*) και τους προφητας‖Mt 5 17: (Mcn^{Ep}) *Le* b(c)ff^{2}ilq(*om* και^2: r^2 vg^1)(30 vg^2)(^{1} *om* κ. τ. προφ.) | φο. Κ. δ.] Κ. φο. δ.‖20 22: *Rpl* (Κ. δ. φο.: σ954 *pc*) Eu(τω Κ.) Thd^C *S*h — φο δ. Κ.: D Cr *L*⟨r^1(*om* Κ.)⟩ — δ. φο. Κ.‖Mt22 17: *C* *Arm* *Aeth* — *txt*: 𝔓^{75} 𝔋T-**0124** CAp Vic *S*' | φορον‖20 22: λ2193 σM-1223 A K R Π *al* Eu | διδ.] δουναι‖←: 1241 λ2193 *pc* Mcn^{Ep}

Jo 18,31 ● κριν. + αυτον: 𝔓^{60v} *Rpl* Cr^{1m} *L*' *S*,j *C*sb'^{B}(^{1} αυτους)a^s — *txt*: 𝔓^{66v} ℵ*W-579 28 **λ**⟨118⟩ **087** *pc* Cr^{cmt} *Lc* *Arm*

Mt27 9 *cf.* EN(?) (Hi Mt): Legi nuper in quodam hebraico volumine, quem Nazarenae sectae mihi Hebraeus obtulit, Hieremiae apocryphum, in quo haec (sc. Mt27 9b.10) ad verbum scripta repperi.

(244)

259. Das Verhör vor Pilatus. *The Trial before Pilate.*

Matth 27 11–14

[11] Ὁ δὲ Ἰησοῦς ἐστάθη ἔμπροσθεν τοῦ ἡγεμόνος· καὶ ἐπηρώτησεν αὐτὸν ὁ ἡγεμὼν λέγων· σὺ εἶ ὁ βασιλεὺς τῶν Ἰουδαίων; ὁ δὲ Ἰησοῦς ἔφη· σὺ λέγεις. [12] καὶ ἐν τῷ κατηγορεῖσθαι αὐτὸν ὑπὸ τῶν ἀρχιερέων καὶ πρεσβυτέρων οὐδὲν ἀπεκρίνατο. [13] τότε λέγει αὐτῷ ὁ Πιλᾶτος· οὐκ ἀκούεις πόσα σου καταμαρτυροῦσιν; [14] καὶ οὐκ ἀπεκρίθη αὐτῷ πρὸς οὐδὲ ἓν ῥῆμα, ὥστε θαυμάζειν τὸν ἡγεμόνα λίαν.

Mark 15 2–5

[2] Καὶ ἐπηρώτησεν αὐτὸν ὁ Πιλᾶτος· σὺ εἶ ὁ βασιλεὺς τῶν Ἰουδαίων; ὁ δὲ ἀποκριθεὶς αὐτῷ λέγει· σὺ λέγεις. [3] καὶ κατηγόρουν αὐτοῦ οἱ ἀρχιερεῖς πολλά. [4] ὁ δὲ Πιλᾶτος πάλιν ἐπηρώτα αὐτὸν λέγων· οὐκ ἀποκρίνῃ οὐδέν; ἴδε πόσα σου κατηγοροῦσιν. [5] ὁ δὲ Ἰησοῦς οὐκέτι οὐδὲν ἀπεκρίθη, ὥστε θαυμάζειν τὸν Πιλᾶτον.

Luk 23 3–5

[3] Ὁ δὲ Πιλᾶτος ἠρώτησεν αὐτὸν λέγων· σὺ εἶ ὁ βασιλεὺς τῶν Ἰουδαίων; ὁ δὲ ἀποκριθεὶς αὐτῷ ἔφη· σὺ λέγεις. *cf. 260.* *cf. 260.* [4] ὁ δὲ Πιλᾶτος εἶπεν πρὸς τοὺς ἀρχιερεῖς καὶ τοὺς ὄχλους·

Jo 18 33–38

18 33–38: Εἰσῆλθεν οὖν πάλιν εἰς τὸ πραιτώριον ὁ Πιλᾶτος καὶ ἐφώνησεν τὸν Ἰησοῦν καὶ εἶπεν αὐτῷ· σὺ εἶ ὁ βασιλεὺς τῶν Ἰουδαίων; [34] ἀπεκρίνατο ὁ Ἰησοῦς· ἀφ' ἑαυτοῦ σὺ τοῦτο λέγεις, ἢ ἄλλοι σοι εἶπον περὶ ἐμοῦ; [35] ἀπεκρίθη ὁ Πιλᾶτος· μήτι ἐγὼ Ἰουδαῖός εἰμι; τὸ ἔθνος τὸ σὸν καὶ οἱ ἀρχιερεῖς παρέδωκάν σε ἐμοί· τί ἐποίησας; [36] ἀπεκρίθη Ἰησοῦς· ἡ βασιλεία ἡ ἐμὴ οὐκ ἔστιν ἐκ τοῦ κόσμου τούτου. εἰ ἐκ τοῦ κόσμου τούτου ἦν ἡ ἐμὴ βασιλεία, οἱ ὑπηρέται οἱ ἐμοὶ ἠγωνίζοντο ἄν, ἵνα μὴ παραδοθῶ τοῖς Ἰουδαίοις· νῦν δὲ ἡ βασιλεία ἡ ἐμὴ οὐκ ἔστιν ἐντεῦθεν. [37] εἶπεν οὖν αὐτῷ ὁ Πιλᾶτος· οὐκοῦν βασιλεὺς εἶ σύ; ἀπεκρίθη ὁ Ἰησοῦς· σὺ λέγεις ὅτι βασιλεύς εἰμι. ἐγὼ εἰς τοῦτο γεγέννημαι καὶ εἰς τοῦτο ἐλήλυθα εἰς τὸν κόσμον, ἵνα μαρτυρήσω τῇ ἀληθείᾳ· πᾶς ὁ ὢν ἐκ τῆς ἀληθείας ἀκούει μου τῆς φωνῆς. [38] λέγει αὐτῷ ὁ Πιλᾶτος· τί ἐστιν ἀλήθεια; *cf. 19 9f. (261.)* καὶ τοῦτο εἰπὼν πάλιν ἐξῆλθεν πρὸς τοὺς Ἰουδαίους καὶ λέγει αὐτοῖς· ἐγὼ

Mt 27,11 ο ηγ.] ο Πιλατος‖**p**: *Lr*¹30 — *om*‖p: W Θ Or *S*s[c] *Geo*¹ | *om* I.²‖p: L 700 σ1010 *pc* | εφη + αυτω‖p: *Rpl* Or *L*'[ek](-οις: g²) *S Cs*¹ *Geo*ᴬ — *txt*: 𝔥〈B〉 700 *pc* Chr *L*ad *S*j *Cs*⁶b *Arm Geo*' *Aeth* | λεγ.] ειπας‖**26**64: Chr *L*dq Hil *S*s[c]pj^bck?1 *C*b¹ **13** ποσα] τι‖26 62: σ945-990 *S*h | σου] ουτοι σου(∼)‖←: σ(945)-990 (157 Chr) *S*j^abckv (*C*^1:7b³) | καταμ.] κατηγορουσιν‖Mk: Φ **λ**-1582 *L*Or *Aeth*

Mk 15,2 επηρ.] ηρωτησεν‖Lk: 60 | Π. + λεγων‖p4: 579 WΘ-565-700 **ϕ** *pc* *L*k[e] cz *S*j *Cs*^2:8 *Arm* (+ αυτω) *Geo Aeth* | ο δε + Ιησους‖Mt: NΣ *pc Geo Aeth* | *om* αποκ.‖Mt: 56 *L*c | *om* αυτω‖Mt Jo: W-565 σ71 *pc L*k[e] cff²q *Cs*^1:8 **3** πολ. + αυτος δε ουδεν απεκρινατο‖p Lk23 9: ΔΨ-33-579 NW ΘΣ-565-1071 **ϕ**-*l*547 **σ**〈954〉-1194 U *mu l*48 *l*49 Or *L*ac vg² *S*s[c](+ αυτοις)hj *Cs*^1:8 *Arm Aeth* **4** *om* παλ.‖p: 544 σ517-1424 U *pc L*vg¹ *Cs*^1:9b¹ | ● *om* λεγ.‖2: ℵ* 565 λ209-1582 *L*a *Cs*^8:9 *Arm* | ουκ αποκ. ουδεν] ουδ. απ.‖Mt12 26 62 Lk←: ϕ983*ᵛ-1689? — ουκ απ.: B*-579 | κατηγορ.] καταμαρτυρ.‖p: *Rpl S Cs Geo*ᴬ — *txt*: ℵBCΨ-892 W-700 **λ**-22-1278*ᵛ σ267 D 697 *l*48 *L S*j *C*b *Geo*' *Aeth* **5** *om* ουκετι‖**p**: 106 *pc l*184 *L*ff² *C*sb⁹ | απεκρινατο‖Mt12 Lk←: **λ ϕ**-*l*547 G 495

Lk 23,3 επηρωτ.‖Mt Mk: *Rpl* — *txt*: 𝔓⁷⁵ ℵBT R *l*48 | ο δε² αποκ.] αυτος‖Mt: W — *om*‖Mt: W *S*cp(εφη αυτω ο Ιησους) — ο δε I. αποκ.‖Mt: *L*f — αποκ. ο I.: *Lr*¹ — αποκ.: *S*s | *om* αυτω‖Mt: 𝔓⁷⁵ 544 W **047** *pc l*13 *L*〈a〉 *C*sb² | εφη] λεγει‖Mk: ℵ 1279(∼ λ. αυ.) *L*〈ac30 vg¹〉

Jo 18,33 ● ∼ εις το πρ. παλ.: *Rpl* (∼ ο Π. παλ.: N Ψ) *S*h — *om* παλ.: Cᶜ-33 *S*[sc]p *Cs*⁶ *Δ*a — *txt* (∼ ο Π. εις το πρ.): 𝔓^52.66 𝔥'〈ℵ-1241〉C*X-**0109** 1071 **ϕ**'(69) σ71 Dˢ Y Δ **0141** *al* Cr *L*'(30) *S*j *Cs*⁴(b⁺ᴮ) *Arm* (*Aeth*) *Δ*ad l(i md n^〈L〉) **34** απεκριθη‖35.36.37: *Rpl* — *txt*: 𝔓⁶⁶ W-33-1241 N **λ**〈118〉 σ1223 A Dˢ U Π Ψ **087** 157 *al* | απεκ. + αυτω‖Mk Lk: *Rpl L*c *S*[sc]pj *Cs*¹ b^B1 — *txt*: 𝔓⁶⁶ 𝔥〈ℵ〉CX N-544-700 λ1 σM A Dˢ E G H U Y Θ Π Ψ **0141** *mu* Cr *L*' *S*h *Cs*¹⁰b'aˢ *Arm* | ● *om* ο: 𝔓^66v BLX-**0109** 1071 λ1 σ1194 **0141** *al* Cr — *txt*: 𝔓^60v *Rpl* | αφ εαυ.] ● απο σεαυ.: 𝔓⁶⁶ ℵBC* L-**0109**-579 N Ψ 1820 Chr(σαυ.) Cr **36** εμη βασ.²] ● β. η εμη‖36a.c: 𝔓^66v *Rpl* Or *L*,CP — *txt*: ℵ N ϕ124 Dˢ Θ *pc* Chr | ● ∼ αν οι εμοι ηγ.: *Rpl* Or *L*a Hi — *om* αν: {𝔓^66v} B* σ1424 713 *L*' — *txt*: {} ℵBᵐLW X-**0109**-33-579 1071 λ1-1582 **ϕ**-*l*547 Ψ **0141** *pc* Chr Or *L*cfff²g²r¹ vg¹² **37** τη αλ.] περι της αληθειας‖17.8: ℵ*

οὐδὲν εὑρίσκω αἴτιον ἐν τῷ ἀνθρώπῳ τού- | οὐδεμίαν αἰτίαν εὑρίσκω ἐν αὐτῷ.
τῳ. [5] οἱ δὲ ἐπίσχυον λέγοντες ὅτι ἀνασείει τὸν λαόν, διδάσκων καθ' ὅλης τῆς Ἰουδαίας, καὶ ἀρξάμενος ἀπὸ τῆς Γαλιλαίας ἕως ὧδε.

(245)

260. Jesus vor Herodes. *Jesus before Herod.* Luk 23 6–12

[6] Πιλᾶτος δὲ ἀκούσας ἐπηρώτησεν εἰ ὁ ἄνθρωπος Γαλιλαῖός ἐστιν, [7] καὶ ἐπιγνοὺς ὅτι ἐκ τῆς ἐξουσίας Ἡρῴδου ἐστίν, ἀνέπεμψεν αὐτὸν πρὸς Ἡρῴδην, ὄντα καὶ αὐτὸν ἐν Ἱεροσολύμοις ἐν ταύταις ταῖς ἡμέραις. *cf.259.* [8] ὁ δὲ Ἡρῴδης ἰδὼν τὸν Ἰησοῦν ἐχάρη λίαν· ἦν γὰρ ἐξ ἱκανοῦ θέλων ἰδεῖν αὐτὸν διὰ τὸ ἀκούειν περὶ αὐτοῦ, καὶ ἤλπιζέν τι σημεῖον ἰδεῖν ὑπ' αὐτοῦ γινόμενον. [9] ἐπηρώτα δὲ αὐτὸν ἐν λόγοις ἱκανοῖς· αὐτὸς δὲ οὐδὲν *cf.259.* ἀπεκρίνατο αὐτῷ. [10] εἱστήκεισαν δὲ οἱ ἀρχιερεῖς καὶ οἱ γραμματεῖς εὐτόνως κατηγοροῦντες αὐτοῦ. [11] ἐξουθενήσας δὲ αὐτὸν καὶ ὁ Ἡρῴδης σὺν τοῖς στρατεύμασιν αὐτοῦ καὶ ἐμπαίξας, περιβαλὼν ἐσθῆτα λαμπρὰν ἀνέπεμψεν αὐτὸν τῷ Πιλάτῳ. [12] ἐγένοντο δὲ φίλοι ὅ τε Ἡρῴδης καὶ ὁ Πιλᾶτος ἐν αὐτῇ τῇ ἡμέρᾳ μετ' ἀλλήλων· προϋπῆρχον γὰρ ἐν ἔχθρᾳ ὄντες πρὸς αὐτούς.

(245. 246)

261. Die Verurteilung. *The Sentence of Death.*

Matth 27 15–26 — Mark 15 6–15 — Luk 23 13–25

[13] Πιλᾶτος δὲ συγκαλεσάμενος τοὺς ἀρχιερεῖς καὶ τοὺς ἄρχοντας καὶ τὸν λαὸν [14] εἶπεν πρὸς αὐτούς· προσηνέγκατέ μοι τὸν ἄνθρωπον τοῦτον ὡς ἀποστρέφοντα τὸν λαόν, καὶ ἰδοὺ ἐγὼ ἐνώπιον ὑμῶν ἀνακρίνας οὐθὲν εὗρον ἐν τῷ ἀνθρώπῳ τούτῳ αἴτιον ὧν κατηγορεῖτε κατ' αὐτοῦ. [15] ἀλλ' οὐδὲ Ἡρῴδης· ἀνέπεμψεν γὰρ αὐτὸν πρὸς ἡμᾶς· καὶ ἰδοὺ οὐδὲν ἄξιον θανάτου ἐστὶν πεπραγμένον αὐτῷ· [16] παιδεύσας οὖν αὐτὸν ἀπολύσω.

Matth	Mark	Luk
[15] Κατὰ δὲ ἑορτὴν εἰώθει ὁ ἡγεμὼν	[6] Κατὰ δὲ ἑορτὴν	18 39 f. : ἔστιν δὲ συνήθεια ὑμῖν

Lk 23,4 αιτιαν‖Jo: ϕ69 433 **5** λαον] οχλον‖Mk15 11: ℵL λ131 *pc* | *om* και‖24 47: 𝔓^{75} *Rpl* *L*vl'⟨z⟩g^{2}36^{v} vg^{1} *C'* — *txt*: ℌ⟨892⟩T-**0124** Θ *L*r^{2} vg' *S* *C*b^{8} **8** ικαν.] ικ. χρονου *cf.* 8 27 Act8 11 *etc.*: X N-1604 **λ**-1582-2193(ικ. + του) **ϕ**-*l*547 σM-71-1194 H W Π Ψ *al* *l*184 *L*'⟨a vg^{1}⟩ *C*s^{1}(*om* ικ.){b *Δ*⟨me n^{Hg}⟩}^{1} — ● ικανων χρονων‖20 9: ℌT-**0124** 1071 D Θ 157 *L*c {*C*s$^{9+1?}$}^{2} — *txt*: 𝔓^{75} *Rpl* {}$^{1.2}$ | υπ] παρ‖11 16 Mk8 11: L 28 245 — απ‖Mt12 38: 579 λ1278 ϕ983-1689 *pc* | *om* γιν.‖←: X G *pc* *S*p *C*s$^{1:11}$ *Δ*a md n$^{C\,Hg\,L}$ p **11** ● *om* και^{1}: *Rpl* *L*' *S*'(s *om* 10-12) *C*' *Δ* — *txt*: 𝔓^{75} ℵLTX-**0124**(∼ κ. αυ.)-579 N **ϕ** Ψ *pc* *L*ad *S*h^{m} *C*b^{8} *Arm* *Geo*^{1} | περιβ. + αυτον (*et om* αυτον^{2})‖Jo19 2 Mk15 17: *Rpl* (σ1194 *pc*) *L*e b(c)f(ff^{2}l)qr^{1}(30) {*S* *C*} *Geo*^{A} — + αυτω (*et om* αυτον^{2})‖Mt27 28: ϕ69-983 σ(1194)-1223 R S U Γ **047** *pc* {} — *txt* (*et om* αυτον^{2}): 𝔓^{75} ℵBLT-**0124**-579 544 **σ**⟨1675⟩-659 *pc* *L*(ar^{2}z vg')^{1} *Geo*^{1} **12** ● εαυτους: *Rpl* — *txt*: 𝔓^{75} ℵBLT *al* *l*184 **13** κ. τ. λαον] του λαου‖Mt26 47 27 1: 348 *pc* *L*e abfff^{2}lr^{1} vg^{1} *S*p^{3} *C*s$^{7:9}$ *Aeth* *Δ*a i$^{T⟨P⟩V}$ md n$^{⟨L⟩}$ p — κ. παντα τον λαον‖Mt25: D *L*c *S*sc *Δ*me **14** διαστρεφ.‖23 2: 1241 **λλ**⟨22-1278⟩ **ϕ**-*l*547 σ945 *pc* | λαον + και κωλυοντα Καισαρι φορους διδοναι‖←: ϕ1689 | *om* εγω‖23 4: **λλ**⟨22-1278⟩ σ1194 H Γ *pc* *L*vg^{1} *C*s *Arm* | ευρισκω‖←Jo18 38 19 4.6: 579-1241 *L*e bff^{2} lqr^{1}30 vg^{8} | τ. αν. τουτω] αυτω‖22 Jo18 38 19 6: **ϕ**-*l*547 D *L*r^{1}(αυ.] τουτω) *S*sc *C*s | αιτιαν‖Jo18 38 19 4.6: E F G^{c} 440 *l*184 | *om* ων—αυ.‖23 4: D *pc* | *om* κατ‖23 2.10 6 7 Mt27 13: ℵLT-**0124**-892-1241 ΘΛ-28 **λλ**⟨22-1278⟩ A *pc* **16** ● 16.(19) + [17]αναγκην δε ειχεν απολυειν αυτοις κατα εορτην ενα *vel sim.*‖p: *Rpl* (D 1574) Eu^{can} *L* *S*(sc)' *C*b^{10} *Geo* (*Aeth*) ⟦αναγκ.] συνηθειαν‖Jo39: N *S*scp *C*b^{5} | ∼ κ. εορ. απολ. αυ.‖Mk6: (∼ ενα αυ.: 579-892^{m}) Θ-1071(*om* αυ.) D Ψ *pc* *L*q *Geo* | αυτοις] τω οχλω‖Mt15: ϕ1689 | ενα + δεσμιον(+ ον ηθελον)‖←Mk6: σ71-1194 (472) *al* *L*c(+ ον ηθελεν ο λαος: l)q vg^{2} *S*sh^{-} *C*b^{2}⟧ — *txt*: 𝔓^{75} BLT-**0124**-892^{t}-1241 K L Π *pc* *l*185 vg^{1} *C*'

Jo 18,38 ● ∼ ευρ. εν αυ. αιτ.‖19 6 Lk23 14.4: BLX-**054**(*om* εν αυ.)-**0109**-579 σ954 **0141** *pc* *L*'(ευρον: r^{1}) — ευρ. αιτ. εν αυ.‖Lk4: 𝔓^{66} *L*f — *txt* (∼ εν αυ. ευρ.): *Rpl* (D *pc*) *L*(a)q30 vg^{1} | αιτ. + θανατου‖Lk23 15: ϕ69 *L*30 vg^{1}

Matthew

ἀπολύειν ἕνα τῷ ὄχλῳ δέσμιον ὃν ἤθελον. [16] εἶχον δὲ τότε δέσμιον ἐπίσημον λεγόμενον Βαραββᾶν.

[17] συνηγμένων οὖν αὐτῶν εἶπεν αὐτοῖς ὁ Πιλᾶτος· τίνα θέλετε ἀπολύσω ὑμῖν, Βαραββᾶν ἢ Ἰησοῦν τὸν λεγόμενον Χριστόν; · [18] ᾔδει γὰρ ὅτι διὰ φθόνον παρέδωκαν αὐτόν. [19] καθημένου δὲ αὐτοῦ ἐπὶ τοῦ βήματος ἀπέστειλεν πρὸς αὐτὸν ἡ γυνὴ αὐτοῦ λέγουσα· μηδὲν σοὶ καὶ τῷ δικαίῳ ἐκείνῳ· πολλὰ γὰρ ἔπαθον σήμερον κατ' ὄναρ δι' αὐτόν. [20] οἱ δὲ ἀρχιερεῖς καὶ οἱ πρεσβύτεροι ἔπεισαν τοὺς ὄχλους ἵνα αἰτήσωνται

Mark

ἀπέλυεν αὐτοῖς ἕνα δέσμιον ὅνπερ ᾐτοῦντο. [7] ἦν δὲ ὁ λεγόμενος Βαραββᾶς μετὰ τῶν στασιαστῶν δεδεμένος, οἵτινες ἐν τῇ στάσει φόνον πεποιήκεισαν. [8] καὶ ἀναβὰς ὁ ὄχλος ἤρξατο αἰτεῖσθαι καθὼς ἐποίει αὐτοῖς. [9] ὁ δὲ Πιλᾶτος ἀπεκρίθη αὐτοῖς λέγων· θέλετε ἀπολύσω ὑμῖν τὸν βασιλέα τῶν Ἰουδαίων; [10] ἐγίνωσκεν γὰρ ὅτι διὰ φθόνον παραδεδώκεισαν αὐτὸν οἱ ἀρχιερεῖς.

[11] οἱ δὲ ἀρχιερεῖς ἀνέσεισαν τὸν ὄχλον ἵνα

Luke

cf. v. 19 ↓

[18] ἀνέκραγον δὲ παμπληθεὶ λέγοντες· αἶρε τοῦτον, ἀπόλυ-

John

ἵνα ἕνα ἀπολύσω ὑμῖν ἐν τῷ πασχα· βούλεσθε οὖν ἀπολύσω ὑμῖν τὸν βασιλέα τῶν Ἰουδαίων;

[40] ἐκραύγασαν οὖν πάλιν πάντες λέγοντες· μὴ τοῦτον,

Mt 27,15 ∼ τω οχ. ενα δ.‖Mk: φ⟨828⟩-*l*547 σM-1402 *al l*47 *l*50 *l*54 *L*'[ek](vg^1 *om* ενα) *S*s[c]j | τω οχ.] *om*‖Mk: 544 — αυτοις‖Mk: *S*j^{c1} | ηθ.] παρητουντο‖Mk: ℵ* **16** B. + οστις(ος: Φ) δια φονον (φθο.: φ13-346; + και στασιαν: Φ 443 *L*32 *S*h^{Brs}) ην βεβλημενος (∼ β. ην: φ346) εις φυλακην‖Lk19.25: (Φ) **φ**'⟨69-788⟩(13-346 443 *L*32) vg^2 Σ(*sim.*: s[c])(h^{Brs}) — + οστις ην δια στασιν τινα γενομενην εν τη πολει και φονον βεβλημενον(!) εις φυ.‖←: φ124-*l*547^1 (^{26}Βαρ. + οστις ην—γενομ. κ. φον. βεβλημενος εις φυ.: φ174-788) **18** ηδει] εγινωσκεν‖Mk: σ945-1010-1223-1293

Mk 15,6 απελ.] ειωθει ο ηγεμων(*om* ο ηγ.) απολυειν‖**p**: W **φ**-*l*547 *L*(k[e] cdff^{2}lr^2)z (vg *S*p')^1 *C*s^8{(^{2})} | ονπ. ητ.] ον ητ.‖p: W λ1 φ983-1689 σ115-659 *pc l*47 — ● ον παρητ.‖p: ℵ*B* A *pc* — ον αν ητ. (ηθελον)‖p: Θ(ονπερ αν)-565 **φ**'-*l*547 D G *pc* (*l*47 *Lz*) {} — *txt*: *Rpl* {*L*'} **7** δε + τοτε‖p: W **φ** *C*s$^{7:10}$ **8** αναβοησας‖13f. Mt23 Lk18.21.23 Jo40.6.12: *Rpl S*,j *Δ*a p — ανασεισας‖11: φ543 — *txt*: ℵ*B-892 D *L*'(k[e] *om*) *C* | ● καθως + αει: *Rpl L*'⟨k[e] c⟩ *S*h — *txt*: 𝔋⟨33⟩ WΘ-565-700 λ1278 **σ**⟨954⟩-1082 1342 1396 *Lz Sp C Aeth* | εποιει] εθος ην (+ αυτοις) ινα τον Βαραββαν απολυση‖11 Mt15 Jo39: Θ-565-(700) *Arm* — ειωθεν ποιειν‖Mt15: *Lz Sp Δ*a **10** επεγινωσκεν‖Lk237: σ1223 A K Y Π *al* — ηδει‖p: WΘ-565-700 λ1-872 **φ**⟨124⟩ D *pc* | παρεδωκαν‖**p**: WΘ-565-700 λ1 **φ**-*l*547 σ517 D H S *pc* | *om* οι αρ.‖**p**: B-579 544 λ1-872 σ115-349 *pc l*10 *l*13 *l*47 *S*s[c] *C*b$^{\langle 1\rangle}$ **11** ανεσ.] επεισαν‖Mt: Θ(εποιησαν)-565 D *L*vl[e]⟨lr^2⟩r^1 *S*s[c] *C*s — ανεπεισαν‖Mt: 544-1071 σ827-945-1194-1223 Γ *al l*18 *l*48

Lk 23,18 ανεκραξαν‖Mk13f.: *Rpl* — *txt*: 𝔓^{75} 𝔋T-**0124** φ124-*l*547 157 *pc* Cr | δε + παλιν‖Jo: 1355 | τουτ.] απο της γης τον τοιουτον‖Act2222: Or *L* Or

Jo 18,39 ● ∼ υμ.^{2} απολ.^{1}: *Rpl* (*om* υμ.^{2}: φ1689 Ψ *S*p^1) — *txt*: 𝔓^{66v} 𝔋⟨1241⟩X-**0109** 544-1071 **λ** σ1675 D^s K U Δ Π *al* Cr^{cmt} *L*'(*om* υμ.^{2}: bcff^{2}j^v) | ∼ υμ.^{3} απολ.^{2}: *Rpl* (*om* υμ.^{3}: Θ) — *txt*: 𝔓^{66} 𝔋X-**054-0109** N-544-1071 **λ** **φ**-*l*547 σ1675 A D^s K U Y Π Ψ **0141** *pc L*'(υμ.^{2}⌒^{3}: a; *om* υμ.^{3}: vg^1) **40** *om* παλ.‖Lk18 Mt22: 33 N-28-700 **φ**-*l*547 σ1223 G K U Π **053** *pm* Chr *L*vl'j^{v}r^1 *S*[sc]pj *C*$^{+B}$ *Δ*a — *om* παλ. παν.: 1241 Ψ *C*a^s — ● *om* παν.‖Mk13 Lk21: 𝔋'X-**0109** σ71 **0141** *al* — *txt*: 𝔓^{66v} *Rpl* (∼ παλ. λεγ. παν.: D^s) *L*f vg *S*h

---

Mt27 16pJo18 40 *cf.* EN frgm.20 (Hi Mt *ad* 27 16): Iste (*sc.* Barabbas) in evangelio quod scribitur iuxta Hebraeos *filius magistri* eorum interpretatur qui propter seditionem et homicidium fuerat condemnatus.

Matth	Mark	Luk	Joh
τὸν Βαραββᾶν, τὸν δὲ Ἰησοῦν ἀπολέσωσιν.	μᾶλλον τὸν Βαραββᾶν ἀπολύσῃ αὐτοῖς.	σον δὲ ἡμῖν τὸν Βαραββᾶν· 19 ὅστις ἦν διὰ στάσιν τινὰ	ἀλλὰ τὸν Βαραββᾶν. ἦν δὲ ὁ Βαραββᾶς λῃστής.
21 ἀποκριθεὶς δὲ ὁ ἡγεμὼν εἶπεν αὐτοῖς· τίνα θέλετε ἀπὸ τῶν δύο ἀπολύσω ὑμῖν; οἱ δὲ εἶπον· τὸν Βαραββᾶν. 22 λέγει αὐτοῖς ὁ Πιλᾶτος· τί οὖν ποιήσω Ἰησοῦν τὸν λεγόμενον Χριστόν; λέγουσιν πάντες·	cf. v. 7 ↑ 12 ὁ δὲ Πιλᾶτος πάλιν ἀποκριθεὶς εἶπεν αὐτοῖς· τί οὖν ποιήσω ὃν λέγετε τὸν βασιλέα τῶν Ἰουδαίων; 13 οἱ δὲ πάλιν ἔκραξαν·	γενομένην ἐν τῇ πόλει καὶ φόνον βληθεὶς ἐν τῇ φυλακῇ. 20 πάλιν δὲ ὁ Πιλᾶτος προσεφώνησεν, θέλων ἀπολῦσαι τὸν Ἰησοῦν. 21 οἱ δὲ ἐπεφώνουν λέγοντες·	19 4–16: ἐξῆλθεν πάλιν ἔξω ὁ Πιλᾶτος καὶ λέγει αὐτοῖς· ἴδε ἄγω ὑμῖν αὐτὸν ἔξω, ἵνα γνῶτε ὅτι ἐν αὐτῷ οὐδεμίαν αἰτίαν εὑρίσκω. 5 ἐξῆλθεν οὖν ὁ Ἰησοῦς ἔξω, φορῶν τὸν ἀκάνθινον στέφανον καὶ τὸ πορφυροῦν ἱμάτιον. καὶ λέγει αὐτοῖς· ἰδοὺ ὁ ἄνθρωπος. 6 ὅτε οὖν εἶδον αὐτὸν οἱ ἀρχιερεῖς καὶ οἱ ὑπηρέται, ἐκραύγασαν λέγοντες· σταύρωσον σταύρωσον. λέγει αὐτοῖς ὁ Πιλᾶτος· λάβετε αὐτὸν ὑμεῖς καὶ σταυρώσατε· ἐγὼ γὰρ οὐχ εὑρίσκω ἐν αὐτῷ αἰτίαν. 7 ἀπεκρίθησαν οἱ Ἰουδαῖοι· ἡμεῖς νόμον ἔχομεν, καὶ κατὰ τὸν νόμον ὀφείλει ἀποθανεῖν, ὅτι υἱὸν θεοῦ ἑαυτὸν ἐποίησεν. 8 ὅτε οὖν ἤκουσεν ὁ Πιλᾶτος τοῦτον τὸν λόγον, μᾶλλον ἐφοβήθη, 9 καὶ εἰσῆλθεν εἰς τὸ πραιτώριον

Mt 27,22 *om* παντ.‖Mk: σ1402 *pc* *Geo*^{1}

Mk 15,12 παλιν αποκ.] αποκ.‖Mt: W ϕ13 σ517-1207 D Γ *al* *Lk*[e] ff^2 vg^2 *C*b' — αποκ. πα.: *Rpl* *Laz* vg^1 *Ss*[c](∼ απεκριθη πα. ο Π. *et*+ και)j — *om*‖Lk: *Sp* — *txt* (απεκριθη): ℌ'⟨Δ⟩C (Θ-565-700)-1071 σ115 1342 (1574) *pc* *L*(c)lr$^{1.2}$ vg' Au *S*h *C*(s)b^8 (*Geo*) | ειπ. αυ.] ● ελεγεν αυ.‖14: ℵBC σ115 1342 *S*h — αυτοις: Θ-565-700 *Lc*(+ λεγων) — αυ. λεγει‖Mt22: Γ 1574 (αυ. και λ.) *L*'(∼)⟨ff^2 (*om* αυ.)⟩ — *txt*: *Rpl* *Lk*[e] Au *S*'j | ● ουν + θελετε(+ ινα)‖9 Mt21.17: *Rpl* (σ517 *pc* *l*15) *L*'(c vg^3) Au *S*,j — *txt*: BCΔΨ W λ1 ϕ⟨124-346⟩ σ115 A 1342 *pc* *C* *Geo* | ον λεγ.] *om*‖Jo39: W Θ-565-700 **λ** ϕ⟨124-346⟩ σ115 A D *pc* *l*13 *L*'Au *Ss*[c] *Cs*^{4} *Arm* — λεγετε μοι(ημιν): B(*om* μοι) *Cs*^{3}(^{1}) — *txt*: *Rpl* *L*vg^1 *S*'j *C*b **13** *om* παλ.‖Lk Mt: 544 *L*acff^{2}z *Ss*[c] *Cs*$^{1:9}$b^{3}f^v | εκραζον (εκραυγαζον)‖Mt23 Lk: (565-700) λ1 ϕ σ954-1675 G *pc* (*pc*) *l*15 *L*vg^3 *S*hj *Cs*$^{1:9}$b^{4}f^v *Arm* | εκρα. + λεγοντες‖←: 565-700 λ872 σM-7-945-1082-1223-1391 A D K Y Π *al* *l*48 *l*49 *L*⟨k[e] lr^2⟩ *S*j *Cs*$^{5:9}$ *Aeth*

Lk 23,19 *om* τινα‖25: 157 *Δ*a | *om* γεν. εν τη πολ.‖25: 1241 *S*sc — *om* εν τη π.‖25: 28 348^c | βεβλημενος‖25: *Rpl* (ℵ* *om*) — *txt*: 𝔓^{75} BLT-**0124**-579-892 | εν τ. φυ.] εις (+ την) φυλακην‖25: *Rpl* (1241 **λλ**⟨1278⟩ σ1194 W *pc* *l*48 *l*49) *L*' — *txt*: 𝔓^{75} ℌ'TX-**0124** 1071 Ψ *pc* *L*fq30 vg^2 **20** ● προσεφ. + αυτοις‖p: 𝔓^{75} ℌ'T-**0124** 1071 ϕ⟨69⟩-*l*547 Ψ 157 *pc* *L*a *S*p {*C*} — + αυτους: 579 D{} — + αυτους και ειπεν αυτοις: *S*sc — + προς αυτους: ϕ69 *L*'{} — *txt*: *Rpl* *S*h *Arm* | τον Ι.] αυτον‖Jo12: **λλ**⟨22-1278⟩ H **21** επεφ.] εκραξαν‖Mk13f.: D *Lc* *C*⟨b^4⟩ | *om* λεγ.‖Mk: D *Ss*

Jo 19,4 παλ. εξω ο Π.] ● παλ.(*om*) ο Π. εξω‖18 29: ℵL(W)X-1241 1071 ϕ'(346-*l*547) σ945 *pc* (*pc* *l*47) *L*'(παλ.] ουν: b ff^2, δε: a) (vg^1) *S*j *Arm*' *Geo*^{2} — ο Π. παλ. εξω(*om*)‖←: (579) *pc* *S*[sc]p'(^{1}) *Arm*^{pc} — εξω παλ. ο Π.: **054** σ1424 Y 245 — παλ. ο Π.: 28-544 **0141** *pc* *L*e *Cs*$^{1:14}$b^1 *Geo*^{1} | ● ∼ ουδ. αι. ευ. εν αυ.‖18 38: ℵ*(*om* εν αυ.)^a(∼ αι. ουδ.)B-33 565 **λ** 131(= ℵ*) *pc* Cr^{cmt} *L*vg^1 *Aeth* — ουδ. αι. (∼ αι ουδ.) εν αυ. ευ.‖←: 892^s (1071) Ψ **0141** (213) *pc* *L*z — ουδ. εν αυ. αι. ευ.‖←: λ2193 A — ● αι. εν αυ. ουδ.(ουχ) ευ.‖6: (𝔓^{66v}) L(W)X-**054** Y 157 *pc* (*pc* *l*253 *L*r^1 *Arm*) *Geo*^{1} — ουχ ευ. εν αυ. αι.‖6: *L*a(∼ αι. εν αυ.: bfj^v *S*p) — αι. ουχ ευ. εν αυ.‖6: *S*j — εν αυ. ουχ ευ. αι.‖6: 579(*om* εν *et* ∼ αι. ουχ ευ.) ϕ⟨346⟩-*l*547 (∼ αι. ουχ ευ.: *L*e cff^{2}q) — *txt*: *Rpl* *L*vg' *S*[sc]h *Geo*^{2} **5** *om* κ. λεγ.—ανθ.‖p: 𝔓^{66} *L*e aff^{2}r^1 *C*a^s **6** αυτον^1 + ο οχλος και‖Mk11 Mt20: **054** 700 Y *pc* | *om* κ. οι υπ.‖p: σ71 *Cs*$^{1?:13}$ | υπ.] πρεσβυτεροι‖Mt20: **054** Y — + συμβουλιον ποιησαντες‖Mk15 1: 1093 — + παλιν‖18 40 Mk13: **053** | εκραυγαζον‖12 Mt23: σ1188 *L*bff^{2}z vg$^{⟨1⟩}$ Au — εκραξαν‖Mk13: ℵ* | *om* λεγον.‖←: ℵ Y 91 *L*e abff^2 Hil *Cs*$^{1:13}$b^3 | *om* σταυρωσον^2‖Mk Mt: 𝔓^{66*v} σ7-1010 (-ρωθητω: *L*e r^1; -ρωσαι: a^v) Au$^{1:2}$ *Cs*$^{1:13}$ | σταυρωσον^2(*et*^{1}) + αυτον‖Mk13.14 Lk21: *Rpl* *L*b(cj)fff^{2}q30 vg^2(^{1}) Au^2 *S*[sc](p) h(j^{abc1}) *Cs*^{1}(^{12}b^{+B}a^s) *Arm* — *txt*: 𝔓^{66v} BLW **λ** Ψ 245 Chr Cr *L*r^{1}z vg' Au^1 Hil *S*j^{c1} **7** ● απεκρ. + αυτω: 𝔓^{60v} *Rpl* *L*'⟨vg^2⟩ *S*[sc] *C*' — *txt*: 𝔓^{66v} ℵW-579 544 **λ** **0141** *pc* Or *L*e a^{v}bcfff^2 vg^1 *C*b^{B1}a^s *Aeth* | ● νομον^2 + ημων‖18 31: 𝔓^{60v} *Rpl* *L* *S*[sc] *C*'$^{+B}$ *Δ*a i$^{T1.V}$ n^L p — *txt*: 𝔓^{66} ℵBLW-579 N D^s Δ Ψ Or *L*'⟨vg^1⟩ Hil *S*j *C*b^1 *Δ*'⟨me⟩ | ∼ θε. υι.‖Mt27 43.54: *Rpl* — *txt* (του θε.): 𝔓$^{60.66}$ ℌX NΛ-1071 **λ** ϕ-(*l*547) σM-7-71-1223 A D^s E H K U Θ Π Ψ Ω **053** **0141** *pm* Or *L* σταυρωθήτω. [23] ὁ δὲ ἔφη· τί γὰρ κακὸν ἐποίησεν; οἱ δὲ περισσῶς ἔκραζον λέγοντες· σταυρωθήτω. [24] ἰδὼν δὲ ὁ Πιλᾶ-

σταύρωσον αὐτόν. [14] ὁ δὲ Πιλᾶτος ἔλεγεν αὐτοῖς· τί γὰρ ἐποίησεν κακόν; οἱ δὲ περισσῶς ἔκραξαν· σταύρωσον αὐτόν. [15] ὁ δὲ Πιλᾶ-

σταύρου σταύρου αὐτόν. [22] ὁ δὲ τρίτον εἶπεν πρὸς αὐτούς· τί γὰρ κακὸν ἐποίησεν οὗτος; οὐδὲν αἴτιον θανάτου εὗρον ἐν αὐτῷ· παιδεύσας οὖν αὐτὸν ἀπολύσω. [23] οἱ δὲ ἐπέκειντο φωναῖς μεγάλαις αἰτούμενοι αὐτὸν σταυρωθῆναι, καὶ κατίσχυον αἱ φωναὶ αὐτῶν. [24] καὶ Πιλᾶ-

πάλιν καὶ λέγει τῷ Ἰησοῦ· πόθεν εἶ σύ; ὁ δὲ Ἰησοῦς ἀπόκρισιν οὐκ ἔδωκεν αὐτῷ. [10] λέγει αὐτῷ ὁ Πιλᾶτος· ἐμοὶ οὐ λαλεῖς; οὐκ οἶδας ὅτι ἐξουσίαν ἔχω ἀπολῦσαί σε καὶ ἐξουσίαν ἔχω σταυρῶσαί σε; [11] ἀπεκρίθη Ἰησοῦς· οὐκ ἔχεις ἐξουσίαν κατ' ἐμοῦ οὐδεμίαν εἰ μὴ ἦν δεδομένον σοι ἄνωθεν· διὰ τοῦτο ὁ παραδιδούς με σοὶ μείζονα ἁμαρτίαν ἔχει. [12] ἐκ τούτου ὁ Πιλᾶτος ἐζήτει ἀπολῦσαι αὐτόν· οἱ δὲ Ἰουδαῖοι ἐκραύγαζον λέγοντες· ἐὰν τοῦτον ἀπολύσῃς, οὐκ εἶ φίλος τοῦ Καίσαρος· πᾶς ὁ βασιλέα ἑαυτὸν ποιῶν ἀντιλέγει τῷ Καίσαρι. [13] ὁ οὖν Πιλᾶτος ἀκούσας τῶν λόγων τούτων ἤγαγεν ἔξω τὸν Ἰησοῦν, καὶ ἐκάθισεν ἐπὶ

Mt 27,22 σταυ. + σταυρωθητω ‖ Lk Jo6: K Π *pc* *Sj*^b1 **23** ο δε εφη] ● ο δε ηγεμων εφη ‖ Mk: *Rpl* *S*h *Geo*^A — λεγει αυτοις ο ηγ. (Πιλατος) ‖ p: L-892 1604 **λ**-1582 D (213) 1295 *L*'[ek](z vg²) Au *S*(*om* ο ηγ.: s[c])p'(⁵) *C*b *Aeth* — *txt*: ℵB-33 ϕ69-788 Θ Chr *Sj* *Cs* *Arm* *Geo*' | εκραξαν ‖ Mk: D *L*vg¹ Or *S*p *C*^1:8 *Aeth* | *om* λεγ. ‖ Mk: 544 **λ**-1582 **σ**-71 K Y Π *pc* *l*47 Chr *L*[ek] abr^1.2 *Cs*^4:6b¹ | σταυ.] σταυρωσον αυτον ‖ Mk Jo6: 157 — σταυρωσον σταυρωσον ‖ Lk21 Jo6: *Aeth*

Mk 15,13 σταυ. αυ.] σταυρωθητω ‖ Mt: σ827 | σταυ. + σταυρωσον ‖ Jo6 Lk: 28 *pc* *L*30 — + αυτον σταυ.: *S*s[c] | *om* αυτ. ‖ Jo6: 700 **14** ελεγ.] λεγει ‖ Mt22: N-565 330 — εφη *vel* ειπεν ‖ p: *Lk*[e] a {*S*s[c]p} *C*sf | *om* αυτοις ‖ Mt: ℵ*Ψ *Cf*^v | ∼ κακ. εποι. ‖ Mt Lk: *Rpl* *L*,Au *S*,j — *txt*: BCΔΨ-892 Θ-565 λ872 σ7-517-659-827-1082-1391 1342 *pc* *l*49 | ● περισσοτερως (-ρον): *Rpl* (*pc*) — *txt*: 𝔥C Θ-565-700-1071 **λ** **ϕ**⟨124⟩ σM-827-945-954-1223-1424-1606 A D G H K Y Π 1342 *mu* | εκραζον (εκραυγαζον) ‖ Mt: (565-700) **λ** **ϕ**⟨124⟩ σM-267-945-954-1194-1223-1606 A D G K P Y Π 1342 *mu* *L*⟨vg¹⟩Au *S*s[c]pj *C*bf | εκρ. + λεγοντες ‖ Mt: ℵ 565 *Sj* *Cs*^1:7 *Geo* | σταυ. + σταυρωσον ‖ Jo6: 1071 *l*48

Lk 23,21 στ. στ.] σταυρωσον σταυρωσον ‖ Jo11 16 Mk: *Rpl* {} — σταυρωσον ‖ Mk: 1604 U W 21 157 *L*e abfff²l vg¹ *C*b¹ *Arm* *Aeth* — *txt*: 𝔓^75 ℵB-**0124** D F^c Cr Eu Or {*L*' *S* *C*'} **22** ειπ.] εφη ‖ Mt: 579 | *om* ουτος ‖ **p**: 579 *L*vg¹ *Cs*^1:11 | ουδ. αιτ.] ουδ. αξιον ‖ 15: L-892-1241 1071 σ7 Ψ *L*ac *S*sch^m — ουδεμιαν αιτιαν ‖ Jo5.6.39: D *L*' *S*p (+ αξιαν) h^t | ευρισκω ‖ ←234: 1071 D 243 *L*⟨a 30 vg⁵⟩ *S*sc **23** σταυρωσαι ‖ Mk13f. Jo6: B 2533 *L*δ *S*p {*Δ*a n^L p} | αυτων + και των αρχιερεων (+ μετ αυτων) ‖ Mt20 Mk11: *Rpl* *L*cf *S*s(+ και οι αρχιενεις μετ αυτων)(c)ph *C*b¹ *Aeth*(*om* αυ. και) *Δ*a p(= *Aeth*) — *txt*: 𝔓^75 ℵBL-**0124**-1241 130 *l*241 *L*' *C*' *Δ*md^MV n^⟨L⟩ **24** και¹] ο δε ‖ p: *Rpl* (επεκρ. δε ο Πιλ.: D) Phlp *L*c(εκρ. ουν ο Π.)f *S*' *Cs* — *txt*: 𝔓^75 ℵBL-**0124**-579 157(ο Π.) *L*' *S*sc Cr *C*b *Arm* *Aeth*

Jo 19,10 λεγ.] ● + ουν: 𝔓^66 *Rpl* *L*'⟨vg¹⟩ *S*h *Cs*^8 *Δ*'⟨me⟩ — + δε: *Sj*^⟨b1⟩ *Δ*a i^T l^A p — και λεγ.: *Aeth* — *txt*: ℵ* 28 **ϕ**-*l*547 σ71-659-1194 A V *al* Cr *L*qr¹ vg¹ *S*[sc]p *Cs*^4 b^+B | ● ∼ σταυ. ... απολ.: *Rpl* *L*' *S*hj *C*^+B a^sv *Arm* *Δ*' — *txt*: 𝔓^60 ℵB N A E 821 *L*e j(στ. ... απ. ... στ.) *S*[sc]p *Δ*a me p **11** ● απεκ. + αυτω: 𝔓^60 𝔥⟨1241⟩ 1071 **λ** D^s Γ Ψ **0141** *al* Cr *L*acj30 *S*[sc]p *Cs*^12 — *txt*: 𝔓^66v *Rpl* *L*' *S*hj *Cs*¹b⁺a^s *Arm* | I.] ● ο I.: 𝔓^60v ℵL W-**054**^c-33-579 NΛ-1071 **λ** **ϕ**-*l*547 σM A Y^c Δ Θ **0141** *al* Cr | I. + και ειπεν αυτω(*om*): **ϕ**-*l*547 (*L*acff²) *S*[sc]j *Cs*^1:13b^B *Aeth* | εχ.] ● ειχες: *Rpl* Chr¹ Thd^C *Cs*^7 — *txt*: ℵLX-**054**-33-579 NΛ-544-565-1071 λ2193 A D^s V Y Π Ψ *pc* Chr¹ *Cs*³b^+B | παραδι.] ● παραδους ‖ Mt10 4: ℵB Λ E Δ Θ *pc* *l*47 *l*251 *L*⟨vg¹⟩ *S*[sc] *C*^+B *Geo*¹ **12** ● εκραυγασαν ‖ 6.15 Mk13f. Lk18: 𝔓^60? B-33 544-700-1071 σ1223 D^s Ψ **0141** *al* *L*a *Sj*^ac *C*b¹ — εκραζον ‖ Mt: *Rpl* Chr Cr {} — ελεγον *et om* λεγ.: ℵ* — *txt* (-αυαζον): 𝔓^60? 𝔥'(L)-**054**-**065** N **λ**-22 **ϕ**⟨13⟩-(1689)-*l*547 σ(M)-7-1194 A Θ Π *al* Or {*L*' *S*[sc],j^b *C*'^+B} **13** τουτ. + μαλλον εφοβηθη ‖ 8: σ1424 | επι + του ‖ Mt19: *Rpl* Chrn¹ *Cs*b^⟨1⟩+B a^s — *txt*: 𝔓^66 ℵBX-**065**-33-579 N-1071 **λ** A D^s U Π Ψ **0141** *al* Chrn¹ Cr^cmt

---

Mt27 24 *cf.* EP 1,1f.: (... Πειλᾶτος ... ἀπενίψατο τὰς χεῖρας ...?)τ[ῶν] δὲ Ἰουδαίων οὐδεὶς ἐνίψατο τὰς χεῖρας, οὐδὲ Ἡρῴδης οὐδέ τις [τ]ῶν κριτῶν αὐτοῦ. κ[αὶ μὴ] βουληθέντων νίψασθαι ἀνέσ[τ]η Πειλᾶτος· [2] καὶ τότε κελεύει Ἡρῴδης ὁ βασιλεὺς παρ[αλη]μφθῆναι τὸν κύριον, εἰπὼν αὐτοῖς ὅτι 'ὅσα ἐκέλευσα ὑμῖν ποιῆσαι αὐτῷ ποιήσατε.' (2) [3] Εἱστήκει ... (*cf. ad 266.*)

Matth: τος ὅτι οὐδὲν ὠφελεῖ ἀλλὰ μᾶλλον θόρυβος γίνεται, λαβὼν ὕδωρ ἀπενίψατο τὰς χεῖρας ἀπέναντι τοῦ ὄχλου λέγων· ἀθῷός εἰμι ἀπὸ τοῦ αἵματος τούτου· ὑμεῖς ὄψεσθε. 25 καὶ ἀποκριθεὶς πᾶς ὁ λαὸς εἶπεν· τὸ αἷμα αὐτοῦ ἐφ' ἡμᾶς καὶ ἐπὶ τὰ τέκνα ἡμῶν. 26 τότε ἀπέλυσεν αὐτοῖς τὸν Βαραββᾶν, τὸν δὲ Ἰησοῦν φραγελλώσας παρέδωκεν ἵνα σταυρωθῇ.

Mark: τος βουλόμενος τῷ ὄχλῳ τὸ ἱκανὸν ποιῆσαι ἀπέλυσεν αὐτοῖς τὸν Βαραββᾶν, καὶ παρέδωκεν τὸν Ἰησοῦν φραγελλώσας ἵνα σταυρωθῇ.

Luk: τος ἐπέκρινεν γενέσθαι τὸ αἴτημα αὐτῶν· 25 ἀπέλυσεν δὲ τὸν διὰ στάσιν καὶ φόνον βεβλημένον εἰς τὴν φυλακήν, ὃν ᾐτοῦντο, τὸν δὲ Ἰησοῦν παρέδωκεν τῷ θελήματι αὐτῶν.

Joh: βήματος εἰς τόπον λεγόμενον Λιθόστρωτον, Ἑβραϊστὶ δὲ Γαββαθα. 14 ἦν δὲ παρασκευὴ τοῦ πασχα, ὥρα ἦν ὡς ἕκτη· καὶ λέγει τοῖς Ἰουδαίοις· ἴδε ὁ βασιλεὺς ὑμῶν. 15 ἐκραύγασαν οὖν ἐκεῖνοι· ἆρον ἆρον, σταύρωσον αὐτόν. λέγει αὐτοῖς ὁ Πιλᾶτος· τὸν βασιλέα ὑμῶν σταυρώσω; ἀπεκρίθησαν οἱ ἀρχιερεῖς· οὐκ ἔχομεν βασιλέα εἰ μὴ Καίσαρα. 16 τότε οὖν παρέδωκεν αὐτὸν αὐτοῖς ἵνα σταυρωθῇ . . .

(247)

262. Verspottung des Judenkönigs. *The Mocking by the Soldiers.*

Matth 27 27–31a

27 Τότε οἱ στρατιῶται τοῦ ἡγεμόνος παραλαβόντες τὸν Ἰησοῦν

Mark 15 16–20a

16 Οἱ δὲ στρατιῶται ἀπήγαγον αὐτὸν

19 1–3: Τότε οὖν ἔλαβεν ὁ Πιλᾶτος τὸν Ἰησοῦν καὶ ἐμαστίγωσεν.

Mt 27,24 ● κατεναντι: B D | τουτ.] τουτ. του δικαιου‖Lk23 47: Φ A Δ **064** *pc l*1231 *L*fhr^{2}z vg^{1} Au^{2} *S*pj{} *Geo*^{1}(^{2} *om* τ. δι.) — ● του δικ. τουτ. ‖←: *Rpl* CAp Cr Cr^{I} Thd^{M} *L*'[ek] Au^{2} *S*h {*C*s^{2}b'} *Arm* — *txt* (+ του ανθρωπου): B D Θ 229 PsAth Chr Hip(τουτ.] αυτ.) *L*abff^{2}r^{1} vg^{1} Cp Or *S*s[c] *C*s^{1+1v}(^{3}b^{1}) **26** *cf. ad* 16

Mk 15,15 *om* βουλ.—ποι.‖p: D *L*k[e] ff^{2}r^{1v} | ∼ και τον Ι. παρεδ. φρα.‖p: σ1402 *C*b^{1}(τον δε Ι. *et* φραγελλωθηναι) — τον(και) δε(τον) Ι. φρα. παρ.‖p: 565-(700) D *pc* *L*k[e] (*om* δε) *C*sf^{v} (*Arm*) *Aeth* | παρεδ. + αυτοις‖Jo16: F *pc* *L*cg^{2}30 vg^{4} *S* **16** απηγ.] απηνεγκαν‖15 1: *l*260

Lk 23,25 δε + αυτοις‖p: 1071-1604 **λλ**⟨2193⟩ **φ**⟨788⟩ σM-7-659-1207-1223 K Π *mu* *L*⟨a⟩ *S*'h^{-} | τον^{1} + Βαραββαν τον‖p: **λλ**⟨1278⟩ **φ**-*l*547 σ7-71-659-692-1207-1223 1064 *al* *Arm* | στασ. + τινα‖19: σ659 | ● *om* την‖22 23 Mt5 25p: ℵB-**0124** 28-1071-1604 φ69-983 σ692 D F K Θ *pc l*49 Or {} — εν τη φυλακη‖19: 579 W 235 *l*184 *L*vg^{2} — *txt*: 𝔓^{75} *Rpl* {*L*'} | Ι. + φραγελλωσας‖p: φ69

Jo 19,1 ελαβ.—και] ● ο Π. λαβων(∼λαβων ο Π.) τ. Ι.: (ℵW)LX-33-579 1071 *pc* *L*a — *txt*(∼ ο Π. ελ.): (𝔓^{66v}) *Rpl* (**054** σM Y **0141**) (∼ ελ. τ. Ι. ο Π.: N) *L*' | εμασ. + αυτον‖Mk10 34: σ659 *pc* *L*e acj^{v}r^{1v} vg^{4} *S*[sc]hj *C*$^{+B}$a^{s} *Geo* *Aeth* **14** ωσει‖Lk23 44: *Rpl* Chrn Cr Thd^{C} — *txt*: 𝔓^{66c}(^{1}?)(* *om* ην ως) 𝔋⟨1241⟩X-**054**-**065** Λ-544 λ2193 σ7-945-1010-1424 A E K S V Y Γ Θ Ψ Ω **053** *al* | εκτη] τριτη‖Mk15 25: ℵ^{c} LX D^{s} Δ Ψ **053** Chrn Ep **15** εκρ. ουν εκ.] οι(εκ.) δε εκρ.‖Mt23 Mk14 Lk23: *Rpl* (+ ουν: 33) *L*'(fz vg) *S*[sc],j *C*$^{+B}$a^{sv} *Geo*^{2} — και εκ. εκρ.: *Arm* *Geo*^{1} — *txt*: ℵ^{c}BLX 1071 Ψ *pc* Cr^{cmt} *L*e(*om* εκ.) bjn^{v}q(ουν] δε) | εκραυαζον‖12 Mt23: **054**-1241 N λ2193 D^{s} K Y Θ Π (-ασον: A 1346) *pc* — εκραζον‖←: *l*135 *l*^{a1} — ελεγον: 𝔓^{66*v} ℵ*W *S*[sc]j | εκ.] παντες‖18 40 Mt23 Lk18: **0141** 1321 | *om* αυτον‖6: φ13-543-826-828 *Geo*

Mt27 26p *cf.* EN frgm.34 (HPass fol.44r°): Legitur in evangelio Nazareorum quod Judei appreciaverunt quattuor milites ad flagellandum dominum tam dure usque ad effusionem sanguinis de toto corpore. Eosdem eciam milites appreciaverunt quod ipsum crucifix(ere)nt sicut dicitur Jo19.

cf. EP 2,5: ... καὶ παρέδωκεν αὐτὸν τῷ λαῷ πρὸ μιᾶς τῶν ἀζύμων τῆς ἑορτῆς αὐτῶν ... (*cf. ad 262.*)

262. cf. EP 3,6-9: (*cf. ad 266.*) ... Οἱ δὲ λαβόντες τὸν κύριον ὤθουν αὐτὸν τρέχοντες καὶ ἔλεγον· [7]'σύρωμεν τὸν υἱὸν τοῦ θεοῦ ἐξουσίαν αὐτοῦ ἐσχηκότες'. καὶ πορφύραν αὐτὸν περιέβαλον καὶ ἐκάθισαν αὐτὸν ἐπὶ καθέδραν κρίσεως λέγοντες· 'δικαίως κρῖνε, βασιλεῦ τοῦ Ισραηλ'. [8]καί τις αὐτῶν ἐνεγκὼν στέφανον ἀκάνθινον ἔθηκεν ἐπὶ τῆς κεφαλῆς τοῦ κυρίου. [9]καὶ ἕτεροι ἑστῶτες ἐνέπτυον αὐτοῦ ταῖς ὄψεσι καὶ ἄλλοι τὰς σιαγόνας αὐτοῦ ἐράπισαν, ἕτεροι καλάμῳ ἔνυσσον αὐτὸν καί τινες αὐτὸν ἐμάστιζον λέγοντες· 'ταύτῃ τῇ τιμῇ τιμήσωμεν τὸν υἱὸν τοῦ θεοῦ.' (4)[10]Καὶ ἤνεγκον ... (*cf. ad 264.*)

Matth: εἰς τὸ πραιτώριον συνήγαγον ἐπ' αὐτὸν ὅλην τὴν σπεῖραν. [28] καὶ ἐκδύσαντες αὐτὸν χλαμύδα κοκκίνην περιέθηκαν αὐτῷ, [29] καὶ πλέξαντες στέφανον ἐξ ἀκανθῶν ἐπέθηκαν ἐπὶ τῆς κεφαλῆς αὐτοῦ καὶ κάλαμον ἐν τῇ δεξιᾷ αὐτοῦ, καὶ γονυπετήσαντες ἔμπροσθεν αὐτοῦ ἐνέπαιζον αὐτῷ λέγοντες· χαῖρε, βασιλεῦ τῶν Ἰουδαίων· [30] καὶ ἐμπτύσαντες εἰς αὐτὸν ἔλαβον τὸν κάλαμον καὶ ἔτυπτον εἰς τὴν κεφαλὴν αὐτοῦ. cf. v. 29 b ↑

Mark: ἔσω τῆς αὐλῆς, ὅ ἐστιν πραιτώριον, καὶ συγκαλοῦσιν ὅλην τὴν σπεῖραν. [17] καὶ ἐνδιδύσκουσιν αὐτὸν πορφύραν καὶ περιτιθέασιν αὐτῷ πλέξαντες ἀκάνθινον στέφανον· cf. v. 19 b ↓ [18] καὶ ἤρξαντο ἀσπάζεσθαι αὐτόν· χαῖρε, βασιλεῦ τῶν Ἰουδαίων· [19] καὶ ἔτυπτον αὐτοῦ τὴν κεφαλὴν καλάμῳ καὶ ἐνέπτυον αὐτῷ, καὶ τιθέντες τὰ γόνατα προσεκύνουν αὐτῷ.

Joh 19: [2] καὶ οἱ στρατιῶται πλέξαντες στέφανον ἐξ ἀκανθῶν ἐπέθηκαν αὐτοῦ τῇ κεφαλῇ, καὶ ἱμάτιον πορφυροῦν περιέβαλον αὐτόν, [3] καὶ ἤρχοντο πρὸς αὐτὸν καὶ ἔλεγον· χαῖρε, ὁ βασιλεὺς τῶν Ἰουδαίων· καὶ ἐδίδοσαν αὐτῷ ῥαπίσματα.

Matth: [31a] καὶ ὅτε ἐνέπαιξαν αὐτῷ, ἐξέδυσαν αὐτὸν τὴν χλαμύδα καὶ ἐνέδυσαν αὐτὸν τὰ ἱμάτια αὐτοῦ.

Mark: [20a] καὶ ὅτε ἐνέπαιξαν αὐτῷ, ἐξέδυσαν αὐτὸν τὴν πορφύραν καὶ ἐνέδυσαν αὐτὸν τὰ ἱμάτια τὰ ἴδια.

(247. 248)

263. Der Todesgang. *The Road to Calvary.*

Matth 27 31b–32: [31b] Καὶ ἀπήγαγον αὐτὸν εἰς τὸ σταυρῶσαι. [32] ἐξερχόμενοι

Mark 15 20b–21: [20b] Καὶ ἐξάγουσιν αὐτὸν ἵνα σταυρώσωσιν αὐτόν. [21] καὶ

Luk 23 26–32: [26] Καὶ ὡς ἀπήγαγον αὐτόν, ἐπιλαβόμενοι Σίμωνά τινα Κυ-

19 16f.: ... Παρέλαβον οὖν τὸν

Mt 27,28 ενδυσαντες‖p: ℵ^{ca}B D 157 348 *L*[ek] abcff^{2}q Or *Ss*[c]j *Aeth* | αυτον + ιματιον πορφυρουν‖JoMk: D 157(*om* και) 348 *L*[ek] abcff^{2} *Sj* — + περιεβαλον αυτον ιμ. πορ. και: *L*fhr^{2}30 | κοκ. + και πορφυραν‖p: *L*q(∼ περ. αυτω και πορ.) Or *Ss*[c] **29** επεθ.—αυτου^{1}] αυτου τη κεφαλη επεθ.‖Jo: 33 H (∼ τ. κ. αυ.) | περιεθηκαν‖28Mk: B 131 | ● ενεπαιξαν‖31Mk20: ℌ D Γ *pc* — *txt*: *Rpl* Chr Eu *L*,Or *S*,j | λεγ.] δεροντες‖Jo18 23: A | βασ.] ● ο βασιλευς‖Jo: *Rpl* Eu — *txt*: B Φ **λ**-1582 σ7 D Y Δ Θ Π *al* **30** εις αυτον] αυτω‖Mk: 33 σ659 *pc* | *om* εις^{2}‖Mk: 348 1279 *L* **31** χλ. + και το ιματιον το πορφυρουν‖p: 157 *L*h *Sj* | αυτου] τα ιδια‖p: σ659 *Geo*

Mk 15,16 εσω] εως‖14 54 Mt26 58: 157 *pc l*15 *l*32^{1} *l*251^{1} | εσω τ. αυλ.] εσω(*om*) εις την αυλην‖14 54: (C^{3}) Θ-565-700 **λ**-22-1278 **φ**'⟨124⟩(69-346-826 σM) D P *pc* (*pc l*31 *l*47 *l*63 *l*183^{1} *l*^{a1}) *L*vg$^{⟨10⟩}$ (*S*j) | αυλ. + του Καιαφα‖Mt26 3: Θ σM *pc l*63 *l*67 *l*183^{1} *l*184 *l*^{a1} | ο εστ. πραι.] του αρχιερεως‖←: 1200 | πραι.] το πραι.‖pJo18 28: 1241 U 127 | συγκ. + επ αυτον‖p: 1574 1579 *C*⟨f⟩ **17** αυτον + χλαμυδα κοκκινην και‖p: Θ-565-700-1071 **φ** σ1606 *pc* (*et om* πορφ. και: *pc*) *l*251^{1} *Sj Arm* | επιτιθε.‖p: D *Sj* | ακ. στε.] στε. εξ ακανθων‖MtJo: Θ λ1-872 **047** 1342 *pc l*49 *Lk*[e] d **18** αυτ. + και λεγειν‖p: ℵC^{2}-33-579 NΣ **λ**⟨1⟩-1278 **φ**346 σ1194-1402-1606 U 157 *al Sj Arm* — + λεγοντες‖p: **φ***l*547 σM-1082-1391 157 *pm L*cz vg^{1} *Cf* | βασ.] ο βασιλευς‖Jo: *Rpl* (-λευ: Ω) — *txt*: ℵBXΨ Θ-28-565-700 **λ**-22 **φ**230 σM-349-1207-1606 D P S V **047** 1342 *pc l*1629 **19** ∼ τ. κεφ. αυ.‖p: C-892 Σ σ1207 **047** *pc* | αυτου—καλ.] αυτον καλ. εις τ. κεφ.‖p: 565 D *Lk*[e] cff^{2} *S*(∼ εις τ. κεφ. καλ.: s[c]ph)j *Aeth* | *om* κ. τιθ.—αυτω^{2}‖p: σ71-692 D 253 *pc Lk*[e](*om* κ. ενεπτ.—αυτω^{2}) | αυτω^{2}] αυτον‖5 7: 579 472 **20** πορφ.] χλαμυδα‖p: λ1-22-872 *pc* — χλ. και την πορφ.‖p: Θ-565-700-1071 **φ** *pc Sj Arm* | ιμ. τα ιδ.] ● ιμ. αυτου‖p: BCΔΨ 1342 *C*,f^{v} — ● ιδ. ιμ. (+ αυτου)‖p: (ℵ)-**0215**^{v}-892 Θ σ115 282 (472) — ιμ. αυτου τα ιδ.‖p: λ2193 1279(∼ τα ιδ. αυ.) *pc* — *txt*: *Rpl* (*om* τα ιδ.: D **φ** *l*547) *Ss*[c]h | ινα στ. αυ.] ινα σταυρωθη‖15 15 Mt27 26 Jo19 16: 28 131 — ωστε σταυρωσαι‖Mt31 27 1: λ1-872 72(+ αυτον) *pc Geo*^{1} | ● *om* αυτον^{4}‖Mt: ℵ 700 **σ**⟨954⟩ D 122^{c} *l*47 *Lk*[e] ff^{2} *Sp*^{1} *Geo*

Lk 23,26 *om* ως‖p: 660 | αυτον + εις το σταυρωσαι‖p: 1071 *Geo* | Σιμωνος τινος Κυρηναιου ερχομενου(-ον): *Rpl* (565 H *pc l*184) — *txt*: ℌ'(C)(*om* τινα: L-**0124**) **φ**'(ερχομενου: 13-69-346-543-788-826)-*l*547 (D) 213 1342 *l*7 | ∼ τινα Σ.‖Mk: C D *Lr*^{1}

Jo 19,2 περιεθηκαν‖Mk: 1355 | ∼ τη κεφ. αυ.‖Mt: G **0141** *pc L* | τη κεφ.] επι την κεφαλην‖Mt: λ2193 A G U Π **0141** *al L*cqr^{1} vg^{1} **3** *om* και^{1}—αυτον‖p: *Rpl Lfq Sp* — *txt*: 𝔓$^{60.66v}$ ℌ⟨1241⟩X NΛ-28-544-700 λ2193 **φ**-230-*l*547 σ659 U Θ Π **0141** *al* Cr^{cmt} Non *L' S*[sc]hj *C*$^{+B}$a^{s} *Arm Aeth* | ελεγ.] ηρξαντο λεγειν‖Mk: 544 | ο βασ.] βασιλευ‖p: 𝔓^{66} ℵ **16** παρελ.] παραλαβοντες‖Mt27 27: 𝔓^{66v} ℵ^{c}(*λαβ.)W-579 N-700 **λ** **φ**-*l*547 σM-7 U Π^{c} *mu l*135 *l*260 *l*1599 Or *S*[sc]j *Cs*(*om*: b^{B})a^{s} | τ. Ι.] αυτον‖p: 𝔓^{66} **λ** **φ**-*l*547 σM *pc* Or *Geo*$^{⟨B⟩}$

Matth 27: δὲ εὗρον ἄνθρωπον Κυρηναῖον, ὀνόματι Σίμωνα· τοῦτον ἠγγάρευσαν ἵνα ἄρῃ τὸν σταυρὸν αὐτοῦ.

Mark 15: ἀγγαρεύουσιν παράγοντά τινα Σίμωνα Κυρηναῖον ἐρχόμενον ἀπ᾽ ἀγροῦ, τὸν πατέρα Ἀλεξάνδρου καὶ Ῥούφου, ἵνα ἄρῃ τὸν σταυρὸν αὐτοῦ.

Luk 23: ρηναῖον ἐρχόμενον ἀπ᾽ ἀγροῦ ἐπέθηκαν αὐτῷ τὸν σταυρὸν φέρειν ὄπισθεν τοῦ Ἰησοῦ. [27] ἠκολούθει δὲ αὐτῷ πολὺ πλῆθος τοῦ λαοῦ καὶ γυναικῶν αἳ ἐκόπτοντο καὶ ἐθρήνουν αὐτόν. [28] στραφεὶς δὲ πρὸς αὐτὰς ὁ Ἰησοῦς εἶπεν· θυγατέρες Ἰερουσαλημ, μὴ κλαίετε ἐπ᾽ ἐμέ· πλὴν ἐφ᾽ ἑαυτὰς κλαίετε καὶ ἐπὶ τὰ τέκνα ὑμῶν, [29] ὅτι ἰδοὺ ἡμέραι ἔρχονται ἐν αἷς ἐροῦσιν· μακάριαι αἱ στεῖραι, καὶ αἱ κοιλίαι αἳ οὐκ ἐγέννησαν, καὶ μαστοὶ οἳ οὐκ ἔθρεψαν. [30] τότε ἄρξονται **λέγειν τοῖς ὄρεσιν· πέσετε ἐφ᾽ ἡμᾶς, καὶ τοῖς βουνοῖς· καλύψατε ἡμᾶς·** [31] ὅτι εἰ ἐν τῷ ὑγρῷ ξύλῳ ταῦτα ποιοῦσιν, ἐν τῷ ξηρῷ τί γένηται; [32] ἤγοντο δὲ καὶ ἕτεροι δύο κακοῦργοι σὺν αὐτῷ ἀναιρεθῆναι.

(Margin: Hos10 8; *cf. 264.*)

Jo 19: Ἰησοῦν· [17] καὶ βαστάζων ἑαυτῷ τὸν σταυρὸν ἐξῆλθεν ...

(249)

264. Die Kreuzigung. *The Crucifixion.*

Matth 27 33–44	Mark 15 22–32	Luk 23 33–43	
[33] Καὶ ἐλθόντες εἰς τόπον λεγόμενον Γολγοθα,	[22] Καὶ φέρουσιν αὐτὸν ἐπὶ τὸν Γολγοθᾶν	[33] Καὶ ὅτε ἀπῆλθον ἐπὶ τὸν	19 17–24: ... ἐξῆλθεν εἰς

Mt 27,32 *om* ανθ.‖Mk: 700 | Κ. + ερχομενον απ αγρου‖MkLk: 33 **33** τοπ.] τον τοπ. τον‖LkMk: B *l*47(*om* τον²) | *om* λεγομενον‖Mk: ℵ*

Mk 15,21 *om* παραγ.‖p: ΝΣ 1342 *S*s[c] *C*b¹ | ∼ Σ. τινα‖Lk: 579 **λ**⟨118⟩-872 1542 **22** επι] εις‖MtJo: **ϕ** | *om* τον‖Mt: *Rpl Cs*² — *txt*: 𝔥C² ΝΘΣ-565-1071 λ872 **ϕ** σ517-1402-1424 F 1342 *al Cs*⁴b | ∼ τοπ. Γ.‖Mt: D

Lk 23,26 φερ.] αιρειν‖p 9 23p: ℵᵃ(* *om*) | οπισω‖9 23p: σ-7-115-659 *pc l*18 *l*19 *l*48 | τ. Ι.] αυτου‖p: **λ** *Lc Cb*⁷ **27** γυναικες‖23 49p.55: 1071 D 243 *L*cfr¹ *S*scp *Aeth Δ*a n⟨L⟩ **28** ● *om* ο: 𝔓⁷⁵ ℵ*BL **29** ● ∼ ερχ. (+ αι) ημ. *cf.* 5 35p 17 22 *etc.*: 𝔓⁷⁵(ερχεται) *Rpl* (579) *L* — *txt*: ℵCX-**0124**-1241 1071-1604 σ71-692 *pc* | εθρ.] εθηλασαν‖11 27: *Rpl L*fz{} vg *S*' *Cs Geo*¹ — εξεθρ.: C²-579-1241 **λλ**'⟨22-1278⟩ D' F G Γ Θ Ψ 655 *La* — *txt*: 𝔓⁷⁵ 𝔥'⟨33⟩C*-**0124** λ131 Γ *pc* {*L*vl'r¹ᵛ} *S*hᵐ Cr *Geo*² *Aeth* **31** ● *om* τω¹: BC-**0124** 1574 **32** *om* ετερ.‖Mt 27 38 Mk 15 27: *Le* c *Sc* | ● ∼ κακ. δυο: 𝔓⁷⁵ ℵB — δυο λησται‖Mt←Mk←: *L* vl⟨cz⟩ **33** απηλθ.] ● ηλθ.‖Mt: 𝔓⁷⁵ 𝔥'C-**0124** Θ-1071 ϕ69-124-788 D Q Ψ *pc* Mchᴱᵖ(και ελθοντες) *L S*'hᵐj — *txt*: *Rpl* (εισηλθ.: 579) Da *S*hᵗ

Jo 19,16 Ι. + απηγαγον (*prm* και)‖MtLk: 𝔓⁶⁰·⁶⁶ᵛ ℵW-579 N-700 **λ** (ϕ230) σM (A) U Πᶜ (*mu*) *al* (*L*vg') *Csb*¹(¹)ᴮ (∼ απ. τ. Ι.) *Geo*² — + και(*om*) ηγαγον‖Mt: *Rpl* (**ϕ**' σ7 *al l*135 *l*1599) Chr *L*fq vg⁹ *S*[sc] *Geo*¹ ⟦απηγ./ηγαγον + αυτον‖p: ℵ Chr¹:² *S*[sc] *Csb*² — + οι στρατιωται‖Mt 27 27p: σ659 — + εις το πραιτωριον‖←: 700 σM-7-1194 U(∼ εις—πρ. απηγ.) Γ *pm l*135 *l*1599 Cr — + εις το σταυρωσαι‖MtMk: 28ˢ *pc* — + και επεθηκαν αυτω τον σταυρον‖Lk: **ϕ**⟨69-124-788⟩⟧ — + επεθηκαν—σταυ.(+ αυτου)‖Lk: ϕ69-124-788-*l*547 (*Sj*ᵇᶜ; ᵃ *et prm* εις το πραι.) Or — *txt*: 𝔥'⟨1241⟩X Ψ **0141** *pc* Cr *L*vl'jᵛr¹ *C*b' **17** *om* και—εξηλ.‖MtMkLk: 𝔓⁶⁶* | εαυτω τ. στ.] τ. στ. αυτου(*om*)‖Mt 16 24p: *Rpl L*q {Or} *S*[sc] *Csb*'(ᴮ¹)aᵇⱽ — τ. στ. εαυτου‖←: **054-065** N-700 A U **0141** *pc* Chr Cr *L*'{} | εαυτου (αυτ.) τ. στ.‖←: (700) σ1223 Dˢ Θ(482) *pc l*1599 — τ. στ. εαυτω(αυτω): **λ**-(1582) 565 — αυτον: **ϕ**-*l*547 *Sj* — *txt* (αυτω): 𝔓⁶⁰·⁶⁶ᶜ 𝔥'(BX-33)(εβασταζον αυτω τ. στ.: 579) (1071) λ2193 Π Ψ (1093) *pc* Crᶜᵐᵗ Or *L*' | εις τον] εις τοπον(τον τ.)‖Mt: 𝔓⁶⁶ *Rpl* (ϕ346 *pc*) *L*vlr¹30 vg³ Or *S*[sc]ph⁺j *Cs*⁹⁽⁺²?⁾(b⁺ᴮ) — *txt*: 𝔓⁶⁰ 𝔥⟨1241⟩X-**054-065** N-28ˢ **λ** ϕ69-788-*l*547 σM-1194-1223 A Dˢ K U Y(το) Θ Π Ψ **0141** *pm* Cr *L*vg' *Cs*¹

Lk 23 29 *cf.* ETh^II 79: (*cf. ad 165.*) ... *ἡμέραι γὰρ ἔσονται, ἐν αἷς ἐρεῖτε· μακαρία ἡ κοιλία ἣ οὐ συνέλαβεν καὶ οἱ μαστοὶ οἳ οὐκ ἔθρεψαν(ἐθήλασαν?)*

264. cf. EP 4,10-14: (*cf. ad 262.*) ... Καὶ ἤνεγκον δύο κακούργους καὶ ἐσταύρωσαν ἀνὰ μέσον αὐτῶν τὸν κύριον· αὐτὸς δὲ ἐσιώπα ὡς μηδένα πόνον ἔχων· [11] καὶ ὅτε ὤρθωσαν τὸν σταυρὸν ἐπέγραψαν ὅτι ‘οὗτός ἐστιν ὁ βασιλεὺς τοῦ Ἰσραηλ’. [12] καὶ τεθεικότες τὰ ἐνδύματα ἔμπροσθεν αὐτοῦ διεμερίσαντο, καὶ λαχμὸν ἔβαλον ἐπ᾽ αὐτοῖς. [13] εἷς δέ τις τῶν κακούργων ἐκείνων ὠνείδισεν αὐτοὺς λέγων· ‘ἡμεῖς διὰ τὰ κακὰ ἃ ἐποιήσαμεν οὕτω πεπόνθαμεν, οὗτος δὲ σωτὴρ γενόμενος τῶν ἀνθρώπων τί ἠδίκησεν ὑμᾶς;’ [14] καὶ ἀγανακτήσαντες ἐπ᾽ αὐτῷ ἐκέλευσαν ἵνα μὴ σκελοκοπηθῇ, ὅπως βασανιζόμενος ἀποθάνῃ. (5) [15] Ἦν δὲ ... (*cf. ad 265.*)

<table>
<tr><td>ὅ ἐστιν κρανίου τόπος λεγόμενος, 34 ἔδωκαν αὐτῷ πιεῖν οἶνον μετὰ χολῆς μεμιγμένον· καὶ γευσάμενος οὐκ ἠθέλησεν πιεῖν. 35 σταυρώσαντες δὲ αὐτὸν
cf. v. 38 ↓</td><td>τόπον, ὅ ἐστιν μεθερμηνευόμενον κρανίου τόπος.
23 καὶ ἐδίδουν αὐτῷ ἐσμυρνισμένον οἶνον· ὃς δὲ οὐκ ἔλαβεν. 24 καὶ σταυρώσαντες αὐτόν,
cf. v. 27 ↓</td><td>τόπον τὸν καλούμενον Κρανίον,
ἐκεῖ ἐσταύρωσαν αὐτὸν καὶ τοὺς κακούργους, ὃν μὲν ἐκ δεξιῶν ὃν δὲ ἐξ ἀριστερῶν. 34 ὁ δὲ Ἰησοῦς ἔλεγεν· πάτερ, ἄφες αὐτοῖς· οὐ γὰρ οἴδασιν τί ποιοῦσιν.</td><td>τὸν λεγόμενον Κρανίου τόπον, ὃς λέγεται Ἑβραϊστὶ Γολγοθα, (Ps69 22)
18 ὅπου αὐτὸν ἐσταύρωσαν ... 23 οἱ οὖν στρατιῶται, ὅτε ἐσταύρωσαν τὸν Ἰησοῦν, ἔλαβον τὰ ἱμάτια αὐτοῦ καὶ ἐποίησαν τέσσερα μέρη, ἑκάστῳ στρατιώτῃ μέρος, καὶ τὸν χιτῶνα. ἦν δὲ</td></tr>
<tr><td colspan="4">ὁ χιτὼν ἄρραφος, ἐκ τῶν ἄνωθεν ὑφαντὸς δι᾽ ὅλου. 24 εἶπον οὖν πρὸς ἀλλήλους· μὴ σχίσωμεν αὐτόν, ἀλλὰ λάχωμεν περὶ</td></tr>
<tr><td></td><td></td><td></td><td>αὐτοῦ τίνος ἔσται· ἵνα ἡ γραφὴ πληρωθῇ ἡ λέγουσα·</td></tr>
<tr><td>διεμερίσαντο τὰ ἱμάτια αὐτοῦ
βάλ-</td><td>διαμερίζονται τὰ ἱμάτια αὐτοῦ,
βάλ-</td><td>διαμεριζόμενοι δὲ τὰ ἱμάτια αὐτοῦ
ἔβαλον</td><td>διεμερίσαντο τὰ ἱμάτιά μου ἑαυτοῖς καὶ ἐπὶ τὸν ἱματισμόν μου ἔβαλον (Ps22 19)</td></tr>
</table>

Mt 27,33 ο] ος‖Jo: Φ ϕ124 σ71-349-517-990-1223-1675 A E^{c} S V Y Δ Θ Π Ω *al* | ∼ λεγομενος(-ον) κρα. τοπος(-ον)‖Mk Jo: *Rpl* (N*Σ W *l*52 *l*54 *pm*) (-ον κρα. -ος: ϕ*l*547^{1}) *L*vg^{1} *S*hj^{ab1}(^{1}*om* τοπ.)^{c} — μεθερμηνευομενος(-ον) κρα. τοπος‖Mk: N^{c}(ερμην.)-(1604) σM 252^{c} (348 476 *l*183^{1}) *L*r^{1} (*om* τοπ.‖Lk: *S*pj^{k}) (*sim*: *Aeth*) — *om* λεγομενος *cf.* Mk3 17 7 11: ℵ^{ca} 544-700 ϕ124 σ1424^{c} D Θ *pc* *L*'[ek] *C* *Arm* — *txt*: ℌ⟨1241⟩ λ⟨118⟩-1582 157 713(λεγομενον) *L*ff^{1} vg^{2} **34** εδωκαν] και εδ.‖Mk: D *L*[ek]⟨f⟩ Or *S*s[c]pj | *om* πειν^{1}‖Mk: L σ27 *S*p^{1} *C*b *Arm*^{pc} *Geo*^{2} | οιν.] οξος‖27 48p Lk 36: *Rpl* *L*cfhq Or *S*'j^{a1} Ef *C*b^{2} *Geo*^{2} — *txt*: ℵBL-33 λ⟨118⟩-22-1582 ϕ69-543-788-826 D K Θ Π *pc* Or *L*[ek]⟨ff^{2}(*om*)⟩ Or *S*s[c]h^{m}j^{a1bck} *C*' *Arm* *Geo*^{1} *Aeth*

Mk 15,22 ● μεθερμηνευομενος: ℵB-892 NΣ *pc* **23** αυτω + πειν‖Mt: *Rpl* *L*' Au *S*'j *C*s^{3} *Geo*^{2} — *txt*: ℵBC*LΔΨ 700 1342 *pc* *L*n *S*s[c] *C*s^{2}bf *Arm* *Geo*^{1} | ος δε] ● ο δε: *Rpl* {} — και‖Mt: λ D *L*,Au *S*s[c] — *txt*: ℵB-33-579-892 Σ σ517-1675 Γ^{v} {*S*' *C*} | ουκ] γευσαμενος ουκ‖Mt: λ G | ελα.] ηθελεν‖Mt: 213 1342 — ηθ. λαβειν‖Mt: *C*b^{1}f^{v} **24** κ. σταυ. αυ.] ● κ. σταυρουσιν(εσταυρωσαν) αυ. και‖27: BL(*om* και^{2}) Ψ-892 (*L*k[e] cff^{1}r^{1})(*et om* και^{2}: d) (*S*s[c]) *C*s^{1}bf *Arm*'(^{pc}) — *txt* (σταυρουντες): *Rpl* (στ. + δε: 1071) *L*l(nz vg Au) *S*ph(^{m})j *C*s^{3}(στ. + δε) | διεμερισαντο‖Mt: 1071(-σαν) ϕ983-1689 *pc* *l*13 *l*44 *l*253 *L*,Au | βαλλ.—αυτα] και επι τον ιματισμον αυτου βαλλ. κλ.‖Jo Ps21 19 LXX: 157 — *om*: σ349 — *om* επ αυτα‖Mt Lk: *L*k[e] cff^{2}nr^{1} *S*j^{c}

Lk 23,33 καλ.] λεγομενον‖Mt Jo: CX Λ G 157 *al* Mcn^{Ep} *L*ff^{2}30 vg^{2} | Κρ.] κρανιου τοπον‖Jo Mt Mk: **047** Mcn^{Ep}(τοπος) | ∼ αυ. εσταυ.‖Jo: ϕ69 *L*fl | κακ.] δυο κακ.‖23 32: 28 157 1012 *L*vg^{1} {} — κακ. δυο‖←: **0124** *L*vg^{1} {*C*s} — ληστας‖p: *L*'⟨c⟩ | ον ... ον] ενα ... ετερον‖p *cf.* 17 34f. Mt 6 24p: 1355 | αρι.] ευωνυμων‖p: *C**L-**0124**-33 N-28-544-1604 λ2193 ϕ Q Ψ 157 **34** *om* ο δε—ποιου.‖p: 𝔓^{75} ℵ^{a}B-**0124**-579-1241 D* W Θ *pc* Cr *L*a *S*s *C*sb^{12} — *om* ου γ. οιδ.: 1012 — *txt*: *Rpl* (E^{+}) APh APi Bas CAp Chr Cl PsCl Da Eu^{can} (Hgs^{Eu}) HM PsIg Iu Mcn Thd^{C} *L*'Am Amph Amst Au PsAu Hi Hil Ir Or *S*'j Ef LG *C*b' *Δ*, E^{sa} | διεμεριζοντο ... βαλλοντες(-λ-)‖p: D *L*c (*C*b^{6})

Jo 19,17 λεγο.] καλουμενον‖Lk: σ954 *L*acr^{1}z *S*[sc]pj | Κρ. τοπ.] Κρανιον‖Lk: 1071 | *om* τοπ.‖Lk: 𝔓^{66} Γ *pc* *L*cff^{2}z30 vg^{1} *S*[sc]pj | ος] ● ο‖13 9 20 16 Mt Mk: 𝔓^{66} ℵBW-579 1071 A K **0141** *al* *l*135 *l*1599 Cr *L*acfff^{2}qz *S*[sc]j **18** ∼ εσταυ. αυ.‖Lk: λ σ945 *pc* *L*ff^{2} *Arm* **23** οτε εστ.] οι σταυρωσαντες‖Mt Mk: ℵ-579 1170(*om* οι) | τ. Ι.] αυτον‖p: 1071 ϕ124 713 *L*32 vg$^{\langle 1\rangle}$ Au *C*s$^{5:13}$ **24** ∼ πλη. η γρ.‖19 28 Mk 28(*cf. ad* 27) 14 49: 579 1170 Eu *L*f vg^{1} *S*[sc]p | ● *om* η λεγ.‖**13** 18 **19** 36: ℵB 249 *L*e abcff^{2}r^{1} *C*s$^{6:12}$ b^{B}a^{s} | *om* εαυτ.‖Mt Mk Lk: W-579 Λ Ep *L*bn*

Lk23 34 *cf.* EN frgm.24 (Haimo Is *ad* 53 12): Sicut enim in evangelio Nazaraeorum habetur, ad hanc vocem domini (*sc.* Lk23 34) multa milia Judaeorum astantium circa crucem crediderunt.

frgm.35 (Hist. pass. dom. fol.55^{r}): Pater ignosce eis. Non enim sciunt quid faciunt. Et nota, quod in evangelio Nazareorum legitur quod ad virtuosam istam Christi oracionem VIII milia conversi sunt postea ad fidem. scilicet tria milia in die pentecostes. sicut habetur Actuum 2° et postea quinque milia de quibus dicitur Actuum X.

Matth	Mark	Luk	Jo
λοντες κλῆρον, 36 καὶ καθήμενοι ἐτήρουν αὐτὸν ἐκεῖ.	**λοντες κλῆρον ἐπ'** αὐτὰ τίς τί ἄρῃ. 25 ἦν δὲ ὥρα τρίτη καὶ ἐσταύρωσαν αὐτόν. 26 καὶ ἦν ἡ ἐπιγραφὴ	**κλήρους.**	**κλῆρον.** οἱ μὲν οὖν στρατιῶται ταῦτα ἐποίησαν …
37 καὶ ἐπέθηκαν ἐπάνω τῆς κεφαλῆς αὐτοῦ τὴν αἰτίαν αὐτοῦ γεγραμμένην· οὗτός ἐστιν Ἰησοῦς ὁ βασιλεὺς τῶν Ἰουδαίων.	τῆς αἰτίας αὐτοῦ ἐπιγεγραμμένη· ὁ βασιλεὺς τῶν Ἰουδαίων.	38 *ἦν δὲ καὶ ἐπιγραφὴ γεγραμμένη ἐπ' αὐτῷ γράμμασιν Ἑλληνικοῖς καὶ Ῥωμαϊκοῖς καὶ Ἑβραϊκοῖς· ὁ βασιλεὺς τῶν Ἰουδαίων οὗτος.*	19 ἔγραψεν δὲ καὶ τίτλον ὁ Πιλᾶτος καὶ ἔθηκεν ἐπὶ τοῦ σταυροῦ· ἦν δὲ γεγραμμένον· Ἰησοῦς ὁ Ναζωραῖος ὁ βασιλεὺς τῶν Ἰουδαίων.

20 τοῦτον οὖν τὸν τίτλον πολλοὶ ἀνέγνωσαν τῶν Ἰουδαίων, ὅτι ἐγγὺς ἦν ὁ τόπος τῆς πόλεως ὅπου ἐσταυρώθη ὁ Ἰησοῦς· καὶ ἦν γεγραμμένον Ἑβραϊστί, Ῥωμαϊστί, Ἑλληνιστί. 21 ἔλεγον οὖν τῷ Πιλάτῳ οἱ ἀρχιερεῖς τῶν Ἰουδαίων· μὴ γράφε· ὁ βασιλεὺς τῶν Ἰουδαίων, ἀλλ' ὅτι ἐκεῖνος εἶπεν· βασιλεύς εἰμι τῶν Ἰουδαίων. 22 ἀπεκρίθη ὁ Πιλᾶτος· ὃ γέγραφα, γέγραφα… 18 ὅπου

Matth	Mark	Luk	Jo
38 τότε σταυροῦνται σὺν αὐτῷ δύο λῃσταί, εἷς ἐκ δεξιῶν καὶ εἷς ἐξ εὐωνύμων.	27 καὶ σὺν αὐτῷ σταυροῦσιν δύο λῃστάς, ἕνα ἐκ δεξιῶν καὶ ἕνα ἐξ εὐωνύμων αὐτοῦ.	33 … *ἐσταύρωσαν αὐτὸν καὶ τοὺς κακούργους, ὃν μὲν ἐκ δεξιῶν ὃν δὲ ἐξ ἀριστερῶν.* *cf. 263.*	αὐτὸν ἐσταύρωσαν, καὶ μετ' αὐτοῦ ἄλλους δύο ἐντεῦθεν καὶ ἐντεῦθεν, μέσον δὲ τὸν Ἰησοῦν.

	Matth	Mark	Luk
Ps22 8 Thr2 15	39 οἱ δὲ παραπορευόμενοι ἐβλασφήμουν αὐτὸν **κινοῦντες τὰς κεφαλὰς αὐτῶν** 40 καὶ λέγοντες·	29 καὶ οἱ παραπορευόμενοι ἐβλασφήμουν αὐτὸν **κινοῦντες τὰς κεφαλὰς αὐτῶν** καὶ λέγοντες·	35 καὶ εἱστήκει ὁ λαὸς **θεωρῶν …** 36 … *οἱ στρατιῶται* … 37 … *λέγοντες·*

Mt 27,35 κληρον(39αυτων) + ινα πληρωθη το ρηθεν δια του προφητου· διεμερισαντο τα ιματια μου εαυτοις και επι τον ιματισμον μου εβαλον κληρον ‖ Jo24: Φ **λ**-22-1582 **φ**⟨828⟩(983-1689)-*l*547¹ **σ**-349 Δ Θ *al* PsAth Eu *L*'[ek]⟨ff¹·²g¹l vg¹¹⟩ *S*h⁻j^abc⟨k⟩ *Geo* [[δια‖υπο: **λ**-22-1582 **φ***l*547¹ | προφ. + λεγοντος: *L*b vg¹⁰ *Sj* — + λεγον: φ983 *Geo*² | διεμ.] διεμερισαν: Δ Θ *pc* | εαυ.] αυτοις: Δ]] — + επ αυτα ‖ Mk: 892 Σ *Ss*[c] — + τις τι αρη ‖ Mk: 238 **37** επεθ.] εθηκαν ‖ Jo: 229 | *om* l. ‖ **Mk**Lk: 544-700 λ118-1278 φ230-346-*l*547¹ σ945-1010-1194-1207-1223-1293-1424 *al* *l*47 *l*183 *l*184¹ Eu *L*abff¹qr¹30 vg⁵ *Cs*^4:8b⟨2⟩ **38** δεξ. + αυτου(*om*) *et* ευων. + αυτου ‖ Mk *cf.* Mt20 21p.23p: (*l*48) *Ss*[c]pj^c1 *Δ*a (ad l^FG) n^L (p) **39** αυτων: *cf. ad* 35 **40** λεγ. + ουα ‖ Mk: ΣΦ-1604 σM D Δ Θ Eu Or *L*[ek]⟨ff¹g¹ vg¹⁰⟩ *S*hj *Arm*

Mk 15,24 κληρους ‖ Lk: φ13-346-543-826-828 *L*Au^2:5 *Sj*⟨fv⟩ *Arm* | *om* τις τι αρη ‖ MtLk: D 157 *l*185¹ *L*k[e] ff²nr^1v *Ss*[c] **25** τριτη] εκτη ‖ 15 33p Jo19 14: Θ 478^c APh Cat^Mo Ox *L*Hi *S*h^m *Aeth* | εσταυ.] **26** και εφυλασσον ‖ Mt: D *L*k[e] ff²nr¹ — εστ. αυτον και εφυλαξαν ‖ Mt: *L*vg¹(-ασσον) *Cs*^3:6 | επιγε.] γεγραμ. ‖ p: ην—επιγεγ.] κ. ην γεγραμμενον ‖ Jo: *l*183 *Sj*^c | *om* η ‖ LkJo: Δ φ13 D *pc* | επιγεγ. + ουτος εστιν ‖ Mt: Ψ σ1391 1342 *pc* *l*44 *l*48 *l*184 *l*253 *l*260 — *om*: 213 *pc* *L*k[e] c | επιγεγ. + ουτος εστιν ‖ Mt: D *Lr*^1v z *Ss*[c]p — + Ιησους ‖ MtJo: *Lc* — + χαιρε ‖ 15 18p: 76 *pc* | Ιου. + ουτος ‖ Lk: 33 1071 **27** εσταυρωσαν ‖ Lk Jo: B 565 372 1342 *L*vl'[e]⟨l⟩ vg² | σταυρουνται … λησται ‖ Mt: D' *Sp*¹ | *om* αυτου ‖ MtLk: C³ Θ-565 **λ** σ-71-179-349-692-1194 D *pc* *l*36 *L*vl'[e]⟨l⟩30 vg¹ *Sj*^ab⟨c⟩f *Cb*² | ● 27 + ²⁸και επληρωθη η γραφη η λεγουσα· και μετα ανομων ελογισθη ‖ Lk22 37: *Rpl* (λεγ. + το: V 76) Eu^can PsHip Or L, Vig^v *S*'j *Cb*' — *txt*: ℵBC* *et* ³XΨ 544 φ*l*547 σ27-71-179-692-1207 A D Y **047** 157 *pc* *l*^pl Amm Eus^can *L*k[e] 30 *Ss*[c] *Csb*⁸f^v

Lk 23,34 κληρον ‖ p: 𝔓75 *Rpl* *Lc* vg³ Au¹ — *txt*: X-33 N **λλ**⟨22-1278⟩ σ1194 A Θ Ψ *pc* *L*'(b *om* διαμ.—κλη.) Au² *Sj*

Jo 19,18 ∼ εσταυ. αυ. ‖ Lk: **λ** σ945 *pc* *L*ff² *Arm* | δυο + λῃστας ‖ **Mk**Mt: 1071 1321 *La* vg¹ *C*b^+B | εντ.^1.2 + ενα ‖ p: 348 1579 *S*[sc]h^m **19** επεθηκ. ‖ Mt: 544 λ2193 σ1223 A K Θ Π *al* *l*135 | γεγ. + Εβραιστι, Ελληνιστι, Ρωμαιστι ‖ 20 Lk: 579 **φ**'(∼ Ρω. … Ελ.: 13-346-543-788-826-828-*l*547)-1689 | *om* l. ο N. ‖ MkLkMt: φ69 4 **20** και ην—Ελ.] *om*: **φ**-*l*547 — ∼ Ελ. (+ και) Ρω. ‖ Lk: *Rpl* (1241 φ230 660 *L*') (και Ελ. και Ρω.: c *S*[sc]p)h — ∼ Ρω. Εβ. ‖ Lk: {} W(*om* Ελ.) σ1194 — *txt* (Ρω. + και): {𝔓66v} 𝔥'⟨1241⟩X N σ945 Ψ *pc* Cr (*Le* ff²) *Sj*(και Ρω. και) *C*^+B (*Arm*) *Aeth* **21** των Ιου.³] εγω ‖ 18 37: 477 **24** κληρους ‖ Lk: 482

Mt27 40p *cf.* ETh^II 71 (*cf. ad 256.* Mt26 61)

ὁ καταλύων τὸν ναὸν καὶ
ἐν τρισὶν ἡμέραις οἰκοδομῶν,
σῶσον σεαυτόν· εἰ υἱὸς εἶ τοῦ θεοῦ,
κατάβηθι ἀπὸ τοῦ σταυροῦ. 41 ὁμοίως
καὶ οἱ ἀρχιερεῖς ἐμπαίζοντες
μετὰ τῶν γραμματέων καὶ πρεσβυτέρων ἔλεγον· 42 ἄλλους ἔσωσεν,
ἑαυτὸν οὐ δύναται σῶσαι·
βασιλεὺς Ισραηλ ἐστιν, καταβάτω νῦν ἀπὸ τοῦ σταυροῦ
καὶ πιστεύσομεν ἐπ' αὐτόν.
43 **πέποιθεν ἐπὶ τὸν θεόν, ῥυσάσθω** νῦν, **εἰ θέλει αὐτόν**· εἶπεν γὰρ ὅτι θεοῦ εἰμι υἱός.
cf. v. 37 ↑ 44 τὸ δ' αὐτὸ καὶ οἱ

οὐὰ ὁ καταλύων τὸν ναὸν καὶ οἰκοδομῶν ἐν τρισὶν ἡμέραις,
30 σῶσον σεαυτὸν
καταβὰς ἀπὸ τοῦ σταυροῦ. 31 ὁμοίως
καὶ οἱ ἀρχιερεῖς ἐμπαίζοντες πρὸς ἀλλήλους μετὰ τῶν γραμματέων
ἔλεγον· ἄλλους ἔσωσεν,
ἑαυτὸν οὐ δύναται σῶσαι· 32 ὁ
Χριστὸς ὁ βασιλεὺς Ισραηλ καταβάτω νῦν ἀπὸ τοῦ σταυροῦ, ἵνα ἴδωμεν καὶ πιστεύσωμεν. *cf. 265.*
cf. v. 26 ↑

*εἰ σὺ εἶ ὁ βασιλεὺς τῶν Ἰουδαίων,
σῶσον σεαυτόν.*
35b **ἐξεμυκτήριζον** δὲ καὶ οἱ ἄρχοντες (Ps22 8)
λέγοντες· ἄλλους ἔσωσεν, σωσάτω ἑαυτόν, εἰ οὗτός ἐστιν ὁ
Χριστὸς τοῦ θεοῦ ὁ ἐκλεκτός.
36 ἐνέπαιζον δὲ αὐτῷ καὶ οἱ στρατιῶται προσερχόμενοι, **ὄξος** προσφέροντες αὐτῷ (Ps69 22) 37 καὶ λέγοντες· εἰ σὺ εἶ ὁ βασιλεὺς τῶν Ἰουδαίων, σῶσον (Ps22 9)
σεαυτόν. 38 ἦν δὲ καὶ ἐπιγραφὴ γεγραμμένη ἐπ' αὐτῷ γράμμασιν Ἑλληνικοῖς
καὶ Ῥωμαϊκοῖς καὶ Ἑβραϊκοῖς· ὁ βασιλεὺς τῶν Ἰουδαίων οὗτος. 39 εἷς

Mt 27,40 ναον + του θεου ‖ 26 61: Φ *L*[ek] abcfff$^{1.2}$qr^{2}30 vg^{11} Hil Or *S*j^{abck1} *C*b | καταβ.] ● και κ.: ℵ* A D 1295 *L*[ek] abchr$^{1.2}$ *S*s[c]pj *Δ*a i$^{T(S)}$ p **41** και^1] δε και ‖ Lk: *Rpl* Eu^1 *L*ff^{1}30 *S*hj^k *C*s(*om* και) — ● *om*: ℵL ϕ*l*547 σ71-1207 A W Π *S*j^{b1c1} *C*b' — *txt*: B-33 700 **λ**⟨118⟩-1582 **ϕ**⟨124⟩-174 σ349-1391 K Θ *pc l*49 Eu^1 *L*'[ek] Au Or *S*s[c](*om* ομ.)pj^{ab1c1} *C*b^8 | εμπ. + προς αλληλους ‖ Mk: 474 | *om* και πρε. ‖ Mk: Γ *l*183^1 *l*253^1 *Arm*$^{\langle pc \rangle}$ | ελεγ.] λεγοντες ‖ Lk: D 273 569 *L*ff^{1}g$^{1.2}$ Au$^{1:2}$ *S*h *C*s$^{7:8}$b **42** βασ. *prm* ει ‖ 40 Lk: *Rpl* Eu *L*[ek], Or *S*,j^{abc} *C*b — *txt*: ℌ⟨1241⟩ D 566 *S*j^k *C*s | σταυρ. + ινα ιδωμεν ‖ Mk: 1574 *L*f *S*p^4

Mk 15,29 ουα] *om* ‖ Mt: ℵ^{ca}LΔΨ-892 **σ**⟨954⟩ 59 *L*d *C*b$^{\langle 5 \rangle}$ — hic est (= ουτος?) ‖ Lk38: *L*k[e] | ∼ εν τρ. ημ. οικ. ‖ Mt: *Rpl* Ddy Eu *L*l 30 vg *S*hj *Arm* — *txt*: BLΨ-**059**-**0112** 565 D **0192** *L*' *S*' | ● *om* εν(⌒?): Θ-28-565 λ872 A D P V Ŷ *al l*48 **30** καταβ.] και καταβηθι ‖ Mt: 579 1071 **λ**-22-872 ϕ*l*547 σ179-267-517-1606 P Eu {} — και(*om*) καταβα ‖ Mt: *Rpl* (544) {*L*cdff^2 (vg^1) *C*s(∼)(f)} — και καταβατω ‖ 32 Mt42: σ827 *pc* — *txt*: ℵBLΔΨ-**059**-**0112** Θ D **0192** 1342 *L*' *C*b **31** πρ. αλλ.] *om* ‖ Mt: 28 **ϕ**⟨124-346⟩ σ1606 *pc l*36 Eu — αυτον: *L*k[e] cz **32** ο X.] ει ο X. ‖ Lk: 1071 1093(*om* ο) *L*c vg^1 *C*b^4 — *om* ‖ Mt: 544 σ827 *l*253 | ο^2] εστιν ο: 348 *pc S*h *C*s^{1}b^{10} — ει: 544 *l*253 *L*c(= es) — *om* ο ‖ Mt: ϕ13-346 *pc* | Ισ.] του Ισ. ‖ Jo1 49 12 13: *Rpl* Eu — *txt*: ℵBLΔΨ-**0112**-892 544 **λ**⟨118⟩ **ϕ**⟨124⟩ D K Π 1342 *al* | Ισ. + εστιν: 544-1071 1093 *l*253 *L*30 vg^1 *S*j *C*b^4 | *om* ινα ιδ. ‖ Mt: *l*253 *L*k[e] cz | πιστ. + αυτω(-ον) ‖ Jo6 30 Mt: *Rpl* (ϕ230 *l*26 *l*49^1) Eu *L*vl'[e]30 vg^3 — + εις αυτον ‖ Mt18 6 Jo12 42 *etc.*: 544 *pc l*49^1 {} — + επ αυτω ‖ Mt: 90 483 *l*184 {*S*p *C*s} — *txt*: ℌC*X-**059**^{v}-**0112** 28 λ872 σM^c-115-1207-1223-1402 A E K S U V Y Π Ω **047** **0192** *mu L*vg' *S*'j *C*bf

Lk 23,35 αρχ. + συν αυτοις ‖ p: *Rpl* Eu *L*fz vg' *S*' *Arm* — + συν τοις πρεσβυτεροις ‖ Mt: 1200 *pc* — + συν τ. Σαδδουκαιοις(Φαρισ.): *L*30 vg^2(^{1}) — *txt*: 𝔓^{75} ℌCX-**0124** ϕ69-788 D Q Ψ **047** 157 *pc l*47 *L*vl'r^1 *S*pj *C* | λεγ.] και ελεγον αυτω ‖ p: D *L*c(*om* αυ.) *Aeth* | εσω.—θε.] εσωσας, σεαυτον σωσον ει υιος ει του θε., ει X. ει ‖ Mt46p: D *L*c(*om* ει^1—θε.) (*Δ*me) | σω. εαυ.] και αυτον ου δυναται σωσαι ‖ p: σ267 | ουτ.] υιος ‖ Mt40: B | του] ο υιος του ‖ ←: 𝔓^{75} **0124**(*om* ο)-579(*om* ο X.) λ131 **ϕ**-174-230 1071 *pc* Eu *L*lr^1 *S*hj *C Arm* **36** ● ενεπαιξαν ‖ Mt27 31p: 𝔓^{75} ℵBL-**0124**-1241 *S*j *C*sb^1 — *txt*: *Rpl L S*,j *C*b' | προσευχομ. ‖ Mt27 29p: W **37** ει συ ει] συ ει ‖ Mt42 Mk32: **λ** A *pc L*e abff^{2}l — χαιρε ‖ Mt27 29p: D *L*c — χαιρε ει συ ει: *S*sc — ει συ ει ο Χριστος ‖ 35.39: **ϕ** *Arm*^{pc} | σεαυ. + περιθεντες αυτω και ακανθινον στεφανον ‖ Mk15 17p: D(*om* σω. σεαυ.) *L*c (περ. + δε) *S*sc — + και καταβα απο του σταυρου ‖ Mt40 Mk30: 1071 **38** επιγρ.] η επ. ‖ Mk: C-579(+ αυτη) 1071 λ22 σ7-659-1207-1675 D G S U *mu* | γεγ.] επιγεγ. ‖ ←: A D Q *l*950 *L*bq vg' — ● *om*: 𝔓^{75} ℵBL-**0124**-1241 *C*s^{9}b' — ∼ επ αυ. γεγ.: C*X-33 **ϕ** Ψ *pc C*s^1 — *txt*: *Rpl* (*om* επ αυ.: 579) APi Cr *L*vl'g^{2}r^1 vg^3 *S*'(*om* και^1: s)j(*om* και επιγ.) *C*b^1 | ● *om* γραμ.—Εβ. ‖ p: 𝔓^{75} ℵ^{a}BC*L-**0124**-579-1241 *L*a *S*sc *C*'s — *txt*: *Rpl L*' *S*'j *C*b^5(^{1}∼ ο—ουτ. γραμ.—Εβ.) | *om* και$^{2.3}$ ‖ Jo20: ℵ* D *pc C*b^6 — *om* και^2: H *l*60 APi Cr | ∼ Εβ. ... Ελ. ... Ρω. ‖ ←: *l*60 *L*c — ∼ Εβ. ... Ρω. ... Ελ.: *C*b^4 | ∼ Εβ. ... Ρω.: 157 | ο—ουτ.] *om* ουτ. ‖ Mk Jo: C *L*c — + εστιν ‖ Mt: ϕ124 D *L*e ff^{2}r^1 — ουτ. εστιν ο—Ιου. ‖ Mt: *Rpl* Or *L*'(l) *S*,j {*C*} — *txt*: 𝔓^{75} ℵBL-**0124**-579 *L*a {} | ο βασ.] Ιησους ο β. ‖ Mt Jo: X-33 N-28 **λ**-22-1278 239 *l*183^1 *L*l *C*s$^{1:11}$

Matth: λησταὶ οἱ συσταυρωθέντες σὺν αὐτῷ ὠνείδιζον αὐτόν. cf. v. 40 ↑

Mark: καὶ οἱ συνεσταυρωμένοι σὺν αὐτῷ ὠνείδιζον αὐτόν. cf. v. 30 ↑

Luk: δὲ τῶν κρεμασθέντων κακούργων ἐβλασφήμει αὐτὸν λέγων· οὐχὶ σὺ εἶ ὁ Χριστός; σῶσον σεαυτὸν καὶ ἡμᾶς. [40] ἀποκριθεὶς δὲ ὁ ἕτερος ἐπετίμα αὐτῷ λέγων· οὐδὲ φοβῇ σὺ τὸν θεόν, ὅτι ἐν τῷ αὐτῷ κρίματι εἶ; [41] καὶ ἡμεῖς μὲν δικαίως, ἄξια γὰρ ὧν ἐπράξαμεν ἀπολαμβάνομεν· οὗτος δὲ οὐδὲν ἄτοπον ἔπραξεν. [42] καὶ ἔλεγεν· Ἰησοῦ, μνήσθητί μου ὅταν ἔλθῃς ἐν τῇ βασιλείᾳ σου. [43] καὶ εἶπεν αὐτῷ· αμην σοι λέγω, σήμερον μετ᾽ ἐμοῦ ἔσῃ ἐν τῷ παραδείσῳ.

Jo: 19 25-27: εἱστήκεισαν δὲ παρὰ τῷ σταυρῷ τοῦ Ἰησοῦ ἡ μήτηρ αὐτοῦ καὶ ἡ ἀδελφὴ τῆς μητρὸς αὐτοῦ, Μαριαμ ἡ τοῦ Κλωπᾶ καὶ Μαριαμ ἡ Μαγδαληνή. [26] Ἰησοῦς οὖν ἰδὼν τὴν μητέρα καὶ τὸν μαθητὴν παρεστῶτα ὃν ἠγάπα, λέγει τῇ μητρί· γύναι, ἴδε ὁ υἱός σου. [27] εἶτα λέγει τῷ μαθητῇ· ἴδε ἡ μήτηρ σου. καὶ ἀπ᾽ ἐκείνης τῆς ὥρας ἔλαβεν ὁ μαθητὴς αὐτὴν εἰς τὰ ἴδια.

(250)

265. Der Tod Jesu. *The Death on the Cross.*

Matth 27 45–56

[45] Ἀπὸ δὲ ἕκτης ὥρας σκότος ἐγένετο ἐπὶ πᾶσαν τὴν γῆν ἕως ὥρας ἐνάτης. cf. v. 51a ↓ [46] περὶ δὲ τὴν ἐνάτην ὥραν ἀνεβόησεν ὁ Ἰησοῦς

Mark 15 33–41

[33] Καὶ γενομένης ὥρας ἕκτης σκότος ἐγένετο ἐφ᾽ ὅλην τὴν γῆν ἕως ὥρας ἐνάτης. cf. v. 38 ↓ [34] καὶ τῇ ἐνάτῃ ὥρᾳ ἐβόησεν ὁ Ἰησοῦς

Luk 23 44–49

[44] Καὶ ἦν ὡσεὶ ὥρα ἕκτη καὶ σκότος ἐγένετο ἐφ᾽ ὅλην τὴν γῆν ἕως ὥρας ἐνάτης [45] τοῦ ἡλίου ἐκλιπόντος· ἐσχίσθη δὲ τὸ καταπέτασμα τοῦ ναοῦ

Mt 27,44 *om* συν‖Jo19 32: *Rpl* (μετ αυτου: **090** 157) — *txt*: ℵBL-892 (σταυρ.: ϕ124-*l*547^{1}) D Θ **45** επι πα.] εφ ολην‖p: ℵ^{a} σ1424 245 **46** ανεβ.] ● εβοησεν‖Mk: BL-33 Σ-700 ϕ69-124-788 W *pc*

Mk 15,32 συν αυτω] αυτω‖Jo19 32: *Rpl* — μετ αυτου: Ψ — *om*: σ827-1402-1424 D — *txt*: ℵBL-**059**-**0112**-579-892 Θ σ517 **0192**^{c} 713 **33** εφ ολ.] επι πασαν‖Mt: 238(εν παση τη γη) 1574 *l*183 **34** ανεβο.‖Mt: N λ118-209 σM-827 1342 *pc* — εφωνησεν‖Lk46: D

Lk 23,39 *om* λεγ.—ημ.‖p: D *Le* — ● *om* λεγ.: BL-1241 *Ll* 30 — *txt*: 𝔓^{75} *Rpl* (λεγω: 579) *L*'Or *S*,j *C* *Δ*⟨me⟩ | ουχι] ει‖37 Mt40: *Rpl* *L*'⟨e l⟩ Or *S*'j^{b} *C*b^{5} *Δ* — *om*‖Mk32: 1574 — *txt*: 𝔓^{75} ℵBC*L-**0124**-1241 Ψ 597 *L*abff^{2}r^{1} *S*scj^{ac} *C*' *Δ*E^{a} **40** επετ. ... λεγ.] ● επιτιμων ... εφη: 𝔓^{75} 𝔋⟨33⟩C*X-**0124** Ψ *pc* *S*Cr *Arm* *Aeth* — *txt*: *Rpl* (-τιμησεν: E) *L* *S*(αποκ. δε] και: scp)hj *Δ*ad i^{V}(= *S*c)^{T} l **42** ● εις την βασιλειαν: 𝔓^{75} BL Chr *L*'Hi Hil Or *Δ*a ad l md me — *txt*: *pl* (βασ.] ημερα της ελευσεως *et om* οτ. ελ.: D) Chr Ep Eu Or *L*abq Hi Hil *S*,j *C* *Δ*p(∼ εν—σου οτ. ελ.) E^{a} **43** αμ.—λεγω] θαρσει‖Mt9 2.22: D **44** ● ην + ηδη: 𝔓^{75} BC*L-**0124**-892-1241 *L*Or^{1} *S*h *C*b' — *txt*: *Rpl* *L*,Or^{1} *S*'j *C*sb^{1} | *om* ωσει‖p: 157 *l*184 *L*vg^{1} *C* | εφ ολ.] επι πασαν‖Mt: **0117** **45** *om* του ηλ. εκλ.‖p: 33 *pc* *L*vg^{1} | εσχ. δε] και εσχ.‖p: *Rpl* APi^{v} *L*(∼ το—ναου εσχ.) *S*,j — *txt*: 𝔓^{75} 𝔋'⟨892⟩(+ και: 579) C*-**0124** 1071 λ1-131-1582 *C*s^{1}(*om* δε: s^{9}b) | ∼ [46]και—εξεπν. [45]εσχ.—μεσον‖p: D (∼ [45]το—ναου εσχ.‖Mt Mk *et om* μεσ.) Ψ 475

Jo 19,27 ● ∼ αυ. ο μαθ.: ℵW-1241 544-1071 **λ** **ϕ**'(αυτης: 13)-*l*547 σ659-1194 D^{s} U Γ **053** **0141** *pm* *L*' — *txt*: 𝔓^{66} *Rpl* *Le* | μαθητης + εκεινος‖**21** 7.23: 1241 700 λ209 ϕ983-1689 U Γ Ω *pm* *L*acnz *S*[sc] *Geo*^{2}

---

265. *cf.* EP 5,15—6,22: (*cf. ad 264.*) ... Ἦν δὲ μεσημβρία καὶ σκότος κατέσχε πᾶσαν τὴν Ἰουδαίαν· καὶ ἐθορυβοῦντο καὶ ἠγωνίων μήποτε ὁ ἥλιος ἔδυ, ἐπειδὴ ἔτι ἔζῃ· γέγραπται ⟨γὰρ⟩ αὐτοῖς, ἥλιον μὴ δῦναι ἐπὶ πεφονευμένῳ. [16] καί τις αὐτῶν εἶπεν· 'ποτίσατε αὐτὸν χολὴν μετὰ ὄξους·' καὶ κεράσαντες ἐπότισαν. [17] καὶ ἐπλήρωσαν πάντα καὶ ἐτελείωσαν κατὰ τῆς κεφαλῆς αὐτῶν τὰ ἁμαρτήματα. [18] περιήρχοντο δὲ πολλοὶ μετὰ λύχνων ⟨καὶ⟩ νομίζοντες ὅτι νύξ ἐστι⟨ν ἀν⟩επαύσαντο. [19] καὶ ὁ κύριος ἀνεβόησε λέγων· 'ἡ δύναμίς μου, ἡ δύναμίς ⟨μου⟩, κατέλειψάς με'. καὶ εἰπὼν ἀνελήφθη. [20] καὶ αὐτοσώρας διεράγη τὸ καταπέτασμα τοῦ ναοῦ τῆς Ιερουσαλημ εἰς δύο. (6) [21] καὶ τότε ἀπέσπασαν τοὺς ἥλους ἀπὸ τῶν χειρῶν τοῦ κυρίου καὶ ἔθηκαν αὐτὸν ἐπὶ τῆς γῆς· καὶ ἡ γῆ πᾶσα ἐσείσθη καὶ φόβος μέγας ἐγένετο. [22] τότε ἥλιος ἔλαμψε καὶ εὑρέθη ὥρα ἐνάτη· [23] ἐχάρησαν ... (*cf. ad 266.*)

Matthew

φωνῇ μεγάλῃ λέγων· **ηλι ηλι λεμα σαβαχθανι;** τοῦτ' ἔστιν· **θεέ μου θεέ μου, ἱνατί με ἐγκατέλιπες;** [47] τινὲς δὲ τῶν ἐκεῖ ἑστηκότων ἀκούσαντες ἔλεγον· Ἠλίαν φωνεῖ οὗτος. [48] καὶ εὐθέως δραμὼν εἷς ἐξ αὐτῶν καὶ λαβὼν σπόγγον πλήσας τε **ὄξους** καὶ περιθεὶς καλάμῳ **ἐπότιζεν** αὐτόν. [49] οἱ δὲ λοιποὶ ἔλεγον· ἄφες ἴδωμεν εἰ ἔρχεται Ἠλίας σώσων αὐτόν. [50] ὁ δὲ Ἰησοῦς πάλιν κράξας φωνῇ μεγάλῃ

Mark

φωνῇ μεγάλῃ· **ελωι ελωι λαμα σαβαχθανι;** ὅ ἐστιν μεθερμηνευόμενον· **ὁ θεός μου ὁ θεός μου, εἰς τί ἐγκατέλιπές με;** [35] καί τινες τῶν παρεστηκότων ἀκούσαντες ἔλεγον· ἴδε Ἠλίαν φωνεῖ. [36] δραμὼν δὲ εἷς γεμίσας σπόγγον **ὄξους** περιθεὶς καλάμῳ **ἐπότιζεν** αὐτόν, λέγων· ἄφετε ἴδωμεν εἰ ἔρχεται Ἠλίας καθελεῖν αὐτόν. [37] ὁ δὲ Ἰησοῦς ἀφεὶς φωνὴν μεγάλην

Luke

μέσον. *cf. 264.* [46] καὶ φωνήσας φωνῇ μεγάλῃ ὁ Ἰησοῦς εἶπεν· πάτερ, **εἰς χεῖράς σου παρατίθεμαι τὸ πνεῦμά μου.** τοῦτο

John

19 28–30: μετὰ τοῦτο εἰδὼς ὁ Ἰησοῦς ὅτι ἤδη πάντα τετέλεσται, ἵνα τελειωθῇ ἡ γραφή, λέγει· διψῶ. [29] σκεῦος οὖν ἔκειτο ὄξους μεστόν· σπόγγον οὖν μεστὸν τοῦ ὄξους ὑσσώπῳ περιθέντες προσήνεγκαν αὐτοῦ τῷ στόματι. [30] ὅτε οὖν ἔλαβεν τὸ ὄξος ὁ Ἰησοῦς εἶπεν· τετέλεσται, καὶ κλίνας τὴν κεφαλὴν

Ps22 2 — Ps69 22 — Ps31 6

Mt 27,46 *om* λεγ.‖p: Φ σ1402 | ηλι$^{1.2}$] • ελωι$^{1.2}$‖p: ℵB-33 *L*vg^{9} *C Aeth* | ινατι] εις τι‖p: 1295 Te$^{1:2}$ | ∼ εγκ. με‖Mk Ps211 LXX: Ir **47** • ελεγ. + οτι: *Rpl L*fq *S*h — + ιδε‖Lk: *Geo*^{1} — *txt*: ℌ⟨B⟩ 700 **σ**-659 D Θ 59 *L*'[ek] Or *S*'j **48** *om* εξ αυ.‖Mk: ℵ | *om* και^{3}‖Mk: *l*55 vg^{1} **49** ελεγ.] • ειπαν: B **φ**⟨346⟩ D *L*[ek] abff^{2}qr^{2} | αφετε‖p: 33 **090** 157 713 *L*l *S*s[c]pj | σωσ.] καθελων‖p: 544 — σωσαι‖p: ℵ* φ69 σ1010-1293 Θ 1241 *l*184^{1} *L*fg^{2}30 vg^{2} *Arm Aeth* | • αυτ. + αλλος δε λαβων λογχην ενυξεν αυτου την πλευραν, και εξηλθεν υδωρ και αιμα‖Jo1934: ℵBCL σ115-1010-1293 U Γ *pc* Chr^{Sev} *L*r^{2}30 vg^{7} *S*j$^{a1\,b1\,c1}$ *Aeth* ⟦*om* δε: *S*j^{b1} | ενυξ. + και ηνοιξεν: *L*30 | και^{1} + ευθεως: U | ∼ αι. κ. υδ.: U 1555 *Aeth*⟧ — *txt*: *Rpl* CAp Eu *L*'[ek] Au Hi Hil Or *S*,j$^{a1\,b1\,c1\,1}$ *C Aeth* **50** *om* παλ.‖Mk Lk: L Φ σ1402 F *pc* Chr *S*s[c]j^{1} *C*s$^{4:11}$b^{3} *Geo*^{2}

Mk 15,34 μεγ. + λεγων‖Mt: *Rpl* Eu *L*clz vg *S*h *C*f — + και ειπεν: 579 *S*p — *txt*: **ℵBLΨ-059-0112**-892 Θ-565-700 σ517 D **0192** *pc L*k[e] ff^{2}in *S*s[c] *C* | ελ.$^{1.2}$] ηλι$^{1.2}$‖p: **059** Θ-565 D 131 Eu | *om* μεθερ.‖**p**: σ517(*om* μεθ.—τι) 1342 *L*k[e](*om* ο^{2}—μεθ.) *S*p | εις] ινα‖p: σ349-1424 *pc l*4 *L*cdlz vg Ir | ∼ με εγκ.‖p: *Rpl* Ir *L*vl'[e] vg^{7} Ir — *txt* (εγκ.] ωνειδισας): **ℵBLΨ-059-0112**-892 565 **φ**124λ(κατελ.) σ517 (D) **0192** *pc* Eu Ir *L*(c i) vg' **35** των + εκει‖p: A 213 *C*s$^{2:3}$ *Aeth* | τ. παρε.] τ. εστηκοτων‖p: B (A *Aeth*) — εστωτες‖p: (213) | ιδε] *om*‖p: Θ-700 D Eu *L*k[e] cff^{2} *S*p *C*s^{1}f^{v} *Arm*^{pc} — ιδου: *Rpl* {} — οτι ιδου(*om*): (C 565 σ72-659)-945-1223-(1402) K Y Π *al* (*pc l*13 *l*17 *S*s[c] *Arm*') — *txt*: ℌ 1071 λ1 **φ** σ7-115-517-1188-1291 F U *pc* {*L*' *S*h *C*(s^{2})b *Geo*} | φων. + ουτος‖**p**: D *L*cff^{2}30 vg^{2} **36** δρα.—λεγ.] και δραμοντες εγεμισαν σπογγον(*om*) οξ. και περιθεντες καλ. εποτιζον αυ. λεγοντες‖Lk2336 Jo: **φ**'(346) 1542 *Geo* | δρα. δε] και δρα.(-οντες)‖p: Θ-565-700 λ1 (**φ**) σ1606(*om* και) D (1542) *L*vl[e]⟨lz⟩ (vg^{1}) *S*s[c] *C*b^{1} *Arm* (*Geo*) *Aeth* | εις] • τις: ℌ⟨33⟩**-0112** — *txt*: *Rpl L*Au | εις + εξ αυτων‖p: σ1402 74^{c} *L*30 vg^{1} | γεμ.] • και γ.‖p: *Rpl* ⟨**φ** 1542⟩ {*L*'Au *S*p$^{\langle 1\rangle}$} — και πλησας‖p: Θ-565-700 D 495 {} — *txt*: BLΨ *L*cff^{2}(εγεμισεν)i vg^{2} | περιθ.] και π.‖p: Θ λ1 (**φ** 1542) σ27-827-954-1207 V(+ τε) {*L*k[e n]ff^{2} vg^{3}} — π. τε‖p: *Rpl* {*L*'Au} — *txt*: **ℵBLΨ-0112-33-892** N-565-700-1071 σ517 D(επιθεις) *pc l*13 *l*17 *L*c(*om* π. καλ.: d)i vg^{1} | λεγ.] οι δε λοιποι ελεγον‖p: 28 | αφες‖p: ℵ-579 Θ-28-544-565-700 λ1 **φ** D V Ω *pc l*49 *L*vl⟨ff^{2}l⟩ Au *Arm*$^{\langle 0\rangle}$ | καθ.] ινα σωση‖p: σ1424 — σωσων και καθ.‖p: φ69 *C*s

Jo 19,28 τετ. + τα(*om*) περι αυτου‖Lk2237 2427: 700 (φ828) σM^{m}-(7) U (Θ) **0141** *pc* (*al*) | τελ. η γρ.] πληρωθη η γρ.‖Mt2654 Mk1449: ℵ **φ**-*l*547 D^{s} Θ **0141** 157 *pc* Eu *L*e bfqr^{1} — η γρ. πλη.‖24.36 **17**12: **λ** φ828 σ659 **053** *pc L*cff^{2}n **29** σκ. ουν] σκ. δε: ℵ *S*j^{abc} *C*s^{7}b^{+B} — • *om* ουν: 𝔓^{66v} BLWX-579 A Ψ Eu(σκ.] λεκανη) *L*e abr^{1}v *C*s^{3}a^{s} — και σκ.: *L*ff^{2}n *S*[sc]p — *txt*: *Rpl* Cr^{cmt} *L*' *S*hj^{f} | σπο.—οξ.^{2}] οι δε πλησαντες σπο. οξ. και‖Mt Mk: *Rpl*(του οξ.: Θ; *om* και: λ209) *L*f *S*[sc], (*om* υσσ. περ.: j^{bc})^{f} — πλησ. (+ ουν) σπο. οξ: *C*b'$^{(4)}$ — *txt*: 𝔓^{66} ℌ⟨1241⟩X λ1 Ψ **0141** Cr^{cmt} Eu *L*e(∼ τ. οξ. μεσ.) bff^{2}r^{1}v Hil *C*s$^{9:10}$b^{B}(*om* ουν)a^{s} | του] • *om*‖Mt Mk: *Rpl C*s^{7}b^{+B} — και: 579 — *txt*: 𝔓^{66v} ℵ^{c}BLW-33 λ1 Θ Ψ *pc C*s^{5}a^{s} | μεσ.^{2} + ποιησαντες‖Mt Mk: Eu | οξ.^{2} + μετα χολης και(*om*)‖Mt2734: 892^{s} **φ**-*l*547 Θ *pc* Eu *L*(c)q(μετα] και)r^{1} Or *S*[sc]h(και] μεμιγμενου)j (*Arm*) *Geo*^{1} | περιθ. + καλαμω‖Mt Mk: Θ *pc L*Or **30** οξ. + μετα (+ της) χολης‖Mt2734: (**φ**')-69-346-983-*l*547 Ep Eu *L*vg^{1} *S*[sc]j *Arm*

Matthew 27 50–55

ἀφῆκεν τὸ πνεῦμα. 51 καὶ ἰδοὺ τὸ καταπέτασμα τοῦ ναοῦ ἐσχίσθη εἰς δύο, ἀπ' ἄνωθεν ἕως κάτω καὶ ἡ γῆ ἐσείσθη, καὶ αἱ πέτραι ἐσχίσθησαν, 52 καὶ τὰ μνημεῖα ἀνεῴχθησαν καὶ πολλὰ σώματα τῶν κεκοιμημένων ἁγίων ἠγέρθησαν· 53 καὶ ἐξελθόντες ἐκ τῶν μνημείων μετὰ τὴν ἔγερσιν αὐτοῦ εἰσῆλθον εἰς τὴν ἁγίαν πόλιν καὶ ἐνεφανίσθησαν πολλοῖς. 54 ὁ δὲ ἑκατόνταρχος καὶ οἱ μετ' αὐτοῦ τηροῦντες τὸν Ἰησοῦν ἰδόντες τὸν σεισμὸν καὶ τὰ γινόμενα ἐφοβήθησαν σφόδρα, λέγοντες· ἀληθῶς θεοῦ υἱὸς ἦν οὗτος.

Ps38 12 — 55 ἦσαν δὲ ἐκεῖ γυναῖκες πολλαὶ ἀπὸ μακρόθεν θεωροῦσαι, cf. v. 56 ↓

Mark 15 37–40

ἐξέπνευσεν. 38 καὶ τὸ καταπέτασμα τοῦ ναοῦ ἐσχίσθη εἰς δύο ἀπ' ἄνωθεν ἕως κάτω· 39 ἰδὼν δὲ ὁ κεντυρίων ὁ παρεστηκὼς ἐξ ἐναντίας αὐτοῦ ὅτι οὕτως κράξας ἐξέπνευσεν, εἶπεν· ἀληθῶς οὗτος ὁ ἄνθρωπος υἱὸς θεοῦ ἦν. 40 ἦσαν δὲ καὶ γυναῖκες ἀπὸ μακρόθεν θεωροῦσαι, ἐν αἷς καὶ Μαρία ἡ Μαγδαληνὴ

Luke 23 46–49

δὲ εἰπὼν ἐξέπνευσεν. 45 … *ἐσχίσθη δὲ τὸ καταπέτασμα τοῦ ναοῦ μέσον.* 47 ἰδὼν δὲ ὁ ἑκατοντάρχης τὸ γενόμενον ἐδόξαζεν τὸν θεὸν λέγων· ὄντως ὁ ἄνθρωπος οὗτος δίκαιος ἦν. 48 καὶ πάντες οἱ συμπαραγενόμενοι ὄχλοι ἐπὶ τὴν θεωρίαν ταύτην, θεωρήσαντες τὰ γενόμενα, τύπτοντες τὰ στήθη ὑπέστρεφον. 49 **εἱστήκεισαν** δὲ πάντες **οἱ γνωστοὶ** αὐτῷ **μακρόθεν,** καὶ γυναῖκες *cf. 8 2f.* ↓

John

παρέδωκεν τὸ πνεῦμα.

19 25: εἱστήκεισαν δὲ παρὰ τῷ σταυρῷ τοῦ Ἰησοῦ ἡ μήτηρ αὐτοῦ καὶ ἡ ἀδελφὴ τῆς μητρὸς αὐτοῦ, Μαριαμ ἡ

Mt 27,50 αφη.] παρεδωκεν‖Jo: 472 **51** *om* ιδου‖Mk: σ1010-1293 *S*j *C*b² | ● ∼ απ—κατω εις δυο: BC*L-33 *C Aeth Δ*n^L p — *om* εις δυο‖Lk: σ1424 1170 Or *S*s[c] — *txt*: *Rpl* (δυο + μερη: D) *L*[ek],Au Or *S*'j *Δ*'⟨me⟩ **54** ∼ υι. θε.‖Mk: B D' *L*[ek] bhlr²z vg⁵ Or **55** εκει] και‖Mk: σ7 D *l*48 *L*z — κακει‖Mk: ℵ *S*p⁸ — εκει και‖Mk: L-33 λ1278ᶜ σ27-945-1207-1223-1293-1391 F K Π *l*52 *l*54 *l*183 *pm* *S*p⁶hᵐj *Geo*² | *om* απο‖Lk: σ954-1424 A K W Y Δ Π *al* Chr

Mk 15,38 και + ιδου‖Mt: NΣ *L*n vg¹ **39** εξ εν. αυ.] εκει‖Mt47: Θ-565 D *L*inq Or *Arm* | ουτ. κραξ.] ● ουτως‖p: ℵBLΨ-(**0112**)-892 (*L*k[e]) *C*sf — *om*: 2148 *C*b — κραξας: WΘ-565 1542 *L*Or *S*s[c] *Arm* — *txt*: *Rpl* (ουτ. αυτον κραξαντα και *et om* οτι: D) *L*'(∼: i) Au *S*' | εξεπ.] αφηκεν το πνευμα‖Mt50 Jo30: σ1424 *L*cff²nq vg¹ — εκραξεν: **0112** *L*k[e] | ∼ ο ανθ. ουτ.‖Lk: *Rpl* *L*l vg Au *S*h *Arm* — *om* ο ανθ.‖Mt: **0112** *S*s[c] — *txt*: 𝕳⟨579⟩ Θ-565-700 σ517 D 1342 *L*vl'[e]30 Or *S*p | ∼ θε. υι. ην ο ανθ. ουτ.‖Mt: 1071 | ∼ θε. υι.‖Mt: (1071) σ115-1606-1675 D *L*k[e] ff²iq **40** δε + εκει‖Mt: C 16 713 *S*p¹ *Geo*¹ | *om* και¹‖Mt: 506 *pc* *L*n *S*s[c]p¹ *C*s | αις + ην‖Mt: *Rpl* *L*vl[e] 30 vg¹⁰ Au *S*h — *txt*: ℵBL-**0112**-892 482 1352 *L*vg' | *om* και²‖Mt: C³-33-579 WΘΣ-28-565-700-1071 **λ**-22 φ⟨346⟩ σ349-517 D G U Γ 157 *pm* *L*vl[e]⟨l⟩ vg⟨10⟩ Au *S*(*om* εν αις και: s[c]p)h *C*,f *Geo*

Lk 23,47 τα γενομενα‖48 Mt: Θ R *l*48 Cr(γεγενημ.) *L*Or | ∼ δικ. ην ο ανθ. ουτ.‖Mt: D *L*Or^1:2 *C*s *Aeth* **49** αυτω¹] ● αυτου‖Jo18 16: *Rpl L* — *txt*: 𝔓⁷⁵ 𝕳⟨ℵ-892⟩-**0124** A P Ω *pc* APi | μακρ.] ● απο μ.‖Mt Mk: 𝔓⁷⁵ ℵBL-**0124**-579-1241 **λ** D *pc* APi

Jo 19,30 πνευ. + ως δε εξεπνευσεν εσχισθη το καταπετασμα του ναου μεσον απο ανωθεν εως κατω‖p: 37 *pc* (εξεπ.] εξενευσθη: *pc* *l*48) Cr^cmt *L*r¹ vg² *S*[sc]h⁺j^a1 bcf

---

Mt27 51p *cf.* EN frgm.21 (Hi Mt *ad* 27 51): In evangelio cujus saepe facimus mentionem superliminare templi infinitae magnitudinis fractum esse ac divisum legimus.

(Hi ep. 120, 8, 2): In evangelio autem, quod Hebraicis litteris scriptum est, legimus non velum templi scissum, sed superliminare templi mirae magnitudinis conruisse.

EN frgm.36 (Hist. pass. dom. fol.65^r): Item in ewangelio Nazareorum legitur superliminare templi infinite magnitudinis in morte Christi scissum.

EN frgm.24 (*cf. ad 264.* Lk23 34)

Mt27 55f. p *cf.* *Δ*g (=**0212**): … Ζεβεδ]αίου καὶ Σαλώμη κ[α]ὶ αἱ γυναῖκες [τῶν συ]νακολουθησάντων α[ὐτ]ῷ ἀπὸ τῆς [Γαλιλαί]ας ὁρῶσαι τὸν στ[αυρωθέντ]α. ἦν δὲ [ἡ ἡμέρ]α παρασκευή· σάββατον ἐπέφω[σκεν … (*cf. ad 266.* Mt27 57p)

Lk23 48 *cf.* EP 7,25: (*cf. ad 266.*) … Τότε οἱ Ἰουδαῖοι καὶ οἱ πρεσβύτεροι καὶ οἱ ἱερεῖς γνόντες οἷον κακὸν ἑαυτοῖς ἐποίησαν ἤρξαντο κόπτεσθαι καὶ λέγειν· 'οὐαὶ ταῖς ἁμαρτίαις ἡμῶν· ἤγγισεν ἡ κρίσις καὶ τὸ τέλος Ἰερουσαλημ.' 26 Ἐγὼ … (*cf. ad 275.*)

Matth 27,55–56: αἵτινες ἠκολούθησαν τῷ Ἰησοῦ ἀπὸ τῆς Γαλιλαίας διακονοῦσαι αὐτῷ· [56] ἐν αἷς ἦν Μαρία ἡ Μαγδαληνὴ καὶ Μαρία ἡ τοῦ Ἰακώβου καὶ Ἰωσῆ μήτηρ καὶ ἡ μήτηρ τῶν υἱῶν Ζεβεδαίου.

Mark 15,40–41: καὶ Μαρία ἡ Ἰακώβου τοῦ μικροῦ καὶ Ἰωσῆτος μήτηρ καὶ Σαλώμη, [41] αἳ ὅτε ἦν ἐν τῇ Γαλιλαίᾳ ἠκολούθουν αὐτῷ καὶ διηκόνουν αὐτῷ, καὶ ἄλλαι πολλαὶ αἱ συναναβᾶσαι αὐτῷ εἰς Ἱεροσόλυμα. cf. v. 40 ↑

Luk 23,49: αἱ συνακολουθοῦσαι αὐτῷ ἀπὸ τῆς Γαλιλαίας, ὁρῶσαι ταῦτα. *8 2f (97.): ... Μαρία ἡ καλουμένη Μαγδαληνή, ἀφ' ἧς δαιμόνια ἑπτὰ ἐξεληλύθει, [3] καὶ Ἰωάννα γυνὴ Χουζα ἐπιτρόπου Ἡρῴδου καὶ Σουσάννα καὶ ἕτεραι πολλαί, αἵτινες διηκόνουν αὐτοῖς ἐκ τῶν ὑπαρχόντων αὐταῖς.*

John 19,25: τοῦ Κλωπᾶ καὶ Μαριαμ ἡ Μαγδαληνή.

19 31-37: Οἱ οὖν Ἰουδαῖοι, ἐπεὶ παρασκευὴ ἦν, ἵνα μὴ μείνῃ ἐπὶ τοῦ σταυροῦ τὰ σώματα ἐν τῷ σαββάτῳ, ἦν γὰρ μεγάλη ἡ ἡμέρα ἐκείνου τοῦ σαββάτου, ἠρώτησαν τὸν Πιλᾶτον ἵνα κατεαγῶσιν αὐτῶν τὰ σκέλη καὶ ἀρθῶσιν. [32] ἦλθαν οὖν οἱ στρατιῶται, καὶ τοῦ μὲν πρώτου κατέαξαν τὰ σκέλη καὶ τοῦ ἄλλου τοῦ συσταυρωθέντος αὐτῷ· [33] ἐπὶ δὲ τὸν Ἰησοῦν ἐλθόντες, ὡς εἶδον αὐτὸν ἤδη τεθνηκότα, οὐ κατέαξαν αὐτοῦ τὰ σκέλη, [34] ἀλλ' εἷς τῶν στρατιωτῶν λόγχῃ αὐτοῦ τὴν πλευρὰν ἔνυξεν, καὶ ἐξῆλθεν εὐθὺς αἷμα καὶ ὕδωρ. [35] καὶ ὁ ἑορακὼς μεμαρτύρηκεν, καὶ ἀληθινὴ αὐτοῦ ἐστιν ἡ μαρτυρία, κἀκεῖνος οἶδεν ὅτι ἀληθῆ λέγει, ἵνα καὶ ὑμεῖς πιστεύσητε. [36] ἐγένετο γὰρ ταῦτα ἵνα ἡ γραφὴ πληρωθῇ· **ὀστοῦν οὐ συντριβήσεται αὐτοῦ.** [37] καὶ πάλιν ἑτέρα γραφὴ λέγει· **ὄψονται εἰς ὃν ἐξεκέντησαν.** Ex12 46 Zch12 10

(251)

266. Das Begräbnis Jesu. *The Burial of Jesus.*

Matth 27 57–61: [57] Ὀψίας δὲ γενομένης

Mark 15 42–47: [42] Καὶ ἤδη ὀψίας γενομένης, ἐπεὶ ἦν παρασκευή, ὅ

Luk 23 50–56 a: [50] Καὶ ἰδοὺ

19 38-42: Μετὰ δὲ ταῦτα ἠρώτησεν τὸν Πιλᾶτον Ιωσηφ ὁ

Mt 27,55 τω Ι.] αυτω‖p: σ1424 F 80 Eu **56** ην + και‖Mk: C* | *om* του‖Mk Lk24 10: 892 *l*48 — *om* η του: 1604 σ71-692-1424 E *l*184 *pc* Eu | Ια. + του μικρου‖Mk: *l*183 | Ιω. μη.] η Μαρια η Ιω.‖Mk15 47: ℵ* *C*b^{1} | ● Ιωσηφ‖13 55: ℵL D* W Θ 59^{c} 157 *L*[ek],Au Or *S*s[c]h^{m}j *C*s^{4}b — Ιωσητος‖Mk: D^{c} {} — *txt*: *Rpl* Eu {*S*ph^{t} *C*s^{2}}

Mk 15,40 η Ια.] η του Ια.‖16 1 Mt: *Rpl* — Ια.: LΨ-33-579 Θ-28-565 ϕ'σ517 D F^{W*} *al* — του Ια.: σ827-1606 — *txt*: ℌ'C-**0112** NWΣ-1071 λ ϕ983 σ349-517 K U Π 1342 *al* | Ιω.] Ιωση‖Mt: *Rpl* {} — Ιωσηπος‖Mt13 55: Δ(-σηβτος) λ1 *L*'Au Or *S*s[c] — *txt*: ℵ^{c}BL-**0112**-33 Θ ϕ⟨124⟩ D *L*k[e]n {*S*' *C*s}b$^{\langle 1\rangle}$ **41** ηκολουθησαν‖Mt: Σ D *pc* *C*s$^{3:4}$ | κ. διηκ. αυ.] διακονουσαι αυ.‖Mt: 28 — *om*‖Lk: *C*Δ-579 σ349-659 D *al* *L*n | αλ.] ετεραι‖Lk8 3: A **42** *om* επει—προσα.‖Mt: 472 | ∼ παρ. ην‖Jo19 31: 245 *mu* *L*n30 | *om* ο—προσα.‖←: 213

Jo 19,33 ● ∼ ηδη αυ.: 𝔓^{66} BLW Or — *om* ηδη: *L*cff^{2}qr^{1} vg^{1} *Arm* *Geo*^{2} *Aeth* **35** *om* και^{3}‖20 31: *Rpl* *L*vg^{1} *C*b^{4} *Arm*'(*^{pc}* ∼ και ινα) *Geo*^{B} — *txt*: 𝔓^{66v} ℌX NΛ-544-1071 λ-22 ϕ σ1194 A D^{s} H K U Θ Π Ψ **0141** *mu* Cr^{cmt} Or *L*'⟨e(*om* 35)⟩ *S*[sc],j *C*'$^{+B}$ *Geo*' | ● πιστευητε: ℵ*B Ψ Or **38** Ιω. ο] ο Ιω. ο: *Rpl* Cr — ● Ιω.: {𝔓^{66v}} BL-579 D^{s} Ψ *pc* — ο Ιω.: {} A — *txt*: ℌ'X N-700-1071 λ ϕ⟨346⟩-*l*547 σM-7-71-659-945-1223 E G K U Π **053 0141** *pm* Chr Thd^{C}

---

266. cf. EP 2,3-5; 6,23-24: (*cf. ad 261.* Mt27 24) ... Εἱστήκει δὲ ἐκεῖ Ιωσηφ, ὁ φίλος Πειλάτου καὶ τοῦ κυρίου. καὶ εἰδὼς ὅτι σταυρίσκειν αὐτὸν μέλλουσιν ἦλθεν πρὸς τὸν Πειλᾶτον καὶ ᾔτησε τὸ σῶμα τοῦ κυρίου πρὸς ταφήν. [4] καὶ ὁ Πειλᾶτος πέμψας πρὸς Ἡρῴδην ᾔτησεν αὐτοῦ τὸ σῶμα· [5] καὶ ὁ Ἡρῴδης ἔφη· 'ἄδελφε Πειλᾶτε, εἰ καὶ μή τις αὐτὸν ᾐτήκει, ἡμεῖς αὐτὸν ἐθάπτομεν, ἐπεὶ καὶ σάββατον ἐπιφώσκει. γέγραπται γὰρ ἐν τῷ νόμῳ ἥλιον μὴ δῦναι ἐπὶ πεφονευμένῳ' (*cf.* 5,15: *ad 265.*). καὶ παρέδωκεν αὐτὸν τῷ λαῷ πρὸ μιᾶς τῶν ἀζύμων τῆς ἑορτῆς αὐτῶν ... (*cf. ad 262.*). (6) (*cf. ad 265.*) ... [23] ἐχάρησαν δὲ οἱ Ἰουδαῖοι καὶ δεδώκασι τῷ Ιωσηφ τὸ σῶμα αὐτοῦ ἵνα αὐτὸ θάψῃ, ἐπειδὴ θεασάμενος ἦν ὅσα ἀγαθὰ ἐποίησεν. [24] λαβὼν δὲ τὸν κύριον ἔλουσε καὶ ⟨ἐν⟩είλησε σινδόνι καὶ εἰσήγαγεν εἰς ἴδιον τάφον καλούμενον κῆπον Ιωσηφ. (7) [25] Τότε ...

Mt27 57p *cf.* *Δ*g(= **0212**): (*cf. ad 265.* Mt27 55f.) ... ὀ]ψίας δὲ γενομένης ἐπὶ τ[ῇ π]αρ[α]σ[κευῇ], ὅ ἐστιν προσάββατον, προσ[ῆλθεν] ἄνθρωπος βουλευτὴ[ς ὑ]πάρ[χων ἀ]πὸ Ἐρινμαθαία[ς] π[ό]λεως τῆς [Ἰουδαί]ας ὄνομα Ιω[σηφ] ἀ[γ]αθὸς δί[καιος] ὢν μαθητὴς [το]ῦ Ἰησοῦ, κα[τακεκρυμ]μένος δὲ διὰ τὸν φόβον τῶν [Ἰουδαίω]ν καὶ αὐτὸς προσεδέχετο [τὴν] β[ασιλείαν] τοῦ θεοῦ. οὗτος οὐκ [ἦν συνκατατ]ιθέμενος τῇ β[ουλῇ].

Matth 27:

ἦλθεν ἄνθρωπος πλούσιος ἀπὸ Ἀριμαθαίας, τοὔνομα Ιωσηφ, ὃς καὶ αὐτὸς ἐμαθήτευσεν τῷ Ἰησοῦ· [58] οὗτος προσελθὼν τῷ Πιλάτῳ ᾐτήσατο τὸ σῶμα τοῦ Ἰησοῦ. τότε ὁ Πιλᾶτος ἐκέλευσεν ἀποδοθῆναι. [59] καὶ λαβὼν τὸ σῶμα ὁ Ιωσηφ ἐνετύλιξεν αὐτὸ σινδόνι καθαρᾷ, [60] καὶ ἔθηκεν

Mark 15:

ἐστιν προσάββατον, [43] ἐλθὼν Ιωσηφ ὁ ἀπὸ Ἀριμαθαίας, εὐσχήμων βουλευτής, ὃς καὶ αὐτὸς ἦν προσδεχόμενος τὴν βασιλείαν τοῦ θεοῦ, τολμήσας εἰσῆλθεν πρὸς Πιλᾶτον καὶ ᾐτήσατο τὸ σῶμα τοῦ Ἰησοῦ. [44] ὁ δὲ Πιλᾶτος ἐθαύμασεν εἰ ἤδη τέθνηκεν, καὶ προσκαλεσάμενος τὸν κεντυρίωνα ἐπηρώτησεν αὐτὸν εἰ πάλαι ἀπέθανεν· [45] καὶ γνοὺς ἀπὸ τοῦ κεντυρίωνος ἐδωρήσατο τὸ πτῶμα τῷ Ιωσηφ. [46] καὶ ἀγοράσας σινδόνα καθελὼν αὐτὸν ἐνείλησεν τῇ σινδόνι καὶ κατέθηκεν αὐ-

Luk 23:

ἀνὴρ ὀνόματι Ιωσηφ βουλευτὴς ὑπάρχων, καὶ ἀνὴρ ἀγαθὸς καὶ δίκαιος, [51] — οὗτος οὐκ ἦν συγκατατιθέμενος τῇ βουλῇ καὶ τῇ πράξει αὐτῶν, — ἀπὸ Ἀριμαθαίας πόλεως τῶν Ἰουδαίων, ὃς προσεδέχετο τὴν βασιλείαν τοῦ θεοῦ· [52] οὗτος προσελθὼν τῷ Πιλάτῳ ᾐτήσατο τὸ σῶμα τοῦ Ἰησοῦ, [53] καὶ καθελὼν ἐνετύλιξεν αὐτὸ σινδόνι, καὶ ἔθηκεν αὐ-

Joh 19:

ἀπὸ Ἀριμαθαίας, ὢν μαθητὴς τοῦ Ἰησοῦ κεκρυμμένος δὲ διὰ τὸν φόβον τῶν Ἰουδαίων, ἵνα ἄρῃ τὸ σῶμα τοῦ Ἰησοῦ· καὶ ἐπέτρεψεν ὁ Πιλᾶτος. ἦλθεν οὖν καὶ ἦρεν τὸ σῶμα αὐτοῦ. [39] ἦλθεν δὲ καὶ Νικόδημος, ὁ ἐλθὼν πρὸς τὸν Ἰησοῦν νυκτὸς τὸ πρῶτον, φέρων μίγμα σμύρνης καὶ ἀλόης ὡς λίτρας ἑκατόν. [40] ἔλαβον οὖν τὸ σῶμα τοῦ Ἰησοῦ καὶ ἔδησαν αὐτὸ ὀθονίοις μετὰ τῶν ἀρωμάτων, καθὼς ἔθος ἐστὶν τοῖς Ἰουδαίοις ἐνταφιάζειν. [41] ἦν δὲ ἐν τῷ τόπῳ ὅπου ἐσταυρώθη κῆπος, καὶ ἐν τῷ κήπῳ μνημεῖον καινόν, ἐν ᾧ οὐδέπω

Mt 27,57 Α. + πολεως των Ιουδαιων‖Lk: Σ *l*184 | ● εμαθητευθη ‖1352: ℵC-33-892 Σ-700 **λ**-2193 D Θ *pc* **58** πρ. τω Π.] προσηλθεν τω Π. και‖Mk: D {*L*[ek], Or} | *om* τω‖Mk: Y Π *pc* | τοτε ο] ο δε‖Mk: 237 *pc* | αποδ. + το σωμα‖Mk: *Rpl* (*et* + του Ιησου: Σ 1170; *et* + του Χριστου: λ118^{cv}; *et* + τω Ιωσηφ: **σ**-349) *L*'(vg^{1} = Σ; ^{1}*et* + αυτου) Au Or *S*p(αυτω το σωμα)h(^{m} = Σ) — *txt* (+ αυτω): 𝔋 **λ**'-1582 *pc* (*S*s[c]j *C*s)b (*Geo*^{1}) **59** ενετ.] ενειλησεν‖Mk: **φ**⟨826⟩-*l*547 **60** ● εθη. + αυτο(-ον)‖(p): *Rpl* *L*'[ek] (abcfff^{2}hqr^{1} vg^{2} Or) *S*,j^{b} *C* *Geo*^{2} — *txt*: ℵL-892 **φ**⟨124-346⟩ Θ 243 *S*j^{ac} *Arm* *Geo*^{1}

Mk 15,43 ελθ.] ηλθεν‖Mt: *Rpl* *L* — *txt*: 𝔋C-**0112** WΣ-1071 **λ**-22-1278 **φ**⟨124⟩ **σ**⟨954⟩-M-349-659-945-1223-1402 A K U Y Γ Π 1342 *pm* *Arm* | Ιωσης‖1540 Mt2756: W *L*k[e] | Α. + πολεως‖Lk: 282 | Π.] ● τον Π.‖p: ℵBLΔΨ-33 W *pc* | σω.] πτωμα‖45: D *L*k[e] *S*s[c] *Geo*^{1} **45** πτ.] σωμα‖43p Mt59 Jo38; *Rpl* *S*'j *C*b *Geo*^{2} — *txt*: ℵBL Θ-565 D *S*s[c] *Geo*^{1} *Aeth* | Ιωση‖1540 Mt2756: B W **46** καθ.] και κ.‖Lk: *Rpl* *L*'Au *S*h — και(*om*) λαβων‖Mt: D (*L*dn) — *txt*: ℵBLΨ-**0112** 1342 *pc* *L*(καθειλεν *et* αυ.^{1} + και: k[e ff^{2}] c) vg^{1} *C*b | αυ. ενειλ.] ειλησεν αυ.‖p: 565 | αυτον^{1}] αυτο‖p: λ872 σ659 *pc* *l*14 *l*183^{1} | ενειλ. + αυτον‖p: 28 *S*,j *C* | κατεθ. ● εθηκεν‖MtLk: 𝔋⟨Δ-579⟩C^{2}-**0112** WΘΣ-565 **λ** **φ**-*l*547^{1} **σ**⟨954⟩-71-179-692-1194-1207 D 1342 *pc* *l*184 | αυτον^{2}] αυτο‖Mt59 Lk53a: **0112** λ872 σM-659 A 1342 *pc*

Lk 23,50 ον.] ω ονομα‖127 225 861: 544 **λλ**⟨22-1278⟩ 25 | και^{2} αν.] ● ανηρ: *Rpl* *L*fz vg *S*'s^{v}j *C* — *om*: D Γ *L*vl'r^{1} — *txt*: 𝔓^{75} ℵC(κ. ο αν.)LX-**0124**-33 σ7-659 W *pc* *l*150 *l*185 *L*c(homo) **51** ● -τεθειμενος: 𝔓^{75} *Rpl* (-θεμενος: 579 1071 Π 477; -τεθεις: 1241) — *txt*: ℵCLX-**0124**-33-892 28-544-1604 **λ**-22 **φ**'(κατα-: 13) σ267 D A Ψ **0117** 157 *pc* | ος πρ.] ος και αυτος πρ.‖p: X σM-71-692-1207 K P U Π 157 *al* *L*ff^{2} *Arm* *Aeth* — ος και πρ. κ. αυ.‖p: *Rpl* *S*h — ος πρ. κ. αυ.‖p: 33 **λ**-1582 *pm* *L*fz vg — ος και πρ.‖p: 544(+ αυτος) **φ**'⟨124⟩-230 σ1223 Γ *L*q *Geo* — *txt*: 𝔓^{75} 𝔋'⟨892⟩C-**0124** φ69-788 D *L*e(οι … -οντο) ablr^{1v} *S*'(ος] και) *C*s^{8}(ος] ουτος: s^{2}b^{2})' **52** *om* τω‖Mk: λ131 472 — *om* τω Π.: 213 *S*c **53** καθ. + αυτον‖Mk: 1071 U 157 *pc* *L*bq {*S*'s^{v} *C*} — + το σωμα‖Mt: *L*c *Aeth* — + αυτο‖p: *Rpl* {} — *txt*: 𝔓^{75} 𝔋⟨892⟩C-**0124** **φ**⟨124⟩-174-230 D 258 *L*' | αυτο] αυτον‖Mk: φ983 *L*aff^{2} {} — το σωμα του Ιησου‖52 Mt: D — *om*‖Mk: X 544-1071 **λ**-1278 σ7 H W Γ Θ Ψ 157 *pc* *L*' *Arm* — *txt*: 𝔓^{75} *Rpl* {*S* *C*} | σινδ.] τη σ.‖Mk: λ22 H *pc* — σ. καθαρα‖Mt: **φ**⟨124⟩-230 157 *L*b(καθ.] καινη) vg^{1} *S*p^{1} | αυτον] αυτο‖Mt59: 𝔓^{75} *Rpl* *L*c {} — *om*‖Mt: **λ**-22-1582 **φ**'⟨124⟩ *pc* *L*e vg^{1} *Arm* — *txt*: ℵBC-33 1071 φ983 D 157 475 *L*' {*S* *C*}

Jo 19,38 ● ηλθον … ηραν‖40: ℵ*W N *L*e abcff^{2}jnr^{1}v *S*[sc]j *C*s$^{7(8?):8(9?)}$ *Arm*$^{\langle 0\rangle}$ *Geo*^{2} *Δ*a | το σω.^{2} αυ.] ● αυτον‖Mk46: ℵ*W *pc* *L*e abcff^{2}j^{v}nv *S*[sc]j *Arm* **39** τ. l.] ● αυτον‖32: 𝔓^{66v} BLX-**054** 1071 A U Y Ψ **0141** 1321 Cr^{cmt} *C*s$^{1:7}$ **40** εδησ.] ενειλησαν‖Mk: Θ *S*s[c]pj *C*b^{+B} **41** ∼ ουδεις ουδεπω‖Lk: ℵ σ1424 *S*p — ουδεις πωποτε‖Lk1930: N

ἐν τῷ καινῷ αὐτοῦ μνημείῳ ὃ ἐλατόμησεν ἐν τῇ πέτρᾳ, καὶ προσκυλίσας λίθον μέγαν τῇ θύρᾳ τοῦ μνημείου ἀπῆλθεν. [61] ἦν δὲ ἐκεῖ Μαριαμ ἡ Μαγδαληνὴ καὶ ἡ ἄλλη Μαρία, καθήμεναι ἀπέναντι τοῦ τάφου.

τὸν ἐν μνημείῳ ὃ ἦν λελατομημένον ἐκ πέτρας, καὶ προσεκύλισεν λίθον ἐπὶ τὴν θύραν τοῦ μνημείου. [47] ἡ δὲ Μαρία ἡ Μαγδαληνὴ καὶ Μαρία ἡ Ἰωσῆτος ἐθεώρουν ποῦ τέθειται.

τὸν ἐν μνήματι λαξευτῷ, οὗ οὐκ ἦν οὐδεὶς οὔπω κείμενος. [54] καὶ ἡμέρα ἦν παρασκευῆς, καὶ σάββατον ἐπέφωσκεν. [55] κατακολουθήσασαι δὲ αἱ γυναῖκες, αἵτινες ἦσαν συνεληλυθυῖαι ἐκ τῆς Γαλιλαίας αὐτῷ, ἐθεάσαντο τὸ μνημεῖον καὶ ὡς ἐτέθη τὸ σῶμα αὐτοῦ, [56a] ὑποστρέψασαι δὲ ἡτοίμασαν ἀρώματα καὶ μύρα.

οὐδεὶς ἐτέθη· [42] ἐκεῖ οὖν διὰ τὴν παρασκευὴν τῶν Ἰουδαίων, ὅτι ἐγγὺς ἦν τὸ μνημεῖον, ἔθηκαν τὸν Ἰησοῦν.

(252) *267.* Die Grabeswächter. *The Guard at the Tomb.* **Matth 27** 62–66

[62] Τῇ δὲ ἐπαύριον, ἥτις ἐστὶν μετὰ τὴν παρασκευήν, συνήχθησαν οἱ ἀρχιερεῖς καὶ οἱ Φαρισαῖοι πρὸς Πιλᾶτον [63] λέγοντες· κύριε, ἐμνήσθημεν ὅτι ἐκεῖνος ὁ πλάνος εἶπεν ἔτι ζῶν· μετὰ τρεῖς ἡμέρας ἐγείρομαι.

Mt 27,60 εν τη π.] εκ πετρας ‖ Mk: **047** | τη θυ.] επι τη(-ην) θυρα(-αν) ‖ Mk: A 242 243 (1515) **62** Φ.] πρεσβυτεροι ‖ 27 20.3.12: 59 1574 *Sj* *C*s(b^{2} Φ. και πρ.)

Mk 15,46 μνημειω] + λαξευτω ‖ Lk: σ115 — τω καινω αυτου μν. ‖ Mt: *l*253 — τω μν. ‖ Mt: σ267 D 569 *C*s^{2}(^{1} + αυτου) — ● μνηματι ‖ Lk: ℵB 1342 | εκ πετ.] εκ της π. ‖ Mt: WΘ-565 λ1 D 300 *l*253 {} *C*s^{2}b^{1} — εν τη(*om*) πετρα ‖ Mt: ϕ-*l*547^{1} (1574) *L*k[e] cdff^{2}(εις την πετραν)g^{2}lq vg^{2} *S*'j *C*s^{1}(b^{4}) — *txt*: *Rpl* {*L*'Au *S*h} *C*b'f *Arm* | προσεκ.] προσκυλισας ‖ Mt: λ-22 D' *pc* | λιθ.] + μεγαν ‖ 16 4 Mt: ℵ — τον λ. ‖ 16 3 Mt 28 2 Lk 24 2: σ517-1675 *C*b⟨8⟩ | την θ.] τη θυρα ‖ Mt: 565(εν τη θ.)-700 *pc* | μνημειου + απηλθεν(και απη.) ‖ Mt: λ-22 (σ267 D) G (157 495) *pc* *L*vg^{1}(^{1}) **47** Ιω.] Ιωση ‖ Mt 27 56: *Rpl* {} *C*s^{2}(^{1} -ης)f^{v} — Ιωσηϕ ‖ Mt 13 55: Σ ϕ*l*547^{1} σ1675 A 258 *L*'Au — Ιακωβου και Ιωσητος(Ιωση) ‖ 15 40 16 1 Mt 27 56 Lk 24 10: Θ ϕ'(124-983) 1542 *L*c(Ιωσηϕ; *sim*: g^{2} vg^{1}) *S*j^{ab1}(^{1} = *L*c)$^{c.1}$ (*Arm*) *Geo*^{1} — Ιακωβου ‖ 16 1 Lk ←: D 1342 *pc* *L*ff^{2}nq *S*s[c] — *txt*: ℵ^{c}BLΔΨ-**0112** λ *L*k[e] {*S*'} *C*b *Geo*^{2} | Ιω.] + μητηρ ‖ 15 40 Mt ←: W ϕ 1542 *S*j^{a} — Ιακωβου θυγατηρ: *S*s[c]j$^{bc.1}$ — *prm* Ιακωβου και Σαλωμη και Μαρια ‖ ←: *L*r^{2} — + και Σαλωμη ‖ 15 40 16 1: 472 1515 | εθεω.] εθεασαντο ‖ Lk: Θ-565 D *L*vl[e]⟨lr^{2}⟩ *S*pj

Lk 23,53 μνημειω ‖ Mt Mk: 579-1241 544 D *pc* | λαξ.] λελατομημενω ‖ p: D | ου] εν ω ‖ Jo: σ1194 *pc* *L*⟨ac⟩ *Geo*^{1} | ουδεις ουπω] ουδεπω ουδεις ‖ Jo: *Rpl* (ουδεποτε: Λ *pc*; ουδε εις: λ22 660) {*L*' *S*c *C*b}^{1} — ουπω ουδεις ‖ ←: **0124** D Or {}^{1} — ● ουδεις ουδεπω ‖ ←: ℵC-33-892 1071 λ131 ϕ⟨124⟩ σM-7-659-1207 K P U Θ Π 157 *al* *l*48 *l*49 {}^{2} — ουδεις: *L*c *Geo* *Aeth* — *txt*: 𝔓^{75} BL-579-1241 λλ'⟨1278⟩ A {*S*' *C*s(ουδεποτε)}^{2} | κειμ. + και προσεκυλισε λιθον μεγαν(*om*) επι την θυραν του μνημειου ‖ p: (700) ϕ⟨69⟩-174-230 σ1194 U *pc* *C*b *Aeth* — + και θεντος αυτου επεθηκεν τω μνημειω λιθον ον μογις εικοσι εκυλιον ‖ p: **0124**(επεθηκαν *et* λι. + μεγαν *et* εικ. + ανδρες) 1071 (τεθεντος *et om* ον—εκυ.) D *L*c(∼ τω μν. επεθηκαν) vg^{1}(ον—εικ.] μεγαν) *C*s(τω μν.] τη θυρα του μνημειου)($^{7:11}$ επεθηκαν; $^{6:11}$ λι. + μεγαν) — + εκει εθηκαν το σωμα του Ιησου ‖ Jo: *L*l **54** και^{1}—επεφ.] ην δε η ημερα προσαββατον ‖ Mk 42: D *L*c(ημ. + παρασκευης) | παρασ.] παρασκευη ‖ ← Jo 19 14.31: *Rpl* (D) Eu *L*fff^{2}r^{1}z vg^{7} *S* — *txt*: 𝔓^{75} ℵBC* L-**0124**-579 ϕ⟨69-124-788⟩ *L*'⟨l*(*om* 54f.)⟩ *C* *Aeth* **55** κατακ.] ακολ. ‖ Mt 23 55 Mk 15 41: 713 *L*cd — *om* ‖ p: *S*sc | αι] δυο ‖ p: D 29 Eu *L*vl'r^{1} vg^{1} *Aeth* — ● *om* ‖ 8 2 23 49 p: *Rpl* Eu {} *Aeth* — *txt*: 𝔓^{75} 𝔥⟨ℵ⟩X-**0124** 1071 λλ ϕ⟨124⟩ σ7-659 157 P Θ Ψ *al* {*L*cfl^{c}z vg'} *S* *C* *Arm* | ∼ αυ. εκ τ. Γ. ‖ 23 49 Mt 27 55: *Rpl* Eu^{1} *L*' *S* *C*s^{8}b — *om* αυ.: 1604 D 2533 *L*c *C*s^{1} *Aeth* — *txt*: 𝔓^{75} ℵBCL-**0124**-579-1241 Eu^{1} | εκ] απο ‖ ←: 28-1071 σ945-1194 D **047** *pc* Eu$^{3:5}$ *L*cfr^{1} | εθεα.] εθεωρουν ‖ Mk Mt 28 1: ϕ *Geo*^{1} | μνη.—σωμα] μνημα ‖ 53 Mk 16 1: D **56** *om* κ. μυρα ‖ 24 1 p: λ1-131-1582-2193 *pc* Eu *Aeth*

Jo 19,41 ετεθη] ● ην τεθειμενος ‖ Lk: 𝔓^{66v} ℵBW-579 1071 Cr^{cmt} *S*, j

---

267. cf. EP 8,28—9,34: (*cf. ad 275.*) ... Συναχθέντες δὲ οἱ γραμματεῖς καὶ Φαρισαῖοι καὶ πρεσβύτεροι πρὸς ἀλλήλους, ἀκούσαντες ὅτι ὁ λαὸς ἅπας γογγύζει καὶ κόπτεται τὰ στήθη λέγοντες ὅτι ‘εἰ τῷ θανάτῳ αὐτοῦ ταῦτα τὰ μέγιστα σημεῖα γέγονεν, ἴδετε ὁπόσον δίκαιός ἐστιν’, [29] ἐφοβήθησαν καὶ ἦλθον πρὸς Πειλᾶτον δεόμενοι αὐτοῦ καὶ λέγον-

64 κέλευσον οὖν ἀσφαλισθῆναι τὸν τάφον ἕως τῆς τρίτης ἡμέρας, μήποτε ἐλθόντες οἱ μαθηταὶ αὐτοῦ κλέψωσιν αὐτὸν καὶ εἴπωσιν τῷ λαῷ· ἠγέρθη ἀπὸ τῶν νεκρῶν, καὶ ἔσται ἡ ἐσχάτη πλάνη χείρων τῆς πρώτης. 65 ἔφη αὐτοῖς ὁ Πιλᾶτος· ἔχετε κουστωδίαν· ὑπάγετε ἀσφαλίσασθε ὡς οἴδατε. 66 οἱ δὲ πορευθέντες ἠσφαλίσαντο τὸν τάφον σφραγίσαντες τὸν λίθον μετὰ τῆς κουστωδίας.

Mt 27,64 ● *om* αυτου: ℵB *Arm Geo*^{B} | κλ. αυ.] νυκτος κλ. αυ.‖**28**13: *Rpl* *S*s[c] *Arm Geo*^{1} — κλ. αυ. νυκ.‖←: 28 λ1278 S Ω *pc* *S*p *Δ*a^{AE} — *txt*: ℵBC*-33 Φ-544-1071-1604 **λ**-22-1582 **ɸ**⟨69-893⟩-174-230 σ71-517-692-1424 A D E H K V W Y Δ Θ Π **047** *al l*211 Chr Da EP↓ *L*[ek],Or *S*hj *C Geo*^{2} *Got Δ*' **65** ● εφη + δε: *Rpl* *L*Or *S*h^{+} *C*b' — *txt*: BL-33 544-700 **ɸ**-230 σM^{c}-7-27-71-692-945-1194-1207-1391-1402 E F G H K Γ Θ **045** 157 *pm l*47 *l*48 *l*183 *l*184 *L*[ek],Au *S*'j *C*sb^{7} *Δ*a l p

---

τες· [30]'παράδος ἡμῖν στρατιώτας, ἵνα φυλάξω⟨μεν⟩ τὸ μνῆμα αὐτοῦ ἐπὶ τρεῖς ἡμ[έρας], μήποτε ἐλθόντες οἱ μαθηταὶ αὐτοῦ κλέψωσιν αὐτὸν καὶ ὑπολάβῃ ὁ λαὸς ὅτι ἐκ νεκρῶν ἀνέστη, καὶ ποιήσωσιν ἡμῖν κακά'. [31] ὁ δὲ Πειλᾶτος παραδέδωκεν αὐτοῖς Πειρώνιον τὸν κεντυρίωνα μετὰ στρατιωτῶν φυλάσσειν τὸν τάφον. καὶ σὺν αὐτοῖς ἦλθον πρεσβύτεροι καὶ γραμματεῖς ἐπὶ τὸ μνῆμα. [32]καὶ κυλίσαντες λίθον μέγαν μετὰ τοῦ κεντυρίωνος καὶ τῶν στρατιωτῶν ὁμοῦ πάντες οἱ ὄντες ἐκεῖ ἔθηκαν ἐπὶ τῇ θύρᾳ τοῦ μνήματος, [33]καὶ ἐπέχρισαν ἑπτὰ σφραγῖδας, καὶ σκηνὴν ἐκεῖ πήξαντες ἐφύλαξαν. (9) [34]πρωΐας δὲ ἐπιφώσκοντος τοῦ σαββάτου ἦλθον ὄχλος ἀπὸ Ιερουσαλημ καὶ τῆς περιχώρου ἵνα ἴδωσι τὸ μνημεῖον ἐσφραγισμένον. [35]Τῇ δὲ ... (*cf. ad 268.*)

Mt27₆₅ *cf.* EN frgm.22 (Cod. N. T. 1424^{m}): Τὸ Ἰουδαϊκόν· καὶ παρέδωκεν αὐτοῖς ἄνδρας ἐνόπλους, ἵνα καθέζωνται κατ' ἐναντίον τοῦ σπηλαίου καὶ τηρῶσιν αὐτὸν ἡμέρας καὶ νυκτός.

IV. Der Auferstandene. *The Risen Jesus.*

Matth 28 = Mark 16 = Luk 24

(251.253)

268. Das leere Grab. *The Resurrection.*

Matth 28 1–8	**Mark 16** 1–8	**Luk 23** 56b — **24** 12	
¹ Ὀψὲ	¹ Καὶ διαγενομένου τοῦ	56b Καὶ τὸ	20 1–10: Τῇ δὲ μιᾷ τῶν σαβ-
δὲ σαββάτων,	σαββάτου	μὲν σάββατον ἡσύχασαν κα-	βάτων Μαριαμ ἡ Μαγδαληνὴ
τῇ ἐπιφω-		τὰ τὴν ἐντολήν, ¹ τῇ δὲ	ἔρχεται πρωῒ σκοτίας ἔτι
σκούσῃ εἰς μίαν σαββά-		μιᾷ τῶν σαββά-	οὔσης εἰς τὸ μνημεῖον, καὶ
των, ἦλθεν Μαριαμ ἡ Μαγ-	Μαρία ἡ Μαγ-	των ὄρθρου βαθέως	βλέπει τὸν λίθον ἠρμένον ἐκ
δαληνὴ καὶ ἡ ἄλλη Μαρία θε-	δαληνὴ καὶ Μαρία ἡ	cf. v. 10 ↓	τοῦ μνημείου. ² τρέχει οὖν
ωρῆσαι τὸν τάφον.	τοῦ Ἰακώβου καὶ Σαλώμη	ἐπὶ τὸ μνῆμα ἦλθαν φέρου-	καὶ ἔρχεται πρὸς Σίμωνα

Mt 28,1 σαβ.^{1}] σαββατω‖Mk: L σ692 Δ *pc l*184 *L*vg^{1} *Geo* — σαββατου‖Mk: 1515 *L*[ek],Or *Cs Aeth* | εις μιαν] μια‖Lk Jo: 243 | θεωρουσαι‖27 55 Mk15 40: W 240

Mk 16,1 Μαρ^{1}] ● η Μ.‖15 47: B*L 566 | η^{2} του] ● η‖15 40.47 Lk 10: ℵ*CXΨ WΘ-700 ϕ983 σM-1194 G S U V Γ *pc* — του: L *al l*253 — *om*: *Rpl* — *txt*: ℵ^{c}BΔ-33-892 Σ λ⟨1⟩ σ349-827 A K Π *al*

Lk 24,1 ορθ.—μνη.] ∼ ηλθ. ο. β. επι το μν. ‖ Jo 1: 1071 Eu^{1} *L*vl'(*om* βαθ.: c30 vg^{1}; ∼ ηλθ. επι το μν. ορθ.: c) *C*b^{6} — ο. β. ηλθ. επι τ. μν.‖Mk: *Rpl* (ηλθ.] ηρχοντο: D) *L*fr^{1v}z vg' *C*' — *txt*: 𝔓^{75} ℵBL-**0124** ϕ124-*l*547 Dio^{A1} Eu^{1} | μνημειον‖22 23 55 Mk: 𝔓^{75} ℵC*X-**0124**(-αν!)-579 1071 ϕ346 F Δ 157 *pc* Eu$^{1:2}$

Jo 20,1 ∼ ερχ. Μ. η Μ.‖Mt: 33 σ659 280 Eu *L*abcfj *S*s[c]pj *C*b^{1} | εις] επι‖Mk Lk: W | εκ] απο της θυρας (+ εκ)‖Mk 3: (ℵ*W)-579 λ-22 (138) 157 *pc L*dfr^{1} vg^{1} *S*s[c]j *C*b$^{\langle 1\rangle +B}$ *Arm Aeth* — εκ τ. θυ.‖←: ϕ*l*547 — απο‖Lk 2: ϕ69

---

268. cf. EP 9,35—10,42; 12,50—13,57: (*cf. ad 267.*) ... Τῇ δὲ νυκτὶ ᾗ ἐπέφωσκεν ἡ κυριακή, φυλασσόντων τῶν στρατιωτῶν ἀνὰ δύο κατὰ φρουράν, μεγάλη φωνὴ ἐγένετο ἐν τῷ οὐρανῷ, [36] καὶ εἶδον ἀνοιχθέντας τοὺς οὐρα[ν]οὺς καὶ δύο ἄνδρας κατελθόντας ἐκεῖθεν πολὺ φέγγος ἔχοντας καὶ ἐγγίσαντας τῷ τάφῳ. [37] ὁ δὲ λίθος ἐκεῖνος ὁ βεβλημένος ἐπὶ τῇ θύρᾳ ἀφ' ἑαυτοῦ κυλισθεὶς ἀπεχώρησε παρὰ μέρος, καὶ ὁ τάφος ἠνοίγη καὶ ἀμφότεροι οἱ νεανίσκοι εἰσῆλθον. (10) [38] ἰδόντες οὖν οἱ στρατιῶται ἐκεῖνοι ἐξύπνισαν τὸν κεντυρίωνα καὶ τοὺς πρεσβυτέρους (παρῆσαν γὰρ καὶ αὐτοὶ φυλάσσοντες), [39] καὶ ἐξηγουμένων αὐτῶν ἃ εἶδον πάλιν ὁρῶσιν ἐξελθόντας ἀπὸ τοῦ τάφου τρεῖς ἄνδρας, καὶ τοὺς δύο τὸν ἕνα ὑπορθοῦντας καὶ σταυρὸν ἀκολουθοῦντα αὐτοῖς, [40] καὶ τῶν μὲν δύο τὴν κεφαλὴν χωροῦσαν μέχρι τοῦ οὐρανοῦ, τοῦ δὲ χειραγωγουμένου ὑπ' αὐτῶν ὑπερβαίνουσαν τοὺς οὐρανούς· [41] καὶ φωνῆς ἤκουον ἐκ τῶν οὐρανῶν λεγούσης· 'ἐκήρυξας τοῖς κοιμωμένοις;' [42] καὶ ὑπακοὴ ἠκούετο ἀπὸ τοῦ σταυροῦ ὅτι 'ναί'. (11) [43] συνεσκέπτοντο ... (*cf. ad 270.*) ... (12) [50] Ὄρθρου δὲ τῆς κυριακῆς Μαριαμ ἡ Μαγδαληνή, μαθήτρια τοῦ κυρίου (⟨ἣ⟩ φοβουμένη διὰ τοὺς Ἰουδαίους, ἐπειδὴ ἐφλέγοντο ὑπὸ τῆς ὀργῆς, οὐκ ἐποίησεν ἐπὶ τῷ μνήματι τοῦ κυρίου ἃ εἰώθεσαν ποιεῖν αἱ γυναῖκες ἐπὶ τοῖς ἀποθνῄσκουσι τοῖς καὶ ἀγαπωμένοις αὐταῖς) [51] λαβοῦσα μεθ' ἑαυτῆς τὰς φίλας ἦλθεν ἐπὶ τὸ μνημεῖον ὅπου ἦν τεθείς. [52] καὶ ἐφοβοῦντο μὴ ἴδωσιν αὐτὰς οἱ Ἰουδαῖοι καὶ ἔλεγον· 'εἰ καὶ μὴ ἐν ἐκείνῃ τῇ ἡμέρᾳ ᾗ ἐσταυρώθη ἐδυνήθημεν κλαῦσαι καὶ κόψασθαι, κἂν νῦν ἐπὶ τοῦ μνήματος αὐτοῦ ποιήσωμεν ταῦτα. [53] τίς δὲ ἀποκυλίσει ἡμῖν καὶ τὸν λίθον τὸν τεθέντα ἐπὶ τῆς θύρας τοῦ μνημείου, ἵνα εἰσελθοῦσαι παρακαθεσθῶμεν αὐτῷ καὶ ποιήσωμεν τὰ ὀφειλόμενα; [54] μέγας γὰρ ἦν ὁ λίθος, καὶ φοβούμεθα μή τις ἡμᾶς ἴδῃ. καὶ εἰ μὴ δυνάμεθα, κἂν ἐπὶ τῆς θύρας βάλωμεν ἃ φέρομεν εἰς μνημοσύνην αὐτοῦ, ⟨καὶ⟩ κλαύσωμεν καὶ κοψώμεθα ἕως ἔλθωμεν εἰς τὸν οἶκον ἡμῶν'. (13) [55] καὶ ἐπελθοῦσαι εὗρον τὸν τάφον ἠνεῳγμένον· καὶ προσελθοῦσαι παρέκυψαν ἐκεῖ, καὶ ὁρῶσιν ἐκεῖ τινα νεανίσκον καθεζόμενον ⟨ἐν⟩ μέσῳ τοῦ τάφου ὡραῖον καὶ περιβεβλημένον στολὴν λαμπροτάτην, ὅστις ἔφη αὐταῖς· [56] 'τί ἤλθατε; τίνα ζητεῖτε; μὴ τὸν σταυρωθέντα ἐκεῖνον; ἀνέστη καὶ ἀπῆλθεν· εἰ δὲ μὴ πιστεύετε, παρακύψατε καὶ ἴδετε τὸν τόπον ἔνθα ἔκειτο, ὅτι οὐκ ἔστιν· ἀνέστη γὰρ καὶ ἀπῆλθεν ἐκεῖ ὅθεν ἀπεστάλη'. [57] τότε αἱ γυναῖκες φοβηθεῖσαι ἔφυγον. (14) [58] Ἦν δὲ ... (*cf. ad 275.*)

Matth 28 2-5

2 καὶ ἰδοὺ σεισμὸς ἐγένετο μέγας· ἄγγελος γὰρ κυρίου καταβὰς ἐξ οὐρανοῦ καὶ προσελθὼν ἀπεκύλισεν τὸν λίθον καὶ ἐκάθητο ἐπάνω αὐτοῦ. 3 ἦν δὲ ἡ εἰδέα αὐτοῦ ὡς ἀστραπή, καὶ τὸ ἔνδυμα αὐτοῦ λευκὸν ὡς χιών. 4 ἀπὸ δὲ τοῦ φόβου αὐτοῦ ἐσείσθησαν οἱ τηροῦντες καὶ ἐγενήθησαν ὡς νεκροί.

cf. v. 2f. ↑

5 ἀποκριθεὶς δὲ ὁ ἄγγελος εἶπεν ταῖς γυναιξίν· μὴ φοβεῖσθε ὑμεῖς· οἶδα

Mark 16 1-6

ἠγόρασαν ἀρώματα ἵνα ἐλθοῦσαι ἀλείψωσιν αὐτόν. 2 καὶ λίαν πρωῒ τῆς μιᾶς τῶν σαββάτων ἔρχονται ἐπὶ τὸ μνημεῖον, ἀνατείλαντος τοῦ ἡλίου.

cf. v. 5 ↓

3 καὶ ἔλεγον πρὸς ἑαυτάς· τίς ἀποκυλίσει ἡμῖν τὸν λίθον ἐκ τῆς θύρας τοῦ μνημείου; 4 καὶ ἀναβλέψασαι θεωροῦσιν ὅτι ἀποκεκύλισται ὁ λίθος· ἦν γὰρ μέγας σφόδρα. 5 καὶ εἰσελθοῦσαι εἰς τὸ μνημεῖον εἶδον νεανίσκον καθήμενον ἐν τοῖς δεξιοῖς περιβεβλημένον στολὴν λευκήν, καὶ ἐξεθαμβήθησαν. 6 ὁ δὲ λέγει αὐταῖς· μὴ ἐκθαμβεῖσθε·

Luk 24 1-5

σαι ἃ ἡτοίμασαν ἀρώματα.

cf. v. 4 ↓

2 εὗρον δὲ τὸν λίθον ἀποκεκυλισμένον ἀπὸ τοῦ μνημείου, 3 εἰσελθοῦσαι δὲ οὐχ εὗρον τὸ σῶμα τοῦ κυρίου Ἰησοῦ. 4 καὶ ἐγένετο ἐν τῷ ἀπορεῖσθαι αὐτὰς περὶ τούτου καὶ ἰδοὺ ἄνδρες δύο ἐπέστησαν αὐταῖς ἐν ἐσθῆτι ἀστραπτούσῃ· 5 ἐμφόβων δὲ γενομένων αὐτῶν καὶ κλινουσῶν τὰ πρόσωπα εἰς τὴν γῆν, εἶπαν πρὸς αὐτάς·

Jo 20 2-7

Πέτρον καὶ πρὸς τὸν ἄλλον μαθητὴν ὃν ἐφίλει ὁ Ἰησοῦς, καὶ λέγει αὐτοῖς· ἦραν τὸν κύριον ἐκ τοῦ μνημείου, καὶ οὐκ οἴδαμεν ποῦ ἔθηκαν αὐτόν. 3 ἐξῆλθεν οὖν ὁ Πέτρος καὶ ὁ ἄλλος μαθητής, καὶ ἤρχοντο εἰς τὸ μνημεῖον. 4 ἔτρεχον δὲ οἱ δύο ὁμοῦ· καὶ ὁ ἄλλος μαθητὴς προέδραμεν τάχιον τοῦ Πέτρου καὶ ἦλθεν πρῶτος εἰς τὸ μνημεῖον, 5 καὶ παρακύψας βλέπει κείμενα τὰ ὀθόνια, οὐ μέντοι εἰσῆλθεν. 6 ἔρχεται οὖν Σίμων Πέτρος ἀκολουθῶν αὐτῷ, καὶ εἰσῆλθεν εἰς τὸ μνημεῖον· καὶ θεωρεῖ τὰ ὀθόνια κείμενα, 7 καὶ τὸ σουδάριον, ὃ ἦν ἐπὶ τῆς κεφαλῆς

Mt 28,2 λιθ. + απο της θυρας (+ του μνημειου) ‖ Mk3 Lk2 Jo1: *Rpl* (L-33 Σ-28-1604 **λ**-22-1582 **φ**⟨69-124-788⟩-*l*547 σM^{c}-7-27-945-990-1010-1194-1293-1402 E^{c} F U Γ Θ **047** 157 *al l*53 *l*184 *l*1837 Chr Eu) (απο] εκ: 28 213) *L*fnq *S*p'(hj^{abc})^{k} (*C*b *Geo*^{2})^{1} *Δ*a — + απο του μν. ‖ ←: 485 *S*p^{1} *Δ*md me n p — *txt*: ℵB-892 544-700 D 1555 *L*'[ek] *S*s[c] *C*sf *Aeth Δ*ad i

Mk 16,1 ηγ. *prm* πορευθεισαι ‖ Mt25 9: Θ-565 D 1542 *L*k[e] (∼ πορ. Μαρ^{1}—Σα.: cff^{2})nz *S*j *C*b$^{⟨5⟩}$ *Arm Δ*me | ηγ.] ητοιμασαν ‖ Lk1 23 56: Θ-565 — ηνεγκον ‖ Lk1: *L*k [e] c | *om* ελθ.: D *L*vl'⟨lq⟩ *C*b^{3} *Arm* **2** *om* λιαν ‖ Jo: W D *L*k[e] c(*et om* πρωι)n *S*s[c]pj^{b1c} | της μ.] ● τη μια ‖ Lk Jo: ℵ(B)LΔΨ-**0112**^{v}-33-892 (W)Θ-565-1071 λ(1)-22-1278 1342 *l*1602 Eu *L S*s[c]pj | ● *om* της/τη ‖ Mt: BX W λ1 D | *om* των ‖ Mt: *Rpl* — *txt*: ℌ⟨Δ*-579⟩ WΘ-565-1071 λ872 **φ**-230-*l*547 K 157 1342 *pc l*1602 Eu *C*s^{3}(^{1}του σαββατου)bf | ● μνη.] μνημα ‖ Lk: ℵ*C* WΘ-565 | ανατ. *prm* ετι ‖ Jo1: WΘ-565 **λ**⟨118⟩ K Y Π *pc l*1602 Eu — *prm* ουκετι: *C*s$^{3:4}$ — + ηδη: *L*lr^{2}z32 vg **3** εκ] απο ‖ Lk: CΨ WΘ **φ**⟨124⟩ σ517 D 157 *pc l*54 *l*260 Eu | του μν. ^{4}και] subito autem ad horam tertiam tenebrae diei facti sunt per totum orbem terrae et descenderunt de caelis angeli et surgent in claritate vivi dei; simul ascenderunt cum eo et continuo lux facta est. tunc illae ‖ Mt: *L*k[e] EP↓ **4** ∼ ην—σφοδ. και—λιθ. ‖ Lk: Θ-565 D Eu *L*cff^{2}nz vg^{2}(+ ην—σφ.) *S*s[c]j *Δ*a ad i l^{FG} md n | αναβ. θεω.] ερχονται και ευρισκουσιν ‖ Lk: Θ-565 D Eu *L*cff^{2}(ηλθον κ. ευρον)n *S*j — ελθουσαι βλεπουσιν ‖ Jo1: *C*s$^{1:4}$ — ερχ. εις το μνημειον κ. βλεπ. ‖ ←: *L*k[e] *S*s[c](*om* εις—μν.) | οτι—λιθ.] αποκεκυλισμενον τον λιθον ‖ Lk: (ℵ) Θ-565 D *L*' *S*j(∼ τ. λι. απ.) — αυτον αποκ.: Eu *L*r^{2} | ● ανακεκ.: ℵBL **5** ειδ.] θεωρουσιν ‖ Jo20 12: W *L*vg^{1} **6** ο δε λε. αυ.] και λε. αυ. ο αγγελος ‖ Mt Lk2 10: D *L*ff^{2} | εκθ.] φοβεισθε ‖ ←: WΘ-565 σ115 D Eu$^{2:3}$ *L*n *S*s[c]pj *Geo*^{1}

Lk 24,1 αρω. + και(+ μυρα και) τινες συν αυταις ‖ 10 (23 56a): *Rpl* (λ⟨1⟩) Eu^{1} *L*qr^{1v} *S*j^{bc} *Aeth Δ*a — + και(+ ηλθον) αλλαι σ. αυ. ‖ 10: *L*f *S*(sc)(και + ησαν: pj^{av})h *C*sb^{6} *Arm* — *txt*: 𝔓^{75} ℵBCL-33 φ124 Dio^{A1} Eu^{1} *L*' *C*b' *Aeth* **2** ευρ. *prm* ελογιζοντο δε εν εαυταις τις αρα απολισει ημιν(*om*) τον λιθον ‖ 10 Mk3: **0124** (D *L*c *C*s^{3})^{8} | απο] εκ ‖ Jo1 Mk3: C* H Eu — + της θυρας ‖ Mk3: X 1604 *pc S*j *C*b^{1} **3** εισελ. δε] και εισ. ‖ Mk: *Rpl L*fz vg Or *S*,j(+ δε) — *txt*: 𝔓^{75} ℌC*-**0124** 1071 **λλ**⟨22-1278⟩ D Eu *L*vl'r^{1v} *C*⟨b^{1}⟩ *Aeth* | *om* κυ. ‖ 23 52p Jo19 38.40 20 12: 579-1241 1071 42 *S*scp *C*b^{1} **4** ∼ δυο αν. ‖ Jo20 12: D Eu *L*⟨af vg^{1}⟩ *S*scpj | ● εσθησεσιν αστραπτουσαις(λευκαις) ‖ ←Act1 10: *Rpl* (L) Eu^{1} *S*hj *C Arm Δ*md n — *txt*: 𝔓^{75} ℵB-**0124**(-ητι -αις!) D Eu^{1} Mcn^{Ep} *L*⟨l⟩ *S*' *Δ*'⟨me⟩ | αστρ.] λαμπρα ‖ 23 11 Act10 30: Mcn^{Ep} *L*ff^{2} — αστραπτοντες: *L*l

Jo 20,2 εφιλ.] ηγαπα ‖ **13** 23 19 26 **21** 7.20: 1071 77 *l*31 *l*260 **4** εις] επι ‖ Mk2 Lk1: W **5** τα οθ.] + μονα ‖ Lk12: σ1223 397 — μονα τ. οθ. ‖ ←: Ψ(∼ οθ. κει.) 245 | ● μεντοι + γε(+ και): L(X)-579 λ1 Ψ *pc* **6** ● ουν + και: 𝔓66 ℵ^{c}(*^{5}∩^{6}οθ.)BLWX-33 Ψ *pc L*r^{1} vg^{2} *C*$^{+B}$a^{sv} *Arm* | κειμ. + μονα ‖ Lk12: 348 *pc*

Matth 28

γὰρ ὅτι Ἰησοῦν τὸν ἐσταυρωμένον ζητεῖτε· 6 οὐκ ἔστιν ὧδε· ἠγέρθη γὰρ καθὼς εἶπεν· δεῦτε ἴδετε τὸν τόπον ὅπου ἔκειτο. 7 καὶ ταχὺ πορευθεῖσαι εἴπατε τοῖς μαθηταῖς αὐτοῦ ὅτι ἠγέρθη ἀπὸ τῶν νεκρῶν, καὶ ἰδοὺ προάγει ὑμᾶς εἰς τὴν Γαλιλαίαν, ἐκεῖ αὐτὸν ὄψεσθε. ἰδοὺ εἶπον ὑμῖν.

8 καὶ ἀπελθοῦσαι ταχὺ ἀπὸ τοῦ μνημείου μετὰ φόβου καὶ χαρᾶς μεγάλης ἔδραμον ἀπαγγεῖλαι τοῖς μαθηταῖς αὐτοῦ.

cf. v. 1↑

Mark 16

Ἰησοῦν ζητεῖτε τὸν Ναζαρηνὸν τὸν ἐσταυρωμένον· ἠγέρθη, οὐκ ἔστιν ὧδε· ἴδε ὁ τόπος ὅπου ἔθηκαν αὐτόν. 7 ἀλλὰ ὑπάγετε εἴπατε τοῖς μαθηταῖς αὐτοῦ καὶ τῷ Πέτρῳ ὅτι προάγει ὑμᾶς εἰς τὴν Γαλιλαίαν· ἐκεῖ αὐτὸν ὄψεσθε, καθὼς εἶπεν ὑμῖν. **136.** cf. 254.

8 καὶ ἐξελθοῦσαι ἔφυγον ἀπὸ τοῦ μνημείου, εἶχεν γὰρ αὐτὰς τρόμος καὶ ἔκστασις· καὶ οὐδενὶ οὐδὲν εἶπον· ἐφοβοῦντο γάρ.

cf. v. 1↑ cf. 275.

Luk 24

τί ζητεῖτε τὸν ζῶντα μετὰ τῶν νεκρῶν; 6 οὐκ ἔστιν ὧδε, ἀλλὰ ἠγέρθη. μνήσθητε ὡς ἐλάλησεν ὑμῖν ἔτι ὢν ἐν τῇ Γαλιλαίᾳ, 7 λέγων τὸν υἱὸν τοῦ ἀνθρώπου ὅτι δεῖ παραδοθῆναι εἰς χεῖρας ἀνθρώπων ἁμαρτωλῶν καὶ σταυρωθῆναι καὶ τῇ τρίτῃ ἡμέρᾳ ἀναστῆναι. 8 καὶ ἐμνήσθησαν τῶν ῥημάτων αὐτοῦ, 9 καὶ ὑποστρέψασαι ἀπὸ τοῦ μνημείου ἀπήγγειλαν πάντα ταῦτα τοῖς ἕνδεκα καὶ πᾶσι τοῖς λοιποῖς. 10 ἦσαν δὲ ἡ Μαγδαληνὴ Μαρία καὶ Ἰωάννα καὶ Μαρία ἡ Ἰακώβου· καὶ αἱ λοιπαὶ σὺν αὐταῖς ἔλεγον πρὸς τοὺς ἀποστόλους ταῦτα. 11 καὶ ἐφάνησαν ἐνώπιον αὐτῶν ὡσεὶ λῆρος τὰ ῥήματα ταῦτα, καὶ ἠπίστουν αὐταῖς. 12 ὁ δὲ Πέτρος ἀναστὰς ἔδραμεν ἐπὶ τὸ μνημεῖον· καὶ παρακύψας βλέπει τὰ ὀθόνια μόνα, καὶ ἀπῆλθεν πρὸς ἑαυτὸν θαυμάζων τὸ γεγονός.

Joh 20

αὐτοῦ, οὐ μετὰ τῶν ὀθονίων κείμενον ἀλλὰ χωρὶς ἐντετυλιγμένον εἰς ἕνα τόπον. 8 τότε οὖν εἰσῆλθεν καὶ ὁ ἄλλος μαθητὴς ὁ ἐλθὼν πρῶτος εἰς τὸ μνημεῖον, καὶ εἶδεν καὶ ἐπίστευσεν· 9 οὐδέπω γὰρ ᾔδεισαν τὴν γραφήν, ὅτι δεῖ αὐτὸν ἐκ νεκρῶν ἀναστῆναι. 10 ἀπῆλθον οὖν πάλιν πρὸς ἑαυτοὺς οἱ μαθηταί.

Mt 28,5 I. + τον Ναζαρηνον‖Mk: Sh^{+} | ∼ ζη. (+ τον Ν.) τ. εστ.‖Mk: (28) σ1424 *pc* Lr^{1} *Aeth* **6** γαρ] απο των νεκρων‖7 27 64: σ Lff^{2} — *om*‖Mk: 33 1604 σ692-945-1010-1194-1293-1391 Δ *al* l53 l54 l184 Ss[c]j^{k} Cb^{1} Δa ad **7** αυτου + και τω Πετρω‖Mk: φ l547 | *om* απο τ. νε.‖6p: D *pc* Cr^{I} Or Le[k] abff^{1}g^{1}hl vg$^{\langle 6\rangle}$ Au Or Ss[c]j^{k} *Arm* | *om* ιδ.^{1}‖Mk: D *pc* Labcff^{2}h vg^{1} | ιδ.^{2} ειπ.] καθως ειπεν‖Mk: 126 472(*om* εκει αυ. οψ.) Lf vg^{2} **8** εξελθ.‖Mk: *Rpl* L' — *txt*: ℵBCL-33 1604 φ-174-l547 σ1402 Θ *pc*

Mk 16,6 I.] οιδα γαρ οτι I.‖Mt: W l1602 Cs$^{2:4}$ | τ. Ναζωραιον‖Mt 26 71 Jo 19 19: LΔ Lk[e] ff^{2} Cs$^{2:4}$f — τ. Ναζωρηνον: 579 1071 φ69 σ115-954 *pc* Lq — *om*‖Mt: ℵ* D | ιδετε‖Mt: W D Lc — ιδετε ιδε: Lvl'⟨k[e] l⟩30 | ο τοπ.] εκει(*om*) τοπον αυτου‖Mt: D* L(c)ff^{2} **7** οτι + ηγερθη απο των νεκρων και‖Mt: λ-22-1278 *pc* Geo^{A}(*om* απο τ. ν.) | προα.] ιδου πρ.‖Mt: WΘ-565 λ-22-1278 D *pc* Lff^{2}n vg^{2} Ss[c]pj Geo^{2ch} | προαγω‖14 28: W D Lk[e] Sj^{b} | αυτον] με‖← Mt 28 10: D Lk[e] Eug Sj^{c1} | ειπον‖Mt: 1241 D(ειρηκα) *pc* Lk[e] a^{s}ff^{2}qr^{2} vg^{1} Cb^{1} **8** εξε. + ταχυ‖Mt: 1071 E *pc* — εφυ. + ταχυ‖Mt: Cb^{1} | τρο.] φοβος‖Mt: W D Π*^{v} 1375 Lvl⟨k[e] a^{s}l⟩ vg^{1}(*et* εκστ.] τρο.)

Lk 24,7 ∼ οτι δει τον—ανθ.‖9 22p: *Rpl* (∼ οτι δει παραδ. τ.—ανθ.: 579) Eu Mcn^{Ep} L(∼ οτι τον—ανθ. δει: a) Mcn^{Te}(= 579) S,j — *txt*: 𝔓^{75} ℵ*BC*L-0124 | *om* αμαρ.‖9 44p: D Le bff^{2}lr^{1} | αναστ.] εγερθ.‖9 22 Mt 16 21 17 23 20 19: 33 Δ 1038 **9** ● ∼ ταυ. παντα *cf.* Mt 13 34.51 *etc.*: 𝔓^{75} *Rpl* L' S'j {Cb} — *om* παντα: φ543 *pc* Cs *Aeth* — τα ρηματα ταυ.‖11 2 19: Ssc — *txt*: ℵX-0124-1241 Λ φ124-174 σ115-945-1194-1207 D E F H K U V Γ Δ Θ Π *al* l183 l1602 Cr Eu Lc {} **10** ησ. δε] ην δε‖Mt 27 61: λλ⟨1278⟩ φ69-l547 σ1207-1223(+ και‖Mk 15 40) K U Π Ψ *al* Cr L' — *om*: 1241 φ788 σ7-27-71-659-692-1010-1194 A D W Γ *al* l44 l48 l49 l183 Le Ssch^{+} *Aeth* | ∼ Μαρ. η Μαγ.‖Mk Mt Jo: 579 D *pc* l1602 L | *om* και^{3}—αυτ.‖←: 1216 *pc* **12** ● *om* 12‖p: D Eu^{can}? Le ablr^{1} Sj Cb^{1} Δmd me n p — *txt*: 𝔓^{75} *Rpl* Cr Eu L' S'j C' | *om* παρακ.‖Jo 6: 300 | μονα] κειμενα‖←: 579 544 φ69-l547 A K Π *al* Lvg^{7} — κει. μονα‖←: *Rpl* (∼ κει. τα οθ.: 1038‖Jo 5) Lff^{2}30 S'j^{a1} Cb^{1} — *om*‖Jo 5f.: ℵ* Cs^{2} — + κει.‖←: L Lcfz vg'(^{3} *prm* και) — *txt*: 𝔓^{75} ℵ^{cb}B-0124 W 243 l44 l47^{1} Eu Sscj^{a1bc} Cs^{7}b' | απηλθον‖Jo 10: A

A. Die matthäische Nachgeschichte. *The Matthean Post-Resurrection Narrative.*

Matth 28 9–20

(253) *269.* Die Erscheinung des Auferstandenen vor den Frauen. **Matth 28** 9–10
The Appearance of the Risen Jesus to the Women.

[9] Καὶ ἰδοὺ Ἰησοῦς ὑπήντησεν αὐταῖς λέγων· χαίρετε. αἱ δὲ προσελθοῦσαι ἐκράτησαν αὐτοῦ τοὺς πόδας καὶ προσεκύνησαν αὐτῷ. [10] τότε λέγει αὐταῖς ὁ Ἰησοῦς· μὴ φοβεῖσθε· ὑπάγετε ἀπαγγείλατε τοῖς ἀδελφοῖς μου ἵνα ἀπέλθωσιν εἰς τὴν Γαλιλαίαν, κἀκεῖ με ὄψονται.

20 11-18: Μαριαμ δὲ εἱστήκει πρὸς τῷ μνημείῳ ἔξω κλαίουσα. ὡς οὖν ἔκλαιεν, παρέκυψεν εἰς τὸ μνημεῖον, [12] καὶ θεωρεῖ δύο ἀγγέλους ἐν λευκοῖς καθεζομένους, ἕνα πρὸς τῇ κεφαλῇ καὶ ἕνα πρὸς τοῖς ποσίν, ὅπου ἔκειτο τὸ σῶμα τοῦ Ἰησοῦ. [13] καὶ λέγουσιν αὐτῇ ἐκεῖνοι· γύναι, τί κλαίεις; λέγει αὐτοῖς ὅτι ἦραν τὸν κύριόν μου, καὶ οὐκ οἶδα ποῦ ἔθηκαν αὐτόν. [14] ταῦτα εἰποῦσα ἐστράφη εἰς τὰ ὀπίσω, καὶ θεωρεῖ τὸν Ἰησοῦν ἑστῶτα, καὶ οὐκ ᾔδει ὅτι Ἰησοῦς ἐστιν. [15] λέγει αὐτῇ ὁ Ἰησοῦς· γύναι, τί κλαίεις; τίνα ζητεῖς; ἐκείνη δοκοῦσα ὅτι ὁ κηπουρός ἐστιν, λέγει αὐτῷ· κύριε, εἰ σὺ ἐβάστασας αὐτόν, εἰπέ μοι ποῦ ἔθηκας αὐτόν, κἀγὼ αὐτὸν ἀρῶ. [16] λέγει αὐτῇ ὁ Ἰησοῦς· Μαριαμ. στραφεῖσα ἐκείνη λέγει αὐτῷ Ἑβραϊστί· ραββουνι, ὃ λέγεται διδάσκαλε. [17] λέγει αὐτῇ ὁ Ἰησοῦς· μή μου ἅπτου, οὔπω γὰρ ἀναβέβηκα πρὸς τὸν πατέρα· πορεύου δὲ πρὸς τοὺς ἀδελφούς μου καὶ εἰπὲ αὐτοῖς· ἀναβαίνω πρὸς τὸν πατέρα μου καὶ πατέρα ὑμῶν καὶ θεόν μου καὶ θεὸν ὑμῶν. [18] ἔρχεται Μαριαμ ἡ Μαγδαληνὴ ἀγγέλλουσα τοῖς μαθηταῖς ὅτι ἑόρακα τὸν κύριον, καὶ ταῦτα εἶπεν αὐτῇ. *cf. 275.*

(A1) *270.* Der Betrug der Hierarchen. *The Bribing of the Soldiers.* **Matth 28** 11–15

[11] Πορευομένων δὲ αὐτῶν ἰδού τινες τῆς κουστωδίας ἐλθόντες εἰς τὴν πόλιν ἀπήγγειλαν τοῖς ἀρχιερεῦσιν ἅπαντα τὰ γενόμενα. [12] καὶ συναχθέντες μετὰ τῶν πρεσβυτέρων συμβούλιόν τε λαβόντες ἀργύρια ἱκανὰ ἔδωκαν τοῖς στρατιώταις, [13] λέγοντες· εἴπατε ὅτι οἱ μαθηταὶ αὐτοῦ νυκτὸς ἐλθόντες ἔκλεψαν αὐτὸν ἡμῶν κοιμωμένων. [14] καὶ ἐὰν ἀκουσθῇ τοῦτο ἐπὶ τοῦ ἡγεμόνος, ἡμεῖς πείσομεν καὶ ὑμᾶς ἀμερίμνους ποιήσομεν. [15] οἱ δὲ λαβόντες τὰ ἀργύρια ἐποίησαν ὡς ἐδιδάχθησαν. καὶ διεφημίσθη ὁ λόγος οὗτος παρὰ Ἰουδαίοις μέχρι τῆς σήμερον.

Mt 28,9 αυτω] αυτον‖Mk5 6: *l*53 **10** αδελ.] μαθηταις‖28 8[Mk16 7]: 157 1555 | κακει] εκει‖28 7[Mk16 7]: 481 1574 *L*⟨fff^{2}hqr^{1} vg^{1}⟩ *S*[sc]p^{1} *C*s | οψεσθε‖28 7[Mk←]: D *l*260 *L*e[k] h **14** ● πει. + αυτον: *Rpl* *L*' *S*[sc] *C* — *txt*: ℵB-33 Θ Or *L*e[k] *S*j *Aeth* **15** ● *om* τα‖12: ℵ*B* W 1574 | μεχρι] εως‖27 8: ℵ*σ1424 D 213 | ● σημ. + ημερας *cf.* Act20 26 R11 8 2K3 14: BL D Θ 569 *l*7 Chr

Jo 20,12 l.] κυριου l.‖Lk24 3: N G *l*184 *S*j **13** οιδαμεν‖20 2: λ Θ 565 *L*30 vg^{2} *C*s$^{1:7}$ **15** ● *om* ο^{1}: 𝔓^{66} ℵBLW *pc* **16** ● *om* ο^{1}: BL D Θ **050** 1187 | *om* Εβ.‖13 8: *Rpl* Cr *L*' *S*s[c] *Δ*' — *txt*: 𝔓$^{5v.66v}$ ℌ⟨1241⟩X N λ2193 ϕ*l*547 σ71 D Δ Θ Π Ψ **050** 157 *pc* *l*253 *L*e bcff^{2}r^{1} vg^{2}(^{1}∼ ρα. ο Εβ.) *S*'j *C*$^{+B}$a^{s} *Δ*a p **17** ● *om* ο: BL σM D Ψ **18** απαγγ.‖Mt28 8.10 Lk24 9: 𝔓^{66c} *Rpl* — αναγγ.: 33 E G S Δ *pc* — *txt*: 𝔓^{66*} ℵBX λ1582 A **078** | εορακαμεν‖20 25: 33 S — εορακεν: *Rpl* *L*vl'r^{1} *S*'{j} *C*s^{4}b^{1} — *txt*: 𝔓^{66} ℵBWX N-1071 *L*az vg *S*s[c]{} *C*s^{4}b^{1+B}a^{s} *Aeth*

---

270. cf. EP 11,43-49: (*cf. ad 268.*) ... συνεσκέπτοντο οὖν ἀλλήλοις ἐκεῖνοι ἀπελθεῖν καὶ ἐνφανίσαι ταῦτα τῷ Πειλάτῳ· [44] καὶ ἔτι διανοουμένων αὐτῶν φαίνονται πάλιν ἀνοιχθέντες οἱ οὐρανοὶ καὶ ἄνθρωπός τις κατελθὼν καὶ εἰσελθὼν εἰς τὸ μνῆμα. [45] ταῦτα ἰδόντες οἱ περὶ τὸν κεντυρίωνα νυκτὸς ἔσπευσαν πρὸς Πειλᾶτον, ἀφέντες τὸν τάφον ὃν ἐφύλασσον, καὶ ἐξηγήσαντο πάντα ἅπερ εἶδον, ἀγωνιῶντες μεγάλως καὶ λέγοντες· 'ἀληθῶς υἱὸς ἦν θεοῦ.' [46] ἀποκριθεὶς ὁ Πειλᾶτος ἔφη· 'ἐγὼ καθαρεύω τοῦ αἵματος τοῦ υἱοῦ τοῦ θεοῦ, ὑμῖν δὲ τοῦτο ἔδοξεν.' [47] εἶτα προσελθόντες πάντες ἐδέοντο αὐτοῦ καὶ παρεκάλουν κελεῦσαι τῷ κεντυρίωνι καὶ τοῖς στρατιώταις μηδενὶ εἰπεῖν ἃ εἶδον· [48] 'συμφέρει γάρ,' φασίν, 'ἡμῖν ὀφλῆσαι μεγίστην ἁμαρτίαν ἔμπροσθεν τοῦ θεοῦ καὶ μὴ ἐμπεσεῖν εἰς χεῖρας τοῦ λαοῦ τῶν Ἰουδαίων καὶ λιθασθῆναι.' [49] ἐκέλευσεν οὖν ὁ Πειλᾶτος τῷ κεντυρίωνι καὶ τοῖς στρατιώταις μηδὲν εἰπεῖν. (12) [50] Ὄρθρου ... (*cf. ad 268.*)

(A 2) ***271.*** Die Offenbarung des Auferstandenen in Galiläa. **Matth 28** 16–20
The Command to Baptize.

16 Οἱ δὲ ἕνδεκα μαθηταὶ ἐπορεύθησαν εἰς τὴν Γαλιλαίαν, εἰς τὸ ὄρος οὗ ἐτάξατο αὐτοῖς ὁ Ἰησοῦς, 17 καὶ ἰδόντες αὐτὸν προσεκύνησαν αὐτῷ, οἱ δὲ ἐδίστασαν. 18 καὶ προσελθὼν ὁ Ἰησοῦς ἐλάλησεν αὐτοῖς λέγων· ἐδόθη μοι πᾶσα ἐξουσία ἐν οὐρανῷ καὶ ἐπὶ τῆς γῆς. 19 πορευθέντες οὖν μαθητεύσατε πάντα τὰ ἔθνη, βαπτίζοντες αὐτοὺς εἰς τὸ ὄνομα τοῦ πατρὸς καὶ τοῦ υἱοῦ καὶ τοῦ ἁγίου πνεύματος, 20 διδάσκοντες αὐτοὺς τηρεῖν πάντα ὅσα ἐνετειλάμην ὑμῖν· καὶ ἰδοὺ ἐγὼ μεθ' ὑμῶν εἰμι πάσας τὰς ἡμέρας ἕως τῆς συντελείας τοῦ αἰῶνος. *cf. 275.*

B. Die lukanische Nachgeschichte. *The Lucan Post-Resurrection Narraitve.* **Luk 24** 13–53

(B 1) ***272.*** Die Emmausjünger. *The Road to Emmaus.* **Luk 24** 13–35

13 Καὶ ἰδοὺ δύο ἐξ αὐτῶν ἦσαν πορευόμενοι ἐν αὐτῇ τῇ ἡμέρᾳ εἰς κώμην ἀπέχουσαν σταδίους ἑξήκοντα ἀπὸ Ιερουσαλημ, ᾗ ὄνομα Εμμαους, 14 καὶ αὐτοὶ ὡμίλουν πρὸς ἀλλήλους περὶ πάντων τῶν συμβεβηκότων τούτων. 15 καὶ ἐγένετο ἐν τῷ ὁμιλεῖν αὐτοὺς καὶ συζητεῖν, καὶ αὐτὸς Ἰησοῦς ἐγγίσας συνεπορεύετο αὐτοῖς· 16 οἱ δὲ ὀφθαλμοὶ αὐτῶν ἐκρατοῦντο τοῦ μὴ ἐπιγνῶναι αὐτόν. 17 εἶπεν δὲ πρὸς αὐτούς· τίνες οἱ λόγοι οὗτοι οὓς ἀντιβάλλετε πρὸς ἀλλήλους περιπατοῦντες; καὶ ἐστάθησαν σκυθρωποί. 18 ἀποκριθεὶς δὲ εἷς ὀνόματι Κλεοπᾶς εἶπεν πρὸς αὐτόν· σὺ μόνος παροικεῖς Ιερουσαλημ καὶ οὐκ ἔγνως τὰ γενόμενα ἐν αὐτῇ ἐν ταῖς ἡμέραις ταύταις; 19 καὶ εἶπεν αὐτοῖς· ποῖα; οἱ δὲ εἶπαν αὐτῷ· τὰ περὶ Ἰησοῦ τοῦ Ναζαρηνοῦ, ὃς ἐγένετο ἀνὴρ προφήτης δυνατὸς ἐν ἔργῳ καὶ λόγῳ ἐναντίον τοῦ θεοῦ καὶ παντὸς τοῦ λαοῦ, 20 ὅπως τε παρέδωκαν αὐτὸν οἱ ἀρχιερεῖς καὶ οἱ ἄρχοντες ἡμῶν εἰς κρίμα θανάτου καὶ ἐσταύρωσαν αὐτόν. 21 ἡμεῖς δὲ ἠλπίζομεν ὅτι αὐτός ἐστιν ὁ μέλλων λυτροῦσθαι τὸν Ισραηλ· ἀλλά γε καὶ σὺν πᾶσι τούτοις τρίτην ταύτην ἡμέραν ἄγει ἀφ' οὗ ταῦτα ἐγένετο. 22 ἀλλὰ καὶ γυναῖκές τινες ἐξ ἡμῶν ἐξέστησαν ἡμᾶς, γενόμεναι ὀρθριναὶ ἐπὶ τὸ μνημεῖον, 23 καὶ μὴ εὑροῦσαι τὸ σῶμα αὐτοῦ ἦλθαν λέγουσαι καὶ ὀπτασίαν ἀγγέλων ἑορακέναι, οἳ λέγουσιν αὐτὸν ζῆν. 24 καὶ ἀπῆλθόν τινες τῶν σὺν ἡμῖν ἐπὶ τὸ μνημεῖον, καὶ εὗρον οὕτως καθὼς καὶ αἱ γυναῖκες εἶπον, αὐτὸν δὲ οὐκ εἶδον. 25 καὶ αὐτὸς εἶπεν πρὸς αὐτούς· ὦ ἀνόητοι καὶ βραδεῖς τῇ καρδίᾳ τοῦ πιστεύειν ἐπὶ πᾶσιν οἷς ἐλάλησαν οἱ προφῆται· 26 οὐχὶ ταῦτα ἔδει παθεῖν τὸν Χριστὸν καὶ εἰσελθεῖν εἰς τὴν δόξαν αὐτοῦ; 27 καὶ ἀρξάμενος ἀπὸ Μωυσέως καὶ ἀπὸ πάντων

> 21 4: ... οὐ μέντοι ᾔδεισαν οἱ μαθηταὶ ὅτι Ἰησοῦς ἐστιν.

Mt 28,17 αυτω] αυτον: 28-700* σ954-990 Γ **074** 157 *al l*32 *l*183 *l*184 *l*303 *l*950 *l*1231 *l*1634 {} — ● *om*: ℵB-33 700 D Chr *L*' *S*j^{b} — *txt*: *Rpl* (αυτου: ϕ346) Ddy {*L*q vg^{1}(∼ αυ. πρ.) *S*[sc],j^{ac} Eu *C*}
18 γης + καθως απεστειλεν(-αλκεν) με ο πατηρ καγω αποστελω(-λλω) υμας ‖ Jo20 21: (1604) Θ (*S*[sc]p *Geo*^{1}) *Δ*a p
19 ● *om* ουν ‖ [Mk16 15]: *Rpl* Amph Ath Bas CAp Cr Cr^{I} Eu Gr^{Ny} Hip Or *L* Luc Or Te Vic^{P} *S*p^{1} Af Ef Eu *C*b^{4}(^{2} δε; ^{3} και πορ.) *Δ*a(= *C*b^{3}) ad i^{T} l^{FG} md n — *txt* (ουν] νυν): B-33-892 ΣΦ-28-1604 **λ**-1582 ϕ13-174-346-543 σ1010-1293 (D) W Δ Θ Π **074** *al* Eu *L*'(abhnz)(ουν νυν: 30 vg^{5} Faustin Leo) Cp Hil(^{1}) *S*'[sc]j *C*' *Arm* *Δ*i^{V} l^{AD}

Lk 24,13 και—ημ.] ● και—αυτων εν—ημ. ησ. πορ.: 𝔓^{75} ℵ(* ησ. + δε)B Eu *S*pj — και ωφθη δυσιν εξ αυ. εν—ημ. πορευομενοις: *S*sc — ησ. δε δυο πορευομενοι εξ αυ. εν—ημ.: D *L*e(∼ εξ αυ. πορ.) — *txt*: *Rpl* (ημ.] ωρα: 579; ∼ ησ. εξ αυ.: X; *om* ησ.: ϕ346) *L*'(= X: ar^{1}; *om* εν—ημ.: a; *om* ησ.: c)⟨vg^{1}⟩ *S*h *C*s(∼ εις κω. εν—ημ.)b **19** Ναζωραιου *cf.* Mt26 71 *etc.*: *Rpl* *L*l(-ζα-: bff^{2}) *C*s *Geo*^{1}(^{2} -ζα-) — *txt*: 𝔓^{75} ℵBL-**0124** **079** 372 Or *L*'(-ζω-: fr^{1}) Au **20** ∼ αυτον(του-) παρεδ. ‖ Mt26 16 Mk14 11: 1071 λ1-1582 ϕ ⟨983⟩ A (D) K P W Θ Π 157 *pc* *L*(vl'⟨l(*om* αυ.)z⟩r^{1}30)cf vg^{9}(^{1} Au^{1})^{1} **22** μνημα ‖ 24 1: 127 1200

---

272. cf. EH frgm.7 (Hi vir. inl. 2): Evangelium quoque quod appellatur secundum Hebraeos et a me nuper in Graecum sermonem Latinumque translatum est, quo et Origenes saepe utitur, post resurrectionem salvatoris refert: Dominus autem, cum dedisset sindonem servo sacerdotis, ivit ad Jacobum et apparuit ei – iuraverat enim Jacobus se non comesurum panem ab illa hora qua biberat calicem domini, donec videret eum resurgentem a dormientibus – rursusque post paululum: Adferte, ait dominus, mensam et panem, statimque additur. tulit panem et benedixit et fregit et dedit Jacobo iusto et dixit ei: Frater mi, comede panem tuum, quia resurrexit filius hominis a dormientibus.

τῶν προφητῶν διηρμήνευσεν αὐτοῖς ἐν πάσαις ταῖς γραφαῖς τὰ περὶ ἑαυτοῦ. [28] καὶ ἤγγισαν εἰς τὴν κώμην οὗ ἐπορεύοντο, καὶ αὐτὸς προσεποιήσατο πορρωτέρω πορεύεσθαι. [29] καὶ παρεβιάσαντο αὐτὸν λέγοντες· μεῖνον μεθ' ἡμῶν, ὅτι πρὸς ἑσπέραν ἐστὶν καὶ κέκλικεν ἤδη ἡ ἡμέρα. καὶ εἰσῆλθεν τοῦ μεῖναι σὺν αὐτοῖς. [30] καὶ ἐγένετο ἐν τῷ κατακλιθῆναι αὐτὸν μετ' αὐτῶν λαβὼν τὸν ἄρτον εὐλόγησεν καὶ κλάσας ἐπεδίδου αὐτοῖς· [31] αὐτῶν δὲ διηνοίχθησαν οἱ ὀφθαλμοί, καὶ ἐπέγνωσαν αὐτόν· καὶ αὐτὸς ἄφαντος ἐγένετο ἀπ' αὐτῶν. [32] καὶ εἶπαν πρὸς ἀλλήλους· οὐχὶ ἡ καρδία ἡμῶν καιομένη ἦν ἐν ἡμῖν, ὡς ἐλάλει ἡμῖν ἐν τῇ ὁδῷ, ὡς διήνοιγεν ἡμῖν τὰς γραφάς; [33] καὶ ἀναστάντες αὐτῇ τῇ ὥρᾳ ὑπέστρεψαν εἰς Ἰερουσαλημ, καὶ εὗρον ἠθροισμένους τοὺς ἕνδεκα καὶ τοὺς σὺν αὐτοῖς, [34] λέγοντας ὅτι ὄντως ἠγέρθη ὁ κύριος καὶ ὤφθη Σίμωνι. [35] καὶ αὐτοὶ ἐξηγοῦντο τὰ ἐν τῇ ὁδῷ καὶ ὡς ἐγνώσθη αὐτοῖς ἐν τῇ κλάσει τοῦ ἄρτου. *cf. 275.*

(B 2)

273. Die Offenbarung des Auferstandenen in Jerusalem. Luk 24 36–49
The Appearance of the Risen Jesus in Jerusalem.

[36] Ταῦτα δὲ αὐτῶν λαλούντων αὐτὸς ἔστη ἐν μέσῳ αὐτῶν. [37] πτοηθέντες δὲ καὶ ἔμφοβοι γενόμενοι ἐδόκουν πνεῦμα θεωρεῖν. [38] καὶ εἶπεν αὐτοῖς· τί τεταραγμένοι ἐστέ, καὶ διὰ τί διαλογισμοὶ ἀναβαίνουσιν ἐν ταῖς καρδίαις ὑμῶν; [39] ἴδετε τὰς χεῖράς μου καὶ τοὺς πόδας, ὅτι ἐγώ εἰμι αὐτός· ψηλαφήσατέ με καὶ ἴδετε, ὅτι πνεῦμα σάρκα καὶ ὀστέα οὐκ ἔχει καθὼς ἐμὲ θεωρεῖτε ἔχοντα. [41] ἔτι δὲ ἀπιστούντων αὐτῶν ἀπὸ τῆς χαρᾶς καὶ θαυμαζόντων, εἶπεν αὐτοῖς· ἔχετέ τι βρώσιμον ἐνθάδε; [42] οἱ δὲ ἐπέδωκαν αὐτῷ ἰχθύος ὀπτοῦ μέρος· [43] καὶ λαβὼν ἐνώπιον αὐτῶν ἔφαγεν. *cf. 275.*

20 19-23: Οὔσης οὖν ὀψίας τῇ ἡμέρᾳ ἐκείνῃ τῇ μιᾷ σαββάτων, καὶ τῶν θυρῶν κεκλεισμένων ὅπου ἦσαν οἱ μαθηταὶ διὰ τὸν φόβον τῶν Ἰουδαίων, ἦλθεν ὁ Ἰησοῦς καὶ ἔστη εἰς τὸ μέσον, καὶ λέγει αὐτοῖς· εἰρήνη ὑμῖν. [20] καὶ τοῦτο εἰπὼν ἔδειξεν τὰς χεῖρας καὶ τὴν πλευρὰν αὐτοῖς. ἐχάρησαν οὖν οἱ μαθηταὶ ἰδόντες

Lk 24,27 αυτοις + τι ην(+ γεγραμμενον) *cf.* 2017 Mt127p Jo1617f.: ℵL-33-892 λ1-22-1582-2193 Θ *S*j *C*b(τινα ην) (*Arm*; *et* ην] εστιν: *Arm*$^{\langle pc\rangle}$) — *txt*: *Rpl L S*scp *C*s *Δ*⟨me⟩ **28** ● πορρωτερον: B-579 A 382 **29** ● *om* ηδη‖912: *Rpl L*cl *C*s *Arm* — *om* και^2—ημ.: *S*sc *Δ*p — *txt*: 𝔓^{75} ℵBL-0139-33 **λλ**⟨118-209-1278⟩ ϕ124-174 Ψ *pc L' S*'h$^-$(∼ ηδη προς—κεκ.)j *C*b *Δ*'⟨me⟩ **30** λαβ.] και λ.‖2219 Mt2627 Mk1423: σ1675 *C*b^2 | *om* τον‖2219p: λ131 D 1093 Eu *C*s *Δ*a **32** ημιν^3] ημων τον νουν του συνιεναι‖2445: 472 **36** αυτων] ◆ + και λεγει αυτοις· ειρηνη υμιν‖Jo2019.26: 𝔓^{75} *Rpl* Chr Cr Eu *L*Au^2 *S*sc *C*sb' (^{1}*om* και) — + και—υμιν. εγω ειμι· μη φοβεισθε‖Mt1427p: 579(∼ μη φοβ. εγω ειμι)-1241 1604 G P W (∼ εγω—φοβ. ειρ. υμ.) *pc L*z(λεγ.] εφη: cf30 vg^7)' Am Au^2 *S*'j *C*b^7 *Aeth Δ* — *txt*: D *L*e abff^{2}lr^1 **37** πνευ.] φαντασμα‖Mt1426p: D Ad(-ασιαν) Ap *L*Mcn^{Te} **38** ● εν τη καρδια‖2425.32: 𝔓^{75} B D *L*abff^{2}l 30 vg^1 Au Hil Mcn^{Te} *C*s — εις την -ιαν‖←: Ad *L*e c **39** ποδ.] ● + μου: *Rpl* Ad Cr Mcn^{Ep} *L*vl'j^{v}30 vg^4 Am Au Hil *S*'j *C Slav*Meth — + μου και τους τοπους των ηλων‖Jo2025: 579(*om* και) Ath^{Ep} *S*Ath — *txt*: 𝔓^{75} L-33 1071 λ1 ϕ13-543-788-826-983 W Θ 300 Eu Mcn^{Ep} Thd^C *L*e cfz vg' Au Hi Mcn^{Te} *S*h *Arm*, Ath | εγω ειμι αυ.] *om* αυτος‖Mt1427p: 4 300 Ep *L*a vg^1 Te *S*(∼ ψη.—ιδ.^{2} οτι—αυ.: sc)pj *C* — αυ. εγω ειμι: *Rpl* Eu Thd^C *L*z vg' Hi Hil Mcn^{Te} *S*h — εγω αυ. ειμι: D *L*e c Au *Arm*, Ath — *txt*: 𝔓^{75} ℵBL-33-579(αυ.] ο αυ.) Ad Ath Cr *L*vl'(αυτοι: al*) Am *S*Ath | ◆ εχοντα + $^{(40)}$και τουτο ειπων επεδειξεν αυτοις τας χειρας(+ αυτου) και τους ποδας(+ αυτου)‖Jo2020: 𝔓^{75} *Rpl* (υπεδ.: 1604) Ath^{Ep} Cr Da Eu *L* (*S*phj Ath *C*) *Arm*, Ath [[επεδ.] ● εδειξεν‖Jo←: 𝔓^{75} 𝔥CX N **λ** ϕ230-983-1689-*l*547 σ267 G H *al* Ath Cr Da | τ. ποδ.] την πλευραν αυτου‖Jo←: 1579]] — *txt*: D *L*e abff^{2}jlr^1 Mcn$^{Te v}$ *S*sc **43** εφαγ. + και(+ λαβων) τα επιλοιπα εδωκεν αυτοις‖Jo2113: ϕ⟨69-124-788⟩ K Θ(*om* και^1 *et* ^{2} *et om* ενω.—εφαγ.) Π (88 713) *al* (*L*cr^{1}z vg) Au (*S*ch και^1 εφ. ενω. αυ. λαβ. δε τα—αυτοις$^+$j) *C*b^{11} *Arm Aeth* — + λαβων τα επ. απεδ. αυ.: PsAth — + και εδωκε τοις μαθηταις *et om* ενω. αυτων: Ep

Jo 20,19 μια + των‖201 Lk241 Mk162: *Rpl C*b^{+B} — *txt*: 𝔓^{66v} 𝔥⟨1241⟩ A **078 0250** 1321 | ● μαθ. + συνηγμενοι *cf.* Act431 208: 𝔓^{66v} *Rpl* Cr Ep Eu *L*vl'g^{2}r^1 vg^{11} *S*h$^+$j *C*' *Arm Geo*^{1} *Δ*' — κεκρυμμενοι: *Geo*^{2ch} — *txt*: ℵ*BWΛ A D **078** *pc L*qz vg' *S*' *C*b^{B}a^s *Δ*a i^V(^{T}*om* οπου—μαθ.) l^{FG} p **20** ● εδειξ. + και: B A *S*h | ∼ αυτοις τ. χ. κ. τ. πλ.‖*cf. ad* Lk2420: *Rpl* Eu *L*' *S*,j {*C*$^{+B}$a^s} — *txt*: 𝔓^{5v} ℵBWA D **078 0250** *L*q{} | χει. + και τους ποδας‖Lk39: ϕ13-346-543-826-983 Non *L*z *Arm*^{pc} | τ. πλ.] τους ποδας‖←: 138 565 | πλ. + αυτου: 𝔓^{66v} *Rpl* Cr Eu *L*bcr^{1}30 vg^1 *S*,j *C*$^{+B}$ a^s *Geo*^{ch} — *txt*: 𝔓^{5v} ℵBW N λ1 A D **078 0141 0250** *pc L Geo*

44 εἶπεν δὲ πρὸς αὐτούς· οὗτοι οἱ λόγοι μου οὓς ἐλάλησα πρὸς ὑμᾶς ἔτι ὢν σὺν ὑμῖν, ὅτι δεῖ πληρωθῆναι πάντα τὰ γεγραμμένα ἐν τῷ νόμῳ Μωυσέως καὶ προφήταις καὶ ψαλμοῖς περὶ ἐμοῦ. 45 τότε διήνοιξεν αὐτῶν τὸν νοῦν τοῦ συνιέναι τὰς γραφάς· 46 καὶ εἶπεν αὐτοῖς ὅτι οὕτως γέγραπται παθεῖν τὸν Χριστὸν καὶ ἀναστῆναι ἐκ νεκρῶν τῇ τρίτῃ ἡμέρᾳ, 47 καὶ κηρυχθῆναι ἐπὶ τῷ ὀνόματι αὐτοῦ μετάνοιαν καὶ ἄφεσιν ἁμαρτιῶν εἰς πάντα τὰ ἔθνη, — ἀρξάμενοι ἀπὸ Ιερουσαλημ. 48 ὑμεῖς ἐστε μάρτυρες τούτων. 49 κἀγὼ ἐξαποστέλλω τὴν ἐπαγγελίαν τοῦ πατρός μου ἐφ' ὑμᾶς· ὑμεῖς δὲ καθίσατε ἐν τῇ πόλει ἕως οὗ ἐνδύσησθε ἐξ ὕψους δύναμιν.

τὸν κύριον. 21 εἶπεν οὖν αὐτοῖς πάλιν· εἰρήνη ὑμῖν· καθὼς ἀπέσταλκέν με ὁ πατήρ, κἀγὼ πέμπω ὑμᾶς. 22 καὶ τοῦτο εἰπὼν ἐνεφύσησεν καὶ λέγει αὐτοῖς· λάβετε πνεῦμα ἅγιον. 23 ἄν τινων ἀφῆτε τὰς ἁμαρτίας, ἀφέωνται αὐτοῖς· ἄν τινων κρατῆτε, κεκράτηνται.

(B 3) *274.* Die Himmelfahrt. *The Ascension.* **Luk 24 50–53**

50 Ἐξήγαγεν δὲ αὐτοὺς ἕως πρὸς Βηθανίαν, καὶ ἐπάρας τὰς χεῖρας αὐτοῦ εὐλόγησεν αὐτούς. 51 καὶ ἐγένετο ἐν τῷ εὐλογεῖν αὐτὸν αὐτοὺς διέστη ἀπ' αὐτῶν. 52 καὶ αὐτοὶ ὑπέστρεψαν εἰς Ιερουσαλημ μετὰ χαρᾶς μεγάλης, 53 καὶ ἦσαν διὰ παντὸς ἐν τῷ ἱερῷ εὐλογοῦντες τὸν θεόν. *cf. 275.*

Lk 24,44 ελαλ. πρ. υμ.] αντιβαλλετε πρ. αλληλους‖2417: 1579 | πλησθηναι‖2122: D | προφ.] ● τοις πρ.‖1629.31: 𝔓^{75} B-579 *C* — εν τ. πρ.‖←: ℵL *L*c30 Au$^{1:2}$ | *om* κ. ψαλ.‖←2427: λ1-22-1582 F *pc* *Δ*i^{V} **45** *om* τον—συνι.‖2432: Λ **46** γεγρ. + και ουτως εδει‖922 1725 2426 Mt1621 Mk831: *Rpl* *L*fqz vg$^{\langle 1\rangle}$ Au^{20} *S'* *Δ*⟨me⟩ — + εδει‖←: 579 *C*s^{1}(*prm* οτι) — εδει‖←: 237 *pc* *S*s[c] Eu *Arm* — *txt*: 𝔓^{75} ℵBCL D *L*vl'(*om* ουτ.: e cr^{1})30 Au^{1} Hil Ir Te *S*j *C*s^{6}b'(^{1} = e) *Aeth* | *om* εκ νεκ.‖922p 1833p 247 Mt1723p: σ27-71-692-1194 D *pc* *L*Au$^{15:31}$ *C*s *Δ*n **47** και^{2}] ● εις‖33 Mk14: 𝔓^{75} ℵB *S*pj(και εις) *C* *Δ*a i l^{A} n^{CHr} **48** ● *om* εστε *cf.* Act1039 1Th210: 𝔓^{75}B D *pc* *L*Au$^{1:3}$ *S*j *Aeth* **49** καγω] ● και ιδου εγω‖103p 727 Mk12: *Rpl* (*om* και: σ1675) *L*fq *S*hj *Arm* — κ. εγω ιδ.‖←: λ1-1582-2193 W *pc* — *txt* (και εγω): (𝔓^{75}) ℵL-33-579 (D) *pc* *L'*Au *S'*h^{Brs}(*om* και) *C*⟨b^{1}⟩ *Δ*⟨me⟩ | εξαπ.] αποστ.‖←: 𝔓^{75} *Rpl* — *txt*: ℵ^{c}BLX-33-892 Δ 157 472 **50** αυτους^{1} + εξω‖Mt2117: *Rpl* *L'*Au^{1} *S*h *Δ*lp — *txt*: 𝔓^{75} ℵBC*L-33-579 λ1-1582 157 Co *L*e a Au^{1} *S'*j *C* *Δ*a | *om* εως‖←: D 157 1012 *L*⟨e a30⟩ Au$^{1:2}$ {*Δ*⟨me p⟩} | προς] εις‖←: *Rpl* *L'*Au^{1} — *om*: W* *pc* *l*253 *L*vg^{1} Au^{1} — *txt*: 𝔓^{75} ℵBC*L-33-579 λ1-1582 D 237 *L*e(εως] ως) a30 **51** ● αυτων + και ανεφερετο εις τον ουρανον‖[Mk1619] Act19f.: 𝔓^{75} *Rpl* Co Cr *L'*Au^{1} *S'*j *C* *Geo*^{2} *Δ*⟨me⟩ — *txt*: ℵ* D *L*e abff^{2}jl Au^{1} *S*s[c](διεστη] υψωθη‖Jo1232.34) *Geo*^{1} **52** ● αυτοι + προσκυνησαντες αυτον(*om*)‖Mt2817: 𝔓^{75} *Rpl* (700 *pc*) *L*vl'(c)r^{1v} vg^{4}(') *S'*j *C* — *txt*: D *L*e abff^{2}jl Au *S*s[c] | *om* μεγ.‖1017: B* **53** ευλογ.] ● αιν.‖Act247: D *L*vl'r^{1v} Au {} — ● αιν. και ευλ.‖←: *Rpl* *L*cfqz vg *S'* *Aeth*(∼ ευ. κ. αι.) — *txt*: 𝔓^{75} ℵBC*L *S*s[c]j {*C*} *Geo*^{1}[^{2}]

Jo 20,21 απεστειλεν‖657: L *l*253 Chr Cr | πεμ.] αποστελλω‖21a 1718 Mt1016: ℵ^{ca}L-33 D* **050** *pc* Cr **23** αφεωνται] αφιενται‖Mt92 Mk25: *Rpl* (-εται: φ69*^{v} 127) PsAth Bas^{2} Cr Cr^{I} Eu Or *L'*Cp^{3} Or *C*b *Δ*ad l — αφεθησεται(-ονται)‖Mt1231f.p 1818p: ℵ*Δ (Or *L*e adff^{2}r^{1}30)q (vg^{6}) Cp^{1}(^{4} Nov *S*)j *C*sb^{B}a^{s} *Δ'* *Geo* *Aeth* — *txt*: ℵ^{c}LX-33^{v} O **λ** **φ'** A D **050** 157 *pr* Bas^{2} Chr Cr *L*vg^{1} *Arm*

C. Der unechte Markusschluß. *The Longer Ending of Mark.*

(C) **275. Mark 16** 9-20

[9] Ἀναστὰς δὲ πρωῒ πρώτῃ σαββάτου ἐφάνη πρῶτον Μαρίᾳ τῇ Μαγδαληνῇ, παρ' ἧς ἐκβεβλήκει ἑπτὰ δαιμόνια. *cf. 269.* [10] ἐκείνη πορευθεῖσα ἀπήγγειλεν τοῖς μετ' αὐτοῦ γενομένοις πενθοῦσι καὶ κλαίουσιν· [11] κἀκεῖνοι ἀκούσαντες ὅτι ζῇ καὶ ἐθεάθη ὑπ' αὐτῆς ἠπίστησαν (*cf. 268.*).

[12] μετὰ δὲ ταῦτα δυσὶν ἐξ αὐτῶν περιπατοῦσιν ἐφανερώθη ἐν ἑτέρᾳ μορφῇ πορευομένοις εἰς ἀγρόν· [13] κἀκεῖνοι ἀπελθόντες ἀπήγγειλαν τοῖς λοιποῖς· οὐδὲ ἐκείνοις ἐπίστευσαν (*cf. 272.*).

[14] ὕστερον ἀνακειμένοις αὐτοῖς τοῖς ἕνδεκα ἐφανερώθη, καὶ ὠνείδισεν τὴν ἀπιστίαν αὐτῶν καὶ σκληροκαρδίαν ὅτι τοῖς θεασαμένοις αὐτὸν ἐγηγερμένον ἐκ νεκρῶν οὐκ ἐπίστευσαν (*cf. 273.*). [15] καὶ εἶπεν αὐτοῖς· πορευθέντες εἰς τὸν κόσμον ἅπαντα κηρύξατε τὸ εὐαγγέλιον πάσῃ τῇ κτίσει. [16] ὁ πιστεύσας καὶ βαπτισθεὶς σωθήσεται, ὁ δὲ ἀπιστήσας κατακριθήσεται (*cf. 271.*). [17] σημεῖα δὲ τοῖς πιστεύσασιν ταῦτα παρακολουθήσει· ἐν τῷ ὀνόματί μου δαιμόνια ἐκβαλοῦσιν, γλώσσαις

Mk 16,9-20 *om* 9-20: **ℵ**B 137^{+} 138^{+} 340 (*cf.* ^{sch} *ad* 9-20: **099** λ1-22-209-1582 20; ^{sch} *ad* Jo21₁₂: 237 239 259) Amm^{can} Cl Eu Eu^{can} Euthy Hes Or Sev Vic^{A} *L*(k[e]) Hi *S*s *C*s$^{1:7}$b^{2} *Arm*^{pc} *Geo*⟨B⟩ *Aeth* **9** 9 *prm* παντα δε τα παρηγγελμενα τοις περι τον Πετρον συντομως εξηγγειλαν. μετα δε ταυτα και αυτος ο Ιησους απο ανατολης και αχρι δυσεως εξαπεστειλεν δι αυτων το ιερον και αφθαρτον κηρυγμα της αιωνιου σωτηριας ‖ Mt24₁₇₋₂₀ Lk24₄₇₋₄₉: LΨ-**099**-**0112**-579 274^{m} *l*1602 *L*k[e](*om* 9-20) *S*h^{m} *C*s^{2}b^{2} *Aeth* ⟦παντα] *prm* φερεται που και ταυτα: L *S*[c]h^{m} — *prm* εν τισι των αντιγραφων ταυτα φερεται: **099**^{sch} *C*s^{1}b^{1}(τινι *et om* ταυ. φε.) | *om* παντα—δε^{2}, *et spat.*: **0112** | τοις—Π.] τω Πετρω: *C*b^{1} | ο Ι.] Ι.: Ψ-**0112** | Ι. + εφανη(+ αυτοις): Ψ-(**099**) 274^{m} *l*1602 *L*k (*C*s^{2}b^{2} *Aeth*) | απο] και απο: *L*k[e] *C*s^{1} | ανατολων ‖ Mt24₂₇: 274^{m} — + του ηλιου: **099** *C*s^{2}b^{2} | *om* και^{2}: **0112** *L*k[e] *S*[c]h^{m} *C*s^{2}b^{2} | μεχρι: Ψ | δυσεως + και: *C*b^{1} | σωτηρ. + αμην(+ αμην): Ψ-**0112**-579 274^{m} *l*1602 *L*k[e] *S*[c]h^{m} (*Aeth*) — + αμην. εστιν δε(+ και) ταυτα φερομενα(+ μετα το εφοβουντο γαρ): (L) **099**^{sch}(*et* + 16₈!) — + (*transl.*) *αμην. ταυτα δε και καταλεγεται αυτων·(+ και μετα ταυτα) ειχεν(εσχεν) δε(om) αυτας τρομος* ... (16₈): *C*s^{2}(b^{1})⟧ | πρωτης ‖ 16₂: ϕ1689 *pc* *l*183 — τη μια ‖ 16₂p: Eu | σαββατων ‖ ←: 28-544-700 **λ**-22 σ267-659-827-945-1223-1391-1402 K Y Π *mu* Eu PsGr^{Ny} *C*b | παρ] ● αφ ‖ Lk8₂: *Rpl*⟨ℵB⟩ Eu *L*Hi — *txt*: C*LΨ-**0112**-579-892 W D^{s} *pc* **10** πορ.] απελθουσα ‖ 13 Mt28₈ 8₃₃: 579-892 σ517 K Π *al* | μετ] μαθηταις ‖ Mt28₈: Θ 1573 **12** εφα.] εφανη ‖ 9: Θ **13** απελ.] πορευθεντες ‖ 10 Mt11₄p: Θ **14** ● υστ. + δε ‖ Mt25₁₁: 579-892 ΘΣ-565 λ872-1582 σ115-954-1402-1424 A D^{s} *L*cff^{2}oqz vg^{4} *S*[c]ph^{+}j *C*b — *txt*: *Rpl* ⟨ℵB⟩ *La*^{s}lr^{2}32 vg' *C*s⟨1⟩ *Geo*^{B} | ● *om* εκ νεκ. ‖ 16₆p Mt16₂₁ 17₂₃ 20₁₉ Lk9₂₂: *Rpl* ⟨ℵB⟩ *L*⟨k[e]⟩ *S*[c] pj *C*s^{5}b' *Geo*^{B} — *txt* (εκ των ν.): C*X(*om* εγη.)Δ-33-579-892 28-565-(1071) λ1-22 **ϕ**-230-*l*547 σ827 A *al* *S*h (*C*b^{5}) | επιστ. + κακεινοι απελογουντε(-το) λεγοντες οτι ο αιων ουτος της ανομιας και της απιστιας υπο τον σαταναν εστιν ο μη εων τα (ο—τα] τον μη εωντα) υπο των πνευματων ακαθαρτα(-των) την αληθειαν(-ινην) του θεου καταλαβεσθαι δυναμιν· δια τουτο αποκαλυψον σου την δικαιοσυνην ηδη. εκεινοι ελεγον (+ ταυτα) τω Χριστω. και ο Χριστος εκεινοις προσελεγεν οτι πεπληρωται ο ορος των ετων της εξουσιας του σατανα, αλλα εγγιζει αλλα δινα(= δει), και υπερ των(ων) αμαρτησαντων εγω (∼ εγω αμ.) παρεδοθην εις θανατον, ινα υποστρεψωσιν εις την αληθειαν και μηκετι αμαρτησωσιν· ινα την εν τω ουρανω πνευματικην και αφθαρτον της δικαιοσυνης δοξαν κληρονομησωσιν: W (*cj* Swete) *L*Hi↓ **15** και ειπ. αυ.] αλλα: W **17** ● ∼ παρακ./ακ. ταυτα: 𝔋'⟨Δ⟩C-**099** A — *txt*: *Rpl* ⟨ℵB⟩ *La*^{s}cloz vg Δad1 | παρακ.] ● ακολ.: 𝔋'⟨33⟩C* — *txt*: *Rpl*⟨ℵB⟩ (ρακολ.!: Δ)

---

275. cf. EP 7,26-27; 14,58-59: (*cf. ad 265.* Lk23₄₈) ... ἐγὼ δὲ μετὰ τῶν ἑταίρων μου ἐλυπούμην, καὶ τετρωμένοι κατὰ διάνοιαν ἐκρυβόμεθα· ἐζητούμεθα γὰρ ὑπ' αὐτῶν ὡς κακοῦργοι καὶ ὡς τὸν ναὸν θέλοντες ἐμπρῆσαι. [27] ἐπὶ δὲ τούτοις πᾶσιν ἐνηστεύομεν καὶ ἐκαθεζόμεθα πενθοῦντες καὶ κλαίοντες νυκτὸς καὶ ἡμέρας ἕως τοῦ σαββάτου. (8) [28] Συναχθέντες ... (*cf. ad 267.*). (14) (*cf. ad 268.*) ... [58] Ἦν δὲ τελευταία ἡμέρα τῶν ἀζύμων, καὶ πολλοί τινες ἐξήρχοντο ὑποστρέφοντες εἰς τοὺς οἴκους αὐτῶν τῆς ἑορτῆς παυσαμένης. [59] ἡμεῖς δὲ οἱ δώδεκα μαθηταὶ τοῦ κυρίου ἐκλαίομεν καὶ ἐλυπούμεθα, καὶ ἕκαστος λυπούμενος διὰ τὸ συμβὰν ἀπηλλάγη εἰς τὸν οἶκον αὐτοῦ. [60] ἐγὼ δὲ ... (*cf. ad 29.* Jo21₂f.)

Mk16₁₄ *cf.* Hi c. Pelag. 2,15: In quibusdam exemplaribus et maxime in Graecis codicibus iuxta Marcum in fine eius evangelii scribitur: [14] Postea, quum accubuissent undecim, apparuit eis Jesus et exprobavit incredulitatem et duritiam cordis eorum, quia his, qui viderant eum resurgentem, non crediderunt. et illi satisfaciebant dicentes: saeculum istud iniquitatis et incredulitatis sub satana (> substantia: ms) est, qui non sinit per immundos spiritus veram dei apprehendi virtutem: idcirco iam nunc revela iustitiam tuam.

λαλήσουσιν καιναῖς, [18] ὄφεις ἀροῦσιν κἂν θανάσιμόν τι πίωσιν οὐ μὴ αὐτοὺς βλάψῃ, ἐπὶ ἀρρώστους χεῖρας ἐπιθήσουσιν καὶ καλῶς ἕξουσιν. [19] ὁ μὲν οὖν κύριος Ἰησοῦς μετὰ τὸ λαλῆσαι αὐτοῖς **ἀνελήμφθη εἰς τὸν οὐρανὸν** καὶ **ἐκάθισεν ἐκ δεξιῶν** τοῦ θεοῦ *(cf. 274.)*. [20] ἐκεῖνοι δὲ ἐξελθόντες ἐκήρυξαν πανταχοῦ, τοῦ κυρίου συνεργοῦντος καὶ τὸν λόγον βεβαιοῦντος διὰ τῶν ἐπακολουθούντων σημείων.

2Rg2 11 Ps110 1

Mk 16,17 ● *om* καιν.‖Act10 46 1K12 30 14 2-27: C*LΔΨ *Cs*$^{5+1v}$b Sch *Arm*$^{\langle pc\rangle}$ — *txt*(∼ καιν. λαλ.): *Rpl* ⟨ℵB⟩ (CAp Hip Iac) *L*'⟨k[e ff^{2}]⟩(o) Am Au {*S*cphj *Geo*^{B}} ({}) *Δ* **18** ● οφ. αρ.] *prm* και εν ταις χερσιν(+ αυτων)‖Act28 3f.: 𝔥'CX-**099** 565 λ1-22 **σ**⟨954⟩-M^{m}-115 *pc l*6 *l*253 APi Phlst *S*h^{+} *Arm*$^{\langle pc\rangle}$ *Geo*^{B}(∼ οφ. εν τ. χ. *et om* και) — και(*om*) αρ. οφ. εν τ. χ. αυτων: (*S*c; *et* ∼ οφ. αρ.) *Cs*^{2}(^{3}) (^{1v}*om* αυτων)b(∼ οφ. αρ.) (Sch) — *txt*: *Rpl* ⟨ℵB⟩ APi Hip *L*⟨k[e ff^{2}]⟩ *S*pj *Δ*⟨me⟩ **19** ● *om* Ι.: *Rpl*⟨ℵB⟩ *L*] vg Ir *Geo*^{B} *Δ*a — *om* κυ.: H 474 *Δ*n^{CHrL} — *txt* (+ Χριστος): C*LΔ-33-579-892^{m} (W)-565-1071 λ1-22-872-1582 ϕ124-983-*l*547 σ954-1424 K *al* Ir *L*'⟨k[e]⟩(o) Ir *S*cp(∼ Ι. κυ.)hj *Cs*^{5}b'(^{2}) *Arm*$^{\langle pc\rangle}$ *Aeth* *Δ*p(= *S*p)

Alttestamentliche Zitate. *Old Testament Quotations.*

Verzeichnis der im 2. Apparat abgedruckten Texte.
List of the Texts given in the Second Apparatus.

Verzeichnis der im 2. Apparat abgedruckten Texte. *List of the Texts given in the Second Apparatus.*

Parallelenregister. *List of Parallels.*

Perikope. *Pericope*	Fortlaufender Text *Continuous Text*			Parallelen. *Parallels* Kursiv: Verweise (ohne Text). *Italics: References (without Text)*				Seite *Page*
	Matth	**Mark**	**Luk**	Matth	Mark	Luk	Joh	
Die Vorgeschichten. *The Infancy Narratives 1.–12.*								
A. Die matthäische Vorgeschichte. *The Matthean Infancy Narrative 1.–4.*								
1. Die Ahnentafel Jesu. *The Genealogy of Jesus*	**1** 1–17					3 23–34		1
2. Die Geburt Jesu. *The Birth of Jesus*	18–25							2
3. Die Weisen aus dem Morgenland. *The Visit of the Magi*	**2** 1–12					7 41f.		3
4. Von Bethlehem nach Nazareth. *The Flight into Egypt, the Massacre of the Innocents, and the Return*	13–23							4
B. Die lukanische Vorgeschichte. *The Lucan Infancy Narrative 5.–12.*								
5. Der Prolog *The Prologue*			**1** 1–4				15 27	4
6. Verheißung der Geburt des Täufers. *The Promise of the Baptist's Birth*			5–25					5
7. Verheißung der Geburt Jesu. *The Annunciation*			26–38					6
8. Besuch der Maria bei Elisabeth. *The Visitation*			39–56					6
9. Die Geburt des Täufers. *The Birth of the Baptist*			57–80					7
10. Die Geburt Jesu. *The Birth of Jesus*			**2** 1–20					8
11. Beschneidung Jesu und Darstellung im Tempel. *The Circumcision of Jesus and the Presentation in the Temple*			21–40					9
12. Der zwölfjährige Jesus. *The Child Jesus in the Temple*			41–52					10
I. Die galiläische Periode. *The Galilean Period 13.–150.*								
13. Der Täufer. *John the Baptist*	**3** 1–6	**1** 1–6	**3** 1–6	11 10 *4 17*	*1 15*	7 27	1 6.23	12
14. Bußpredigt des Täufers. *John's Preaching of Repentance*	7–10		7–9	7 19 23 33			8 39 15 5f.	13
15. Standespredigt des Täufers. *John's Ethical Teaching*			10–14					14
16. Messianische Verkündigung des Täufers. *John's Messianic Preaching*	11–12	7–8	15–17				1 5.19f. 25–27. 30f. 33	14
17. Die Gefangennahme des Täufers. *John's Imprisonment*			18–20	*14 3f.*	*6 17f.*			16
18. Die Taufe Jesu. *The Baptism of Jesus*	13–17	9–11	21–22				1 32–33	16
19. Die Ahnentafel Jesu. *The Genealogy of Jesus*			23–28	1 1–16				18
20. Die Versuchung Jesu. *The Temptation*	**4** 1–11	12–13	**4** 1–13					19

	Perikope. *Pericope*	Fortlaufender Text *Continuous Text*			Parallelen. *Parallels* Kursiv: Verweise (ohne Text). *Italics: References (without Text)*				Seite *Page*
		Matth	**Mark**	**Luk**	Matth	Mark	Luk	Joh	
21.	Jesu Auftreten in Galiläa. *Jesus' First Preaching in Galilee*	**4 12–17**	**1 14–15**	**4 14–15**	3 1f.	*1 21*	3 2 *4 31*	4 1–3 *2 12*	21
22.	Verwerfung in Nazareth. *The Rejection at Nazareth*			**16–30**	*13 53–58*	*6 1–6a*		7 30 10 39 *4 44 6 42*	22
23.	Berufung der ersten Jünger. *The Call of the First Disciples*	**18–22**	**16–20**				5 10f.	1 38f.	23
24.	Jesus in der Synagoge zu Kapernaum. *Jesus in the Synagogue at Capernaum*		**21–28**	**31–37**	4 13.24 7 28f.		4 14	2 12 6 69 7 46	24
25.	Heilung der Schwiegermutter des Petrus. *The Healing of Peter's Wife's Mother*		**29–31**	**38–39**	8 14f.				26
26.	Krankenheilungen am Abend. *The Sick Healed at Evening*		**32–34**	**40–41**	4 24 8 16 14 35	6 55 *3 11f.*			26
27.	Aufbruch von Kapernaum. *Jesus' Departure from Capernaum*		**35–38**	**42–43**					27
28.	Wanderpredigt in Galiläa. *Preaching and Healing in Galilee*	**23–25**	**39**	**44**	9 35 *8 16* *10 1 12 15* *14 35*	6 6b *1 28.32.34* *3 10 6 55*	8 1 *4 14.37.40* *6 18*		28
29.	Der Fischzug des Petrus. *The Miraculous Draught of Fishes*			**5 1–11**	*13 2*	*3 9* *4 1*		21 1–11	28
	Die Bergpredigt. *The Sermon on the Mount 30.–56.*								
30.	Einleitung. *Introduction*	**5 1–2**				*3 13*	6 *12.17.*20a		30
31.	Die Seligpreisungen *The Beatitudes*	**3–12**					6 20b–23	*16 2*	30
32.	Gleichnisse vom Salz und vom Licht. *Parables about Salt and Light*	**13–16**				9 50 *4 21*	11 33 14 34f. *8 16*	8 12	31
33.	Jesu Stellung zum Gesetz. *The Law and the Prophets*	**17–20**			*24 35*	*13 31*	16 17 *21 33*		31
34.	Vom Töten. *On Murder*	**21–26**				11 25	12 58f.		32
35.	Vom Ehebruch. *On Adultery*	**27–30**			*18 8f.*	*9 43–47*			32
36.	Von der Ehescheidung. *On Divorce*	**31–32**			*19 9*	*10 11f.*	16 18		33
37.	Vom Schwören. *On Swearing*	**33–37**							33
38.	Von der Wiedervergeltung. *On Retaliation*	**38–42**					6 29–30		34
39.	Von der Feindesliebe. *On Loving One's Enemies*	**43–48**					6 27f.32f.35f.		34
40.	Vom Almosen. *On Almsgiving*	**6 1–4**							35
41.	Vom Beten. *On Prayer*	**5–6**							36
42.	Das Unser-Vater. *The Lord's Prayer*	**7–15**			*6 32*	11 25	11 2–4 *12 30*		36
43.	Vom Fasten. *On Fasting*	**16–18**							37
44.	Vom Schätzesammeln. *On Treasures*	**19–21**						12 33f.	38
45.	Parabel vom Auge. *The Single Eye*	**22–23**						11 34–36	38
46.	Vom Doppeldienst. *On Serving Two Masters*	**24**					16 13		38

Perikope. *Pericope*	Fortlaufender Text *Continuous Text*			Parallelen. *Parallels* Kursiv: Verweise (ohne Text). *Italics: References (without Text)*				Seite *Page*
	Matth	**Mark**	**Luk**	Matth	Mark	Luk	Joh	
47. Vom Sorgen. *On Earthly Cares*	**6** 25–34			6 8		12 22–31		39
40. Vom Richten. *On Judging*	**7** 1–5				4 24	6 37f. 41f.		40
49. Von der Entweihung des Heiligen. *On Casting Pearls before Swine*	6							40
50. Von der Gebetserhörung. *The Answer to Prayer*	7–11					11 9–13	16 24	41
51. Die Goldene Regel. *The Golden Rule*	12					6 31		41
52. Die enge Pforte. *The Two Ways*	13–14					13 24		42
53. Falsche Propheten. *False Prophets*	15–20			*3 10* *12 33*		6 43f. *9*	15 *6*	42
54. Warnung vor Selbsttäuschung. *Warning against Self-Deception*	21–23					6 46 13 26f.		43
55. Schlußgleichnisse. *Hearers and Doers of the Word*	24–27					6 47–49		43
56. Nachwort. *The End of the Sermon*	28–29				*1 22*	7 1 *4 32*	*7 46*	44
57. Heilung des Aussätzigen. *The Healing of a Leper*	**8** 1–4	**1** 40–45	**5** 12–16					44
58. Der Hauptmann von Kapernaum. *The Centurion's Servant*	5–13					7 1–19 13 28f	4 46–53	45
59. Heilung der Schwiegermutter des Petrus. *The Healing of Peter's Wife's Mother*	14–15				*1 29–31*	*4 38f.*		47
60. Krankenheilungen am Abend. *The Sick Healed at Evening*	16–17			*4 24 12 15* *14 35*	*1 32–34 3 10* *6 55*	*4 40* *6 18*		47
61. Verschiedene Nachfolger. *Two Claimants to Discipleship*	18–22				*4 35*	9 57–60 *8 22*		47
62. Der Seesturm. *Stilling the Tempest*	23–27				*4 35–41*	*8 22–25*		48
63. Die Besessenen von Gadara. *The Gadarene Demoniacs*	28–34				*5 1–20*	*8 26–29*		48
64. Heilung des Gichtbrüchigen. *The Healing of the Man Sick of the Palsy*	**9** 1–8	**2** 1–12	17–26		*5 18*	*8 38*	5 8f.	49
65. Berufung des Levi und Zöllnermahl. *The Call of Levi*	9–13	13–17	27–32	*12 7*		15 1f.		51
66. Die Fastenfrage. *The Question about Fasting*	14–17	18–22	33–39					53
67. Die Tochter des Jairus und das blutflüssige Weib. *Jairus' Daughter and the Woman with the Issue of Blood*	18–26				*5 21–43*	*8 40–56*		55
68. Heilung zweier Blinder. *Two Blind Men Healed*	27–31			*20 29–34*	*10 46–52*	*18 35–43*		56
69. Heilung eines stummen Dämonischen. *The Healing of a Dumb Demoniac*	32–34			*12 22–24*	*3 22*	*11 14f.*	*7 31*	56
70. Die Aussendung der Zwölf. *The Mission ot the Twelve*	35– **10** 16			*4 23 11 24* *14 14* *15 24.32*	*1 39 3 13–19* *6 6b–13.34* *8 1f.*	*4 44 6 13–16* *8 1 9 1–6* *10 1–12* *Act 1 13*	*1 42* *4 35*	56
71. Das Schicksal der Jünger. *The Afflictions of the Disciples*	17–25			*24 9–13*	*13 9–13*	*6 40 12 11f.* *21 12–19*	*13 16 14 26* *15 19–21 16 2*	58
72. Aufforderung zum furchtlosen Bekenntnis. *Exhortation to Fearless Confession*	26–33				*4 22* *8 38*	12 2–9 21 18 *8 17 9 26*		58
73. Zwiespalt unter den Nächsten. *Division in Households*	34–36					12 51–53		59

Perikope. *Pericope*	Fortlaufender Text *Continuous Text*			Parallelen. *Parallels* Kursiv: Verweise (ohne Text). *Italics: References (without Text)*				Seite *Page*
	Matth	**Mark**	**Luk**	Matth	Mark	Luk	Joh	
74. Bedingungen der Nachfolge. *The Conditions of Discipleship*	**10** 37–39			*16 24f.*	*8 34f.*	14 26f. 17 33 *9 23f.*	*12 25f.*	60
75. Schluß der Rede. *End of the Discourse*	**11** 40– 1			*18 5*	*9 37*	9 41 *9 48 10 16*	*12 44f. 13 20*	60
76. Anfrage des Täufers. *The Baptist's Question*	**11** 2–6					7 18–23		61
77. Jesu Zeugnis über den Täufer. *Jesus' Testimony to the Baptist*	7–19			*11 14 17 9–13*	*1 2 9 9–13*	7 24–28.31–35 16 16		61
78. Wehe über die galiläischen Städte. *Woes on the Cities of Galilee*	20–24			10 15		10 12–15		62
79. Jubelruf. *Jesus' Thanksgiving to the Father*	25–27					10 21f.	3 35 10 15 17 2.25f.	63
80. Heilandsruf. *Comfort for the Heavy-laden*	28–30							64
81. Das Ährenraufen am Sabbat. *Plucking Corn on the Sabbath*	**12** 1–8	**2** 23–28	**6** 1–5	9 13			5 10	64
82. Die Heilung der verdorrten Hand. *The Healing of the Man with the Withered Hand*	9–14	**3** 1–6	6–11			13 15 14 3–5		66
83. Berufung der zwölf Apostel. *The Call of the Twelve*			12–16	*10 1–4*	*3 13–19*	*Act 1 13*	*1 42*	68
84. Zulauf und Heilungen. *Jesus Heals the Multitudes*	15–21	7–12	17–19	4 24f. 8 16 14 36	1 34 6 56	4 40f.		69
85. Berufung der zwölf Apostel. *The Call of the Twelve*		13–19		5 1 10 1–4 *3 13–15 4 23 9 35*	*6 6b.7*	6 12–16 *9 1f. 10 1* Act 1 13	1 42	70
Die Feldrede. *The Sermon on the Plain 86.–91.*								
86. Die Seligpreisungen. *The Beatitudes*			20–23	5 3f. 6 11f.			16 2	72
87. Die Weherufe. *The Woes*			24–26					73
88. Von der Feindesliebe. *On Loving One's Enemies*			27–36	5 39f.42.44–48				73
89. Vom Richten. *On Judging*			37–42	7 1–5 10 24f. 15 14	*4 24*		13 16 15 20	74
90. Baum und Frucht. *The Tree and Its Fruit*			43–46	7 6.18.21 12 33–35				75
91. Schlußgleichnisse. *Hearers and Doers of the Word*			47–49	7 24–27				76
92. Der Hauptmann von Kapernaum. *The Centurion's Servant*			**7** 1–10	*7 28 8 5–13*			*4 46–53*	77
93. Der Jüngling von Nain. *The Window's Son at Nain*			11–17					78
94. Anfrage des Täufers. *The Baptist's Question*			18–23	*11 2–6*				78
95. Jesu Zeugnis über den Täufer. *Jesus' Testimony to the Baptist*			24–35	21 32 *11 7–19*	*1 2*			78
96. Die große Sünderin. *The Woman Who Was a Sinner*			36–50	*26 6f.*	*14 3*		*12 1–3*	79
97. Die dienenden Frauen. *The Ministering Women*			**8** 1–3	*4 23 9 35 27 56*	*1 39 6 6 15 40*	*4 44*		80
98. „Er ist von Sinnen". *"He is out of His Mind"*		20–21				8 19		81
99. Die Lästerung der Schriftgelehrten. *The Beelzebul Controversy*	22–37	22–30		9 32–34 *7 16.18*	*9 40*	11 14–23 12 10 *6 43 9 50*	7 31	81

Parallelenregister. *List of Parallels.*

	Perikope. *Pericope*	Fortlaufender Text *Continuous Text* Matth	Mark	Luk	Parallelen. *Parallels* Kursiv: Verweise (ohne Text). *Italics: References (without Text)* Matth	Mark	Luk	Joh	Seite *Page*
100.	Die Zeichenforderung der Pharisäer. *The Pharisees Seek a Sign*	**12** 38–42			16 1f.4	8 11f.	11 16.29f.31f.	2 18 6 30	83
101.	Spruch vom Rückfall. *The Return of the Evil Spirit*	43–45					11 24–26		84
102.	Jesu wahre Verwandte. *Jesus' Real Brethren*	46–50	**3** 31–35			*3 21*	8 19–21	15 14	85
103.	Das Gleichnis vom Säemann. *The Parabel of the Sower*	**13** 1–9	**4** 1–9	**8** 4–8		*3 9*	*5 3*		86
104.	Zweck der Gleichnisrede. *The Reason for Parables*	10–15	10–12	9–10	*25 29*	*4 25*	*8 18* *19 26*	12 39f.	88
105.	Seelige Augenzeugen. *The Blessedness of the Disciples*	16–17					10 23f.		89
106.	Deutung des Gleichnisses vom Säemann. *The Interpretation of the Parable of the Sower*	18–23	13–20	11–15					90
107.	Sprüche über das rechte Hören der Parabeln. *The Right Use of Parables*		21–25	16–18	5 15 10 26 13 12 25 29 *7 2*		11 33 12 2 19 26 *6 38*		91
108.	Das Gleichnis von der selbstwachsenden Saat. *The Parable of the Seed Growing Secretly*		26–29						93
109.	Das Gleichnis vom Unkraut unter dem Weizen. *The Parable of the Tares*	24–30							93
110.	Das Gleichnis vom Senfkorn. *The Parable of the Mustard Seed*	31–32	30–32				13 18f.		94
111.	Das Gleichnis vom Sauerteig. *The Parable of the Leaven*	33					13 20f.		94
112.	Gebrauch der Gleichnisrede. *The Use of Parables*	34–35	33–34						95
113.	Deutung des Gleichnisses vom Unkraut. *The Interpretation of the Parable of the Tares*	36–43							95
114.	Die Gleichnisse vom Schatz und von der Perle. *The Parables of the Hidden Treasure and of the Pearl of Great Price*	44–46							95
115.	Das Gleichnis vom Fischnetz. *The Parable of the Drag-net*	47–50							96
116.	Abschluß der Gleichnisrede. *The End of the Parables*	51–52							96
117.	Jesu wahre Verwandte. *Jesus' Real Brethren*			19–21	*12 46–50*	*3 20.31–35*		*15 14*	96
118.	Der Seesturm. *The Stilling of the Tempest*		35–41	22–25	8 18.23–27				97
119.	Der gerasenische Besessene. *The Gerasene Demoniac*		**5** 1–20	26–39	8 28– 9 1				98
120.	Die Tochter des Jairus und das blutflüssige Weib. *Jairus' Daugther and the Woman with the Issue of Blood*		21–43	40–56	9 18–26				101
121.	Verwerfung in Nazareth. *The Rejection at Nazareth*	**13** 53–58	**6** 1–6a				4 16–30	4 44 6 42 7 15 *7 30 10 39*	104
122.	Die Aussendung der Zwölf. *The Mission of the Twelfe*		6b–13	**9** 1–6	9 37f. 10 1. 5–16a *4 23* *9 35 15 29*	3 13–15	10 1–12	4 35	106
123.	Urteil des Herodes über Jesus. *Herod's Opinion of Jesus*	**14** 1–2	14–16	7–9	16 14	8 28	9 19	1 21.25	109
124.	Der Tod des Täufers. *The Death of the Baptist*	3–12	17–29				3 19f.		110
125.	Rückkehr der Jünger und Speisung der Fünftausend. *The Return of the Twelve and the Feeding of the Five Thousand*	13–21	30–44	10–17	9 36 15 32–38	8 1–9		6 1–13	112

Perikope. *Pericope*	Fortlaufender Text *Continuous Text*			Parallelen. *Parallels* Kursiv: Verweise (ohne Text). *Italics: References (without Text)*				Seite *Page*
	Matth	Mark	Luk	Matth	Mark	Luk	Joh	
126. Das Wandeln auf dem See. *The Walking on the Water*	**14** 22–33	**6** 45–52					6 15–21	117
127. Heilungen in Gennesaret. *Healings in Gennesaret*	34–36	53–56		*4 24* *8 16*	*1 32* *3 10*	*4 40* *6 19*		119
128. Rein und Unrein. *Clean and Unclean*	**15** 1–20	**7** 1–23		*16 9*	*8 17*	11 38 *6 39*		119
129. Die Kanaanitin. *The Syro-phoenician Woman*	21–28	24–30		10 6				122
130. Heilung vieler Kranker (Matth) – eines Taubstummen (Mark). *The Healing of Many Sick Persons (Matth) – of the Deaf Mute (Mark)*	29–31	31–37						123
131. Die Speisung der Viertausend. *The Feeding of the Four Thousand*	32–39	**8** 1–10		*9 36* *14 13–21*	*6 30–44*	*9 10–17*	*6 1–13*	124
132. Die Zeichenforderung der Pharisäer. *The Pharisees Seek a Sign*	**16** 1–4	11–13		*12 38f.*		12 54–56 *11 16.29*	*2 18* *6 30*	126
133. Vom Sauerteig der Pharisäer. *The Leaven of the Pharisees*	5–12	14–21		*15 17*	*7 18*	12 1		126
134. Der Blinde von Bethsaida. *The Blind Man of Bethsaida*		22–26		*9 27–30* *20 29–34*	*10 46–52*	*18 35–43*	9 1–17	128
135. Das Petrusbekenntnis. *Peter's Confession*	13–20	27–30	**9** 18–21	*14 1f.* *18 18*	*6 14–16*	*9 7–9*	6 68f. *1 21.* *25 20 22f.*	128
136. Erste Leidensverkündigung. *The First Prediction of the Passion*	21–23	31–33	22	17 22f. 20 17–19	9 31f. 10 33f.	9 44f. 18 31– 34 24 6–8 *17 25*		132
137. Die Leidensnachfolge der Jünger. *The Conditions of Discipleship*	24–28	34– **9** 1	23–27	10 33.38f. *24 34*	*13 30*	12 9 14 27 17 33 *21 32*	12 25f.	130
138. Die Verklärung. *The Transfiguration*	**17** 1–8	2–8	28–36	3 17	1 11	3 22	1 14	135
139. Das Kommen des Elias. *The Coming of Elijah*	9–13	9–13		11 14		*9 37*		137
140. Heilung des epileptischen Knaben. *The Healing of an Epileptic Child*	14–20	14–29	37–43a	*17 9* *21 21*	*9 9* *11 22f.*	*17 6*	14 19	138
141. Zweite Leidensverkündigung. *The Second Prediction of the Passion*	22–23	30–32	43b–45	*16 21–23* *20 17–19*	*8 31–33* *10 33f.*	*9 22 18 31–34* *24 6–8*	7 1 16 6	140
142. Die Tempelsteuer. *The Tempel Tax*	24–27							141
143. Der Rangstreit. *The Dispute about Greatness*	**18** 1–5	33–37	46–48	10 40 20 26f. 23 11 *17 24* 23 12	10 43f. *10 15*	10 16 22 26 *14 11 18 14.17* *22 24*	12 44f. 13 20 *3 3.5.*	141
144. Der fremde Exorzist. *The Strange Exorcist*		38–41	49–50	12 30 *10 42*		11 23		143
145. Vom Ärgernis. *About Offences*	6–9	42–48		5 29f.		17 1f.		143
146. Vom Salz. *About Salt*		49–50		*5 13*		*14 34f.*		145
147. Das Gleichnis vom verlornen Schaf. *The Lost Sheep*	10–14					15 3–7		145
148. Vom Mahnen und Beten unter Brüdern. *On Reproving One's Brother*	15–20			16 19 *21 22*	*11 24*	17 3	20 22f. *14 13f. 15 7* *16 23*	146
149. Von der Versöhnlichkeit. *On Reconciliation*	21–22					17 4		147
150. Das Gleichnis vom Schalksknecht. *The Parable of the Unmerciful Servant*	23–35			*6 14f.*	*11 25*			147

Perikope. *Pericope*	Fortlaufender Text *Continuous Text*			Parallelen. *Parallels* Kursiv: Verweise (ohne Text). *Italics: References (without Text)*				Seite *Page*
	Matth	**Mark**	**Luk**	Matth	Mark	Luk	Joh	
II. Der lukanische Reisebericht. *The Lucan Travel Narrative 151.–200.*								
151. Die Samariterherberge. *The Samaritan Villages*			**9** 51–56					148
152. Verschiedene Nachfolger. *Claimants to Discipleship*			57–62	*8 18–22*				148
153. Die Aussendung der Zweiundsiebzig. *The Mission of the Seventy Two*			**10** 1–16	*9 37f. 10 1.5–16a.40 11 20–24 18 5*	*3 13–15 6 6b–13 9 37*	*9 1–6.48*	5 23 15 23 *12 44f. 13 20*	149
154. Die Rückkehr der Zweiundsiebzig. *The Return of the Seventy Two*			17–20		*6 30*	*9 10*	12 31	150
155. Jubelruf. *Jesus' Gratitude to His Father*			21–22	*11 25–27*			*3 35 10 15 17 25f.*	150
156. Selige Augenzeugen. *The Blessedness of the Disciples*			23–24	*13 16f.*				150
157. Die Frage nach dem großen Gebot. *The Great Commandment*			25–28	*7 12 22 34–40*	*12 28–34*			151
158. Der barmherzige Samariter. *The Good Samaritan*			29–37					151
159. Martha und Maria. *Martha and Mary*			38–42				12 2	151
160. Das Unser-Vater. *The Lord's Prayer*			**11** 1–4	*6 7–15 18 35*	*11 25*			152
161. Gleichnis vom bittenden Freund. *The Friend at Midnight*			5–8					152
162. Von der Gebetserhörung. *The Answer to Prayer*			9–13	*7 7–11*			*16 24*	153
163. Gegen den Vorwurf des Teufelsbündnisses. *The Beelzebul Controversy*			14–23	*9 32–34 12 22–38 16 1*	*3 22–30 8 11 9 40*	*9 50*	*2 18 6 30 7 31*	153
164. Spruch vom Rückfall. *The Return of the Evil Spirit*			24–26	*12 43–45*				154
165. Seligpreisung der Mutter Jesu. *The Blessedness of Jesus' Mother*			27–28					154
166. Das Zeichen für dieses Geschlecht. *The Sign for this Generation*			29–32	*12 39–42 16 4*	*8 12*			155
167. Vom Licht. *About Light*			33–36	*5 15 6 22f.*	*4 21*	*8 16*		155
168. Rede gegen Pharisäer und Schriftgelehrte. *Discourse against the Scribes and Pharisees*			37–54	*23 1–36*	*7 2 12 37b–40*	*20 45–47*	*13 13*	156
169. Aufforderung zum furchtlosen Bekenntnis. *Exhortation to Fearless Confession*			**12** 1–12	*10 19f.26–33 12 32 16 6.27*	*3 28f. 4 22 8 15.38 13 11*	*8 17 9 26 21 14f.18*	*14 26*	157
170. Der törichte Reiche. *The Rich Fool*			13–21					158
171. Vom Sorgen und Schätzesammeln. *On Earthly Cares*			22–34	*6 8.19–21.25–34*				159
172. Von der Wachsamkeit und Treue. *Watchfulness and Faithfulness*			35–46	24 43–51 *25 1–13*	*13 35f.*		13 4f.	160
173. Vom Knechtslohn. *The Servant's Wages*			47–48					161
174. Vom Ernst der Zeit. *Signs for this Age*			49–56	*10 34–36 16 2f.*	*10 38f.*			161
175. Empfehlung rechtzeitigen Ausgleichs. *Agreement with One's Adversary*			57–59	*5 25f.*				162
176. Bußruf. *The Call to Repentance*			**13** 1–9					162

	Perikope. *Pericope*	Fortlaufender Text *Continuous Text*			Parallelen. *Parallels* Kursiv: Verweise (ohne Text). *Italics: References (without Text)*				Seite *Page*
		Matth	**Mark**	**Luk**	Matth	Mark	Luk	Joh	
177.	Heilung der verkrümmten Frau. *The Healing of the Woman with a Spirit of Infirmity*			**13** 10–17	*12 11*	*14 5*			163
178.	Gleichnisse vom Senfkorn und Sauerteig. *The Parables of the Mustard Seed and Leaven*			18–21	*13 31–33*	*4 30–32*			163
179.	Ausschließung aus dem Reiche Gottes. *Exclusion from the Kingdom of God*			22–30	25 10f. *7 13f. 22f. 8 11f. 19 30 20 16*	*10 31*			164
180.	Abschied von Galiläa. *The Departure from Galilee*			31–33					164
181.	Weissagung über Jerusalem. *The Lament over Jerusalem*			34–35	23 37–39				165
182.	Heilung eines Wassersüchtigen. *Healing of a Man with the Dropsy*			**14** 1–6	*12 11f.*	*3 4*	*6 9*		165
183.	Gastmahlsreden. *Teaching on Humility*			7–14	18 4 23 12		18 14		166
184.	Das Gleichnis vom Abendmahl. *The Parable of the Great Supper*			15–24	22 1–10				166
185.	Bedingungen der Jüngerschaft. *The Cost of Discipleship*			25–35	*5 13 10 37f. 16 24*	*8 34 9 50*	*9 23*	*12 26*	167
186.	Die Gleichnisse vom verlorenen Schaf und vom verlorenen Groschen. *The Lost Sheep and the Lost Coin*			**15** 1–10	*9 10f. 18 10–14*	*2 15f.*	*5 29f.*		168
187.	Das Gleichnis vom verlorenen Sohn. *The Prodigal Son*			11–32				17 10	169
188.	Das Gleichnis vom ungerechten Haushalter. *The Unjust Steward*			**16** 1–13	*6 24*				170
189.	Verurteilung des pharisäischen Hochmuts. *The Hypocrisy of the Pharisees*			14–15					170
190.	Vom Gesetz und von der Ehescheidung. *About the Law and about Divorce*			16–18	*5 18 11 12f. 24 35*	*13 31*	*21 33*		170
191.	Vom reichen Mann und armen Lazarus. *Dives and Lazarus*			19–31				5 46	171
192.	Vom Ärgernis. *On Offences*			**17** 1–2	*18 6f.*	*9 42*			171
193.	Von der Versöhnlichkeit. *On Forgiveness*			3–4	*18 15.21f.*				172
194.	Vom Glauben. *On Faith*			5–6	*17 20 21 21*	*11 22f.*			172
195.	Vom Knechtslohn. *The Servant's Wages*			7–10					172
196.	Heilung von zehn Aussätzigen. *The Healing of the Ten Lepers*			11–19					172
197.	Vom Reiche Gottes. *On the Kingdom of God*			20–21	*24 23*	*13 21*			173
198.	Der Tag des Menschensohns. *The Day of the Son of Man*			22–37	24 26–28. 37–41 *10 39 16 21–25 24 17.23*	*8 31.35 13 15.21*	*9 22.24 21 21*	*12 25*	173
199.	Das Gleichnis vom gottlosen Richter. *The Parable of the Unjust Judge*			**18** 1–8					175
200.	Pharisäer und Zöllner. *The Pharisee and the Publican*			9–14	*18 4 23 12*		*14 11*		175

Perikope. *Pericope*	Fortlaufender Text *Continuous Text*			Parallelen. *Parallels* Kursiv: Verweise (ohne Text). *Italics: References (without Text)*				Seite *Page*
	Matth	**Mark**	**Luk**	Matth	Mark	Luk	Joh	
III. Die judäische Periode. *The Judean Period 201.–267.* **1. Der Zug nach Jerusalem. *The Journey to Jerusalem 201.–209.***								
201. Verbot der Ehescheidung. *The Forbidding of Divorce*	**19** 1–12	**10** 1–12		5 32		16 18		176
202. Segnung der Kinder. *"Suffer Little Children"*	13–15	13–16	**18** 15–17	18 3			3 3.5	178
203. Von der Gefahr des Reichtums. *The Rich Young Man*	16–30	17–31	18–30	20 16 *19 19*		13 30 22 28–30		179
204. Das Gleichnis von den Arbeitern im Weinberg. *The Parable of the Labourers in the Vineyard*	**20** 1–16			*19 30* *20 18*	*10 31*	*13 30*		183
205. Dritte Leidensverkündigung. *The Third Prediction of the Passion*	17–19	32–34	31–34	*16 21* *17 23*	*8 31* *9 31f.*	*9 22.44f.* *24 6–8*		184
206. Jesus und die Zebedaiden. *Jesus and the Sons of Zebedee*	20–28	35–45		*23 11*	*9 35*	12 50 22 25–27		185
207. Die Heilung des Bartimäus. *The Healing of Bartimaeus*	29–34	46–52	35–43	9 27–30	*8 25*		*9 7*	187
208. Zakchäus. *Zacchaeus*			**19** 1–10					189
209. Das Gleichnis von den Minen. *The Parable of the Pounds*			11–27	25 14–30 *13 12*	*4 25*	*8 19*		189
2. Die jerusalemischen Tage. *The Days in Jerusalem 210.–242.*								
210. Der Einzug in Jerusalem. *The Entry into Jerusalem*	**21** 1–9	**11** 1–10	**19** 28–38				12 13–15	191
211. Weissagung von der Zerstörung Jerusalems. *Prediction of the Destruction of Jerusalem*			39–44	*21 16*				194
212. Jesus im Tempel; (Tempelreinigung); Rückkehr nach Bethanien. *Jesus in the Temple; (the Cleansing of It); Return to Bethany*	10–17	11			*11 15–17*	*19 40.45f.* *21 37*	*12 13–16* [*8 1f.*]	195
213. Die Verfluchung des Feigenbaums. *The Cursing of the Fig Tree*	18–19	12–14						195
214. Die Tempelreinigung. *The Cleansing of the Temple*		15–19	45–48	21 12f 22 3		*21 37*	[*8 1f.*]	196
215. Von der Kraft des Glaubens. *The Power of Faith*	20–22	20–25		17 20 18 19 *5 23 6 14*		17 6	14 13f. 15 7 16 23	197
216. Die Vollmachtsfrage. *The Question about Authority*	23–27	27–33	**20** 1–8				2 18	199
217. Das Gleichnis von den ungleichen Söhnen. *The Parable of the Two Sons*	28–32					*7 28–30*		201
218. Das Gleichnis von den bösen Winzern. *The Parable of the Wicked Husbandmen*	33–46	**12** 1–12	9–19	*22 22*			7 30	202
219. Das Gleichnis vom Hochzeitsmahl. *The Parable of the Marriage Feast*	**22** 1–14					*14 15–24*		205
220. Die Pharisäerfrage. *The Question concerning Tribute to Caesar*	15–22	13–17	20–26		*12 12*	*20 19*	3 2 *7 30*	205
221. Die Sadduzäerfrage. *The Question concerning the Resurrection*	23–33	18–27	27–40	22 46	12 34 *11 18 12 32*	*19 48*		207
222. Die Frage nach dem großen Gebot. *The Great Commandment*	34–40	28–34		7 12 *19 19 22 46*		10 25–28 *20 39f.*		210
223. Der Davidssohn. *About David's Son*	41–46	35–37a	41–44		*12 34*	*20 40*	7 42	211
224. Rede gegen Pharisäer und Schriftgelehrte. *Discourse against the Scribes and Pharisees*	**23** 1–36	37b–40	45–47	*3 7 5 34* *18 4 20 26*	*9 35* *10 43*	11 39–44. 46–52 *3 7 14 11* *18 14 22 26*	13 13	213

Perikope. *Pericope*	Fortlaufender Text *Continuous Text*			Parallelen. *Parallels* Kursiv: Verweise (ohne Text). *Italics: References (without Text)*				Seite *Page*
	Matth	**Mark**	**Luk**	Matth	Mark	Luk	Joh	
225. Weissagung über Jerusalem. *The Lament over Jerusalem*	**23** 37–39					*13 34f.*		216
226. Die Scherflein der Witwe. *The Widow's Mites*		**12** 41–44	**21** 1–4					216
Die synoptische Apokalypse. *The Synoptic Apocalypse 227.–242.*								
227. Einleitung. Die Zerstörung des Tempels. *Introduction. The Destruction of the Temple*	**24** 1–3	**13** 1–4	5–7					217
228. Der Anfang der Wehen. *The Beginning of Woes*	4–8	5–8	8–11	*24 11.24*	*13 22*			218
229. Die Verfolgung der Jünger. *The Persecution of the Disciples*	9–14	9–13	12–19	*10 17–22.30* *24 5.24*	*13 6.22*	*12 7.11f.* *21 8*	14 26 15 19.21 16 2	219
230. Die Bedrängnis in Judäa. *The Abomination of Desolation*	15–22	14–20	20–24			17 31		221
231. Warnung vor falschen Messias- und Prophetengestalten. *Against False Messiahs and False Prophets*	23–28	21–23		*24 5.11*	*13 6*	17 23 *17 21.24 21 8*	13 19 14 29 16 4	223
232. Die Parusie des Menschensohns. *The Parousia of the Son of Man*	29–31	24–27	25–28	*26 64*	*14 62*	*22 69*		224
233. Das Gleichnis vom Feigenbaum. *The Parable of the Fig Tree*	32–33	28–29	29–31					225
234. Das „Wann" der Parusie. *The Time of the Parousia*	34–36	30–32	32–33	5 18		16 17		225
235. Unverhofft kommt das Gericht. *The Unexpected Judgement*	37–41					*17 26f. 34f.*		226
236. Das Gleichnis vom verreisten Hausherrn. *Watch and Pray*	42	33–37		25 13–15		12 38		227
237. Das Gleichnis vom wachenden Hausherrn. *The Watchful Householder*	43–44					*12 39f.*		227
238. Der treue und kluge Knecht. *The Faithful and Wise Servant*	45–51					*12 42–46*		227
239. Das Gleichnis von den zehn Jungfrauen. *The Parable of the Ten Virgins*	**25** 1–13				*13 33*	12 35f. *13 25–27*		228
240. Das Gleichnis von den Talenten. *The Parable of the Talents*	14–30			*13 12*	*4 25* *13 34*	*8 18* *19 11–27*		229
241. Die große Scheidung. *The Sheep and the Goats*	31–46						5 29	230
242. Schluß der Rede nach Lukas. *The Lucan Ending of the Discourse*			34–38	*21 17* *26 30*	*11 11.19* *14 26*	*22 39*	[*8 1f.*]	230
3. Die Leidensgeschichte. *The Passion Narrative 243.–267*								
243. Der Todesanschlag. *The Conspiracy of the Jews*	**26** 1–5	**14** 1–2	**22** 1–2				11 47–53	231
244. Die Salbung in Bethanien. *The Anointing at Bethany*	6–13	3–9				7 37f.	12 1–8	232
245. Der Verrat des Judas. *The Betrayal by Judas*	14–16	10–11	3–6		*14 20*		6 71 13 2.27	234
Die letzte Mahlzeit. *The Last Supper 246.–252.*								
246. Zurüstung zum Passahmal. *Preparation for the Passover*	17–19	12–16	7–13					235
247. Ankündigung des Verrats. *The Foretelling of the Betrayal*	20–25	17–21	14	*26 14*	*14 10*	22 21–23 *22 3*	6 70 13 18. 21–27.30	237
248. Die Stiftung des Herrnmahls. *The Institution of the Lord's Supper*	26–29	22–25	15–20			1 K 11 23–25	6 51.53–58	238

Perikope. *Pericope*		Fortlaufender Text *Continuous Text*			Parallelen. *Parallels* Kursiv: Verweise (ohne Text). *Italics: References (without Text)*				Seite *Page*
		Matth	**Mark**	**Luk**	Matth	Mark	Luk	Joh	
249.	Ankündigung des Verrats. *The Foretelling of the Betrayal*			**22** 21–23	*26 21–24*	*14 18–21*		6 *70* *13 21–26*	241
250.	Die Rangordnung im Reiche Gottes. *Greatness in the Kingdom of God*			24–30	*18 1 20 25–28* *23 11*	*9 33.35* *10 42–45*	*9 46*	13 4f. 12–14	241
251.	Vorhersage der Verleugnung des Petrus. *The Prophecy of Peter's Denial*			31–34	*26 33–34*	*14 29f.*		*13 37f.*	242
252.	Rückblick und Ausblick. *The Two Swords*			35–38					242
253.	Auf dem Wege nach Gethsemane; Vorhersage der Verleugnung des Petrus. *On the Way to Gethsemane; Prophecy of Peter's Denial*	**26** 30–35	**14** 26–31	39			22 31–34 *21 37*	11 16 13 36–38 16 32 18 1 [*8 1f.*]	243
254.	Jesus in Gethsemane. *Jesus in Gethsemane*	36–46	32–42	40–46			*24 7*	12 27 14 31 18 1.11	244
255.	Die Gefangennahme Jesu. *Jesus Taken Captive*	47–56	43–52	47–53				18 2–11.20	247
256.	Jesus vor dem Hohen Rat; Verleugnung des Petrus. *Jesus before the Sanhedrin; Peter's Denial*	57–75	53–72	54–71	*24 30*	*13 26*	*21 27*	2 19 10 24f. 18 12–27	249
257.	Übergabe des Verurteilten an Pilatus. *Jesus Delivered to Pilate*	**27** 1–2	**15** 1	**23** 1–2			22 66	18 28–32	255
258.	Das Ende des Judas. *The Death of Judas*	3–10							256
259.	Das Verhör vor Pilatus. *The Trial before Pilate*	11–14	2–5	3–5			*23 9f.*	18 33–38 *19 9f.*	257
260.	Jesus vor Herodes. *Jesus before Herod*			6–12	*27 12.14*	*15 3.5*			258
261.	Die Verurteilung. *The Sentence of Death*	15–26	6–15	13–25				18 39f. 19 4–16	258
262.	Verspottung des Judenkönigs. *The Mocking by the Soldiers*	27–31a	16–20a					19 1–3	262
263.	Der Todesgang. *The Road to Calvary*	31b–32	20b–21	26–32	*27 38*	*15 27*		16f.	263
264.	Die Kreuzigung. *The Crucifixion*	33–44	22–32	33–43	*27 48*	*15 36*	*23 32*	19 17–24	264
265.	Der Tod Jesu. *The Death on the Cross*	45–56	33–41	44–49			*8 2f.* *23 36*	19 25.28–37	268
266.	Das Begräbnis Jesu. *The Burial of Jesus*	57–61	42–47	50–56a				19 38–42	271
267.	Die Grabeswächter. *The Guard at the Tomb*	62–66							273

IV. Der Auferstandene. *The Risen Jesus 268.–275.*

		Matth	Mark	Luk	Matth	Mark	Luk	Joh	Page
268.	Das leere Grab. *The Resurrection*	**28** 1–8	**16** 1–8	**23** 56b–**24** 12	*16 21* *17 22f.* *20 18f. 26 45*	*8 31 9 31* *10 33f. 14 41* [*16 11*]	*9 22.44* *18 31f.*	20 1–10	275

A. Die matthäische Nachgeschichte. *The Matthean Post-Resurrection Narrative 269.–271.*

		Matth	Mark	Luk	Matth	Mark	Luk	Joh	Page
269.	Die Erscheinung des Auferstandenen vor den Frauen. *The Appearence of the Risen Jesus to the Women*	**28** 9–10				[*16 9f.*]		20 11–18	278
270.	Der Betrug der Hierarchen *The Bribing of the Soldiers*	11–15							278
271.	Die Offenbarung des Auferstandenen in Galiläa. *The Command to Baptize*	16–20				[*16 15f.*]			279

Perikope. *Pericope*	Fortlaufender Text *Continuous Text* Matth	Mark	Luk	Parallelen. *Parallels* Kursiv: Verweise (ohne Text). *Italics: References (without Text)* Matth	Mark	Luk	Joh	Seite *Page*
B. Die lukanische Nachgeschichte. *The Lucan Post-Resurrection Narrative 272.–274.*								
272. Die Emmausjünger. *The Road to Emmaus*			**24** 13–35		[*16 12f.*]		21 4	279
273. Die Offenbarung des Auferstandenen in Jerusalem. *The Appearence of the Risen Jesus in Jerusalem*			36–49		[*16 14*]		20 19–23	280
274. Die Himmelfahrt. *The Ascension*			50–53		[*16 19*]			281
C. Der unechte Markusschluß. *The Longer Ending of Mark*								
275. Mark 16, 9–20		[**16** 9–20]		*28 9f. 19f.*		*24 11.13–42. 50–53*	20 *11–18*	282

Verzeichnis der abgedruckten Johannestexte.
List of the Texts printed from John.

Joh	Pk. Nr.	Joh	Pk. Nr.	Joh	Pk. Nr.	Joh	Pk. Nr.	Joh	Pk. Nr.	Joh	Pk. Nr.
1 6	*13.*	35	*79.*	14	*214.*	31	*154.*	7	*215.*	28–32	*257.*
14	*138.*	4 1–3	*21.*	15	*121.*	39f.	*104.*	14	*102.*	33–38	*259.*
15	*16.*	35	*122.*	30	*22.218.*	44f.	*143.*	19	*229.*	39f.	*261.*
19f.	*16.*	44	*121.*	31	*99.*	13 2	*245.*	20	*89.*	19 1–3	*262.*
21	*123.*	46–53	*58.*	41f.	*3.*	4f.	*172.250.*	21	*229.*	4–16	*261.*
23	*13.*	5 8f.	*64.*	42	*223.*	12–14	*250.*	23	*153.*	16f.	*263.*
25–27	*16.*	10	*81.*	46	*24.*	13	*224.*	27	*5.*	17–27	*264.*
25	*123.*	23	*153.*	8 [1f.]	*242.*	16	*89.*	16 2	*86.229.*	25	*265.*
30f.	*16.*	29	*241.*	12	*32.*	18	*247.*	4	*231.*	28–37	*265.*
32–34	*18.*	46	*191.*	39	*14.*	19	*231.*	6	*141.*	38–42	*266.*
33	*16.*	6 1–13	*125.*	9 1–7	*134.*	20	*143.*	23	*215.*	20 1–10	*268.*
38f.	*23.*	15–21	*126.*	10 15	*79.*	21–27	*247.*	24	*50.*	11–18	*269.*
42	*85.*	30	*100.*	24f.	*256.*	27	*245.*	32	*253.*	19–23	*273.*
49	*135.*	42	*121.*	39	*22.*	30	*247.*	17 2	*79.*	22f.	*148.*
2 12	*24.*	51	*248.*	11 16	*253.*	36–38	*253.*	10	*187.*	21 1–11	*29.*
13–16	*214.*	53–58	*248.*	47–53	*243.*	14 9	*140.*	25f.	*79.*	4	*272.*
18	*100.216.*	68f.	*135.*	12 1–8	*244.*	13f.	*215.*	18 1	*253.254.*		
19	*256.*	69	*24.*	2	*159.*	26	*229.*	2–11	*255.*		
3 2	*220.*	70	*247.*	12–15	*210.*	29	*231.*	11	*254.*		
3.5	*202.*	71	*245.*	25f.	*137.*	14 31	*254.*	12–27	*256.*		
29	*8.*	7 1	*141.*	27	*254.*	15 5f.	*14.*	20	*255.*		

Außerdem/*in addition:* **Act 1** 13 *85.*; **1 K 11** 25 *248.*